SUZUKI

GSF1200 BANDIT • 1996-2003

WHAT'S IN YOUR TOOLBOX?

More information available at Clymer.com

Phone: 805-498-6703

Haynes Publishing Group
Sparkford Nr Yeovil
Somerset BA22 7JJ England

Haynes North America, Inc
861 Lawrence Drive
Newbury Park
California 91320 USA

ISBN 10: 0-89287-800-2
ISBN-13: 978-0-89287-800-0
Library of Congress: 2002111262

Printed in the U.S.A.

M353, 12R1, 13-488 **ABCDEFGHIJKLMNOPQRS**

Common spark plug conditions

NORMAL

Symptoms: Brown to grayish-tan color and slight electrode wear. Correct heat range for engine and operating conditions.
Recommendation: When new spark plugs are installed, replace with plugs of the same heat range.

WORN

Symptoms: Rounded electrodes with a small amount of deposits on the firing end. Normal color. Causes hard starting in damp or cold weather and poor fuel economy.
Recommendation: Plugs have been left in the engine too long. Replace with new plugs of the same heat range. Follow the recommended maintenance schedule.

CARBON DEPOSITS

Symptoms: Dry sooty deposits indicate a rich mixture or weak ignition. Causes misfiring, hard starting and hesitation.
Recommendation: Make sure the plug has the correct heat range. Check for a clogged air filter or problem in the fuel system or engine management system. Also check for ignition system problems.

ASH DEPOSITS

Symptoms: Light brown deposits encrusted on the side or center electrodes or both. Derived from oil and/or fuel additives. Excessive amounts may mask the spark, causing misfiring and hesitation during acceleration.
Recommendation: If excessive deposits accumulate over a short time or low mileage, install new valve guide seals to prevent seepage of oil into the combustion chambers. Also try changing gasoline brands.

OIL DEPOSITS

Symptoms: Oily coating caused by poor oil control. Oil is leaking past worn valve guides or piston rings into the combustion chamber. Causes hard starting, misfiring and hesitation.
Recommendation: Correct the mechanical condition with necessary repairs and install new plugs.

GAP BRIDGING

Symptoms: Combustion deposits lodge between the electrodes. Heavy deposits accumulate and bridge the electrode gap. The plug ceases to fire, resulting in a dead cylinder.
Recommendation: Locate the faulty plug and remove the deposits from between the electrodes.

TOO HOT

Symptoms: Blistered, white insulator, eroded electrode and absence of deposits. Results in shortened plug life.
Recommendation: Check for the correct plug heat range, over-advanced ignition timing, lean fuel mixture, intake manifold vacuum leaks, sticking valves and insufficient engine cooling.

PREIGNITION

Symptoms: Melted electrodes. Insulators are white, but may be dirty due to misfiring or flying debris in the combustion chamber. Can lead to engine damage.
Recommendation: Check for the correct plug heat range, over-advanced ignition timing, lean fuel mixture, insufficient engine cooling and lack of lubrication.

HIGH SPEED GLAZING

Symptoms: Insulator has yellowish, glazed appearance. Indicates that combustion chamber temperatures have risen suddenly during hard acceleration. Normal deposits melt to form a conductive coating. Causes misfiring at high speeds.
Recommendation: Install new plugs. Consider using a colder plug if driving habits warrant.

DETONATION

Symptoms: Insulators may be cracked or chipped. Improper gap setting techniques can also result in a fractured insulator tip. Can lead to piston damage.
Recommendation: Make sure the fuel anti-knock values meet engine requirements. Use care when setting the gaps on new plugs. Avoid lugging the engine.

MECHANICAL DAMAGE

Symptoms: May be caused by a foreign object in the combustion chamber or the piston striking an incorrect reach (too long) plug. Causes a dead cylinder and could result in piston damage.
Recommendation: Repair the mechanical damage. Remove the foreign object from the engine and/or install the correct reach plug.

CONTENTS

QUICK REFERENCE DATA

MOTORCYCLE INFORMATION

MODEL:____________________YEAR:__________

VIN NUMBER:____________________

ENGINE SERIAL NUMBER:____________________

CARBURETOR SERIAL NUMBER OR I.D. MARK:____________________

TIRE AND WHEEL SPECIFICATIONS

Item	Front	Rear
Tire type	Tubeless	Tubeless
Size	120/70 ZR17	180/55 ZR17
Minimum tread depth	1.6 mm (0.06 in.)	2.0 mm (0.08 in.)
Inflation pressure (cold)*		
U.S. models		
Solo	225 kPa (33 psi)	250 kPa (36 psi)
Rider and passenger	225 kPa (33 psi)	250 kPa (36 psi)
All models except U.S. models		
Solo	250 kPa (36 psi)	250 kPa (36 psi)
Rider and passenger	250 kPa (36 psi)	250 kPa (36 psi)
Wheel rim size	J17 × MT 3.50	J17 × MT5.50

*Tire inflation pressure is for original equipment tires. Aftermarket tires may require different inflation pressure. The use of tires other than those specified by Suzuki may cause instability.

RECOMMENDED LUBRICANTS AND FLUIDS

Fuel	Unleaded
Octane	87 [(R + M)/2 method] or research octane of 91 or higher
Fuel tank capacity, including reserve	
1996-2000	19.0 L (5.0 U.S. gal., 4.2 Imp gal.)
2001-on	
California models	19.0 L (5.0 U.S. gal., 4.2 Imp gal.)
All models except California	20.0 L (5.2 U.S. gal., 4.4 Imp. gal.)
Fuel tank reserve capacity	4.5 L (1.2 U.S. gal., 1.0 Imp. gal.)
Engine oil	
Grade	API SF or SG
Viscosity	SAE 10W-40
Capacity	
Oil change only	3.3 L (3.5 U.S. qt., 2.9 Imp. qt.)
Oil and filter change	3.5 L (3.7 U.S. qt., 3.1 Imp. qt.)
Brake fluid	DOT 4
Fork oil viscosity	Suzuki #10 fork oil or equivalent
Capacity per leg	
1996-2000	514 ml (17.3 U.S. oz., 18.1 Imp. oz.)
2001-on	508 ml (17.1 U.S. oz., 17.9 Imp.oz.)

MAINTENANCE AND TUNE-UP SPECIFICATIONS

Battery	
Type	YTX12-BS Yuasa maintenance-free
Capacity	12 volt 10 amp hour
Spark plug	
Standard	NGK: JR9B
Hot type	NGK: JR8B
Cold type	NGK: JR10B
Spark plug gap	0.6-0.7 mm (0.024-0.028 in.)
Idle speed	
Switzerland models	1150-1300 rpm
U.S. models	1150-1250 rpm
All models except Switzerland and U.S.	1100-1300 rpm
Valve clearance (cold)	
Intake	0.10-0.15 mm (0.004-0.006 in.)
Exhaust	0.18-0.23 mm (0.007-0.090 in.)
Compression pressure (at sea level)	
Standard	1250 kPa (181 psi)
Service limit	875 kPa (126 psi)
Maximum difference between cylinders	200 kPa (29 psi)
Brake pedal height	55 mm (2.2 in.)
Throttle cable free play	
1996-2000 models	
Return (push) cable	0.5-1.0 mm (0.02-0.04 in.)
Pull cable	0.5-1.0 mm (0.02-0.04 in.)
2001-on models	2.0-4.0 mm (0.08-0.16 in.)
Drive chain 21-pin length (service limit)	319.4 mm (12.6 in.)
Drive chain free play	20-30 mm (0.8-1.2 in.)

MAINTENANCE AND TUNE UP TORQUE SPECIFICATIONS

Item	N•m	in.-lb.	ft.-lb.
Brake hose banjo bolt	23	–	17
Cylinder base nut	9	80	–
Cylinder head bolt, 6 mm	10	88	–
Cylinder head cover			
banjo bolt	10	88	–
Cylinder head cover bolt	14	–	10
Cylinder head nut, 10 mm	38	–	28
Exhaust pipe bolt	23	–	17
Engine sprocket nut	115	–	85
Front axle	65	–	48
Front axle pinch bolt	23	–	17
Handlebar clamp bolt	23	–	17
Main oil gallery plug	40	–	29
Muffler mounting bolt	29	–	21
Oil cooler			
Hose banjo bolt			
1996-2000 models	28	–	21
2001-on models	23	–	17
Mounting bolts	10	88	–
Oil drain plug	23	–	17
Oil pan bolt	14	–	10
Rear axle nut	100	–	74

(continued)

MAINTENANCE AND TUNE UP TORQUE SPECIFICATIONS (continued)

Item	N•m	in.-lb.	ft.-lb.
Rear brake master cylinder rod locknut	18	–	13
Rear torque link nut	35	–	26
Removable frame down tube mounting bolt	32	–	23
Spark plug	11	97	–

REPLACEMENT BULBS

Item	Wattage
Headlight (high/low beam)	
1996-2000 models	60/55 W
2001-on models	60/50 W
Position light*	4 W
Tail/brake light	
1996-2000	5/21 W
2001-on models	5/21 W × 2
Turn signal	21 W
License plate light	5 W
Tachometer light	
1996-2000 models	1.7 W
2001-on models	LED
Speedometer light	
1996-2000 models	1.7 W
2001-on models	LED
Neutral indicator light	
1996-2000 models	3 W
2001-on models	LED
High beam indicator light	
1996-2000 models	1.7 W
2001-on models	LED
Turn signal indicator light	
1996-2000 models	4 W
2001-on models	LED
Oil pressure indicator light	
1996-2000 models	3.4 W
2001-on	LED

*Not used on U.S.A., California, Canada and Australia models

1

CHAPTER ONE

GENERAL INFORMATION

This detailed and comprehensive manual covers the Suzuki GSF1200 (1996-2003) and GSF1200S (1997-2003) Bandit.

The text provides complete information on maintenance, tune-up, repair and overhaul. Hundreds of original photos and drawings guide the reader through every job.

A shop manual is a reference tool and as in all Clymer manuals, the chapters are thumb tabbed for easy reference. Important items are indexed at the end of the book. All procedures, tables and figures are designed for the reader who may be working on the motorcycle for the first time. Frequently used specifications and capacities from individual chapters are summarized in the *Quick Reference Data* at the front of the manual.

Tables 1-8 are at the end of this chapter.

Table 1 lists frame serial numbers.

Table 2 lists motorcycle dimensions.

Table 3 lists motorcycle weight.

Table 4 lists conversion formulas.

Table 5 lists general torque specifications.

Table 6 lists technical abbreviations.

Table 7 lists decimal and metric equivalents.

Table 8 lists metric tap and drill sizes.

MANUAL ORGANIZATION

All dimensions and capacities are expressed in metric and U.S. standard units of measurement.

This chapter provides general information on shop safety, tool use, service fundamentals and shop supplies. The tables at the end of the chapter include general motorcycle information.

Chapter Two provides methods for quick and accurate diagnosis of problems. Troubleshooting procedures present typical symptoms and logical methods to pinpoint and repair the problem.

Chapter Three explains all routine maintenance necessary to keep the motorcycle running well.

Chapter Three also includes recommended tune-up procedures, eliminating the need to constantly consult the chapters on the various assemblies.

Subsequent chapters describe specific systems such as engine, transmission, clutch, drive system, fuel and exhaust systems, suspension and brakes. Each disassembly, repair and assembly procedure is discussed in step-by-step form.

Some of the procedures in this manual specify special tools. In most cases, the tool is illustrated in use. Well-equipped mechanics may be able to substitute similar tools or fabricate a suitable replacement. However, in some cases, the specialized equipment or expertise may make it impractical for the home mechanic to attempt the procedure. When necessary, such operations are identified in the text with the recommendation to have a dealership or specialist perform the task. It may be less expensive to have a professional perform these jobs, especially when considering the cost of the equipment.

WARNINGS, CAUTIONS AND NOTES

The terms WARNING, CAUTION and NOTE have specific meanings in this manual.

A WARNING emphasizes areas where injury or even death could result from negligence. Mechanical damage may also occur. WARNINGS *are to be taken seriously.*

A CAUTION emphasizes areas where equipment damage could result. Disregarding a CAUTION could cause permanent mechanical damage, though injury is unlikely.

A NOTE provides additional information to make a step or procedure easier or clearer. Disregarding a NOTE could cause inconvenience, but would not cause equipment damage or personal injury.

SAFETY

Professional mechanics can work for years and never sustain a serious injury or mishap. Follow these guidelines and practice common sense to safely service the motorcycle.

1. Do not operate the motorcycle in an enclosed area. The exhaust gasses contain carbon monoxide, an odorless, colorless, and tasteless poisonous gas. Carbon monoxide levels build quickly in small enclosed areas and can cause unconsciousness and death in a short time. Make sure the work area is properly ventilated or operate the motorcycle outside.
2. *Never* use gasoline or any extremely flammable liquid to clean parts. Refer to *Cleaning Parts* and *Handling Gasoline Safely* in this chapter.
3. *Never* smoke or use a torch in the vicinity of flammable liquids, such as gasoline or cleaning solvent.
4. If welding or brazing on the motorcycle, remove the fuel tank, carburetor and shocks to a safe distance at least 50 ft. (15 m) away.
5. Use the correct type and size of tools to avoid damaging fasteners.
6. Keep tools clean and in good condition. Replace or repair worn or damaged equipment.
7. When loosening a tight fastener, be guided by what would happen if the tool slips.
8. When replacing fasteners, make sure the new fasteners are of the same size and strength as the original ones.
9. Keep the work area clean and organized.
10. Wear eye protection *anytime* the safety of the eyes is in question. This includes procedures involving drilling, grinding, hammering, compressed air and chemicals.
11. Wear the correct clothing for the job. Tie up or cover long hair so it can not get caught in moving equipment.
12. Do not carry sharp tools in clothing pockets.
13. Always have an approved fire extinguisher available. Make sure it is rated for gasoline (Class B) and electrical (Class C) fires.
14. Do not use compressed air to clean clothes, the motorcycle or the work area. Debris may be blown into the eyes or skin. *Never* direct compressed air at anyone. Do not allow children to use or play with any compressed air equipment.
15. When using compressed air to dry rotating parts, hold the part so it cannot rotate. Do not allow the force of the air to spin the part. The air jet is capable of rotating parts at extreme speed. The part may be damaged or disintegrate, causing serious injury.
16. Do not inhale the dust created by brake pad and clutch wear. These particles may contain asbestos. In addition, some types of insulating materials and gaskets may contain asbestos. Inhaling asbestos particles is hazardous to people's health.
17. Never work on the motorcycle while someone is working under it.

18. When placing the motorcycle on a stand, make sure it is secure before walking away.

Handling Gasoline Safely

Gasoline is a volatile flammable liquid and is one of the most dangerous items in the shop.

Because gasoline is used so often, many people forget that it is hazardous. Only use gasoline as fuel for gasoline internal combustion engines. Keep in mind, when working on a motorcycle, gasoline is always present in the fuel tank, fuel line and carburetors. To avoid a disastrous accident when working around the fuel system, carefully observe the following precautions:

1. *Never* use gasoline to clean parts. See *Cleaning Parts* in this chapter.
2. When working on the fuel system, work outside or in a well-ventilated area.
3. Do not add fuel to the fuel tank or service the fuel system while the motorcycle is near open flames, sparks or where someone is smoking. Gasoline vapor is heavier than air, it collects in low areas and is more easily ignited than liquid gasoline.
4. Allow the engine to cool completely before working on any fuel system component.
5. When draining the carburetors, catch the fuel in a plastic container and then pour it into an approved gasoline storage device.
6. Do not store gasoline in glass containers. If the glass breaks, a serious explosion or fire may occur.
7. Immediately wipe up spilled gasoline with rags. Store the rags in a metal container with a lid until they can be properly disposed of, or place them outside in a safe place for the fuel to evaporate.
8. Do not pour water onto a gasoline fire. Water spreads the fire and makes it more difficult to put out. Use a class B, BC or ABC fire extinguisher to extinguish the fire.
9. Always turn off the engine before refueling. Do not spill fuel onto the engine or exhaust system. Do not overfill the fuel tank. Leave an air space at the top of the tank to allow room for the fuel to expand due to temperature fluctuations.

Cleaning Parts

Cleaning parts is one of the more tedious and difficult service jobs performed in the home garage. There are many types of chemical cleaners and solvents available for shop use. Most are poisonous and extremely flammable. To prevent chemical exposure, vapor buildup, fire and serious injury, observe each product warning label and note the following:

1. Read and observe the entire product label before using any chemical. Always know what type of chemical is being used and whether it is poisonous and/or flammable.
2. Do not use more than one type of cleaning solvent at a time. If mixing chemicals is called for, measure the proper amounts according to the manufacturer.
3. Work in a well-ventilated area.
4. Wear chemical-resistant gloves.
5. Wear safety glasses.
6. Wear a vapor respirator if the instructions call for it.
7. Wash hands and arms thoroughly after cleaning parts.
8. Keep chemical products away from children and pets.
9. Thoroughly clean all oil, grease and cleaner residue from any part that must be heated.
10. Use a nylon brush when cleaning parts. Metal brushes may cause a spark.
11. When using a parts washer, only use the solvent recommended by the manufacturer. Make sure the parts washer is equipped with a metal lid that will lower in case of fire.

Warning Labels

Most manufacturers attach information and warning labels to the motorcycle. These labels contain instructions that are important to personal safety when operating, servicing, transporting and storing the motorcycle Refer to the owner's manual for the description and location of labels. Order replacement labels from the manufacturer if they are missing or damaged.

SERIAL NUMBERS

Serial numbers are stamped on various locations on the frame, engine, transmission and carburetor. Record these numbers in the *Quick Reference Data* section in the front of the manual. Have these numbers available when ordering parts.

The frame serial number (**Figure 1**) is stamped on the right side of the frame steering head.

The VIN number label (**Figure 2**) is attached to the right side frame rail under the fuel tank.

The engine serial number (**Figure 3**) is stamped on the right side top surface of the crankcase next to the engine oil fill cap.

The carburetor serial number (**Figure 4**) is located on the right side of the carburetor body above the float bowl.

FASTENERS

Proper fastener selection and installation is important to ensure that the motorcycle operates as designed and can be serviced efficiently. The choice of original equipment fasteners is not arrived at by chance. Make sure that replacement fasteners meet all the same requirements as the originals.

Threaded Fasteners

Threaded fasteners secure most of the components on the motorcycle. Most are tightened by turning them clockwise (right-hand threads). If the normal rotation of the component being tightened would loosen the fastener, it may have left-hand threads. If a left-hand threaded fastener is used, it is noted in the text.

Two dimensions are required to match the thread size of the fastener: the number of threads in a given distance and the outside diameter of the threads.

Two systems are currently used to specify threaded fastener dimensions: the U.S. Standard system and the metric system. Although fasteners may appear similar, close inspection shows that the thread design are not the same (**Figure 5**).

Pay particular attention when working with unidentified fasteners; mismatching thread types can damage threads.

CAUTION

To ensure that the fastener threads are not mismatched or cross-threaded, start all fasteners by hand. If a fastener is hard to start or turn, determine the cause before tightening with a wrench.

The length (L, **Figure 6**), diameter (D) and distance between thread crests (pitch) (T) classify met-

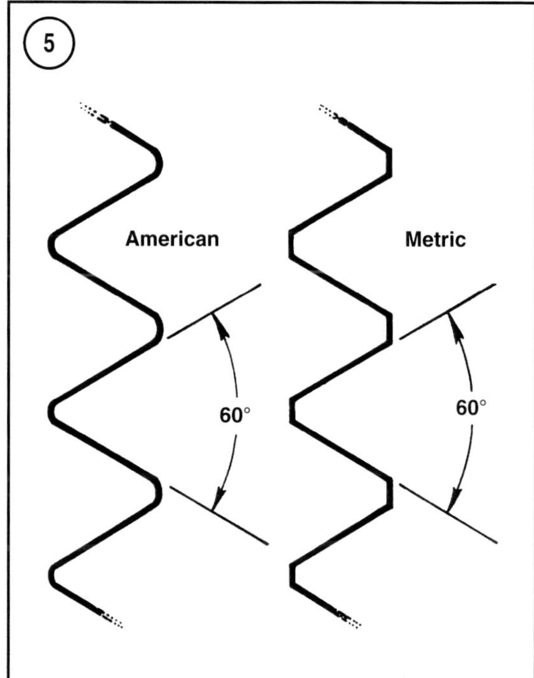

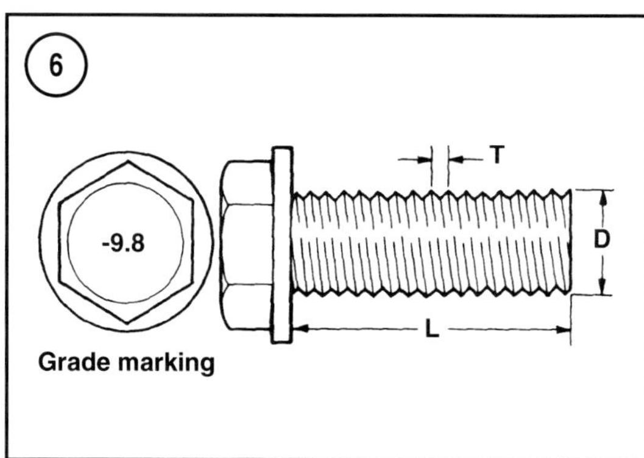

ric screws and bolts. A typical bolt may be identified by the numbers, 8—1.25 × 130. This indicates the bolt has diameter of 8 mm, the distance between thread crests is 1.25 mm and the length is 130 mm. Always measure bolt length as shown in **Figure 6** to avoid purchasing replacements of the wrong length.

The numbers located on the top of the fastener (**Figure 6**) indicate the strength of metric screws and bolts. The higher the number, the stronger the fastener is. Unnumbered fasteners are generally the weakest.

Many screws, bolts and studs are combined with nuts to secure particular components. To indicate the size of a nut, manufacturers specify the internal diameter and the thread pitch.

The measurement across two flats on a nut or bolt indicates the wrench size.

WARNING
Do not install fasteners with a strength classification lower than what was originally installed by the manufacturer. Doing so may cause equipment failure and/or damage.

Torque Specifications

The materials used in the manufacture of the motorcycle may be subjected to uneven stresses if the fasteners of the various subassemblies are not installed and tightened correctly. Fasteners that are improperly installed or work loose can cause extensive damage. It is essential to use an accurate torque wrench, described in this chapter, with the torque specifications in this manual.

Specifications for torque are provided in Newton-meters (N•m), foot-pounds (ft.-lb.) and inch-pounds (in.-lb.). Refer to **Table 5** for general torque specifications. To use **Table 5**, first determine the size of the fastener as described in *Fasteners* in this chapter. Torque specifications for specific components are at the end of the appropriate chapters. Torque wrenches are covered in the *Basic Tools* section.

Self-Locking Fasteners

Several types of bolts, screws and nuts incorporate a system that creates interference between the two fasteners. Interference is achieved in various ways. The most common type is the nylon insert nut and a dry adhesive coating on the threads of a new bolt.

Self-locking fasteners offer greater holding strength than standard fasteners, which improves their resistance to vibration. Most self-locking fasteners cannot be reused. The materials used to form the lock become distorted after the initial installation and removal. It is a good practice to discard and replace self-locking fasteners after their removal. Do not replace self-locking fasteners with standard fasteners.

Washers

There are two basic types of washers: flat washers and lockwashers. Flat washers are simple discs with a hole to fit a screw or bolt. Lockwashers are used to prevent a fastener from working loose. Washers can be used as spacers and seals, or to help distribute fastener load and to prevent the fastener from damaging the component.

As with fasteners, when replacing washers make sure the replacement washers are of the same design and quality.

Cotter Pins

A cotter pin is a split metal pin inserted into a hole or slot to prevent a fastener from loosening. In certain applications, such as the rear axle on some motorcycles, the fastener must be secured in this way. For these applications, a cotter pin and castellated (slotted) nut is used.

To use a cotter pin, first make sure the diameter is correct for the hole in the fastener. After correctly tightening the fastener and aligning the holes, insert the cotter pin through the hole and bend the ends over the fastener (**Figure 7**). Unless instructed to do so, never loosen a torqued fastener to align the holes. If the holes do not align, tighten the fastener just enough to achieve alignment.

Cotter pins are available in various diameters and lengths. Measure length from the bottom of the head to the tip of the shortest pin.

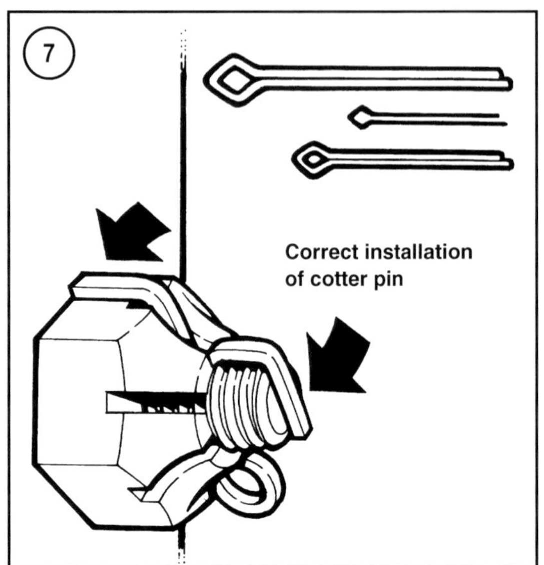

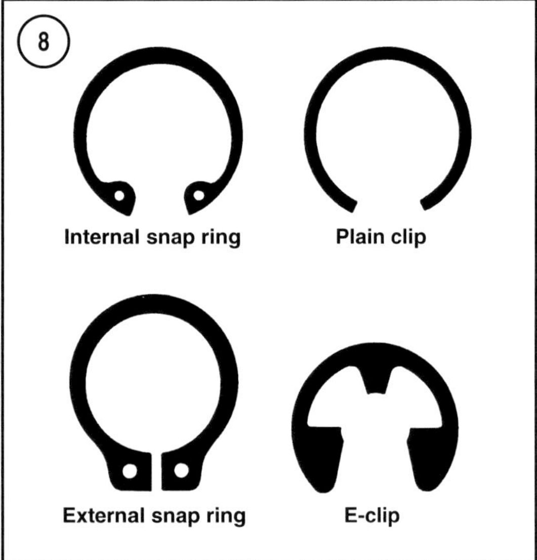

Snap Rings and E-clips

Snap rings (**Figure 8**) are circular-shaped metal retaining clips. They are required to secure parts and gears in place on parts such as shafts, pins or rods. External type snap rings are used to retain items on shafts. Internal type snap rings secure parts within housing bores. In some applications, in addition to securing the component(s), snap rings of varying thickness also determine endplay. These are usually called selective snap rings.

Two basic types of snap rings are used: machined and stamped. Machined snap rings (**Figure 9**) can be installed in either direction, since both faces have sharp edges. Stamped snap rings (**Figure 10**) are manufactured with a sharp edge and a round edge. When installing a stamped snap ring in a thrust application, install the sharp edge facing away from the part producing the thrust.

E-clips are used when it is not practical to use a snap ring. Remove E-clips with a flat blade screwdriver by prying between the shaft and E-clip. To install an E-clip, center it over the shaft groove and push or tap it into place.

Observe the following when installing snap rings:

1. Remove and install snap rings with snap ring pliers. See *Snap Ring Pliers* in this chapter.
2. In some applications, it may be necessary to replace snap rings after removing them.

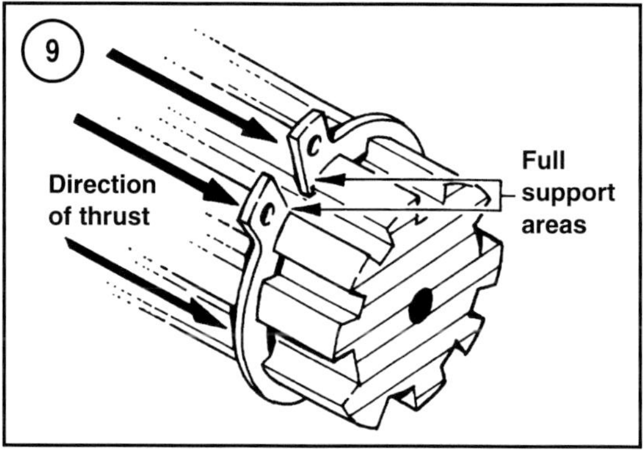

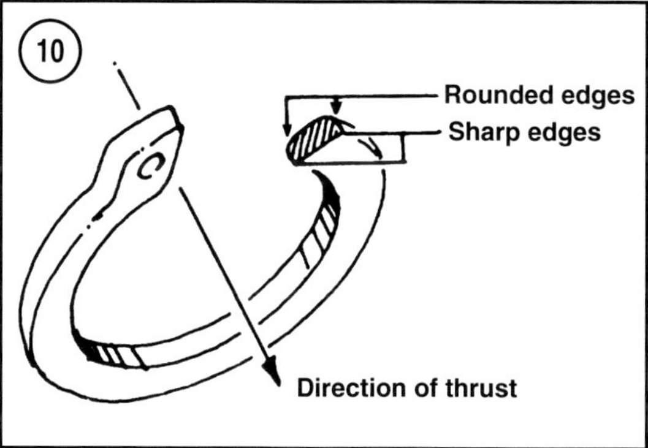

3. Compress or expand snap rings only enough to install them. If overly expanded, they lose their retaining ability.
4. After installing a snap ring, make sure it seats completely.
5. Wear eye protection when removing and installing snap rings.

SHOP SUPPLIES

Lubricants and Fluids

Periodic lubrication helps ensure a long service life for any type of equipment. Using the correct type of lubricant is as important as performing the lubrication service, although in an emergency the wrong type is better than none. The following section describes the types of lubricants most often required. Make sure to follow the manufacturer's recommendations for lubricant types.

Engine oils

Engine oil is classified by two standards: the American Petroleum Institute (API) service classification and the Society of Automotive Engineers (SAE) viscosity rating. This information is on the oil container label. Two letters indicate the API service classification. The number or sequence of numbers and letter (10W-40, for example) is the oil's viscosity rating. The API service classification and the SAE viscosity index are not indications of oil quality.

The service classification indicates that the oil meets specific lubrication standards. The first letter in the classification (*S*) indicates that the oil is for gasoline engines. The second letter indicates the standard the oil satisfies.

Always use an oil with a classification recommended by the manufacturer. Using an oil with a different classification can cause engine damage.

Viscosity is an indication of the oil's thickness. Thin oils have a lower number while thick oils have a higher number. Engine oils fall into the 5- to 50-weight range for single-grade oils.

Most manufacturers recommend multi-grade oil. These oils perform efficiently across a wide range of operating conditions. Multi-grade oils are identified by a *W* after the first number, which indicates the low-temperature viscosity.

Engine oils are most commonly mineral (petroleum) based; however, synthetic and semi-synthetic types are used more frequently. When selecting engine oil, follow the manufacturer's recommendation for type, classification and viscosity.

Greases

Grease is lubricating oil with thickening agents added to it. The National Lubricating Grease Institute (NLGI) grades grease. Grades range from No. 000 to No. 6, with No. 6 being the thickest. Typical multipurpose grease is NLGI No. 2. For specific applications, manufacturers may recommend water-resistant type grease or one with an additive such as molybdenum disulfide (MoS_2).

Brake fluid

Brake fluid is the hydraulic fluid used to transmit hydraulic pressure (force) to the wheel brakes. Brake fluid is classified by the Department of

Transportation (DOT). Current designations for brake fluid are DOT 3, DOT 4 and DOT 5. This classification appears on the fluid container.

Each type of brake fluid has its own definite characteristics. Do not intermix different types of brake fluid. DOT 5 fluid is silicone-based. DOT 5 brake fluid is not compatible with other brake fluids or in systems for which it is not designed. Mixing DOT 5 fluid with other fluids may cause brake failure. When adding brake fluid, *only* use the fluid recommended by the manufacturer.

Brake fluid will damage any plastic, painted or plated surface it contacts. Use extreme care when working with brake fluid and remove any spills immediately with soap and water.

Hydraulic brake systems require clean and moisture free brake fluid. Never reuse brake fluid. Keep containers and reservoirs properly sealed.

WARNING

Never put a mineral-based (petroleum) oil into the brake system. Mineral oil will cause rubber parts in the system to swell and break apart, resulting in complete brake failure.

Cleaners, Degreasers and Solvents

Many chemicals are available to remove oil, grease and other residue from the motorcycle. Before using cleaning solvents, consider how they will be used and disposed of, particularly if they are not water-soluble. Local ordinances may require special procedures for the disposal of many types of cleaning chemicals. Refer to *Safety and Cleaning Parts* in this chapter for more information on their use.

Use brake parts cleaner to clean brake system components when contact with petroleum-based products will damage seals. Brake parts cleaner leaves no residue. Use electrical contact cleaner to clean electrical connections and components without leaving any residue. Carburetor cleaner is a powerful solvent used to remove fuel deposits and varnish from fuel system components. Use this cleaner carefully, as it may damage finishes.

Generally, degreasers are strong cleaners used to remove heavy accumulations of grease from engine and frame components.

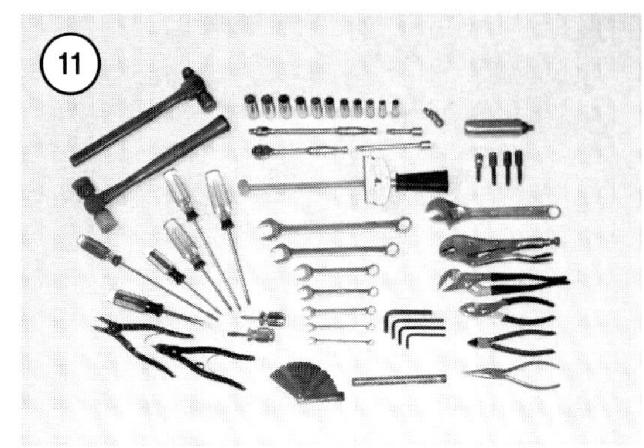

Most solvents are designed to be used in a parts washing cabinet for individual component cleaning. For safety, use only nonflammable or high flash point solvents.

Gasket Sealant

Sealants are used in combination with a gasket or seal and are occasionally alone. Follow the manufacturer's recommendation when using sealants. Use extreme care when choosing a sealant different from the type originally recommended. Choose sealants based on their resistance to heat, various fluids and their sealing capabilities.

One of the most common sealants is RTV, or room temperature vulcanizing sealant. This sealant cures at room temperature over a specific time period. This allows the repositioning of components without damaging gaskets.

Moisture in the air causes the RTV sealant to cure. Always install the tube cap as soon as possible after applying RTV sealant. RTV sealant has a limited shelf life and will not cure properly if the shelf life has expired. Keep partial tubes sealed and discard them if they have surpassed the expiration date.

Applying RTV sealant

Clean all old gasket residue from the mating surfaces. Remove all gasket material from blind threaded holes; it can cause inaccurate bolt torque. Spray the mating surfaces with aerosol parts cleaner and then wipe with a lint-free cloth. The area must be clean for the sealant to adhere.

Apply RTV sealant in a continuous bead 2-3 mm (0.08-0.12 in.) thick. Circle all the fastener holes

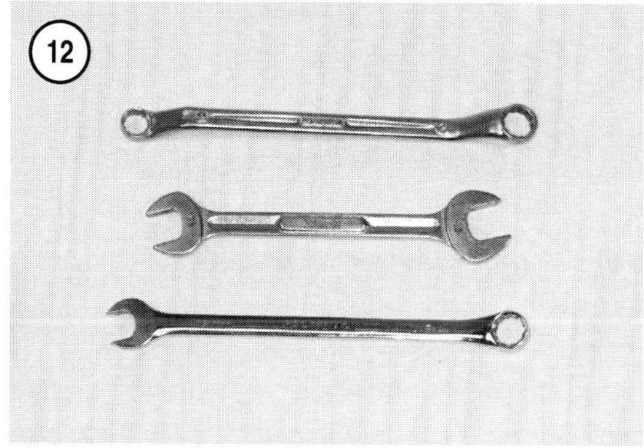
12

unless otherwise specified. Do not allow any sealant to enter these holes. Assemble and tighten the fasteners to the specified torque within the time frame recommended by the RTV sealant manufacturer.

Gasket Remover

Aerosol gasket remover can help remove stubborn gaskets. This product can speed up the removal process and prevent damage to the mating surface that may be caused by using a scraping tool. Most of these types of products are very caustic. Follow the gasket remover manufacturer's instructions for use.

Threadlocking Compound

A threadlocking compound is a fluid applied to the threads of fasteners. After tightening the fastener, the fluid dries and becomes a solid filler between the threads. This makes it difficult for the fastener to work loose from vibration, or heat expansion and contraction. Some threadlocking compounds also provide a seal against fluid leakage.

Before applying threadlocking compound, remove any old compound from both thread areas and clean them with aerosol parts cleaner. Use the compound sparingly. Excess fluid can run into adjoining parts.

Threadlocking compounds are available for a wide range of strength, temperature and repair applications. Follow the particular manufacturer's recommendations regarding compound selection.

BASIC TOOLS

Most of the procedures in this manual can be carried out with simple hand tools and test equipment familiar to the home mechanic. Always use the correct tools for the job at hand. Keep tools organized and clean. Store them in a tool chest with related tools organized together.

Quality tools are essential. The best are constructed of high-strength alloy steel. These tools are light, easy to use and resistant to wear. Their working surface is devoid of sharp edges and the tool is carefully polished. They have an easy-to-clean finish and are comfortable to use. Quality tools are a good investment.

When purchasing tools to perform the procedures covered in this manual, consider the tool's potential frequency of use. If a tool kit is just now being started, consider purchasing a basic tool set (**Figure 11**) from a large tool supplier. These sets are available in many tool combinations and offer substantial savings when compared to individually purchased tools. As work experience grows and tasks become more complicated, specialized tools can be added.

Screwdrivers

Screwdrivers of various lengths and types are mandatory for the simplest tool kit. The two basic types are the slotted tip (flat blade) and the Phillips tip. These are available in sets that often include an assortment of tip sizes and shaft lengths.

As with all tools, use a screwdriver designed for the job. Make sure the size of the tip conforms to the size and shape of the fastener. Use them only for driving screws. Never use a screwdriver for prying or chiseling metal. Repair or replace worn or damaged screwdrivers. A worn tip may damage the fastener, making it difficult to remove.

Wrenches

Open-end, box-end and combination wrenches (**Figure 12**) are available in a variety of types and sizes.

The number stamped on the wrench refers to the distance between the work areas. This size must match the size of the fastener head.

The box-end wrench is an excellent tool because it grips the fastener on all sides. This reduces the chance of the tool slipping. The box-end wrench is designed with either a 6- or 12-point opening. For stubborn or damaged fasteners, the 6-point provides superior holding ability by contacting the fastener across a wider area at all six edges. For general use, the 12-point works well. It allows the wrench to be removed and reinstalled without moving the handle over such a wide arc.

An open-end wrench is fast and works best in areas with limited overhead access. It contacts the fastener at only two points, and is subject to slipping under heavy force, or if the tool or fastener is worn. A box-end wrench is preferred in most instances, especially when breaking loose and applying the final tightness to a fastener.

The combination wrench has a box-end on one end, and an open-end on the other. This combination makes it a very convenient tool.

Adjustable Wrenches

An adjustable wrench or Crescent wrench (**Figure 13**) can fit nearly any nut or bolt head that has clear access around its entire perimeter. Adjustable wrenches are best used as a backup wrench to keep a large nut or bolt from turning while the other end is being loosened or tightened with a box-end or socket wrench.

Adjustable wrenches contact the fastener at only two points, which makes them more subject to slipping off the fastener. The fact that one jaw is adjustable and may loosen only aggravates this shortcoming. Make certain the solid jaw is the one transmitting the force.

Socket Wrenches, Ratchets and Handles

Sockets that attach to a ratchet handle (**Figure 14**) are available with 6-point (A, **Figure 15**) or 12-point (B) openings and different drive sizes. The drive size indicates the size of the square hole that accepts the ratchet handle. The number stamped on the socket is the size of the work area and must match the fastener head.

As with wrenches, a 6-point socket provides superior-holding ability, while a 12-point socket needs to be moved only half as far to reposition it on the fastener.

Sockets are designated for either hand or impact use. Impact sockets are made of thicker material for

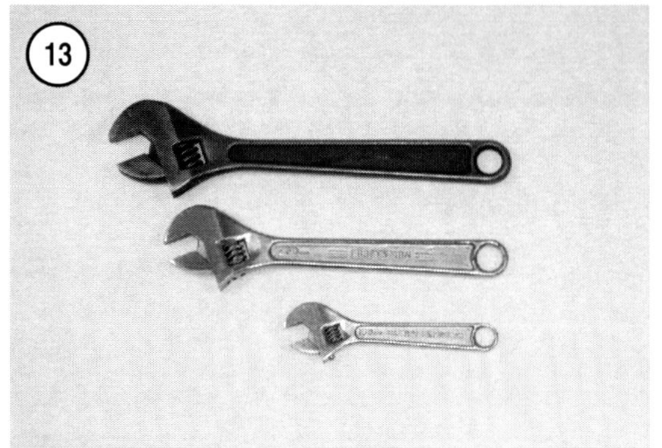

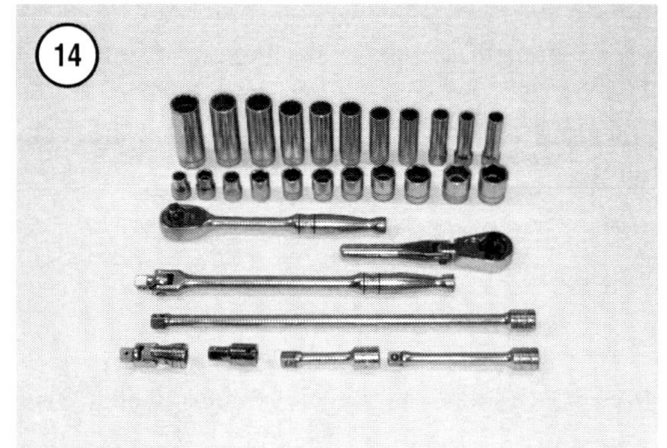

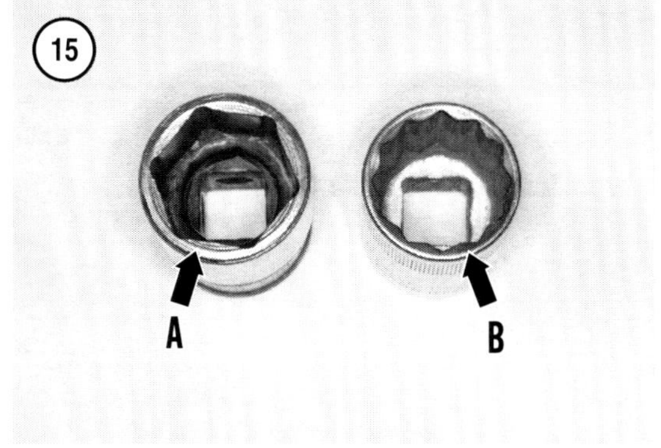

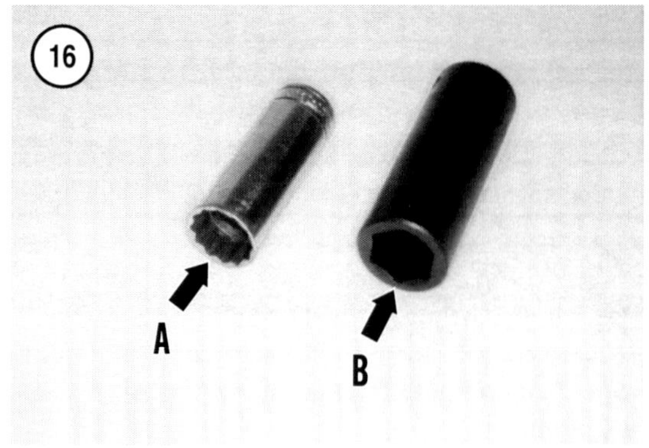

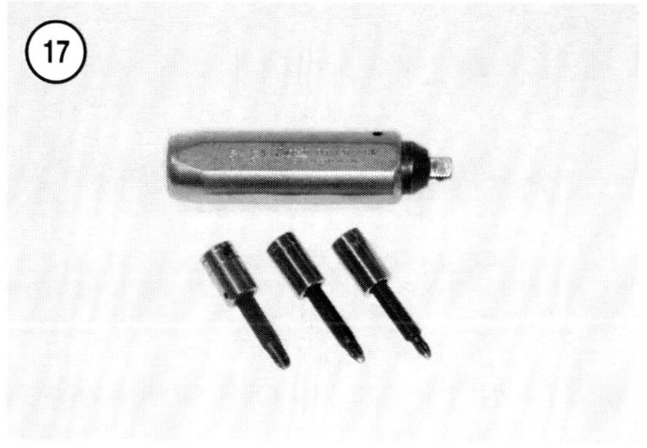
17

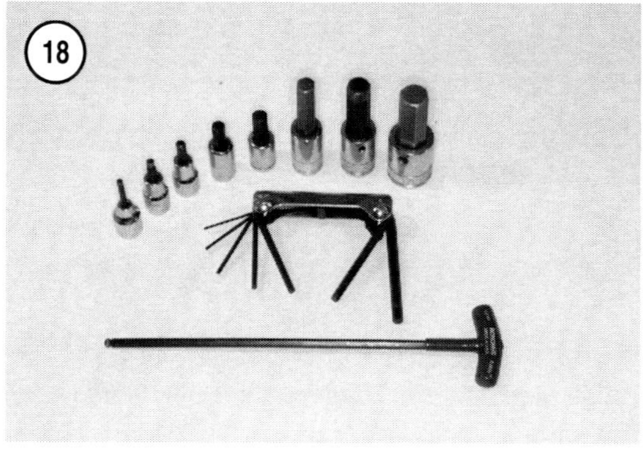
18

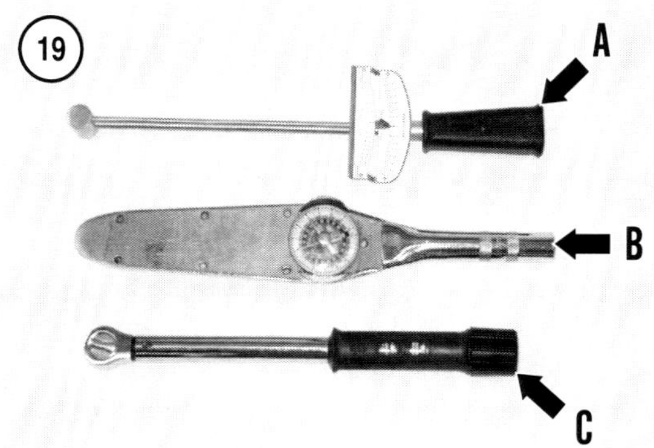

19

more durability. Compare the size and wall thickness of a 19-mm hand socket (A, **Figure 16**) and the 19-mm impact socket (B). Use impact sockets when using an impact driver or air tools. Use hand sockets with hand-driven attachments.

WARNING
Do not use hand sockets with air or impact tools, as they may shatter and cause injury. Always wear eye protection when using impact or air tools.

Various handles are available for sockets. The speed handle is used for fast operation. Flexible ratchet heads in varying lengths allow the socket to be turned with varying force, and at odd angles. Extension bars allow the socket setup to reach difficult areas. The ratchet is the most versatile. It allows the user to install or remove the nut without removing the socket.

Sockets combined with any number of drivers make them undoubtedly the fastest, safest and most convenient tool for fastener removal and installation.

Impact Driver

An impact driver provides extra force for removing fasteners, by converting the impact of a hammer into a turning motion. This makes it possible to remove stubborn fasteners without damaging them. Impact drivers and interchangeable bits (**Figure 17**) are available from most tool suppliers. When using a socket with an impact driver, make sure the socket is designed for impact use. Refer to *Socket Wrenches, Ratchets and Handles* in this section.

WARNING
Do not use hand sockets with air or impact tools as they may shatter and cause injury. Always wear eye protection when using impact or air tools.

Allen Wrenches

Allen or setscrew wrenches (**Figure 18**) are used on fasteners with hexagonal recesses in the fastener head. These wrenches are available in L-shaped bar, socket and T-handle types. A metric set is required when working on most motorcycles. Allen bolts are sometimes called socket bolts.

Torque Wrenches

A torque wrench is used with a socket, torque adapter or similar extension to tighten a fastener to a measured torque. Torque wrenches come in several drive sizes (1/4, 3/8, 1/2 and 3/4) and have various methods of reading the torque value. The drive size indicates the size of the square drive that accepts the socket, adapter or extension. Common methods of reading the torque value are the deflecting beam (A, **Figure 19**), the dial indicator (B) and the audible click (C).

When choosing a torque wrench, consider the torque range, drive size and accuracy. The torque specifications in this manual provide an indication of the range required.

A torque wrench is a precision tool that must be properly cared for to remain accurate. Store torque wrenches in cases or separate padded drawers within a toolbox. Follow the manufacturer's instructions for their care and calibration.

Torque Adapters

Torque adapters or extensions extend or reduce the reach of a torque wrench. The torque adapter shown in **Figure 20** is used to tighten a fastener that cannot be reached due to the size of the torque wrench head, drive, and socket. If a torque adapter changes the effective lever length (**Figure 21**), the torque reading on the wrench will not equal the actual torque applied to the fastener. It is necessary to recalibrate the torque setting on the wrench to compensate for the change of lever length. When a torque adapter is used at a right angle to the drive head, calibration is not required, since the effective length has not changed.

To recalculate a torque reading when using a torque adapter, use the following formula, and refer to **Figure 21**.

$$TW = \frac{TA \times L}{L + A}$$

TW is the torque setting or dial reading on the wrench.

TA is the torque specification and the actual amount of torque that will be applied to the fastener.

A is the amount that the adapter increases (or in some cases reduces) the effective lever length as measured along the centerline of the torque wrench (**Figure 21**).

L is the lever length of the wrench as measured from the center of the drive to the center of the grip.

The effective length is the sum of L and A (**Figure 21**).

Example:

TA = 20 ft.-lb.

A = 3 in.

L = 14 in.

$$TW = \frac{20 \times 14}{14 + 3} = \frac{280}{17} = 16.5 \text{ ft. lb.}$$

In this example, the torque wrench would be set to the recalculated torque value (TW = 16.5 ft.-lb.) .

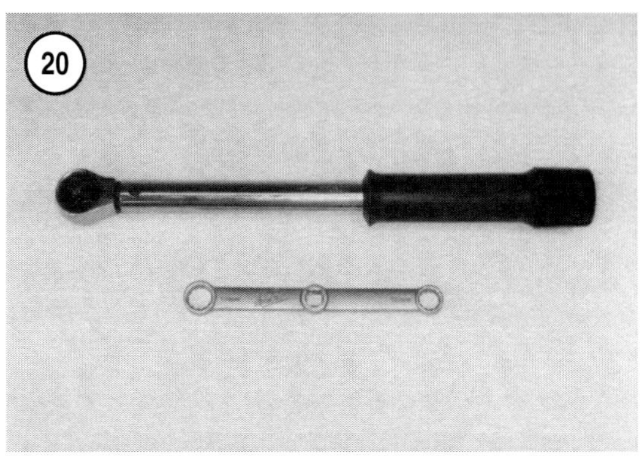

When using a beam-type wrench, tighten the fastener until the pointer aligns with 16.5 ft.-lb. In this example, although the torque wrench is preset to 16.5 ft.-lb., the actual torque is 20 ft.-lb.

Pliers

Pliers come in a wide range of types and sizes. Pliers are useful for holding, cutting, bending, and crimping. Do not use them to turn fasteners. **Figure 22** and **Figure 23** show several types of useful pliers. Each design has a specialized function. Slip-joint pliers are general-purpose pliers used for gripping and bending. Diagonal cutting pliers are needed to cut wire and can be used to remove cotter pins. Needlenose pliers are used to hold or bend small objects. Locking pliers (**Figure 23**), sometimes called vise-grips, are used to hold objects very tightly. They have many uses, ranging from holding two parts together to gripping the end of a broken stud. Use caution when using locking pliers, as the sharp jaws will damage the objects they hold.

Snap Ring Pliers

Snap ring pliers are specialized pliers with tips that fit into the ends of snap rings to remove and install them.

Snap ring pliers are available with a fixed action (either internal or external) or convertible (one tool works on both internal and external snap rings). They may have fixed tips or interchangeable ones of various sizes and angles. For general use, select a convertible type pliers with interchangeable tips.

21

HOW TO MEASURE TORQUE WRENCH EFFECTIVE LENGTH

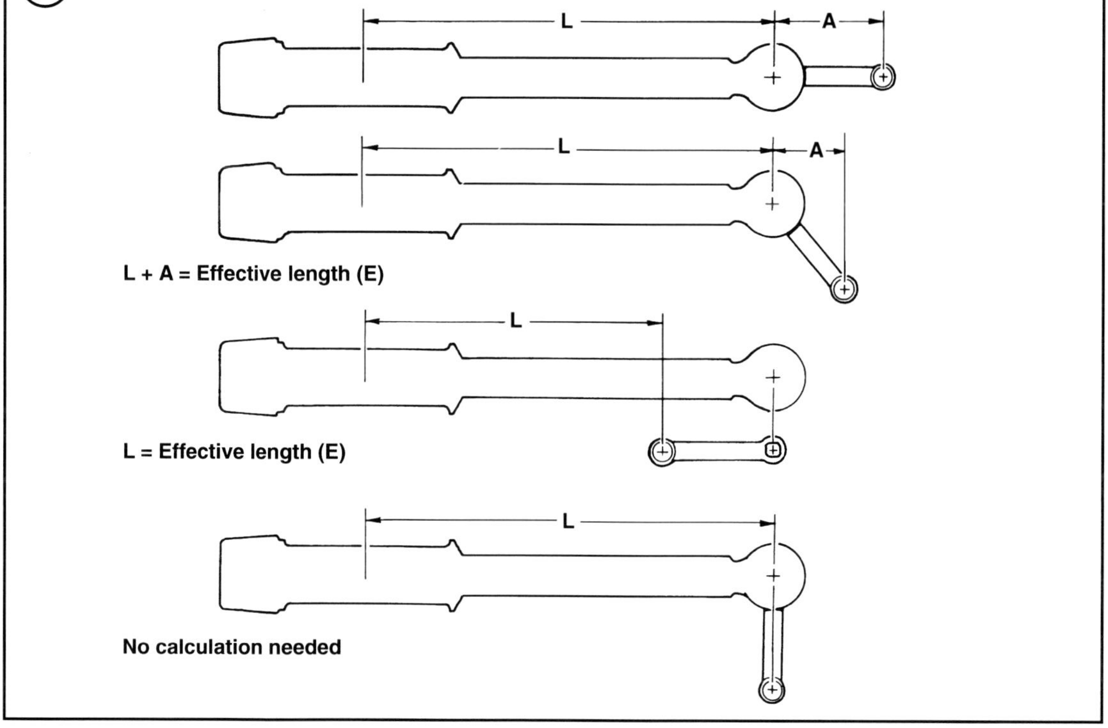

L + A = Effective length (E)

L = Effective length (E)

No calculation needed

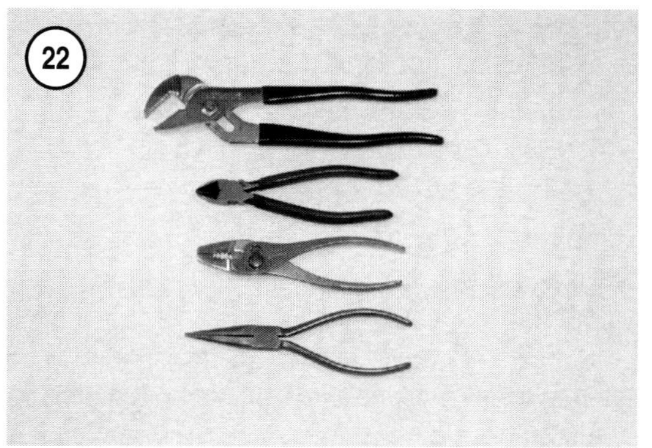

22

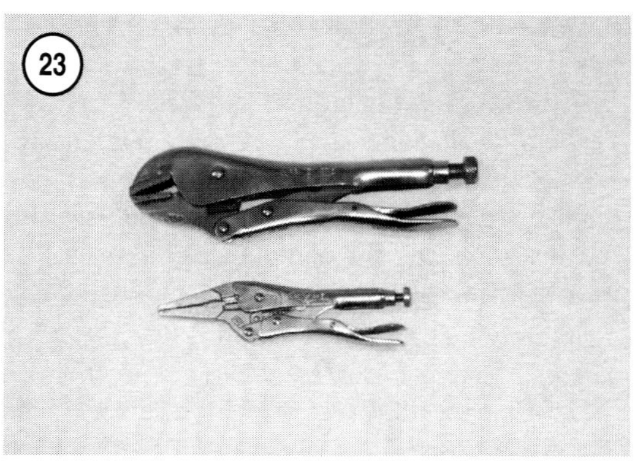

23

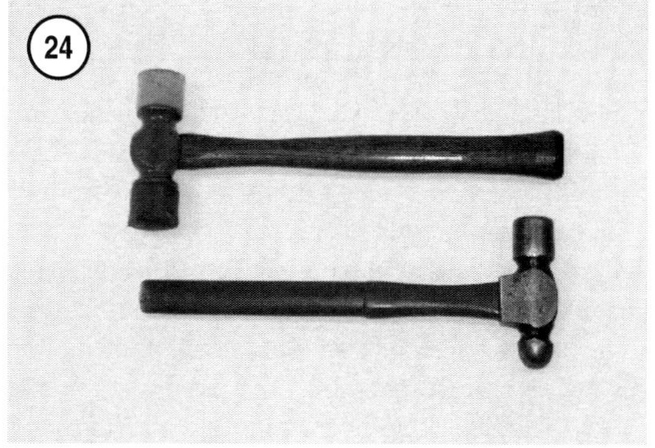

24

WARNING

Snap rings can slip and fly off when removing and installing them. Also, the snap ring pliers tips may break. Always wear eye protection when using snap ring pliers.

Hammers

Various types of hammers (**Figure 24**) are available to fit a number of applications. A ball-peen hammer is used to strike another tool, such as a punch or chisel. Soft-faced hammers are required when a metal object must be struck without damaging it. *Never* use a metal-faced hammer on engine and suspension components, as damage will occur in most cases.

Always wear eye protection when using hammers. Make sure the hammer face is in good condition and the handle is not cracked. Select the correct hammer for the job and make sure to strike the object squarely. Do not use the handle or the side of the hammer to strike an object.

PRECISION MEASURING TOOLS

The ability to accurately measure components is essential to successfully rebuild an engine. Equipment is manufactured to close tolerances, and obtaining consistently accurate measurements is essential to determining which components require replacement or further service.

Each type of measuring instrument is designed to measure a dimension with a certain degree of accuracy and within a certain range. When selecting the measuring tool, make sure it is applicable to the task.

As with all tools, measuring tools provide the best results if cared for properly. Improper use can damage the tool and result in inaccurate readings. If any measurement is questionable, verify the measurement using another tool. A standard gauge is usually provided with measuring tools to check accuracy and calibrate the tool if necessary.

Precision measurements can vary according to the experience of the person performing the procedure. Accurate results are only possible if the mechanic possesses a feel for using the tool. Heavy-handed use of measuring tools will produce less accurate results. Hold the tool gently by the fingertips so the point at which the tool contacts the object is easily felt. This feel for the equipment will produce more accurate measurements and reduce the risk of damaging the tool or component. Refer to the following sections for specific measuring tools.

Feeler Gauge

The feeler or thickness gauge (**Figure 25**) is used for measuring the distance between two surfaces.

A feeler gauge set consists of an assortment of steel strips of graduated thickness. Each blade is marked with its thickness. Blades can be of various lengths and angles for different procedures.

25

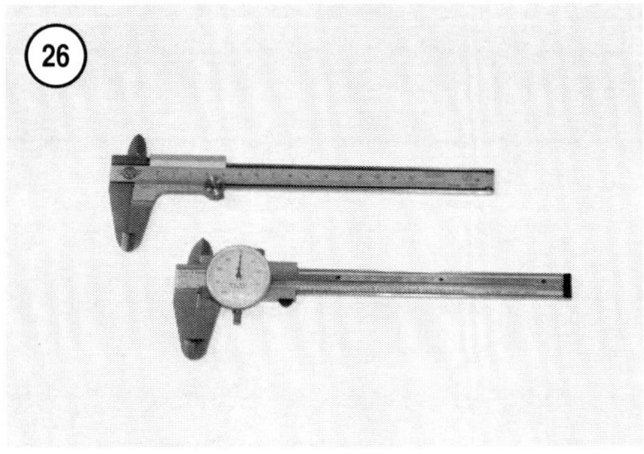
26

A common use for a feeler gauge is to measure valve clearance. Wire (round) type gauges are used to measure spark plug gap.

Calipers

Calipers (**Figure 26**) are excellent tools for obtaining inside, outside and depth measurements. Although not as precise as a micrometer, they allow reasonable precision, typically to within 0.05 mm (0.001 in.). Most calipers have a range up to 150 mm (6 in.).

Calipers are available in dial, vernier or digital versions. Dial calipers have a dial readout that provides convenient reading. Vernier calipers have marked scales that must be compared to determine the measurement. The digital caliper uses an LCD to show the measurement.

Properly maintain the measuring surfaces of the caliper. There must not be any dirt or burrs between the tool and the object being measured. Never force the caliper closed around an object; close the caliper

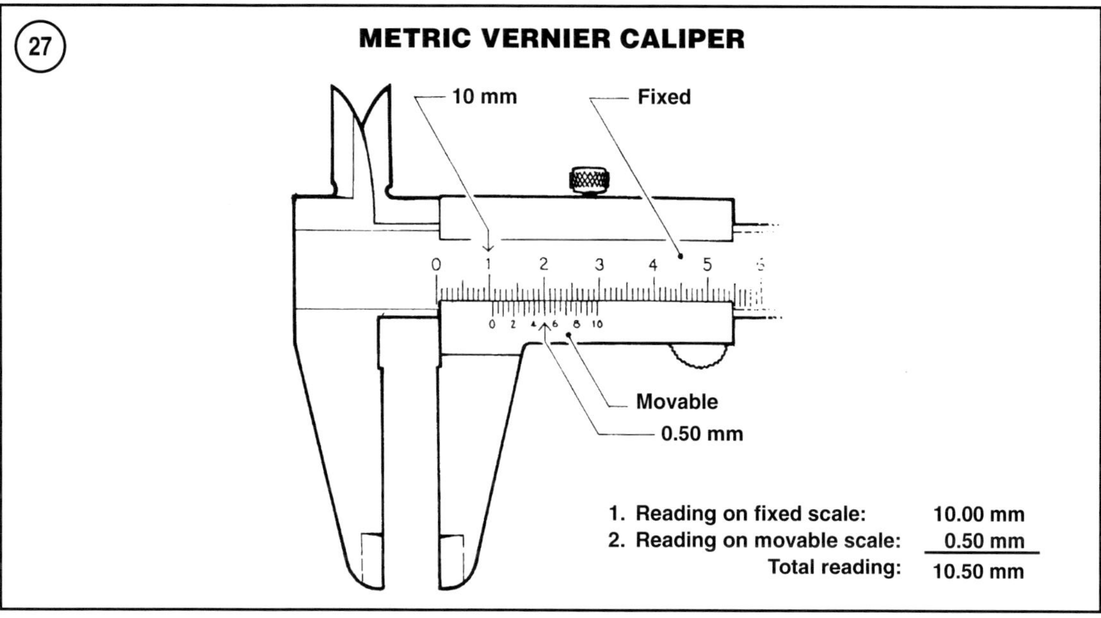

28

DECIMAL PLACE VALUES*

0.1	Indicates 1/10 (one tenth of an inch or millimeter)
0.010	Indicates 1/100 (one one-hundreth of an inch or millimeter)
0.001	Indicates 1/1,000 (one one-thousandth of an inch or millimeter)

*This chart represents the values of figures placed to the right of the decimal point. Use it when reading decimals from one-tenth to one one-thousandth of an inch or millimeter. It is not a conversion chart (for example: 0.001 in. is not equal to 0.001 mm).

around the highest point so it can be removed with a slight drag. Some calipers require calibration. Always refer to the manufacturer's instructions when using a new or unfamiliar caliper.

To read a vernier caliper refer to **Figure 27**. The fixed scale is marked in 1 mm increments. Ten individual lines on the fixed scale equal 1 cm. The moveable scale is marked in 0.05 mm (hundredth) increments. To obtain a reading, establish the first number by the location of the 0 line on the movable scale in relation to the first line to the left on the fixed scale. In this example, the number is 10 mm. To determine the next number, note which of the lines on the movable scale align with a mark on the fixed scale. A number of lines will seem close, but only one will align exactly. In this case, 0.50 mm is the reading to add to the first number. The result of adding 10 mm and 0.50 mm is a measurement of 10.50 mm.

Micrometers

A micrometer is an instrument designed for linear measurement using the decimal divisions of the inch or meter (**Figure 28**). While there are many types and styles of micrometers, most of the procedures in this manual call for an outside micrometer. The outside micrometer is used to measure the outside diameter of cylindrical forms and the thickness of materials.

A micrometer's size indicates the minimum and maximum size of a part that it can measure. The usual sizes (**Figure 29**) are 0-1 in. (0-25 mm), 1-2 in. (25-50 mm), 2-3 in. (50-75 mm) and 3-4 in. (75-100 mm).

Micrometers that cover a wider range of measurements are available. These use a large frame with interchangeable anvils of various lengths. This type of micrometer offers a cost savings; however, its overall size may make it less convenient.

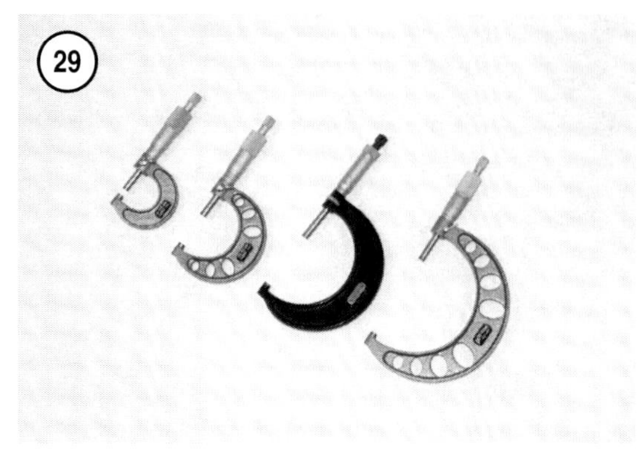

29

Reading a Micrometer

When reading a micrometer, numbers are taken from different scales and added together. The following sections describe how to read the measurements of various types of outside micrometers.

For accurate results, properly maintain the measuring surfaces of the micrometer. There cannot be any dirt or burrs between the tool and the measured object. Never force the micrometer closed around an object. Close the micrometer around the highest point so it can be removed with a slight drag. **Figure 30** shows the markings and parts of a standard inch micrometer. Be familiar with these terms before using a micrometer in the follow sections.

Standard inch micrometer

The standard inch micrometer is accurate to one-thousandth of an inch or 0.001. The sleeve is marked in 0.025 in. increments. Every fourth sleeve mark is numbered 1, 2, 3, 4, 5, 6, 7, 8, 9. These numbers indicate 0.100, 0.200, 0.300, and so on.

The tapered end of the thimble has twenty-five lines marked around it. Each mark equals 0.001 in. One complete turn of the thimble will align its zero mark with the first mark on the sleeve or 0.025 in.

When reading a standard inch micrometer, perform the following steps while referring to **Figure 31**.

1. Read the sleeve and find the largest number visible. Each sleeve number equals 0.100 in.

2. Count the number of lines between the numbered sleeve mark and the edge of the thimble. Each sleeve mark equals 0.025 in.

3. Read the thimble mark that aligns with the sleeve line. Each thimble mark equals 0.001 in.

NOTE

If a thimble mark does not align exactly with the sleeve line, estimate the amount between the lines. For accurate readings in ten-thousandths of an inch (0.0001 in.), use a vernier inch micrometer.

4. Add the readings from Steps 1-3.

Vernier inch micrometer

A vernier inch micrometer is accurate to one ten-thousandth of an inch or 0.0001 in. It has the same marking as a standard inch micrometer with an additional vernier scale on the sleeve (**Figure 32**).

The vernier scale consists of 11 lines marked 1-9 with a 0 on each end. These lines run parallel to the thimble lines and represent 0.0001 in. increments.

When reading a vernier inch micrometer, perform the following steps while referring to **Figure 32**.

1. Read the micrometer in the same way as a standard micrometer. This is the initial reading.

2. If a thimble mark aligns exactly with the sleeve line, reading the vernier scale is not necessary. If they do not align, read the vernier scale in Step 3.

3. Determine which vernier scale mark aligns with one thimble mark. The vernier scale number is the amount in ten-thousandths of an inch to add to the initial reading from Step 1.

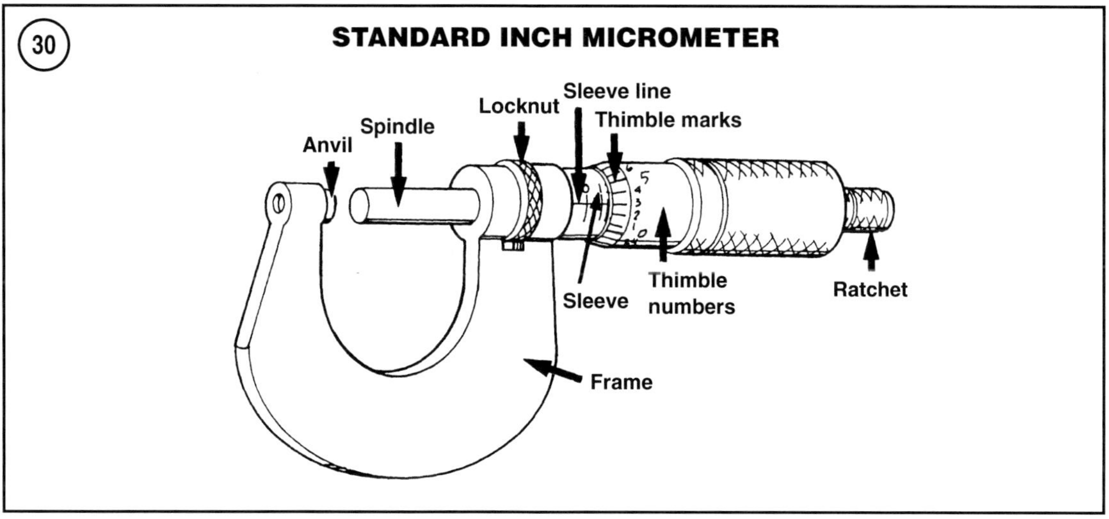

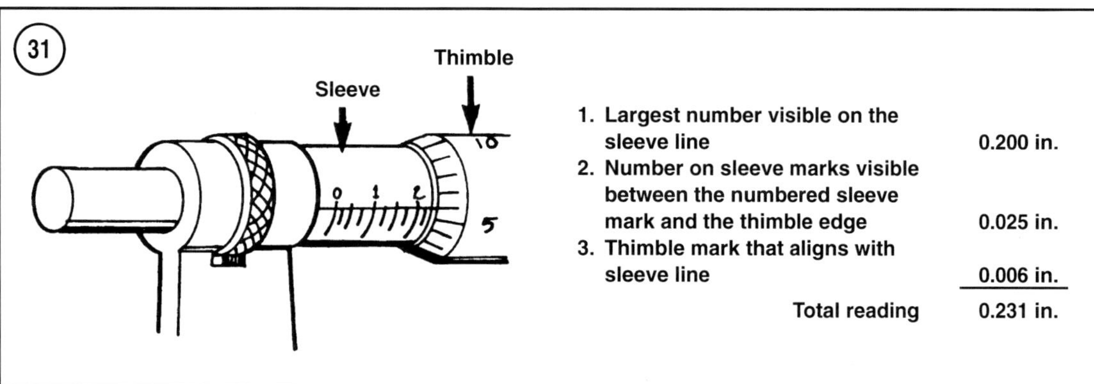

1. Largest number visible on the sleeve line	0.200 in.
2. Number on sleeve marks visible between the numbered sleeve mark and the thimble edge	0.025 in.
3. Thimble mark that aligns with sleeve line	0.006 in.
Total reading	0.231 in.

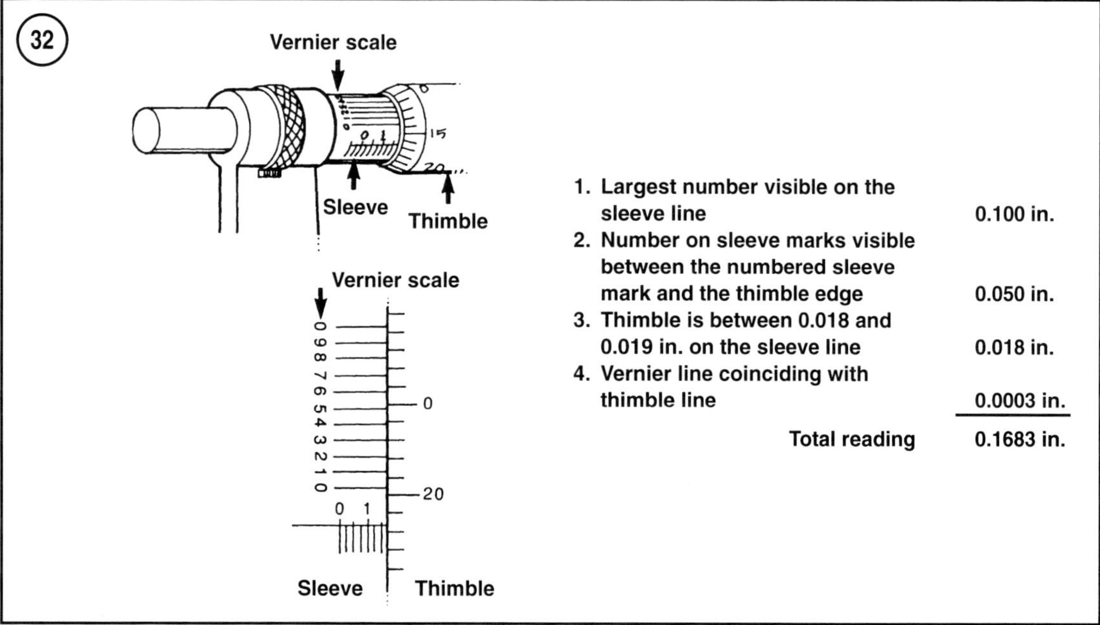

1. Largest number visible on the sleeve line	0.100 in.
2. Number on sleeve marks visible between the numbered sleeve mark and the thimble edge	0.050 in.
3. Thimble is between 0.018 and 0.019 in. on the sleeve line	0.018 in.
4. Vernier line coinciding with thimble line	0.0003 in.
Total reading	0.1683 in.

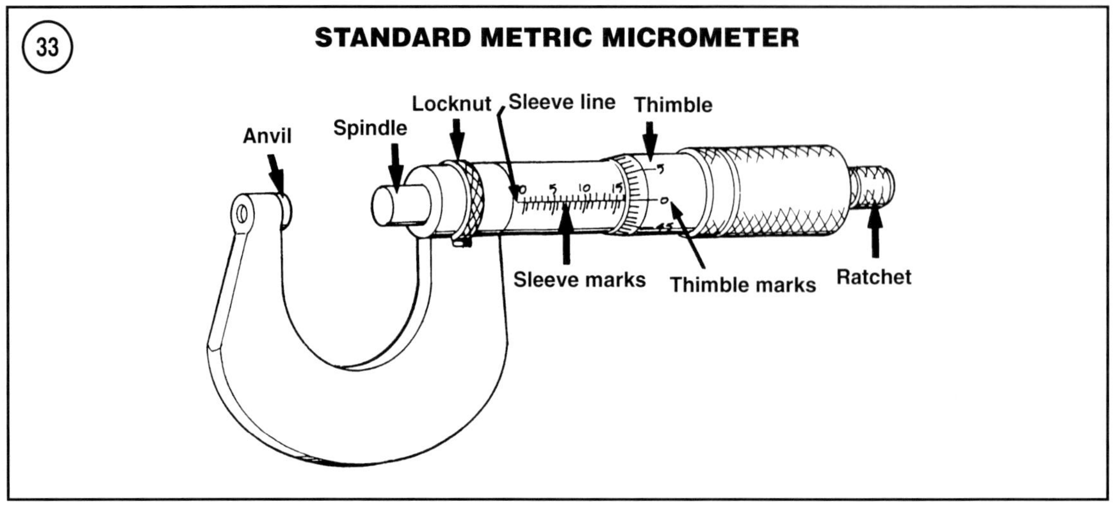

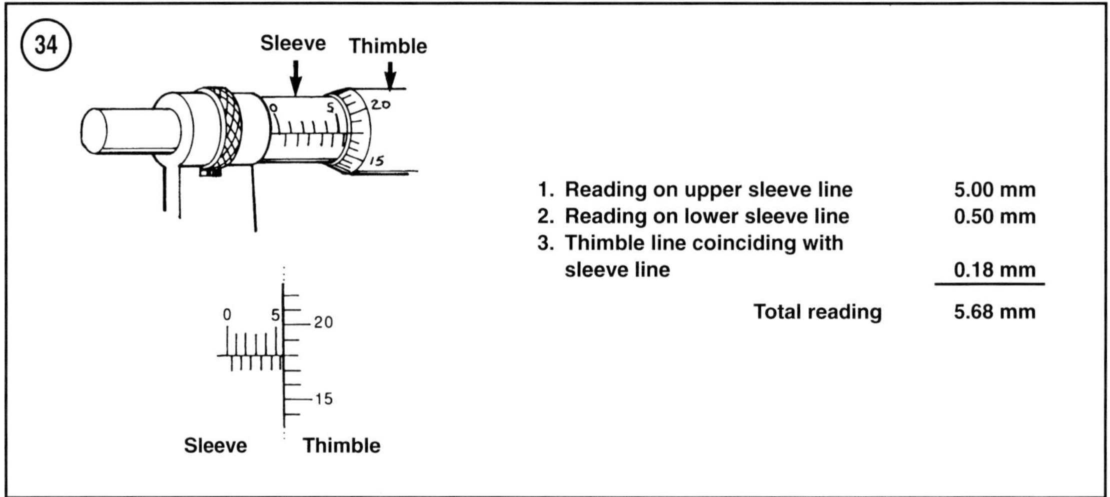

Metric micrometer

The standard metric micrometer (**Figure 33**) is accurate to one one-hundredth of a millimeter (0.01-mm). The sleeve line is graduated in millimeter and half millimeter increments. The marks on the upper half of the sleeve line equal 1.00 mm. Every fifth mark above the sleeve line is identified with a number. The number sequence depends on the size of the micrometer. A 0-25 mm micrometer, for example, will have sleeve marks numbered 0 through 25 in 5 mm increments. This numbering sequence continues with larger micrometers. On all metric micrometers, each mark on the lower half of the sleeve equals 0.50 mm.

The tapered end of the thimble has fifty lines marked around it. Each mark equals 0.01 mm. One complete turn of the thimble aligns its 0 mark with the first line on the lower half of the sleeve line or 0.50 mm.

When reading a metric micrometer, add the number of millimeters and half-millimeters on the sleeve line to the number of one one-hundredth millimeters on the thimble. Perform the following steps while referring to **Figure 34**.

1. Read the upper half of the sleeve line and count the number of lines visible. Each upper line equals 1 mm.

2. See if the half-millimeter line is visible on the lower sleeve line. If so, add 0.50 mm to the reading in Step 1.

3. Read the thimble mark that aligns with the sleeve line. Each thimble mark equals 0.01 mm.

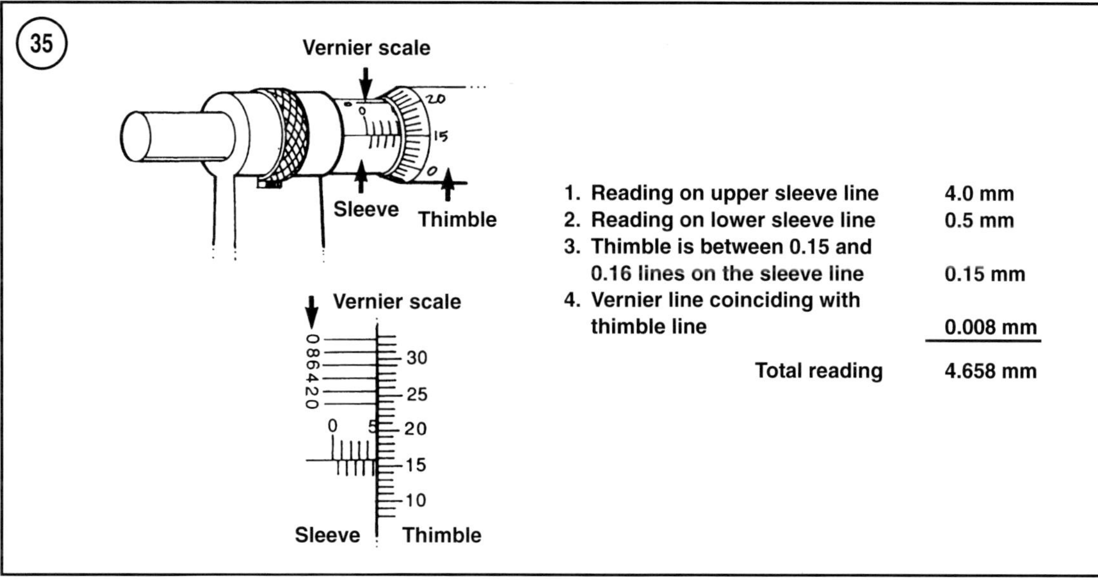

NOTE

If a thimble mark does not align exactly with the sleeve line, estimate the amount between the lines. For accurate readings in two-thousandths of a millimeter (0.002 mm), use a metric vernier micrometer.

4. Add the readings from Steps 1-3.

Metric vernier micrometer

A metric vernier micrometer is accurate to two-thousandths of a millimeter (0.002 mm). It has the same markings as a standard metric micrometer with the addition of a vernier scale on the sleeve. The vernier scale consists of five lines marked 0, 2, 4, 6, and 8. These lines run parallel to the thimble lines and represent 0.002 mm increments.

When reading a metric vernier micrometer, refer to **Figure 35** and perform the following steps.

1. Read the micrometer in the same way as a standard metric micrometer. This is the initial reading.

2. If a thimble mark aligns exactly with the sleeve line, reading the vernier scale is not necessary. If they do not align, read the vernier scale in Step 3.

3. Determine which vernier scale mark aligns exactly with one thimble mark. The vernier scale number is the amount in two-thousandths of a millimeter to add to the initial reading from Step 1.

Micrometer Adjustment

Before using a micrometer, check its adjustment as follows.

1. Clean the anvil and spindle faces.

2A. To check a 0-1 in. or 0-25 mm micrometer:

a. Turn the thimble until the spindle contacts the anvil. If the micrometer has a ratchet stop, use it to ensure that the proper amount of pressure is applied.

b. If the adjustment is correct, the 0 mark on the thimble will align exactly with the 0 mark on the sleeve line. If the marks do not align, the micrometer is out of adjustment.

c. Follow the manufacturer's instructions to adjust the micrometer.

2B. To check a micrometer larger than 1 in. or 25 mm use the standard gauge supplied by the manufacturer. A standard gauge is a steel block, disc or rod that is machined to an exact size.

a. Place the standard gauge between the spindle and anvil, and measure its outside diameter or length. If the micrometer has a ratchet stop, use it to ensure that the proper amount of pressure is applied.

b. If the adjustment is correct, the 0 mark on the thimble will align exactly with the 0 mark on the sleeve line. If the marks do not align, the micrometer is out of adjustment.

c. Follow the manufacturer's instructions to adjust the micrometer.

Micrometer Care

Micrometers are precision instruments. They must be used and maintained with great care. Note the following:

1. Store micrometers in protective cases or separate padded drawers in a toolbox.
2. When in storage, make sure the spindle and anvil faces do not contact each other or another object. If they do, temperature changes and corrosion may damage the contact faces.
3. Do not clean a micrometer with compressed air. Dirt forced into the tool will cause wear.
4. Lubricate micrometers with WD-40 to prevent corrosion.

Telescoping and Small Bore Gauges

Use telescoping gauges (**Figure 36**) and small hole gauges (**Figure 37**) to measure bores. Neither gauge has a scale for direct readings. An outside micrometer must be used to determine the reading.

To use a telescoping gauge, select the correct size gauge for the bore. Compress the movable post and carefully insert the gauge into the bore. Carefully move the gauge in the bore to make sure it is centered. Tighten the knurled end of the gauge to hold the movable post in position. Remove the gauge and measure the length of the posts. Telescoping gauges are typically used to measure cylinder bores.

To use a small-bore gauge, select the correct size gauge for the bore. Carefully insert the gauge into the bore. Tighten the knurled end of the gauge to carefully expand the gauge fingers to the limit within the bore. Do not overtighten the gauge, as there is no built-in release. Excessive tightening can damage the bore surface and damage the tool. Remove the gauge and measure the outside dimension (**Figure 38**). Small hole gauges are typically used to measure valve guides.

Dial Indicator

A dial indicator (A, **Figure 39**) is a gauge with a dial face and needle used to measure variations in dimensions and movements. Measuring brake rotor runout is a typical use for a dial indicator.

Dial indicators are available in various ranges and graduations and with three basic types of mounting bases: magnetic, clamp, or screw-in stud. When

36

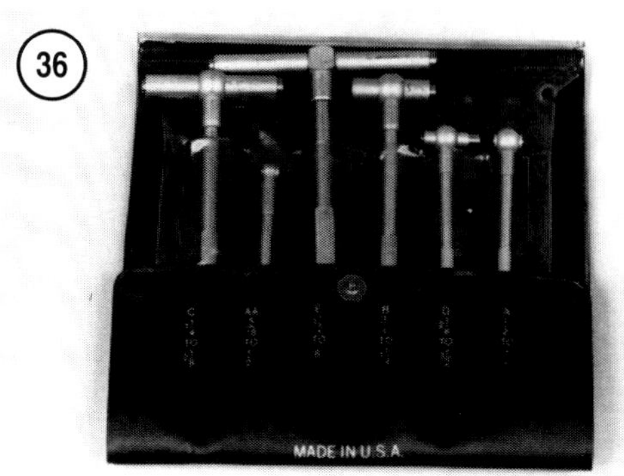

37

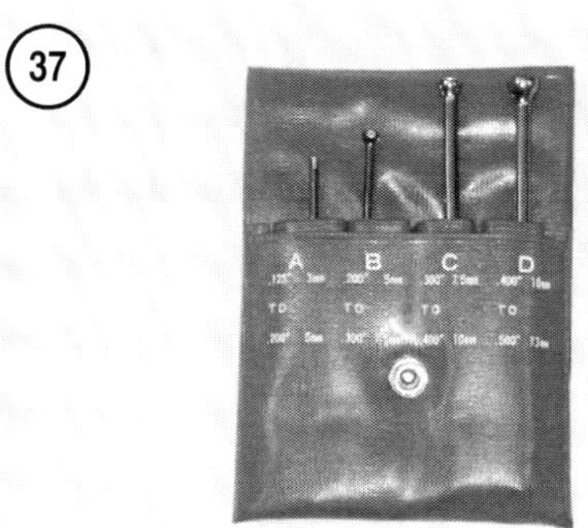

38

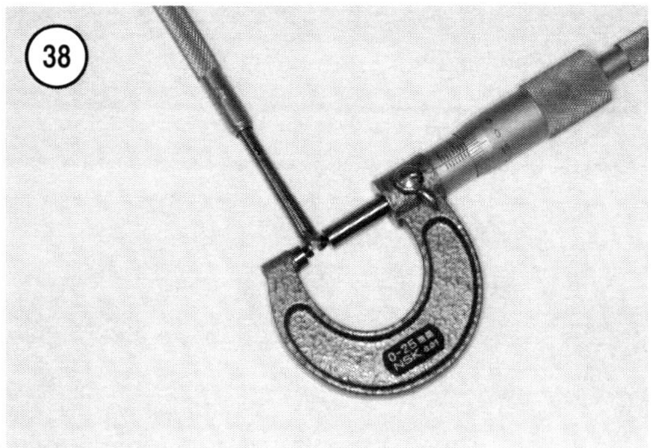

39

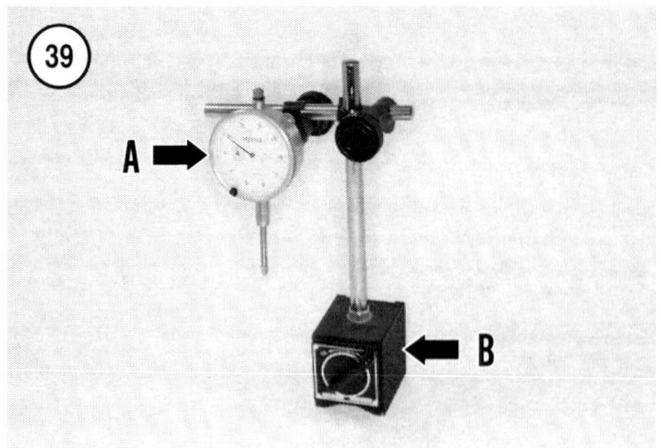

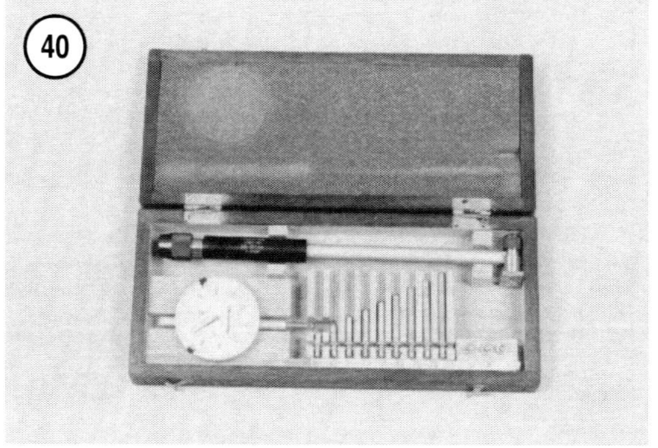

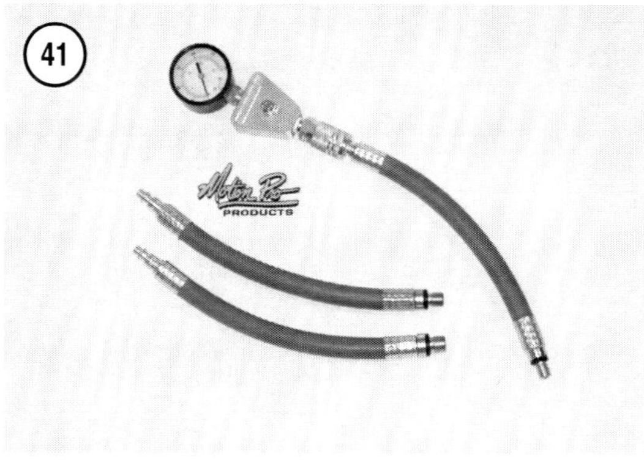

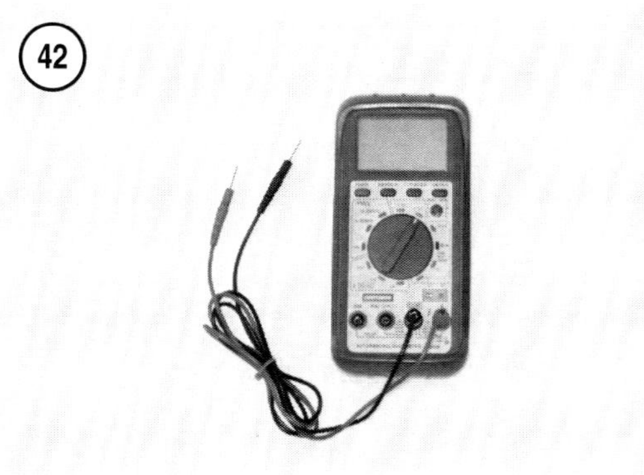

purchasing a dial indicator, select the magnetic stand type (B, **Figure 39**) with a continuous dial.

Cylinder Bore Gauge

A cylinder bore gauge is similar to a dial indicator. The gauge set shown in **Figure 40** consists of a dial indicator, handle and different length adapters (anvils) to fit the gauge to various bore sizes. The bore gauge is used to measure bore size, taper and out-of-round. When using a bore gauge, follow the manufacturer's instructions.

Compression Gauge

A compression gauge (**Figure 41**) measures combustion chamber (cylinder) pressure, usually in psi or kg/cm^2. The gauge adapter is either inserted or screwed into the spark plug hole to obtain the reading. Disable the engine so it will not start and hold the throttle in the wide-open position when performing a compression test. An engine that does not have adequate compression cannot be properly tuned. See Chapter Three.

Multimeter

A multimeter (**Figure 42**) is an essential tool for electrical system diagnosis. The voltage function indicates the voltage applied or available to various electrical components. The ohmmeter function tests circuits for continuity, or lack of continuity, and measures the resistance of a circuit.

Some manufacturers' specifications for electrical components are based on results using a specific test meter. Results may vary if using a meter not recommend by the manufacturer is used. Such requirements are noted when applicable.

Ohmmeter (analog) calibration

Each time an analog ohmmeter is used or if the scale is changed, the ohmmeter must be calibrated. Digital ohmmeters do not require calibration.

1. Make sure the meter battery is in good condition.
2. Make sure the meter probes are in good condition.
3. Touch the two probes together and observe the needle location on the ohms scale. The needle must align with the 0 mark to obtain accurate measurements.
4. If necessary, rotate the meter ohms adjust knob until the needle and 0 mark align.

ELECTRICAL SYSTEM FUNDAMENTALS

A thorough study of the many types of electrical systems used in today's motorcycles is beyond the scope of this manual. However, a basic understanding of electrical basics is necessary to perform simple diagnostic tests.

Voltage

Voltage is the electrical potential or pressure in an electrical circuit and is expressed in volts. The more pressure (voltage) in a circuit, the more work that can be performed.

Direct current (DC) voltage means the electricity flows in one direction. All circuits powered by a battery are DC circuits.

Alternating current (AC) means that the electricity flows in one direction momentarily then switches to the opposite direction. Alternator output is an example of AC voltage. This voltage must be changed or rectified to direct current to operate in a battery powered system.

Measuring voltage

Unless otherwise specified, perform all voltage tests with the electrical connectors attached.

When measuring voltage, select the meter range that is one scale higher than the expected voltage of the circuit to prevent damage to the meter. To determine the actual voltage in a circuit, use a voltmeter. To simply check if voltage is present, use a test light.

NOTE
When using a test light, either lead can be attached to ground.

1. Attach the negative meter test lead to a good ground (bare metal). Make sure the ground is not insulated with a rubber gasket or grommet.
2. Attach the positive meter test lead to the point being checked for voltage (**Figure 43**).
3. Turn on the ignition switch. The test light should light or the meter should display a reading. The reading should be within one volt of battery voltage. If the voltage is less, there is a problem in the circuit.

Voltage drop test

Resistance causes voltage to drop. This resistance can be measured in an active circuit by using a voltmeter to perform a voltage drop test. A voltage drop

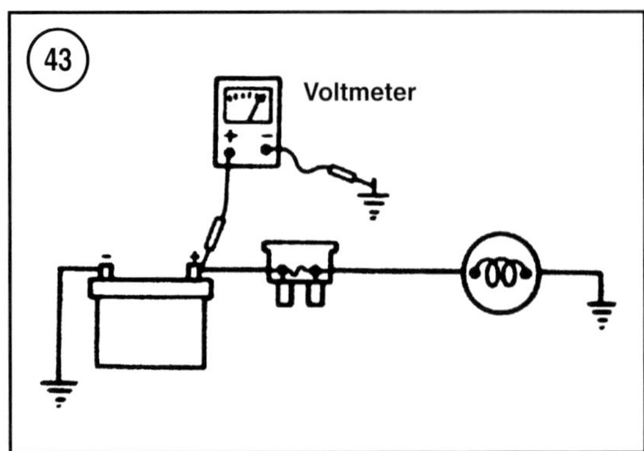

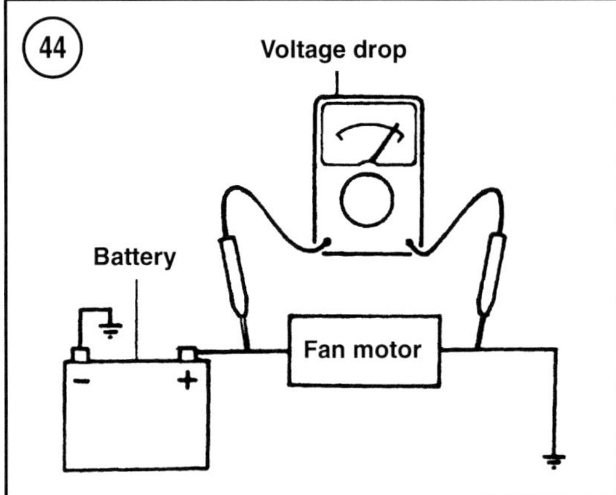

test compares the difference between the voltage available at the start of a circuit to the voltage at the end of the circuit while the circuit is operational. If the circuit has no resistance, there will be no voltage drop. The greater the resistance, the greater the voltage drop will be. A voltage drop of one volt or more indicates excessive resistance in the circuit.

1. Connect the positive meter test lead to the electrical source (where electricity is coming from).
2. Connect the negative meter test lead to the electrical load (where electricity is going). See **Figure 44**.
3. If necessary, activate the component(s) in the circuit.
4. A voltage reading of 1 volt or more indicates excessive resistance in the circuit. A reading equal to battery voltage indicates an open circuit.

Resistance

Resistance is the opposition to the flow of electricity within a circuit or component and is mea-

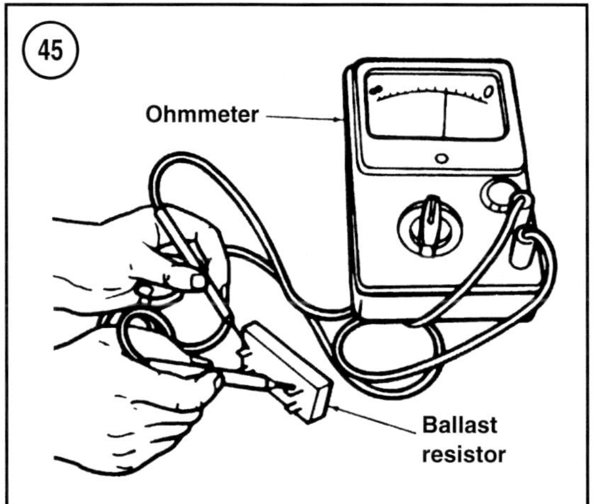

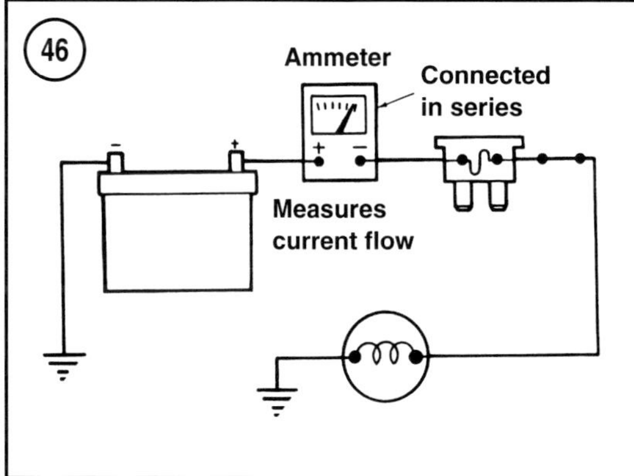

sured in ohms. Resistance causes a reduction in available current and voltage.

Resistance is measured in a inactive circuit with an ohmmeter. The ohmmeter sends a small amount of current into the circuit and measures how difficult it is to push the current through the circuit.

An ohmmeter, although useful, is not always a good indicator of a circuit's actual ability under operating conditions. This is due to the low voltage (6-9 volts) that the meter uses to test the circuit. The voltage in an ignition coil secondary winding can be several thousand volts. Such high voltage can cause the coil to malfunction, even though it tests acceptable during a resistance test.

Resistance generally increases with temperature. Perform all testing with the component or circuit at room temperature. Resistance tests performed at high temperatures may indicate high resistance readings and result in the unnecessary replacement of a component.

Measuring resistance and continuity testing

CAUTION

*Only use an ohmmeter on a circuit that has no voltage present. The meter will be damaged if it is connected to a live circuit. An analog meter must be calibrated each time it is used or the scale is changed. See **Multimeter** in this chapter.*

A continuity test can determine if the circuit is complete. This type of test is performed with an ohmmeter or a self-powered test lamp.

1. Disconnect the negative battery cable.
2. Attach one test lead (ohmmeter or test light) to one end of the component or circuit.
3. Attach the other test lead to the opposite end of the component or circuit (**Figure 45**).
4. A self-powered test light will come on if the circuit has continuity or is complete. An ohmmeter will indicate either low or no resistance if the circuit has continuity. An open circuit is indicated if the meter displays infinite resistance.

Amperage

Amperage is the unit of measure for the amount of current within a circuit. Current is the actual flow of electricity. The higher the current, the more work that can be performed up to a given point. If the current flow exceeds the circuit or component capacity, the system will be damaged.

Measuring amps

An ammeter measures the current flow or amps of a circuit (**Figure 46**). Amperage measurement requires that the circuit be disconnected and the ammeter be connected in series to the circuit. Always use an ammeter that can read higher than the anticipated current flow to prevent damage to the meter. Connect the positive test lead to the electrical source and the negative test lead to the electrical load.

SPECIAL TOOLS

Some of the procedures in this manual require special tools. These are described in the appropriate chapter and are available from either the manufacturer or a tool supplier.

In many cases, an acceptable substitute may be found in an existing tool kit. Another alternative is to make the tool. Many schools with a machine shop curriculum welcome outside work that can be used as practical shop applications for students.

BASIC SERVICE METHODS

Most of the procedures in this manual are straightforward and can be performed by anyone reasonably competent with tools. However, consider personal capabilities carefully before attempting any operation involving major disassembly of the engine.

1. Front, in this manual, refers to the front of the motorcycle. The front of any component is the end closest to the front of the motorcycle. The left and right sides refer to the position of the parts as viewed by the rider sitting on the seat facing forward.
2. Whenever servicing an engine or suspension component, secure the motorcycle in a safe manner.
3. Tag all similar parts for location and mark all mating parts for position. Record the number and thickness of any shims as they are removed. Identify parts by placing them in sealed and labeled plastic sandwich bags.
4. Tag disconnected wires and connectors with masking tape and a marking pen. Do not rely on memory alone.
5. Protect finished surfaces from physical damage or corrosion. Keep gasoline and other chemicals off painted surfaces.
6. Use penetrating oil on frozen or tight bolts. Avoid using heat where possible. Heat can warp, melt or affect the temper of parts. Heat also damages the finish of paint and plastics.
7. When a part is a press fit or requires a special tool for removal, the information or type of tool is identified in the text. Otherwise, if a part is difficult to remove or install, determine the cause before proceeding.
8. To prevent objects or debris from falling into the engine, cover all openings.
9. Read each procedure thoroughly and compare the illustrations to the actual components before starting the procedure. Perform the procedure in sequence.
10. Recommendations are occasionally made to refer service to a dealership or specialist. In these cases, the work can be performed more economically by the specialist than by the home mechanic.

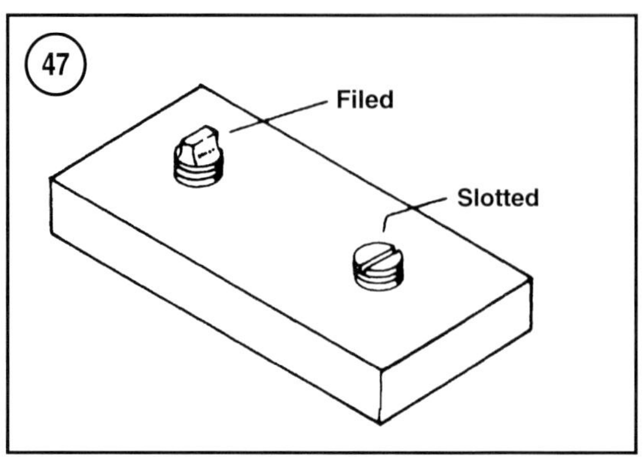

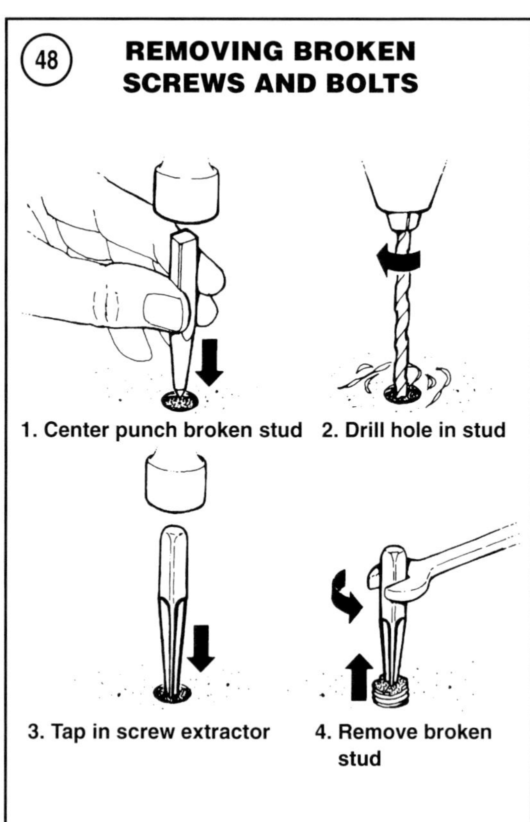

11. The term *replace* means to discard a defective part and replace it with a new part. *Overhaul* means to remove, disassemble, inspect, measure, repair and/or replace parts as required to recondition an assembly.
12. Some operations require the use of a hydraulic press. If a press is not available, have these operations performed by a shop equipped with the necessary equipment. Do not use makeshift equipment that may damage the motorcycle.
13. Repairs are much faster and easier if the motorcycle is clean before starting work. Degrease the

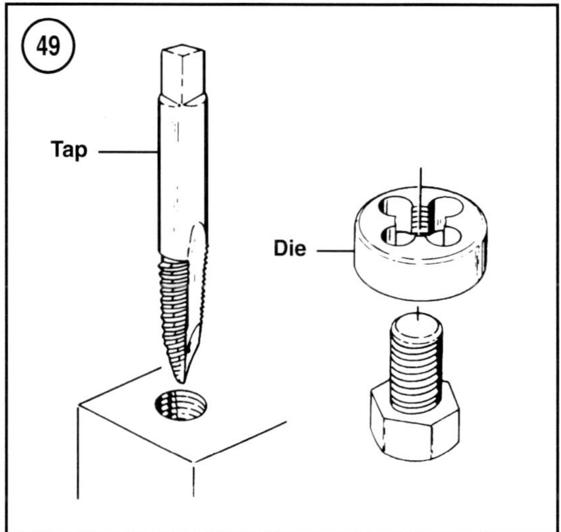

motorcycle with a commercial degreaser; follow the directions on the container for the best results. Clean all parts with cleaning solvent while removing them.

CAUTION
Do not apply a chemical degreaser to an O-ring chain. These chemicals damage the O-rings. Use kerosene to clean O-ring type chains.

CAUTION
Do not direct high-pressure water at steering bearings, carburetor hoses, wheel bearings, suspension and electrical components. The water will force the grease out of the bearings and possibly damage the seals.

14. If special tools are required, have them available before starting the procedure. When special tools are required, they will be described at the beginning of the procedure.
15. Make diagrams of similar-appearing parts. For instance, crankcase bolts are often not the same lengths. Do not rely on memory alone. It is possible that carefully laid out parts will become disturbed, making it difficult to reassemble the components correctly without a diagram.
16. Make sure all shims and washers are reinstalled in the same location and position.
17. Whenever rotating parts contact a stationary part, look for a shim or washer.
18. Use new gaskets if there is any doubt about the condition of old ones.
19. If self-locking fasteners are used, replace them with new ones. Do not install standard fasteners in place of self-locking ones.
20. Use grease to hold small parts in place if they tend to fall out during assembly. Do not apply grease to electrical or brake components.

Removing Frozen Fasteners

If a fastener cannot be removed, several methods may be used to loosen it. First, apply penetrating oil such as Liquid Wrench or WD-40. Apply it liberally and let it penetrate for 10-15 minutes. Rap the fastener several times with a small hammer. Do not hit it hard enough to cause damage. Reapply the penetrating oil if necessary.

For frozen screws, apply penetrating oil as described, then insert a screwdriver in the slot and rap the top of the screwdriver with a hammer. This loosens the rust so the screw can be removed in the normal way. If the screw head is too damaged to use this method, grip the head with locking pliers and twist the screw out.

Avoid applying heat unless specifically instructed, as it may melt, warp or remove the temper from parts.

Removing Broken Fasteners

If the head breaks off a screw or bolt, several methods are available for removing the remaining portion. If a large portion of the remainder projects out, try gripping it with locking pliers. If the projecting portion is too small, file it to fit a wrench or cut a slot in it to fit a screwdriver (**Figure 47**).

If the head breaks off flush, use a screw extractor. To do this, centerpunch the exact center of the remaining portion of the screw or bolt. Drill a small hole in the screw and tap the extractor into the hole. Back the screw out with a wrench on the extractor (**Figure 48**).

Repairing Damaged Threads

Occasionally, threads are stripped through carelessness or impact damage. Often the threads can be repaired by running a tap (for internal threads) or die (for external threads) through the threads (**Figure 49**). To clean or repair spark plug threads, use a spark plug tap.

If an internal thread is damaged, it may be necessary to install a Helicoil or some other type of thread insert. Follow the manufacturer's instructions when installing their insert.

If it is necessary to drill and tap a hole, refer to **Table 7** for metric tap and drill sizes.

Stud Removal/Installation

A stud removal tool is available from most tool suppliers. This tool makes the removal and installation of studs easier. If one is not available, thread two nuts onto the stud and tighten them against each other. Remove the stud by turning the lower nut (**Figure 50**).

1. Measure the height of the stud above the surface.
2. Thread the stud removal tool onto the stud and tighten it, or thread two nuts onto the stud.
3. Remove the stud by turning the stud remover or the lower nut.
4. Remove any threadlocking compound from the threaded hole. Clean the threads with an aerosol parts cleaner.
5. Install the stud removal tool onto the new stud or thread two nuts onto the stud.
6. Apply threadlocking compound to the threads of the stud.
7. Install the stud and tighten with the stud removal tool or the top nut.
8. Install the stud to the height noted in Step 1 or its torque specification.
9. Remove the stud removal tool or the two nuts.

Removing Hoses

When removing stubborn hoses, do not exert excessive force on the hose or fitting. Remove the hose clamp and carefully insert a small screwdriver or pick tool between the fitting and hose. Apply a spray lubricant under the hose and carefully twist the hose off the fitting. Clean the fitting of any corrosion or rubber hose material with a wire brush. Clean the inside of the hose thoroughly. Do not use any lubricant when installing the hose (new or old). The lubricant may allow the hose to come off the fitting, even with the clamp secure.

Bearings

Bearings are used in the engine and transmission assembly to reduce power loss, heat and noise resulting from friction. Because bearings are precision parts, they must be maintained by proper

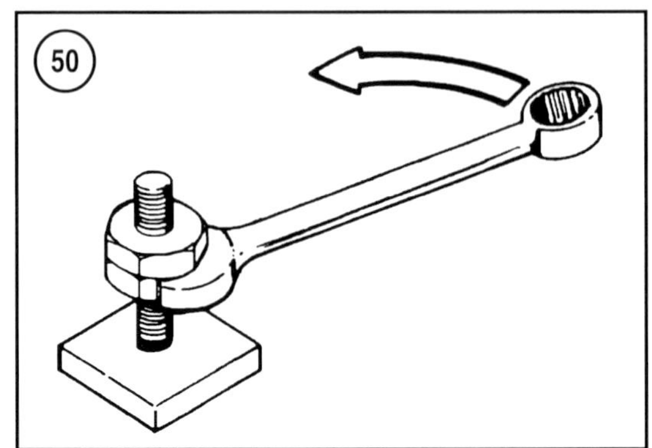

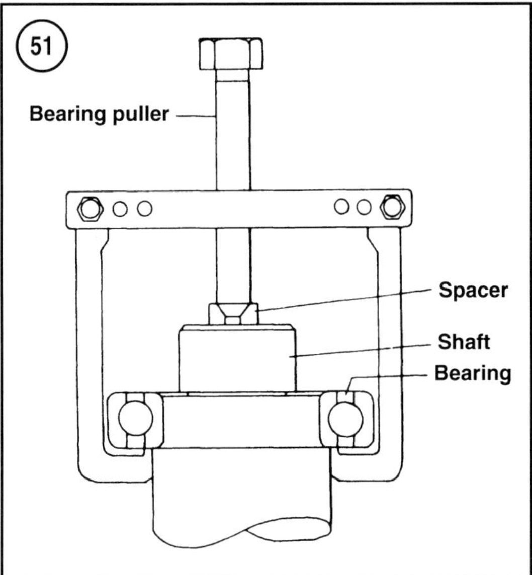

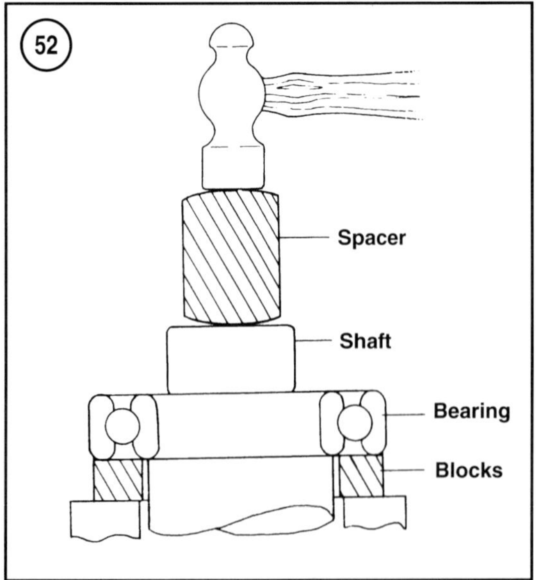

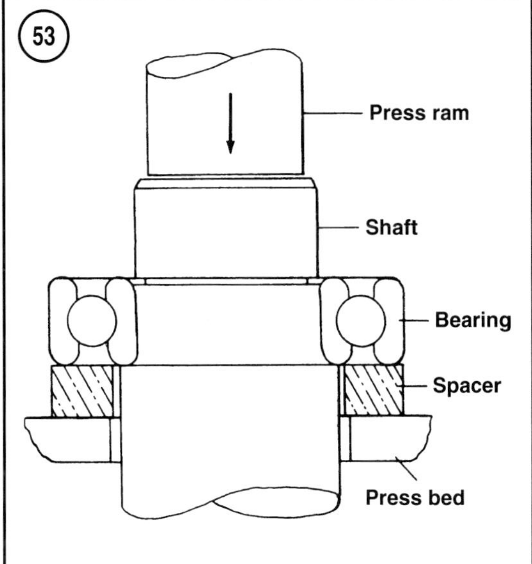

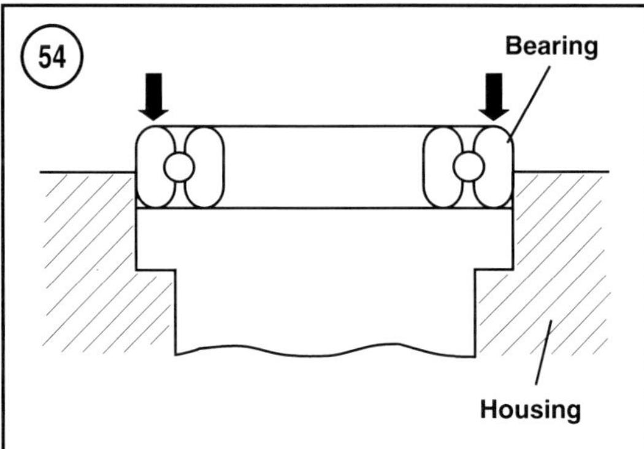

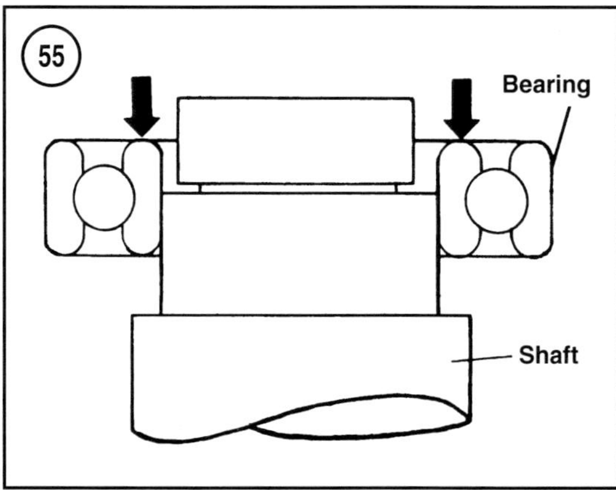

lubrication and maintenance. If a bearing is damaged, replace it immediately. When installing a new bearing, take care to prevent damaging it. Bearing replacement procedures are included in the individual chapters where applicable; however, use the following sections as a guideline.

NOTE
Unless otherwise specified, install bearings with the manufacturer's mark or number facing outward.

Removal

While bearings are normally removed only when damaged, there may be times when it is necessary to remove a bearing that is in good condition. However, improper bearing removal will damage the bearing and may damage the shaft or case half. Note the following when removing bearings.

1. When using a puller to remove a bearing from a shaft, take care that the shaft is not damaged. Always place a piece of metal between the end of the shaft and the puller screw. In addition, place the puller arms next to the inner bearing race. See **Figure 51**.
2. When using a hammer to remove a bearing from a shaft, do not strike the hammer directly against the shaft. Instead, use a brass or aluminum rod between the hammer and shaft (**Figure 52**) and make sure to support both bearing races with wooden blocks as shown.
3. The ideal method of bearing removal is with a hydraulic press. Note the following when using a press:
   a. Always support the inner and outer bearing races with a suitable size wooden or aluminum spacer ring (**Figure 53**). If only the outer race is supported, pressure applied against the balls and/or the inner race will damage them.
   b. Always make sure the press ram (**Figure 53**) aligns with the center of the shaft. If the ram is not centered, it may damage the bearing and/or shaft.
   c. The moment the shaft is free of the bearing, it will drop to the floor. Secure or hold the shaft to prevent it from falling.

Installation

1. When installing a bearing in a housing, apply pressure to the *outer* bearing race (**Figure 54**). When installing a bearing on a shaft, apply pressure to the *inner* bearing race (**Figure 55**).
2. When installing a bearing as described in Step 1, some type of driver is required. Never strike the bearing directly with a hammer or the bearing will

be damaged. When installing a bearing, use a piece of pipe or a driver with a diameter that matches the bearing inner race. **Figure 56** shows the correct way to use a driver and hammer to install a bearing.

3. Step 1 describes how to install a bearing in a case half or over a shaft. However, when installing a bearing over a shaft and into a housing at the same time, a tight fit will be required for both outer and inner bearing races. In this situation, install a spacer underneath the driver tool so that pressure is applied evenly across both races. See **Figure 57**. If the outer race is not supported as shown, the balls will push against the outer bearing race and damage it.

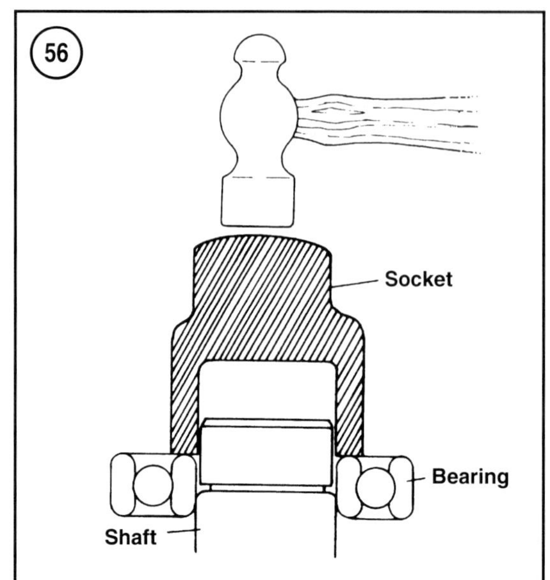

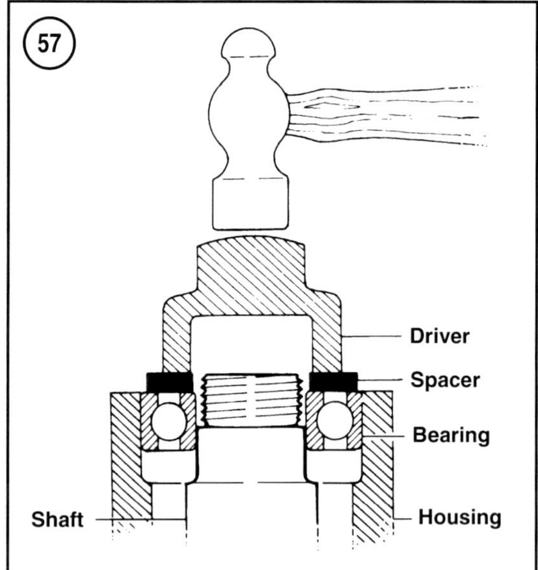

Interference fit

1. Follow this procedure when installing a bearing over a shaft. When a tight fit is required, the bearing inside diameter will be smaller than the shaft. In this case, driving the bearing on the shaft using normal methods may cause bearing damage. Instead, heat the bearing before installation. Note the following:

   a. Secure the shaft so it is ready for bearing installation.
   b. Clean all residues from the bearing surface of the shaft. Remove burrs with a file or sandpaper.
   c. Fill a suitable pot or beaker with clean mineral oil. Place a thermometer rated above 120° C (248° F) in the oil. Support the thermometer so that it does not rest on the bottom or side of the pot.
   d. Remove the bearing from its wrapper and secure it with a piece of heavy wire bent to hold it in the pot. Hang the bearing in the pot so it does not touch the bottom or sides of the pot.
   e. Turn the heat on and monitor the thermometer. When the oil temperature rises to approximately 120° C (248° F), remove the bearing from the pot and quickly install it. If necessary, place a socket on the inner bearing race and tap the bearing into place. As the bearing chills, it will tighten on the shaft, so installation must be done quickly. Make sure the bearing is installed completely.

2. Follow this step when installing a bearing in a housing. Bearings are generally installed in a housing with a slight interference fit. Driving the bearing into the housing using normal methods may damage

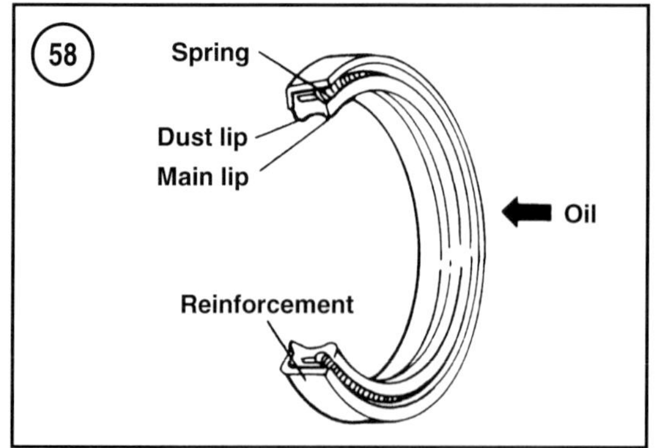

the housing or cause bearing damage. Instead, heat the housing before the bearing is installed. Note the following:

CAUTION

Before heating the housing in this procedure, wash the housing thoroughly with detergent and water. Rinse and rewash the cases as required to remove all traces of oil and other chemical deposits.

a. Heat the housing to approximately 100° C (212° F) in an oven or on a hot plate. An easy way to check that it is the proper temperature is to place tiny drops of water on the housing; if they sizzle and evaporate immediately, the temperature is correct. Heat only one housing at a time.

CAUTION

Do not heat the housing with a propane or acetylene torch. Never bring a flame into contact with the bearing or housing. The direct heat will destroy the case hardening of the bearing and will likely warp the housing.

b. Remove the housing from the oven or hot plate, and hold onto the housing with a kitchen potholder, heavy gloves or heavy shop cloth. It is hot!

NOTE

Remove and install the bearings with a suitable size socket and extension.

c. Hold the housing with the bearing side down and tap the bearing out. Repeat for all bearings in the housing.
d. Before heating the bearing housing, place the new bearing in a freezer if possible. Chilling a bearing slightly reduces its outside diameter while the heated bearing housing assembly is slightly larger due to heat expansion. This will make bearing installation easier.

NOTE

Always install bearings with the manufacturer's mark or number facing outward.

e. While the housing is still hot, install the new bearing(s) into the housing. Install the bearings by hand, if possible. If necessary, lightly tap the bearing(s) into the housing with a socket placed on the outer bearing race (**Figure 54**). Do not install new bearings by driving on the inner-bearing race. Install the bearing(s) until it seats completely.

Seal Replacement

Seals (**Figure 58**) are used to contain oil, water, grease or combustion gasses in a housing or shaft. Improper removal of a seal can damage the housing or shaft. Improper installation of the seal can damage the seal. Note the following:

1. Prying is generally the easiest and most effective method of removing a seal from a housing. However, always place a rag underneath the pry tool (**Figure 59**) to prevent damage to the housing.
2. Pack waterproof grease in the seal lips before the seal is installed.
3. In most cases, install seals with the manufacturer's numbers or marks face out.
4. Install seals with a socket placed on the outside of the seal as shown in **Figure 60**. Drive the seal squarely into the housing. Never install a seal by hitting against the top of the seal with a hammer.

STORAGE

Several months of non-use can cause a general deterioration of the motorcycle. This is especially true in areas of extreme temperature variations. This deterioration can be minimized with careful preparation for storage. A properly stored motorcycle will be much easier to return to service.

Storage Area Selection

When selecting a storage area, consider the following:

1. The storage area must be dry. A heated area is best, but not necessary. It should be insulated to minimize extreme temperature variations.
2. If the building has large window areas, mask them to keep sunlight off the motorcycle.
3. Avoid buildings in industrial areas where corrosive emissions may be present. Avoid areas close to saltwater.
4. Consider the area's risk of fire, theft or vandalism. Check with an insurer regarding coverage while in storage.

Preparing the Motorcycle for Storage

The amount of preparation a motorcycle should undergo before storage depends on the expected length of non-use, storage area conditions and personal preference. Consider the following list the minimum requirement:

1. Wash the motorcycle thoroughly. Make sure all dirt, mud and road debris are removed.
2. Start the engine and allow it to reach operating temperature. Drain the engine oil regardless of the riding time since the last service. Fill the engine with the recommended type of oil.
3. Drain all fuel from the fuel tank, and run the engine until all the fuel is consumed from the lines and carburetors.
4. Remove the spark plugs and pour a teaspoon of engine oil into the cylinder. Place a rag over the openings and slowly turn the engine over to distribute the oil. Reinstall the spark plugs.
5. Remove the battery. Store the battery in a cool and dry location.
6. Cover the exhaust and intake openings.
7. Reduce the normal tire pressure by 20%.
8. Apply a protective substance to the plastic and rubber components, including the tires. Make sure to follow the manufacturer's instructions for each type of product being used.
9. Place the motorcycle on a stand or wooden blocks so the wheels are off the ground. If this is not possible, place a piece of plywood between the tires and the ground. Inflate the tires to the recommended pressure if the motorcycle can not be elevated.
10. Cover the motorcycle with old bed sheets or a similar cover. Do not cover it with any plastic material that will trap moisture.

Returning the Motorcycle to Service

The amount of service required when returning a motorcycle to service after storage depends on the length of non-use and storage conditions. In addition to performing the reverse of the above procedure, make sure the brakes, clutch, throttle and engine stop switch work properly before operating the motorcycle. Refer to Chapter Three and evaluate the service intervals to determine which areas require service.

Table 1 FRAME SERIAL NUMBERS

Model	Frame number
1996 models	
GSF1200T, GSF1200ST	
U.K.	JS1GV75A 000500001-on
1997 models	
GSF1200SV, GSF1200SAV	
U.S.A, California and Canada	JS1GV5A V2100001-on
GSF1200V, GSF1200SV, GSF1200SAV	
U.K.	JS1GV75A 000510752-on

(continued)

Table 1 FRAME SERIAL NUMBERS (continued)

Model	Frame number
1998 models	
GSF1200SW	
U.S.A, California and Canada	JS1GV5A W2100001-on
GSF1200W, GSF1200SW, GSF1200SAW	
U.K.	JS1GV75A 000523033-on
1999 models	
GSF1200SX	
U.S.A, California and Canada	JS1GV5A X2100001-on
GSF1200X, GSF1200SX, GSF1200SAX	
U.K.	JS1GV75A 000533931-on
2000 models	
GSF1200SY	
U.S.A, California and Canada	JS1GV5A Y2100001-on
GSF1200Y, GSF1200SY, GSF1200SAY	
U.K.	JS1GV75A 000547330-on
2001-on models	
GSF1200K1, GSF1200SK1	
U.S.A, California and Canada	JS1GV77A 12100001-on
SF1200K1	
England	JS1A911220010001-on
European markets	JS1A911210010001-on
SF1200SK1	
England	JS1A911120010001-on
European markets	JS1A911110010001-on
Australia	JS1A911130010001-on

Table 2 MOTORCYCLE DIMENSIONS

1996-2000 models (Non-ABS)	
Overall length	
Finland, Norway, Sweden and Germany models	2165 mm (85.2 in.)
Switzerland, Austria	2180 mm (85.8 in.)
All models except Finland, Norway, Sweden, Germany, Switzerland and Austria	2095 mm (82.5 in.)
1997-2000 models (ABS equipped)	
Overall length	
Sweden and Germany models;	2175 mm (85.6 in.)
Switzerland	2235 mm (88.0 in.)
All models except Sweden, Germany and Switzerland	2105 mm (82.9 in.)
Overall width	790 mm (31.1 in.)
Overall height	
1996-2000 GSF1200	1100 mm (43.3 in.)
1996-2000 GSF1200S	1205 mm (47.4 in.)
Seat height	835 mm (32.9 in.)
Wheelbase	
Non ABS	1435 mm (56.5 in.)
ABS equipped	1465 (57.7 in.)
Ground clearance	130 mm (5.1 in.)
2001-on models	
Overall length	2070 mm (81.5 in.)
Overall width	765 mm (30.1 in.)
Overall height	1220 mm (48.0 in.)
Seat height	790 mm (31.1 in.)
Wheelbase	1430 mm (56.3 in.)
Ground clearance	130 mm (5.1 in.)

Table 3 MOTORCYCLE WEIGHT

Dry mass	
Non ABS	
1996-2000 GSF1200	211 kg (465 lb.)
1996-2000 GSF1200S	214 kg (471 lb.)
ABS equipped	
1997 California	224 kg (493 lb.)
1997-2000 all models except California	221 kg. (487 lb.)
2001-on	220 kg (485 lb.)

Table 4 CONVERSION FORMULAS

Multiply:	By:	To get the equivalent of:
Length		
Inches	25.4	Millimeter
Inches	2.54	Centimeter
Miles	1.609	Kilometer
Feet	0.3048	Meter
Millimeter	0.03937	Inches
Centimeter	0.3937	Inches
Kilometer	0.6214	Mile
Meter	3.281	Mile
Fluid volume		
U.S. quarts	0.9463	Liters
U.S. gallons	3.785	Liters
U.S. ounces	29.573529	Milliliters
Imperial gallons	4.54609	Liters
Imperial quarts	1.1365	Liters
Liters	0.2641721	U.S. gallons
Liters	1.0566882	U.S. quarts
Liters	33.814023	U.S. ounces
Liters	0.22	Imperial gallons
Liters	0.8799	Imperial quarts
Milliliters	0.033814	U.S. ounces
Milliliters	1.0	Cubic centimeters
Milliliters	0.001	Liters
Torque		
Foot-pounds	1.3558	Newton-meters
Foot-pounds	0.138255	Meters-kilograms
Inch-pounds	0.11299	Newton-meters
Newton-meters	0.7375622	Foot-pounds
Newton-meters	8.8507	Inch-pounds
Meters-kilograms	7.2330139	Foot-pounds
Volume		
Cubic inches	16.387064	Cubic centimeters
Cubic centimeters	0.0610237	Cubic inches
Temperature		
Fahrenheit	(F – 32°) × 0.556	Centigrade
Centigrade	(C × 1.8) + 32	Fahrenheit
Weight		
Ounces	28.3495	Grams
Pounds	0.4535924	Kilograms
Grams	0.035274	Ounces
Kilograms	2.2046224	Pounds

(continued)

Table 4 CONVERSION FORMULAS (continued)

Multiply:	By:	To get the equivalent of:
Pressure		
Pounds per square inch	0.070307	Kilograms per square centimeter
Kilograms per square centimeter	14.223343	Pounds per square inch
Kilopascals	0.1450	Pounds per square inch
Pounds per square inch	6.895	Kilopascals
Speed		
Miles per hour	1.609344	Kilometers per hour
Kilometers per hour	0.6213712	Miles per hour

Table 5 GENERAL TORQUE SPECIFICATIONS

Fastener size or type	N•m	in.-lb.	ft.-lb.
5 mm screw	4	35	–
5 mm bolt and nut	5	44	–
6 mm screw	9	80	–
6 mm bolt and nut	10	88	–
6 mm flange bolt (8 mm head, small flange)	9	80	–
6 mm flange bolt (10 mm head) and nut	12	106	–
8 mm bolt and nut	22	–	16
8 mm flange bolt and nut	27	–	20
10 mm bolt and nut	35	–	26
10 mm flange bolt and nut	40	–	29
12 mm bolt and nut	55	–	41

Table 6 TECHNICAL ABBREVIATIONS

ABDC	After bottom dead center
ATDC	After top dead center
BBDC	Before bottom dead center
BDC	Bottom dead center
BTDC	Before top dead center
C	Celsius (centigrade)
cc	Cubic centimeters
cid	Cubic inch displacement
CDI	Capacitor discharge ignition
cu. in.	Cubic inches
DOHC	Dual overhead cam
F	Fahrenheit
ft.	Feet
ft.-lb.	Foot-pounds
gal.	Gallons
H/A	High altitude
hp	Horsepower
in.	Inches
in.-lb.	Inch-pounds
I.D.	Inside diameter
kg	Kilograms
kgm	Kilogram meters

(continued)

Table 6 TECHNICAL ABBREVIATIONS (continued)

km	Kilometer
kPa	Kilopascals
L	Liter
m	Meter
MAG	Magneto
ml	Milliliter
mm	Millimeter
N•m	Newton-meters
O.D.	Outside diameter
oz.	Ounces
psi	Pounds per square inch
PTO	Power take off
pt.	Pint
qt.	Quart
rpm	Revolutions per minute
TSCC	Twin Swirl Combustion Chambers

Table 7 DECIMAL AND METRIC EQUIVALENTS

Fractions	Decimal in.	Metric mm	Fractions	Decimal in.	Metric mm
1/64	0.015625	0.39688	33/64	0.515625	13.09687
1/32	0.03125	0.79375	17/32	0.53125	13.49375
3/64	0.046875	1.19062	35/64	0.546875	13.89062
1/16	0.0625	1.58750	9/16	0.5625	14.28750
5/64	0.078125	1.98437	37/64	0.578125	14.68437
3/32	0.09375	2.38125	19/32	0.59375	15.08125
7/64	0.109375	2.77812	39/64	0.609375	15.47812
1/8	0.125	3.1750	5/8	0.625	15.87500
9/64	0.140625	3.57187	41/64	0.640625	16.27187
5/32	0.15625	3.96875	21/32	0.65625	16.66875
11/64	0.171875	4.36562	43/64	0.671875	17.06562
3/16	0.1875	4.76250	11/16	0.6875	17.46250
13/64	0.203125	5.15937	45/64	0.703125	17.85937
7/32	0.21875	5.55625	23/32	0.71875	18.25625
15/64	0.234375	5.95312	47/64	0.734375	18.65312
1/4	0.250	6.35000	3/4	0.750	19.05000
17/64	0.265625	6.74687	49/64	0.765625	19.44687
9/32	0.28125	7.14375	25/32	0.78125	19.84375
19/64	0.296875	7.54062	51/64	0.796875	20.24062
5/16	0.3125	7.93750	13/16	0.8125	20.63750
21/64	0.328125	8.33437	53/64	0.828125	21.03437
11/32	0.34375	8.73125	27/32	0.84375	21.43125
23/64	0.359375	9.12812	55/64	0.859375	22.82812
3/8	0.375	9.52500	7/8	0.875	22.22500
25/64	0.390625	9.92187	57/64	0.890625	22.62187
13/32	0.40625	10.31875	29/32	0.90625	23.01875
27/64	0.421875	10.71562	59/64	0.921875	23.41562
7/16	0.4375	11.11250	15/16	0.9375	23.81250
29/64	0.453125	11.50937	61/64	0.953125	24.20937
15/32	0.46875	11.90625	31/32	0.96875	24.60625
31/64	0.484375	12.30312	63/64	0.984375	25.00312
1/2	0.500	12.70000	1	1.00	25.40000

Table 8 METRIC TAP AND DRILL SIZES

Metric size	Drill equivalent	Decimal fraction	Nearest fraction
3 × 0.50	No. 39	0.0995	3/32
3 × 0.60	3/32	0.0937	3/32
4 × 0.70	No. 30	0.1285	1/8
4 × 0.75	1/8	0.125	1/8
5 × 0.80	No. 19	0.166	11/64
5 × 0.90	No. 20	0.161	5/32
6 × 1.00	No. 9	0.196	13/64
7 × 1.00	16/64	0.234	15/64
8 × 1.00	J	0.277	9/32
8 × 1.25	17/64	0.265	17/64
9 × 1.00	5/16	0.3125	5/16
9 × 1.25	5/16	0.3125	5/16
10 × 1.25	11/32	0.3437	11/32
10 × 1.50	R	0.339	11/32
11 × 1.50	3/8	0.375	3/8
12 × 1.50	13/32	0.406	13/32
12 × 1.75	13/32	0.406	13/32

CHAPTER TWO

TROUBLESHOOTING

Diagnosing mechanical problems is relatively simple if an orderly procedure is used. The first step in any troubleshooting procedure is to define the symptoms closely and then localize the problem. Subsequent steps involve testing and analyzing those areas that could cause the symptoms. A haphazard approach may eventually solve the problem, but it can be very costly with wasted time and unnecessary parts replacement.

Proper lubrication, maintenance and periodic tune-ups as described in Chapter Three will reduce the necessity for troubleshooting. However, even with the best of care, the motorcycle may require troubleshooting.

Never assume anything; do not overlook the obvious. If the engine will not start, the engine stop switch or start button may be shorted out or damaged. When trying to start the engine, it may be flooded.

If the engine suddenly quits, consider the easiest, most accessible system first. If the engine sounded as if it ran out of fuel, make sure there is fuel in the tank and that it is reaching the carburetors. Make sure the fuel shutoff valve is turned to the ON position (**Figure 1**).

If a quick check does not reveal the problem, proceed with one of the troubleshooting procedures described in this chapter. Gather as many symptoms as possible to aid in determine where to start. For example, note whether the engine lost power gradually or all at once, what color smoke came from the exhaust, or other symptoms.

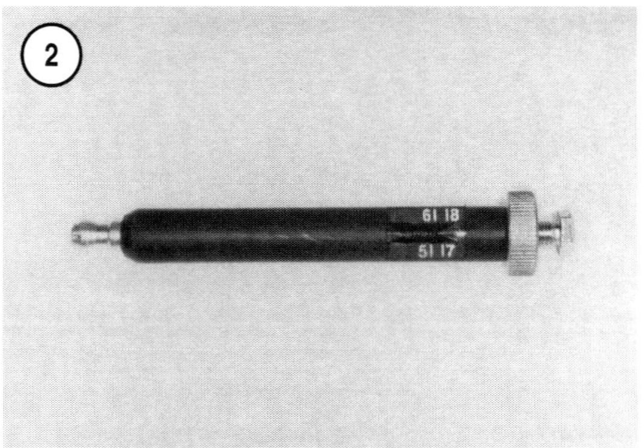

After defining the symptoms, follow the procedure that most closely relates to the condition(s). Guessing at the cause of the problem may provide a solution, but it can easily lead to wasted time and unnecessary parts replacement.

Expensive equipment or complicated test gear is not required to determine whether repairs can be attempted at home. A few simple checks could save a large repair bill and lost time while the motorcycle sits in a dealership's service department. On the other hand, be realistic and do not attempt repairs beyond personal capabilities. Dealership service departments tend to charge heavily when working on equipment that has been abused. Some will not even take on such a job. Use common sense to avoid getting involved in a procedure that cannot be completed satisfactorily.

If the decision has been made to refer troubleshooting to a repair facility, describe problems accurately and fully.

OPERATING REQUIREMENTS

An engine needs three basics to run properly: correct air/fuel mixture, compression and a spark at the right time. If one basic requirement is missing, the engine will not run. Four-stroke engine operating principles are described in Chapter Four under *Engine Principles*.

If the motorcycle has been sitting for any time and refuses to start, check and clean the spark plugs. If the plugs are not fouled, look to the fuel delivery system. This includes the fuel tank, fuel shutoff valve, fuel filter and fuel lines. If the motorcycle sat for a while with fuel in the carburetors, fuel deposits may have gummed up carburetor jets and air passages. Gasoline tends to lose its potency after standing for long periods. Condensation may contaminate it with water. Drain the old gas and try starting with a fresh tank.

STARTING THE ENGINE

Engine Fails to Start (Spark Test)

Perform the following spark test to determine if the ignition system is operating properly.

CAUTION

Before removing the spark plugs in Step 1, clean all dirt and debris away from the plug base. Dirt that falls into the cylinder will cause rapid engine wear.

1. Refer to Chapter Three and disconnect a spark plug wire and remove the spark plug.

NOTE

A spark tester is a useful tool for testing spark output. ***Figure 2*** *shows the Motion Pro Ignition System Tester (part No. 08-0122). This tool is inserted in the spark plug cap and its base is grounded against the cylinder head. The tool's air gap is adjustable and it allows the visual inspection of the spark while testing the intensity of the spark. This tool is available through motorcycle repair shops.*

2. Cover the spark plug hole with a clean shop cloth to lessen the chance of gasoline vapors being emitted from the hole.

3. Insert the spark plug (**Figure 3**), or spark tester (**Figure 4**), into its plug cap and ground the spark

plug base against the cylinder head. Position the spark plug so the electrode is visible.

WARNING
Mount the spark plug, or tester, away from the spark plug hole in the cylinder so that the spark or tester cannot ignite the gasoline vapors in the cylinder. If the engine is flooded, do not perform this test. The firing of the spark plug can ignite fuel that is ejected through the spark plug hole.

NOTE
If a spark plug is used, perform this test with a new spark plug.

4. Turn the ignition switch to the ON position.

WARNING
*Do **not** hold the spark plug, wire or connector, or a serious electrical shock may result.*

5. Turn the engine over with the electric starter. A crisp blue spark should be evident across the spark plug electrode or spark tester terminals. If there is strong sunlight on the plug, shade the plug by hand to better see the spark.
6. If the spark is good, check for one or more of the following possible malfunctions:
   a. Obstructed fuel line or fuel filter.
   b. Low compression or engine damage.
   c. Flooded engine.
7. If the spark is weak or if there is no spark, refer to *Engine is Difficult to Start* in this chapter.

NOTE
If the engine backfires during starting, the ignition timing may be incorrect due to a defective ignition component.

Engine is Difficult to Start

Check for one or more of the following possible malfunctions:
1. Fouled spark plug(s).
2. Improperly adjusted starter (choke) cable.
3. Intake manifold air leak.
4. Plugged fuel tank filler cap.
5. Clogged fuel line.
6. Contaminated fuel system.

7. Improperly adjusted carburetor(s).
8. Defective ignitor unit.
9. Defective ignition coil(s).
10. Damaged ignition coil primary and secondary wires.
11. Incorrect ignition timing.
12. Low engine compression.
13. Engine oil viscosity too heavy for ambient temperature.
14. Discharged battery.
15. Defective starter motor.
16. Loose or corroded starter and/or battery cables.
17. Loose signal generator and ignitor unit electrical connectors.

Engine Will Not Crank

Check for one or more of the following possible malfunctions:
1. Ignition switch turned off.
2. Faulty ignition switch.
3. Engine stop switch in off position.
4. Defective engine stop switch.
5. Loose or corroded starter and battery cables.
6. Discharged or defective battery.
7. Defective starter motor.
8. Defective starter relay.
9. Slipping starter clutch assembly.
10. Seized piston(s).
11. Seized crankshaft bearings.
12. Broken connecting rod(s).

ENGINE PERFORMANCE

In the following checklist, it is assumed that the engine runs, but is not operating at peak performance. This will serve as a starting point from which to isolate a performance malfunction.

Fouled Spark Plugs

If the spark plugs continually foul, check for the following:
1. Severely contaminated air filter element.
2. Incorrect spark plug heat range. See Chapter Three.
3. Rich fuel mixture.
4. Worn or damaged piston rings.
5. Worn or damaged valve guide oil seals.
6. Excessive valve stem-to-guide clearance.
7. Incorrect carburetor float level.

Engine Runs but Misfires

1. Fouled or improperly gapped spark plugs.
2. Damaged spark plug cables.
3. Incorrect ignition timing.
4. Defective ignition components.
5. Obstructed fuel line or fuel shutoff valve.
6. Obstructed fuel filter.
7. Clogged carburetor jets.
8. Loose battery connection.
9. Wiring or connector damage.
10. Water or other contaminants in the fuel.
11. Weak or damaged valve springs.
12. Incorrect camshaft/valve timing.
13. Damaged valve(s).
14. Dirty electrical connections.
15. Intake manifold or carburetor air leak.
16. Plugged carburetor vent hose.
17. Plugged fuel tank vent system.

Engine Overheating

1. Incorrect carburetor adjustment or jet selection.
2. Incorrect ignition timing or defective ignition system components.
3. Improper spark plug heat range.
4. Clogged or dirty cooling fins on cylinder block and cylinder head.
5. Clogged or dirty cooling fins on the oil cooler.
6. Low oil level.
7. Oil not circulating properly.
8. Leaking valves.
9. Heavy engine carbon deposits.

Engine Runs Rough with Excessive Exhaust Smoke

1. Clogged air filter element.
2. Incorrect rich carburetor adjustment.
3. Starter plunger (choke) not operating correctly.
4. Water or other fuel contaminants.
5. Clogged fuel line and/or filter.
6. Spark plug(s) fouled.
7. Defective ignition coil(s).
8. Defective signal generator and/or ignitor unit.
9. Loose or defective ignition circuit wire.
10. Short circuits from damaged wire insulation.
11. Loose battery cable connections.
12. Incorrect camshaft/valve timing.
13. Intake manifold or air filter air leaks.

Engine Loses Power

1. Incorrect carburetor adjustment.
2. Engine overheating.
3. Incorrect ignition timing.
4. Incorrectly gapped spark plug(s).
5. Obstructed muffler.
6. Dragging brake(s).

Engine Lacks Acceleration

1. Incorrect carburetor adjustment.
2. Clogged fuel line.
3. Incorrect ignition timing.
4. Dragging brake(s).

Valve Train Noise

1. Bent valve.
2. Worn or damaged camshaft bearing(s).
3. Worn or damaged camshaft gear(s).

STARTING SYSTEM

The starting system consists of the battery, starter motor, starter relay, start switch and related wiring.

When the ignition switch is turned on and the start button is pushed in, current is transmitted from the battery to the solenoid coil. This causes the coil contacts to close, allowing electricity to flow from the battery to the starter motor.

Troubleshooting Preliminaries

Before troubleshooting the starting system, check the following:

1. Make sure the battery is fully charged.
2. Battery cables are the proper size and length. Replace damaged or undersize cables.
3. All electrical connections are clean and secure. High resistance caused from dirty or loose connectors can affect voltage and current levels.
4. The wiring harness is in good condition, with no worn or frayed insulation or loose harness sockets.
5. The fuel tank is filled with an adequate supply of fresh gasoline.
6. The spark plugs are in good condition and properly gapped.
7. The ignition system is working correctly.

Basic Starting System Malfunctions

The basic starter related troubles are:

1. Starter motor does not spin.
2. Starter motor spins but does not engage.
3. The starter motor will not disengage after the start button is released.
4. Loud grinding noises when starter motor turns.
5. Starter motor stalls or spins too slowly.

CAUTION
Never operate the starter motor for more than 30 seconds at a time. Allow the starter to cool before reusing it. Failing to allow the starter motor to cool after continuous starting attempts can damage the starter.

Starter motor does not spin

1. Check for a blown fuse (Chapter Nine). If the fuses are good, continue with Step 2.
2. Check the starter motor cable for an open circuit and for dirty or loose-fitting terminals.
3. Check the starter relay connector for dirty or loose-fitting terminals. Clean and repair the connector as required.
4. Check the starter relay as follows. Turn the ignition switch ON and depress the starter switch button. When the starter button is depressed, the starter relay switch should click once.
   a. If the relay clicks, continue with Step 5.
   b. If the relay does not click, go on to Step 6.

CAUTION
Because of the large amount of current that flows from the battery to the starter, use a large diameter cable when performing Step 5.

5. Remove the starter from the motorcycle as described in Chapter Nine. Using an auxiliary battery, apply battery voltage directly to the starter. The starter should turn when battery voltage is directly applied. Note the following:
   a. If the starter motor did not turn, disassemble and inspect the starter motor as described in Chapter Nine. Replace worn or damaged parts as required.
   b. If the starter motor turned, check for loose or damaged starter motor cables. If the cables are good, perform Step 6.
6. Perform the *Starter Relay Voltage Test* as described in Chapter Nine. If the voltage equals or exceeds battery voltage, proceed to Step 7. If the voltage is less than battery voltage, refer to Chapter Nine and check the following items:
   a. Check the ignition switch.
   b. Check the engine stop switch.
   c. Check the neutral switch.
   d. Check the diode.
   e. Check the sidestand relay.
   f. Check the clutch switch.
   g. Check for a poor contact in the starting system wiring.
   h. Check for an open in the starting system wiring.
7. Perform the *Starter Relay Continuity and Resistance Test* as described in Chapter Nine. Replace the relay if it is faulty. Check for dirty or poor terminals in the starter relay.

Component Testing

Refer to Chapter Nine.

CHARGING SYSTEM

The charging system consists of the battery, alternator and a solid state rectifier/voltage regulator.

The alternator generates alternating current (AC) which the rectifier converts to direct current (DC). The regulator maintains the voltage to the battery and load (lights, ignition and accessories) at a constant voltage despite variations in engine speed and load.

A malfunction in the charging system generally causes the battery to remain undercharged.

Charging System Precautions

Before servicing the charging system, observe the following precautions to prevent damage to any charging system component.

1. Never reverse battery connections. Damage will occur to the motorcycle's electrical systems.
2. Do not short across any connection.
3. Never start the engine with the alternator disconnected from the voltage regulator/rectifier, unless instructed to do so during testing.
4. Never attempt to start or run the engine with the battery disconnected.
5. Never attempt to use a high-output battery charger to help start the engine.
6. Before charging the battery, remove it from the motorcycle as described in Chapter Nine.
7. Never disconnect the voltage regulator/rectifier connector with the engine running. The voltage regulator and the rectifier are an integral part of the alternator.
8. Make sure the negative battery terminal is connected to the engine and frame.

Troubleshooting Preliminaries

Before testing the charging system, visually check the following:

1. Check the battery connections at the battery. If polarity is reversed, check for a damaged regulator/rectifier.
2. Check for loose or corroded battery cable connectors.
3. Inspect all wiring between the battery and the alternator stator for worn or cracked insulation or loose connections. Replace wiring or clean and tighten connections as required.
4. Check the battery condition. Clean and recharge as described in Chapter Three.

IGNITION SYSTEM

All models are equipped with a transistorized ignition system. Because of the solid state design, problems with the transistorized system are rare. If a problem occurs, it generally causes a weak spark or no spark at all. An ignition system with a weak spark or no spark is relatively easy to troubleshoot. It is difficult, however, to troubleshoot an ignition system that only malfunctions when the engine is hot or under load.

Ignition System Precautions

Certain measures must be taken to protect the ignition system.

1. Never disconnect any of the electrical connectors while the engine is running.
2. Apply dielectric grease to all electrical connectors prior to reconnecting them. This will help seal out moisture.
3. Make sure all electrical connectors are free of corrosion and are completely coupled to each other.
4. The ignitor unit must always be mounted securely to the top of the rear fender under the seat.

Troubleshooting Preliminaries

1. Refer to the wiring diagrams at the end of this manual for the specific model.
2. Check the wiring harness for visible signs of damage.
3. Make sure all connectors are properly attached to each other and locked in place.
4. Check all electrical components for a good ground to the engine.
5. Check all wiring for short circuits or open circuits.
6. Remove the seat as described in Chapter Fourteen.
7. Make sure the fuel tank has an adequate supply of fresh gasoline.
8. Check spark plug cable routing and their connections at the spark plugs. If there is no spark or only a weak one, repeat the test with new spark plugs. If the condition remains the same with new spark plugs and if all external wiring connections are good, the problem is most likely in the ignition system. If a strong spark is present, the problem is probably not in the ignition system. Check the fuel system.
9. Remove the spark plugs and examine them as described in Chapter Three.

Ignitor Unit Testing and Replacement

There are no test procedures for the ignitor unit. If the ignitor unit is suspect, have a Suzuki dealership check it out with the Digital Ignition Checker and Extension test wire or by installing a test ignitor unit to ensure the suspect unit is faulty. Make sure that nothing has been overlooked before purchasing a new ignitor unit. Most parts suppliers will not accept returns on electrical components.

Ignition Cable and Cap Inspection

All models are equipped with resistor- or suppression-type spark plug cables. These cables reduce radio interference. The cable's conductor consists of a carbon-impregnated fabric core material instead of solid wire.

If a plug cable becomes damaged, either due to corrosion or conductor breaks, its resistance increases. Excessive cable resistance will cause engine misfire and other ignition or driveability problems.

When troubleshooting the ignition system, inspect the spark plug cables (**Figure 5**) for:

1. Corroded or damaged connector ends.
2. Breaks in the cable insulation that could allow arcing.
3. Split or damaged plug caps that could allow arcing to the cylinder head.

Replace any damaged or questionable spark plug cable assembly.

FUEL SYSTEM

Many riders automatically assume that the carburetors are at fault when the engine does not run properly. While fuel system problems are not uncommon, carburetor adjustment is seldom the answer. In many cases, adjusting will only compound the problem by making the engine run worse.

Begin fuel system troubleshooting with the fuel tank and work through the system, reserving the carburetors as the final point. Most fuel system problems result from an empty fuel tank, a plugged fuel filter or fuel valve, sour fuel, a dirty air filter or clogged carburetor jets.

The following procedures assume that the ignition system is working properly and is correctly adjusted.

Identifying Carburetor Conditions

Refer to the following conditions to identify whether the engine is running lean or rich.

Rich

1. Fouled spark plugs.
2. Engine misfires and runs rough under load.
3. Excessive exhaust smoke as the throttle is increased.
4. An extreme rich condition results in a choked or dull sound from the exhaust and an inability to clear the exhaust with the throttle held wide open.

Lean

1. Blistered or very white spark plug electrodes.
2. Engine overheats.
3. Slow acceleration, engine power is reduced.
4. Flat spots on acceleration that are similar in feel to when the engine starts to run out of fuel.
5. Engine speed fluctuates at full throttle.

Fuel Level System

Proper carburetor operation depends on a constant and correct carburetor fuel level. As fuel is drawn from the float bowl during engine operation, the float level in the bowl drops. As the float drops, the fuel valve moves away from its seat and allows fuel to flow through the seat into the float bowl.

Fuel entering the float bowl will cause the float to rise and push against the fuel valve. When the fuel level reaches a predetermined level, the fuel valve is pushed against the seat to prevent the float bowl from overfilling.

If the fuel valve fails to close, the engine will run too rich or flood with fuel. Symptoms of this problem are rough running, excessive black smoke and poor acceleration. This condition will sometimes clear up when the engine is run at wide-open throttle, as the fuel is being drawn into the engine before the float bowl can overfill. As the engine speed is reduced, however, the rich running condition returns.

Several things can cause fuel overflow. In most instances, it can be as simple as a small piece of dirt trapped between the fuel valve and seat or an incorrect float level. If fuel is flowing out of the overflow tube connected to the bottom of the float bowl, the fuel valve inside the carburetor is being held open. First check the position of the fuel shutoff valve lever. Turn the fuel shutoff valve lever OFF. Then lightly tap on the carburetor float bowl and turn the fuel shutoff valve lever ON. If the fuel flow stops running out of the overflow tube, whatever was holding the fuel valve off of its seat now has been dislodged. If fuel continues to flow from the overflow tube, remove and service the carburetor. See Chapter Eight.

Starting Enrichment (Choke) System

A cold engine requires a rich mixture to start and run properly. A cable-actuated starter enrichment lever (**Figure 6**) on the handlebar and the valve on the carburetor are used for cold starting.

If the engine is difficult to start when cold, check the starting enrichment (choke) cable adjustment as described in Chapter Three.

ENGINE NOISES

1. Knocking or pinging during acceleration can be caused by using a lower octane fuel than recommended or a poor grade of fuel. Incorrect carburetor jetting and an incorrect (hot) spark plug heat range can cause pinging. Refer to *Spark Plug Heat Range* in Chapter Three. Check also for excessive carbon buildup in the combustion chamber or a defective ignitor unit.
2. Slapping or rattling noises at low speed or during acceleration can be caused by excessive piston-to-cylinder wall clearance. Check also for a bent connecting rod or worn piston pin and/or piston pin hole in the piston.
3. Knocking or rapping while decelerating is usually caused by excessive rod bearing clearance.
4. Persistent knocking and vibration or other noises are usually caused by worn main bearings. If the main bearings are in good condition, consider the following:
   a. Loose engine mounts.
   b. Cracked frame.
   c. Leaking cylinder head gasket.
   d. Exhaust pipe leakage at cylinder head ports.
   e. Stuck piston ring(s).
   f. Broken piston ring(s).
   g. Partial engine seizure.
   h. Excessive connecting rod bearing clearance.
   i. Excessive connecting rod side clearance.
   j. Excessive crankshaft runout.
5. Rapid on-off squeal indicates a compression leak around the cylinder head gasket or spark plugs.
6. Valve train noise is usually caused by the following:
   a. Valve sticking in guide.
   b. Worn camshaft gears and/or camshafts.

ENGINE LUBRICATION

An improperly operating engine lubrication system will quickly lead to serious engine damage. Check the engine oil level weekly as described in Chapter Three. Oil pump service is covered in Chapter Five.

Oil Consumption High or Engine Smokes Excessively

1. Worn valve guides.
2. Worn valve guide seals.
3. Worn or damaged piston rings.
4. Oil pan overfilled.
5. Oil filter restricted.
6. Leaking cylinder head surfaces.

Engine Oil Leaks

1. Loose engine parts.
2. Damaged gasket sealing surfaces.
3. Restricted oil filter.
4. Damaged oil cooler, fittings or oil lines.

CLUTCH

All clutch troubles require partial clutch disassembly to identify and cure the problem. Refer to Chapter Six for clutch service procedures.

Clutch Chatter or Noise

This problem is usually caused by worn or warped friction and/or steel plates.

Clutch Slippage

1. Worn friction plates.
2. Weak or damaged diaphragm springs.
3. Damaged pressure plate.

Clutch Dragging

1. Incorrect clutch adjustment.
2. Warped clutch plates.
3. Worn or damaged clutch outer housing or clutch hub.
4. Worn or incorrectly assembled clutch push piece release mechanism.

TRANSMISSION

Transmission symptoms are sometimes hard to distinguish from clutch symptoms. Refer to Chapter Seven transmission service procedures.

Jumping Out of Gear

1. Worn or damaged gear shifter parts.
2. Severely worn or damaged gears and/or shift forks.

Difficult Shifting

1. Worn or damaged shift forks.
2. Worn or damaged shift fork dogs.
3. Weak or damaged shift lever return spring.
4. Clutch drag.

Excessive Gear Noise

1. Worn or damaged bearings.
2. Worn or damaged gears.
3. Excessive gear backlash.

LIGHTING SYSTEM

If bulbs burn out frequently, check for excessive vibration, loose connections that permit sudden current surges, or the installation of the wrong type of bulb.

Most light and ignition problems are caused by loose or corroded ground connections. Check these prior to replacing a bulb or electrical component.

EXCESSIVE VIBRATION

Excessive vibration is usually caused by loose engine mounting hardware. A bent axle shaft or loose suspension component will cause high-speed vibration problems. Vibration can also be caused by the following conditions:

1. Engine balance shaft incorrectly aligned with the crankshaft.
2. Cracked or broken frame.
3. Loose or damaged engine mounts.
4. Improperly balanced wheel(s).
5. Defective or damaged wheel(s).
6. Defective or damaged tire(s).
7. Internal engine wear or damage.
8. Loose or worn steering head bearings.
9. Loose swing arm pivot shaft nut.

FRONT SUSPENSION AND STEERING

Poor handling may be caused by improper tire inflation pressure, a damaged or bent frame or front steering components, worn wheel bearings or dragging brakes. Possible causes for suspension and steering malfunctions are listed below.

Irregular or Wobbly Steering

1. Loose front axle.
2. Loose or worn steering head bearings.
3. Excessive wheel bearing play.
4. Wheel out of alignment.
5. Unbalanced wheel assembly.
6. Bent or damaged steering stem or frame at steering neck.
7. Tire incorrectly seated on rim.

Stiff Steering

1. Low front tire air pressure.
2. Bent or damaged steering stem or frame.
3. Loose or worn steering head bearings.

Stiff or Heavy Fork Operation

1. Incorrect fork springs.
2. Incorrect fork oil viscosity.
3. Excessive amount of fork oil.
4. Bent fork sliders.

Poor Fork Operation

1. Worn or damage fork tubes and sliders.
2. Fork oil capacity low due to leaking fork seals.
3. Bent or damaged fork tubes or sliders.
4. Contaminated fork oil.
5. Incorrect fork springs.

Poor Rear Shock Absorber Operation

1. Weak or worn spring.
2. Damper unit leaking.
3. Shock shaft worn or bent.
4. Incorrect rear shock spring.
5. Rear shock adjusted incorrectly.

BRAKE PROBLEMS

All models are equipped with front and rear disc brakes. Good brakes are vital to the safe operation of any motorcycle. Perform the maintenance specified in Chapter Three to minimize brake system problems. Brake system service is covered in Chapter Thirteen. When refilling the front and rear master cylinders, use only DOT 4 brake fluid.

Insufficient Braking Power

Worn brake pads or discs, air in the hydraulic system, glazed or contaminated pads, low brake fluid level, or a leaking brake line or hose can cause this problem. Visually check for leaks. Check for worn brake pads. Check also for a leaking seal in the caliper(s). Bleed and adjust the brakes. Replace a leaking master cylinder or brake caliper. Brake drag will result in excessive heat and brake fade. See *Brake Drag* in this section.

Spongy Brake Feel

This problem is generally caused by air in the hydraulic system. Bleed the brakes as described in Chapter Thirteen

Brake Drag

Check for worn, loose or missing parts in the brake calipers. Check the brake discs for excessive runout.

Brakes Squeal or Chatter

Check brake pad thickness and disc condition. Check that the caliper anti-rattle springs are properly installed and in good condition. Clean off any dirt on the pads. Loose components can also cause this. Check for:

1. Warped brake disc.
2. Loose brake disc.
3. Loose caliper mounting bolts.
4. Loose front axle nut.
5. Worn wheel bearings.
6. Damaged hub.

CHAPTER THREE

LUBRICATION, MAINTENANCE AND TUNE-UP

The service life and operation of the Suzuki GSF1200 Bandit depends on the maintenance it receives. This is easy to understand once it is realized that a motorcycle, even in normal use, is subjected to tremendous heat, stress and vibration. When neglected, any motorcycle becomes unreliable and dangerous to ride. **Figure 1** and **Figure 2** show the location of various components relating to service.

All motorcycles require attention before and after riding them. The time spent on basic maintenance and lubrication will give the utmost in safety and performance. Minor problems found during these inspections are simple and can be corrected inexpensively. If they are not found and corrected at this time, they can lead to major and more expensive problems.

Start by doing simple tune-up, lubrication and maintenance procedures. Tackle more involved jobs after becoming more familiar with the machine.

Perform critical maintenance tasks and checks weekly. Perform others at specific time or mileage intervals or if certain symptoms appear. The *Tune-up* section at the end of this chapter lists procedures that affect driveability and performance. If a procedure requires more than minor disassembly, it is covered in a subsequent chapter.

Periodic maintenance intervals are listed in **Table 1** at the end of the chapter. Subsequent tables provide capacities, recommendations and specifications.

Record all service performed in the maintenance log at the back of this manual.

SAFETY CHECKS

Perform the following safety checks before the first ride of the day.

General Inspection

1. Inspect the engine and oil tank hoses for leakage.

(1)

COMPONENT LOCATION

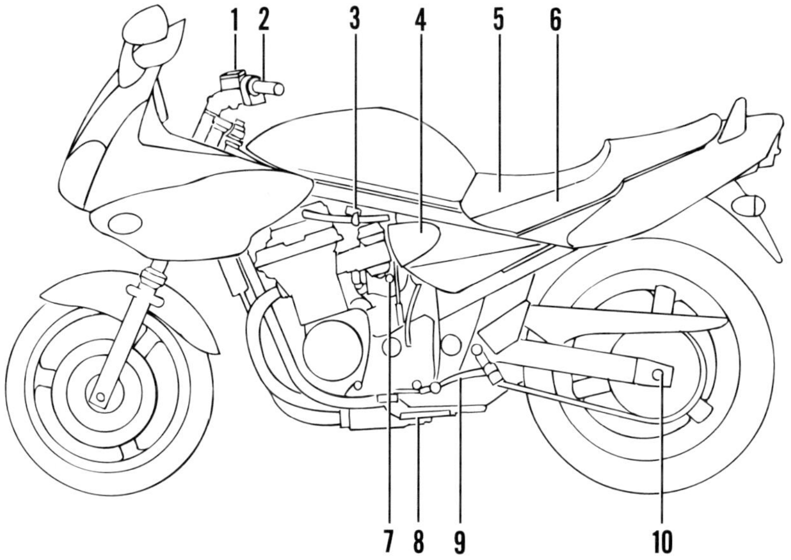

1. Clutch master cylinder reservoir
2. Clutch lever
3. Fuel shutoff valve
4. Main fuse
5. Battery
6. Fuse panel
7. Idle adjust screw
8. Side stand
9. Gearshift lever
10. Drive chain adjust

(2)

COMPONENT LOCATION

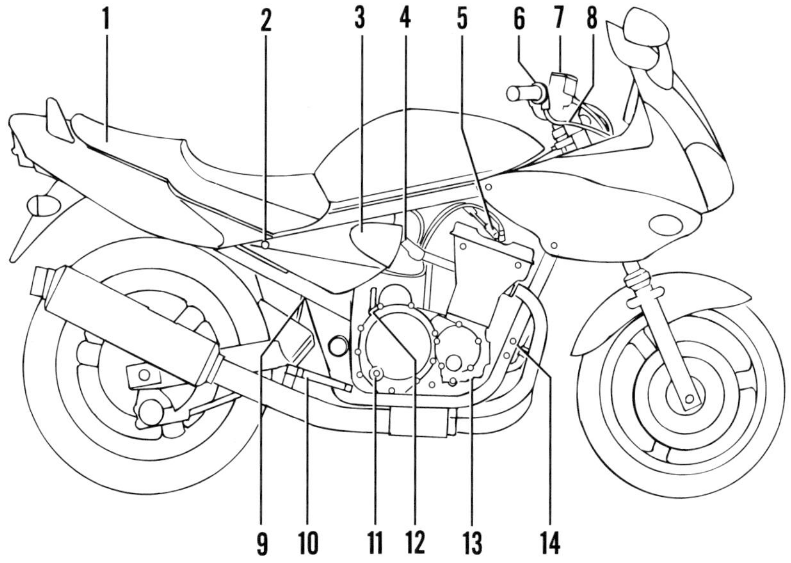

1. Tool kit
2. Rear brake master cylinder reservoir
3. Air filter
4. Carburetors
5. Spark plugs
6. Throttle cable adjust
7. Front brake master cylinder reservoir
8. Fork spring preload adjuster
9. Rear shock absorber adjusters
10. Rear brake light switch
11. Engine oil level check window
12. Engine oil filler cap
13. Engine oil drain plug
14. Engine oil filter

2. Check the tires for embedded stones. Pry them out with a suitable tool.
3. Check tire pressure (**Table 2**) when the tires are cold. Refer to *Tire and Wheels* in this chapter for more information.
4. Make sure *all* lights work.
5. Inspect the fuel lines and fittings for leakage.
6. Check the fuel level in the fuel tank. Top off, if required.
7. Check the operation of the front and rear brakes. Add DOT 4 brake fluid to the front and rear master cylinders as required.
8. Check clutch operation. Add DOT 4 brake fluid to the clutch master cylinder as required.
9. Check the throttle operation. The hand throttle must move smoothly with no roughness, sticking or tightness. The throttle must snap back when released. Adjust throttle free play, if necessary, as described in this chapter.
10. Check the rear brake pedal. It must move smoothly.
11. Inspect the front and rear suspension. Make sure they have a good solid feel with no looseness.
12. Check the exhaust system for leakage or damage.

Lights and Horn

With the engine running, check the following.

1. Pull the front brake lever and check that the brake light comes on.
2. Push the rear brake pedal down and check that the brake light comes on soon after the pedal has been depressed.
3. Make sure the headlight and taillight are on.
4. Move the dimmer switch up and down between the high and low positions and make sure both headlights or elements are working.
5. Push the turn signal switch to the left and right positions and make sure all four turn signal lights are working.
6. Check the horn button operation.
7. If the horn or any light fails to work properly, refer to Chapter Nine.

MAINTENANCE INTERVALS

The recommended service intervals are listed in **Table 1**. Strict adherence to these recommendations will go a long way toward ensuring long service from the motorcycle. To prevent damage when operating the motorcycle in areas of high humidity or when riding near the ocean, increase the lubrication service intervals.

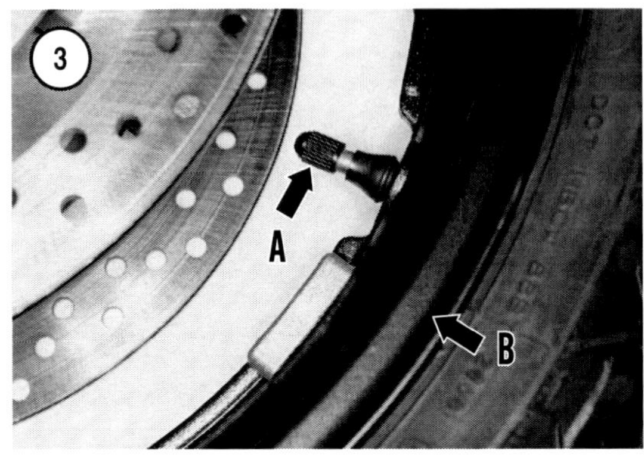

This chapter describes most of the services shown in **Table 1**. The remaining chapters cover those procedures that require more than minor disassembly or adjustment.

TIRES AND WHEELS

Tire Pressure

Check the tire pressure often to maintain tire profile, traction, and handling and to get the maximum life out of the tire. Carry a tire gauge in the motorcycle's tool kit. **Table 2** lists the cold tire pressures for the original equipment tires.

NOTE

*After checking and adjusting the air pressure, reinstall the air valve caps (A, **Figure 3**). These caps prevent small debris from collecting in the valve stems and causing air leakage or incorrect tire pressure readings.*

Tire Inspection

The tires take a lot of punishment, so inspect them periodically for excessive wear, deep cuts and imbedded objects such as stones or nails. If a nail or other object is found in a tire, mark its location with a light crayon prior to removing it. This will help locate the hole for repair.

Refer to Chapter Nine for tire changing and repair information. Check local traffic regulations concerning minimum tread depth. Measure with a tread

depth gauge or a small ruler in the center of the tire and to the center of the tire tread. Replace the tire when the tread is worn to the dimension specified in **Table 2**.

Wheel Inspection

Check the wheel rims (B, **Figure 3**) for cracks and other damage. A damaged wheel can make the motorcycle handle poorly. Refer to Chapter Ten for wheel service.

BATTERY

The battery is an important component in the motorcycle's electrical system, yet most electrical system troubles can be traced to battery neglect. Clean and inspect the battery at periodic intervals. All models are equipped with a maintenance-free battery. This is a sealed battery and the electrolyte level cannot be checked.

On all models covered in this manual, the negative side is grounded. When removing the battery, disconnect the negative cable first and then disconnect the positive cable. This minimizes the chance of a tool shorting to ground when the battery positive cable is disconnected.

Battery Negative Cable

Some of the component replacement procedures and some of the test procedures in this chapter require disconnecting the negative battery cable as a safety precaution.

1. Remove the seat as described in Chapter Fourteen.
2. On 2001-on models, remove the screws securing the document tray (**Figure 4**) and remove the tray.
3. Remove the bolt (**Figure 5**) securing the negative cable to the battery and disconnect it. Move the cable away from the battery to avoid making accidental contact with the battery post.
4. Connect the negative cable onto the battery, reinstall the bolt and tighten securely.
5. On 2001-on models, install the document tray (**Figure 4**).
6. Install the seat.

Battery Cable Service

To ensure good electrical contact between the battery and the electrical cables, the cables must be clean and free of corrosion.

1. If the electrical cable terminals are badly corroded, disconnect them from the motorcycle's electrical system.
2. Thoroughly clean each connector with a wire brush and then with a baking soda solution. Rinse thoroughly with clean water and wipe dry with a clean cloth.
3. After cleaning, apply a thin layer of dielectric grease to the battery terminals before reattaching the cables.
4. If disconnected, attach the electrical cables to the motorcycle's electrical system.
5. After connecting the electrical cables, apply a light coat of dielectric grease to the terminals to retard corrosion and decomposition of the terminals.

Battery

Removal/installation

1. Turn the ignition switch to the OFF position.

2. Remove the seat as described in Chapter Fourteen.
3. On 2001-on models, remove the screws securing the document tray (**Figure 4**) and remove the tray.
4. Remove the bolt securing the negative cable to the battery and disconnect it (A, **Figure 6**).
5. Move the negative cable out of the way so it will not accidentally contact the battery negative terminal.
6. Remove the red terminal cap from the positive battery terminal (B, **Figure 6**). Disconnect the positive battery cable from the positive battery terminal.
7. Remove the battery (C, **Figure 6**) from the motorcycle.
8. To install the battery, set the battery into the battery compartment. Make sure the negative terminal (D, **Figure 6**) is on the left side of the motorcycle.

CAUTION
Be sure the battery cables are connected to their proper terminals. The red battery cable must be connected to the positive battery terminal and the black battery cable must be connected to the negative battery terminal. Connecting the battery backwards reverses the polarity and will damage the rectifier.

9. Install and tighten the positive battery cable.
10. Install and tighten the negative battery cable (A, **Figure 6**).
11. Coat the battery connections with dielectric grease to retard corrosion. Reinstall the red terminal cap (B, **Figure 6**) over the positive battery terminal.
12. On 2001-on models install the document tray (**Figure 4**) and tighten the screws securely.
13. Install the seat as described in Chapter Fourteen.

Inspection and testing

The battery electrolyte level cannot be serviced. *Never* attempt to remove the sealing bar from the top of the battery. This bar was removed for the initial filling of electrolyte prior to delivery of the motorcycle or the installation of a new battery. It is not to be removed thereafter. The battery does not require periodic electrolyte inspection or water refilling.

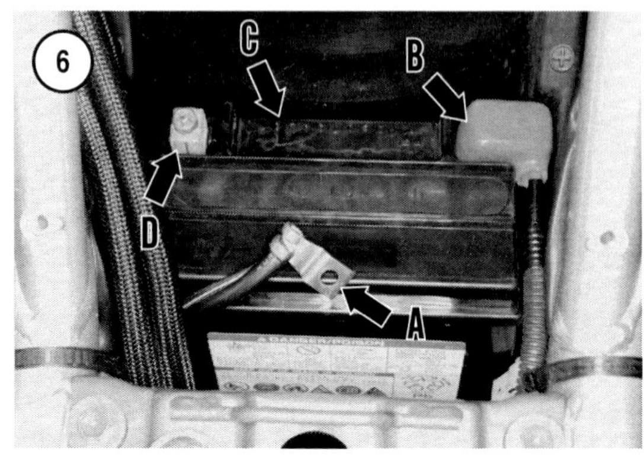

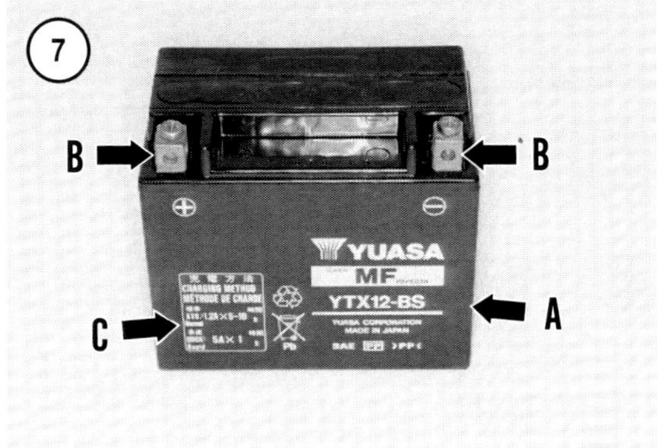

Even though the battery is sealed, protect eyes, skin and clothing in the event that the battery is cracked and leaking electrolyte. Battery electrolyte is very corrosive and can cause severe chemical burns and permanent injury. If electrolyte spills onto clothing or skin, immediately neutralize the electrolyte with a solution of baking soda and water, and then flush the area with an abundance of clean water.

WARNING
Electrolyte splashed into the eyes is extremely harmful. Safety glasses must always be worn while working with a battery. If electrolyte gets into one's eyes, call a physician immediately. Force the eyes open and flush them with cool, clean water for approximately 15 minutes or until medical help arrives.

1. Remove the battery as described in this chapter. Do not clean the battery while it is mounted in the frame.
2. Inspect the battery pads in the battery compartment for contamination or damage. Clean the pads

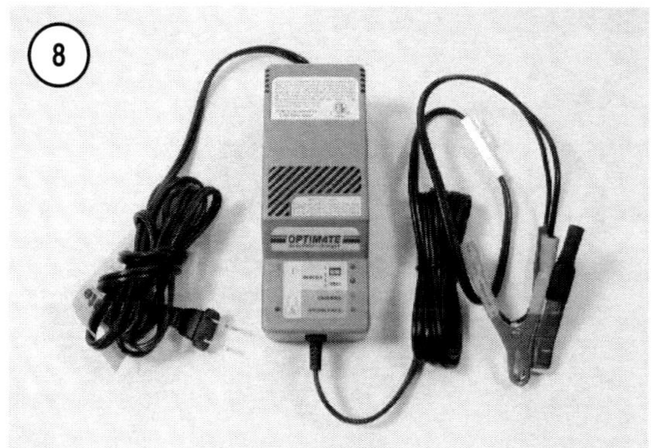

and compartment with a solution of baking soda and water.

3. Set the battery on a stack of newspapers or shop cloths to protect the workbench surface.

4. Check the entire battery case (A, **Figure 7**) for cracks or other damage. If the battery case is warped, discolored or has a raised top, the battery has overheated from overcharging.

5. Check the battery terminals (B, **Figure 7**) and bolts for corrosion or damage. Clean parts thoroughly with a solution of baking soda and water. Replace severely corroded or damaged parts.

6. If corroded, clean the top of the battery with a stiff bristle brush using the baking soda and water solution.

7. Check the battery cable clamps for corrosion and damage. If corrosion is minor, clean the battery cable clamps with a stiff wire brush. Replace severely worn or damaged cables.

8. Connect a digital voltmeter across the battery negative and positive terminals. Note the following:
   a. If the battery voltage is 12.6 volts (at 20° C, 68° F), or greater, the battery is fully charged.
   b. If the battery voltage is 12.0 to 12.5 volts (at 20° C, 68° F), or greater, the battery is undercharged. Recharge it as described in this chapter.
   c. Once the battery is fully charged, test the charging system as described in Chapter Nine.

Battery Charging

Refer to *Battery Initialization* in this chapter if the battery is new.

If recharging is required on a maintenance free battery, a digital voltmeter and a charger with an adjustable amperage output are required. If this equipment is not available, entrust the battery charging to a shop with the proper equipment. Excessive voltage and amperage from an unregulated charger can damage the battery and shorten service life.

The battery should only self-discharge approximately one percent each day. If a battery not in use, with no loads connected, loses it charge within a week after charging, the battery is defective.

If the motorcycle is not used for long periods of time, an automatic battery charger (**Figure 8**) with variable voltage and amperage outputs is recommended for optimum battery service life.

WARNING

During charging, highly explosive hydrogen gas is released from the battery.

Only charge the battery in a well-ventilated area that has no open flames (including pilot lights on some gas home appliances). Do not allow any smoking in the area. Never check the charge of the battery by arcing across the terminals. The resultant spark can ignite the hydrogen gas.

CAUTION

Always disconnect the battery cables from the battery and remove the battery from the motorcycle before connecting charging equipment. If the cables are left connected, the charger may destroy the diodes within the voltage regulator/rectifier.

1. Remove the battery from the motorcycle as described in this chapter.

2. Set the battery on a stack of newspapers or shop cloths to protect the surface of the workbench.

3. Make sure the charger is turned to the OFF position prior to attaching the charger leads to the battery.

4. Connect the positive charger lead to the positive battery terminal and the negative charger lead to the negative battery terminal.

5. Set the charger to 12 volts. If the output of the charger is variable, it is best to select the low setting.

CAUTION

Never set the battery charger to more than 4 amps. The battery will be damaged if the charge rate exceeds 4 amps.

6. The charging rate (C, **Figure** 7) depends on the discharged condition of the battery. Refer to **Table 6** for the suggested charging rate/time. Normally, a battery should be charged at a slow charge rate of 1/10th its given capacity.
7. Turn the charger to the ON position.
8. After the battery has been charged for the pre-determined time, turn the charger OFF and disconnect the leads. Wait 30 minutes, and then measure the battery voltage. Refer to the following:
   a. If the battery voltage is 12.6 volts (at 20° C, 68° F), or greater, the battery is fully charged.
   b. If the battery voltage is 12.0 to 12.5 volts (at 20° C, 68° F), or greater, the battery is undercharged and requires additional charging time.
9. If the battery remains stable for one hour, the battery is charged.
10. Install the battery into the motorcycle as described in this chapter.

Battery Initialization

A new battery must be *fully* charged (12.6 volts for a maintenance-free type) before installation. To bring the battery to a full charge, give it an initial full charge. Using a new battery without an initial full charge will cause permanent battery damage. That is, the battery will never be able to hold more than an 80% charge. Charging a new battery after it has been used will not bring its charge to 100%. When purchasing a new battery, verify its charge status.

NOTE

***Recycle the old battery**. When a new battery is purchased, turn in the old one for recycling. Most motorcycle dealerships will accept the old battery in trade when purchasing a new one. Never place an old battery in the household trash since it is illegal, in most states, to place any acid or lead (heavy metal) contents in landfills.*

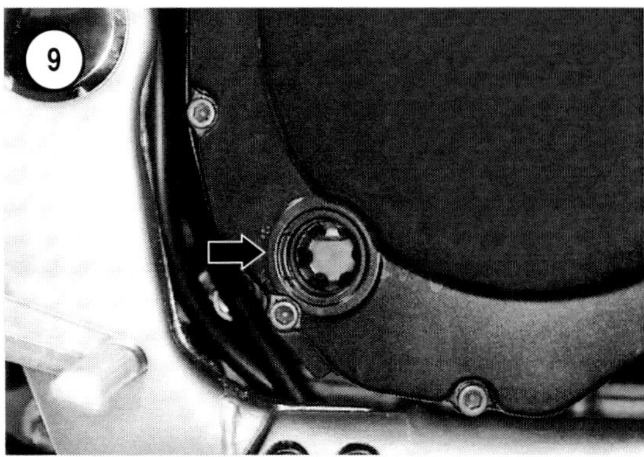

PERIODIC LUBRICATION

Perform the services listed in this section at the maintenance intervals in **Table 1**. If the motorcycle is exposed to harder than normal use or constant exposure to water and high humidity, perform the services more frequently.

Engine Oil Level Check

Engine oil level is checked with the oil level gauge located on the clutch cover.

1. If the motorcycle has not been run, start the engine and let it warm up for two to three minutes.
2. Park the motorcycle on level ground on the centerstand.
3. Shut off the engine and let the oil settle for two to three minutes.

CAUTION

Do not take this oil level reading with the motorcycle on the sidestand as the oil will flow away from the gauge, giving a false reading.

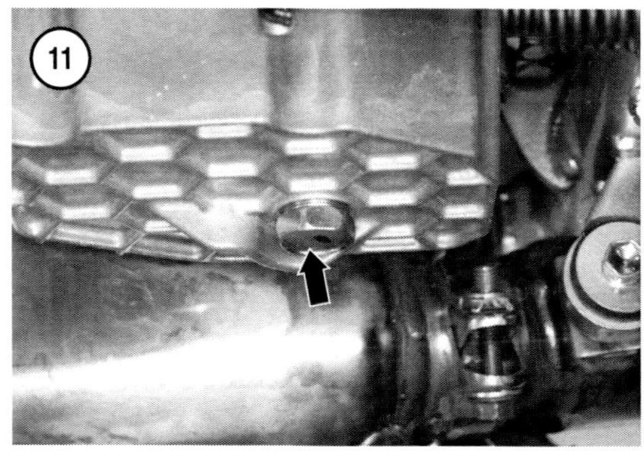

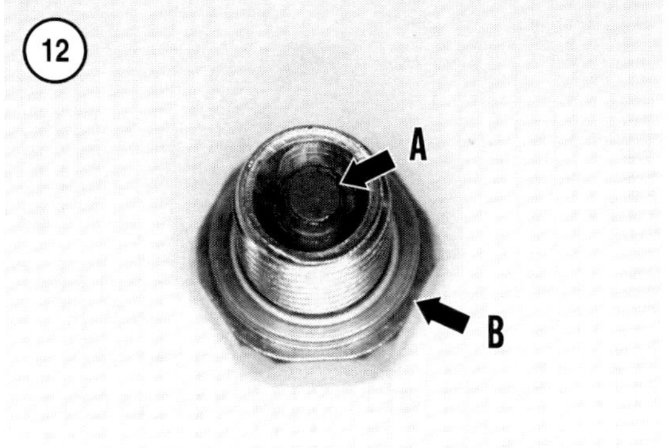

4. Check the engine oil level in the oil inspection window (**Figure 9**) on the clutch cover. The oil level must be between the upper and lower lines.
5. If the oil level is low, unscrew the oil filler cap (**Figure 10**) from the clutch cover. Insert a small funnel into the hole. Correct the oil level by adding the recommended grade and viscosity oil listed in **Table 3**.
6. Inspect the O-ring seal on the oil filler cap. Replace the O-ring if it is starting to deteriorate or harden.
7. Install the oil filler cap, and tighten it securely.

NOTE
*Refer to **Engine Oil and Filter Change** in this chapter for additional information on oil selection.*

8. If the oil level is too high, remove the oil filler cap and draw out the excess oil with a syringe or suitable pump.
9. Recheck the oil level. Adjust it if necessary.

Engine Oil and Filter Change

Regular oil and filter changes contribute more to engine longevity than any other maintenance service. The recommended oil and filter change interval is in **Table 1**. This assumes that the motorcycle is operated in moderate climates. If it is operated under dusty conditions, the oil will get dirty more quickly and should be changed more frequently than recommended.

Use only a high-quality detergent motor oil with an API classification of SF or SG. The classification is listed on the container. Use SAE 10W-40 weight oil in all models. Use a lighter viscosity oil in cool climates and the heavier viscosity oil in warm climates. Use the same brand of oil at each oil change.

NOTE
A socket type oil filter wrench (Suzuki part No. 09915-40610, Vector part No. 17070c or equivalent) is required to remove the oil filter because of the small working area between the oil filter, the exhaust system and the engine.

NOTE
Never dispose of the motor oil in the trash, on the ground, or down the storm drain. Many service stations accept used engine oil and some local waste haulers provide curbside used motor oil collection. Do not combine other fluids with the motor oil to be recycled. To locate a recycler, contact the American Petroleum Institute (API) at www.recycleoil.org.

NOTE
Warming up the engine heats the oil so it flows freely and carries out contamination and sludge.

1. Securely support the motorcycle on level ground on the centerstand.
2. Start the engine and let it warm up for two to three minutes. Shut the engine off.
3. Place a drain pan under the engine.
4. Remove the oil drain plug (**Figure 11**) and gasket from the bottom of the oil pan.
5. Loosen the oil filler cap (**Figure 10**). This speeds up the flow of oil.
6. Allow the oil to completely drain.
7. Inspect the oil drain plug for an accumulation of metal debris on its magnet (A, **Figure 12**). Clean off all debris.
8. Inspect the condition of the drained oil for contamination. After it has cooled down, check for any

metal particles or clutch friction disc particles. If any debris is found, remove the oil pan from the bottom of the engine. Clean the pan and the pick up screen as described in this chapter.

WARNING
The exhaust system must be completely cool before removing the oil filter. The oil cooler hoses and fittings, as well as the exhaust system, surround the oil filter. The working area is very small. The oil filter is hot, so protect hands accordingly.

9. To replace the oil filter, perform the following:
   a. Move the drain pan under the oil filter so it will catch residual oil that drains from the filter.
   b. Install a socket-type oil filter wrench (A, **Figure 13**) and socket handle onto the oil filter (B). Turn the filter *counterclockwise* until oil begins to run out. Wait until the oil stops draining, then loosen the filter until it is easy to turn.
   c. Due to limited space, remove the oil filter wrench from the end of the filter. Completely unscrew the filter by hand and remove it. Hold it with the open end facing up.
   d. Hold the filter over the drain pan and pour out any remaining oil. Place the old filter in a reclosable plastic bag and close the bag. Discard the old filter properly.
   e. Thoroughly clean the oil filter sealing surface on the crankcase. This surface must be clean to achieve a good seal with the oil filter.
   f. Apply a light coat of clean engine oil to the rubber seal on the new filter.
   g. Install a new oil filter onto the engine's threaded fitting.
   h. Tighten the filter by hand until the rubber seal contacts the crankcase surface and then tighten it an additional two full turns.

10. Inspect the drain plug gasket (B, **Figure 12**) for damage. Replace the gasket if necessary.
11. Install the drain plug (**Figure 11**) and its gasket. Tighten the oil drain plug to 23 N•m (17 ft.-lb.).
12. Insert a funnel into the oil filler hole and add the quantity of oil specified in **Table 3**.
13. Remove the funnel and screw in the oil filler cap securely (**Figure 10**).

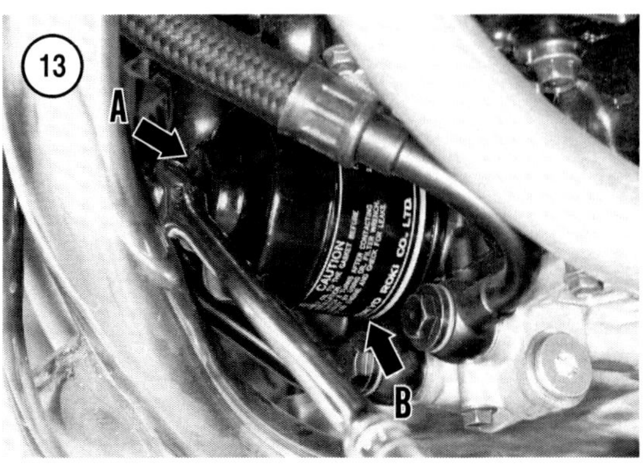

14. If oil drips onto the exhaust pipes during this procedure, wipe off as much as possible with a shop rag. Then spray some aerosol parts cleaner onto the pipes to remove the oil residue. This will help eliminate the burned oil smoke and smell when the motorcycle is first started.

NOTE
If servicing a rebuilt engine, inspect the lubrication system. Check the engine oil pressure as described in this chapter.

15. Start the engine and let it idle.
16. Check the oil filter and drain plug for leaks. Tighten either if necessary.
17. Turn off the engine and check the engine oil level as described in this chapter. Adjust the oil level if necessary.

WARNING
Prolonged contact with oil may cause skin cancer. Wash hands thoroughly with soap and water as soon as possible after handling or coming in contact with engine oil.

Engine Oil Pan, Oil Strainer and Oil Pressure Regulator

The engine oil pan, oil sump strainer and oil pressure regulator can be removed, inspected and installed with the engine in the frame. Refer to the procedure in Chapter Five.

Engine Oil Pressure Test

To check the pressure a Suzuki oil pressure gauge (part No. 09915-74510), gauge attachment (part

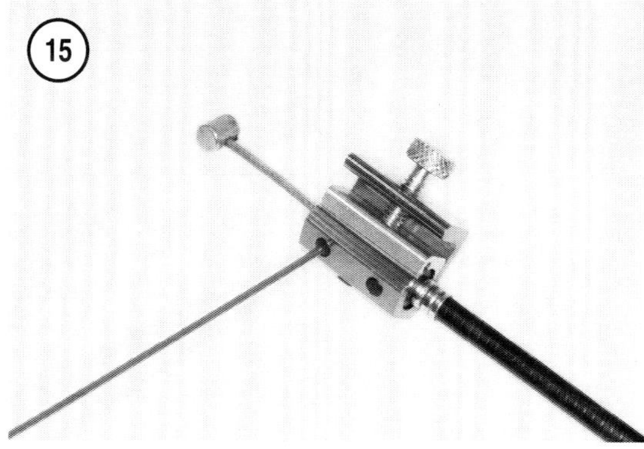

No. 09915-74540) and high-pressure meter (part No. 09915-77330) are required.

1. Check that the engine oil level is correct as described in this chapter. Add oil if necessary.

2. Start the engine and allow it to reach normal operating temperature. Turn off the engine.

3. Place a drain pan under the main oil gallery plug (**Figure 14**) to catch the oil that drains out during the test.

4. Unscrew and remove the main oil gallery plug from the crankcase.

5. Install the adapter and then the gauge into the main oil gallery. Make sure the fitting is tight to avoid oil loss.

CAUTION

Keep the gauge hose away from the exhaust pipe during this test. If the hose contacts the exhaust pipes, it will probably melt and spray hot oil onto the hot exhaust pipe, resulting in a dangerous fire.

6. Start the engine and warm it up to test temperature (60° C [140° F]). In the summer, run the engine at 2000 rpm for approximately ten minutes. In the winter, run it at 2000 rpm for 20 minutes.

7. Increase engine speed to 3000 rpm and measure the oil pressure. The oil pressure should be within the range specified in **Table 4** when the oil temperature is 60° C (140° F).

8. If the oil pressure is lower than specified, check the following:

   a. Clogged oil filter.
   b. Clogged oil cooler.
   c. Oil leak from oil passageway.
   d. Damaged oil seal(s).
   e. Defective oil pump.
   f. Combination of the above.

9. If the oil pressure is higher than specified check the following:

   a. Oil viscosity too heavy (drain oil and install lighter weight oil).
   b. Clogged oil passageway.
   c. Combination of the above.

10. Shut off the engine and remove the test equipment.

11. Apply a light coat of gasket sealer to the main oil gallery plug. Install the plug (**Figure 14**) onto the crankcase and tighten it securely.

12. Check oil level and adjust if necessary.

General Lubrication

At the service intervals in **Table 1**, lubricate the drive chain with Suzuki chain lube, its equivalent or with SAE 20W-50 engine oil. Lubricate the brake pedal pivot, gearshift lever pivot, footpeg pivots, brake lever holder, clutch lever holder and the sidestand/centerstand pivot and springs with waterproof grease.

Control Cable Lubrication (Non-Nylon Lined Cables)

Lubricate the throttle cables at the intervals indicated in **Table 1**. In addition, check the cables for kinks and signs of wear and damage or fraying that could cause the cables to fail or stick.

The most positive method of control cable lubrication involves the use of a cable lubricator like the one shown in **Figure 15**. A can of cable lube or an aerosol general lubricant is required. Do *not* use chain lube as a cable lubricant.

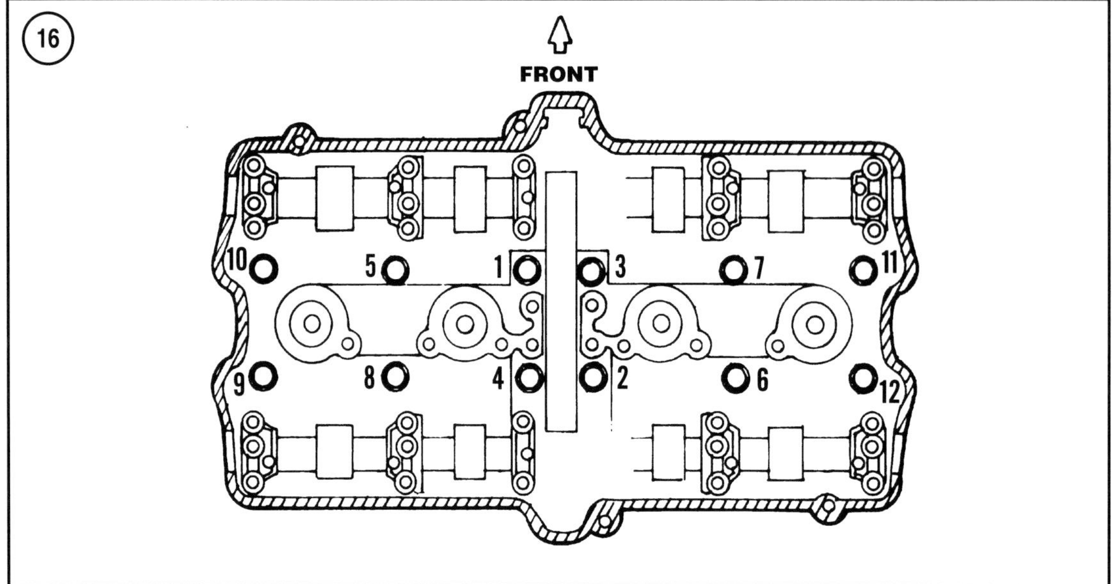

1. Remove the fuel tank as described in Chapter Eight. This is necessary to gain access to the lower end of the cables being lubricated.
2. Disconnect both throttle cables from the right handlebar switch. Refer to *Throttle Cable Replacement* in Chapter Eight.
3. Disconnect the starter (choke) cable from the left handlebar switch. Refer to *Starter (Choke) Cable Replacement* in Chapter Eight.
4. Attach a cable lubricator to the end of the cable, following the manufacturer's instructions.

NOTE
Place a shop cloth at the end of the cables to catch the oil as it runs out.

5. Insert the lubricant can nozzle into the lubricator. Press and hold the button on the can until the lubricant begins to flow out of the other end of the cable. If unable to get the cable lube to flow through the cable at one end, remove the lubricator from the cable end. Disconnect the cable from the carburetor assembly and try at the opposite end of the cable.
6. Disconnect the lubricator.
7. Apply a light coat of grease to the cable ends before reconnecting them. Reconnect the cable(s), and adjust them as described in this chapter.
8. After lubricating the throttle cables, operate the throttle at the handlebar. It should open and close smoothly with no binding.
9. After lubricating the starter (choke) cable, operate the lever at the left handlebar. It should move back and forth with no binding.

Drive Chain Cleaning and Lubrication

Clean and lubricate the drive chain at the interval indicated in **Table 1** or whenever it becomes dry. If the drive chain tends to rust between cleanings, clean and lubricate the chain at more frequent intervals. A properly maintained drive chain will provide maximum service life and reliability.

NOTE
On O-ring type drive chains, the chain lubrication described in this procedure is used mainly to keep the side plates and rollers from rusting. The actual chain lubrication is trapped within each chain roller cavity by the O-rings.

1. Securely support the motorcycle on level ground on the centerstand.
2. Shift the transmission into NEUTRAL.
3. If necessary, place a suitable size jack or wooden blocks under the engine to securely support the motorcycle with the rear wheel off the ground.

CAUTION
Do not use gasoline or solvent to clean the chain. Only use kerosene. Other fluids can damage the chain O-rings.

4. Carefully and thoroughly clean the drive chain with kerosene and a brush. Dry with a clean cloth and then with compressed air.

CAUTION
Lubricate the drive chain with Suzuki chain lube, its equivalent or with SAE 20W-50 engine oil. If using engine oil, do not use a lighter weight oil. It will not stay on the chain as long.

5. Apply the lubricant to the bottom chain run. Concentrate on getting the oil down between the side plates on both sides of the chain. Do not over-lubricate the chain. This will cause dirt to collect on the chain and sprockets.

6. Rotate the wheel and continue applying lubricant until the entire chain is lubricated.

7. Turn the wheel slowly, and wipe excess oil from the chain with a clean shop cloth. Also wipe off any oil that got onto the rear hub, wheel and tire.

Swing Arm Bearing Lubrication

Periodic lubrication of the swing arm bearings is vital to keep the rear suspension in peak condition. Lubricate the swing arm bearing assemblies whenever they are disassembled. Use a good grade waterproof grease.

The swing arm must be removed and partially disassembled to lubricate the needle bearings and collars. Remove the swing arm as described in Chapter Twelve. Clean, inspect and lubricate the bearings while they are still installed in the swing arm. Do *not* remove the bearings. They are damaged during removal.

Shock Lever Lubrication

The shock lever assembly must be removed and partially disassembled to lubricate the needle bearings and collars.

To clean, examine and lubricate the shock lever bearings and collars, remove the shock lever as described in Chapter Twelve. Clean, inspect and lubricate the bearings while they are still installed in the shock lever. Do *not* remove the bearings during lubrication. The bearings will be damaged during removal.

PERIODIC MAINTENANCE

Periodic maintenance intervals are listed in **Table 1**.

Cylinder Head Fasteners

The cylinder head (not the cylinder head cover) is held in place with 12 nuts (**Figure 16**), one cylinder head bolt (**Figure 17**) and one cylinder base nut (**Figure 18**).

NOTE
***Figure 18** is shown with the engine removed and partially disassembled to better illustrate the step.*

Tighten the cylinder head fasteners after the first 600 miles (1000 km) of operation, after the cylinder head has been removed for service or at the interval specified in **Table 1**.

NOTE
This procedure is shown with the engine removed from the frame for clarity. Do not remove the engine for this procedure.

NOTE
This procedure must be performed with the engine cool, at room temperature (below 35° C [95° F]).

1. Remove the cylinder head cover as described in Chapter Four.
2. Reverse the torque pattern shown in **Figure 16** and loosen all cylinder head nuts.
3. Tighten all cylinder head nuts in the torque pattern to 38 N•m (28 ft.-lb.).
4. Tighten the cylinder head bolt (**Figure 17**) and the cylinder base nut (**Figure 18**) to 10 N•m (88 in.-lb.) and 9 N•m (80 in.-lb.), respectively.
5. Check the valve clearance as described in this chapter.

Air Filter Cleaning

Remove and clean the air filter at the interval indicated in **Table 1**. Replace the element at the specified interval or whenever it is damaged or starting to deteriorate.

The air filter removes dust and abrasive particles from incoming air before it enters the carburetors and the engine. *Never* run the motorcycle without the air filter element installed.

1. Securely support the motorcycle on level ground on the centerstand.
2. Remove the seat as described in Chapter Fourteen.
3. Remove the fuel tank as described in Chapter Eight.
4. Thoroughly clean any debris from the area surrounding the air filter housing cover.

5A. On 1996-2000 models, perform the following:

a. Move the vent hoses away from the air filter cover.
b. Remove the screws (**Figure 19**) securing the cover to the air filter housing.
c. Pivot the cover toward the rear and disengage the cover's rear lower tabs from the two notches in the bottom of the air box.

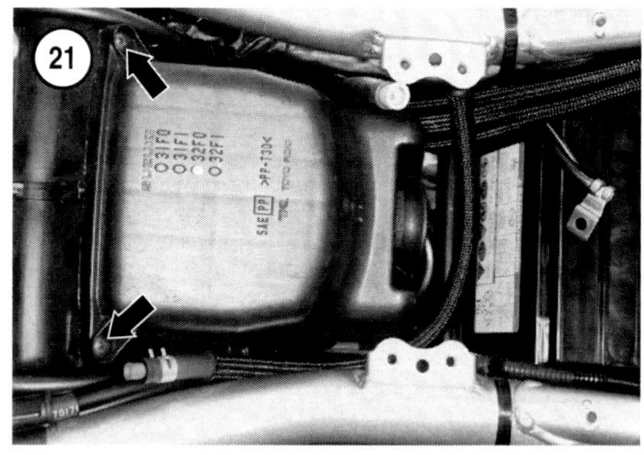

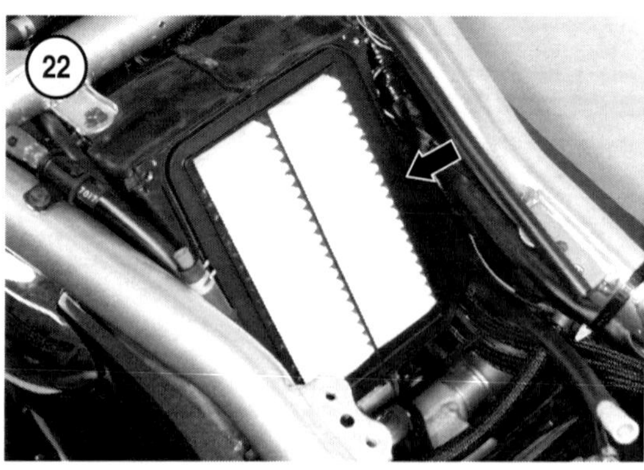

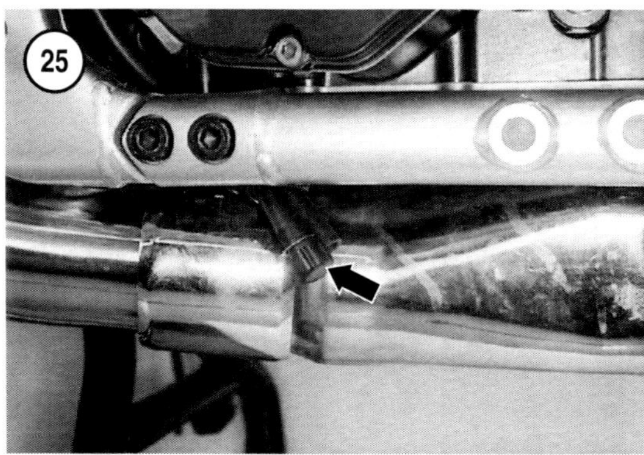

   d. Remove the cover.

5B. On 2001-on models, perform the following:

   a. Remove the bolts securing the fuel tank mounting bracket and remove the bracket (**Figure 20**).
   b. Remove the screws (**Figure 21**) securing the cover to the air filter housing
   c. Pivot the cover toward the rear and disengage the cover's rear lower tabs from the two notches in the bottom of the air box.
   d. Remove the cover.

6. Remove the air filter element (**Figure 22**) from the air box.
7. Cover the air filter air box with a heavy towel to prevent the entry of objects or debris.

NOTE
If the air filter element is extremely dirty or if it has any holes, wipe out the interior of the air filter housing with a shop rag dampened in cleaning solvent. Remove any debris that may have passed through a broken element.

8. Gently tap the air filter to loosen the trapped dirt and dust.

CAUTION
In the next step, do not apply compressed air toward the outside surface of the filter. Air directed at the outside surface will force the dirt and dust into the pores of the element, thus restricting air flow.

9. Apply compressed air to the *inside surface* (**Figure 23**) of the air filter element and remove all loosened dirt and dust.
10. Thoroughly and carefully inspect the filter element. If it is torn or broken in any area, replace it. Do not run the motorcycle with a damaged air filter element. If the element is good, it can be used until the indicated time for replacement in **Table 1**.
11. Inspect the air box screen (**Figure 24**) for dirt and damage. Clean off all debris that may have passed through the air filter element. If the screen is damaged, replace the air box assembly.
12. Remove the plug (**Figure 25**) from the air filter drain hose and drain out any water and debris. Securely reinstall the plug into the drain hose.
13. Install the air filter into the housing so the Suzuki *S* mark (**Figure 26**) on the filter frame is located at the top of the housing and is facing out.

14A. On 1996-2000 models, install the air filter cover as follows:

a. Insert the two lower tabs (**Figure 27**) into the two notches in the bottom of the air box.
b. Secure the carburetor vent hoses with the hose guides on the side of the cover. Make sure to capture the vent hoses, and do *not* pinch them.
c. Install the air filter cover and tighten the screws (**Figure 19**) securely.

14B. On 2001-on models, install the air filter cover as follows:

a. If necessary, install a new air-filter-cover gasket
b. Insert the two lower tabs (A, **Figure 28**) into the two notches in the bottom of the air box.
c. Pivot the cover forward and seat it against the air box.
d. Secure the carburetor vent hoses with the hose guides (B, **Figure 28**) on the side of the cover. Make sure to capture the vent hoses, and do *not* pinch them.
e. Tighten the screws securely.

15. On 2001-on models, reinstall the fuel tank bracket (**Figure 20**).
16. Install the fuel tank and the seat.

27

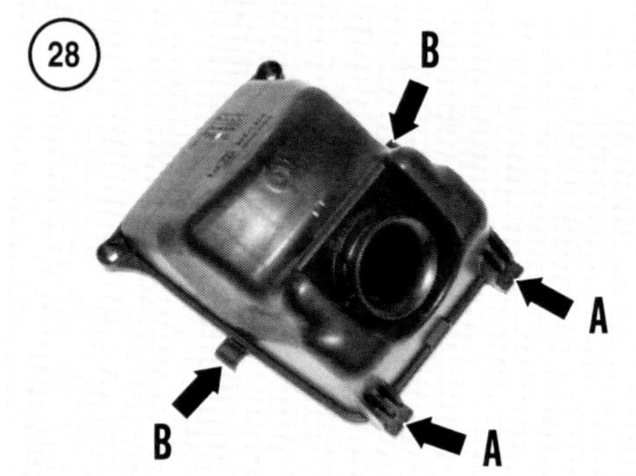

28

Drive Chain and Sprocket Wear Inspection

Check the drive chain frequently and replace it when it is excessively worn or damaged. The following simple test quickly indicates the condition of the drive chain.

At the rear sprocket, pull one of the links away from the sprocket. If the link pulls away more than 1/2 the height of a sprocket tooth as shown in **Figure 29**, the chain is probably worn beyond the service limit. Confirm this by measuring drive chain length as described below.

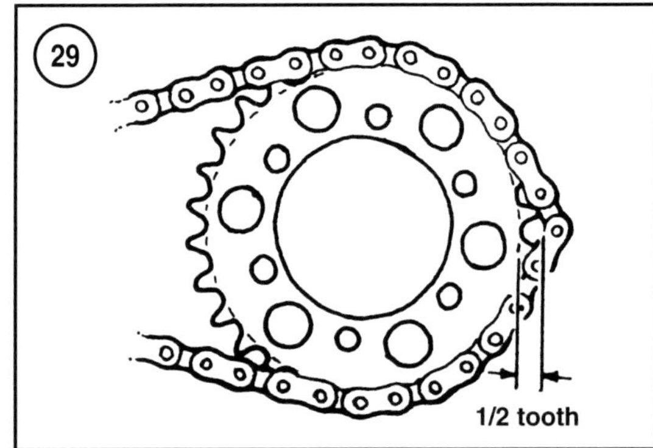

29

Drive Chain Length Inspection

1. Securely support the motorcycle on level ground on the centerstand.
2. On models so equipped, remove the cotter pin (A, **Figure 30**) from the rear axle nut. Discard the cotter pin. A new one must be installed during assembly.
3. Have an assistant apply the rear brake, then loosen the rear axle nut (B, **Figure 30**).

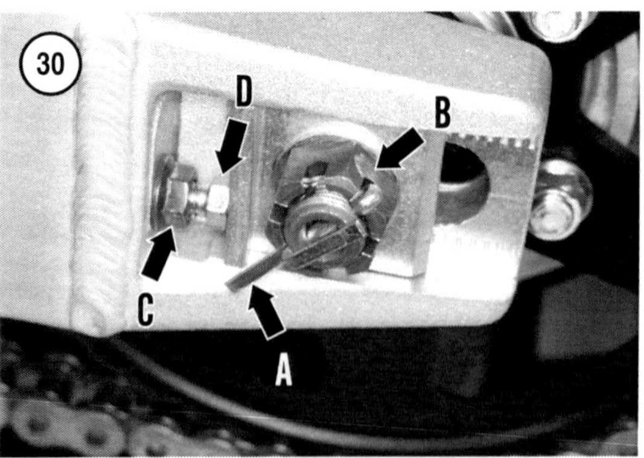

30

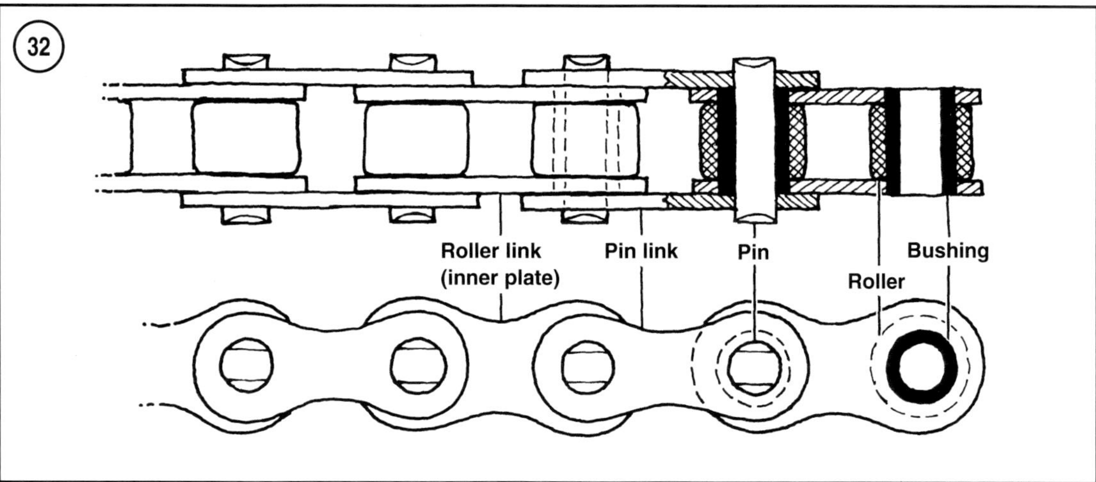

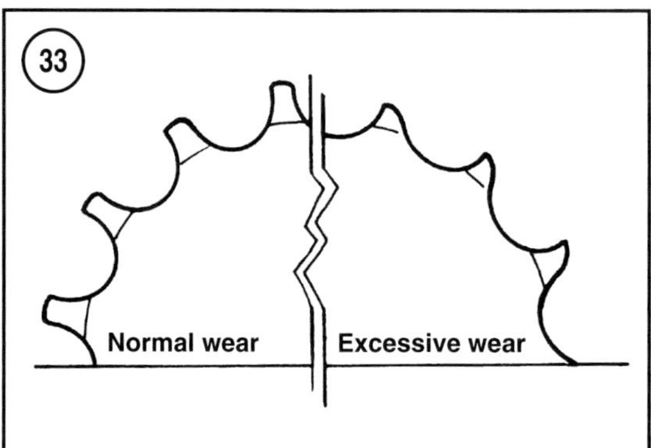

4. Loosen the drive chain locknut (C, **Figure 30**) on both sides of the swing arm.
5. Tighten the chain adjuster (D, **Figure 30**) on each side of the swing arm and move the wheel rearward until the chain is tight with no slack.
6. Place a vernier caliper along the chain run and measure the distance between 21 pins (20 links) in the chain as shown in **Figure 31**. If the 21-pin length exceeds the specification in **Table 4**, install a new drive chain as described in Chapter Ten.
7. Inspect the faces of the inner chain plates (**Figure 32**). They should be lightly polished on both sides. If they show considerable uneven wear on one side, the engine and rear sprockets are not aligned properly. Severe wear requires replacement of not only the drive chain, but also the engine and rear sprockets.
8. If the drive chain is severely worn, remove the engine sprocket cover as described in Chapter Seven. Inspect both the engine sprocket and rear sprocket for the following defects:
   a. Undercutting or sharp teeth (**Figure 33**).

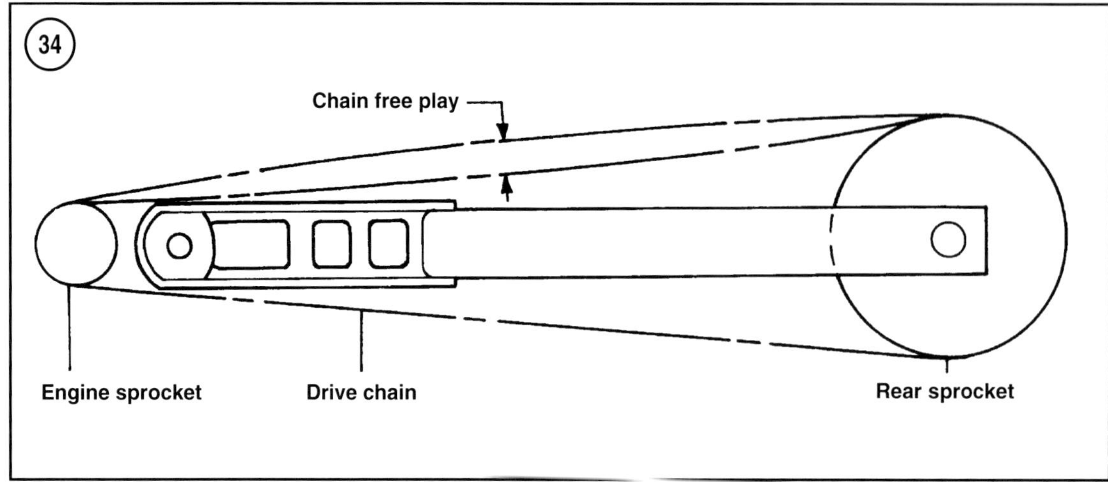

b. Broken teeth.

CAUTION
On a new motorcycle or after a new rear sprocket has been installed, check the torque on the rear sprocket nuts after 10 minutes of riding and after each 10-minute riding period until the nuts have seated and remain tight. Failure to keep the sprocket nuts correctly tightened will damage the rear hub.

9. If wear is evident, replace the drive chain and sprockets as a set. If only the drive chain is replaced, the worn sprockets will quickly wear out the new chain. Refer to Chapter Seven for *Engine Sprocket Removal/Installation*. Refer to Chapter Ten for *Rear Sprocket Removal/Installation*.
10. Adjust the drive chain as described in this chapter.
11. Install the engine sprocket cover as described in Chapter Seven.

Drive Chain Free Play Adjustment

The drive chain must have adequate play so that the chain is not strung tightly when the swing arm is horizontal. On the other hand, too much slack may cause the chain to jump off the sprockets with potentially dangerous consequences.

Check and adjust the drive chain at the interval in **Table 1**. A properly lubricated and adjusted drive chain provides maximum service life and reliability.

When adjusting the chain, check the free play at several places along its length by rotating the rear wheel. The chain rarely wears uniformly and as a result will be tighter at some places than at others. Measure the chain free play when the chain's tightest point is halfway between the sprockets.

1. Roll the motorcycle back and forth and check the chain for tightness at several points on the chain. Identify the tightest point and mark this spot with a piece of chalk.
2. Turn the wheel until this mark is on the lower chain run, midway between the engine and drive sprockets.
3. Securely support the motorcycle on level ground on the centerstand.
4. With thumb and forefinger, grasp the chain at the center of the chain run and move the chain up and down. Measure the distance the chain moves vertically (**Figure 34**). Compare the measurement to the drive chain free play specified in **Table 5**. If necessary, adjust the free play by performing the following.
5. On models so equipped, remove the cotter pin (A, **Figure 30**) from the rear axle nut. Discard the cotter pin. A new one must be installed during assembly.
6. Loosen the rear axle nut (B, **Figure 30**).

NOTE
Always maintain rear wheel alignment when adjusting drive chain free play. A mis-aligned rear wheel can cause poor handling. For alignment purposes, all models are equipped with an alignment scale and an ad-

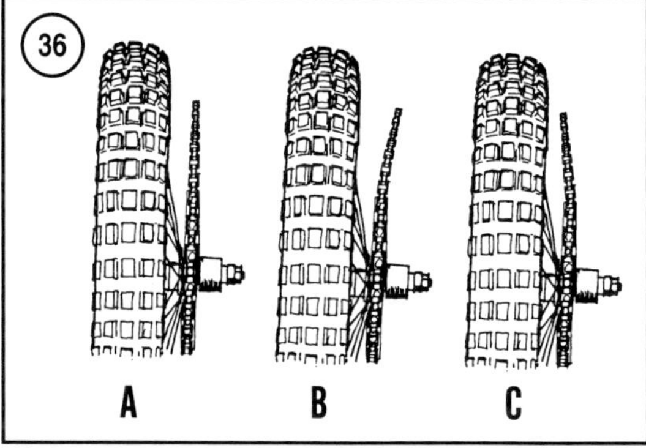

*juster plate (**Figure 35**) on each side of the swing arm.*

7. Loosen the drive chain locknut (C, **Figure 30**) on both sides of the swing arm.

8. Tighten or loosen the chain adjuster (D, **Figure 30**) on each side an equal amount until the chain free play is within the range specified in **Table 4**. Make sure the indexing mark on the left adjuster plate aligns with the same point on its alignment scale as the indexing mark on the right side of the swing arm (**Figure 35**).

9. When drive chain free play is correct, check the wheel alignment by sighting along the top of the drive chain from the rear sprocket. The chain should form a straight line as it leaves the rear sprocket and travels to the engine sprocket (A, **Figure 36**). If the chain veers to one side or the other (B and C, **Figure 36**), perform the following:
   a. Check that the indexing marks on the left and right adjuster plates (**Figure 35**) align with the same points on their respective alignment scales.
   b. If not, readjust the drive chain so the adjuster plates are at the same positions on their respective scales and the free play is within specification.

10. Tighten the rear axle nut to 100 N•m (74 ft.-lb.).

11. On models so equipped, install a *new* cotter pin (A, **Figure 30**) and bend the ends over completely.

12. If the drive chain cannot be adjusted to the correct measurement, the drive chain is excessively worn and must be replaced as described in Chapter Ten. Replace both the engine drive and rear driven sprockets when replacing the drive chain. Never install a new drive chain over worn sprockets.

Drive Chain Slider Inspection

Inspect the drive chain slider (**Figure 37**) on the left side of the swing arm for wear. Replace the slider if it is excessively worn.

Routine inspection and replacement of the drive chain slider prevents the drive chain from damaging the swing arm. A drive chain with too much free play causes rapid wear of the chain slider.

To replace the drive chain slider, remove the swing arm as described in Chapter Twelve and remove the slider. Whenever the swing arm is removed for slider replacement, inspect and lubricate the swing arm bearings. Use a good grade of waterproof grease such as Suzuki Super Grease A or equivalent.

Throttle Operation

Check throttle operation at the interval indicated in **Table 1**.

Operate the throttle grip. Check for smooth throttle operation from fully closed to fully open and then back to the fully closed position. The throttle should automatically return to the fully closed position without any hesitation.

Check the throttle cables for damage, wear or deterioration. Make sure the throttle cables are not kinked at any place.

If the throttle does not return to the fully closed position smoothly and if the exterior of the cable sheaths appears to be in good condition, lubricate the throttle cables as described in this chapter. Also apply a light coat of grease to the throttle cable spool at the hand grip.

If cable lubrication does not solve the problem, the throttle cables must be replaced as described in Chapter Eight.

Throttle Cable Free Play

Check the throttle cable free play at the interval indicated in **Table 1**.

In time, the throttle cable free play becomes excessive from cable stretch. This delays throttle response and affects low speed operation. On the other hand, insufficient throttle cable free play can lead to an excessively high idle.

NOTE
The pull cable is located at the front fitting on the right side switch housing. The return cable is located at the back fitting.

1. Securely support the motorcycle on level ground on the centerstand.
2. Shift the transmission into NEUTRAL.
3. Start the engine and allow it to idle.
4. With the engine at idle speed, slowly twist the throttle to raise engine speed. Note the amount of rotational movement (**Figure 38**) required to raise the idle. This amount of movement is the throttle cable free play.
5. If throttle cable free play is outside the range specified in **Table 4**, adjust it by performing the following procedure.
6. Shut off the engine.

7A. On 1996-2000 models, perform the following:
  a. Loosen the locknut (A, **Figure 39**) on the return cable and turn the adjuster (B) in either direction until there is 0.5-1.0 mm (0.02-0.04 in.) of free play in the return cable.
  b. Hold onto the return cable adjuster (B, **Figure 39**) and tighten the locknut (A).

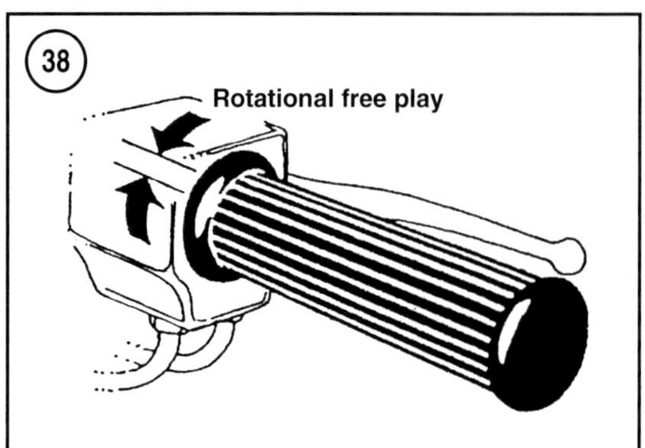

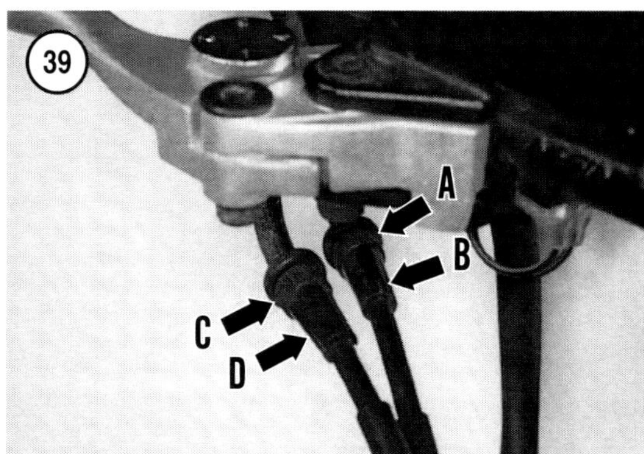

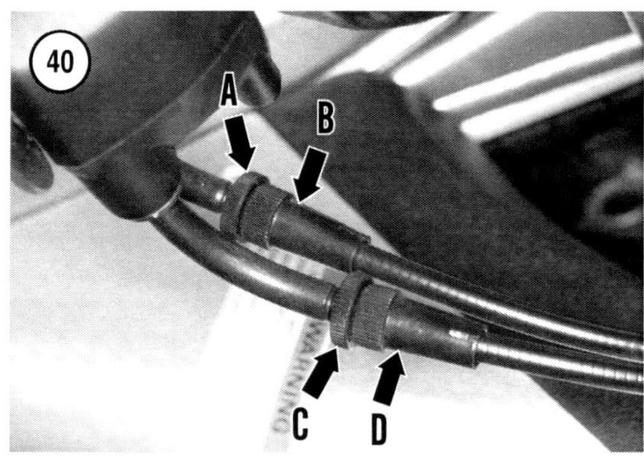

  c. Loosen the locknut (C, **Figure 39**) on the pull cable and turn the adjuster (D) in either direction until there is 0.5-1.0 mm (0.02-0.04 in.) of free play in the pull cable.
  d. Hold onto the pull cable adjuster (D, **Figure 39**) and tighten the locknut (C).

7B. On 2001-on models, perform the following:
  a. Loosen the locknut (A, **Figure 40**) on the return cable and turn the adjuster (B) all the way in onto the threads.
  b. Loosen the locknut (C, **Figure 40**) on the pull cable and turn the adjuster (D) in either direc-

tion until there is 2-4 mm (0.08-16 in.) of free play in the pull cable. Hold the pull cable adjuster (D, **Figure 40**), and tighten the locknut (C) securely.

c. Twist the throttle grip in the fully closed position and hold it there.
d. Loosen the locknut (A, **Figure 40**) on the return cable and slowly turn the adjuster (B) until resistance is felt then stop.
e. Hold onto the return cable adjuster (B, **Figure 40**) and tighten the locknut (A).

8. Restart the engine and repeat Steps 4 and 5 to make sure the adjustment is correct.

9. If the throttle cable free play cannot be adjusted to specification at the throttle grip, the cable(s) is stretched beyond the wear limit and must be replaced. Refer to Chapter Eight for this service procedure.

10. Check the operation of the throttle. Make sure it opens and closes smoothly and crisply.

11. Check the throttle cables from grip to carburetor. Make sure they are not kinked or chafed. Replace as necessary.

WARNING
*With the engine idling, move the handlebar from side to side. If the idle speed increases during this movement, the throttle cables may need adjusting or may be incorrectly routed through the frame. Correct this problem immediately. Do **not** ride the motorcycle in this unsafe condition.*

12. Test ride the motorcycle, slowly at first, and make sure the throttle cables are operating correctly. Readjust if necessary.

Brake Fluid Level

Check the hydraulic brake fluid in each brake master cylinder at the interval in **Table 1**. Check the brake pads for wear at the same time. Bleeding the system, servicing the brake system components and replacing the brake pads are covered in Chapter Thirteen.

Keep the hydraulic brake fluid in the reservoir above the lower mark on the reservoir. If the fluid level drops to the low level line on the front brake reservoir (A, **Figure 41**) or the rear brake reservoir (A, **Figure 42**), correct the level by adding fresh brake fluid.

CAUTION
Be careful when adding brake fluid. Do not spill it on plastic, painted or plated surfaces. Brake fluid damages these surfaces. Immediately wash off spilled brake fluid with soapy water. Thoroughly rinse the area with clean water.

1. Securely support the motorcycle on level ground on the centerstand.
2. On the front master cylinder, perform the following:
   a. Position the handlebar so the front master cylinder is horizontal.
   b. Clean all debris from the top of the master cylinder reservoir.
   c. Remove the top cover screws, and remove the top cover (B, **Figure 41**), the diaphragm plate and diaphragm from the master cylinder reservoir.

3. On the rear master cylinder, perform the following:
   a. Remove the right side rear frame cover as described in Chapter Fourteen.
   b. Clean all debris from the top of the master cylinder reservoir.
   c. Remove the screws securing the top cover (B, **Figure 42**). Remove the top cover and diaphragm.

WARNING
Use brake fluid clearly marked DOT 4 from a sealed container. Other types may vaporize and cause brake failure. Always use the same brand name of brake fluid. Do not intermix different brands. They may not be compatible. Do not use silicone based (DOT 5) brake fluid. It can cause brake component damage, leading to brake system failure.

NOTE
To control the flow of brake fluid from a new container, punch a small hole in the seal next to the edge of the pour spout. This helps eliminate fluid spillage, especially while adding fluid to the small reservoir.

4. Refill the master cylinder reservoir, if necessary, to maintain the correct fluid level as indicated on the side of the reservoir.
5. On the front master cylinder, install the diaphragm, diaphragm plate and cover. Tighten the cover screws securely.
6. On the rear master cylinder, perform the following:
   a. Install the diaphragm and cover. Tighten the cover screws securely.
   b. Install the rear frame cover as described in Chapter Fourteen.

Brake Fluid Change

Every time the reservoir top cover and diaphragm are removed, a small amount of dirt and moisture enter the brake fluid system. The same thing happens if a leak occurs or if any part of the hydraulic brake system is loosened or disconnected. Dirt can clog the system and cause unnecessary wear. Water in the brake fluid vaporizes at high temperature, impairing the hydraulic action and reducing the brake's stopping ability.

To maintain peak braking efficiency, change the brake fluid at the interval listed in **Table 1**. To change brake fluid, follow the *Bleeding The System* procedure in Chapter Thirteen. Continue adding new brake fluid to the master cylinder and bleed the fluid from the caliper bleeder valve until the brake fluid leaving the caliper is clean and free of contaminants.

WARNING
Use brake fluid clearly marked DOT 4 from a sealed container. Other types may vaporize and cause brake failure. Always use the same brand name of

46

Wear limit Wear limit

Front pads Rear pads

brake fluid. Do not intermix different brands. They may not be compatible. Do not use silicone based (DOT 5) brake fluid. It can cause brake component damage leading to brake system failure.

Brake Hose Inspection

Check the brake hoses between each master cylinder and each brake caliper assembly.

If there is any leakage, tighten the connections and bleed the brakes as described in Chapter Thirteen. If tightening the connection does not stop the leak or if the brake hose(s) is obviously damaged, cracked or chafed, replace the brake hose(s) and bleed the system as described in Chapter Thirteen.

Brake Pad Inspection

Inspect the brake pads for wear at the interval indicated in **Table 1**.

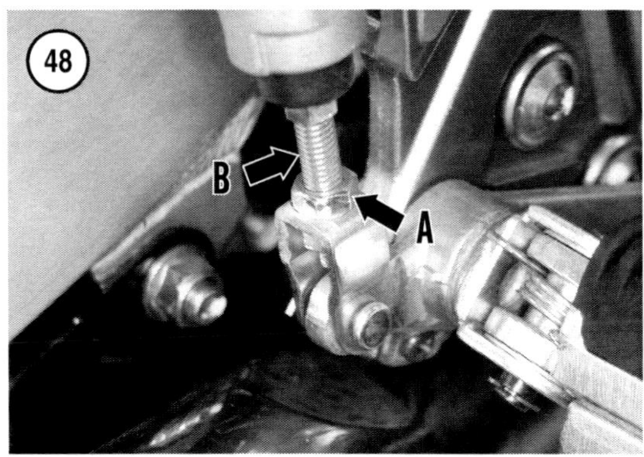

On the front brake caliper, remove the top cover (**Figure 43**) look into the caliper assembly, and inspect the brake pads (**Figure 44**) for excessive or uneven wear.

On the rear caliper, look into the top of the caliper assembly and inspect the brake pads (**Figure 45**) for excessive wear.

If any pad is worn to the wear limit (**Figure 46**), the pads must be replaced. Follow the pad replacement procedure in Chapter Thirteen.

NOTE

Always replace both pads in each caliper at the same time to maintain even pressure on the brake disc. On the front brakes, replace both brake pads in both calipers at the same time to maintain even braking.

Brake Pedal Height Adjustment

The brake pedal height changes as the brake pads wear. The top of the brake pedal should be positioned below the top surface of the footpeg as shown in **Figure 47**. The distance between the top of the brake pedal and the top of the footpeg should equal the specification listed in **Table 4**. If the dimension is incorrect, adjust the brake pedal height by performing the following.

1. Securely support the motorcycle on level ground on the centerstand.
2. Make sure the brake pedal is in the at-rest position.
3. At the rear brake master cylinder, loosen the locknut (A, **Figure 48**) and turn the pushrod (B) in either direction until the brake pedal height equals the listed specification.

4. Tighten the rear brake master cylinder rod locknut to 18 N•m (13 ft.-lb.).

Rear Brake Switch Adjustment

1. Turn the ignition switch to the ON position.
2. Depress the brake pedal. The brake light should come on just as the brake begins to work.

NOTE
Some riders prefer that the brake light turns on a little early. This way, they can tap the pedal without braking to warn drivers who are following too closely.

3. To make the brake light come on earlier, hold the brake light switch body (**Figure 49**) and turn the adjusting nut clockwise as viewed from the top. Turn the adjusting nut counterclockwise to delay the light from coming on.
4. Turn the ignition switch OFF.

Crankcase Breather

1. Remove the fuel tank as described in Chapter Eight.
2. Inspect the breather hose (**Figure 50**) from the cylinder head cover to the air filter housing. If it is cracked or deteriorated it must be replaced. Make sure the hose clamps are in place and are tight.
3. Install the fuel tank.

Evaporative Emission Control System (California Models Only)

The evaporative emissions control system captures fuel vapors and stores them so they will not be released into the atmosphere. The fuel vapors are routed through the roll-over valve and stored in the charcoal canister (**Figure 51**), located on the right side of the frame. When the engine is started, the stored vapors are drawn from the canister. They pass through the purge control valves, flow into the carburetors and then into the engine, where they are burned.

Make sure all evaporative emission control hoses are correctly routed and properly attached to their respective components. Inspect the hoses and replace any if necessary as described in Chapter Eight.

PAIR (Air Supply) System Emission Control System (California Models)

The PAIR system introduces fresh air into the exhaust ports to reduce the exhaust emission level.

Refer to *PAIR (Air Supply) System Emission Control System* in Chapter Eight for complete inspection and service procedures.

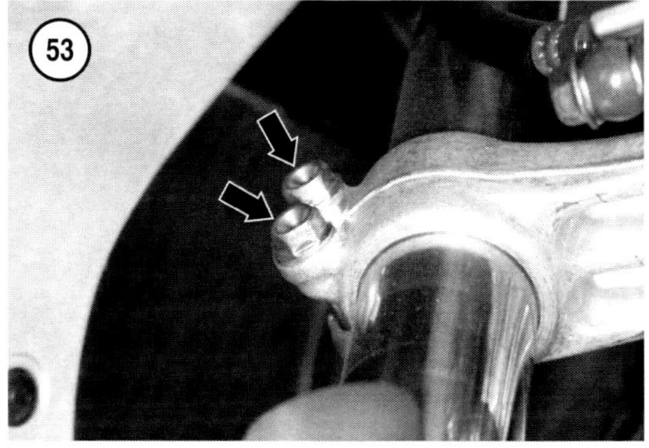

NON-SCHEDULED MAINTENANCE

Exhaust System Inspection

1. Inspect the exhaust system for cracks or dents that could alter performance.
2. Check all exhaust system fasteners and mounting points for loose or damaged parts.
3. Make sure all mounting bolts and nuts are tight. Tighten any loose fasteners.

Fuel Line Inspection

Inspect the fuel lines from the fuel tank to the carburetor assembly and other remaining hoses. Replace any hose that is cracked or starting to deteriorate. Make sure the small hose clamps are in place and holding securely.

WARNING
A damaged or deteriorated fuel line presents a very dangerous fire hazard to both the rider and the motorcycle. Fuel could spill onto the hot engine or exhaust pipe.

Wheel Bearing Inspection

Routinely inspect the front and rear wheel bearings and oil seals for excessive wear or damage. Clean and repack non-sealed bearings once a year with Suzuki Super Grease A or an equivalent waterproof grease. Repack the bearings more often if the motorcycle is operated in wet conditions. The service procedures are covered in Chapter Ten.

Steering Head Inspection

The steering head on all models consists of upper and lower caged roller or ball bearings. A loose bearing adjustment will hamper steering. In severe conditions, a loose bearing adjustment can cause loss of control.

1. Securely support the motorcycle on level ground on the centerstand.
2. Place wooden blocks under the engine.
3. Have an assistant sit on the seat to raise the front wheel off the ground.
4. Hold onto the front fork tubes and gently rock the fork assembly back and forth. If looseness is felt, adjust the steering head as described in *Steering Head Installation* in Chapter Eleven.

Front Suspension Inspection

1. Inspect the handlebar weekly for any signs of damage. Replace a bent or damaged handlebar. Check the tightness of the clamp bolts.
2. Wipe each front fork leg with a soft wet cloth. Remove any dirt, road tar or bugs from the fork legs. This debris will eventually work its way into the seals and cause an oil leak.
3. Check the fork tubes for signs of leaks or damage.
4. Apply the front brake and pump the front fork up and down vigorously. Check for smooth operation and for any oil leaks.
5. Make sure the upper (**Figure 52**) and lower fork bridge clamp bolts (**Figure 53**) are tight.
6. On the right side, make sure the front axle clamp bolts (A, **Figure 54**) are tight and check the tightness of the front axle (B).

Fork Oil

Each front fork leg must be partially disassembled for fork oil replacement and oil level adjustment. Refer to *Front Fork* in Chapter Eleven.

Front Suspension Spring Pre-load Adjustment

WARNING
Set both fork spring pre-load adjusters to the same setting. An unequal setting will result in poor handling and possible loss of control of the motorcycle.

To change the fork spring pre-load adjuster, use a screwdriver (A, **Figure 55**) and rotate the adjuster (B) at the top of the fork cap bolt. Turning the spring seat *clockwise* to the 0 position increases the pre-load and provides a stiffer suspension. Turning the adjuster *counterclockwise* decreases pre-load and provides a softer suspension. Position 3 is the standard setting.

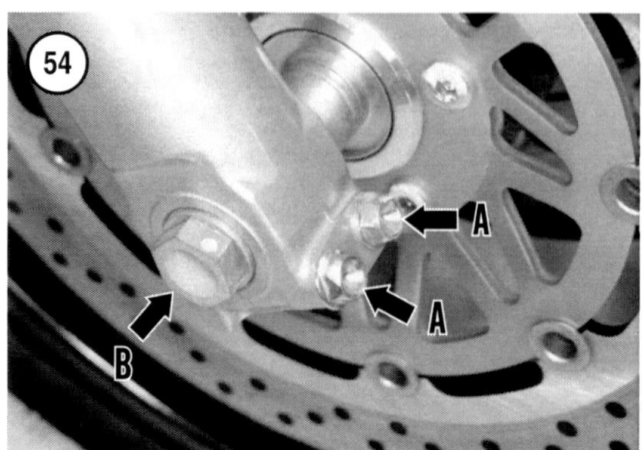

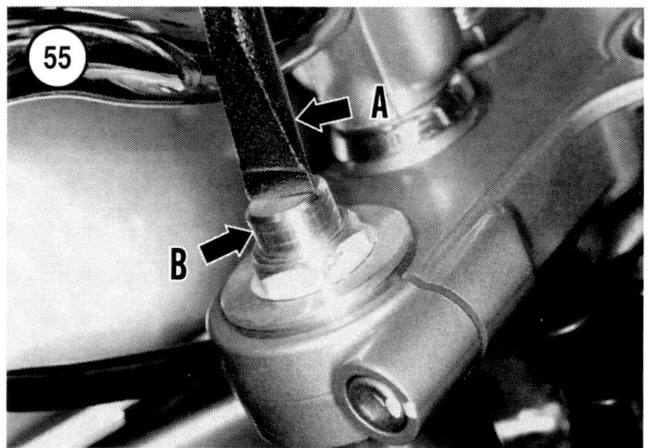

Rear Suspension Inspection

1. With both wheels on the ground, check the shock absorber by bouncing on the seat several times.
2. Securely support the motorcycle on a stand with the rear wheel off the ground.
3. Have an assistant steady the motorcycle.
4. Push hard on the rear wheel (sideways) to check for side play in the rear swing arm bearings.
5. Check the shock absorber for oil leaks, loose mounting fasteners or other damage.
6. Check the rear suspension for loose or missing fasteners.
7. Make sure the rear axle nut is tight.
8. Check the drive chain guard for loose or missing fasteners.

CAUTION
If any fastener is loose, refer to Chapter Twelve for tightening procedures and torque specifications.

Rear Shock Absorber Adjustment

The rear shock can be adjusted to suit the load and rider preference. The spring preload can be adjusted

by varying the spring installed length. The shock absorber rebound damping can also be adjusted.

Spring preload adjustment

CAUTION
Never turn the upper spring seat beyond the maximum or minimum position.

Use the ring nut wrench to adjust the preload by rotating the upper spring seat (**Figure 56**) at the top

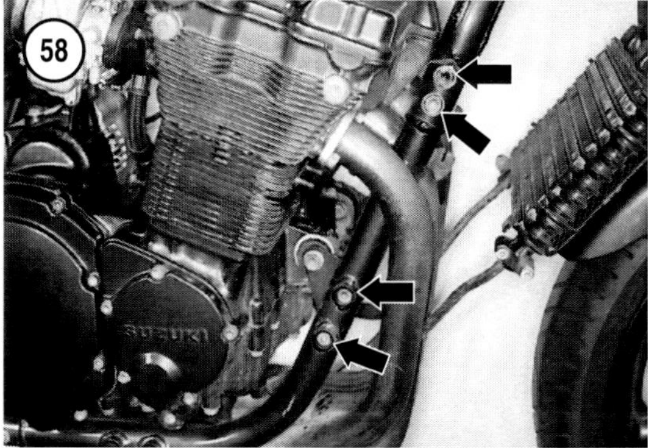

of the shock absorber. Turning the spring seat *clockwise* to a higher numbered setting increases the preload and provides a stiffer suspension. Turning the ring counterclockwise to a lower numbered setting decreases preload and provides a softer suspension. Position 4 is the standard setting.

Rebound damping adjustment

Rebound damping affects the rate at which the shock absorber returns to its extended position after compression. Rebound damping does not affect the action of the shock on compression.

The rebound damping adjuster (**Figure 57**) at the bottom of the shock absorber has four settings. Position 1 is the softest setting. It provides the least amount of rebound damping. Position 4 is the stiffest setting. It provides the greatest amount of rebound damping. Position 2 is the standard setting.

CAUTION
The rebound damping adjuster must click into one of the detent positions. The rebound damping will be at the stiffest setting if the adjuster sits between detent positions.

To adjust the rebound damping, turn the adjuster to the desired setting. Make sure the adjuster clicks into a detent. If the adjuster is not set to a detent, the rebound damping is set to the stiffest setting.

Frame Inspection

Inspect the frame for cracks or other damage. Check all areas where welded sections attach to the main frame spar. Check the tightness of the removable sub-frame down tube mounting bolts. Refer to **Figure 58** and **Figure 59**.

If necessary, refer to Chapter 5 and tighten the bolts to the specification.

Fastener Inspection

Constant vibration can loosen many of the fasteners on a motorcycle. Check the tightness of all fasteners, especially those on:

1. Engine mounting hardware.
2. Engine crankcase covers.
3. Handlebar and front fork.
4. Gearshift lever.
5. Brake pedal and lever.
6. Exhaust system.
7. Removable sub-frame down tube.

ENGINE TUNE-UP

The following section describes tune-up procedures. Perform these tasks in the following order:

1. Clean or replace the air filter element.
2. Check and adjust valve clearances (engine must be cold).

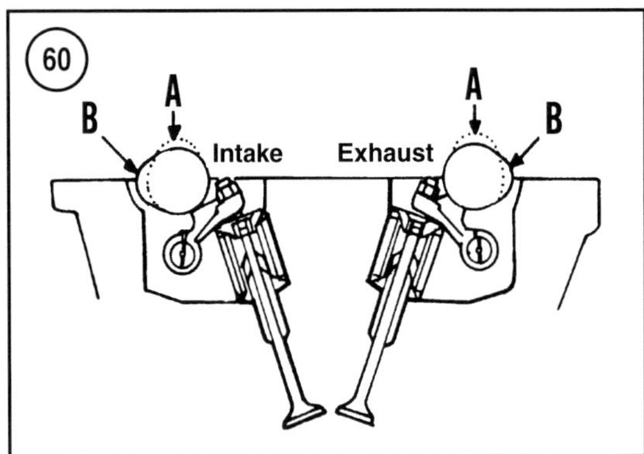

3. Perform a compression test.
4. Check or replace the spark plugs.
5. Check and adjust the carburetor idle speed and synchronization.

Air Filter Element

Clean or replace the air filter element as described in this chapter prior to performing the following tune-up procedures.

Valve Clearance Measurement

The valve clearances are listed in **Table 4**. The exhaust valves are located at the front of the engine and the intake valves are located at the rear.

The cylinders are numbered from left to right 1-4. The left and right sides refer to the engine as viewed by the rider sitting on the seat facing forward.

The figures in this procedure show the engine removed from the frame to better illustrate the steps; it is not necessary to remove the engine to adjust the valves.

The engine *must* be cold (below 35° C [95° F]) to obtain accurate results.

CAUTION
For this procedure the camshaft lobes must point away from the rockers as shown in either position A or B, ***Figure 60****. Clearance dimensions taken with the camshaft in any other position will give a false reading, leading to incorrect valve clearance adjustment and possible engine damage.*

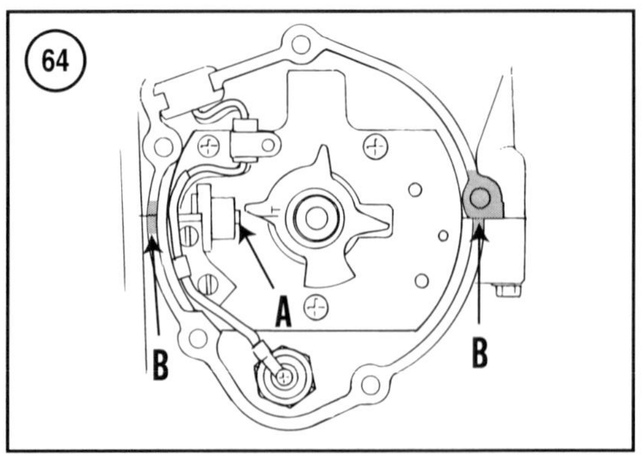

1. Remove the seat as described in Chapter Fourteen.
2. Remove the fuel tank as described in Chapter Eight.

65

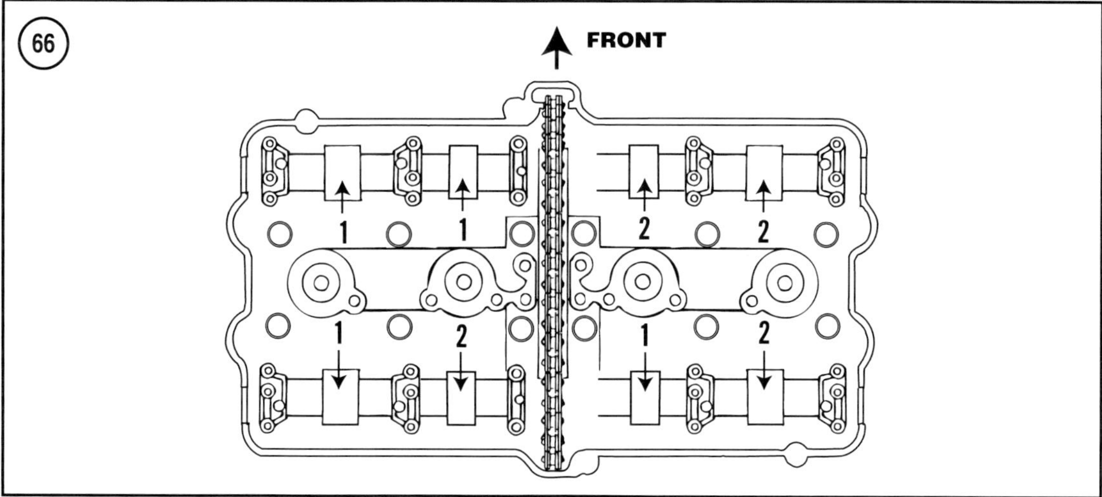

3. Remove all four spark plugs as described in this chapter. This will make it easier to turn the engine by hand.

4. Remove the cylinder head cover as described in Chapter Four.

5. Remove the signal generator cover bolts and remove the cover and its gasket (**Figure 61**). One cover bolt has a sealing washer (**Figure 62**) installed beneath it. Note the position of this bolt. It must be reinstalled in the same location during assembly.

CAUTION

Always use a 19 mm wrench on the flats of the signal generator rotor when rotating the engine. Do not use the Allen bolt that secures the rotor to turn the crankshaft. This bolt may shear off.

6. Correctly position the camshafts by performing the following:
   a. Place a 19 mm wrench on the flats of the signal generator rotor (A, **Figure 63**). Rotate the engine *clockwise* until the T-mark on the signal generator rotor aligns with the center of the pickup coil (A, **Figure 64**).
   b. At the same time, bring the camshaft notches on the right side of each camshaft to the positions shown in **Figure 65**.
   c. If the camshaft notches do not point out as shown, rotate the engine 360° (one full revolution) until the camshaft notches are positioned correctly and the signal generator T-mark aligns with the pickup coil.

7. With the engine in this position, check the valve clearance for each valve indicated by 1, **Figure 66**. These are:

a. No. 1 cylinder: intake and exhaust valves.

b. No. 2 cylinder: exhaust valves.

c. No. 3 cylinder: intake valves.

8. Check the clearance by inserting a flat feeler gauge (**Figure 67**) between the adjusting screw and each valve stem. When the clearance is correct, there will be a slight drag on the feeler gauge when it is inserted and withdrawn.

9. To adjust the clearance, perform the following:

a. Loosen the adjuster locknut (A, **Figure 68**).

b. Screw the adjuster (B, **Figure 68**) in or out so there is a slight resistance felt on the feeler gauge (C).

c. Hold the adjuster to prevent it from turning further and tighten the locknut securely.

d. Recheck the clearance to make sure the adjuster did not turn after the correct clearance was achieved. Readjust if necessary.

e. Repeat for the adjuster of the other valve controlled by the same rocker arm.

f. Repeat this checking/adjustment procedure for all the valves indicated at 1, **Figure 66**.

10. Correctly reposition the camshafts by performing the following:

a. Place a 19 mm wrench on the flats of the signal generator rotor (A, **Figure 63**). Rotate the engine *clockwise* 360° (one full revolution) until the T-mark on the signal generator rotor aligns with the center of the pickup coil (A, **Figure 64**).

b. At the same time, bring the camshaft notches on the right side of each camshaft to the position shown in **Figure 69**.

c. If the camshaft notches do not point inward as shown, rotate the engine 360° (one full revolution) until the camshaft notches are positioned correctly and the signal generator T-mark aligns with the pickup coil (**Figure 70**).

11. With the engine in this position, check the valve clearance for each valve indicated by 2, **Figure 66**. These are:

a. Cylinder No. 2: intake valves.

b. Cylinder No. 3: exhaust valves.

c. Cylinder No. 4: intake and exhaust valves.

12. Check the valve clearances as described in Step 8. If any valve indicated by 2, **Figure 66** is out of specification, adjust it as described in Step 9.

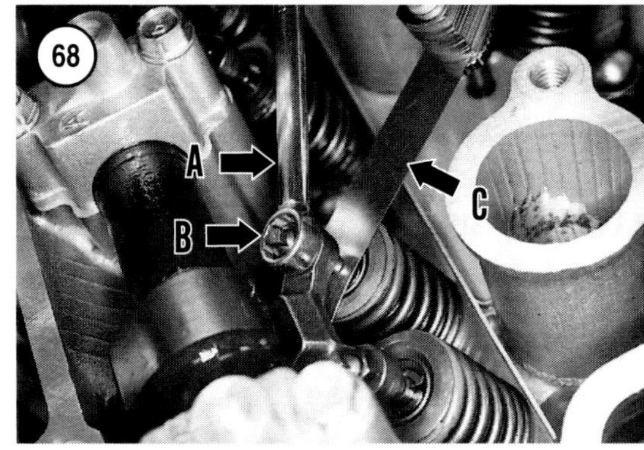

13. Once all valves are within specification, install the cylinder head cover as described in Chapter Four.

14. Install the signal generator cover and a *new* gasket as follows:

a. Apply a light coat of gasket sealer to the groove in the rubber grommet (B, **Figure 63**).

b. Apply gasket sealer to the crankcase mating surfaces where the cover fits (B, **Figure 64**).

c. Tighten the cover bolts securely. Be sure the bolt with the sealing washer is in the location noted during disassembly (**Figure 62**).

Camshaft Chain Adjustment

An automatic camshaft chain tensioner assembly is attached to the backside of the cylinder head. Adjustment is neither possible nor required.

Cylinder Compression

A cylinder cranking compression check is one of the quickest ways to check the internal condition of the engine, including the pistons, piston rings and

69

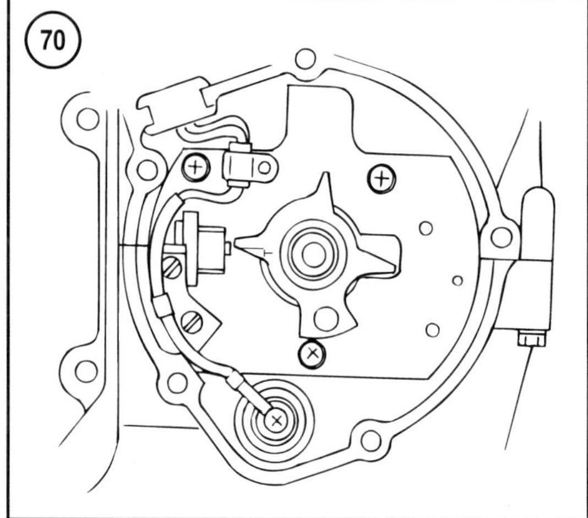

70

71

cylinder head gasket. Check the compression at each tune-up, record the readings in the maintenance log at the back of the manual and compare them with the readings at the next tune-up. This may help reveal developing problems.

1. Prior to starting the compression test, make sure the following items are correct:
   a. The cylinder head bolts are tightened as described in this chapter.
   b. The valves are properly adjusted as described in this chapter.
   c. The battery is fully charged to ensure proper engine cranking speed.
2. Warm the engine to normal operating temperature. Turn the engine off.
3. Remove the fuel tank as described in Chapter Eight.
4. Remove all four spark plugs as described in this chapter.

NOTE

A screw-in type compression gauge with a flexible adapter is required for this procedure. Before using this gauge, check the condition of the rubber gasket on the end of the adapter. Replace the seal if it is cracked, hard or starting to deteriorate.

5. Lubricate the adapter with a *light* coat of antiseize compound to prevent damaging the spark plug hole threads in the cylinder head.
6. Thread the tip of a compression gauge into the No. 4 cylinder (**Figure 71**), following the manufacturer's instructions.

CAUTION

Do not crank the engine more than absolutely necessary. When the spark plug leads are disconnected, the electronic ignition will produce the high-

est voltage possible and the coils may overheat and be damaged.

7. *Open the throttle completely* and turn the engine over until there is no further rise in pressure. Maximum pressure is usually reached within 4-7 seconds. Record the pressure reading for that cylinder. The recommended cylinder compression and the maximum allowable difference between cylinders are listed in **Table 4**.
8. Remove the compression gauge from that cylinder.
9. Repeat Steps 5-8 for the remaining three cylinders and record the readings.
10. Compare the compression readings of the cylinders. Engine service is required if the readings are as follows:
    a. Compression in one cylinder is less than 875 kPa (126 psi).
    b. The difference in readings between any two cylinders exceeds 200 kPa (29 psi).
11. Low compression pressure indicates one or more of the following:
    a. Excessively worn cylinder walls.
    b. Worn piston or piston rings.
    c. Piston ring stuck in its groove.
    d. Poor valve seating.
    e. Defective cylinder head gasket.
12. To determine whether the problem is valve or ring related, pour about a teaspoon of engine oil into the spark plug hole of the low-reading cylinder and repeat Steps 6-7.
    a. If the compression increases significantly, the piston rings are probably worn.
    b. If the compression does not increase, the valves are leaking.
13. Install the spark plugs, plug caps, and the fuel tank.

SPARK PLUGS

Spark Plug Removal

A spark plug can be used to help determine the operating condition of its cylinder when properly inspected. As each spark plug is removed, label it with its cylinder number. If anything turns up during the inspection, knowing which cylinder a plug came from will be useful.

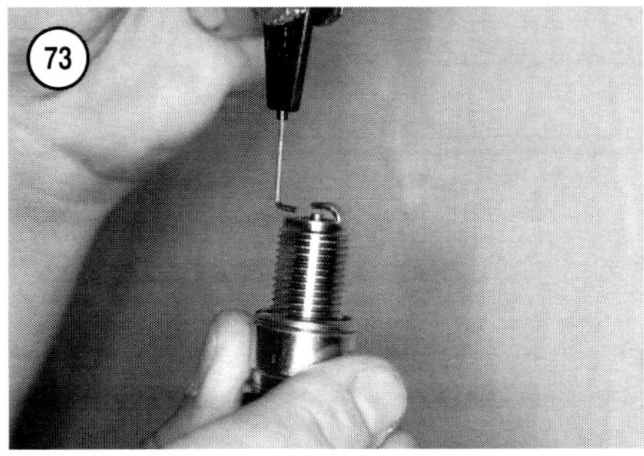

The cylinders are numbered from left to right 1-4. The left and right sides refer to the parts as viewed by the rider sitting on the seat facing forward.

1. Remove the seat as described in Chapter Fourteen.
2. Remove the fuel tank as described in Chapter Eight.

CAUTION
Whenever a spark plug is removed, dirt around it can fall into the spark plug hole. This can cause serious engine damage.

3. Blow away all loose dirt, then wipe off the top surface of the cylinder head cover. Remove all loose debris that could fall into the cylinder head spark plug tunnels.
4. Carefully disconnect the spark plug cap from each spark plug. The plug caps form a tight seal on the cylinder head cover as well as the spark plugs. Grasp the plug cap (**Figure 72**) and twist it from side to side to break the seal loose. Carefully pull the plug cap up and off the spark plug. If it is stuck to the plug, continue to twist it slightly.

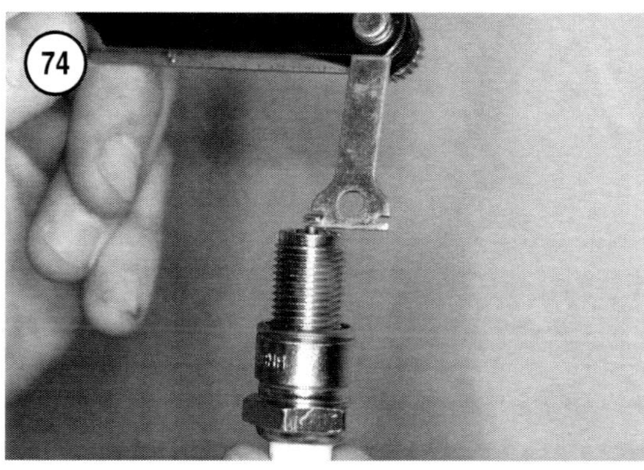

NOTE
If plugs are difficult to remove, apply penetrating oil around the base of the plugs and let it soak in about 10-20 minutes.

5. Remove the spark plugs with an 18 mm spark plug wrench. Label each spark plug by cylinder number.

6. Thoroughly inspect the spark plug. Look for a plug with broken center porcelain, excessively eroded electrodes and excessive carbon or oil fouling. Replace such a plug. If deposits are light, the plug may be cleaned in solvent with a wire brush or in a special spark plug cleaner. Re-gap the plug as explained in this chapter.

Spark Plug Gap and Installation

Carefully gap the spark plugs to ensure reliable, consistent spark with a special spark plug gapping tool and a wire feeler gauge.

1. Insert a wire feeler gauge between the center and side electrodes of the plug (**Figure 73**). The specified gap is in **Table 4**. If the gap is correct, a slight drag will be felt as the wire is pulled through. If there is no drag or if the gauge will not pass through, bend the side electrode with a gaping tool (**Figure 74**) and set the gap to specification.

2. Apply a *light* coat of antiseize compound onto the threads of the spark plug before installing it. Do not use engine oil on the plug threads.

3. If installed, unscrew the terminal nut (A, **Figure 75**) from the end of the plug. This nut is *not* used.

CAUTION
The cylinder head is aluminum. The spark plug hole threads can be easily damaged by cross-threading of the spark plug.

4. Attach a length of vinyl or rubber hose to the top end of the spark plug. Screw the spark plug in by hand until it seats. Very little effort is required. If force is necessary, the plug is cross-threaded. Unscrew it and try again. Once screwed on several complete revolutions, remove the hose.

NOTE
Do not overtighten the spark plug. This will only squash the gasket and destroy its sealing ability.

5. Use the same tool set-up used during removal and hand-tighten the plug until it seats on the spark plug hole in the cylinder head. Tighten the plug to 11 N•m (97 in.-lb.).

CAUTION
Do not use a plastic hammer or any type of tool to tap the plug cap assembly onto the spark plug, as the assembly will be damaged. Use fingers only.

NOTE
Be sure to push the plug cap all the way down to make full contact with the spark plug threaded post. If the cap does not completely contact the plug, the engine may start to falter and cut out at high engine speeds.

6. Refer to the marks made during removal and install each plug cap onto the correct spark plug. Press the cap (**Figure 72**) onto the spark plug, rotate the assembly slightly in both directions and make sure it is attached to the spark plug and to the sealing surface of the cylinder head cover.
7. Install the fuel tank as described in Chapter Eight.
8. Install the seat as described in Chapter Fourteen.

Spark Plug Heat Range

Spark plugs are available in various heat ranges, hotter or colder than the original equipment plugs.

Select a plug with a heat range designed for the loads and conditions under which the motorcycle will be run. A plug with an incorrect heat range can foul, overheat and cause piston damage.

In general, use a hot plug for low speeds and low temperatures. Use a cold plug for high speeds, high engine loads and high temperatures. The plug should operate hot enough to burn off unwanted deposits, but not so hot that it is damaged or causes preignition. To determine if the spark plugs have a proper heat range, remove each spark plug and examine the portion of the insulator that sits inside the combustion chamber. Its color should be light tan.

Do not change spark plug heat range to compensate for adverse engine or carburetion conditions.

The reach (B, **Figure 75**) of a plug is also important. A longer than normal plug could interfere with the piston, causing permanent and severe damage.

Refer to **Table 4** for recommended spark plugs

Spark Plug Reading

Reading the spark plugs can provide a significant amount of information regarding engine performance. Reading plugs that have been in use will give an indication of spark plug operation, air/fuel mixture composition and engine conditions (such as oil consumption or pistons). Before checking the spark plugs, operate the motorcycle under a medium load for approximately 6 miles (10 km). Avoid prolonged idling before shutting off the engine. Remove the spark plugs as described in this chapter. Examine each plug and compare it to those in **Figure 76**.

If the plugs are being read to determine if carburetor jetting is correct, start with new plugs and operate the motorcycle at the load that corresponds to the jetting information desired. For example, if the main jet is in question, operate the motorcycle at full throttle and shut the engine off and coast to a stop.

Normal condition

A light tan- or gray-colored deposit on the firing tip and no abnormal gap wear or erosion indicate good engine, ignition and air/fuel mixture conditions. A plug with the proper heat range is being used. It may be serviced and returned to use.

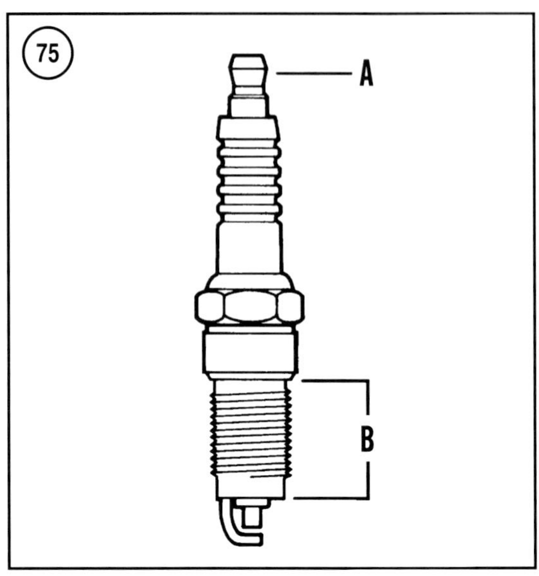

Carbon fouled

Soft, dry, sooty deposits covering the entire firing end of the plug are evidence of incomplete combustion. Even though the firing end of the plug is dry, the deposits decrease the plug's insulation. The carbon forms an electrical path that bypasses the electrodes resulting in a misfire condition. Carbon fouling can be caused by one or more of the following conditions:

1. Rich fuel mixture.
2. Cold spark plug heat.
3. Clogged air filter.
4. Improperly operating ignition component.
5. Ignition component failure.
6. Low engine compression.
7. Prolonged idling.

Oil fouled

An oil fouled plug has a black insulator tip, a damp oily film over the firing end and a carbon layer over the entire nose. The electrodes are not worn. Common causes for this condition are:

1. Incorrect air/fuel mixture.
2. Low idle speed or prolonged idling.
3. Ignition component failure.
4. Cold spark plug heat range.
5. Engine still being broken in.
6. Valve guides worn.
7. Piston rings worn or broken.

(76)

SPARK PLUG CONDITION

NORMAL

GAP BRIDGED

CARBON FOULED

OVERHEATED

OIL FOULED

SUSTAINED PREIGNITION

Oil fouled spark plugs may be cleaned in an emergency, but it is better to replace them. It is important to correct the cause of fouling before the engine is returned to service.

Gap bridging

Plugs with this condition have deposits building up between the electrodes. The deposits reduce the gap and eventually close it entirely. If this condition is encountered, check for excessive carbon or oil in the combustion chamber. Be sure to locate and correct the cause of this condition.

Overheating

Badly worn electrodes and premature gap wear are signs of overheating, along with a gray or white blistered porcelain insulator surface. This condition is commonly caused by a spark plug with a heat range that is too hot. If the plug is overheated, consider the following causes:

1. Lean air/fuel mixture.
2. Improperly operating ignition component.
3. Engine lubrication system malfunction.
4. Air/oil cooling system malfunction.
5. Engine air leak.
6. Improper spark plug installation (for example, overtightening).
7. No spark plug gasket.

Worn out

Corrosive gases formed by combustion and high voltage sparks have eroded the electrodes. A spark plug in this condition requires more voltage to fire under hard acceleration. Install a new spark plug.

Preignition

If the electrodes are melted, preignition is almost certainly the cause. Check for carburetor mounting or intake manifold leaks and advanced ignition timing. The plug heat range may also be too hot. Find the cause of the preignition before returning the engine into service. For additional information on preignition, refer to Chapter Two.

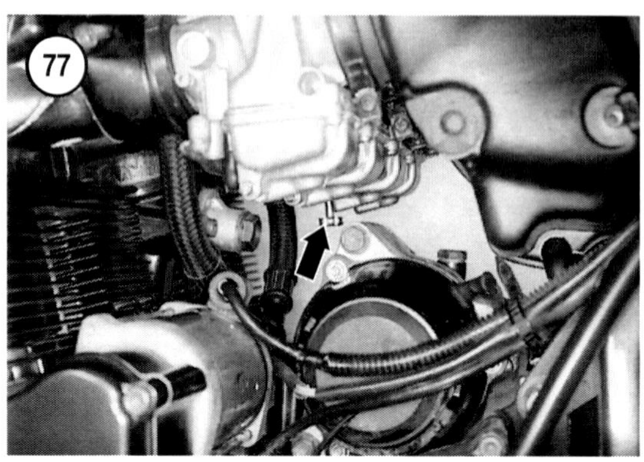

Ignition Timing

The engine is equipped with a fully transistorized solid state ignition system. Ignition timing is not adjustable.

Because of the solid-state design, problems with the transistorized system are rare. If there is an ignition-related problem, inspect the ignition components as described in Chapter Nine.

Incorrect ignition timing can cause a drastic loss of engine performance and efficiency. It may also cause overheating.

Idle Speed Adjustment

Before making this adjustment, clean the air filter element and check engine compression as described in this chapter. Idle speed cannot be properly set unless the filter is clean and the engine has adequate compression.

1. Make sure the throttle cable free play is adjusted correctly. If necessary, adjust free play as described in this chapter.
2. Connect a tachometer, following the manufacturer's instructions.
3. Start the engine and let it warm up approximately two to three minutes. Make sure the choke lever is all the way forward in the OFF position.

4A. On 1996-2000 models, the idle speed knob (**Figure 77**) is located under the carburetor assembly, between the second and third carburetors.

4B. On 2001-on models, the idle speed knob (**Figure 78**) is located on the left side of the carburetor assembly.

5. Turn the idle speed knob in or out to adjust the idle speed to the specification in **Table 4**.

6. Open and close the throttle two or three times. Check for variations in idle speed, and readjust if necessary.

WARNING
With the engine running at idle speed, move the handlebar from side to side. If idle speed increases during this movement, the throttle cables need adjusting or may be incorrectly routed through the frame. Correct this problem immediately. Do not ride the motorcycle in this unsafe condition.

7. Turn off the engine.
8. Disconnect the tachometer.

Carburetor Idle Mixture

The idle mixture (pilot screw) is pre-set by the manufacturer and *is not to be reset*. Do not adjust the pilot screws unless the carburetors have been overhauled. If so, refer to Chapter Eight.

Carburetor Synchronization

To ensure maximum engine performance, the carburetors must be synchronized. This procedure ensures that each carburetor is opening the same amount throughout the throttle range.

Synchronization tools are available in a number of different styles; some measure engine vacuum with a traditional vacuum gauge or by the movement of mercury within a glass tube, while some perform this function electronically. In addition to the synchronization tool, an auxiliary fuel tank and portable tachometer are required for this procedure. If this equipment is not available, have a Suzuki dealership or motorcycle specialist perform this procedure. Do not attempt to synchronize the carburetors without the proper equipment. Doing so will result in mis-adjustment and poor engine performance.

NOTE
Prior to synchronizing the carburetors, clean the air filter element and adjust the valve clearance.

1. Start the engine and let it reach normal operating temperature.
2. Adjust the idle speed as described in this chapter, then shut off the engine.
3. Install a portable tachometer, following the manufacturer's instructions.
4. Remove the fuel tank as described in Chapter Eight.

WARNING
When using an auxiliary fuel tank, make sure the tank is secure and that all fuel lines are tight to prevent leaks.

NOTE
Fuel tanks from small displacement motorcycles, ATV's and lawn mowers make excellent auxiliary fuel tanks. Make sure the tank is mounted securely and positioned so that the connecting fuel hose is not kinked or obstructed.

5. Install an auxiliary fuel tank onto the motorcycle, and attach its fuel hose to the carburetor assembly.
6. Balance the vacuum gauge set, following the manufacturer's instructions.

7A. On 1996-2000 models, perform the following:
   a. Label and disconnect the vacuum hose or vacuum cap from the vacuum fitting on each carburetor.
   b. On models with a PAIR system, disconnect the PAIR vacuum hose from the vacuum fitting on the No. 2 carburetor.

7B. On 2001-on models, perform the following:
   a. Label and disconnect the vacuum hose or vacuum cap from the vacuum fitting on each carburetor.
   b. On models with a PAIR system, disconnect the PAIR vacuum hose from the vacuum fitting on the No. 4 carburetor.

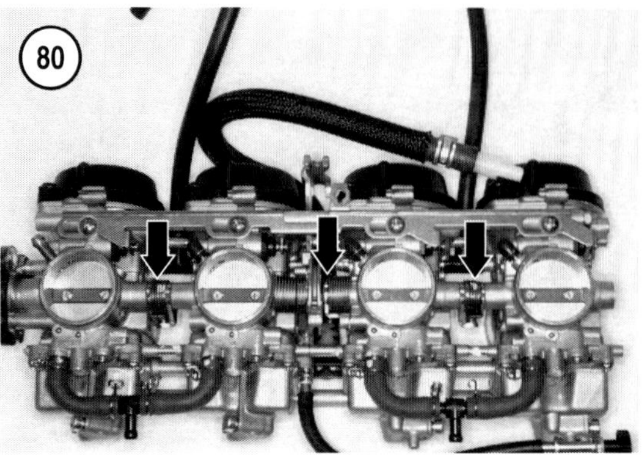

8. Connect the vacuum gauge set to the vacuum fittings, following the manufacturer's instructions.
9. Start the engine. Turn the idle adjust knob until the engine idles at 1750 rpm. Refer to **Figure 77** for 1996-2000 models or **Figure 78** for 2001-on models.
10. If the carburetors are correctly balanced, the steel balls in the vacuum gauge set will all be at the same level.

NOTE
On all models, the No. 4 carburetor is the base carburetor. It has no synchronizing screw. The other carburetors must be synchronized to the No. 4 carburetor.

11A. On 1996-2000 models, turn the synchronizing screws (**Figure 79**), and adjust the No. 1, 2 and 3 carburetors so they each have the same gauge reading as the No. 4 carburetor. Snap the throttle a few times and recheck the synchronization readings. Readjust synchronization if required.

11B. On 2001-on models, turn the synchronizing screws (**Figure 80**) and adjust the No. 1, 2 and 3 carburetors so they each have the same gauge reading as the No. 4 carburetor. Snap the throttle a few times and recheck the synchronization readings. Readjust synchronization if required.
12. Reset the idle speed to the specification in **Table 4**.
13. Shut off the engine.
14. Disconnect the auxiliary fuel tank and the vacuum gauge set from the carburetors.
15. Install the vacuum hoses or plugs to the correct fittings. Make sure they are properly seated to avoid a vacuum leak.
16. Install the fuel tank as described in Chapter Eight.
17. Restart the engine and reset the engine idle speed to the value specified in **Table 4**, if necessary.
18. Shut off the engine.

Table 1 MAINTENANCE SCHEDULE

Weekly/fuel stop
Check tire pressure cold; adjust to suit load (Table 2)
Check condition of tires
Check brakes for a solid feel
Check throttle grip for smooth operation and return
Check for smooth but not loose steering
Check axles, suspension, controls, linkage nuts, bolts and fasteners; tighten if necessary
Check engine oil level; add oil if necessary
Check lights and horn operation, especially brake light
Check for any abnormal engine noise and leaks
Check engine stop switch operation
Initial 600 miles (1000 km) or 1 month
Check the valve clearance; adjust if necessary
Change engine oil and replace oil filter
(continued)

Table 1 MAINTENANCE SCHEDULE (continued)

Initial 600 miles (1000 km) or 1 month (continued)
Check idle speed; adjust if necessary
Check throttle cable free-play; lubricate and adjust if necessary
Clean, lubricate and adjust the drive chain
Check brake pads for wear
Check brake discs for rust and corrosion; clean if necessary
Check brake fluid in both master cylinders; add fluid if necessary
Check clutch hydraulic fluid in the master cylinder; add fluid if necessary
Check steering play; adjust if necessary
Check and tighten all cylinder head and exhaust system fasteners
Check tightness of all chassis bolts and nuts; tighten if necessary
On California models, inspect the EVAP system and synchronize the carburetors
Every 4000 miles (6000 km) or 6 months
Check air filter element for contamination; clean or replace if necessary
Check air filter housing drain tube
Check spark plugs; replace if necessary
Check all fuel system hoses for leakage; repair or replace if necessary
On California models, inspect the EVAP system
Replace the engine oil
Check idle speed; adjust if necessary
Check throttle cable free-play; lubricate and adjust if necessary
Check clutch hydraulic system for leakage; repair if necessary
Check battery charge and condition of battery
Clean and lubricate the drive chain
Check drive chain and sprockets for wear or damage
Check drive chain free play; adjust if necessary
Check brake pads for wear
Check brake discs thickness; replace if necessary
Check brake discs for rust and corrosion; clean if necessary
Check brake system for leakage; repair if necessary
Check brake fluid level in both master cylinders; add fluid if necessary
Check clutch hydraulic fluid in the master cylinder; add fluid if necessary
Check tire and wheel rim condition
Lubricate all pivot points
Check and tighten all cylinder head and exhaust system fasteners
Check tightness of all chassis fasteners; tighten if necessary
Every 7500 miles (12,000 km) or 12 months
All of the checks listed in 4000 miles (6000 km) or 6 months and the following:
Check the valve clearance; adjust if necessary
Replace all four spark plugs
Synchronize carburetors
Check front fork operation and for leakage
Check PAIR (air supply) system (models so equipped)
Check steering play; adjust if necessary
Check the rear suspension
Lubricate control cables
Every 11,000 miles (18,000 km) or 18 months
All of the checks listed in 4000 miles (6000 km) or 12 months and the following:
Replace air filter element
Replace engine oil filter
Every 15,000 miles (24,000 km) or 24 months
All of the checks listed in 7500 miles (12,000 km) or 24 months
Replace all four spark plugs
Every 2 years
Replace brake fluid
Replace clutch hydraulic fluid
Every 4 years
Replace all brake hoses
Replace EVAP hoses (California models)
Replace all fuel hoses

Table 2 TIRE AND WHEEL SPECIFICATIONS

Item	Front	Rear
Tire type	Tubeless	Tubeless
Size	120/70 ZR17	180/55 ZR17
Minimum tread depth	1.6 mm (0.06 in.)	2.0 mm (0.08 in.)
Inflation pressure (cold)*		
U.S. models		
Solo	225 kPa (33 psi)	250 kPa (36 psi)
Rider and passenger	225 kPa (33 psi)	250 kPa (36 psi)
All models except U.S. models		
Solo	250 kPa (36 psi)	250 kPa (36 psi)
Rider and passenger	250 kPa (36 psi)	250 kPa (36 psi)
Wheel rim size	J17 × MT 3.50	J17 × MT5.50

*Tire inflation pressure is for original equipment tires. Aftermarket tires may require different inflation pressure. The use of tires other than those specified by Suzuki may cause instability.

Table 3 RECOMMENDED LUBRICANTS AND FLUIDS

Fuel	Unleaded
Octane	87 ([R + M]/2 method) or research octane of 91 or higher
Fuel tank capacity, including reserve	
1996-2000	19.0 L (5.0 U.S. gal., 4.2 Imp gal.)
2001	
California models	19.0 L (5.0 U.S. gal., 4.2 Imp gal.)
All models except California	20.0 L (5.2 U.S. gal., 4.4 Imp. gal.)
Fuel tank reserve capacity	4.5 L (1.2 U.S. gal., 1.0 Imp. gal.)
Engine oil	
Grade	API SF or SG
Viscosity	SAE 10W-40
Capacity	
Oil change only	3.3 L (3.5 U.S. qt., 2.9 Imp. qt.)
Oil and filter change	3.5 L (3.7 U.S. qt., 3.1 Imp. qt.)
When engine completely dry	4.6 L (4.9 U.S. qt., 4.0 Imp. qt.)
Brake fluid	DOT 4
Fork oil	
Viscosity	Suzuki #10 fork oil or equivalent
Capacity per leg	
1996-2000	514 ml (17.3 U.S. oz., 18.1 Imp. oz.)
2001	508 ml (17.1 U.S. oz., 17.9 Imp.oz.)

Table 4 MAINTENANCE AND TUNE-UP SPECIFICATIONS

Battery	
Type	YTX12-BS Yuasa Maintenance free
Capacity	12 volt 10 amp hour
Spark plug	
Standard	NGK: JR9B
Hot type	NGK: JR8B
Cold type	NGK: JR10B
Spark plug gap	0.6-0.7 mm (0.024-0.028 in.)

(continued)

Table 4 MAINTENANCE AND TUNE-UP SPECIFICATIONS (continued)

Idle speed	
Switzerland models	1150-1300 rpm
U.S. models	1150-1250 rpm
All models except Switzerland and U.S.	1100-1300 rpm
Firing order	1-2-4-3
Valve clearance (cold)	
Intake	0.10-0.15 mm (0.004-0.006 in.)
Exhaust	0.18-0.23 mm (0.007-0.090 in.)
Compression pressure (at sea level)	
Standard	1250 kPa (181 psi)
Service limit	875 kPa (126 psi)
Maximum difference between cylinders	200 kPa (29 psi)
Engine oil pressure (@ 60° C / 140° F)	300-600 kPa (43-87 psi) @ 3000 rpm
Brake pedal height	55 mm (2.2 in.)
Throttle cable free play	
1996-2000 models	
Return (push) cable	0.5-1.0 mm (0.02-0.04 in.)
Pull cable	0.5-1.0 mm (0.02-0.04 in.)
2001 models	2.0-4.0 mm (0.08-0.16 in.)
Rim runout (front and rear)	
Axial	2.0 mm (0.08 in.)
Radial	2.0 mm (0.08 in.)
Drive chain 21-pin length (service limit)	319.4 mm (12.6 in.)
Drive chain free play	20-30 mm (0.8-1.2 in.)

Table 5 MAINTENANCE AND TUNE UP TORQUE SPECIFICATIONS

Item	N•m	in.-lb.	ft.-lb.
Brake hose banjo bolt	23	–	17
Cylinder base nut	9	80	–
Cylinder head bolt, 6 mm	10	88	–
Cylinder head cover			
banjo bolt	10	88	–
Cylinder head cover bolt	14	–	10
Cylinder head nut, 10 mm	38	–	28
Exhaust pipe bolt	23	–	17
Engine sprocket nut	115	–	85
Front axle	65	–	48
Front axle pinch bolt	23	–	17
Handlebar clamp bolt	23	–	17
Main oil gallery plug	40	–	29
Muffler mounting bolt	29	–	21
Oil cooler			
Hose banjo bolt			
1996-2000 models	28	–	21
2001 models	23	–	17
Mounting bolts	10	88	–
Oil drain plug	23	–	17
Oil pan bolt	14	–	10
Rear axle nut	100	–	74
Rear brake master			
cylinder rod locknut	18	–	13
Rear torque link nut	35	–	26
Removable frame down			
tube mounting bolt	32	–	23
Spark plug	11	97	–

Table 6 BATTERY CHARGING RATES/TIMES (APPROXIMATE)

Voltage	% of charge	3 amp charger	6 amp charger	10 amp charger	20 amp charger
12.8	100%	–	–	–	–
12.6	75%	1.75 hours	50 minutes	30 minutes	15 minutes
12.3	50%	3.5 hours	1.75 hours	1 hour	30 minutes
12.0	25%	5 hours	2.5 hours	1.5 hours	45 minutes
11.8	0%	6 hours and 40 minutes	3 hours and 20 minutes	2 hours	1 hour

CHAPTER FOUR

ENGINE TOP END

This chapter provides complete service and overhaul procedures for the engine top end components: the camshafts, valves, cylinder head, pistons, piston rings and the cylinder block.

The 1200cc Bandit is powered by an air/oil-cooled, in-line four-cylinder, DOHC, 16-valve engine. A single camshaft chain drives the dual overhead camshafts. Valve actuation is via rocker arms operating directly on the valves.

Cooling is provided by a unique oil system that helps dissipate the engine heat. In addition to the normal engine components that require lubrication, engine oil is also routed through the cylinder head, sprayed onto the lower potion of the pistons and piston pins and directed to any portion of the engine where there is normal heat build-up.

The oil is pumped from the engine and into the frame-mounted oil cooler in front of the engine. From here, the cooled oil returns to the engine. Lubrication system service is covered in Chapter Five.

The cylinder head cover, cylinder head and cylinder block have shallow cooling fins that also help to dissipate engine heat.

Tables 1-3 are located at the end of the chapter.

ENGINE SERVICE NOTES

An important part of successful engine service is preparation. Before servicing the engine, note the following:

1. Review the information in Chapter One, especially the *Service Methods* and *Precision Measuring Tools* sections. Accurate measurements are critical to a successful engine rebuild.
2. Clean the entire engine and frame with a commercial degreaser before removing engine components. A clean motorcycle is easier to work on and this will help prevent the possibility of dirt and debris falling into the open engine.
3. Have all the necessary tools and parts on hand before starting the procedure(s). Store parts in boxes, plastic bags and containers. Use masking tape and a permanent, waterproof marking pen to label parts. Record the location, position and thickness of all shims and washers as they are removed.

1 FOUR-STROKE OPERATING PRINCIPLES

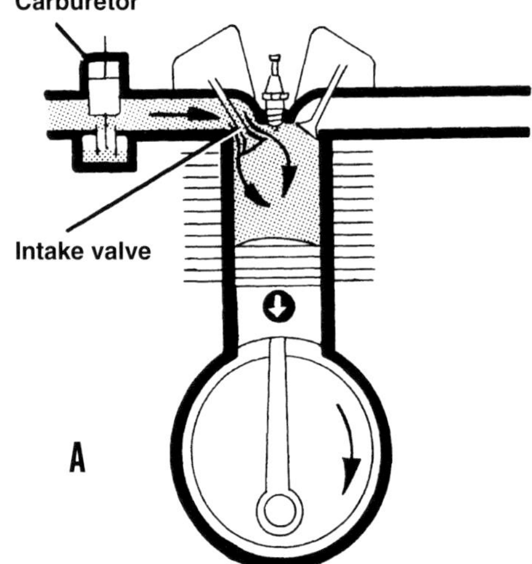

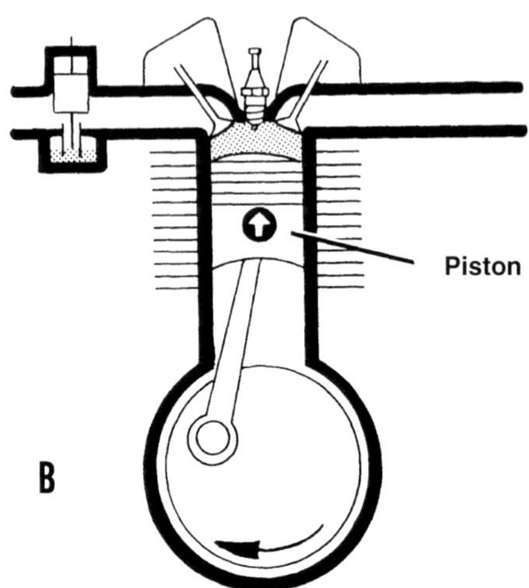

As the piston travels downward, the exhaust valve closes and the intake valve opens, allowing the new air-fuel mixture from the carburetor to be drawn into the cylinder. When the piston reaches the bottom of its travel, (BDC) the intake valve closes and remains closed for the next 1 1/2 revolutions of the crankshaft.

While the crankshaft continues to rotate, the piston moves upward, compressing the air-fuel mixture.

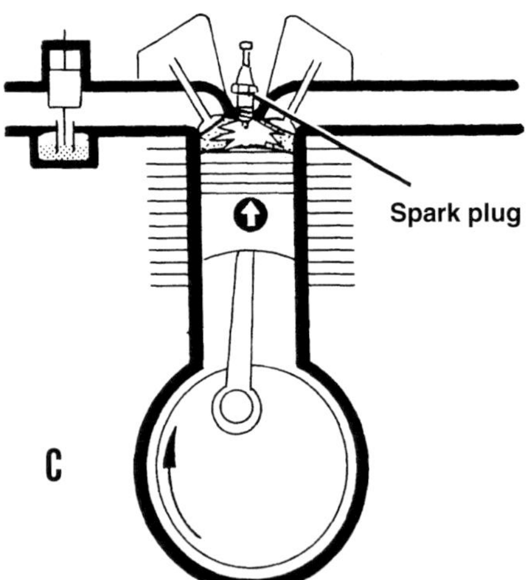

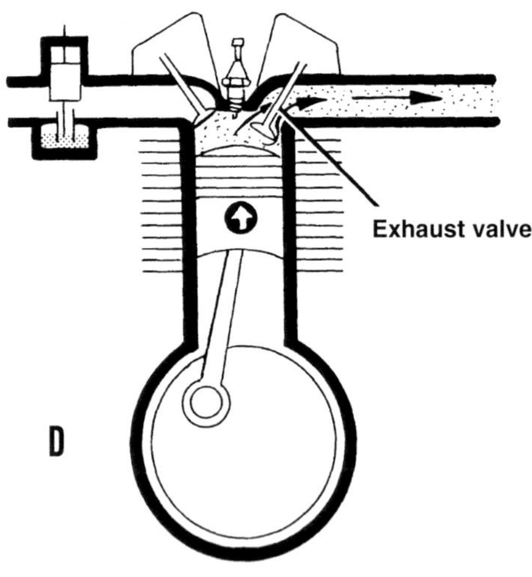

As the piston nears the top of its travel, the spark plug fires, igniting the compressed air-fuel mixture. The piston continues to top dead center (TDC) and is pushed down by the expanding gasses.

As the piston nears BDC, the exhaust valve opens and remains open until the piston is near TDC. The upward travel of the piston forces the exhaust gasses out of the cylinder. After the piston has reached TDC, the exhaust valve closes and the cycle repeats.

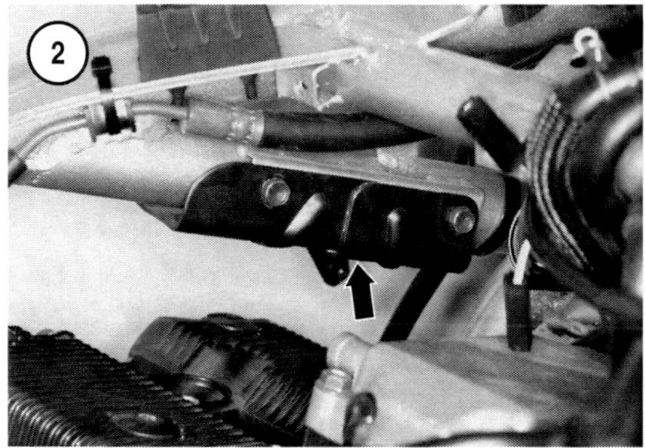

4. Use a box of assorted size and color vacuum hose identifiers (Lisle part No. 74600) for identifying hoses and fittings during engine services.
5. Throughout the text there are references to the left and right side of the engine. This refers to the engine as it is mounted in the frame, not how it may sit on the workbench.
6. When inspecting components described in this chapter, compare the measurements to the service specifications listed in **Table 2**. Replace any part that is out of specification, worn to the service limit or damaged.
7. Always replace worn or damaged fasteners with those of the same size, type and torque requirements. If a specific torque value is not listed in **Table 3**, refer to the general torque specification table in Chapter One.
8. Use a vise with protective jaws to hold parts.
9. Use a press or special tools when force is required to remove and install parts. Do not try to pry, hammer or otherwise force them on or off.
10. Replace all O-rings and oil seals during reassembly. Set aside old seals and O-rings so they can be compared with the *new* ones if necessary. Apply a small amount of grease to the inner lips of each *new* oil seal to prevent damage when the engine is first started.

ENGINE PRINCIPLES

Figure 1 explains basic four-stroke engine operation. This will be helpful when troubleshooting or repairing the engine.

CYLINDER HEAD COVER

The cylinder head cover can be removed with the engine mounted in the frame.

Removal

1. Place the motorcycle securely on level ground on the centerstand.
2. On GSF1200S models, remove the fairing as described in Chapter Fourteen. Remove the bolts securing the side fairing panel mounting bracket (**Figure 2**) on each side.
3. Disconnect the negative battery cable as described in Chapter Three.
4. Remove the fuel tank as described in Chapter Eight.
5. On models with a PAIR system, remove the PAIR valve assembly as described in Chapter Eight.
6. Disconnect the spark plug wires and caps (A, **Figure 3**).
7. Remove the two shouldered cylinder head cover bolts (**Figure 4**) from the mounts on the front and rear of the cylinder head cover.
8. Disconnect the crankcase breather hose (B, **Figure 3**) from the breather cover.

9. Remove the breather cover (A, **Figure 5**) and gasket from the top of the cylinder head cover. Note the location of any clamps under the mounting bolts.

10. Remove the mounting bolts securing the oil hose fittings (B, **Figure 5**) to the cylinder head cover and move the hoses out of the way. Discard the O-rings from each hose fitting. Install *new* O-rings during installation to prevent oil leaks.

11. Using a crisscross pattern, loosen the ten cylinder head cover bolts (A, **Figure 6**) and the cylinder head cover banjo bolts (B). Remove the bolts and their washers.

12. Pull the cover (C, **Figure 6**) straight up and off the cylinder head and remove the cover and the gasket. Do not lose the two locating dowels or the small rubber gasket that surrounds each spark plug hole in the cover.

13. Inspect the cylinder head cover and replace the gasket as described in the following procedure.

Inspection and Gasket Replacement

1. Remove the old gaskets from the cylinder head or cover.

2. Make sure the gasket sealing surfaces in the cover are clean and free of any oil buildup from a previously leaking gasket. These surfaces must be clean and smooth to provide an oil tight seal.

3. Remove all old gasket sealer residue from the gasket sealing surface around the perimeter of the cylinder head and from the grooves around the spark plug holes. Be sure to clean off all old sealer from the crescent-shaped machined surfaces at each end of the cylinder head.

4. Apply ThreeBond Liquid Gasket 1104 or an equivalent to the grooves in the cylinder head cover. Follow the sealant manufacturer's instructions.

5. Install a *new* gasket around the perimeter of the cover (A, **Figure 7**) and around each spark plug hole (B). Be sure the holes in the spark plug gaskets align with the holes in the cylinder head cover.

6. Apply ThreeBond Liquid Gasket 1104 or equivalent to the half-round camshaft end caps (C, **Figure 7**) on the cylinder head gasket.

7. Ensure that all gaskets are installed correctly; reposition if necessary.

8. Check the cylinder head cover for warp, cracks or damage. Replace the cover if necessary.

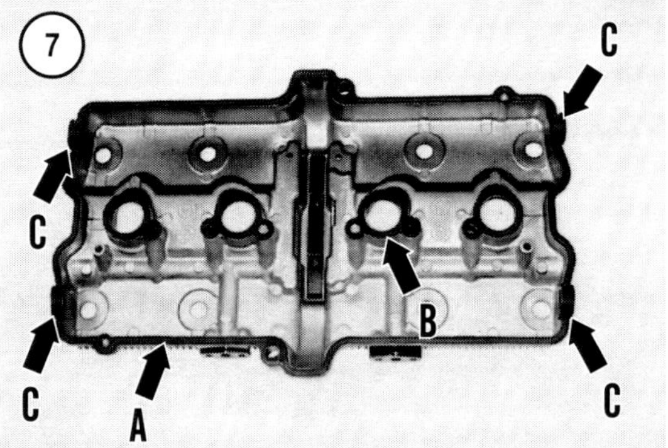

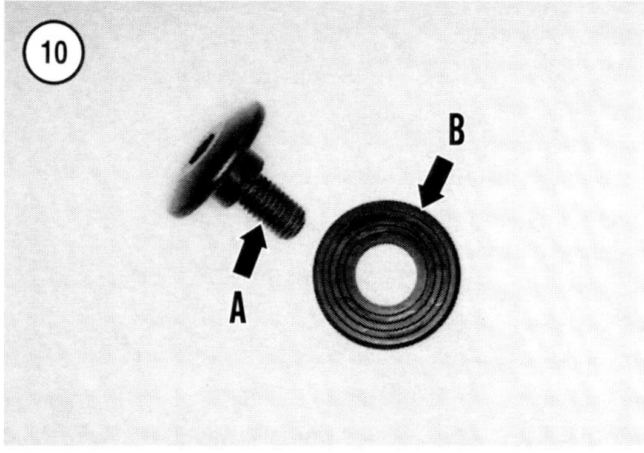

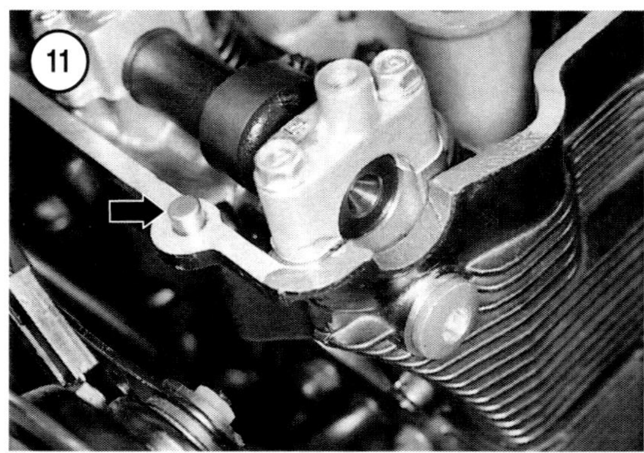

9. Inspect the camshaft chain guide No. 2 (**Figure 8**) for wear or damage. Replace the chain guide if worn half-way through the material. Remove the screws (**Figure 9**) and the guide. Install a new chain guide and apply a medium strength threadlocking compound to the screw threads prior to installation, then tighten the screws securely.

10. Inspect the cover bolts (A, **Figure 10**) for thread damage. Replace the bolts as necessary. Check the cover bolt gaskets (B, **Figure 10**) for harness or deterioration and replace them if necessary.

11. Inspect the cover banjo bolts for thread damage. Make sure the oil flow holes are clear. Replace the banjo bolts as necessary.

Installation

1. Install *new* gaskets onto the cylinder head cover as previously described.
2. If removed, install the two locating dowels (**Figure 11**) into the cylinder head.
3. Install the cylinder head cover into place on the cylinder head. Make sure the gaskets remain in place on the cover and that they properly mate with the cylinder head. Pay particular attention to the camshaft end caps. Oil will leak if the half-round end caps do not properly mate with the cylinder head.
4. Install a *new* sealing washer onto the four cylinder head cover banjo bolts. Install the banjo bolts (**Figure 12**) into the holes beside the spark plug holes and finger-tighten the bolts.

NOTE
The two bolts in Step 5 do not use washers.

5. Install the two shouldered cylinder head cover bolts (**Figure 4**) into the mounts on the front and rear of the cylinder head cover.
6. Install a *new* gasket (**Figure 13**) onto the eight remaining cylinder head cover bolts. Install and finger-tighten the bolts.
7. Tighten the cylinder head cover banjo bolts to 16 N•m (12 ft.-lb.).
8. Using a crisscross pattern, tighten the cylinder head cover bolts to 14 N•m (10 ft.-lb.).
9. Install a *new* O-ring into each fitting on the oil hoses.

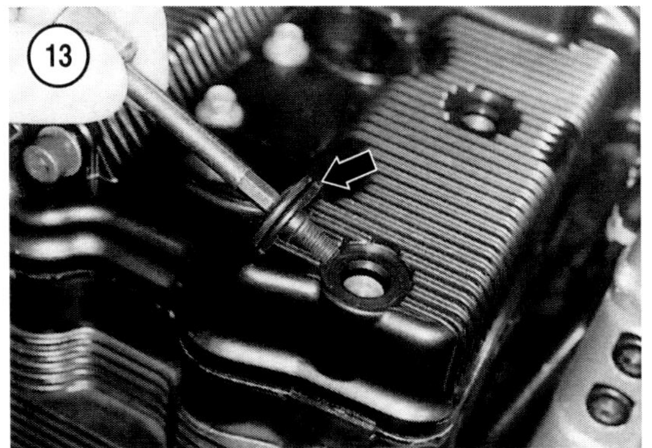

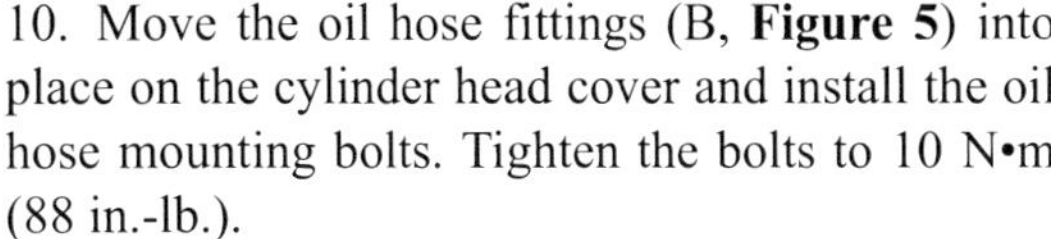

10. Move the oil hose fittings (B, **Figure 5**) into place on the cylinder head cover and install the oil hose mounting bolts. Tighten the bolts to 10 N•m (88 in.-lb.).
11. Install the gasket (**Figure 14**) onto the breather cover and set the cover in place on the cylinder head cover (A, **Figure 5**). Install any clamps (B, **Figure 5**) under the mounting bolts as noted during removal.
12. Spray the breather cover bolts with a rust inhibitor. Install and tighten the bolts securely.
13. Connect the crankcase breather hose (B, **Figure 3**) to the port on the breather cover.
14. Connect the spark plug wires (A, **Figure 3**) to the spark plugs. Make sure each cap securely engages the cylinder head cover.
15. On models with a PAIR system, install the PAIR valve assembly as described in Chapter Eight.
16. Install the fuel tank as described in Chapter Eight.
17. Connect the negative battery cable as described in Chapter Three.
18. On GSF1200S models, install the side fairing panel mounting bracket (**Figure 2**) and bolts on each side. Tighten the bolts securely. Install the fairing as described in Chapter Fourteen.

CAMSHAFTS

Removal

1. Remove the cylinder head cover as described in this chapter.
2. Remove all four spark plugs as described in Chapter Three. This makes it easier to turn the engine by hand.
3. Remove the camshaft chain tensioner as described in this chapter.
4. Remove the signal generator cover bolts and remove the cover (**Figure 15**) and its gasket. One bolt

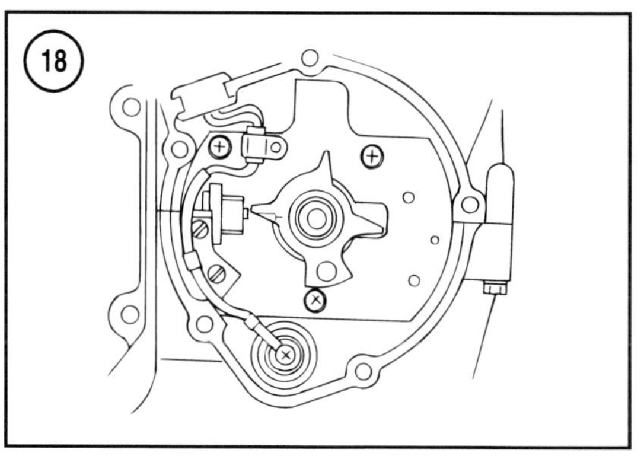

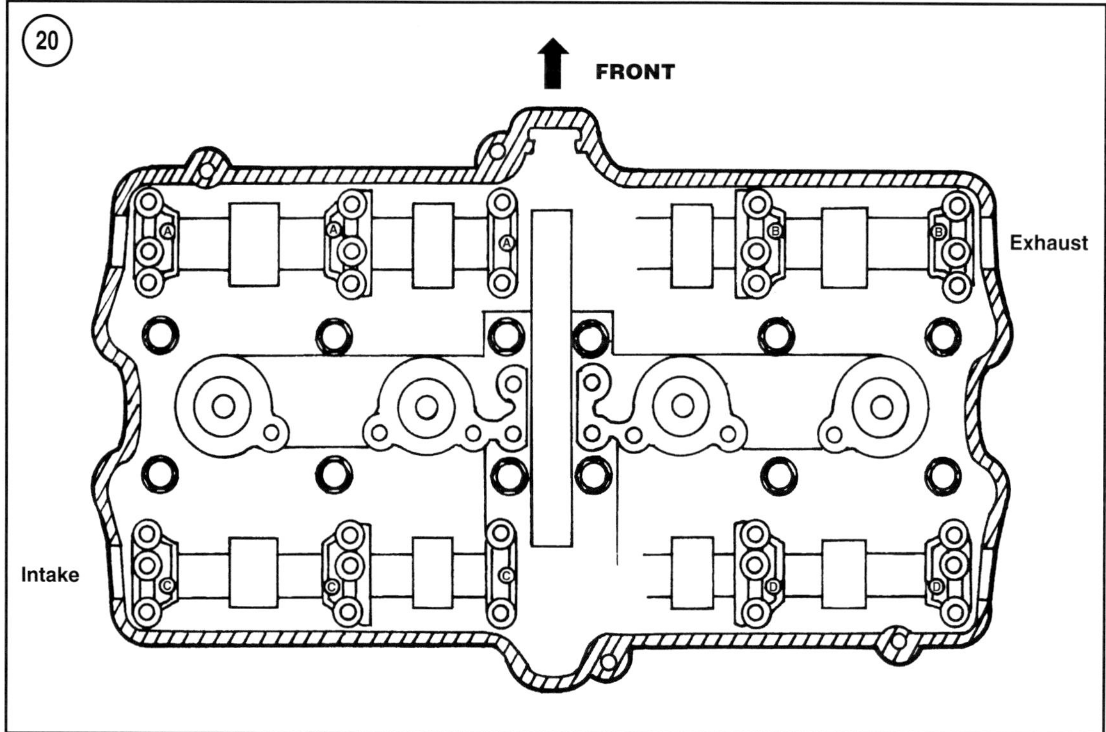

has a sealing washer installed beneath it (**Figure 16**). Note the position of this bolt. It must be reinstalled in the same location during assembly.

CAUTION
*Always use a 19 mm wrench on the flats of the signal generator rotor when rotating the engine. Do **not** use the Allen bolt that secures the rotor to the crankshaft. This Allen bolt may shear off.*

5. Place a 19 mm wrench on the flats of the signal generator rotor (**Figure 17**). Rotate the engine *clockwise* until the T-mark on the signal generator rotor aligns with the center of the pickup coil (**Figure 18**).

6. Using a crisscross pattern, evenly loosen the bolts securing the camshaft bearing caps (A, **Figure 19**) on the intake camshaft.

7. Using a crisscross pattern, loosen the bolts securing the camshaft bearing caps (B, **Figure 19**) on the exhaust camshaft.

NOTE
*Note the identification marks on each camshaft bearing cap (**Figure 20**).*

Each camshaft bearing cap must be reinstalled in its original location in the cylinder head.

8. Remove all the bearing caps from both camshafts. Do not lose the locating dowel beneath each bearing cap.
9. Disengage the camshaft chain from the camshaft sprockets and remove both the intake and exhaust camshafts.

CAUTION
If the crankshaft must be rotated while the camshafts are removed, pull up the camshaft chain so it properly engages the crankshaft timing sprocket. Hold the chain taut on the timing sprocket while rotating the crankshaft. If this is not done, the camshaft chain could become kinked, which could cause damage to the chain, timing sprocket and surrounding crankcase area.

10. Tie a piece of wire to the camshaft chain and secure the loose end of the wire to the engine or frame.
11. Inspect both camshafts as described in this chapter.

Installation

1. Pull the camshaft chain taut and make sure it properly engages the crankshaft timing sprocket.

CAUTION
*Always use a 19 mm wrench on the flats of the signal generator rotor when rotating the engine. Do **not** use the Allen bolt that secures the rotor to the crankshaft. This Allen bolt may shear off.*

2. Place a 19 mm wrench on the flats of the signal generator rotor (**Figure 17**). Rotate the engine *clockwise* until the T-mark on the signal generator rotor aligns with the center of the pickup coil (**Figure 18**).
3. Check the camshaft sprocket bolts (**Figure 21**) on both camshafts. If either sprocket bolt is loose on a camshaft, remove and reinstall both bolts. Apply ThreeBond Threadlock No. 1303 or an equivalent to the threads of each bolt and tighten the camshaft sprocket bolts to 25 N•m (18 ft.-lb.).

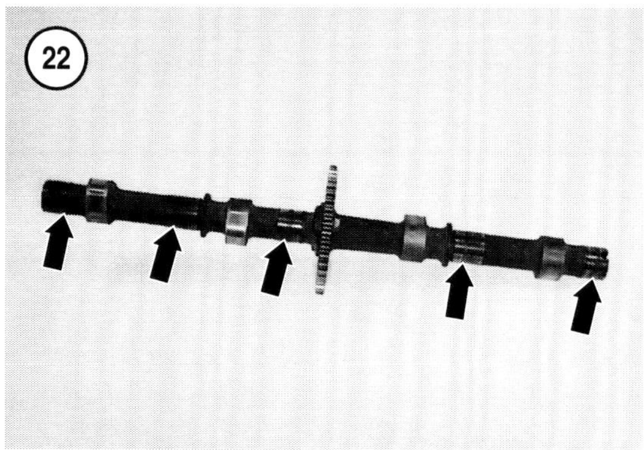

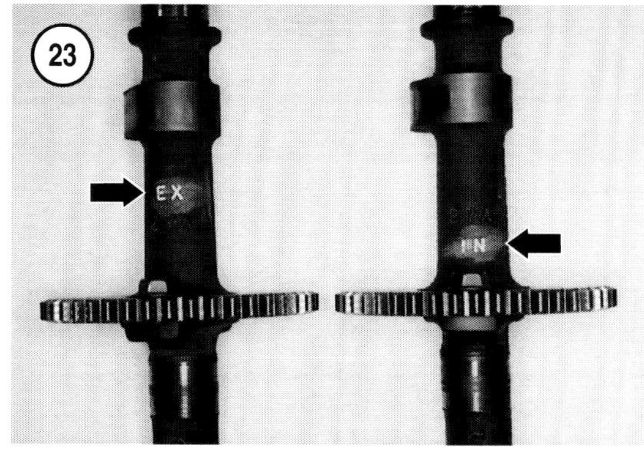

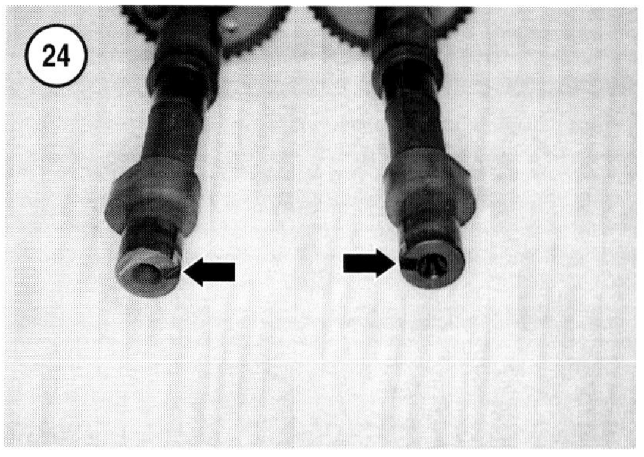

25

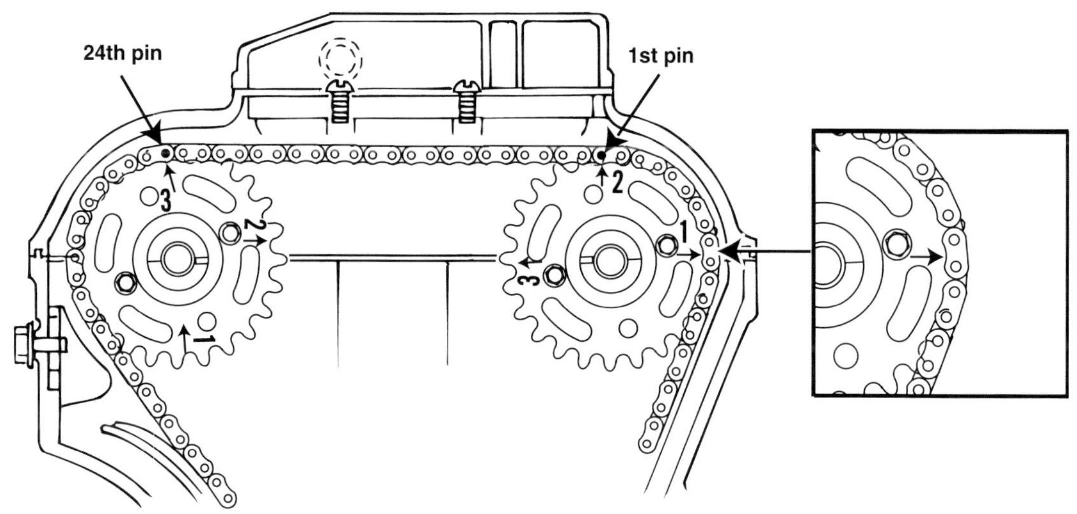

24th pin

1st pin

4. Apply a light but complete coat of molybdenum disulfide grease to each camshaft bearing journal (**Figure 22**) on both camshafts.

5. Coat all camshaft bearing surfaces in the cylinder head and the bearing surfaces of the bearing caps with clean engine oil.

6. Each camshaft is identified by an IN (intake) or EX (exhaust) embossed (**Figure 23**) on the shaft. Also, the right side of each shaft is identified by a notch (**Figure 24**) on the end of the camshaft.

7. Position the exhaust camshaft so the notched end faces the right side of the engine. Insert the camshaft through the camshaft chain and set the camshaft into place in the cylinder head.

8. Rotate the exhaust camshaft until the No. 1 arrow on the camshaft sprocket aligns with the top surface of the cylinder head as shown in **Figure 25**.

9. Lift the front of the camshaft chain and mesh the chain with the exhaust camshaft sprocket (**Figure 26**).

10. Use a white grease pencil and highlight the pin on the camshaft chain opposite the No. 2 arrow (**Figure 27**) on the exhaust camshaft sprocket. This is the 1st pin.

11. Starting at this first pin, count toward the rear along the camshaft chain and identify the 24th pin. Also highlight this pin with a white grease pencil.

12. Recheck to make sure the No. 1 arrow on the exhaust camshaft sprocket (**Figure 25**) is still aligned with the top surface of the cylinder head. If the alignment is not correct, readjust the camshaft chain on the sprocket at this time.

13. Position the intake camshaft so the notch faces the right side of the engine. Install the camshaft through the camshaft chain and set the camshaft into place in the cylinder head.

14. Rotate the intake camshaft so the No. 3 arrow points straight up. Mesh the camshaft chain onto the intake sprocket so the chain's 24th pin is opposite the No. 3 arrow on the intake camshaft sprocket as shown in **Figure 28**.

15. Recheck the following:

a. Make sure the T-mark on the signal generator rotor points to the center of the pickup coil (**Figure 18**).

b. Make sure the No. 1 arrow on the exhaust camshaft sprocket points to the top surface of the cylinder head and that its No. 2 arrow points to the first pin (**Figure 27**) on the camshaft chain.

c. Make sure the No. 3 arrow on the intake camshaft sprocket points to the 24th pin (**Figure 28**) on the camshaft chain.

d. Insert a finger into the tensioner receptacle in the cylinder block, push on the chain and take out the chain slack. Recheck all of the timing marks to make sure all marks are still aligned properly. If incorrect, reposition the drive chain on the driven sprockets at this time.

CAUTION

Very expensive damage could result from improper camshaft drive chain to camshaft installation and alignment. Recheck the alignment several times to make sure all timing marks are aligned correctly.

NOTE

Each camshaft bearing cap is identified by a unique identification mark. Make sure each cap is installed in its proper location as shown in ***Figure 20****.*

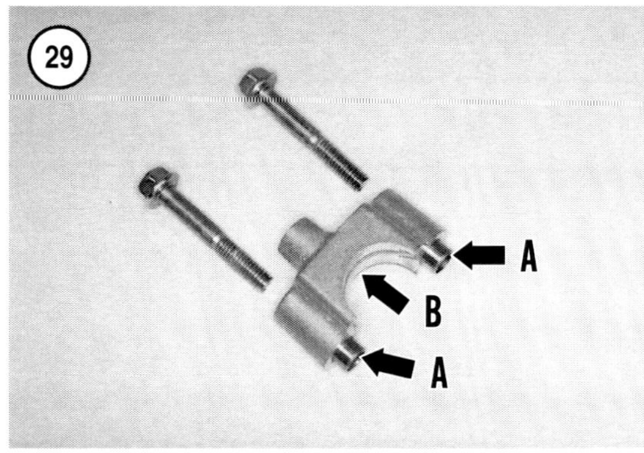

16. If removed, install two locating dowels (A, **Figure 29**) into each camshaft bearing cap and install the cap in its correct location in the cylinder head.

NOTE

The camshaft bearing cap bolts are identified with the numeral 9 embossed on the heads. Only use these bolts to secure the camshaft bearing caps.

17. Loosely install the camshaft bearing cap bolts.

NOTE

The camshaft may move down slightly when the camshaft bearing cap bolts are tightened and the camshaft chain could jump a tooth. Observe the camshaft chain while tightening the camshaft bearing cap bolts.

18. Following a crisscross pattern, evenly tighten the bolts on the exhaust camshaft in two to three stages and then tighten the camshaft bearing cap bolts to 10 N•m (88 in.-lb.).

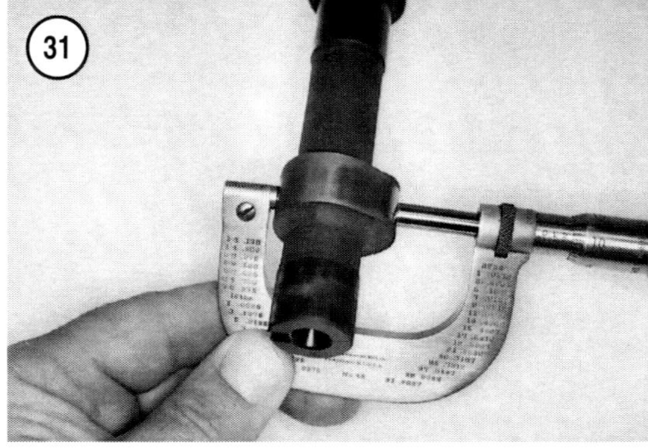

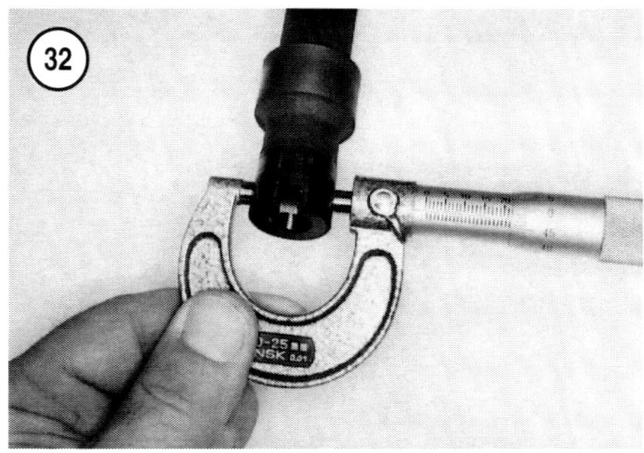

19. Repeat this procedure and tighten the cap bolts on the intake camshaft to 10 N•m (88 in.-lb.).

20. Install the camshaft chain tensioner as described in this chapter.

21. Recheck the camshaft timing as follows:

   a. Make sure the No. 2 arrow on the exhaust camshaft sprocket still points to the first pin (**Figure 25**) on the camshaft chain.

   b. Make sure the No. 3 arrow on the intake camshaft sprocket points to the 24th pin (**Figure 25**) on the camshaft chain.

22. Fill the oil pockets in the cylinder head with new engine oil so the camshaft lobes are submerged in fresh oil.

CAUTION

*Always use a 19 mm wrench on the flats of the signal generator rotor when rotating the engine. Do **not** use the Allen bolt that secures the rotor to the crankshaft. This Allen bolt may shear off.*

23. Place a 19 mm wrench on the signal generator rotor (**Figure 17**) and rotate the crankshaft clockwise several times.
24. Adjust the valves as described in Chapter Three.
25. Install the spark plugs.
26. Install the signal generator cover and a *new* gasket as follows:
   a. Apply a light coat of gasket sealer to the groove in the rubber grommet (A, **Figure 30**).
   b. Also apply gasket sealer to the crankcase mating surfaces (B, **Figure 30**) and install the *new* gasket.
   c. Install the bolt with the sealing washer in the location noted during disassembly (**Figure 16**). Tighten the cover bolts securely.
27. Install the cylinder head cover as described in this chapter.

Inspection

When measuring the camshafts in this section, compare the measurements to the specifications listed in **Table 2**. Replace parts that are out of specification or that show damage as described in this section.
1. Check the camshaft lobes for wear. The lobes should not be scored and the edges should be square.
2. Measure the height of each lobe (**Figure 31**) with a micrometer.
3. Check each camshaft bearing journal (**Figure 22**) for wear and scoring.
4. Measure the diameter of each camshaft bearing journal with a micrometer (**Figure 32**). Replace the camshaft if any journal diameter is out of specification. Record each camshaft journal diameter. These measurements are needed when checking camshaft bearing clearance.

5. If the bearing journals are severely worn or damaged, check the camshaft bearing surfaces in the cylinder head (**Figure 33**) and in the camshaft bearing caps (B, **Figure 29**). They should not be scored or excessively worn. If any of the bearing surfaces are worn or scored, the cylinder head assembly and camshaft bearing caps must be replaced as a set.

6. Place each camshaft on a set of V-blocks or truing stand (**Figure 34**) and check the runout with a dial indicator.

NOTE
If the camshaft sprockets are worn, check the camshaft drive chain, chain guides, crankshaft driven sprocket and chain tensioner for damage.

7. Inspect the camshaft sprockets (**Figure 35**) for broken or chipped teeth. Also check the teeth for cracking or rounding. If the camshaft sprocket is damaged or severely worn, replace the camshaft. Also, inspect the timing sprocket mounted on the crankshaft as described in Chapter Five.

8. Measure the camshaft bearing clearance as described in the following procedure.

Camshaft Bearing Clearance Measurement

This procedure requires the use of Plastigage. The camshafts must be installed into the cylinder head. Before installing the camshafts, wipe all oil residue from each camshaft bearing journal and from the bearing surface of the cylinder head and camshaft bearing caps.

1. Do not install the camshaft chain onto the camshafts for this procedure.

2. Install the camshafts into the cylinder head in the correct location. Install the exhaust camshaft in the front of the engine and the intake camshaft in the rear. Make sure the notch on the end of each camshaft faces the right side of the engine.

3. Place a strip of Plastigage onto each bearing journal (**Figure 36**). The Plastigage must parallel the camshaft.

NOTE
Each camshaft bearing cap is identified by a unique identification mark. Make sure each cap is installed in its proper location as shown in ***Figure 20****.*

33

34

35

4. If removed, install two locating dowels (A, **Figure 29**) into each camshaft bearing cap and install the caps into their proper location in the cylinder head.

NOTE
The camshaft bearing cap bolts are identified with the numeral 9 embossed on the heads. Only use these bolts to secure the camshaft bearing caps.

5. Loosely install the camshaft bearing cap bolts.

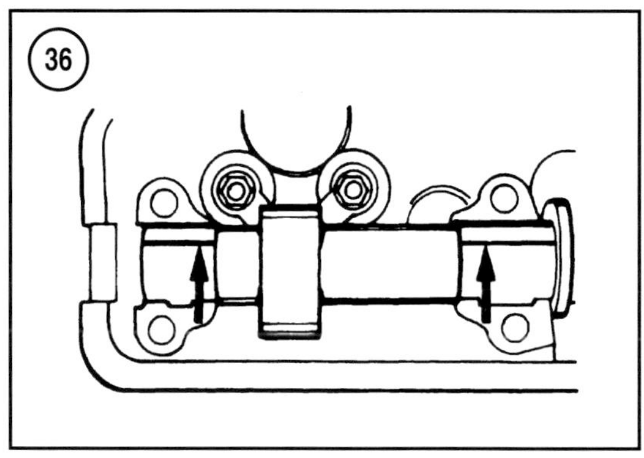

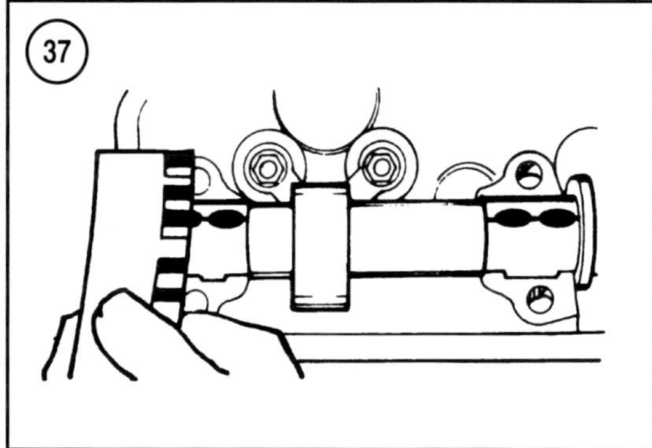

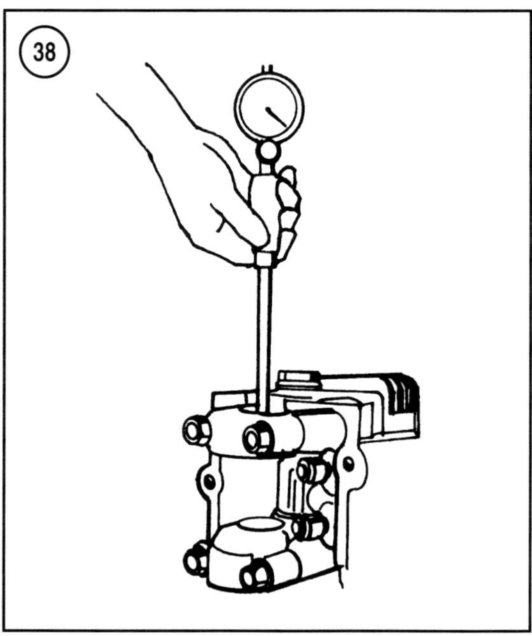

6. Following a crisscross pattern, evenly tighten the bolts on the exhaust camshaft in two to three stages and then tighten the camshaft bearing cap bolts to 10 N•m (88 in.-lb.).

7. Repeat this procedure and tighten the cap bolts on the intake camshaft to 10 N•m (88 in.-lb.).

CAUTION
Do not rotate the camshafts with the Plastigage in place.

8. Following a crisscross pattern, evenly loosen the bearing cap bolts in two to three stages.
9. Pull straight up and carefully remove each bearing cap.
10. Measure the flattened Plastigage (**Figure 37**) at the widest point, according to the manufacturer's instructions.

CAUTION
Be sure to remove all traces of Plastigage from the camshaft bearing caps and from the camshaft bearing journals. If any Plastigage is left in the engine, it can plug up an oil control orifice and cause severe engine damage.

11. Remove *all* Plastigage from the camshafts and bearing caps.
12. If the camshaft bearing oil clearance is greater than specified in **Table 2**, perform the following:
   a. Remove both camshafts from the cylinder head.

NOTE
*Each camshaft bearing cap is identified by a unique identification mark. Make sure each cap is installed in its proper location as shown in **Figure 20**.*

   b. Place the bearing caps in their correct location in the cylinder head and install the camshaft bearing cap bolts. Tighten the bolts to 10 N•m (88 in.-lb.).
   c. Use a bore gauge and measure the inside diameter of each camshaft journal holder (**Figure 38**). Record each measurement.
   d. Refer to the camshaft journal outside diameter dimensions taken during camshaft *Inspection* (Step 4).
   e. Replace the camshaft if the outside diameter of a camshaft journal is outside the range specified in **Table 2**. Replace the cylinder head and the camshaft caps as a set if the in-

(39)

CAMSHAFT CHAIN AND TENSIONER

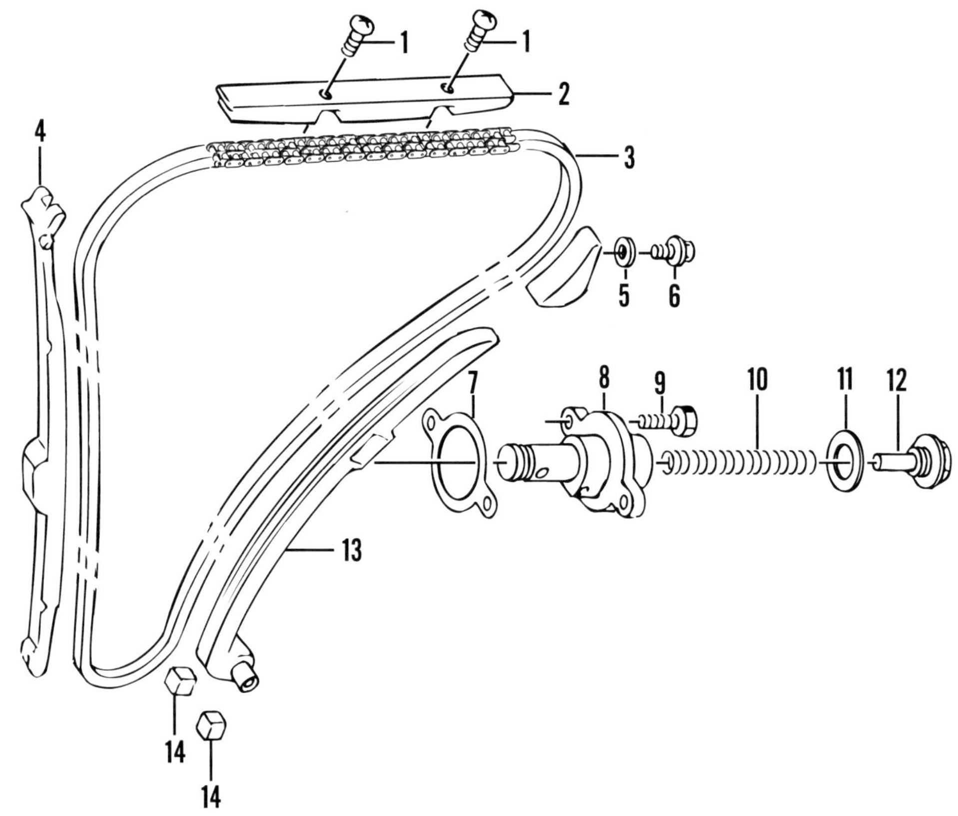

1. Screw
2. Chain guide No. 2
3. Camshaft chain
4. Chain guide No. 1
5. Washer
6. Screw
7. Gasket
8. Tensioner body
9. Bolt
10. Spring
11. Gasket
12. Spring holder bolt
13. Tensioner guide
14. Cushion

side diameter of a camshaft journal holder is out of specification.

CAMSHAFT CHAIN TENSIONER

Removal/Installation

Refer to **Figure 39** for this procedure.

1. Remove the spring holder bolt (A, **Figure 40**) and gasket from the camshaft chain tensioner.
2. Withdraw the spring (B, **Figure 40**) from the tensioner body.

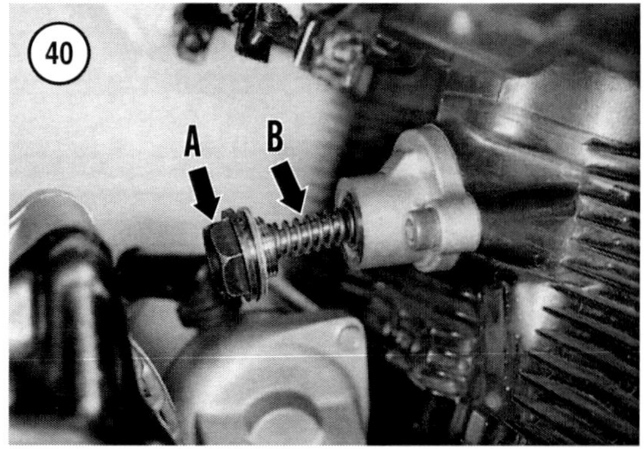

41

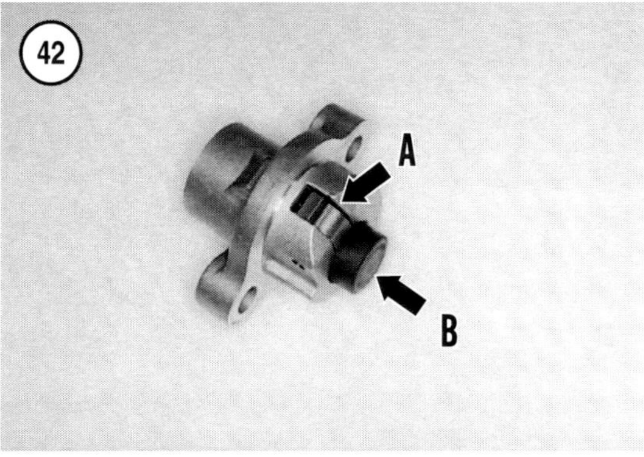

42

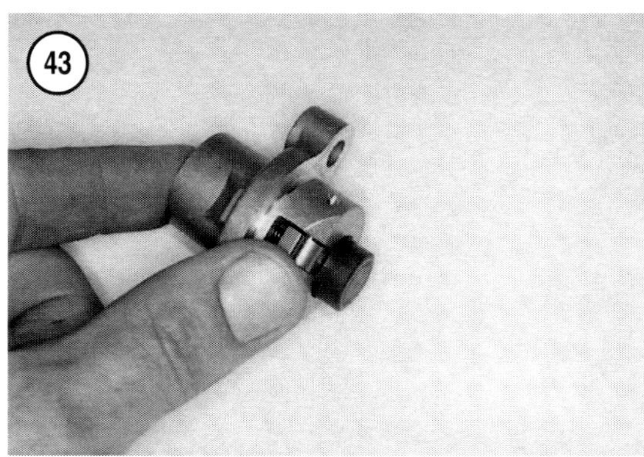

43

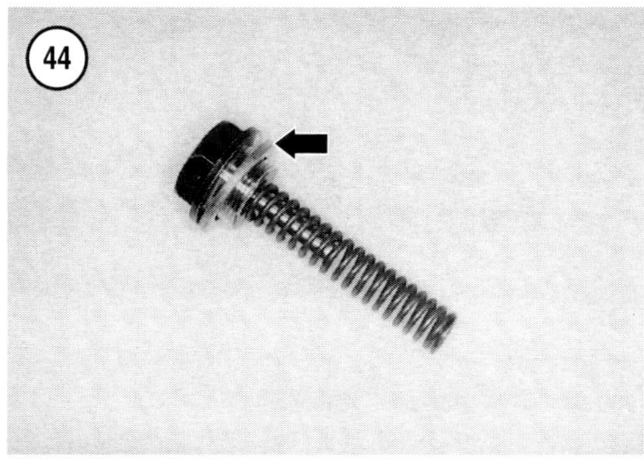

44

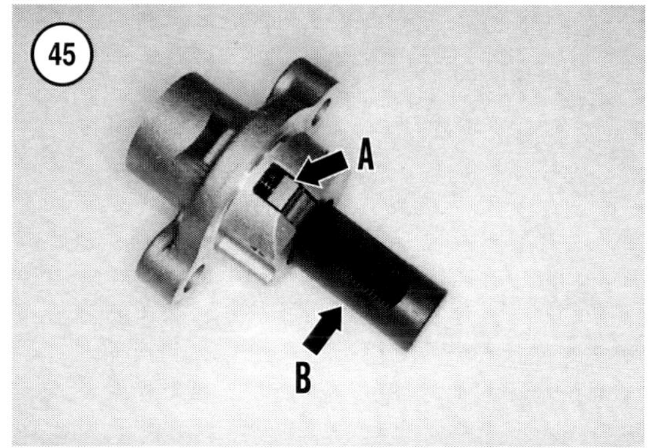

45

3. Remove the camshaft chain tensioner bolts and remove the tensioner body and gasket (**Figure 41**).
4. Inspect the chain tensioner as described in this section.

CAUTION
Reset the ratchet pushrod before installing the tensioner. Correct tension will not be applied to the camshaft chain unless the pushrod is reset.

5. To reset the ratchet pushrod, perform the following:
   a. Push the spring ratchet pawl (A, **Figure 42**) and press the pushrod (B) all the way into the body.
   b. Release the ratchet pawl (**Figure 43**). The pushrod should stay within the body. If it does not, replace the tensioner body.
6. Install the tensioner body and a *new* gasket (**Figure 41**) onto the cylinder block.
7. Install the tensioner mounting bolts and tighten to 7 N•m (62 in.-lb.).
8. Install the washer and spring onto the spring holder bolt (**Figure 44**).
9. Install the spring holder bolt washer and spring into the tensioner body. Tighten the spring holder bolt to 35 N•m (26 ft-lb.).
10. Once the chain tensioner is installed, the camshaft chain will be slightly loose. To correct this, rotate the crankshaft clockwise slightly. A distinct click should be heard as the chain is tensioned.

Inspection

1. Release the ratchet pawl (A, **Figure 45**) and check the movement of the pushrod (B). If it does not slide smoothly in and out of the housing, replace the tensioner body.

2. Check the condition of the spring, washer and spring holder bolt. Replace any part that is worn or damaged.

CAMSHAFT CHAIN

A continuous camshaft chain is used on all models. Do not cut the chain; replacement link components are not available. The camshaft chain comes out with the crankshaft. Refer to crankshaft removal in Chapter Five for camshaft chain removal and inspection procedures.

ROCKER ARMS

NOTE
The rocker arms can be serviced while the engine is in the frame. This procedure is shown with the engine removed from the frame to better illustrate the steps.

Removal

1. Remove both camshafts as described in this chapter.
2. Unscrew the cylinder head plug (**Figure 46**) and remove the plug and the washer.
3. Remove the rocker arm shaft securing bolt (**Figure 47**) from the cylinder head.

NOTE
Each rocker arm assembly must be reinstalled in its original position in the cylinder head. Mark the shafts and rocker arms with an I (intake) or E (exhaust) and with the cylinder number. The cylinders are numbered from left to right, 1-4. The left and right sides refer to the position of parts as viewed by the rider sitting on the seat facing forward.

4. Screw an 8 mm bolt (**Figure 48**) into the end of the rocker arm shaft.
5. Use the 8 mm bolt and slowly withdraw the rocker arm shaft (**Figure 49**) out from the cylinder head.
6. Remove the rocker arms and springs (**Figure 50**). Keep all parts in order and reinstall them onto their respective shaft to avoid the intermixing of parts.

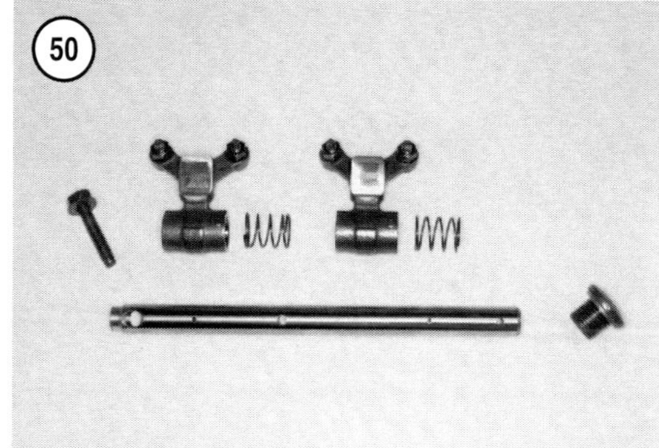

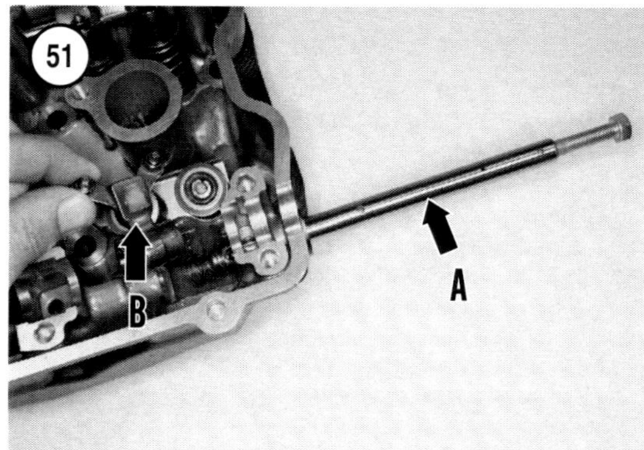

7. Repeat this for the remaining rocker arm shaft assemblies.

8. Wash all parts in solvent and thoroughly dry them with compressed air.

9. Inspect the parts as described in the following procedure.

Installation

1. Apply clean engine oil to the rocker arm shaft, rocker arm bore and the cylinder head receptacles.

2. Refer to the marks made during disassembly so each rocker arm assembly will be reinstalled in its original location in the cylinder head.

3. Position the rocker arm shaft so the bolt hole is vertical.

4. Partially install the rocker arm shaft into the cylinder head (A, **Figure 51**).

5. Position the rocker arm with the rocker arm pad facing up and install it into the cylinder head (B, **Figure 51**).

6. Install a spring (**Figure 52**) on the outboard side of the rocker arm (the side away from the camshaft chain tunnel).

7. Slowly push the rocker arm shaft through the first spring and rocker arm.

8. Repeat Steps 5 and 6 and install the other rocker arm and spring set.

9. Slowly push the rocker arm shaft through the second spring and rocker arm.

10. Rotate the rocker arm shaft so the bolt hole aligns with the securing bolt hole in the cylinder head.

11. Push the shaft into the cylinder head until it bottoms. If necessary, rotate the shaft slightly to align the shaft's bolt hole with the bolt hole in the cylinder head.

12. Install the rocker arm shaft set bolt (**Figure 53**) and tighten to 9 N•m (80 in.-lb.).

13. Inspect the sealing washer on the cylinder head plug. Replace the washer if necessary.

14. Install the cylinder head plug and sealing washer. Tighten the plug to 28 N•m (21 ft.-lb.).

15. Repeat this for all remaining rocker arm assemblies.

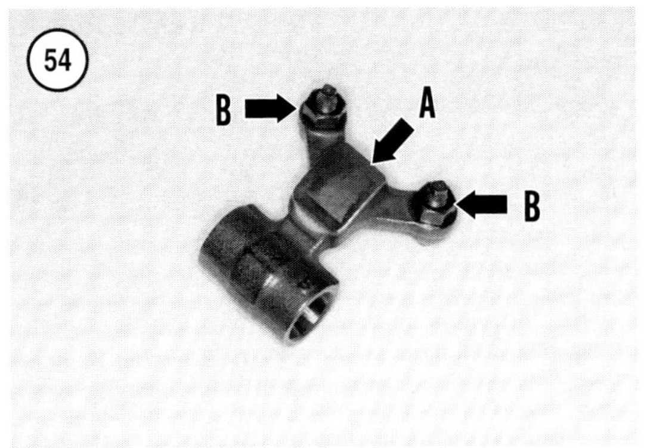

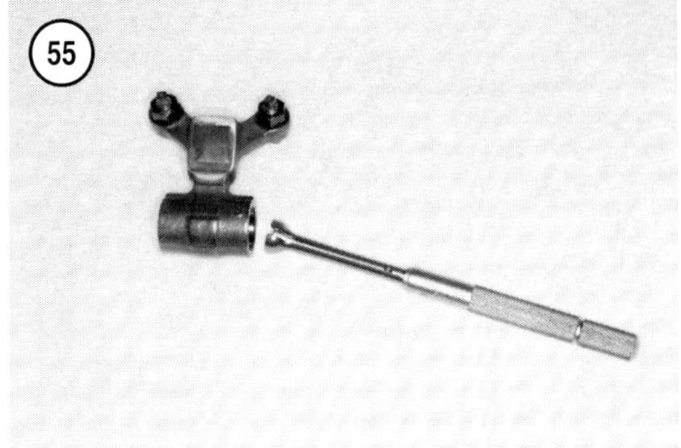

Inspection

Compare all measurements to the specifications in **Table 2**. Replace parts that are damaged or out of specification.

1. Inspect the rocker arm pad (A, **Figure 54**) where it rides on the camshaft lobe. If the pad is scratched or unevenly worn, inspect the camshaft lobe for scoring, chipping or flat spots. Replace the rocker arm as necessary.
2. Inspect the adjusters and locknuts (B, **Figure 54**) for wear or damage. Inspect the opposite end of the valve adjusters where they contact the valve stems. If the adjuster end is pitted or worn, replace it.
3. Measure the inside diameter of the rocker arm bore with an inside micrometer or a small hole gauge (**Figure 55**). Measure the bore in two places that are at right angles to each other.
4. Inspect each rocker arm shaft for signs or wear or damage.
5. Measure the shaft's outside diameter (**Figure 56**) with a micrometer.
6. Check the rocker arm springs for cracks or distortion. Replace the springs as necessary.

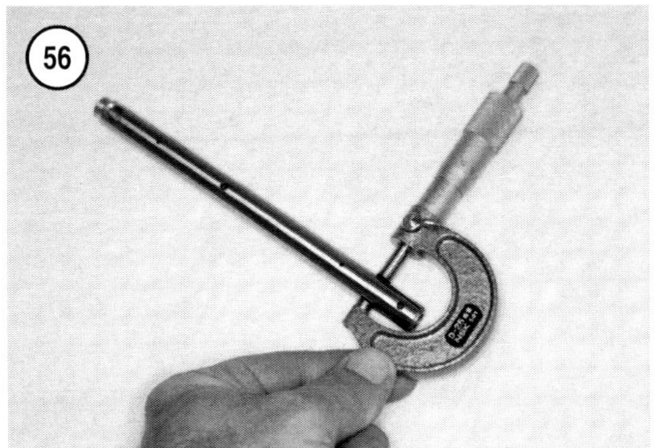

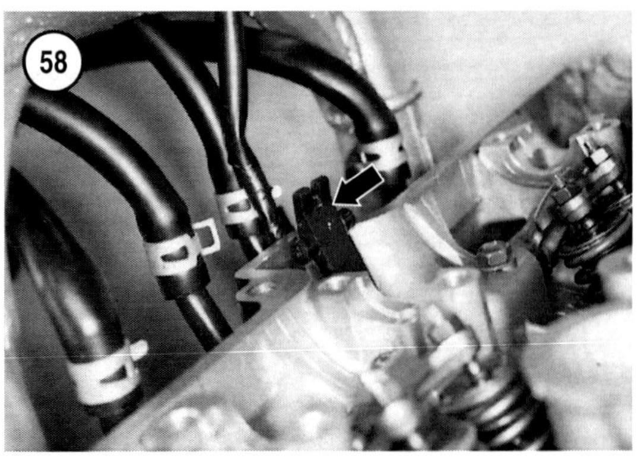

CYLINDER HEAD

The cylinder head can be serviced with the engine mounted in the frame.

CAUTION
To prevent warping and damage, remove the cylinder head only when the engine is at room temperature.

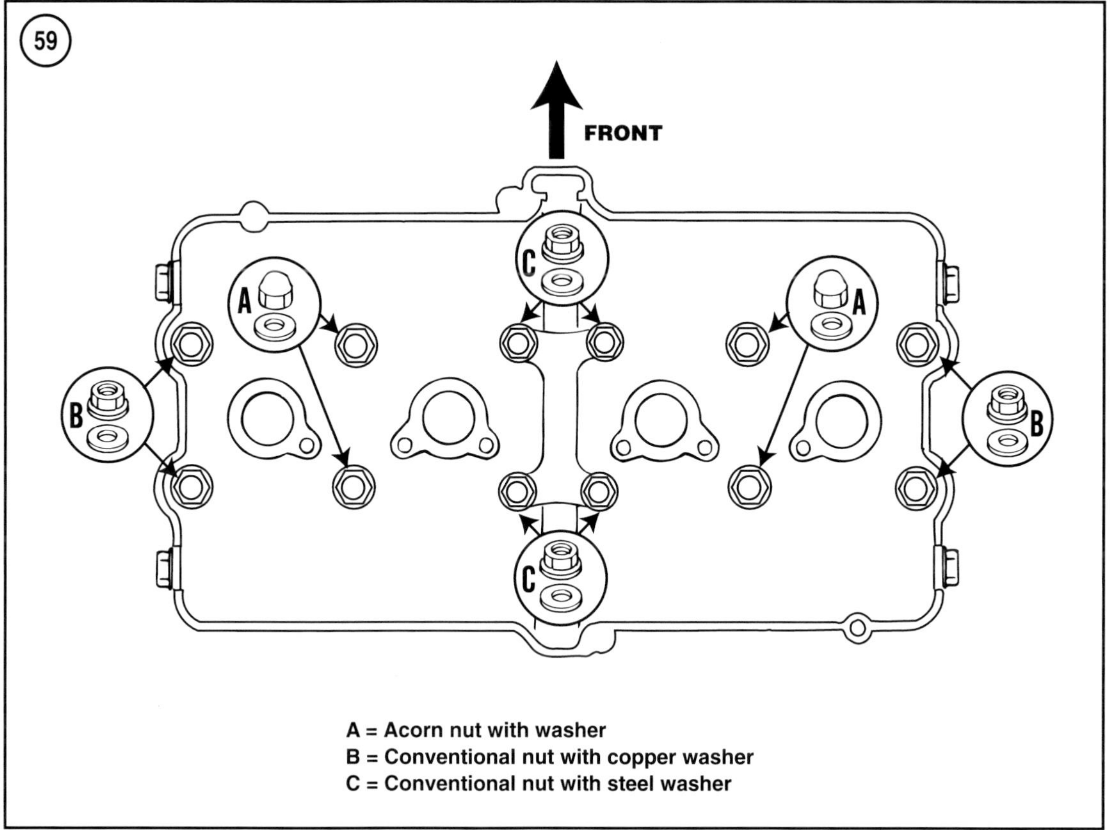

Removal

1. Remove the carburetor assembly and the exhaust system as described in Chapter Eight.
2. Remove the cylinder head cover as described in this chapter.
3. Remove the camshafts and rocker arm assemblies as described in this chapter.
4. Remove the lower bolt (**Figure 57**) securing the front of the cylinder head to the cylinder block.
5. Remove the camshaft front chain guide No. 1 (**Figure 58**).

CAUTION
*The nuts securing the cylinder head are of different design (**Figure 59**). The No. 1-4 nuts are conventional nuts with steel washers, the No. 5-8 nuts are acorn nuts with steel washers and the No. 9-12 nuts are conventional nuts with copper washers. All nuts and washers must be reinstalled in the correct location during assembly.*

6. Following the reverse of the tightening sequence shown in **Figure 60**, evenly loosen the cylinder head nuts in two to three stages. Remove the nuts along with their washers.
7. Remove the reinforcement plate (**Figure 61**) from under the camshaft chain.

CAUTION
The cooling fins are fragile and may be damaged if tapped or pried too hard. Never use a metal hammer to loosen the cylinder head.

8. Loosen the cylinder head by tapping around the perimeter with a soft-faced mallet. If necessary, gently pry the head loose.
9. Lift the cylinder head straight up and remove the head from the cylinder block and crankcase studs. Guide the camshaft chain through the camshaft chain tunnel in the cylinder head and retie the wire to the exterior of the engine. This prevents the camshaft chain from falling into the crankcase.
10. Remove the cylinder head gasket. Do not lose the locating dowels.

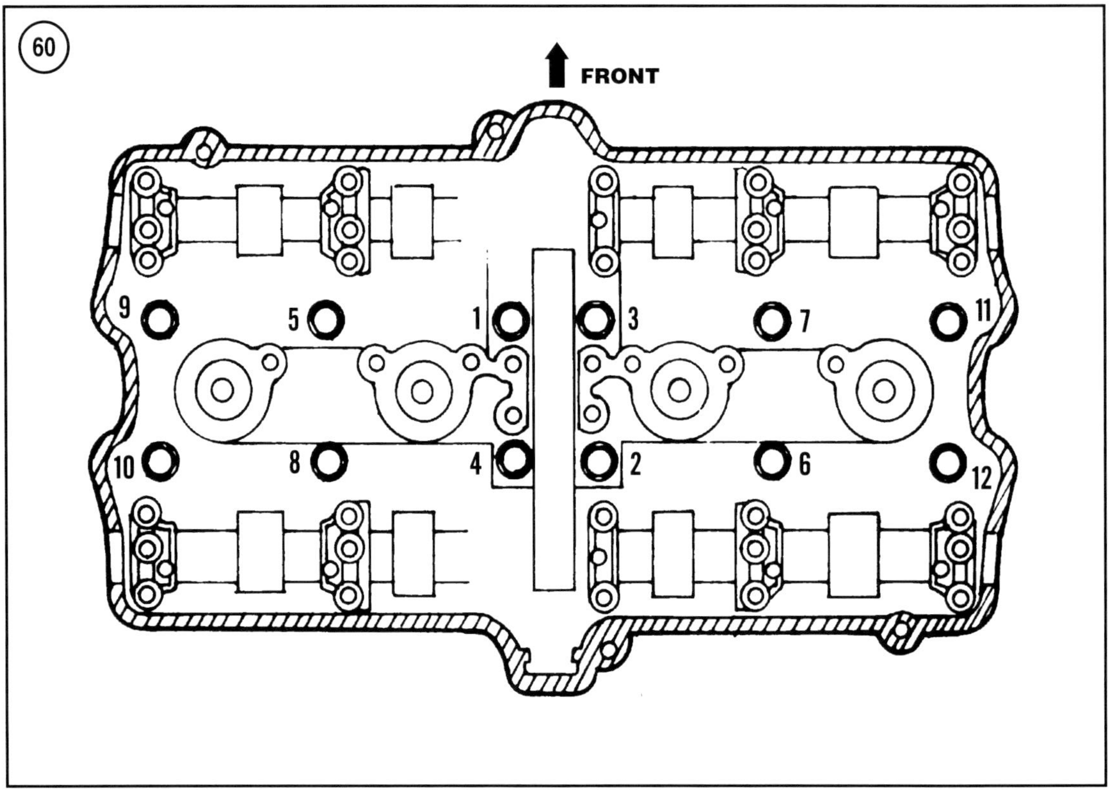

11. Place a clean shop cloth into the camshaft chain tunnel in the cylinder block to keep objects and debris out of the crankcase.

12. Remove and discard the six O-rings from the cylinder block. *New* O-rings must be installed during assembly to prevent oil leaks.

13. Remove the external oil pipes (**Figure 62**) from the crankcase. Discard the O-rings from the oil pipes. *New* O-rings must be installed during assembly to prevent oil leaks.

14. Inspect the cylinder head as described in this section.

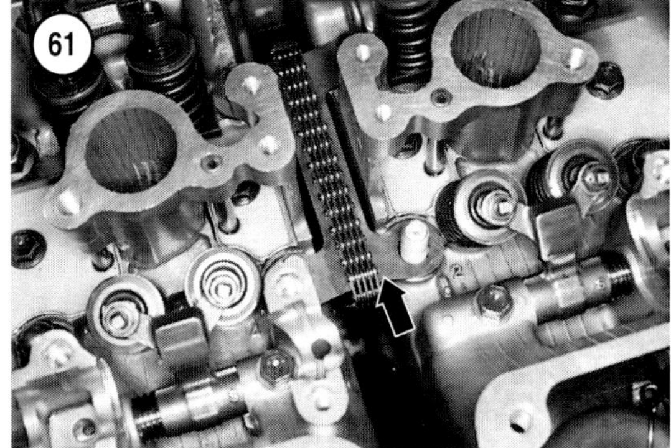

Installation

1. Apply Suzuki Super Grease A to *new* O-rings and install the O-rings (**Figure 63**) at each end of both front external oil pipes.

2. Install both oil pipes (**Figure 62**) into the receptacles in the crankcase. Push them in until they bottom.

3. Apply Suzuki Super Grease A to *new* O-rings and install the six O-rings (A, **Figure 64**) into the crankcase studs on the cylinder block.

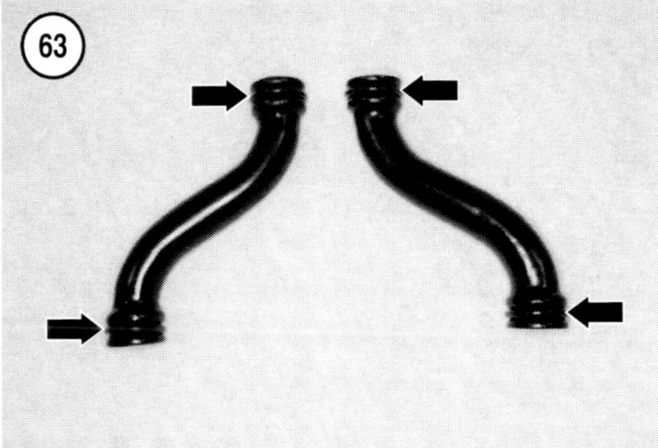

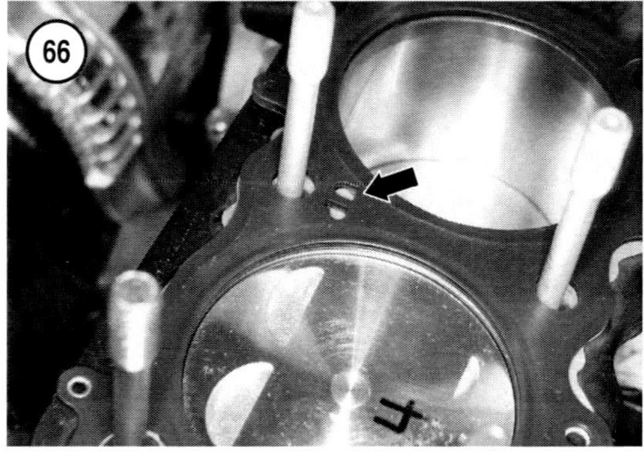

4. If removed, install a locating dowel (B, **Figure 64**) at each end of the cylinder block.
5. Remove the shop rag from the camshaft chain tunnel in the cylinder block.

NOTE
If a Suzuki gasket kit is being used, carefully inspect the cylinder head gasket. A small oil jet can become lodged between the laminated layers of this gasket.

6. Install a *new* cylinder head gasket (**Figure 65**) with the UP mark (**Figure 66**) facing up.
7. Carefully slide the cylinder head onto the cylinder block and onto the external oil pipes. Make sure the oil pipes' upper O-rings seat correctly in the cylinder head receptacles. An oil leak will occur if they are not seated correctly.
8. Feed the camshaft chain through the tunnel in the cylinder head and secure the wire to the exterior of the engine.
9. Install the reinforcement plate (**Figure 61**) onto the crankcase studs and rest the camshaft chain on top of it.

CAUTION
*The nuts securing the cylinder head are of different design (**Figure 59**). The No. 1-4 nuts are conventional nuts with steel washers, the No. 5-8 nuts are acorn nuts with steel washers and the No. 9-12 nuts are conventional nuts with copper washers. All nuts and washers must be installed in the correct location during assembly.*

10. Apply oil to the crankcase stud washers.
11. Install the cylinder head nuts and washers. Install the copper washers with the acorn nuts and install the other steel and copper washers with the conventional nuts. Refer to **Figure 59** for the correct location of the different washers, conventional nuts and the acorn nuts.
12. Evenly tighten the cylinder head nuts in two to three stages. Following the tightening sequence shown in **Figure 60**, tighten the nuts to 38 N•m (28 ft.-lb.).
13. Install the camshaft front chain guide No. 1 and make sure it seats correctly into the cylinder head receptacle (**Figure 67**).
14. Install the lower cylinder head bolt (**Figure 57**) and tighten to 10 N•m (88 in.-lb.).

15. Install the rocker arm assemblies and the camshafts as described in this chapter.
16. Adjust the valves as described in Chapter Three.
17. Install the carburetor assembly and exhaust system as described in Chapter Eight.

Inspection

Compare all measurements to the specifications in **Table 2**. Replace any part that is damaged or out of specification.

1. Before cleaning the head or removing the valves, perform the following leak test:
   a. Position the cylinder head so the exhaust ports face up. Pour solvent or kerosene into each port opening (**Figure 68**).
   b. Turn the head over slightly and check each exhaust valve area on the combustion chamber side. If the valve and seats are in good condition, there should be no leakage past the valve seats. If an area is wet, the valve seat is not sealing correctly. This can be caused by a damaged valve seat or valve face or by a bent or damaged valve. Remove the leaking valve and inspect the valve and seat for wear.
   c. Repeat this test for the intake valves.
2. Remove all traces of gasket residue from the cylinder head and cylinder block mating surfaces. Do not scratch the gasket surfaces.

CAUTION
Cleaning the combustion chamber with the valves removed can damage the valve seat surfaces. A damaged or even slightly scratched valve seat will cause poor valve seating.

3. *Without removing the valves*, remove all carbon deposits from the combustion chamber (A, **Figure 69**). Use a fine wire brush or wooden scraper. Take care not to damage the cylinder head, valves or spark plug threads.

NOTE
When using a tap to clean spark plug threads, coat the tap with an aluminum tap cutting fluid or kerosene.

NOTE
Aluminum spark plug threads are commonly damaged due to galling, cross-threading and overtightening. To prevent galling, apply an anti-seize compound to the plug threads before installation. Do not overtighten the plug.

4. Examine the spark plug threads (B, **Figure 69**) in the cylinder head for damage. If damage is minor

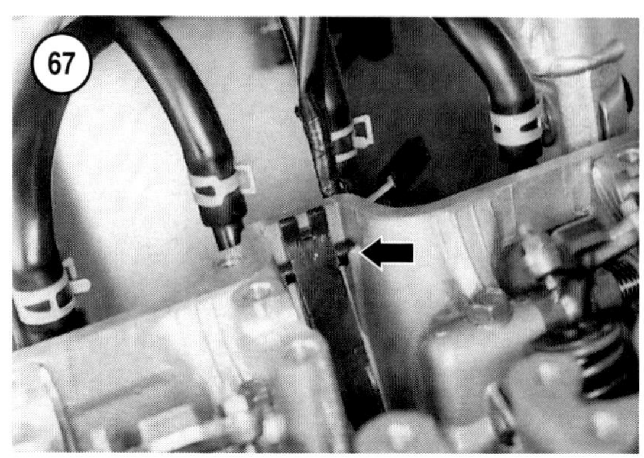

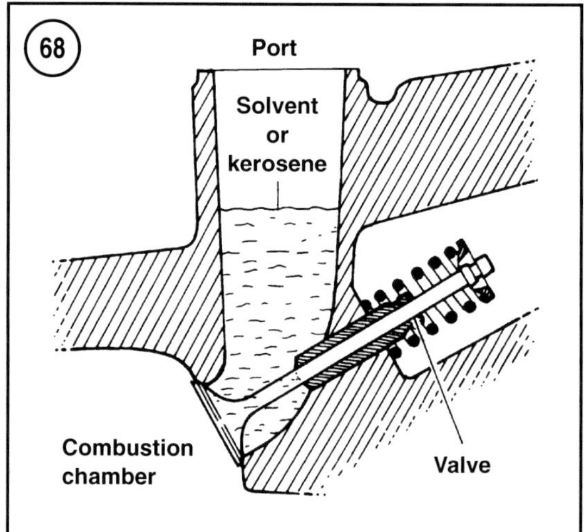

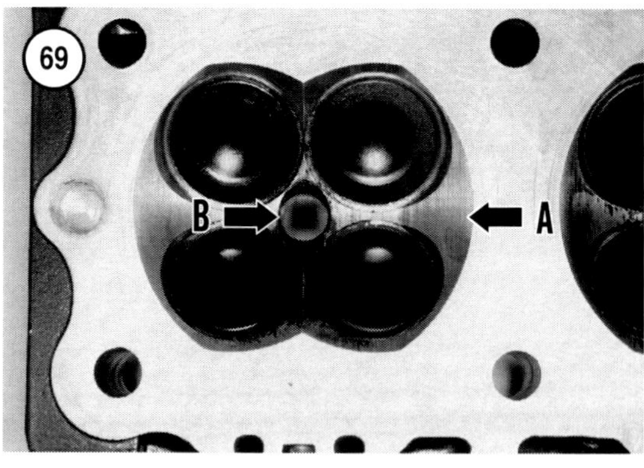

70

71

72

or if the threads are dirty or clogged with carbon, use a spark plug thread tap to clean the threads. If thread damage is severe, the threads can be restored by installing a steel thread insert. Purchase thread insert kits from an automotive supply store or have the inserts installed by a Suzuki dealership or machine shop.

NOTE

If the cylinder head was bead-blasted, clean the cylinder head thoroughly with solvent and then with hot, soapy water. Residual grit can be hard to get out of small crevices and other areas. Also chase each exposed thread with a tap to remove grit between the threads, or the threads may be damaged later. Residue grit left in the engine will contaminate the oil and cause premature piston, ring and bearing wear.

5. After all carbon is removed from the combustion chambers and valve ports and the spark plug thread hole is repaired, clean the entire cylinder head in solvent. Blow it dry with compressed air.
6. Check for cracks in the combustion chambers and the exhaust ports. A cracked cylinder head must be replaced.

CAUTION

Do not clean the piston crowns while the pistons are installed in the cylinders. Carbon will fall between the cylinder wall and piston and collect on the piston rings. Because carbon grit is very abrasive, premature cylinder, piston and ring wear will occur. If the piston crowns have heavy carbon deposits, remove the pistons as described in this chapter and clean them. Excessive carbon buildup on the piston crowns reduces piston cooling, raises engine compression and causes overheating.

7. Examine the crown on all four pistons (**Figure 70**). A crown should show no signs of wear or damage. If a crown appears pecked or spongy-looking, also check the spark plug, valves and combustion chamber for aluminum deposits. If these deposits are found, the cylinder is overheating due to a lean fuel mixture or preignition.
8. Place a straightedge across the gasket surface at several points. Measure warp by attempting to insert a feeler gauge between the straightedge and cylinder head at each location (**Figure 71**). Maximum allowable warp is listed in **Table 2**. Warp or nicks in the cylinder head surface could cause an air leak and result in overheating. If the amount of warp exceeds the limit, the cylinder head must be resurfaced or replaced. Consult a Suzuki dealership or machine shop experienced in this type of work.
9. Inspect the hole in each oil pipe (**Figure 72**). Make sure it is clean and unobstructed. If necessary,

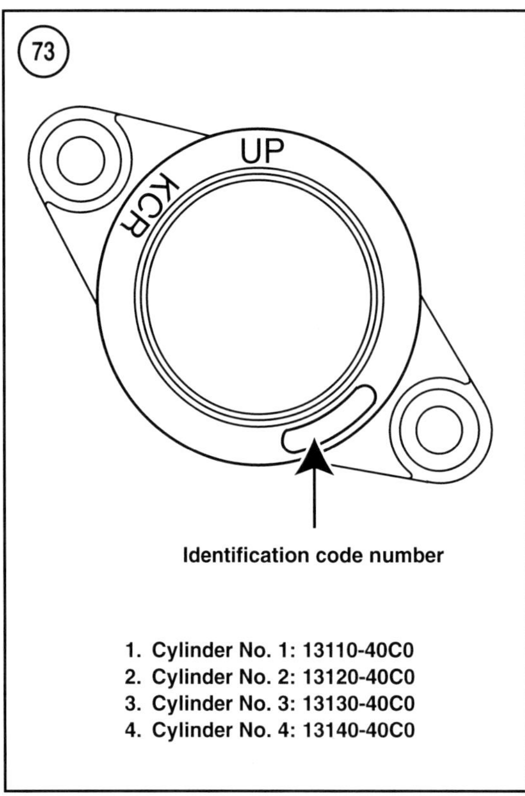

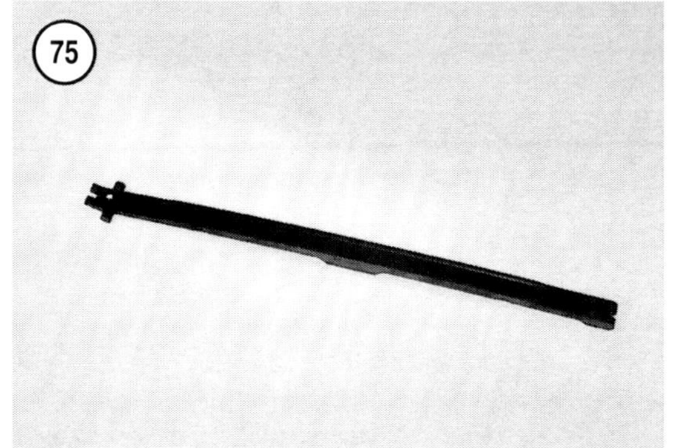

remove the oil pipe. Clean it with solvent, dry it with compressed air and install the pipe with its large end going in last.

NOTE
*Each intake manifold must be reinstalled in its original location. Mark each manifold prior to removal. If new intake manifolds are required, refer to **Figure 73** for correct identification numbers and cylinder location.*

10. Inspect the intake manifolds (**Figure 74**) for cracks or other damage that would allow unfiltered air to enter the engine. If necessary, remove the intake manifolds and discard the O-rings. To prevent a vacuum leak, install a *new* O-ring between the intake manifold and the cylinder head. Lubricate the O-ring with Suzuki Super Grease A and install each manifold in its original location. Tighten the screws securely.
11. Inspect the camshaft front chain guide No. 1 (**Figure 75**) for wear or damage.
12. Inspect the camshaft rear chain guide No. 3 (**Figure 76**) for wear or damage. If necessary, remove the bolt and washer (**Figure 77**) and replace

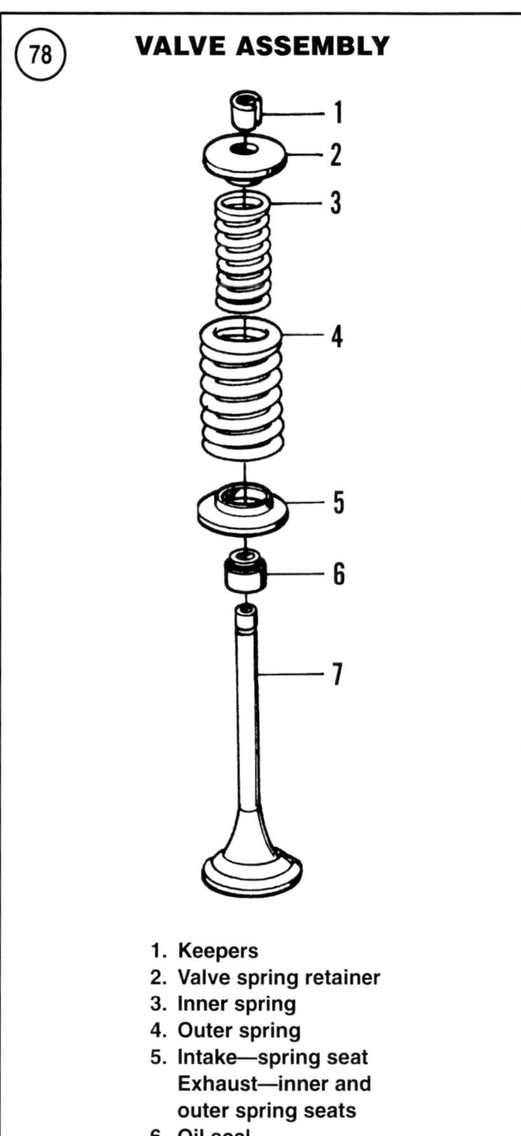

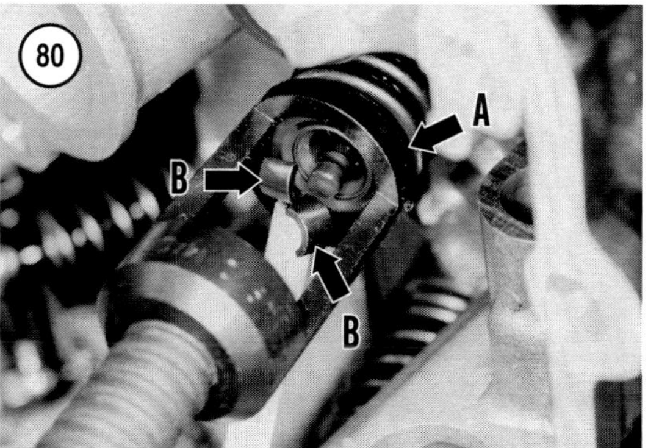

the guide. Apply a medium strength threadlocking compound to the threads prior to installation, then tighten securely.

13. Inspect the threads on the exhaust pipe mounting bolts for damage. Clean the threads with an appropriate size metric tap if necessary.

14. Check the valves and valve guides as described in this chapter.

VALVES AND VALVE COMPONENTS

Refer to **Figure 78** when servicing the valves.

Complete valve service requires a number of special tools and considerable skill to use them. Consequently, even experienced mechanics that perform their own service generally remove the cylinder head and have a machine shop or dealership perform inspection and service.

The following procedures describe how to check for valve component wear and to determine what type of service is required. In most cases, valve troubles are caused by poor valve seating, worn valve guides and burned valves. A valve spring compressor is required to remove and install the valves.

Valve Removal

1. Remove the cylinder head as described in this chapter.

2. Install a valve spring compressor (**Figure 79**) squarely over the valve spring retainer (A, **Figure 80**). Place the other end of the tool against the valve head.

CAUTION

To avoid loss of spring tension, do not compress the spring any more than necessary to remove the valve keepers.

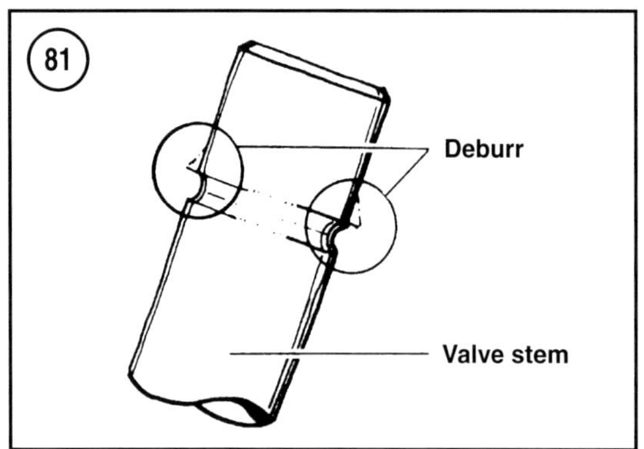

3. Tighten the valve spring compressor until the valve keepers separate from the valve stem. Lift the valve keepers (B, **Figure 80**) out through the valve spring compressor with a magnet or needlenose pliers.

4. Gradually loosen the valve spring compressor and remove it from the cylinder head.

5. Remove the spring retainer and the two valve springs.

6. Remove any burrs from the valve stem groove before removing the valve (**Figure 81**). Otherwise the valve guide will be damaged as the valve stem passes through it.

7. Remove the valve from the cylinder while rotating it slightly.

8A. On intake valves, remove the spring seat.

8B. On exhaust valves, remove the inner and outer spring seats.

9. Pull the oil seal off the valve guide. Discard the oil seal.

CAUTION

*All component parts of each valve assembly must be kept together (**Figure 82**). Place each set in a divided carton, into separate small boxes or into small reclosable plastic bags. Label each valve set. Identify a valve set by its cylinder number and either intake or exhaust valves. This avoids parts getting mixed up and makes installation simpler. Do not intermix components from the valve assemblies or excessive wear may result.*

10. Repeat Steps 2-9 and remove the remaining valves. Keep all valve sets separate.

11. Remove both exhaust valve seat plates (**Figure 83**) from the cylinder head.

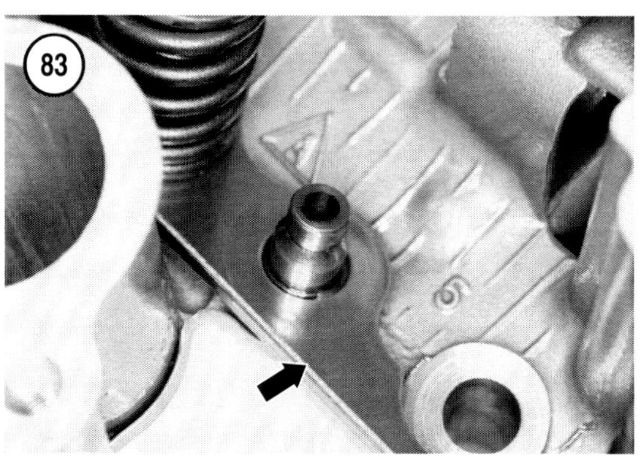

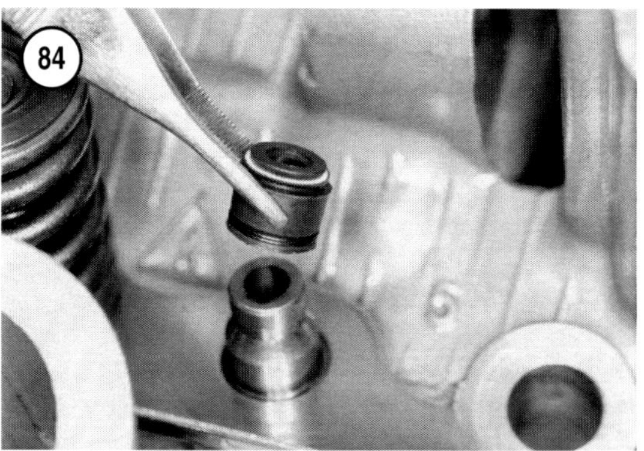

86

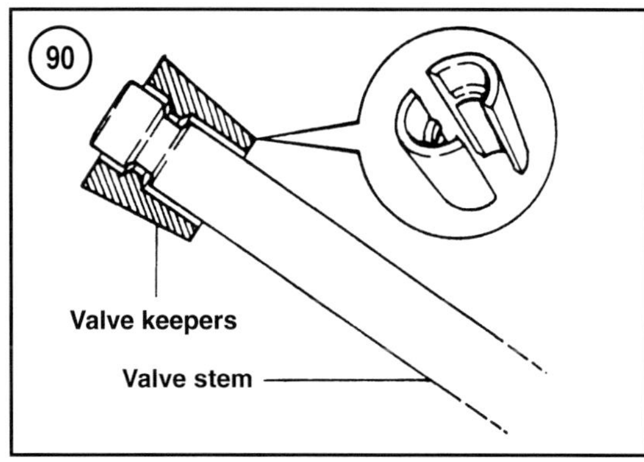

90

87

88

89

Valve Installation

1. Clean the end of the valve guides.
2. Install both exhaust valve seat plates (**Figure 83**) onto the exhaust side of the cylinder head.
3. Oil the inside of the *new* oil seal and install the seal onto the valve guide (**Figure 84**). Push it down until it bottoms.
4. Coat the valve stem with molybdenum disulfide paste. Partially install the valve into the guide. Slowly turn the valve as it enters the oil seal and continue turning it until the valve is completely installed.
5A. On intake valves, install the spring seat.
5B. On exhaust valves, install the outer (**Figure 85**) and the inner (**Figure 86**) spring seats.
6. Position the valve springs with their *closer* wound coils (**Figure 87**) facing the cylinder head.
7. Install the outer valve spring (A, **Figure 88**) and make sure it is properly seated on the spring seat.
8. Install the inner valve spring (B, **Figure 88**) and make sure it is properly seated on the spring seat.
9. Install the spring retainer (C, **Figure 88**) on top of both valve springs.

CAUTION
To avoid loss of spring tension, do not compress the springs any more than necessary to install the valve keepers.

10. Compress the valve springs with a valve spring compressor and install the valve keepers.
11. Make sure both keepers are seated around the valve stem prior to releasing the compressor.
12. Slowly release the tension from the compressor and remove it. After removing the compressor, inspect the valve keepers (**Figure 89**) to make sure they are properly seated (**Figure 90**). Tap the end of

the valve stem with a drift and hammer. This ensures that the keepers are properly seated.

13. If the valve stem end has been resurfaced, check that the end of the valve (A, **Figure 91**) extends above the valve keepers (B). If it does not, replace the valve.

14. Repeat Steps 3-12 for the remaining valves.

15. Install the cylinder head as described in this chapter.

16. After installing the cylinder head, adjust the valve clearance as described in Chapter Three.

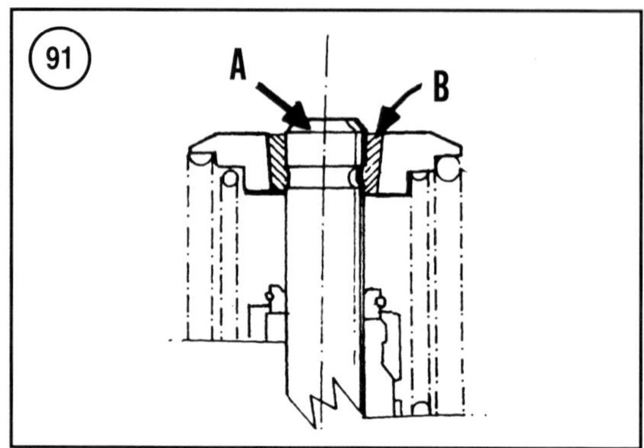

Valve Inspection

Compare all measurement to the specifications in **Table 2**. Replace any component that is out of specification, worn to the wear limit or damaged.

1. Clean the valves in solvent. Do not gouge or damage the valve-seating surface.

2. Inspect the valve face (**Figure 92**). Minor roughness and pitting can be removed by lapping the valve as described in this chapter. Excessive unevenness to the contact surface is an indication that the valve is not serviceable.

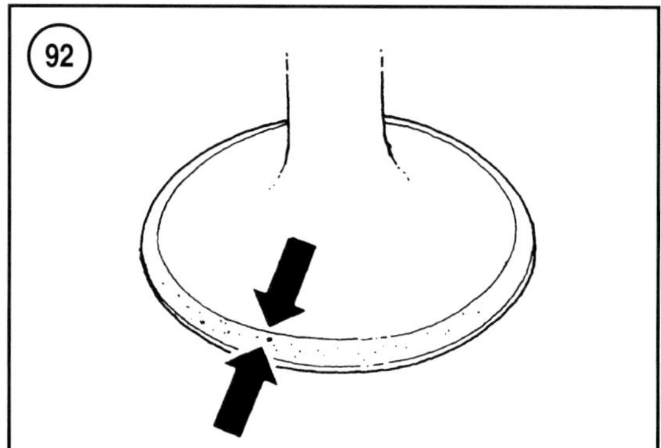

3. Inspect the valve stem for wear and roughness. Measure the valve head radial runout as shown in **Figure 93**.

4. Measure the valve stem runout as shown in **Figure 94**.

5. Measure the valve stem outside diameter with a micrometer (**Figure 95**).

   a. If the valve stem is out of specification, discard the valve.

   b. If the valve stem is within specification, record the measurement so it can be used to determine valve stem-to-guide clearance in Step 9.

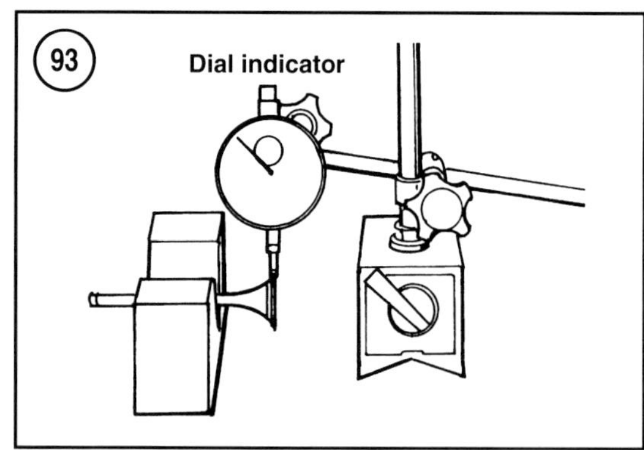

6. Measure the valve head thickness (**Figure 96**) with a vernier caliper.

7. Before measuring wear, remove all carbon and varnish from the valve guides (**Figure 97**) with a stiff spiral wire brush.

NOTE

If the required measuring tools are unavailable, proceed to Step 10.

8. Measure the valve guide inside diameter with a small hole gauge. Measure the diameter at the top, center and bottom of the guide. Measure the small

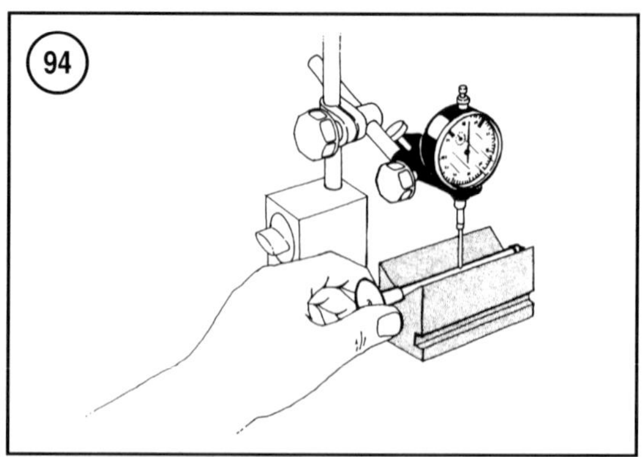

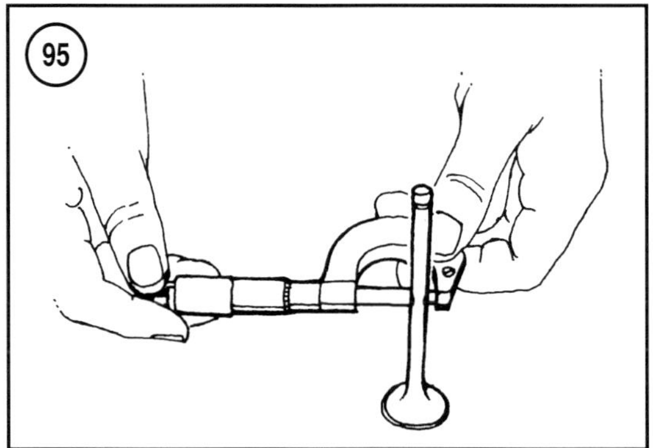

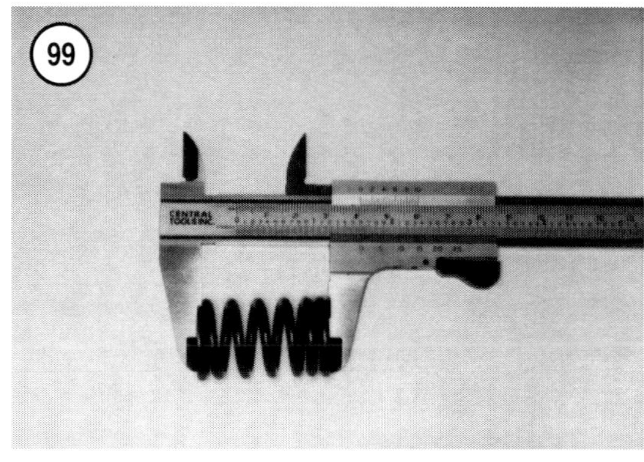

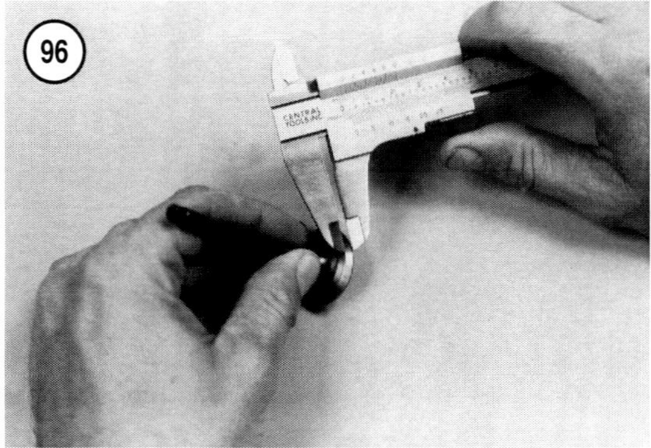

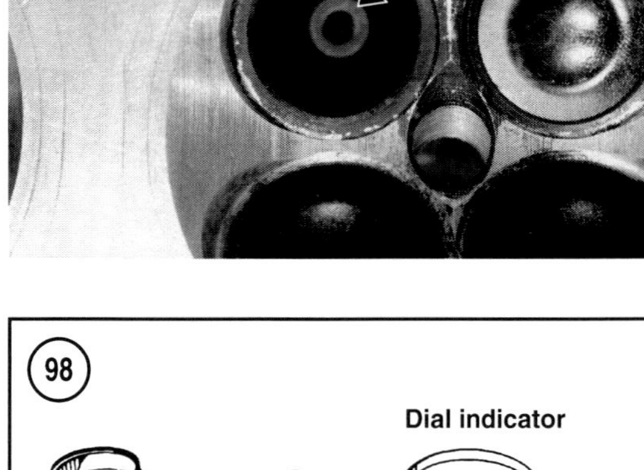

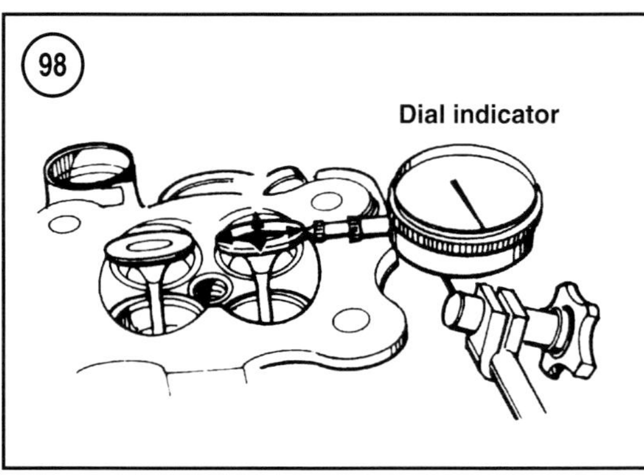

hole gauge and compare the largest measurement to the specification in **Table 2**:

a. If the valve guide is out of specification, replace it as described in this chapter.
b. If the valve guide is within specification, record the measurement so it can be used to calculate valve stem-to-guide clearance in Step 9.

9. Subtract the valve stem outside diameter (Step 5) from the valve guide inside diameter (Step 8). The difference is the valve stem-to-guide clearance. If the clearance is out of specification, replace the valve and guide as a set.

10. If a small bore gauge is not available, measure the valve stem deflection as follows:

a. Insert each valve into its guide.
b. Hold the valve slightly off its seat (about 10 mm or 0.39 in.).
c. Attach a dial indicator to the valve head (**Figure 98**) and rock the valve sideways in two directions 90° to each other. If the valve stem deflection in either direction exceeds the service limit in **Table 2** and the valve stem outside diameter is within specification, the valve guide is probably worn. However, as a final check, take the cylinder head to a Suzuki dealership or machine shop and have the valve guides measured.

11. Check the inner and outer valve springs as follows:

a. Visually inspect each valve spring for cracks, distortion or other damage.
b. Measure the valve spring free length with a vernier caliper (**Figure 99**).
c. Repeat for each valve spring.
d. Replace defective springs as a set (inner and outer).

12. Check the valve spring retainer and valve keepers for cracks or other damage.

13. Inspect the valve stem end for pitting or wear. If necessary, resurface the valve stem end and measure the valve stem end length (**Figure 100**). The valve must be replaced if the valve stem end length is worn to the service limit in **Table 2**.

14. Inspect the valve seats. If worn or burned, they may be reconditioned as described in this chapter.

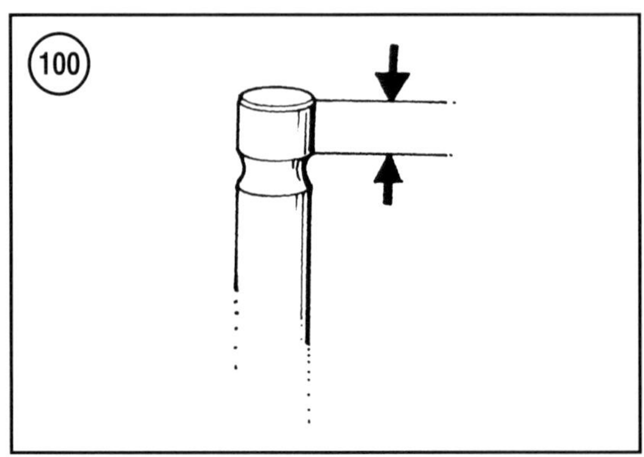

Valve Guide Replacement

Special tools and considerable experience are required to properly replace the valve guides in the cylinder head. If these tools are unavailable, have a Suzuki dealership or machine shop perform this procedure. The following procedure is provided for those who choose to perform this task. When a valve guide is replaced, the valve must also be replaced.

NOTE
*Each intake manifold must be reinstalled in its original location. Mark each manifold prior to removal. If new intake manifolds are required, refer to **Figure 73** for correct identification numbers and cylinder location.*

1. Remove the screws and remove all of the intake manifolds (**Figure 74**) from the cylinder head.

CAUTION
Do not heat the cylinder head with a torch (propane or acetylene). Never bring a flame into contact with the cylinder head. The direct heat will destroy the case hardening and may warp the head.

2. The valve guides are installed with a slight interference fit. Heat the cylinder head in a shop oven or on a hot plate. Heat the cylinder head to a temperature of 100-150° C (212-300° F). Use temperature indicator sticks, available at welding supply stores, to monitor the cylinder head temperature.

3. Place the *new* valve guides in the freezer. The cold temperature will reduce the guides' outside diameter and ease installation.

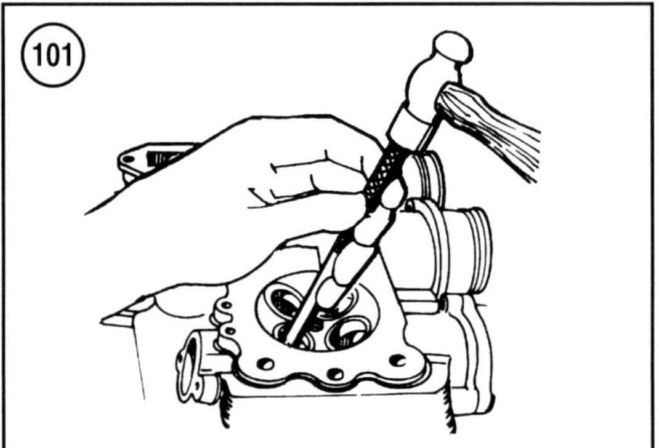

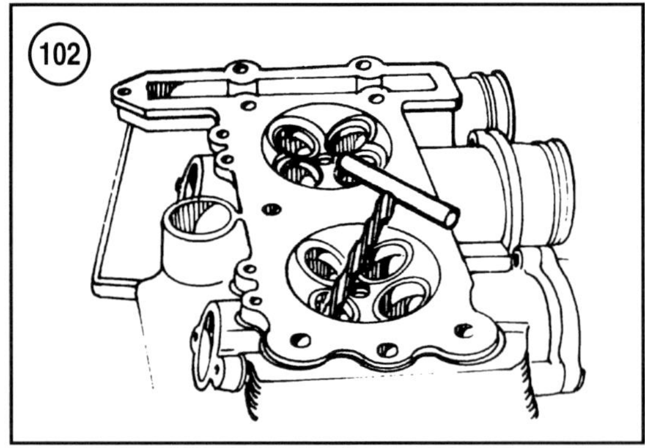

WARNING
Wear welding gloves when performing the following procedure. The cylinder head will be very hot.

4. Remove the cylinder head from the oven or hot plate. Place it on wooden blocks with the combustion chambers facing up.

CAUTION
Do not attempt to remove the valve guides if the head is not hot enough.

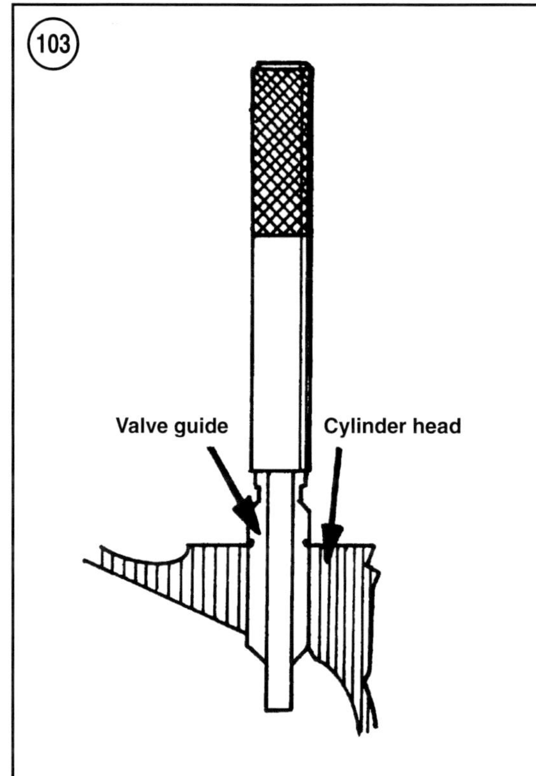

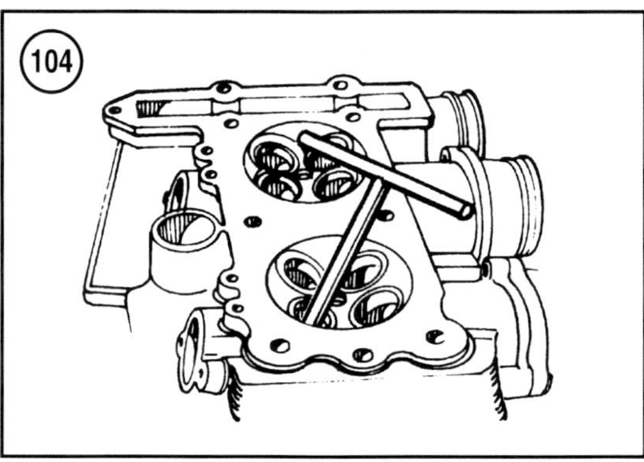

Doing so may damage the valve guide bore.

5. From the combustion side of the cylinder head, drive out the old valve guide (**Figure 101**) with a hammer and the Suzuki valve guide remover/installer (part No. 09916-44310) or an equivalent.

6. Remove and discard the valve guide and the ring. Never reuse a valve guide or ring. They are no longer true nor within tolerance.

7. Insert the valve guide reamer from the combustion chamber side, and rotate the reamer *clockwise* through the valve guide bore (**Figure 102**). Continue to rotate the reamer and work it through the entire length of the bore. Use the Suzuki valve guide bore reamer (part No. 09916-34580) and reamer handle (part No. 09916-34542) or an equivalent.

8. Rotate the reamer *clockwise* and withdraw it from the valve guide bore. Remove the reamer and handle.

9. Remove a *new* valve guide from the freezer and install a *new* ring onto the guide.

10. Apply fresh engine oil to the valve guide and to the valve guide bore in the cylinder head.

11. From the top side (valve side) of the cylinder head, drive the valve guide into place with a hammer and the Suzuki valve guide remover/installer (**Figure 103**). Drive the valve guide until the ring completely seats in the cylinder head.

12. After installation, ream the valve guide by performing the following:

   a. Use the Suzuki valve guide reamer (part No. 09916-34570) and the reamer handle (part No. 09916-34542) or equivalent.
   b. Apply cutting oil to both the valve guide and the valve guide reamer.

CAUTION

*Always rotate the reamer **clockwise**. The valve guide will be damaged if the reamer is rotated counterclockwise.*

   c. Insert the reamer from the combustion chamber side and rotate it *clockwise* through the valve guide (**Figure 104**). Continue to rotate the reamer and work it down through the entire length of the *new* valve guide. Apply additional cutting oil during this procedure.
   d. While rotating the reamer *clockwise*, withdraw the reamer from the valve guide.
   e. Measure the valve guide inside diameter with a small hole gauge. This measurement must be within the specification listed in **Table 2**.

13. Repeat for the other valve guides.

14. Thoroughly clean the cylinder head and valve guides with solvent to remove all metal particles. Clean the cylinder head with hot, soapy water, rinse the cylinder head completely and thoroughly dry it with compressed air.

15. Lubricate the valve guides with engine oil.

16. Recondition the valve seats as described in this chapter.

17. Install the intake manifolds in their original locations on the cylinder head. To prevent a vacuum leak, install a *new* O-ring with each intake manifold. If new intake manifolds are installed, refer to **Figure 73** for correct identification numbers and cylinder location

Valve Seat Inspection

The most accurate method for checking the valve seat is to use a marking compound, available from auto parts and tool stores. Marking compounds are used for locating high or irregular spots when checking or making close fits and when scraping bearing surfaces. Follow the manufacturer's directions.

NOTE
Because of the close operating tolerances within the valve assembly, the valve stem and guide must be in good condition (within tolerance); otherwise, the inspection results will be inaccurate.

1. Remove the valves as described in this chapter.
2. Clean the valve seat in the cylinder head and valve mating areas with contact cleaner.
3. Thoroughly clean off all carbon deposits from the valve face with solvent or detergent. Dry the valve thoroughly.
4. Spread a thin layer of marking compound evenly on the valve face.
5. Moisten the end of a suction cup valve tool and attach it to the valve. Insert the valve into the guide.
6. Using the valve lapping tool, tap the valve against the valve seat so the marking compound transfers to the valve contact area (**Figure 105**).
7. Remove the valve and examine the impression left by the marking compound. If the impression (on the valve or on the cylinder head) is not even and continuous and if the valve seat width (**Figure 106**) is not within the specified tolerance, the valve seat must be reconditioned.
8. Closely examine the valve seat in the cylinder head. It should be smooth and even with a polished seating surface.
9. If the valve seat is good, install the valve as described in this chapter.
10. If the valve seat is not correct, it must be reconditioned.

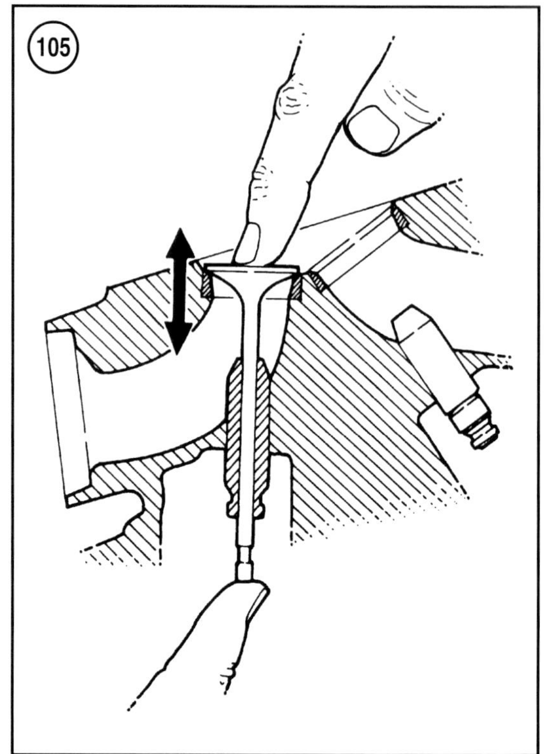

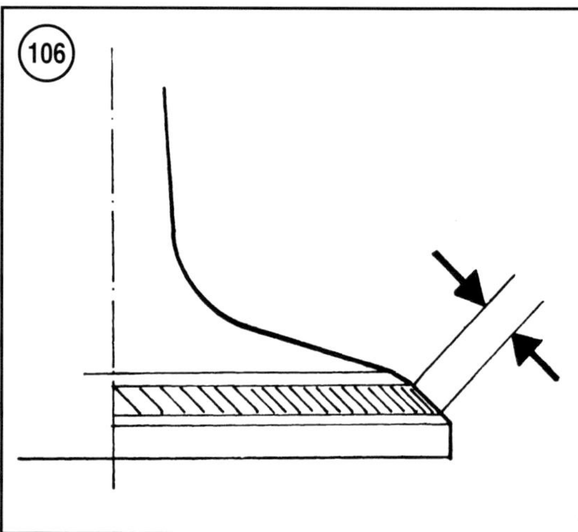

11. Repeat for the other valves.

Valve Seat Reconditioning

Special valve cutters and considerable experience are required to properly recondition the valve seats in the cylinder head. If these tools are unavailable, have a Suzuki dealership or machine shop perform

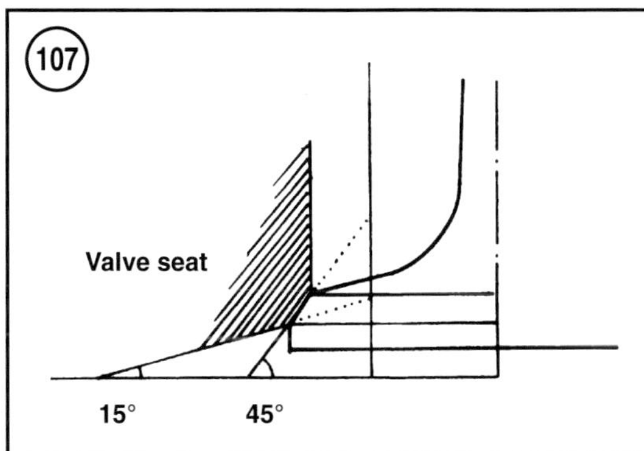

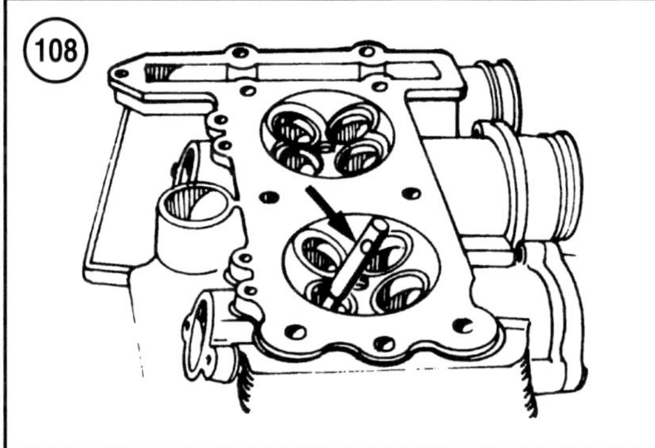

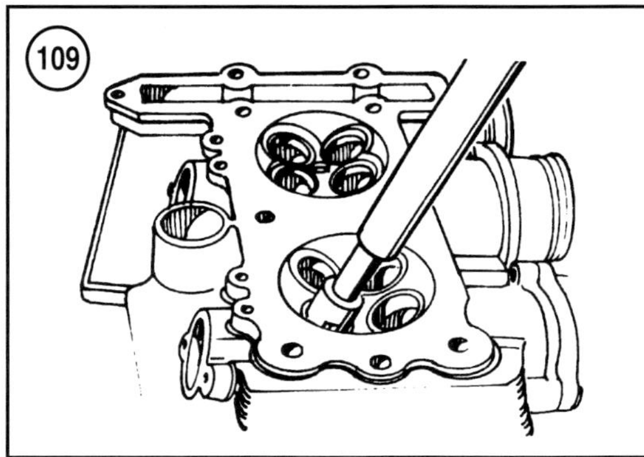

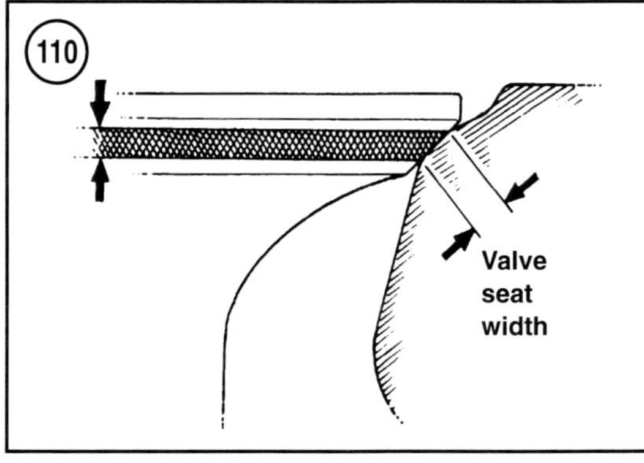

this procedure. The following procedure is provided for those who choose to perform this task.

The Suzuki solid pilot (N-100-5.0) and valve cutters (N-121 or N-122) or equivalent are required to recondition the valve seats.

The valve seat for both the intake and exhaust valves are machined to the same angles. The valve contact surface is cut to a 45° angle and the area above the contact surface (closest to the combustion chamber) is cut to a 15° angle (**Figure 107**).

1. Carefully rotate and insert the solid pilot into the valve guide (**Figure 108**). Be sure the pilot is correctly seated.
2. Install the 45° cutter and T-handle onto the solid pilot.
3. Using the 45° cutter, de-scale and clean the valve seat with one or two turns (**Figure 109**).

CAUTION

When cutting valve seats, work slowly. Measure the valve seat contact area in the cylinder head after each cut to make sure the contact area is correct and to avoid removing too much material. Over-cutting will sink the valve too far into the cylinder head resulting in replacing the cylinder head.

4. If the seat is still pitted or burned, turn the 45° cutter additional turns until the surface is clean. Refer to the previous CAUTION to avoid removing too much material from the cylinder head.
5. Inspect the valve seat by performing the following:
   a. Spread a thin layer of marking compound evenly on the valve face.
   b. Moisten the end of a suction cup valve tool and attach it to the valve. Insert the valve into the guide.
   c. Using the valve lapping tool, tap the valve against the valve seat (**Figure 105**).
   d. Measure the valve seat width (**Figure 110**) with a vernier caliper. It should be within the range specified in **Table 2**.
6. If the contact area is too *high* on the valve (**Figure 111**) or if it is too wide, use the 15° cutter to remove a portion of the top area of the valve seat. This lowers and narrows the contact area on the valve.

7. If the contact area is too *low* on the valve or too narrow (**Figure 111**), use the 45° cutter to remove a portion of the lower area of the valve seat. This raises and widens the contact area on the valve.
8. Once the desired valve seat position and width are obtained, use the 45° cutter to lightly clean off any burrs that may have been caused by previous cuts.

CAUTION
Do not use any valve lapping compound after the final cut has been made.

9. Check that the finish has a smooth, velvety surface. It should not be shiny or polished. Final seating will take place when the engine is run.
10. Repeat for the remaining valve seats.
11. Thoroughly clean the cylinder head and all valve components in solvent or detergent and hot water.
12. Install the valve assemblies as described in this chapter. Check the seal at each valve seat by pouring solvent into the intake and exhaust ports (**Figure 112**). There should be no leaking past the seat in the combustion chamber. If leakage occurs, the combustion chamber will appear wet. If fluid leaks past any of the seats, the valve seats must be inspected for foreign matter or burrs that are preventing a proper seal.
13. Apply a light coat of engine oil to all bare metal surfaces to prevent rust.

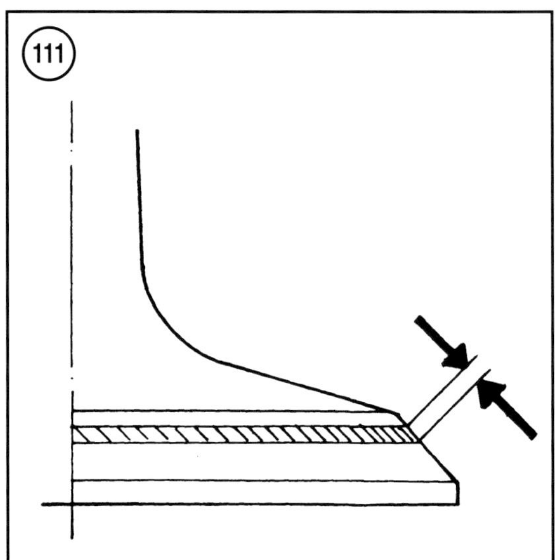

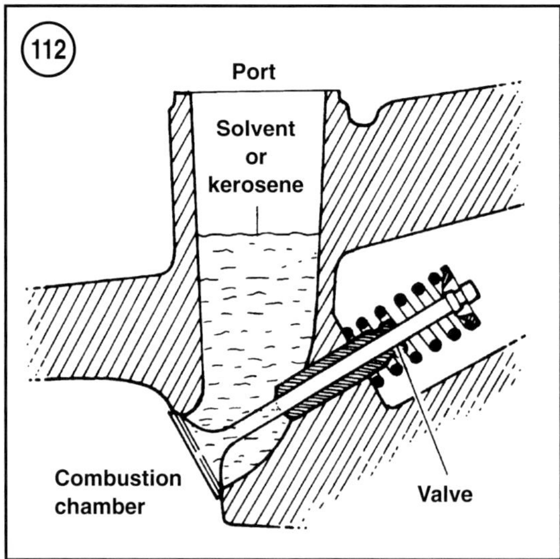

Valve Lapping

Valve lapping is a simple operation which can restore the valve seal without machining if the amount of wear or distortion is not too great.

This procedure should only be performed after determining that valve seat width and outside diameter are within specifications. A valve lapping tool is required.

1. Smear a light coat of fine grade valve lapping compound onto the seating surface of the valve.
2. Insert the valve into the cylinder head.
3. Wet the suction cup of the lapping tool and stick in onto the head of the valve. Spin the tool in both directions, while pressing it against the valve seat and lap the valve to the seat. Every 5 to 10 seconds, rotate the valve 180° in the valve seat. Continue with this action until the mating surfaces on the valve and seat are smooth and equal in size.
4. Closely examine the valve seat in the cylinder head. It should be smooth and evenly polished.
5. Repeat Steps 1-4 for the other valves.
6. Thoroughly clean the valves and cylinder head in solvent or detergent and hot water to remove all valve lapping compound. Dry the components thoroughly.

CAUTION
Any compound left on the valves or the cylinder head will end up in the engine and cause excessive wear and damage.

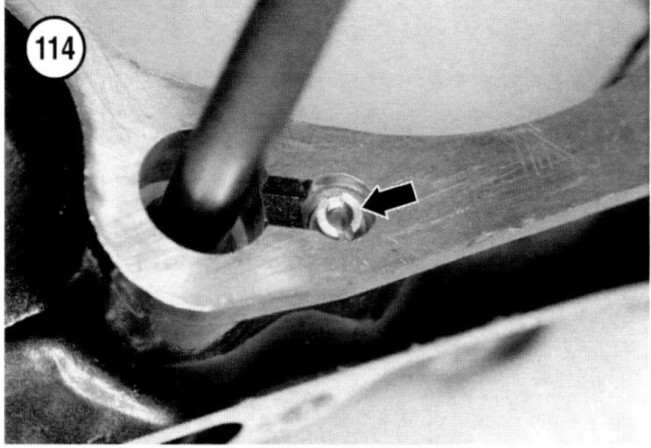

7. Install the valve assemblies as described in this chapter.

8. After the lapping has been completed and the valves have been reinstalled into the head, the valve seats should be tested as described in Step 12 in *Valve Seat Reconditioning*. If fluid leaks past any of the seats, disassemble that valve assembly and repeat this procedure until there is no leakage.

NOTE
This solvent test does not ensure long-term durability or maximum power. It merely ensures maximum compression will be available on initial start-up after reassembly.

9. Apply a light coat of engine oil to all bare metal surfaces to prevent rust.

CYLINDER BLOCK

Removal

1. Remove the cylinder head as described in this chapter.

2. Remove the cylinder head gasket and the locating dowels.

3. If still installed, remove the external oil pipes from the front of the crankcase. Discard the O-rings.

4. On PAIR equipped models, remove the PAIR air pipes from the cylinder block as described in Chapter Eight.

5. Remove the cylinder base nut (**Figure 113**) from the stud at the front of the crankcase.

CAUTION
The cooling fins are fragile and may be damaged if tapped or pried too hard. Do not strike the fins with a metal-faced hammer.

6. Loosen the cylinder block by tapping around its perimeter with a soft-faced mallet. If necessary, pry the cylinder block loose from the crankcase.

7. Push the rear camshaft chain guide forward so it is out of the way.

8. Pull the cylinder block straight up and off of the pistons and crankcase studs. Work the camshaft chain wire through the camshaft chain tunnel in the cylinder block. Reattach the wire to the exterior of the crankcase.

9. Remove and discard the base gasket.

10. Remove the locating dowels from the crankcase.

11. Use tweezers or needlenose pliers to remove the two oil jets (**Figure 114**) from the top of the crankcase. The oil jets are located adjacent to each rear crankcase stud on the left and right corners of the crankcase.

12. Inspect the cylinder block as described in the following procedure.

Installation

A set of piston holding fixtures and piston ring compressors make installation of the cylinder block over the pistons safer and easier. Cylinder block installation can be accomplished without these tools, but it is a lot more difficult and also increases the chance of damage to both the cylinder wall surfaces and to the piston rings and skirts. These tools are available from a Suzuki dealership or tool supplier.

1. Check the top surface of the crankcase and the bottom surface of the cylinder block. Both must be clean.

2. Install a *new* O-ring seal (**Figure 115**) on each oil jet. Apply clean engine oil to the O-ring.

3. Install the two oil jets (**Figure 114**) adjacent to the rear crankcase stud on the left and right corners of the crankcase.

4. Install the locating dowels (A, **Figure 116**) onto the two front center crankcase studs.

5. Install a *new* base gasket (B, **Figure 116**) onto the crankcase. Make sure the UP mark on the gasket faces up.

6. Rotate the crankshaft so the No. 2 and No. 3 pistons (**Figure 117**) are at top dead center. Install a 19 mm (3/4 in.) thick wooden piston holding fixture (A, **Figure 118**) onto the No. 2 and No. 3 pistons.

7. Install the piston ring compressor tools (B, **Figure 118**) onto the No. 2 and No. 3 pistons.

8. Lubricate the cylinder walls, pistons and rings liberally with clean engine oil prior to installation.

9. Feed the camshaft chain and wire up through the camshaft chain tunnel in the cylinder block. Carefully align the cylinder block with the two raised pistons.

10. Slowly slide the cylinder block over the rear camshaft chain guide and lower the block down onto the No. 2 and No. 3 pistons until the cylinder liners *lightly* touch the top piston rings.

11. On the No. 2 and No. 3 pistons, compress each piston ring as it enters the cylinder bore. Slide the cylinder block all the way down until it passes by the piston rings.

CAUTION

In the following step, do not damage the No. 2 and No. 3 pistons when removing the piston ring compressors and piston holding fixtures.

12. Support the cylinder block and remove the piston ring compressors and piston holding fixtures.

13. Slowly lower the cylinder block and insert the No. 1 and No. 4 pistons into the cylinder bores. Compress each piston ring as it enters the cylinder bore. Slide the cylinder block all the way down until it passes by the piston rings.

14. Carefully push the cylinder block down until it bottoms on the upper crankcase. Make sure the locating dowels correctly engage the cylinder block.

15. Install the cylinder base nut (**Figure 113**) onto the stud at the front of the crankcase. Tighten the nut to 9 N•m (80 in.-lb.).

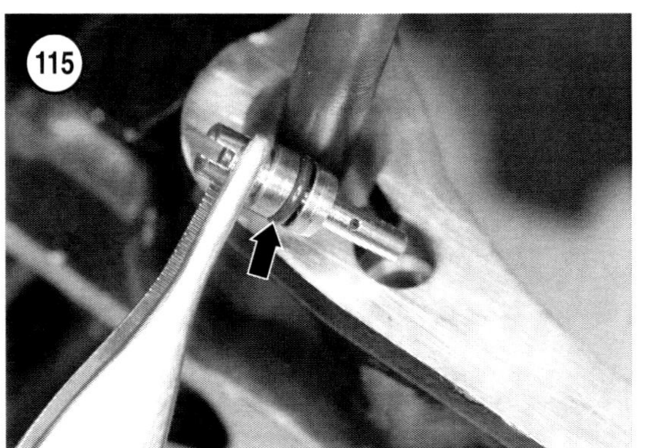

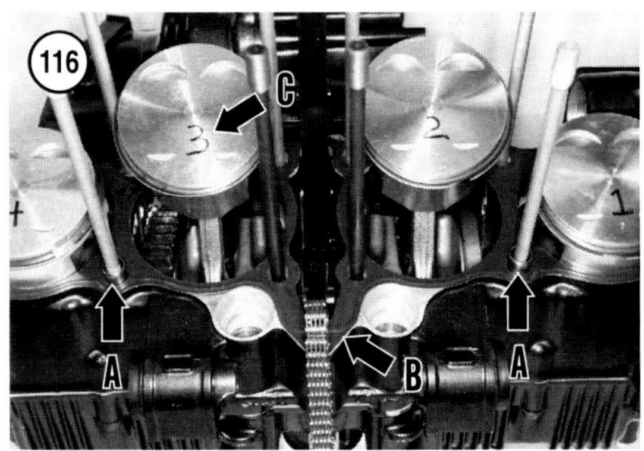

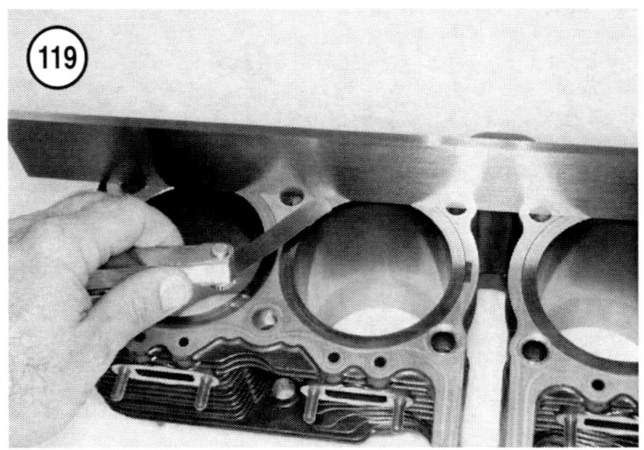

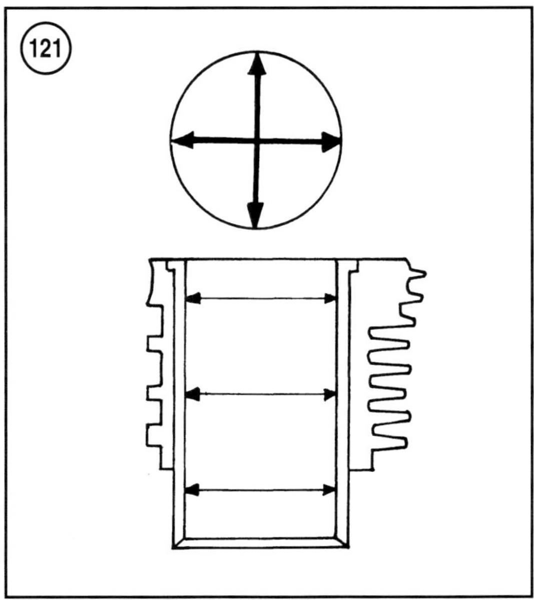

16. Place *new* O-rings into the external oil pipes and install them into the crankcase receptacles.
17. On PAIR equipped models, install the PAIR air pipes onto the cylinder block as described in Chapter Eight.
18. Install the cylinder head gasket and the locating dowels.
19. Install the cylinder head and cylinder head cover as described in this chapter.

Inspection

A bore gauge and micrometer are required to accurately measure the cylinder bore. If these tools are not available, have the measurements performed by a Suzuki dealership or machine shop.

Compare all measurement to the specifications in **Table 2**. Replace or re-bore the cylinder block if it is damaged or out of specification.

1. Soak any old gasket material with solvent. Remove all gasket residue from the cylinder block top and bottom gasket surfaces. If necessary, gently scrape away any gasket residue. Both surfaces must be free of all residue.
2. Wash the cylinder block in solvent. Dry it with compressed air.
3. Check the cylinder block surfaces for cracks or damage.
4. Check the cylinder block for warp with a straightedge and flat feeler gauge. Check for warp at several spots across the cylinder block. (**Figure 119**). The block must be replaced if cylinder warp exceeds the wear limit.
5. Check the locating dowel holes for cracks or other damage.
6. Check each cylinder bore (**Figure 120**) for deep scratches, scoring, or other visible damage.
7. Measure the inside diameter or each cylinder bore with a bore gauge or inside micrometer at the points shown in **Figure 121**. Measure in line with the piston pin and 90° to the pin. If any measurement is out of specification, the cylinder block must be rebored to the next oversize and *new* pistons and piston rings installed. Rebore all four cylinders even though only one may be worn.

CAUTION

*Never re-bore a cylinder if the finished diameter will exceed the cylinder diameter wear limit in **Table 2**.*

NOTE

Purchase the new pistons before boring the cylinders so the pistons can be measured. Each cylinder must be bored to match one piston only.

8. Wash each cylinder bore in hot, soapy water and rinse it completely. This is the only way to clean the cylinder walls of the fine grit material left from the bore or honing job. After washing the walls, run a clean white cloth through each cylinder. The cloth should show no traces of grit or other debris. If the cloth is dirty, rewash the cylinder walls. Once the cylinder walls are completely clean, lubricate them with clean engine oil to prevent rust.

PISTON AND PISTON RINGS

The pistons are made of an aluminum alloy. The piston pin is made of steel and is a precision fit in the pistons. The piston pins are held in place by a circlip at each end.

Piston Removal

1. Remove the cylinder head and cylinder block as described in this chapter.
2. Mark the top of each piston with its identification number (C, **Figure 116**). Start with the No. 1 cylinder on the left side. The pistons must be reinstalled onto the correct connecting rods and into the correct cylinder bores during installation.
3. Cover the crankcase below the piston with a clean shop cloth to keep the piston pin circlips from falling into the crankcase.
4. Before removing a piston, hold the rod tightly and rock the piston (**Figure 122**). Any rocking motion (do not confuse with the normal sliding motion) indicates wear on the piston pin, rod bushing, pin bore, or more likely, a combination of all three.
5. Remove the circlip from each side of the piston pin bore (**Figure 123**). When removing the clip, hold a thumb over one clip edge so the clip will not spring out.

NOTE
*Discard the piston circlips. **New** circlips must be installed during assembly.*

6. Push the piston pin out of the bore by hand. If the pin is tight, remove it with a home made tool (**Figure 124**). Do not drive the piston pin out, as this action could damage the piston pin, connecting rod or piston.
7. Lift the piston off the connecting rod.
8. Repeat for the other three pistons.

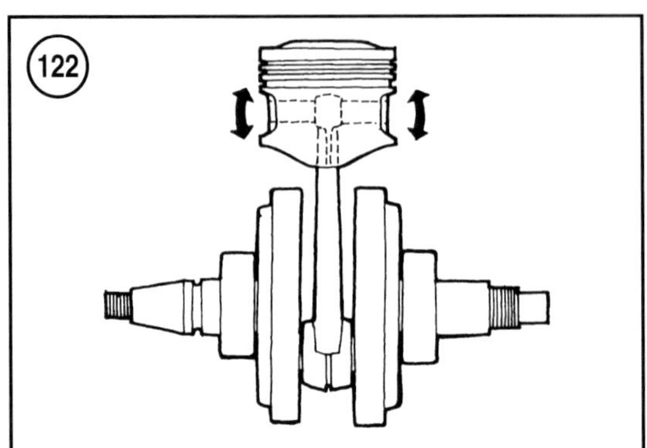

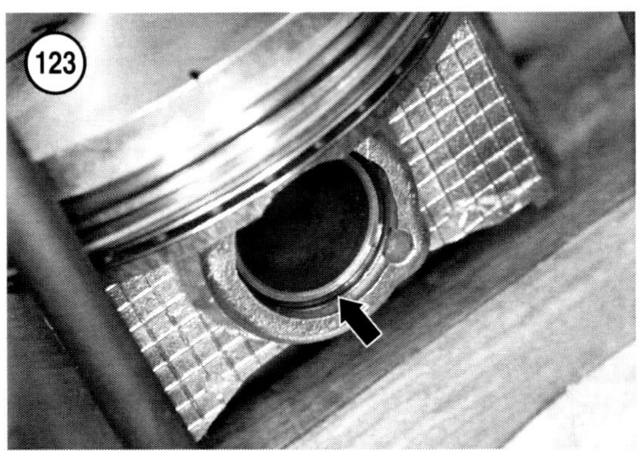

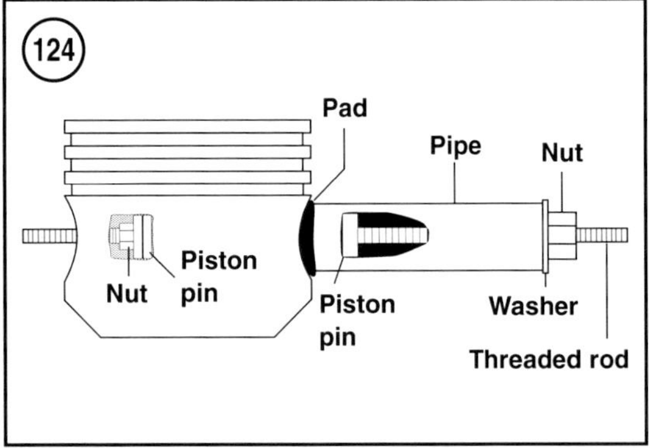

9. Inspect the pistons and piston pins as described in this chapter.

Piston Installation

1. Apply molybdenum disulfide grease to the inside of the connecting rod small end bushing.

NOTE
The pistons must be installed with the arrow facing forward toward the exhaust side, or front, of the engine.

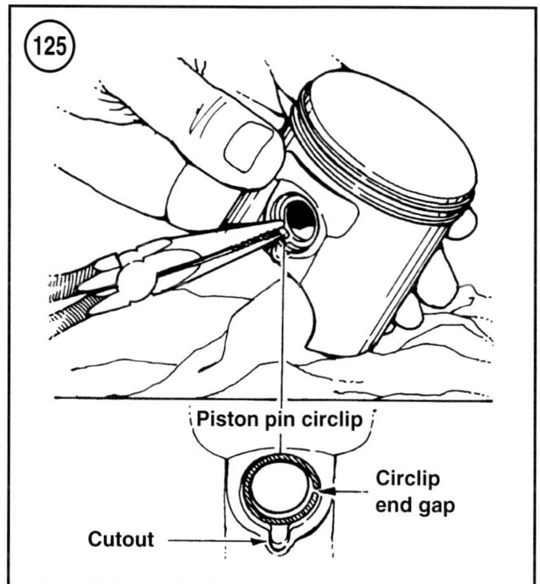

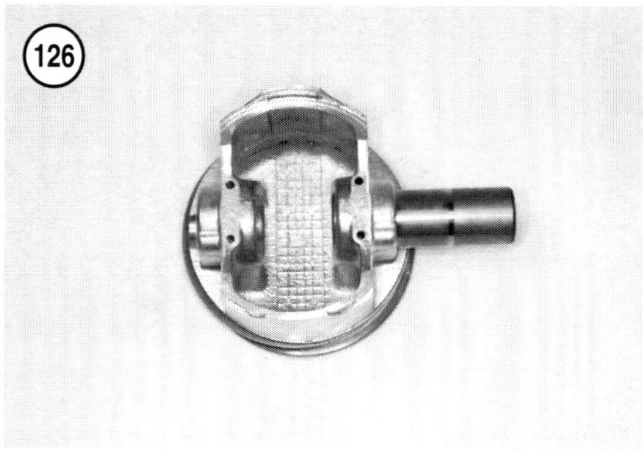

2. Install a *new* circlip into the side of the piston that will face the center line of the cylinder block. Make sure the clip is correctly seated in the piston groove. The circlip ends must not align with the cutout in the piston (**Figure 125**)

3. Apply molybdenum disulfide grease to the piston pin and slide the pin into the piston until the pin is flush with the piston pin boss (**Figure 126**).
4. Place the correct piston over the connecting rod.
   a. Refer to the reference numbers marked on the pistons during removal and install the pistons onto their original connecting rods. If the cylinders were rebored, match each piston with the correct connecting rod.
   b. Install each piston so the arrow on the crown points to the exhaust side, or front, of the engine.
5. Align the piston pin with the hole in the connecting rod. Push the piston pin through the connecting rod (**Figure 127**) and into the other side of the piston. Do not use force when installing the piston pin. Push the pin until it clears the pin circlip groove in the near side of the piston or until it touches the pin clip in the other side.
6. Once the pin is installed, check that the arrow on the piston crown points to the exhaust side, or front of the engine. Also make sure the piston is installed on the correct connecting rod.
7. Install a *new* piston pin circlip into the other side of the pin boss. Make sure the circlip is seated correctly in the piston groove (**Figure 123**).
8. Check the installation by rocking the piston back and forth around the pin axis and from side to side along the axis. The piston should rotate freely back and forth but not from side to side.
9. Repeat Steps 1-8 for the remaining pistons.
10. If removed, install the piston rings as described in this chapter.
11. Install the cylinder block and cylinder head as described in this chapter.

Piston Inspection

1. If necessary, remove the piston rings as described in this chapter.

CAUTION

Be careful not to gouge or otherwise damage the piston when removing carbon. Never use a wire brush to clean the piston skirt or ring grooves. Do not attempt to remove the carbon ridge from the sides of the piston, above the top ring or from the cylinder bore near the top. Removal of car-

bon from these two areas may cause increased oil consumption.

2. Carefully clean the carbon from the piston crown (**Figure 128**) with a soft scraper. Large carbon accumulations reduce piston cooling and result in detonation and piston damage. Re-number the piston as soon as it is cleaned so the piston can be properly identified during assembly.
3. After cleaning the piston, examine the crown. The crown should show no signs of wear or damage. If the crown appears pecked or spongy-looking, also check the spark plug, valves and combustion chamber for aluminum deposits. If these deposits are found, the engine is overheating.
4. Examine each ring groove for burrs, dented edges or other damage. Pay particular attention to the top compression ring groove. It usually wears more than the others. Because the oil rings are constantly bathed in oil, these rings and grooves wear little compared to compression rings and their grooves. If there is evidence of oil ring groove wear or if the oil ring assembly is tight and difficult to remove, the piston skirt may have collapsed due to excessive heat and is permanently deformed. Replace the piston.
5. Check the oil control holes (**Figure 129**) in the piston for carbon or oil sludge buildup. Clean the holes with wire and blow them clear with compressed air.
6. Check the piston skirt (A, **Figure 130**) for galling and abrasion which may have been caused by piston seizure. If a piston shows signs of partial seizure (bits of aluminum build-up on the piston skirt), the piston should be replaced (and cylinders rebored if necessary) to reduce the possibility of engine noise and further piston seizure.

NOTE

If the piston skirt is worn or scuffed unevenly from side-to-side, the connecting rod may be bent or twisted.

7. Check the circlip groove (B, **Figure 130**) on each side for wear, cracks or other damage. If the grooves are questionable, check the circlip fit by installing a *new* circlip into each groove and then attempt to move the circlip from side to side. If the circlip has any side play, the groove is worn and the piston must be replaced.
8. Measure piston-to-cylinder clearance as described in *Piston Clearance* in this chapter.

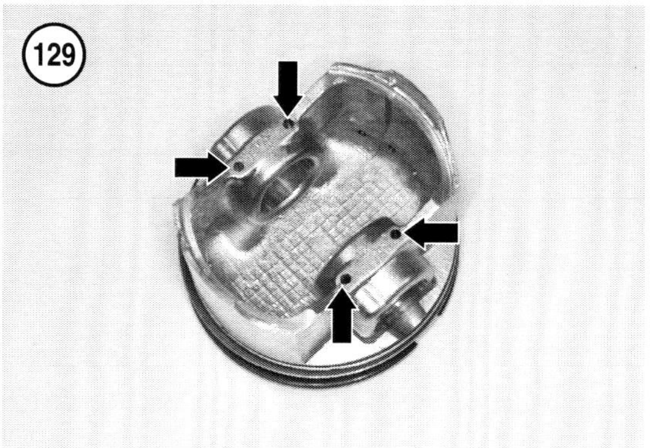

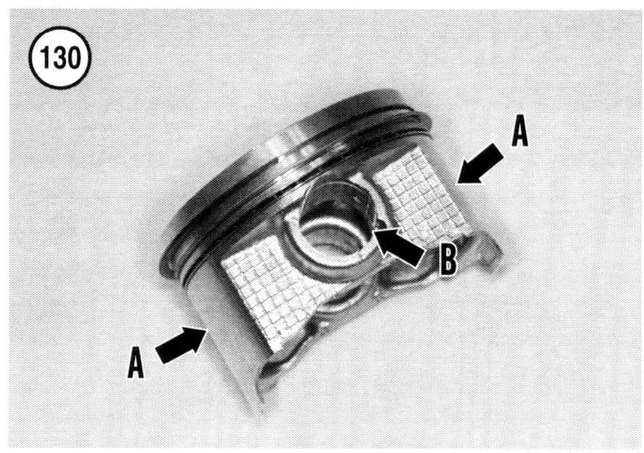

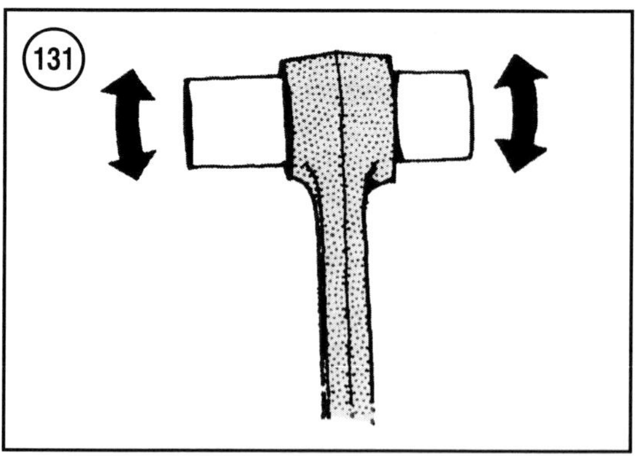

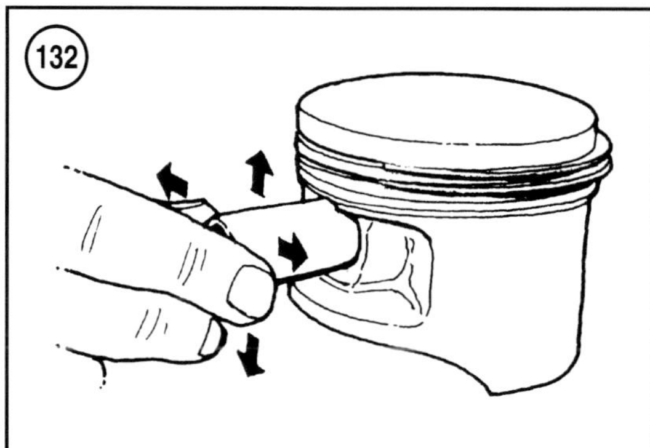

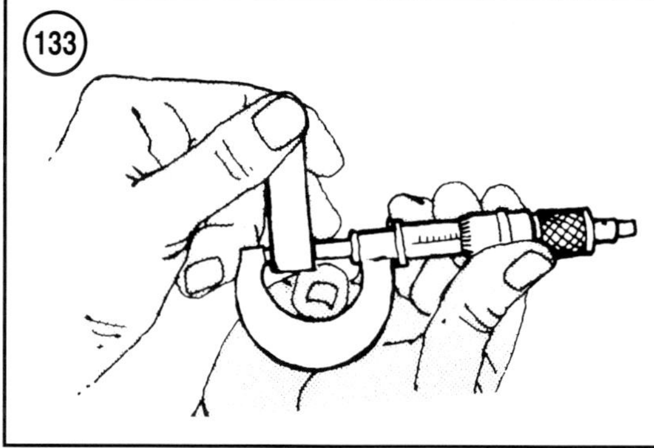

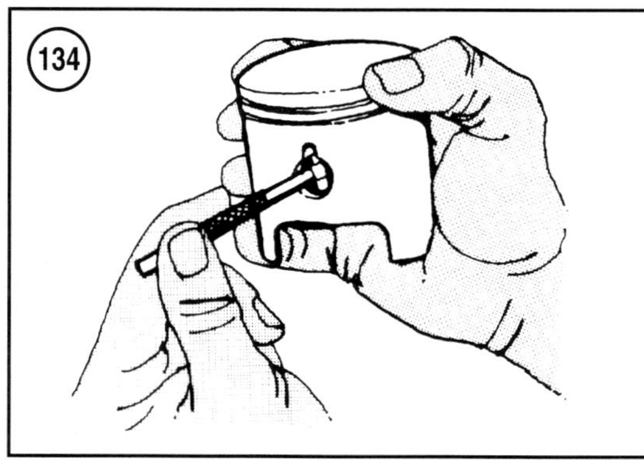

9. If damage or wear indicates piston replacement, select a *new* piston as described under *Piston Clearance* in this chapter. If the piston, rings and cylinder are not damaged and are dimensionally correct, they can be reused.

Piston Pin Inspection

Compare all measurements to the specification in **Table 2**. Replace any part that is damaged, worn to the service limit or out of specification.

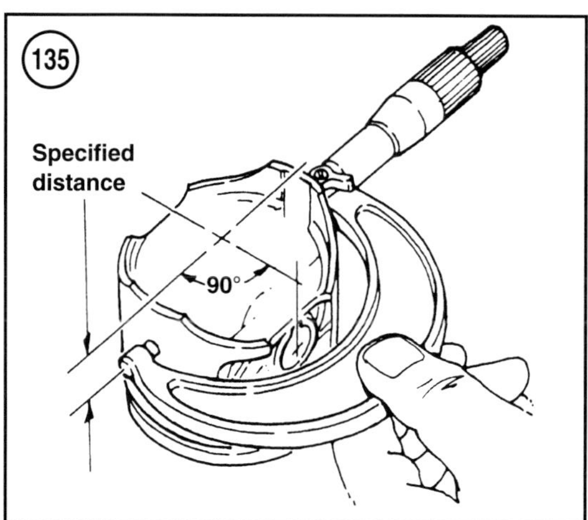

1. Clean the piston pin in solvent, and dry it thoroughly.
2. Inspect the piston pin for chrome flaking or cracks. Replace if necessary.
3. Oil the piston pin and install it into the connecting rod (**Figure 131**). Slowly rotate the piston pin and check for radial play.
4. Oil the piston pin and partially install it into the piston. Check the piston pin for excessive play (**Figure 132**).
5. Measure the piston pin outside diameter at three places with a micrometer (**Figure 133**). Replace the piston pin if any one measurement is out of specification.
6. Measure the inside diameter of the piston pin bore (**Figure 134**) with a small hole gauge. Measure the small hole gauge with a micrometer.
7. Replace the piston pin and/or piston or connecting rod if necessary.

Piston Clearance Measurement

1. Make sure the piston skirt and cylinder wall are clean and dry.
2. Measure the cylinder bore with a bore gauge or inside micrometer. Measure the cylinder bore at the three positions, measured from the top surface, as shown in **Figure 121**. Measure in line with the piston pin and 90° to the pin. Write down the bore inner diameter measurements.
3. Measure the piston outside diameter with a micrometer at a right angle to the piston pin bore (**Figure 135**). Measure up 15 mm (0.590 in.) from the bottom edge of the piston skirt (**Figure 136**).

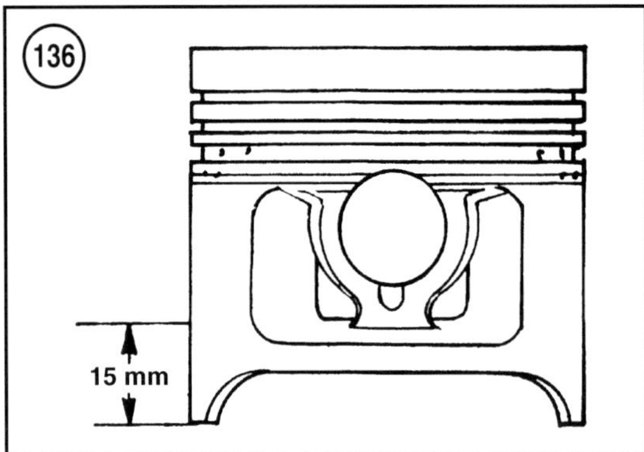

4. Subtract the piston outside diameter from the largest bore diameter; the difference is piston-to-cylinder clearance. If clearance exceeds the service limit specified in **Table 2**, replace the pistons and cylinder block.

Piston Ring Inspection and Removal

The piston and ring assembly is a three-ring type (**Figure 137**). The top and second rings are compression rings. The lower ring is an oil control ring assembly, consisting of two ring rails and an expander spacer.

When measuring the piston rings and piston in this section, compare the actual measurements to the new and service limit specifications in **Table 2**. Replace parts that are out of specification or show damage as described in this section.

1. Measure the side clearance of each compression ring in its groove with a flat feeler gauge (**Figure 138**). If the clearance is greater than specified, the rings must be replaced. If the clearance is still excessive with the *new* rings installed, replace the piston.

WARNING
The edges of all piston rings are very sharp. Be careful when handling them to avoid cutting fingers.

NOTE
Store the old rings in the order in which they are removed.

2. Remove the compression rings with a ring expander tool (**Figure 139**) or by spreading the ring ends with two thumbs and lifting the rings up evenly (**Figure 140**).
3. Remove the oil ring assembly by first removing the upper and then the lower ring rails. Then remove the expander spacer.

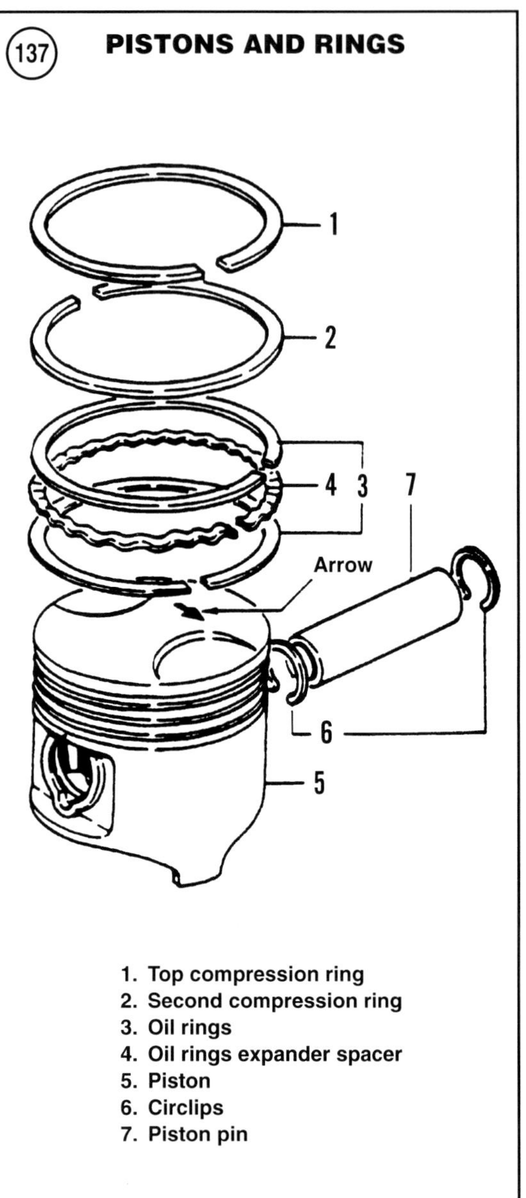

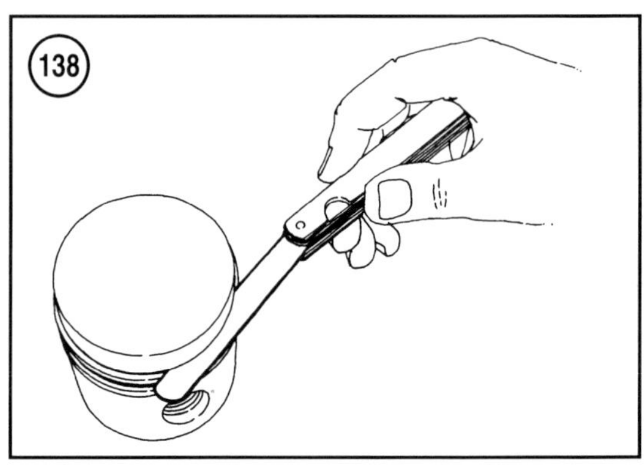

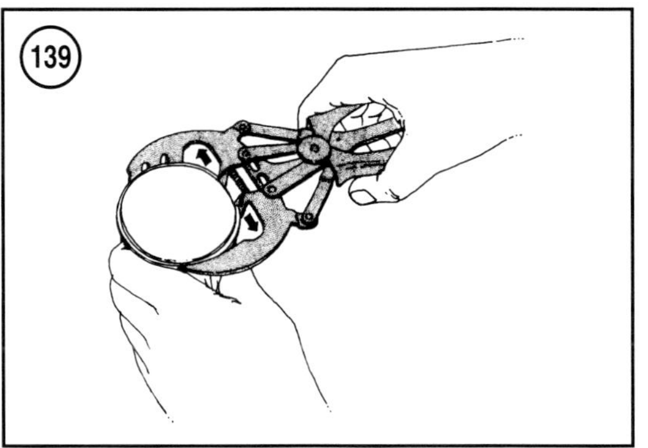

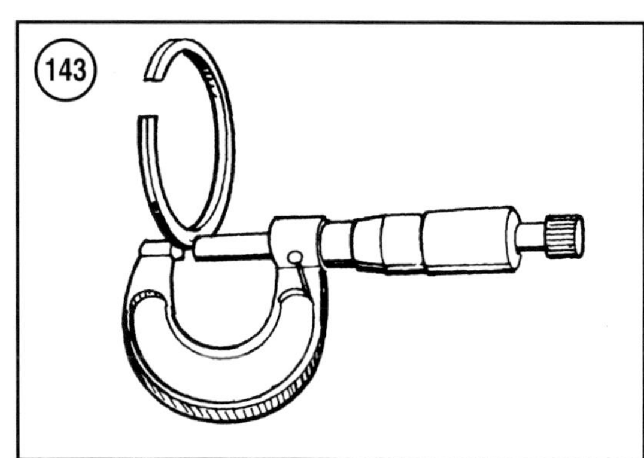

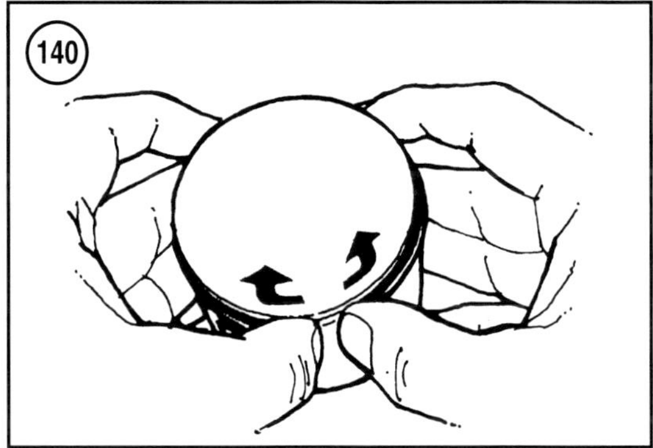

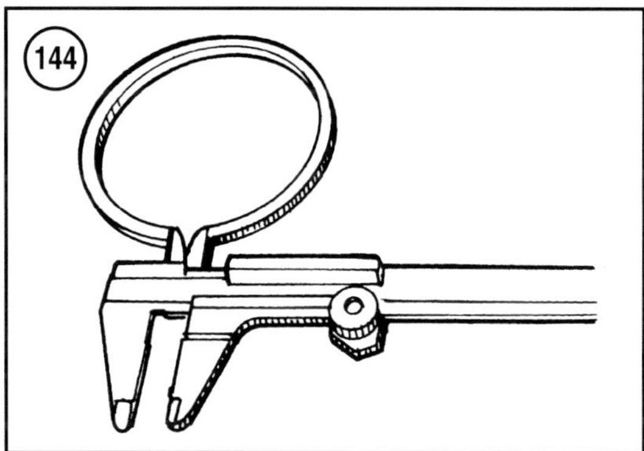

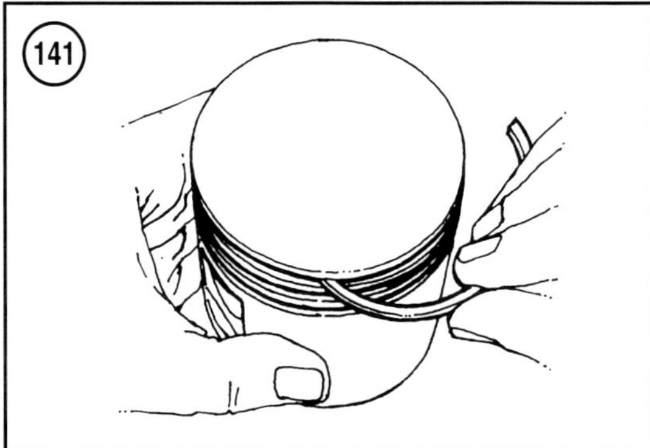

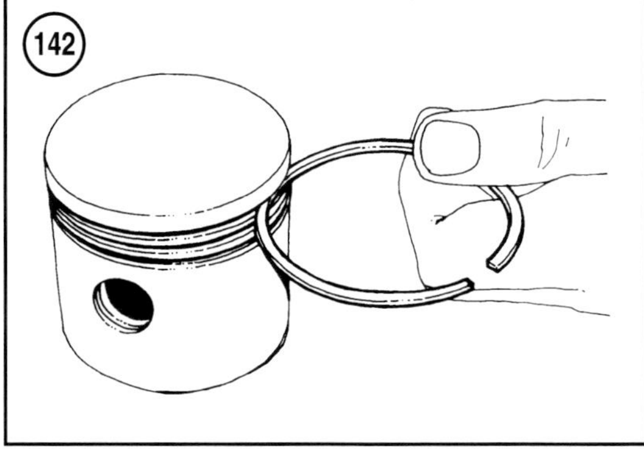

4. Using a broken piston ring, carefully remove carbon and oil residue from the piston ring grooves (**Figure 141**). Do not remove aluminum material from the ring grooves as this will increase ring side clearance.
5. Roll each ring around its piston groove as shown in **Figure 142** to check for binding. Minor binding may be cleaned up with a fine-cut file.
6. Measure each compression ring groove width with a vernier caliper. Measure each groove at several points around the piston. Replace the piston if any groove is outside the specified range.
7. Inspect grooves carefully for burrs, nicks or broken or cracked lands. Replace the piston if necessary.
8. Measure the thickness of each compression ring with a micrometer (**Figure 143**). If the thickness is less than specified, replace the ring(s).
9. Measure the free end gap of each compression ring with a vernier caliper (**Figure 144**). If the free end gap exceeds the service limit, the ring(s) must be replaced.
10. Insert the ring into the bottom of the cylinder bore and square it with the cylinder wall by tapping it with the piston (**Figure 145**). Measure the end gap

with a feeler gauge. Replace the rings if the end gap equals or exceeds the service limit. Also measure the end gap when installing new piston rings. If the gap on a new compression ring is smaller than specified, secure a small file in a vise, grip the ends of the ring and enlarge the gap (**Figure 146**).

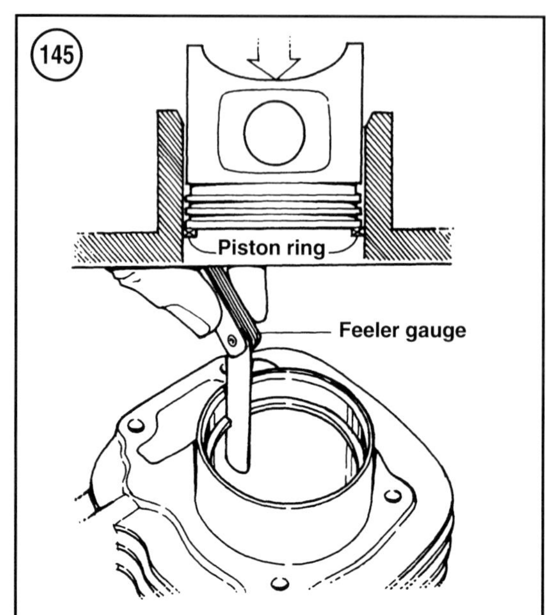

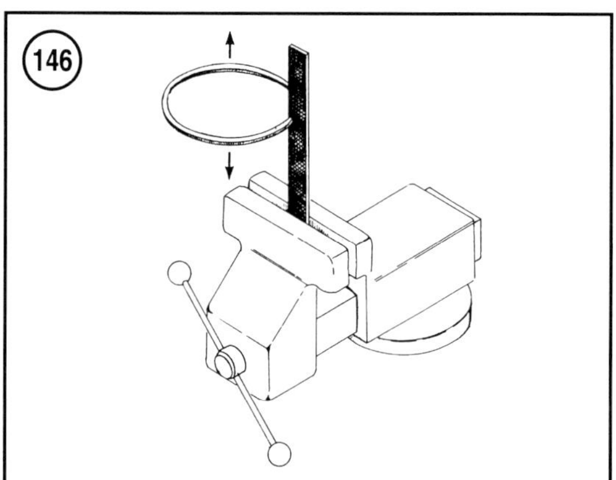

Piston Ring Installation

1. Clean the piston and rings. Dry them with compressed air.
2. Install piston rings as follows:

NOTE
Install the piston rings (first the bottom, then the middle, and then the top ring) by carefully spreading the ends with two thumbs and slipping the rings over the top of the piston. Remember that the piston rings must be installed with the manufacturer's marks facing up toward the top of the piston. Incorrectly installed piston rings can wear rapidly and/or allow oil to escape past them.

   a. Install the oil control ring assembly into the bottom ring groove. Install the oil ring expander spacer first (A, **Figure 147**) and then install each ring rail (B). Be sure the ends of the expander spacer butt together (**Figure 148**). They should not overlap. If reassembling used parts, install the ring rails in their original locations.

NOTE
When installing aftermarket piston rings, follow the manufacturer's directions.

   b. Install the second or middle compression ring with the manufacturer's 2N mark facing up. This ring has a slight taper (**Figure 149**).
   c. Install the top compression ring with the manufacturer's N mark facing up.

3. Make sure the rings are seated completely in their grooves all the way around the piston. Also check that the end gaps are distributed around the piston as shown in **Figure 150**. The ring gaps must not align with each other. This will prevent compression pressures from escaping past them.
4. If new rings are installed, the cylinders must be de-glazed or honed. This helps seat the new rings. Refer honing service to a Suzuki dealership or competent

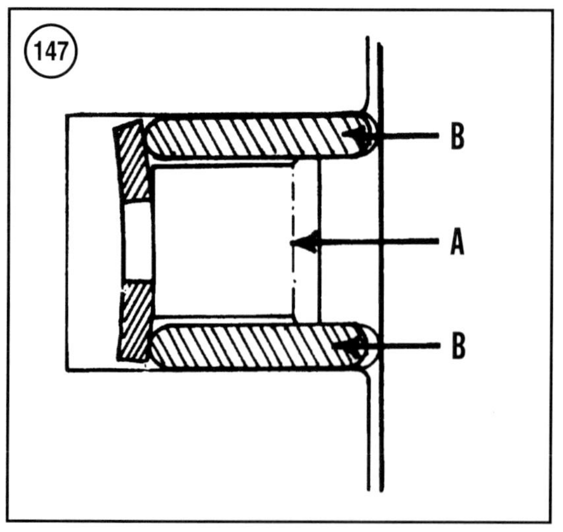

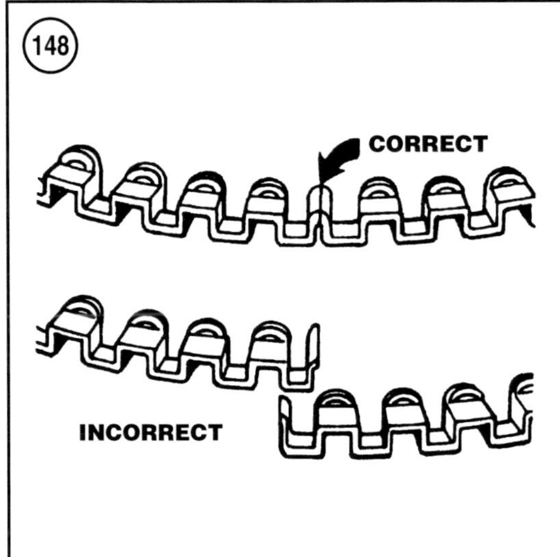

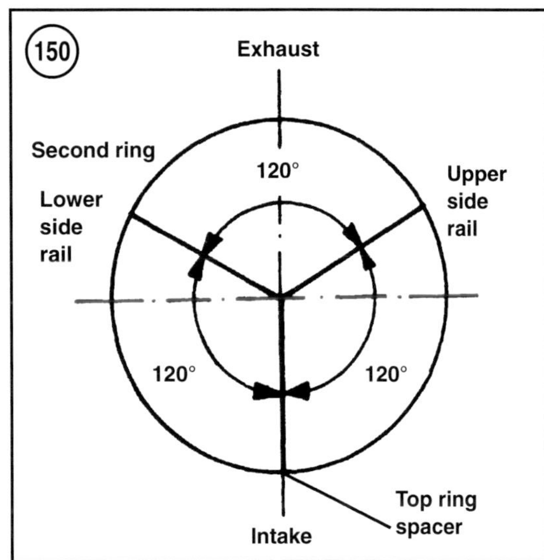

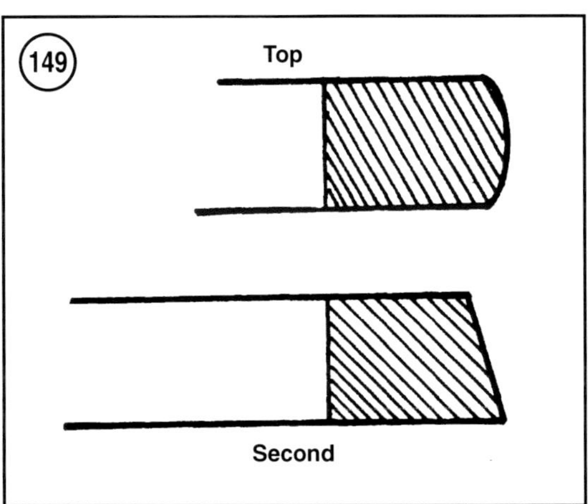

machine shop. After honing, measure the ring end gap (**Figure 145**) for each compression ring.

5. When installing *oversized* compression rings, check the ring number to ensure that the correct rings are installed. The ring oversize number should be the same as the piston oversize number.

6. Paint on the oil ring spacer is used to identify oversized oil rings. When installing oversized oil rings, check the color to assure that the correct size oil rings are being installed. Standard size oil rings have red paint, while 0.5 mm oversize rings have blue.

7. When new parts are installed, the engine should be broken-in just as though it were new. Refer to *Engine Break-in* in Chapter Five.

Table 1 GENERAL ENGINE SPECIFICATIONS

Item	Specification
Engine type	Four-stroke, DOHC, TCSS, four-valve head, inline four cylinders
Bore × stroke	79.0 × 59.0 mm (3.110 × 2.323 in.)
Displacement	1157 cc (70.6 cu. in.)
Compression ratio	9.5:1
Compression pressure (at sea level)	
Standard	1250 kPa (181 psi)
Service limit	875 kPa (126 psi)
Maximum difference between cylinders	200 kPa (29 psi)
Ignition type	Electronic
Ignition timing	7° BTDC @ 1500 rpm
Firing order	1-2-4-3
Cooling system	Air/oil cooled
Lubrication system	Wet sump

Table 2 TOP END SPECIFICATIONS

Item	Standard mm (in.)	Wear limit mm (in.)
Camshaft		
Cam lobe height		
Intake	33.58-33.62 (1.3220-1.3236)	33.28 (1.3102)
Exhaust	33.41-33.45 (1.3154-1.3170)	33.11 (1.3035)
Journal oil clearance		
(bearing clearance)	0.032-0.066 (0.0013-0.0026)	0.150 (0.0059)
Journal outside diameter	21.959-21.980 (0.8645-0.8654)	–
Journal holder inside diameter	22.012-22.025 (0.8666-0.8671)	–
Camshaft runout	–	0.10 mm (0.004)
Rocker arm		
Bore inside diameter	12.000-12.018 (0.4724-0.4731)	–
Shaft outside diameter	11.973-11.984 (0.4714-0.4718)	–
Valves and valve springs		
Valve clearance (cold)		
Intake	0.10-0.15 (0.004-0.006)	–
Exhaust	0.18-0.23 (0.007-0.009)	–
Valve stem outside diameter		
Intake	4.965-4.980 (0.1955-0.1961)	–
Exhaust	4.945-4.960 (0.1947-0.1953)	–
Valve stem deflection	–	0.35 (0.014)
Valve stem runout	–	0.05 (0.002)
Valve stem end length	–	2.5 (0.10)
Valve guide inside diameter	5.000-5.012 (0.1969-0.1973)	–
Valve stem-to-guide clearance		
Intake	0.020-0.047 (0.0008-0.0019)	–
Exhaust	0.040-0.067 (0.0016-0.0026)	–
Valve head diameter		
Intake	28.5 (1.12)	–
Exhaust	25 (1.0)	–
Valve head thickness	–	0.5 (0.02)
Valve head radial runout	–	0.03 (0.001)
Valve seat width	0.9-1.1 (0.035-0.043)	–
Valve seat cutter angle		
Intake	15 and 45°	
Exhaust	15 and 45°	
Valve spring free length		
Inner	–	35.0 (1.38)
Outer	–	37.8 (1.49)
Valve spring tension		
Inner	5.6-6.6 kg @ 28 mm (12.3-14.6 lbs.@ 1.10 in.)	–
Outer	12.8-15.0 kg @ 31.5 mm (28.2-33.1 lbs.@ 1.24 in.)	
Cylinder head warp	–	0.20 (0.008)
Cylinder		
Bore	79.000-79.015 (3.1102-3.1108)	79.080 (3.1134)
Distortion	–	0.20 (0.008)
Compression pressure (at sea level)		
Standard	1250 kPa (181 psi)	
Service limit	875 kPa (126 psi)	
Maximum difference between cylinders		200 kPa (29 psi)
Piston		
Outside diameter*	78.945-78.960 (3.1081-3.1087)	78.880 (3.1055)
Piston-to-cylinder clearance	0.040-0.070 (0.0016-0.0028)	0.120 (0.0047)
Piston oversize	0.5 (0.02)	–
Piston-pin bore inside diameter	20.002-20.008 (0.7875-0.7877)	20.030 (0.7886)

(continued)

Table 2 TOP END SPECIFICATIONS (continued)

Item	Standard mm (in.)	Wear limit mm (in.)
Piston pin outside diameter	19.996-20.000 (0.7872-0.7874)	19.980 (0.7866)
Piston rings		
Ring-to groove clearance		
Top	–	0.180 (0.007)
Second	–	0.150 (0.006)
Ring thickness		
Top	0.97-0.99 (0.038-0.039)	–
Second	0.97-0.99 (0.038-0.039)	–
Piston ring groove width		
Top	1.01-1.03 (0.039-0.040)	–
Second	1.01-1.03 (0.039-0.040)	–
Oil ring	2.01-2.03 (0.079-0.080)	–
Ring end gap (installed)		
Top	0.20-0.35 (0.008-0.014)	0.5 (0.02)
Second	0.35-0.50 (0.014-0.020)	1.0 (0.04)
Ring free gap		
First	Approx. 10.0 (0.39)	8.0 (0.31)
Second	Approx. 12.0 (0.47)	9.6 (0.38)

*Measured 15 mm (0.590 in.) from skirt bottom

Table 3 TOP END TORQUE SPECIFICATIONS

Item	N•m	in.-lb.	ft.-lb.
Camshaft bearing cap bolts	10	88	–
Camshaft chain guide mounting bolt	6	53	–
Camshaft chain tensioner body mounting bolt	7	62	–
Camshaft chain tensioner spring holder bolt	35	–	26
Camshaft sprocket bolts	25	–	18
Cylinder base nut	9	80	–
Cylinder head banjo bolt	16	–	12
Cylinder head bolt, 6 mm	10	88	–
Cylinder head cover banjo bolts	16	–	12
Cylinder head cover bolts	14	–	10
Cylinder head cover plug	15	–	11
Cylinder head nuts, 10 mm	38	–	28
Cylinder head plug	28	–	21
Cylinder stud bolt	15	–	11
Oil hose bolts	10	88	–
PAIR hose mounting nuts	10	88	–
Spark plug	11	97	–
Rocker arm shaft set bolt	9	80	–
Valve adjuster locknut	10	88	–

CHAPTER FIVE

ENGINE LOWER END

This chapter describes service procedures for the following lower end components:
1. Crankcase assembly.
2. Crankshaft.
3. Connecting rods.
4. Starter clutch and gears.
5. Oil cooler, oil pump and lubrication system.
6. Transmission shaft assemblies (removal and installation only).
5. Starter and gears.
6. Exhaust system.
7. Signal generator.

Tables 1-7 are located at the end of the chapter.

SERVICING THE ENGINE IN FRAME

Refer to *Engine Service Notes* in Chapter Four.

Many components including the following can be serviced with the engine in the frame.

The motorcycle frame is an excellent holding fixture, especially for breaking loose stubborn bolts and nuts.
1. External gearshift mechanism.
2. Clutch.
3. Carburetor assembly.
4. Alternator.

ENGINE

Removal/Installation

Refer to **Figure 1**.
1. On GSF1200S models, remove the fairing as described in Chapter Fourteen.
2. Remove the seat and frame cover as described in Chapter Fourteen.
3. Remove the fuel tank as described in Chapter Eight.
4. Remove the battery as described in Chapter Three.
5. Remove the exhaust system as described in Chapter Eight.
6. On 2001-on PAIR equipped models, disconnect the hoses and remove the PAIR valve (A, **Figure 2**).
7. Disconnect the crankcase breather hose (B, **Figure 2**) from the breather cover.

1

ENGINE MOUNTING HARDWARE

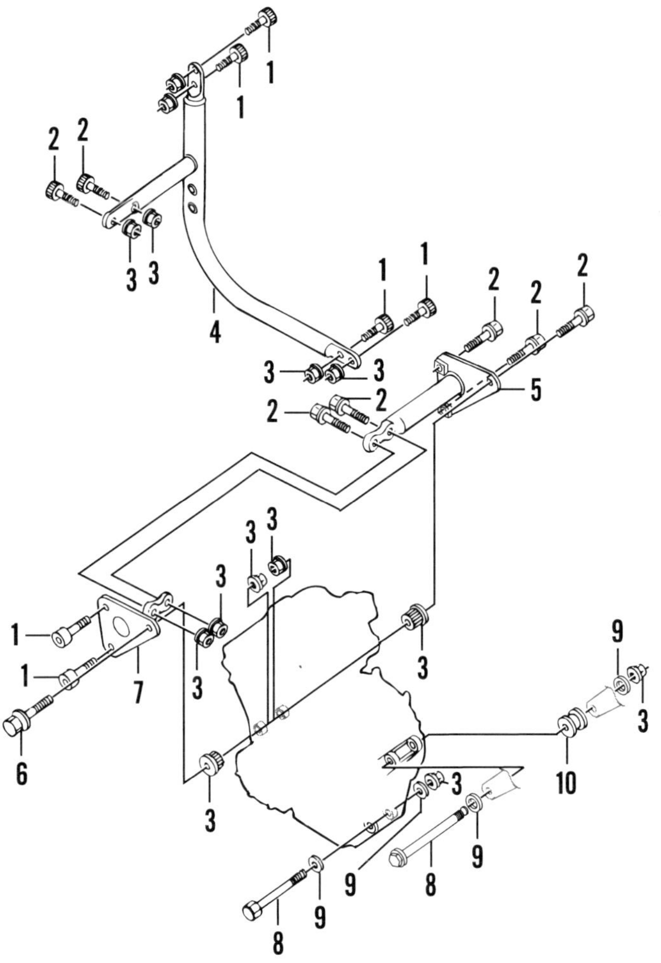

1. Allen bolt
2. Allen bolt
3. Nut
4. Sub-frame
5. Front mount plate
6. Hex bolt
7. Side mount plate
8. Upper and lower through bolts
9. Washer
10. Spacer

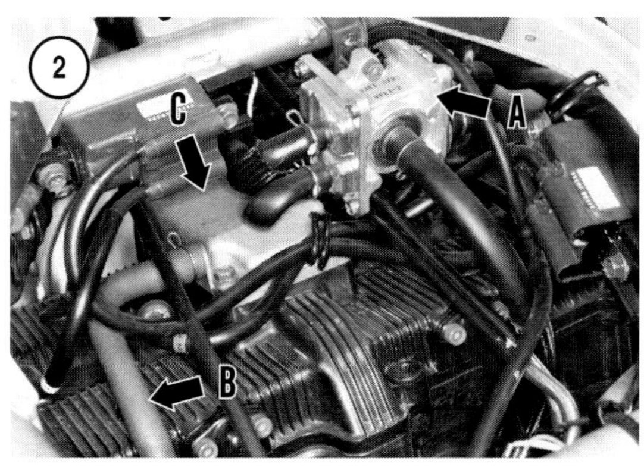

8. Remove the breather cover (C, **Figure 2**) and gasket from the top of the cylinder head cover.

9. Remove the carburetor assembly as described in Chapter Eight.

10. Drain the engine oil and remove the oil filter as described in Chapter Three.

11. Disconnect the spark plug leads and tie them up out of the way.

12. Remove the bolt (A, **Figure 3**) securing the gear-shift lever (B) and remove the lever from the shift shaft. Lower the shift lever linkage out of the way.

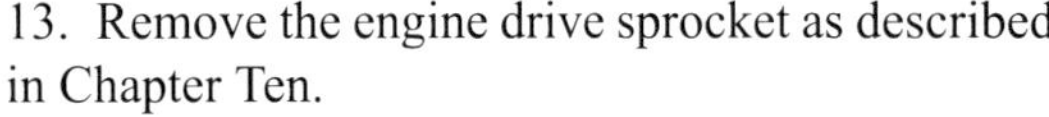

13. Remove the engine drive sprocket as described in Chapter Ten.

14A. On 1996-2000 models, disconnect the following electrical connectors located on the left side of the rear frame (**Figure 4**):

   a. Neutral indicator switch (four-pin connector, blue, red/black and green/blue wires)
   b. Signal generator (two-pin connector, yellow, black/blue wires).
   c. Oil pressure switch (bullet connector, green/yellow wire).
   d. Alternator (two-pin connector, red and orange wires).

14B. On 2001-on models, disconnect the following electrical connectors located on the left side of the rear frame (**Figure 5**):

   a. Gear position switch (four-pin connector, blue, red/black, green/blue and black/white wires).
   b. Signal generator (two-pin connector, yellow/white and black/blue).
   c. Oil pressure switch (bullet connector, green/yellow wire).
   d. Alternator (two-pin connector, red and black/orange wires).

15. Remove the bolt and washer (**Figure 6**) and disconnect the engine ground wire.

16. Disconnect the starter motor lead from the starter motor.

17. Remove the oil cooler as described in this chapter.

18. If the engine is going to be disassembled, remove the following parts while the engine is still in the frame:

   a. Cylinder head (Chapter Four).
   b. Cylinder block (Chapter Four).
   c. Pistons (Chapter Four).
   d. Alternator and starter (Chapter Nine).
   e. Starter clutch and gears.
   f. Signal generator (Chapter Nine).
   g. Clutch assembly (Chapter Six).

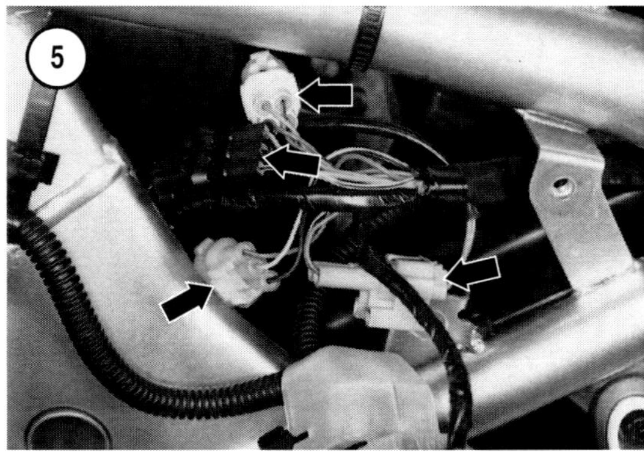

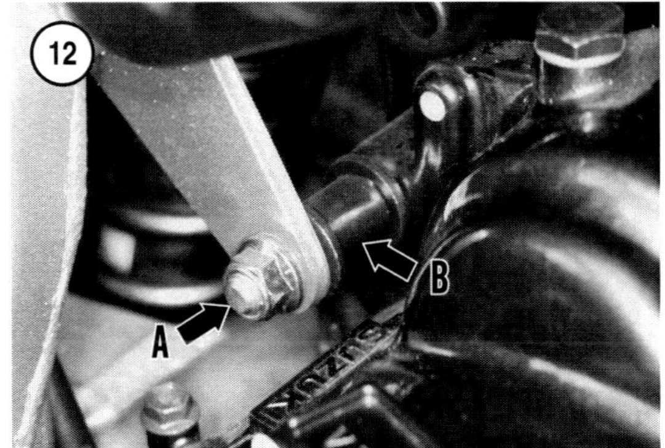

h. External shift mechanism (Chapter Seven).

19. Take a final look over the engine to make sure everything has been disconnected.

20. Place a suitable size jack, with a piece of wood to protect the crankcase, under the engine. Raise the jack and apply a small amount of jack pressure on the engine.

CAUTION
Continually adjust jack pressure during engine removal and installation to prevent damage to the mounting bolt threads and hardware.

CAUTION
Discard all self-locking mounting nuts as they cannot be reused.

21. Remove the lower rear through bolt, washers and nut (**Figure 7**).

22. Remove the front left side Allen bolts (**Figure 8**) from the front mount plate.

23. Remove the rear right side pair of bolts and nuts (A, **Figure 9**) from the sub-frame.

24. Remove the front right side pair bolts and nuts (B, **Figure 9**) from the sub-frame down tube.

25. Remove the sub-frame (C, **Figure 9**).

26. Remove the front left side bolt and nut (**Figure 10**).

27. Remove the front upper bolt and nut (**Figure 11**) from the front mount plate. The front mount plate can remain in place.

WARNING
Due to the weight of the engine, two people are required to safely remove the engine assembly from the frame.

28. Have an assistant secure the engine in place.

29. Remove the rear upper through bolt nut (A, **Figure 12**), then withdraw the through bolt from the

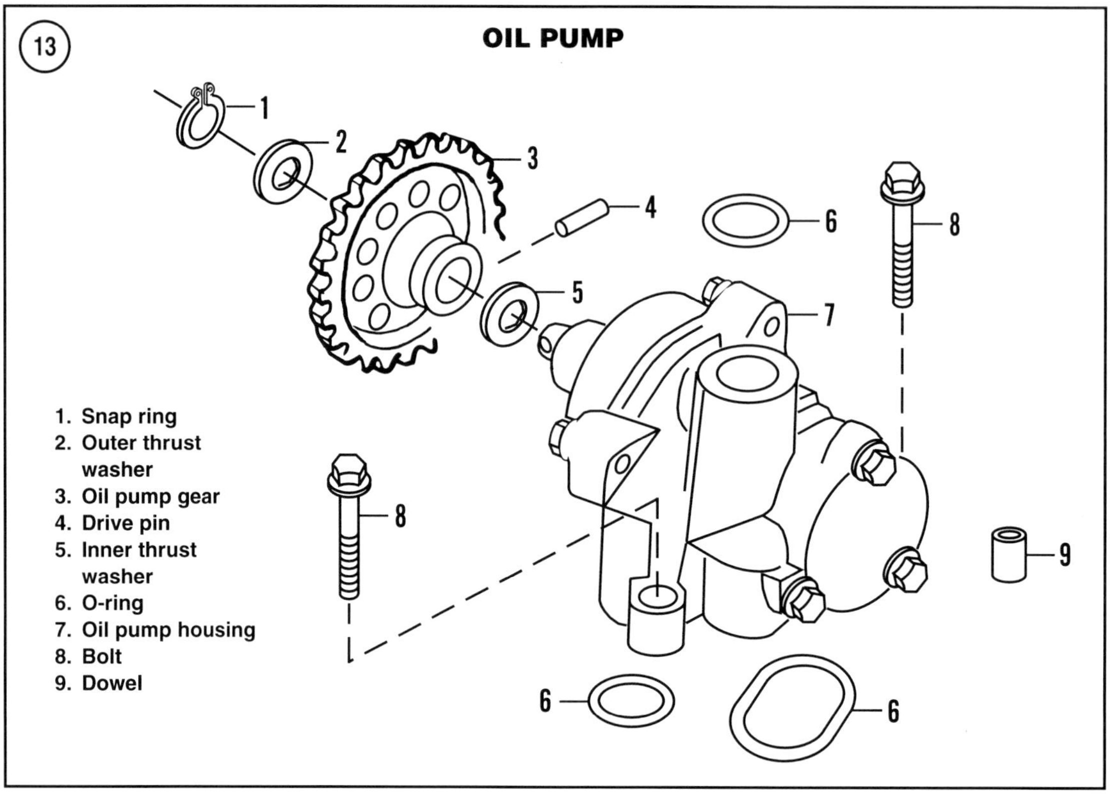

13

OIL PUMP

1. Snap ring
2. Outer thrust washer
3. Oil pump gear
4. Drive pin
5. Inner thrust washer
6. O-ring
7. Oil pump housing
8. Bolt
9. Dowel

left side. Do not lose the spacer (B, **Figure 12**) located on the right side between the engine and frame mount.

30. Gradually lower the engine and remove it from the right side of the frame.

31. Install the engine by reversing these removal steps while noting the following:

CAUTION

*Install **new** self-locking nuts on all engine mounting bolts. Never reuse a self-locking nut. These fasteners lose their locking abilities once they have been removed. Do **not** try to use a locking agent and then re-use an old self-locking nut. This will not be sufficient to keep the nut in place.*

a. Tighten the mounting bolts to the specifications in **Table 2**.
b. Fill the engine with the recommended type and quantity of oil; refer to Chapter Three.
c. Adjust the drive chain as described in Chapter Three.
d. Start the engine and check for leaks.

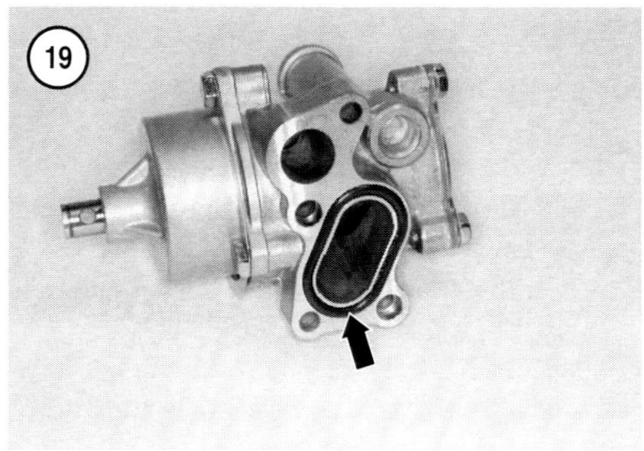

OIL PUMP

Removal/Installation

Refer to **Figure 13**.

1. Remove the clutch assembly as described in Chapter Six.
2. Remove the snap ring and the outer thrust washer (**Figure 14**) from inside the oil pump gear.
3. If only removing the oil pump gear, cover the crankcase opening so parts or debris will not fall into the crankcase.

NOTE
The drive pin is loosely installed in the oil pump shaft. Rotate the oil pump gear so the pin is horizontal before removing the gear. The pin could easily fall into the crankcase during oil pump gear removal.

4. Rotate the oil pump gear so the drive pin in the shaft is horizontal. Remove the oil pump gear (**Figure 15**) from the oil pump shaft.
5. Remove the drive pin (A, **Figure 16**) and the inner thrust washer (B) from the pump shaft.
6. Remove the engine and separate the crankcase as described in this chapter.
7. Use an impact driver and Allen bolt bit and loosen the bolts (**Figure 17**) securing the oil pump to the lower crankcase.
8. Remove the Allen bolts and the oil pump.
9. Remove the O-ring (A, **Figure 18**) and two locating dowels (B) from the crankcase.
10. Remove the O-ring (**Figure 19**) from the oil pump.
11. Inspect the oil pump as described in this chapter.

CAUTION
*To prevent loss of oil pressure and to prevent an oil leak, always install **new** O-rings.*

12. Install the locating dowels (B, **Figure 18**) and *new* O-rings (A) in the crankcase receptacles.
13. Install a *new* O-ring (**Figure 19**) onto the oil pump.
14. Set the oil pump into place in the crankcase.
15. Apply ThreeBond Threadlock No. 1342 to the threads of the oil pump mounting bolts. Install the bolts and tighten to 25 N•m (18 in.-lb.).

16. Assemble the crankcase as described in this chapter.

17. Rotate the oil pump gear shaft until the drive pin pinhole is horizontal.

18. Install the inner thrust washer (B, **Figure 16**) and drive pin (A).

19. Install the oil pump gear (**Figure 15**) onto the oil pump shaft.

NOTE
The oil pump shaft will move in toward the oil pump while trying to install the snap ring in the following step. The outer thrust washer then partially covers the circlip groove in the shaft.

20. Install the outer thrust washer and snap ring as follows:
   a. Install the outer thrust washer (A, **Figure 20**) and snap ring (B) onto the shaft.
   b. Place a magnet onto the end of the shaft and pull the shaft out until it stops.
   c. Push the outer thrust washer in, then, using a scribe, push the snap ring in on the shaft and into the groove. Make sure the snap ring is properly seated in the oil pump shaft.

Inspection

Replacement parts are not available for the oil pump. If the oil pump is not operating properly, the entire oil pump assembly must be replaced.

1. Rotate the drive shaft (A, **Figure 21**). If there is any binding or signs of wear; replace the oil pump assembly.

2. Make sure the locking tabs on the lockwashers are in place and bent up against one side of the bolts (B, **Figure 21**) securing the oil pump together.

3. Inspect the oil pump body for cracks or damage. Make sure all oil flow openings are clear.

4. Inspect the teeth on the oil pump gear (A, **Figure 22**). Replace the gear if any teeth are damaged or missing.

5. Inspect the drive pin (B, **Figure 22**) for cracks, nicks or other signs of wear. If damage is found, replace the drive pin, and inspect the drive-pin-mating surfaces of the oil pump gear and the oil pump shaft.

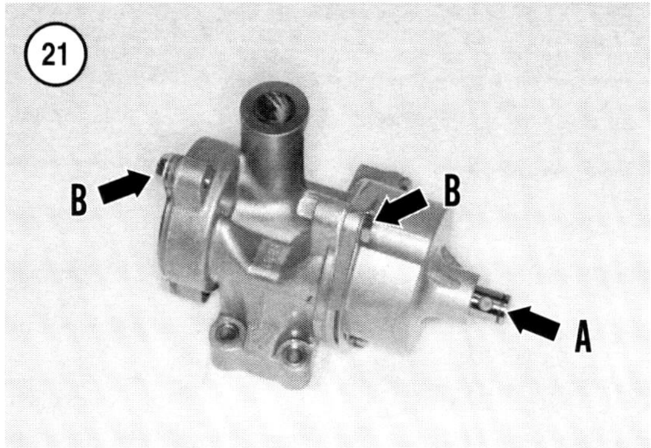

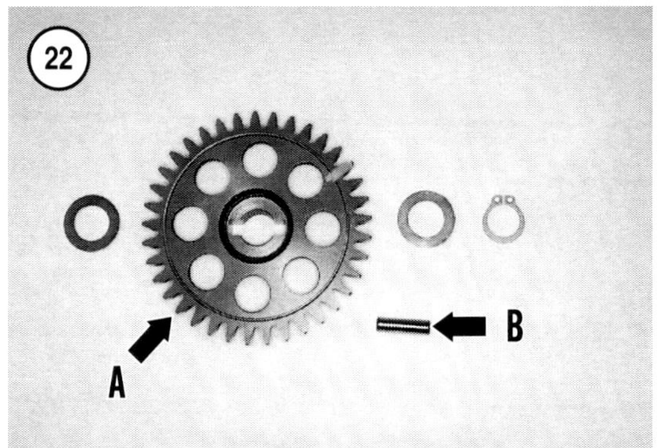

OIL COOLER

Removal/Installation

Refer to **Figure 23**.

1. Drain the engine oil as described in Chapter Three.

2. On GSF1200S models, remove the front fairing as described in Chapter Fourteen.

3. Place an oil pan beneath the lower fittings on the oil cooler hoses to catch oil that drains from the fittings as the hoses are disconnected.

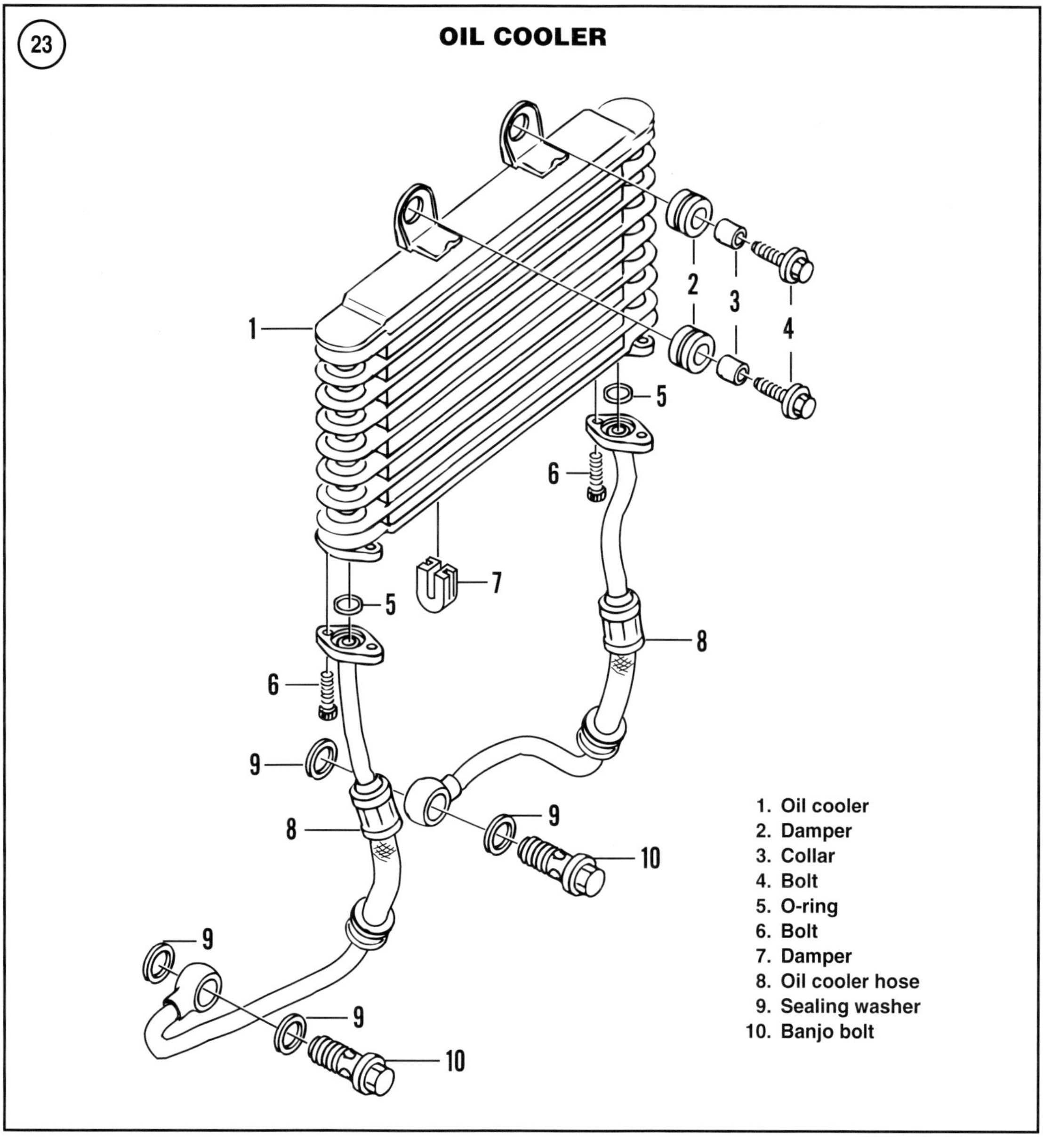

23

OIL COOLER

1. Oil cooler
2. Damper
3. Collar
4. Bolt
5. O-ring
6. Bolt
7. Damper
8. Oil cooler hose
9. Sealing washer
10. Banjo bolt

24

4. Remove the union bolts and sealing washers (**Figure 24**) securing each oil hose fitting to the front of the oil pan. Place the oil hose ends in reclosable plastic bags to prevent the entry of debris.

5. Remove the clamp bolt (**Figure 25**) securing the left side oil line to the frame.

6. Remove the bolts (**Figure 26**) securing the oil cooler mounts to the frame.

7. Pull the oil cooler up to release the lower locating tabs from the dampers in the frame receptacles

and remove the oil cooler from the frame. Do not lose the collar and damper inside each oil cooler mounts.

8. If necessary, remove the bolts securing the hoses to the base of the oil cooler.

9. Clean all dirt and road debris from the oil cooler core with a stiff paint brush. Do not press hard as the cooling fins may be damaged.

10. Install by reversing these removal steps while noting the following:

   a. Clean all road dirt and oil residue from the mating surfaces on the oil pan and the oil hoses.
   b. If the oil hoses were removed, install *new* O-ring seals on the fittings on top of the oil hoses. Tighten these bolts securely.
   c. Install a *new* sealing washer on each side of the oil hose fittings when installing each banjo bolt.
   d. Tighten each banjo bolt to 28 N•m (21 ft.-lb.).
   e. Make sure the collar and damper is in place in each oil cooler mount and install the oil cooler mounting bolts (**Figure 26**). Tighten the bolts to 10 N•m (88 in.-lb.).
   f. Refill the engine with the recommended type and quantity oil as described in Chapter Three.
   g. Start the engine and check for oil leaks.

OIL PAN, OIL STRAINER AND OIL PRESSURE REGULATOR

Removal

NOTE

This procedure is shown with the engine removed from the frame to better illustrate the steps. The oil pan can be removed with the engine installed in the frame.

1. If the engine is still installed in the frame, perform the following:

   a. Remove the exhaust system as described in Chapter Eight.
   b. Remove the banjo bolts and sealing washers (**Figure 24**) securing each oil cooler hose fitting to the front of the oil pan. Place the oil hose ends in reclosable plastic bags to prevent the entry of debris.

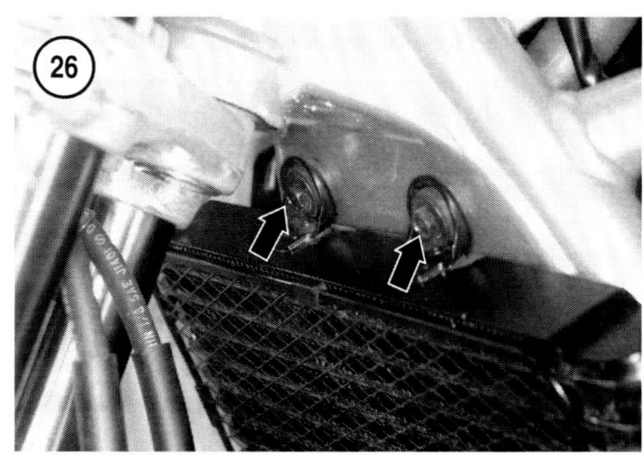

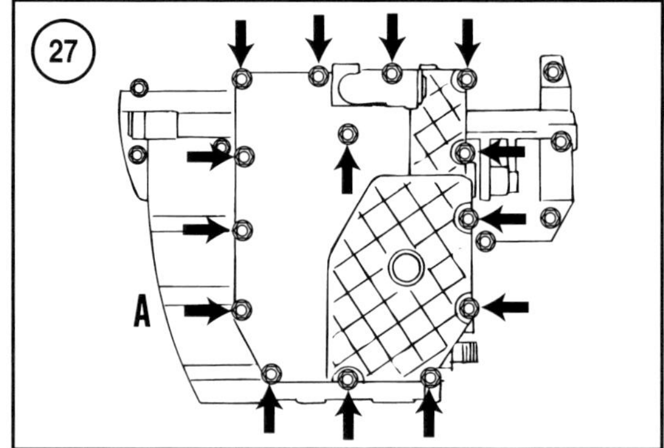

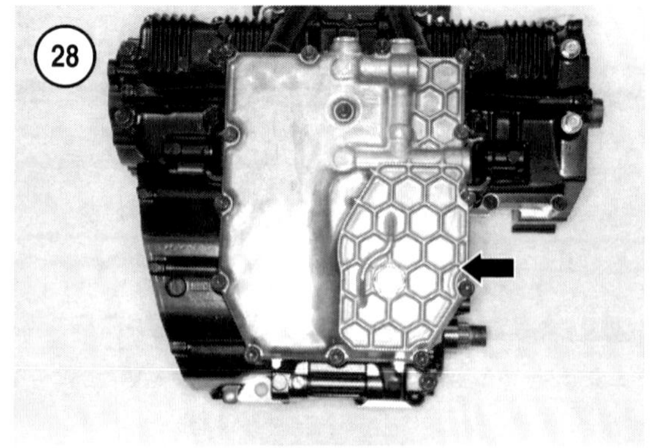

2. Remove the oil pan bolts (**Figure 27**). Note the location of a copper washer installed under one bolt (A, **Figure 27**). A *new* copper washer will have to be installed under this bolt during installation.

3. Remove the oil pan (**Figure 28**) and the gasket from the lower crankcase. Install a *new* gasket during assembly.

4. Remove the oil strainer bolts (A, **Figure 29**) and remove the oil strainer (B) and its gasket from the crankcase.

5. Remove the outlet shim (A, **Figure 30**) and outlet O-ring (A, **Figure 31**).

6. Remove the flat inlet gasket (B, **Figure 30**).

7. Unscrew and remove the oil pressure regulator (**Figure 32**) from the oil pan.

8. Inspect the oil pan, oil strainer and oil pressure regulator as described in the following procedure.

Installation

1. Install the oil pressure regulator (**Figure 32**) onto the oil pan. Tighten to 28 N•m (21 ft.-lb.).

2. Apply a coat of Suzuki Super Grease A to a *new* O-ring and install the O-ring (A, **Figure 31**) into the oil outlet in the crankcase.

3. Apply a coat of Suzuki Super Grease A to the shim (B, **Figure 31**) and install it on top of the oil outlet.

4. Install a *new* flat inlet gasket (B, **Figure 30**).

5. Set the oil strainer in place in the crankcase so the arrow stamped on the strainer cover points toward the front of the engine.

6. Install the oil strainer bolts (A, **Figure 29**) and tighten them securely.

7. Install a *new* oil pan gasket (**Figure 33**) onto the lower crankcase.

8. Install the oil pan and bolts. Install a *new* copper washer (**Figure 34**) under bolt A, **Figure 27**. Tighten the oil pan bolts to 14 N•m (10 ft.-lb.).
9. If the engine is still installed in the frame, perform the following:
   a. Secure the oil cooler lines to the front of the oil pan. Use a *new* sealing washer on both sides of each oil fitting, and tighten each banjo bolt (**Figure 24**) to 28 N•m (21 ft.-lb.).
   b. Install the exhaust system as described in Chapter Eight.

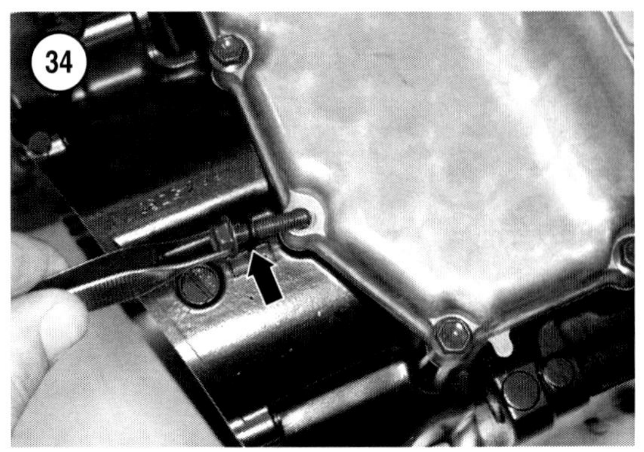

Inspection and Cleaning

Refer to **Figure 35**.
1. Remove all traces of gasket material from the gasket sealing surfaces of the oil pan and the crankcase. This will provide a good, leak-free surface for the oil pan gasket.
2. Remove the oil gallery plugs and their gaskets from the oil pan.
3. If still in place, remove the oil pressure regulator (**Figure 32**) and washer from the oil pan.
4. Wash the oil pan in solvent. Clean out the oil galleries located behind the plug.
5. Thoroughly dry the pan with compressed air. Be sure to remove all solvent residue and any oil sludge loosened by the solvent. Any pieces of sludge left in any oil gallery may clog the gallery or oil control orifices in the lubrication system.
6. Make sure all oil control openings in the oil pan are clear.
7. Inspect the oil drain bolt threads in the oil pan. Clean the threads with the proper size metric thread tap if necessary.
8. Install the oil gallery plugs and gaskets into the oil pan. Tighten the plugs securely.
9. Inspect the oil pressure regulator as follows:
   a. Insert a screwdriver into the end of the oil pressure regulator (**Figure 36**).
   b. Use the screwdriver to push and release the piston and note the piston's movement and spring pressure.
   c. Replace the oil pressure regulator if the piston does not move smoothly within the regulator.
10. Install the oil pressure regulator and washer (**Figure 32**) into the oil pan. Tighten the regulator to 28 N•m (21 ft.-lb.).

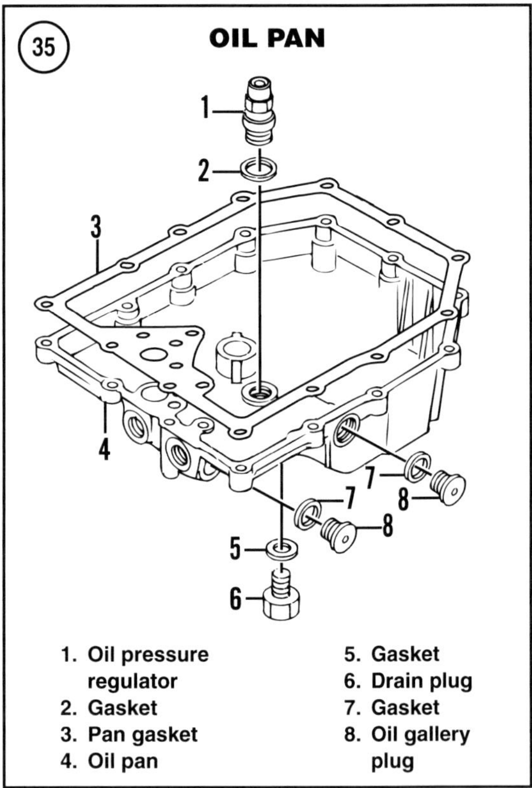

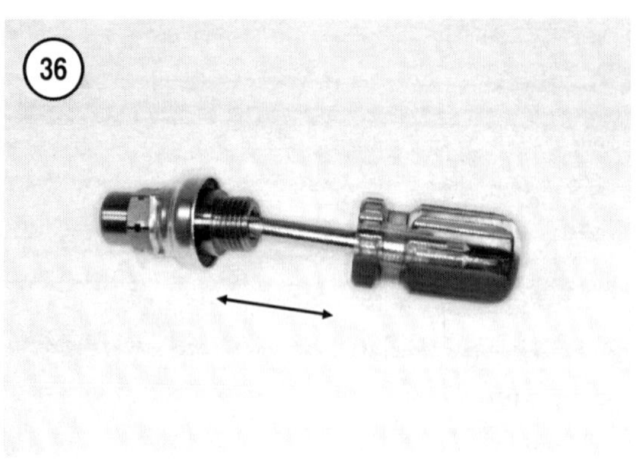

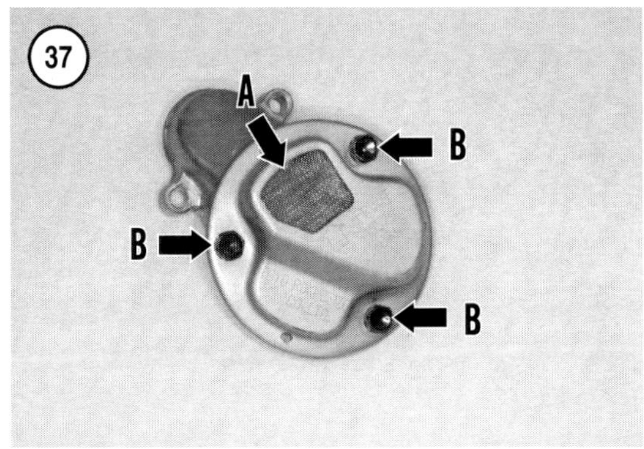

11. Clean the oil strainer with solvent and check the inlet screen (A, **Figure 37**) for broken areas or damage. If necessary, remove the mounting bolts (B, **Figure 37**) and install a *new* oil strainer onto the housing.

STARTER CLUTCH AND GEARS

Removal

The starter gears can be removed with the engine in the frame.

1. Drain the engine oil as described in Chapter Three.
2. Place an oil drain pan under the starter clutch cover.
3. Remove the bolts securing the starter clutch cover (A, **Figure 38**) to the crankcase and remove the cover and gasket. Note the location of the bolt (B, **Figure 38**) with a copper washer under it. Install a *new* copper washer at this location during assembly.
4. If loose, remove the locating dowel (**Figure 39**).
5. Remove the shaft (A, **Figure 40**) and the starter idler gear (B) from the crankcase.

CAUTION

The starter clutch mounting bolt is tightened to 150 N•m (111 ft-lb.). It also has a threadlocking compound on the threads and is very difficult to loosen.

6A. If the engine is installed in the frame, shift the transmission into gear. This prevents the gear from rotating while loosening the mounting bolt. Also have an assistant apply the rear brake.

6B. On 1996-2000 models, if the engine is removed, hold the starter clutch with the Suzuki starter clutch holder (part No. 09920-34810), or an equivalent. Do not overtighten the tool, as it may damage the gear.

6C. On 2001-on models, if the engine is removed, hold the starter clutch with the Suzuki starter clutch holder (part No. 09920-34840), or an equivalent. Do not overtighten the tool, as it may damage the gear.

7. If available, loosen the starter clutch mounting bolt (A, **Figure 41**) with an electric or air impact

driver (**Figure 42**). Do not remove the starter clutch mounting bolt as it must be left in place for use with the special tool in the next step.

8. Install the Suzuki rotor remover (part No. 09930-33720) onto the starter clutch (**Figure 43**), and loosen the starter clutch from the taper on the end of the crankshaft.

9. Remove the rotor remover, unscrew the starter clutch mounting bolt (A, **Figure 41**) and remove the starter clutch (B) from the crankshaft.

Installation

1. Thoroughly clean off all old threadlocking compound from the threaded hole in the crankshaft and from the mounting bolt threads.

2. Clean the tapered end of the crankshaft and the mating surface of the starter clutch with aerosol parts cleaner to remove all traces of oil. Both surfaces must be dry and free of any residue.

3. Install the starter clutch (B, **Figure 41**) onto the crankshaft.

4. Apply ThreeBond Threadlock 1303 to the threads of the starter clutch mounting bolt and install the bolt. (A, **Figure 41**).

5. Hold the starter clutch with the same tool used during removal and tighten the starter clutch mounting bolt to 150 N•m (111 ft.-lb.).

6. Install the starter idler gear (B, **Figure 40**) and shaft (A).

7. Apply a light coat of ThreeBond Liquid Gasket 1104, or an equivalent, to the crankcase surfaces at the point where the upper and lower crankcase halves meet (**Figure 44**). This helps prevent an oil leak.

8. Install a *new* gasket (A, **Figure 45**) and the locating dowel (B) into the crankcase.

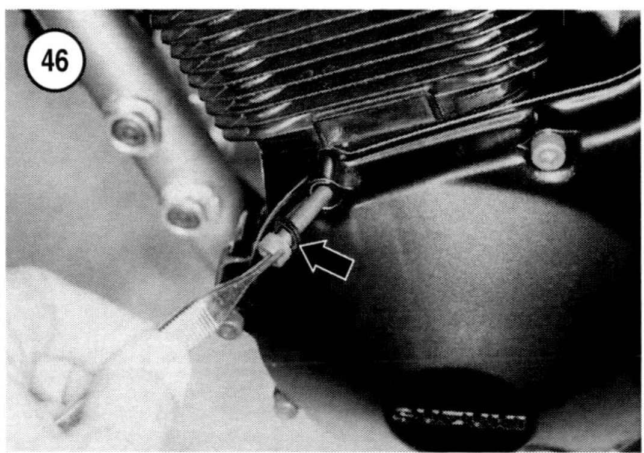

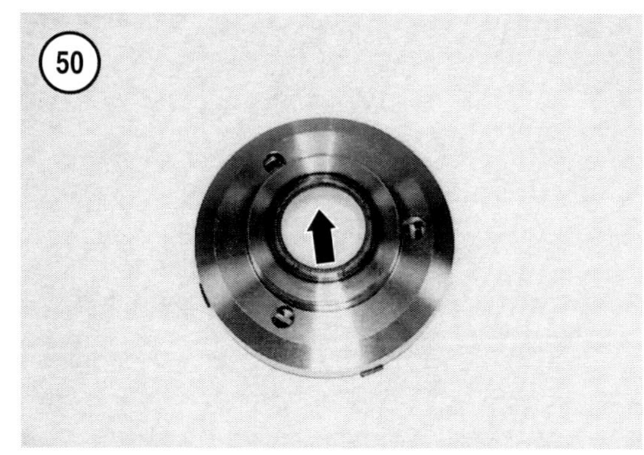

9. Install the starter clutch cover (A, **Figure 38**) and mounting bolts. Install a *new* copper washer under the bolt shown in **Figure 46**. Using a crisscross pattern, securely tighten the cover bolts.

10. Refill the engine with the recommended type and quantity of engine oil as described in Chapter Three.

Disassembly/Inspection/Assembly

1. Check the operation of the starter clutch as follows:
   a. Set the starter clutch down on the bench with the sprague clutch facing up.
   b. Rotate the sprague clutch (A, **Figure 47**) *counterclockwise* around the starter driven gear (B). The sprague clutch should rotate freely when turned counterclockwise.
   c. Rotate the sprague clutch (A, **Figure 47**) *clockwise* around the starter driven gear (B). The sprague clutch should engage the starter driven gear when turned in this direction.
   d. The starter clutch is faulty if it fails either test. Replace both the starter driven gear and sprague clutch as a set.
2. Lift up and remove the sprague clutch from the starter driven gear.
3. Check the rollers (**Figure 48**) in the sprague clutch for uneven or excessive wear.
4. Inspect the outer bearing surface (A, **Figure 49**) of the starter driven gear for wear or abrasion.
5. Inspect the inner bearing surface (B, **Figure 49**) of the starter driven gear for wear or abrasion.
6. Inspect the starter driven gear for chipped or missing teeth (C, **Figure 49**).
7. Inspect the inner bearing surface (**Figure 50**) of the sprague clutch for wear or abrasion.

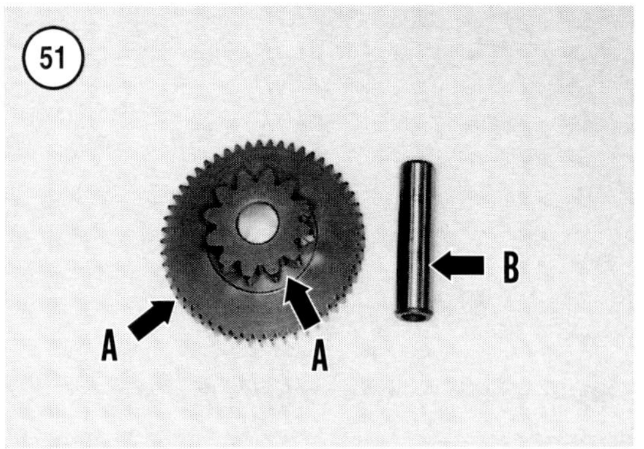

8. If either the sprague clutch or the starter driven gear is worn or damaged, replace both the starter driven gear and sprague clutch as a set.
9. Inspect the starter idler gear (A, **Figure 51**) for chipped or missing teeth. Look for uneven or excessive wear on the gear faces.
10. Inspect the starter idler gear shaft (B, **Figure 51**) for nicks, scratches, or signs of uneven wear.
11. Rotate the sprague clutch (A, **Figure 47**) counterclockwise, and install it onto the starter driven gear (B). Push it down until it bottoms.

CRANKCASE

The engine must be removed from the frame in order to service the lower end.

Disassembly

1. Remove the drive sprocket cover as described in Chapter Seven.
2. Remove the left side clutch pushrod (A, **Figure 52**).
3. Remove the engine drive sprocket (B, **Figure 52**) as described in Chapter Seven.
4. Straighten the locking tabs and remove the bolts securing the oil seal retainer (**Figure 53**). Remove the retainer.
5. Remove the neutral switch, or gear position switch, as described in Chapter Nine.
6. Remove the crankcase from the frame as described in this chapter.
7. Remove the screws (**Figure 54**) securing the mainshaft bearing retainer and remove the bearing retainer.
8. Install a bolt and washer (**Figure 55**) to secure the shift drum in place.

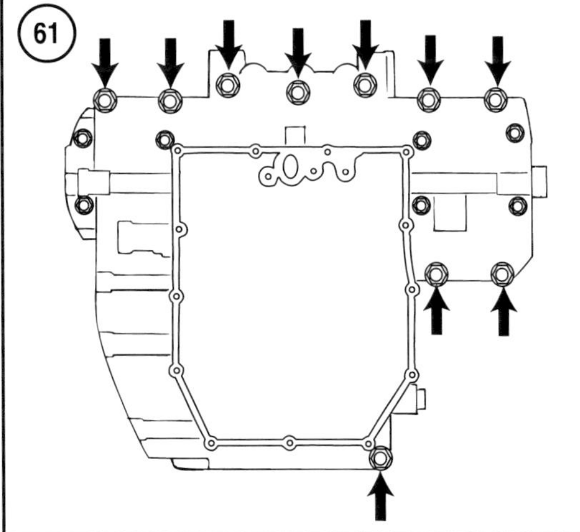

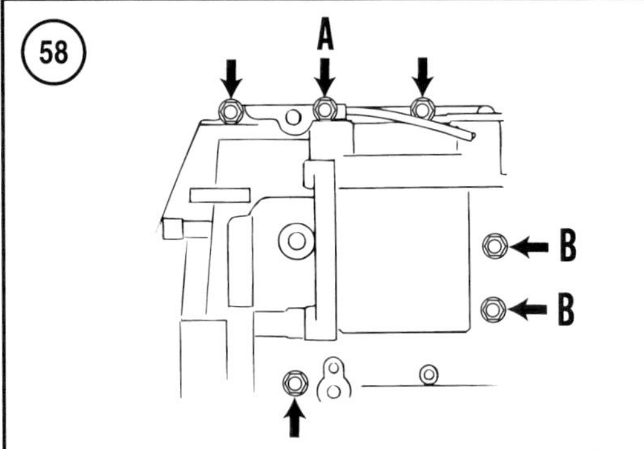

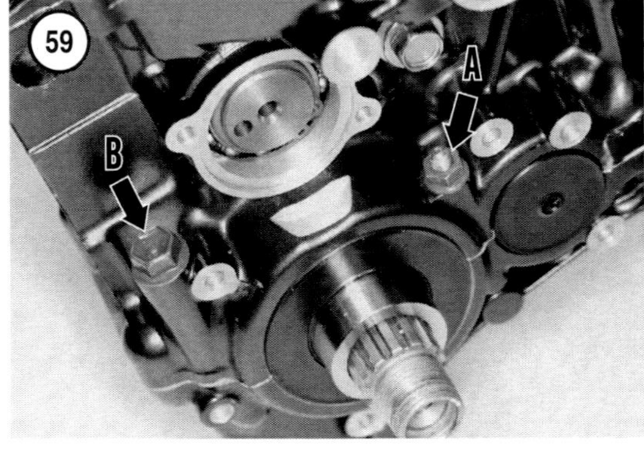

9. Remove the upper crankcase plug bolt and washer (**Figure 56**) to gain access to the upper crankcase bolt (A, **Figure 57**) located below it.

10. Remove the upper crankcase bolt (A, **Figure 57**) and the upper crankcase nut (B).

11. Remove the upper crankcase bolts shown in **Figure 58**. Note the location of the engine ground strap (A, **Figure 58**) and the copper washers (B) under the two bolts.

12. Place the engine upside down on wooden blocks. This protects the connecting rods and the crankcase studs.

13. Remove the oil pan and oil strainer as described in this chapter.

14. Remove the lower crankcase stud nut (A, **Figure 59**) located next to the mainshaft.

15. Remove the main oil gallery plug (**Figure 60**) and its O-ring.

16. Remove the lower crankcase bolts shown in **Figure 61**. Do not forget the single bolt (B, **Figure 59**) at the rear corner.

17. Remove the bolt (A, **Figure 62**) securing the left side oil return pipe to the crankcase and remove the pipe (B).

NOTE
*A tightening sequence number is cast into the lower crankcase next to each main bearing bolt (**Figure 63**).*

18. Evenly loosen the main bearing bolts in descending order of the tightening sequence cast into the lower crankcase (**Figure 63**). Remove the bolts. Note the sealing washer located under bolts No. 9 and No. 11. Install *new* washers under these two bolts during assembly.
19. Remove the oil return pipe (C, **Figure 62**) that was held in place by main bearing bolt No. 1 (D).
20. Double check that all upper and lower crankcase bolts have been removed.
21. Tap the lower crankcase with a plastic mallet and separate the two halves.

CAUTION
If it is necessary to pry the halves apart, do it very carefully. Do not mar the gasket surfaces. If any gasket surface is scratched or otherwise damaged, the cases will leak oil and have to be replaced.

22. Lift the lower crankcase off of the upper crankcase and immediately turn the lower crankcase over. Be careful that the crankshaft main bearing inserts do not fall out of the lower crankcase half. If any do, reinstall them immediately into their original locations if possible.
23. Remove the O-rings (A, **Figure 64**) from the oil galleries.
24. Remove the front locating dowel (B, **Figure 64**) if loose.
25. Remove the mainshaft assembly (A, **Figure 65**) and the countershaft assembly (B) from the upper crankcase half.
26. Remove the rear locating dowel (C, **Figure 65**) if loose.
27. Remove the C-rings (A, **Figure 66**) and the transmission bearing locating dowels (B).
28. Remove the crankshaft side thrust bearings (**Figure 67**) from the crankshaft and the upper crankcase half.

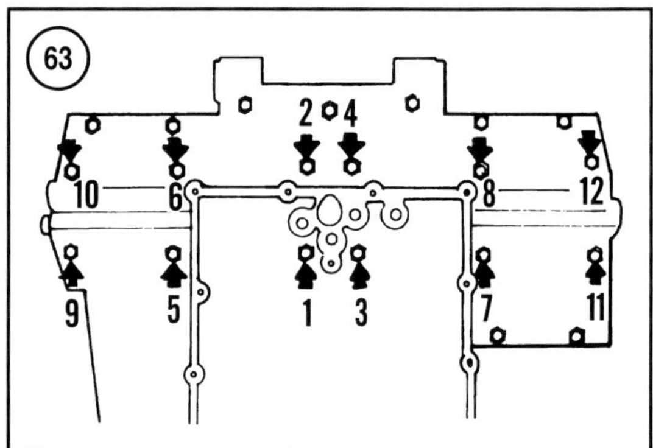

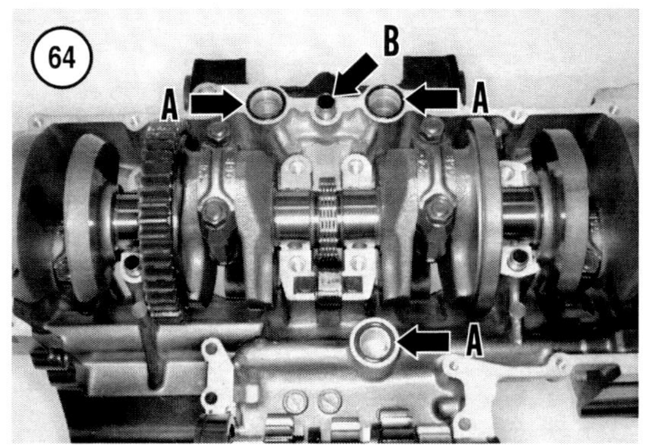

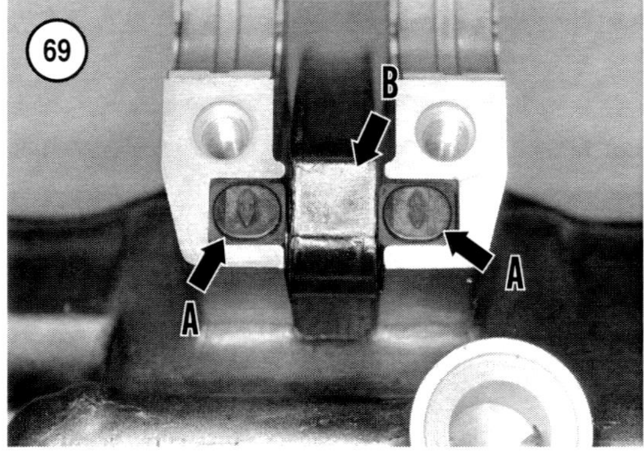

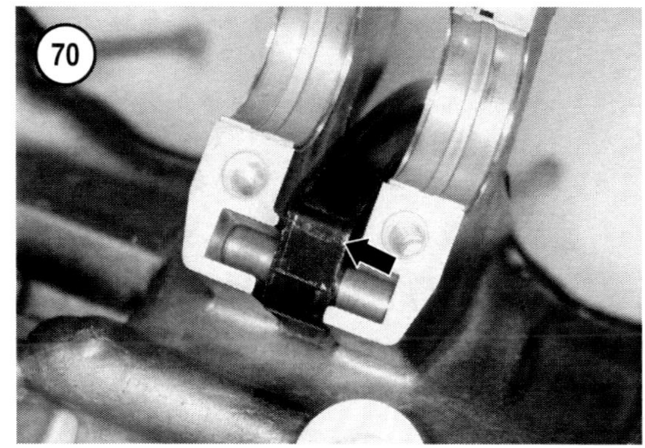

29. Lift the crankshaft/connecting rod assembly (**Figure 68**) out of the upper crankcase.

30. Remove both camshaft chain guide dampers (A, **Figure 69**), then remove the rear camshaft chain guide (B).

31. Remove the oil pump as described in this chapter.

32. Remove the internal shift mechanism as described in Chapter Six.

33. Remove the crankshaft main bearing inserts as described in this chapter.

34. Inspect the crankcase assembly as described in this chapter.

Assembly

NOTE

If reusing the old bearing inserts, make sure they are installed in the same locations noted during removal.

1. Place the upper crankcase upside down on wooden blocks. This protects the crankcase studs and the connecting rods when they are installed later in this procedure .

2. Install the crankshaft main bearing inserts into the crankcase halves as described in this chapter.

3. Install the internal shift mechanism as described in Chapter Six.

4. Install the oil pump as described in this chapter.

5. Install the rear camshaft chain guide (**Figure 70**) into the upper crankcase half receptacles.

6. Position the camshaft chain guide dampers (A, **Figure 69**) so the double-ended arrows point toward the front and rear of the engine. Press them into the crankcase receptacles until they bottom.

5

7. If removed, install the camshaft chain (**Figure 71**) onto the crankshaft timing gear.
8. Apply molybdenum disulfide oil to each crankshaft journal.

NOTE
Prior to installation, coat all bearing surfaces with assembly oil or fresh engine oil.

9. Install the camshaft chain, crankshaft/connecting rod assembly (**Figure 68**) into the upper crankcase.
10. Position the crankshaft side thrust bearings with the grooved sides facing out (**Figure 72**) and install them into upper crankcase half (**Figure 73**).
11. Install the C-rings (A, **Figure 66**) and the transmission bearing locating dowels (B).
12. Install the mainshaft assembly (A, **Figure 65**) as follows:
   a. Align the small bearing end cap hole (A, **Figure 74**) with the locating dowel (B) in the crankcase.
   b. Set the mainshaft assembly into the upper crankcase half so the large bearing properly engages the C-ring (A, **Figure 75**).
   c. Rotate the large bearing so the locating pin (B, **Figure 75**) correctly engages the crankcase receptacle.
   d. If not yet installed, install the end cap (**Figure 76**) onto the end of the mainshaft.
13. Install the countershaft assembly (B, **Figure 65**) as follows:
   a. If removed, install the large end cap (**Figure 77**) onto the transmission shaft.
   b. Align the small bearing end cap hole with the locating dowel in the crankcase.
   c. Set the countershaft assembly into the upper crankcase half so the large bearing properly engages the C-ring (A, **Figure 78**).
   d. Rotate the large bearing so the locating pin (B, **Figure 78**) correctly engages the crankcase receptacle.
14. If removed, install the rear locating dowel (C, **Figure 65**) and the front locating dowel (B, **Figure 64**).
15. Install *new* O-rings (A, **Figure 64**) into the oil galleries.
16. Make sure the crankshaft main bearing inserts are securely in place in the lower crankcase half.
17. Shift the shift drum into NEUTRAL.
18. Level the upper case half so the transmission shafts are parallel to the workbench. This keeps the gears from sliding during lower case half installation.

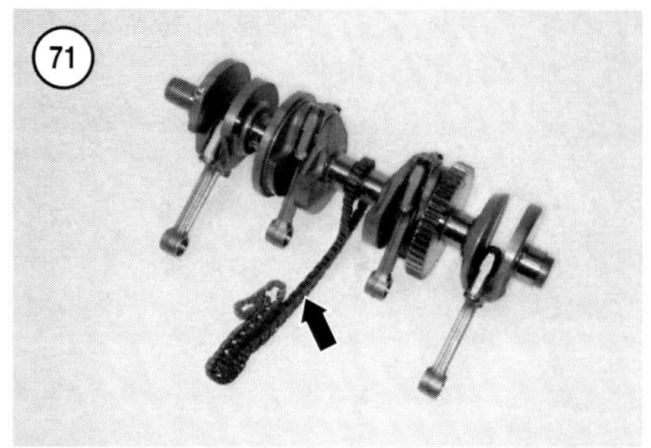

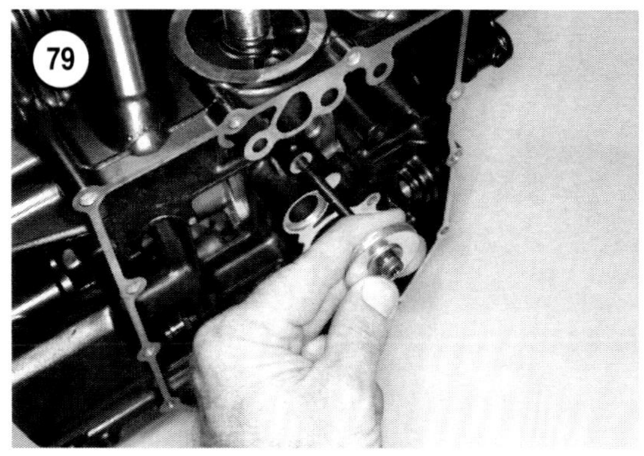

19. Check the shift-fork-and-sliding-gear alignment by partially lowering the lower crankcase half onto the upper half. Be sure that the sliding gears on the transmission shafts align with shift forks. Reposition the gears as necessary and then remove the lower case half.

20. Make sure the camshaft chain guide dampers (A, **Figure 69**) are still in place. If necessary, position them so the double-ended arrows point toward the front and rear of the engine. Press them into the crankcase receptacles until they bottom.

21. Make sure the crankcase half mating surfaces are perfectly clean and dry. Clean them with electrical contact cleaner and wipe them with a lint-free cloth.

NOTE

It is difficult to install the lower crankcase half onto the upper case half with gasket sealer in place and while trying to correctly position the shift forks into the transmission gear grooves. Make an easy to use handle using a long 6 mm bolt and large washer and thread the bolt into the lower crankcase as shown in ***Figure 79****.*

NOTE

Use ThreeBond Liquid Gasket 1104, Gasgacinch Gasket Sealer, or an equivalent gasket sealer. When selecting a sealer, avoid thick and hard setting materials.

22. Apply a light coat of gasket sealer to the mating surfaces of the lower crankcase half (**Figure 80**). Cover only flat surfaces. Do not apply gasket sealer to any curved bearing surfaces. Make the

coating as thin as possible, but be sure the gasket sealer completely covers the mating surfaces. If it does not, the cases can shift and hammer out the bearings.

CAUTION
Crankcase halves should fit together without force. If the crankcase halves do not completely mate with one another, do not attempt to pull them together with the crankcase bolts. Separate the crankcase halves and investigate the cause of the interference. If the transmission shafts were disassembled, recheck to make sure that a gear is not installed backwards. Do not risk damage by trying to force the cases together.

23. Position the lower crankcase onto the upper crankcase. Set the front portion down first and lower the rear area into place. Be sure the shift forks properly engage their respective transmission gears and that the shift fork guide pins still engage in the shift drum grooves. Join both halves and tap them together lightly with a plastic mallet. Do *not* use a metal hammer as it will damage the crankcase half.

24. If installed, remove the temporary 6 mm bolt and washer (**Figure 55**) securing the shift drum.

25. Slowly spin the transmission shafts and shift the transmission with the shift drum. Make sure the shift forks are operating properly and that it is possible to shift through all gears. This is the time to find that something may be installed incorrectly, not after the crankcase is completely assembled.

26. Install the right oil return pipe (A, **Figure 81**) into the lower crankcase half. Be sure its mounting bolt (B, **Figure 81**) hole aligns with the crankcase hole for main bearing bolt No. 1.

NOTE
Prior to tightening the bolts, install all bolts and check that the bolt heads are all the same distance up from the bolt boss on the crankcase. If any bolts are higher or lower than the others, switch the bolts around until all are of the same height.

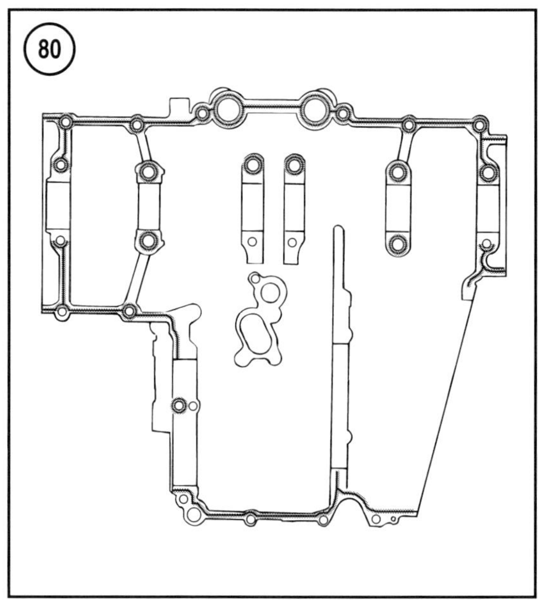

27. Apply a light coat of oil to the main bearing bolts and install the bolts. Place a *new* copper washer under the bolts No. 9 and No. 11 (**Figure 82**).

28. Following the tightening sequence cast into the lower crankcase, evenly tighten the main bearing bolts. Tighten all bolts to the initial specification listed in **Table 2** and then tighten all the bolts to the final specification listed in **Table 2**.

29. Unscrew and remove the long 6 mm bolt and large washer (**Figure 79**) used as a handle.

30. Install the main oil gallery plug (**Figure 60**) and a *new* O-ring. Tighten the plug to 40 N•m (29 ft.-lb.).

31. Install the left side oil return pipe onto the crankcase and install the bolt (A, **Figure 62**). Tighten the bolt securely.

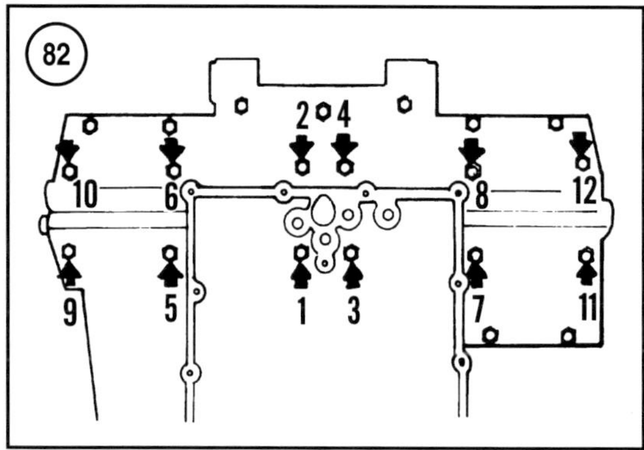

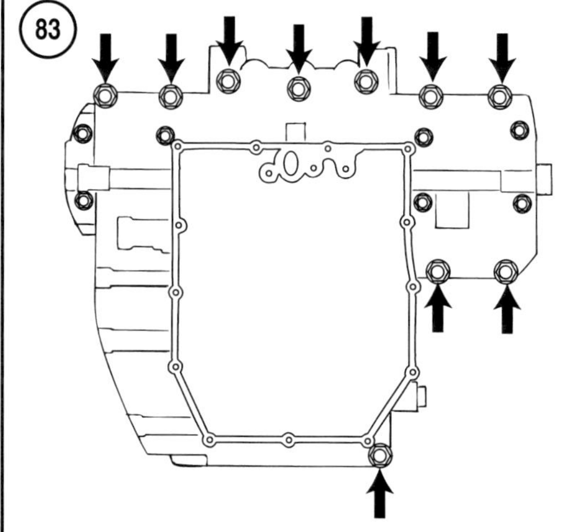

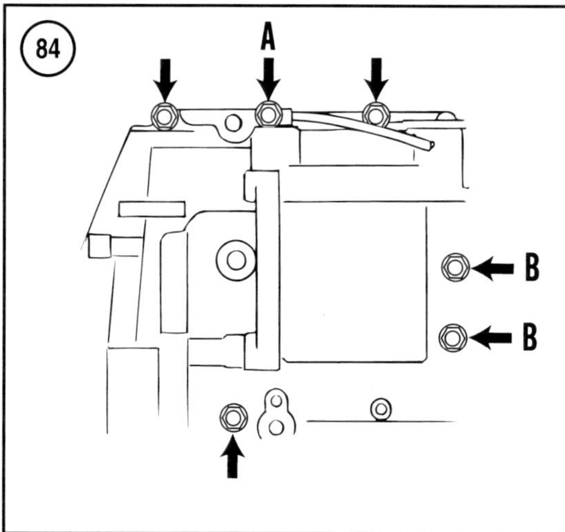

32. Install the lower crankcase bolts shown in **Figure 83**. Do not forget the single bolt (B, **Figure 59**) at the rear corner. Tighten the bolts to the specification in **Table 2**.

33. Install the lower crankcase stud nut (A, **Figure 59**) located next to the mainshaft. Tighten to 16 N•m (12 ft.-lb.).

34. Install the oil pan and oil strainer as described in this chapter.

35. Install the upper crankcase bolts. Note the location of the engine ground strap (A, **Figure 84**) and the copper washers (B) under the two bolts.

36. Install the upper crankcase bolt (A, **Figure 57**) and the upper crankcase nut (B).

37. Install the upper crankcase plug bolt and washer (**Figure 56**).

38. Install the crankcase into the frame as described in this chapter.

39. Apply a light coat of ThreeBond Threadlock 1342 to the mainshaft bearing retainer mounting screw threads. Install the mainshaft bearing retainer and tighten the screws (**Figure 54**) securely.

40. Install the neutral switch, or gear position switch, as described in Chapter Nine.

41. Install the oil seal retainer (**Figure 53**) and install the mounting bolts. Tighten the bolts securely, then bend up the locking tab against the bolts.

42. Install the engine drive sprocket (B, **Figure 52**) as described in Chapter Seven.

43. Install the left side clutch pushrod (A, **Figure 52**).

44. Install the drive sprocket cover as described in Chapter Seven.

45. Install all exterior components removed as described in this and other related chapters.

Inspection

1. Remove the oil gallery plug and O-ring from the upper crankcase.

2. Thoroughly clean the inside and outside of both crankcase halves with cleaning solvent. Dry them with compressed air. Make sure no solvent residue is left in the cases. It will contaminate the new engine oil.

3. Remove all old gasket sealing material from the mating surfaces on both case halves.

4. Carefully inspect the cases for cracks and fractures. Also check the areas around the stiffening ribs, around bearing bosses and threaded holes. If damage is found, have it repaired by a shop special-

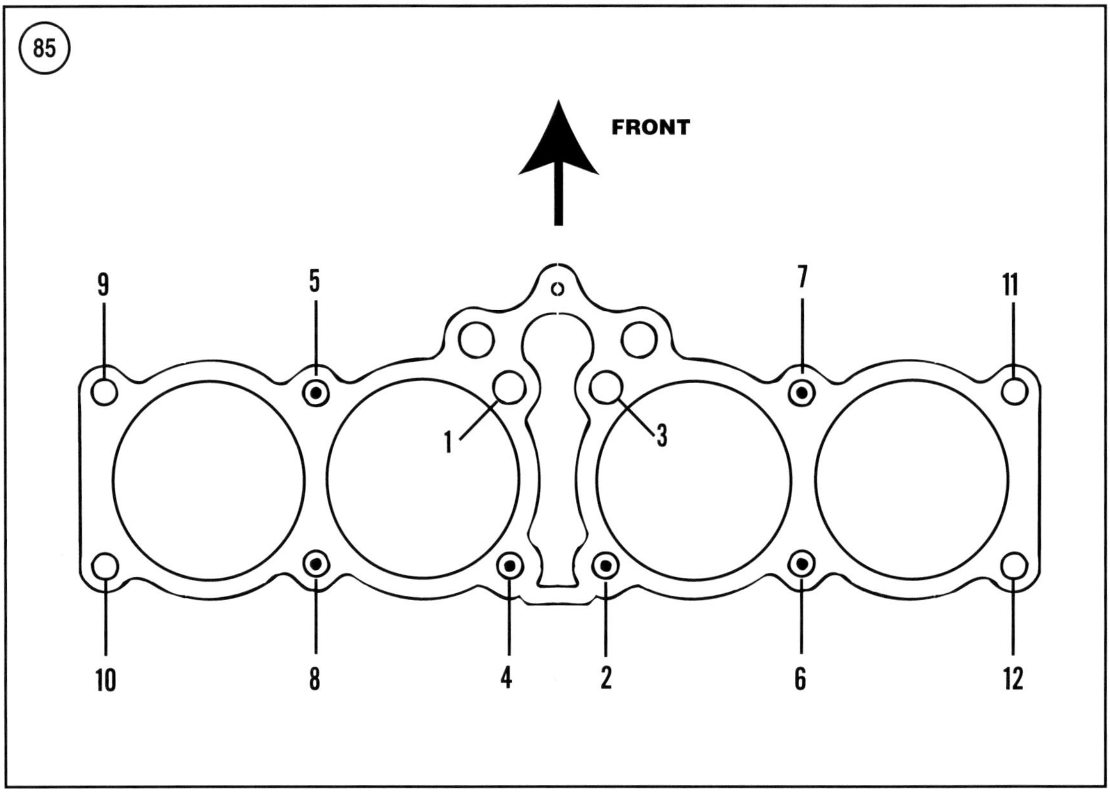

85

FRONT

9 5 7 11

1 3

10 8 4 2 6 12

izing in the repair of precision aluminum castings or replace the crankcase halves as a set.

NOTE

*The engine uses two different length crankcase studs, which are available in either silver or black. If a crankcase stud must be replaced, see a Suzuki dealership to get the proper size and color stud. If stud No. 7 shown in **Figure 85** must be replaced, apply Suzuki Bond 1207B to the threads and tighten the stud to 16 N•m (12 ft.-lb.).*

5. Make sure the crankcase studs are tight. If necessary, tighten the studs to 16 N•m (12 ft.-lb.).

6. Inspect the threads of the crankcase-to-cylinder block threaded stud (**Figure 86**), as well as the studs in the upper crankcase (**Figure 87**) and in the lower crankcase (**Figure 88**). If necessary, clean the threads with the proper size metric die or replace the stud.

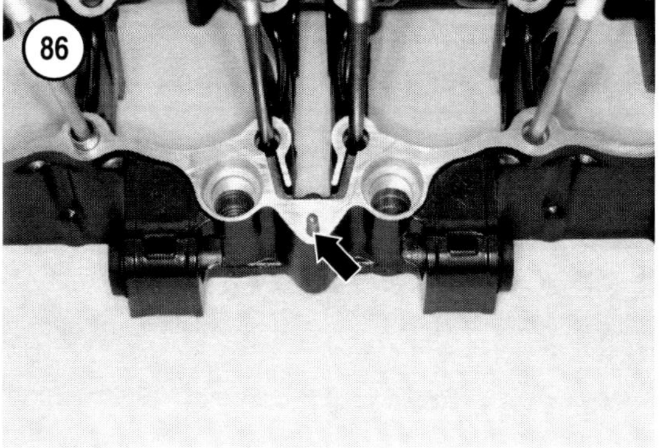

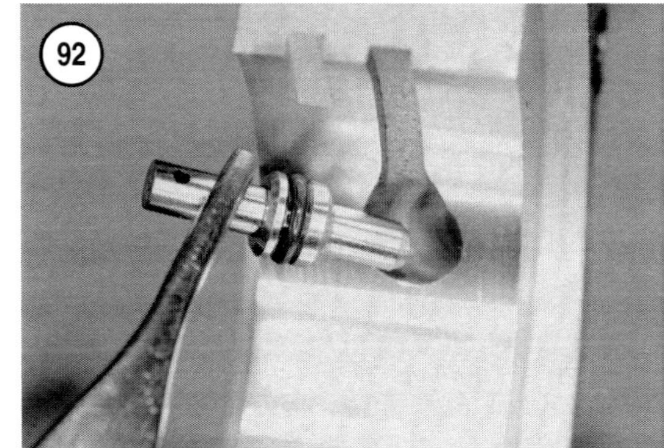

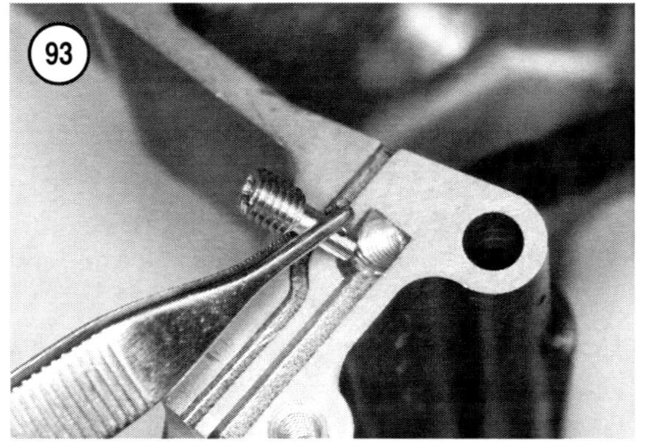

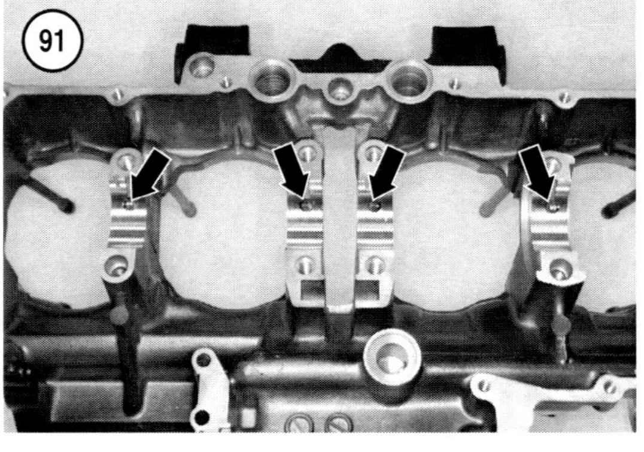

7. Check the transmission bearing C-ring grooves (A, **Figure 89**) at each side of the crankcase for wear or damage.

8. Make sure the transmission bearing locating dowels (B, **Figure 89**) are tight and in place. Replace if necessary.

9. Use needlenose pliers to pull the two oil jets (**Figure 90**) from the cylinder mating surface on the upper crankcase.

10. Remove the four oil jets from the bearing bosses in the upper crankcase (**Figure 91**) as follows:

   a. If still installed, remove the main bearing inserts as described in *Crankshaft*.
   b. Use a round punch to push the oil jets from the base side of the crankcase half and remove the jets from inside the crankcase (**Figure 92**).

11. Unscrew and remove the two threaded oil jets from either side of the transmission shaft area (**Figure 93**) in the lower crankcase.

12. Inspect the oil jets and their O-ring. Refer to **Figure 94** and **Figure 95**. If any wear or damage is found, replace the jet. The O-rings cannot be replaced separately.

13. Make sure all openings (**Figure 96**, typical) in the oil jets are clear. Clean out if necessary and blow out with compressed air.

14. Make sure all oil control openings (**Figure 97**) and galleries are clear.

NOTE

The shift shaft oil seal is very thick (9 mm [0.35 in.]) and is difficult to remove. Follow the oil seal replacement procedure described in Chapter One, prying the oil seal ***(Figure 98)*** *about halfway out, then pull it up evenly the rest of the way. Install the new seal with the closed side facing out and push it in until it bottoms in the mounting bore.*

15. Inspect the shift shaft oil seal (**Figure 99**) in the upper crankcase half. Replace the seal if necessary. Apply Suzuki Super Grease A to the lips of the *new* oil seal before installation.

16. Apply clean engine oil to the oil jet O-rings and install all jets. Push the oil jets into place until they bottom.

17. Install the two threaded oil jets on either side of the transmission shaft area (**Figure 93**) in the lower crankcase and tighten securely.

18. Install the oil gallery plug and *new* O-ring into the upper crankcase and tighten securely.

Shift Drum Bearings Removal/Installation

1. Turn the shift drum bearings by hand and check for damaged races, balls or needles. Refer to **Figure 100** and **Figure 101**. Replace a bearing if it has excessive side play. If the bearings are good, oil the races or needles with fresh engine oil. If necessary, replace the bearings as follows.

NOTE

If bearing replacement is required, purchase the new bearing(s) and place them in a freezer for approximately two hours before installation. Chilling the bearings slightly reduces their overall diameter and heating the crankcase slightly increases the bearing boss's inside diameter. This makes bearing installation much easier.

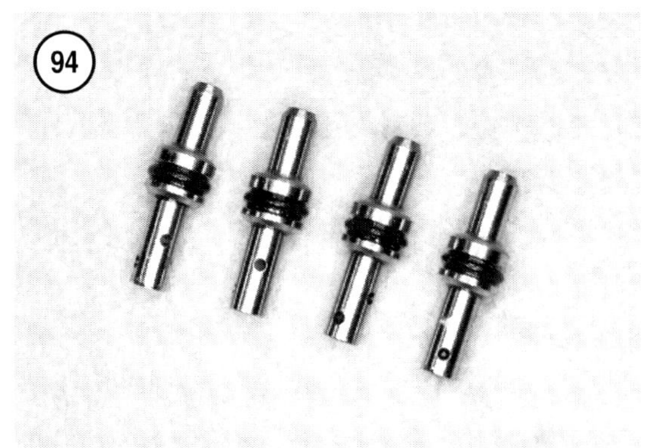

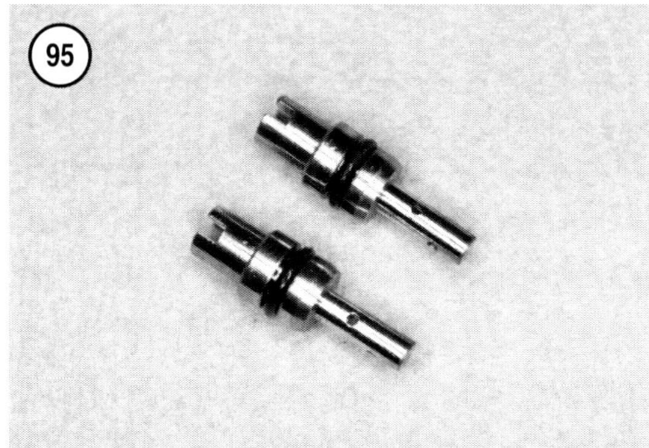

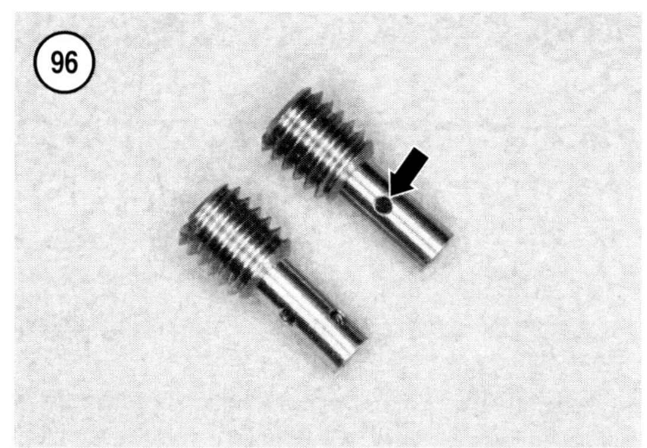

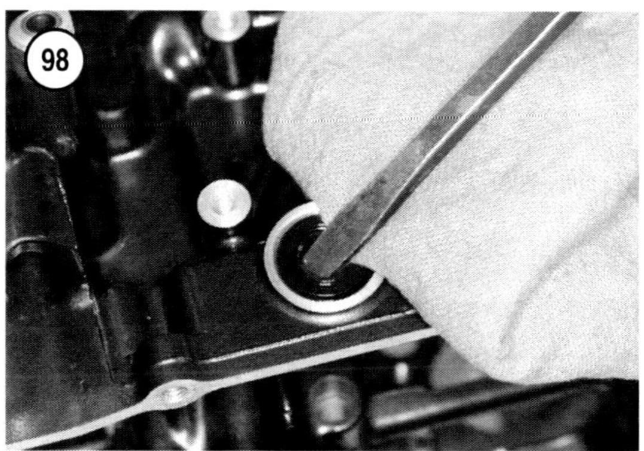

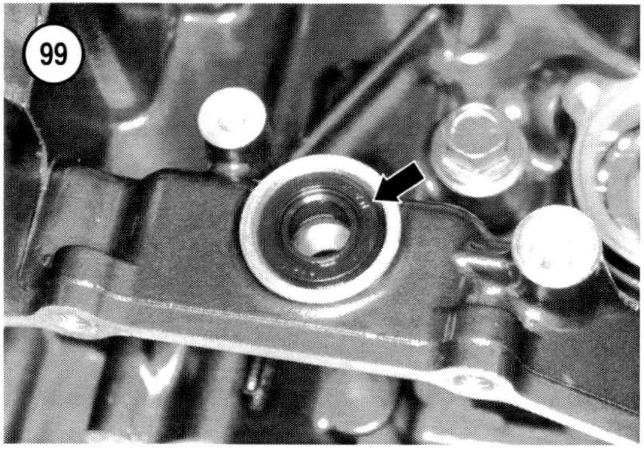

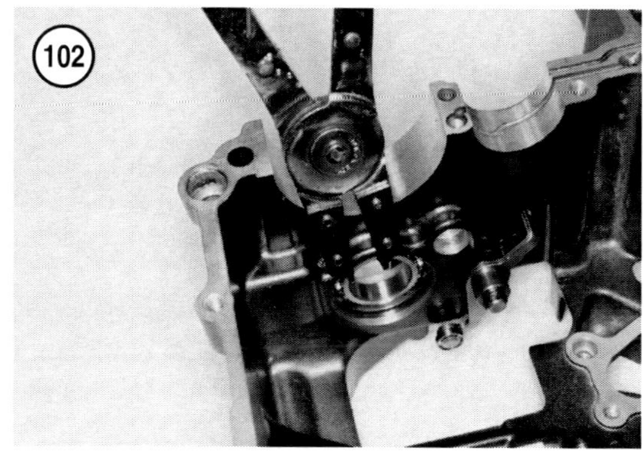

2. Remove the snap ring (**Figure 102**) securing the ball bearing into the inner surface of the crankcase.

WARNING
*Prior to heating the crankcase half as described in Step 3, remove the shift shaft oil seal (**Figure 99**) and thoroughly wash the crankcase in soap and water. Make sure no gasoline or solvent fumes are present.*

3. The bearings are installed with a slight interference fit. The crankcase half must be heated in a shop oven to a temperature of about 100° C (212° F). Use temperature indicator sticks, available at welding supply stores, to monitor the crankcase temperature.

WARNING
Wear welding gloves or insulated gloves (insulated kitchen mitts) when handling heated parts.

CAUTION
Do not heat the cases with a torch (propane or acetylene). Never bring a flame into contact with the bearing or case. The direct heat will destroy the case hardening of the bearing and will likely warp the case.

4. Remove the case from the shop oven, and place it on wood blocks. Hold onto the crankcase with welding gloves or kitchen mitts—it is hot.
5. Carefully tap the bearing(s) out of the crankcase with a block of wood, socket or piece of pipe that matches the diameter of the bearing outer race.

NOTE
If a bearing is difficult to remove or install, do not take a chance on expen-

sive crankcase damage. Have the work performed by a Suzuki dealership or competent machine shop.

6. Reheat the crankcase half in the oven.
7. Remove the case from the oven and place on wood blocks. Hold onto the crankcase with welding gloves or kitchen mitts—it is hot.
8. While the crankcase is still hot, press each *new* bearing into place in the crankcase by hand until it seats completely. Do not hammer it in. If the bearing will not seat, remove it and cool it again. Reheat the crankcase and install the bearing again.
9. Install the snap ring retaining the ball bearing. Make sure the snap ring is seated correctly in the groove.

CRANKSHAFT

Removal/Installation

1. Disassemble the crankcase as described in this chapter.
2. Remove the crankshaft/connecting rod assembly (**Figure 103**) and the camshaft chain from the upper crankcase half. Remove the camshaft chain from the crankshaft.

NOTE
In Step 3, No. 1 refers to the left-most bearing in a crankcase half. This is the bearing that sits to the left (or outside) of the No. 1 cylinder. The bearings are numbered 1-6, counting from left to right across the engine. Left refers to the engine as it sits in the frame, not as it sits on the workbench.

3. If the main bearing inserts are going to be removed for cleaning, perform the following;
   a. Remove each main bearing insert from its bearing boss in the upper (**Figure 104**) and lower (**Figure 105**) crankcase halves.
   b. Mark the backside of the inserts with a 1, 2, 3, 4, 5 or 6 and U (upper) or L (lower) so they can be reinstalled in their original locations. Remember that the inserts with an oil path hole (**Figure 106**) are located in the lower crankcase.

CAUTION
If the old bearings are reused, they must be installed in their original locations.

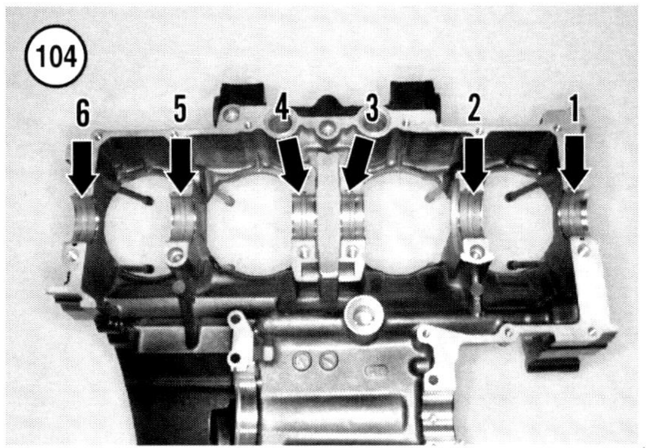

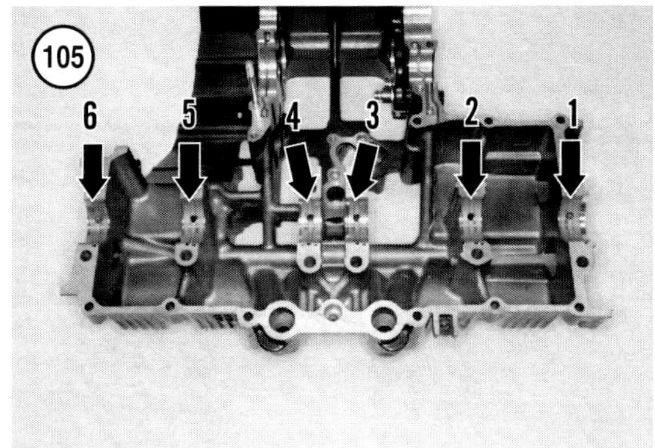

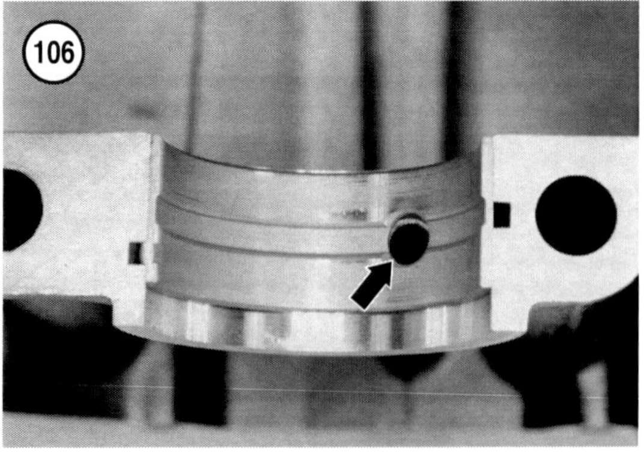

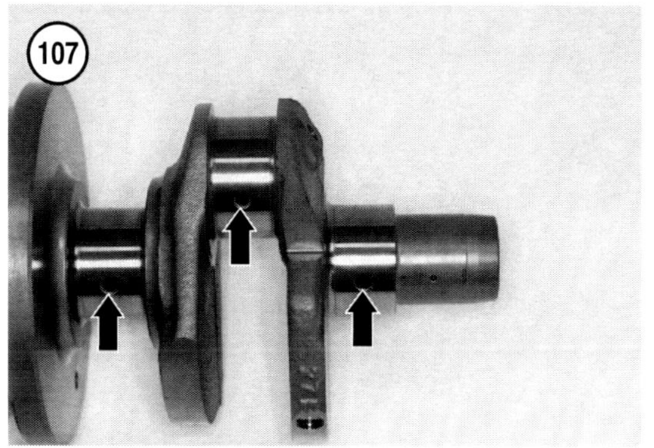

107

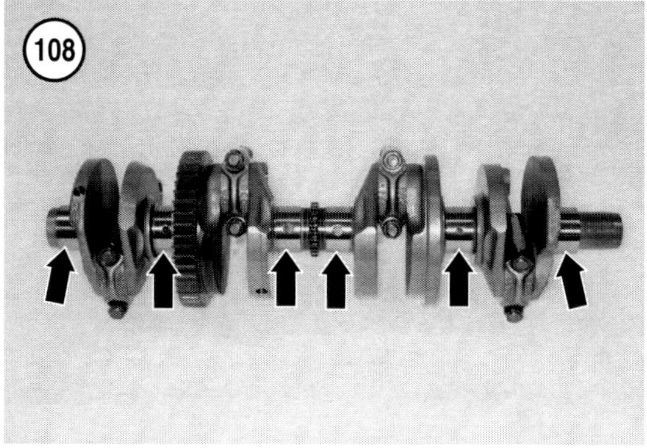

108

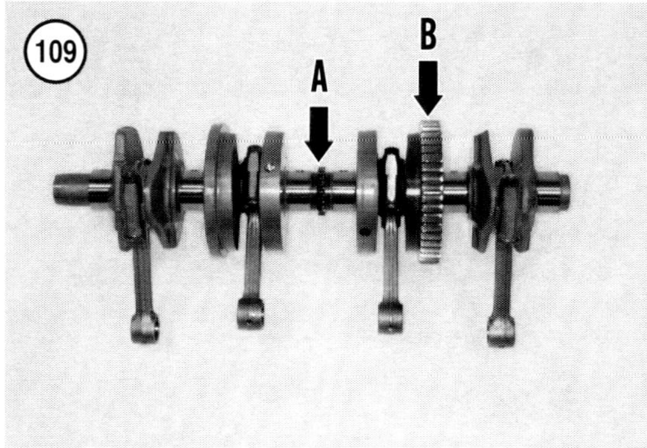

109

110

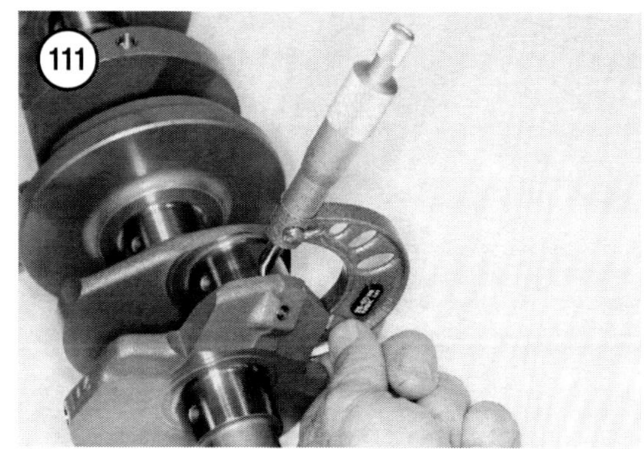

111

4. Remove the connecting rods as described in this chapter.
5. Inspect the crankshaft and main bearings as described in this chapter.
6. Install the crankshaft/connecting rod assembly and camshaft chain (**Figure 103**) into the upper crankcase half.
7. Assemble the crankcase as described earlier in this chapter.

Inspection

Compare all measurements to the specifications in **Table 1**. Replace any component that is damaged or out of specification.

1. Clean the crankshaft thoroughly with solvent. Clean oil path holes (**Figure 107**) with rifle cleaning brushes. Flush thoroughly, and dry the crankshaft with compressed air. Lightly oil all bearing journal surfaces immediately to prevent rust.
2. Carefully inspect each main bearing journal (**Figure 108**) for scratches, ridges, scoring or nicks. Very small nicks and scratches may be removed with crocus cloth. More serious damage may require machine work, a job best left to a machine shop.
3. Inspect the camshaft timing sprocket teeth (A, **Figure 109**). If damaged, the crankshaft must be replaced.
4. Inspect the primary drive gear teeth (B, **Figure 109**). If damaged, the crankshaft must be replaced.
5. If the surface finish on all main bearing journals is satisfactory, measure the journal outside diameter with a micrometer (**Figure 110**).
6. If the surface finish on all connecting rod bearing journals is satisfactory, measure the journal outside diameter with a micrometer (**Figure 111**).

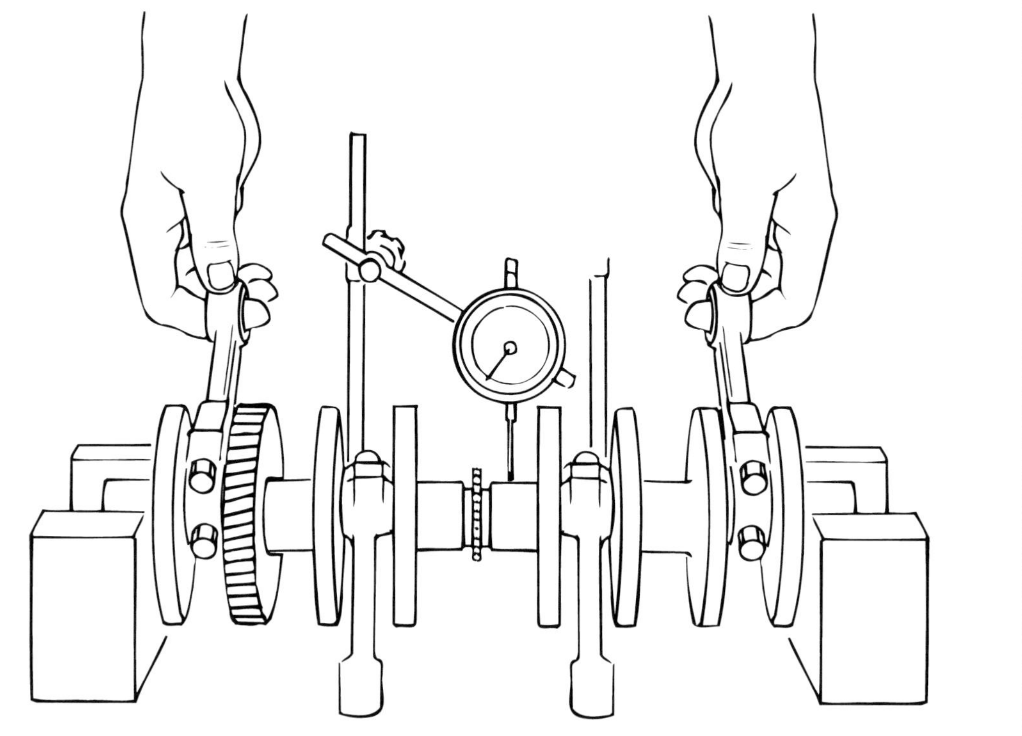

7. Set the crankshaft on V-blocks, and use a dial indicator to check crankshaft runout. See **Figure 112**.
8. Make sure the dowel pin on the right side end of the crankshaft is secure.
9. Check the crankshaft main bearing clearance as described in the following procedure.
10. Inspect the camshaft chain for wear

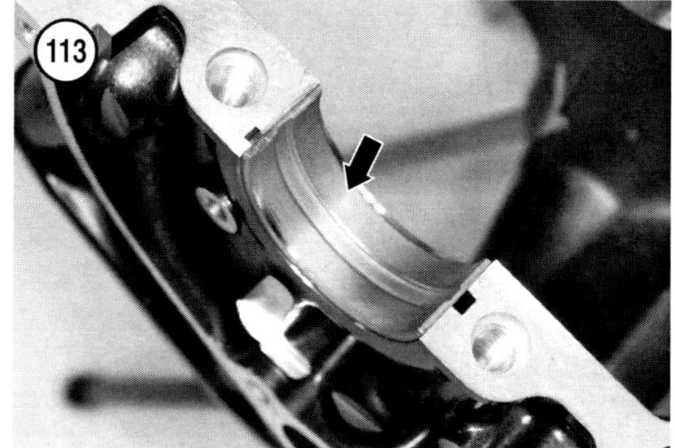

Main Bearing Clearance Measurement

1. Remove the transmission shaft assemblies as described in this chapter.
2. Check each main bearing insert (**Figure 113**) for evidence of wear, abrasion and scoring. If the bearings are good, they may be reused. If any insert is questionable, replace the entire set.
3. Clean the bearing surfaces of the main bearing inserts and clean the crankshaft journals.
4. Place the upper crankcase on a workbench upside down on wooden blocks. This will protect the protruding connecting rod ends and the crankcase studs.
5. Install the existing main bearing inserts into their original positions in the upper (**Figure 104**) and the

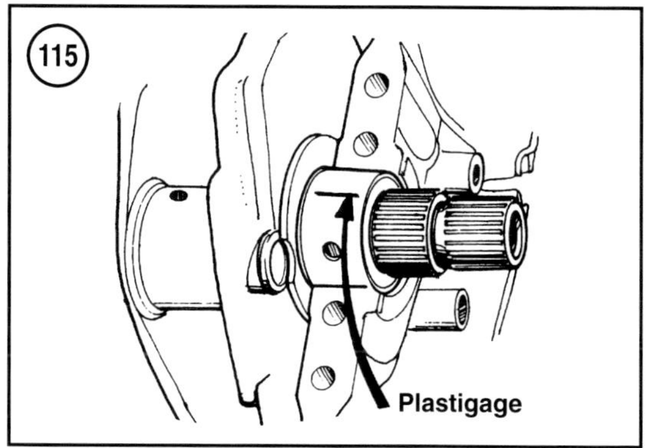

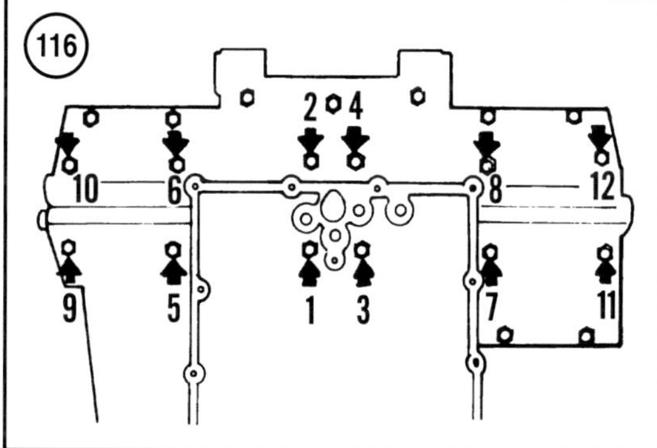

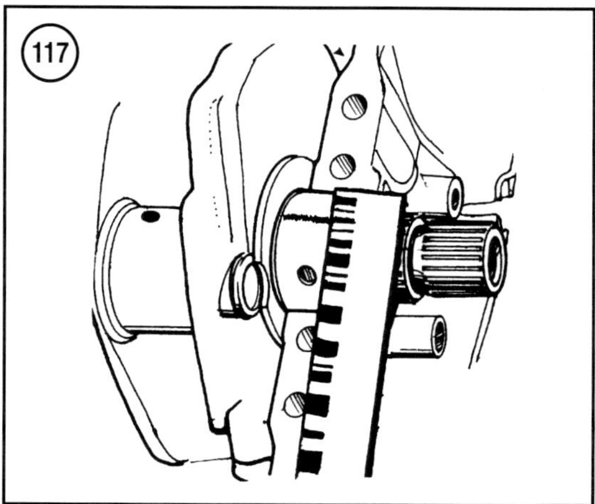

lower (**Figure 105**) crankcase. Carefully press each insert into place with a thumb. Be sure the tab on the insert (**Figure 114**) locks into the cutout in the bearing boss. Remember that the inserts with an oil path hole (**Figure 106**) are located in the lower crankcase.

6. Install the crankshaft into the upper crankcase (**Figure 103**) half.

7. Place a piece of Plastigage over each main bearing journal. Each piece of Plastigage must parallel the crankshaft (**Figure 115**). Do not place any Plastigage over an oil hole in the crankshaft.

CAUTION
Do not rotate the crankshaft while the Plastigage is in place.

8. Position the lower crankcase onto the upper crankcase. Set the front portion down first, then lower the rear. Join both halves and tap them together lightly with a plastic mallet. Do not use a metal hammer, as it will damage the case.

CAUTION
Crankcase halves should fit together without force. If the crankcase halves do not fit together completely, do not attempt to pull them together with the crankcase bolts. Separate the crankcase halves and investigate the cause of the interference. If the transmission shafts were disassembled, recheck them to make sure that a gear is not installed backwards. Do not risk damage by trying to force the cases together.

9. Apply a light coat of oil to the main bearing bolts, and install the bolts. Place a *new* copper washer under the bolts No. 9 and No. 11 (**Figure 116**).

10. Following the tightening sequence cast into the lower crankcase (**Figure 116**), evenly tighten the main bearing bolts. First tighten all the bolts to 13 N•m (115 in.-lb.), and then tighten them all to 22 N•m (16 ft.-lb.).

11. Loosen each main bearing bolt in the descending order of the numbers cast into the lower crankcase (**Figure 116**). Remove the bolts.

12. Carefully remove the lower crankcase half.

13. Measure the width of the flattened Plastigage according to manufacturer's instructions. Measure the Plastigage (**Figure 117**) at its widest point.

14. If any crankshaft main bearing clearance exceeds the wear limit specified in **Table 1**, replace the entire set of main bearings. Select the *new* main bearings as described in the following procedure.

15. Remove the Plastigage strips from the main bearing journals.

CAUTION
Make sure to remove all traces of Plastigage from the main bearing journals and bearing inserts. If any Plastigage is left in the engine, it can

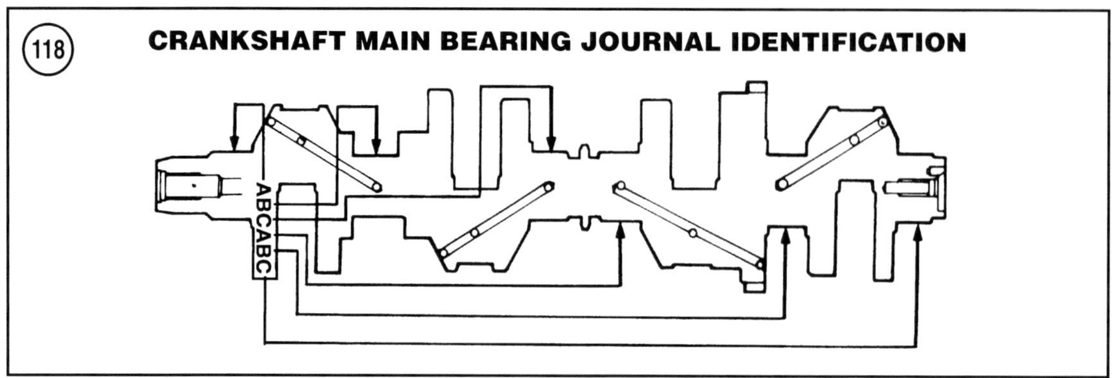

118

plug up an oil control orifice and cause severe engine damage.

119

Main Bearing Selection

1. The crankshaft main bearing journals are identified by an A, B or C stamped into the crank web. The stamped letters relate to the journals as shown in **Figure 118**.

2. The crankcase main bearing boss codes (A or B) are stamped on the rear surface of the upper crankcase (**Figure 119**). The stamped letters are in the same order as the bearing boss locations in the crankcase.

3. Bearing inserts are identified by color codes (**Figure 120**). Refer to **Table 3**, and select *new* bearings by cross-referencing the crankshaft journal codes with the crankcase bearing boss codes (**Figure 119**). **Table 4** lists the bearing insert color, thickness specification and the part number. Always replace bearing inserts as a set.

4. After new bearing inserts have been installed, recheck the clearance by repeating the procedure described in this chapter. If the clearance is still out of specification, either the crankcases or the crankshaft is worn beyond the service limit and requires replacement.

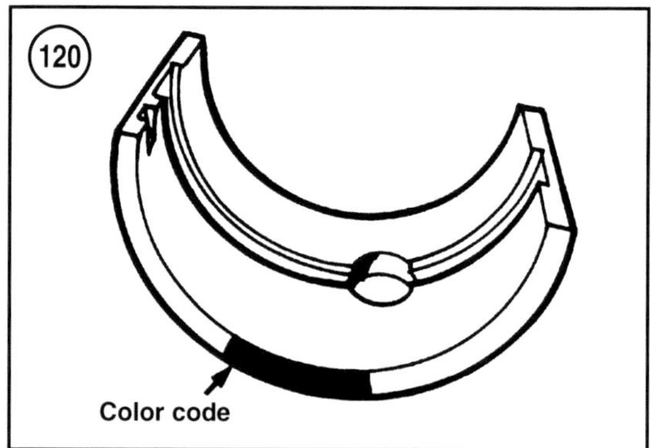

120

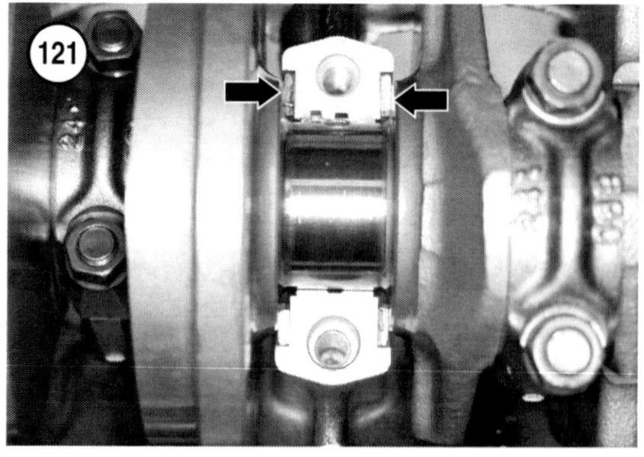
121

Side Thrust Clearance Inspection

1. Disassemble the crankcase as described in this chapter.

2. Leave the crankshaft and both right and left thrust bearings in place in the upper case half (**Figure 121**), perform the following.

122

Upper crankcase half

Push

FRONT

Left-hand bearing

Right-hand bearing

123

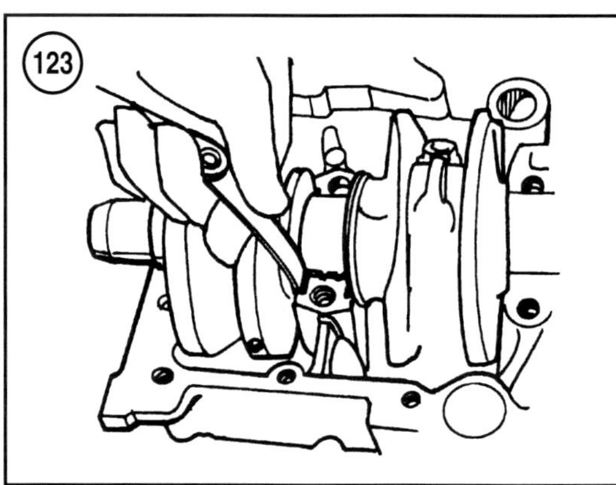

124

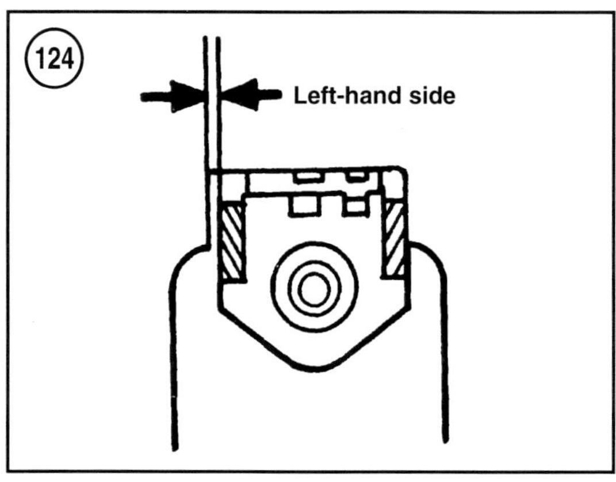

125

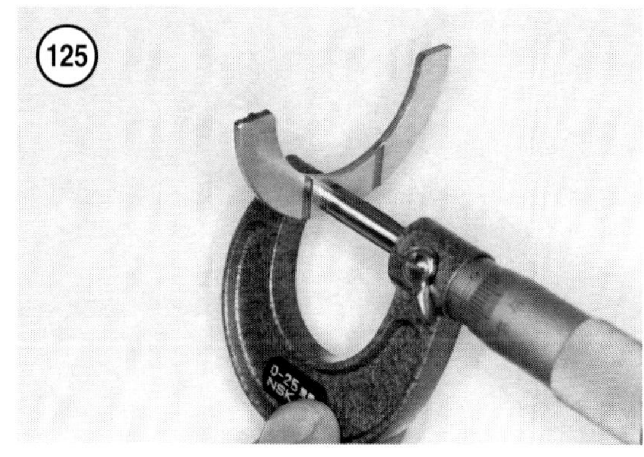

126

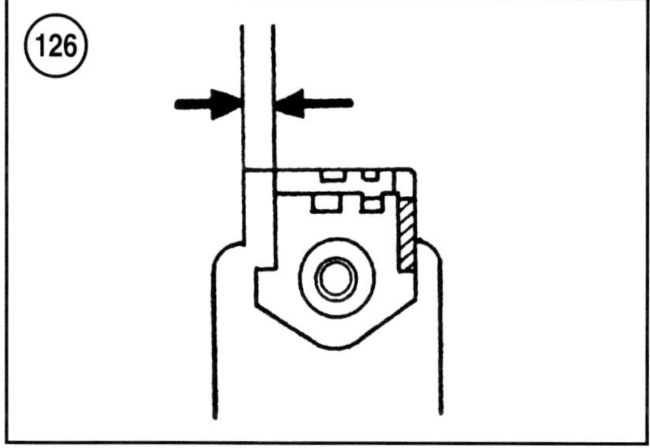

3. Push the crankshaft to the left until there is no clearance between the crankshaft and the right thrust bearing (**Figure 122**).

4. Install a flat feeler gauge between the left thrust bearing and the machined surface of the crankshaft. Refer to **Figure 123** and **Figure 124**. The measurement should equal the crankshaft thrust clearance specification in **Table 1**. If the crankshaft thrust clearance is greater than specified, perform the following:

   a. Remove the right thrust bearing and measure its thickness with a micrometer (**Figure 125**).
   b. If the thickness is within specification, proceed to Step 6. If the thickness is less than specified, replace the right thrust bearing with a *new* one and repeat Step 3 and Step 4.

5. Install the right thrust bearing and measure the thrust bearing clearance.

6. If the clearance is still greater than specified, remove the left thrust bearing.

7. Use a flat feeler gauge to measure the clearance between the machined surface of the crankshaft and the left surface of the crankcase boss (**Figure 126**).

8. Refer to **Table 5** and select the correct thrust bearing based on the clearance measured in Step 7.
9. Install the *new* left thrust bearing, and then repeat Step 3 and Step 4.
10. If the clearance cannot be brought into specification with different thrust bearings, replace the crankshaft.

CAUTION
*Install both the right and left thrust bearings with their oil grooves (**Figure 127**) facing out toward the crankshaft web.*

11. After the clearance has been correctly adjusted, remove both thrust bearings and apply a coat of molybdenum disulfide grease to each side of both bearings. Install both bearings into the crankcase with their oil groove facing the crankshaft web.

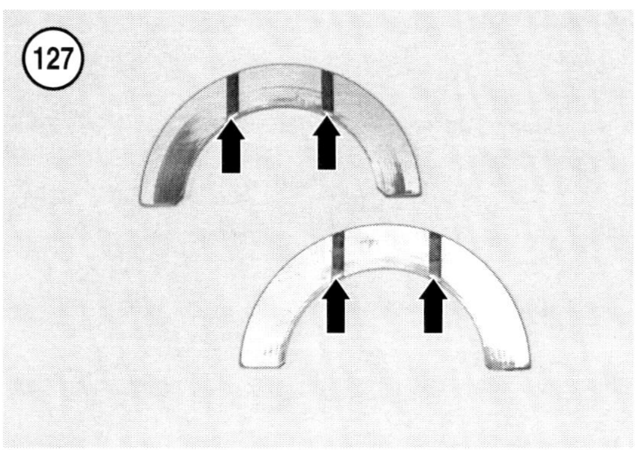

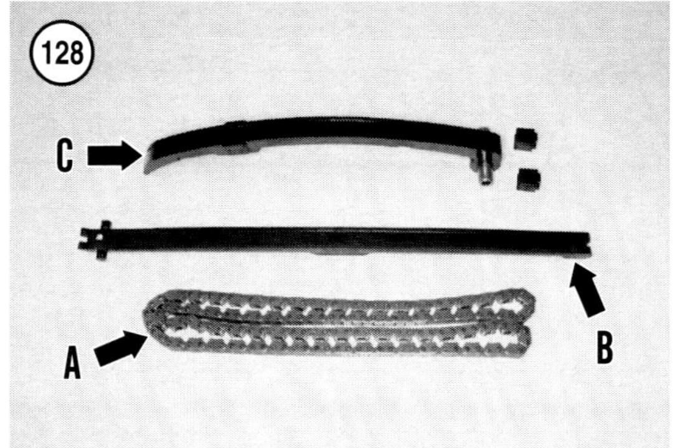

CAMSHAFT CHAIN AND GUIDES

A continuous camshaft drive chain is used on all models. Do not cut the chain; replacement link components are not available.

Removal/Installation

1. Remove the engine from the frame as described in this chapter.
2. Disassemble the crankcase as described in this chapter. Remove both chain guides.
3. Remove the camshaft chain from the crankshaft.
4. Install by reversing these removal steps.

Inspection

If the following procedures show that the cam chain is severely worn or damaged, the automatic chain tensioner may not be tensioning the chain properly; refer to *Camshaft Chain Tensioner Inspection* in Chapter Four. Likewise, the chain guides should be checked for excessive wear and damage.

1. Clean the camshaft chain in solvent and dry with compressed air.
2. Check the camshaft chain (A, **Figure 128**) for:
   a. Worn or damaged pins and rollers.
   b. Cracked or damaged side plates.
3. If the camshaft chain is severely worn or damaged, inspect both camshaft sprockets (**Figure 129**) and the crankshaft chain sprocket (A, **Figure 109**). If the camshaft sprockets show wear or damage, replace them. If the crankshaft chain sprocket is worn, replace the crankshaft.

CAUTION
Do not run a new chain over severely worn or damaged sprockets. Doing so may cause excessive chain wear after only a short service period.

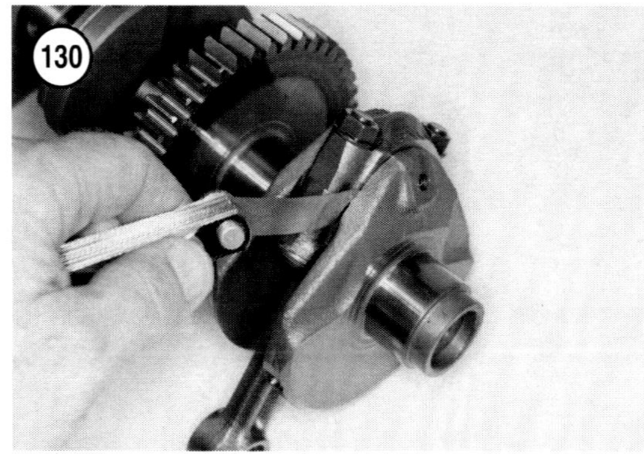

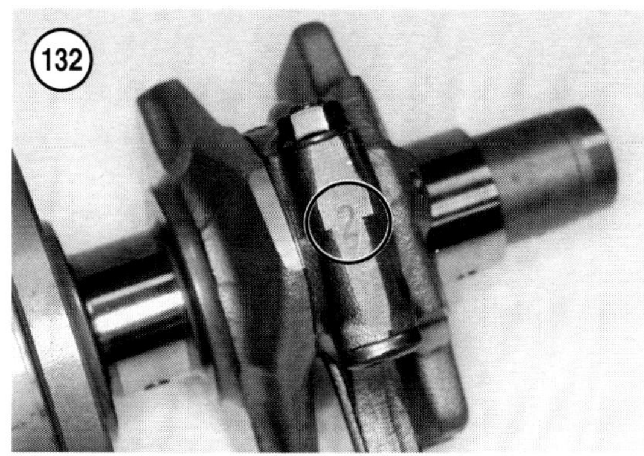

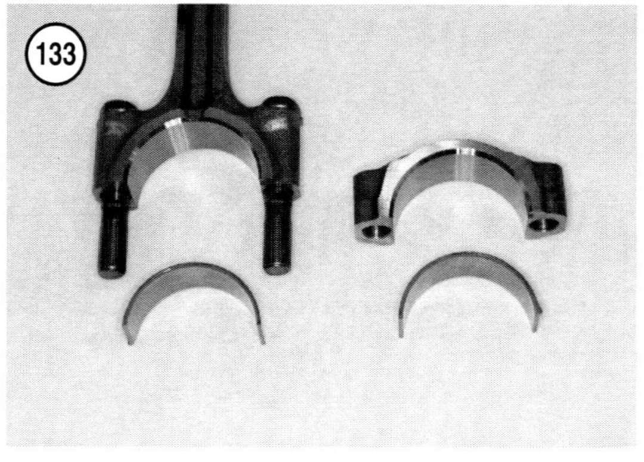

4. Inspect the camshaft chain guide No. 1 (B, **Figure 128**) and No. 3 (C) for wear or damage. Replace as a set even if only one is damaged.

CONNECTING RODS

Removal/Installation

1. Disassemble the crankcase as described in this chapter.
2. Lift the crankshaft/connecting rod assembly and camshaft chain (**Figure 103**) from the upper crankcase half.
3. With the connecting rods correctly attached to the crankshaft, measure the big end side clearance. Insert a flat feeler gauge between a connecting rod big end and either crankshaft machined web (**Figure 130**). Record the clearance for each connecting rod and compare the measurements to the specifications in **Table 1**. If the clearance exceeds the wear limit, inspect the connecting rod width and the crankshaft pin width as described in this chapter.

NOTE
Before disassembling the connecting rods, mark each rod and cap with the rod's cylinder number. Cylinders are numbered 1-4, counting left to right. Left refers to the engine as it sits in the frame, not as it sits on the workbench.

4. Remove the connecting rod cap nuts (**Figure 131**). Carefully tap on the end of the connecting rod studs with a plastic mallet to break the connecting rod loose from the cap and the crankshaft.
5. Separate the rods from the crankshaft. Keep each cap with its original rod so the code on the end of the cap mates with the mark on the rod (**Figure 132**).

NOTE
*Keep each bearing insert in its original location in the connecting rod or rod cap (**Figure 133**). If the bearing inserts are reused, they must be installed in their original locations to prevent rapid wear.*

6. Inspect the connecting rods and bearings as described in this chapter.
7. If new bearing inserts are going to be installed, check the bearing clearance as described in this chapter.

8. Apply a light even coat of molybdenum disulfide grease to the crankpin and to the connecting rod bearing inserts. Make sure the bearing inserts are locked into place (A, **Figure 134**).

9. Install the connecting rod onto the crankshaft with the weight mark facing toward the *rear* of the engine. Be careful not to damage the bearing surface of the crankpin with the threaded studs on the connecting rod.

10. Match the code on the end of the cap with the code on the connecting rod (**Figure 132**) and install the cap.

11. Apply a light coat of molybdenum disulfide grease to the threads of the connecting rod studs and install the cap nuts (**Figure 131**). Tighten both connecting rod cap nuts to 25 N•m (18 ft.-lb.), then to 50 N•m (37 ft.-lb.).

12. After the connecting rods are installed and the cap nuts tightened to the correct torque, rotate the connecting rod on the crankshaft several times and check that the bearings are not too tight. Make sure there is no binding.

Connecting Rod Inspection

CAUTION
Never try to remove the connecting rod studs. If loosened and re-tightened, the bearing cap will not fit properly.

Compare all measurements to the specifications in **Table 1**. Replace the connecting rod assembly if any part is damaged or out of specification.

1. Carefully inspect each crankpin (**Figure 135**) for scratches, ridges, scoring or nicks. Very small nicks and scratches may be removed with crocus cloth. Have more serious damage removed by a machine shop.

2. Check each connecting rod for obvious damage such as cracks and burns. Check the threads of the connecting rod studs (**Figure 136**) for thread damage or stretching.

3. Check the piston pin bushing for wear or scoring.

4. Measure the small end inner diameter with a small hole gauge (**Figure 137**), and measure the gauge with a micrometer.

5. Measure the piston pin outer diameter with a micrometer (**Figure 138**).

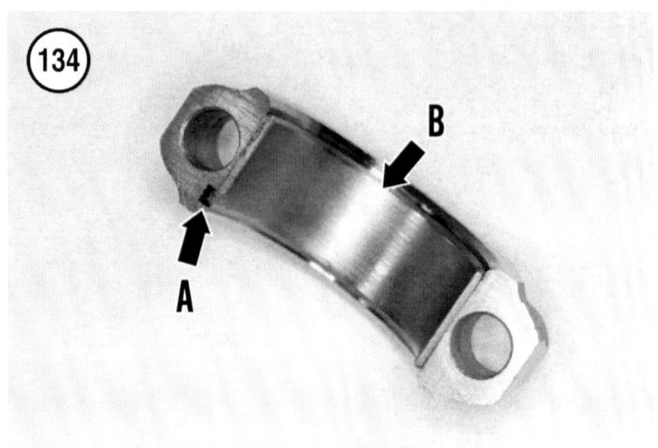

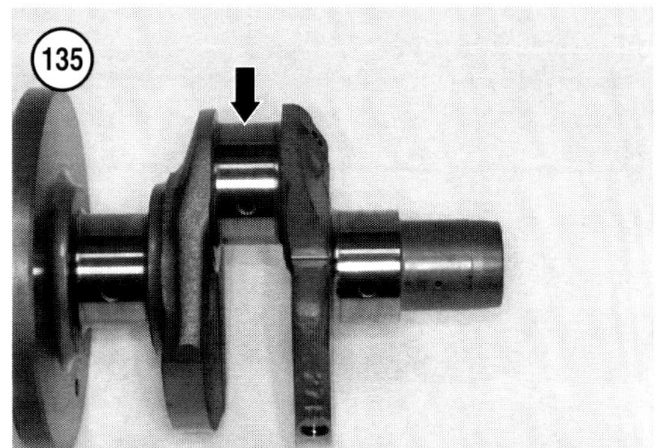

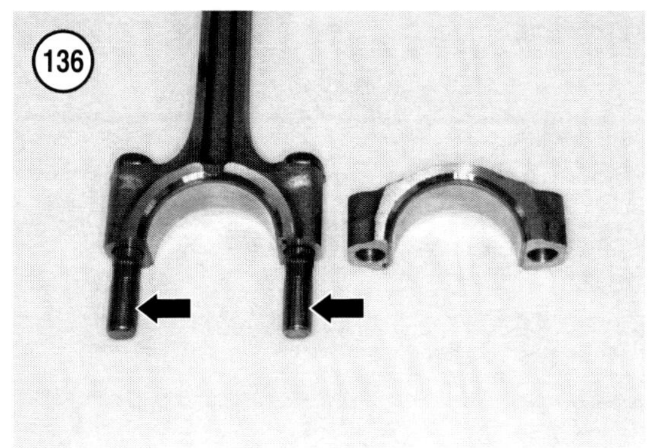

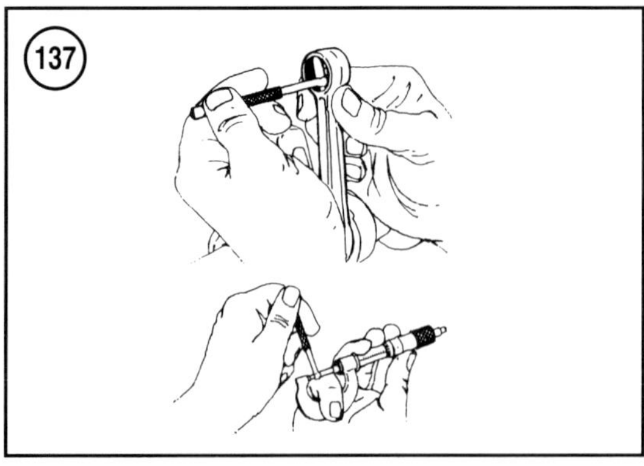

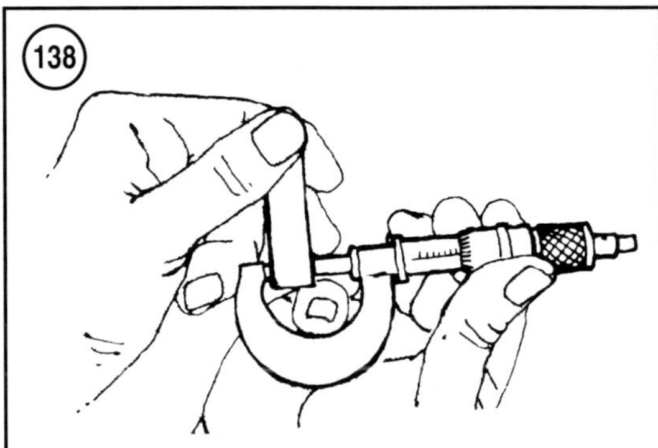

6. Take the connecting rods to a machine shop and check the alignment for twisting and bending.
7. Examine each bearing insert (B, **Figure 134**) for wear, scoring or burning. They are reusable if in good condition. If discarding an insert, make a note of the bearing color code on the side of the insert. A previous owner may have used undersize bearings.
8. Refer to the connecting rod big end clearances measured during removal. If the connecting rod big end clearance exceeds the service limit, perform the following:

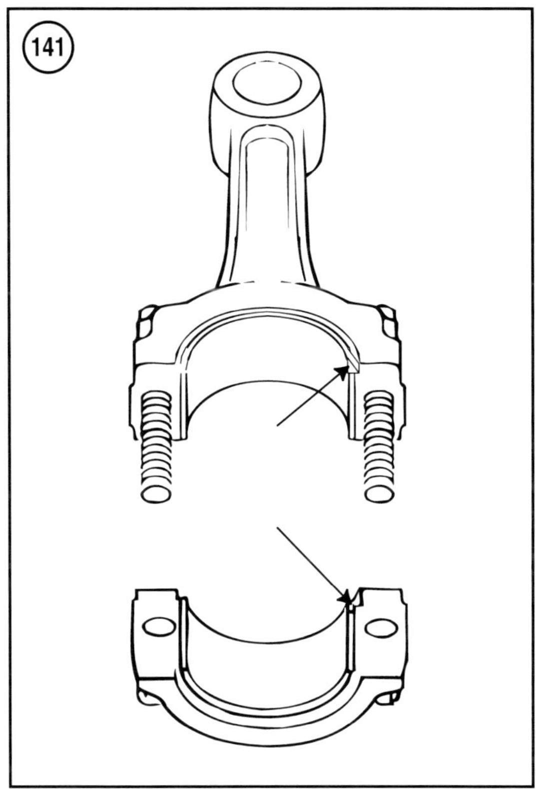

a. Measure the width of the connecting rod big end with a micrometer (**Figure 139**). If the width is less than specified, replace the connecting rod assembly.
b. Measure the crankpin width with a dial caliper (**Figure 140**). If the width is greater than specified, replace the crankshaft.

Connecting Rod Bearing Clearance Measurement

1. Check the bearing inserts (**Figure 133**) in each connecting rod for evidence of wear, abrasion and scoring. If the bearings are good, they may be reused. If any insert is questionable, replace both inserts in that connecting rod as a set.
2. Clean the bearing surfaces of the crankpin and the bearing inserts.
3. Install the bearing inserts in the connecting rod and bearing cap (**Figure 133**). Be sure the tab on the insert locks into the cutout in the cap or in the connecting rod (**Figure 141**). Carefully press each insert into place by hand. Make sure the inserts are locked into place correctly.

4. Install the connecting rod onto the crankshaft, being careful not to damage the bearing surface of the crankpin with the threaded studs.
5. Place a piece of Plastigage over the crankpin parallel to the crankshaft (**Figure 142**). Do not place the Plastigage material over an oil hole in the crankshaft.

CAUTION
Do not rotate the crankshaft while the Plastigage is in place.

6. Match the mark on the end of the cap with the mark on the rod (**Figure 132**) and install the cap.
7. Apply a light coat of molybdenum disulfide grease to threads of the connecting rod studs, and install the cap nuts. Tighten both cap nuts to 25 N•m (18 ft.-lb.) and then to 50 N•m (37 ft.-lb.).
8. Loosen the cap nuts and carefully remove the cap from the connecting rod.
9. Measure the width of the flattened Plastigage according to manufacturer's instructions. Measure at both ends of the Plastigage strip (**Figure 143**) and record the widest measurement.
10. If the connecting rod bearing clearance exceeds the wear limit, select *new* bearings as described in this chapter.
11. Remove the Plastigage strips from the main bearing journals.

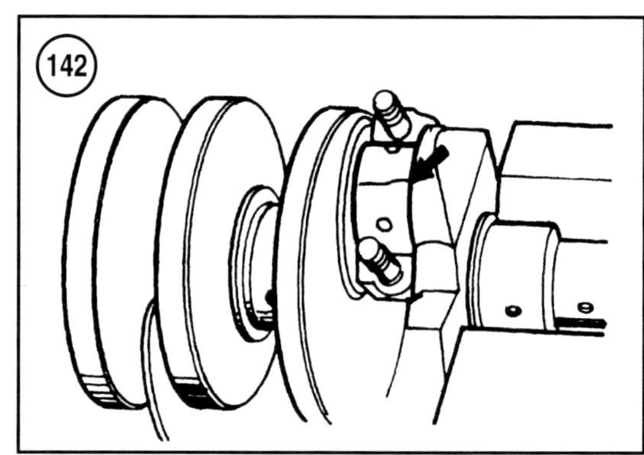

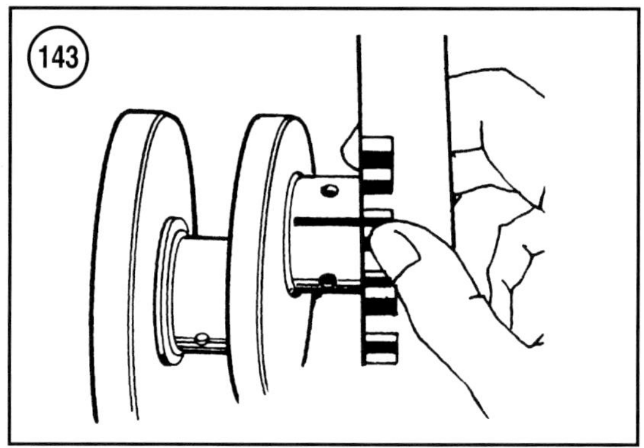

Connecting Rod Bearing Selection

1. A series of code numbers stamped onto the crankshaft web indicate the outside diameter of the crankpins. Refer to **Figure 144** to determine the outside diameter code number for each particular crankpin.
2. The connecting rod code (1 or 2) marked on the side of each connecting rod and cap (**Figure 132**) indicates the inside diameter of the connecting rod.
3. Bearing inserts are identified by color codes (**Figure 145**). Refer to **Table 6** and select a new set of bearing inserts by cross-referencing the connecting rod inner diameter code with the crankpin outer diameter code. **Table 7** lists the bearing insert color, thickness specification and the part number. Always replace bearing inserts as a set.
4. After new bearing inserts have been installed, recheck the clearance by repeating the procedure described in this chapter. If the clearance is still out of specification, either the connecting rod or the crankshaft is worn beyond the service limit and requires replacement.

BREAK-IN

Following cylinder servicing (boring, honing or new rings) and major lower end work, the engine should be broken in just as though it were *new*. The performance and service life of the engine greatly depend upon careful and sensible break-in, particularly during the first 800 km (500 miles) of operation.

For the first 800 km (500 miles) of operation, engine speed should be kept below 6000 rpm. Avoid prolonged, steady running at one engine speed, no matter how moderate, and avoid hard acceleration.

During the period of 800-1600 km (500-1000 miles) of service, engine speed should be kept below 9000 rpm. Again, hard acceleration, as well as prolonged, steady running at one engine speed should be avoided.

144

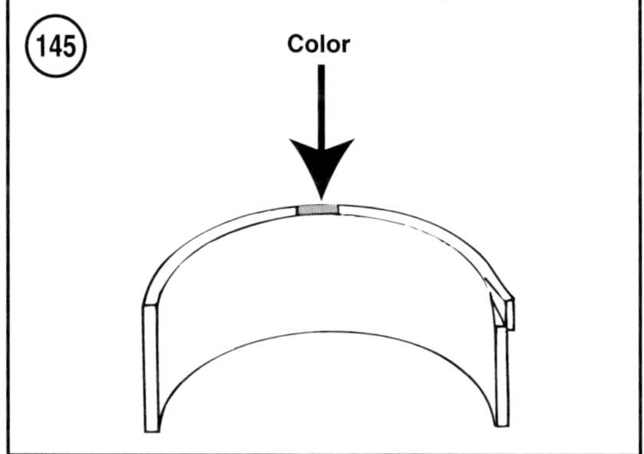

After 1600 km (1000 miles) of operation, the engine can be operated at full throttle, but engine speed should be kept below 12,000 rpm.

During break-in, always take the time to warm up a cold engine before revving the engine or shifting the transmission into gear. This gives the lubrication system time to circulate oil throughout the engine.

At no time, either during or after break-in, should the oil level be allowed to drop below the low level line on the oil inspection window. The oil will become overheated, resulting in insufficient lubrication and increased wear.

1000 km (600 Mile) Service

It is essential that the oil and filter be changed after the first 1000 km (600 miles). In addition, it is a good idea to change the oil and filter at the completion of break-in (about 1600 km/1000 miles) to ensure that all of the particles produced during break-in are removed from the lubrication system. The small added expense may be considered a smart investment that will pay off in increased engine life.

Table 1 LOWER END SPECIFICATIONS

Item	Standard mm (in.)	Wear limit mm (in.)
Connecting rod		
Small end inside diameter	20.010-20.018 (0.7878-0.7881)	20.040 (0.7890)
Big end side clearance	0.10-0.20 (0.004-0.008)	0.30 (0.012)
Big end width	20.95-21.00 (0.825-0.827)	
Connecting rod bearing clearance	0.032-0.056 (0.0013-0.0022)	0.080 (0.0031)
Connecting rod inside diameter		
Code 1	41.000-41.008 (1.6142-1.6145)	
Code 2	41.008-41.016 (1.6145-1.6148)	
Crankshaft		
Crankpin width	21.10-21.15 (0.831-0.833)	–
Crankpin standard outside diameter	37.976-38.000 (1.4951-1.4961)	–

(continued)

Table 1 LOWER END SPECIFICATIONS (continued)

Item	Standard mm (in.)	Wear limit mm (in.)
Crankshaft (continued)		
Crankpin outside diameter		
Code 1	37.992-38.000 mm (1.4957-1.4961 in.)	–
Code 2	37.984-37.992 mm (1.4954-1.4957 in.)	–
Code 3	37.976-37.984 mm (1.4951-1.4954 in.)	–
Crankshaft main bearing clearance	0.020-0.044 ((0.0008-0.0017)	0.080 (0.0031)
Crankshaft journal standard outside diameter	35.976-36.000 (1.4164-1.4173)	–
Code A	35.992-36.000 mm (1.4170-1.4173 in.)	–
Code B	35.984-35.992 mm (1.4167-1.4170 in.)	–
Code C	35.976-35.984 mm (1.4164-1.4167 in.)	–
Crankshaft runout	–	0.05 (0.002)
Crankshaft thrust clearance	0.04-0.08 mm (0.002-0.003 in.)	–
Crankshaft thrust bearing thickness		
Left side	2.36-2.52 mm (0.093-0.099 in.)	–
Right side	2.42-2.44 mm (0.095-0.096 in.)	–
Oil pressure (hot)	300-600 kPa (43-87 psi) @ 3000 rpm	

Table 2 LOWER END TORQUE SPECIFICATIONS

Item	N•m	in.-lb.	ft.-lb.
Connecting rod cap bolt			
Initial	25	–	18
Final	50	–	37
Crankcase bolt and nut			
6 mm			–
Initial	6	53	–
Final	13	115	–
8 mm			
Initial	13	115	–
Final	22	–	16
Crankcase studs	16	–	12
Engine drive sprocket nut	115	–	85
Engine mounting hardware			
Front sub-frame			
Front bolts and nuts	50	–	37
Front side bolts and nuts	23	–	17
Rear side bolt and nut	55	–	41
Left side mounting bracket			
Front side bolts	23	–	17
Rear side bolt	55	–	41
Right side sub-frame bolts and nuts	50	–	37
Main bearing bolts (8 mm)			
Initial	13	115	–
Final	22	–	16
Main oil gallery plug	40	–	29
Oil cooler banjo bolt	28	–	21
Oil cooler hose mounting bolts	10	88	–
Oil cooler mounting bolt	10	88	–

(continued)

Table 2 LOWER END TORQUE SPECIFICATIONS (continued)

Item	N•m	in.-lb.	ft.-lb.
Oil drain plug	23	–	17
Oil pan bolts	14	–	10
Oil pressure regulator	28	–	21
Oil pressure switch	14	–	10
Oil pump mounting bolt	14	–	10
Signal generator rotor bolts	25	–	18
Speed sensor rotor bolt	13	115	–
Starter clutch mounting bolt	150	–	111

Table 3 CRANKSHAFT MAIN BEARING INSERT SELECTION

Crankshaft main bearing journal code	A	B	C
Crankcase main bearing boss code			
A	Green	Black	Brown
B	Black	Brown	Yellow

Table 4 CRANKSHAFT INSERT COLOR, THICKNESS AND PART NO.

Color	Specification mm (in.)	Part No.
Green	1.480-1.484 (0.0583-0.0584)	12164-46E01-0A0
Black	1.484-1.488 (0.0584-0.0586)	12164-46E01-0B0
Brown	1.488-1.492 (0.0586-0.0587)	12164-46E01-0C0
Yellow	1.492-1.496 (0.0587-0.0589)	12164-46E01-0D0

Table 5 THRUST BEARING SELECTION

Clearance before inserting left thrust bearing mm (in.)	Color	Part No.	Thrust bearing thickness mm (in.)
2.42-2.44 (0.0953-0.0961)	Black	12228-48BOO-OHO	2.36-2.38[1] (0.0929-0.0937)
2.44-2.46 (0.0961-0.0969)	Orange	12228-48BOO-OGO	2.38-2.340[1] (0.0937-0.0945)
2.46-2.48 (0.0969-0.0976)	Blue	12228-48BOO-OFO	2.40-2.42[1] (0.0945-0.0953)
2.48-2.50 (0.0976-0.0984)	Green	12228-48BOO-OEO	2.42-2.44[1] (0.0953-0.0961
2.50-2.52 (0.0984-0.0992)	Yellow	12228-48BOO-ODO	2.44-2.46[1] (0.0961-0.0969)
2.52-2.54 (0.0992-0.1000)	Red	12228-48BOO-OCO	2.46-2.48[1] (0.0969-0.0976)
2.54-2.56 (0.1000-0.1008)	Brown	12228-48BOO-OBO	2.48-2.50[1] (0.0976-0.0984)
2.56-2.57 (0.1008-0.1012)	Pink	12228-48BOO-OAO	2.50-2.52[2] (0.0984-0.0992)

1. Thrust clearance = 0.04-0.08 mm (0.0016-0.0031 in.)
2. Thrust clearance = 0.04-0.07 mm (0.0016-0.0027 in.)

Table 6 CONNECTING ROD BEARING INSERT SELECTION

Crankpin outer diameter code	1	2	3
Connecting rod inner diameter code			
1	Green	Black	Brown
2	Black	Brown	Yellow

Table 7 CONNECTING ROD INSERT COLOR, THICKNESS AND PART NO.

Year/color	Specification	Part No.
Green	1.480-1.484 (0.0583-0.0584)	12164-46E01-0A0
Black	1.484-1.488 (0.0584-0.0586)	12164-46E01-0B0
Brown	1.488-1.492 (0.0586-0.0587)	12164-46E01-0C0
Yellow	1.492-1.496 (0.0587-0.0589)	12164-46E01-0D0

6

CHAPTER SIX

CLUTCH

This chapter provides complete service procedures for the clutch and clutch hydraulic release mechanism. When inspecting clutch components, compare any measurements to the clutch specifications in **Table 1**. Replace components that are damaged, worn to the wear limit or out of specification. **Table 1** and **Table 2** are located at the end of this chapter.

The clutch is a wet, multi-plate type that operates immersed in the engine oil. It is mounted on the right end of the transmission mainshaft. The inner clutch hub is splined to the mainshaft. The clutch outer housing rotates freely on the mainshaft and the housing is geared to the crankshaft. The two clutch pushrods sit inside a channel in the transmission mainshaft.

The clutch is activated by hydraulic pressure and is controlled by the clutch master cylinder, located on the left side handlebar. The hydraulic pressure generated by the master cylinder activates the clutch release cylinder, which in turn pushes the clutch push rods against the push piece. This moves the pressure plate that disengages the clutch. The clutch requires no routing adjustment.

CLUTCH

Removal/Disassembly

CAUTION

A Suzuki special tool, the clutch pressure plate holder (part No. 09920-34820 for 1996-2000 models, part No. 09920-34840 for 2001-on models), is required to hold the pressure plate while loosening and tightening the clutch nut. This tool is shown in this procedure. Do not try to loosen the clutch nut without the special tool, as the pressure plate will be damaged.

Refer to **Figure 1**.

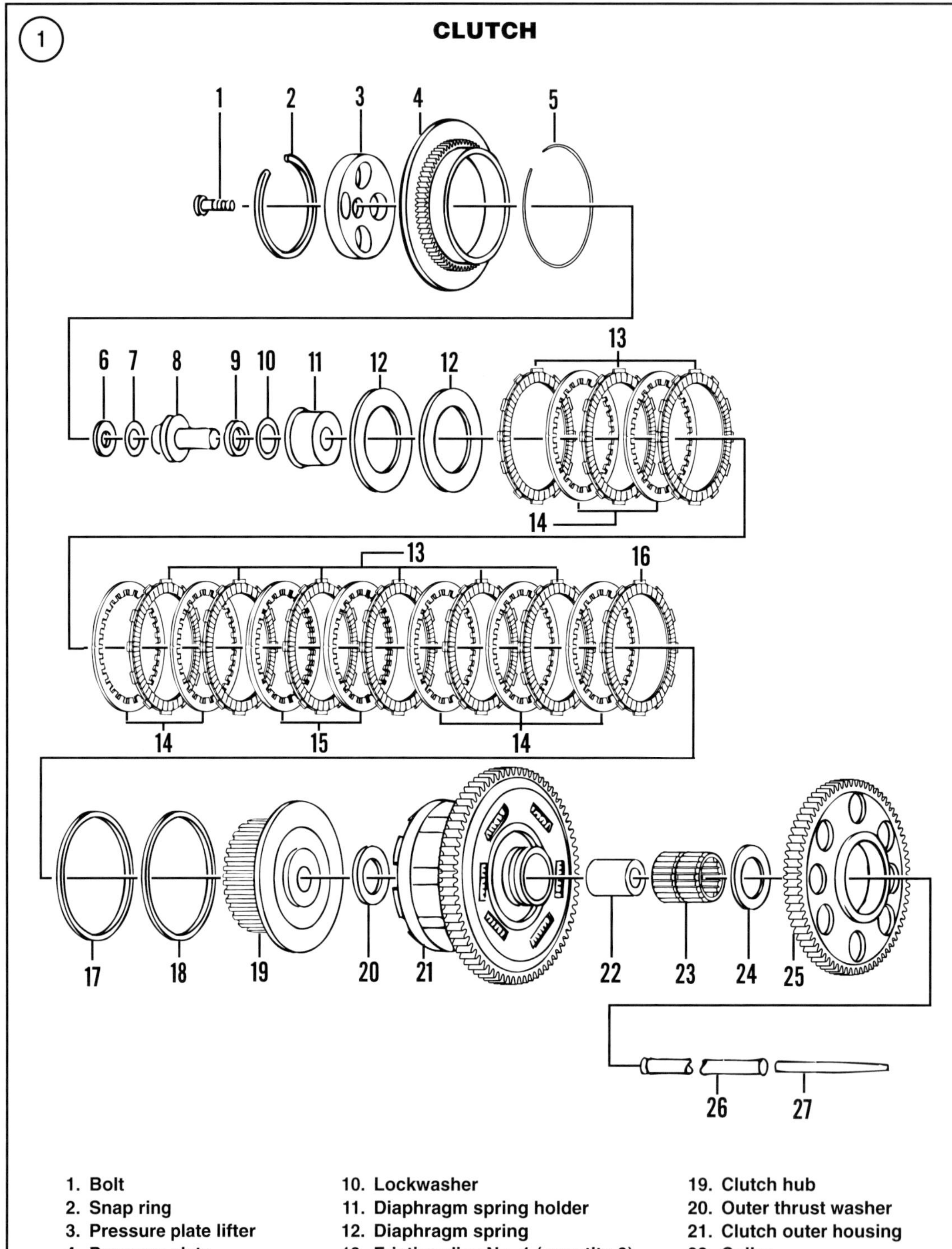

1. Bolt
2. Snap ring
3. Pressure plate lifter
4. Pressure plate
5. Diaphragm spring seat
6. Thrust washer
7. Thrust bearing
8. Push piece
9. Clutch sleeve nut
10. Lockwasher
11. Diaphragm spring holder
12. Diaphragm spring
13. Friction disc No. 1 (quantity 9)
14. Clutch plate No. 1 (quantity 7)
15. Clutch plate No. 2 (quantity 2)
16. Friction disc No. 2 (quantity 1)
17. Clutch plate washer
18. Clutch plate seat
19. Clutch hub
20. Outer thrust washer
21. Clutch outer housing
22. Collar
23. Needle bearing
24. Inner thrust washer
25. Oil pump drive gear
26. Pushrod—right side
27. Pushrod—left side

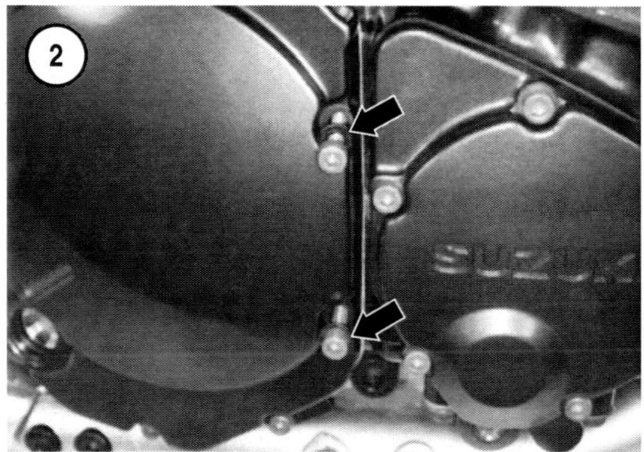

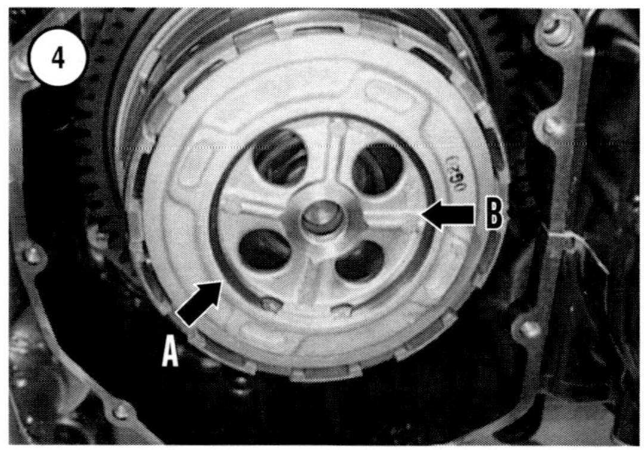

1. Place the motorcycle on level ground on the centerstand.
2. Drain the engine oil as described in Chapter Three.

NOTE
This procedure is shown with the exhaust system removed to better illustrate the steps. It is not necessary to remove the system.

3. Shift the transmission into gear.

NOTE
Mark with a permanent pen the location of the two sealing washers under the bolts ***(Figure 2)*** *securing the clutch cover. During assembly these sealing washers must be reinstalled under both bolts to prevent an oil leak.*

4. Remove the bolts securing the clutch cover (**Figure 3**). Remove the clutch cover and gasket. Do not lose the two locating dowels.
5. Remove the large snap ring (A, **Figure 4**) securing the pressure plate lifter.
6. Remove the pressure plate lifter (B, **Figure 4**).
7. Remove the thrust washer, bearing and clutch push piece (**Figure 5**) from the end of the transmission shaft.
8. Withdraw the right side clutch push rod (**Figure 6**). If necessary, use a magnetic tool and remove the push rod.
9. Install a clutch holding tool (A, **Figure 7**) onto the pressure plate and loosen the clutch nut (B). Remove the tool and the nut and lockwasher.

CAUTION
To avoid rounding off the small Phillips screw head, use the correct size

7

8

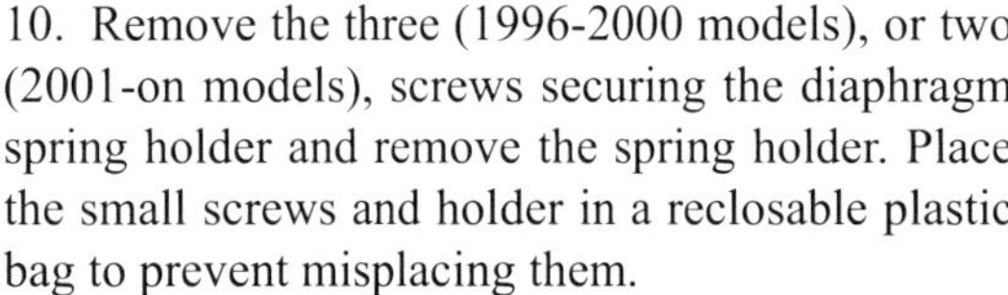
Phillips screw bit and an impact driver. Do not try to loosen the screws with a Phillips screwdriver. If necessary, apply a small amount of valve grinding compound to the Phillips screw bit to help secure the bit within the screw head slots.

10. Remove the three (1996-2000 models), or two (2001-on models), screws securing the diaphragm spring holder and remove the spring holder. Place the small screws and holder in a reclosable plastic bag to prevent misplacing them.
11. Remove the two diaphragm springs (**Figure 8**).
12. Remove the diaphragm spring seat (**Figure 9**) and the pressure plate (**Figure 10**).
13. Install two small bolts into the center of the clutch hub.
14. Pull on the two bolts and withdraw the clutch hub, friction discs and clutch plates as an assembly (**Figure 11**).
15. Remove the thrust washer (**Figure 12**) from the transmission shaft.
16. Pull the clutch outer housing part way out (A, **Figure 13**) and withdraw the collar and needle bearing from the transmission mainshaft.
17. Remove the collar (B, **Figure 13**) and needle bearing (C) from within the clutch outer housing and transmission shaft.
18. Carefully remove the clutch outer housing along with the oil pump drive gear from the transmission shaft. Do not drop the oil pump driven gear (**Figure 14**) that is located on the backside of the outer housing.
19. Remove the inner washer (**Figure 15**) from the transmission shaft.
20. Remove the friction discs, clutch plates and the clutch plate washer and clutch plate seat from the clutch hub. Keep all parts in order of removal.

9

10

11

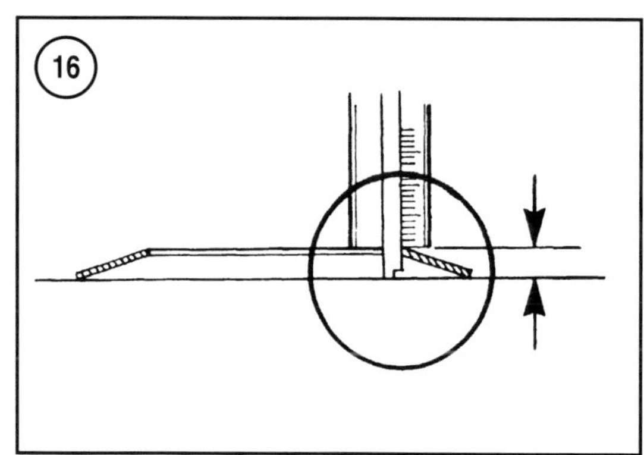

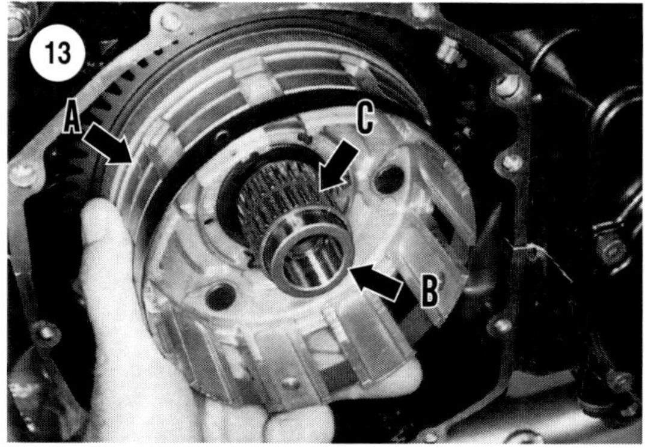

21. Inspect all components as described in this chapter.

Inspection

Compare all measurements to the specifications in **Table 1**. Replace any part that is damaged, worn to the wear limit or out of specification.

1. Clean all clutch parts in petroleum-based solvent such as kerosene and thoroughly dry with compressed air.
2. Check both diaphragm springs for wear or distortion. Measure the free height of each diaphragm spring with a vernier caliper as shown in **Figure 16**.
3. Check the diaphragm spring holder for wear or damage.

NOTE

The thickness of all friction discs is identical.

4. Measure the thickness of each friction disc at several places around the disc as shown in **Figure 17**.
5. Check the bonded material on the friction disc for uneven wear, cracks and other damage.

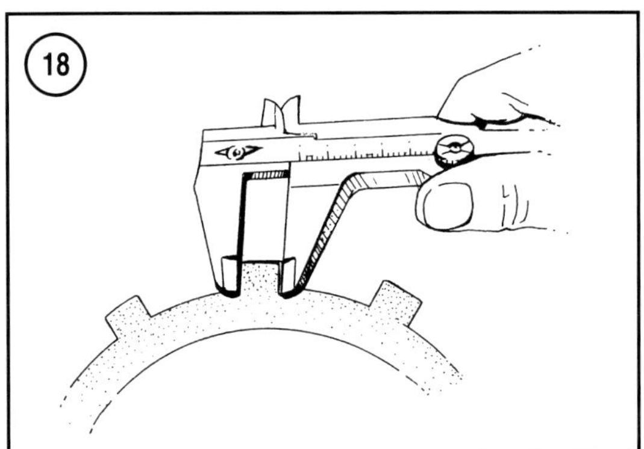

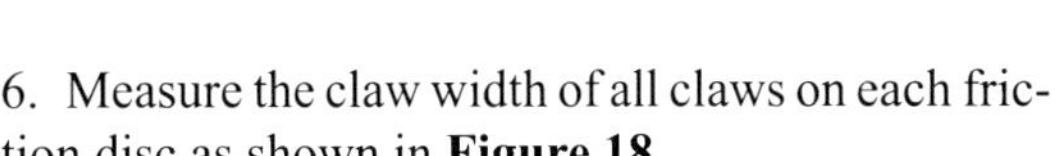

6. Measure the claw width of all claws on each friction disc as shown in **Figure 18**.
7. Check the clutch plates for surface damage from heat or lack of oil. Replace any plate that is damaged.
8. Check the clutch plates for warp with a flat feeler gauge on a surface plate, such as a piece of plate glass (**Figure 19**).

NOTE

If any of the friction discs and clutch plates require replacement, replace all of them as a set to retain maximum clutch performance.

9. Inspect the clutch outer housing slots (A, **Figure 20**) for cracks, nicks or galling where they come in contact with the friction disc tabs. If any severe damage is evident, the housing must be replaced.
10. Inspect the driven gear teeth (A, **Figure 21**) on the clutch outer housing for damage. Remove any small nicks with an oilstone. If damage is severe, the clutch outer housing must be replaced.
11. Inspect the damper springs. If they are sagged, cracked or broken the housing must be replaced.
12. Check the clutch outer housing inner surface (B, **Figure 21**), where the needle bearing rides, for signs of wear or damage. Replace the clutch outer housing if necessary.
13. Inspect the oil pump drive gear teeth (**Figure 14**) for damage. Remove any small nicks with an oilstone.
14. Inspect the outer grooves (B, **Figure 20**) in the clutch hub. If either show signs of wear or galling, replace the clutch hub.
15. Check the splines (**Figure 22**) in the clutch hub for wear or damage. Remove any small nicks with an oilstone.
16. Check the needle bearing (A, **Figure 23**). The bearing must turn smoothly. Replace if necessary.

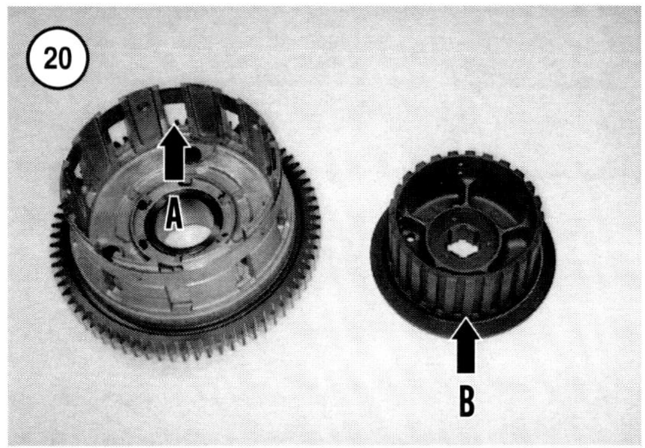

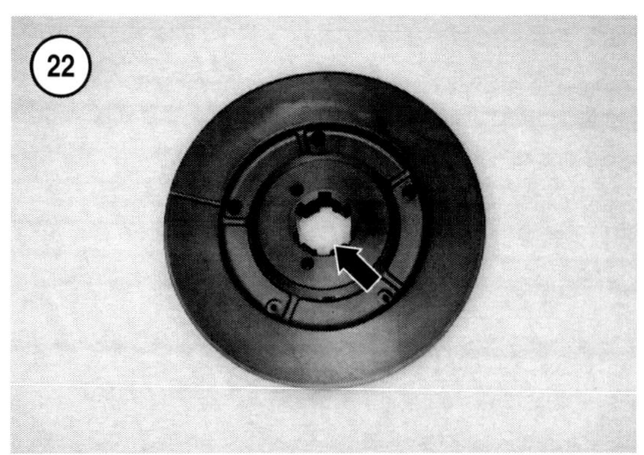

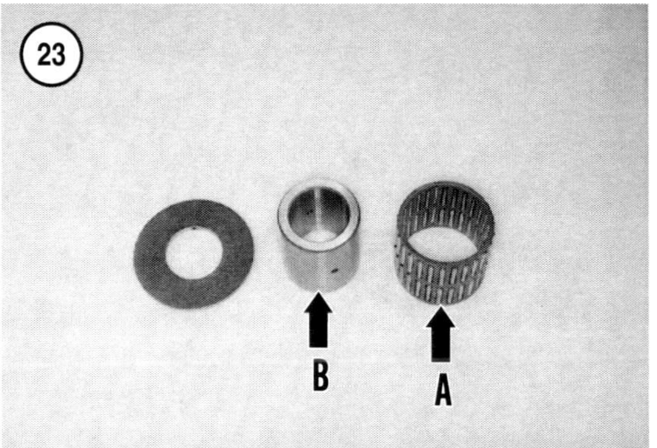

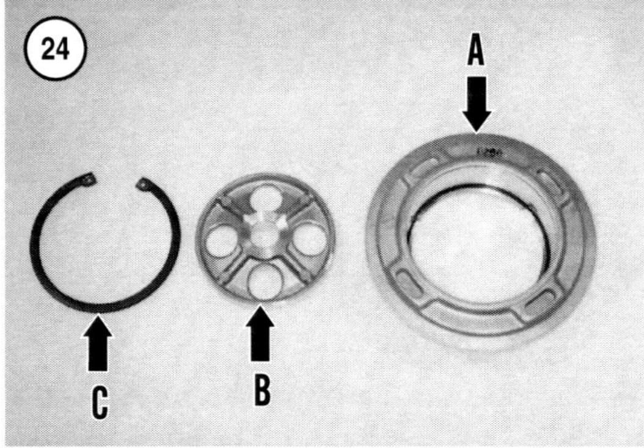

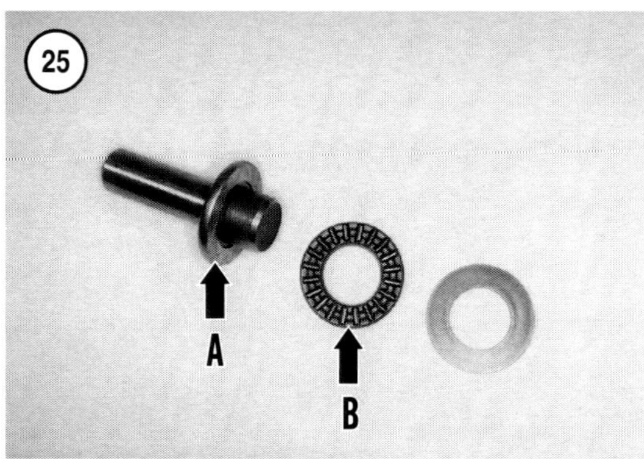

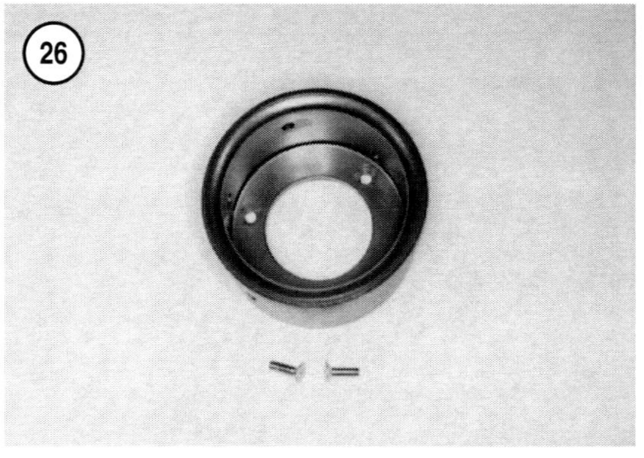

17. Check the inner and outer surfaces of the collar (B, **Figure 23**) for signs of wear or damage. Replace if necessary.
18. Install the collar into the needle bearing. Rotate the spacer and check for wear. Replace either part if necessary.
19. Inspect the pressure plate (A, **Figure 24**) and pressure plate lifter (B) for wear or damage.
20. Check the pressure plate snap ring (C, **Figure 24**) for distortion.
21. Check the clutch push piece (A, **Figure 25**) for wear or damage. Inspect the end that rides against the right-hand push rod. Replace if necessary.
22. Make sure the clutch push piece bearing (B, **Figure 25**) rotates smoothly. Replace if necessary.
23. Install the bearing and washer onto the push piece and rotate them by hand. Make sure all parts rotate smoothly. Replace any worn part.
24. Inspect the diaphragm spring holder (**Figure 26**) for wear or damage. Make sure the small screw holes are not elongated.
25. Check the clutch plate washer and seat for wear or distortion.
26. Inspect the clutch right side push rod and left side push rod for bending. Roll them on a surface plate or piece of plate glass. Suzuki does not provide service information for this component, but if the push rod(s) is bent or deformed in any way it must be replaced. Otherwise, it may hang up within the transmission shaft tunnel, causing erratic clutch operation.

Assembly/Installation

Refer to **Figure 1**.

1. Position the inner thrust washer with the bevel side (**Figure 27**) facing in and install the inner washer (**Figure 15**) onto the transmission shaft.

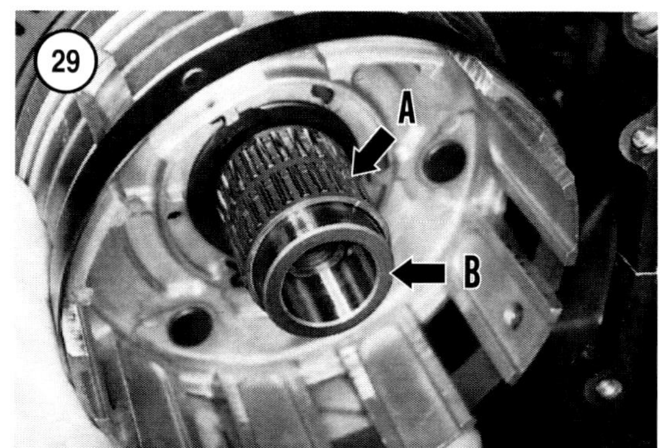

2. If removed, install the oil pump drive gear (**Figure 14**) into the backside of the clutch outer housing.

3. Install the outer housing onto the transmission shaft (**Figure 28**). If necessary, use a scribe or thin screwdriver and slightly rotate the oil pump driven gear back and forth to properly mesh with the outer housing driven gears. Push the outer housing on until it bottoms.

4. Apply clean engine oil to the needle bearing and install the needle bearing (A, **Figure 29**) into the outer housing. Push the needle bearing all the way into the outer housing.

5. Apply clean engine oil to both the inner and outer surfaces of the collar. Center the outer housing and needle bearing on the shaft. Install the collar (B, **Figure 29**) onto the transmission shaft and into the needle bearing. Push the collar on until it bottoms against the inner thrust washer.

6. Install the outer thrust washer (**Figure 30**) onto the transmission shaft.

NOTE

If new friction discs and clutch plates are being installed, apply new engine oil to all surfaces to avoid clutch lock up when the clutch is used for the first time.

7. Assemble the components onto the clutch hub as follows:

   a. Install the clutch plate seat (A, **Figure 31**).

   b. Position the clutch plate washer with the concave, or dished, side facing up and install the clutch plate washer (B, **Figure 31**). Push the clutch plate washer and clutch plate seat all the way on until they bottom.

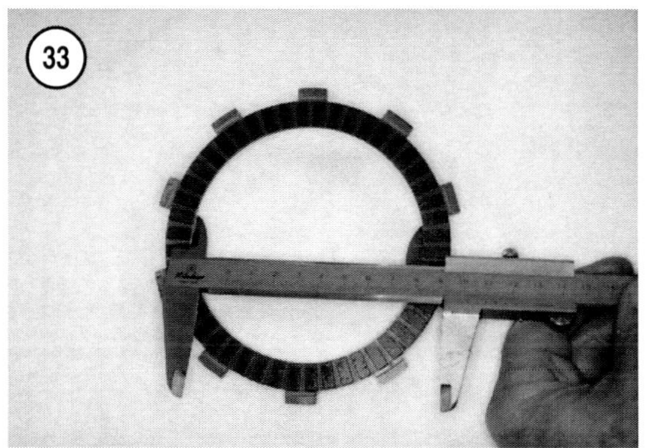

8. Install the clutch hub (**Figure 32**) onto the transmission shaft. Push it on until it stops.

NOTE
*The narrow friction disc has a larger inside diameter of 108 mm (4.3 in.) (**Figure 33**). All other friction discs have a smaller inside diameter of 101 mm (4.0 in.).*

9. Install the narrow inside friction disc No. 2 (larger inside diameter) onto the clutch hub. Seat it correctly next to the clutch plate washer and seat.

10. Onto the clutch hub, install a clutch plate No. 1, then a friction disc. Install three No. 1 clutch plates and three friction discs, alternating them until all are installed.

11. Next install a thick clutch plate No. 2, a friction disc, and then the other thick clutch plate No. 2.

12. Next install a friction disc and clutch plate, alternating them until all are installed. The last item installed is a friction disc (**Figure 34**).

13. Refer to **Figure 1** to ensure all friction discs and clutch plates are installed in the correct order.

14. Install the pressure plate (**Figure 35**) and push it in until it bottoms (**Figure 10**).

15. Install the diaphragm spring seat into the pressure plate (**Figure 9**). Push it in until it seats against the pressure plate flange (**Figure 36**).

16. Position the diaphragm springs (**Figure 37**) with the concave, or dished, side facing out and install the springs. Push the diaphragm springs all the way on until they bottom (**Figure 8**).

17. Install the diaphragm spring holder (**Figure 38**) and push it on until it stops. Align the screw holes,

38

40

39

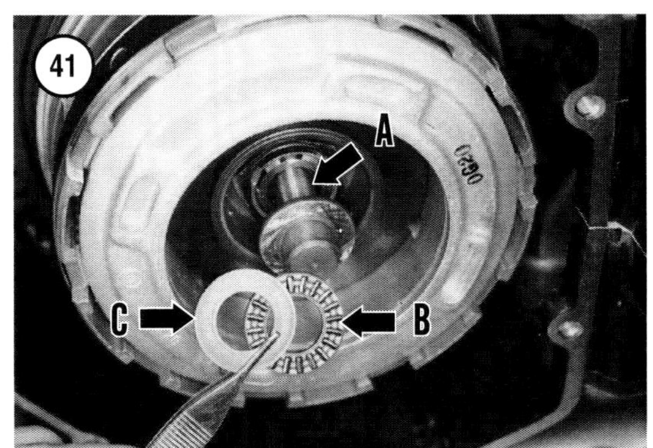

41

install the three (1996-2000 models), or two (2001-on models), screws and tighten securely.

18. Install the lockwasher (A, **Figure 39**) and *new* clutch hub nut (B).

19. Use the same special tool set-up (A, **Figure 7**) used in Step 9 of *Removal/Disassembly* to hold the clutch hub for the following step.

20. Tighten the clutch hub nut (B, **Figure 7**) to 150 N•m (111 ft.-lb.). Use a centerpunch and hammer and stake the clutch nut onto the transmission shaft (**Figure 40**).

21. Remove the special tool from the clutch hub.

22. Install the clutch right side pushrod (**Figure 6**) into the transmission shaft.

23. Install the clutch push piece (A, **Figure 41**), bearing (B) and thrust washer (C) onto the end of the transmission shaft. Push them in until they bottom (**Figure 42**).

24. Install the pressure plate lifter (**Figure 43**) and push it in until it bottoms in the pressure plate.

25. Position the large snap ring with the sharp edge (**Figure 44**) facing outside, away from the engine. Install the large snap ring and make sure it is correctly seated within the pressure plate lifter groove (**Figure 45**).

42

43

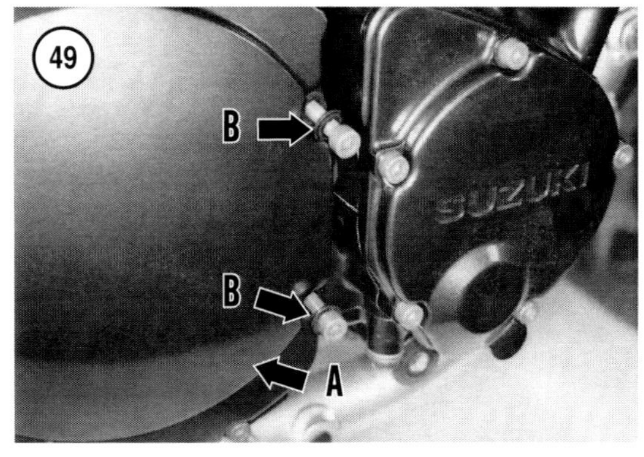

26. If removed, install the left side pushrod (**Figure 46**) into the transmission mainshaft.
27. Apply a light coat of Suzuki Bond No. 1207B, or equivalent sealant, to the mating surfaces of the upper and lower crankcase (**Figure 47**). This will reduce a possible oil leak.
28. Install the locating dowels (A, **Figure 48**) and a new gasket (B) onto the crankcase.
29. Install the clutch cover (A, **Figure 49**). Install the gasket washers (B) under the heads of the front two bolts.
30. Install the bolts securing the clutch cover and tighten securely.
31. Refill the engine oil as described in Chapter Three.

CLUTCH HYDRAULIC SYSTEM

The clutch is actuated by hydraulic fluid pressure and is controlled by the hand lever on the clutch master cylinder. As clutch components wear, the fluid level drops in the master cylinder and automatically adjusts for wear. There is no routine clutch adjustment necessary or possible.

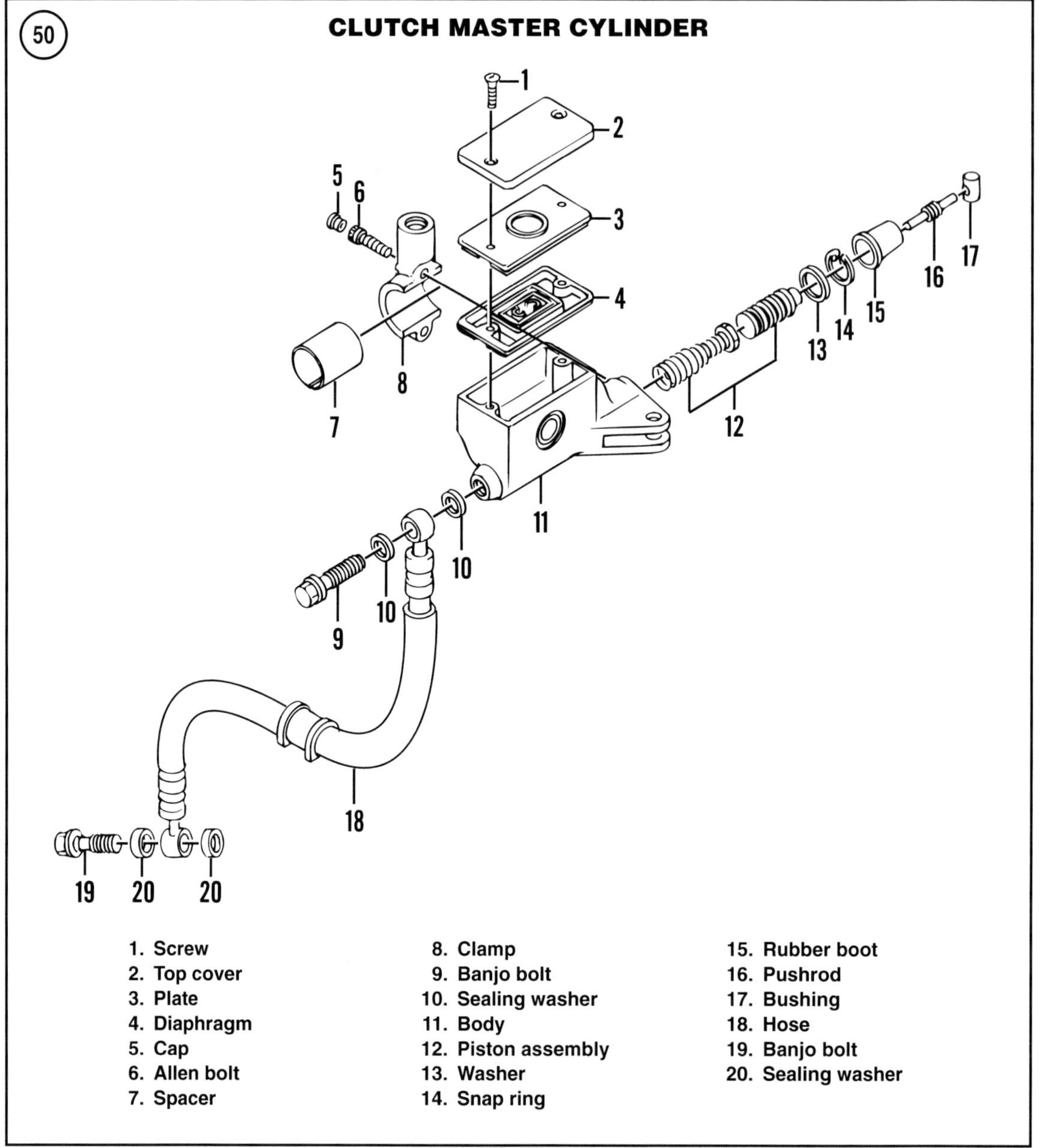

1. Screw
2. Top cover
3. Plate
4. Diaphragm
5. Cap
6. Allen bolt
7. Spacer
8. Clamp
9. Banjo bolt
10. Sealing washer
11. Body
12. Piston assembly
13. Washer
14. Snap ring
15. Rubber boot
16. Pushrod
17. Bushing
18. Hose
19. Banjo bolt
20. Sealing washer

When working on the clutch hydraulic system, the work area and all tools must be absolutely clean. Clutch master cylinder and release cylinder components can be damaged by even tiny particles of grit that enter the clutch system. Also, do not use sharp tools inside the master cylinder or release cylinder or on the pistons.

If there is any doubt about the ability to correctly and safely service the clutch components, refer the job to a Suzuki dealership or other qualified specialist.

CLUTCH MASTER CYLINDER

Removal

CAUTION

Cover the fuel tank and front fairing with a heavy cloth or plastic tarp to protect them from accidental brake fluid spills. Brake fluid will damage the finish on any plastic, painted or plated surface. Immediately wash any spilled brake fluid from the motorcy-

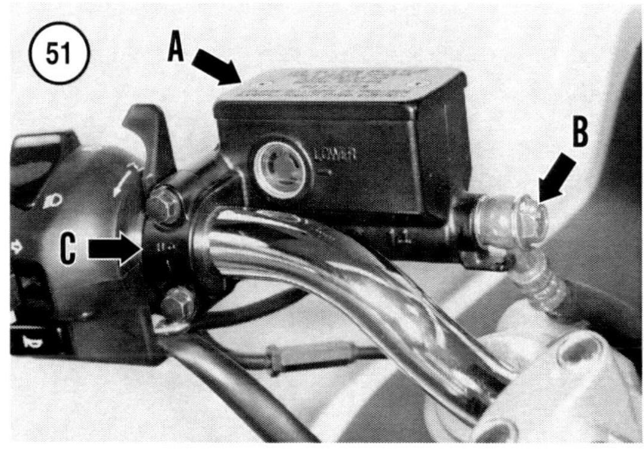

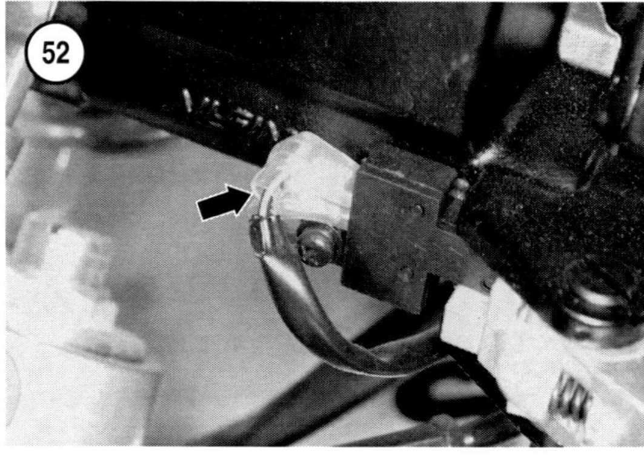

cle. Use soapy water, and rinse the area completely.

Refer to **Figure 50**.

1. Clean all debris from the top of the master cylinder.
2. On GSF1200 models, unscrew and remove the rear view mirror.
3. Remove the screws securing the top cover (A, **Figure 51**). Remove the top cover, plate and diaphragm from the master cylinder reservoir.
4. If a shop syringe is available, draw all of the brake fluid out of the master cylinder reservoir. Temporarily reinstall the diaphragm, plate and cover. Tighten the cover finger-tight.
5. Disconnect the clutch lever position switch electrical connectors from the switch (**Figure 52**).
6. Place a rag beneath the banjo bolt, (B, **Figure 51**) and remove the bolt. Separate the clutch hose from the master cylinder. Do not lose the two sealing washers, one from each side of the clutch hose fitting.
7. Place the loose end of the clutch hose in a reclosable plastic bag to prevent brake fluid from dribbling onto the motorcycle. Tie the loose end of the hose up to the handlebar.
8. Remove the master cylinder clamp bolts and the clamp (C, **Figure 51**).
9. Remove the clutch master cylinder from the handlebar.
10. Drain any residual brake fluid from the master cylinder and reservoir. Dispose of the fluid properly.
11. If the master cylinder is not going to be serviced, place it in a reclosable plastic bag to protect it from contamination.

Installation

1. Position the clutch master cylinder onto the left handlebar, and align the mating surface of the master cylinder with the handlebar punch mark.
2. Position the clamp (C, **Figure 51**) with the UP mark facing up, and install the master cylinder clamp bolts. Tighten the upper mounting bolt first, and then the lower bolt, leaving a gap at the bottom. Tighten the bolts to 10 N•m (88 in.-lb.).
3. Install the clutch hose onto the master cylinder. Install a *new* sealing washer onto each side of the hose fitting. Tighten the banjo bolt (B, **Figure 51**) to 23 N•m (17 ft.-lb.).
4. Reconnect the clutch lever position switch electrical connectors to the switch (**Figure 52**). Make sure the electrical connectors are corrosion-free and secure.
5. Refill the master cylinder and reservoir with fresh DOT 4 brake fluid and bleed the clutch system as described in this chapter.
6. On GSF1200 models, install the rear view mirror and tighten securely.

Disassembly

Refer to **Figure 50**.

1. Remove the clutch master cylinder assembly as described in this chapter.
2. Remove the mounting screw and the clutch lever position switch (**Figure 53**) from the master cylinder assembly.
3. Remove the nut and pivot bolt securing the hand lever to the master cylinder body. Remove the hand lever. Do not lose the bushing (**Figure 54**) on the end of the pushrod.

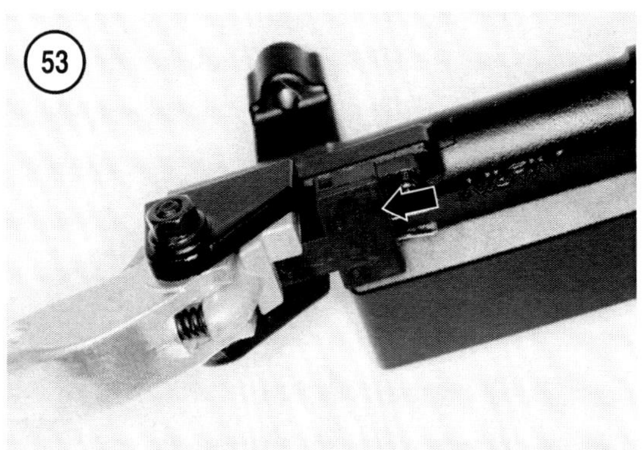

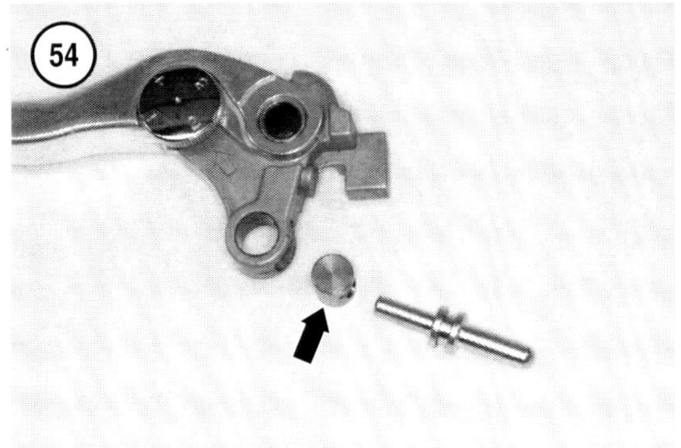

4. Remove the pushrod and rubber boot (**Figure 55**) from the cylinder bore on the master cylinder.

NOTE
*To aid in the removal and installation of the snap ring, thread a bolt and nut into the banjo bolt fitting on the master cylinder. Tighten the nut, then secure the bolt in a vise (**Figure 56**).*

5. Press the piston into the cylinder bore and use snap ring pliers to remove the internal snap ring from the bore.

6. Remove the washer and piston assembly (**Figure 57**) and the spring from the cylinder bore.

7. Inspect the components as described in this chapter.

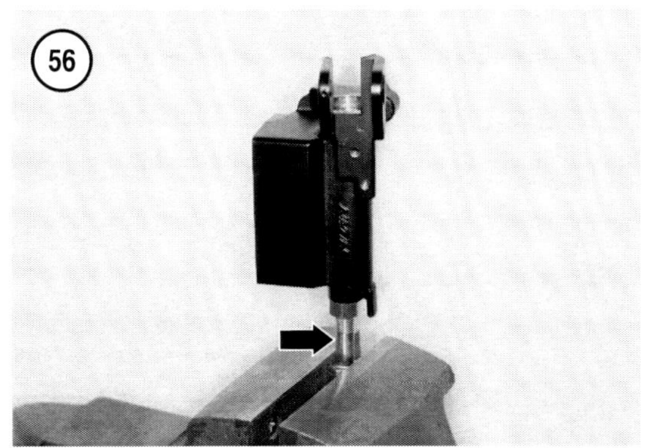

Assembly

Refer to **Figure 50**.

1. Soak the new cups and the new piston assembly in fresh DOT 4 brake fluid for at least 15 minutes to make them pliable. Coat the inside of the cylinder bore with fresh brake fluid prior to the assembly of parts.

2. If removed, install the primary cup onto the spring and install the secondary cup onto the piston (A, **Figure 58**). Position the spring (B, **Figure 58**) with its tapered end facing the piston.

CAUTION
When installing the piston assembly, do not allow the cups to turn inside out. They will be damaged and allow brake fluid leakage within the cylinder bore.

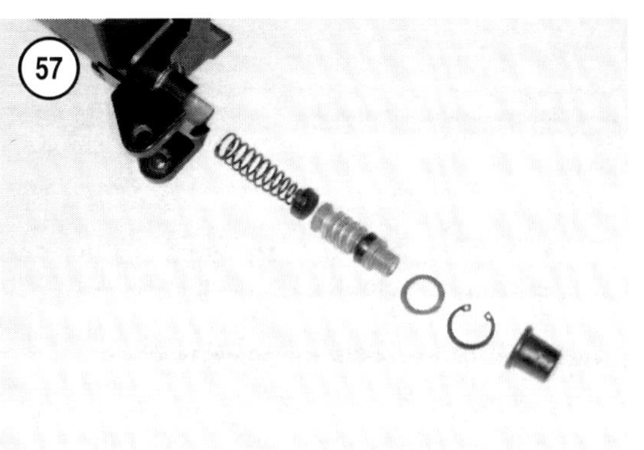

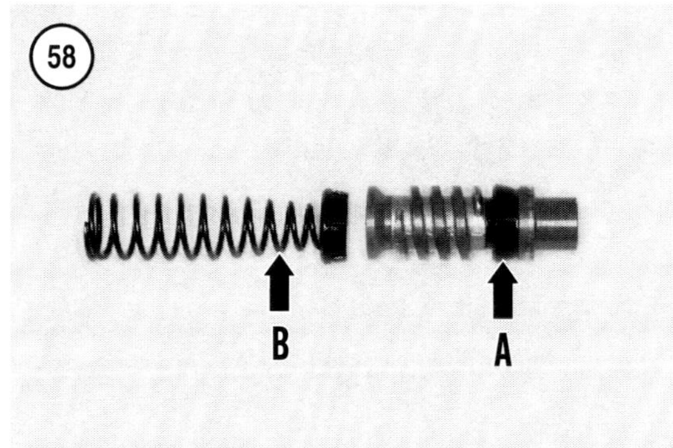

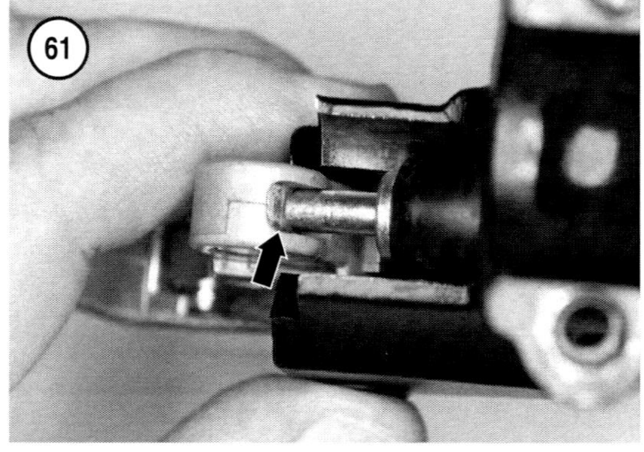

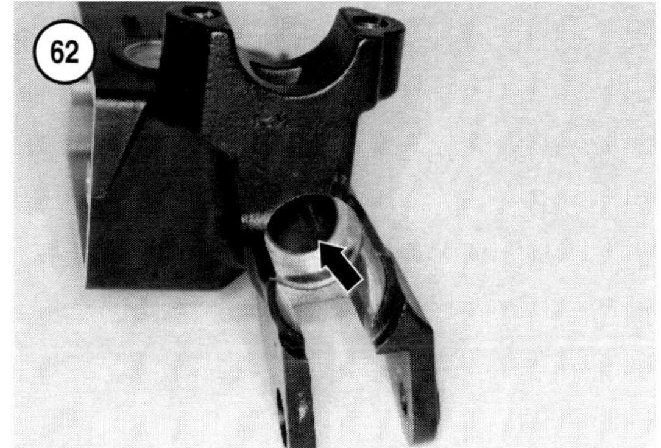

3. Install the spring and piston assembly (**Figure 57**). Push them into the cylinder until they bottom in the bore.

4. Press the piston assembly into the cylinder and install the snap ring. Make sure it is correctly seated in the groove.

5. Position the pushrod with the larger outer diameter end (**Figure 59**) going into the rubber boot. Install the pushrod into the rubber boot (**Figure 60**).

6. Install the pushrod and the rubber boot (**Figure 55**) into place in the cylinder bore.

7. Install the bushing (**Figure 54**) into the clutch lever.

8. Install the hand lever onto the master cylinder. Guide the pushrod into the hole in the bushing (**Figure 61**).

9. Align the bolt holes and install the pivot bolt and nut. Tighten the bolt and nut securely. Make sure the hand lever operates freely within the master cylinder with no binding.

10. Align the projection on the switch with the hole in the master cylinder and install the switch. Tighten the screw securely.

11. Operate the clutch lever and make sure the switch plunger moves in and out with no binding.

12. Install the clutch master cylinder as described in this chapter.

Inspection

Compare all measurements to the specifications in **Table 1**. Replace any part that is damaged or out of specification.

1. Clean all parts in isopropyl alcohol or fresh DOT 4 brake fluid. Inspect the cylinder bore surface (**Figure 62**) for signs of wear or damage. If less than per-

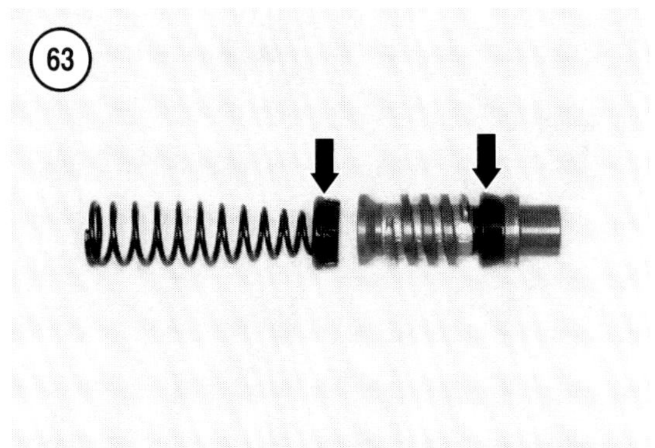

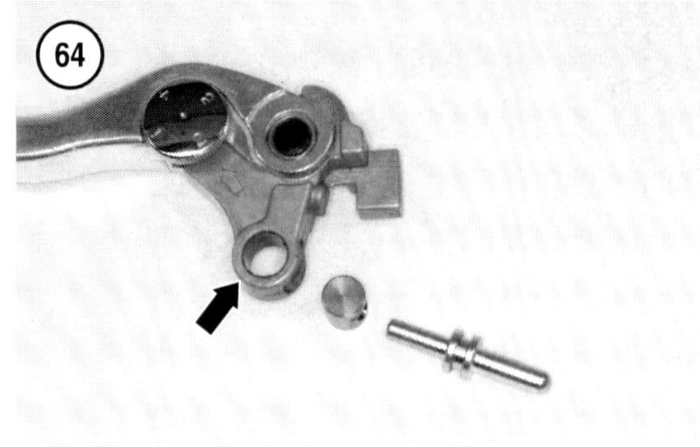

fect, replace the master cylinder assembly. The body cannot be replaced separately.

2. Inspect the piston cups (**Figure 63**) for signs of wear and damage. If less than perfect, replace the piston assembly. Individual cups cannot be replaced.

3. Inspect the piston contact surfaces for signs of wear and damage. If less than perfect, replace the piston assembly.

4. Check the end of the piston for wear caused by the hand lever. If worn, replace the piston assembly.

5. Inspect the pivot hole in the hand lever (**Figure 64**). If worn or elongated, the lever must be replaced.

6. Inspect the hand lever pivot lugs on the master cylinder for cracks or other signs of damage.

7. Make sure the fluid passage (**Figure 65**) in the bottom of the reservoir is clear. Clean it if necessary.

8. Inspect the banjo bolt threads in the cylinder bore. If worn or damaged, clean the threads with a metric thread tap or replace the master cylinder assembly.

9. Measure the cylinder bore with a bore gauge (**Figure 66**) or vernier caliper.

10. Measure the outside diameter of the piston with a micrometer (**Figure 67**).

11. Check the top cover, diaphragm and diaphragm plate for damage and deterioration; replace as necessary.

12. Inspect the adjuster on the hand lever. If worn or damaged, replace the hand lever as an assembly.

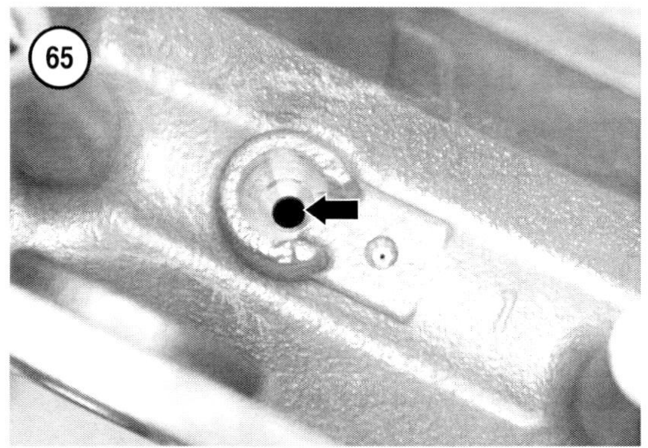

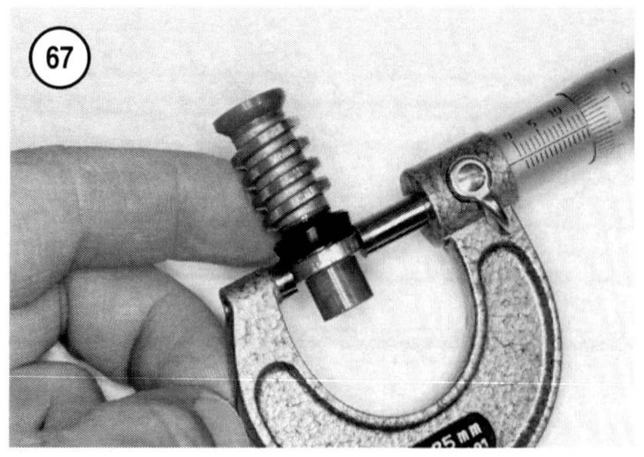

CLUTCH RELEASE CYLINDER

Removal/Installation

1. Place the motorcycle on level ground on the centerstand.

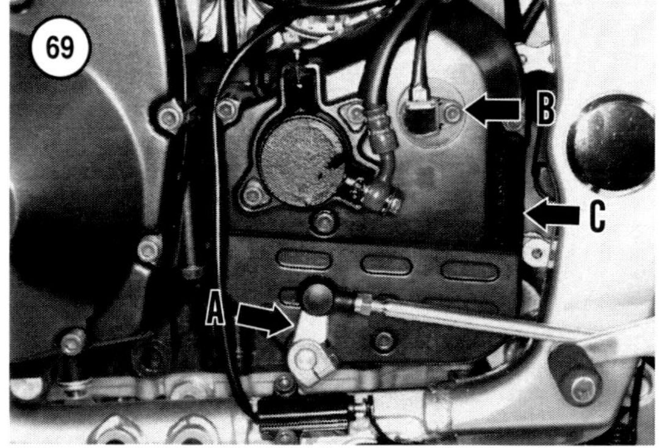

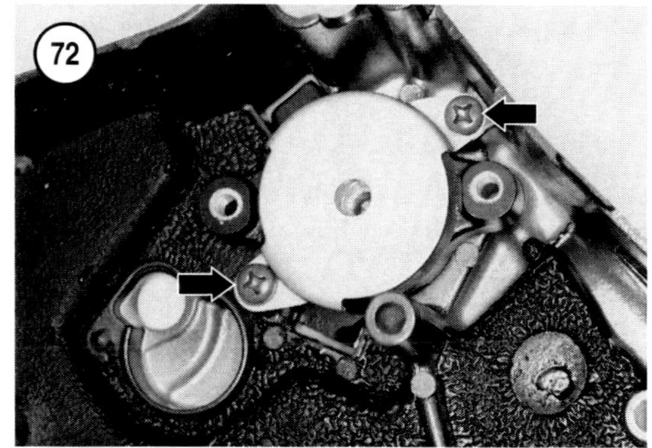

2. Remove the cap (**Figure 68**), then attach a hose to the bleed valve.

3. Place the loose end of the hose in a container and let the brake fluid drain out into the container. Apply the clutch lever several times to force the fluid out of the clutch hose. Dispose of this brake fluid properly; never reuse brake fluid.

4. Remove the hose and tighten the bleed valve.

5. Remove the bolt securing the shift lever and remove the shift lever (A, **Figure 69**).

6. On 2001-on models, remove the screw and the speed sensor (B, **Figure 69**) from the sprocket cover.

7. Remove the bolts securing the engine drive sprocket cover (C, **Figure 69**) and remove the cover.

8. Place several rags beneath the banjo bolt (**Figure 70**) and remove the bolt. Some residual brake fluid will come out when the clutch hose is disconnected. Separate the clutch hose from the release cylinder. Do not lose the two sealing washers, one from each side of the clutch hose fitting.

9. Remove the bolts (**Figure 71**) securing the release cylinder to the engine drive sprocket cover.

10. Turn the drive sprocket cover over on several shop cloths on the workbench to protect the finish.

CAUTION

The Phillips screws are very tight and must be loosened with an impact driver. Do not try to loosen the Phillips screws without placing the sprocket cover on a workbench.

11. Use an impact driver and No. 3 Phillips head bit and loosen the screws (**Figure 72**) securing the piston retainer. Remove the screws.

12. Remove the release cylinder (**Figure 73**) from the engine drive sprocket cover.

13. Install by reversing these removal steps while noting the following:

   a. Tighten all mounting bolts securely.
   b. Install a *new* sealing washer on each side of the clutch hose fitting. Install the banjo bolt and tighten to 23 N•m (17 ft.-lb.).
   c. Bleed the clutch system as described in this chapter.

Disassembly

Refer to **Figure 74**.

1. Remove the release cylinder as described in this chapter.
2. Remove the bleed valve.
3. Place a folded shop cloth on the workbench. Place wooden blocks on the shop cloth and place the release cylinder on the blocks with the piston facing down (A, **Figure 75**).

WARNING
In the next step, the piston may shoot out of the release cylinder with considerable force. Keep hands and fingers out of the way. Wear shop gloves and safety goggles when using compressed air to remove the piston.

4. Apply compressed air in short spurts through the bleed valve hose fitting (B, **Figure 75**) and force the piston out of the release cylinder. Use a service station air hose if compressed air is not available.
5. Inspect the release cylinder assembly as described in this section.

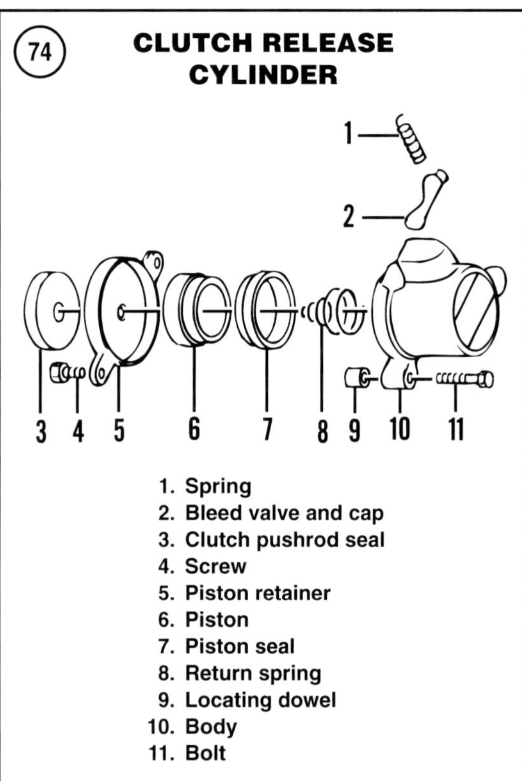

Assembly

NOTE
Never reuse an old piston seal. Very minor damage or age deterioration can make a seal useless.

1. Soak the *new* piston seal in fresh DOT 4 brake fluid.
2. Coat the piston bore and piston with clean DOT 4 brake fluid.

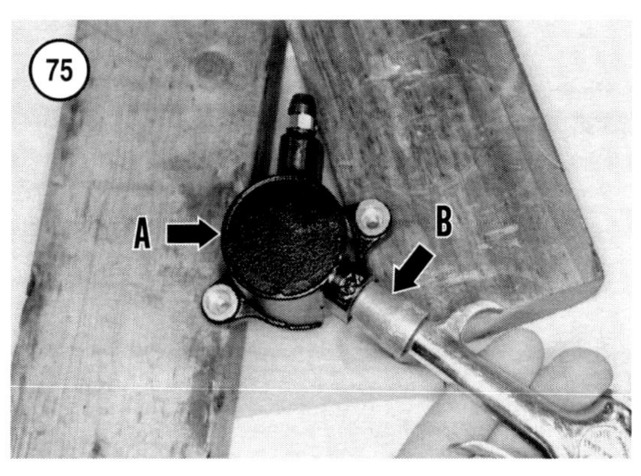

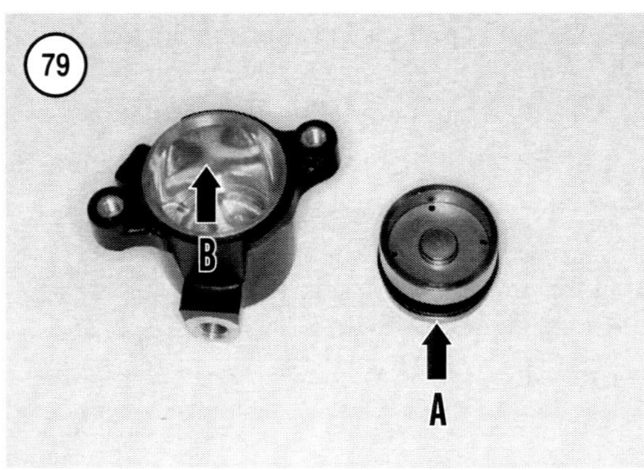

3. Carefully install the new piston seal (**Figure 76**) onto the piston. Make sure the seal is properly seated in the groove.

4. The piston spring has a small and large end. Install the small end into the piston.

5. Install the spring and piston into the release cylinder bore (**Figure 77**). Push the piston all the way into the cylinder until it bottoms (**Figure 78**).

6. Install the bleed valve and tighten securely.

7. Install the release cylinder as described in this chapter.

Inspection

When inspecting the clutch release cylinder, compare any measurements to the specifications in **Table 1**. Replace any part that is damaged or out of specification.

1. Clean the release cylinder body and piston in fresh DOT 4 brake fluid or isopropyl alcohol. Thoroughly dry the parts with compressed air.

2. Make sure the fluid passageway in the base of the cylinder bore is clear. Apply compressed air to the opening to make sure it is clear. Clean out the passage, if necessary, with fresh brake fluid.

3. Inspect the piston (A, **Figure 79**) and seal groove for damage. If the groove is damaged or corroded, replace the release cylinder.

4. Inspect the banjo bolt threaded hole in the cylinder body. If worn or damaged, clean the threads with a metric thread tap or replace the caliper assembly.

5. Inspect the bleed valve. Apply compressed air to the opening and make sure it is clear. Clean out, if necessary, with fresh brake fluid. Install the bleed valve, and tighten it securely.

6. Inspect the piston spring for cracks or other signs of damage.

7. Inspect the cylinder body (B, **Figure 79**) for damage.

8. Inspect the cylinder wall and piston for scratches, scoring or other damage.

9. Measure the cylinder bore with a bore gauge or vernier caliper.

10. Measure the outside diameter of the piston with a micrometer (**Figure 80**) or vernier caliper.

CLUTCH HOSE ASSEMBLY REPLACEMENT

Periodically inspect the clutch hose and replace it if it is cracked or damaged. The clutch hose assembly consists of two flexible hoses and one metal hose. The hose assembly must be replaced as a complete unit.

CAUTION
Drape a heavy cloth or plastic tarp over the front fender to protect it from accidental brake fluid spills. Brake fluid will damage the finish on plastic, painted or plated surfaces. Immediately wash spilled brake fluid off the motorcycle. Use soapy water, and rinse the area completely.

1. Place the motorcycle on level ground on the centerstand.
2. On GSF1200S models, remove the fairing as described in Chapter Fourteen.
3. Remove the seat as described in Chapter Fourteen.
4. Remove the fuel tank as described in Chapter Eight.
5. Attach a hose to the release cylinder bleed valve (A, **Figure 81**).
6. Place the loose end of the hose in a container and let the brake fluid drain out into the container. Apply the clutch lever several times to force the fluid out of the clutch hose. Dispose of this brake fluid properly; never reuse brake fluid.
7. Remove the hose and tighten the bleed valve.
8. Place a rag beneath the banjo bolt (B, **Figure 81**) and remove the bolt. Separate the clutch hose from the release cylinder. Do not lose the two sealing washers, one from each side of the clutch hose fitting. Place the loose end of the brake hose in a reclosable plastic bag to prevent brake fluid from dribbling onto the motorcycle.
9. Remove the banjo bolt (**Figure 82**) and two sealing washers securing the clutch upper hose to the master cylinder. Do not lose the two sealing washers, one from each side of the clutch hose fitting. Place the loose end of the brake hose in a reclosable plastic bag to prevent brake fluid from dribbling onto the motorcycle.
10. Loosen all clamps or guides securing the clutch hose assembly (**Figure 83**) to the frame.
11. Carefully pull the upper end of the upper flexible hose down and out from behind the steering head and fork tube on the left side.

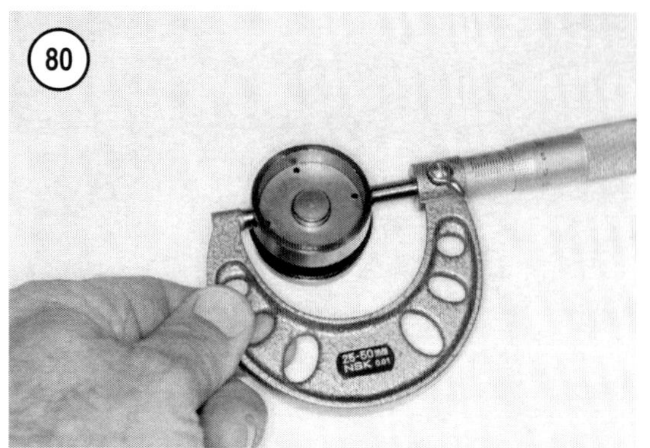

12. Carefully pull the lower end of the lower flexible hose up past the starter wiring harness and out from behind the frame side rail on the left side.
13. Remove the clutch hose assembly from the frame.
14. Wash off any spilled brake fluid that may have drained out of the hoses during removal.
15. Install the new clutch hose assembly in the reverse order of removal while noting the following:
   a. Install *new* sealing washers on each side of the hose fittings at each end.

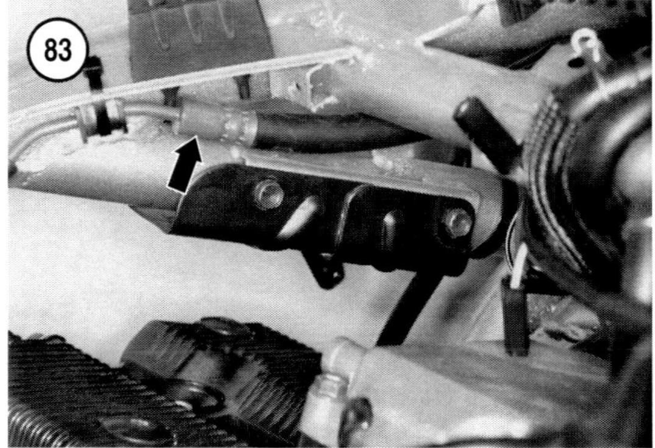

b. Tighten the banjo bolts securely.

c. Refill the clutch master cylinder reservoir and bleed the clutch system as described in this chapter.

BLEEDING THE HYDRAULIC CLUTCH SYSTEM

Bleeding the clutch hydraulic system removes air from the clutch system. Air in the clutch system increases clutch lever travel, and it makes the clutch action feel soft or spongy. Under extreme circumstances, it can cause complete loss of clutch action.

The clutch can be bled manually or with the use of a brake bleeding tool, and this method is described here. Only use fresh DOT 4 brake fluid when bleeding the brakes. Do not reuse old brake fluid, and do not use DOT 5 (silicone-based) brake fluid.

Protect the motorcycle from accidental spills by covering the areas beneath the release cylinder and the master cylinder with a tarp. Brake fluid will damage the finish on most surfaces, so immediately clean up any spilled brake fluid. Wash the affected parts with soapy water, and completely rinse the area with plenty of clean water.

This procedure uses the Mityvac hydraulic brake bleeding kit that is available from automotive or motorcycle supply stores.

1. Remove the dust cap from the caliper bleed valve (**Figure 68**).
2. Place a clean shop cloth over the drive sprocket cover to protect it from accidental brake fluid spills.
3. Open the bleed screw approximately 1/2 turn.
4. Assemble the Mityvac tool according to its manufacturer's instructions. Secure it to the caliper bleed valve (**Figure 84**).
5. Clean the top of the master cylinder of all dirt and debris.
6. Remove the screws securing the clutch master cylinder top cover and remove the cover, plate and diaphragm.
7. Fill the reservoir almost to the top with DOT 4 brake fluid and reinstall the diaphragm, plate and cover. Leave the cover in place during this procedure to prevent the entry of dirt.

NOTE

As brake fluid exits the system, the level in the reservoir drops. Add brake fluid as necessary to keep the fluid level 10 mm (3/8 in.) below the reservoir top so air will not be drawn into the system.

8. Operate the pump several times to create a vacuum in the line, then open the bleed valve (**Figure 85**). Brake fluid will quickly draw from the release cylinder into the pump's reservoir. Tighten the caliper bleed valve before the fluid stops flowing through the hose. To prevent air from being drawn

through the release cylinder, add fluid to maintain its level at the top of the reservoir.

NOTE
Do not allow the master cylinder reservoir to empty during the bleeding operation or more air will enter the system. If this occurs, the procedure must be repeated.

9. Continue the bleeding process until the fluid drawn from the release cylinder is bubble-free. If bubbles are withdrawn with the brake fluid, more air is trapped in the line. Repeat Step 8, making sure to refill the master cylinder to prevent air from being drawn into the system.
10. When the brake fluid is free of bubbles, tighten the bleed valve and remove the brake bleeder assembly. Reinstall the bleed valve dust cap.

NOTE
Dispose of the brake fluid expelled during the bleeding process. Do not reuse the brake fluid.

11. If necessary, add fluid to correct the level in the master cylinder reservoir.

12. Reinstall the diaphragm, plate and cover. Install the screws and tighten securely.

13. Test the feel of the clutch lever. It must be firm and offer the same resistance each time it is operated. If it feels spongy, it is likely that there is still air in the system and it must be bled again. After bleeding the system, check for leaks and tighten all fittings and connections as necessary.

14. Test ride the motorcycle slowly at first to make sure the clutch is operating properly.

Table 1 CLUTCH SPECIFICATIONS

Item	Standard	Wear limit
Friction disc		
Quantity	9 + 1, total 10	–
Thickness	2.92-3.08 mm (0.115-0.121 in.)	–
Claw width	–	13.0 mm (0.51 in.)
Clutch plate		
Quantity	7 + 2, total 9	–
Thickness		
Plate No. 1	1.6 mm (0.06 in.)	–
Plate No. 2	2.0 mm (0.08 in.)	–
Warp	–	0.1 mm (0.004 in.)
Clutch spring free height	–	2.9 mm (0.11 in.)
Clutch master cylinder		
Bore inside diameter	14.00-14.043 mm (0.5511-0.5529 in.)	–
Piston outside diameter	13.957-13.984 mm (0.5495-0.5506 in.)	–
Clutch release cylinder		
Bore inside diameter	35.700-35.762 mm (1.4055-1.4079 in.)	–
Piston outside diameter	35.650-35.675 mm (1.4035-1.4045 in.)	–

Table 2 CLUTCH TORQUE SPECIFICATIONS

Item	N•m	in.-lb.	ft.-lb.
Clutch hub nut	150	–	111
Clutch master cylinder			
Banjo bolts	23	–	17
Clamp bolts	10	88	–
Clutch release cylinder			
Banjo bolts	23	–	17

CHAPTER SEVEN

TRANSMISSION AND GEARSHIFT MECHANISMS

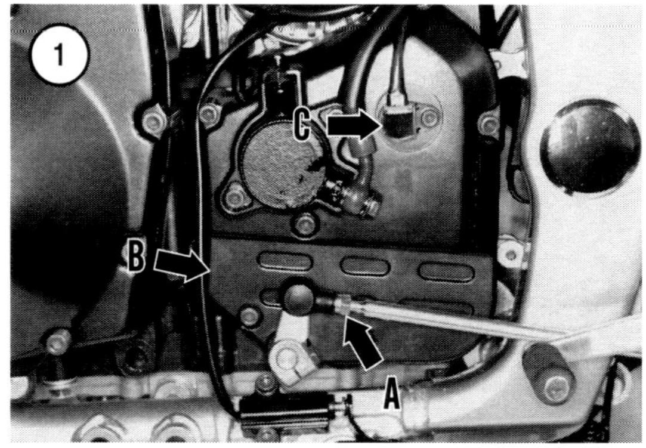

This chapter provides complete service procedures for the transmission and the external and the internal shift mechanisms. During inspection, compare any measurements to the gearshift specifications in **Table 2**. Replace any component that is damaged, worn to the wear limit or out of specification. During assembly, tighten fasteners to the specifications listed. **Tables 1-3** are at the end of the chapter.

ENGINE DRIVE SPROCKET COVER

Removal/Installation

1. Loosen the shift lever clamp bolt and remove the shift lever (A, **Figure 1**) from the shift shaft.
2. Remove the bolts securing the engine drive sprocket cover (B, **Figure 1**) and move the cover out of the way. Do not lose the dowels installed behind the cover.
3. Suspend the cover from the frame with a wire or bungee cord. The clutch hydraulic hose does not have to be disconnected unless the cover must be completely removed. The same applies to the speed sensor (C, **Figure 1**) on 2001-on models. Leave the sensor mounted on the engine sprocket cover unless the cover must be completely removed.
4. Installation is the reverse of removal. Note the following:
   a. If removed, reinstall the dowels into the crankcase.

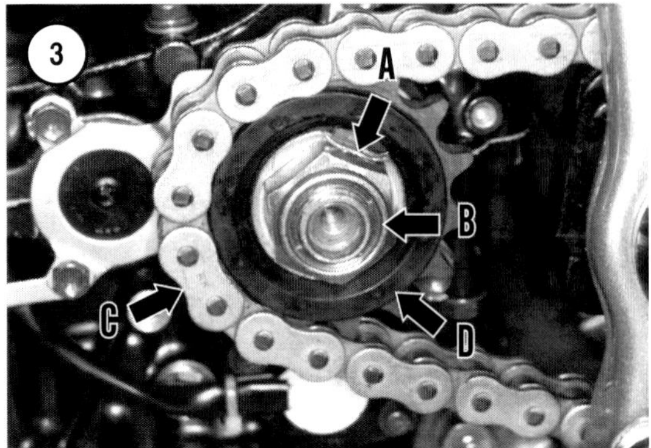

b. Install the shift lever onto the shift shaft so the split in the shift lever clamp aligns with the punch mark on the end of the shift shaft.
c. Tighten the clamp bolt securely.

ENGINE DRIVE SPROCKET

The drive chain is an endless type with no master link. To remove the drive chain, remove the engine drive sprocket from the countershaft and remove the swing arm as described in Chapter Twelve.

Removal/Installation

1. Remove the engine sprocket cover as described in this chapter.
2. Have an assistant apply the rear brake.
3. On 2001-on models, remove the bolt securing the speed sensor rotor (**Figure 2**) and remove the rotor.
4. Straighten the tab on the lockwasher (A, **Figure 3**).
5. Loosen and remove the drive sprocket nut (B, **Figure 3**) and the lockwasher (A).
6. Provide slack in the drive chain at the rear wheel as follows:
   a. On models so equipped, remove the cotter pin (A, **Figure 4**).
   b. Loosen the rear axle nut (B, **Figure 4**).
   c. Loosen the drive chain adjuster locknut (C, **Figure 4**) and adjuster (D) on each side of the swing arm.
   d. Push the rear wheel forward to provide maximum slack in the drive chain.
7. Remove the drive chain (C, **Figure 3**) from the engine sprocket.
8. Slide the engine sprocket (D, **Figure 3**) off the countershaft.

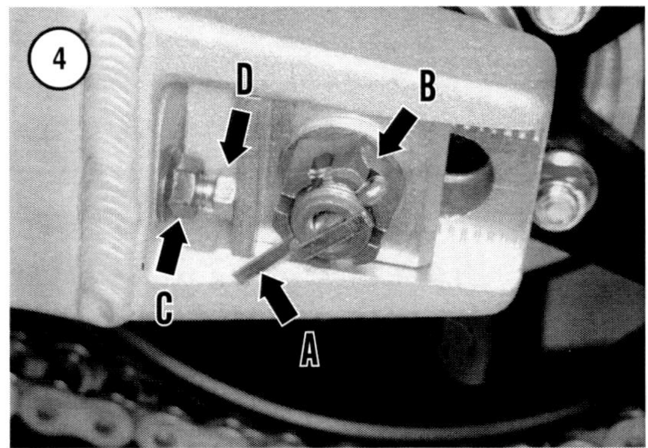

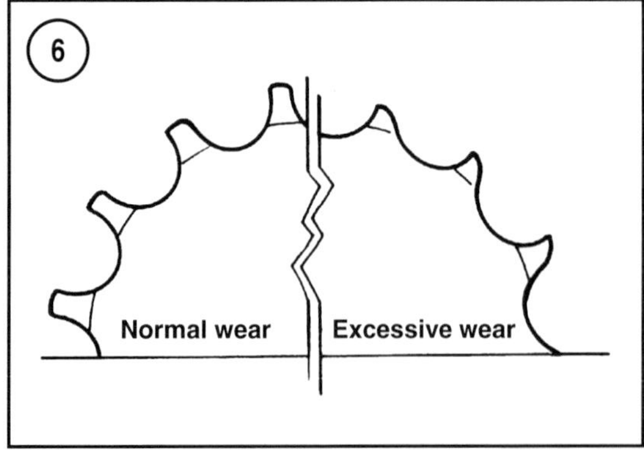

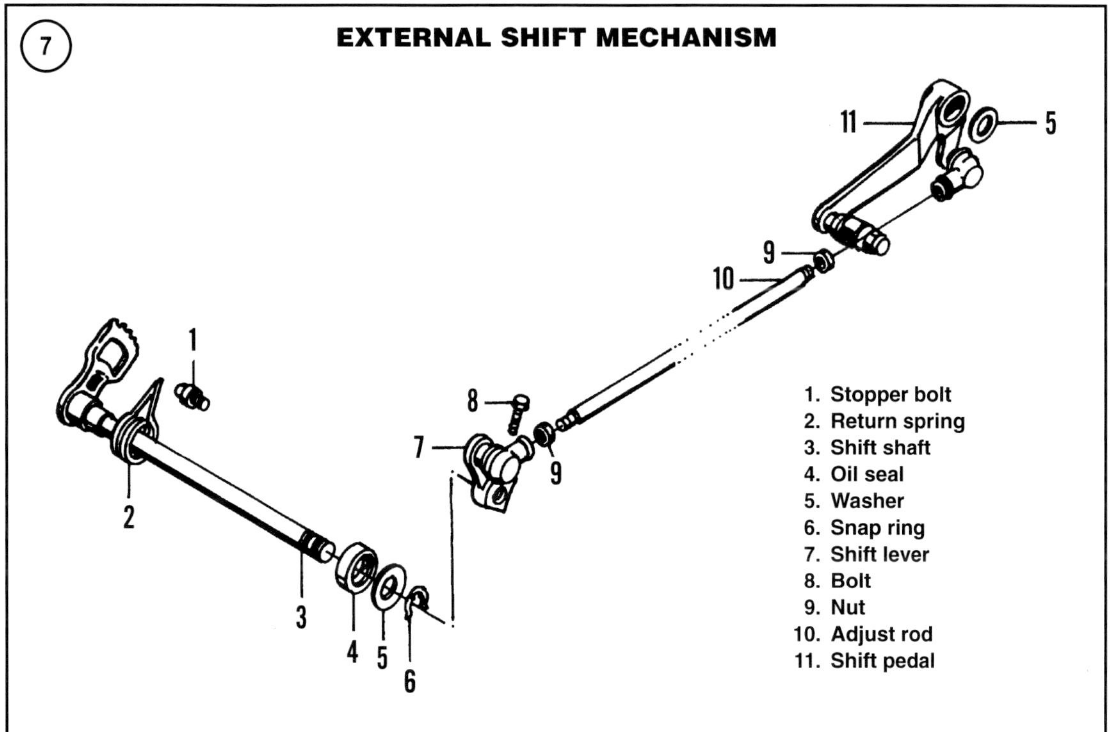

9. If the crankcase is going to be disassembled, remove the bolts securing the oil seal retainer (**Figure 5**) and remove the retainer.

10. Inspect the engine sprocket as described in this section.

11. Install by reversing these removal steps while noting the following:

  a. Position the drive chain onto the engine sprocket and then slide the sprocket onto the countershaft.
  b. Install a new sprocket lockwasher.
  c. Apply a medium strength threadlocking compound to the countershaft threads. Install the sprocket nut and tighten it to 115 N•m (85 ft.-lb.).
  d. On 2001-on models, apply a low strength threadlocking compound to the speed sensor bolt and tighten it to 20 N•m (15 ft.-lb.).
  e. Adjust the drive chain as described in Chapter Three.

Inspection

1. Clean all parts in solvent and thoroughly dry.

2. Inspect the driven sprocket teeth (**Figure 6**). If the teeth are visibly worn or undercut, replace the engine drive sprocket, the rear driven sprocket, and the drive chain. Never replace any one sprocket or the chain separately. Worn parts will cause rapid wear of the new component.

EXTERNAL SHIFT MECHANISM

The shift ratchet mechanism is located on the right side of the crankcase and the shift lever is located on the left side. The shift lever is subject to a lot of abuse. If the motorcycle has been in a hard spill, the gearshift lever may have been hit and the shift shaft bent. It is very hard to straighten the shaft without subjecting the crankcase halves to abnormal stress. If the shaft is bent enough to prevent it from being withdrawn from the crankcase, there is little recourse but to cut the shaft off with a hacksaw very close to the crankcase. It is much cheaper in the long run to replace the shift shaft than to risk damaging a very expensive crankcase assembly.

After the shaft has been cut off, file off any burrs to avoid damaging the shaft's oil seals in the crankcase.

Removal

Refer to **Figure 7**.

1. Remove the engine sprocket cover as described in this chapter.
2. Remove the clutch assembly as described in Chapter Six.
3. Remove the snap ring (A, **Figure 8**) and the washer (B) from the left side of the shift shaft.

NOTE
*During operation, residue thrown from the chain collects on the shift shaft end. Clean the exposed end of the shift shaft (C, **Figure 8**) before removing it through the oil seal.*

4. Pull the shift shaft (A, **Figure 9**) from the right side of the crankcase. See the information regarding a bent shift shaft in the introductory paragraph of this procedure.
5. Remove the screws securing the pawl retainer (A, **Figure 10**), and remove the pawl retainer.
6. Remove the screws securing the cam guide (B, **Figure 10**) and remove the cam guide.
7. Remove the cam gear assembly (**Figure 11**) from the end of the shift drum. Do not lose the pawls, springs and pins in the assembly. Store these small parts in a reclosable plastic bag to avoid misplacing them.
8. Inspect the external shift mechanism as described in this section.

Installation

1. Cover the opening in the base of the crankcase to keep any small parts from falling in should they drop during installation.
2. Compress the spring-loaded shift pawls by hand (**Figure 12**). Install the cam gear assembly (**Figure 11**) into the shift drum.
3. Set the cam guide (B, **Figure 10**) into place on the crankcase. Apply a small amount of ThreeBond Threadlock 1342 to the mounting screws and tighten the screws securely.
4. Set the pawl retainer (A, **Figure 10**) into place. Apply a small amount of ThreeBond Threadlock 1342 to the mounting screws and tighten the screws securely.
5. Apply clean engine oil to the shift shaft and slide the shift shaft part way into the crankcase.
6. Align the center of the cam gear with the center of the shift shaft gear (B, **Figure 9**) and then push the shaft assembly all the way into the crankcase

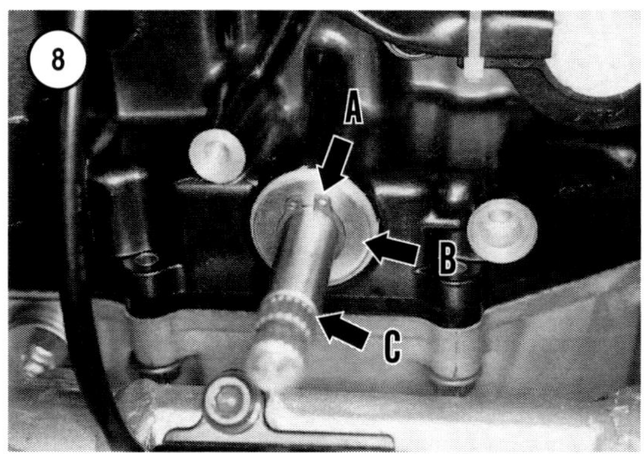

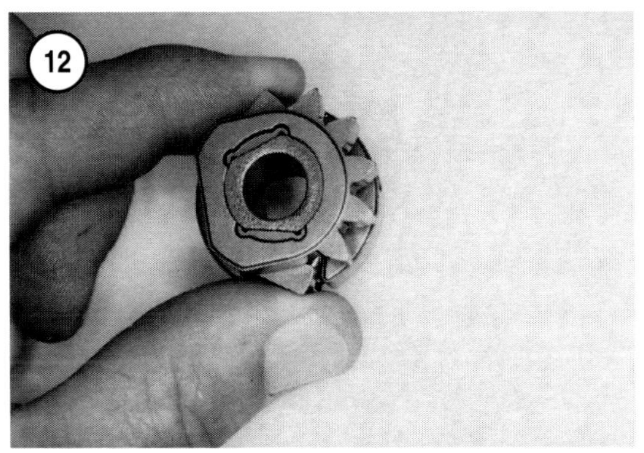

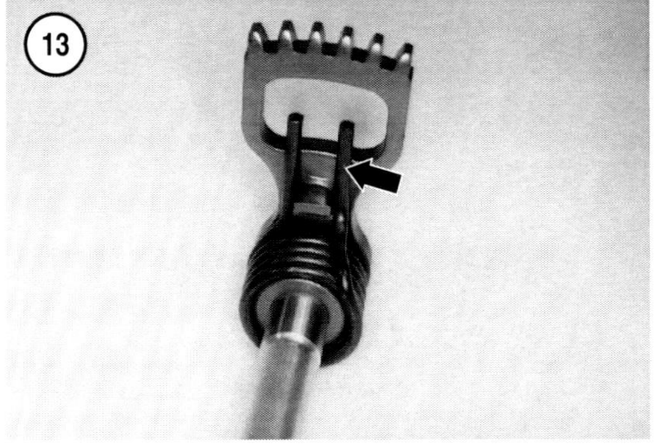

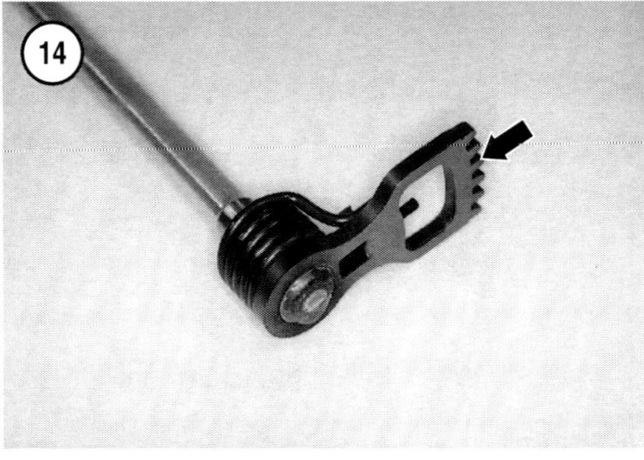

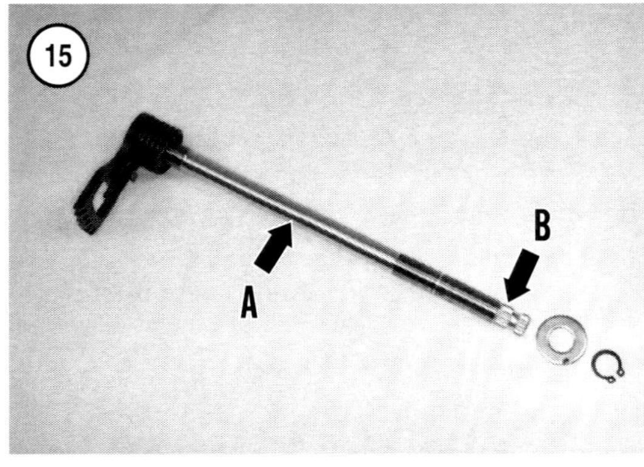

until it bottoms. Make sure the arms of the return spring straddle the stopper bolt (C, **Figure 9**) in the crankcase.

7. On the other side of the crankcase, install the washer (B, **Figure 8**) and the snap ring (A) onto the shift shaft. Make sure the snap ring is correctly seated in the shaft groove.

8. Remove the covering agent on the base of the crankcase opening.

9. Install the clutch assembly as described in Chapter Six.

10. Install the engine sprocket cover as described in this chapter.

Inspection

1. Inspect the return spring (**Figure 13**) on the shift shaft assembly. If broken or weak, it must be replaced.

2. Inspect the gear teeth (**Figure 14**) on the shift shaft assembly. If a tooth is broken or worn, replace the shift shaft assembly.

3. Inspect the shift shaft assembly (A, **Figure 15**) for bending, wear or other damage; replace it if necessary.

4. Check the gearshift lever splines (B, **Figure 15**) for damage. Clean them if necessary.

5. Inspect the pawl retainer and cam guide for damage and/or hole elongation.

6. Disassemble the cam gear assembly (**Figure 16**). Inspect the pawls, springs and pins for wear or damage.

7. Assemble the cam gear assembly as follows:
   a. Install the springs into the cam gear body.
   b. Position the pawl pins with the rounded end facing out, and install them onto the springs.

c. Install the pawls onto the pins and into the cam gear body (**Figure 17**).

d. The pin grooves in the pawls are offset. When the pawls are installed correctly, the wider shoulder (A, **Figure 18**) must face toward the outside of the cam gear body.

e. Hold the pawls in place and place the assembly into a spray paint can top.

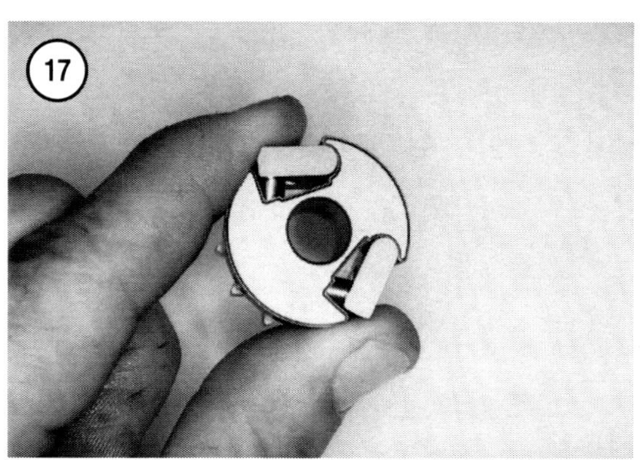

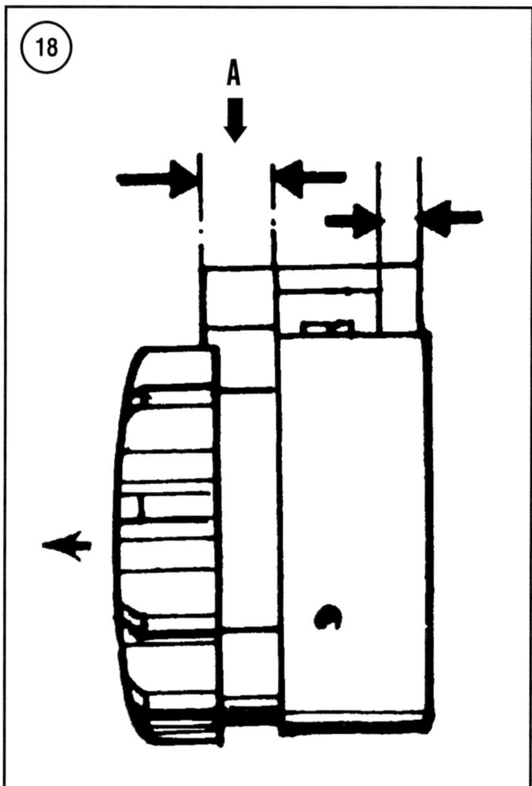

TRANSMISSION

Servicing the transmission and internal gearshift components requires removing the engine and separating the crankcase as described in Chapter Five. Once the crankcase has been disassembled, the transmission assemblies, shift drum and shift fork assemblies can be removed from the crankcase.

These overhaul procedures refer to the transmission mainshaft and countershaft. The term mainshaft refers to the input shaft in the transmission. The mainshaft is connected to the clutch outer housing, which is driven by the primary drive gear on the crankshaft. The term countershaft refers to the output shaft of the transmission. The countershaft drives the engine sprocket.

NOTE
Suzuki's terminology for the transmission shafts is different than most manufacturer's. Suzuki refers to the mainshaft (input) as the countershaft and the countershaft (output) shaft as the driveshaft. Most manufacturers, and the procedures in this manual, refer to the input shaft as the mainshaft and the output shaft as the countershaft. Notice that this is opposite of Suzuki's parts information and keep this in mind when ordering replacement parts.

Removal/Installation

Remove and install the transmission mainshaft and countershaft assemblies as described in Chapter Five.

Preliminary Inspection

1. Clean and inspect the assemblies prior to disassembling them. Place the assembled shaft into a large can or plastic bucket and thoroughly clean the assembly with a petroleum-based solvent, such as kerosene, and a stiff brush. Dry the assembly with compressed air or let it sit on rags to drip dry. Do this for both shaft assemblies.

2. Visually inspect the components for excessive wear. Check the gear teeth for chips, burrs or pitting. Clean up damage with an oilstone. Replace

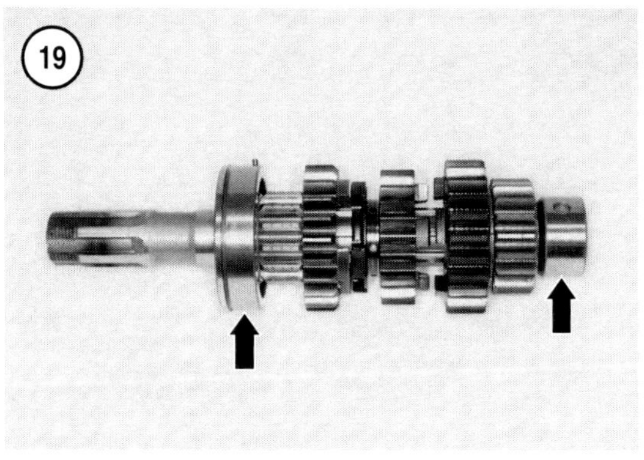

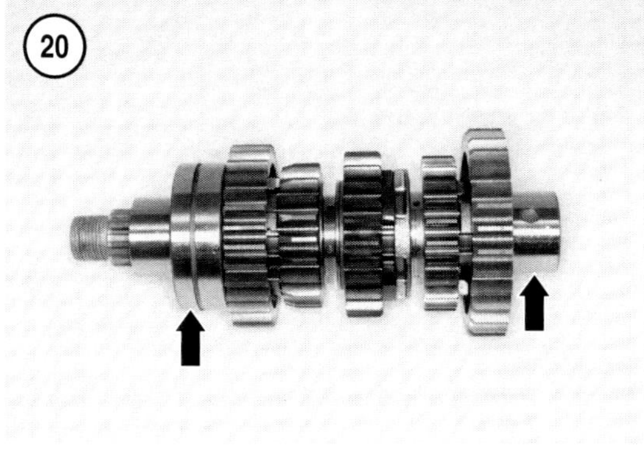

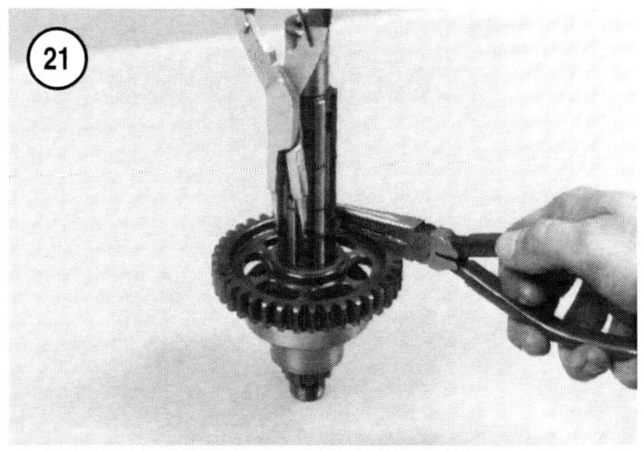

any components with damage that cannot be cleaned up.

NOTE
Replace defective gears and their mating gear on the other shaft as well, even though it may not show as much wear or damage.

3. Carefully check the engagement dogs. If any are chipped, worn, rounded or missing, the affected gear must be replaced.

4. Rotate the transmission bearings by hand. Refer to mainshaft, **Figure 19** and countershaft, **Figure 20**. Check for roughness, noise and radial play. Replace any bearing that is suspect.

5. Slide both clutch pushrods into the mainshaft and check for binding. If binding occurs, check the pushrods for bending or damage. If they are in good condition, inspect the mainshaft tunnel for debris. Clean out the tunnel if necessary.

6. If the transmission shafts are satisfactory and are not going to be disassembled, apply assembly oil or engine oil to all components and reinstall them into the crankcase as described in Chapter Five.

NOTE
If disassembling a used, high-mileage transmission for the first time, pay particular attention to any additional shims not shown in the illustrations or photographs. To compensate for wear, additional shims may have been installed during the previous repair. If the transmission is being reassembled with the old parts, install these shims in their original locations since the shims have developed a wear pattern. If new parts are being used, discard the additional shims.

Transmission Service Notes

1. As each part is removed from the shaft, set it in an egg crate in the exact order of removal and with the same orientation the part had when installed on the shaft. This is an easy way to remember the correct relationship of all parts.

2. The snap rings fit tightly on the transmission shafts. It is recommended that all snap rings be replaced during assembly.

3. Snap rings will turn and fold over, making removal and installation difficult. To ease replacement, open a snap ring with a pair of snap ring pliers. At the same time, grasp the back of the snap ring with another pair of pliers and remove the snap ring (**Figure 21**). Repeat for installation.

Countershaft Disassembly

Refer to **Figure 22**.

1. If not cleaned during *Preliminary Inspection*, place the assembled shaft into a large can or plastic

22

TRANSMISSION

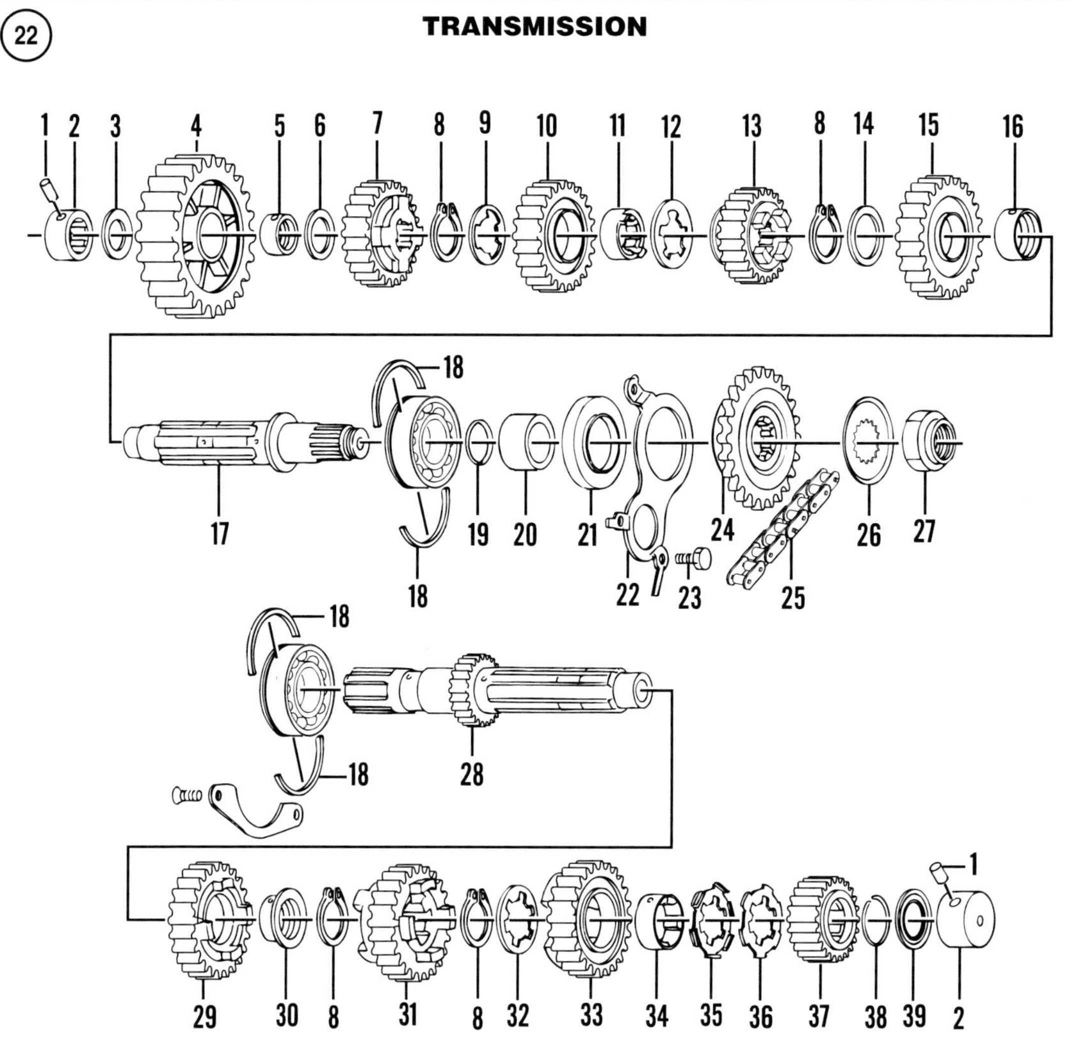

1. Dowel pin
2. Needle bearing
3. Thrust washer
4. Countershaft first gear
5. Countershaft first gear bushing
6. Thrust washer
7. Countershaft fourth gear
8. Snap ring
9. Splined washer
10. Countershaft third gear
11. Countershaft third gear bushing
12. Splined washer
13. Countershaft fifth gear
14. Thrust washer
15. Countershaft second gear
16. Countershaft second gear bushing
17. Countershaft
18. C-clips and ball bearing
19. O-ring
20. Spacer
21. Oil seal
22. Oil seal retainer
23. Bolt
24. Engine drive sprocket
25. Drive chain
26. Splined washer
27. Nut
28. Mainshaft/first gear
29. Mainshaft fourth gear
30. Mainshaft fourth gear bushing
31. Mainshaft third gear
32. Splined washer
33. Mainshaft fifth gear
34. Mainshaft fifth gear bushing
35. Lockwasher No. 1
36. Lockwasher No. 2
37. Mainshaft second gear
38. Circlip
39. Oil seal

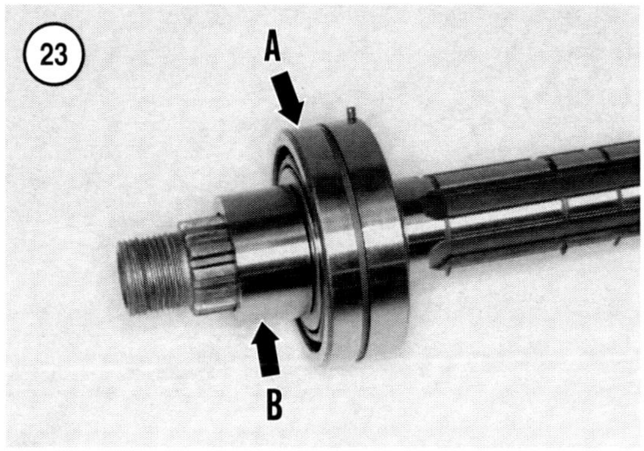

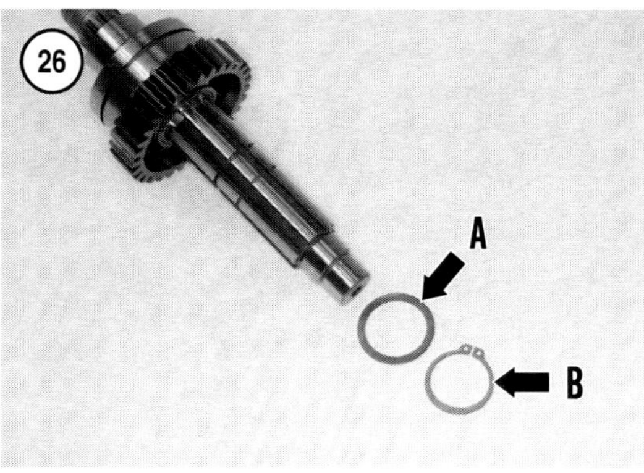

bucket. Thoroughly clean it with solvent and a stiff brush. Dry the shaft assembly with compressed air or let it sit on rags to dry.

2. Remove the outer bearing race, needle bearing and oil seal. Do not lose the locating dowel in the outer bearing race.
3. Slide first gear, first gear bushing and the thrust washer off the countershaft.
4. Slide off the fourth gear.
5. Remove the snap ring and splined washer.
6. Slide off the third gear and third gear bushing.
7. Slide off the splined washer.
8. Slide off the fifth gear.
9. Remove the snap ring and thrust washer.
10. Slide off the second gear and second gear bushing.
11. Remove the oil seal and spacer from the other end of the countershaft.
12. If necessary, remove the ball bearing from the countershaft.
13. Inspect the components as described in this chapter.

7

Countershaft Assembly

NOTE

*Install **new** snap rings during assembly to ensure proper gear alignment. Do not expand a snap ring more than necessary to slide it over the shaft.*

1. Apply a light coat of molybdenum disulfide oil to all sliding surfaces prior to installing any parts.
2. If removed, install the ball bearing (A, **Figure 23**) and the spacer (B).
3. Slide second gear bushing (**Figure 24**) onto the countershaft.
4. Position the second gear with the shift dog receptacle side going on last and install the second gear (**Figure 25**).
5. Install the thrust washer (A, **Figure 26**) and the snap ring (B). Make sure the snap ring is correctly seated in the snap ring groove (**Figure 27**).
6. Position the fifth gear with the shift fork groove side going on last and install the fifth gear (**Figure 28**).
7. Install the splined washer (A, **Figure 29**).
8. Align the oil hole in the third gear bushing (B, **Figure 29**) with the oil hole in the countershaft (C) and slide on the bushing (**Figure 30**). These holes must align to ensure proper gear lubrication.

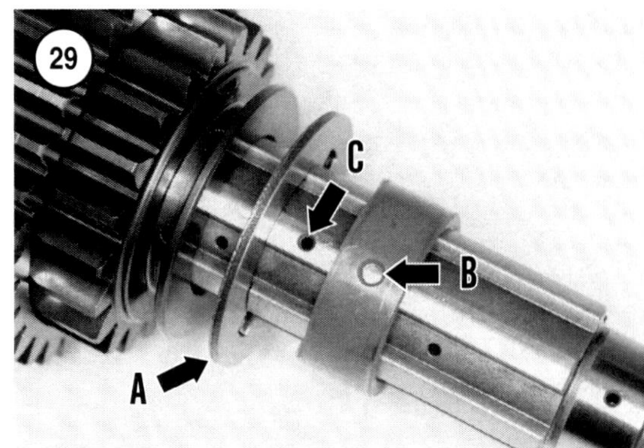

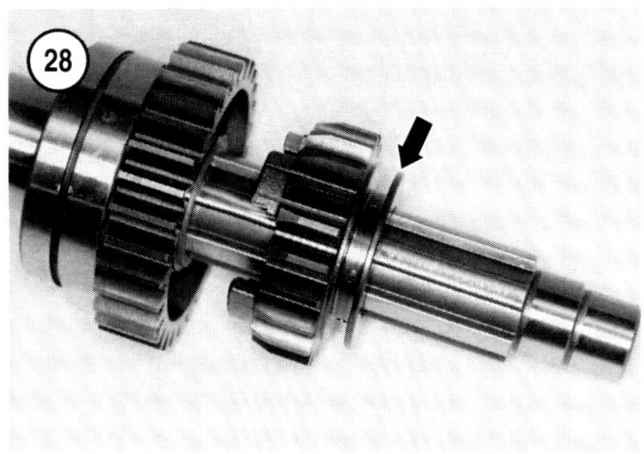

9. Position the third gear with the engagement dog side going on last and install the third gear (**Figure 31**).

10. Install the splined washer (A, **Figure 32**) and the snap ring (B). Make sure the snap ring is correctly seated in the snap ring groove (**Figure 33**).

11. Position the fourth gear with the shift fork groove side going on first and install the fourth gear (**Figure 34**).

12. Install the thrust washer (A, **Figure 35**).

13. Slide on the first gear bushing (B, **Figure 35**).

14. Position the first gear with the engagement dog side going on first (C, **Figure 35**) and install the first gear (A, **Figure 36**) onto the first gear bushing.

15. Install the thrust washer (B, **Figure 36**).

16. Apply a light coat of Suzuki Super Grease A to the lips of a *new* oil seal. Position the oil seal with the dished side facing out and install the oil seal (A, **Figure 37**).

17. Install the needle bearing and outer bearing race (B, **Figure 37**). Make sure the locating dowel is in place in the outer bearing race.

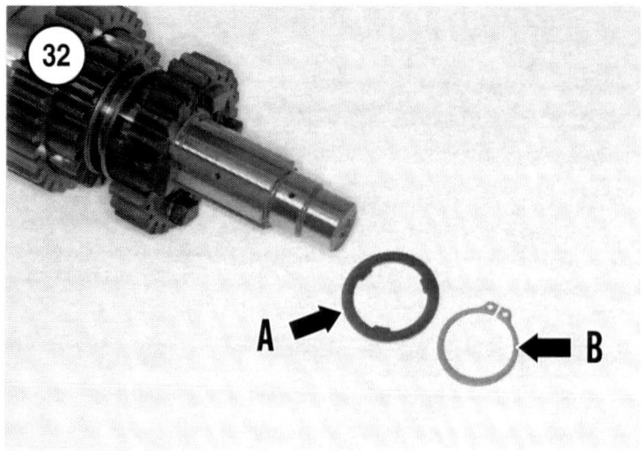

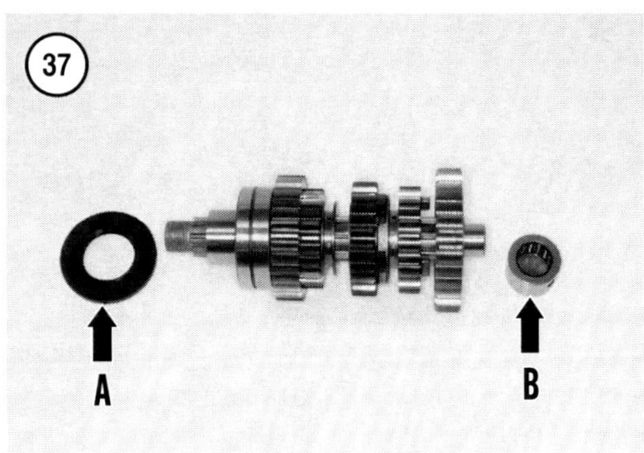

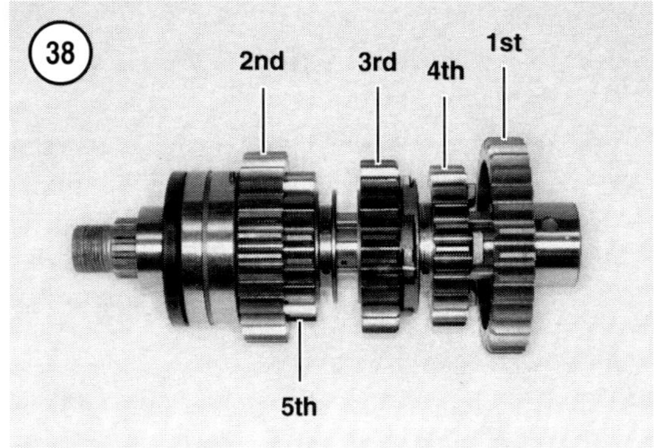

18. Refer to **Figure 38** for correct placement of all gears. Make sure all snap rings are correctly seated in the countershaft grooves.

19. Make sure each gear properly engages an adjoining gear where applicable.

Mainshaft Disassembly

Refer to **Figure 22**.

1. If not cleaned during *Preliminary Inspection*, place the assembled mainshaft into a large can or plastic bucket, and thoroughly clean the assembly with solvent and a stiff brush. Dry with compressed air or let it sit on rags to dry.

2. Remove the outer bearing race, needle bearing and oil seal. Do not lose the locating dowel in the outer bearing race.

NOTE

The snap ring is recessed inside the second gear. Steps 3-5 must be performed to expose this snap ring for removal.

3. Slide the third gear away from the fifth gear to expose the snap ring and splined washer (**Figure 39**).

4. Using angled snap ring pliers, open the snap ring and slide the snap ring (**Figure 40**) and the splined washer away from the fifth gear and toward the third gear.

5. Slide the fifth gear (A, **Figure 41**) toward the third gear (B).

6. Slide the lockwasher No. 1 (A, **Figure 42**) toward the fifth gear.

7. Rotate the lockwasher No. 2 (B, **Figure 42**) in either direction to disengage its tangs from the grooves on the countershaft. Slide the lockwasher No. 2 toward the fifth gear.

8. Slide second gear (A, **Figure 43**) toward the fifth gear and expose the circlip under second gear.

9. Remove the circlip (B, **Figure 43**) and slide off the second gear (A, **Figure 44**).

10. Remove the lockwashers No. 2 (B, **Figure 44**) and No. 1 (C).

11. Slide off the fifth gear and bushing.

12. Slide off the splined washer.

13. Remove the snap ring.

14. Slide off the third gear.

15. Remove the snap ring.

16. Slide off the fourth gear and fourth gear bushing.

17. If necessary, remove the ball bearing (A, **Figure 45**) from the mainshaft.

18. Inspect the components as described in this chapter.

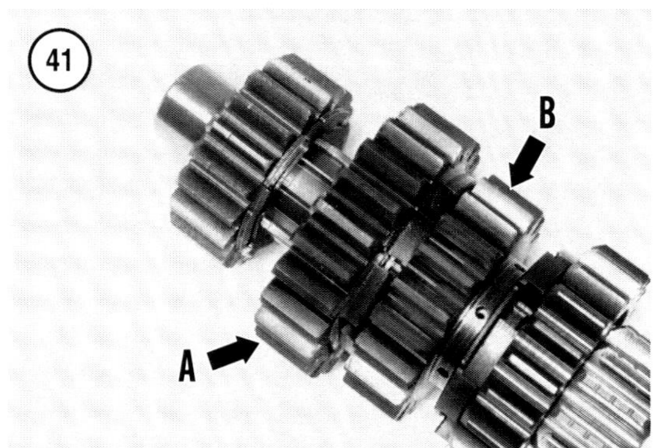

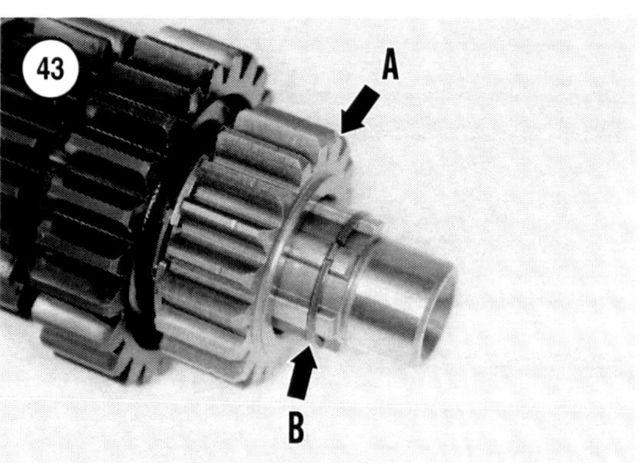

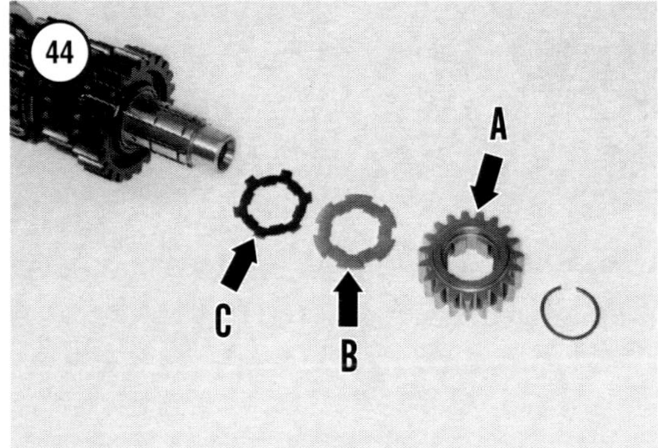

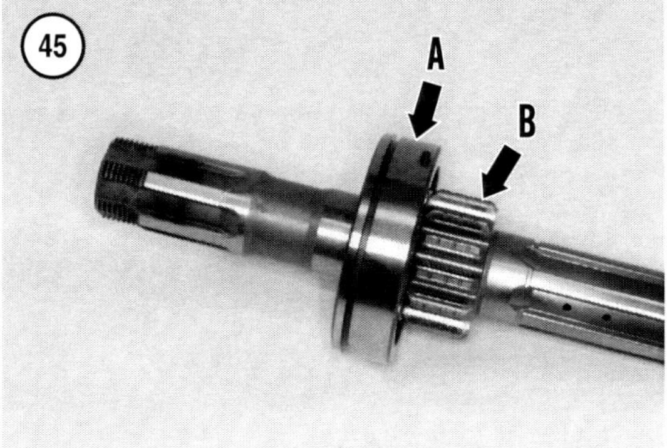

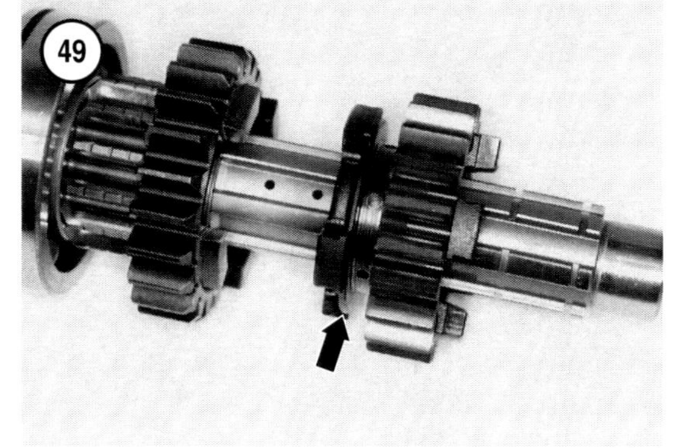

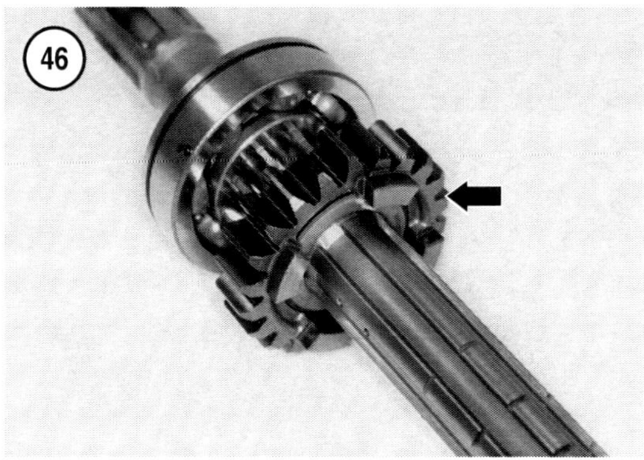

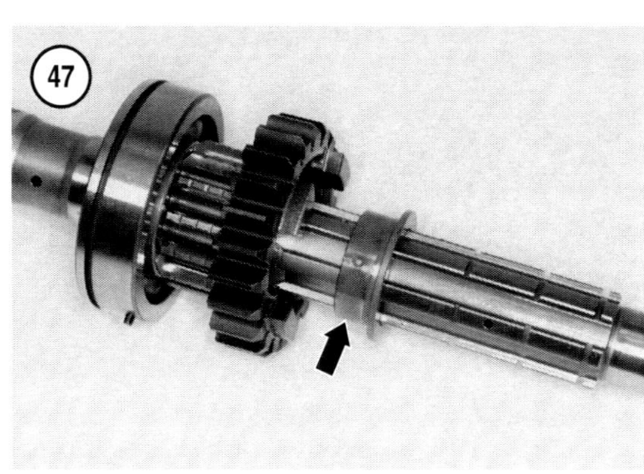

Mainshaft Assembly

NOTE
*The first gear (B, **Figure 45**) is part of the mainshaft. If the gear is defective, replace the mainshaft.*

1. Apply a light coat of molybdenum disulfide oil to all sliding surfaces prior to installing any parts.
2. If removed, install the ball bearing (A, **Figure 45**) onto the mainshaft.
3. Position the fourth gear with the shift dog side going on last and install the fourth gear (**Figure 46**).
4. Install the fourth gear bushing (**Figure 47**) and insert it into the fourth gear.
5. Install the snap ring. Make sure the snap ring is correctly seated (**Figure 48**) in the snap ring groove.
6. Position the third gear with the shift fork groove side going on first and install the third gear (**Figure 49**).

NOTE
*In Step 7 do **not** seat the snap ring in its respective groove at this time. It will be positioned correctly in Step 17.*

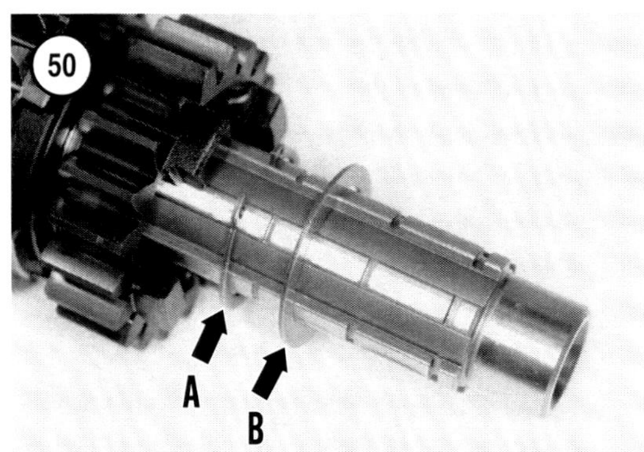

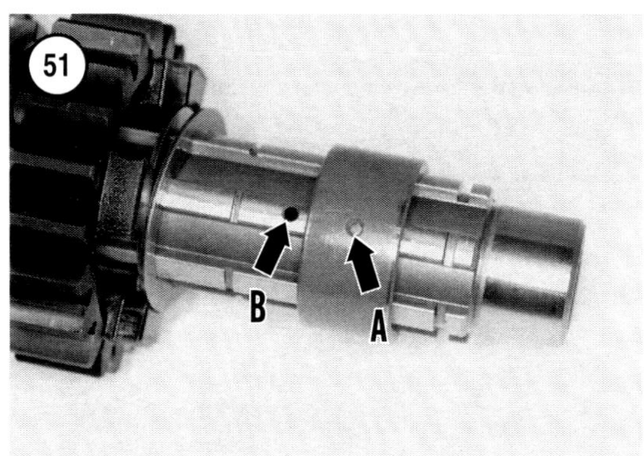

7. Install the snap ring (A, **Figure 50**) but do *not* seat it in its respective groove in the shaft. Move the snap ring *past the snap ring groove* toward the third gear.

8. Install the splined washer (B, **Figure 50**) and move it against the snap ring.

9. Align the oil hole in the fifth gear bushing (A, **Figure 51**) with the oil hole in the countershaft and slide on the bushing (B). These holes must align to ensure proper gear lubrication.

10. Position the fifth gear with the shift dog side going on first and install the fifth gear (**Figure 52**).

11. Position lockwasher No. 1 with the tang side going on last (**Figure 53**). Install lockwasher No. 1 (A, **Figure 54**) and lockwasher No. 2 (B). Move the lockwashers past the lockwasher grooves toward the fifth gear.

12. Position the second gear with the shoulder side going on first. Slide the second gear (A, **Figure 55**) down the shaft toward fifth gear until the circlip groove is exposed (B).

13. Install the circlip. Make sure it is correctly seated in the mainshaft groove (**Figure 56**).

14. Slide the second gear up against the circlip (A, **Figure 57**).

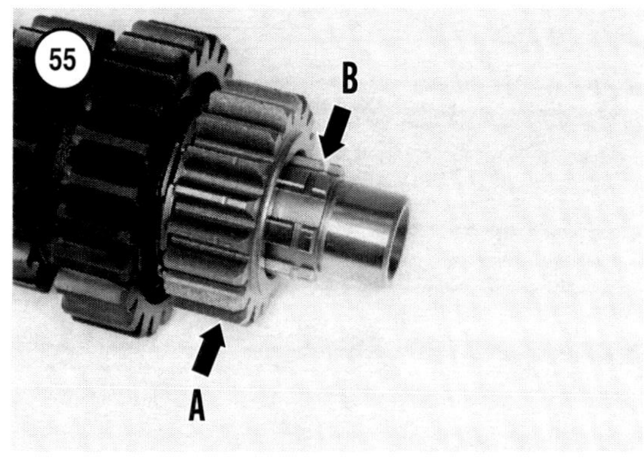

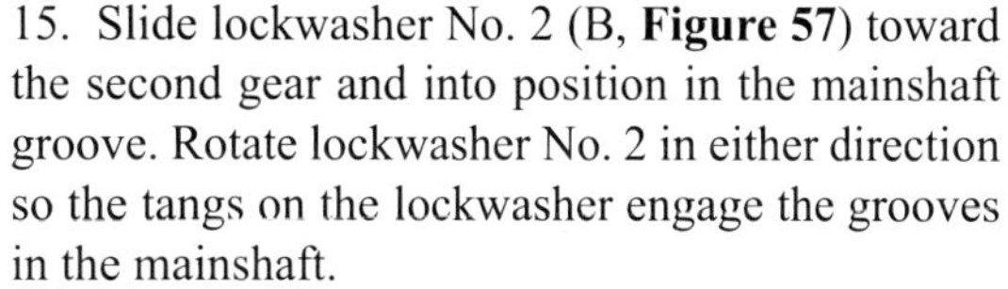

15. Slide lockwasher No. 2 (B, **Figure 57**) toward the second gear and into position in the mainshaft groove. Rotate lockwasher No. 2 in either direction so the tangs on the lockwasher engage the grooves in the mainshaft.

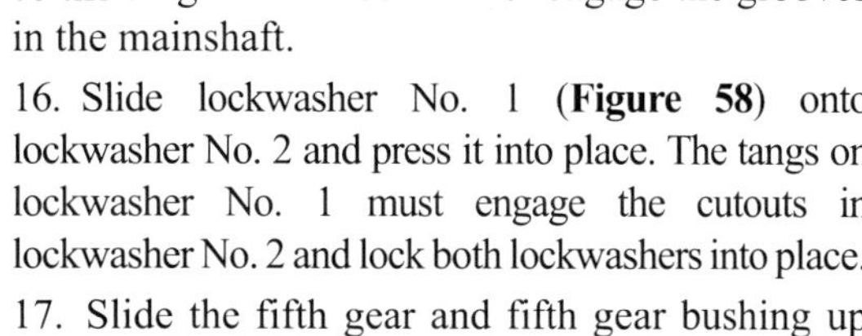

16. Slide lockwasher No. 1 (**Figure 58**) onto lockwasher No. 2 and press it into place. The tangs on lockwasher No. 1 must engage the cutouts in lockwasher No. 2 and lock both lockwashers into place.

17. Slide the fifth gear and fifth gear bushing up against the two lockwashers (A, **Figure 59**).

18. Slide the splined washer (B, **Figure 59**) toward the fifth gear.

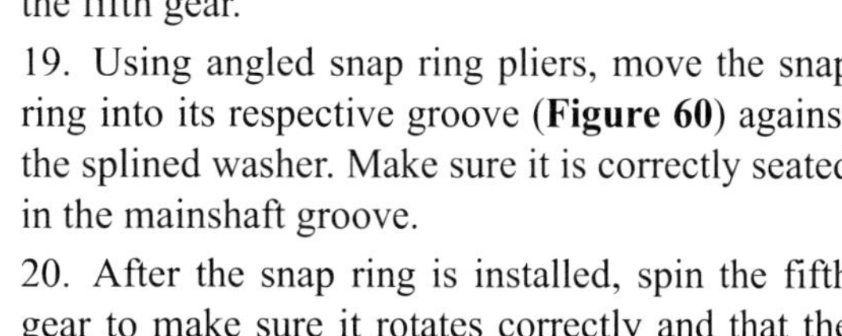

19. Using angled snap ring pliers, move the snap ring into its respective groove (**Figure 60**) against the splined washer. Make sure it is correctly seated in the mainshaft groove.

20. After the snap ring is installed, spin the fifth gear to make sure it rotates correctly and that the splined washer and snap ring are installed correctly. Reposition the snap ring if necessary.

21. Apply a light coat of Suzuki Super Grease A to the lips of a *new* oil seal. Position the oil seal with the dished side out and install the oil seal (**Figure 61**).

22. Install the needle bearing and bearing race (**Figure 62**). Make sure the locating dowel is in place in the outer bearing race.
23. Refer to **Figure 63** for correct placement of all gears. Make sure all snap rings/circlips are correctly seated in the mainshaft grooves.
24. Make sure each gear properly engages an adjoining gear where applicable.
25. After both transmission shafts have been assembled, mesh the two assemblies together in the correct position. Check that each gear properly engages its mate on the opposite shaft. This is the last check prior to installing the shaft assemblies into the crankcase; make sure they are correctly assembled.

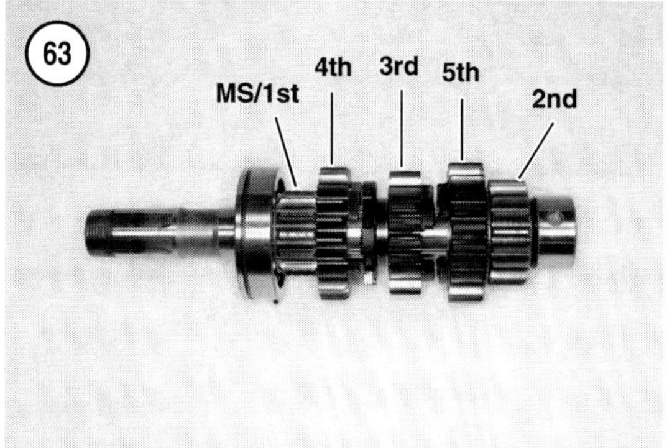

Transmission Inspection

NOTE

Replace defective gears and their mated gear on the other shaft as well, even though it may not show as much wear or damage.

1. Check each gear for excessive wear, burrs, pitting, chipped or missing teeth (A, **Figure 64**). Make sure the engagement dogs (B, **Figure 64**) on the gears are in good condition. Also inspect the engagement slots for wear or damage.
2. On splined gears, check the inner splines for excessive wear or damage. Replace the gear if necessary.
3. On gears with bushings, inspect the inner surface of the gear (A, **Figure 65**) for wear, pitting or damage. Insert the bushing into the gear, and check for smooth operation.
4. Check each bushing (B, **Figure 65**) for excessive wear, pitting or damage. Replace any bushing if necessary.
5. On splined bushings, check the inner splines (**Figure 66**) for excessive wear or damage. Replace if necessary.
6. Make sure that all gears and bushings slide smoothly on the shaft splines.
7. Inspect countershaft lockwashers No. 1 and No. 2 for wear, cracks, or damage. Replace if necessary.
8. Inspect the washers for bending wear or damage. Replace if necessary.
9. Check the needle bearing (**Figure 67**). Make sure the needles rotate smoothly with no signs of wear or damage. Replace the needle bearing as necessary.
10. Inspect the ball bearing (A, **Figure 68**). Make sure the bearing rotates smoothly.

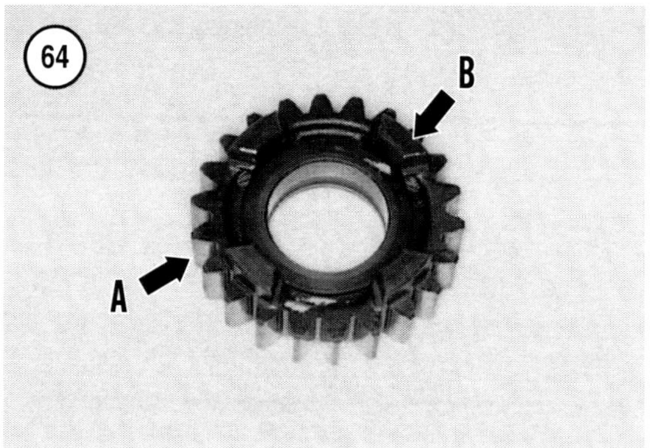

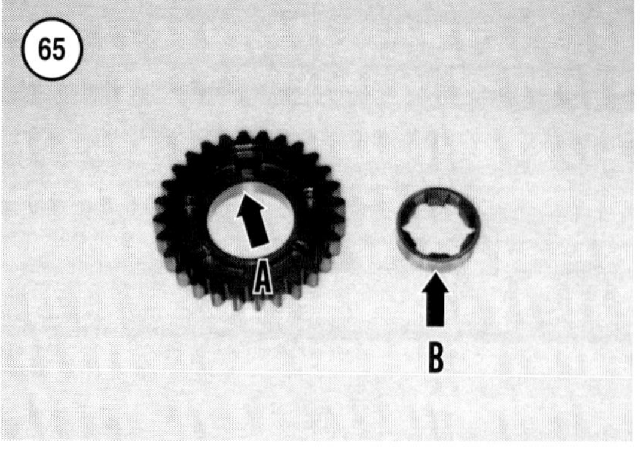

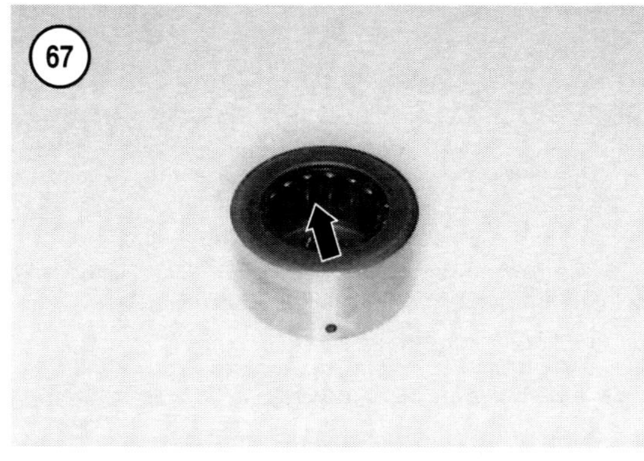

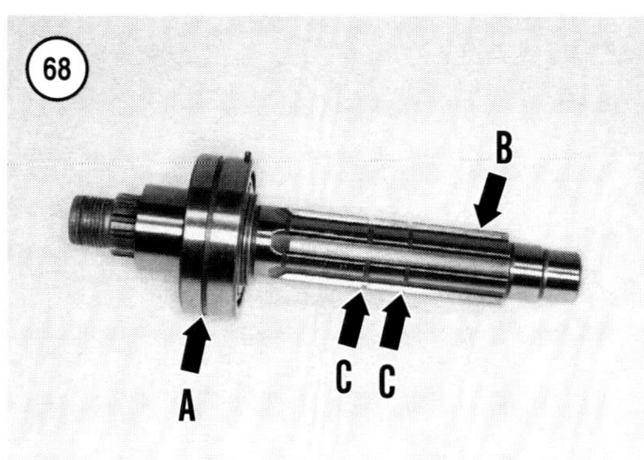

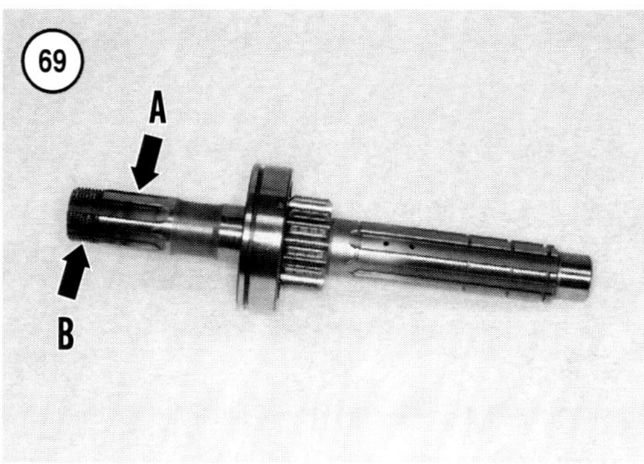

11. Inspect the splines (B, **Figure 68**) and snap ring grooves (C) in a shaft. If any are damaged, replace the shaft.
12. Inspect the clutch hub splines (A, **Figure 69**) and clutch nut threads (B) on the end of the mainshaft. If any of the splines are damaged, the shaft must be replaced.
13. Inspect the shift fork-to-gear clearance as described in *Internal Gearshift Mechanism* later in this chapter.

INTERNAL SHIFT MECHANISM

The internal shift mechanism consists of the shift drum, three shift forks and a shift fork shaft. To service the internal shift mechanism, it is necessary to remove the engine and split the crankcase as described in Chapter Five.

Removal/Disassembly

Refer to **Figure 70**.
1. Remove the engine and split the crankcase as described in Chapter Five.
2. Remove the transmission assemblies as described in Chapter Five.
3. Remove the external shift mechanism as described in this chapter.
4. Hold onto the shift forks and withdraw the shift shaft. Remove each shift fork as it is released from the shaft.
5. Turn the crankcase over.
6. Unhook the shift drum stopper spring (**Figure 71**) from the boss in the crankcase.
7. Turn the crankcase over.
8. Remove the snap ring (A, **Figure 72**) securing the shift drum stopper to the crankcase stud. Remove the shift drum stopper (B, **Figure 72**) and washer (C) from the stud.

NOTE
The neutral switch is referred to as the gear position switch on 2001-on models and performs the same function.

9. Remove the screws (**Figure 73**) securing the switch and remove the switch assembly.
10. The O-ring may come out with the switch or remain in the crankcase. Remove and discard the O-ring. A new one must be installed during assembly.

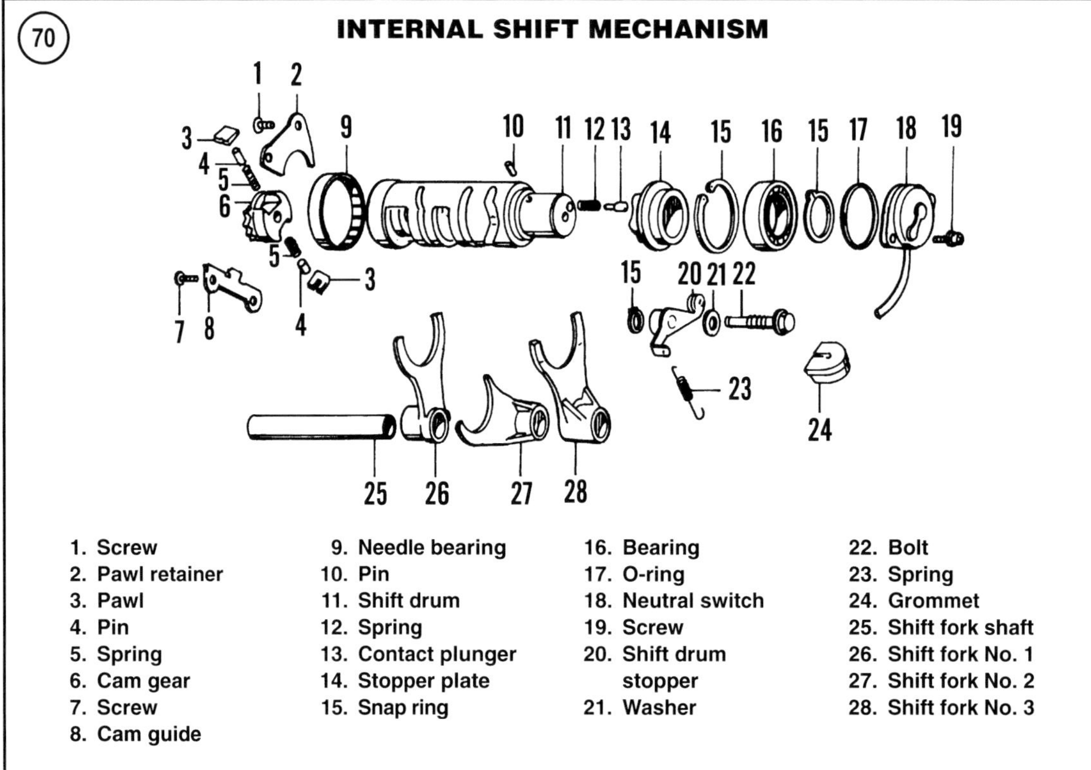

11. Remove the neutral switch, or gear position switch, contact plunger and spring (**Figure 74**) from the end of the shift drum.

12. Remove the snap ring (**Figure 75**) securing the shift drum into the crankcase.

13. Carefully withdraw the shift drum (**Figure 76**) from the crankcase.

14. Thoroughly clean all parts in solvent, and dry them with compressed air.

15. Inspect the internal shift mechanism components as described in this section.

Assembly/Installation

1. Apply a light coat of engine oil to the shift fork shafts, the inside bores of the shift forks, the shift drum bearing surfaces and the bearings in the crankcase prior to installing any parts.

2. If removed, make sure the locating pin (A, **Figure 77**) is in place in the shift drum. Align the pin groove in the stopper plate with the locating pin in the shift drum and push the stopper plate (B) onto the drum until the plate bottoms.

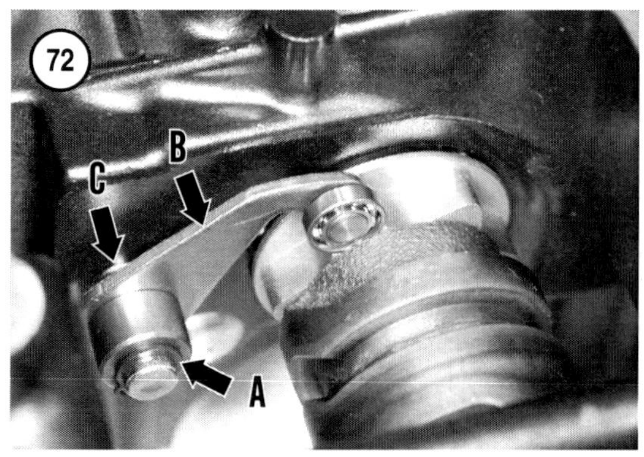

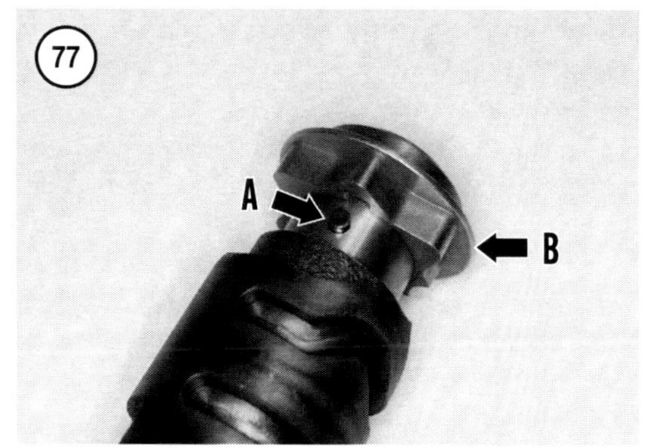

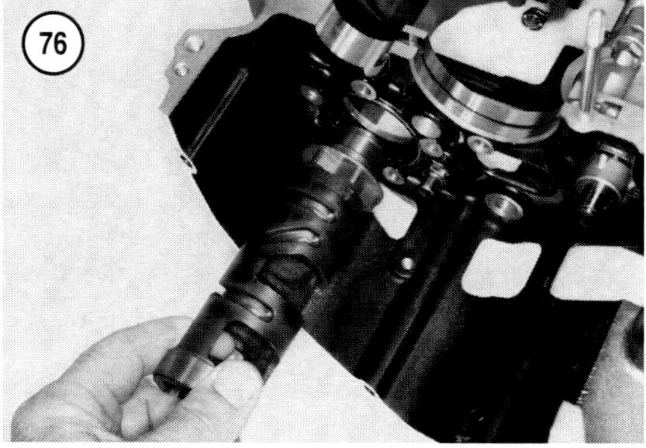

3. Install the shift drum (**Figure 76**) into the crankcase until it stops. Make sure the shift drum rotates smoothly.

NOTE

*To help secure the shift drum during snap ring installation in Step 4, install a 6 mm screw and washer (**Figure 78**) onto the crankcase.*

4. Install the snap ring (**Figure 79**) securing the shift drum into the crankcase. Make sure the

snap ring is correctly seated in the shift drum groove (**Figure 75**). Remove the 6 mm screw and washer.

5. Install the neutral switch contact spring and plunger (**Figure 74**) into the end of the gearshift drum.

6. Install a *new* O-ring into the receptacle in the crankcase or onto the switch (**Figure 80**) and install the neutral, or gear position, switch. Tighten the screws (**Figure 73**) securely.

7. Install the washer (C, **Figure 72**) and shift drum stopper (B) onto the crankcase stud. Secure them in place with the snap ring. Make sure the snap ring (A, **Figure 72**) is correctly seated in the groove.

8. Hook the shift drum stopper spring onto the shift drum stopper.

9. Turn the crankcase over.

10. Hook the shift drum stopper spring (**Figure 71**) onto the mounting boss in the crankcase.

11. Rotate the shift drum back and fourth and make sure the shift drum stopper roller rides correctly on the stopper plate.

12. Rotate the shift drum to the NEUTRAL position and make sure the shift drum stopper roller is correctly seated in the neutral detent of the stopper plate.

13. Turn the crankcase over.

14. Partially install the shift fork shaft (A, **Figure 81**) into the crankcase.

15. Hold shift fork No. 1 (B, **Figure 81**) in position and push the shift fork shaft through it.

16. Hold shift fork No. 2 (**Figure 82**) in position and push the shift fork shaft through it.

17. Hold shift fork No. 3 (**Figure 83**) in position and push the shift fork shaft through it.

18. Push the shift fork all the way through each shift fork until the shaft bottoms in the crankcase boss.

19. The shift fork shaft can slide out of the crankcase at this point. To prevent this from happening, install the external shift mechanism as described in this chapter or temporarily install a spare 6 mm bolt and washer.

20. Install the transmission assemblies as described in this chapter.

21. Assemble the crankcase as described in Chapter Five.

22. Install the engine as described in Chapter Five.

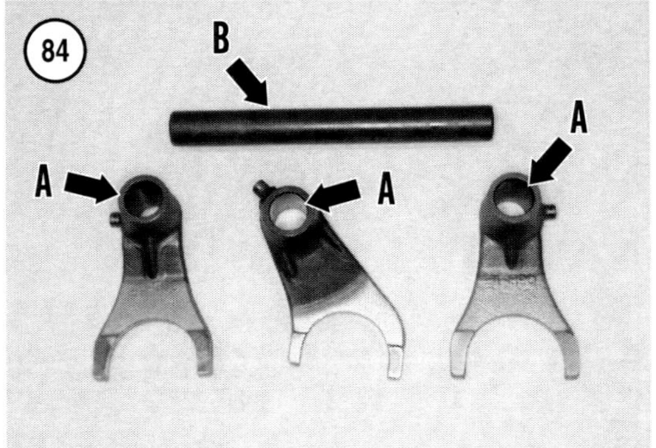

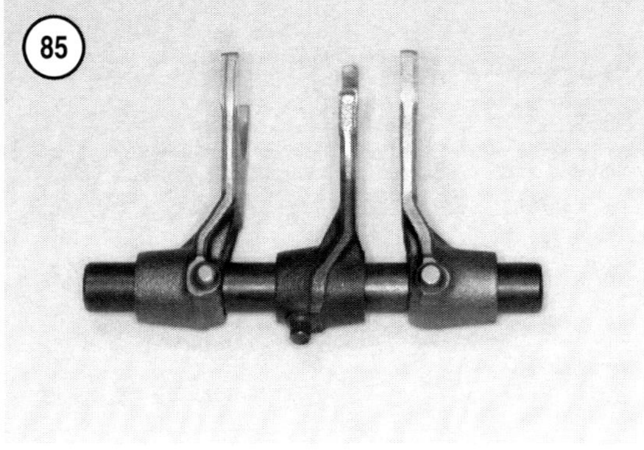

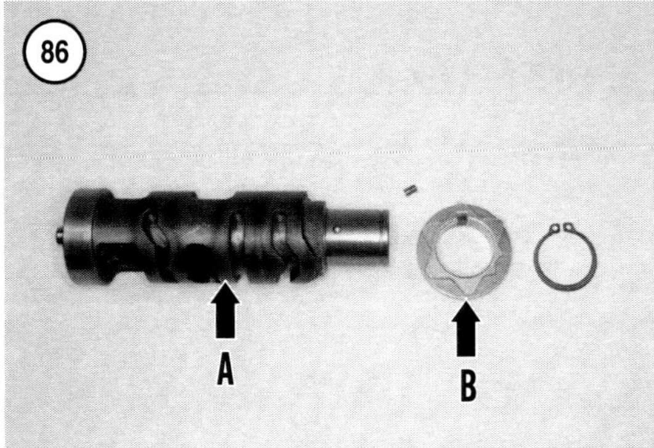

Inspection

Compare any measurements to the specification in **Table 2**. Replace any part that is damaged, worn to the wear limit or out of specification.

1. Inspect each shift fork for signs of wear or cracking. Check for any arc-shaped wear or burned marks on the fingers of the shift forks. This indicates that the shift fork has come in contact with the gear. The fork fingers have become excessively worn and the fork must be replaced.
2. Check the bore of each shift fork (A, **Figure 84**) and the shift fork shaft (B) for burrs, wear or pitting. Replace any worn parts.
3. Install each shift fork onto the shaft (**Figure 85**) and make sure it moves freely on the shaft with no binding.
4. Check the guide pin on each shift fork for wear or damage. Replace the shift fork(s) as necessary.
5. Roll the shift fork shaft on a flat surface, such as a piece of plate glass, and check for any bends. If the shaft is bent, it must be replaced.
6. Check the grooves in the shift drum (A, **Figure 86**) for wear or roughness. If any of the groove profiles have excessive wear or damage, replace the shift drum.
7. Inspect the cam gear receptacle in the end of the shift drum for wear or damage. Replace the shift drum if necessary.
8. Check the shift drum stopper plate (B, **Figure 86**) for wear; replace as necessary.
9. Check the neutral switch, or gear position switch, contact plunger and spring for wear or damage. If the spring has sagged, replace it.
10. Make sure the locating pin fits tightly in the shift drum. If the pin is loose, replace it.
11. Check the shift drum bearings in the crankcase. Make sure they operate smoothly with no signs of wear or damage. If damaged, replace the bearing as described in Chapter Five.
12. Inspect the roller on the end of the shift drum stopper. If worn or damaged, replace the shift drum stopper.

CAUTION
Marginally worn shift forks should be replaced. Worn forks can cause the transmission to slip out of gear, leading to more serious and expensive damage.

13. Inspect the shift fork-to-groove clearance as follows:
    a. Install each shift fork into the shift fork groove in its respective gear. Use a flat feeler gauge and measure the clearance between the fork and the gear as shown in **Figure 87**.
    b. If the clearance is greater than the specification, measure the thickness of the shift fork fingers with a micrometer (**Figure 88**). If the thickness is out of specification, replace the shift fork.
    c. If the shift fork thickness is within tolerance, measure the shift fork groove width in each gear. Replace the gear(s) if the groove width is out of specification.

7

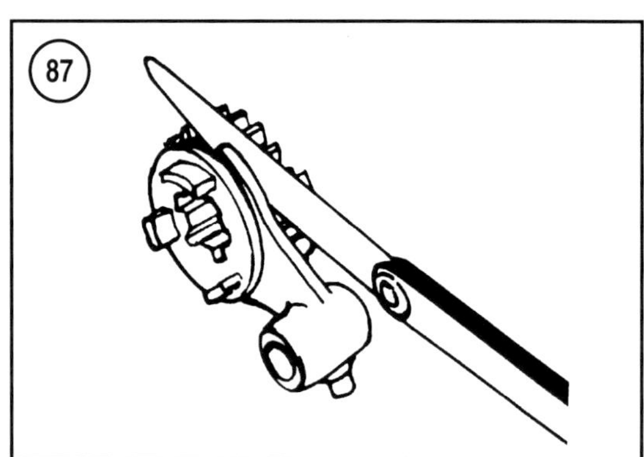

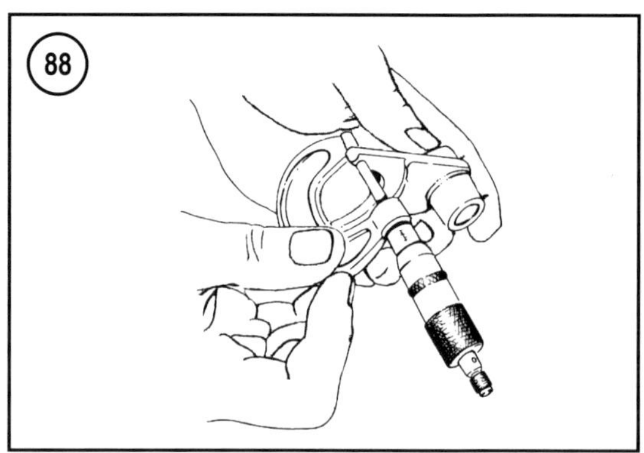

Table 1 TRANSMISSION SPECIFICATIONS

Item	Standard
Transmission gear ratios	
1st gear	2.384 (31/15)
2nd gear	1.631 (31/19)
3rd gear	1.250 (25/20)
4th gear	1.045 (23/22)
5th gear	0.913 (21/23)
Primary reduction ratio	1.565 (72/46)
Final reduction ratio	3.000 (45/15)

Table 2 GEARSHIFT SPECIFICATIONS

Item	Standard mm (in.)	Wear limit mm (in.)
Shift fork-to-groove clearance	0.1-0.3 (0.004-0.012)	0.50 (0.020)
Shift fork groove width	5.0-5.1 (0.197-0.201)	–
Shift fork thickness	4.8-4.9 (0.189-0.193)	–
Shift lever height	55 (2.2)	–

Table 3 ENGINE DRIVE SPROCKET TORQUE SPECIFICATIONS

Item	N•m	in.-lb.	ft.-lb.
Engine drive sprocket nut	115	–	85
Speed sensor mounting bolt	20	–	15

CHAPTER EIGHT

FUEL, EMISSION CONTROL AND EXHAUST SYSTEMS

This chapter includes service procedures for all parts of the fuel system, emission control systems and the exhaust system. Air filter service is covered in Chapter Three.

Refer to **Tables 1-6** at the end of this chapter for carburetor and torque specifications.

The fuel system consists of the fuel tank, the fuel valve, four carburetors and an air filter assembly. The exhaust system consists of a 4-into-1 exhaust pipe and a muffler assembly.

The emission controls consist of a crankcase emission system, an evaporative emission control system, and a PAIR (Air Supply) system on California models.

WARNING

Gasoline is a known carcinogenic, as well as an extremely flammable liquid, and must be handled carefully. Wear latex gloves when working on components that come in contact with gasoline. If gasoline contacts any skin, rinse it off immediately and the thoroughly wash with soap and warm water.

CARBURETOR OPERATION

For proper operation, a gasoline engine must be supplied with air and fuel mixed in proper proportions by weight. A mixture with an excessive amount of fuel is said to be rich. A lean mixture is one that contains insufficient fuel. A properly adjusted carburetor supplies the proper air/fuel mixture under all operating conditions.

A carburetor consists of several major systems. A float and float valve mechanism maintain a constant fuel level in the float bowl. The pilot system supplies fuel at low speeds. The main system supplies fuel at medium and high speeds. A starter (choke) system supplies the very rich mixture needed to start a cold engine.

CARBURETOR SERVICE

If poor engine performance, hesitation and little or no response to mixture adjustment is observed, and if all other factors that could affect performance are correct, perform major carburetor service (removal and cleaning) as described in this chapter. Alterations in jet size and jet needle position should only be attempted by those experienced in this type of tuning work. Do not adjust or modify the carburetors in an attempt to fix a driveability problem caused by another system.

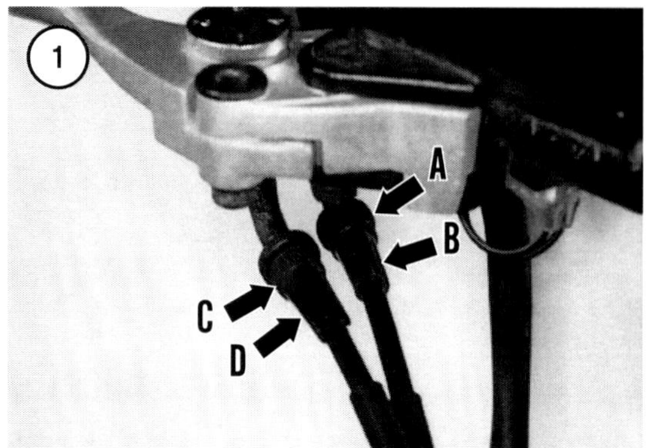

CARBURETOR ASSEMBLY (1996-2000 MODELS)

Removal/Installation

Remove all four carburetors as an assembled unit.

1. Remove the seat as described in Chapter Fourteen.
2. Remove the frame side covers as described in Chapter Fourteen.
3. Remove the fuel tank as described in this chapter.
4. Disconnect the negative lead from the battery as described in Chapter Three.
5. Provide slack in the throttle cables as follows:
   a. Loosen the locknut (A, **Figure 1**) on the return cable adjuster. Turn the cable adjuster (B, **Figure 1**) all the way in to provide cable slack.
   b. Loosen the locknut (C, **Figure 1**) on the pull cable adjuster. Turn the adjuster (D, **Figure 1**) in all the way in to provide cable slack.
6. Disconnect the crankcase breather hose (**Figure 2**) from the air filter housing.
7. Remove the screw (**Figure 3**) securing the air filter housing on each side.
8. On California models, disconnect each EVAP purge hose from its fitting on the bottom of the carburetor assembly.
9. On models so equipped, disconnect the PAIR vacuum hose from the fitting on the No. 3 carburetor.
10. On models so equipped, disconnect the throttle position sensor electrical lead.
11. Loosen the carburetor clamp screw (A, **Figure 4**) on each intake manifold on the cylinder head.
12. Loosen the carburetor clamp screw (B, **Figure 4**) on each air duct from the air filter housing.

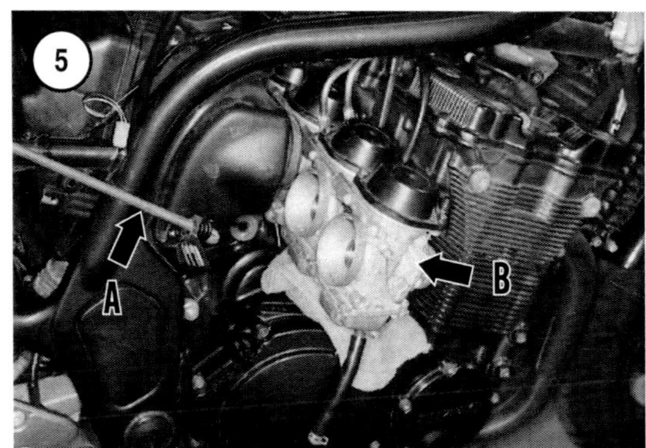

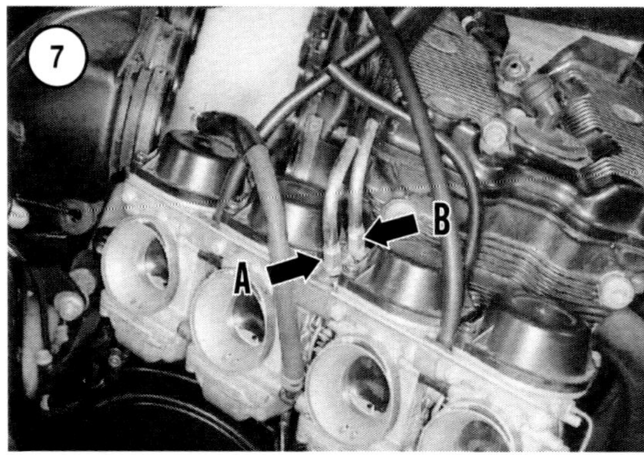

13. Move the air filter housing rearward slightly and disengage each air duct from the carburetor inlet. Secure the air filter rearward with a bungee cord (A, **Figure 5**).

14. Remove the starter (choke) cable as follows:
   a. Disconnect the starter (choke) cable end from the anchor on the starter plate.
   b. Disconnect the starter (choke) cable (**Figure 6**) from the left side of the carburetor assembly.

15. Pull the carburetor assembly rearward and disengage each carburetor from its intake manifold.

16. Carefully move the carburetor assembly (B, **Figure 5**) out from the right side.

NOTE
*Label the throttle pull and return cables before disconnecting them so they can be reinstalled in the proper position during assembly. When the carburetor assembly is installed in the engine, the pull cable is the rear-most cable (A, **Figure** 7). The return cable is the front cable (B, **Figure** 7).*

17. Loosen the cable locknut (A, **Figure 8**) and loosen the cable adjuster (B) until there is sufficient slack in the return cable.

18. Disconnect the return cable end (**Figure 9**) from the throttle wheel.

19. Repeat this procedure for the pull cable.

20. Remove the carburetor assembly from the engine and frame.

21. Place a clean lint-free cloth into each intake manifold on the cylinder head to prevent the entry of debris.

22. Install by reversing these removal steps while noting the following:

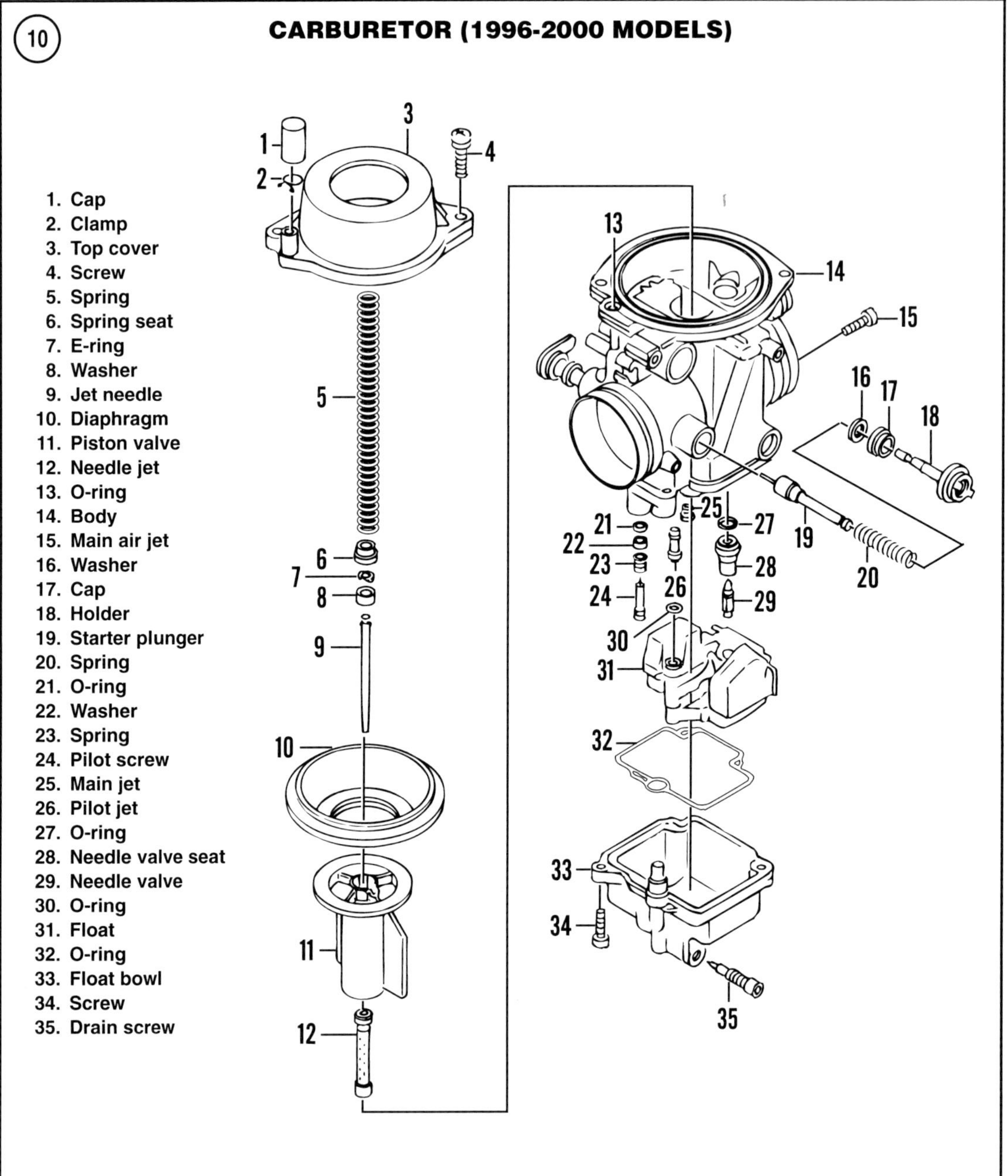

a. Make sure the carburetors are fully seated forward in the intake manifolds on the cylinder head. A solid bottoming out will be felt when they are correctly seated.
b. Make sure each carburetor clamp screw is tight to avoid a vacuum loss and possible valve damage due to a lean fuel mixture.
c. Adjust the throttle cables as described in Chapter Three.

Individual Carburetor

Disassembly

NOTE
On models so equipped, the throttle position sensor is preset by the manufacturer. Do not remove it. If removal is necessary, make an alignment mark on the sensor relating to the center-

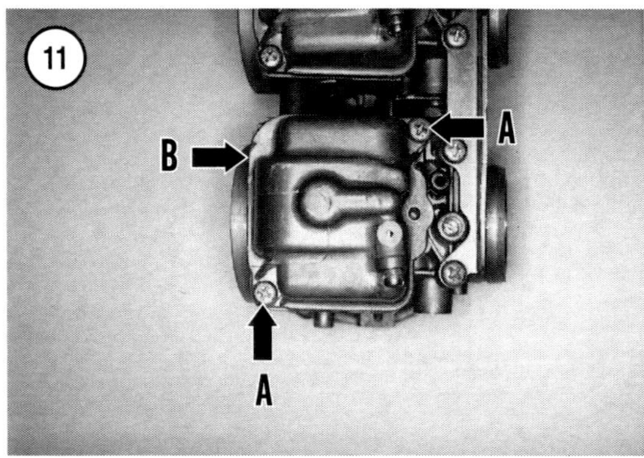

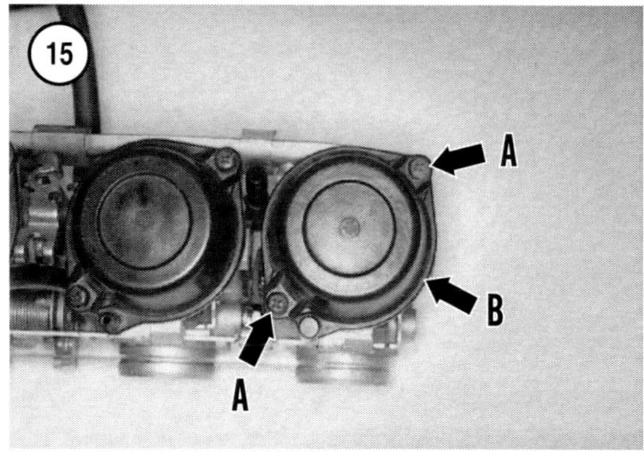

line of the mounting screws. Make corresponding alignment marks on the carburetor body so the sensor can be precisely installed ***in the same position****. Also, check the resistance value prior to removal as described in this chapter.*

Disassemble only one carburetor at a time to prevent the accidental interchange of parts. Refer to **Figure 10**.

1. Remove the float bowl screws (A, **Figure 11**) and remove the float bowl (B). Discard the float bowl O-ring.

2. Pull straight up and remove the float assembly (**Figure 12**). Do not lose the needle valve hanging on the float tang. Make sure the small O-ring comcs out with the float assembly; if not, remove it from the carburetor receptacle.

3A. On U.S.A., California, Canada and some European models, the pilot screw assembly is located under a plug that should not be removed. If removal is necessary, refer to *Pilot Screw* in this chapter.

3B. On models without a pilot-screw plug, screw the pilot screw (A, **Figure 13**) in until it *lightly* seats while counting and recording the number of turns. The pilot screw must be reinstalled to this same position during assembly. Unscrew and remove the pilot screw, spring, washer and O-ring.

4. Unscrew and remove the pilot jet (B, **Figure 13**).

5. Remove the needle valve housing (**Figure 14**).

6. Remove the top cover screws (A, **Figure 15**) and remove the cover (B).

7. Remove the spring (A, **Figure 16**) and the diaphragm/piston valve assembly (B).

8. Unscrew and remove the main jet (**Figure 17**) from the end of the needle jet holder.

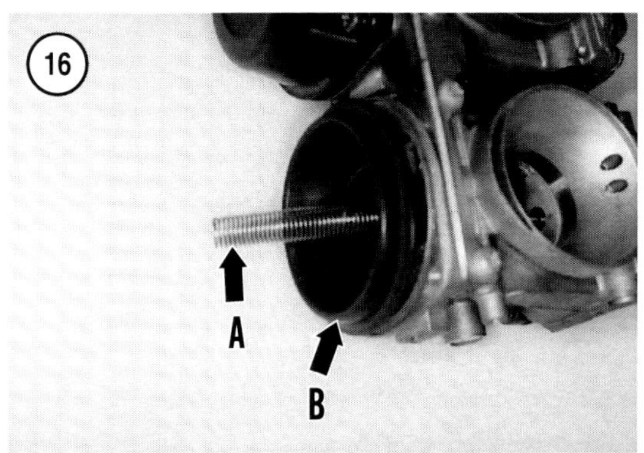

9. Remove the needle jet and holder assembly (**Figure 18**).

10. Disassemble the diaphragm/piston valve as follows:

   a. If still in place, remove the spring (A, **Figure 19**).
   b. Withdraw the jet needle, washer and spring seat assembly (B, **Figure 19**).

NOTE

Further disassembly is neither necessary nor recommended. Do not remove the throttle shaft and butterfly assemblies. If these parts are damaged, the carburetor must be replaced, as these items are not available separately.

11. Clean and inspect all parts as described in this chapter.

Assembly

1. Install a *new* O-ring (**Figure 20**) onto the needle jet holder.

2. Install the needle jet into the holder (**Figure 21**).

3. Align the needle jet flat (**Figure 22**) with the stud (B) on the post. These parts must be correctly aligned during assembly.

4. Slowly install the needle jet assembly (**Figure 23**) into the carburetor body. Guide the needle jet into the carburetor venturi opening (**Figure 24**). Push the assembly in until bottoms (**Figure 18**).

5. Install the main jet (**Figure 17**) and tighten securely.

6. Assemble the diaphragm/piston valve as follows:

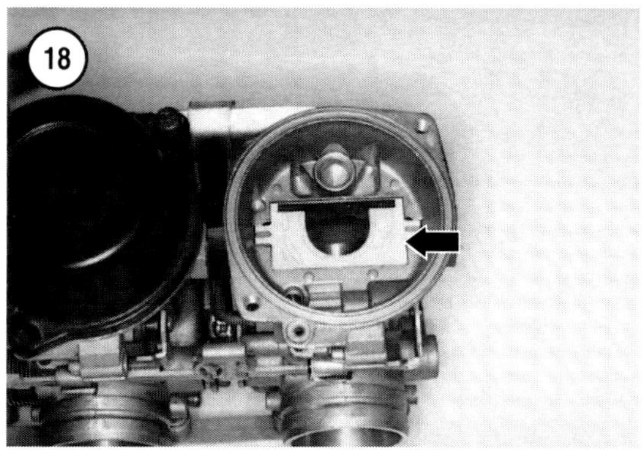

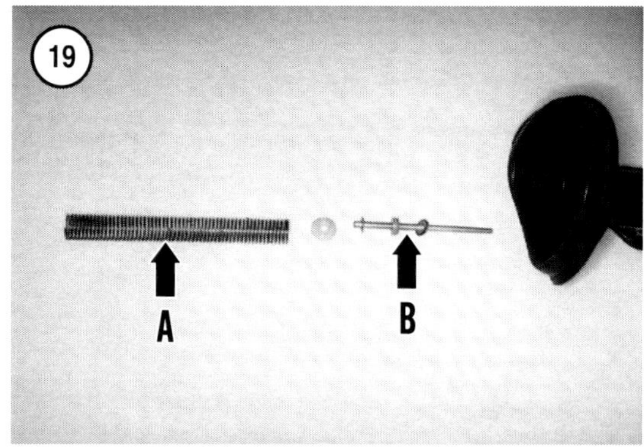

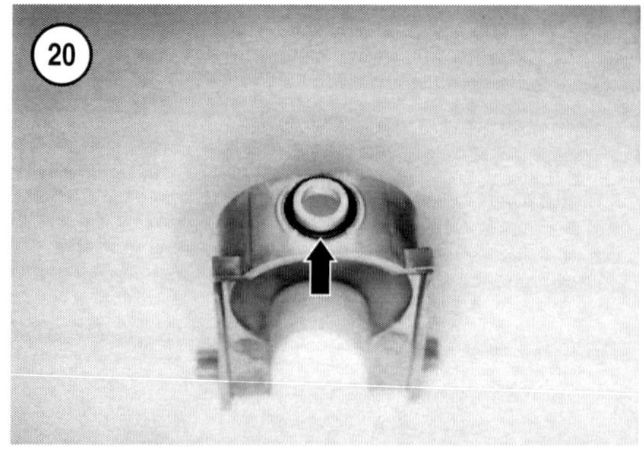

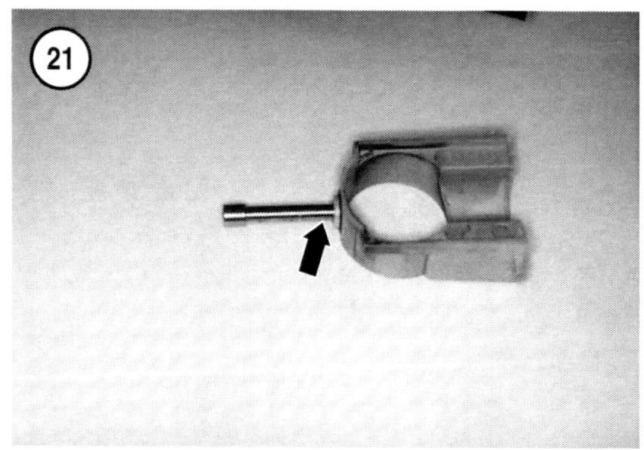
21

25

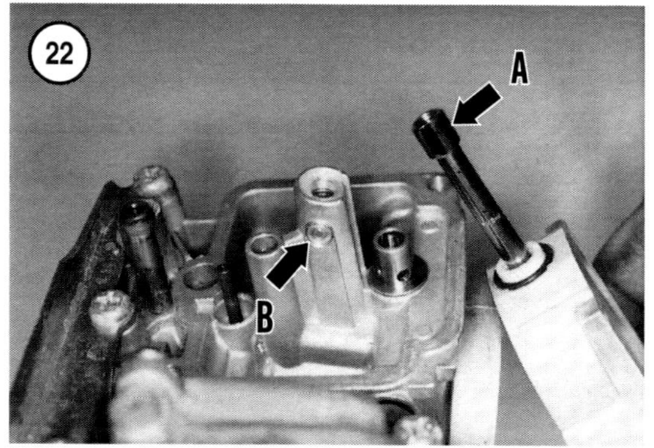
22

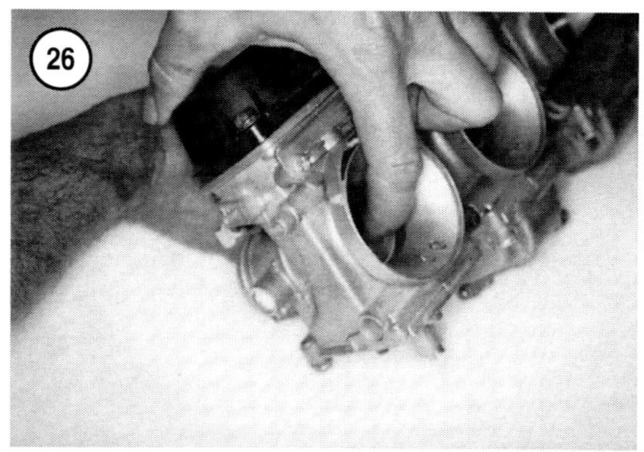
26

23

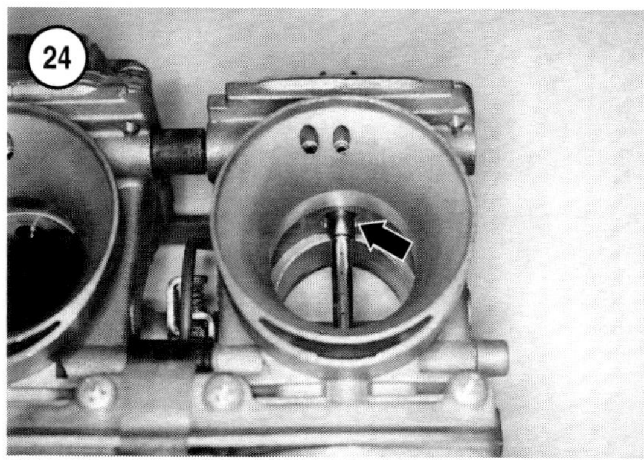
24

a. Install the jet needle, washer and spring seat assembly (B, **Figure 19**) into the piston valve.

b. Install the spring (A, **Figure 19**) into the diaphragm/piston valve assembly.

7. Install the spring (A, **Figure 16**) and the diaphragm/piston valve assembly into the needle jet assembly.

8. Make sure the diaphragm is seated correctly in the sealing groove (**Figure 25**).

9. Make sure the spring is indexed correctly onto the top cover.

10. Install the top cover. Before installing the top cover screws, insert a finger into the venturi and move the piston valve up (**Figure 26**). The piston valve should rise all the way up into the bore and slide back down immediately with no binding. If it binds or if the movement is sluggish, chances are the diaphragm did not seat correctly or the spring is bent or not centered within the top cover.

11. Install the top cover screws (A, **Figure 15**) and tighten securely.

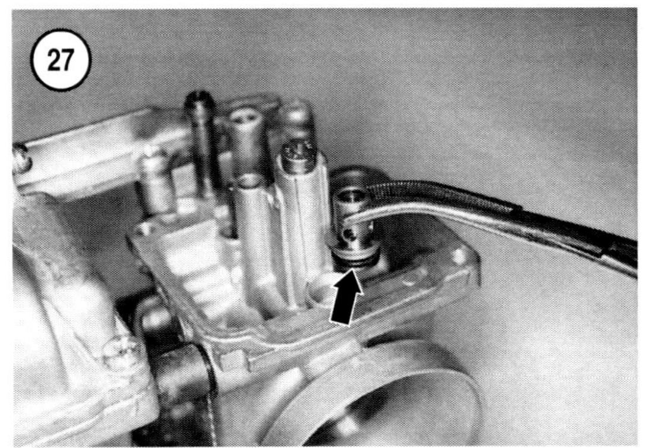

12. Install a *new* O-ring (**Figure 27**) onto the needle valve seat and insert it into the carburetor body. Push it down until it bottoms (**Figure 14**).
13. Install the pilot jet (**Figure 28**) and tighten securely.
14. On models without a pilot-screw plug, install the pilot screw, spring, washer and O-ring. Turn the pilot screw (A, **Figure 13**) to the setting noted during disassembly.
15. Install a *new* O-ring (A, **Figure 29**) onto the float assembly.
16. If removed, install the needle valve (B, **Figure 29**) onto the float tang.
17. Install the float assembly (**Figure 12**) while indexing the needle valve into the housing.
18. Check and adjust the float height as described in this chapter.
19. Install a *new* O-ring (**Figure 30**) in the float bowl.
20. Install the float bowl (B, **Figure 11**) and screws (A). Tighten the screws securely.
21. After the assembly and installation are completed, adjust the carburetors as described in this chapter and in Chapter Three.

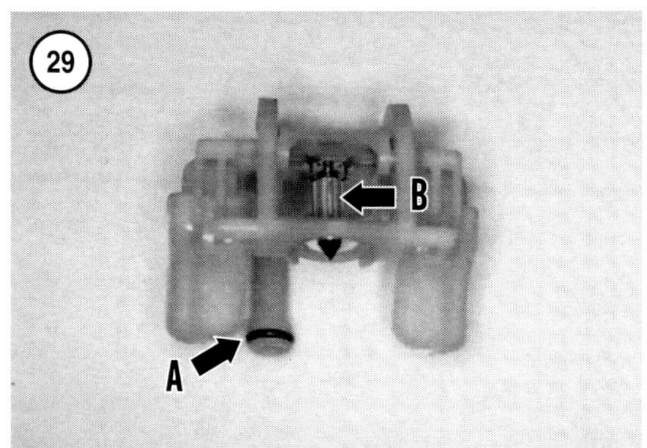

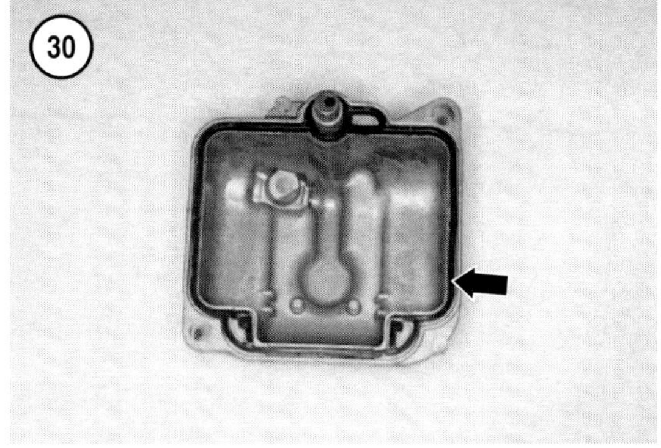

CARBURETOR ASSEMBLY (2001-ON MODELS)

Removal/Installation

Remove all four carburetors as an assembled unit.
1. Remove the seat as described in Chapter Fourteen.
2. Remove the frame side covers as described in Chapter Fourteen.
3. Remove the fuel tank as described in this chapter.
4. Disconnect the negative lead from the battery as described in Chapter Three.
5. Provide slack in the throttle cables as follows:

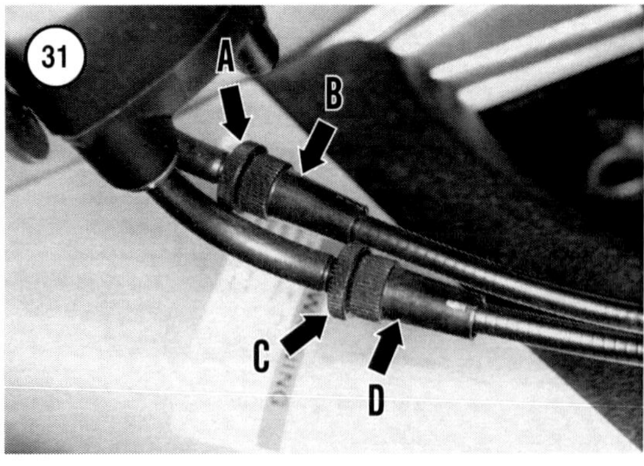

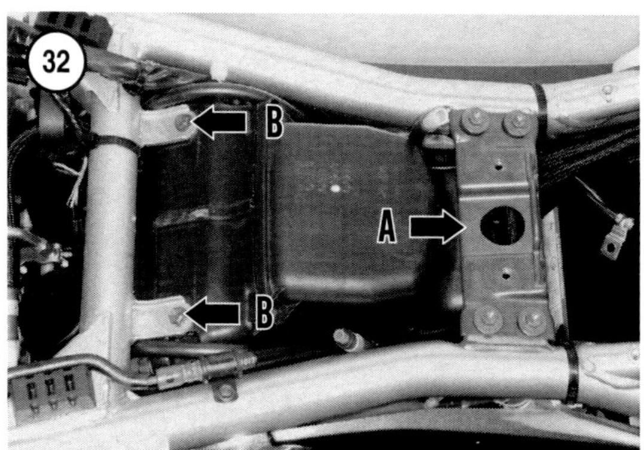

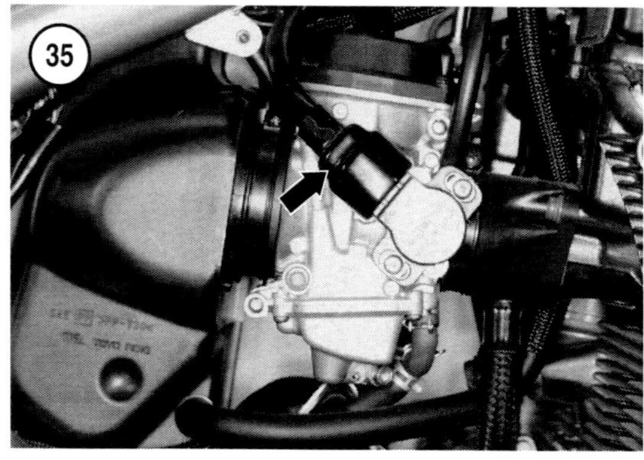

a. Loosen the locknut (A, **Figure 31**) on the return cable adjuster. Turn the cable adjuster (B, **Figure 31**) all the way in to provide cable slack.

b. Loosen the locknut (C, **Figure 31**) on the pull cable adjuster. Turn the adjuster (D, **Figure 31**) all the way in to provide cable slack.

6. Remove the bolts securing the fuel tank mounting bracket (A, **Figure 32**) and remove the bracket.

7. Remove the screws (B, **Figure 32**) securing the air filter housing on each side.

NOTE

*Label the throttle pull and return cables before disconnecting them so they can be reinstalled in the proper position during assembly. When the carburetor assembly is installed in the engine, the pull cable is the rear-most cable (A, **Figure 33**). The return cable is the front cable (B, **Figure 33**).*

8. Loosen the cable locknut (A, **Figure 33**) and loosen the cable adjuster until there is sufficient slack in the pull cable.

9. Loosen the cable locknut (B, **Figure 33**) and loosen the cable adjuster until there is sufficient slack in the return cable.

10. Remove the starter (choke) cable as follows:

a. Disconnect the starter (choke) cable end from the anchor (A, **Figure 34**) on the starter plate.

b. Disconnect the starter (choke) cable (B, **Figure 34**) from the lever.

11. Disconnect the throttle position sensor electrical connector (**Figure 35**). Move the wiring harness out of the way.

12. On U.K. models only, disconnect the electrical connector from the carburetor heaters.

13. Loosen the carburetor clamp screw (A, **Figure 36**) on each intake manifold on the cylinder head.

14. Loosen the carburetor clamp screw (B, **Figure 36**) on each air duct from the air filter housing.
15. Pull the two vent hoses out from the sides of the air filter housing.
16. Pull the fuel inlet hose through the hose guide (**Figure 37**).
17. Disconnect the drain hoses (**Figure 38**) from the float bowls.
18. On California models, disconnect each EVAP purge hose from its fitting on the bottom of the carburetor assembly.
19. On PAIR equipped models, disconnect the PAIR vacuum hose from the fitting on the No. 3 carburetor.
20. Move the air filter housing rearward slightly and disengage each air duct from the carburetor inlets. Secure the air filter with a bungee cord.
21. Pull the carburetor assembly rearward and disengage each carburetor from its intake manifold.
22. Carefully move the carburetor assembly out from the right side.
23. Disconnect the throttle cables from the throttle wheel and cable mounting bracket (**Figure 39**).
24. Remove the carburetor assembly from the engine and frame.
25. Place a clean lint-free cloth into each intake manifold on the cylinder head to prevent the entry of debris.
26. Install by reversing these removal steps while noting the following:
   a. Make sure the carburetors are fully seated forward in the intake manifolds on the cylinder head. A solid bottoming out will be felt when they are correctly seated.
   b. Make sure each carburetor clamp screw is tight to avoid a vacuum loss and possible valve damage due to a lean fuel mixture.
   c. Adjust the throttle cables as described in Chapter Three.

Individual Carburetor

Disassembly

NOTE

The throttle position sensor is preset by the manufacturer. Do not remove it. If removal is necessary, refer to the procedure later in this section.

Disassemble only one carburetor at a time to prevent the accidental interchange of parts. Refer to **Figure 40**.

1. Remove the top cover screws (**Figure 41**).
2. Remove the cover (A, **Figure 42**), the spring (B) and the diaphragm/piston valve assembly (C).
3. Disassemble the diaphragm/piston valve as follows:
   a. Pull straight out and remove the stopper (**Figure 43**) securing the jet needle assembly.

40

CARBURETOR (2001-ON MODELS)

1. Top cover
2. Screw
3. O-ring
4. Spring
5. Stopper
6. O-ring
7. Spring
8. Washer
9. E-clip
10. Spacer
11. Jet needle
12. Diaphragm/piston valve
13. Cap
14. Clamp
15. Pilot air jet
16. Starter plunger
17. Starter assembly
18. O-ring
19. Washer
20. Spring
21. Pilot screw
22. O-ring
23. Needle valve seat
24. Needle valve
25. Float
26. Float pivot pin
27. Needle jet
28. O-ring
29. Screw
30. Screw
31. Pilot jet
32. Main jet holder
33. Main jet
34. Starter jet
35. O-ring
36. Screw
37. Drain screw

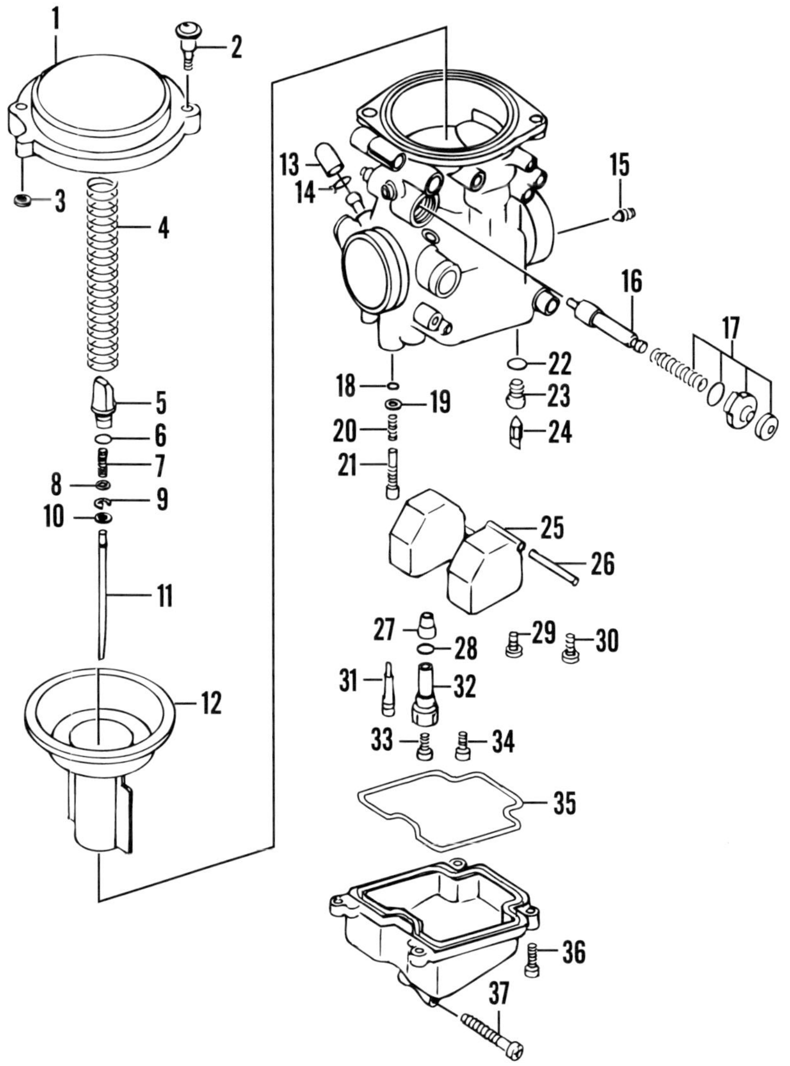

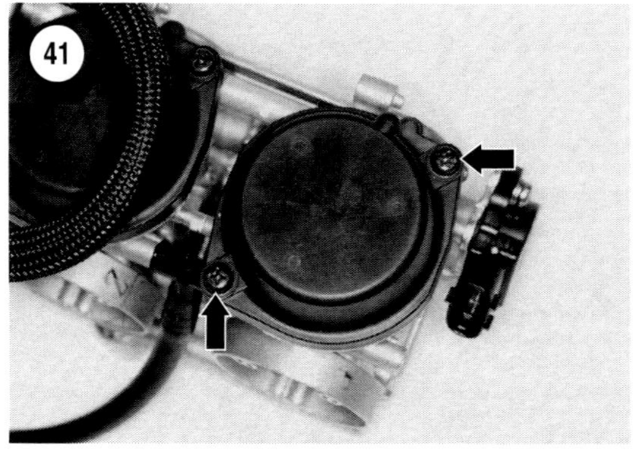

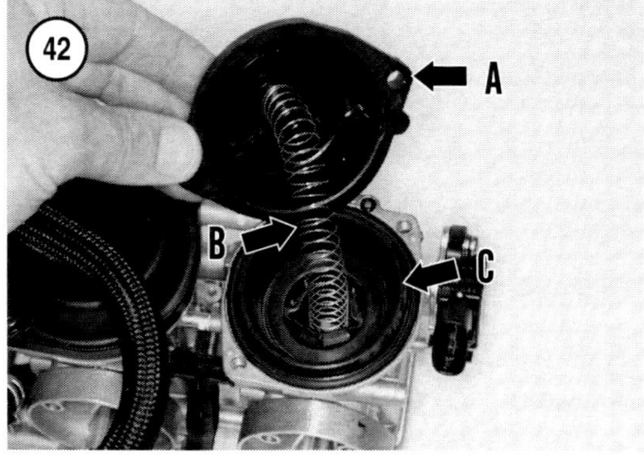

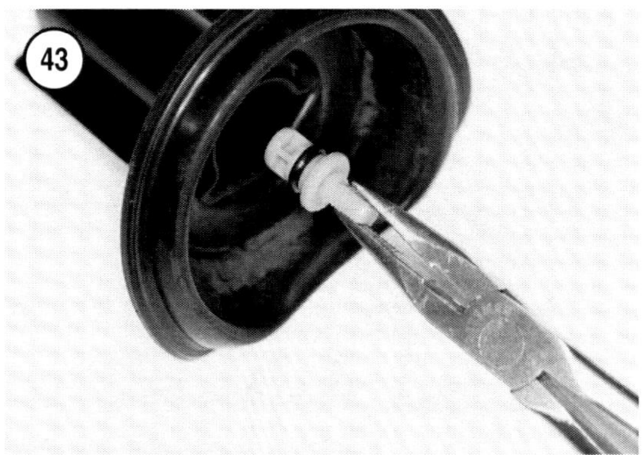

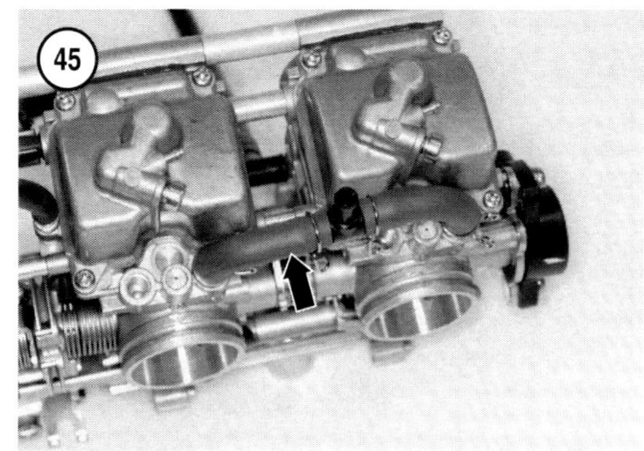

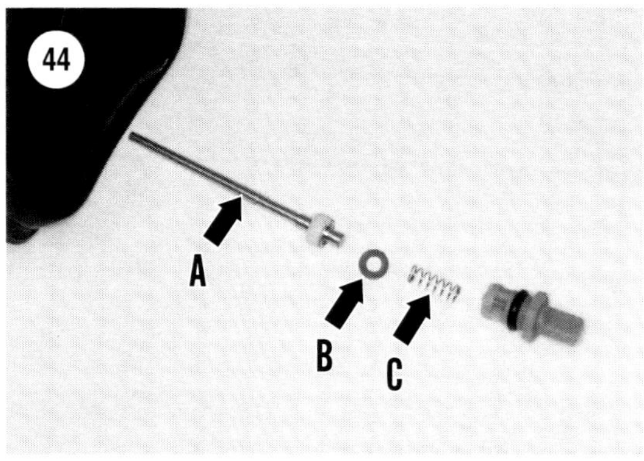

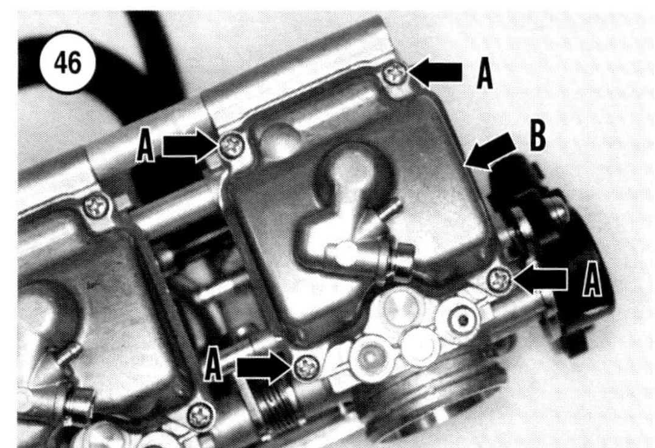

b. Withdraw the jet needle (A, **Figure 44**), washer (B) and spring (C).

4. Remove the interconnecting hoses (**Figure 45**) from the No. 1 and No. 2 carburetors and the No. 3 and No. 4 carburetors.

5. Remove the float bowl screws (A, **Figure 46**) and the float bowl (B). Discard the float bowl O-ring.

6. Remove the float pin retaining screw (**Figure 47**).

7. Pull straight up and remove the float and float pin assembly (**Figure 48**). Do not lose the needle valve hanging on the float tang.

8. Remove the screw (A, **Figure 49**) securing the needle valve seat (B) and remove the housing.

9. Unscrew and remove the main jet (A, **Figure 50**) from the end of the needle jet holder (B).

10. Turn the carburetor assembly over and remove the needle jet (**Figure 51**) from the carburetor post.

11. Unscrew and remove the starter jet (C, **Figure 50**) and the pilot jet (D).

12. Unscrew and remove the pilot air jet (**Figure 52**).

13A. On U.S.A., California, Canada and some European models, the pilot screw assembly is located under a plug (E, **Figure 50**) that should not be removed. If removal is necessary, refer to *Pilot Screw* in this chapter.

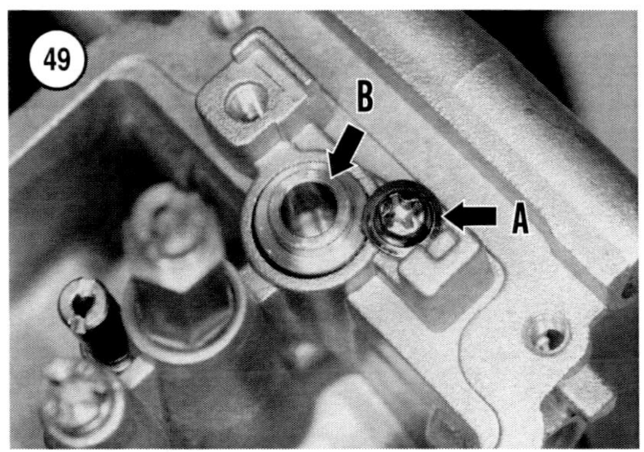

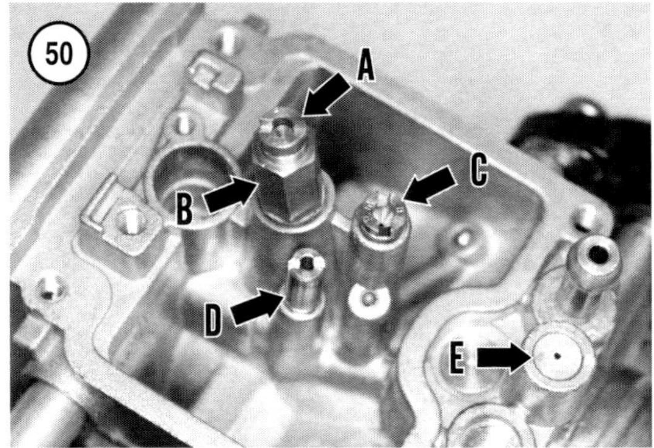

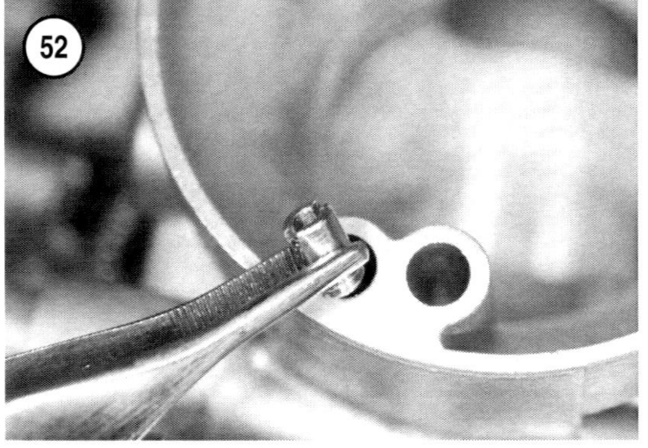

13B. On models without a pilot-screw plug, screw the pilot screw in until it *lightly* seats while counting and recording the number of turns. The pilot screw must be reinstalled to this same position during assembly. Unscrew and remove the pilot screw, spring, washer and O-ring.

NOTE

Further disassembly is neither necessary nor recommended. Do not remove the throttle shaft and butterfly assemblies (A, ***Figure 53****). If these parts are damaged, the carburetor must be replaced, as these items are not available separately.*

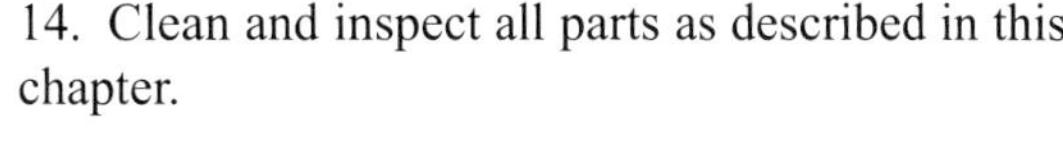

14. Clean and inspect all parts as described in this chapter.

Assembly

1. Install the pilot air jet (**Figure 52**) and tighten securely.
2. Install the pilot jet (**Figure 54**) and the starter jet (**Figure 55**) and tighten securely.

3. Install the needle jet (**Figure 56**) into the post. Make sure it is correctly seated, then install the main jet holder (**Figure 57**) and tighten securely.
4. Install the main jet (**Figure 58**) and tighten securely.
5. Install a *new* O-ring (**Figure 59**) onto the needle valve seat and insert it into the carburetor body. Push it down until it bottoms (B, **Figure 49**), then secure it with the mounting screw (A).
6. If removed, install the needle valve (**Figure 60**) onto the float tang.
7. Install the float and float pin assembly (**Figure 48**) while indexing the needle valve into the housing.
8. Install the float pin mounting screw (**Figure 47**) and tighten securely.
9. Check and adjust the float height as described in this chapter.
10. Install a *new* O-ring (**Figure 61**) into the float bowl.
11. Install the float bowl (B, **Figure 46**) and screws. Tighten the screws securely.
12. Install the interconnecting fuel hoses (**Figure 45**) between the No. 1 and No. 2 carburetors and the No. 3 and No. 4 carburetors.
13. Assemble the diaphragm/piston valve as follows:
    a. Install the jet needle (A, **Figure 44**), washer (B) and spring (C) into the diaphragm/piston valve. Check to make sure the washer and spring are still in place on the end of the jet needle.
    b. Push straight in and install the stopper (**Figure 43**) securing the jet needle assembly. Push it in until it bottoms.
    c. Carefully push on the end of the jet needle and release it. If the spring is installed correctly, it will push the jet needle back out. If not, re-assemble the jet needle and spring correctly.
14. Install the diaphragm/piston valve assembly. Make sure the diaphragm is seated correctly in the sealing groove and vent hole (**Figure 62**).

NOTE

The piston valve spring is very long and is difficult to install while keeping it straight. Use the method listed in Step 15 to avoid having the spring getting cocked within the top cover.

15. Install the top cover and spring as follows:

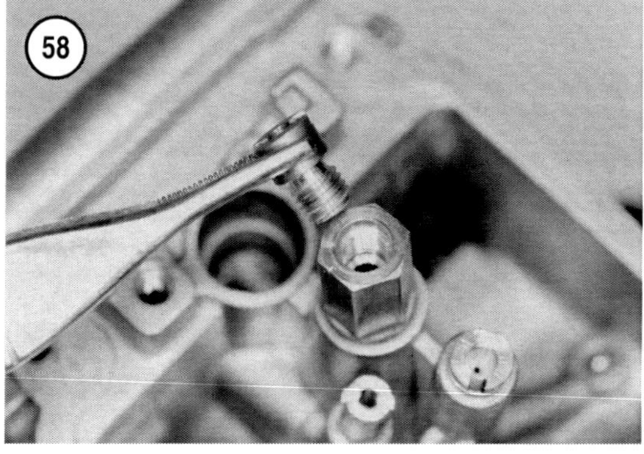

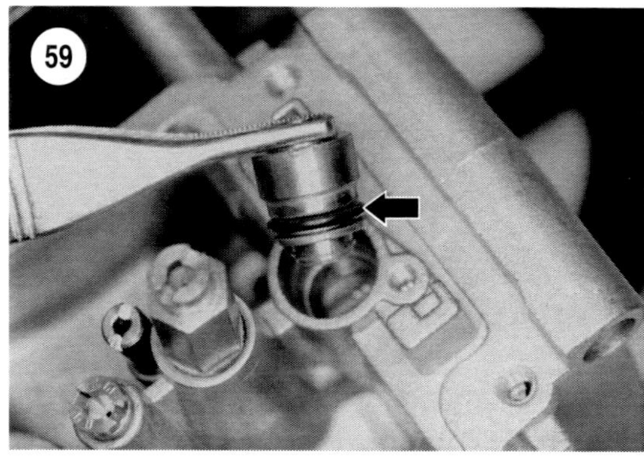
59

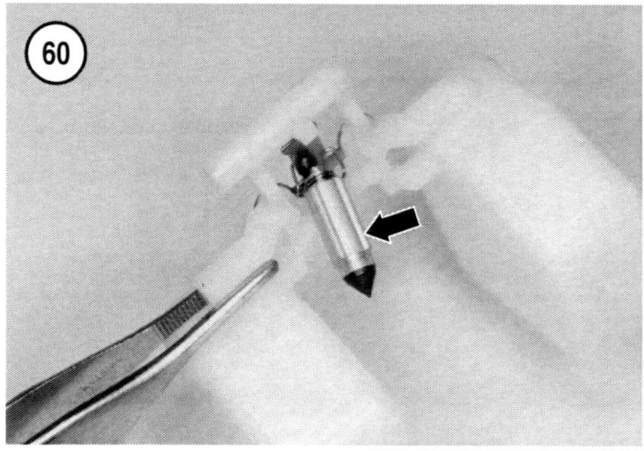
60

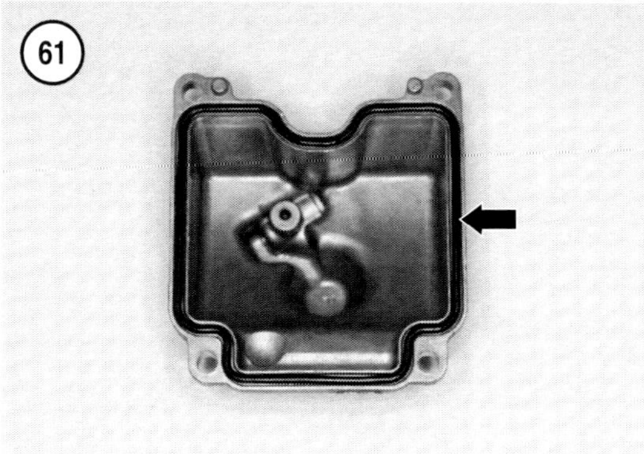
61

62

a. Insert the upper end of the spring into the top cover (A, **Figure 42**) and into the piston valve receptacle.
b. Hold onto the top cover with one hand and raise the piston valve with the other and correctly compress the spring between these two parts.
c. Hold the piston valve in the raised position and install the top cover onto the top of the carburetor.
d. Lower the piston valve and temporarily install the top cover screws.
e. Insert a finger into the venturi area and move the piston valve up in the carburetor body. The piston valve should rise all the way up into the bore and slide back down immediately with no binding. If it binds or if the movement is sluggish, chances are the diaphragm did not seat correctly or the spring is cocked to one side or not centered within the top cover.
f. If the spring is installed correctly, tighten the top cover screws (**Figure 41**) securely.

16. On models without a pilot-screw plug, install the pilot screw, spring, washer and O-ring. Turn the pilot screw to the setting noted during disassembly.
17. After the assembly and installation are completed, adjust the carburetors as described in this chapter and in Chapter Three.

CARBURETOR CLEANING AND INSPECTION (ALL MODELS)

CAUTION
The carburetor bodies are equipped with plastic parts that cannot be removed. Do not dip the carburetor body, O-rings, float assembly, needle valve or piston valve/diaphragm into carburetor cleaner or other harsh solutions that can damage these parts. Suzuki does not recommend the use of a caustic carburetor cleaning solvent. Instead, clean the carburetors and related parts in a petroleum-based solvent.

1. Initially clean all parts in a mild petroleum-based cleaning solution. Wash the parts in hot soap and water and rinse them with cold water. Blow-dry the parts with compressed air.

CAUTION
If compressed air is not available, allow the parts to air-dry or use a clean

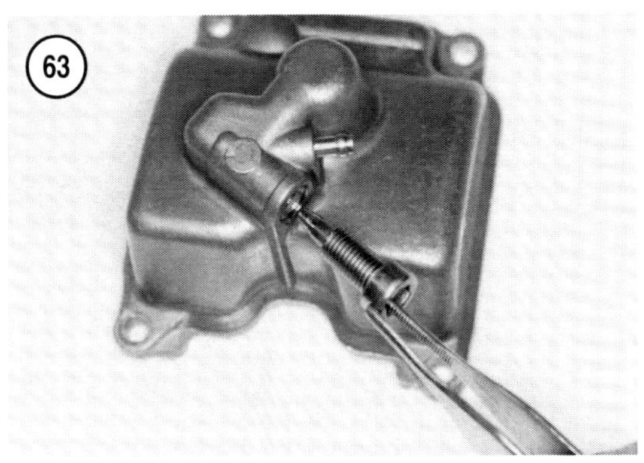

63

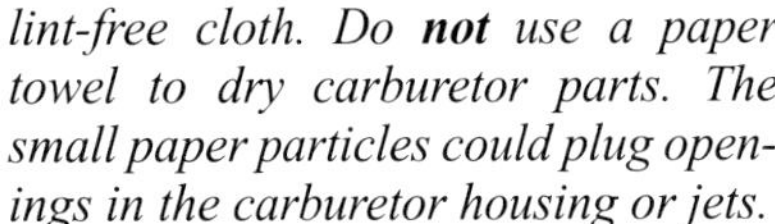

*lint-free cloth. Do **not** use a paper towel to dry carburetor parts. The small paper particles could plug openings in the carburetor housing or jets.*

2. Allow the carburetor body and components to dry thoroughly before assembly. Blow out the jets and the needle jet holder with compressed air.

CAUTION

*Do **not** use wire or drill bits to clean jets. Even minor gouges in a jet can alter flow rate and upset the air/fuel mixture.*

3. Make sure the float bowl drain screw (**Figure 63**) is in good condition and does not leak. Replace the drain screw if necessary.
4. Inspect the diaphragm (A, **Figure 64**) for cracks, deterioration or other damage. Check the sides of the piston valve (B, **Figure 64**) for excessive wear. Install the piston valve into the carburetor body and move it up and down in the bore. The piston valve should move smoothly with no binding or excessive play. Replace the piston valve and/or carburetor body if necessary.
5. Inspect the tapered end of the needle valve (A, **Figure 65**) for steps, uneven wear or damage (**Figure 66**).
6. Inspect the needle valve seat (B, **Figure 65**) for steps, uneven wear or other damage. Insert the needle valve into the valve seat, and slowly move it back and forth and check for smooth operation. If either part is worn or damaged, replace both parts as a pair for maximum performance.
7. Inspect the float for deterioration or damage. Refer to **Figure 67** and **Figure 68**. Place the float in a container of water and push it down. If the float sinks or if bubbles appear (indicating a leak), replace the float.
8. Inspect all of the jets (**Figure 69**, typical). Make sure all holes are open and no part is worn or damaged. Replace the worn or unserviceable parts.

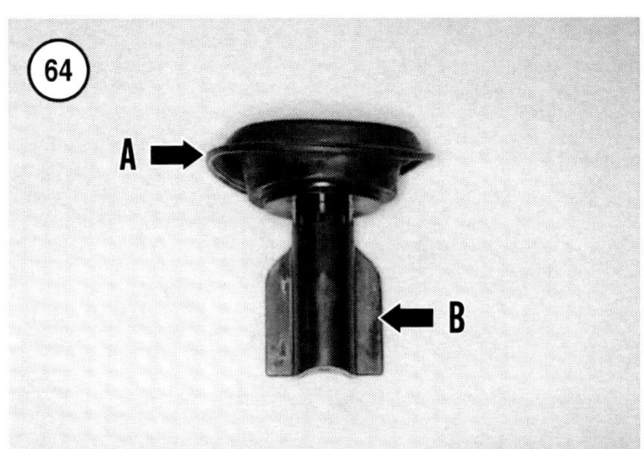

64

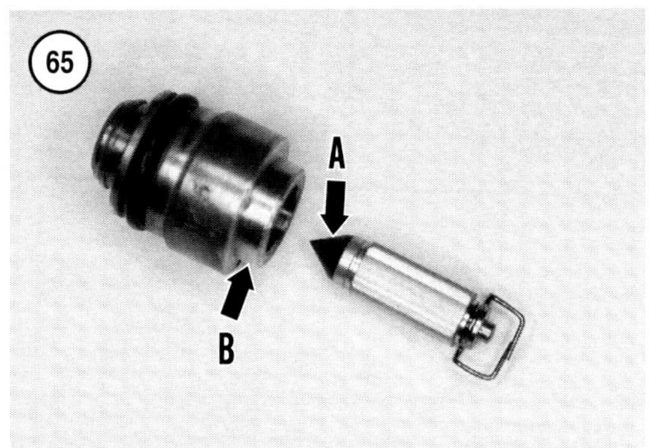

65

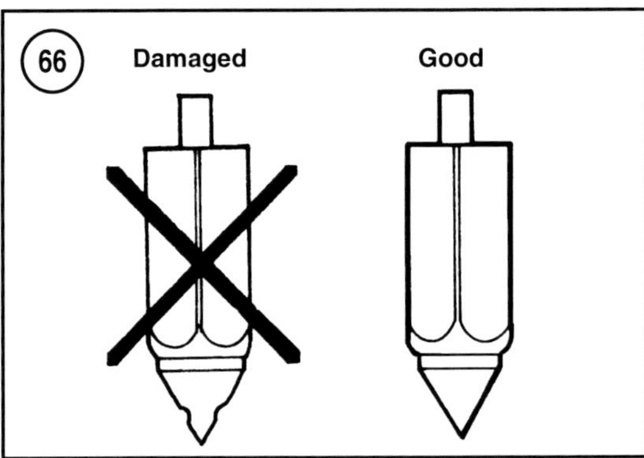

66

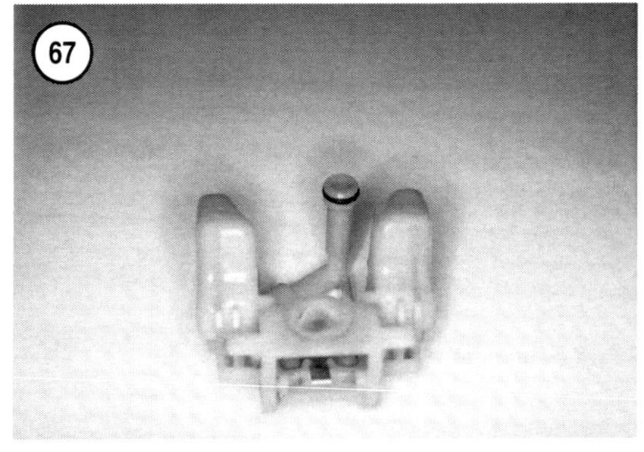

67

68

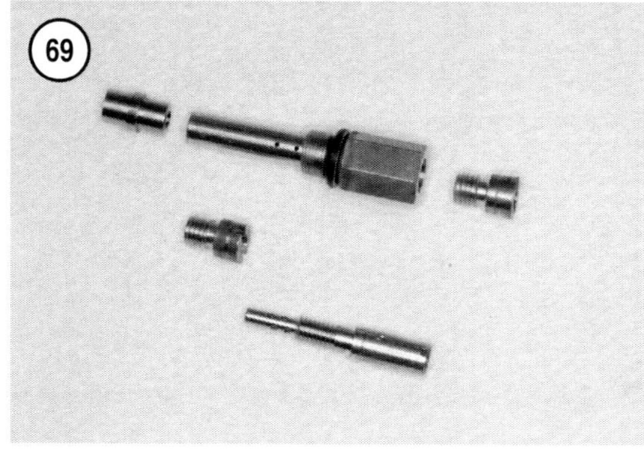
69

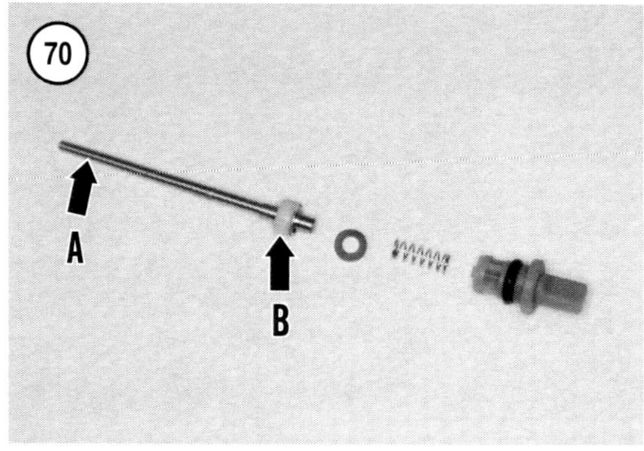

70

71

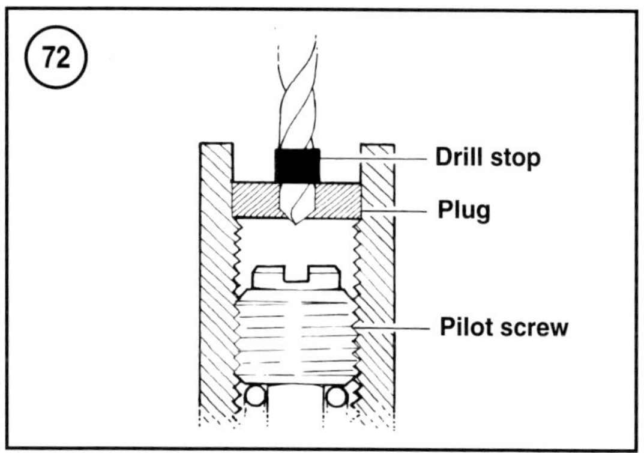

72

9. Inspect the jet needle taper (A, **Figure 70**) for steps, uneven wear or other damage. Make sure the E-clip (B, **Figure 70**) is securely in place.
10. If removed, inspect the pilot screw O-ring. Replace the O-ring if it has become hard or is starting to deteriorate.
11. Make sure all openings in the carburetor housing are clear. Clean them out if they are plugged in any way, and then apply compressed air to all openings.
12. Check the top cover for cracks or damage, replace if necessary.
13. Make sure the throttle plate screws (B, **Figure 53**) are tight.
14. Inspect the carburetor body for internal or external damage. If damaged, replace the carburetor assembly. The body cannot be replaced separately.
15. Move the throttle wheel back and forth from stop to stop. The throttle lever should move smoothly and return under spring tension. If it does not move freely or if it sticks in any position, replace the carburetor.

PILOT SCREW

Removal/Installation (U.S.A., California, Canada and Some European Models)

The pilot screws on these models are sealed. A plug (**Figure 71**) is installed at the top of the pilot screw bore to prevent routine adjustment. A pilot screw does not require adjustment unless the carburetor is overhauled, the pilot screw has been incorrectly adjusted, or if a pilot screw requires replacement. The following procedure describes how to remove and install the pilot screw in these models.

1. Set a stop 6 mm from the end of a 1/8 inch drill bit (**Figure 72**).
2. Carefully drill a hole in the plug at the top of the pilot screw bore on the carburetor body as shown in

Figure 72. Do not drill too deeply. The pilot screw will be difficult to remove if the head is damaged.

3. Screw a sheet metal screw into the plug and pull the plug from the bore.
4. Screw the pilot screw in until it *lightly* seats, while counting and recording the number of turns. The pilot screw must be reinstalled in the same position during assembly.
5. Remove the pilot screw, spring, washer and O-ring from the carburetor body.
6. Inspect the O-ring and the end the pilot screw. Replace the screw and/or O-ring if damaged or worn (grooved).

NOTE
If the pilot screw was incorrectly adjusted, refer to the specifications in ***Tables 1-4***.

7. Install the pilot screw in the same position noted during Step 3 or to the specification listed in the appropriate table.
8. Carefully tap the new plug into place with a punch.
9. Repeat this procedure for the other carburetors, if necessary. Make sure to keep components from each carburetor separate.

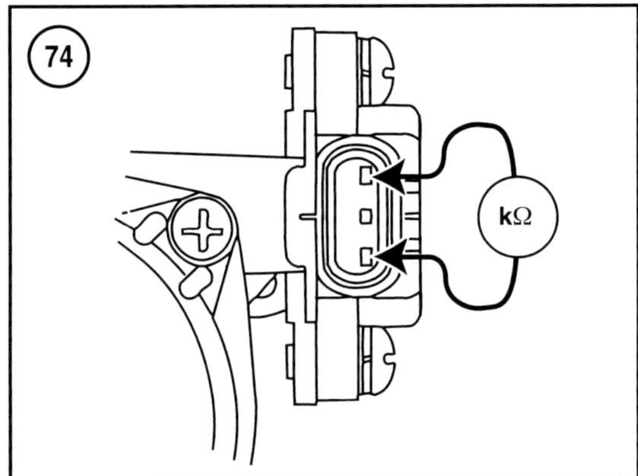

THROTTLE POSITION SENSOR

Inspection

NOTE
Not all 1996-2000 models are equipped with the throttle position sensor.

1. Remove the fuel tank as described in this chapter.
2. Disconnect the electrical connector from the throttle position sensor (**Figure 73**).
3. Set an ohmmeter to the R × 1 k scale. If using an analog meter, calibrate the meter as described in Chapter One.
4. With the throttle lever in the fully-closed position, measure the resistance across the upper and lower terminals on the sensor side of the connector as shown in **Figure 74**.
5. Replace the throttle position sensor if the resistance does not meet the specification in **Table 5**.

Removal/Installation

1. Remove the fuel tank as described in this chapter.

2. Disconnect the electrical connector from the throttle position sensor (**Figure 73**).
3. Prior to removal, check the resistance value as previously described.
4. Make an alignment mark on the sensor relating to the centerline of the mounting screws. Make corresponding alignment marks on the carburetor body so the sensor can be precisely installed *in the same position*.
5. Remove the screws (**Figure 75**) securing the sensor and remove it.

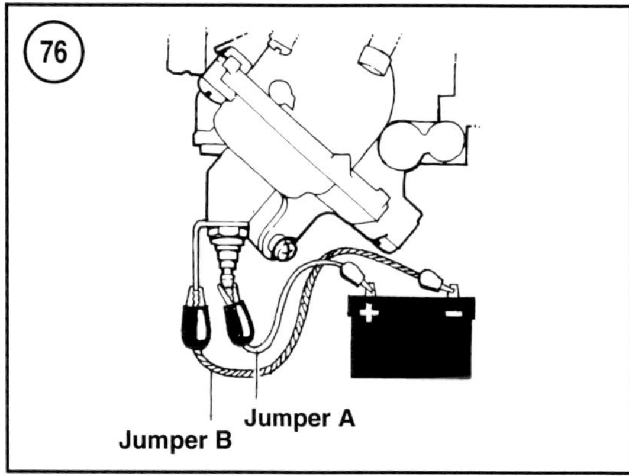

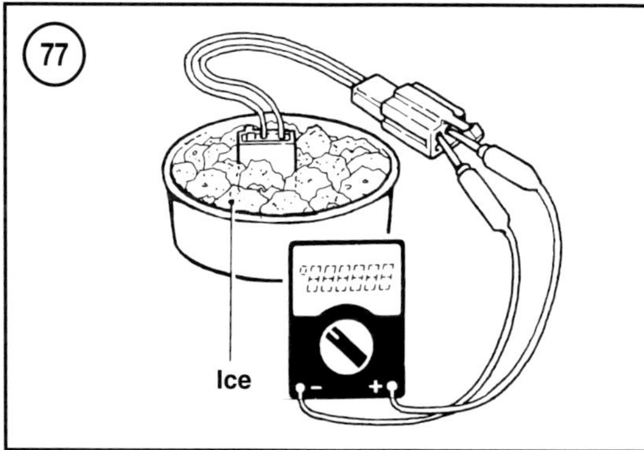

6. Installation is the reverse of removal.

CARBURETOR HEATER AND THERMOSWITCH (2001-ON U.K. MODELS ONLY)

Carburetor Heater Inspection

1. Remove the carburetor assembly as described in this chapter.
2. Disconnect the electrical lead from the carburetor heater on the bottom of the float bowl.

CAUTION
Electrical arcing may occur when the jumpers are connected in the following test. Connect the jumpers in the described order so any arcing will take place away from the carburetors.

3. Connect one end of jumper A to the battery positive terminal. Then connect the other end of jumper A to the carburetor body as shown in **Figure 76**.
4. Connect one end of jumper B to the spade connector on the carburetor heater. Then connect the other end of jumper B to the battery negative terminal as shown in **Figure 76**.

CAUTION
*Do not touch the carburetor heater directly as it is **hot** and can burn.*

5. After 5 minutes, check the temperature of the float bowl by hand. It should be warm. Replace the carburetor heater if the float bowl does not heat up.
6. Disconnect the jumper B from the negative battery terminal and then from the carburetor heater. Then disconnect jumper A.
7. Repeat this test for the remaining carburetor heaters.

Carburetor Heater Removal/Installation

1. Remove the carburetor assembly as described in this chapter.
2. Disconnect the electrical lead from the carburetor heater.
3. Unscrew and remove the carburetor heater from the bottom of the float bowl.
4. Repeat the above procedure for the remaining carburetor heaters.
5. Installation is the reverse of removal. Pay attention to the following:
   a. Apply Suzuki thermo grease (part No. 99000-59029) or an equivalent to the heater threads prior to installation.
   b. Tighten the heater to 3 N•m (26.5 in.-lb.).

Carburetor Thermoswitch Inspection

The carburetor heater controlling thermoswitch is located under the fuel tank.

1. Remove the fuel tank as described in this chapter.
2. Unplug the thermoswitch connector from the wiring harness.
3. Remove the thermoswitch, and immerse it in a pan of ice.
4. After the switch has sat in the ice for about 5 minutes, check the continuity across the two terminals of the thermoswitch connector (**Figure 77**).
5. The chilled switch should have continuity at 8-14° C (46-57° F). There should be no continuity above 15-21° C (59-70° F).
6. Replace the switch if it is out of specification.

78

CARBURETOR FITTINGS (1996-2000 MODELS)

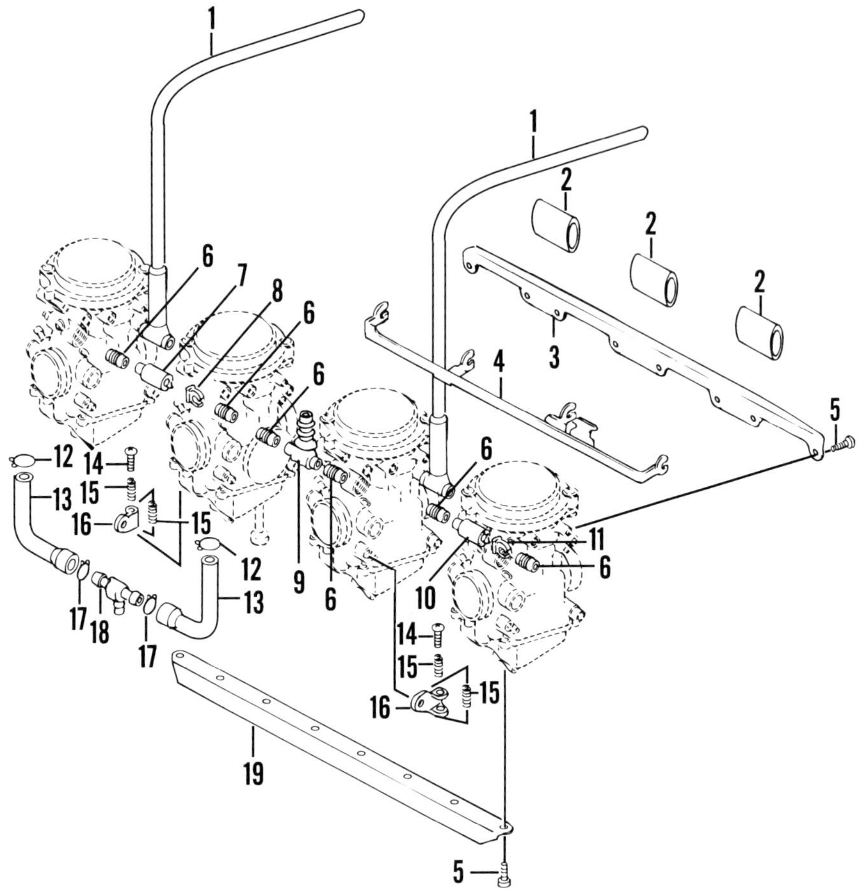

1. Vent hose
2. Hose
3. Upper mounting plate
4. Starter (choke) plate
5. Screw
6. Seal
7. Pipe fitting
8. Holder
9. Nipple
10. Pipe fitting
11. Holder
12. Hose clamp
13. Fuel hose
14. Screw
15. Spring
16. Lever
17. Hose clamp
18. Nipple
19. Lower mounting plate

CARBURETOR SEPARATION

1996-2000 Models

Refer to **Figure 78**.

1. Remove the carburetor assembly as described in this chapter.

2. If still installed, remove any fuel, air, and vacuum hoses from the carburetors. Label each hose and fitting so the hoses can be reinstalled in their original locations during assembly.

80

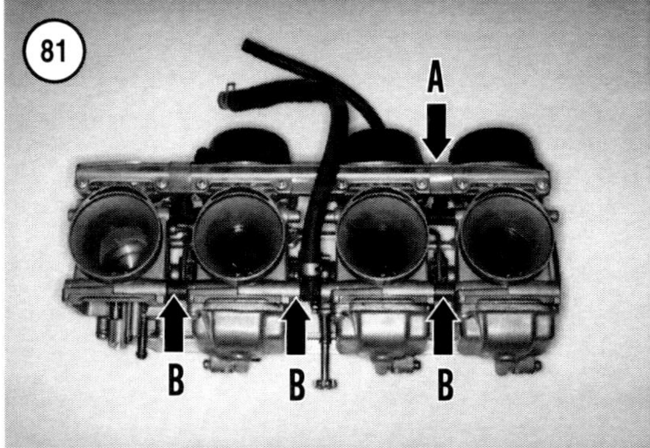

81

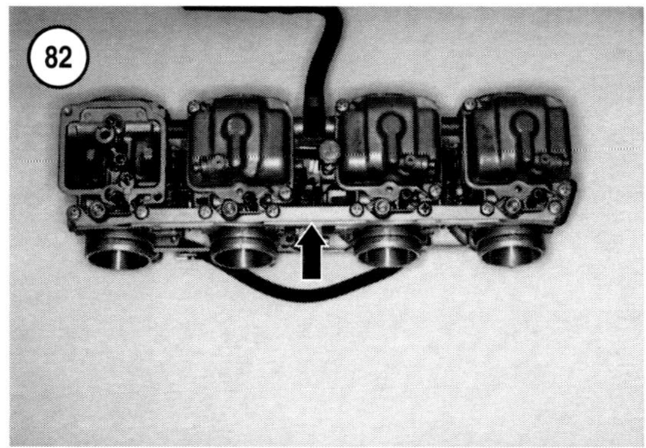
82

3. Remove the mounting screws from the starter plate (A, **Figure 79**).

4. Disengage the starter plate fingers from the starter valve plungers (**Figure 80**) and remove the starter plate.

NOTE
The Phillips head screws in the next step had a threadlocking agent applied prior to assembly. Use an impact driver to loosen the screws to avoid rounding off the screw head slots.

5. Remove the screws securing the upper mounting plate (A, **Figure 81**) and the lower mounting plate (**Figure 82**) to the carburetor bodies.

6. Note the locations of the throttle wheel, spacers and related springs (B, **Figure 79**) prior to carburetor body separation.

7. Carefully pull the two carburetor bodies apart. Separate the following components from their respective ports on the carburetors.
   a. The air vent joint nipples (C, **Figure 79**). Remove and discard the O-rings. New ones must be installed during assembly.
   b. The fuel joint nipples (B, **Figure 81**). Remove and discard the O-rings. New ones must be installed during assembly.

8. Assemble the carburetors by reversing these disassembly steps, noting the following:
   a. Install *new* O-rings on the fuel joints and air vent joint nipples connecting the carburetors.
   b. Place the carburetor assembly on a piece of plate glass.
   c. Tighten the upper and lower interconnecting bolts and nuts securely while pressing down on all four carburetors to maintain proper alignment between all four carburetors.
   d. Connect the air, fuel and vacuum hoses to the proper fittings as noted during disassembly.

2001-on Models

Refer to **Figure 83**.

1. Remove the carburetor assembly as described in this chapter.

2. If still installed, remove all fuel, air and vacuum hoses (A, **Figure 84**) from the carburetors. Label each hose and fitting so the hoses can be reinstalled in their original locations during assembly.

3. Remove the mounting screw securing the idle adjust knob (B, **Figure 84**) and its bracket.

4. Remove the mounting screws and washers (A, **Figure 85**) from the starter plate.

5. Disengage the starter plate fingers from the starter valve plungers (B, **Figure 85**) and remove the starter plate.

NOTE
*Only one of the throughbolts is shown in C, **Figure 85**. Remove both throughbolts.*

(83)

CARBURETOR FITTINGS (2001-ON MODELS)

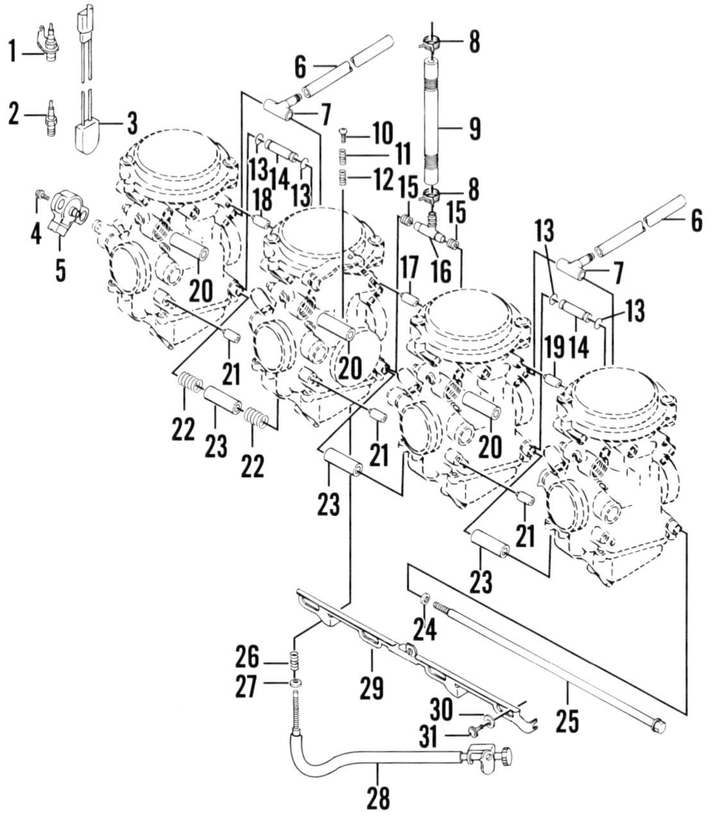

1. Carburetor heater (U.K. models)
2. Carburetor heater (U.K. models)
3. Thermoswitch (U.K. models)
4. Screw
5. Throttle position sensor
6. Vent hose
7. Air vent joint
8. Hose clamp
9. Fuel hose
10. Screw
11. Spring
12. Spring
13. Hose clamp
14. Fuel joint
15. Seal
16. Fuel joint
17. Joint
18. Joint
19. Joint
20. Spacer
21. Spacer
22. Spring
23. Spacer
24. Nut
25. Through bolt
26. Spring
27. Washer
28. Throttle adjust screw cable
29. Starter (choke) plate
30. Washer
31. Screw

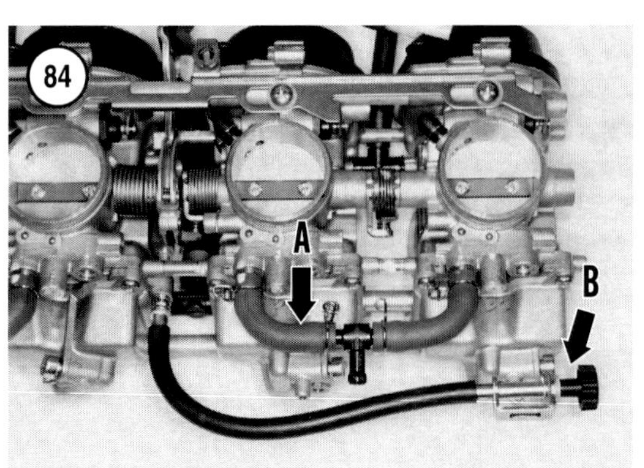

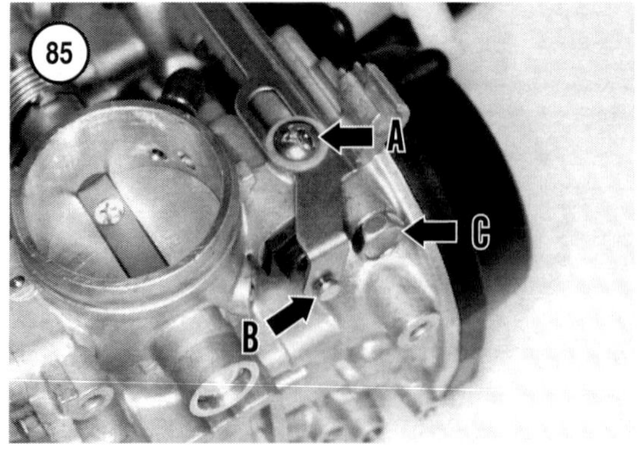

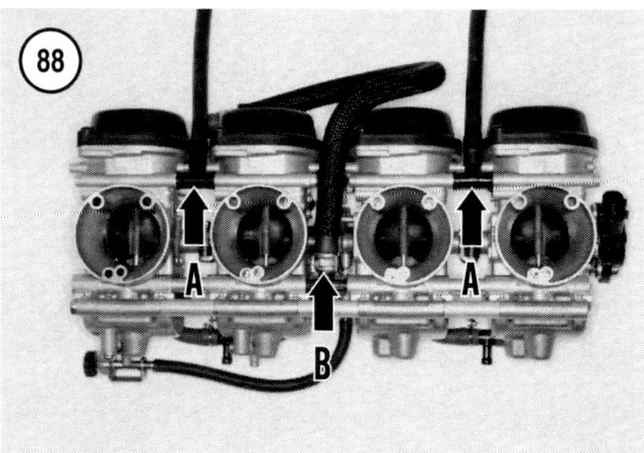

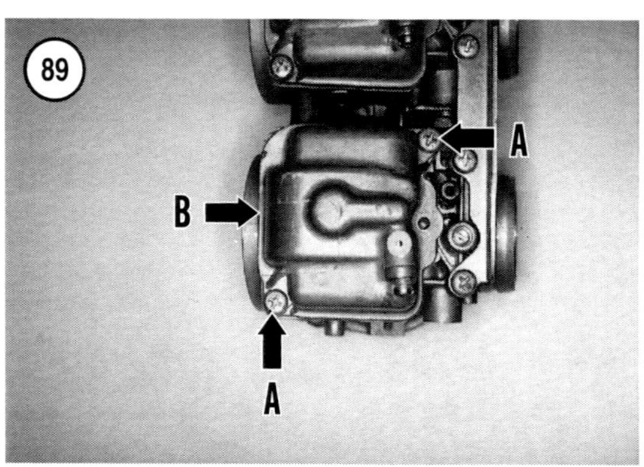

6. On the left side, remove the two through bolts (C, **Figure 85**) securing the four carburetors together.

7. Note the locations of the throttle wheel, spacers and related springs prior to carburetor body separation. Refer to **Figure 86** and **Figure 87**.

8. Carefully separate all four carburetor bodies. Separate the following components from their respective ports on the carburetors.

   a. The air vent joint nipples (A, **Figure 88**). Remove and discard the O-rings. New ones must be installed during assembly.
   b. The fuel joint nipples (B, **Figure 88**). Remove and discard the O-rings. New ones must be installed during assembly.

9. Assemble the carburetors by reversing these disassembly steps. Note the following:

   a. Install *new* O-rings on the fuel joints and air vent joints connecting the carburetors.
   b. Place the carburetor assembly on a piece of plate glass.
   c. Tighten the through bolts securely while pressing down on all four carburetors to maintain proper alignment.
   d. Connect the air, fuel and vacuum hoses to the proper fittings as noted during disassembly.

FLOAT HEIGHT ADJUSTMENT

1996-2000 Models

1. Remove the carburetor assembly as described in this chapter.

2. Remove the screws (A, **Figure 89**) securing the float bowl and remove the bowl (B).

NOTE

The float assembly must be pressed down against the float bowl mating surface in order to achieve a correct reading in Step 3.

3. Use a thumb and press the float assembly down into contact with the float bowl mating surface (A, **Figure 90**).

4. Hold the carburetor assembly with the carburetor inclined until the float arm just touches the float needle—not pushing it down. Use a float level gauge, vernier caliper or small ruler (B, **Figure 90**) and measure the distance from the carburetor body

8

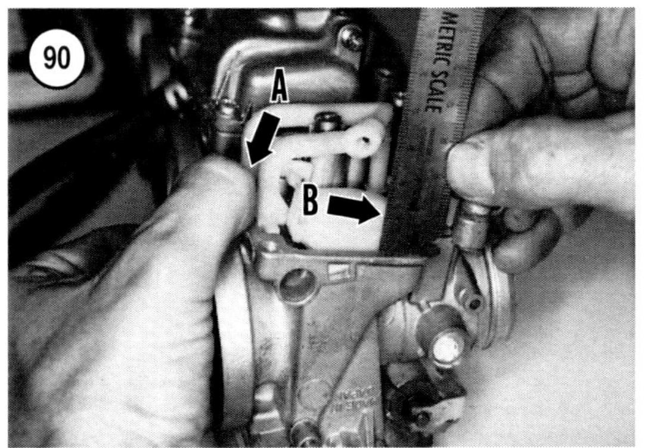

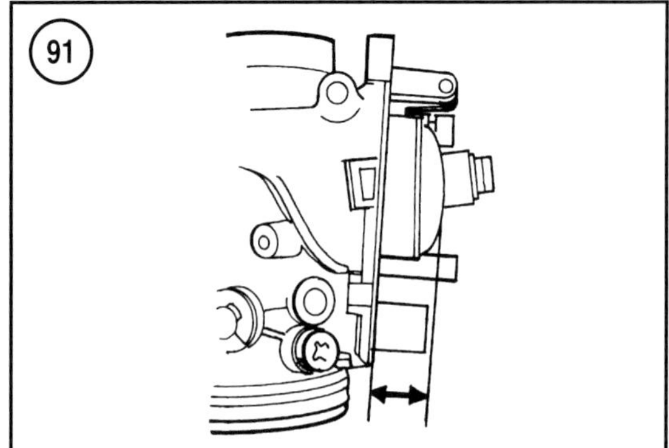

to the bottom surface of the float body (**Figure 91**). The correct float height is listed in **Tables 1-4**.

5. If adjustment is necessary, carefully bend the tang (**Figure 92**) on the float arm. If the float level is too high, the result will be a rich air/fuel mixture. If it is too low, the mixture will be too lean.
6. Repeat Steps 2-5 for the remaining carburetors.

NOTE
The floats on all carburetors must be adjusted to the same height to maintain the same air/fuel mixture.

7. Install the float bowl and install the carburetors.

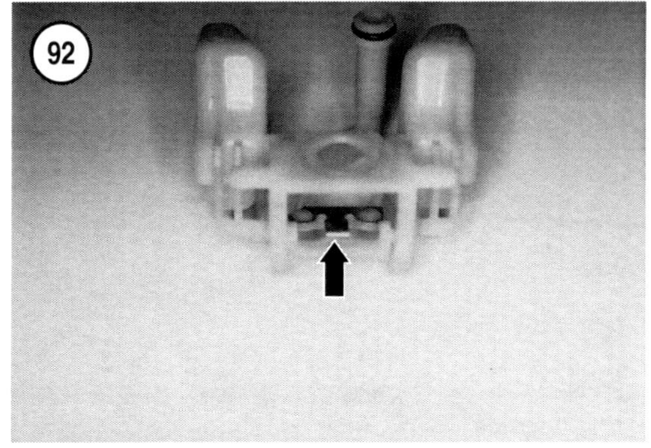

2001-on Models

1. Remove the carburetor assembly as described in this chapter.
2. Remove the screws (A, **Figure 93**) securing the float bowl and remove the bowl (B).
3. Hold the carburetor assembly with carburetor inclined until the float arm just touches the float needle (not pushing it down). Use a float level gauge, vernier caliper or small ruler and measure the distance from the carburetor body to the bottom surface of the float body (**Figure 94**). The correct float height is listed in **Tables 1-4**.
4. To adjust, carefully bend the tang (**Figure 95**) on the float arm. If the fuel level is too high, the result will be a rich air/fuel mixture. If it is too low, the mixture will be too lean.
5. Repeat Steps 2-4 for the remaining carburetors.

NOTE
The floats on all carburetors must be adjusted to the same height to maintain the same air/fuel mixture.

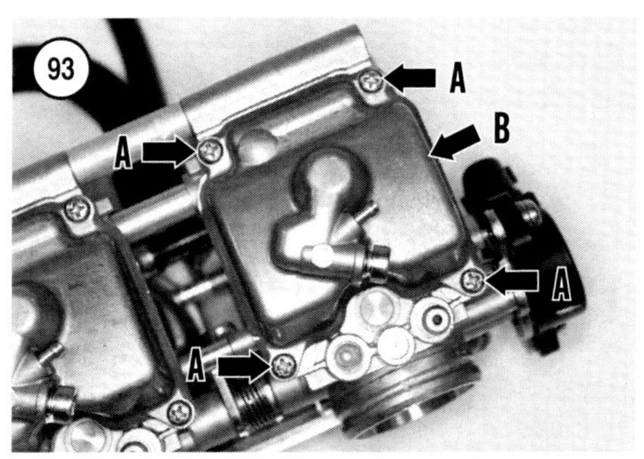

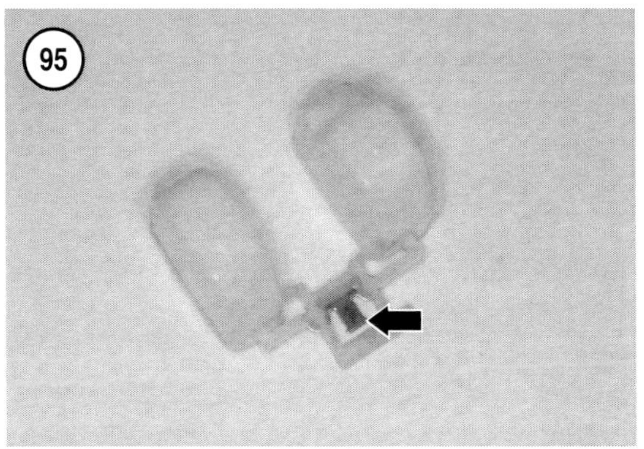

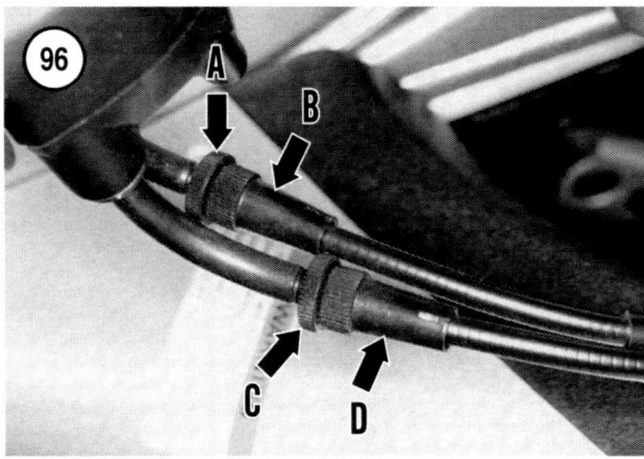

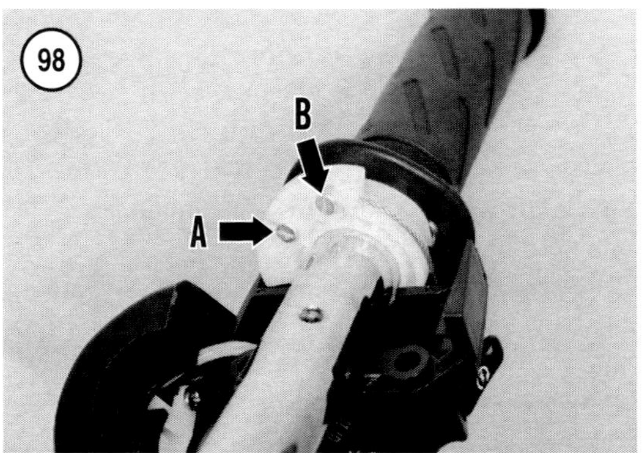

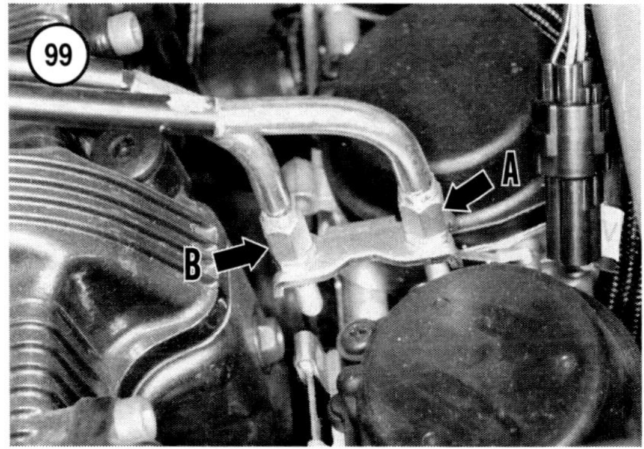

6. Install the float bowls and install the carburetors.

THROTTLE CABLE REPLACEMENT

NOTE

This procedure is shown on a 2001-on model but relates to all models covered in this manual.

1. Remove the seat as described in Chapter Fourteen.
2. Provide slack in the throttle cables as follows:
   a. Loosen the locknut (A, **Figure 96**) on the return cable adjuster. Turn the cable adjuster (B, **Figure 96**) all the way in to provide cable slack.
   b. Loosen the locknut (C, **Figure 96**) on the pull cable adjuster. Turn the adjuster (D, **Figure 96**) in all the way in to provide cable slack.
3. Remove the screws securing the right switch assembly (**Figure 97**) together.
4. At the throttle grip, disengage the pull cable (A, **Figure 98**) and return cable (B) from the throttle grip.
5. Remove the carburetor assembly sufficiently to gain access to the throttle cables as described in this chapter.

NOTE

*Label the throttle pull and return cables before disconnecting them so they can be reinstalled in the proper position during assembly. When the carburetor assembly is installed in the engine, the pull cable is the rear-most cable (A, **Figure 99**). The return cable is the front cable (B, **Figure 99**).*

6. Loosen the cable locknut (A, **Figure 99**) and loosen the cable adjuster until there is sufficient slack in the pull cable.

7. Loosen the cable locknut (B, **Figure 99**) and loosen the cable adjuster until there is sufficient slack in the return cable.

8. Disconnect both throttle cables from the throttle wheel and cable mounting bracket (**Figure 100**).

9. Tie a 7 ft. (2 m) piece of heavy string or cord to the carburetor end of both cables. Wrap this end with masking or duct tape. Do not use an excessive amount of tape as it must be pulled through the frame during removal. Tie the other end of the string to the frame.

10. Visually inspect the route the cable takes through the frame. Loosen any cable ties the cables must pass through.

11. At the throttle grip end of the cable, carefully pull the cable (and attached string) out through the frame. Make sure the attached string follows the same path as the cables through the frame.

12. Remove the tape and untie the string from the old cables.

13. On non-nylon lined cables, lubricate both new cables as described in Chapter Three.

14. Connect the end of the new cables to the carburetor throttle wheel.

15. Tie the string to the carburetor end of the new cables and wrap it with tape.

16. Carefully pull the string back through the frame, routing the new cables along the same path as the old cables.

17. Remove the tape and untie the string from the cables and the frame.

18. At the throttle grip, engage the pull cable (A, **Figure 98**) and return cable (B) onto the throttle grip.

19. Install the right side switch housing and tighten the screws securely.

20. Operate the throttle grip and make sure the carburetor throttle linkage is operating correctly, with no binding. If operation is incorrect or there is binding, carefully check that the cables are attached correctly and there are no tight bends in the cables.

21. Tighten any cable ties that were loosened.

22. Install the carburetor assembly, fuel tank and seat.

23. Adjust the throttle cables as described Chapter Three.

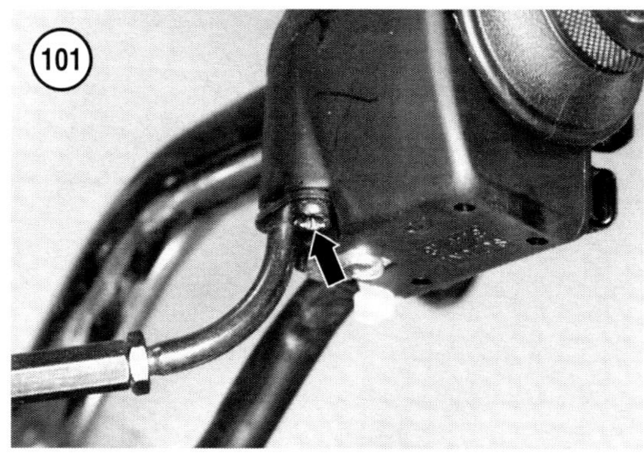

24. Test ride the motorcycle slowly at first and make sure the throttle is operating correctly.

STARTER (CHOKE) CABLE REPLACEMENT

NOTE

This procedure is shown on a 2001-on model but relates to all models covered in this manual.

1. Remove the fuel tank as described in this chapter.

2. Remove the screws securing the left switch assembly together and separate the switch assembly. Note that the starter (choke) cable bracket is secured under one of these screws (**Figure 101**). The bracket will have to be reinstalled in the same location during assembly.

3. Disconnect the starter (choke) cable from the choke lever (**Figure 102**) and from the switch housing.

4. Remove the starter (choke) cable from the carburetor assembly as follows:

a. Disconnect the starter (choke) cable end from the anchor (A, **Figure 103**) on the starter plate.
b. Disconnect the starter (choke) cable (B, **Figure 103**) from the lever.

5. Tie a 7 ft. (2 m) piece of heavy string or cord to the carburetor end of starter cable. Wrap this end with masking or duct tape. Do not use an excessive amount of tape as it must be pulled through the frame during removal. Tie the other end of the string to the frame.

6. Visually inspect the route the cable takes through the frame. Loosen any cable ties the cable must pass through.

7. At the choke lever end of the cable, carefully pull the cable (and attached string) out through the frame. Make sure the attached string follows the same path as the cable through the frame.

8. Remove the tape and untie the string from the old cable.

9. On non-nylon lined cables, lubricate a new starter (choke) cable as described in Chapter Three.

10. Connect the end of the new starter (choke) cable to choke lever.

11. Tie the string to the carburetor end of the new starter (choke) cable and wrap it with tape.

12. Carefully pull the string back through the frame, routing the new cable along the same path as the old cable.

13. Reverse Steps 1-5 to install the new cable. Note the following:
   a. Connect the cable and choke lever to the switch housing.
   b. Align the switch housing locating pin with the hole in the handlebar and fit the switch in place on the handlebar. Tighten the screws securely. Make sure the starter (choke) cable bracket is secured under the mounting screw (**Figure 101**).
   c. Operate the choke lever and make sure the link is operating correctly without binding. If the operation is incorrect or there is binding, carefully check that the cable is attached correctly and that there are no tight bends in the cable.
   d. Start the engine and let it idle. Then turn the handlebar from side to side and listen to the engine. The engine speed should not increase when the handlebars turn. If it does, the cable is improperly routed. Correct the problem before riding.

AIR FILTER HOUSING

Removal/Installation

Refer to **Figure 104** and **Figure 105**.

1. Remove the seat and the rear frame cover as described in Chapter Fourteen.

2. Remove the fuel tank as described in this chapter.

3A. On 1996-2000 models, perform the following:
   a. Disconnect the crankcase breather hose (**Figure 106**) from the air filter housing.
   b. Remove the screw (**Figure 107**) securing the air filter housing on each side.

3B. On 2001-on models, perform the following:
   a. Remove the bolts securing the fuel tank mounting bracket (A, **Figure 108**) and remove the bracket.
   b. Remove the screws (B, **Figure 108**) securing the air filter housing on each side.

4. Remove the carburetor assembly as described in this chapter.

(104)

AIR FILTER HOUSING (1996-2000 MODELS)

FRONT

1. Hose clamp
2. Breather hose
3. Housing
4. Air filter element
5. Screw
6. Cover
7. Inlet tube
8. Rubber cushion
9. Side cover
10. Hose clamp
11. Drain tube and cap
12. Outlet tubes
13. Clamps
14. Washer

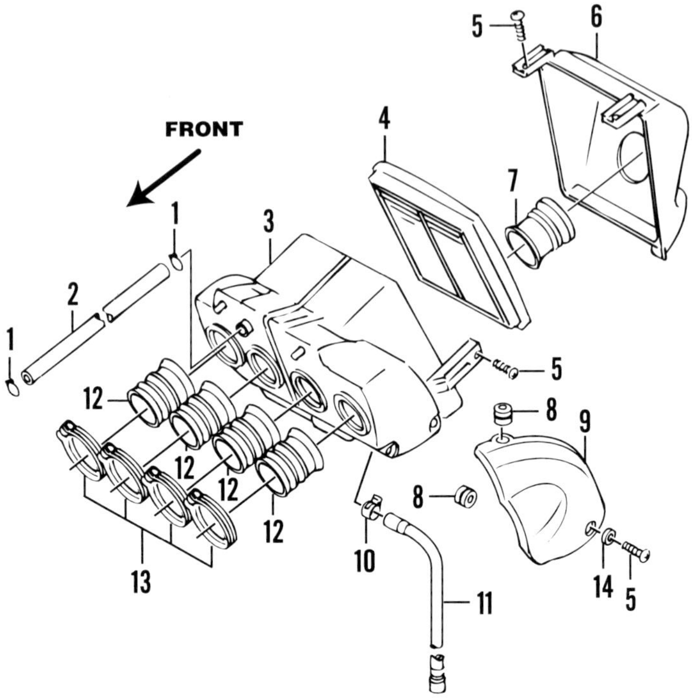

(105)

AIR FILTER HOUSING (2001-ON MODELS)

FRONT

1. Outlet tubes
2. Housing
3. Screw
4. Air filter element
5. Gasket
6. Inlet tube
7. Screw
8. Cover
9. Clamp
10. Hose clamp
11. Breather hose
12. Hose clamp
13. Drain tube and cap

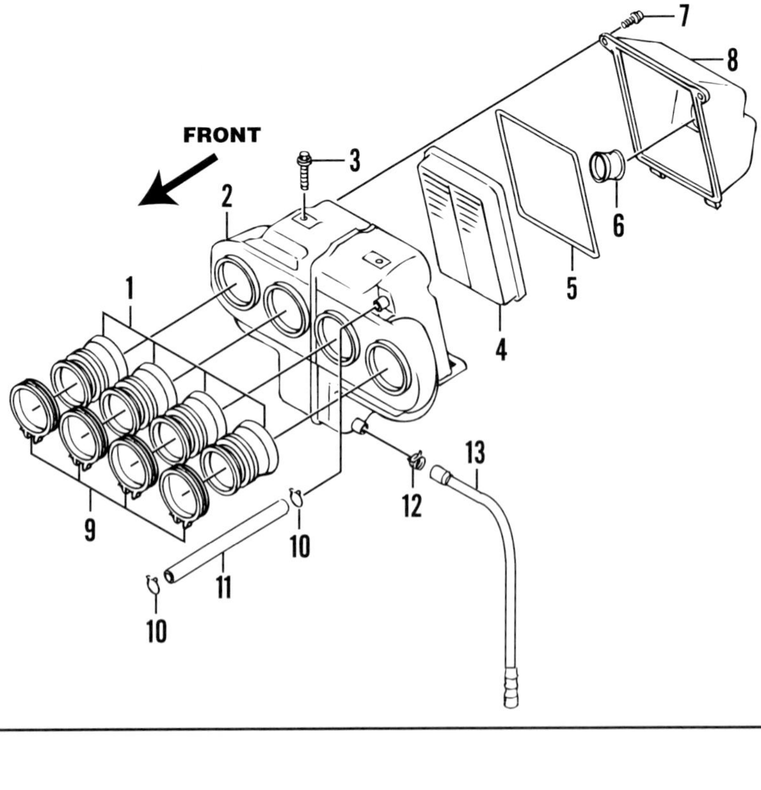

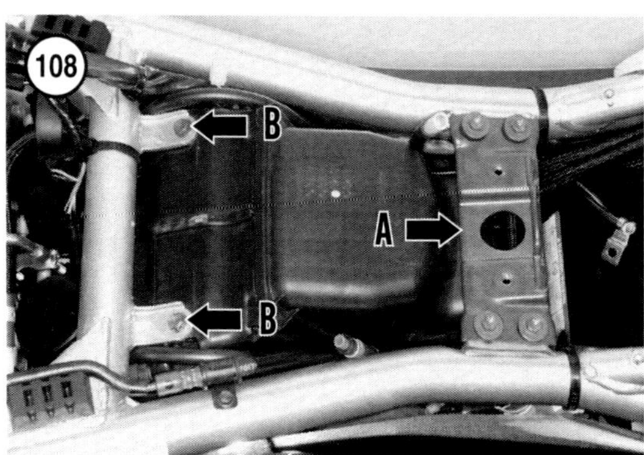

5. Pull the air filter housing forward and remove it from the frame.

6. Install by reversing these removal steps while noting the following:

   a. Make sure the air filter housing air ducts are fully seated against the carburetor inlets. A solid bottoming out must be felt when they are correctly seated.

   b. Make sure the screws on the carburetor clamps are tight to avoid a vacuum loss and possible valve damage due to a lean fuel mixture.

FUEL TANK

Removal/Installation

Refer to **Figure 109**.

1. Remove the seat and rear frame cover as described in Chapter Fourteen.
2. Disconnect the negative lead from the battery as described in Chapter Three.
3. Remove the bolts (**Figure 110**) securing the rear of the fuel tank.
4. Turn the fuel shutoff valve to the OFF position.
5. Remove the screw securing the valve knob and remove the knob (**Figure 111**).
6. Place a shop rag or piece of rubber over the frame tubing in front of the fuel tank to protect the frame finish when the fuel tank is tilted up in the next step.
7. Raise the rear of the fuel tank and place a wooden block (**Figure 112**) under it to keep the tank in the raised position.
8. Reach under the fuel tank and disconnect the fuel level gauge sending unit electrical connector (**Figure 113**).
9. On 2001-on models, disconnect the breather hose (**Figure 114**) from the fuel tank.
10. Disconnect the fuel line (**Figure 115**) and vacuum line from the fuel valve. Plug the end of the lines with golf tees to prevent the entry of foreign matter and to prevent any loss of any residual fuel in the line.
11. Disconnect the drain hose from the fuel tank.
12. On California models, disconnect the evaporative emission system breather line from the fuel tank.
13. Pull the tank toward the rear and lift it off the frame.
14. Install the control knob and mounting screw onto the fuel shutoff valve to avoid misplacing them.
15. If necessary, remove the filler cap as follows:
    a. Remove the bolts (**Figure 116**) securing the filler cap assembly.
    b. Remove the filler cap from the fuel tank.
16. Inspect the fuel tank as described in this chapter.

109

FUEL TANK

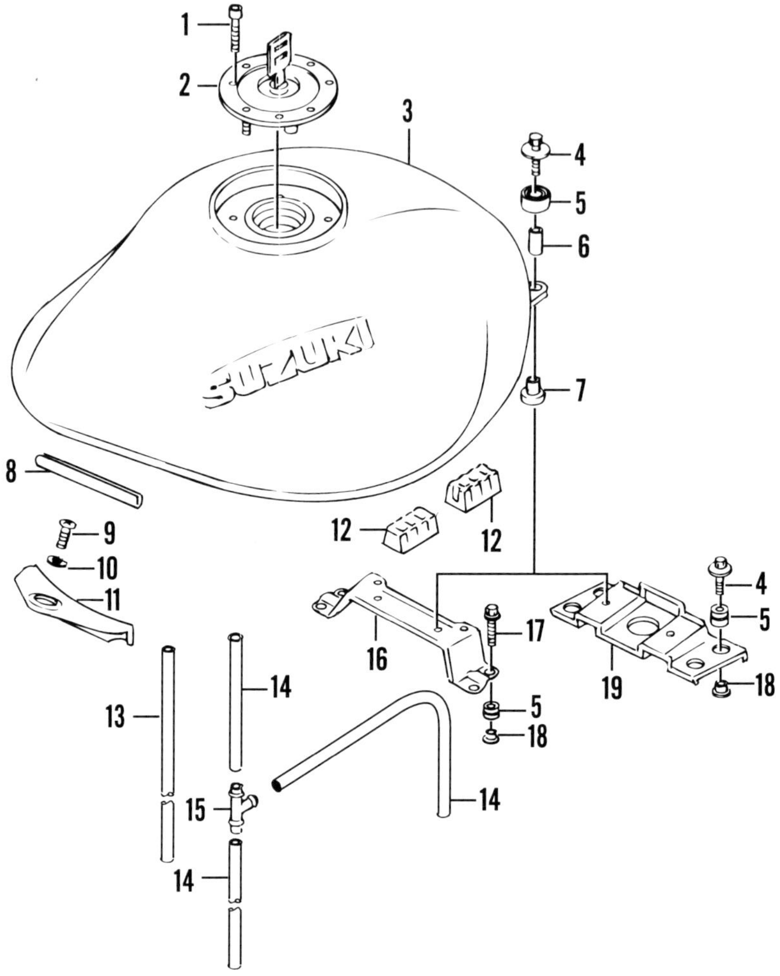

1. Allen bolt
2. Filler cap assembly
3. Fuel tank
4. Bolt
5. Rubber spacer
6. Collar
7. Rear cushion
8. Front trim strip
9. Screw
10. Washer
11. Front cushion
12. Rubber cushion
13. Hose
14. Hose
15. T-fitting
16. Fuel tank mounting bracket (1996-2000 models)
17. Bolt
18. Spacer
19. Fuel tank mounting bracket (2001-on models)

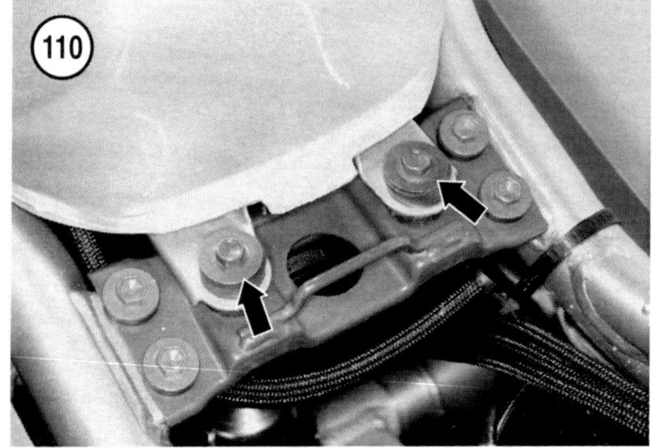

112

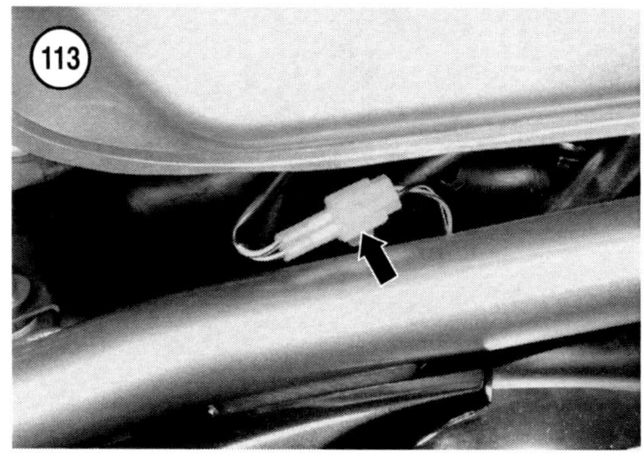
113

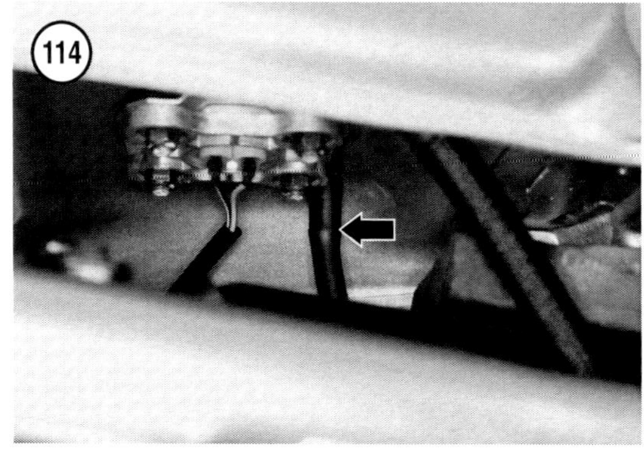
114

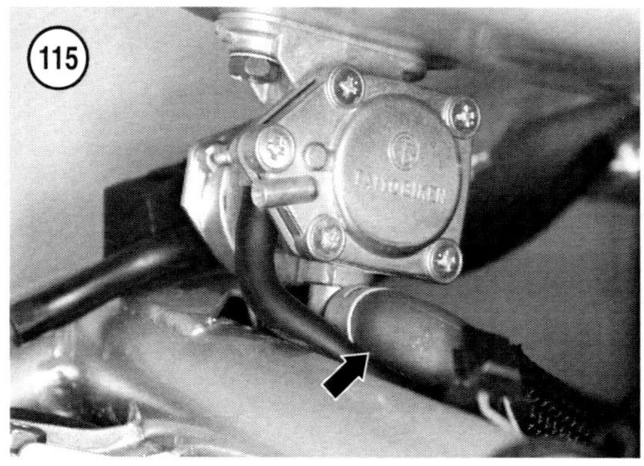
115

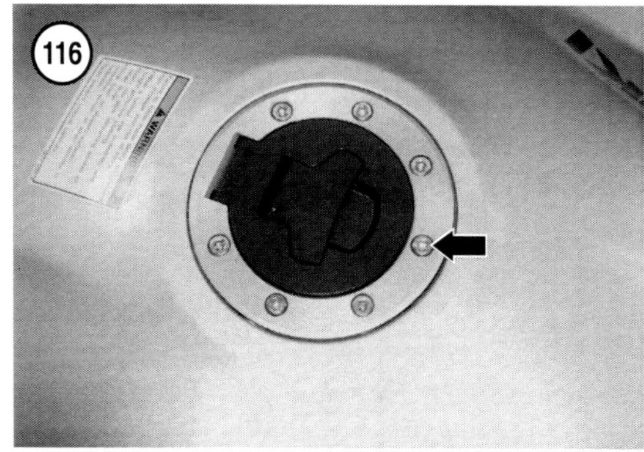
116

17. Install by reversing these removal steps. Note the following:

   a. Make sure the fuel line (**Figure 115**) is secure on the fuel valve.

   b. Be sure the tang at the front of the tank is secured under the frame stop.

   c. Start the engine and check for fuel leaks.

Inspection

1. Inspect the front rubber grommets on the mounting bracket for deterioration. Replace if necessary.

2. Inspect the front cushion where the front of the fuel tank attaches to the frame.

3. Inspect the rear cushions at the rear mounting tabs. Replace either cushion if damaged or starting to deteriorate.

4. Inspect the vinyl molding strips for damage or deterioration. Replace if necessary.

5. Check the fuel and vacuum fittings on the rear of the fuel tank for damage.

6. Use the ignition key and open the fuel filter cap. Inspect the fuel filler cap gaskets. If the cap gasket is damaged or starting to deteriorate, replace the filler cap assembly. The gasket cannot be replaced separately. If the mounting flange gasket is damaged, replace it.

7. Inspect the entire fuel tank for leaks or damage. Repair or replace the fuel tank if any fuel leakage is found.

FUEL SHUTOFF VALVE

Removal/Installation

WARNING
Some fuel may spill during the following procedure. Work in a well-ventilated area at least 50 feet from any sparks or flames, including gas appliance pilot lights. Do not allow anyone to smoke in the area. Keep a BC rated fire extinguisher handy.

Refer to **Figure 117**.

1. Remove the fuel tank as described in this chapter.
2. Cover the workbench with a blanket or several towels to protect the surface of the fuel tank.
3. Turn the fuel tank on its side.
4. If still attached, disconnect the fuel and/or vacuum line(s) from the fuel valve.
5. Remove the bolts and washers (**Figure 118**) securing the fuel valve to the fuel tank and remove the valve.
6. Inspect the fuel valve mounting O-ring; replace it if necessary.
7. Use compressed air to clean the filter screen at the end of the fuel intake on the fuel valve.
8. Install by reversing these removal steps. Pour a small amount of gasoline into the tank after installing the valve and check for leaks. If a leak is present, solve the problem immediately.

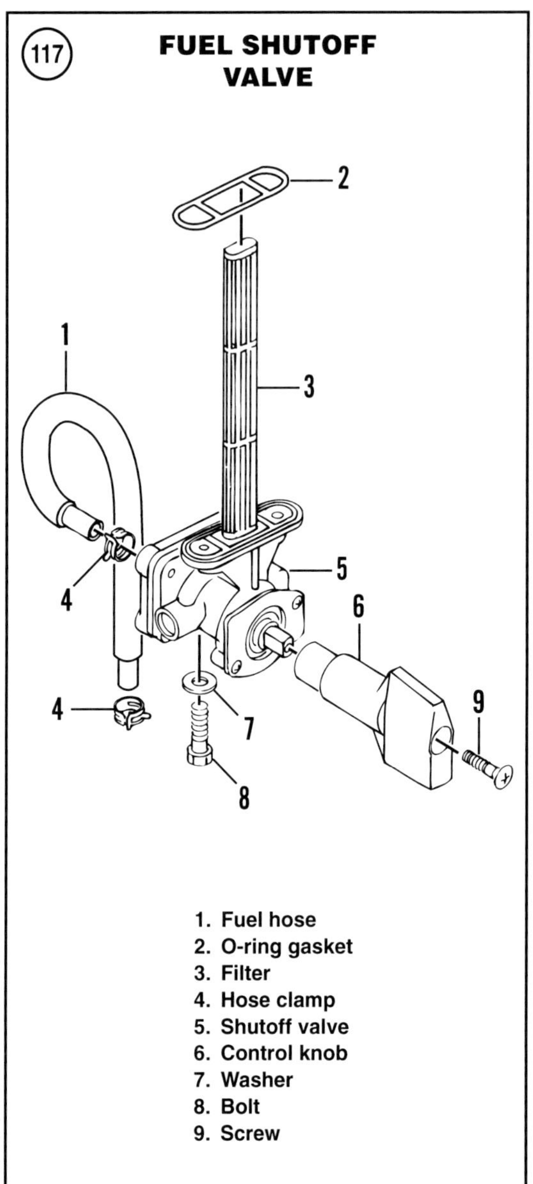

FUEL FILTER

A small fuel filter screen is an integral part of the fuel valve. Consider installing an inline fuel filter on all models.

An inline fuel filter (A.C. part No. GF453 or equivalent) is available at most auto and motorcycle supply stores. Just cut the fuel line from the fuel valve to the carburetor assembly, and install the filter. Cut out a section of the fuel line equivalent to the length of the filter so the fuel line does not kink and restrict fuel flow. Insert the fuel filter and secure the fuel line to each end of the filter. Make sure the direction arrow on the filter points to the carburetor side of the fuel line.

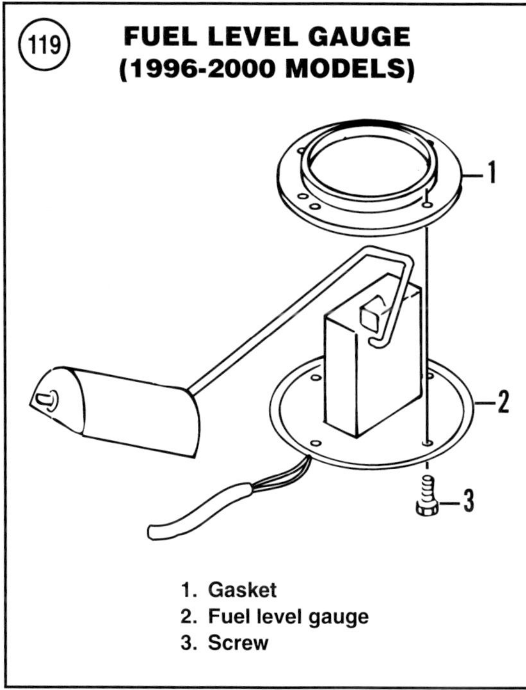

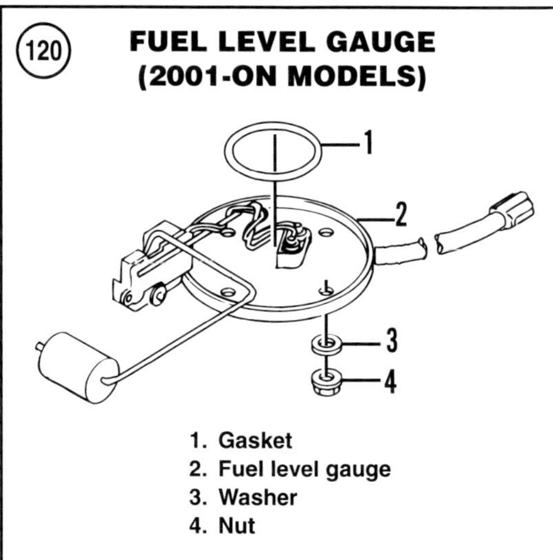

FUEL LEVEL GAUGE

Removal/Installation

WARNING
Some fuel may spill during the following procedure. Work in a well-ventilated area at least 50 feet from any sparks or flames, including gas appliance pilot lights. Do not allow anyone to smoke in the area. Keep a BC rated fire extinguisher handy.

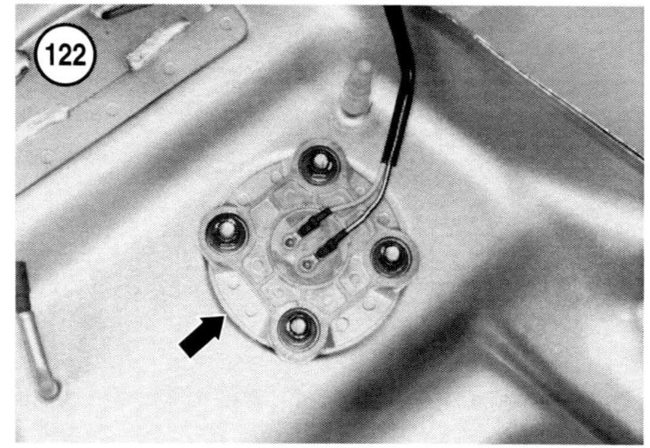

NOTE
Refer to Chapter Nine for fuel level gauge testing.

Refer to **Figure 119** or **Figure 120**.

1. Remove the fuel tank as described in this chapter.
2. Cover the workbench with a blanket or several towels to protect the surface of the fuel tank.
3. Turn the fuel tank on its side.
4. Remove the screws or nuts and washers securing the fuel level gauge to the base of the fuel tank. Refer to **Figure 121** for 1996-2000 models or **Figure 122** for 2001-on models.
5. Carefully remove the fuel level gauge and float assembly and gasket from the fuel tank opening. Be careful not to damage the float during removal.
6. Install by reversing these removal steps. Note the following:
   a. Install a *new* gasket under the assembly.
   b. Tighten the screws or nuts securely.

c. Pour a small amount of gasoline into the fuel tank after installing the gauge and check for fuel leakage. If a leak is present, solve the problem prior to installing the fuel tank.

CRANKCASE BREATHER SYSTEM

All models are equipped with a closed crankcase breather system. The system routs the engine combustion gasses into the air filter housing, where they are burned in the engine.

Inspection/Cleaning

Make sure the hose clamps at each end of the hose are tight. Check the hose for deterioration. Replace it as necessary.

Remove the drain plug (**Figure 123**) on the end of the air filter housing drain hose and drain out all residue. This cleaning procedure should be done more frequently if a considerable amount of riding is done at full throttle or in the rain. Install the drain plug.

EVAPORATIVE EMISSION CONTROL SYSTEM (CALIFORNIA MODELS ONLY)

The evaporative emissions control system (**Figure 124**) captures fuel vapors or hydrocarbons (HC) and stores them so they will not be released into the atmosphere. The fuel vapors are routed through the rollover valve and stored in the charcoal canister, located on the right side of the rear frame. When the engine is started, the stored vapors are drawn from the canister. They pass through the purge control valves, flow into the carburetors and then into the engine, where they are burned.

When removing a hose from any component in the system, mark the hose and the fitting with a piece of masking tape so they can be properly identified during assembly. There are so many vacuum hoses on these models that reconnecting the hoses can be very confusing.

Refer to **Figure 125** for 1996-2000 models or to **Figure 126** for 2001-on models. A hose routing diagram also appears on the emission control label located under the seat.

Inspection

Make sure all evaporative emission control hoses are correctly routed, properly attached to the different components and that all hose clamps are tight. Check all hoses for deterioration and replace them as necessary.

PURGE CONTROL VALVES AND CHARCOAL CANISTER (CALIFORNIA MODELS ONLY)

Removal/Installation

1. Remove the fuel tank as described in this chapter.
2. Remove the seat and right rear frame cover as described in Chapter Fourteen.

NOTE
Prior to removing the hoses from the purge control valves and the charcoal canister, mark the hose and the fitting with a piece of masking tape. Be sure to clearly identify each hose and its fitting.

3. Remove the bolts, lockwashers and washers securing the charcoal canister and the purge control valves assembly to the frame and remove the canister assembly. Refer to **Figure 127** for 1997-2000 models and to **Figure 128** for 2001-on models.
4. Disconnect the hoses going to the charcoal canister (**Figure 129**) and to each purge control valve.
5. Install by reversing these removal steps, noting the following:

(124) EVAPORATIVE EMISSIONS CONTROL SYSTEM (CALIFORNIA MODELS)

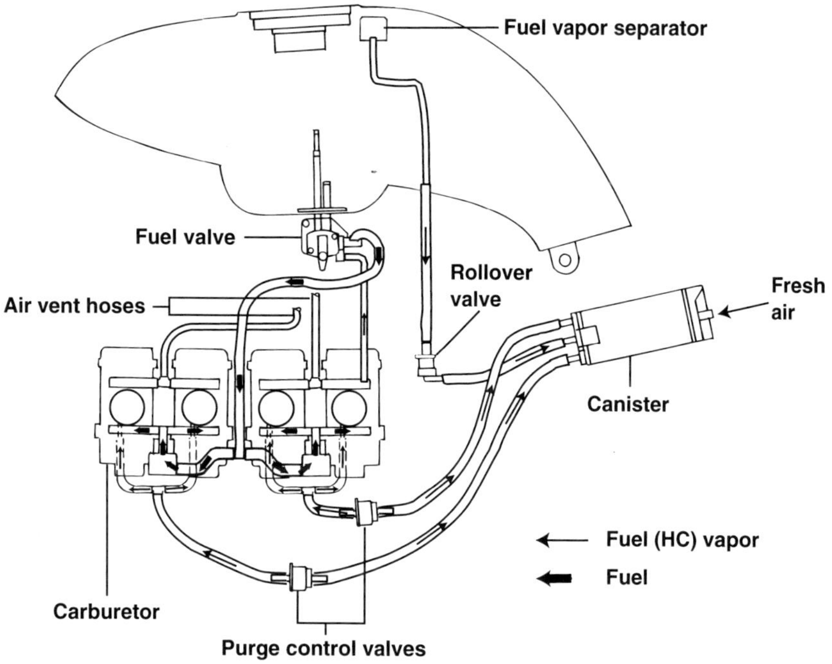

Fuel vapor separator
Fuel valve
Rollover valve
Fresh air
Air vent hoses
Canister
Fuel (HC) vapor
Fuel
Carburetor
Purge control valves

(125) EVAPORATIVE EMISSIONS CONTROL SYSTEM (1997-2000 CALIFORNIA MODELS)

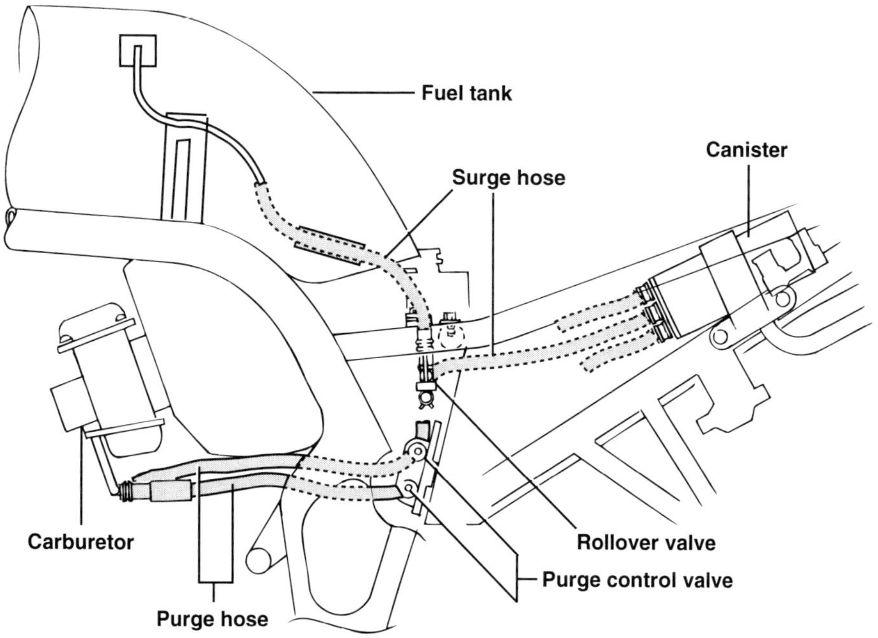

Fuel tank
Canister
Surge hose
Carburetor
Rollover valve
Purge control valve
Purge hose

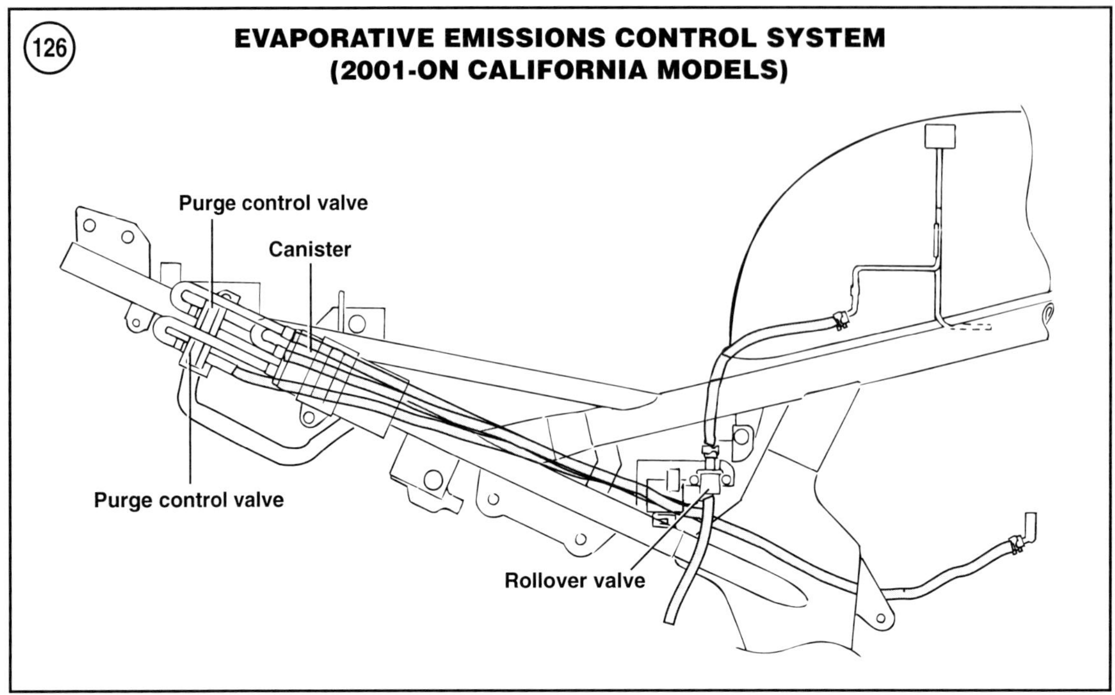

(126) **EVAPORATIVE EMISSIONS CONTROL SYSTEM (2001-ON CALIFORNIA MODELS)**

(127) **EVAPORATIVE SYSTEM (1997-2000 CALIFORNIA MODELS)**

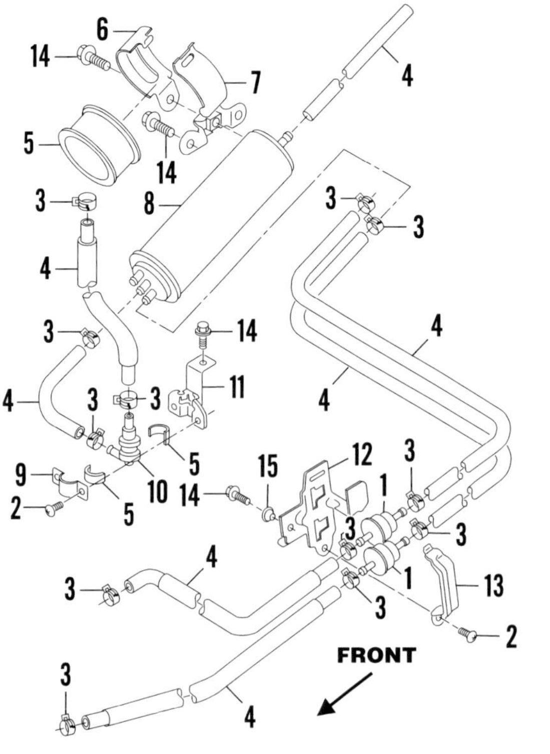

FRONT

1. Purge control valve
2. Screw
3. Clamp
4. Hose
5. Damper
6. Canister holder
7. Canister bracket
8. Canister
9. Rollover valve bracket
10. Rollover valve
11. Rollover valve holder
12. Purge control valve bracket
13. Purge control valve holder
14. Bolt
15. Washer

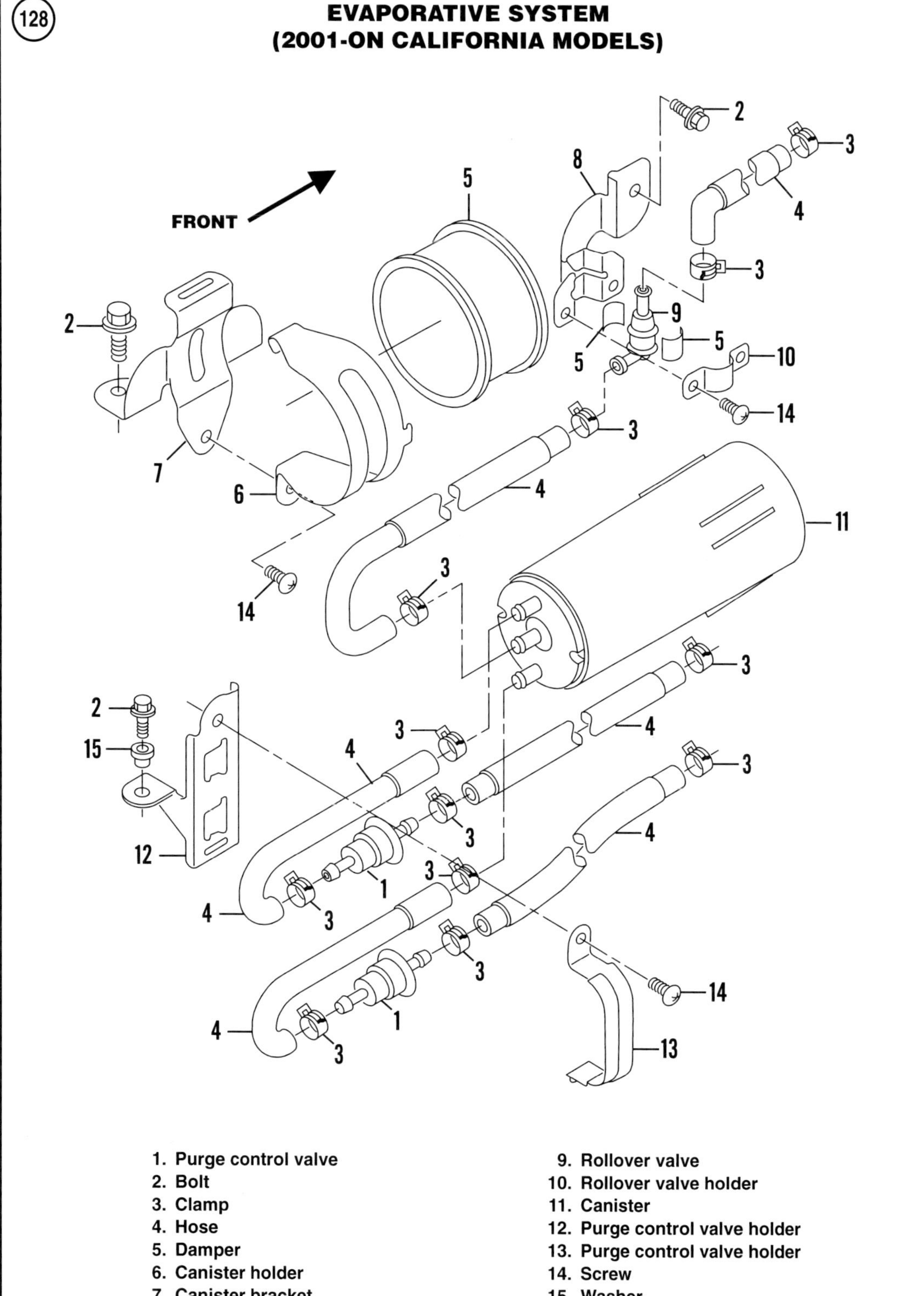

1. Purge control valve
2. Bolt
3. Clamp
4. Hose
5. Damper
6. Canister holder
7. Canister bracket
8. Rollover bracket
9. Rollover valve
10. Rollover valve holder
11. Canister
12. Purge control valve holder
13. Purge control valve holder
14. Screw
15. Washer

a. Be sure to install the hoses onto the correct fittings on the charcoal canister and on the purge control valves.
b. Make sure the hoses are not kinked, twisted or in contact with any sharp surfaces.

PAIR SYSTEM (CALIFORNIA MODELS)

The PAIR (Air Supply) System intake system vacuum pulses to introduce fresh air into the exhaust ports. Refer to **Figure 130** for 1996-2000 models or **Figure 131** for 2001-on models. On 1996-2000 models, the system consists of a PAIR control valve, two reed valves, an air cleaner and air and vacuum hoses. On 2001-on models, the air cleaner, control valve and reed valves are combined into a single PAIR valve assembly.

Make sure all air and vacuum hoses are correctly routed and securely attached to their respective fittings. Inspect the hoses and replace any if necessary.

Removal/Installation

Refer to **Figure 132** for 1996-2000 models and to **Figure 133** for 2001-on models.

1. On GSF1200S models, remove the front fairing as described in Chapter Fourteen.
2. Remove the exhaust system and the fuel tank as described in this chapter.
3. Remove the oil cooler as described in Chapter Five.

NOTE
Label each hose and its fitting during disassembly. This ensures that each hose will be connected to the correct fitting during assembly.

4. Loosen the hose clamps and disconnect the hoses from their respective fittings. Label each hose and its fitting so the hoses can be reinstalled on the correct fittings during assembly.

5A. On 1996-2000 models, remove the PAIR assembly as follows (see **Figure 134**).
a. Disconnect the PAIR vacuum hose on the side of the control valve.
b. Disconnect the PAIR air hose from the fitting on the PAIR air cleaner (**Figure 135**).

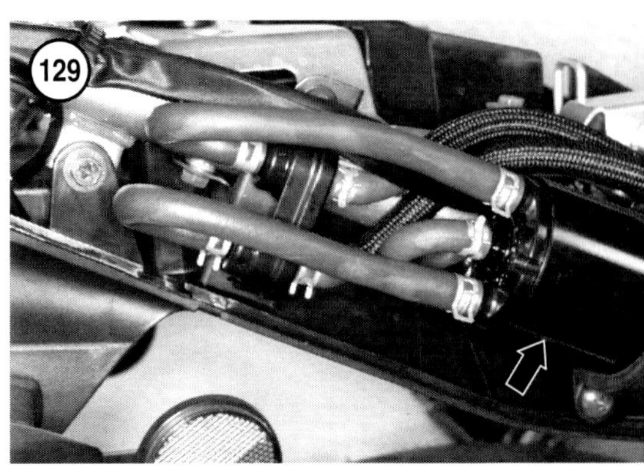

c. Disconnect the two reed valve hoses from each reed valve.
d. Remove the bolts securing the PAIR bracket. Lift the bracket and the PAIR assembly from the frame.
e. Install by reversing these removal steps.

5B. On 2001-on models, remove the PAIR valve assembly as follows (see **Figure 136**):
a. Disconnect the PAIR vacuum hose (A, **Figure 137**) from the PAIR valve assembly.
b. Disconnect the PAIR air inlet hose (B, **Figure 137**) from the PAIR valve assembly.
c. Disconnect the reed valve hoses (C, **Figure 137**) from the outlets on each reed valve.
d. Remove the mounting bolt (D, **Figure 137**) and remove the PAIR valve assembly from the mounting bracket.
e. Install by reversing these removal steps.

6. To remove the air pipes, perform the following:
a. Disconnect the PAIR valve hose from the lower end of the air pipe.
b. Remove the nuts securing the air pipes to the cylinder block.
c. Remove the air pipes and gaskets. New gaskets must be installed during assembly.
d. Install by reversing these removal steps.

7. Install the exhaust system and fuel tank as described in this chapter.
8. Install the oil cooler as described in Chapter Five.
9. Install the fairing as described in Chapter Fourteen.

(130) **PAIR SYSTEM (1997-2000 CALIFORNIA MODELS)**

PAIR air cleaner
PAIR control valve
To PAIR reed valve (No. 1 and No. 2)
To carburetor (vacuum hose)
PAIR reed valve (No. 3 and No. 4)
PAIR reed valve
No. 4 cyl.
No. 3 cyl.
No. 2 cyl.
No. 1 cyl.
PAIR reed valve (No. 1 and No. 2)

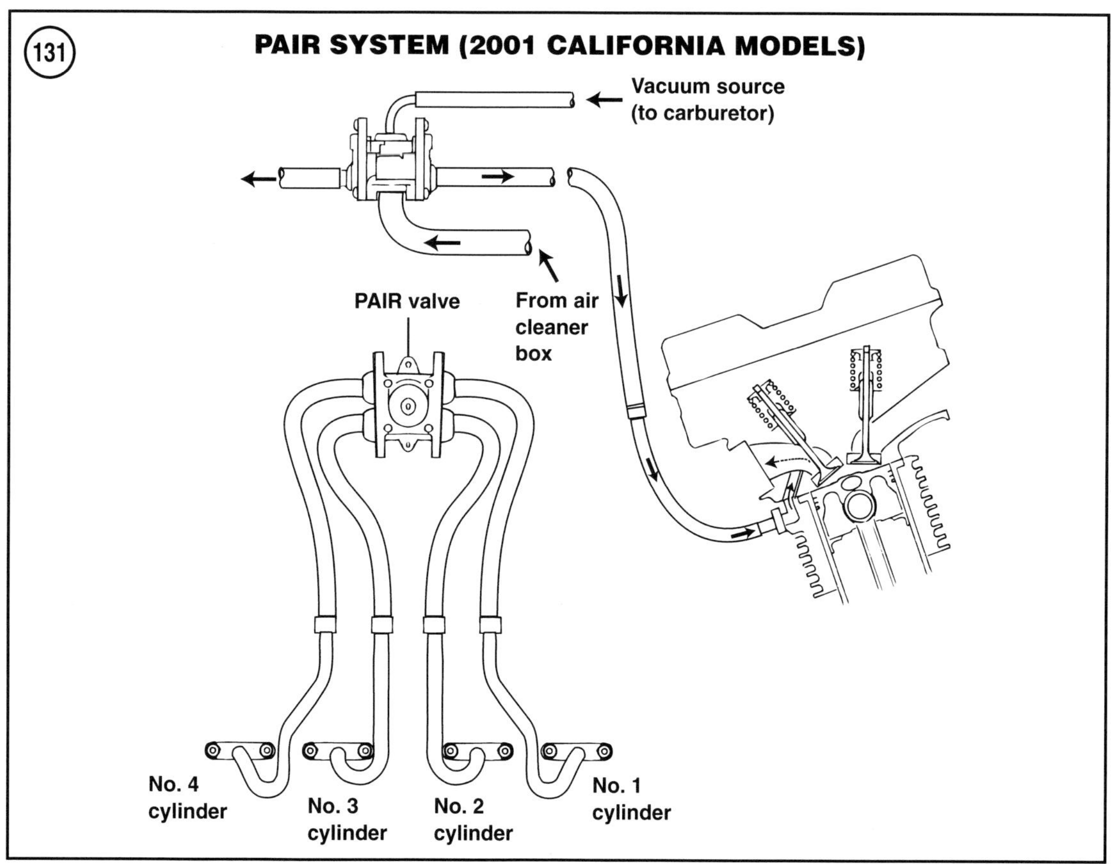

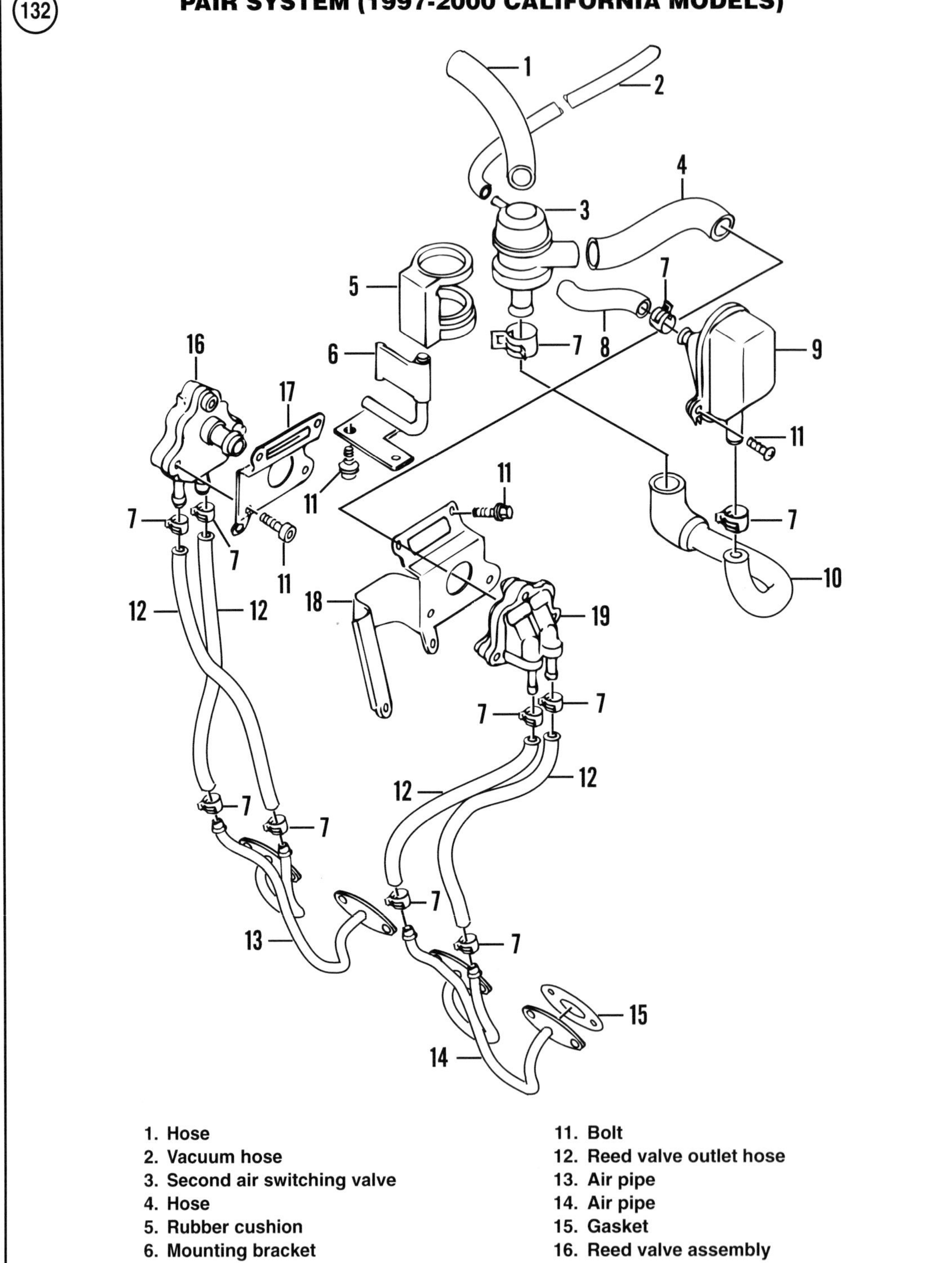

1. Hose
2. Vacuum hose
3. Second air switching valve
4. Hose
5. Rubber cushion
6. Mounting bracket
7. Hose clamp
8. Air cleaner inlet hose
9. Air cleaner
10. Hose
11. Bolt
12. Reed valve outlet hose
13. Air pipe
14. Air pipe
15. Gasket
16. Reed valve assembly
17. Mounting bracket—right side
18. Mounting bracket—left side
19. Reed valve assembly

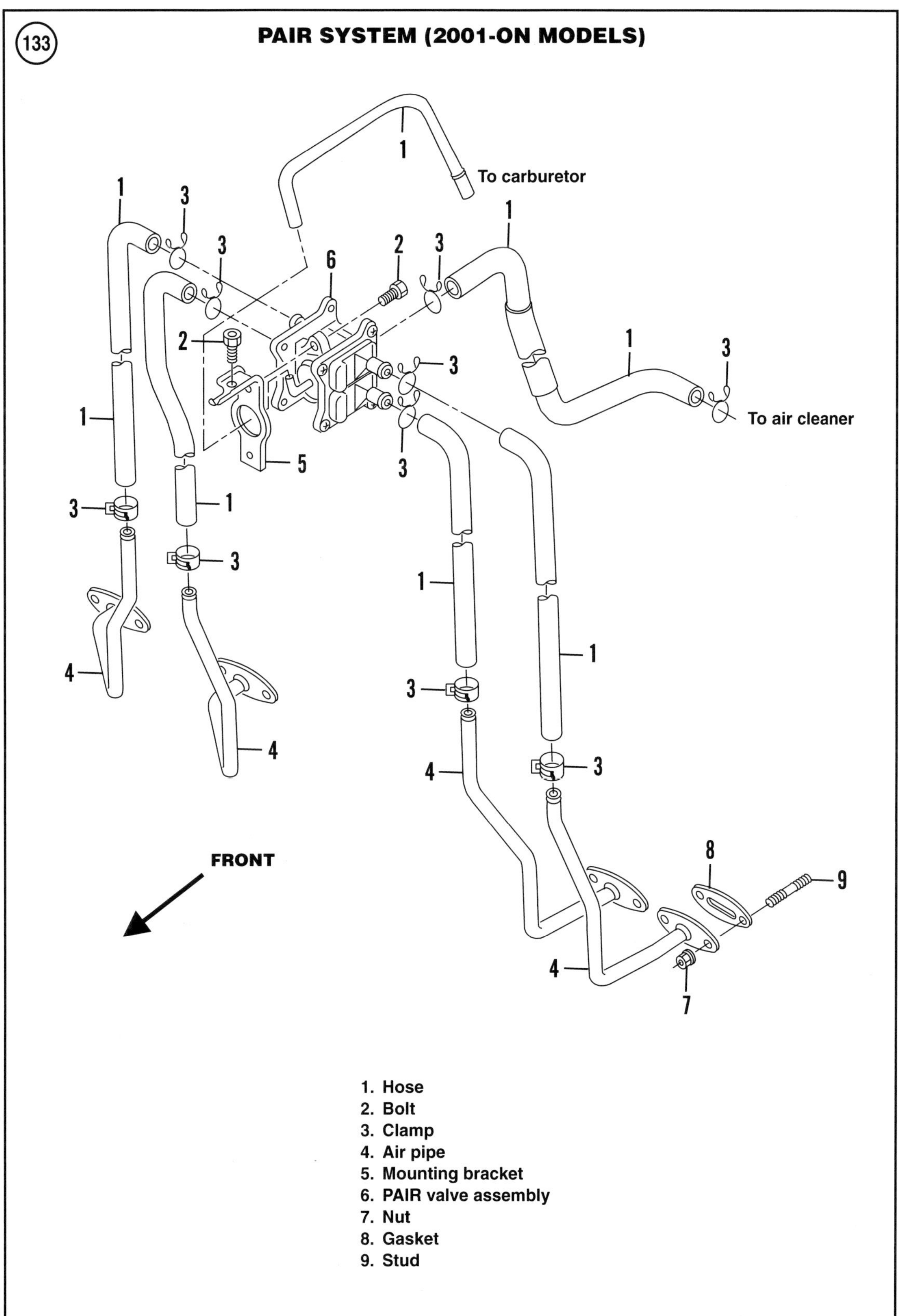
133
PAIR SYSTEM (2001-ON MODELS)
To carburetor
To air cleaner
FRONT
1
2
3
4
5
6
7
8
9
1. Hose
2. Bolt
3. Clamp
4. Air pipe
5. Mounting bracket
6. PAIR valve assembly
7. Nut
8. Gasket
9. Stud

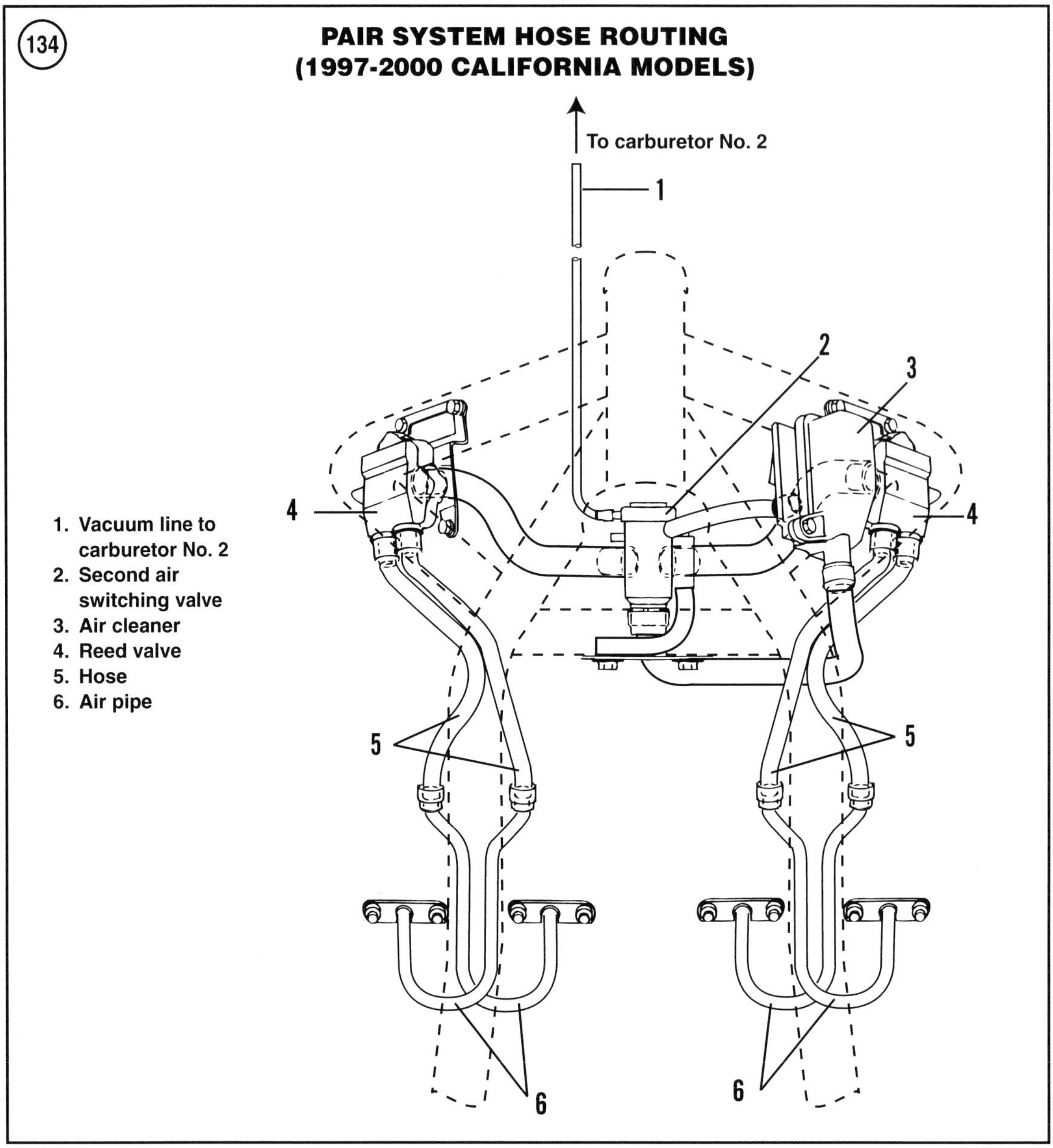

134

PAIR SYSTEM HOSE ROUTING (1997-2000 CALIFORNIA MODELS)

To carburetor No. 2

1. Vacuum line to carburetor No. 2
2. Second air switching valve
3. Air cleaner
4. Reed valve
5. Hose
6. Air pipe

EXHAUST SYSTEM

The exhaust system is a vital performance component. Because of its location, it is a vulnerable piece of equipment. Check the exhaust system for deep dents and fractures. Repair them or replace the defective component immediately. Check the muffler frame mounting flanges for fractures and loose bolts. Check the cylinder head mounting flanges for tightness. A loose exhaust pipe connection can reduce engine performance.

135

136

PAIR SYSTEM HOSE ROUTING (2001-ON CALIFORNIA MODELS)

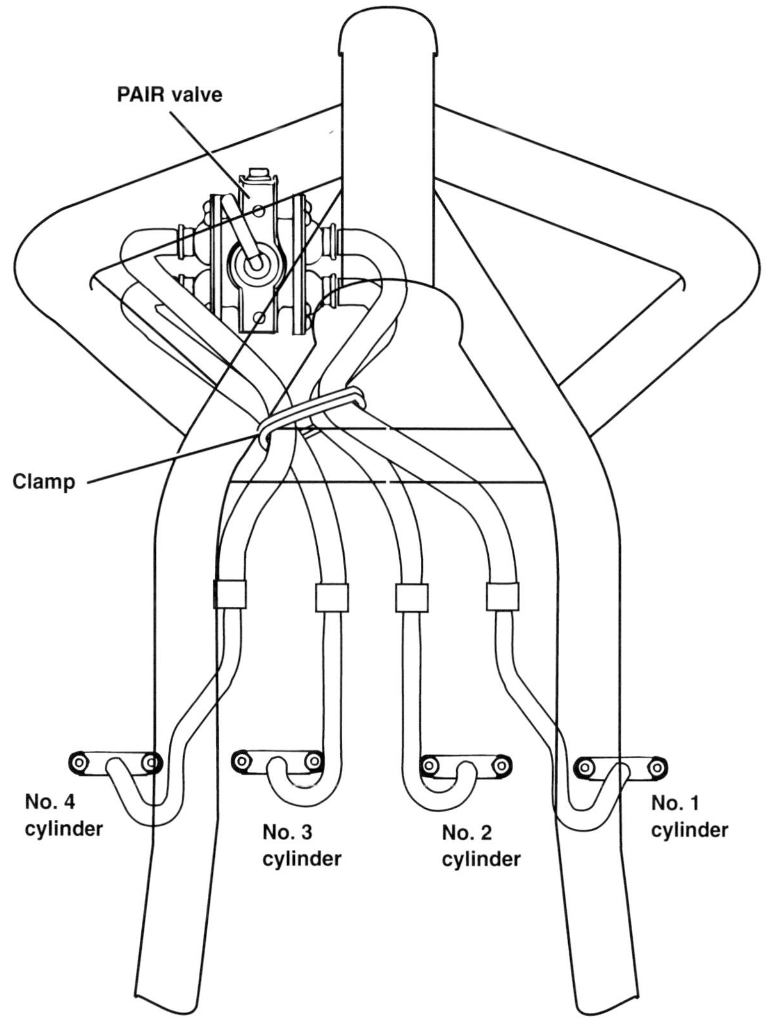

PAIR valve

Clamp

No. 4 cylinder

No. 3 cylinder

No. 2 cylinder

No. 1 cylinder

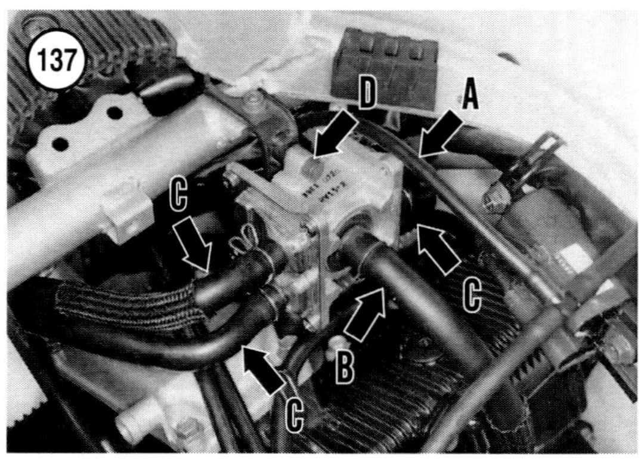

Muffler and Middle Exhaust Pipe Removal/Installation

Refer to **Figure 138**.

1. Securely support the motorcycle on level ground on the centerstand.

2. Loosen the clamp bolt (**Figure 139**) securing the muffler and middle exhaust pipe assembly to the front exhaust pipe.

3. Remove the nut from the muffler mount (A, **Figure 140**) that secures the muffler to the rear footpeg.

138

EXHAUST SYSTEM

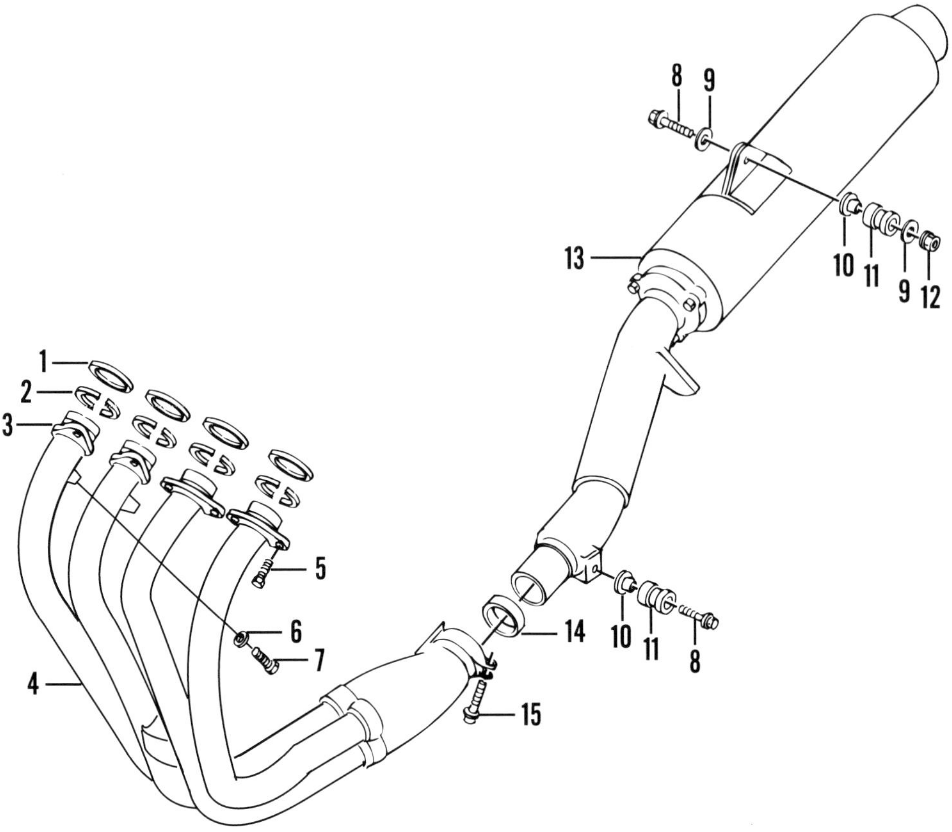

1. Gasket
2. Plate
3. Clamp
4. Front exhaust pipe
5. Bolt
6. Washer
7. Bolt
8. Bolt
9. Washer
10. Spacer
11. Rubber cushion
12. Nut
13. Muffler/middle exhaust pipe assembly
14. Gasket
15. Bolt

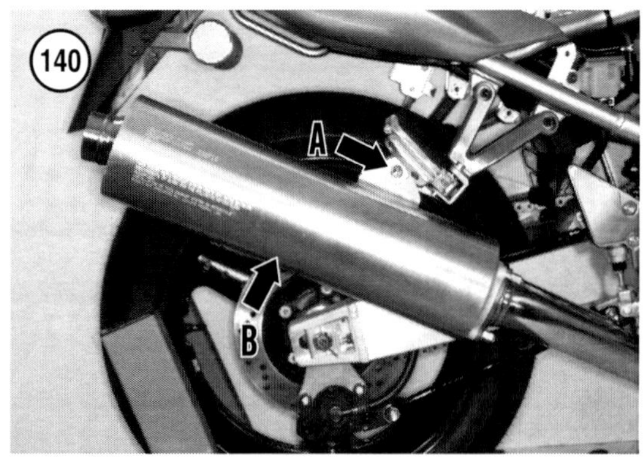

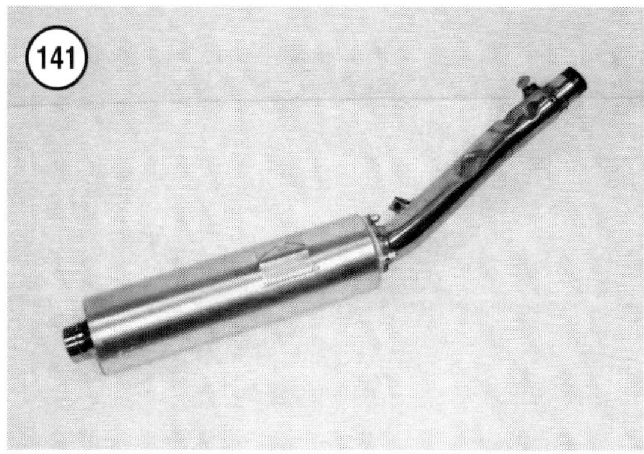

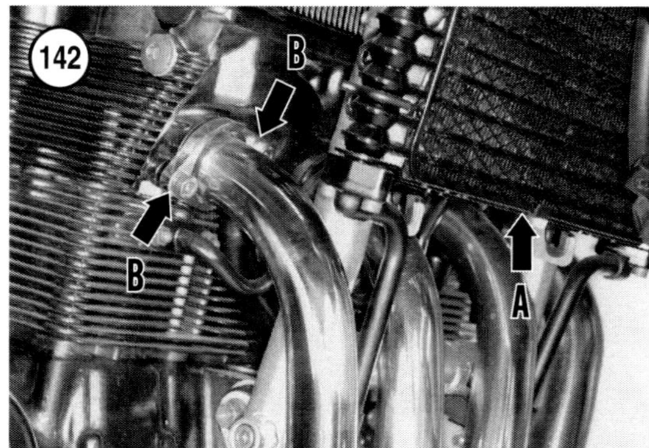

Remove the bolt and washer. Do not lose the collar or damper from this mount.

4. Pull the muffler and middle exhaust pipe (B, **Figure 140**) out of the front exhaust pipe and remove it. Remove the gasket from the front exhaust pipe and discard it.

5. Check the rear mounting bracket rubber grommet. Replace the rubber grommet if it is starting to harden or deteriorate.

6. Inspect the mounting bracket on the muffler and the middle exhaust pipe (**Figure 141**) for cracks or damage.

7. Do not separate the muffler from the middle exhaust pipe, as there is no replacement gasket available for the joint between these two parts.

8. Installation is the reverse of removal. Note the following:

   a. Install a new gasket over the end of the exhaust pipe.
   b. Tighten the mounting fasteners to the specifications in **Table 6**.
   c. After installation is complete, start the engine and check for exhaust leaks.

Front Exhaust Pipe Removal/Installation

Refer to **Figure 138**.

1. Securely support the motorcycle on level ground on the centerstand.

2. If the muffler and middle exhaust pipe assembly has been removed, place a small jack or wooden blocks under the front exhaust pipe to hold it in place.

NOTE
It is necessary to move the front wheel and front fender from side to side to reach all of the header bolts.

NOTE
*The oil cooler (A, **Figure 142**) can be left in place, but partial removal will allow additional working room.*

3. Remove the two header bolts (B, **Figure 142**) from each exhaust port.

4. Pull the front exhaust pipe assembly forward and out of the cylinder head and then remove the front exhaust pipe assembly from the motorcycle. Remove the sealing gasket (**Figure 143**) from the exhaust ports in each cylinder.

5. Check each exhaust pipe-to-cylinder head flange (A, **Figure 144**) for corrosion, burned areas or damage.

6. Inspect all of the welds (B, **Figure 144**) for leakage or corrosion.

7. Install a new exhaust pipe sealing gasket into each exhaust port. Apply a small amount of heavy grease to the gaskets to hold them in place.

8. Install the exhaust pipe assembly onto the cylinder head and frame.

9. Install the exhaust header bolts. Finger-tighten them at this time.

10. Install the muffler and middle exhaust pipe assembly as previously described in this chapter. Finger-tighten the fasteners at this time.

11. Tighten the exhaust system fasteners to the specifications and in the following sequence:
   a. Front exhaust pipe bolts, 23 N•m (17 ft.-lb.).
   b. Front exhaust pipe-to-middle exhaust pipe clamp bolt (securely).
   c. Muffler mounting bolt, 29 N•m (21 ft.-lb.).

12. After installation is complete, start the engine and check for exhaust leaks.

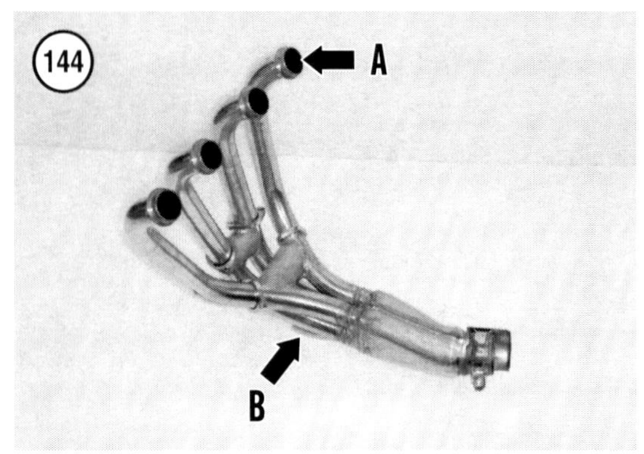

Table 1 CARBURETOR SPECIFICATIONS (1997-2000 U.S. AND CANADA MODELS)

Item	Specification
Carburetor model	Mikuni BST36SS
Carburetor type	Constant velocity
Bore size	36 mm (1.4 in.)
Carburetor identification	
U.S., Canada	27E5
California	27E6
Idle speed	1100-1250 rpm
Float height	13.6-15.6 mm (0.54-0.62 in.)
Main jet	No. 102.5
Jet needle	
1997	5D80
1998-2000	0-8M
Jet needle clip position	
U.S.	Fixed
Canada	4th
Pilot jet	No. 37.5
Pilot screw	Pre-set
Throttle cable free play	0.5-1.0 mm (0.02-0.04 in.)

Table 2 CARBURETOR SPECIFICATIONS (1996-1997 U.K MODELS)

Item	Specification
Carburetor model	Mikuni BST36SS
Carburetor type	Constant velocity
Bore size	36 mm (1.4 in.)
Carburetor identification	
U.K., France, Sweden, Germany, Australia, Netherlands and Italy models	27E1
Switzerland models	27E3
Idle speed	
All models except Switzerland	1100-1300 rpm
Switzerland models	1100-1250 rpm
Float height	13.6-15.6 mm (0.54-0.62 in.)
Main jet	No. 102.5

(continued)

Table 2 CARBURETOR SPECIFICATIONS (1996-1997 U.K MODELS) (continued)

Item	Specification
Jet needle	
All models except Switzerland	5D76
Switzerland models	5D55
Jet needle clip position	
All models except Switzerland	4th
Switzerland models	2nd
Pilot jet	No. 37.5
Pilot screw	Pre-set (1 3/4 turns out)
Throttle cable free play	0.5-1.0 mm (0.02-0.04 in.)

Table 3 CARBURETOR SPECIFICATIONS (1998-2000 U.K MODELS)

Item	Specification
Carburetor model	Mikuni BST36SS
Carburetor type	Constant velocity
Bore size	36 mm (1.4 in.)
Carburetor identification	
U.K., France, Sweden, Germany, Australia, Netherlands and Italy models	27E1
Switzerland models	27E7
Idle speed	
All models except Switzerland	1100-1300 rpm
Switzerland models	1100-1250 rpm
Float height	13.6-15.6 mm (0.54-0.62 in.)
Main jet	No. 102.5
Jet needle	
All models except Switzerland	5D76
Switzerland models	5D55
Jet needle clip position	
All models except Switzerland	4th
Switzerland models	2nd
Pilot jet	No. 37.5
Pilot screw	
All models except Switzerland	Pre-set (1 3/4 turns out)
Switzerland models	Pre-set (1 7/8 turns out)
Throttle cable free play	0.5-1.0 mm (0.02-0.04 in.)

Table 4 CARBURETOR SPECIFICATIONS (2001-ON ALL MODELS)

Item	Specification
Carburetor model	Mikuni BSR36SS
Carburetor type	Constant velocity
Bore size	36 mm (1.4 in.)
Carburetor I.D.	
California	32F2
U.S. and Canada	32F1
All models except California, U.S. and Canada	32F0
Idle speed	1100-1300 rpm
Float height	12.0-14.0 mm (0.47-0.55 in.)

(continued)

Table 4 CARBURETOR SPECIFICATIONS (2001-ON ALL MODELS) (continued)

Item	Specification
Main jet	No. 100
Jet needle	
California, U.S. and Canada	5C71
All models except California, U.S. and Canada	5C70
Jet needle clip position	
California, U.S. and Canada	1st
All models except California, U.S. and Canada	3rd
Pilot jet	No. 15
Pilot screw	Pre-set (3 turns out)
Throttle cable free play	2.0-4.0 mm (0.08-0.16 in.)

Table 5 CARBURETOR TEST SPECIFICATIONS

Item	
Carburetor themoswitch (2001 U.K. models)	
Below 8-14° C (46-57° F)	Continuity
Above 15-21° C (59-70° F)	No continuity
Throttle position sensor	
Wide-open resistance	35,000-65,000 ohms

Table 6 EXHAUST SYSTEM TORQUE SPECIFICATIONS

Item	N•m	in.-lb.	ft.-lb.
Carburetor heater			
(2001-on U.K.)	3	26.5	–
Front exhaust pipe bolts	23	–	17
Muffler mounting bolt	29	–	21

CHAPTER NINE

ELECTRICAL SYSTEM

This chapter contains service and test procedures for all electrical and ignition components. Battery and spark plug information is covered in Chapter Three.

The electrical system includes the following systems:

1. Charging.
2. Ignition.
3. Starting.
4. Lighting.
5. Switches.
6. Combination meter.
7. Horn.
8. Fuses.

Refer to **Figure 1** and **Figure 2** for electrical component location.

PRELIMINARY INFORMATION

Resistance Testing

Resistance readings will vary with temperature. The resistance increases when the temperature increases and decreases when temperature decreases.

Specifications for resistance are based at a specific temperature (68° F [20° C]). If the component is warm or hot, let it cool to room temperature. If a component is tested at a temperature that varies from the specified test temperature, a false resistance reading may result.

The manufacturer specifies the use of a Suzuki Multi Circuit Tester (part No. 09900-25008) for accurate resistance tests. Due to the specific resistance values of the semiconductors in this meter, using another meter may provide inaccurate results.

An equivalent tool is the Motion Pro Ignition Mate (part No. 08-0193). However the test procedures in this chapter use the Suzuki Multi Circuit

① **ELECTRICAL COMPONENT LOCATION**

1. Left side combination switch
2. Ignition coils
3. Fuel level gauge
4. Diode
5. Battery
6. Ignitor unit
7. Fuse box
8. Starter
9. Alternator
10. Neutral, or gear position, switch
11. Side stand switch
12. Starter relay and main fuse
13. Turn signal relay
14. Sidestand relay

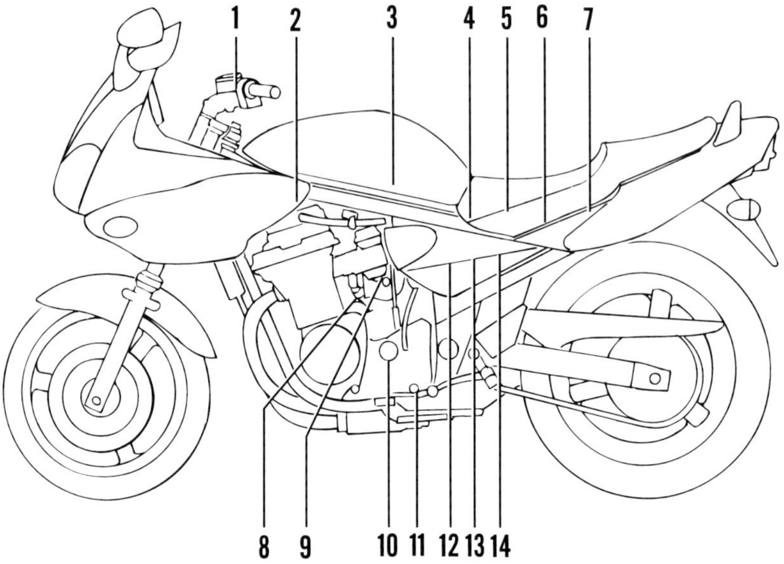

② **ELECTRICAL COMPONENT LOCATION**

1. Taillight/brake light
2. Throttle position sensor
3. Front brake light switch
4. Right side combination switch
5. Combination meter
6. Headlight
7. Rear turn signal
8. Rear brake light switch
9. Ignition signal generator
10. Oil pressure switch
11. Front turn signal

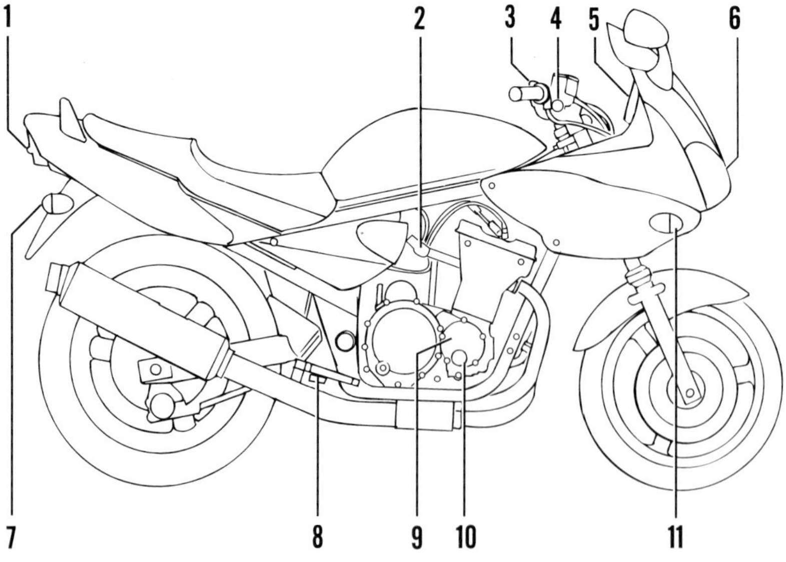

3

4

Tester. If an alternative meter is being used, follow the manufacturer's instructions. Make sure the battery for any tester being used is in good condition. Accurate results depend on the battery having sufficient voltage.

NOTE

Use caution when considering the replacement of an electrical component because it tests slightly out of specification. Resistance tests are performed on inactive circuits and are not always definitive indicators of a component's function under operating conditions.

Electrical Component Replacement

Most motorcycle dealerships and parts suppliers will not accept the return of electrical components. If the exact cause of any electrical system malfunction has not been determined, do not attempt to remedy the problem with guesswork and unnecessary parts replacement. If possible, have the suspect component or system tested by a professional technician *before* purchasing new electrical components.

Electrical Component/Connector Locations and Service

The location of electrical connectors can vary between model years.

The location of the connectors may have been changed during previous repairs. Always confirm the wire color to and from the connector and follow the wiring harness to the various components when performing tests.

Moisture can enter many of the electrical connectors and cause corrosion, which may cause a poor connection. This may result in component failure and possible breakdown on the road. To prevent moisture from entering the various connectors, disconnect them and, after making sure the terminals are clean, pack the terminal with dielectric grease. Do not use a substitute that may interfere with current flow. Dielectric grease is specially formulated to seal the connector and not increase resistance. For best results, the compound should fill the entire inner area of the connector. It is recommended that each time a connector is unplugged that it be cleaned and sealed with dielectric grease.

Ground connections are often overlooked during troubleshooting. Make sure they are corrosion free and tight onto a bare metal surface (where applicable). Apply dielectric grease to the terminals before reconnecting them.

NEGATIVE BATTERY CABLE

Many of the procedures in this chapter require disconnecting the battery negative cable as a safety precaution.

1. Turn the ignition switch to the OFF position.
2. Remove the seat as described in Chapter Fourteen.
3. On 2001-on models, remove the document tray (**Figure 3**).
4. Disconnect the battery negative cable from the battery terminal (**Figure 4**).
5. Move the negative cable out of the way so it will not accidentally make contact with the battery negative terminal.
6. Once the procedure is completed, connect the battery negative lead to the terminal and tighten the bolt securely.
7. On 2001-on models, install the document tray.
8. Install the seat as described in Chapter Fourteen.

5

CHARGING SYSTEM (1996-2000 MODELS)

Ignition switch
IG
B
Load
Alternator
IC Regulator
IG
Stator coil
Fuse
Fuse
Diagram Key
Connectors
Ground
Frame ground
Connection
No connection
F
IC
+
-
Battery
Rotor coil
E

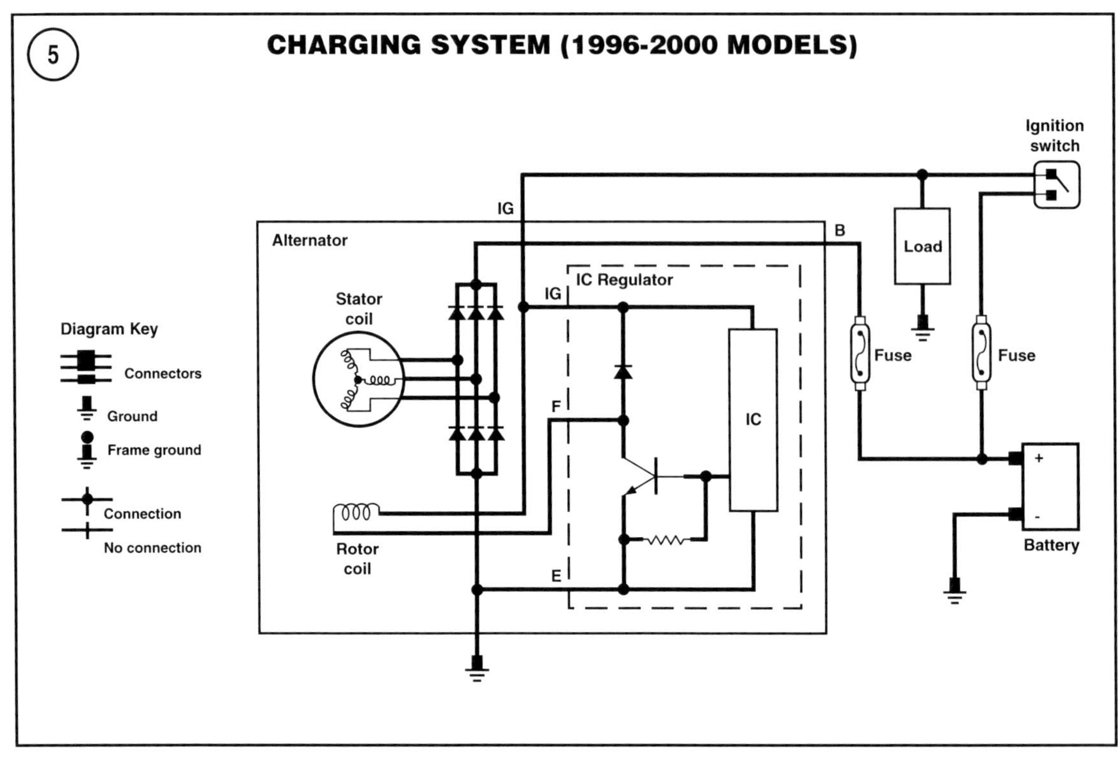

6

CHARGING SYSTEM (2001-ON MODELS)

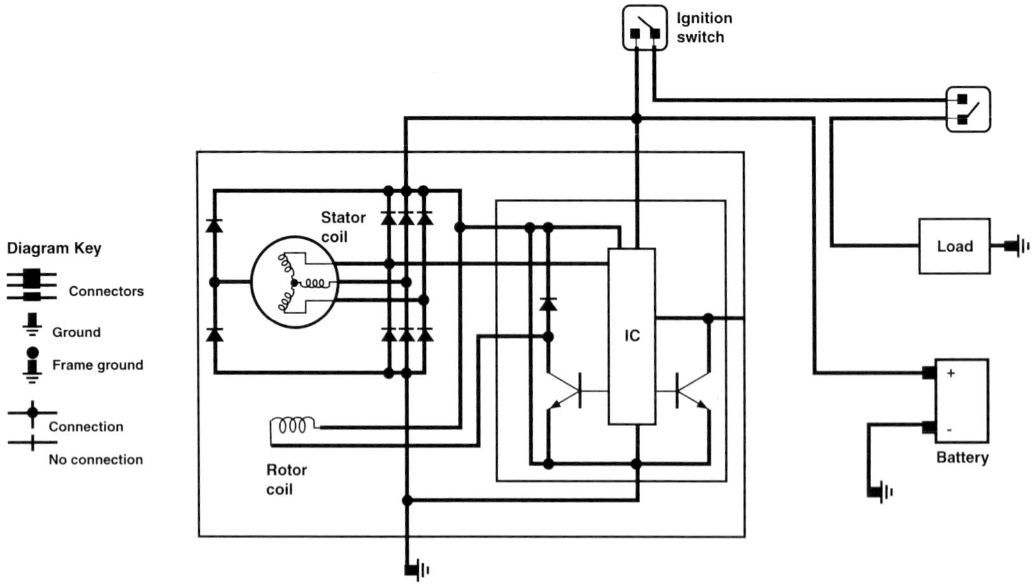

Ignition switch
Stator coil
Load
Diagram Key
Connectors
Ground
Frame ground
IC
Connection
No connection
+
-
Battery
Rotor coil

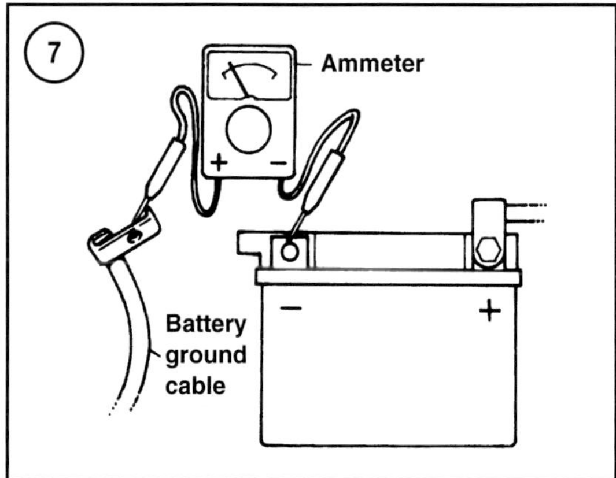

CHARGING SYSTEM

The charging system consists of the battery, alternator, solid-state voltage regulator and rectifier. Refer to **Figure 5** for 1996-2000 models and to **Figure 6** for 2001-on models. Alternating current generated by the alternator is rectified to direct current. The voltage regulator maintains the voltage to the battery and electrical loads (for example, lights and ignition) at a constant voltage regardless of variations in engine speed and load.

Troubleshooting

Refer to Chapter Two.

Current Draw Test

Perform this test prior to performing the regulated voltage test.

1. Turn the ignition switch to the OFF position.
2. Remove the seat as described in Chapter Fourteen.
3. Disconnect the negative battery cable from the battery terminal as described in this chapter.

CAUTION
Before connecting the ammeter into the circuit in Step 5, set the meter to its highest amperage scale. This will prevent a possible large current flow from damaging the meter or blowing the meter's fuse, if so equipped.

4. Connect the ammeter between the battery negative lead and the negative terminal of the battery (**Figure 7**). Switch the ammeter from its highest to lowest amperage scale while reading the meter. If the needle swings even the slightest amount, there is a current draw on the system. If current exceeds 1 mA, the battery will eventually discharge.
5. If the current draw exceeds 1 mA, the probable causes are:
   a. A short circuit in the system.
   b. Loose, dirty or faulty electrical system connectors in the charging system wiring harness system.
   c. Damaged battery.
6. To locate a short circuit, refer to the wiring diagrams at the end of this book. Continue to measure the current draw while disconnecting different connectors in the electrical system one by one. When the current draw returns to normal, that circuit contains the short. Continue testing the defective circuit until the problem is identified.
7. Disconnect the ammeter test leads and reconnect the negative battery cable.

Regulated Voltage Test

Whenever charging system trouble is suspected, make sure the battery is fully charged and in good condition before performing any tests. Clean and test the battery as described in Chapter Three. Make sure all electrical connectors are tight and free of corrosion.

1. Start the engine and let it reach normal operating temperature; shut off the engine.
2. Remove the seat as described in Chapter Fourteen.
3. On 2001-on models, remove the document tray (**Figure 3**).
4. Start the engine and let it idle.
5. Connect a 0-15 DC voltmeter to the battery negative and positive terminals (**Figure 8**).
6. Increase engine speed to 5000 rpm and measure the voltage. It should be within the regulated voltage range specified in **Table 1**. If the voltage is less than specified, test the alternator and the IC regulator as described in this chapter.
7. If the regulated voltage is too high, the IC regulator is probably at fault. Inspect the IC regulator as described in this chapter.
8. After the test is completed, disconnect the voltmeter and shut off the engine.

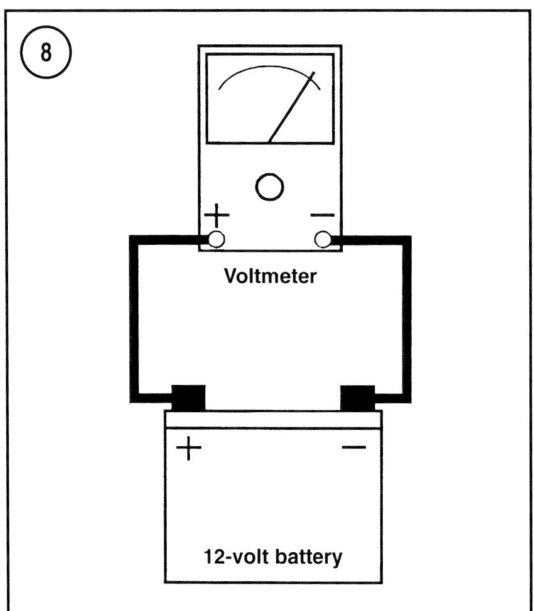

ALTERNATOR

The voltage regulator and IC rectifier are built into the alternator. These two components can be removed and replaced separately.

Removal/Installation

1. Remove the seat as described in Chapter Fourteen.
2. Remove the engine drive sprocket as described in Chapter Seven.
3. Disconnect the negative battery cable from the battery terminal as described in this chapter.

4A. On 1996-2000 models, perform the following:

a. Remove the left, rear frame cover as described in Chapter Fourteen.

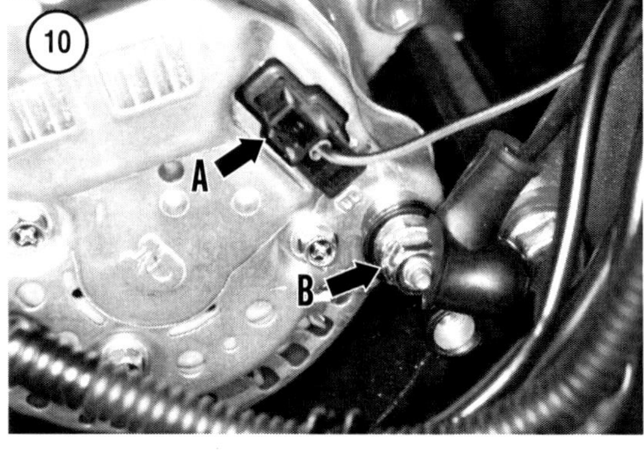

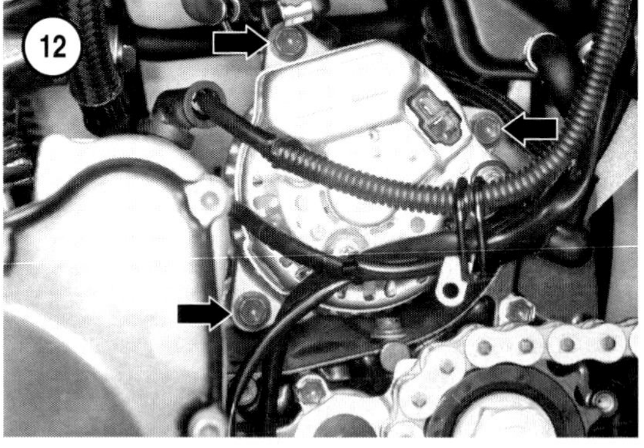

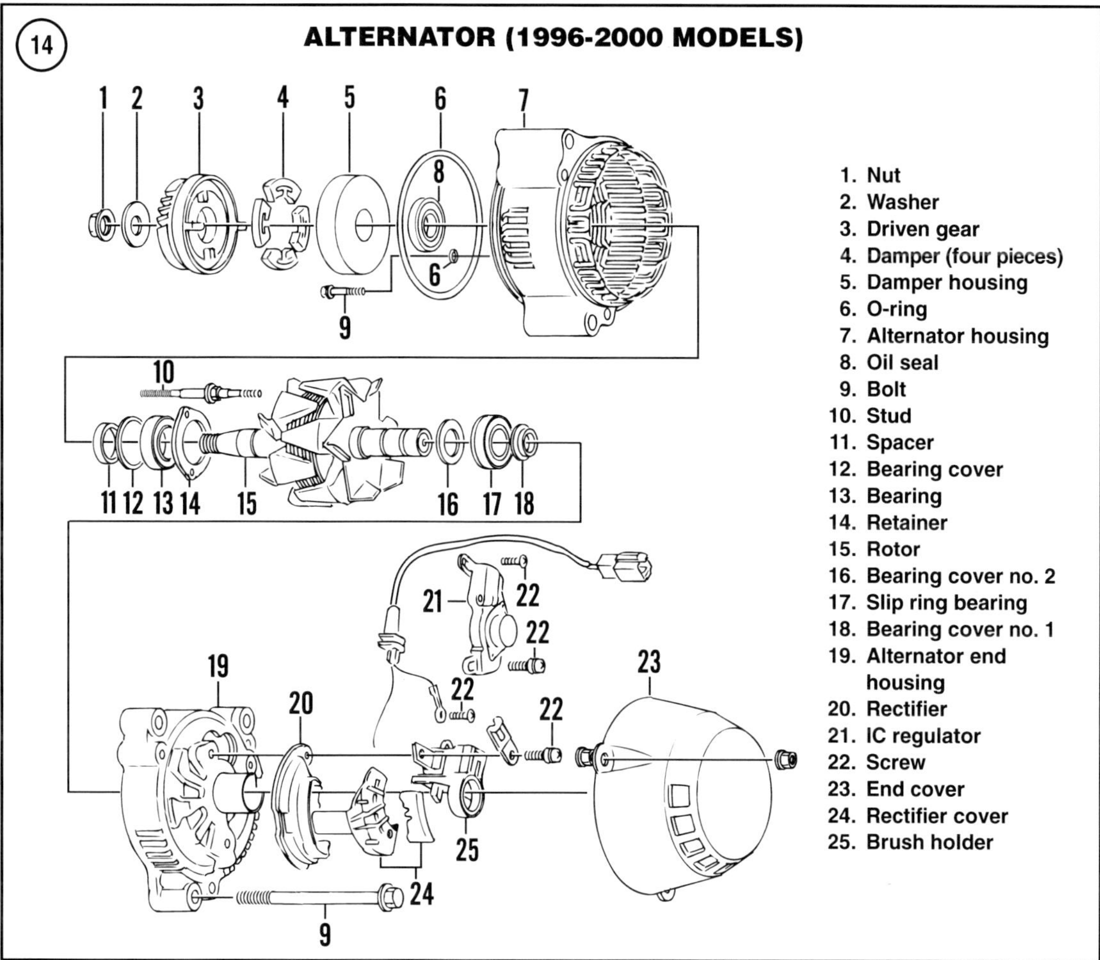

b. Disconnect the two-pin alternator connector (containing one red wire and one orange wire) among the electrical connectors on the left side of the rear frame (**Figure 9**).

c. Remove the starter as described in this chapter.

4B. On 2001-on models, perform the following:

a. Disconnect the connector from the alternator terminal (A, **Figure 10**).

b. Pull back the rubber boot and disconnect the electrical lead from the alternator terminal (B, **Figure 10**).

5A. On 1996-2000 models, remove the alternator mounting bolts (**Figure 11**). Move the wires out of the way and carefully pull the alternator from the crankcase.

5B. On 2001-on models, remove the alternator mounting bolts (**Figure 12**). Move the wires out of the way and carefully pull the alternator from the crankcase.

6. Install by reversing these removal steps. Note the following:

a. Inspect the O-ring (A, **Figure 13**) on the alternator housing. Replace the O-ring if it is starting to harden or deteriorate.

b. Inspect the gear teeth (B, **Figure 13**) for wear or damage. Check for chipped or missing teeth. If damaged, replace the gear.

c. Tighten the alternator mounting bolts to 25 N•m (18 ft.-lb.).

d. Make sure the electrical connector(s) is corrosion-free and secure.

Alternator Testing

The alternator has to be partially disassembled to perform these tests. Refer to **Figure 14** for 1996-2000 models and to **Figure 15** for 2001-on models.

15

ALTERNATOR (2001-ON MODELS)

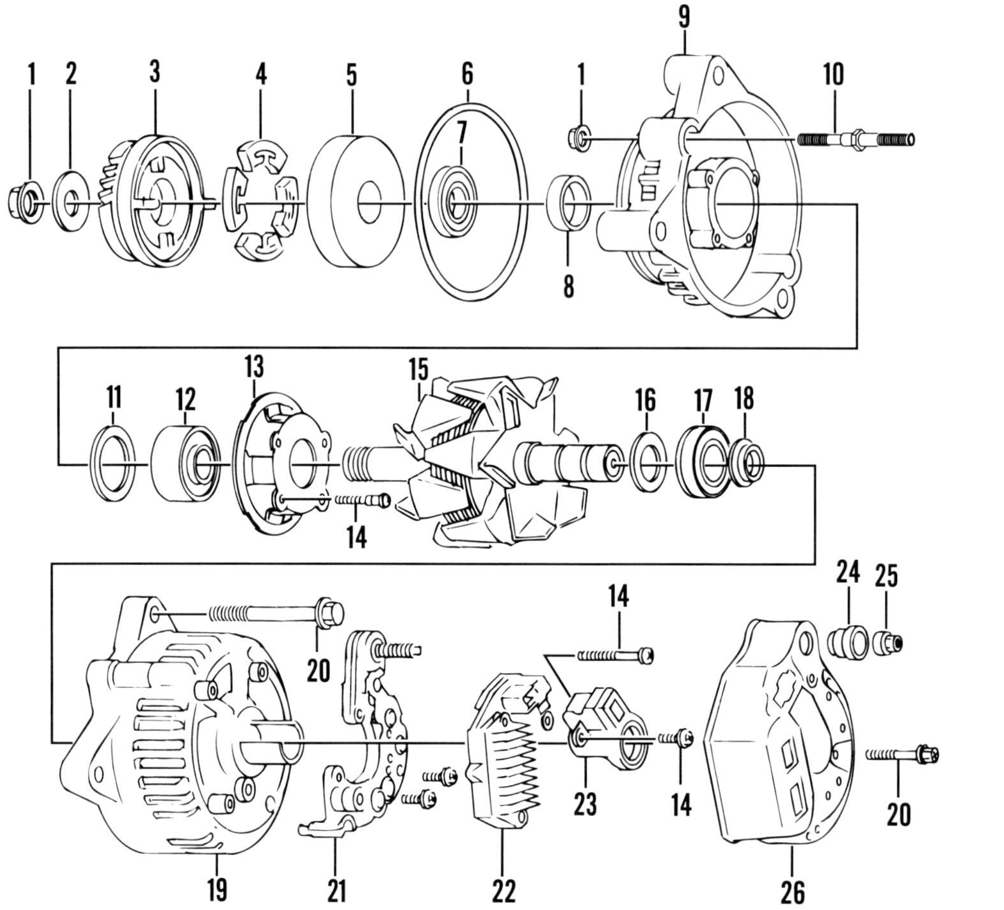

1. Nut
2. Washer
3. Driven gear
4. Damper (four pieces)
5. Damper housing
6. O-ring
7. Oil seal
8. Spacer
9. End housing
10. Stud
11. Bearing cover
12. Bearing
13. Retainer
14. Screw
15. Rotor
16. Bearing cover no. 2
17. Slip ring bearing
18. Bearing cover no. 1
19. Alternator housing
20. Bolt
21. Rectifier
22. IC regulator
23. Brush holder
24. Insulator
25. Terminal
26. End cover

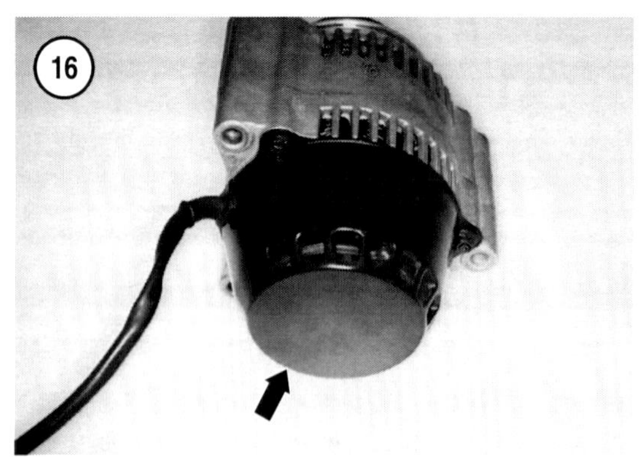

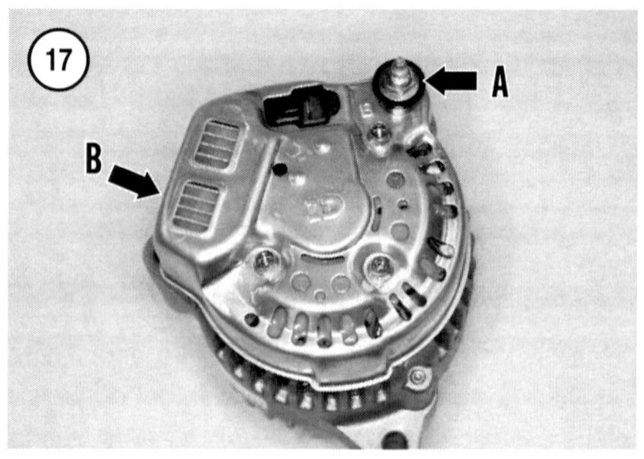

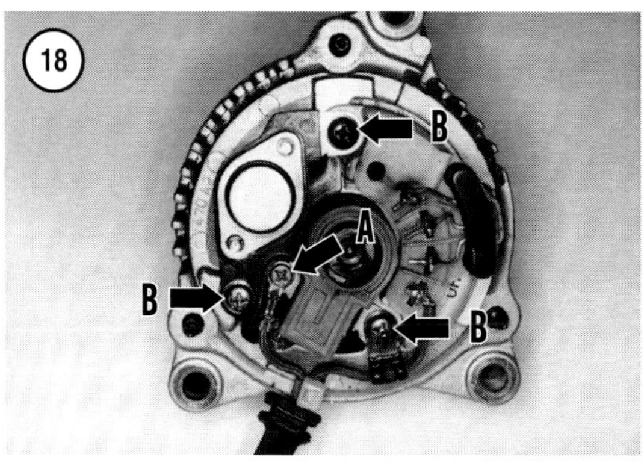

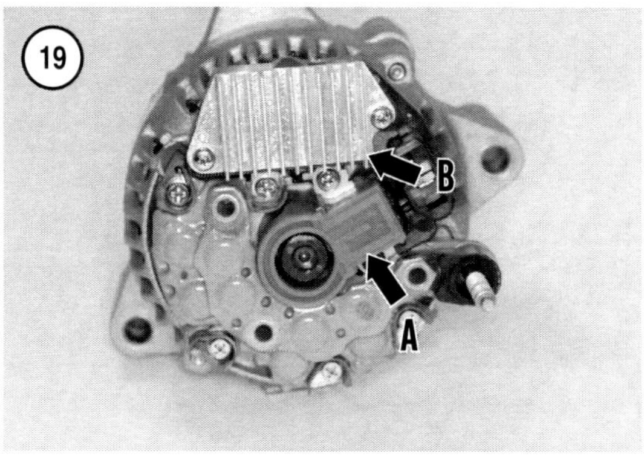

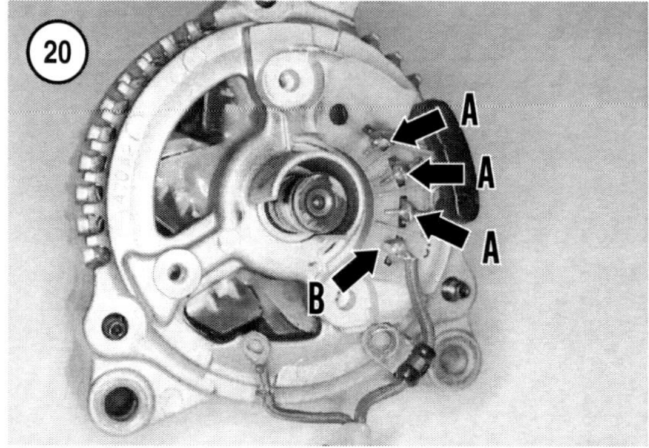

1A. On 1996-2000 models, remove the screws securing the end cover (**Figure 16**) and remove the end cover.

1B. On 2001-on models, perform the following:

a. Remove the nut/terminal and insulator (A, **Figure 17**) from the stud.

b. Remove the screws securing the end cover (B, **Figure 17**) and remove the end cover.

2A. On 1996-2000 models, to remove the brush holder and IC regulator, perform the following:

a. Remove the screw (A, **Figure 18**) securing the electrical lead to the brush holder.

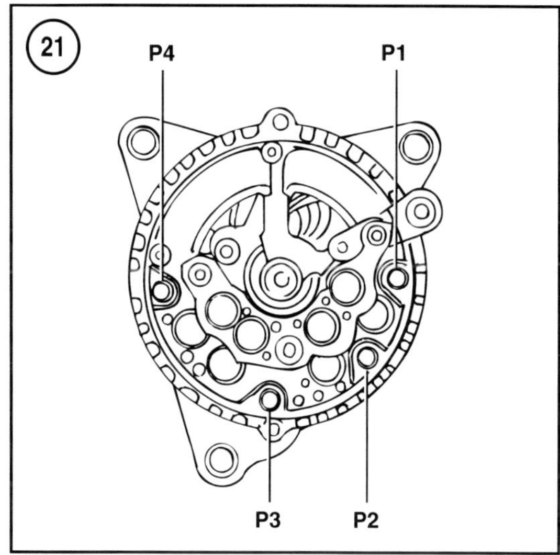

b. Remove the screws (B, **Figure 18**) securing the brush holder and IC regulator. Remove these items.

2B. On 2001-on models, to remove the brush holder and IC regulator, remove the screws securing the brush holder (A, **Figure 19**) and IC regulator (B). Remove these items.

CAUTION

In the following step, do not apply excessive heat from the soldering gun when unsoldering the wires. Excess heat can destroy the components within the rectifier. Place the soldering gun on the terminal just long enough to melt the solder and remove the wire. Remove the solder gun immediately.

3A. On 1996-2000 models, perform the following:

a. Use a solder gun and unsolder the stator coil electrical wires (A, **Figure 20**) and battery lead wire connector (B, **Figure 20**) from the rectifier.

b. Remove the rectifier from the alternator.

3B. On 2001-on models, perform the following:

a. Remove the stator coil mounting screws.

b. Use needlenose pliers to straighten out the stator coil wires P1, P2, P3 and P4 shown in **Figure 21**.

c. Remove the rectifier from the alternator.

4. Test the stator coil by performing the following:

a. Set an ohmmeter to the R × 10 scale, and check the continuity between the stator wires.

9

b. There should be continuity (low resistance) between the wires shown in **Figure 22** on 1996-2000 models or **Figure 23** on 2001-on models. If there is no continuity (infinite resistance), the stator assembly is faulty and must be replaced.

5. Test the rotor by performing the following:

a. Set an ohmmeter to the R × 10 scale, and check the continuity between the two slip rings (**Figure 24**) on the end of the rotor assembly.

b. There should be continuity (low resistance) between the two slip rings. If there is no continuity (infinite resistance), the rotor assembly is faulty and must be replaced.

6. Measure the outside diameter of the slip ring. If the slip ring is worn to the wear limit, replace the rotor assembly.

7. Test the rectifier by performing the following:

a. Set an ohmmeter to the R × 10 scale. For the following continuity tests, refer to **Figure 25** for 1996-2000 models and to **Figure 26** for 2001-on models.

b. Check the continuity between terminal B and ground. Note the continuity shown on the meter.

c. Reverse the connections and note the continuity shown on the meter. The results should be just the opposite of the reading taken in substep b. One of the test readings should show continuity, but the other should show no continuity. Replace the rectifier if both readings are the same.

d. Repeat this test (Steps 7a-c) between terminal B and each of the P terminals. There should be continuity in one direction and no continuity in the other. Replace the rectifier if both readings are the same.

8. Reassemble the alternator by reversing these steps while noting the following:

a. On 1996-2000 models, solder the stator coil electrical wires (A, **Figure 20**) and battery lead wire connector (B) onto the rectifier portion of the alternator.

b. On 2001-on models, install the insulator and nut/terminal (**Figure 27**) and tighten securely.

c. Make sure the electrical connectors are corrosion-free and secure.

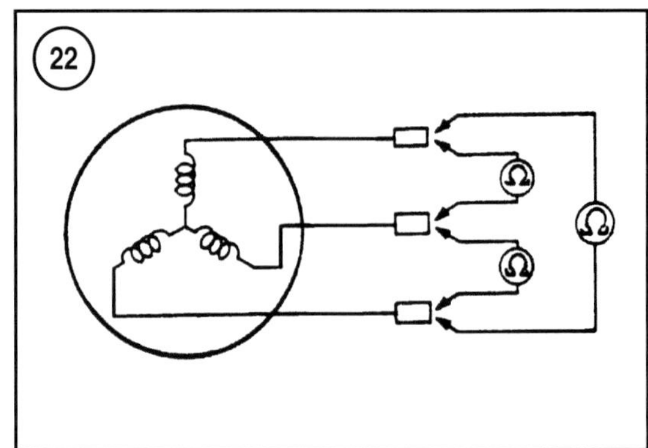

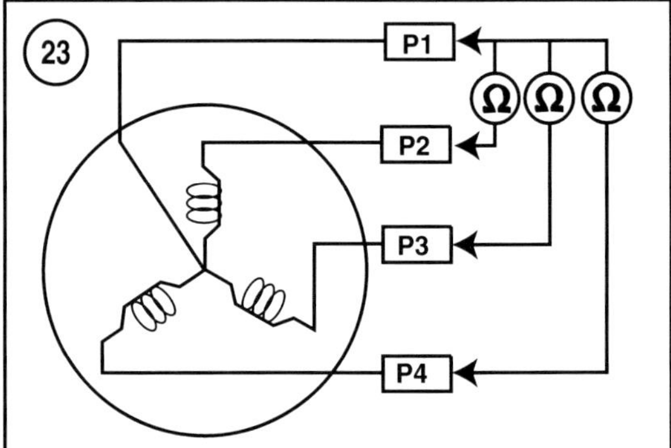

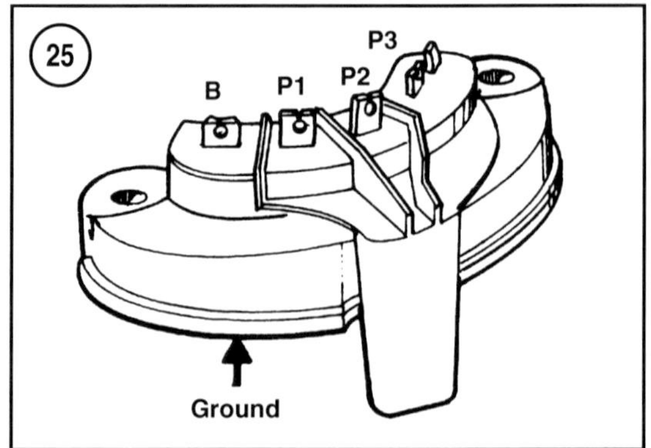

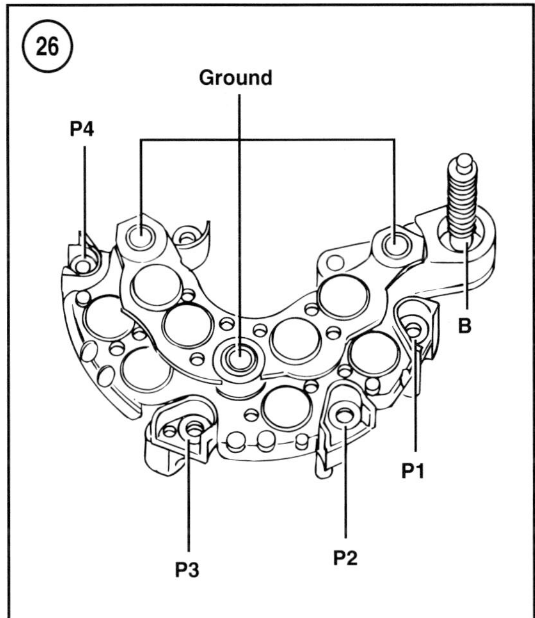

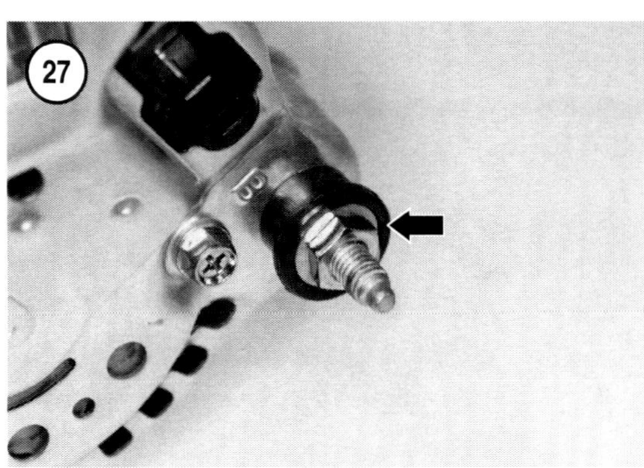

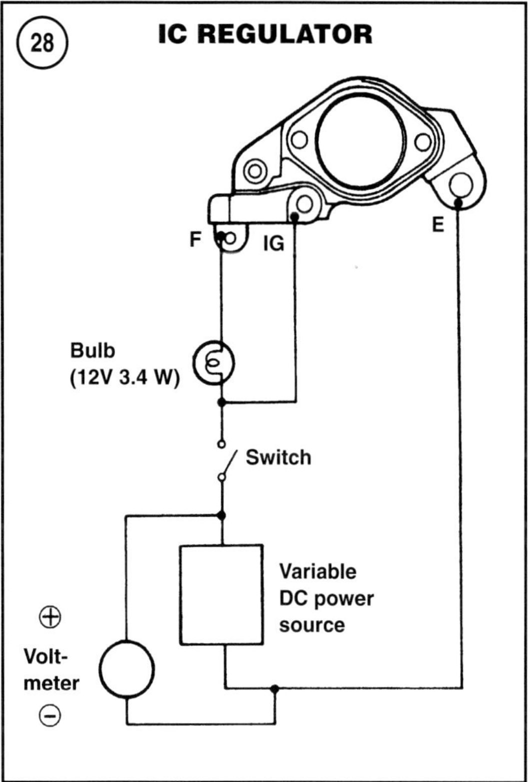

IC Regulator Testing (1996-2000 Models)

Tools

Special test equipment is required for testing the IC voltage regulator in 1996-2000 models. If the required tools and expertise are not available, have the voltage regulator tested by a Suzuki dealership.

The following components are required for this test.

1. A variable DC power source.
2. A 0-25 volt DC voltmeter.
3. A switch.
4. A 12 volt/3.4 watt bulb (a turn signal indicator bulb and socket).
5. Jumper wires.

Test

1. Remove the screws securing the end cover (**Figure 16**) and remove the end cover.
2. Remove the brush holder and IC regulator by performing the following:
   a. Remove the screw (A, **Figure 18**) securing the electrical lead to the brush holder and IC regulator.
   b. Remove the screws (B, **Figure 18**) securing the brush holder and IC regulator, and remove these items.
3. Connect the test components to the IC regulator as shown in **Figure 28**.
4. Turn the variable power supply to 12 volts and turn the switch to the ON position.
5. The test light should be ON. If the light is ON, the regulator is working. If the light is OFF, the regulator is defective and must be replaced.
6. Increase the voltage on the variable power supply to 14.5 volts. The test light should go OFF. If the light goes OFF, the regulator is working. If the light stays ON, the regulator is defective and must be replaced.

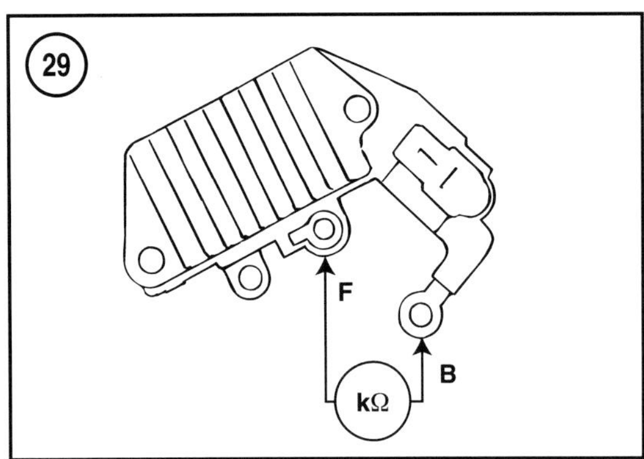

29

30

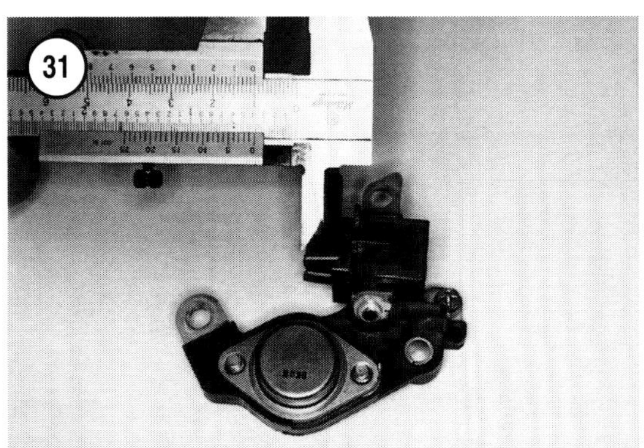

31

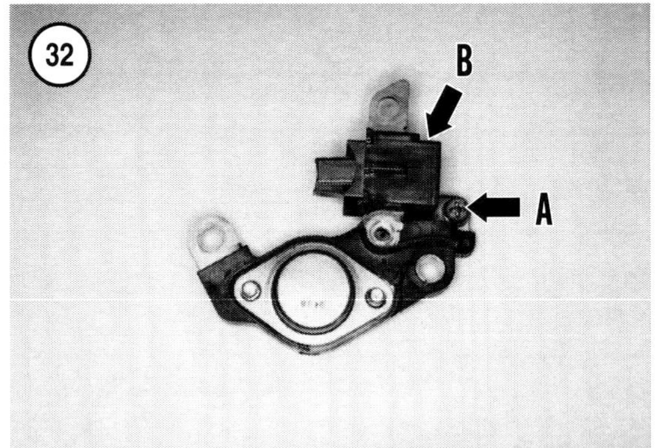

32

33

7. Turn the power supply OFF and disconnect the regulator from the jumper wires.
8. Reassemble by reversing these disassembly steps.

IC Regulator Testing (2001-on Models)

1. Remove the nut/terminal and insulator (A, **Figure 17**) from the stud.
2. Remove the screws securing the end cover (B, **Figure 17**) and remove the end cover.
3. Remove the screws securing the brush holder (A, **Figure 19**) and IC regulator (B). Remove these items.
4. Check the continuity between the rotor coil terminal (F, **Figure 29**) and the battery terminal (B) by performing the following:
   a. Set an ohmmeter to the R × 1k scale.
   b. Connect one test lead to the F terminal on the IC regulator. Connect the other test lead to the B terminal. Note the reading shown on the meter.
   c. Reverse the test leads and again note the reading shown on the meter. The IC regulator should have continuity in one direction, but no continuity in the other. Replace the IC regulator if both readings are the same.

Brush Inspection

1. Remove the nut/terminal and insulator (A, **Figure 17**) from the stud.
2. Remove the screws securing the end cover (B, **Figure 17**) and remove the end cover.
3. Remove the screws securing the brush holder (A, **Figure 19**) and IC regulator (B). Remove these items.

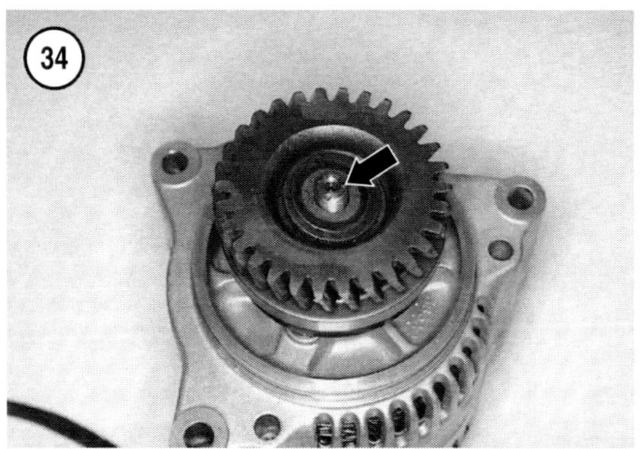
34

35

36

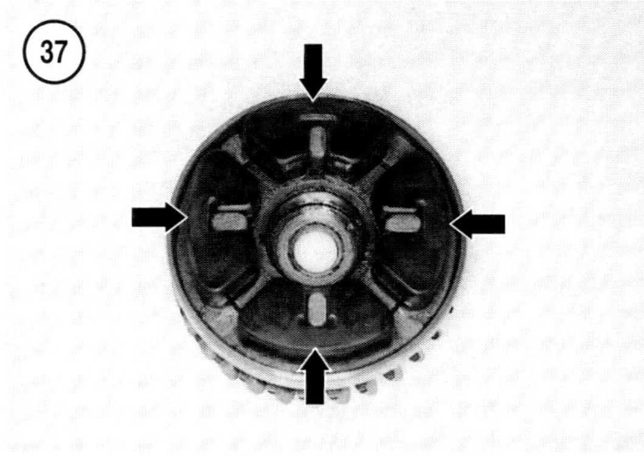
37

38

4. Remove the cover from the brush holder (**Figure 30**).

5. Use a small ruler or vernier caliper to measure the brush length (**Figure 31**). If the brush assembly is worn to the service limit listed in **Table 1**, replace it.

6. If necessary, remove the screw (A, **Figure 32**) securing the brush assembly (B) and remove it from the IC regulator.

7. Reassemble by reversing these disassembly steps.

Driven Gear and Damper Removal/Inspection/Installation

1. Place the driven gear in a vise with soft jaws.
2. Remove the driven gear nut (**Figure 33**).
3. Remove the washer (**Figure 34**).
4. Remove the driven gear (**Figure 35**) and damper from the alternator.
5. Inspect the damper housing for wear or damage. Inspect the damper bosses (**Figure 36**) for wear or damage. Replace the damper housing if necessary.
6. Remove the rubber dampers (**Figure 37**) from the driven gear. Inspect the dampers for wear or deterioration. Replace the dampers as a set if any is worn.
7. Inspect the driven gear (**Figure 38**) for wear or chipped or missing teeth. Replace the driven gear if necessary.
8. Inspect the damper bosses (**Figure 39**) in the backside of the driven gear for wear or damage. Replace the driven gear if necessary.
9. Install by reversing these removal steps. Note the following:

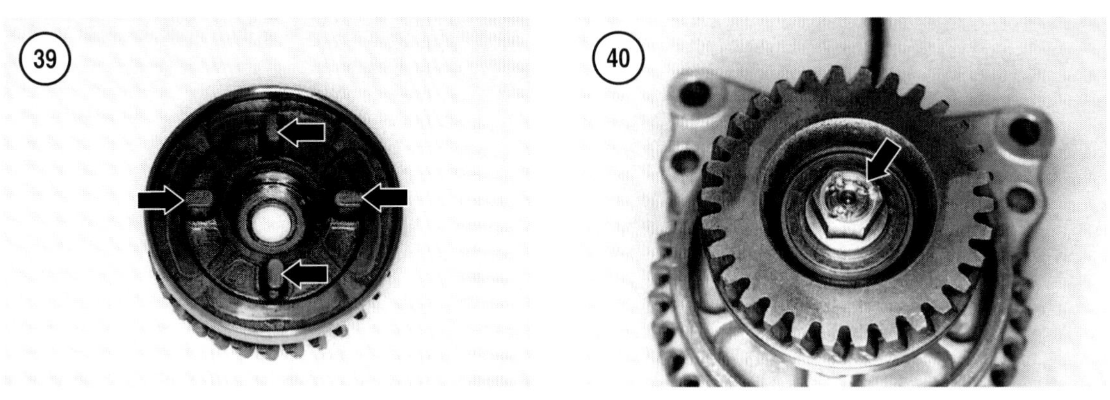

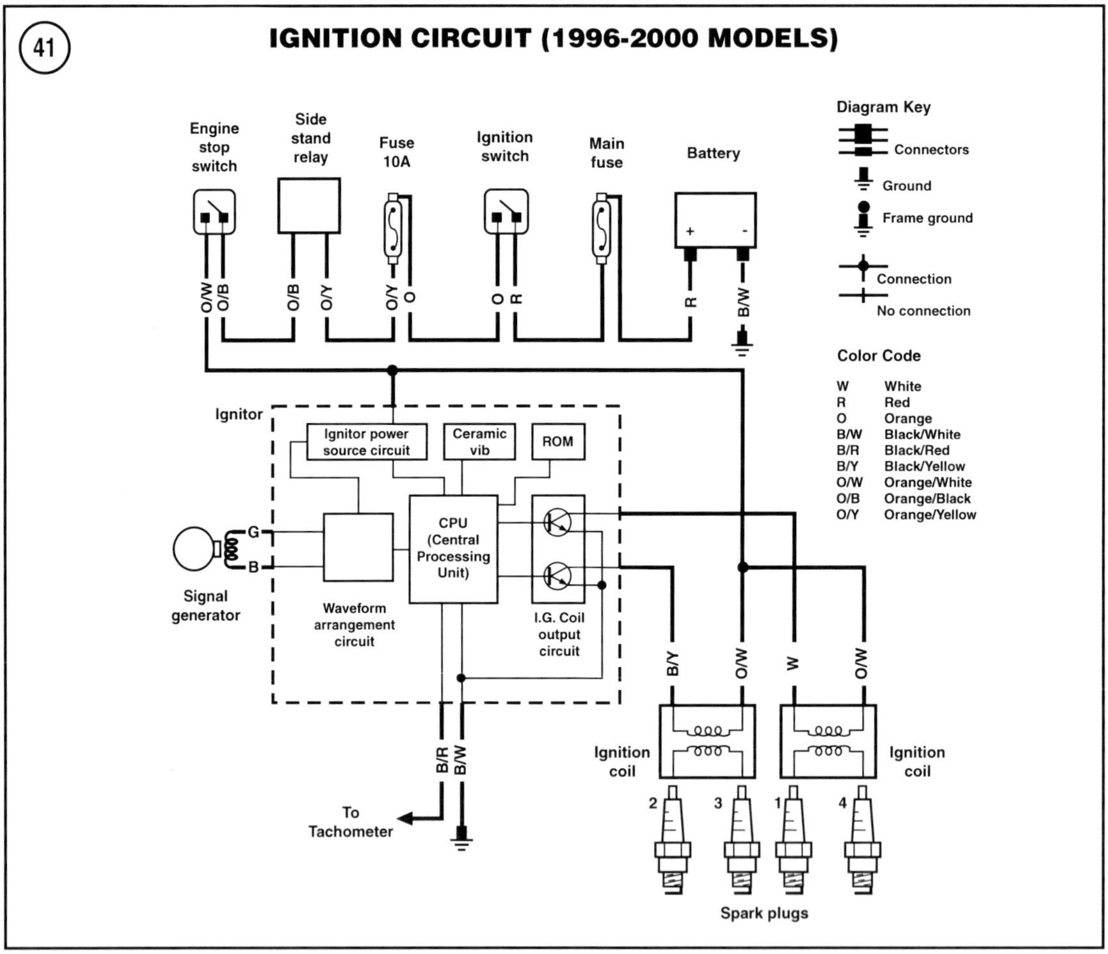

41

IGNITION CIRCUIT (1996-2000 MODELS)

Engine stop switch
Side stand relay
Fuse 10A
Ignition switch
Main fuse
Battery
O/W O/B O/B O/Y O/Y O O R R B/W
Ignitor
Ignitor power source circuit
Ceramic vib
ROM
CPU (Central Processing Unit)
Waveform arrangement circuit
I.G. Coil output circuit
Signal generator
G B
B/R B/W
To Tachometer
B/Y O/W W O/W
Ignition coil
Ignition coil
2 3 1 4
Spark plugs

Diagram Key
Connectors
Ground
Frame ground
Connection
No connection

Color Code

W	White
R	Red
O	Orange
B/W	Black/White
B/R	Black/Red
B/Y	Black/Yellow
O/W	Orange/White
O/B	Orange/Black
O/Y	Orange/Yellow

a. Apply molybdenum disulfide grease to the damper surface (**Figure 37**) prior to installation.
b. Tighten the alternator driven gear nut to the specification in **Table 3**. After the nut is tightened, use a centerpunch and stake the nut in place (**Figure 40**).

IGNITION SYSTEM

The models covered in this manual are equipped with two very similar transistorized electronic ignition systems, which include a signal generator as well as an ignitor unit with an 8-bit central processing unit, a 4 MHz ceramic vibrator and a ROM unit

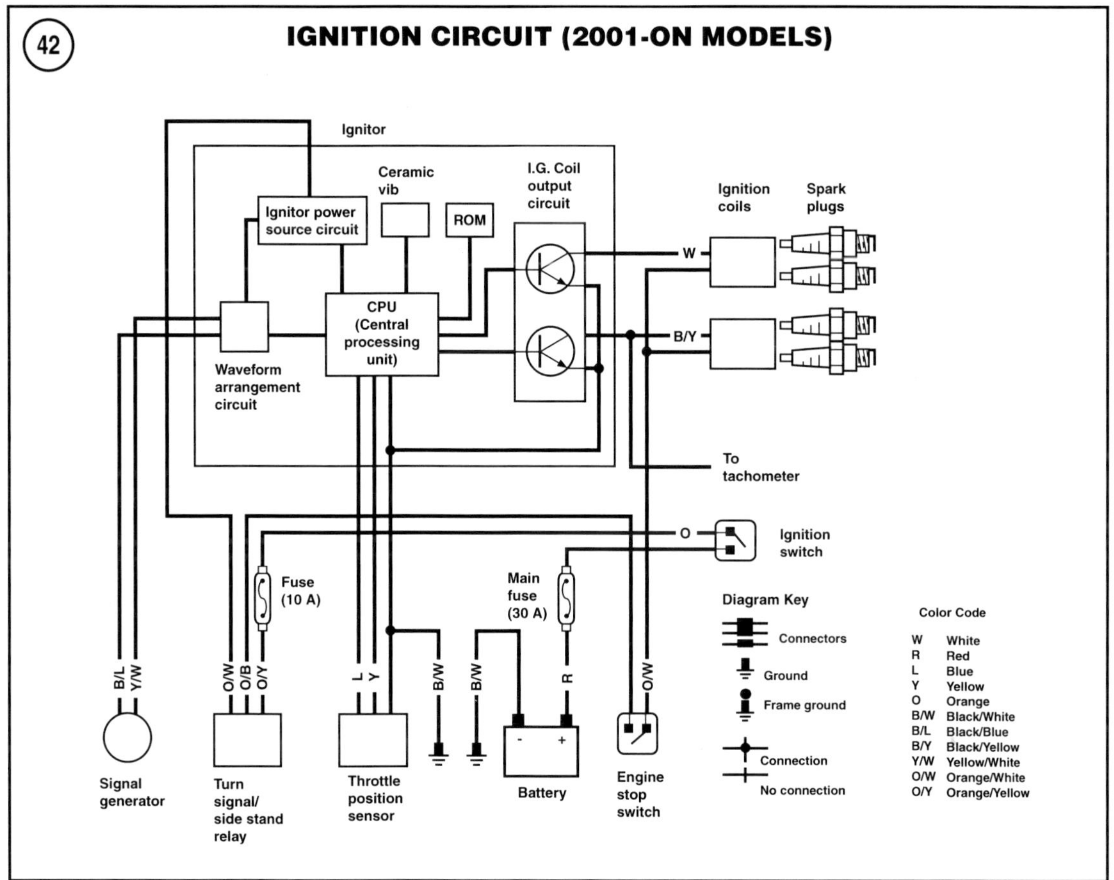

(Read only Memory). The difference between the two ignition systems is the addition of a throttle position sensor on 2001-on models. See **Figure 41** and **Figure 42**.

The ignition system is operated by the digital microprocessor within the ignitor unit. The ignition advance curve is pre-programmed into the ignitor unit's ROM and is closely matched to the engine's requirements. This advance curve cannot be modified to improve performance.

A safe-guard feature is built into both ignition systems to prevent the accidental over-revving of the engine. If the engine speed exceeds 12,000 rpm, the system interrupts the primary current to the No. 1 and No. 4 spark plugs.

CAUTION
Please note that this is not a no-load system. Engine speed can exceed 10,900 rpm without a load, which can lead to engine damage. Take care to avoid operating the engine above 10,900 rpm without a load.

The signal generator is mounted on the right end of the crankshaft. As the signal generator rotor turns via the crankshaft, the rotor sends a signal to the ignitor unit. This signal turns the ignitor unit transistor alternately ON and OFF. As the transistor turns ON and OFF, the current passing through the primary windings of the ignition coil also turns ON and OFF. This induces a secondary current in the ignition coils secondary windings and produces the current necessary to fire the spark plugs.

Ignition System Precautions

To protect the ignition system from damage, observe the following:

1. Never disconnect any of the electrical connections while the engine is running.
2. Keep all connections between the various units clean and tight. Pack the terminal with dielectric

grease and make sure the wiring connectors are pushed together firmly to help keep out moisture.
3. Do not substitute another type of ignition coil.

Signal Generator

Peak voltage test (2001-on models)

Peak voltage test results are based on the use of the Suzuki Multi-Circuit Tester (part No. 09900-25008) with the peak voltage adapter. If these tools are not available, refer testing to a Suzuki dealership.
1. Remove the rear frame cover as described in Chapter Fourteen.
2. Disconnect the electrical connector (**Figure 43**) from the ignitor unit.
3. Turn the tester's knob to voltage.
4. Connect the tester's negative probe to the yellow/white terminal on the connector. Connect the tester's positive probe to the black/blue terminal (**Figure 44**).
5. Shift the transmission into neutral and turn the ignition switch to the ON position.

WARNING
High voltage is present during ignition system operation. Do not touch ignition components, wires or test leads while cranking or running the engine.

6. Pull the clutch lever in, press the starter button and crank the engine for a few seconds while reading the meter. Record the highest meter reading.

NOTE
*The peak voltage specification (**Table 1**) is a **minimum** value. If the measured voltage meets or exceeds the specification, the test results are satisfactory. On some components, the voltage may greatly exceed the minimum specification.*

7. If the signal generator peak voltage is less than the specified value, check the peak voltage at the signal generator coupler (**Figure 45**) by performing the following test:
   a. Remove the left side cover as described in Chapter Fourteen.
   b. Disconnect the two-pin signal generator connector (one blue wire and one yellow wire on

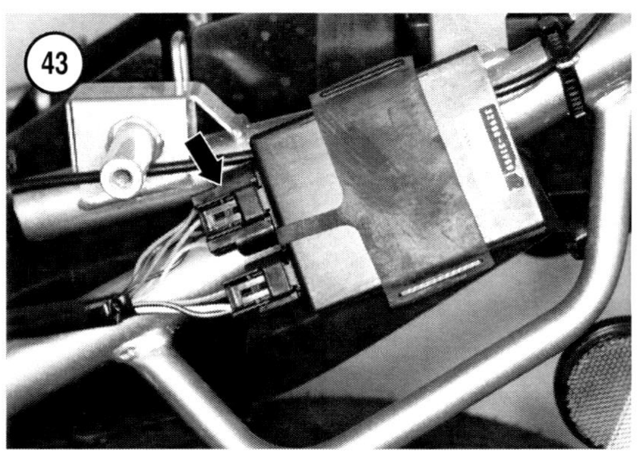

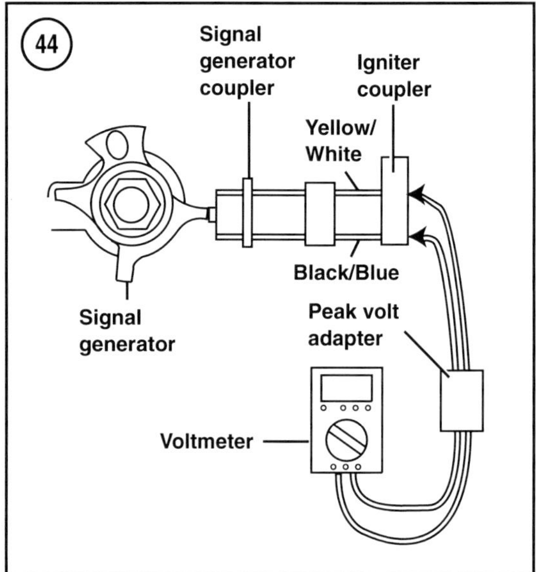

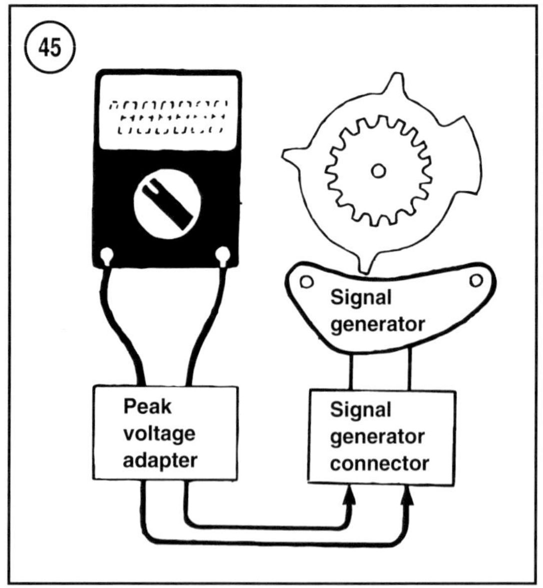

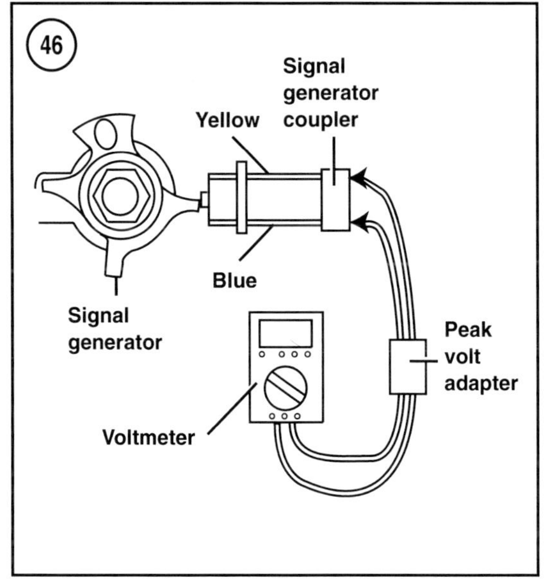

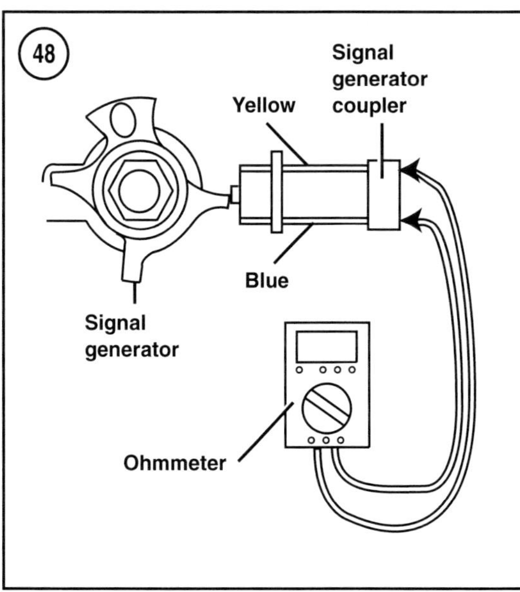

the signal generator side of the connector) from the main harness.

c. Connect the tester's negative probe to the yellow terminal on the signal generator side of the connector and connect the tester's positive probe to the blue terminal (**Figure 46**).

d. Shift the transmission into neutral and turn the ignition switch to the ON position.

e. Pull the clutch lever in, press the starter button and crank the engine for a few seconds while reading the meter. Record the highest meter reading.

8. If the peak voltage measured at the signal generator connector is normal but the peak voltage at the ignitor connector is less than the minimum specified value, replace the wiring.

9. If the peak voltage at both the signal generator connector and the ignitor connector are less than the minimum value specified in **Table 1**, replace the signal generator.

10. If the test results are acceptable, reconnect the electrical connector. Make sure the electrical connector is corrosion-free and secure.

Signal generator resistance test

Suzuki specifies the use of the Suzuki Multi-Circuit Tester (part No. 09900-25008) for accurate resistance tests of the regulator/rectifier unit. Refer to the *Preliminary Information* section at the beginning of this chapter regarding this tester.

1A. On 1996-2000 models, remove the seat and the left rear-frame cover as described in Chapter Fourteen.

1B. On 2001-on models, remove the left side cover as described in Chapter Fourteen.

2. Disconnect the signal generator connector from the main harness (**Figure 47**).

a. On 1996-2000 models, the signal generator is a two-pin connector with one green wire and one black wire on the device side of the connector.

b. On 2001-on models, the signal generator connector is a two-pin connector with one yellow and one blue wire on the device side.

3. Set an ohmmeter to the R × 100 scale and check the resistance between the signal generator terminals in the device side of the connector (**Figure 48**). If the signal generator coil resistance is outside the

specified range (**Table 1**), replace the signal generator.

4. On 2001-on models, check the continuity between the blue terminal on the device side of the connector and ground (**Figure 49**). There should be no continuity (infinite resistance). If the signal generator has continuity to ground, replace the signal generator.

Removal/installation

1A. On 1996-2000 models, remove the seat and the left rear-frame cover as described in Chapter Fourteen.

1B. On 2001-on models, remove the left side cover as described in Chapter Fourteen.

2. Disconnect the signal-generator connector from the wiring harness.
   a. On 1996-2000 models, the signal generator is a two-pin connector with one green and one black wire on the device side of the connector.
   b. On 2001-on models, the signal generator connector is a two-pin connector with one yellow and one blue wire on the device side.

3. Remove the signal generator cover bolts and remove the cover and its gasket (**Figure 50**). One cover bolt has a sealing washer (**Figure 51**) installed beneath it. Note the position of this bolt and washer. It must be reinstalled in the same location during assembly.

4. Loosen the mounting screws (**Figure 52**) securing the signal generator stator plate to the crankcase.

5. Hold onto the signal generator rotor with a wrench (A, **Figure 53**) and loosen the signal-generator-rotor bolt (B). Remove the bolt and rotor (C, **Figure 53**).

6. Disconnect the oil pressure switch wire (D, **Figure 53**).

7. Remove the mounting screws (**Figure 52**) securing the ignition generator stator plate.

8. Carefully remove the rubber grommet (E, **Figure 53**) from the crankcase. Pull the electrical wires through the opening in the crankcase and remove the stator plate assembly.

9. Install by reversing these removal steps. Note the following:
   a. Install the rotor so the notch on the back of the rotor (A, **Figure 54**) engages the locating pin (B) in the crankshaft.

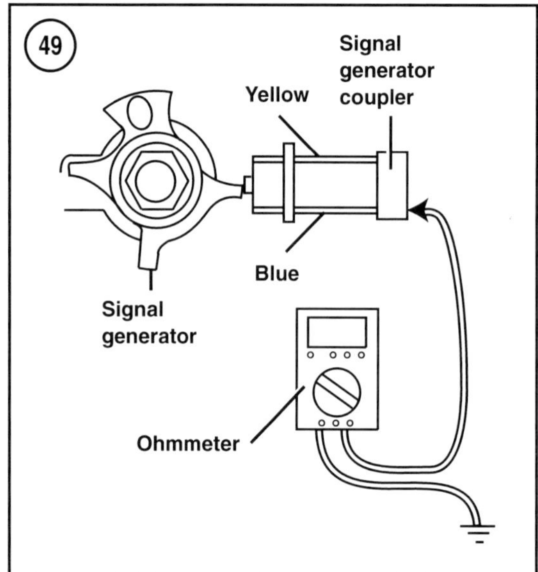

   b. Hold onto the signal generator rotor with a wrench and tighten the signal generator rotor bolt (B, **Figure 53**) to 25 N•m (18 ft.-lb.).
   c. Apply a light coat of gasket sealer to the groove in the rubber grommet.

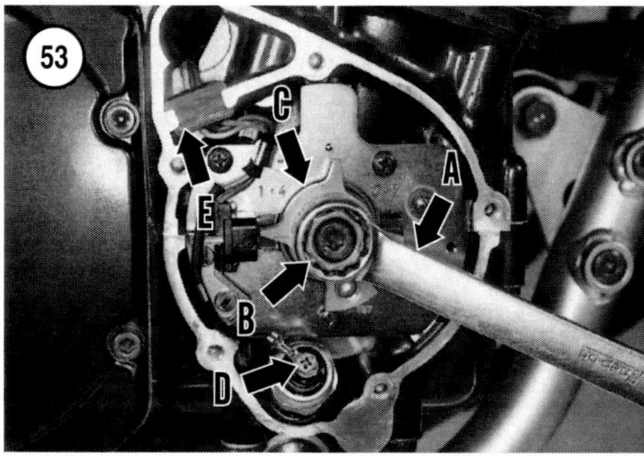

d. Install a new signal-generator-cover gasket and install the cover. Be sure the bolt with the sealing washer (**Figure 51**) is installed in the location noted during disassembly.

e. Make sure the electrical connector is corrosion-free and secure.

Ignition Coils

The ignition coils are a form of transformer which develop the high voltage required to jump the spark plug gap. The only maintenance required is that of keeping the electrical connections clean and tight, and occasionally checking to see that the coils are mounted securely.

Suzuki specifies the use of the Suzuki Multi-Circuit Tester (part No. 09900-25008) for accurate resistance tests of the ignition coil. Refer to the *Preliminary Information* section at the beginning of this chapter regarding this tester.

Primary peak voltage test (2001-on models)

The Suzuki Multi-Circuit Tester (part No. 09900-25008) with the peak voltage adapter, the Motion Pro Ignition Mate (part No. 08-0193), or an equivalent peak voltage tester is required for this test.

1. Remove the fuel tank as described in Chapter Eight.
2. On GSF1200S models, remove the front fairing as described in Chapter Fourteen.
3. Remove all four spark plugs as described in Chapter Three.
4. Connect a new spark plug to each plug cap.
5. Ground all four spark plugs to a bare metal surface of the engine.

WARNING

High voltage is present during ignition system operation. Do not touch ignition components, wires or test leads while cranking or running the engine.

NOTE

*The peak voltage specification (**Table 1**) is a **minimum** value. If the measured voltage meets or exceeds the specification, the test results are satisfactory. On some components, the voltage may greatly exceed the minimum specification.*

NOTE

Do not disconnect the ignition coil primary wire.

6. Check the peak voltage for the No. 1 and No. 4 cylinders by performing the following:
   a. Turn the tester knob to voltage.
   b. Connect the positive test probe to the white terminal on the left ignition coil and connect

9

the negative test probe to ground (**Figure 55**).

c. Shift the transmission into neutral and turn the ignition switch to the ON position.

d. Press the starter button and crank the engine for a few seconds while reading the meter. Record the meter's highest reading.

7. Check the peak voltage for the No. 2 and No. 3 cylinders by performing the following:

a. Turn the tester knob to voltage.

b. Connect the positive test probe to the black/yellow terminal on the right ignition coil and connect the negative test probe to ground (**Figure 55**).

c. Shift the transmission into neutral and turn the ignition switch to the ON position.

d. Press the starter button and crank the engine for a few seconds while reading the meter. Record the meter's highest reading.

8. If the peak voltage reading on either ignition coil is less than specified in **Table 1**, measure the resistance of that ignition coil.

Ignition coil resistance test

The Suzuki Multi-Circuit Tester (part No. 09900-25008) is required for accurate resistance testing of the ignition coil/plug cap. Refer to the *Preliminary Information* section at the beginning of this chapter regarding this tester.

1. Remove the fuel tank as described in Chapter Eight.

2. On GSF1200S models, remove the front fairing as described in Chapter Fourteen.

3. Disconnect all ignition coil wires (including the spark plug leads from the spark plugs) before testing.

4. Set an ohmmeter to the R × 1 scale and measure the primary coil resistance between the positive and the negative terminals on the top of the ignition coil (**Figure 56**). Record the measured resistance.

5. Set the ohmmeter to the R × 1000 scale and measure the secondary coil resistance between the two spark plug leads (with the spark plug caps attached). Record the measured resistance.

6. If either measurement does not meet specification, the coil must be replaced. If the coil exhibits visible damage, replace it.

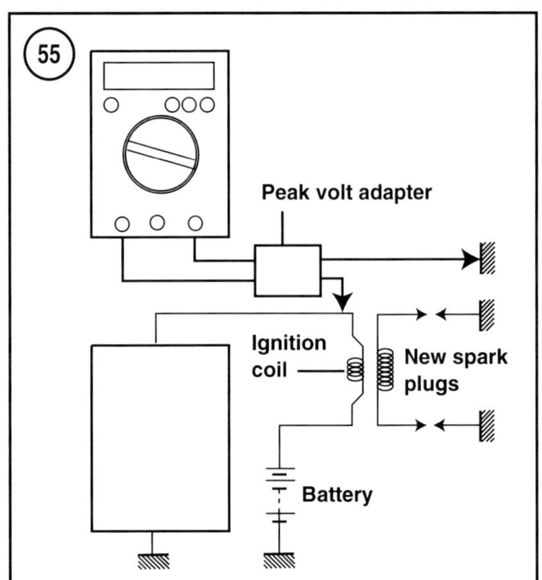

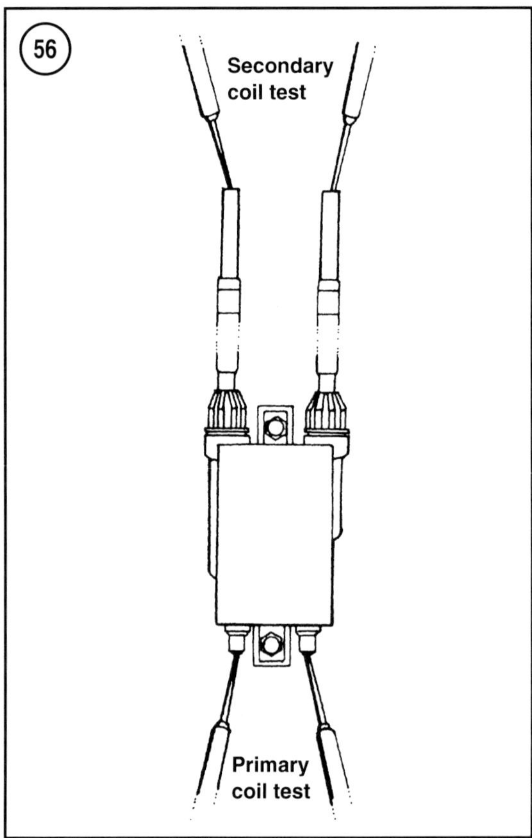

7. Reconnect all ignition coil wires to the ignition coil.

8. Repeat this procedure for the other ignition coil.

Removal/installation

1. Remove the seat as described in Chapter Fourteen.
2. Disconnect the battery negative lead as described in this chapter.
3. Remove the fuel tank as described in Chapter Eight.
4. On GSF1200S models, remove the front fairing as described in Chapter Fourteen.

NOTE
On the original equipment ignition coil and high voltage leads, the cylinder number is marked on each lead. If these marks are no longer legible or are missing, mark each lead with its cylinder number. The No. 1 cylinder is on the left-most cylinder. From left to right the cylinders are numbered No. 1, No. 2, No. 3 and No. 4.

5. Disconnect the high voltage lead (**Figure 57**) from each spark plug.

NOTE
In Step 6 remove only the necessary components to provide easy access to the ignition coils.

6. On 2001-on models so equipped, partially remove the PAIR assembly as described in Chapter Eight.
7. Remove the bolts (A, **Figure 58**) securing the ignition coil to the frame.
8. Carefully pull the ignition coil away from the frame and disconnect the primary electrical wires (B, **Figure 58**) from the coil.
9. If necessary, repeat Steps 6-7 for the other ignition coil.
10. Install by reversing these removal steps. Make sure the electrical connectors are corrosion-free and secure.

Ignitor Unit

Input voltage/ground test

1. Remove the seat as described in Chapter Fourteen.
2A. On 1996-2000 models, connect the probes of a voltmeter to the orange/red terminal and to the black/white terminal of the ignitor electrical connectors (A and B, **Figure 59**).
2B. On 2001-on models, connect the probes of a voltmeter to the orange/yellow terminal and to the black/white terminal of the ignitor electrical connectors (A and B, **Figure 60**).

9

61

STARTING CIRCUIT (1996-2000 MODELS)

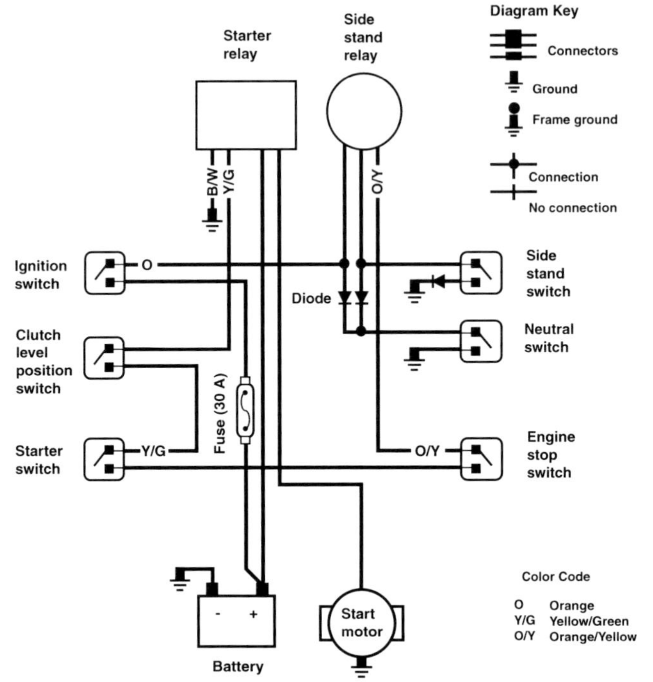

Starter relay

Side stand relay

Diagram Key

Connectors

Ground

Frame ground

Connection

No connection

B/W

Y/G

O/Y

Ignition switch

O

Side stand switch

Diode

Clutch level position switch

Neutral switch

Fuse (30 A)

Starter switch

Y/G

O/Y

Engine stop switch

Color Code

O Orange

Y/G Yellow/Green

O/Y Orange/Yellow

\- +

Battery

Start motor

62

STARTING CIRCUIT (2001-ON MODELS)

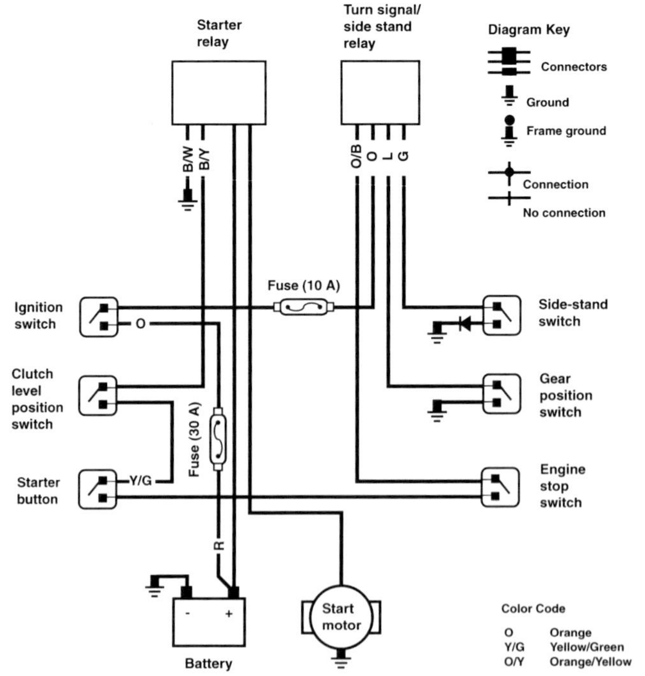

Starter relay

Turn signal/ side stand relay

Diagram Key

Connectors

Ground

Frame ground

Connection

No connection

B/W

B/Y

O/B

O

L

G

Fuse (10 A)

Ignition switch

O

Side-stand switch

Clutch level position switch

Gear position switch

Fuse (30 A)

Starter button

Y/G

Engine stop switch

R

\- +

Battery

Start motor

Color Code

O Orange

Y/G Yellow/Green

O/Y Orange/Yellow

3. Turn the ignition switch ON and check the voltage on the meter. It should read battery voltage.

NOTE
*Further testing of the ignitor unit requires the Suzuki Digital Ignitor Checker (part No. 09931-94490). Refer this testing to a Suzuki dealership. Most parts suppliers do not accept returns on electrical components. If the exact cause of any electrical system malfunction has not been determined, do no attempt to remedy the problem with guesswork and possibly unnecessary parts replacement. If possible, have the suspected component or system tested by a professional technician **before** purchasing new electrical components.*

Replacement

1. Remove the seat and rear frame covers as described in Chapter Fourteen. On 2001-on models, remove the document tray.
2. Disconnect the battery negative lead as described in this chapter.
3A. On 1996-2000 models, perform the following:
   a. Disconnect both ignitor electrical connectors (A and B, **Figure 59**) from the ignitor.
   b. Remove the ignitor unit from its rubber damper (C, **Figure 59**).
3B. On 2001-on models, perform the following:
   a. Disconnect both ignitor electrical connectors (A and B, **Figure 60**) from the ignitor.
   b. Remove the ignitor unit from its rubber damper (C, **Figure 60**).
4. Install a new ignitor unit into the damper. Attach both electrical connectors to it. Make sure the electrical connectors are corrosion-free and secure.
5. Install all removed parts.

STARTING SYSTEM

The starting system consists of the starter motor, starter relay, clutch position switch, sidestand switch, sidestand relay (a combined turn signal/sidestand relay on 2001-on models), neutral switch, engine stop switch and the starter button. When the starter button is pressed, it engages the starter relay that completes the circuit, allowing electricity to flow from the battery to the starter motor.

Refer to **Figure 61** for the1996-2000 starting system or **Figure 62** for the 2001-on models.

CAUTION
Do not operate the starter for more than 5 seconds at a time. Let it cool approximately 10 seconds between starting attempts.

Troubleshooting

Refer to Chapter Two.

STARTER

Removal/Installation

NOTE
The starter mounting bolts are difficult to reach with the carburetor assembly in place. There are two options: either remove the sprocket cover and alternator, or remove the two oil pipe Allen bolts and move the oil pipe out of the way.

1. Remove the seat as described in Chapter Fourteen.
2. Disconnect the battery negative cable as described in this chapter.
3. Slide back the rubber boot on the electrical cable connector (**Figure 63**).
4. Disconnect the electrical cable from the starter terminal.

5. Insert a socket cap set (A, **Figure 64**) into a 5 mm Allen bit (B).

6. Use a 12-point box wrench, along with the tool set-up from Step 5, and remove the two Allen bolts (A, **Figure 65**) securing the oil pipe to the top of the crankcase and move the oil pipe (B) aside.

7. Use a 90° hex driver (**Figure 66**) and No. 3 Phillips bit and loosen and remove both starter mounting bolts.

8. Move the starter toward the right side and withdraw it from the top of the crankcase. Remove the starter.

9. Inspect the O-ring (A, **Figure 67**). O-rings tend to harden after prolonged use and heat and therefore lose their ability to seal properly. Replace the O-ring as necessary.

10. Inspect the gear (B, **Figure 67**) for chipped or missing teeth. If damaged, the starter assembly must be replaced.

11. Install by reversing these removal steps. Tighten the mounting bolts to 6 N•m (53 in.-lb.).

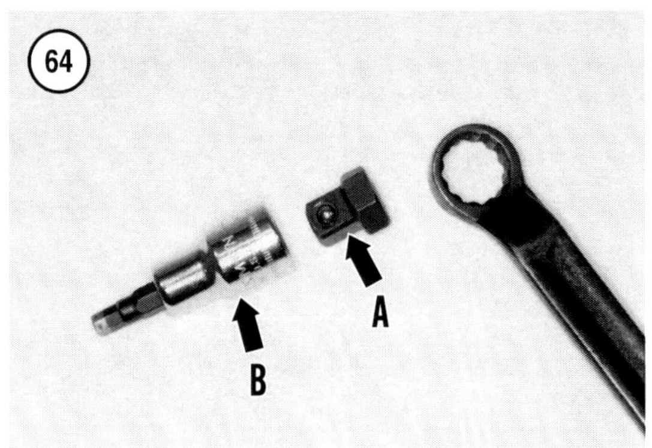

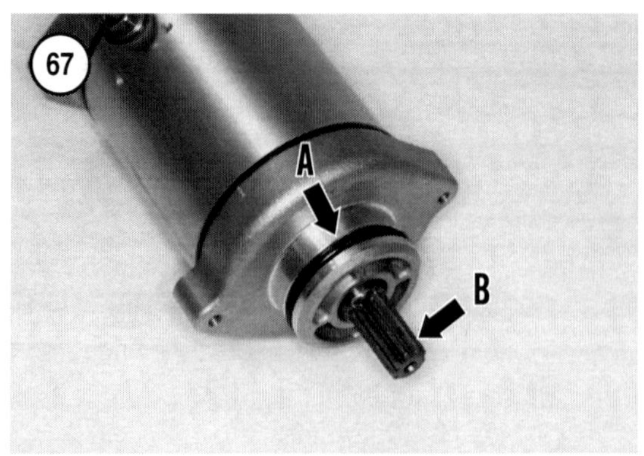

Disassembly

Refer to **Figure 68**.

As the starter is disassembled, lay the parts out in the order of removal. As each part is removed from the starter, set it next to the one previously removed. This is an easy way to remember the correct relationship of all parts.

1. Remove both case bolts.

2. Remove the left cover (A, **Figure 69**) from the case.

3. Slide the tab washer and washers (B and C, **Figure 69**) off the armature shaft.

4. Remove the right cover (A, **Figure 70**) from the case.

5. Slide the washers (B, **Figure 70**) off the armature shaft.

6. Slide the armature out of the case and the brush holder.

NOTE

Before removing the nut and insulated washer assembly, record the washer order and descriptions. They must be reinstalled in the same order to insulate the positive brush plate holder from the case.

68

STARTER

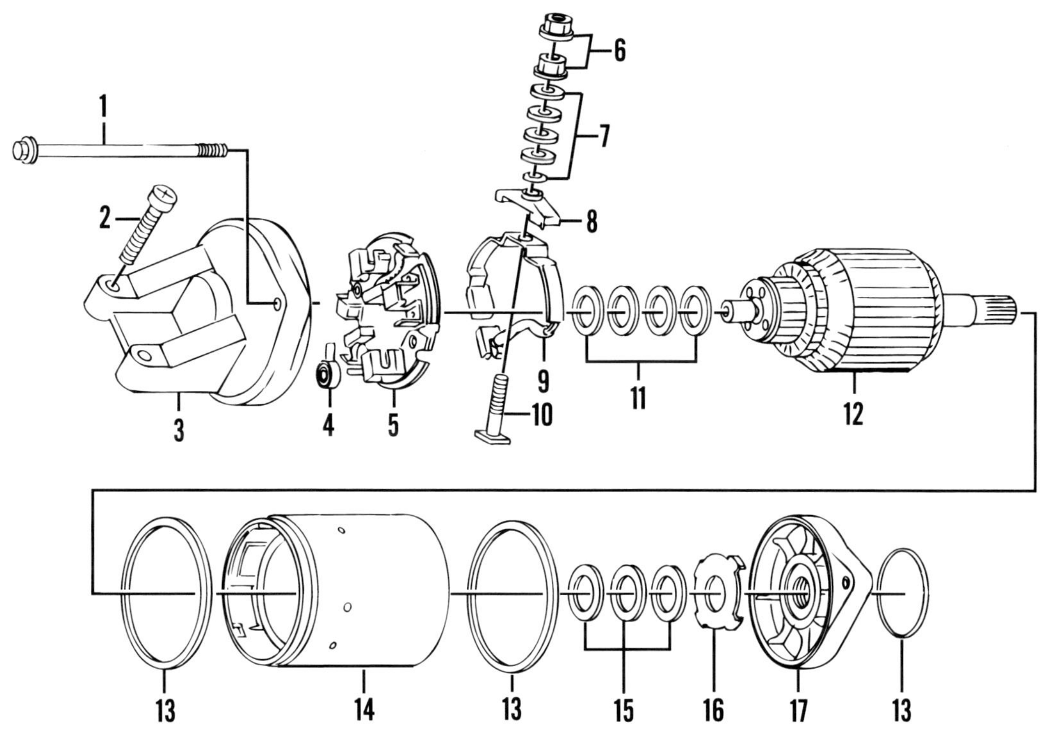

1. Case bolt
2. Mounting bolt
3. Right cover
4. Brush spring
5. Negative brush holder
6. Nuts
7. Insulated washer set
8. Insulator bar
9. Positive brush holder
10. Bolt
11. Shims
12. Armature
13. O-ring
14. Case
15. Washers
16. Tab washer
17. Left cover

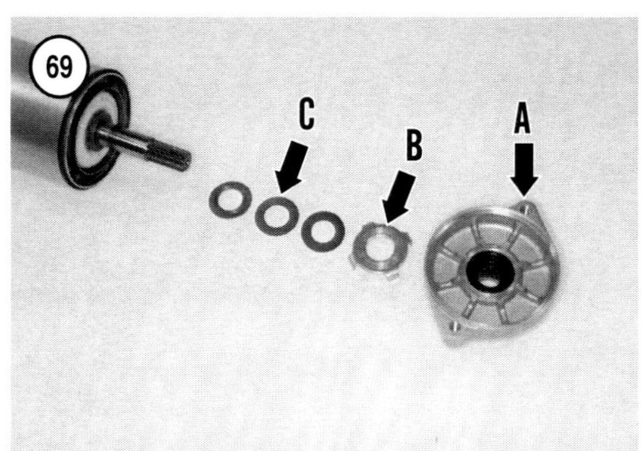

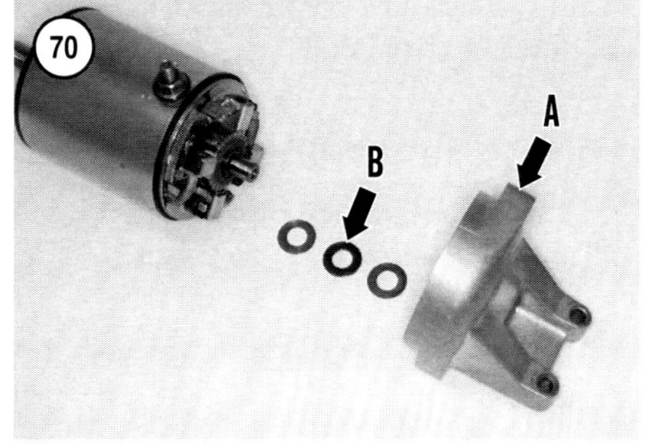

7. Remove the nut and insulated washer assembly (**Figure 71**) securing the brush holder assembly. Keep all parts in the same order as removal (**Figure 72**).
8. Remove the brush holder assembly (**Figure 73**) from the case. Do not lose the O-ring on the positive brush holder bolt. Separate the positive brush holder from the negative brush holder (**Figure 74**).

CAUTION
Do not immerse the wire windings in the case or the armature coil in solvent, as the insulation may be damaged. Wipe the windings with a cloth lightly moistened with solvent and dry thoroughly.

9. Clean all grease, dirt and carbon from all components.
10. Inspect all starter components as described in this chapter.

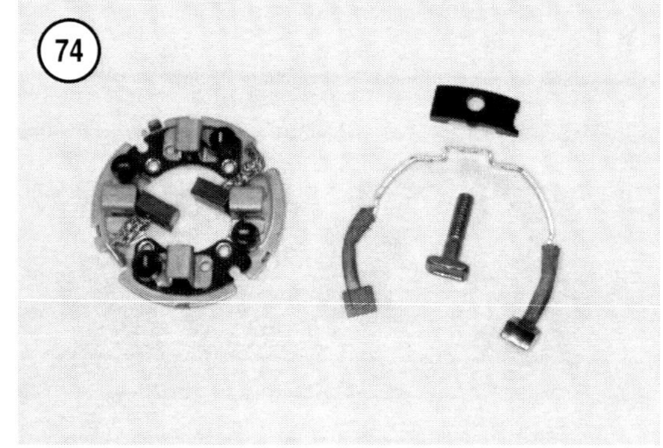

Assembly

1. Assemble the positive brush holder, bolt, insulated bar and O-ring (**Figure 75**).
2. Install the positive brush holder assembly into the case (A, **Figure 76**).

NOTE
*In the next step, reinstall all parts in the same order as noted during removal (**Figure** 72). This is essential in order to insulate the positive brush holder from the case.*

3. Install the insulated washer assembly and nut (B, **Figure 76**) securing the brush holder assembly. Tighten the nut securely.

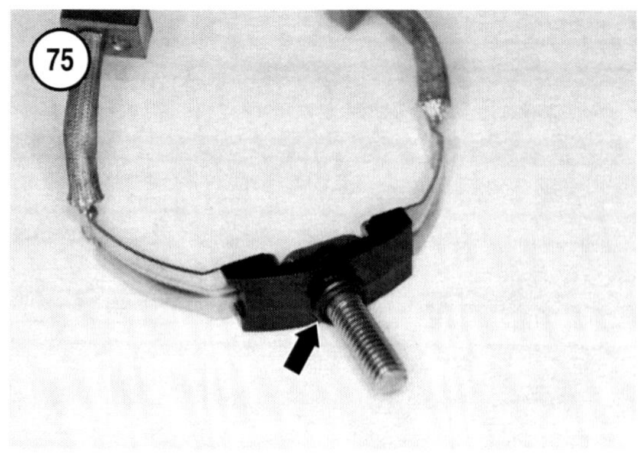

76

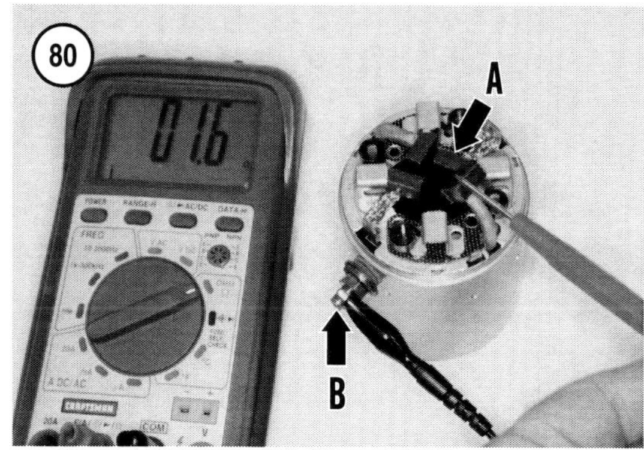

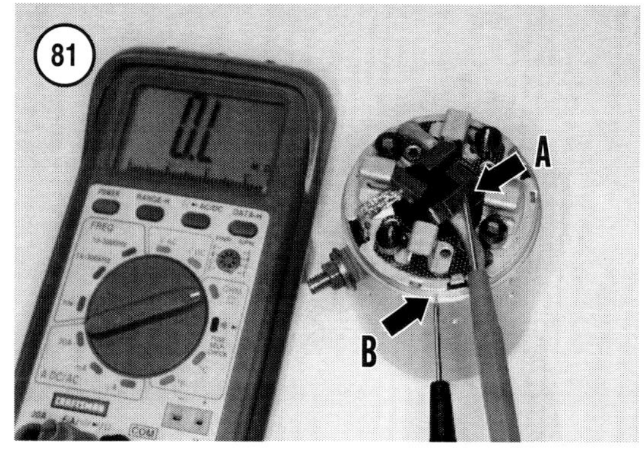

79

4. Install the negative brush holder into the case and the positive brush holder (**Figure 77**). Align the index tab with the case notch (**Figure 78**).
5. Install all four brushes into their receptacles against the springs.
6. To release spring pressure on the brushes, move the spring off of the brush and rest it on the backside of the brush holder. Install a small plastic strip (**Figure 79**) between the spring and the brush holder. Push the brushes back into the plastic strip to allow them to pass by the commutator during the next steps.

NOTE
The following step ensures that the positive brush holder assembly has been installed into the case correctly.

7. Use an ohmmeter and test the following:
   a. Place one ohmmeter test lead on one of the positive brushes (A, **Figure 80**) and the other to the insulated brush terminal (B). There should be continuity.
   b. Place one ohmmeter test lead on one of the positive brushes (A, **Figure 81**) and the other to the case (B). There should be no continuity.

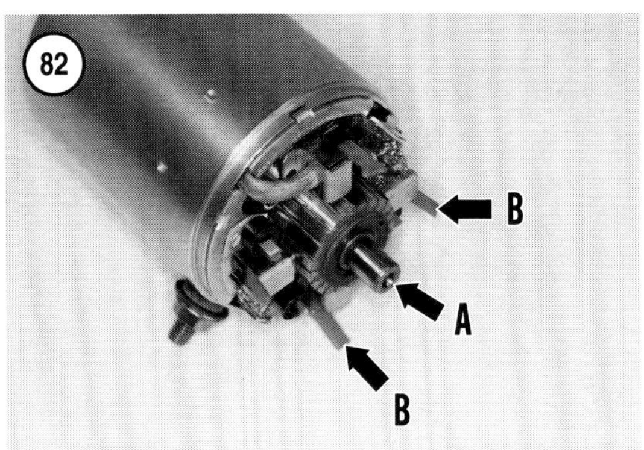

8. Insert the commutator (A, **Figure 82**) into the case and past the brush assemblies.

9. Remove the plastic strips (B, **Figure 82**) from between the brushes and their springs. Make sure the springs press the brushes against the commutator.

10. Keep the assembly in this position and slowly rotate the armature coil assembly to make sure it rotates freely with the brushes in place.

11. Check that the negative brush holder tab is still aligned into the case notch (**Figure 78**).

12. If removed, install the O-ring (**Figure 83**) onto each end of the case.

13. Install the washers (B, **Figure 70**) onto the right end of the commutator.

14. Install the right cover (A, **Figure 70**) and align the cover groove (A, **Figure 84**) with the brush holder tab (B). Push the right cover on until it bottoms against the case.

15. Apply Suzuki Super Grease A (part No. 99000-25030) to the lips of the oil seal (A, **Figure 85**) in the left cover.

16. Install the tab washer (B, **Figure 85**) over the oil seal and index it into the slots in the cover.

17. Install the washers (C, **Figure 69**) onto the left end of the commutator and install the left cover (A). Push the left cover on until it bottoms against the case. Align the left cover index mark with the case index mark.

18. Check that the cover index marks are still aligned with the case index marks (A, **Figure 86**). Realign if necessary.

19. Install both case bolts (B, **Figure 86**) and tighten them securely. After the bolts are tightened, check the seams to ensure both end covers are pulled tight against the case.

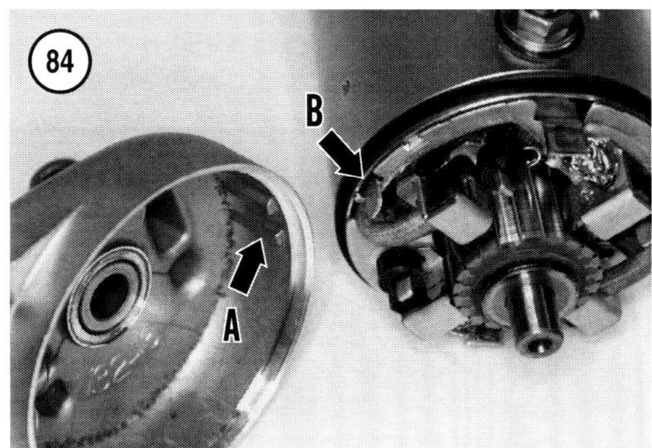

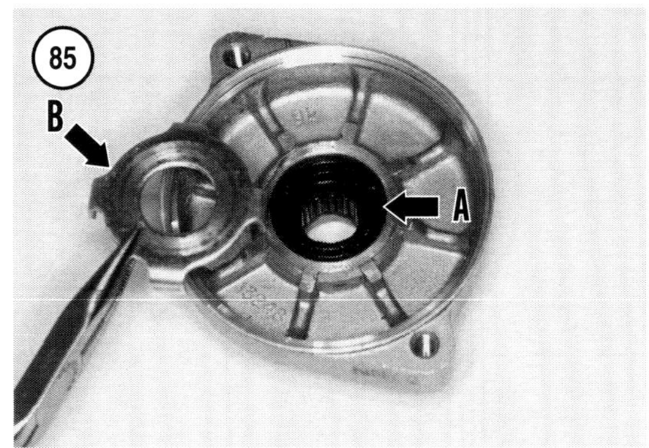

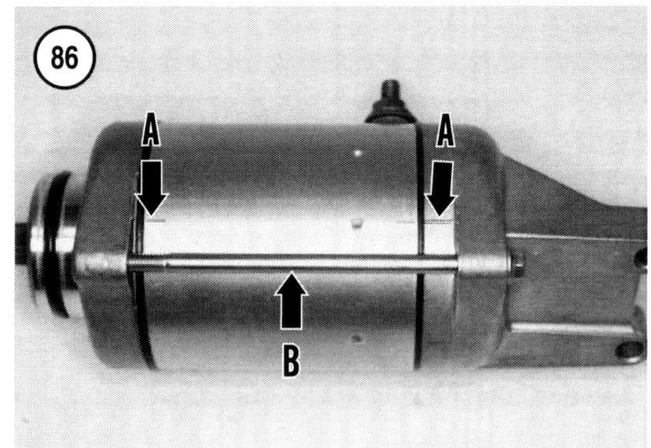

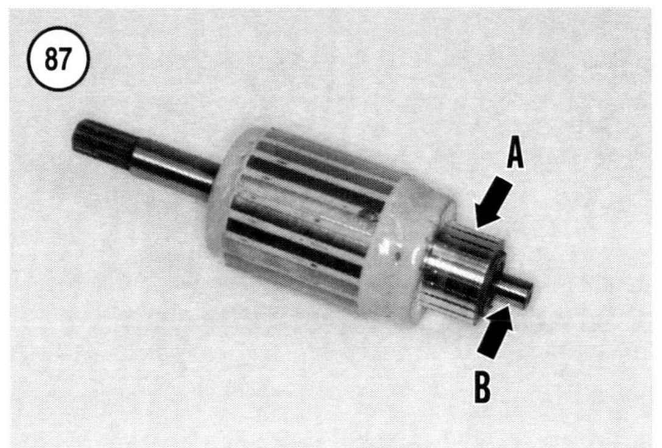

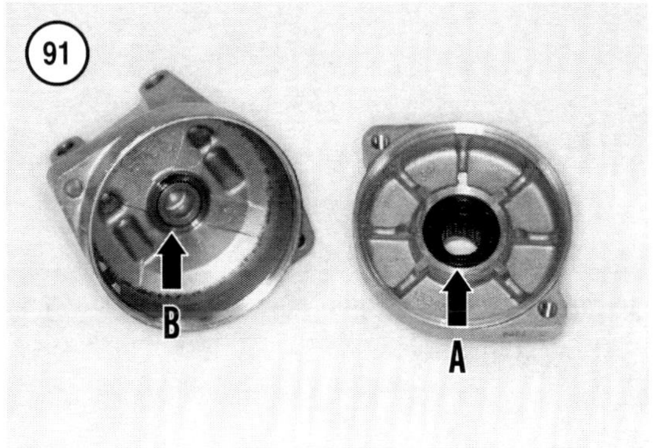

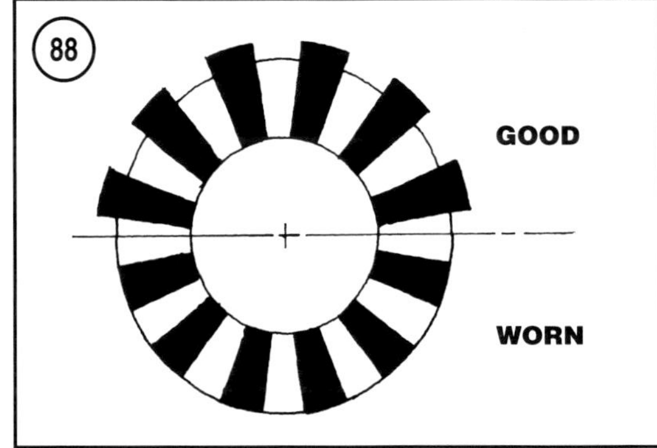

89

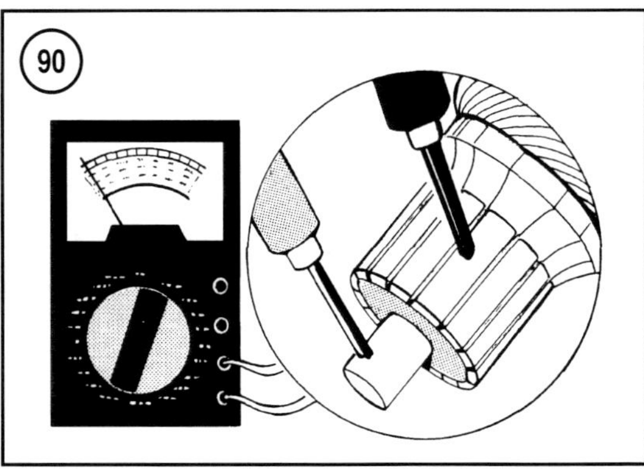

Inspection

1. Inspect each brush for abnormal wear. Service specifications are not available from Suzuki. Replace the brush assemblies as necessary.
2. Inspect the commutator (A, **Figure 87**). The mica in a good commutator is below the surface of the copper bars. On a worn commutator, the mica and copper bars may be worn to the same level (**Figure 88**). If necessary, have the commutator serviced by a Suzuki dealership or electrical repair shop.
3. Check the entire length of the armature coil assembly for straightness or heat damage.
4. Inspect the armature shaft where it rides on the bushing (B, **Figure 87**). Check for wear, burrs or damage.
5. Inspect the commutator copper bars (A, **Figure 87**) for discoloration. If a pair of bars are discolored, grounded armature coils are indicated.
6. Use an ohmmeter and perform the following:
   a. Check for continuity between the commutator bars (**Figure 89**); there should be continuity (indicated resistance) between pairs of bars.
   b. Check for continuity between the commutator bars and the shaft (**Figure 90**); there should be no continuity (infinite resistance).
   c. If the armature fails either test, replace it.
7. Inspect the oil seal (A, **Figure 91**) in the left cover for wear, hardness or damage. If the oil seal is worn or damaged, replace it.
8. Inspect the needle bearing (**Figure 92**) in the left cover. It must turn smoothly without excessive play or noise. Replace the cover as necessary.
9. Inspect the bushing (B, **Figure 91**) in the right cover for wear or damage. The bushing cannot be replaced. If it is damaged, replace the left cover.
10. Inspect the magnets within the case assembly. Make sure they have not picked up any small metal

particles. If so, remove them prior to assembly. Also inspect the case for loose, chipped or damaged magnets.
11. Inspect the brush holder and springs (**Figure 93**) for wear or damage. If necessary, replace the holder or springs.
12. Inspect both end covers for wear or damage. Replace either end cover if it is damaged.
13. Check the case bolts for thread damage. Clean the threads with the appropriate size metric die if necessary. Inspect the O-ring seals for hardness, deterioration or damage. Replace as necessary.

STARTER RELAY

Removal/Installation

The starter relay is located behind the frame left side cover.
1. Remove the seat and the frame left side cover as described in Chapter Fourteen.
2. Disconnect the negative battery cable as described in this chapter.
3. Pinch the two tabs and remove the cover (**Figure 94**) from starter relay.
4A. On 1996-2000 models, perform the following:
   a. Disconnect the starter relay primary connector (A, **Figure 95**).
   b. Disconnect the terminal screws (B, **Figure 95**) and remove the negative (black) starter motor lead and the positive (red) battery lead. Remove the relay.
4B. On 2001-on models, perform the following:
   a. Disconnect the starter relay primary connector (A, **Figure 96**).
   b. Disconnect the terminal screws (B, **Figure 96**) and remove the negative (black) starter motor lead and the positive (red) battery lead. Remove the relay.
5. Install by reversing these removal steps while noting the following:
   a. Install both electrical cables to the relay and tighten the screws securely.
   b. Make sure the electrical connectors are corrosion-free and secure.
   c. Install the cover.

Voltage Test

1A. On 1996-2000 models, remove the seat and the frame left side cover as described in Chapter Fourteen.

92

93

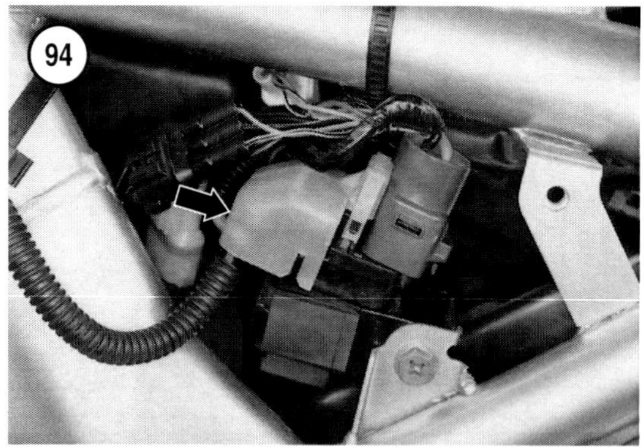

94

95

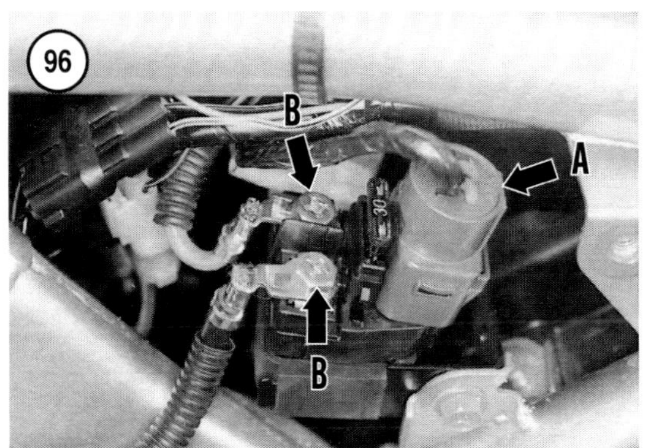

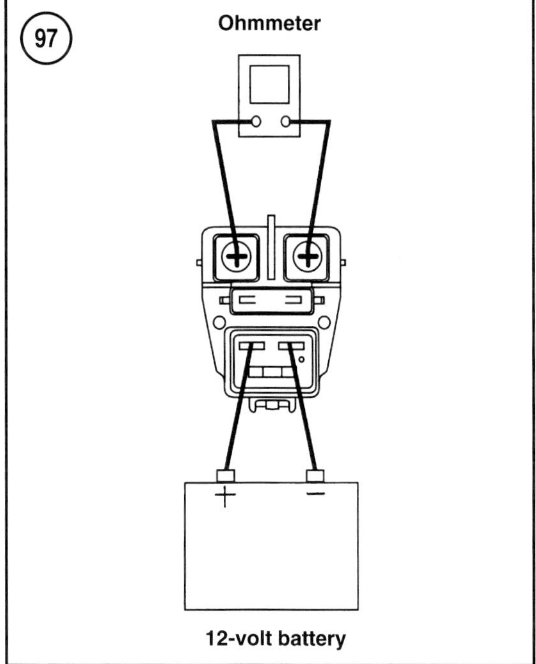

1B. On 2001-on models, remove the frame left side cover as described in Chapter Fourteen.

2. Remove the cover from the starter relay.

3A. On 1996-2000 models, connect a voltmeter's positive test lead to the yellow/green terminal on the starter relay. Connect the negative test lead to the black/white terminal.

3B. On 2001-on models, connect a voltmeter's positive test lead to the black/yellow terminal on the starter relay. Connect the negative test lead to the black/white terminal.

4. Make sure the engine stop switch is in the RUN position.

5. Shift the transmission to neutral and disengage the clutch.

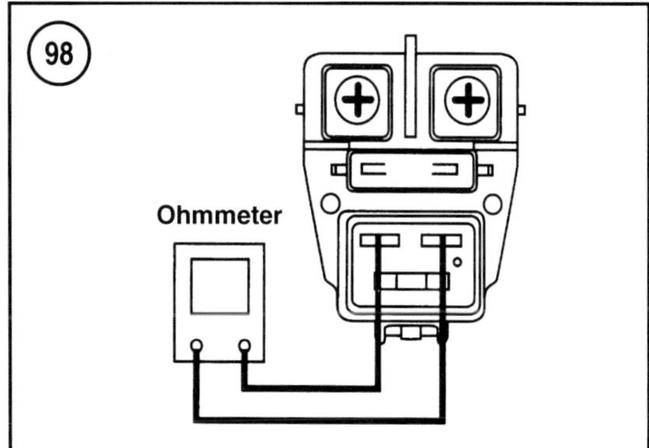

6. Press the starter button and read the voltage displayed on the voltmeter. It should show battery voltage.

7. Turn the ignition OFF and disconnect the voltmeter.

Continuity and Resistance Test

1A. On 1996-2000 models, remove the seat and the left rear-frame cover as described in Chapter Fourteen.

1B. On 2001-on models, remove the left side cover as described in Chapter Fourteen.

2. Disconnect the negative battery cable as described in this chapter.

3. Pinch the two tabs and remove the cover (**Figure 94**) from the starter relay.

4A. On 1996-2000 models, perform the following:

  a. Disconnect the starter relay primary connector (A, **Figure 95**).
  b. Disconnect the terminal screws (B, **Figure 95**) and remove the negative (black) starter motor lead and the positive (red) battery lead. Remove the relay.

4B. On 2001-on models, perform the following:

  a. Disconnect the starter relay primary connector (A, **Figure 96**).
  b. Disconnect the terminal screws (B, **Figure 96**) and remove the negative (black) starter motor lead and the positive (red) battery lead. Remove the relay.

5. Connect an ohmmeter and a 12-volt battery to the starter relay terminals as shown in **Figure 97**. When the battery is connected, there should be continuity (low to zero ohms) across the two load terminals. When the battery is disconnected, there should be no continuity (infinity).

6. Connect an ohmmeter to the starter relay terminals as shown in **Figure 98** and measure the resistance across these terminals. If the resistance is

(99)

HEADLIGHT (1996-2000 GSF1200 MODELS)

1. Screw
2. Washer
3. Trim ring
4. Spring
5. Nut
6. Bezel
7. Lens
8. Clip
9. Bulb
10. Boot
11. Position light (except U.S.A., California and Canada models)

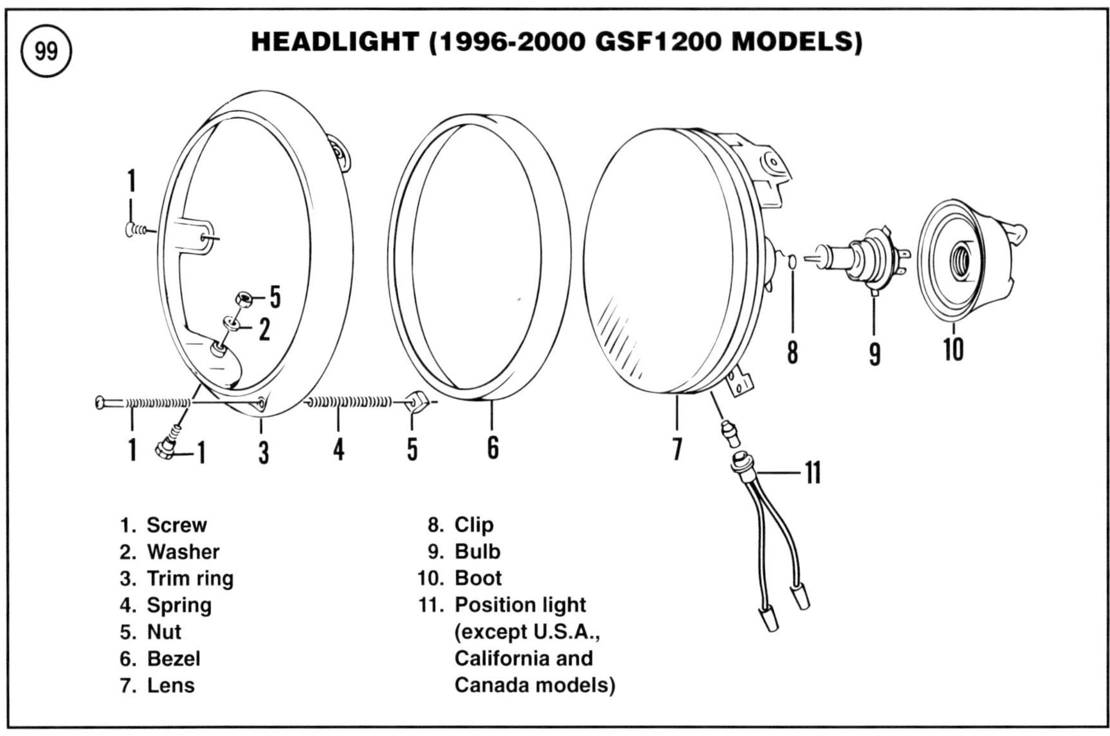

(100)

HEADLIGHT (2001-ON GSF1200 MODELS)

1. Mounting ear
2. Bracket
3. Bolt
4. Damper
5. Collar
6. Nut
7. Housing
8. Washer
9. Spring
10. Vertical adjuster
11. Adjuster plate
12. Horizontal adjuster
13. Screw
14. Trim ring
15. Lens
16. Bulb
17. Boot
18. Position light

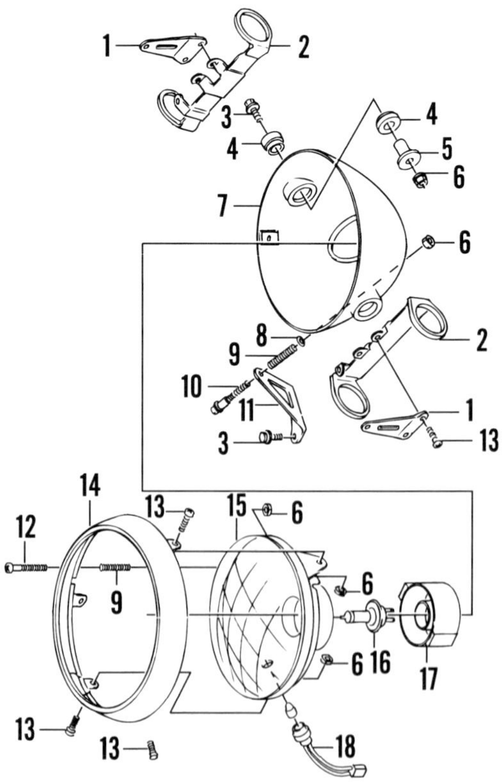

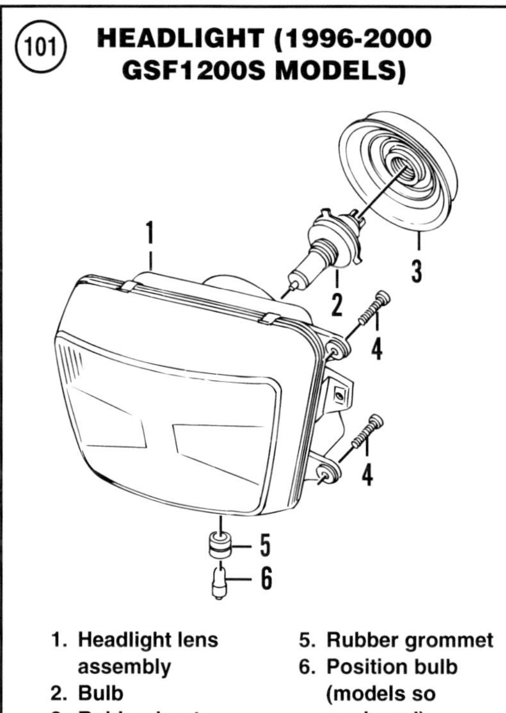

1. Headlight lens assembly
2. Bulb
3. Rubber boot
4. Screw
5. Rubber grommet
6. Position bulb (models so equipped)

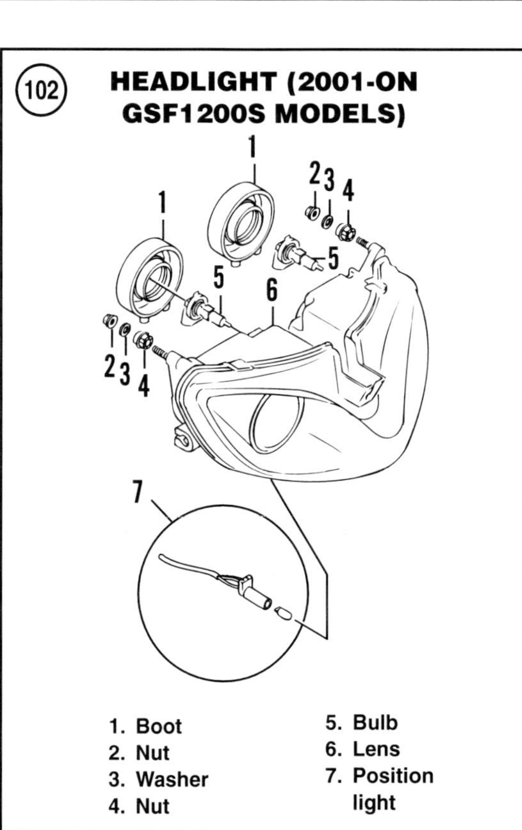

1. Boot
2. Nut
3. Washer
4. Nut
5. Bulb
6. Lens
7. Position light

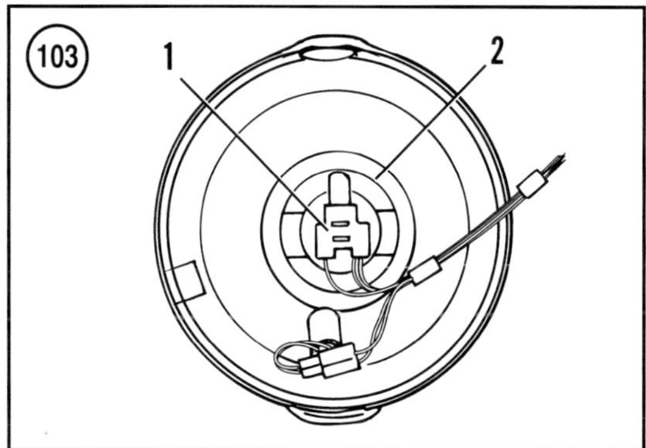

outside the specified range in **Table 1**, replace the starter relay.

LIGHTING SYSTEM

The lighting system consists of a headlight, taillight/brake light, directional lights, indicator lights and meter illumination lights. **Table 2** lists replacement bulb wattage for these components.

Always use the correct wattage bulb as indicated in this section. The use of a larger wattage bulb will give a dim light and a smaller wattage bulb will burn out prematurely.

Headlight Bulb Replacement

WARNING

*If the bulb has just burned out or has just been turned off, it will be **very hot**! Do not touch the bulb, as it will burn fingers. Wait for the bulb to cool before removing it.*

CAUTION

All models are equipped with quartz-halogen bulbs. Do not touch the bulb glass with any fingers because traces of oil on the bulb will drastically reduce the life of the bulb. Clean any traces of oil or other chemicals from the bulb with a cloth moistened in alcohol or lacquer thinner.

Refer to **Figures 99-102**.

1. On GSF1200 models, perform the following:
   a. Remove the headlight lens assembly as described in this chapter.
   b. Disconnect the electrical socket (1, **Figure 103**) from the bulb and remove the rubber boot (2).

c. Unhook the retaining clip (1, **Figure 104**) from the bulb.

d. Remove the light bulb (2, **Figure 104**) and install a new bulb.

2. On 1996-2000 GSF1200S models, perform the following:

a. Disconnect the electrical socket (A, **Figure 105**) from the bulb and remove the rubber boot (B).

b. Unhook the retaining clip (A, **Figure 106**) from the bulb.

c. Remove the light bulb (B, **Figure 106**) and install a new bulb.

NOTE

On 2001-on GSF1200S models, the high beam bulb is located on the right side and the low beam on the left side.

3. On 2001-on GSF1200S, perform the following:

a. Turn the handlebar to the full lock position in one direction to allow access to the blown bulb.

b. Press the electrical connector arm (**Figure 107**) in at the top and at the same time pull the connector up and disconnect it from the bulb.

c. Turn the bulb and holder (**Figure 108**) counterclockwise and remove it from the housing.

d. Remove the light bulb (**Figure 109**) and install a new bulb and holder.

e. Repeat for the other bulb if necessary.

4. Install by reversing these removal steps.

5. On GSF1200 models, be sure to position the rubber boot with the TOP mark facing up.

Headlight Assembly Removal/Installation (GSF1200 Models)

Refer to **Figure 99** and **Figure 100**.

1. Remove the screws securing the trim ring to the headlight housing.

2. Move the lens assembly partially out of the housing and disconnect the electrical socket (1, **Figure 103**) from the bulb.

3. Remove the fasteners securing the headlight housing to the mounting bracket on the front fork assemblies and remove the housing.

4. Install by reversing these removal steps.

5. Adjust the headlight as described in this chapter.

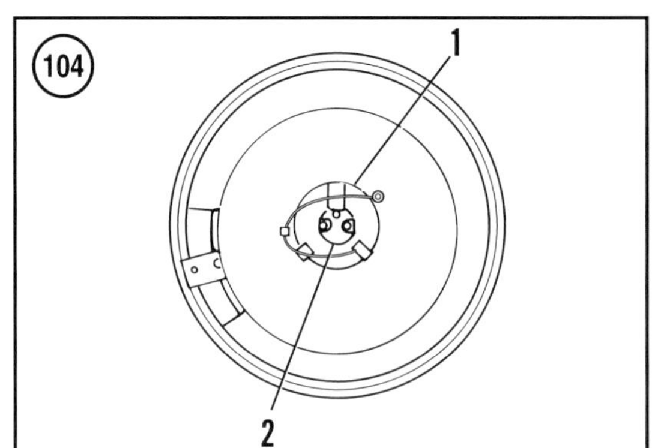

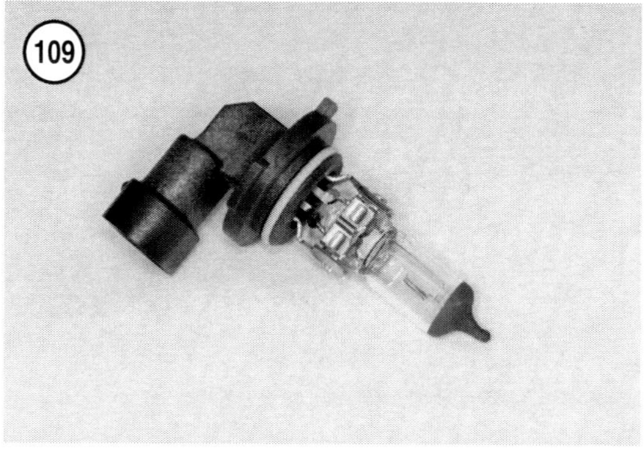

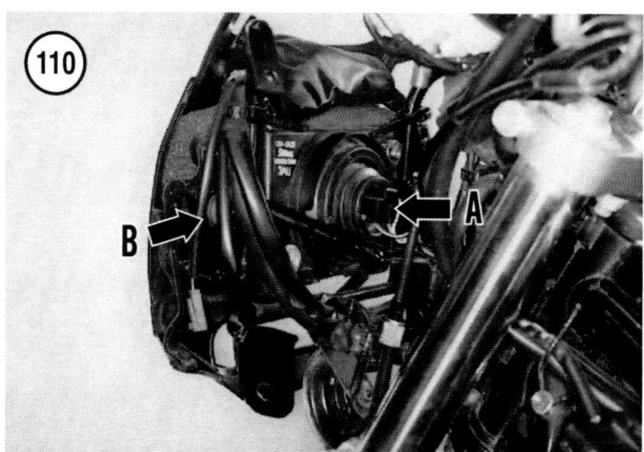

Headlight Assembly Removal/Installation (1996-2000 GSF1200S Models)

Refer to **Figure 101**.

1. Remove the front fairing as described in Chapter Fourteen.
2. If still connected, disconnect the headlight electrical connector (A, **Figure 110**) from the headlight.
3. On models with a position light, disconnect the position light connector.
4. Remove the bolts securing the headlight housing (B, **Figure 110**) to the front fairing mounting bracket and remove the housing.
5. Install by reversing these removal steps while noting the following:
   a. Tighten all bolts securely but do not overtighten. The plastic mounting tabs on the housing may fracture.
   b. Adjust the headlight as described in this chapter.

Headlight Assembly Removal/Installation (2001-on GSF1200S Models)

Refer to **Figure 102**.

1. Remove the front fairing as described in Chapter Fourteen.
2. If still connected, disconnect the headlight electrical connector (A, **Figure 111**) from both headlights.
3. On models with a position light, disconnect the position light electrical connector.
4. Remove the bolts (B, **Figure 111**) securing the headlight housing to the front fairing mounting bracket and remove the housing.
5. Install by reversing these removal steps while noting the following:
   a. Tighten all bolts securely but do not overtighten. The plastic mounting tabs on the housing may fracture.
   b. Adjust the headlight as described in this chapter.

Headlight Adjustment

Adjust the headlight horizontally and vertically according to Department of Motor Vehicle regulations.

9

GSF1200 models

To adjust the headlight horizontally, turn the adjuster on the front right side of the trim ring (A, **Figure 112**) either clockwise or counterclockwise until the aim is correct.

To adjust the headlight vertically, turn the adjuster beneath the trim ring (B, **Figure 112**) either clockwise or counterclockwise until the aim is correct.

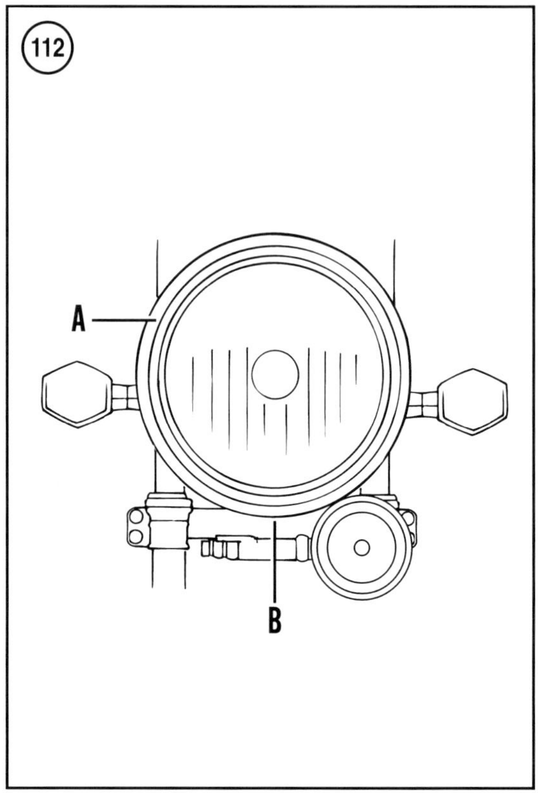

1996-2000 GSF1200S models

To adjust the headlight horizontally, turn the upper right side adjuster (A, **Figure 113**) either clockwise or counterclockwise until the aim is correct.

To adjust the headlight vertically, turn the lower left side adjuster (B, **Figure 113**) either clockwise or counterclockwise until the aim is correct.

2001-on GSF1200S models

Adjust the headlight from the rear of the headlight assembly.

To adjust the headlight horizontally, turn the upper screw (A, **Figure 114**). Turn the screw either clockwise or counterclockwise until the aim is correct.

For vertical adjustment, turn the lower screw (B, **Figure 114**) clockwise or counterclockwise until the aim is correct.

Taillight/Brake Light Bulb Replacement (1996-2000 Models)

Refer to **Figure 115**.

1. Remove the seat as described in Chapter Fourteen.
2. Reach into the rear cowl area and turn the bulb socket assembly (A, **Figure 116**) counterclockwise and remove the socket assembly from the backside of the taillight/brake light lens assembly.
3. Push the bulb into the socket and turn the bulb counterclockwise. Remove the bulb from the socket (**Figure 117**).
4. Replace the bulb and install the socket assembly.
5. Install the seat.

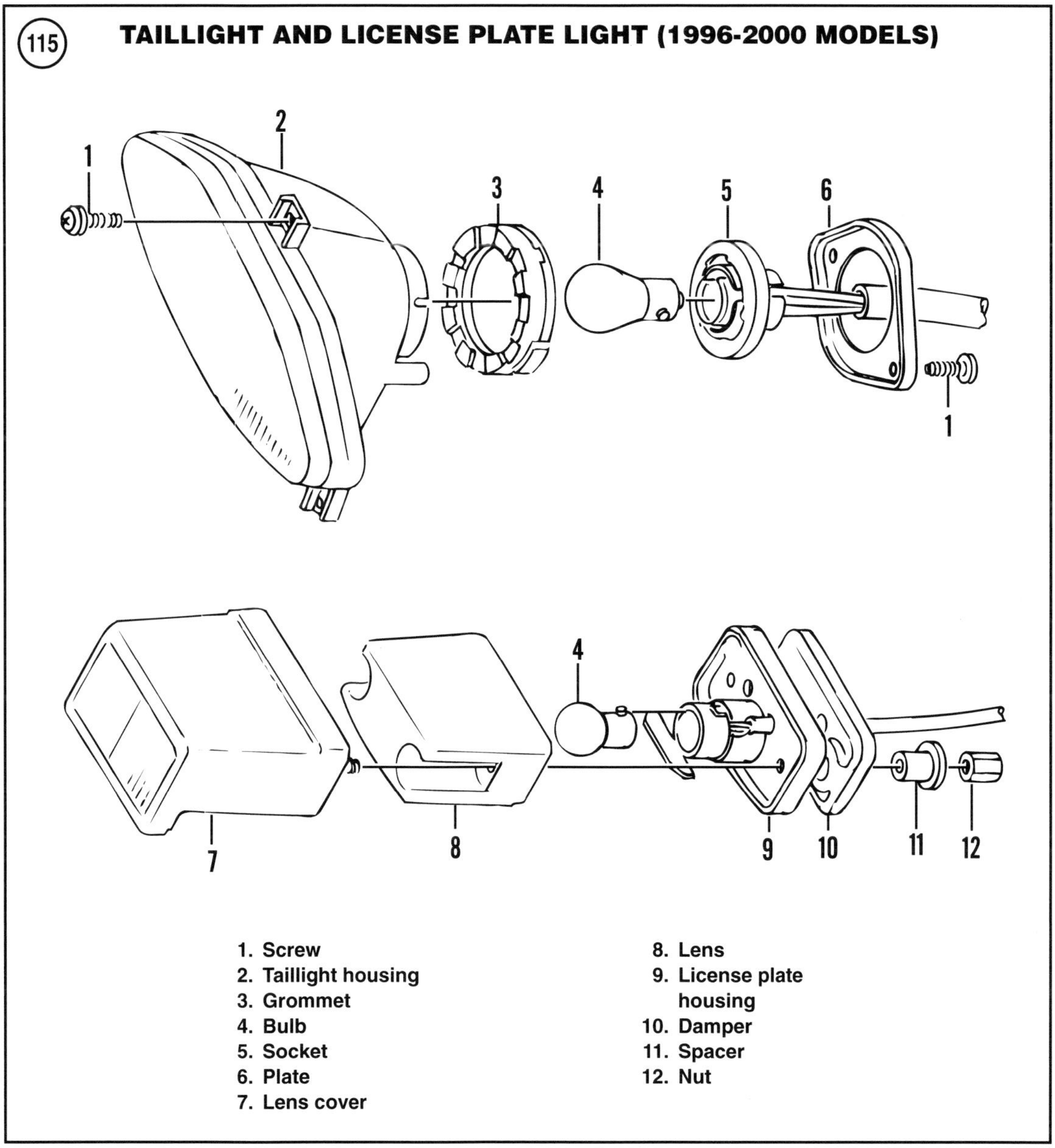

115
TAILLIGHT AND LICENSE PLATE LIGHT (1996-2000 MODELS)
1
2
3
4
5
6
1
4
7
8
9
10
11
12
1. Screw
2. Taillight housing
3. Grommet
4. Bulb
5. Socket
6. Plate
7. Lens cover
8. Lens
9. License plate housing
10. Damper
11. Spacer
12. Nut

116
A
B
B

117

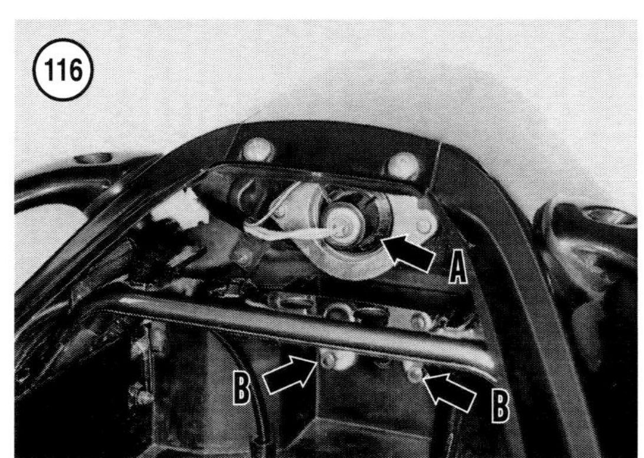

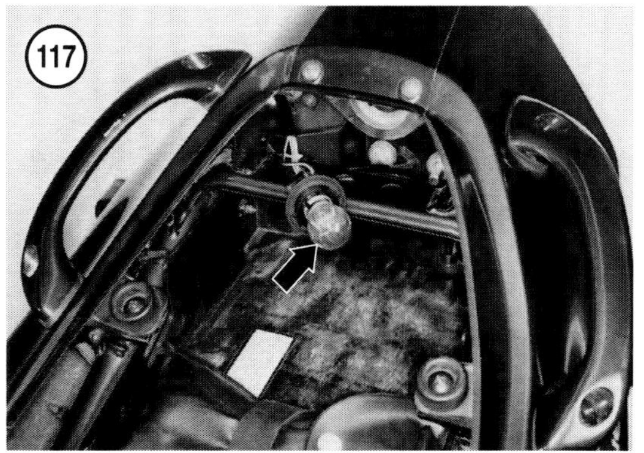

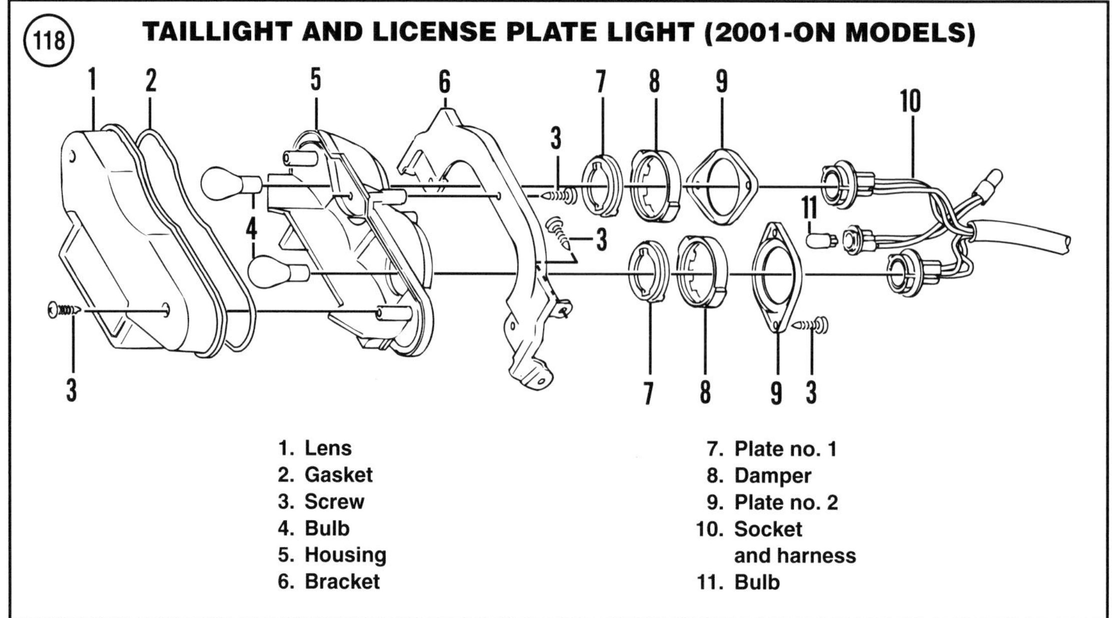

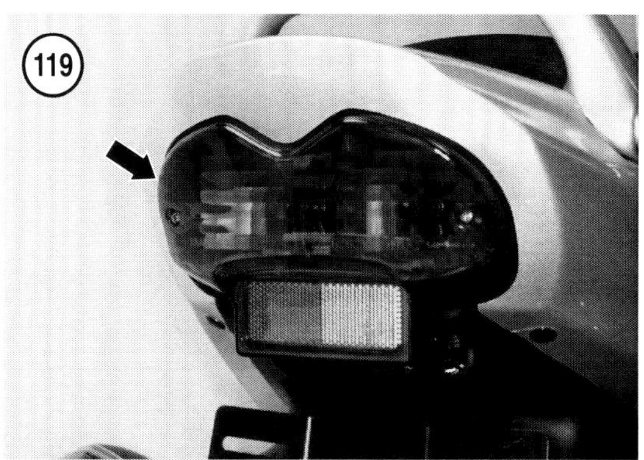

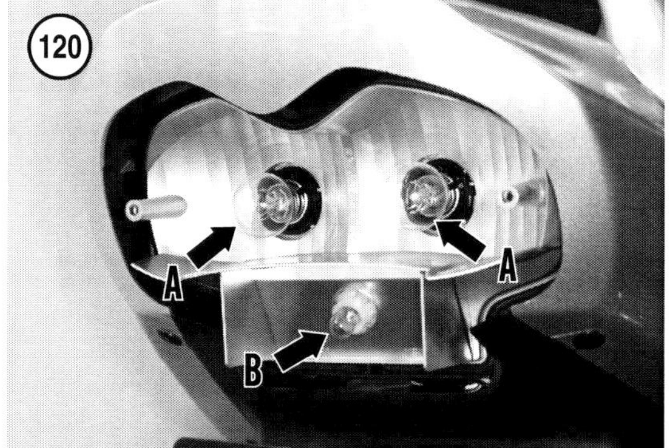

Taillight/Brake Light Bulb Replacement (2001-on Models)

Refer to **Figure 118**.

1. Remove the screws securing the lens (**Figure 119**).
2. Push the bulb into the socket and turn the bulb (A, **Figure 120**) counterclockwise. Remove the bulb from the socket.
3. Replace the bulb and repeat for the other bulb if necessary.
4. Install the lens. Do not overtighten the screws, as the lens may crack.

License Plate Light Bulb Replacement (1996-2000 Models)

Refer to **Figure 115**.

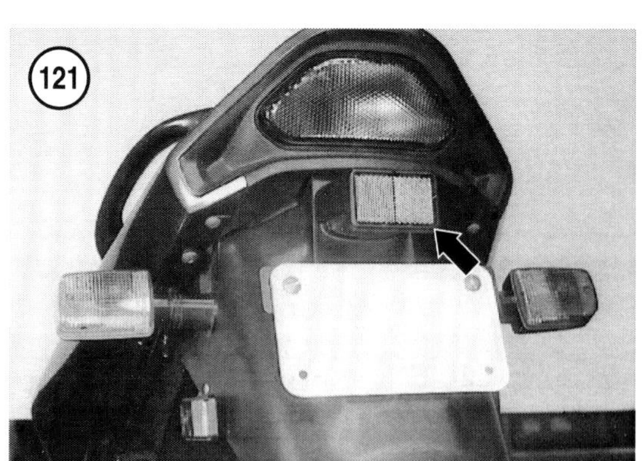

1. Remove the seat as described in Chapter Fourteen.
2. Reach into the rear cowl area and remove the nuts (B, **Figure 116**) securing the lens cover and lens (**Figure 121**). Remove the lens and lens cover.

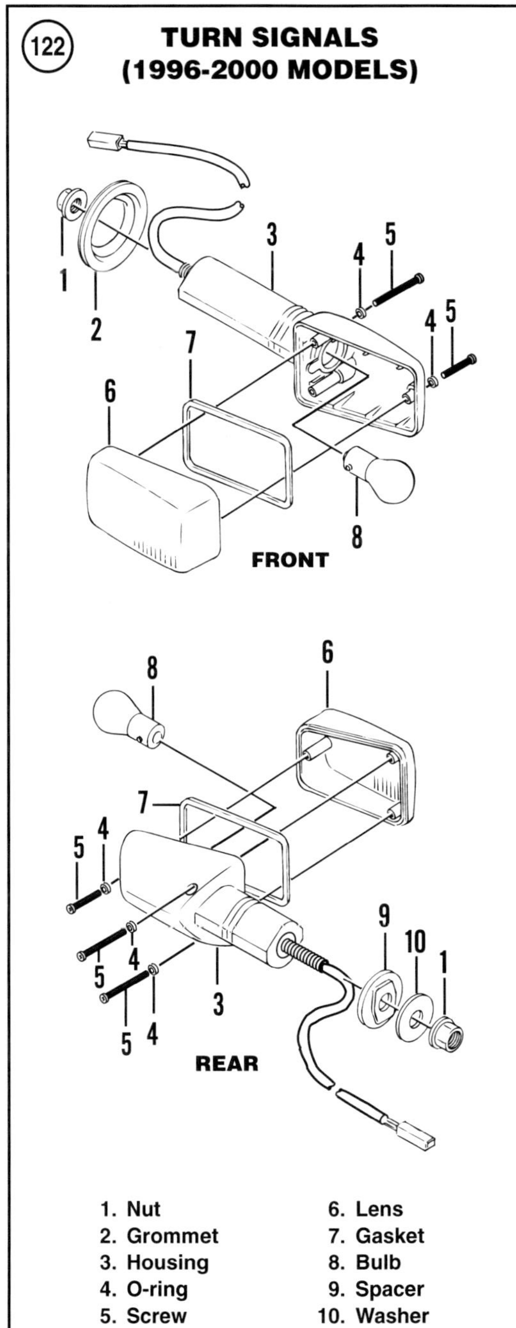

(122) **TURN SIGNALS (1996-2000 MODELS)**

1. Nut
2. Grommet
3. Housing
4. O-ring
5. Screw
6. Lens
7. Gasket
8. Bulb
9. Spacer
10. Washer

3. Push the bulb into the socket and turn the bulb counterclockwise. Remove the bulb from the socket and replace the bulb.
4. Install the lens and lens cover, then install the mounting nuts. Do not overtighten the nuts, as the threaded studs on the lens cover may be damaged.
5. Install the seat.

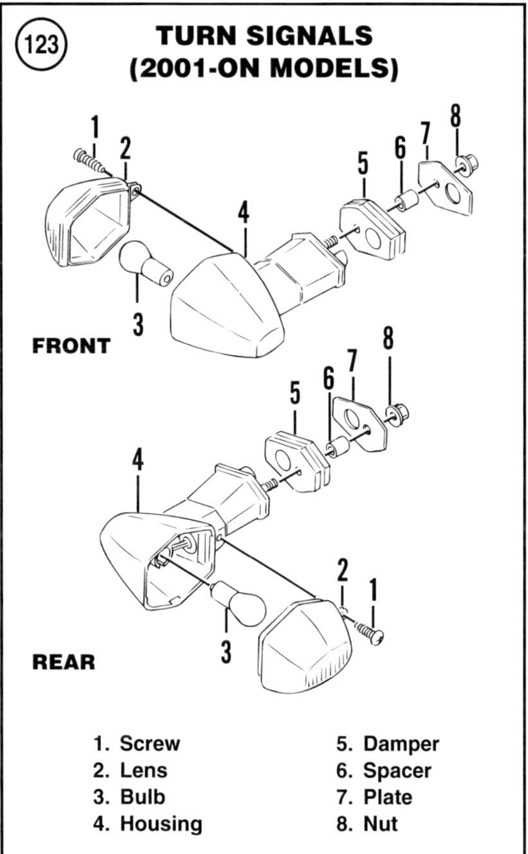

(123) **TURN SIGNALS (2001-ON MODELS)**

1. Screw
2. Lens
3. Bulb
4. Housing
5. Damper
6. Spacer
7. Plate
8. Nut

License Plate Light Bulb Replacement (2001-on Models)

Refer to **Figure 118**.

1. Remove the screws securing the lens (**Figure 119**).
2. Pull straight out and remove the license plate bulb (B, **Figure 120**).
3. Install a new bulb and push it in until it bottoms.
4. Install the lens. Do not overtighten the screws, as the lens may crack.

Turn Signal Bulb Replacement (All Models)

Refer to **Figure 122** and **Figure 123**.

NOTE

On 1996-2000 models, the screws are located on the backside of the turn-signal housing. On 2001-on models, the single screw is located on the front of the turn-signal housing.

1A. On 1996-2000 models, remove the screws securing the lens to the turn-signal housing and remove the lens (**Figure 124**).

1B. On 2001-on models, remove the screw (**Figure 125**) securing the lens to the turn-signal housing and remove the lens.

2. Push the bulb (**Figure 126**) into the socket and turn the bulb counterclockwise. Remove the bulb from the socket.
3. Replace the bulb.
4. Wash out the inside and outside of the lens with mild detergent and wipe dry.
5. Install the lens. Do not overtighten the screws, as the lens may crack.

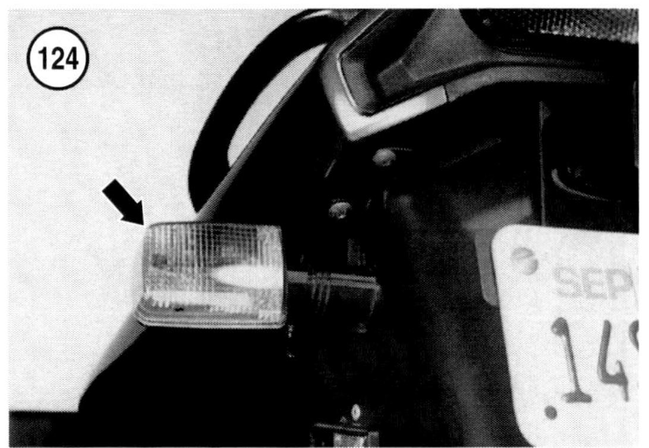
124

125

Turn Signal Assembly Removal/Installation

Refer to **Figure 122** and **Figure 123**.

1. Working within the front fairing or the license plate holder, disconnect the electrical connector.
2. Unscrew the nut and related washers and carefully slide off the electrical wires and connector.
3. Remove the turn signal assembly from the front fairing (**Figure 127**) or the license plate holder.
4. On 2001-on models, do not lose the damper located between the front turn signal assembly and the fairing body panel.
5. Install by reversing these removal steps. Note the following:
   a. When installing the front turn signals, make sure the rubber grommet, or damper, is properly seated in the fairing receptacle.
   b. Make sure the electrical connector is corrosion-free and secure.

126

Speedometer and Tachometer Illumination Light and Indicator Light Replacement (1996-2000 Models)

Illumination lights

1. Remove the front fairing as described in Chapter Fourteen.
2. On the speedometer, disconnect the cable (A, **Figure 128**) from the fitting on the backside of the cover.
3. Remove the screws securing the cover (B, **Figure 128**) and remove the cover.

127

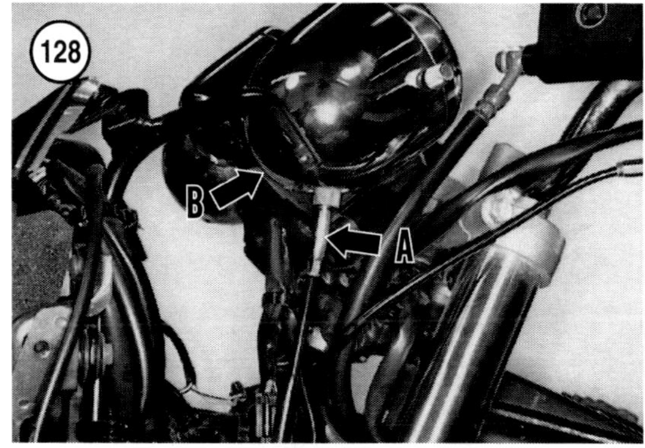

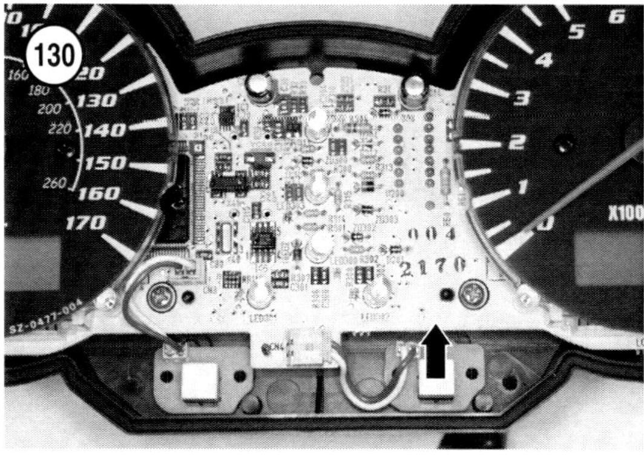

4. Carefully pull the defective lamp holder/electrical wire assembly (A, **Figure 129**) from the backside of the housing.

5. Remove and replace the defective bulb.

6. Push the lamp socket/electrical wire assembly back into the housing. Make sure it is completely seated to prevent the entry of water and moisture.

7. Install the cover and tighten the screws securely.

8. Connect the speedometer cable to the fitting on the backside of the cover.

9. Install the front fairing as described in Chapter Fourteen.

Indicator lights

1. Remove the front fairing as described in Chapter Fourteen.

2. Working on the backside of the meter assembly, remove the screws securing the indicator panel cover (B, **Figure 129**) and remove the cover.

3. Pull straight out and remove the defective bulb(s).

4. Install a new bulb and push it in until it bottoms.

NOTE
If the new bulb will not work, check the wire connections for loose or broken wires. Also check the bulb socket for corrosion.

5. Install the cover and tighten the screws securely.

6. Install the front fairing as described in Chapter Fourteen.

Speedometer and Tachometer Illumination Light and Indicator LED Replacement (2001-on Models)

1. Remove the combination meter as described in this chapter.

2. Partially disassemble the combination meter to gain access to the bulbs or LED's.

3. Pull straight out and remove the defective bulb(s).

4. Install a new bulb and push it in until it bottoms.

5. Carefully pull the defective LED from the front of the printed circuit board (**Figure 130**).

6. Install a new LED and push it in unit it bottoms.

NOTE
If the LED will not work, check the wire connections for loose or broken wires. Also check the LED socket for corrosion.

7. Reassemble the meter assembly.

8. Install the combination meter assembly as described in this chapter.

9

131 **IGNITION SWITCH (AUSTRALIA MODELS)**

Color / Position	R	O	O/Y	B/W
OFF				
ON	●	●	●	●
LOCK				

132 **IGNITION SWITCH (EXCEPT AUSTRALIA MODELS)**

Color / Position	R	O	Gr	Br	O/Y or O/R	B/W
OFF						
ON	●	●	●	●	●	●
LOCK						
PARK	●	—	—	●		

SWITCHES

Check and Testing

Switches can be tested for continuity with an ohmmeter (see Chapter One), or a test light at the switch connector plug by operating the switch in each of its operating positions and comparing the results with its switch operation diagram. For example, **Figure 131** shows a continuity diagram for the ignition switch. The horizontal line indicates which terminals should show continuity when the switch is in a given position.

When the ignition switch in is in the ON position, there should be continuity between the terminals indicated by the line on the operation diagram. An ohmmeter connected between these two terminals should indicate little or no resistance or a test light should light. When the ignition switch is in the OFF position, there should be no continuity between any of the terminals.

Color codes are in **Table 4** at the end of the chapter.

If the switch button does not perform properly, replace it. Refer to **Figures 131-145** for each individual switch.

133 **LIGHTING SWITCH (EXCEPT U.S.A. AND CANADA MODELS)**

Color / Position	O/L	Gr	O/R	Y/W
OFF				
●	●	●		
ON	●	●	●	●

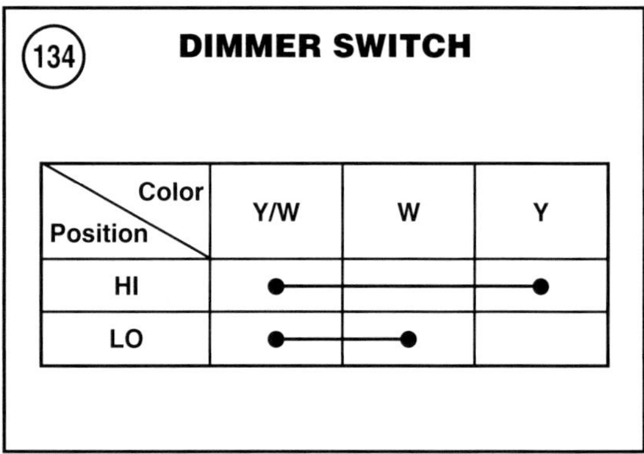

134 **DIMMER SWITCH**

Color / Position	Y/W	W	Y
HI	●	—	●
LO	●	●	

135 **TURN SIGNAL SWITCH**

Color / Position	Lg	Sb	B
L		●	●
PUSH			
R	●	●	

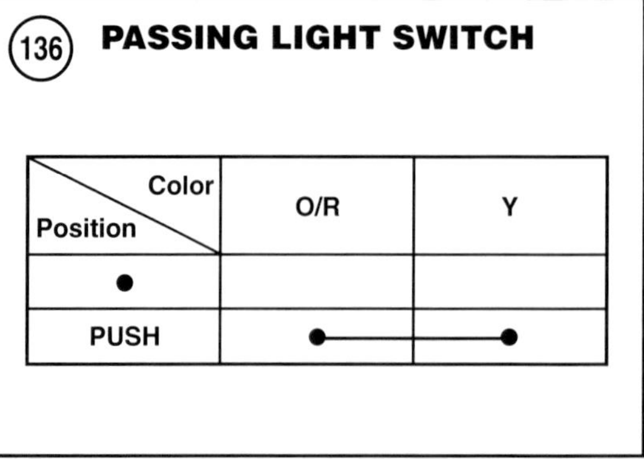

136 **PASSING LIGHT SWITCH**

Color / Position	O/R	Y
●		
PUSH	●	●

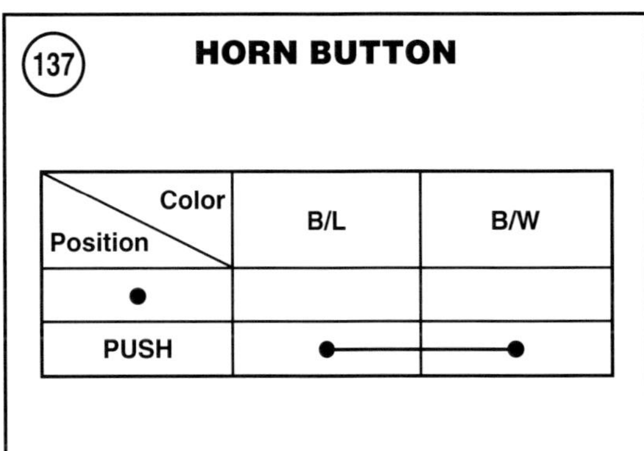

137 **HORN BUTTON**

Position \ Color	B/L	B/W
●		
PUSH	●	●

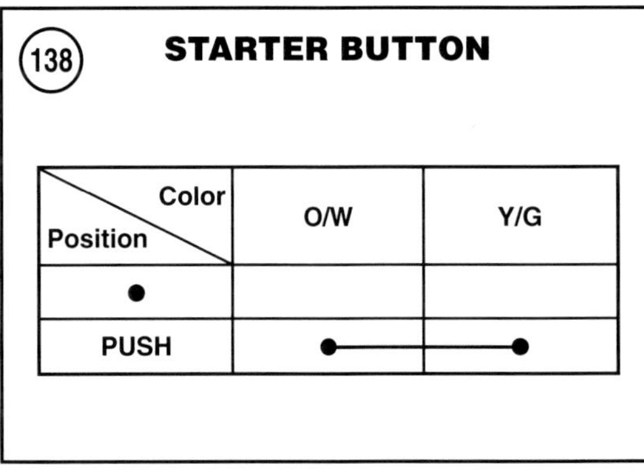

138 **STARTER BUTTON**

Position \ Color	O/W	Y/G
●		
PUSH	●	●

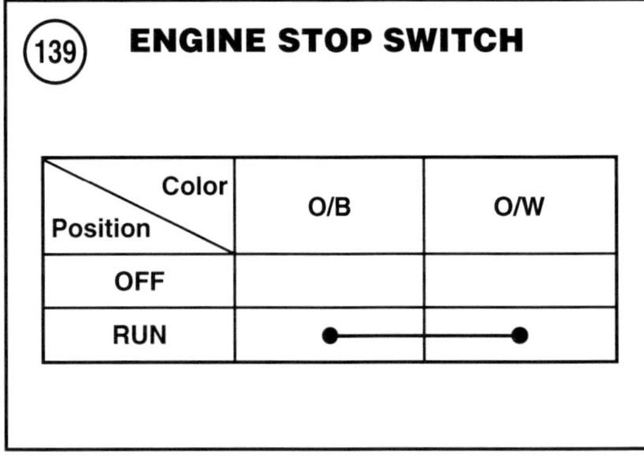

139 **ENGINE STOP SWITCH**

Position \ Color	O/B	O/W
OFF		
RUN	●	●

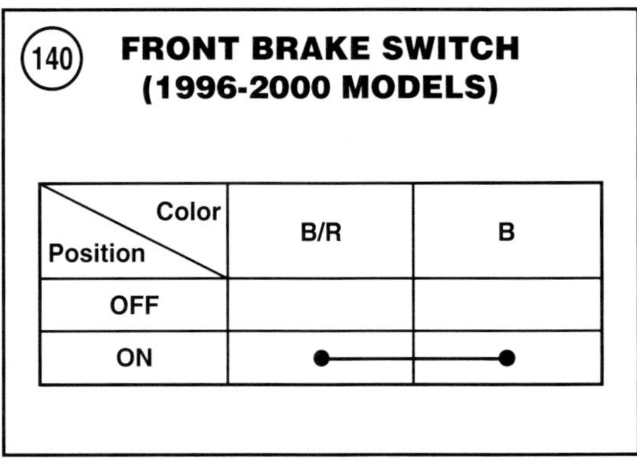

140 **FRONT BRAKE SWITCH (1996-2000 MODELS)**

Position \ Color	B/R	B
OFF		
ON	●	●

141 **FRONT BRAKE SWITCH (2001-ON MODELS)**

Position \ Color	B/R	B/L
OFF		
ON	●	●

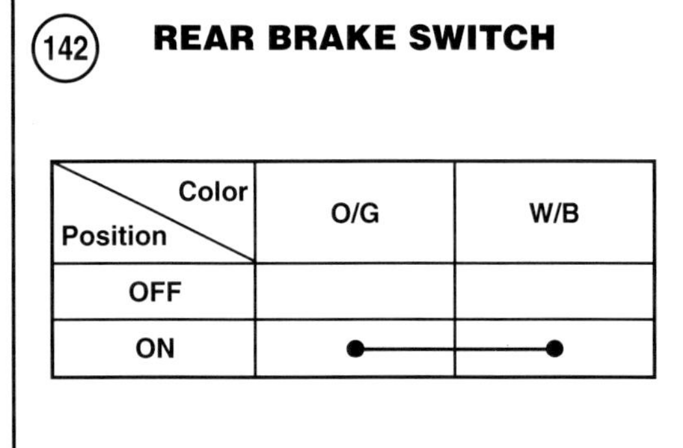

142 **REAR BRAKE SWITCH**

Position \ Color	O/G	W/B
OFF		
ON	●	●

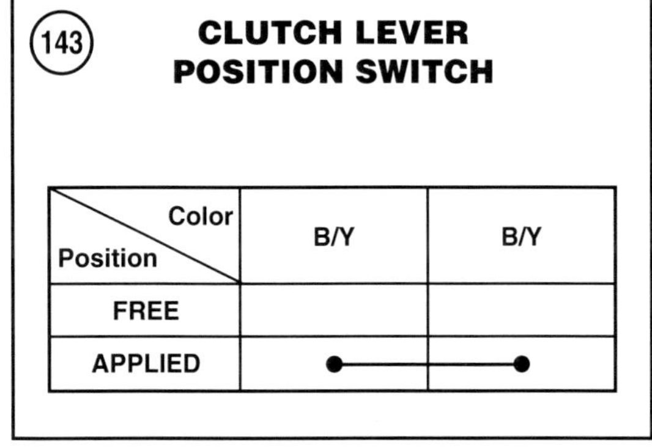

143 **CLUTCH LEVER POSITION SWITCH**

Position \ Color	B/Y	B/Y
FREE		
APPLIED	●	●

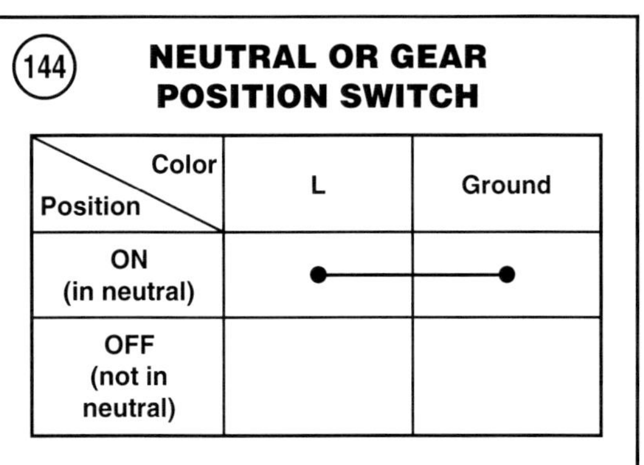

144 **NEUTRAL OR GEAR POSITION SWITCH**

Position \ Color	L	Ground
ON (in neutral)	●	●
OFF (not in neutral)		

When testing switches, note the following:

1. First check the fuse as described in *Fuse* in this chapter.
2. Check the battery as described in *Battery* in Chapter Three. Charge the battery to the correct state of charge, if required.
3. Disconnect the negative battery lead from the battery if the switch connectors are not disconnected in the circuit.

CAUTION
Do not attempt to start the engine with the battery disconnected.

4. When separating two connectors, pull the connector housings and not the wires.
5. After locating a defective circuit, check the connectors to make sure they are clean and properly connected. Check all wires going into a connector housing to make sure each wire is properly positioned and that the wire end is not loose.
6. When reconnecting electrical connector halves, push them together until they click or snap into place.

Ignition Switch Removal/Installation

1. On GSF1200S models, remove the front fairing as described in Chapter Fourteen.
2. Remove the headlight assembly as described in this chapter.
3. Disconnect the four-pin or six-pin ignition switch electrical connector from the wiring harness.
4. Remove the upper fork bridge as described in Chapter Eleven.

NOTE
The ignition switch is held in place with two Torx bolts. On this type of bolt, the head either shears off or rounds off during installation as a theft deterrent.

5. Remove the ignition switch mounting Torx bolts from the upper fork bridge as follows:
   a. Center punch a dimple into the bolt shoulder.
   b. Place the centerpunch in this dimple.
   c. Use a hammer and carefully tap the bolt counterclockwise and remove the bolt.
   d. If the bolt cannot be loosened in this manner, drill a small hole in the center of the bolt and use a screw extractor to loosen and remove the bolt (Chapter One).
   e. Repeat for the remaining bolt.

145 **SIDESTAND SWITCH**

Position \ Color	G	B/W
ON (UP position)	●	●
OFF (DOWN position)		

6. Remove the switch assembly (**Figure 146**) from the underside of the upper fork bridge.
7. Install the new ignition switch onto the upper fork bridge and install new Torx bolts. Tighten the bolts until the head shears off or rounds off the point where the Torx tool slips off the head.
8. Reconnect the four-pin or six-pin electrical connector. Make sure the electrical connector is free of corrosion and is tight.
9. Install the upper fork bridge as described in Chapter Eleven.
10. Install the headlight assembly as described in this chapter.
11. On GSF1200S models, install the front fairing as described in Chapter Fourteen.

Right Handlebar Switch Housing Replacement

The front brake light switch is the only switch in the right handlebar switch assembly that can be re-

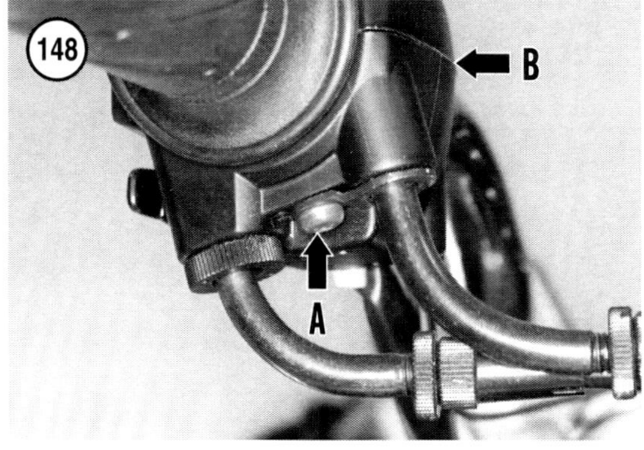

placed separately. The remaining switches are not available individually. If any portion of the switch assembly is faulty, the entire switch housing must be replaced.

The right handlebar switch housing includes the following switches:

1. Engine stop switch.
2. Start button.
3. Front brake light switch (electrical connectors only—the switch is separate).
4. Headlight switch (except U.S. and Canada models).

Replacement

1. Remove the seat as described in Chapter Fourteen.
2. Disconnect the negative battery cable as described in this chapter.
3. Remove the fuel tank as described in Chapter Eight.
4. Unhook the tie wrap and locate the right-handlebar-switch ten-pin electrical connector. Refer to the appropriate wiring diagram at the end of this book to identify colors of the wires in this connector.
5. Disconnect the two connectors (**Figure 147**) from the front brake switch.
6. Remove the electrical wire harness from any clips on the frame and carefully pull the harness out from the frame.

NOTE

*The throttle cable bracket is secured under one of these screws (A, **Figure 148**). The bracket must be reinstalled in the same location during assembly.*

7. Remove the screws securing the right handlebar switch housing together and remove the switch assembly (B, **Figure 148**).
8. Install by reversing the removal steps. Note the following:
   a. Install a new switch and tighten the screws securely. Do not overtighten the screws or the plastic switch housing may crack. Be sure to install the cable bracket under the correct screw (A, **Figure 148**).
   b. Make sure the electrical connectors are corrosion-free and secure.
   c. Install the tie wrap(s) securing the electrical wires to the front of the frame. The wires must be retained in this manner to allow room for the fuel tank.
   d. Check the operation of the front brake switch before riding the motorcycle.

Left Handlebar Switch Housing Replacement

The clutch lever position switch is the only switch in the left handlebar switch assembly that can be replaced separately. The remaining switches are not available individually. If any portion of the switch assembly is faulty, the entire switch housing must be replaced.

The left handlebar switch housing includes the following switches:

1. Headlight dimmer switch.
2. Turn signal switch.
3. Horn button.
4. Passing button (except U.S.A. and Canada models).
5. Clutch lever position switch (electrical connectors only; the switch is separate).

NOTE

The starter (choke) control lever is an integral part of the left handlebar switch and the cable must be disconnected for switch removal.

Replacement

1. Remove the seat as described in Chapter Fourteen.
2. Disconnect the negative battery cable as described in this chapter.
3. Remove the fuel tank as described in Chapter Eight.
4. Unhook the tie wrap(s) and remove any plastic clamps securing the left handlebar switch cable to the frame.
5. Locate and disconnect the left handlebar switch 12-pin electrical connector. Refer to the appropriate wiring diagram at the end of this book to identify colors of the wires in this connector.
6. Disconnect the clutch lever position switch, disconnect the two connectors (**Figure 149**) from the clutch position switch on the clutch lever.

NOTE
*The starter (choke) cable bracket is secured under one of these screws (A, **Figure 150**). The bracket must be reinstalled in the same location during assembly.*

7. Remove the screws securing the left handlebar switch housing (B, **Figure 150**) together and separate the housing halves.
8. Disconnect the starter (choke) cable from the choke lever (**Figure 151**) and remove the switch housing.
9. Install by reversing these removal steps while noting the following:
   a. Connect the starter (choke) cable to the choke lever in the switch housing.
   b. Align the switch locating pin (A, **Figure 152**) with the hole (B) in the handlebar. Install the switch onto the handlebar and tighten the screws securely. Be sure to install the cable bracket under the correct screw (A, **Figure 150**).
   c. Make sure the electrical connector is corrosion-free and secure.
   d. Check the operation of each switch mounted in the left handlebar switch.
   e. Operate the choke lever and make sure the linkage is operating correctly without bind-

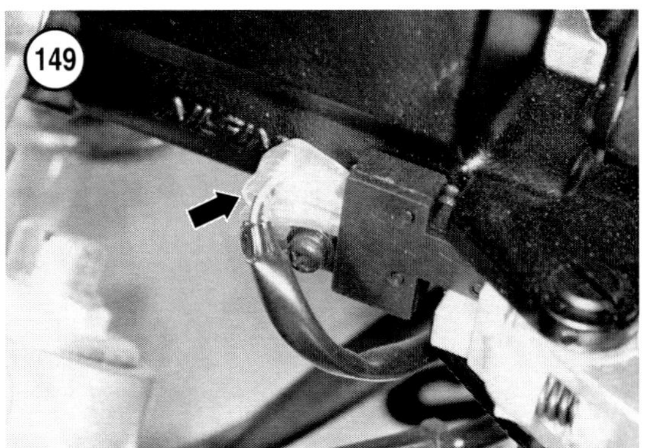

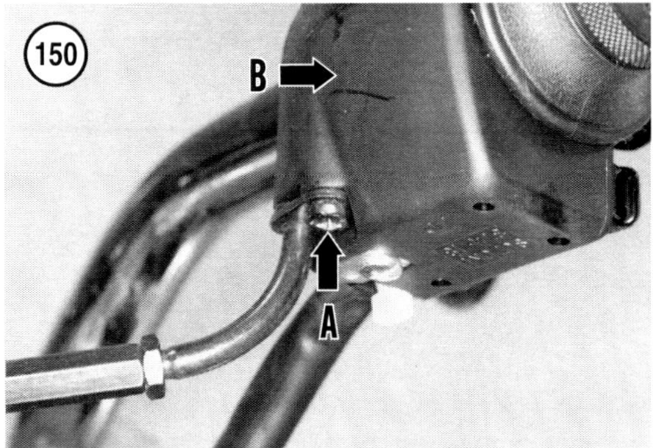

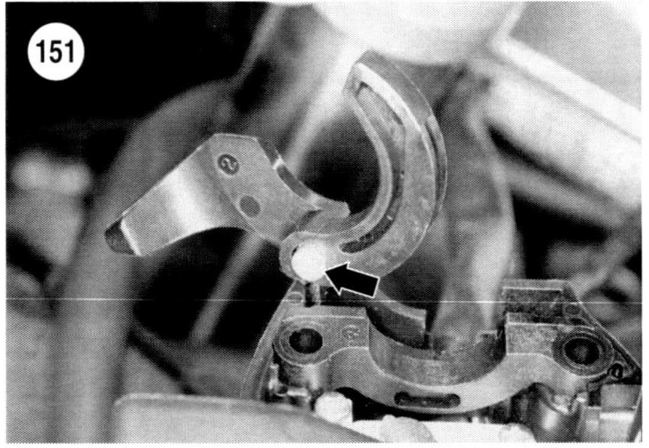

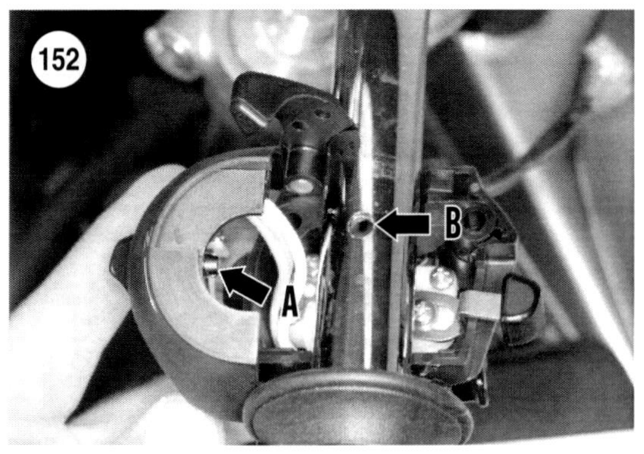

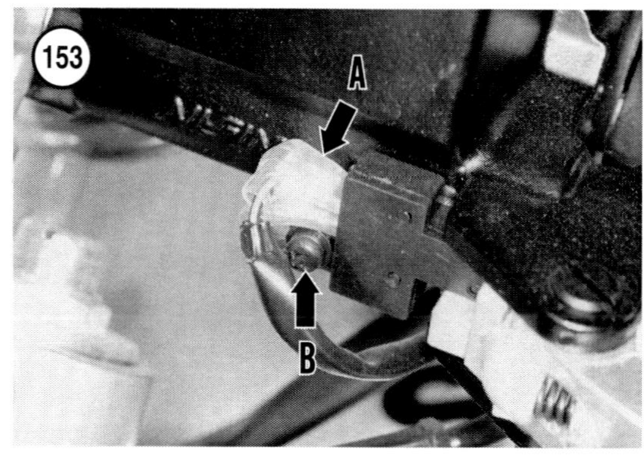

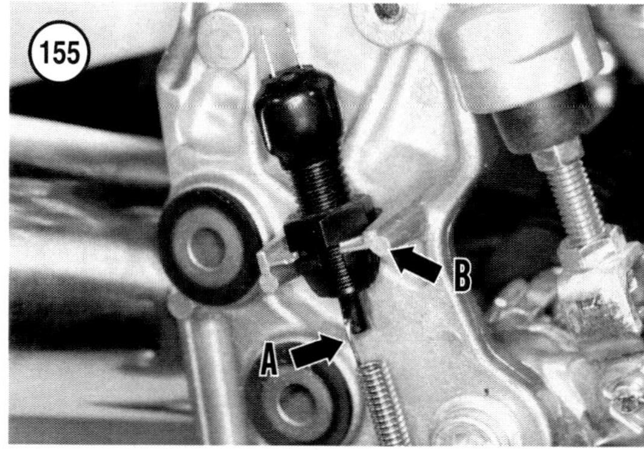

ing. If operation is incorrect or if there is binding, check that the cable is attached correctly and that there are no tight bends in the cable.

Clutch Lever Position Switch

Testing

1. Disconnect the two connectors (**Figure 149**) from the clutch lever position switch.
2. Connect an ohmmeter to the switch connectors.
3. Apply the clutch lever. There should be continuity.
4. If there is no continuity, replace the switch.

Removal/installation

1. Disconnect the two connectors (A, **Figure 153**) from the clutch lever position switch.
2. Remove the switch mounting screw (B, **Figure 153**) and remove the switch from the clutch lever.
3. Secure the new switch to the clutch lever.
4. Tighten the screw and connect the clutch switch connectors.

Front Brake Switch

Testing

1. Disconnect the two connectors (**Figure 147**) from the front brake lever switch.
2. Connect an ohmmeter to the switch connector.
3. Apply the brake lever. There should be continuity.
4. If there is no continuity, replace the switch.

Removal/installation

1. Disconnect the two connectors (**Figure 147**) from the front brake lever switch.
2. Remove the switch mounting screw (**Figure 154**) and remove the switch from the front brake lever.
3. Secure the new switch to the brake lever.
4. Tighten the screw and connect the front brake switch connectors.

Rear Brake Switch Removal/Installation

1. Remove the right side front foot peg and brake pedal assembly as described in Chapter Thirteen.
2. If still attached, disconnect the electrical connector from the top of the brake switch.
3. Disconnect the spring (A, **Figure 155**) from the brake switch body.
4. Withdraw the switch from the mounting boss (B, **Figure 155**) on the front foot peg and brake pedal assembly.
5. Install by reversing these removal steps. Adjust the new brake switch as described in Chapter Three.

Neutral (Gear Position) Switch

Switch inspection

1. Remove the left side cover as described in Chapter Fourteen.
2. Disconnect the gear position switch four-pin electrical connector (A, **Figure 156**).
3. Shift the transmission into NEUTRAL.
4. Connect an ohmmeter between the blue wire and ground (**Figure 157**). There should be continuity.
5. If there is no continuity, replace the switch.

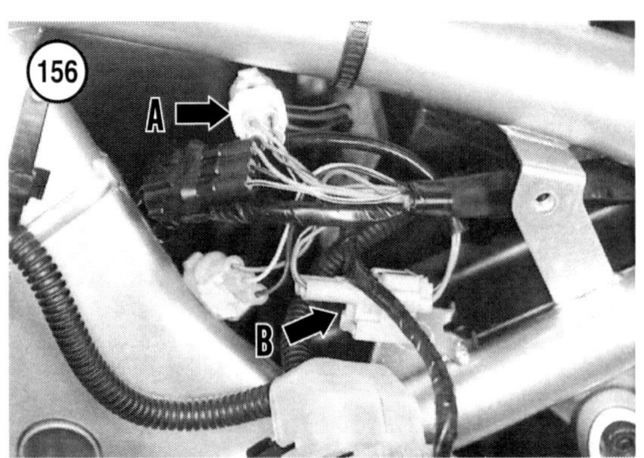

Removal/installation

1. Remove the engine drive sprocket and cover as described in Chapter Seven.
2. Remove any tie wraps securing the electrical wire to the frame.
3. From the neutral, or gear position, switch, follow the single black wire (**Figure 158**) to the electrical connector and disconnect the connector (A, **Figure 156**).
4. Remove the screws (**Figure 159**) securing the switch and remove the switch assembly.
5. The O-ring may come out with the neutral switch or it may remain behind in the crankcase. Remove and discard the O-ring. A new one must be installed during assembly.
6. Do not lose the switch contact plunger and spring (**Figure 160**) from the end of the shift drum.
7. Carefully remove the electrical wire. Note how the wire is routed through the engine. The wire from the new switch will have to follow the same path.
8. Install by reversing these removal steps. Note the following:
   a. Install a new O-ring (**Figure 161**).
   b. Make sure the electrical connector is corrosion-free and secure.
   c. Attach any tie wraps securing the electrical wire to the frame.

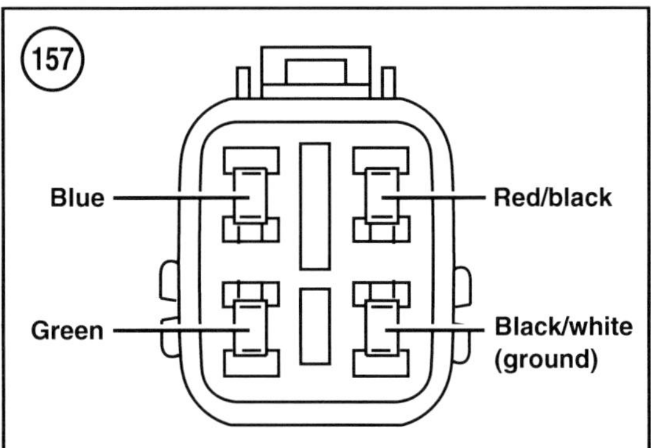

Sidestand Switch

Switch inspection

1. Remove the left side cover as described in Chapter Fourteen.
2. Disconnect the two-pin sidestand switch connector (one green wire and one black/white wire) from the wiring harness (B, **Figure 156**).

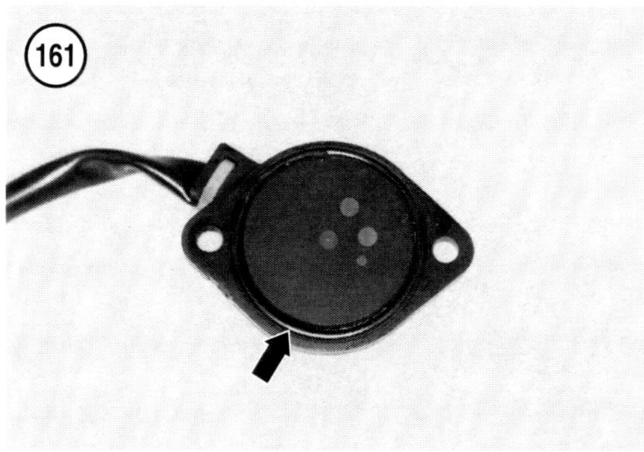

3. Set the Suzuki multi-tester (part No. 09900-25008) to diode test.
4. Connect the positive test probe to the green terminal on the switch side of the connector, and connect the negative test probe to the black/white terminal.
5. Move the sidestand up and note the reading on the meter. Move the sidestand down, and note the voltage reading.
6. Replace the switch if either reading is outside the test-voltage range listed in **Table 1**.

Removal/installation

1. Securely support the motorcycle on level ground.
2A. On 1996-2000 models, remove the seat and the left rear-frame cover as described in Chapter Fourteen.
2B. On 2001-on models, remove the left side cover as described in Chapter Fourteen.
3A. On 1996-2000 models, disconnect the two-pin sidestand switch connector (one green wire and one black/white wire) from the wiring harness (**Figure 162**).
3B. On 2001-on models, disconnect the two-pin sidestand switch connector (one green wire and one black/white wire) from the wiring harness (B, **Figure 156**).
4. Remove the screws securing the sidestand switch (**Figure 163**) to the frame and remove the switch. Note how the cable is routed through the frame. The cable for the new switch must follow the same path.
5. Install by reversing these removal steps. Note the following:
   a. Tighten the sidestand switch mounting screws securely.
   b. Route the electrical wire harness through the frame and install new tie wraps securing the harness to the frame.

Oil Pressure Switch Removal/Installation

1. Drain the engine oil as described in Chapter Three.
2. Remove the signal generator cover bolts, and remove the cover and its gasket (**Figure 164**). One cover bolt has a sealing washer (**Figure 165**) installed beneath it. Note the position of this bolt. It

must be reinstalled in the same location during assembly.

3. Disconnect the oil pressure switch wire (A, **Figure 166**).

4. Unscrew the oil pressure switch (B, **Figure 166**) from the crankcase.

5. Install the oil pressure switch by reversing these removal steps. Note the following:

   a. Apply a light coat of gasket sealer to the switch threads prior to installation. Install the switch and tighten it to 14 N•m (10 ft.-lb.).

   b. Install a new signal generator cover gasket and install the cover. Make sure the bolt with the sealing washer is installed in the location noted during disassembly (**Figure 165**).

   c. Refill the engine oil as described in Chapter Three.

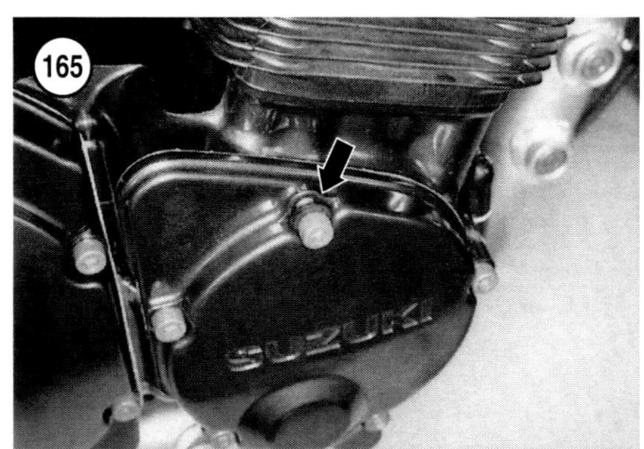

RELAYS

On 2001-on models, the turn-signal relay, sidestand relay and diode are combined into a single component called the turn signal/sidestand relay.

Turn Signal Relay Testing

If a turn signal lamp does not light, first inspect for a blown bulb. If the bulb is good, check the turn signal switch and all electrical connections within the turn signal circuit.

If all of these items are in good working order, replace the turn signal relay on 1996-2000 models. On 2001-on models, replace the turn signal/sidestand relay.

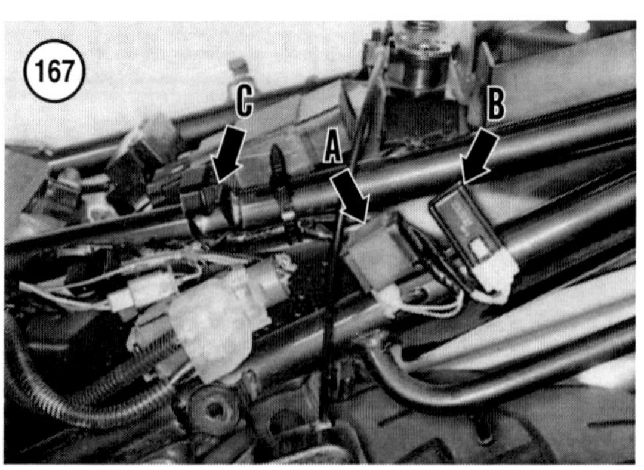

Turn Signal Relay Replacement (1996-2000 Models)

1. Remove the rear frame cover as described in Chapter Fourteen.

2. Unhook the turn signal relay (A, **Figure 167**) from the frame clip.

3. Disconnect the turn signal relay electrical connector and remove the relay.

4. Connect the connector to the new relay, and install the relay onto the frame clip.

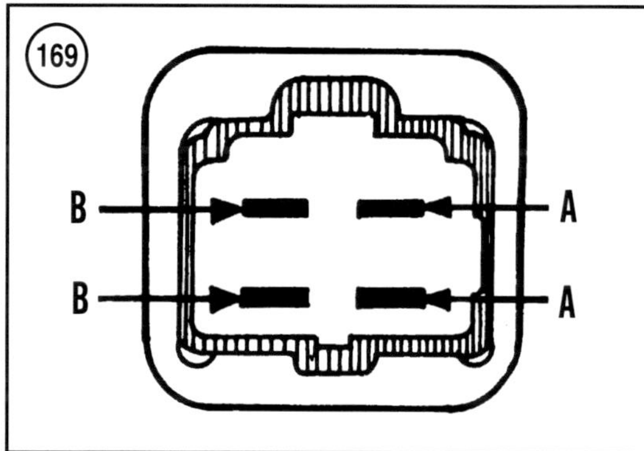

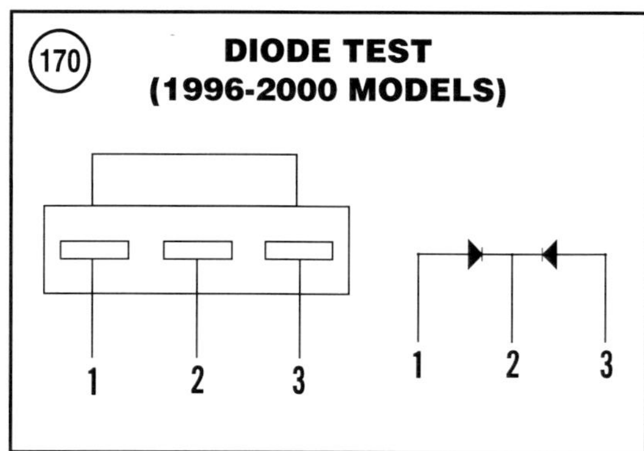

Turn Signal/Sidestand Relay Replacement (2001-on Models)

1. Remove the seat as described in Chapter Fourteen.
2. Remove the turn signal/sidestand relay (**Figure 168**) from the mounting clip.
3. Disconnect the electrical connector from the relay assembly.
4. Connect the connector to a new relay assembly.
5. Install the relay assembly onto the mounting clip.

Sidestand Relay Testing (1996-2000 Models)

1. Remove the seats and rear frame cover as described in Chapter Fourteen.

2. Disconnect the battery negative lead as described in this chapter.

3. Pull straight up and remove the sidestand relay (B, **Figure 167**) from the rubber mount on the rear frame.

4. Disconnect the electrical connector from the relay.

5. Connect a 12-volt battery to the A terminals on the relay (**Figure 169**).

6. Use an ohmmeter and check the continuity between the B terminals on the relay. There should be continuity.

7. If the relay fails this test, the relay is faulty and must be replaced. If the relay is good, reconnect the electrical connector and install the relay onto the rubber mount on the rear frame.

Sidestand/Ignition Interlock Diode Testing (1996-2000 Models)

1. Remove the seats and rear cowl as described in Chapter Fifteen.

2. Disconnect the negative battery cable as described in this chapter.

3. Disconnect the electrical connector from the diode (C, **Figure 167**) and remove the diode.

4. Use an ohmmeter and check the continuity between terminals 1 and 2 (**Figure 170**) in the diode. Reverse the test probes and again check the continuity. The diode should have continuity in one direction but no continuity in the other. Replace the diode if these two readings are the same.

5. Use an ohmmeter and check the continuity between terminals 2 and 3 (**Figure 170**). Reverse the test probes and again check the continuity. The diode should have continuity in one direction but no continuity in the other. Replace the diode if these two readings are the same.

6. If the diode fails this test, it must be replaced. If the diode is good, reconnect the electrical connector and install the relay onto the rubber mount on the rear frame.

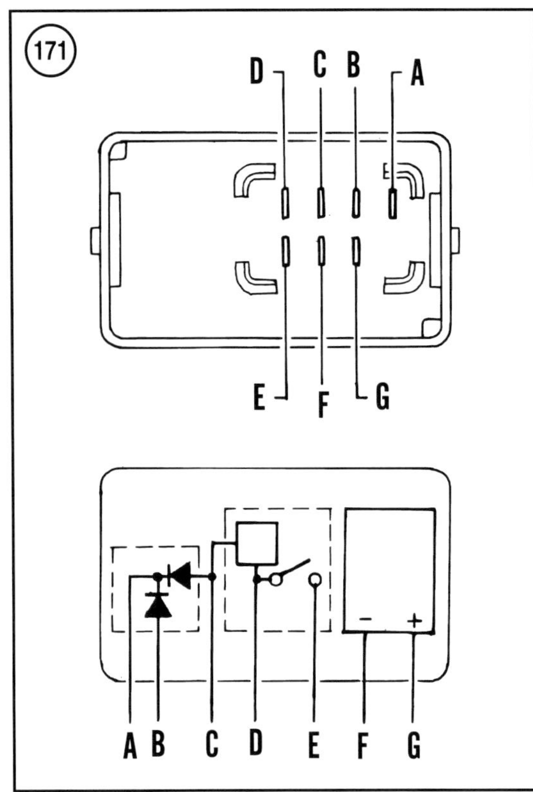

172

TURN SIGNAL/SIDESTAND SWITCH RELAY TEST (2001-ON MODELS)

	+ Probe of tester to:	
- Probe of tester to:	C, B	A
C, B		1.4-1.5
A	0.4-0.6	

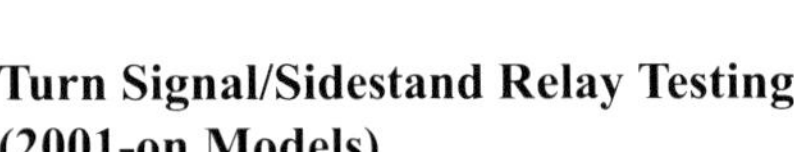

Turn Signal/Sidestand Relay Testing (2001-on Models)

1. Remove the turn-signal/sidestand relay as previously described in this chapter.
2. Set the Suzuki Multi-Circuit Tester (part No. 09900-25008) to diode test.
3. Refer to **Figure 171** and measure the voltage across the diode terminals indicated in **Figure 172**.
4. Replace the turn-signal/sidestand relay if any measurement is outside the range specified in **Figure 172**.

ELECTRICAL COMPONENTS

This section contains information on all electrical components except switches and relays.

COMBINATION METER

Inspection

1. On GSF1200S models, remove the front fairing as described in Chapter Fourteen.

2A. On 1996-2000 models, disconnect the 12-pin electrical connector (**Figure 173**).

2B. On 2001-on models, disconnect the ten-pin and six-pin electrical connectors (**Figure 174**) from the wiring harness.

3. Refer to the table in **Figure 175** or **Figure 176** and check the continuity in the affected circuit.

   a. Set an ohmmeter to the R × 1 scale, and connect the test probes to the terminals indicated in the table.

   b. The circuit should have continuity.

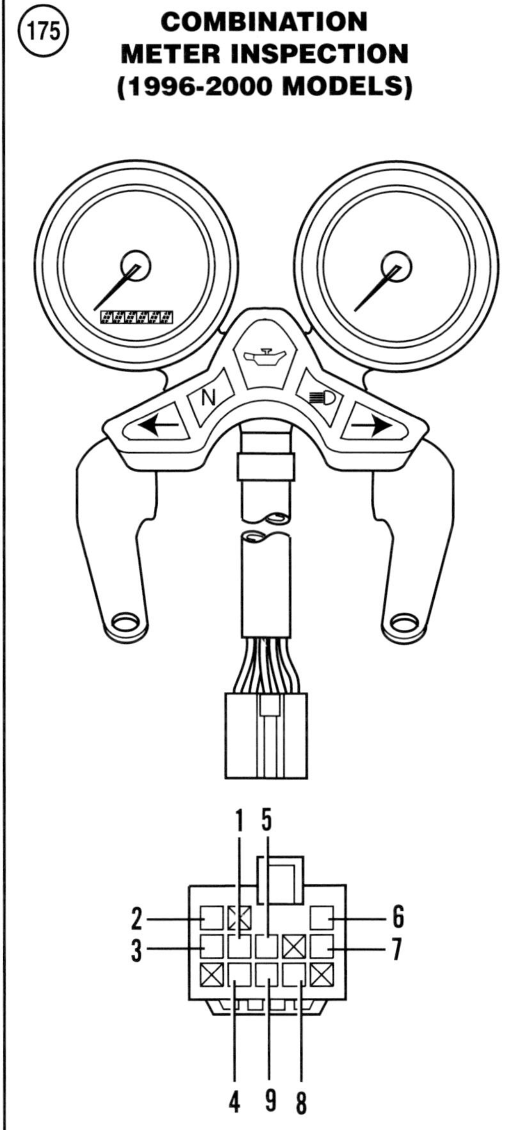

ITEM	Positive (+) test probe	Negative (-) test probe
Oil	2	5
Turn (L)	6	8
Turn (R)	7	8
Tachometer signal	3	8
High beam	1	8
Neutral	2	9
Illumination	4	8
Tachometer	2	8

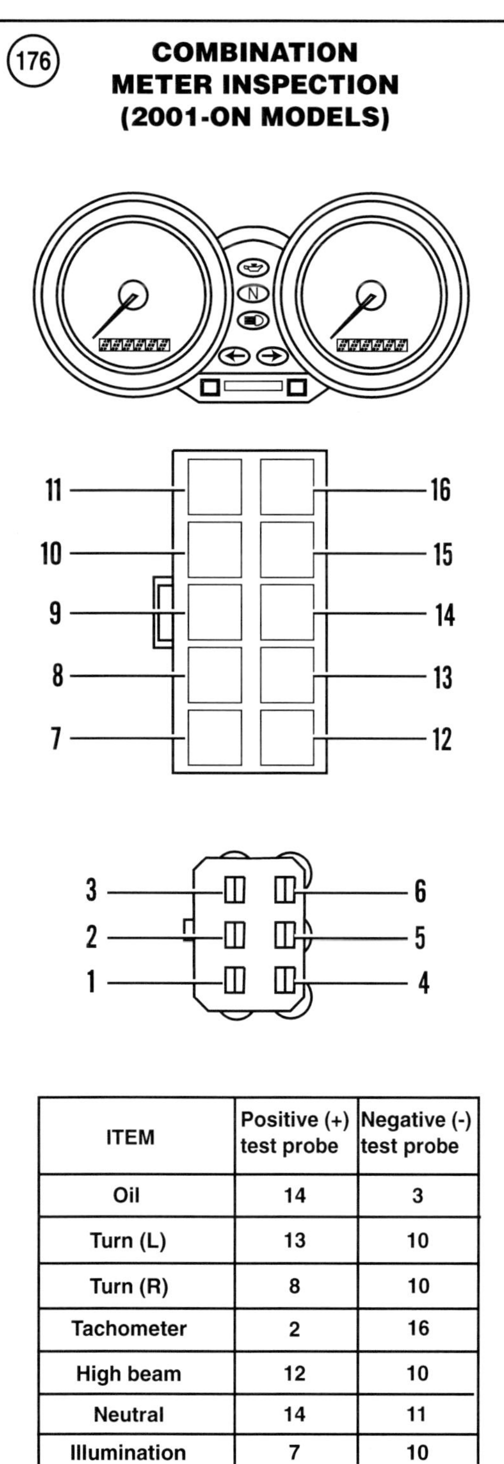

ITEM	Positive (+) test probe	Negative (-) test probe
Oil	14	3
Turn (L)	13	10
Turn (R)	8	10
Tachometer	2	16
High beam	12	10
Neutral	14	11
Illumination	7	10

177

COMBINATION METER (1996-2000 MODELS)

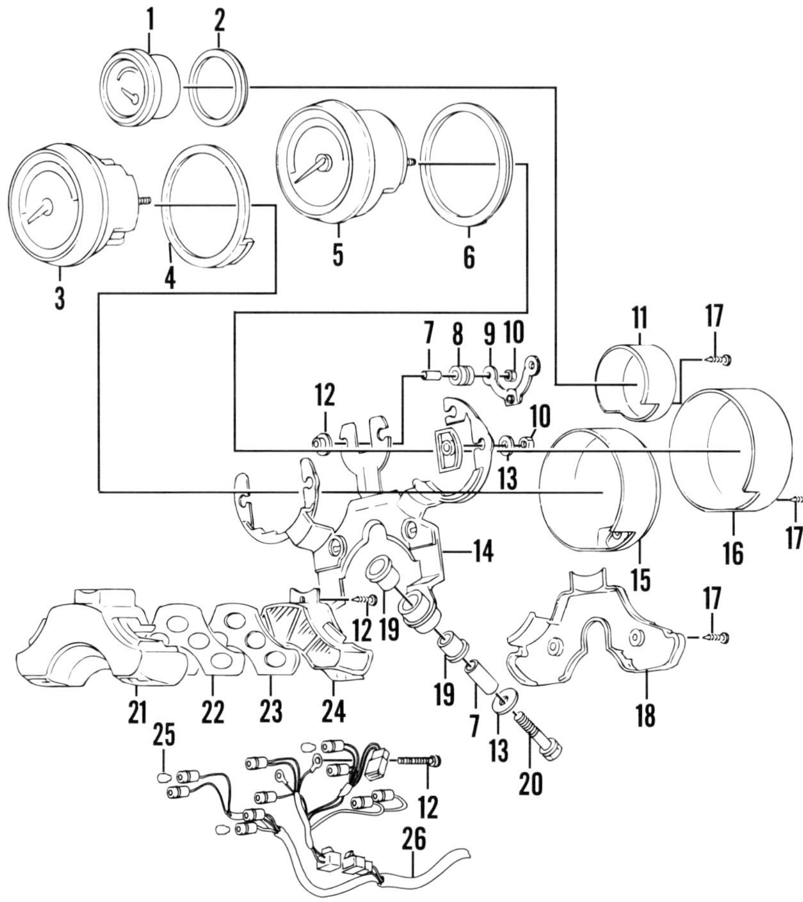

1. Fuel level gauge
2. Damper
3. Speedometer
4. Damper
5. Tachometer
6. Damper
7. Collar
8. Rubber cushion
9. Setting plate
10. Nut
11. Fuel level gauge cover
12. Nut
13. Washer
14. Meter mounting bracket
15. Speedometer cover
16. Tachometer cover
17. Screw
18. Indicator panel cover
19. Cushion
20. Bolt
21. Indicator panel upper case
22. Lens
23. Gasket
24. Indicator panel lower case
25. Bulb
26. Electrical harness

4. If the circuit does not have continuity, replace the indicator bulb, or LED, and repeat the continuity test.
5. If the circuit still does not have continuity, inspect the connector for loose or broken wires.
6. If this does not resolve the problem, replace the combination meter.

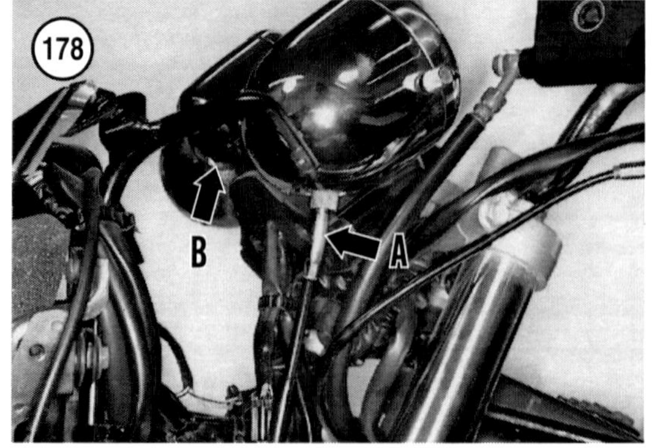

Removal/Installation (1996-2000 Models)

Refer to **Figure 177**.

(179) **COMBINATION METER (2001-ON MODELS)**

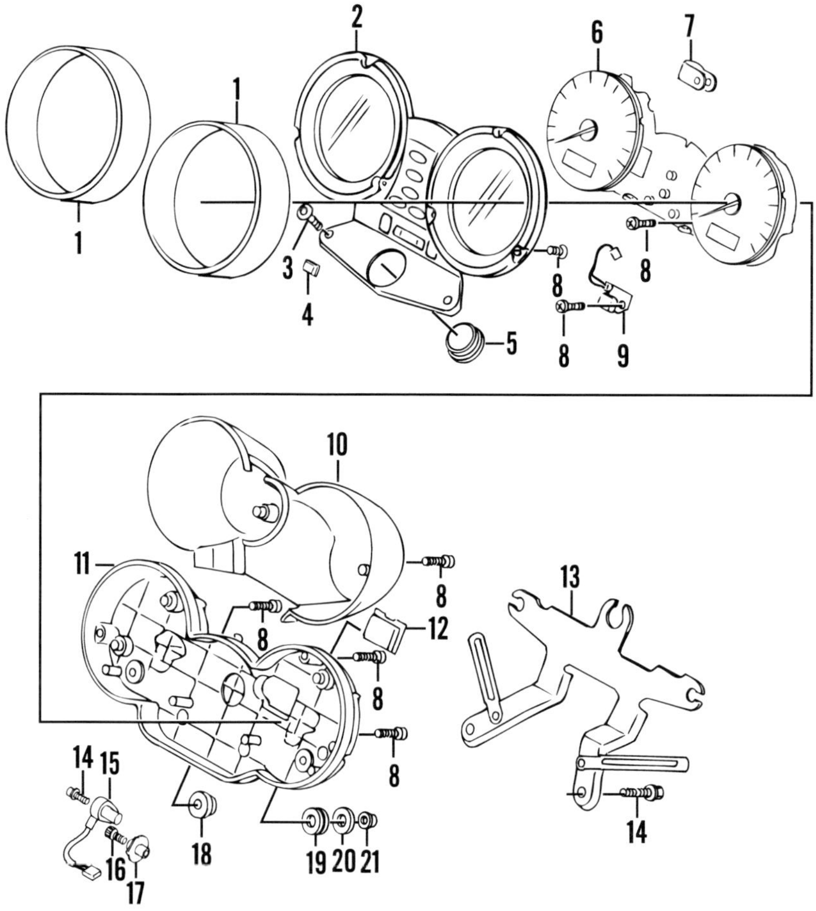

1. Trim ring
2. Upper case
3. Screw
4. Switch cover
5. Damper
6. Meter assembly/ printed circuit board
7. Cable clamp
8. Screw
9. Switch
10. Cover
11. Lower case
12. Grommet
13. Mounting bracket
14. Bolt
15. Speed sensor (at transmission shaft)
16. Bolt
17. Speed rotor
18. Nut
19. Damper
20. Washer
21. Nut

1. Disconnect the negative battery cable.

2A. On GSF1200 models, remove the headlight assembly as described in this chapter.

2B. On GSF1200S models, remove the front fairing as described in Chapter Fourteen.

3. Disconnect the combination meter 14-pin electrical connector.

4. Unscrew the speedometer drive cable (A, **Figure 178**) from the back of the speedometer.

5. Remove the fasteners securing the mounting bracket to the fork bridge.

6. Remove the combination meter assembly (B, **Figure 178**).

7. Install by reversing these removal steps while noting the following:

   a. Tighten all fasteners securely.

   b. Make sure the electrical connector is corrosion-free and secure.

Removal/Installation (2001-on Models)

Refer to **Figure 179**.

1. Disconnect the negative battery cable.

2A. On GSF1200 models, remove the headlight assembly as described in this chapter.

2B. On GSF1200S models, perform the following:

a. Remove the front fairing as described in Chapter Fourteen.

b. Remove the headlight assembly as described in this chapter.

3. Disconnect the two combination meter ten-pin and six-pin electrical connectors (**Figure 174**).

4. Remove the two nuts (**Figure 180**) securing the combination meter to the bracket and remove the meter assembly.

5. Install by reversing these removal steps while noting the following:

a. Tighten the nuts securely.

b. Make sure the electrical connectors are corrosion-free and secure.

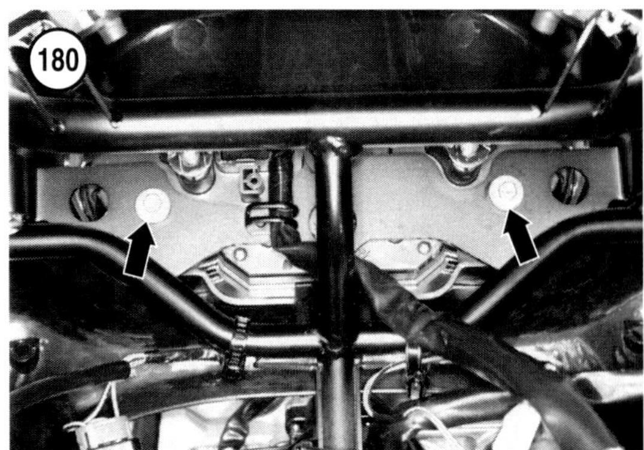

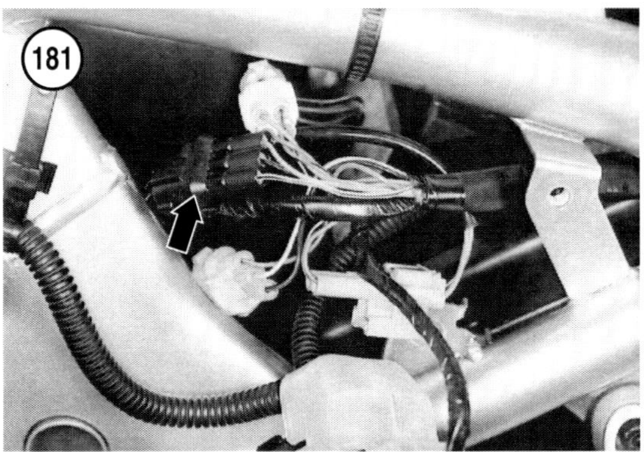

Speedometer Inspection (2001-on Models)

If the speedometer, odometer or trip meter do not function properly, inspect the speed sensor and its connectors as in this chapter. If the speed sensor functions properly, replace the combination meter.

Speed Sensor Inspection (2001-on Models)

1. Remove the left side cover as described in Chapter Fourteen.

2. Disconnect the three-pin speed sensor connector (one black/red wire, one black/white wire and one black wire) (**Figure 181**).

3. Remove the mounting screw and remove the speed sensor (**Figure 182**) from the engine sprocket cover.

4. Connect the negative battery terminal to the black/white terminal in the sensor side of the connector and connect the positive battery terminal to the black terminal (**Figure 183**).

5. Connect a 10 k ohm resistor to the black/red and black terminals on the sensor side of the connector.

6. Connect a voltmeter across the resistor as shown in **Figure 183**.

NOTE

When testing, the highest voltage reading should be the same as battery voltage (12 volts).

7. Move a screwdriver across the pick-up surface of the sensor and watch the voltmeter. The voltage reading should change from 0 to 12 volts or from 12 to 0 volts. If it does not, replace the sensor.

Oil Pressure Indicator Inspection (2001-on Models)

1. Drain the engine oil as described in Chapter Three.

2. Remove the signal generator cover bolts and remove the cover and its gasket (**Figure 164**). One

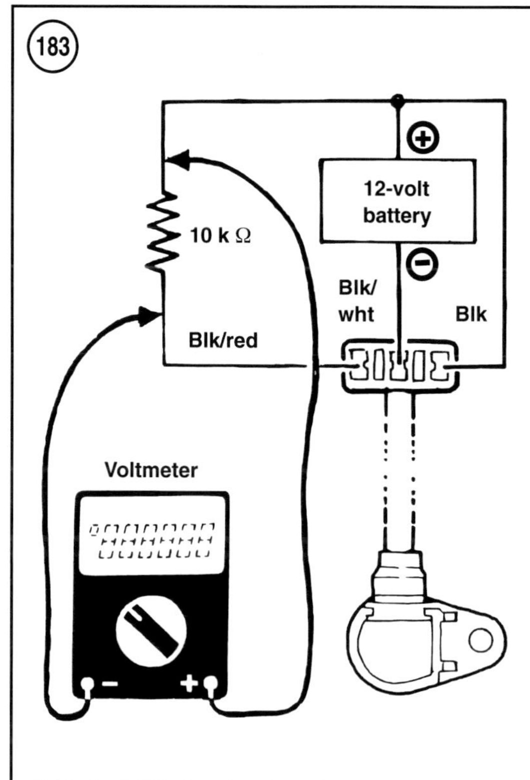

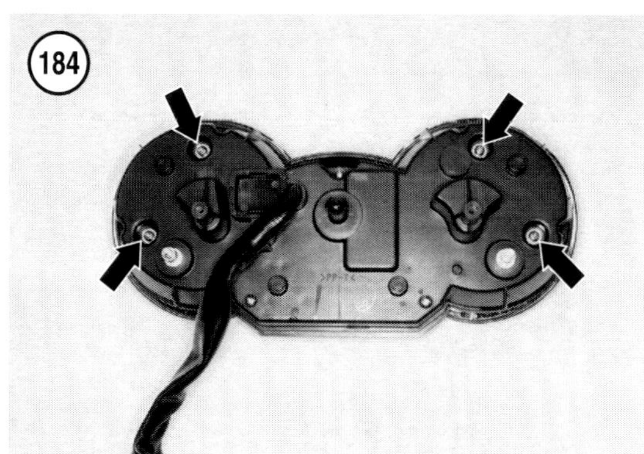

cover bolt has a sealing washer (**Figure 165**) installed beneath it. Note the position of this bolt. It must be reinstalled in the same location during assembly.

3. Disconnect the oil pressure switch green/yellow wire (A, **Figure 166**).

4. Turn the ignition switch to the ON.

5. Ground the oil pressure green/yellow wire and watch the oil pressure indicator. It should turn on.

6. If the oil pressure indicator does not turn on, check all electrical connections. If the connections are clean and tight, replace the oil pressure indicator lamp.

7. After replacing the lamp, repeat this test inspection. If the indicator lamp still does not come on; replace the oil pressure sending unit as described in this chapter.

8. Install the signal generator cover by performing the following:

   a. Apply a light coat of gasket sealer to the groove in the rubber grommet.
   b. Install a new signal generator cover gasket and install the cover. Install the bolt with the sealing washer (**Figure 165**) in the location noted during disassembly.
   c. Refill the engine oil as described in Chapter Three.

Speedometer/Tachometer Removal/Installation (1996-2000 Models)

Refer to **Figure 177**.

1A. On GSF1200 models, remove the headlight assembly as described in this chapter.

1B. On GSF1200S models, remove the front fairing as described in Chapter Fourteen.

2. Disconnect the combination meter 14-pin electrical connector.

3. Unscrew the speedometer drive cable (A, **Figure 178**) from the back of the speedometer.

4. Remove the fasteners securing the mounting bracket to the fork bridge.

5. Remove the combination meter assembly (B, **Figure 178**).

6. Remove the screw from the rear of the cover and remove the meter from its cover.

7. If the meter is being replaced, remove the indicator bulb socket and remove the screws securing the wiring to the meter.

8. Install by reversing the removal steps. Make sure the mounting boss on the meter aligns with the cutout in the meter cover, then install the meter cover screw.

Speedometer/Tachometer Removal/Installation (2001-on Models)

Refer to **Figure 179**.

1. Remove the combination meter as described in this chapter.

2. Remove the fasteners securing the upper case and remove the upper case assembly.

3. Remove the screws (**Figure 184**) securing the lower case to the meter assembly. Remove the lower case.

4. Replace the meter assembly (**Figure 185**) as a unit. Separate parts are not available.
5. Install by reversing the removal steps.

FUEL LEVEL GAUGE (1996-2000 MODELS)

Testing

To test the fuel level gauge, two separate tests must be performed. One additional test must be performed on the fuel level gauge sending unit.

Test No. 1

1. Remove the seat as described in Chapter Fourteen.
2. Remove the bolts securing the rear of the fuel tank.
3. Turn the fuel shutoff valve to the ON position.
4. Remove the screw securing the valve control knob and remove the knob (**Figure 186**).
5. Raise the rear of the fuel tank and place a wooden block under it to keep the tank in the raised position.
6. Reach under the fuel tank and disconnect the fuel level gauge sending unit electrical connector (**Figure 187**).
7. Turn the ignition switch to the ON position.
8. Connect a jumper wire to the harness side of the electrical connector (**Figure 188**). The gauge needle should indicate F (full).
9. If the gauge needle does not indicate F (full), perform Test No. 2.

Test No. 2

To check the fuel level gauge sending unit, perform the following:
1. Remove the fuel level gauge sending unit as described in Chapter Eight.
2. Connect an ohmmeter to the fuel level gauge sending unit and check in both the full and empty positions (**Figure 189**).
3. Record the ohmmeter readings in both positions and compare to those listed in **Table 1**.
4. If the readings are not within specification, replace the fuel level gauge sending unit as described in Chapter Eight.

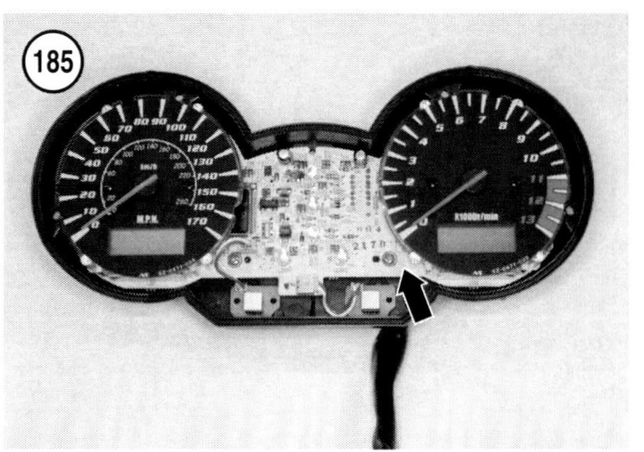
185

186

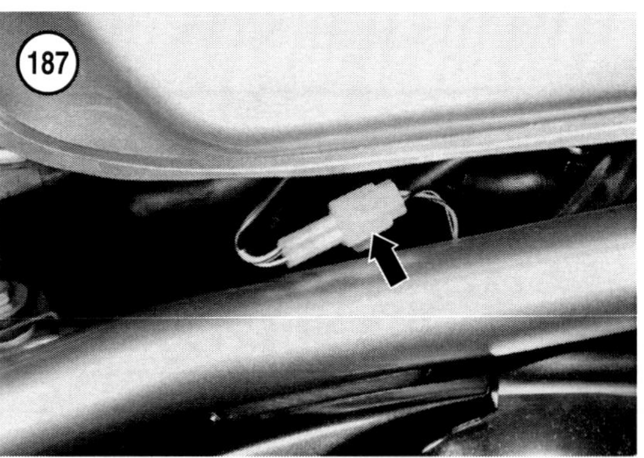
187

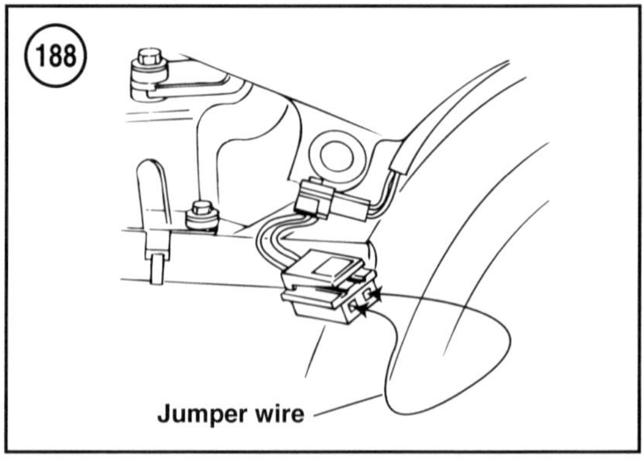

188

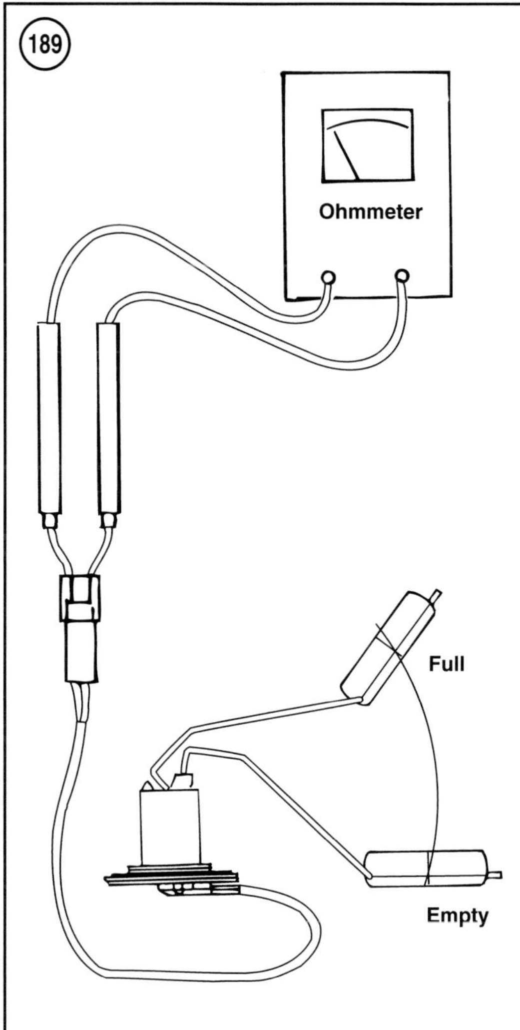

Test No. 3

1. Connect a known good fuel level gauge sending unit to the harness side of the electrical connector (**Figure 190**).
2. With the float in the lower position, the gauge should read E (empty).
3. With the float in the upper position, the gauge should read F (full).
4. If the fuel gauge does not indicate these readings with a good fuel level gauge sending unit, replace the fuel level gauge.
5. Remove the wooden block, lower the fuel tank and install the mounting bolts. Tighten the bolts securely.
6. Install the control valve knob and tighten the screw securely.

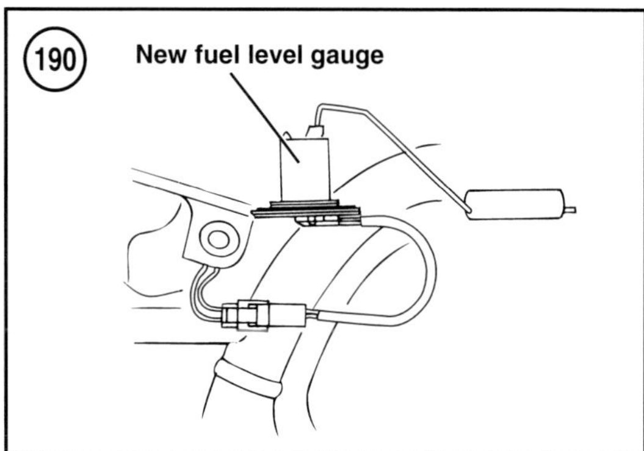

7. Install the seat as described in Chapter Fourteen.

FUEL LEVEL GAUGE (2001-ON MODELS)

Testing

To test the fuel level gauge, two separate tests must be performed. One additional test must be performed on the fuel level gauge sending unit.

9

Test No. 1

1. Remove the seat as described in Chapter Fourteen.
2. Remove the bolts securing the rear of the fuel tank.
3. Turn the fuel shutoff valve to the ON position.
4. Remove the screw securing the control valve knob and remove the knob (**Figure 186**).
5. Raise the rear of the fuel tank and place a wooden block under it to keep the tank in the raised position.
6. Reach under the fuel tank and disconnect the fuel level gauge sending unit electrical connector (**Figure 187**).
7. Turn the ignition switch to the ON position.
8. Connect a jumper wire to the harness side of the electrical connector (**Figure 191**). All five bars should indicate F (full).
9. If the gauge bars do not indicate F (full), perform Test No. 2.

Test No. 2

To check the fuel level gauge sending unit, perform the following:

1. Remove the fuel level gauge sending unit as described in Chapter Eight.
2. Connect an ohmmeter to the fuel level gauge sending unit and check in both the full and empty positions.
3. Record the ohmmeter readings in both positions and compare to those listed in **Table 1**.
4. If the readings are not within specification, replace the fuel level gauge sending unit as described in Chapter Eight.

Test No. 3

1. Connect a known good fuel level gauge sending unit to the harness side of the electrical connector (**Figure 192**).
2. With the float in the lower position, the gauge should read E (empty).
3. With the float in the upper position, the gauge should read F (full).
4. If the fuel gauge does not indicate these readings with a good fuel level gauge sending unit, replace the fuel level gauge.
5. Remove the wooden block, lower the fuel tank and install the mounting bolts. Tighten the bolts securely.
6. Install the control valve knob and tighten the screw securely.
7. Install the seat as described in Chapter Fourteen.

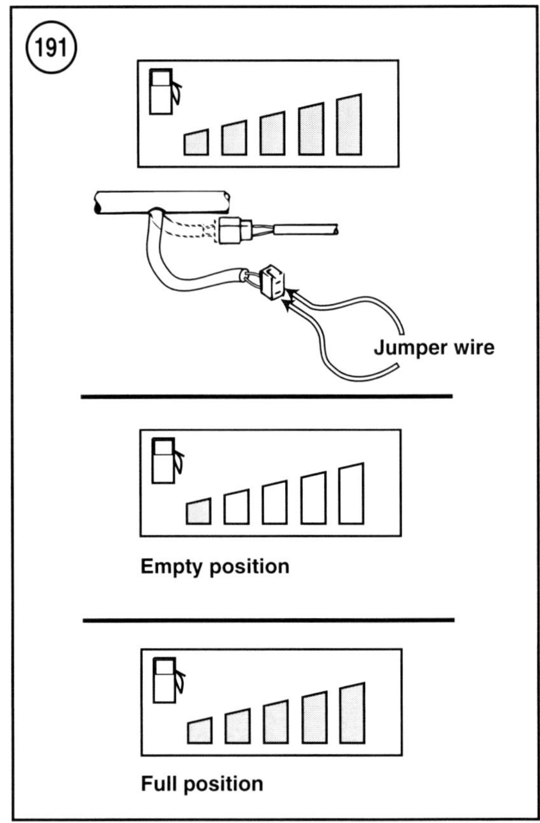

3. Remove the horn mounting bolt and remove the horn (B, **Figure 193**, typical).
4. Install by reversing these removal steps. Make sure the electrical connectors are corrosion-free and secure.

HORN

Testing

1. Disconnect the horn wires from the harness.
2. Connect a 12-volt battery to the horn.
3. If the horn is good, it will sound. If not, replace it.

Removal/Installation

1. The horn is located in various locations as follows:
   a. On GSF1200 models, the horn is on the left side of the lower fork bridge.
   b. On GSF1200S models, the horn is on the left side frame down tube below the front fairing.
2. Disconnect the electrical connector (A, **Figure 193**, typical) from the spade connectors on the horn.

FUSE BOX

On 1996-2000 models, the fuse box (**Figure 194**) is located under the seat, just behind the battery. On 2001-on models, it is located behind the seat latch (**Figure 195**).

Whenever a fuse blows, determine the reason for the failure before replacing the fuse. Usually, the trouble is a short circuit in the wiring. This may be caused by worn-through insulation or a disconnected wire shorted to ground.

CAUTION

Never substitute metal foil or wire for a fuse. Never use a higher amperage fuse than specified. An overload could result in a fire and complete loss of the motorcycle.

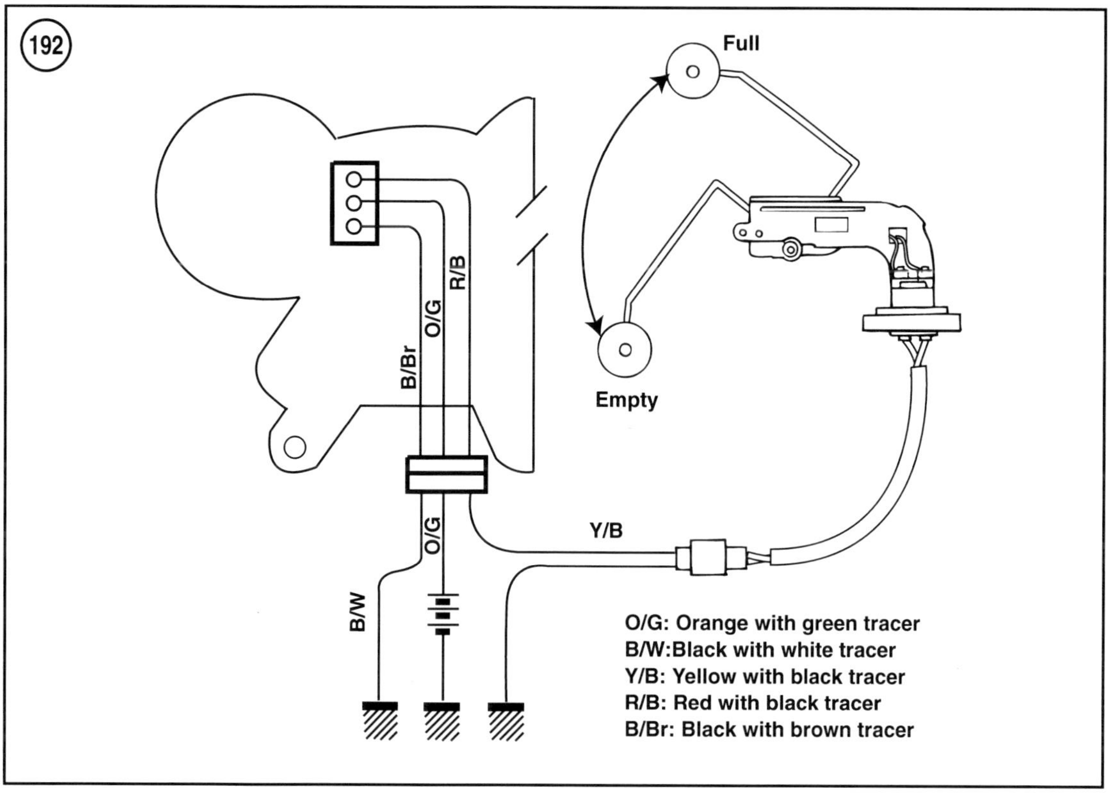

192

Full

Empty

B/Br O/G R/B

O/G

Y/B

B/W

O/G: Orange with green tracer
B/W:Black with white tracer
Y/B: Yellow with black tracer
R/B: Red with black tracer
B/Br: Black with brown tracer

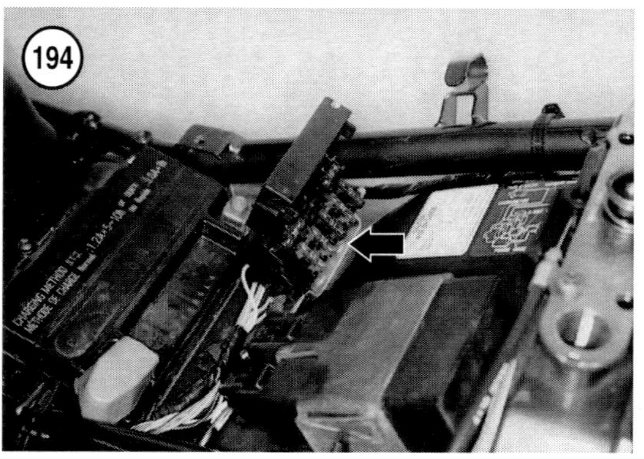

CAUTION
When replacing a fuse, make sure the ignition switch is in the OFF position. This will lessen the chance of a short circuit.

Fuse Replacement

1. Remove the seat as described in Chapter Fourteen.
2. Remove the fuse box cover (**Figure 195**, typical).

3. Remove the fuse (**Figure 196**) and inspect it. There is a spare fuse inside the fuse box.
4. Install the new fuse and push it all the way down until it seats completely, then install the cover.
5. Install the seat.
6. Replace the spare fuse as soon as possible.

MAIN FUSE

A 30-amp main fuse protects all electrical circuits. This fuse is located on the starter relay on the left side behind the left side cover.

1. Remove the seat and the left side cover as described in Chapter Fourteen.
2. Disconnect the negative battery cable as described in this chapter.
3. Pinch the two tabs and remove the cover (**Figure 197**) from the starter relay.
4. Remove the fuse (**Figure 198**) and inspect it.
5. Install the new fuse and push it all the way down until it seats completely, then install the starter relay cover.

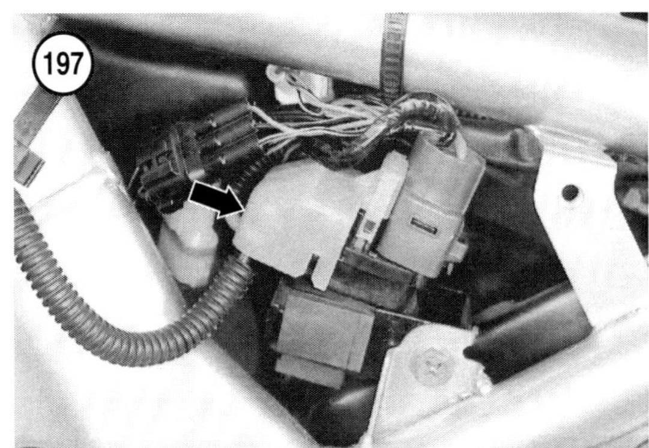

6. Install the left side cover and seat as described in Chapter Fourteen.
7. Replace the main fuse as soon as possible.

WIRING DIAGRAMS

Wiring diagrams for all models are located at the end of this manual.

Table 1 ELECTRICAL SYSTEM SPECIFICATIONS

Alternator	
Type	Three-phase AC
Regulated voltage (charging voltage)	
1996-2000 models	13.5 V @ 5000 rpm
2001 models	13.5-15 V @ 5000 rpm
Maximum output (2001 models)	
More than 550 W @ 5000 rpm	
Rotor slip ring outside diameter wear limit	14.0 mm (0.55 in.)
Brush length wear limit	4.5 mm (0.18 in.)
Battery	
Type	YTX12-BS Yuasa Maintenance-free
Capacity	12 volt 10 amp hour

(continued)

Table 1 ELECTRICAL SYSTEM SPECIFICATIONS (continued)

Circuit breaker (ABS models)	30 amp
Fuel level gauge (1996-2000)	
F (full) position	1-5 ohms
E (empty) position	103-117 ohms
Fuel level gauge (2001-on)	
F (full) position	8-10 ohms
E (empty) position	90-93 ohms
Fuse size	
Headlight (high and low beam)	15 amp
Turn signal	15 amp
Ignition	10 amp
Taillight	10 amp
Main	30 amp
ABS	10 amp
Ignition system	
Type	Fully transistorized
Firing order	1-2-4-3
Ignition timing	7° BTDC @1500 rpm
Ignition coil resistance	
Primary	2-4 ohms
Secondary	30,000-40,000 ohms
Coil primary peak voltage (2001-on models)	140 volts
Signal generator coil resistance	Approx. 135-200 ohms
Side stand switch	
Up position	04.-0.6 volts
Down position	1.4-1.5 volts
Signal generator peak voltage	1.0 V or greater
Starter relay resistance	3-5 ohms

9

Table 2 REPLACEMENT BULBS

Item	Wattage
Headlight (high/low beam)	
1996-2000 models	60/55 W
2001-on models	60/50 W
Position light*	4 W
Tail/brake light	
1996-2000	5/21 W
2001-on models	5/21 W × 2
Turn signal	21 W
License plate light	5 W
Tachometer light	
1996-2000 models	1.7 W
2001-on models	LED
Speedometer light	
1996-2000 models	1.7 W
2001-on models	LED
Neutral indicator light	
1996-2000 models	3 W
2001-on models	LED
High beam indicator light	
1996-2000 models	1.7 W
2001-on models	LED

(continued)

Table 2 REPLACEMENT BULBS (continued)

Item	Wattage
Turn signal indicator light	
1996-2000 models	4 W
2001-on models	LED
Oil pressure indicator light	
1996-2000 models	3.4 W
2001-on	LED

*Not used on U.S.A. California, Canada and Australia models

Table 3 ELECTRICAL SYSTEM TORQUE SPECIFICATIONS

Item	N•m	in.-lb.	ft.-lb.
Alternator driven gear nut			
1996-2000 models	60	–	44
2001-on models	55	–	41
Alternator mounting bolts	25	–	18
Oil pressure switch	14	–	10
Signal generator			
rotor bolt	25	–	18
Starter mounting bolts	6	53	–

Table 4 COLOR CODES

B	Black
W	White
O	Orange
R	Red
L	Blue
Y	Yellow
Sb	Sky blue or light blue
Lg	Light green

CHAPTER TEN

WHEELS, TIRES AND DRIVE CHAIN

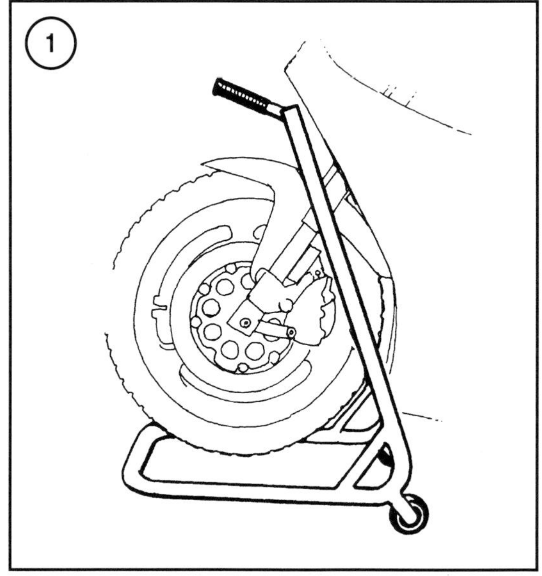

This chapter describes repair and maintenance procedures for the front and rear wheels, tires and the drive chain.

When inspecting any of the components addressed in this chapter, compare all measurements to the wheel, tire and drive chain specifications in **Table 1**. Replace any component that is damaged, worn to the wear limit or out of specification. During assembly, tighten fasteners to the torque specifications listed. **Table 1** and **Table 2** appear at the end of this chapter.

MOTORCYCLE STAND

Many procedures in this chapter require that the motorcycle be supported with a wheel off the ground. A quality motorcycle front end stand (**Figure 1**) or a swing arm stand does this safely and effectively. Before purchasing or using a stand, check the manufacturer's instructions to make sure the stand is designed for these models. If the motorcycle or the stand require any adjustment or accessories, perform the required modifications before lifting the motorcycle. When using a motorcycle stand, have an assistant standing by.

Regardless of the method used to lift a motorcycle, be sure the motorcycle is properly supported before walking away.

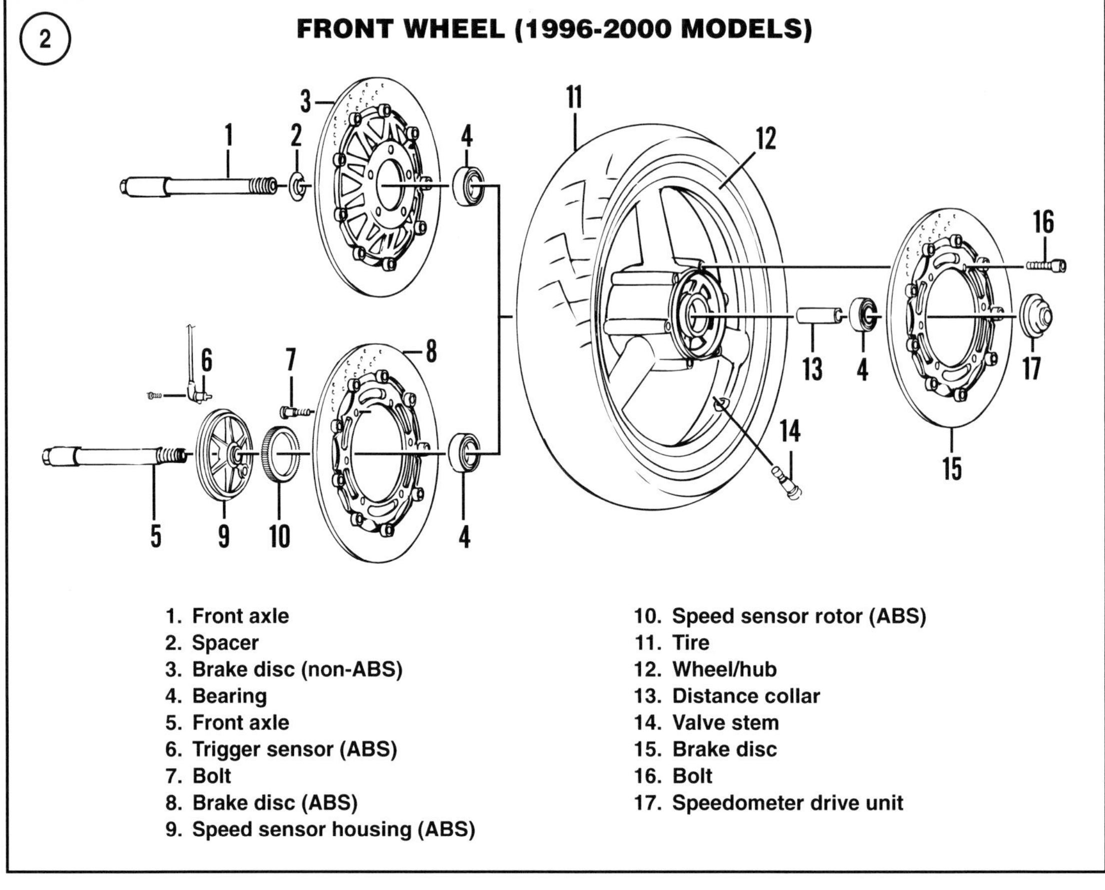

2 FRONT WHEEL (1996-2000 MODELS)

1. Front axle
2. Spacer
3. Brake disc (non-ABS)
4. Bearing
5. Front axle
6. Trigger sensor (ABS)
7. Bolt
8. Brake disc (ABS)
9. Speed sensor housing (ABS)
10. Speed sensor rotor (ABS)
11. Tire
12. Wheel/hub
13. Distance collar
14. Valve stem
15. Brake disc
16. Bolt
17. Speedometer drive unit

ABS MODELS

On ABS equipped models, take extra precautions when removing and installing both wheels to avoid damaging the ABS trigger speed sensors and speed sensor rotors attached to the hub. These components are relatively fragile and expensive to replace.

FRONT WHEEL

Refer to **Figure 2** and **Figure 3**.

Removal

CAUTION

Use care when removing, handling and installing a wheel with disc brake rotors. The rotors are relatively thin in order to dissipate heat and to minimize un-sprung weight. The rotor can withstand tremendous rotational loads, but it can be damaged when subjected to side impact loads. If the rotor is knocked out of true by a side impact, a pulse will be felt at the brake lever when braking. Motorcycle rotors are too thin to be trued and must be replaced. Protect the rotors when transporting a wheel to a dealership or tire specialist for tire service. Do not place a wheel in a car trunk or pickup bed without protecting both rotors from side impact.

1. Support the motorcycle on level ground on the centerstand.
2. Shift the transmission into gear to prevent the motorcycle from rolling in either direction.

CAUTION

On ABS equipped models, the ABS trigger sensor is attached to the right side fork slider. Do not damage the sensor or the wire attached to it during right side caliper and wheel removal. The speed sensor rotor and

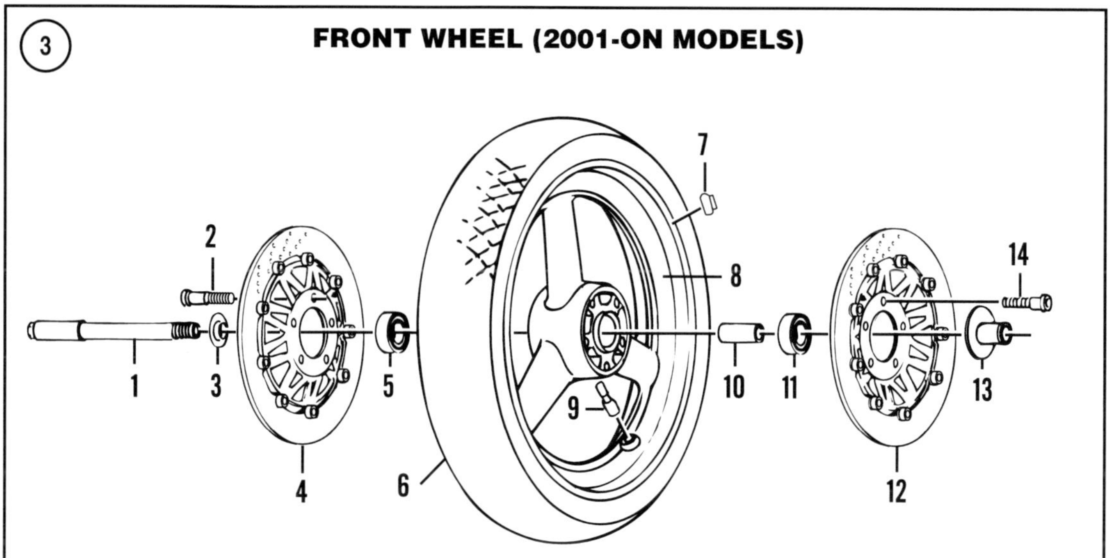

3

FRONT WHEEL (2001-ON MODELS)

1. Front axle
2. Bolt
3. Spacer
4. Brake disc
5. Bearing
6. Tire
7. Balance weight
8. Wheel/hub
9. Valve stem
10. Distance collar
11. Bearing
12. Brake disc
13. Spacer
14. Bolt

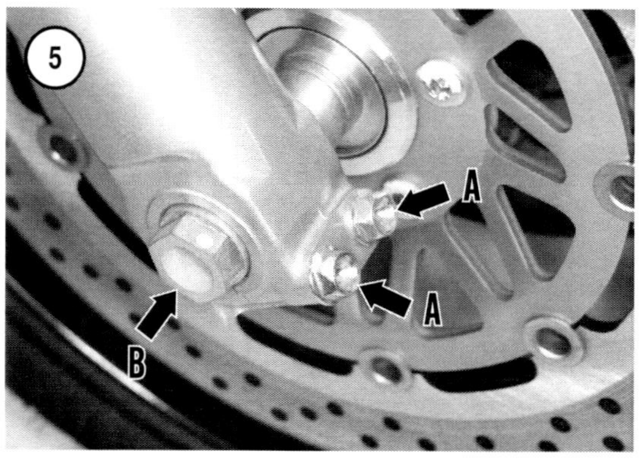

housing are very close to the sensor and can be easily damaged.

NOTE

Insert a piece of vinyl tubing or wood between the pads of each caliper once the caliper is removed. If the brake lever is inadvertently squeezed, the pistons will not be forced out of the cylinder. If this does happen, the caliper may have to be disassembled to reseat the pistons and the system will have to be bled. By using the wood, bleeding the brake is not necessary when installing the wheel.

3. Remove both brake calipers as described in Chapter Thirteen. Support the calipers with wire or bungee cords. Do not allow the calipers to hang from the hydraulic hoses.
4. On 1996-2000 models, remove the speedometer cable (**Figure 4**) from the speedometer drive housing.
5. On the right fork leg, loosen both axle pinch bolts (A, **Figure 5**) and then loosen the front axle (B).

CAUTION

If using a jack, place a piece of wood on the jack pad to protect the oil pan.

6. Place a suitable size jack or wooden blocks under the oil pan to support the motorcycle securely with the front wheel off the ground.
7. Completely unscrew the axle from the left fork slider and remove the axle.
8. Pull the wheel down and forward and remove the wheel from the front fork.
9. On ABS equipped models, pull straight up and remove the speed sensor housing from the right side of the hub.
10A. On 1996-2000 models, perform the following:
   a. Remove the right side spacer (non-ABS models).
   b. Remove the speedometer drive unit from the left side of the hub.
10B. On 2001-on models, perform the following:
   a. Remove the right side spacer (**Figure 6**).
   b. Remove the left side spacer (**Figure 7**).

CAUTION
Set the tire sidewalls on two wooden blocks. Do not set the wheel down on the disc surface. The disc could be scratched or warped.

11. Inspect the wheel as described in this chapter.

6

7

Installation

1. Make sure the bearing surfaces of each fork slider, the spacer(s) and the axle are free of burrs and nicks.
2. Correctly position the wheel so the directional arrow points in the direction of normal wheel rotation (**Figure 8**).
3. On ABS equipped models, install the speed sensor housing into the right side of the hub. Push it down until it bottoms.
4A. On 1996-2000 models, perform the following:
   a. Install the right side spacer (non-ABS models).
   b. Align the arms of the speedometer drive gear with the cutouts in the front hub and install the speedometer drive housing onto the left side of the hub.
4B. On 2001-on models, perform the following:
   a. Install the right side spacer (**Figure 6**).
   b. Install the left side spacer (**Figure 7**).
5. Apply a light coat of grease to the front axle.
6. Position the wheel between the fork legs, lift the wheel and insert the front axle through the right side

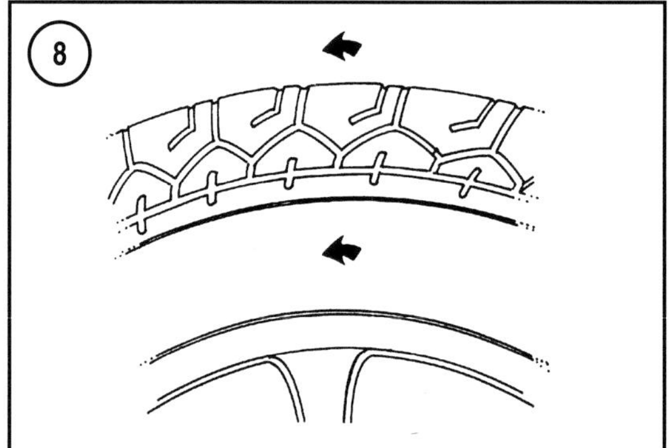
8

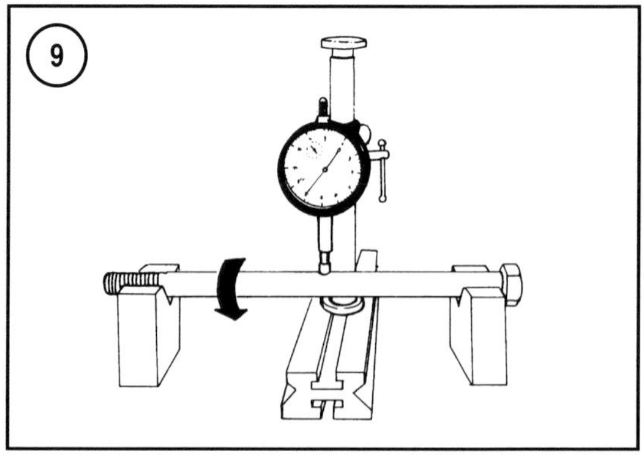
9

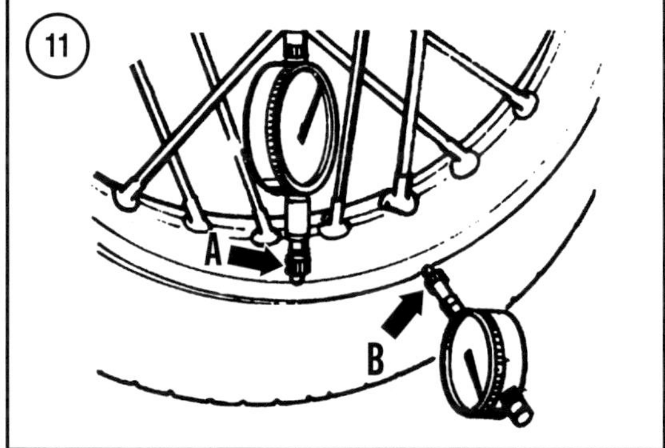

fork slider, the wheel hub and into the left fork slider.

7. On 1996-2000 models, rotate the speedometer drive housing until it rests against the boss on the left fork slider.

8. On ABS equipped models, align the groove on the speed sensor housing with the stopper on the right side fork slider.

9. Screw the axle (B, **Figure 5**) into the left fork slider and tighten the axle to 65 N•m (48 ft.-lb.).

10. Install both brake calipers as described in Chapter Thirteen.

11. Remove the jack or wooden block(s) from under the oil pan.

12. Apply the front brake, push down hard on the handlebars, and pump the fork four or five times to seat the front axle.

13. Tighten the front axle pinch bolts (A, **Figure 5**) to 23 N•m (17 ft.-lb.).

14. Shift the transmission into neutral.

15. Roll the motorcycle back and forth several times. Apply the front brake as many times as necessary to make sure all brake pads seat against the brake disc correctly.

Inspection

1. Remove any corrosion from the front axle with a piece of fine emery cloth. Clean the axle with solvent and then wipe the axle clean with a lint-free cloth.
2. Set the axle on V-blocks and place the tip of a dial indicator in the middle of the axle (**Figure 9**). Rotate the axle and check its runout. If axle runout exceeds the specified value, replace the axle; do not attempt to straighten it.
3. Check the disc brake bolts (**Figure 10**) for tightness on each disc. Tighten the brake disc bolts to 23 N•m (17 ft.-lb.) if necessary.
4. Check rim runout as follows:
   a. Measure the radial (up and down) runout of the wheel rim with a dial indicator as shown at A, **Figure 11**. If runout exceeds the specification in **Table 1**, check the wheel bearings.
   b. Measure the axial (side to side) runout of the wheel rim with a dial indicator as shown at B, **Figure 11**. If runout exceeds specification, check the wheel bearings.
   c. If necessary, replace the front wheel bearings as described in *Front and Rear Hubs* in this chapter.
5. Inspect the wheel rim for dents, bending or cracks. Check the rim and rim sealing surface for scratches that are deeper than 0.5 mm (0.01 in.). If any of these conditions are present, replace the rim.
6. Inspect the cover (**Figure 12**) portion of the right side spacer. Replace the spacer if the cover is bent, buckled or otherwise damaged.
7. On ABS equipped models, inspect the speed sensor rotor for worn or damaged teeth.

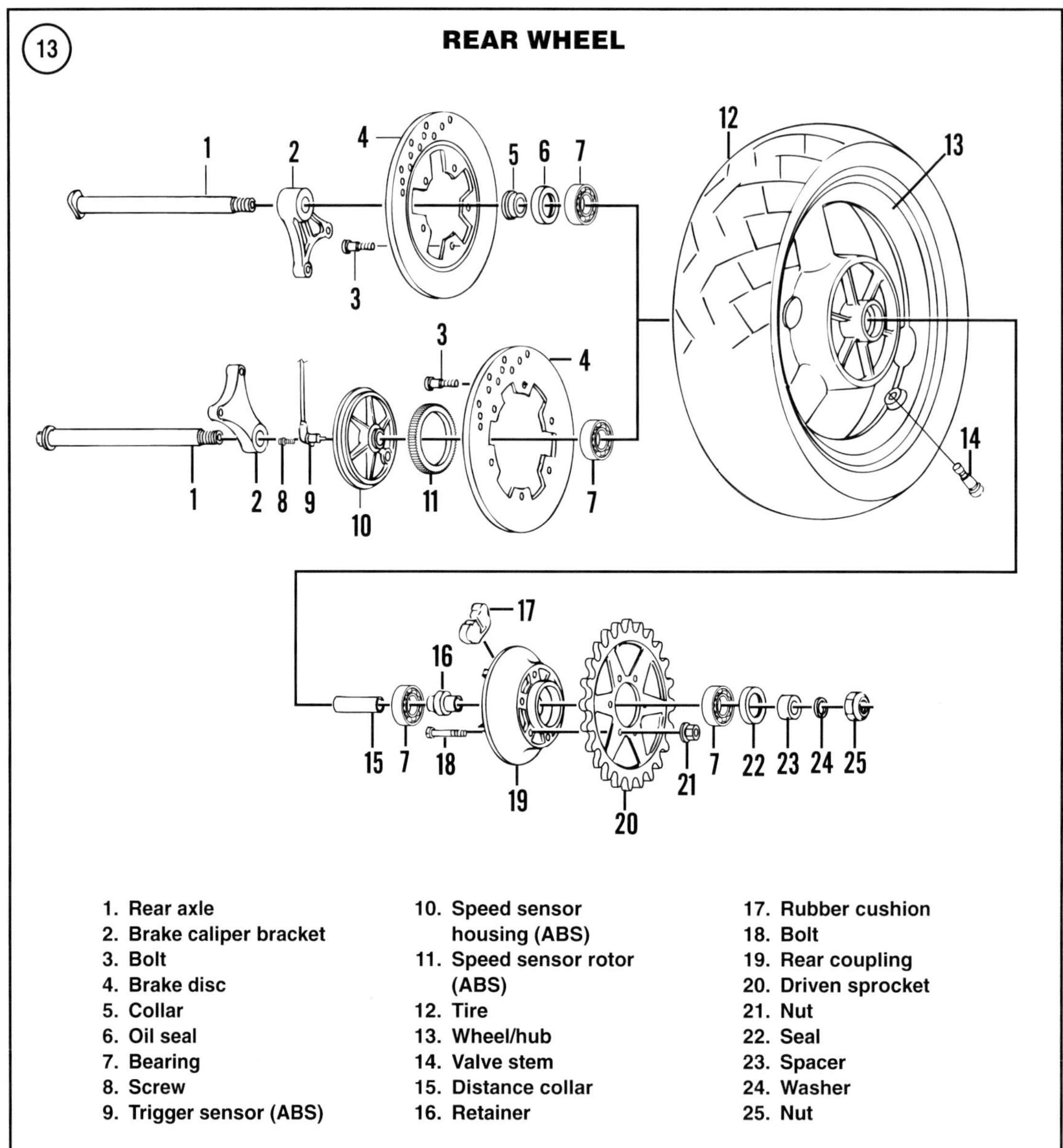

8. Since both front calipers are off the discs at this time, check the brake pads for wear. Refer to Chapter Thirteen.

Speedometer Drive Unit Inspection and Lubrication (1996-2000 Models)

NOTE

The speedometer drive unit is a sealed assembly. No replacement parts are available. If any part of the drive unit is defective, the entire assembly must be replaced.

1. Remove the front wheel as described in this chapter.
2. Inspect the seal for leakage.
3. Inspect the arms of the speedometer drive gear for wear or damage.
4. Inspect the cutouts in the front hub for wear or damage. Repair the hub or replace the wheel.
5. Install the front wheel as described in this chapter.

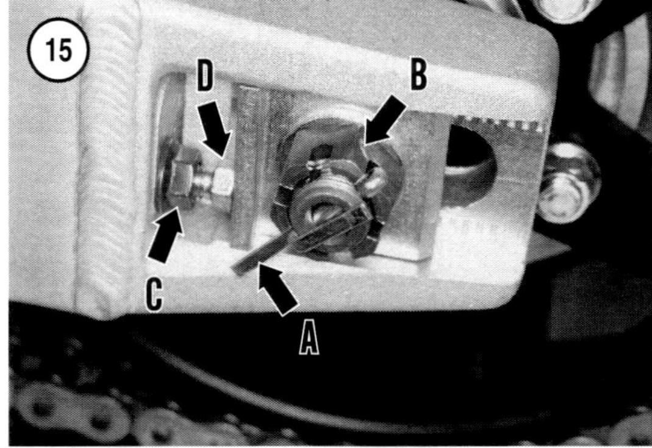

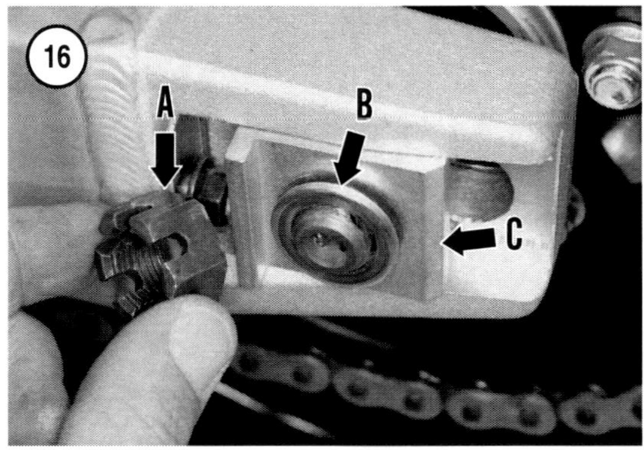

REAR WHEEL

Removal

Refer to **Figure 13**.

CAUTION
On ABS equipped models, the ABS trigger sensor is attached to the right side of the swing arm. The sensor must be removed prior to removing the wheel to prevent damage to the sensor.

NOTE
Insert a piece of vinyl tubing or wood into the caliper in place of the brake disc. If the brake pedal is inadvertently pressed, the pistons will not be forced out of the cylinders. If this does happen, the caliper may have to be disassembled to reseat the pistons and the system will have to be bled. By using the wood, bleeding the brake is not necessary when installing the wheel.

1. Support the motorcycle on level ground on the centerstand.
2. Remove the screws securing the drive chain guard (**Figure 14**). This allows for easy removal of the drive chain from the driven sprocket.
3. On models so equipped, remove the cotter pin (A, **Figure 15**) from the rear axle nut. Discard the cotter pin. A new one must be installed during assembly.
4. Have an assistant apply the rear brake, then loosen the rear axle nut (B, **Figure 15**).
5. Loosen the drive chain locknut (C, **Figure 15**) on both sides of the swing arm.
6. Loosen the chain adjuster (D, **Figure 15**) on each side of the swing arm and provide the maximum amount of slack in the drive chain.
7. Block the front wheel so the motorcycle will not roll in either direction while the motorcycle is on the centerstand.

CAUTION
If using a jack, place a piece of wood on the jack pad to protect the oil pan.

8. If necessary, place a suitable size jack or wooden blocks under the oil pan to support the motorcycle securely with the rear wheel off the ground.

WARNING
If the motorcycle has just been run, the muffler will be very ***hot****. If possible, wait for the muffler to cool down. If not, wear heavy gloves.*

9. Remove the rear axle nut (A, **Figure 16**) and washer (B).
10. Remove the drive chain adjuster plate (C, **Figure 16**) from the axle end.
11. Push the wheel forward and derail the drive chain from the rear sprocket.

12. Withdraw the rear axle (A, **Figure 17**) and drive chain adjuster plate (B).

13. Partially pull the wheel rearward and remove the spacer from the right side (**Figure 18**) (non-ABS models) and the left side (**Figure 19**) of the wheel.

14. The rear wheel rim is very wide and can be easily scratched if it makes contact with the brake caliper. Pivot the bottom of the wheel toward the left side and away from the caliper assembly and remove the wheel.

15. Lower the rear caliper and carrier to the ground.

16. On ABS equipped models, pull straight up and remove the speed sensor housing from the right side of the hub.

CAUTION

Set the tire sidewalls onto two wooden blocks. Do not set the wheel down on the disc surface, as it may get scratched or warped.

17. Inspect the wheel as described in this chapter.

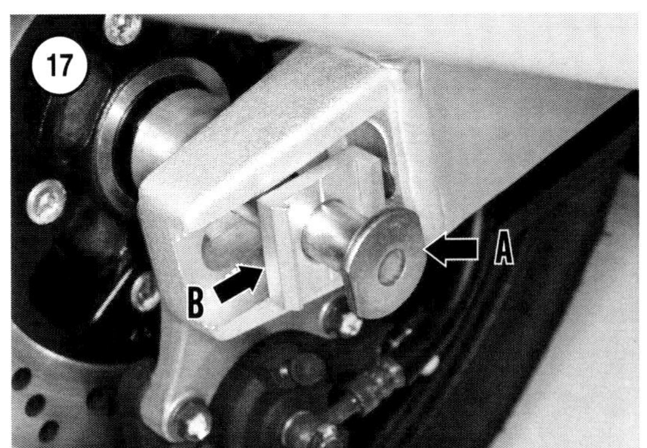

Installation

NOTE

*The drive chain adjuster plates are not symmetrical and must be installed on the correct side of the swing arm. Refer to A, **Figure 20** for the left side and B for the right side.*

1. Make sure all contact surfaces on the axle, swing arm, drive chain adjuster plates and spacers are free of dirt and burrs.
2. Apply a light coat of grease to the axle, bearings, spacers and grease seals.
3. On ABS equipped models, install the speed sensor housing into the right side.
4. Move the caliper assembly into place on the swing arm.
5. Partially position the wheel into place and roll it forward. Pivot the bottom of the wheel toward the left side and away from the caliper assembly and into position within the swing arm.
6. Install the spacer into the right side (**Figure 18**) (non-ABS models) and the left side (**Figure 19**) of the wheel.
7. Roll the wheel forward and install the drive chain onto the rear sprocket.
8. Raise the rear wheel up and into alignment with the swing arm.
9. Install the rear axle (A, **Figure 17**) and the drive chain adjuster plate (B). Push the rear axle through the caliper bracket, the wheel and the other side of the swing arm.

10. On ABS equipped models, align the lug on the speed sensor housing with the grooved stopper on the caliper mounting bracket.

11. Install the drive chain adjuster plate (C, **Figure 16**), washer (B) and the rear axle nut (A). Finger-tighten the nut at this time.

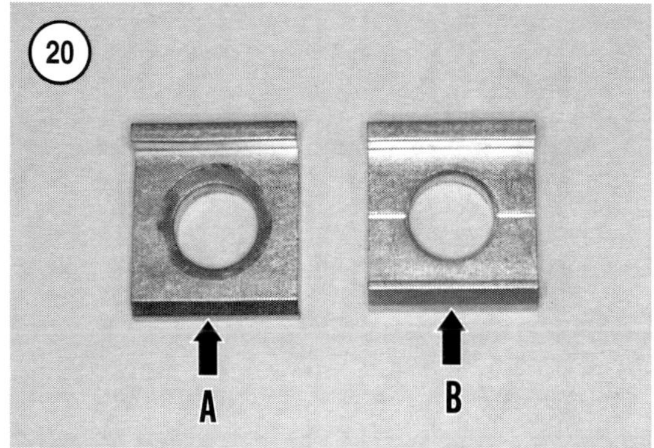

12. Adjust the drive chain as described in Chapter Three.

13. Tighten the rear axle nut to 100 N•m (74 ft.-lb.).

14. Install a new cotter pin onto the rear axle nut and bend both ends over completely.

15. If used, remove the jack or wooden block(s) from under the oil pan. Remove the blocks from the front wheel.

16. Roll the motorcycle back and forth several times. Apply the rear brake as many times as necessary to make sure the brake pads are against the brake disc correctly.

Inspection

NOTE
The rear wheel hub is equipped with a single oil seal that is located on the right side of the hub. The other oil seal is located in the rear coupling assembly on the left side.

1. If still in place, remove the right and left side axle spacers from the hub.
2. Clean the axle, spacers and caliper bracket in solvent to remove all old grease and dirt. Make sure all axle contact surfaces are clean and free of dirt and old grease prior to installation. If these surfaces are not cleaned, the axle may be difficult to remove later on.
3. Place the axle on V-blocks and place the tip of a dial indicator in the middle of the axle (**Figure 9**). Rotate the axle and check the runout. If axle runout exceeds specification, replace the axle; do not attempt to straighten it.
4. Check the disc brake bolts (**Figure 21**) for tightness. Tighten the bolts to 23 N•m (17 ft.-lb.).
5. Check the rear sprocket nuts (A, **Figure 22**) for tightness. Tighten the nuts to specification in **Table 2** if necessary.
6. Check rim runout as follows:
   a. Measure the radial (up and down) runout of the wheel rim with a dial indicator as shown at A, **Figure 11**. If runout exceeds specification, check the wheel bearings.
   b. Measure the axial (side to side) runout of the wheel rim with a dial indicator as shown at B, **Figure 11**. If runout exceeds specification, check the wheel bearings.
   c. If necessary, replace the rear wheel and/or rear coupling bearings as described in *Front and Rear Hubs* in this chapter.
7. Inspect the wheel rim for dents, bending or cracks. Check the rim and rim sealing surface for scratches that are deeper than 0.5 mm (0.01 in.). If any of these conditions are present, replace the rim.
8. On ABS equipped models, inspect the speed sensor rotor for worn or damaged teeth.

9. Since the rear caliper is off the disc at this time, check the brake pads for wear. Refer to Chapter Thirteen.

REAR COUPLING AND REAR SPROCKET

Refer to **Figure 13**.

Removal/Disassembly/Assembly/Installation

1. Remove the rear wheel as described in this chapter.
2. If still in place, remove the left axle spacer.
3. If the rear sprocket is going to be removed, loosen and remove the nuts (A, **Figure 22**) securing the rear sprocket to the rear coupling at this time.

NOTE

If the rear coupling assembly is difficult to remove from the hub, tap on the backside of the sprocket (from the opposite side of the wheel through the wheel spokes) with the wooden handle of a hammer. Tap evenly around the perimeter of the sprocket until the coupling assembly is free of the hub and the rubber dampers.

4. Pull straight up and remove the rear coupling assembly (B, **Figure 22**) from the rear hub.
5. Remove the retainer (**Figure 23**) from the rear coupling assembly.
6. Install by reversing these removal steps. Note the following:
   a. Align the rear coupling bosses (**Figure 24**) with the rubber damper receptacles (**Figure 25**) and install the rear coupling.
   b. If removed, install the rear sprocket so the side with the stamping faces away from the rear coupling.

CAUTION

On a new motorcycle or after a new rear sprocket has been installed, check the torque on the rear sprocket nuts after 10 minutes of riding and after each 10-minute riding period until the nuts have seated and remain tight. Failure to keep the sprocket nuts correctly tightened will cause the destruction of a very expensive rear hub.

23

24

25

26

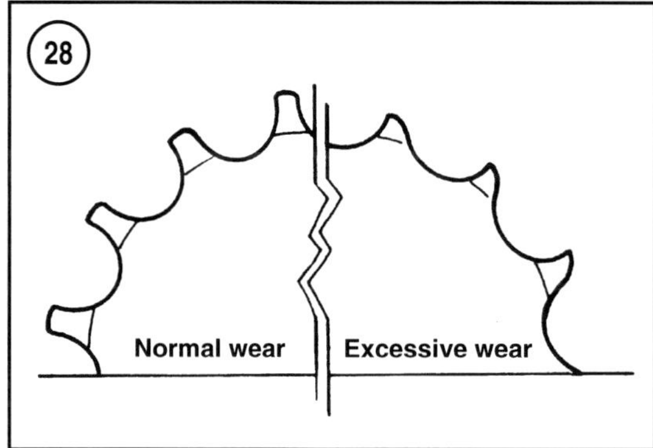

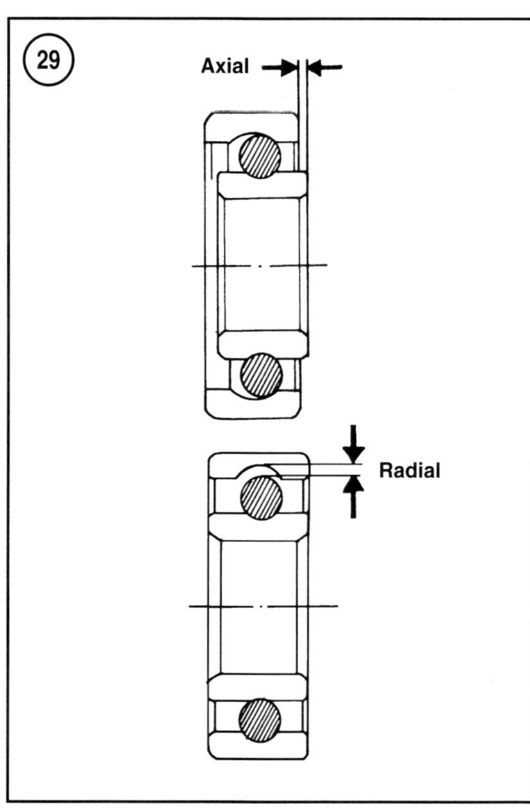

c. Tighten the rear sprocket nuts to the specification in **Table 2** after the assembly has been reinstalled in the rear wheel.

Inspection

1. Inspect the rubber dampers (A, **Figure 26**) for signs of damage or deterioration. If damaged, replace as a complete set.

2. Inspect the raised webs (B, **Figure 26**) in the rear hub. Check for cracks or wear. If any damage is visible, replace the rear wheel.

3. Inspect the rear coupling assembly for cracks or damage, and replace if necessary.

4. Inspect the rear sprocket teeth (**Figure 27**). If the teeth are visibly worn or undercut (**Figure 28**), replace the rear sprocket as described in this chapter.

CAUTION

If the rear sprocket requires replacement, also replace the engine drive sprocket and the drive chain. Never install a new drive chain over work sprockets or worn drive chain over new sprockets. The old part will wear out the new part prematurely.

5. If the rear sprocket requires replacement, also inspect the drive chain (Chapter Three) and engine sprocket (Chapter Seven). They also may be worn and need replacing.

6. Inspect the bearing for excessive axial play and radial play (**Figure 29**). Replace the bearing if it has an excess amount of free play.

7. On a non-sealed bearing, check the balls for evidence of wear, pitting or excessive heat (bluish tint). Turn the inner race by hand. The bearing must turn smoothly without excessive play or noise. A questionable bearing should be replaced. When replacing the bearing, be sure to take the old bearing along to ensure a perfect match.

NOTE

Fully sealed bearings are available from many bearing specialty shops. Fully sealed bearings provide better protection from dirt and moisture that passes through worn or damaged oil seals.

FRONT AND REAR HUBS

Preliminary Inspection

Inspect each wheel bearing prior to removing it from the wheel hub.

CAUTION
Do not remove the wheel bearings for inspection purposes. The bearings will be damaged during removal. Remove the wheel bearings only if they are to be replaced.

1. Perform Steps 1-3 of *Disassembly* in the following procedure.
2. Turn each bearing by hand. The bearings must turn smoothly with no roughness.
3. Inspect the play of the inner race of each wheel bearing. Check for excessive axial play and radial play (**Figure 29**). Replace the bearing if it has an excessive amount of free play.
4. On non-sealed bearings, check the balls for evidence of wear, pitting or excessive heat (bluish tint). Replace the bearings if necessary; always replace bearings as a complete set. When replacing the bearings, be sure to take the old bearings along to ensure a perfect match-up.

NOTE
Fully sealed bearings are available from many bearing specialty shops. Fully sealed bearings provide better protection from dirt and moisture that may get into the hub.

Disassembly

Refer to **Figures 2, 3** and **13**.

This procedure applies to both the front- and rear-wheel hub assemblies. Any differences between the two hubs are identified.

1A. Remove the front wheel as described in this chapter.

1B. Remove the rear wheel as described in this chapter.

2. On the rear wheel perform the following:
   a. If still in place, remove the left and right spacers from the hub.
   b. Remove the rear coupling from the hub as described in this chapter.

30

31

   c. Carefully pry the oil seal out of the right side of the rear hub and from the rear coupler (**Figure 30**). Place a shop cloth under the seal remover to protect the hub and coupling. Discard all removed oil seals. They cannot be reinstalled.

3. If necessary, remove the brake disc bolts (**Figure 21**) and remove the disc(s) from the wheel.

4. Before proceeding further, inspect the wheel bearings (**Figure 31**) as described in this chapter. If they must be replaced, proceed as follows.

5A. If the special tools are not used, perform the following:
   a. To remove the right and left bearings and distance collar, insert a soft aluminum or brass drift into one side of the hub.
   b. Push the distance collar over to one side, and place the drift on the inner race of the lower bearing.
   c. Tap the bearing out of the hub with a hammer, working around the perimeter of the inner race (**Figure 32**). Remove the bearing and distance collar.
   d. Repeat for the bearing on the other side.

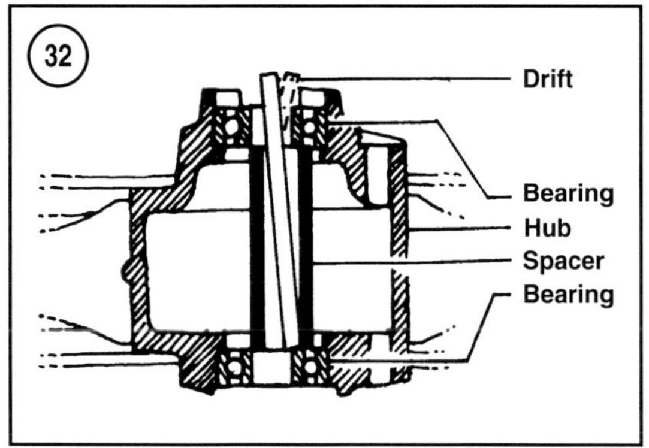

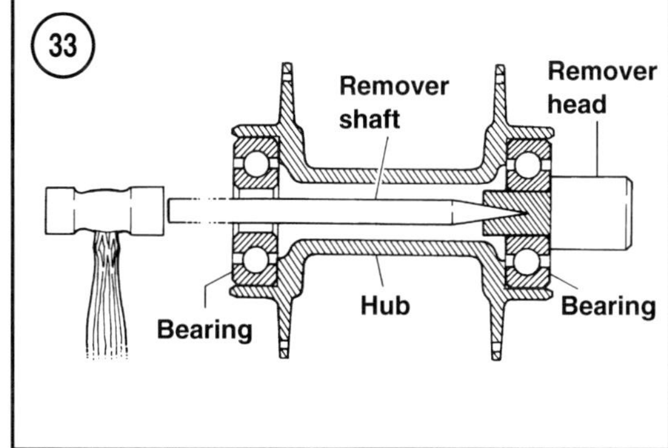

WARNING
Be sure to wear safety glasses while using the wheel bearing remover set.

NOTE
The Kowa Seiki Wheel Bearing Remover set can be ordered by any K & L Supply Co. dealer.

5B. To remove the bearings with the Kowa Seiki Wheel Bearing Remover set, perform the following:

a. Select the correct size remover head tool and insert it into the bearing.
b. Turn the wheel over and insert the remover shaft into the backside of the adapter. Tap the shaft and force it into the slit in the adapter (**Figure 33**). This will force the adapter against the bearing inner race.
c. Tap on the end of the shaft (**Figure 34**) with a hammer and drive the bearing out of the hub. Remove the bearing and the distance collar.
d. Repeat for the bearing on the other side.

6. Clean the inside and the outside of the hub with solvent. Dry with compressed air.

Assembly

CAUTION
*Always reinstall **new** bearings. The bearings are damaged during removal and must not be reused.*

NOTE
Replace bearings as a set. If any one bearing in a wheel is worn, replace all the bearings in that wheel. On the front wheel, replace both wheel bearings. On the rear wheel, replace both wheel bearings, as well as the rear coupling bearing.

1. On non-sealed bearings, pack the bearings with Suzuki Super Grease A or an equivalent good quality, waterproof bearing grease. To pack the bearings, spread some grease in the palm of your hand and scrape the open side of the bearing across your palm until the bearing is completely packed full of grease. Spin the bearing a few times to determine if there are any open areas; repack if necessary.
2. Blow any dirt or foreign matter out of the hub prior to installing the new bearings.
3. Apply a light coat of wheel bearing grease to the bearing seating areas of the hub. This will make bearing installation easier.

CAUTION
Install non-sealed bearings with the single sealed side facing outward. Tap the bearings squarely into place, tapping on the outer race only. Do not tap on the inner race or the bearing might be damaged. Be sure that the bearings are completely seated.

4A. A Suzuki bearing installer (part No. 09924-84510) can be used to install the *front wheel bearings* as follows:

NOTE
Install the left bearing into the hub first, and then install the right bearing.

a. Position the left bearing onto the hub with the sealed side facing out.
b. Set the old bearing on top of the new bearing and install the bearing installer as shown in **Figure 35**.
c. Tighten the bearing installer (**Figure 36**) and pull the left bearing into the hub until it is completely seated. Remove the bearing installer.
d. Turn the wheel over (right side up) on the workbench, and install the distance collar.
e. Position the right bearing onto the hub with the sealed side facing out.
f. Set the old bearing on top of the new bearing, and install the bearing installer as shown in **Figure 37**.
g. Tighten the bearing installer and pull the right bearing into the hub until there is a slight clearance between the inner race and the distance collar (**Figure 38**).
h. Remove the bearing installer.

4B. The Suzuki bearing installer (part No. 09941-34513) can be used to install the *rear wheel bearings* as follows:

NOTE
Install the right bearing into the hub first, and then install the left bearing.

a. Set the right bearing into the hub with the sealed side facing out and install the bearing installer as shown in **Figure 39**.
b. Tighten the bearing installer (**Figure 36**) and pull the right bearing into the hub until it is completely seated. Remove the bearing installer.
c. Turn the wheel over (left side up) on the workbench and install the distance collar.
d. Set the left bearing into the hub with the sealed side facing out and install the bearing installer as shown in **Figure 40**.
e. Tighten the bearing installer and pull the left bearing into the hub until there is a slight

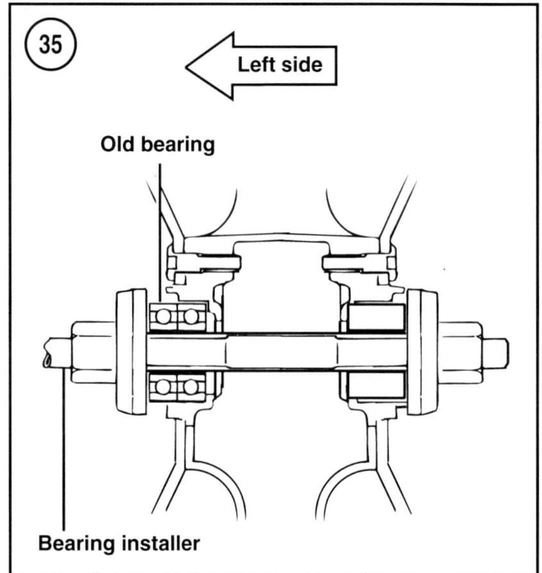

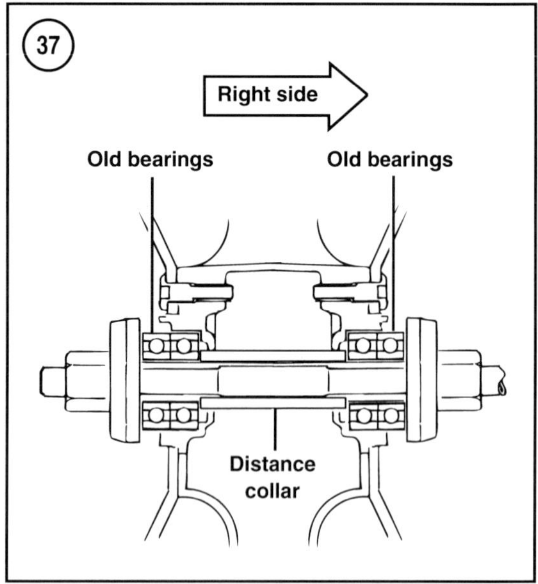

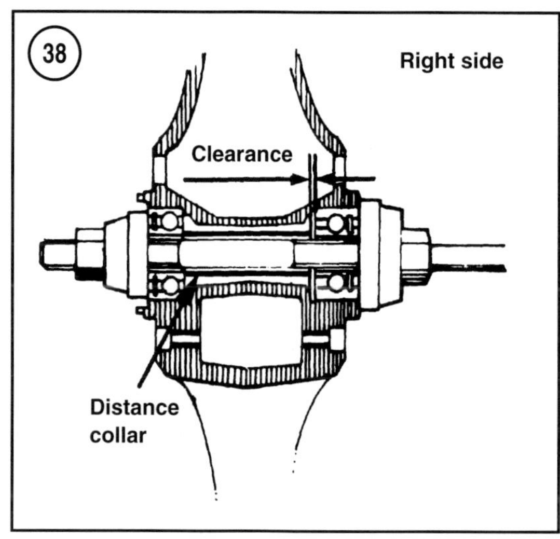

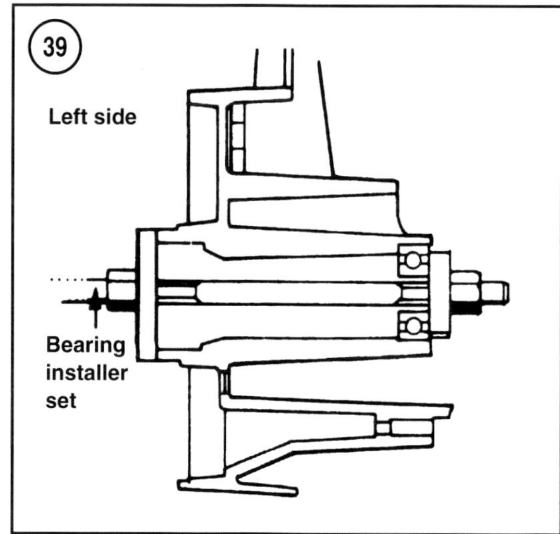

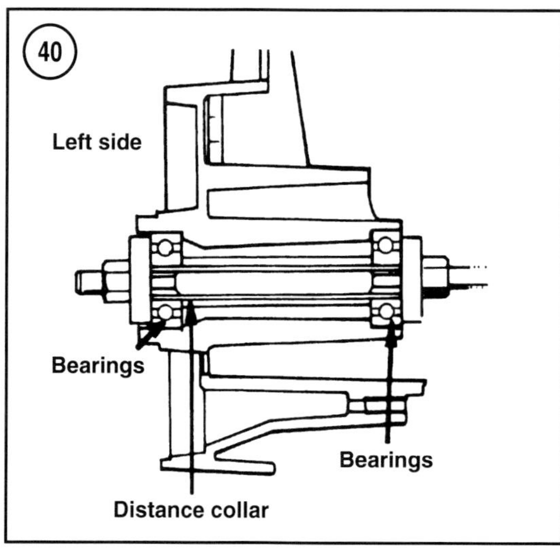

clearance between the inner race and the distance collar.

f. Remove the bearing installer.

4C. The Suzuki bearing installer (part No. 09913-75520) can be used to install the bearing into the rear coupling.

a. Set the bearing into the coupling with the sealed side facing out.
b. Place the bearing installer on top of the bearing.
c. Tap the installer and drive the bearing squarely into place in the rear coupling. Be sure that the bearing is completely seated.

4D. If Suzuki special tools are not used, use a socket or an aftermarket bearing installer tool and perform the following:

NOTE
On the front wheel, install the left bearing first.

a. Using a socket that matches the outer race diameter, tap the first bearing (left bearing on front wheel; right bearing on rear wheel) squarely into place in the hub. Tap on the outer race only (**Figure 41**). Do not tap on the inner race or the bearing might be damaged. Be sure that the bearing is completely seated.
b. Turn the wheel over on the workbench and install the distance collar.
c. Use the same tool set-up and drive the second bearing (right bearing on the front wheel; left bearing on the rear wheel) into the hub until there is a slight clearance (**Figure 38**) between the inner race and the distance collar.
d. Using a socket that matches the outer race diameter, tap the rear coupling bearing squarely into place in the rear coupling. Tap on the

outer race only. Do not tap on the inner race or the bearing might be damaged. Be sure that the bearing is completely seated.

5. Install a *new* seal into the hubs or into the rear coupling by performing the following:
   a. Pack grease to the lips of the new seal.
   b. Position the seal with the manufacturer's marks facing out.
   c. Use a tool with the same diameter as the seal and drive the seal into the mounting bore until it is flush with the top surface of the bore (**Figure 42**) or until it bottoms.
6. If the brake disc was removed, perform the following:
   a. Apply a small amount of a locking compound, such as ThreeBond No. TB1360 or Loctite No. 271, to the brake disc bolt threads prior to installation.
   b. Install the brake disc. Tighten the brake disc bolts 23 N•m (17 ft.-lb.).
7. Install the rear coupler onto the rear wheel.

8A. Install the front wheel as described in this chapter.

8B. Install the rear wheel as described in this chapter.

42

43

WHEELS

Wheel Balance

An unbalanced wheel is unsafe. Depending upon the degree of imbalance and the speed of the motorcycle, the rider may experience anything from a mild vibration to a violent shimmy that could lead to loss of control.

The balance weights attach to the rim on the Bandit. Weight kits are available from a motorcycle dealership. These kits contain test weights and strips of adhesive-backed weights that can be cut to the desired weight and attached to the rim.

Before attempting to balance the wheel, make sure that the wheel bearings are in good condition and properly lubricated. Also make sure that the brakes do not drag. The wheel must rotate freely.

NOTE

When balancing the wheels, do so with the brake disc(s) and the rear coupling attached. Also, on ABS equipped wheels, leave the speed sensor housing in place. These components rotate with the wheel and they affect the balance.

1A. Remove the front wheel as described in this chapter.

1B. Remove the rear wheel as described in this chapter.

2. Mount the wheel on a fixture such as the one shown in **Figure 43** so the wheel can rotate freely.

3. Give the wheel a spin and let it coast to a stop. Mark the tire at the lowest point with chalk or light colored crayon.

4. Spin the wheel several more times. If the wheel keeps coming to rest at the same point, it is out of balance.

5. Attach a test weight to the upper (or light) side of the wheel.

6. Experiment with different weights until the wheel, when spun, comes to rest at a different position each time.

7. Remove the test weight, thoroughly clean the rim surface, and then install the correct size weight onto the rim. Make sure it is secured in place so it will not fly off when riding.

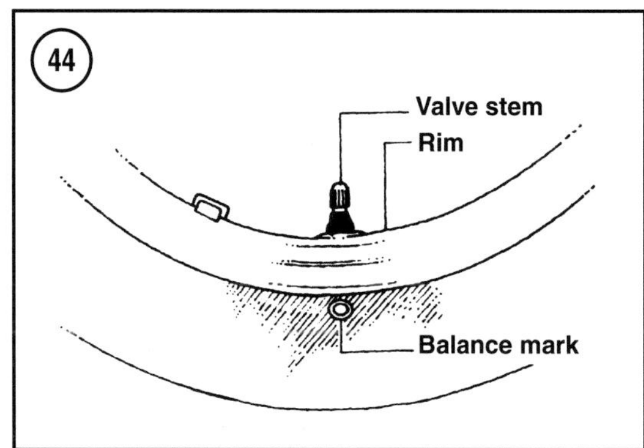

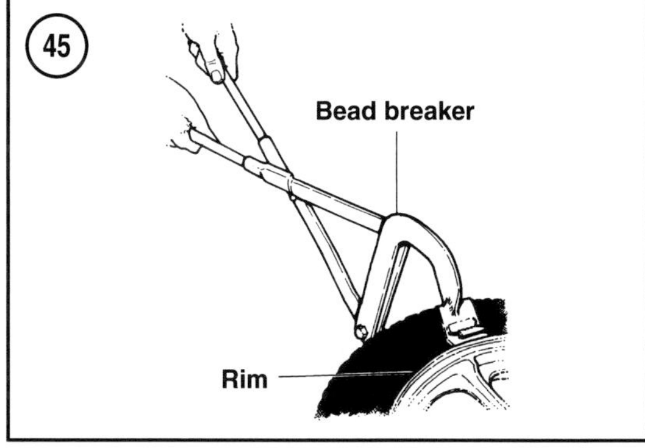

TIRES

Tire wear and performance is greatly affected by tire pressure. Have a good tire pressure gauge on hand and make a habit of frequent pressure checks. Maintain the tire pressure recommended in **Table 1** for original equipment tires. If using another tire brand, follow their recommendations.

Follow a sensible break-in period when running on new tires. New tires will exhibit significantly less adhesion ability. Do not subject a new tire to hard cornering, hard acceleration or hard braking for the first 100 miles (160 km).

Removal

The original equipment cast alloy wheels are designed for use with tubeless tires only. These wheels can easily be damaged during tire removal. Take special care to avoid scratching and gouging the outer rim surface, especially when using tire irons. Insert scraps of leather between the tire iron and the rim to protect the rim from damage.

When removing a tubeless tire, take care not to damage the tire beads, inner liner of the tire or the wheel rim flange. Use tire levers or flat-handle tire irons with rounded heads.

Many experienced riders who perform most of their own service choose to have tire service performed by a Suzuki dealership or sportbike specialist.

CAUTION

Suzuki recommends that the tires be removed with a tire changer. Due to the large and rigid tires, tire removal with tire irons can be difficult and result in rim damage. On the other hand, a pneumatic tire changer can easily break the beads loose, as well as remove and install the tire without damaging the cast wheel. The following procedure is provided if this alternative is not chosen.

NOTE

To make tire removal easier, warming the tire will make it softer and more pliable. Place the wheel and tire assembly in the sun. If possible, place the wheel assembly in a completely closed motorcycle. At the same time, place the new tire in the same location.

1A. Remove the front wheel as described in this chapter.

1B. Remove the rear wheel as described in this chapter.

2. If not already marked by the tire manufacturer, mark the valve stem location on the tire (**Figure 44**) so the tire can be installed in the same location for easier balancing.

3. Remove the valve core from the valve stem and deflate the tire.

NOTE

*Removal of tubeless tires from their rims can be very difficult because of the exceptionally tight tire bead-to-rim seal. Breaking the bead seal may require the use of a special tool (**Figure 45**). If the seal does not break loose, take the wheel to a motorcycle dealership or repair shop and have them break it loose on a tire changing machine.*

CAUTION

The inner rim and bead area are the sealing surfaces on the tubeless tire.

10

Do not scratch the inside of the rim or damage the tire bead.

4. Press the entire bead on both sides of the tire away from the rim and into the center of the rim.
5. Lubricate both beads with soapy water.

CAUTION

Use rim protectors or insert scraps of leather between the tire iron and the rim to protect the rim from damage.

NOTE

Use only quality tire irons without sharp edges. If necessary, file the ends of the tire irons to remove rough edges.

6. Insert a tire iron under the top bead next to the valve stem (**Figure 46**). Force the bead on the opposite side of the tire into the center of the rim and pry the bead over the rim with the tire iron.
7. Insert a second tire iron next to the first iron to hold the bead over the rim. Then work around the tire with the first tire iron, prying the bead over the rim (**Figure 47**).
8. Stand the wheel upright. Insert a tire iron between the second bead and the side of the rim that the first bead was pried over (**Figure 48**). Force the bead on the opposite side from the tire iron into the center of the rim. Pry the back bead off the rim, working around as with the first.
9. Inspect the valve stem seal. Because rubber deteriorates with age, it is advisable to replace the valve stem when replacing the tire.
10. Remove the old valve stem and discard it. Inspect the valve stem hole (**Figure 49**) in the rim. Remove any dirt or corrosion from the hole and wipe it dry with a clean cloth. Install a new valve stem and make sure it is properly seated in the rim.
11. Carefully inspect the tire and wheel rim for any damage as described in the following procedure.

Tire and Wheel Rim Inspection

1. Wipe off the inner surfaces of the wheel rim. Clean off any rubber residue or oxidation.

WARNING

Carefully consider whether a tire should be replaced. If there is any doubt about the quality of the existing tire, replace it with a new one. Do not take a chance on a tire failure at any speed.

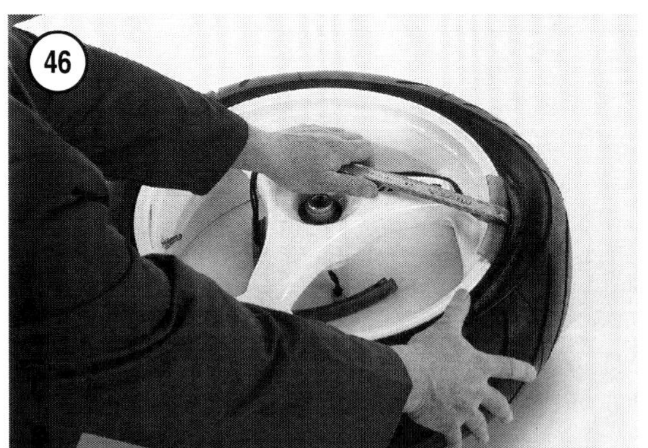
46

47

48

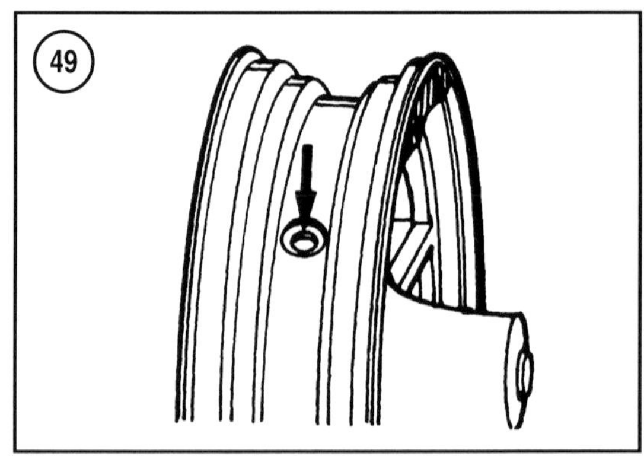
49

50

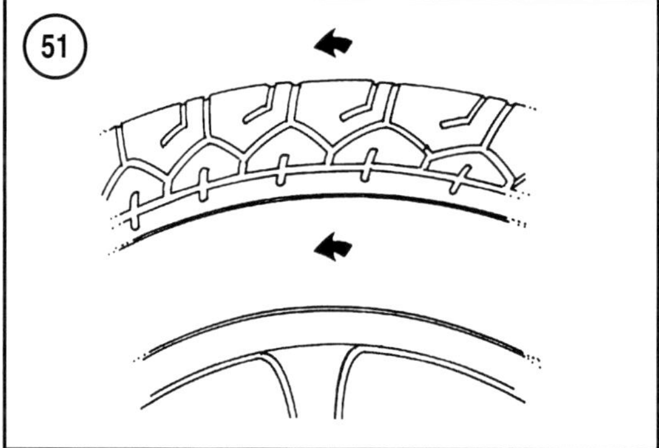

2. If any one of the following is observed, replace the tire:
   a. A puncture or split whose total length or diameter exceeds 6 mm (0.24 in.).
   b. A scratch or split on the side wall.
   c. Any type of ply separation.
   d. Tread separation or excessive abnormal wear pattern.
   e. Tread depth of less than the minimum value specified in **Table 1** on original equipment tires. Aftermarket tires tread depth minimum may vary.
   f. Scratches on either sealing bead.
   g. The cord is cut in any place.
   h. Flat spots in the tread from skidding.
   i. Any abnormality in the inner liner.
3. Inspect the valve stem hole in the rim. Remove any dirt or corrosion from the hole and wipe it dry with a clean cloth.

Installation

1. Inspect the valve stem core rubber seal (**Figure 50**) for hardness or deterioration. Replace the valve core if necessary.
2. A new tire may have balancing rubbers inside. These are not patches and should be left in place. Most tires are marked with a colored spot near the bead (**Figure 44**) that indicates a lighter point on the tire. This should be placed next to the valve stem.
3. Lubricate both beads of the tire with soapy water.
4. When installing the tire on the rim, make sure the correct tire (front or rear) is installed on the correct wheel. Also, install the tire so the direction arrow faces the normal direction of wheel rotation (**Figure 51**).
5. If remounting the old tire, align the mark made in Step 2, *Removal* with the valve stem. If a new tire is being installed, align the colored stop near the bead (indicating the lightest point of the tire) with the valve stem. See **Figure 44**.
6. Place the backside of the tire onto the rim so the lower bead sits in the center of the rim while the upper bead remains outside the rim (**Figure 52**). Work around the tire in both directions and press the lower bead, by hand, into the center of the rim. Use a tire iron for the last few inches of bead.
7. Press the upper bead into the rim opposite the valve stem. Working on both sides of this initial point, pry the bead into the rim with a tire tool, and work around the rim to the valve stem (**Figure 53**).

If the tire wants to pull up on one side, either use another tire iron or one of your knees to hold the tire in place. The last few inches are usually the toughest to install. If possible, continue to push the tire into the rim by hand. Re-lubricate the bead if necessary. If the tire bead wants to pull out from under the rim use both of your knees to hold the tire in place. If necessary, use a tire iron for the last few inches (**Figure 54**).

8. Bounce the wheel several times, rotating it each time. This will force the tire bead against the rim flanges.

9. Once the tire beads are in contact with the rim, place an inflatable band around the circumference of the tire. Slowly inflate the band until the tire beads are pressed against the rim. Inflate the tire enough to seat it. Deflate the band and remove it.

WARNING
In the next step, never exceed 400 kPa (56 psi) inflation pressure as the tire could burst, causing severe injury. Never stand directly over a tire while inflating it.

10. After inflating the tire, check to see that the beads are fully seated and that the rim lines are the same distance from the rim all the way around the tire. If the beads will not seat, deflate the tire and lubricate the rim and beads with soapy water.

11. Re-inflate the tire to the required pressure as listed in **Table 1**. Install the valve stem cap.

12. Balance the wheel as described in this chapter.

13A. Install the front wheel as described in this chapter.

13B. Install the rear wheel as described in this chapter.

TIRE REPAIRS

WARNING
Do not install an inner tube inside a tubeless tire. The tube will cause an abnormal heat buildup in the tire.

NOTE
Changing or patching on the road is very difficult. A can of pressurized tire sealant may inflate the tire and seal the hole, although this is only a temporary fix.

54

Tubeless tires have the word "TUBELESS" molded into the sidewall and the rims have "SUITABLE FOR TUBELESS TIRES" or equivalent cast on them.

If the tire is punctured, remove it from the rim, inspect the inside of the tire, and apply a combination plug/patch from inside the tire (**Figure 55**). Never attempt to repair a tubeless motorcycle tire using a plug or cord patch applied from outside the tire. This type of repair might be acceptable for automobiles, but they are not safe on a motorcycle tire, especially on a high-performance motorcycle like the Bandit.

After repairing a tubeless tire, do not exceed 30 mph (50 kph) for the first 24 hours. Do not exceed 80 mph (130 kph) and never race (canyon or otherwise) on a repaired tubeless tire. The patch could work loose because of tire flex and heat, resulting in a possible serious accident.

Repair

Do not rely on a plug or cord patch applied from outside the tire. Use a combination plug/patch applied from inside the tire (**Figure 55**).

1. Remove the tire from the wheel rim as described in this chapter.

2. Inspect the rim inner flange. Smooth any scratches on the sealing surface with emery cloth. If a scratch is deeper than 0.5 mm (0.020 in.), the wheel should be replaced.

3. Inspect the tire inside and out. Replace a tire if any of the following conditions is found:

   a. A puncture larger than 6 mm (1/4 in) diameter.
   b. A punctured or damaged side wall.
   c. More than two punctures in the tire.

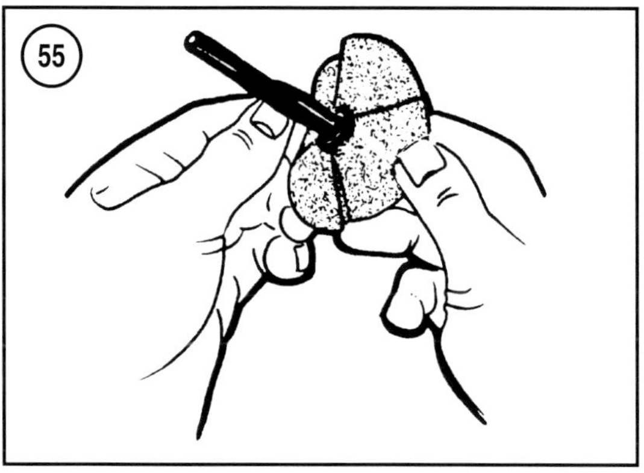

d. Tread depth less than the minimum value specified in **Table 1**.

e. Ply or tread separation.

f. Flat spots.

g. Scratches on the bead.

h. Cuts in the cord.

4. Apply the plug/patch, following the manufacturer's instructions with the patch kit.

DRIVE CHAIN

Removal/Installation

1. Remove the swing arm as described in Chapter Thirteen.
2. Remove the engine sprocket cover as described in Chapter Seven.
3. Slide the drive chain off the engine sprocket and remove it from the motorcycle.
4. Inspect the chain as described in Chapter Three.
5. Installation is the reverse of removal. Adjust the chain as described in Chapter Three.

Table 1 WHEELS, TIRES AND DRIVE CHAIN SPECIFICATIONS

Item	Specification
Wheel rim size	
Front	J17 × MT 3.50
Rear	J17 × MT 5.50
Rim runout limit	
Axial	2.0 mm (0.08 in.)
Radial	2.0 mm (0.08 in.)
Axle runout limit	
Front	0.25 mm (0.010 in.)
Rear	0.25 mm (0.010 in.)
Tire size	
Front	120/70 ZR17
Rear	180/55 ZR17
Tire tread minimum depth	
Front	1.6 mm (0.06 in.)
Rear	2.0 mm (0.08 in.)
Tire inflation pressure (cold)*	
U.S. models	
Front	
Solo	225 kPa (33 psi)
Rider and passenger	225 kPa (33 psi)
Rear	
Solo	250 kPa (36 psi)
Rear	
Rider and passenger	250 kPa (36 psi)
All models except U.S.	
Front	
Solo	250 kPa (36 psi)
Rider and passenger	250 kPa (36 psi)
Rear	
Solo	250 kPa (36 psi)
Rider and passenger	250 kPa (36 psi)

(continued)

Table 1 WHEELS, TIRES AND DRIVE CHAIN SPECIFICATIONS (continued)

Item	Specification
Drive chain	
Type	
1996-2000 models	
All models except ABS	RK GB50MFOZ1 (110 links, continuous)
ABS models	RK GB50MFOZ1 (114 links, continuous)
2001-on models	RK50MFOZ1 (112 links, continuous)
21-pin length	319.4 mm (12.6 in.)
Chain slack	20-30 mm (0.80-1.20 in.)

*Tire inflation pressure is for original equipment tires. Aftermarket tires may require different inflation pressure. The use of tires other than those specified by Suzuki may cause instability.

Table 2 WHEELS, TIRES AND DRIVE CHAIN TORQUE SPECIFICATIONS

Item	N•m	in.-lb.	ft.-lb.
Brake disc bolts	23	–	17
Engine sprocket nut	115	–	85
Front axle	65	–	48
Front axle pinch bolts	23	–	17
Rear axle nut	100		74
Rear caliper mounting bolt	25	–	18
Rear sprocket nuts			
1995-1999 models	60	–	44
2000 models	50	–	37
Rear brake torque link nut	35	–	26
Speedometer sensor rotor bolt (2001-on models)	13	115	–

CHAPTER ELEVEN

FRONT SUSPENSION AND STEERING

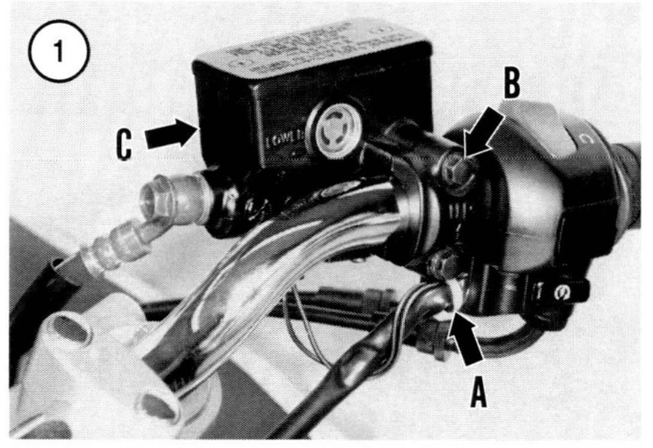

This chapter describes repair and maintenance procedures for the front fork and steering components. Front wheel removal, front hub service, tire changing, tire repair and wheel balancing are covered in Chapter Ten.

When inspecting components described in this chapter, compare all measurements to the front suspension specifications in **Table 1**. Replace any component that is damaged, worn to the wear limit or out of specification. During assembly, tighten fasteners to the torque specifications listed.

Table 1 and **Table 2** are located at the end of the chapter.

HANDLEBAR

Removal/Installation

CAUTION
Cover the frame and fuel tank with a heavy cloth or plastic tarp to protect it from brake fluid spills. Brake fluid damages plastic, painted and plated surfaces. Wash off spilled brake fluid immediately.

NOTE
This procedure is shown on a GSF1200S with the fairing removed to better illustrate the steps.

NOTE
If handlebar replacement is not required, proceed to Step 12.

1. On GSF1200 models, remove the rear view mirrors from the brake and the clutch master cylinder clamps.
2. Disconnect the front brake switch (A, **Figure 1**) from the brake master cylinder.
3. Remove the brake master cylinder clamp bolts (B, **Figure 1**). Remove the clamp and the brake

master cylinder (C, **Figure 1**) from the handlebar. Secure the master cylinder to the frame with a bungee cord. Be sure the master cylinder is in an upright position. Do not disconnect the hydraulic brake line.

4. Loosen the handlebar right side balance weight assembly (**Figure 2**) and slide the weight assembly off the handlebar.

NOTE

By removing the right side weight, it is not necessary to disconnect the throttle cables from the switch assembly.

5. Disconnect the clutch lever position switch (**Figure 3**) from the clutch master cylinder.

6. Remove the clutch master cylinder clamp bolts. Remove the clamp (A, **Figure 4**) and the brake master cylinder (B) from the handlebar. Secure the master cylinder to the frame with a bungee cord. Be sure the master cylinder is in an upright position. Do not disconnect the hydraulic clutch line.

7. Remove the screws securing the left switch assembly and separate the switch assembly. Note that the starter (choke) cable bracket is secured under one of these screws (**Figure 5**). The bracket will have to be reinstalled in the same location during assembly.

8. Remove the trim caps (**Figure 6**) from the upper handlebar holders bolts.

9. Remove the clamp bolts and remove the upper handlebar holders.

10. Lift the handlebar from the lower handlebar holders.

11. To properly secure the handlebar and prevent it from slipping, clean the knurled section of the handlebar with a wire brush. Clean the handlebar holders of any metal debris that may have been gouged loose by handlebar slippage.

12. Install the handlebar by reversing these steps. Note the following:

   a. Replace the handlebar if it is bent.
   b. Position the handlebar so its punch mark aligns with the mating surface of the lower handlebar holder (**Figure 7**).
   c. On 1996-2000 models, tighten the handlebar clamp bolts so the gap at the front of the handlebar holders equals the gap behind the holders (**Figure 8**).

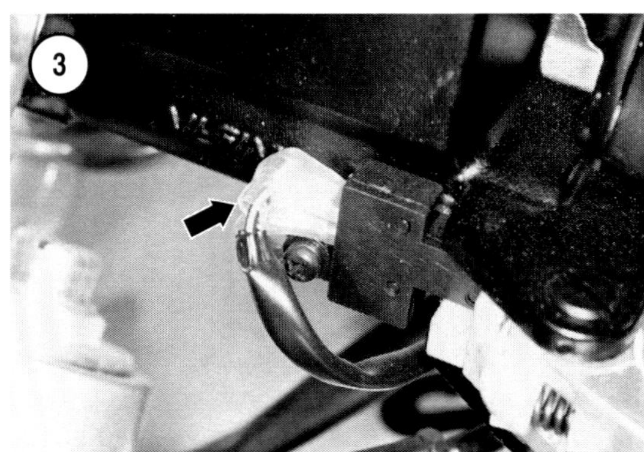

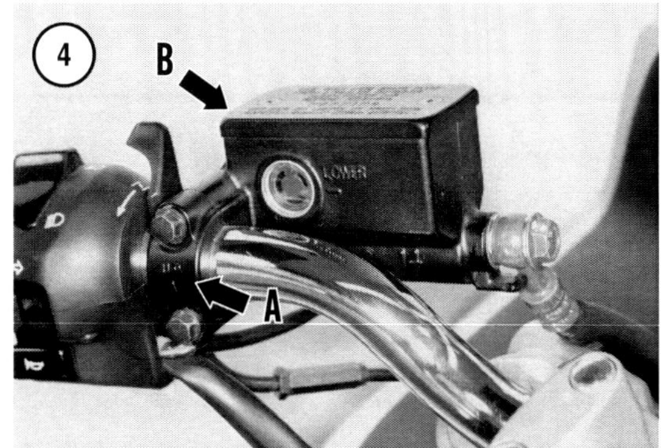

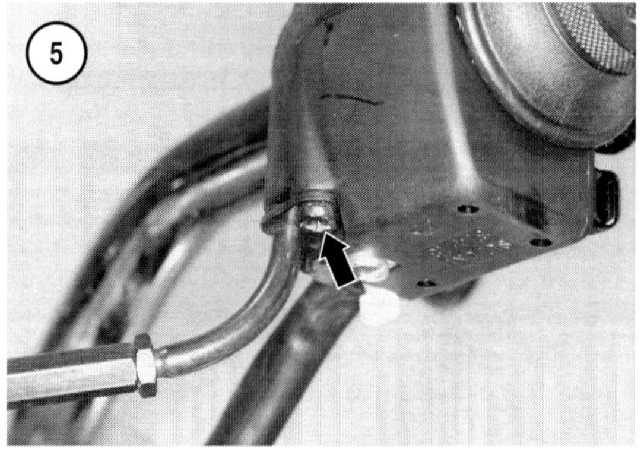

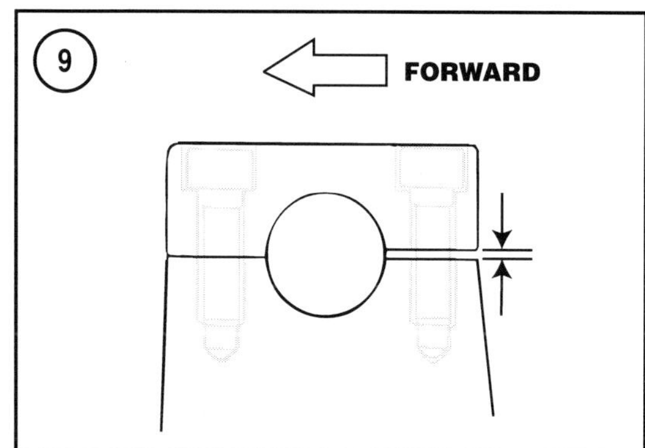

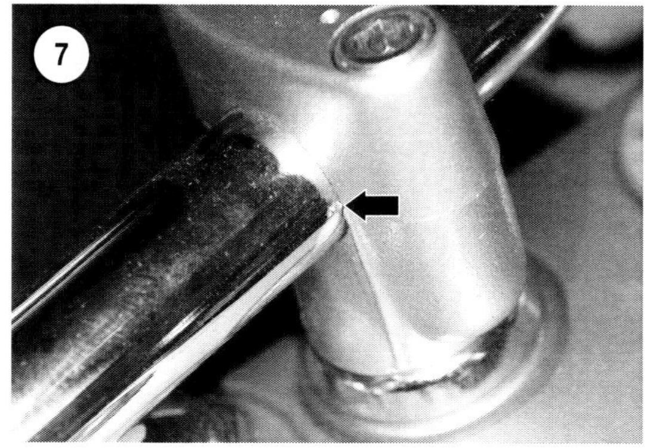

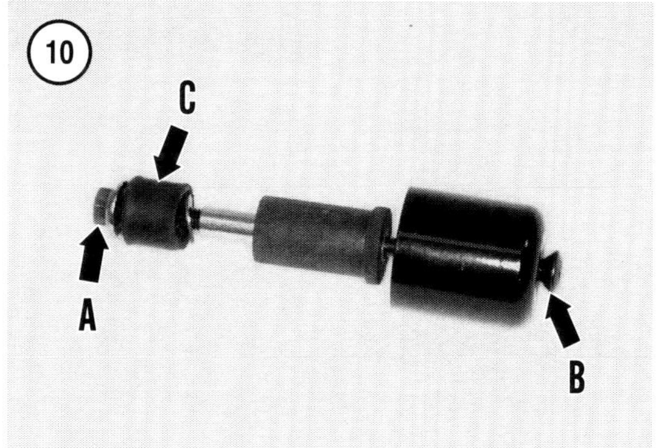

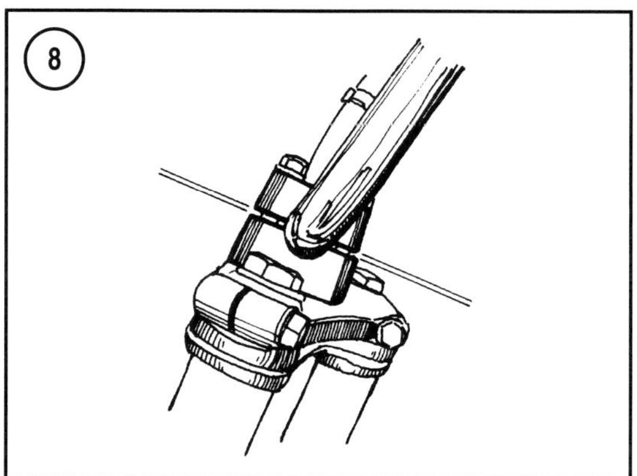

d. On 2001-on models, tighten the front handlebar clamp bolt first, and then tighten the rear handlebar clamp bolt so the gap between the handlebar holders faces the rear of the motorcycle (**Figure 9**).
e. Tighten the handlebar clamp bolts and the brake and clutch master cylinder clamp bolts to 23 N•m (17 ft.-lb.).
f. Apply a light coat of multipurpose grease to the right handlebar end before installing the throttle grip assembly.
g. If removed, install the left handlebar grip as described in this chapter.
h. If disassembled, assemble the balance weights. Hold onto the inner nut (A, **Figure 10**) and tighten the long screw (B) until tension is applied to the inner rubber (C) and spread it slightly. Do *not* lubricate rubber parts. Install the weight assembly into the handlebar and tighten the long screw securely.
i. After installation is complete, make sure the clutch and brake levers do not come in contact with the respective grips. If contact is made, the fluid in the master cylinder(s) may be low; refill as necessary. Refer to Chapter Three.

Inspection

1. Check the handlebar along the entire mounting area for cracks or damage. Replace a bent or damaged handlebar immediately. If the motorcycle is involved in a crash, examine the handlebars, steering stem and front fork carefully.

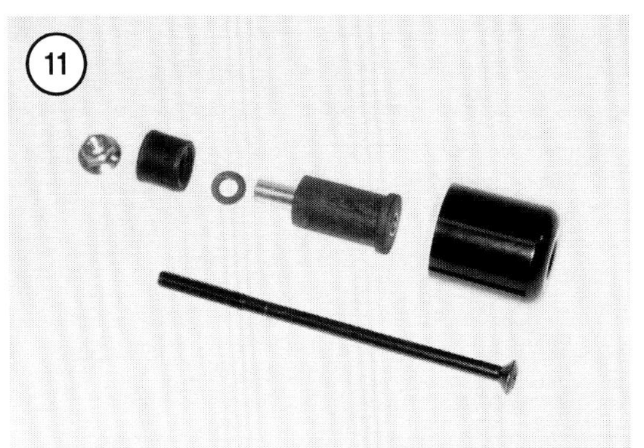
11

12

13

STEERING STEM (1996-2000 MODELS)

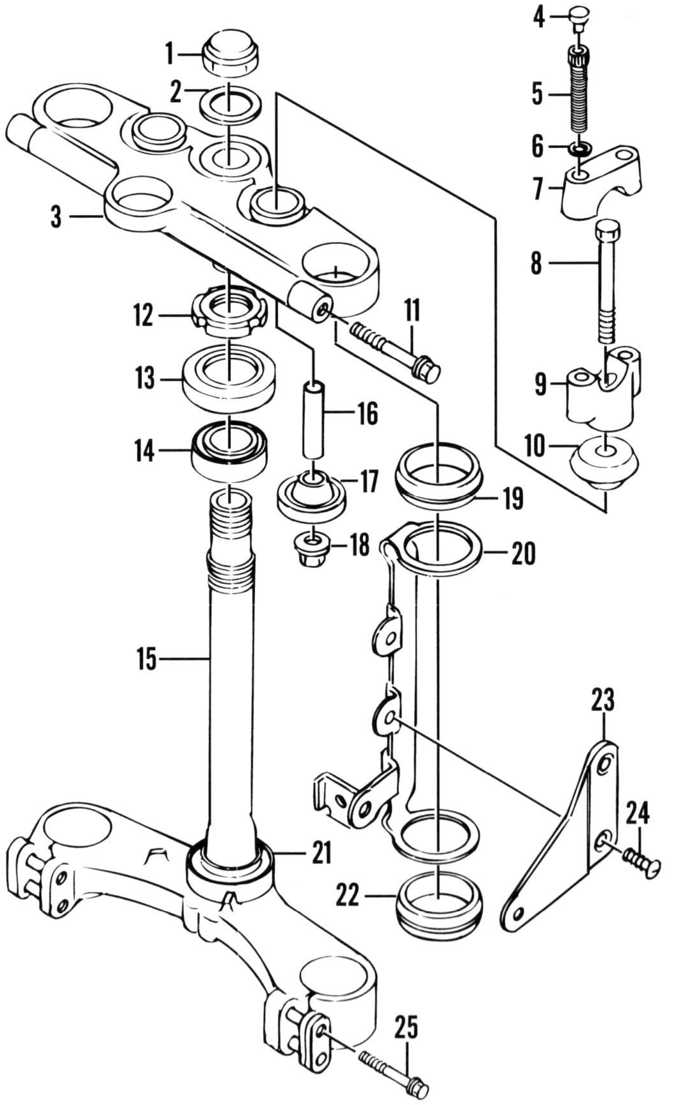

1. Steering stem nut
2. Washer
3. Upper fork bridge
4. Cap
5. Allen bolt
6. Washer
7. Upper clamp
8. Bolt
9. Lower clamp
10. Upper cushion
11. Bolt
12. Steering stem adjust nut
13. Dust seal
14. Upper roller bearing
15. Steering stem/lower fork bridge
16. Collar
17. Lower cushion
18. Nut
19. Rubber bushing
20. Turn signal mounting bracket
21. Lower roller bearing
22. Rubber bushing
23. Turn signal bracket
24. Screw
25. Bolt

(14) **STEERING STEM (2001-ON MODELS)**

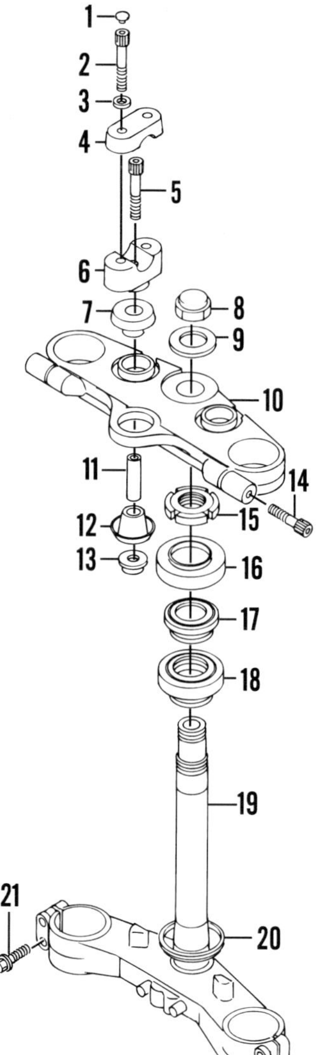

1. Cap
2. Allen bolt
3. Washer
4. Upper clamp
5. Bolt
6. Lower clamp
7. Upper cushion
8. Steering stem nut
9. Washer
10. Upper fork bridge
11. Collar
12. Lower cushion
13. Nut
14. Bolt
15. Steering stem adjust nut
16. Dust seal
17. Upper ball bearing
18. Lower ball bearing
19. Steering stem/ lower fork bridge
20. Dust seal
21. Bolt

2. Inspect the balance weight components (**Figure 11**) for wear or damage.

HANDLEBAR LEFT GRIP REPLACEMENT

NOTE
The original equipment right grip is part of the throttle grip assembly and cannot be replaced separately.

1. Remove the screw securing the left balance set (A, **Figure 12**) and remove the parts from the handlebar end.
2. Slide a thin screwdriver between the left grip (B, **Figure 12**) and handlebar. Spray electrical contact cleaner into the opening under the grip.
3. Pull the screwdriver out and quickly twist the grip to break its bond with the handlebar, and then slide off the grip.
4. Clean the handlebar of all rubber or sealer residue.
5. Install the new grip, following the manufacturer's directions. Apply an adhesive, such as ThreeBond Griplock, between the grip and handlebar. When applying an adhesive, follow the manufacturer's instructions for drying time before operating the motorcycle.

STEERING HEAD AND STEM

Removal

Refer to **Figure 13** and **Figure 14**.

1. On GSF1200S models, remove the front fairing as described in Chapter Fourteen.
2. Remove the front wheel as described in Chapter Ten.
3. Remove the handlebar as described in this chapter.
4. On GSF1200 models, perform the following:
   a. Remove the headlight lens, then disconnect the connectors inside the headlight housing. Remove the headlight housing.
   b. Remove the turn signals and the headlight housing holders from the mounting bracket.
   c. Remove the mounting brackets.
5. Remove the combination meter as described in Chapter Nine.

6. Remove the bolt (**Figure 15**) securing the brake hose joint to the lower fork bridge. Move the hose assembly out of the way.
7. If still connected, disconnect the ignition switch connector from the wiring harness.
8. Loosen and remove the steering stem nut (A, **Figure 16**) and washer.
9. Loosen the upper fork bridge clamp bolts on the fork legs (**Figure 17**).
10. Pull the upper fork bridge (B, **Figure 16**) and the ignition switch wiring harness straight up and off the steering stem and fork assemblies (**Figure 18**).
11. Remove both front assemblies as described in this chapter.
12. Loosen the steering stem adjust nut (A, **Figure 19**) with a spanner wrench, a hammer and drift, or fabricate a tool like the one shown in **Figure 20**.

NOTE
Support the weight of the steering stem while removing the adjust nut or the assembly will drop out of the steering head.

13. Hold onto the steering stem assembly and remove the adjust nut.
14. Gently lower the steering stem assembly (B, **Figure 19**) out of the frame. Do not worry about catching any loose steel balls. Both bearings are caged with no loose parts.
15. Remove the dust seal (C, **Figure 19**) from the top of the frame.
16A. On 1996-2000 models, carefully remove the upper bearing from the upper bearing race in the steering head (**Figure 21**).
16B. On 2001-on models, carefully remove the inner race and the upper caged ball bearing from the upper bearing race in the steering head.

CAUTION
Do not attempt to remove the lower roller bearing (1996-2000 models), or the ball bearing inner race (2001-on models), from the steering stem unless the bearing is going to be replaced. The bearing, or race, is pressed onto the steering stem and will be damaged during removal.

17. Inspect the steering stem as described in this chapter.

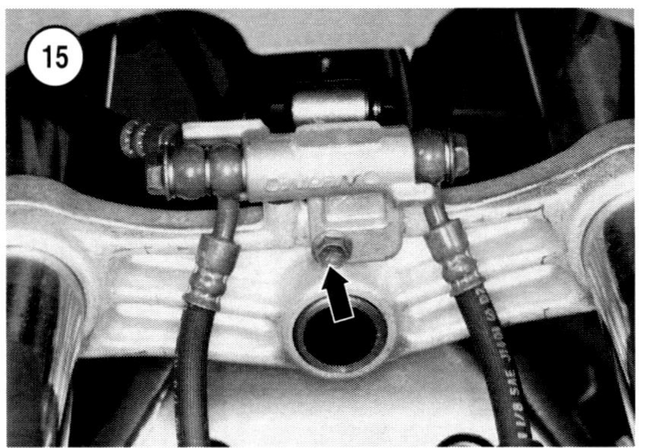

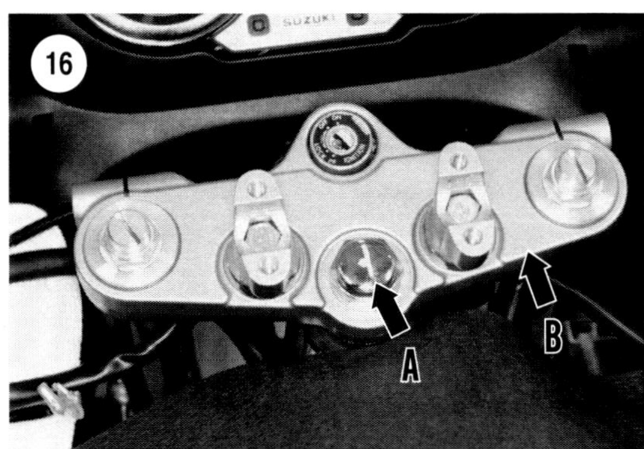

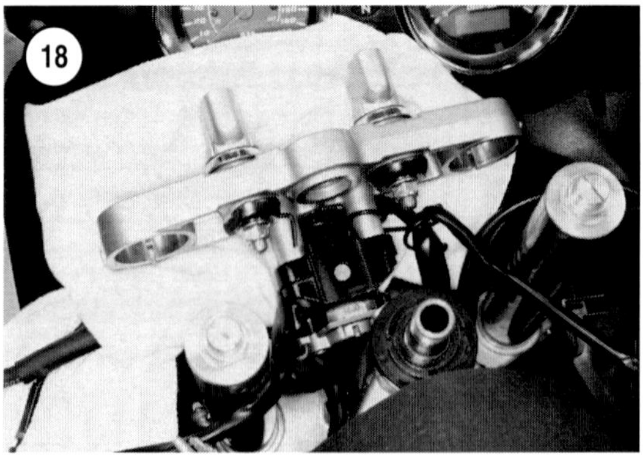

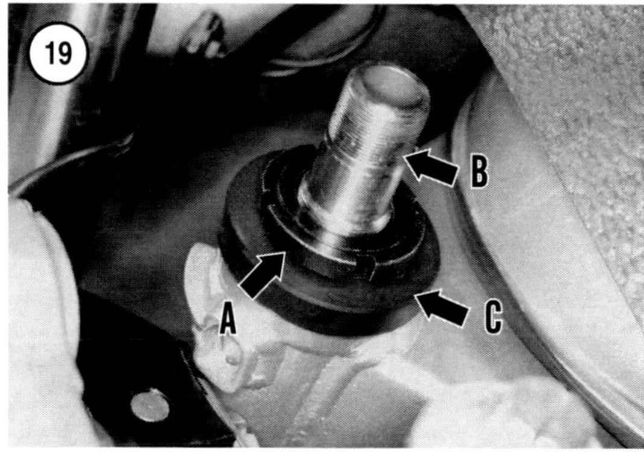

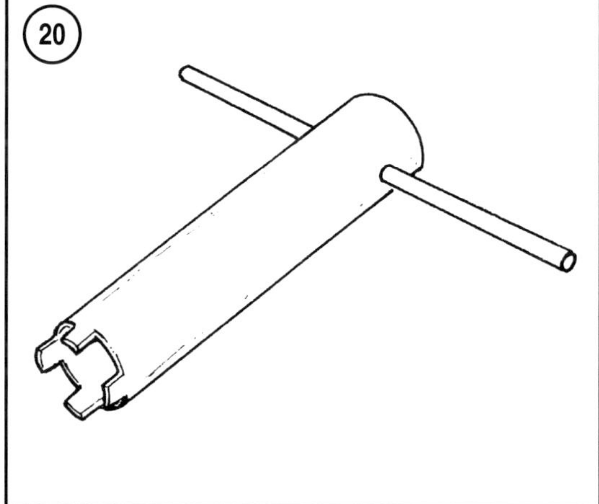

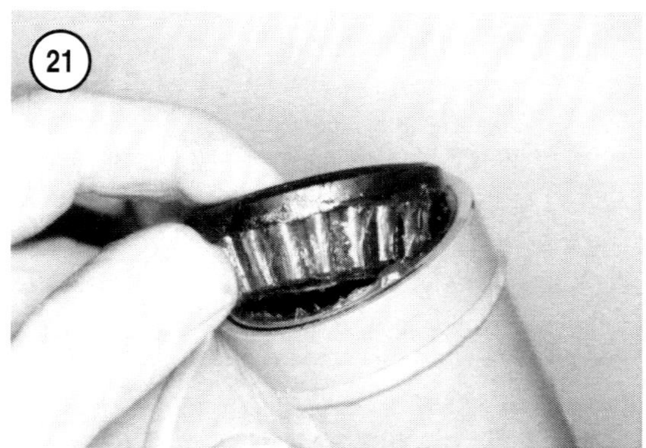

Installation

Refer to **Figure 13** and **Figure 14**.

1. Make sure the steering head outer races are clean and properly seated in the steering head.
2. Apply an even, complete coat of Suzuki Super Grease A or equivalent to the steering head outer races, both bearings, the dust seal and the steering stem nut and adjust nut.

NOTE
The fork receptacles in the steering stem are offset and must face toward the front of the motorcycle. This is necessary for proper alignment with the fork receptacles in the upper fork bridge.

3A. On 1996-2000 models, install the upper bearing and the inner race into the outer race in the top of the steering head (**Figure 21**).

NOTE
On 2001-on models, the caged ball bearings differ in size. The lower bearing is the largest of the two. Make sure to install the bearings into the correct location.

3B. On 2001-on models, perform the following:
   a. Install the inner race and the small upper caged ball bearing onto the upper bearing race in the steering head.
   b. If removed, install the large lower caged ball bearing onto the outer race on the lower fork bridge.

4. Position the lower fork bridge so its fork receptacles face toward the front of the motorcycle. Carefully slide the steering stem up into the steering head. Take care not to dislodge the upper bearing or race. If this happens, reseat the bearing.
5. Pack the underside of the dust seal with grease. Install the dust seal (C, **Figure 19**) and steering stem adjust nut (A), then perform the following:
   a. Tighten the steering stem adjust nut (A, **Figure 19**) to 45 N•m (33 ft.-lb.).
   b. Turn the steering stem from side to side five or six times to help seat the bearings.

NOTE
In substep C, the amount adjustment varies from motorcycle to motorcycle. After loosening the adjust nut 1/4 to 1/2 of a turn, there must be no play detected in the steering stem.

   c. Loosen the adjust nut 1/4 to 1/2 turn.

6. Once again, turn the steering stem from side to side five or six times. The steering stem should move freely with no looseness or stiffness. If necessary, repeat Steps 5 and 6 as necessary until the steering stem moves properly.

7. Install the upper fork bridge (B, **Figure 16**) onto the steering stem.

8. Install the washer and the steering stem nut (A, **Figure 16**). Tighten the nut finger-tight at this time.

NOTE
Steps 9-13 must be performed in this order to ensure proper upper and lower fork bridge to fork alignment.

9. Temporarily slide the fork legs into position until they are just above the top surface of the upper fork bridge. Securely tighten only the lower fork bridge clamp bolts.

10. Temporarily install the front axle into the fork legs and tighten securely.

11. Properly locate the fork tubes in the upper fork bridge and tighten the upper and lower clamp bolts to 23 N•m (17 ft.-lb.).

12. Tighten the steering stem nut (A, **Figure 16**) to 65 N•m (48 ft.-lb.).

13. Remove the front axle.

14. Install the brake hose joint and mounting bolt (**Figure 15**) onto the lower fork bridge. Tighten the bolt securely.

15. Install the combination meter as described in Chapter Nine.

16. Install the handlebar assembly as described in this chapter.

17. Check the movement of the front fork and steering stem assembly. The steering stem must turn freely from side to side, but without any binding or free play when the fork legs are moved fore and aft.

18. Connect the ignition switch electrical connector to the main wiring harness.

19. On GSF1200 models, perform the following:
   a. Install the turn signals and headlight holders onto the mounting bracket.
   b. Reinstall the headlight housing and reconnect the electrical connectors.
   c. Reinstall the headlight as described in Chapter Nine.

20. Install the front wheel as described in Chapter Ten.

21. On GSF1200S models, reinstall the front fairing as described in Chapter Fourteen.

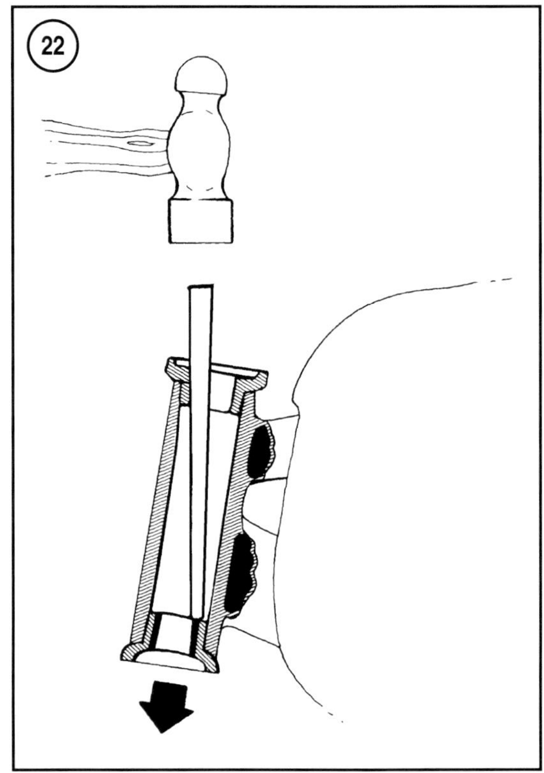

Inspection

1. Clean the upper and lower bearings in a bearing degreaser. Make certain that the bearing degreaser is compatible with the rubber covers on each bearing. Hold the bearing so it will not spin and thoroughly dry both bearings with compressed air. On 1996-2000 models, make sure all solvent is removed from the lower bearing still installed on the steering stem.

2. Wipe the old grease from the outer races located in the steering head and then clean the outer races with a rag soaked in solvent. Thoroughly dry the races with a lint-free cloth.

3. Check the steering stem outer races for pitting, galling and corrosion. If any race is worn or damaged, replace the race and bearing as an assembly. Follow the procedure described in this chapter.

4. Check the welds around the steering head for cracks and fractures. If any damage is found, have the frame repaired at a competent frame or welding shop.

5. Check the balls/needles for pitting, scratches or discoloration indicating wear or corrosion. Replace the bearing if any balls/needles are less than perfect.

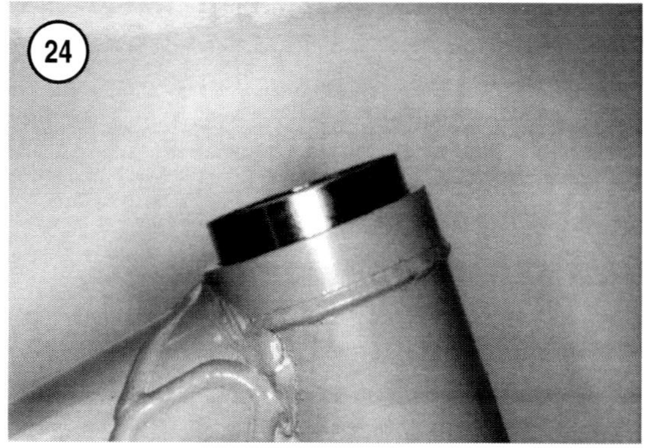

6. If the bearings are in good condition, pack them thoroughly with Suzuki Super Grease A or an equivalent good-quality, waterproof bearing grease. To pack the bearings, spread some grease in the palm of the hand and scrape the open side of the bearing across the palm until the bearing is packed completely full of grease. Spin the bearing a few times to determine if there are any open areas; repack if necessary.
7. Thoroughly clean all mounting parts in solvent. Dry them completely.
8. Inspect the steering stem head nut and steering stem adjust nut for wear or damage. Inspect the threads. If necessary, clean them with an appropriate size metric tap or replace the nut(s). If the threads are damaged, inspect the appropriate steering stem thread(s) for damage. If necessary, clean the threads with an appropriate size metric die.
9. Inspect the steering stem nut and washer for damage; replace if necessary. If damaged, check the underside of the steering stem head nut for damage; replace as necessary.
10. Inspect the steering stem and the lower fork bridge for cracks or other damage. Make sure the fork bridge clamping areas are free of burrs and that the bolt holes are in good condition.
11. Inspect the upper fork bridge for cracks or other damage. Check both the upper and lower surface of the fork bridge. Make sure the fork bridge clamping areas are free of burrs and that the bolt holes are in good condition.

STEERING HEAD BEARING RACE REPLACEMENT

The upper and lower bearing outer races must not be removed unless they are going to be replaced. These races are pressed into place and are damaged during removal. If removed, replace both the outer race along with the bearings at the same time. Never reuse an outer race that has been removed. It is no longer true and will damage the bearings if reused.

NOTE
The following procedure describes simple home techniques to remove the bearing races for both types of bearings used on these models. If removal is difficult, do not chance damage to the motorcycle or new bearing races. Have the task performed by a Suzuki dealership or a qualified specialist.

1. Remove the steering stem as described in this chapter.
2. Insert an aluminum drift into the steering head and carefully tap the lower race out from the steering head (**Figure 22**). Repeat this procedure for the upper race.
3. Chill the new bearing races in a freezer for a few hours to shrink the outer diameter of the race as much as possible.
4. Clean the race seats in the steering head. Check for cracks or other damage.
5. Insert the new race into the steering head with the tapered side facing out (**Figure 23**) and square the race with the race bore (**Figure 24**).

CAUTION
To avoid damage to the races and to the race seats in the steering head, install the races as described below.

6. Assemble a puller tool as shown in **Figure 25**. The block mounted at the bottom of the threaded rod is used as a T-handle to hold the rod stationary when the bearing race is being installed from the opposite end. If the handle is not available, hold the bottom of the rod with two nuts locked together. The hole drilled through the block should be large enough to accept a suitable rod for the T-handle. Two or more *thick* washers are also required. The outer diameter of the washers must be greater than the outer diameter of the bearing races.

CAUTION
When installing the bearing outer races with the threaded rod or similar tool, do not let the rod or tool contact the face of the bearing race. It could damage the race.

7. To install the upper race, insert the puller through the bottom of the steering head. Seat the lower washer or plate against the steering head.
8. At the top of the steering stem, slide the large washer down and seat it squarely on top of the bearing race. Install the required washers and coupling nut onto the rod.
9. Hand-tighten the coupling nut and center the washer on the upper bearing race.
10. Hold the threaded rod to prevent it from turning and tighten the coupling nut with a wrench (**Figure 26**). Continue to tighten the coupling until the race is completely drawn into the steering head. Remove the puller assembly and inspect the bearing race. It should be bottomed in the steering head as shown in **Figure 27**.
11. Turn the special tool over and repeat this procedure for the lower bearing race.

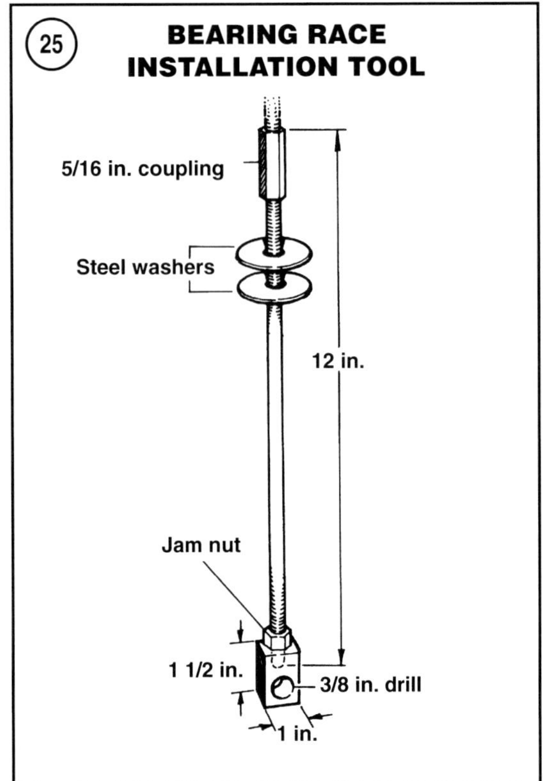

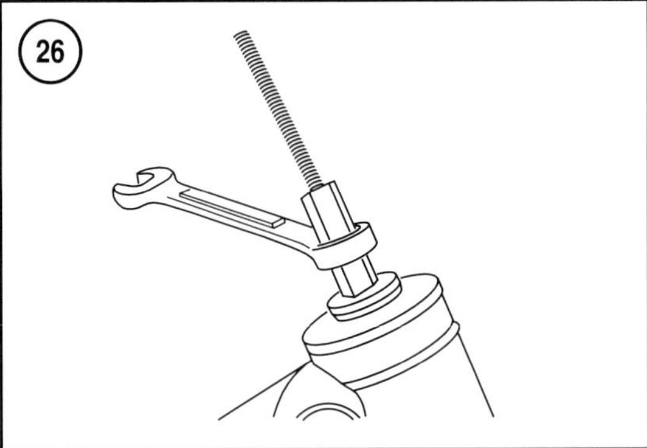

STEERING STEM BEARING REPLACEMENT

Do not remove the steering stem lower roller bearing (1996-2000 models) or the lower bearing outer race and dust seal (2001-on models) unless they are going to be replaced. The lower bearing, or bearing outer race, can be difficult to remove. If it cannot be removed as described in this procedure, have a Suzuki dealership service department replace the bearing and seal.

Never reinstall a lower bearing, or lower bearing outer race, that has been removed. It is no longer true and will damage the rest of the bearing assembly if reused.

1. Install the steering stem nut onto the top of the steering stem to protect the threads.
2. Loosen the lower bearing assembly, or lower bearing outer race, from the shoulder at the base of the steering stem with a chisel as shown in **Figure 28**. Slide the lower bearing, or lower bearing race, and dust seal off the steering stem. Discard them both.
3. Clean the steering stem with solvent and dry it thoroughly.

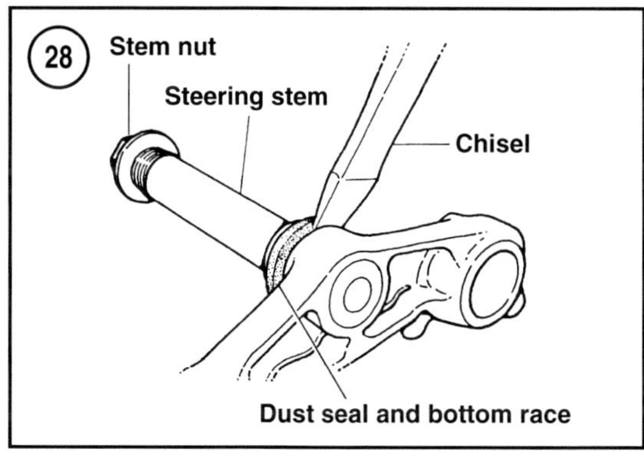

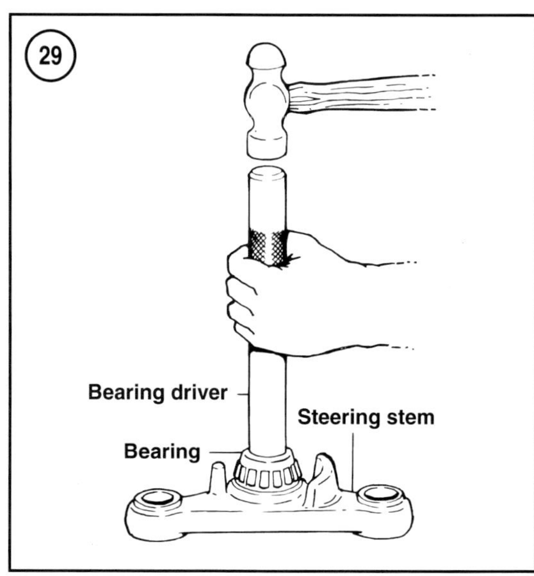

4A. On 1996-2000 models, perform the following:

a. Position the lower bearing outer race onto the steering stem until it stops on the raised shoulder.

b. Align the lower bearing with the machined shoulder on the steering stem.

c. Slide the Suzuki steering bearing installer (part No. 09941-74910), or a piece of pipe (**Figure 29**), over the steering stem until it seats against the inner portion of the *inner* race of the lower bearing.

d. Drive the lower bearing onto the steering stem until it bottoms.

4B. On 2001-on models, perform the following:

a. Position the new grease seal with the flange side facing up.

b. Slide a new grease seal and the lower bearing outer race onto the steering stem until it stops on the raised shoulder.

c. Align the lower bearing outer race with the machined shoulder on the steering stem.

d. Slide the Suzuki steering bearing installer (part No. 09941-74911), or a piece of pipe (**Figure 29**), over the steering stem until it seats against the inner portion of the lower bearing outer race. Drive the lower bearing outer race onto the steering stem until it bottoms.

5. Pack the bearing, or bearing outer race, with Suzuki Super Grease A or an equivalent waterproof wheel bearing grease.

FRONT FORK

Front Fork Service

Before disassembling the fork, drain the front fork oil and refill each fork leg with the specified type and quantity of fork oil as described in this chapter. If trouble persists, such as poor damping, a tendency to bottom or top out, or leakage around the oil seals, perform the service procedures in this section.

To simplify fork service and to prevent the mixing of parts, each fork leg should be removed, serviced and installed individually.

Front Fork Oil Change

To change fork oil, the fork assemblies must be removed and partially disassembled as described in this chapter.

1. Remove the fork assemblies as described in this chapter.
2. Perform *Disassembly* Steps 1-7.
3. Perform *Assembly* Steps 18-32.
4. Install the fork assemblies as described in this chapter.

Removal

CAUTION
The fork legs can be removed and installed with the front fairing in place. However, the fairing should be removed so it will not be damaged during fork removal and installation.

NOTE
For fork assembly removal only, do not perform Step 6. This step is only necessary if the fork assembly is going to be disassembled for service.

1. Remove the front wheel as described in Chapter Ten.
2. Remove the front fender as described in Chapter Fourteen. On 1996-2000 models, remove the front fender brace as described in Chapter Fourteen.
3. Remove the brake hose clamp from the fork leg.
4. On ABS-equipped models, remove the ABS sensor electrical harness from the right fork slider.
5. Remove the brake caliper as described in Chapter Thirteen. Suspend the caliper from the frame with wire or a bungee cord.
6. If the fork is going to be disassembled, or the fork oil is going to be replaced, perform the following:
   a. Place a drain pan under the fork slider to catch the fork oil.
   b. Apply coarse grit valve lapping compound to the end of the Allen wrench. This will create a better bond between the wrench and the Allen bolt head.

CAUTION
Press very hard on the wrench in the next step to ensure the wrench is completely seated within the Allen bolt head. If the Allen wrench starts to rotate within the socket, it will damage the Allen bolt head.

   c. Loosen the damper rod Allen bolt at the base of the slider with an Allen wrench (**Figure 30**). Remove the Allen bolt and washer.
   d. Drain the fork oil and dispose of it properly.
   e. On 2001-on models, move the protector up and off the slider.
   f. Pry the dust seal up and out of the slider groove.

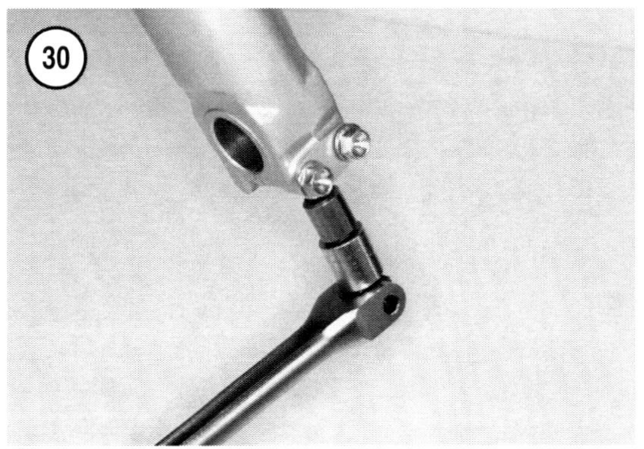

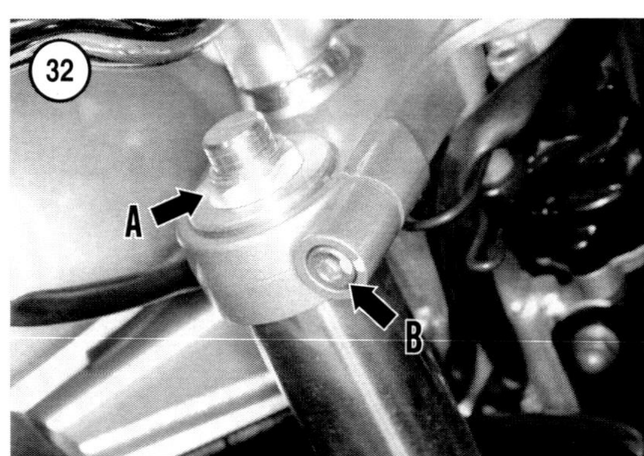

   g. Pry the stopper ring (**Figure 31**) from the slider groove.
   h. There is an interference fit between the bushing in the fork slider and the bushing on the fork tube. In order to remove the fork tube from the slider, pull hard on the fork tube using quick up-and-down strokes. Doing so will withdraw the bushing and the oil seal from the slider.
   i. Remove the fork slider from the fork tube. On 2001-on models, remove the fork protector above the dust seal.

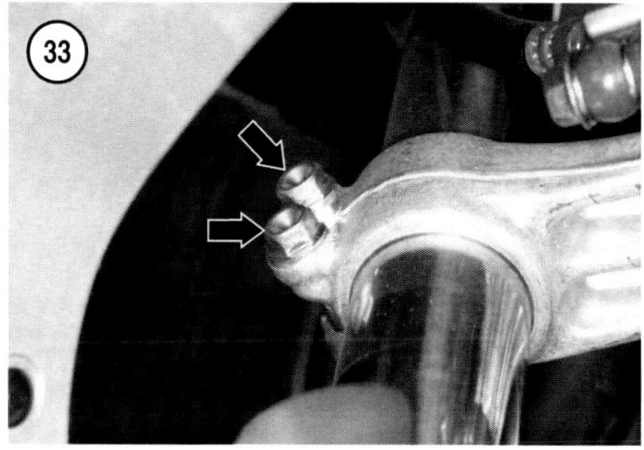

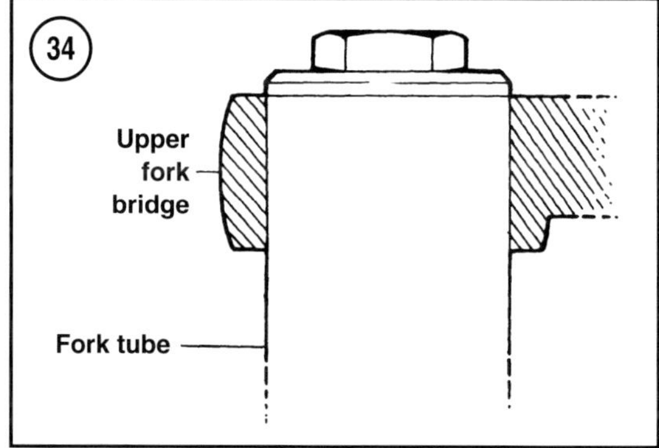

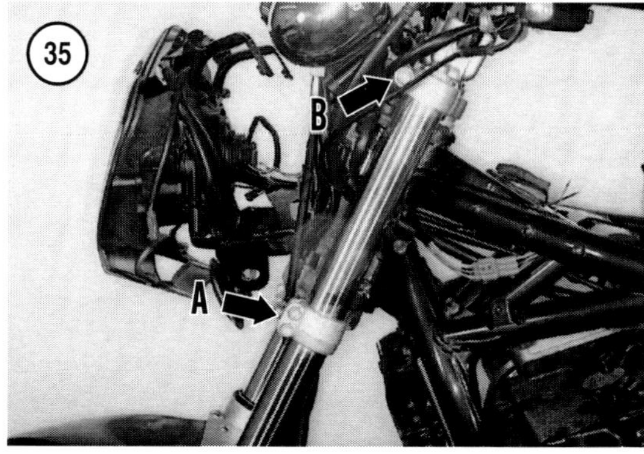

 j. Loosen the clamp bolt (**Figure 17**) on the upper fork bridge.
 k. If the fork leg is going to be disassembled, loosen the cap bolt (A, **Figure 32**).

7. On 2001-on models, measure the distance from the top of the fork tube to the top surface of the upper fork bridge and record this measurement. The fork tube must be reinstalled in the same location.
8. Loosen the clamp bolt (B, **Figure 32**) on the upper fork bridge.
9. Loosen both clamp bolts (**Figure 33**) on the lower fork bridge.
10. Carefully pull the fork assembly from the upper and lower fork bridges. It may be necessary to rotate the fork tube slightly while pulling it down and out. On GSF1200 models, remove the fork tube through the headlight mounting bracket located between the fork bridges.
11. Take the fork assembly to a workbench for service. If the fork is not going to be serviced, wrap it in a towel or blanket to protect the surface from damage.
12. If both fork leg assemblies are going to be removed, mark them with an R (right side) and L (left side) so they will be reinstalled on the correct side.

Installation

NOTE

*If both fork assemblies are removed, be sure to install the fork assembly on the correct side of the motorcycle. Refer to the marks made during **Removal** Step 12.*

1. Slowly install the fork tube into the lower fork bridge and then the upper fork bridge. On GSF1200 models, make sure the fork tube also passes through the headlight mounting bracket located between the fork bridges.

2A. On 1999-2000 models, slide the fork tube assembly into position until the top edge of the fork tube aligns with the top surface of the upper fork bridge (**Figure 34**).

2B. On 2001-on models, slide the fork tube assembly into position until the top edge of the fork tube is above the top surface of the upper fork bridge to the same dimension noted in *Removal* Step 7.

3. Tighten the lower fork bridge clamp bolts (A, **Figure 35**) to 23 N•m (17 ft.-lb.).
4. If the fork was disassembled for service, tighten the cap bolt (A, **Figure 32**) to 23 N•m (17 ft.-lb.).
5. Tighten the upper fork bridge clamp bolt (B, **Figure 35**) to 23 N•m (17 ft.-lb.).
6. On 1996-2000 models, install the fender brace as described in Chapter Fourteen.
7. Install the front fender as described in Chapter Fourteen.
8. Install the front wheel as described in Chapter Ten.
9. Install the brake caliper as described in Chapter Thirteen.

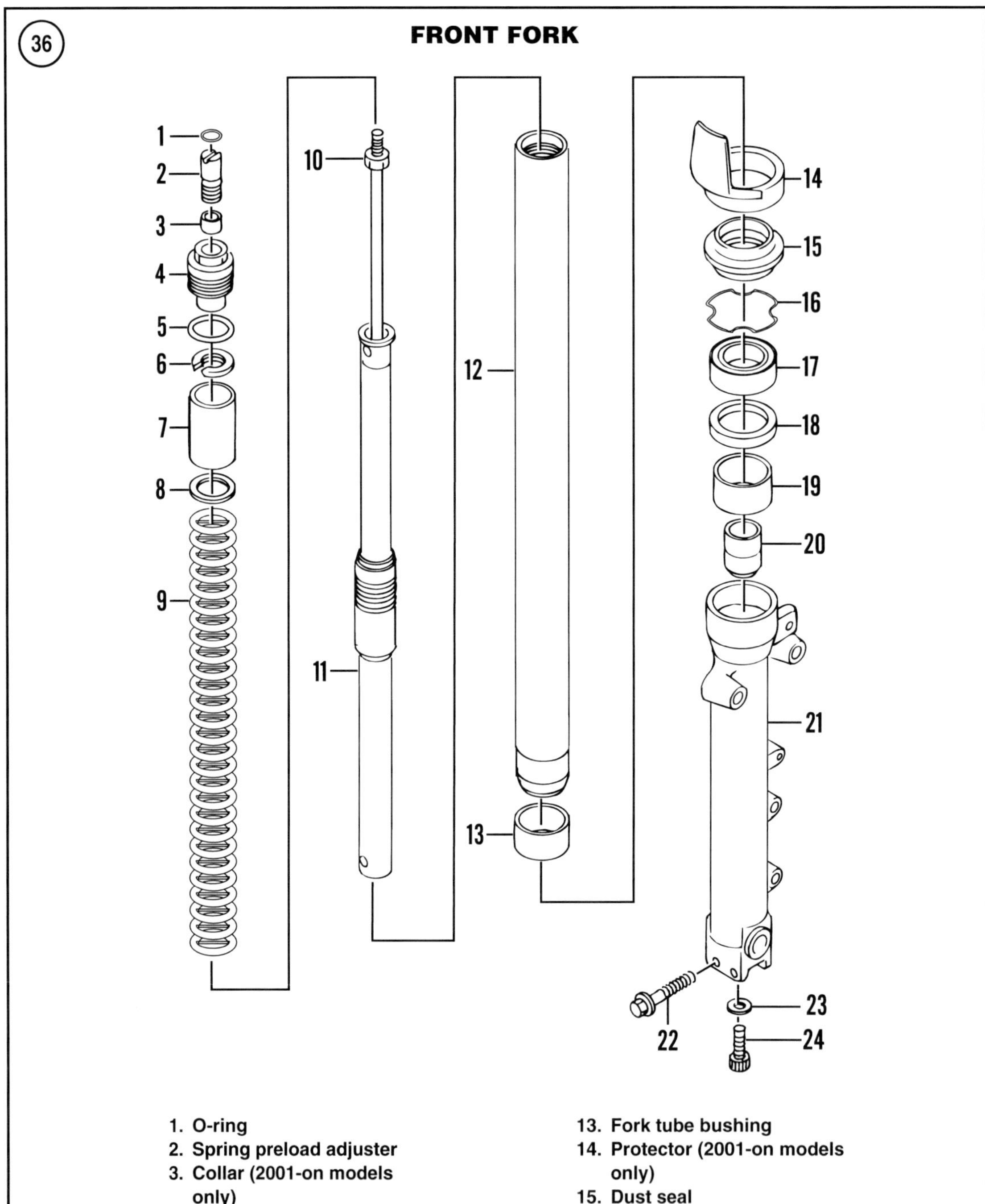

1. O-ring
2. Spring preload adjuster
3. Collar (2001-on models only)
4. Fork cap bolt
5. O-ring
6. Spring seat
7. Spacer
8. Washer
9. Spring
10. Nut
11. Damper rod cartridge
12. Fork tube
13. Fork tube bushing
14. Protector (2001-on models only)
15. Dust seal
16. Stopper ring
17. Oil seal
18. Oil seal retainer
19. Slider bushing
20. Oil lock piece
21. Slider
22. Bolt
23. Gasket
24. Allen bolt

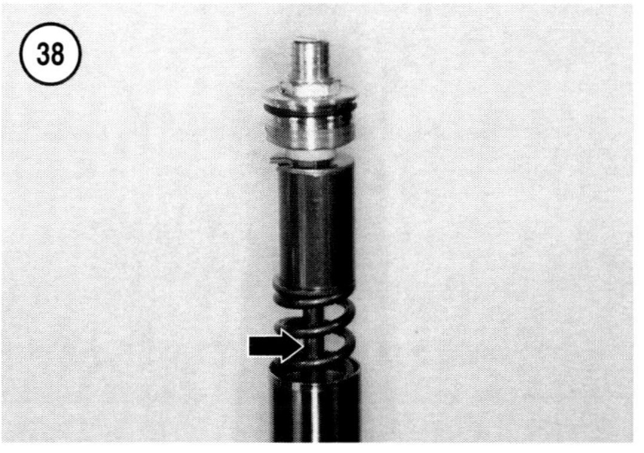

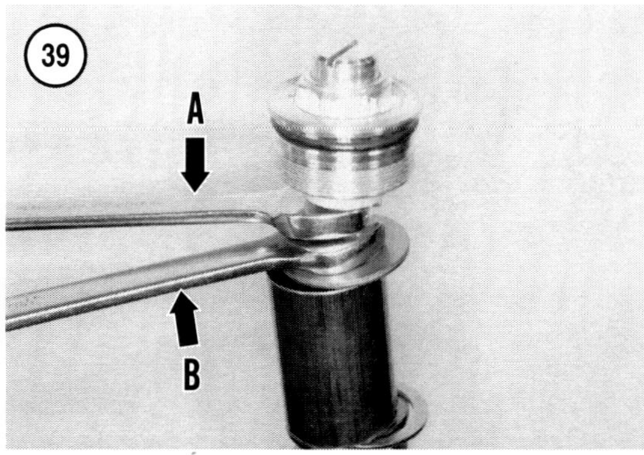

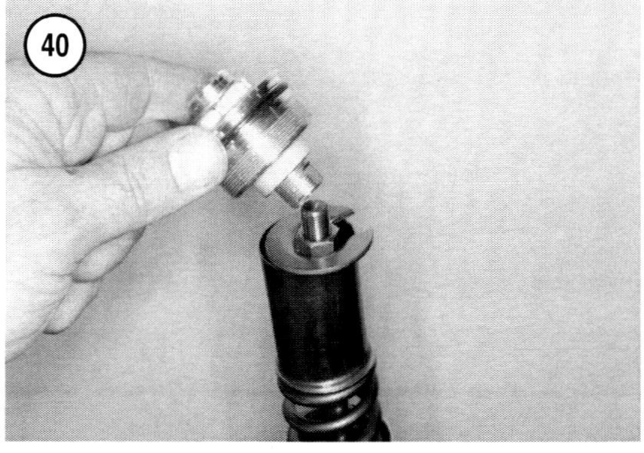

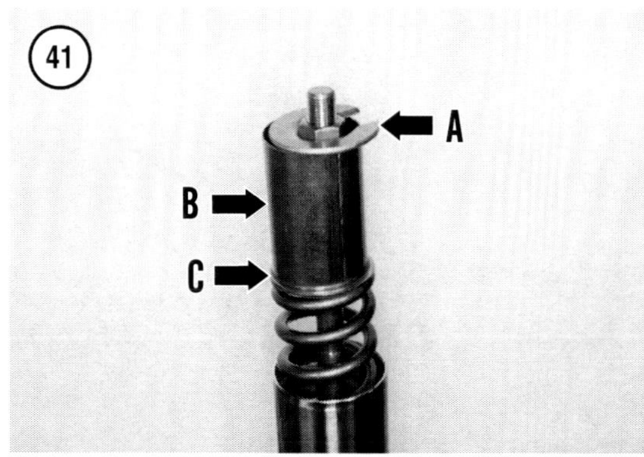

Disassembly

Refer to **Figure 36**.

1. Hold the fork in a vertical position and completely unscrew the fork cap bolt (**Figure 37**) from the fork tube. The fork cap bolt cannot be removed at this time as it is still attached to the damper rod cartridge (**Figure 38**).
2. Turn the fork assembly upside down and drain any residual fork oil into a suitable container. Dispose of the fork oil properly.
3. Install an open-end wrench on the flats on the fork cap bolt (A, **Figure 39**) and the other on the damper rod cartridge nut (B).
4. Hold onto the fork cap bolt and loosen the damper rod cartridge locknut.
5. Completely unscrew the fork cap bolt (**Figure 40**) from the damper rod cartridge.
6. Remove the spring seat (A, **Figure 41**), the spacer (B) and the washer (C).
7. Withdraw the fork spring (**Figure 42**) and the damper rod cartridge (**Figure 43**).
8. Slide the slider bushing, oil seal retainer, oil seal, stopper ring and dust seal from the fork tube.

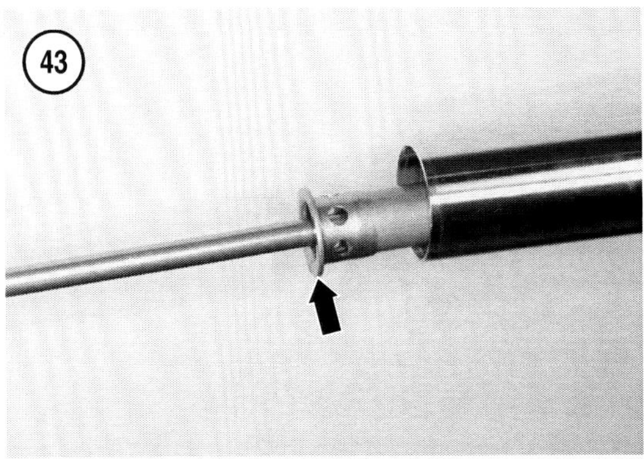

9. Remove the oil lock piece (**Figure 44**) from the damper rod cartridge. If the lock piece is stuck in place, perform the following:

   a. Screw a bolt into the base of the damper rod cartridge past the oil lock piece (A, **Figure 45**).
   b. Place a split bearing puller (B, **Figure 45**) next to the oil lock piece. Tighten the puller sufficiently to rest against the oil lock piece but not tight against the damper rod cartridge.
   c. Tap the end of the bolt and separate the oil lock piece from the damper rod cartridge

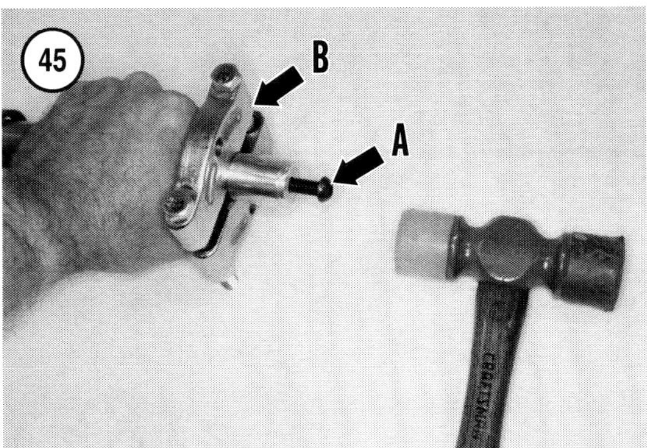

NOTE
Do not remove the fork tube bushing unless it is going to be replaced. Inspect it as described in this chapter.

10. If necessary, remove the fork tube bushing (**Figure 46**).

11. Inspect the components as described in this chapter.

Inspection

Replace any damaged or excessively worn components. Repair damaged threads with an appropriate size metric tap or die. Simply cleaning and reinstalling unserviceable components will not improve performance of the front suspension.

1. Thoroughly clean all parts in solvent and dry them. Check the fork tube for signs of wear or scratches.

2. Check the damper rod cartridge (**Figure 47**) for straightness and damage.

3. Check the threads and nut at the top of the damper rod cartridge for damage.

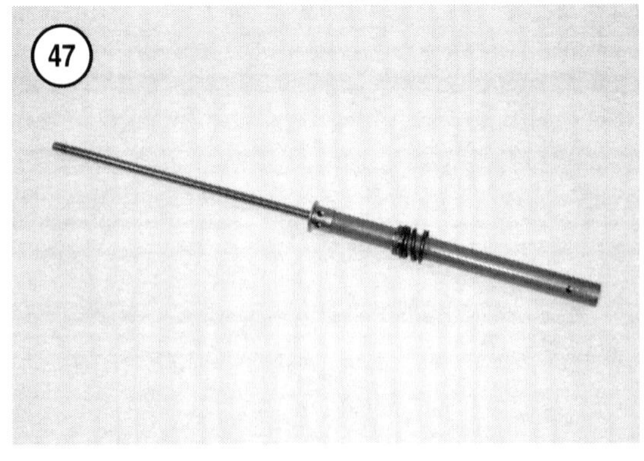

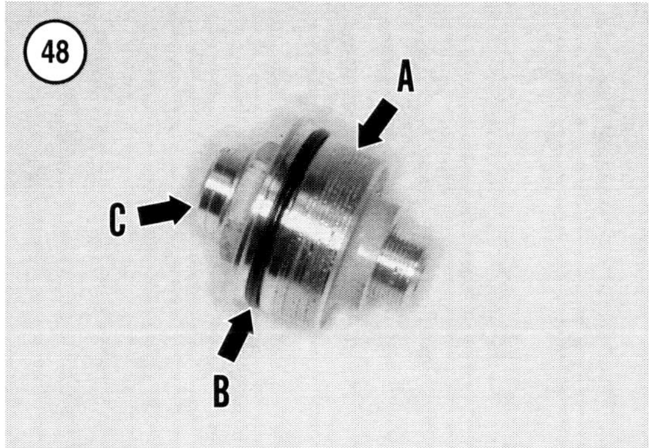

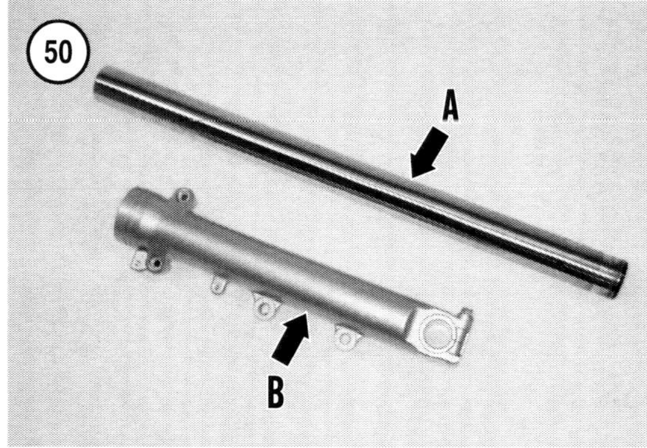

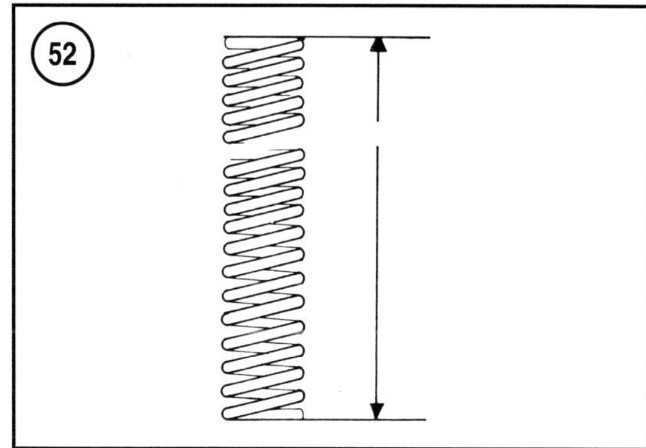

4. Make sure the oil hole in the damper rod cartridge is clear. Clean out if necessary.
5. Inspect the damper rod cartridge threads for the Allen bolt for wear or damage.

NOTE
Do not disassemble the fork cap bolt and rebound adjuster. Internal replacement parts are not available. If faulty, replace the unit as an assembly.

6. Inspect the fork cap bolt threads (A, **Figure 48**) for wear or damage.
7. Install a new O-ring (B) on the fork cap bolt.
8. If necessary, unscrew the spring adjuster (C, **Figure 48**) and inspect the O-ring (**Figure 49**). Replace if necessary.
9. Check the fork tube (A, **Figure 50**) for straightness.
10. Inspect the fork cap bolt threads in the fork tube for wear or damage.
11. Make sure the oil hole in the fork tube is clear. Clean out if necessary.
12. Check the slider (B, **Figure 50**) for dents or exterior damage that may cause the upper fork tube to stick.
13. Inspect the brake caliper mounting bosses on the slider for cracks or other damage.
14. Check the front axle bore in the slider for burrs or damage.
15. Inspect the oil seal seating area in the slider for damage or burrs.
16. Inspect the slider and fork tube bushings (**Figure 51**). If either is scratched or scored, they must be replaced.
17. Measure the uncompressed length of the fork spring as shown in **Figure 52**. Replace the spring if it has sagged to the service limit listed in **Table 1**.

Assembly

1. Coat all parts with fresh Suzuki fork oil prior to installation.
2. If removed, install a new bushing (A, **Figure 53**) onto the fork tube.

NOTE
Place a clinging-type plastic wrap over the end of the slider and coat it with fork oil. This will prevent damage to the dust seal and the oil seal lips when installing them over the top of the slider. These parts can then be carefully slid over the fork slider and the plastic wrap without damaging the seal inner sealing surfaces.

3. Coat the new seal with fresh SAE 10W fork oil.

NOTE
Position the new oil seal with the open groove facing upward.

4. Slide the fork slider bushing (B, **Figure 53**), oil seal retainer (C) and new oil seal (D) down into the fork tube.
5. Insert the fork tube into the slider (**Figure 54**) until the slider bushing reaches the slider.
6. Move the slider bushing (A, **Figure 55**) and the oil seal retainer (B) into position.

NOTE
A 43 mm fork seal driver is required to install the fork tube bushing and oil seal into the fork tube. A number of different aftermarket fork seal drivers are available that can be used for this purpose. Another method is to use a piece of pipe or metal collar with correct dimensions to slide over the fork tube and seat against the seal. When selecting or fabricating a driver tool, it must have sufficient weight to drive the bushing and oil seal into the fork tube. A 43 mm fork seal driver (Motion Pro part No. 088-0124) is used in this procedure,

7. Slide the fork seal driver down the fork tube and seat it against the slider bushing and oil seal retainer (**Figure 56**).
8. Operate the driver and drive the slider bushing and oil seal retainer into the fork tube.

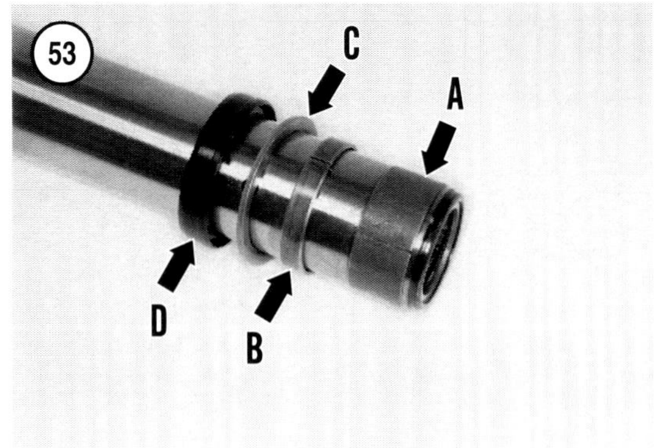

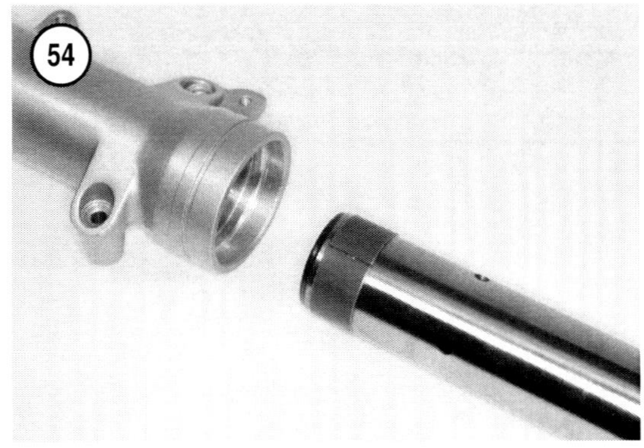

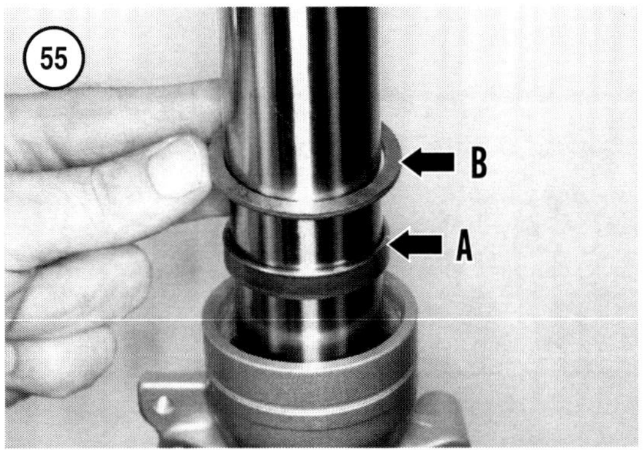

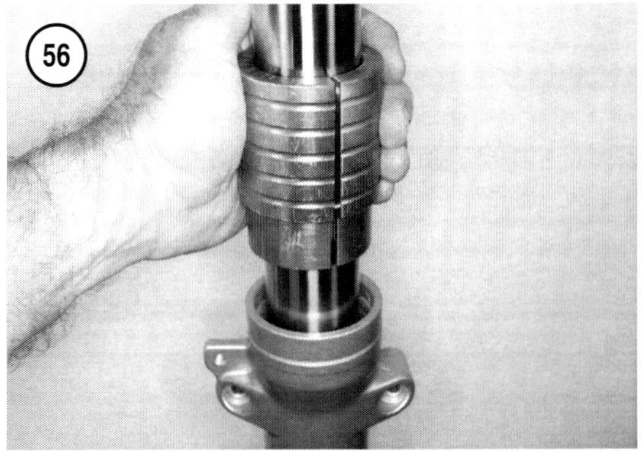

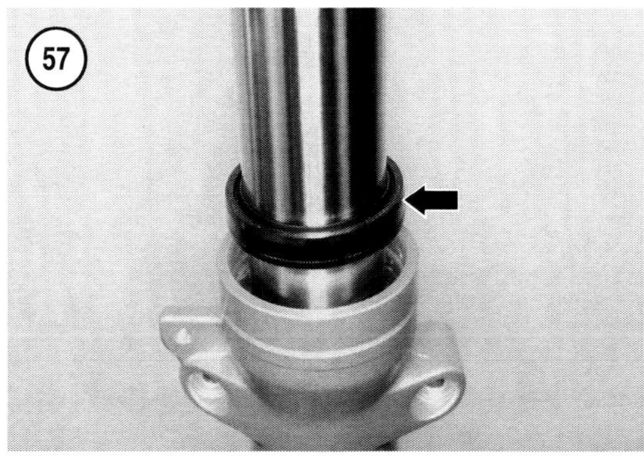
57

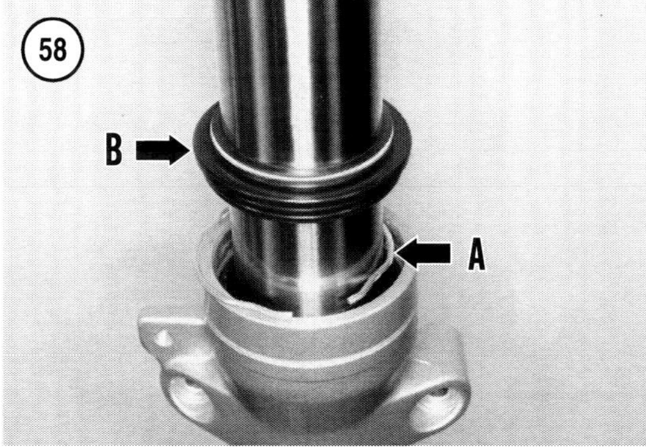

58

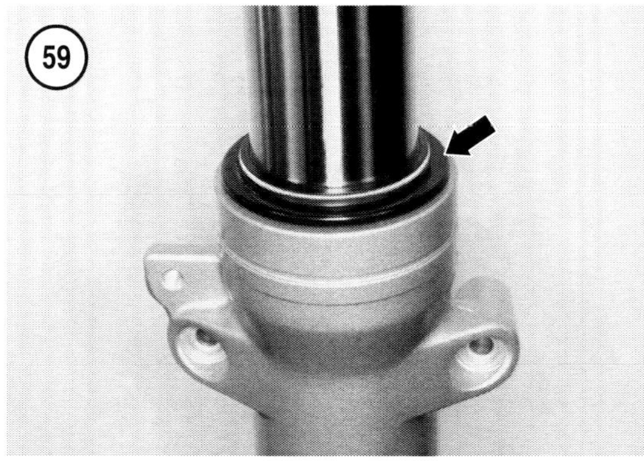
59

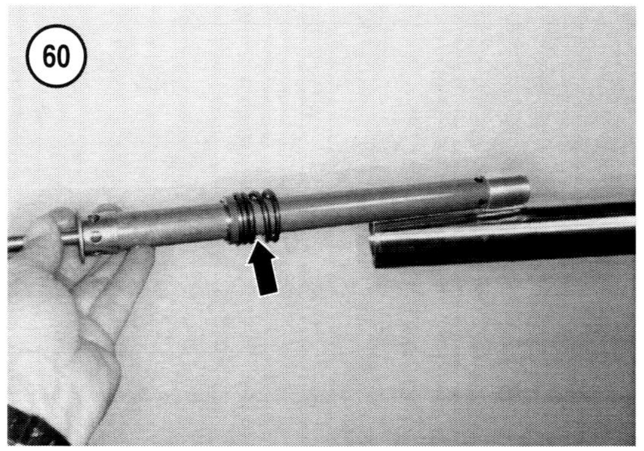
60

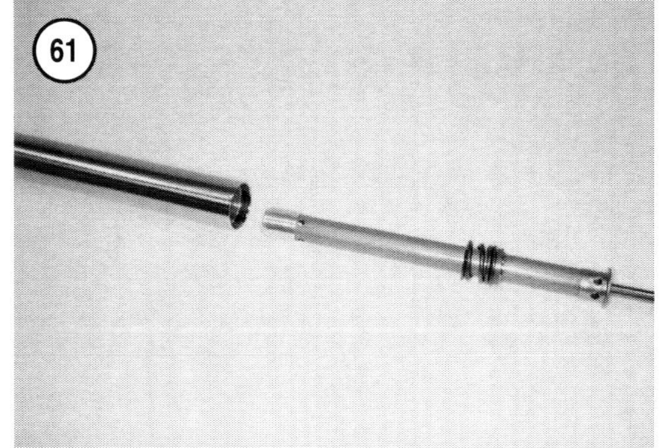
61

9. Slide the new oil seal (**Figure 57**) into position. Use the fork seal driver and drive the oil seal into the fork tube until the fork tube stopper ring groove is visible above the fork oil seal.
10. Slide the stopper ring down the fork tube.
11. Install the stopper ring (A, **Figure 58**) and make sure it is completely seated in the groove in the fork slider.
12. Install the dust seal (B, **Figure 58**) into the slider. Index it into the groove in the slider (**Figure 59**).
13. Install the oil lock piece (**Figure 44**) onto the end of the damper rod cartridge.
14. Make sure the rebound spring (**Figure 60**) is in place and insert the damper rod cartridge into the fork tube (**Figure 61**).

NOTE
The lower end of the damper rod cartridge must be guided into the lower stop in the base of the slider. If not aligned correctly, the Allen bolt can not be installed in Step 16.

15. Insert a scribe or thin screwdriver into the hole in the base of the slider to guide the lower end of the damper rod cartridge into the lower stop in the base of the slider.

NOTE
If the damper rod cartridge rotates while tightening the Allen bolt, temporarily install the fork spring, spacer and the fork cap bolt to hold it stationary.

16. Apply a medium strength threadlocking compound to the Allen bolt threads prior to installation.
17. Install a *new* washer (A, **Figure 62**) on the Allen bolt (B). Install it in the fork slider and tighten to

11

20 N•m (15 ft.-lb.). If installed, remove the fork cap bolt, spacer and fork spring.

NOTE
The following special tool is necessary to bleed the damper rod. One can be fabricated that is approximately 2 inches long with an inner metric thread of 10 × 1.0. This tool is to extend the length of the damper rod for the fork oil bleeding process.

18. Install the special tool extension (**Figure 63**) onto the damper rod cartridge.
19. Secure the fork assembly in a vertical position.

NOTE
To measure the correct amount of fluid, use a plastic baby bottle. These bottles have measurements in milliliters (ml) on the side.

20. Completely compress the fork tube into the slider.
21. Add one-half of the recommended amount (**Table 1**) of Suzuki fork oil to the fork assembly.

NOTE
During the bleeding procedure, maintain the fork oil level above the sliding portion of the damper rod cartridge. If the oil level drops below this level, air may enter the cartridge, nullifying the bleeding procedure.

22. Bleed air from the damper rod cartridge as follows:
    a. Hold the fork assembly in a vertical position during this step.
    b. Hold onto the special tool extension installed in Step 18 and *slowly* move the damper rod cartridge up and down within the fork oil using full travel strokes.
    c. Repeat this at least 10 times, or until the fork oil is free of bubbles.
    d. If necessary, add additional fork oil until the oil is almost level with the top of the compressed fork tube.
    e. Slowly move the fork tube up and down several strokes or until bubbles do not come from the oil.
    f. Secure the fork assembly in this vertical position for 5-10 minutes to allow any additional trapped air to escape. Tap on the side of the fork assembly to break away any bubbles adhering to the side of the fork.

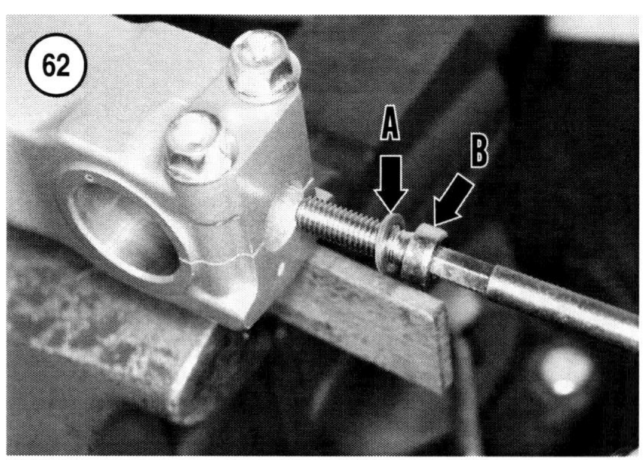

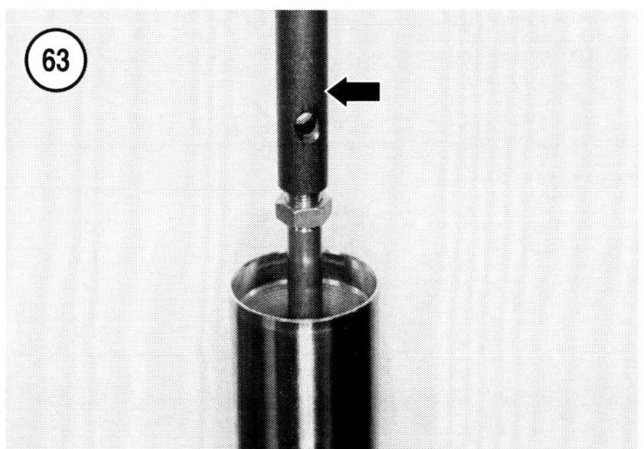

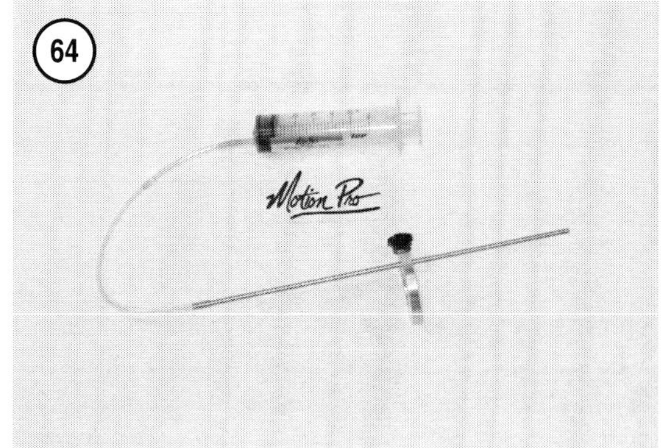

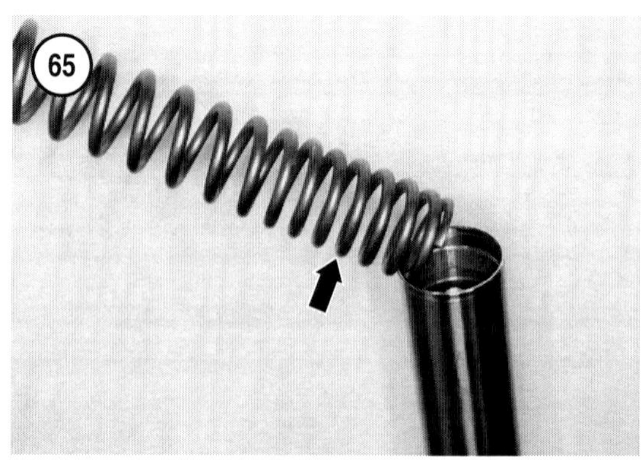

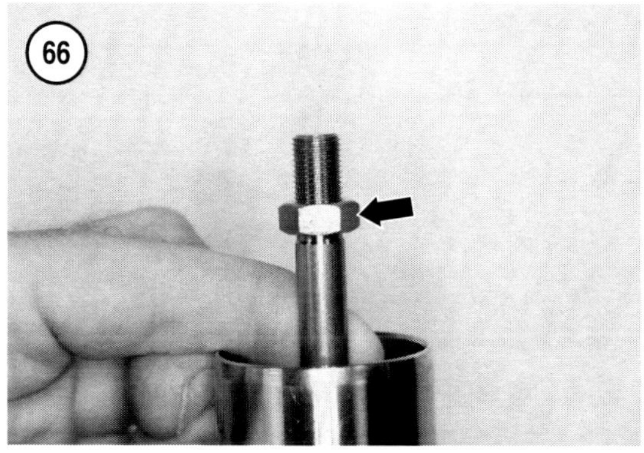

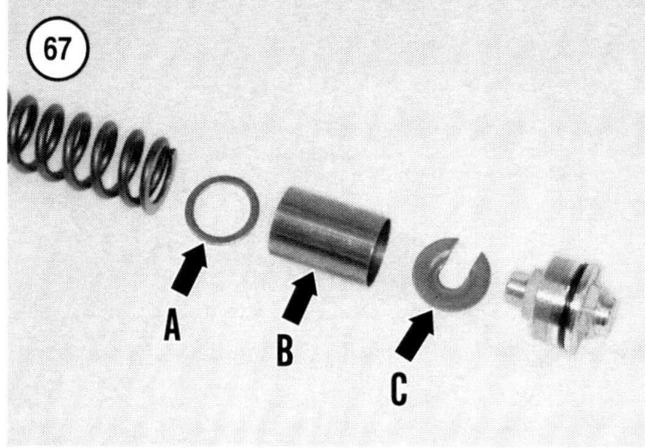

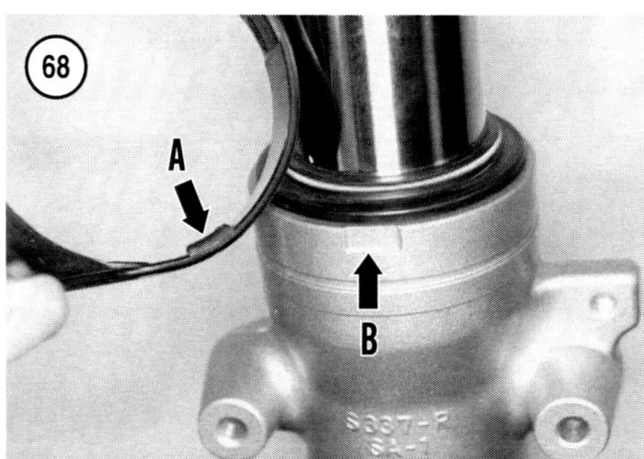

g. Add the remaining amount of the fork oil.

NOTE
Suzuki recommends that the fork oil level be measured, if possible, to ensure a more accurate filling.

23. Adjust the fork oil as follows:
  a. Hold the fork assembly vertically and fully compress the fork tube.
  b. Use an accurate ruler or the Motion Pro oil gauge (part No. 08-0121) (**Figure 64**), or an equivalent, to achieve the correct oil level listed in **Table 1**.
  c. Allow the oil to settle completely and recheck the oil level measurement. Adjust the oil level if necessary.
  d. Remove the special tool.
24. Fully extend the fork tube.
25. Position the fork spring with the closer wound coils (**Figure 65**) going in first and install the fork spring.
26. Keep the fork assembly upright so the fork oil will not drain out and slightly compress the fork so the top of the damper rod is extended up through the top of the spring.
27. Turn the locknut down to the bottom of the damper rod threads (**Figure 66**).
28. Install the washer (A, **Figure 67**), spacer (B) and spring seat (C) onto the top of the damper rod.
29. Screw the fork cap bolt assembly (**Figure 40**) onto the damper rod cartridge until the spring adjuster, within the fork cap bolt, seats on the damper rod.
30. Install an open-end wrench on the flats on the fork cap bolt (A, **Figure 39**) and the other on the damper rod cartridge nut (B).
31. Hold onto the fork cap bolt and tighten the damper rod cartridge locknut to 20 N•m (15 ft.-lb.). Remove the wrenches.
32. Pull the fork tube up against the fork cap bolt and screw the cap bolt into the fork tube and tighten securely. Do not try to tighten to the correct torque at this time.
33. On 2001-on models, align the locating tab (A, **Figure 68**) on the protector with the notch (B) on the fork slider and install the protector. Push it down until it seats completely (**Figure 69**).
34. Install the fork assemblies as described in this chapter and tighten the cap bolt to 23 N•m (17 ft.-lb.).

Table 1 FRONT SUSPENSION SPECIFICATIONS

Item	Specification	Service limit
Front fork stroke	130 mm (5.12 in.)	–
Fork oil capacity		
U.S. and Canada		
1997-2000	514 ml (17.3 U.S. oz./18.1 Imp. oz.)	
2001-on	507 ml (17.1 U.S. oz./17.9 Imp. oz.)	
Other than U.S. and Canada		
1997-2000	514 ml (17.3 U.S. oz./18.1 Imp. oz.)	
2001-on	509 ml (17.2 U.S. oz./17.9 Imp. oz.)	
Fork oil level		
U.S. and Canada		
1997-2000	101 mm (4.0 in.)	
2001-on	107 mm (4.2 in.)	
Other than U.S. and Canada		
1997-2000	99 mm (3.9 in.)	
2001-on	105 mm (4.1 in.)	
Fork spring free length		
U.S. and Canada		
1997-2000	–	360 mm (14.2 in.)
2001-on	–	366 mm (14.4 in.)
Other than U.S. and Canada		
1996-2000	–	362 mm (14.26 in.)
2001-on	–	370 mm (14.6 in.)

Table 2 FRONT SUSPENSION AND STEERING TORQUE SPECIFICATIONS

Item	N•m	in.-lb.	ft.-lb.
Damper rod Allen bolt	20	–	15
Fork bridge			
Lower clamp bolts	23	–	17
Upper clamp bolt	23	–	17
Front axle	100	–	74
Front axle pinch bolt	23	–	17
Front caliper mounting bolt	39	–	29
Front fork			
Cap bolt	23	–	17
Damper rod locknut	20	–	15
Front clutch and master cylinder clamp bolts	10	88	–
Handlebar clamp bolts	23	–	17
Steering stem nut	65	–	48
Steering stem adjust nut	45	–	33

CHAPTER TWELVE

REAR SUSPENSION

This chapter contains procedures for the removal, disassembly, lubrication and repair of the rear suspension components. Rear wheel removal, rear hub service, tire changing, tire repair and wheel balancing are covered in Chapter Ten.

The rear suspension features the Suzuki link-type suspension, which consists of the swing arm, a single shock absorber and a shock-lever and tie-rod assembly. The pivot joints on all components must be disassembled, inspected and lubricated frequently to provide proper operation of the suspension, as well as maximum service life.

The swing arm is supported by a caged roller bearing on each side where the pivot mounts to the frame. The lower end of the shock absorber is connected to the swing arm via the shock linkage.

When inspecting rear suspension components, compare all measurements to the rear suspension specifications listed in **Table 1**. Replace any component that is damaged, worn to the wear limit or out of specification. During assembly, tighten fasteners to the specifications listed. **Table 1** and **Table 2** are located at the end of the chapter.

SHOCK ABSORBER

Removal

1. Securely support the motorcycle on level ground on the centerstand. If necessary, place wooden blocks under the crankcase to support the motorcycle with the rear wheel off the ground.
2. Remove the frame left side cover as described in Chapter Fourteen.
3. Remove the muffler as described in Chapter Eight. Wrap a plastic bag around the exhaust pipe opening to keep out debris.
4. Remove the rear wheel as described in Chapter Ten.
5. Place a box under the swing arm to support it and take the weight off the shock absorber.

6. Remove the lower shock mounting nut (A, **Figure 1**) on the left side.
7. Remove the bolt and nut (B, **Figure 1**) securing the tie rods to the shock lever. On 2001-on models, do not lose the washer between each tie rod and the shock lever.
8. Remove the lower shock mounting bolt from the left side and separate the shock absorber from the shock lever.
9. Lower the swing arm to allow more working room.
10. Working on the left side, insert a socket and long extension through the frame hole (**Figure 2**) and remove the upper mounting nut.
11. Hold onto the shock absorber and remove the upper shock mounting bolt from the right side.
12. Lower the shock absorber from the frame (**Figure 3**) and remove the shock absorber from the hole in the swing arm.
13. Inspect the shock absorber as described in this chapter.

Installation

1. Clean the mounting bolts and nuts in solvent and dry them thoroughly.
2. Apply a light coat of waterproof grease to the shock absorber upper and lower mounts. Also apply a light coat to the upper mount on the frame.
3. On 2001-on models, position the shock so the index punch mark (**Figure 4**) on the lower shock mount faces toward the rear of the motorcycle.

NOTE

It is difficult to install the shock absorber and upper mounting bolt at the same time due to limited working area in the frame. Attach the shock absorber to the swing arm first and then to the frame mount as described in the following steps.

4. Fit the shock absorber through the hole in the swing arm and into the shock mounting area in the frame. Do not install the upper bolt at this time.
5. Move the swing arm up into position and install the shock lower mounting bolt in from the right side, then install the nut (A, **Figure 1**). Finger-tighten the nut at this time.
6. Raise or lower the swing arm as necessary to align the tie rods with the center mount on the shock

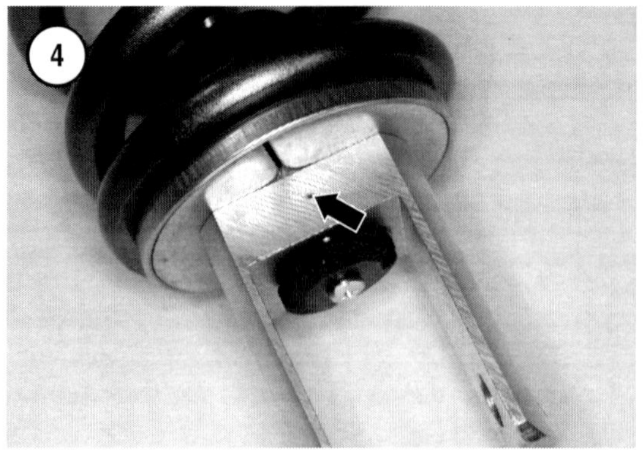

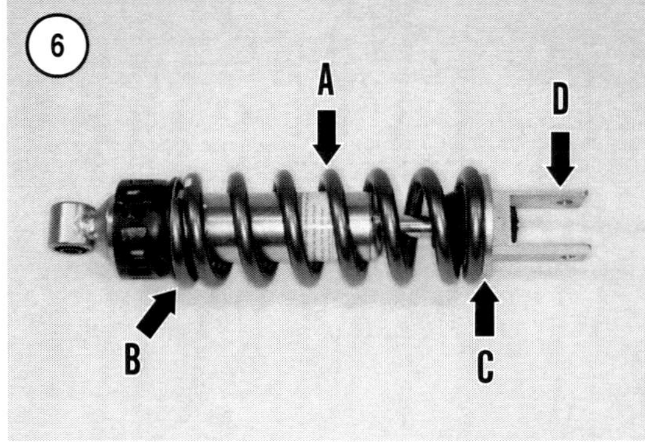

lever. On 2001-on models, install a washer (**Figure 5**) between each tie rod and the shock lever. Install the bolt (B, **Figure 1**) and nut. Finger-tighten the nut at this time.

7. Working on the right side of the motorcycle, raise or lower the swing arm as necessary to align the shock absorber upper mount with the frame mount. Install the bolt through the frame mount and the shock absorber upper mount. Install the nut, and finger-tighten it at this time.

8. Remove the box from under the swing arm.

9. Tighten the lower tie rod bolt and nut, then the lower shock absorber bolt and nut and then the shock absorber upper bolt and nut. Tighten the bolts and nuts to the specifications in **Table 1**.

10. Install the rear wheel as described in Chapter Ten.

11. Install the muffler as described in Chapter Eight.

12. Install the frame left side cover as described in Chapter Fourteen.

13. Take the motorcycle off the centerstand, jack or stand, and push down on the rear of the motorcycle to make sure the linkage is operating correctly with no binding.

Inspection

Replacement parts are not available for the original equipment shock absorber. If any part of the shock absorber is faulty, replace the shock absorber.

1. Inspect the shock absorber for oil leaks.
2. Check the spring (A, **Figure 6**) for cracks or other damage.
3. Check the upper (B, **Figure 6**) and lower spring seats (C) for cracks or looseness.
4. Inspect the shock absorber upper mount bushing (**Figure 7**) for elongation, cracks or other damage.
5. Inspect the shock absorber lower mount (D, **Figure 6**) for elongation, cracks or other damage.
6. If any damage is noted, replace the shock absorber.

SHOCK LEVER ASSEMBLY

Removal/Installation

Refer to **Figure 8**.

NOTE

In this procedure the shock lever assembly is removed, leaving the swing arm in place. If the swing arm is going to be removed, it is easier to disconnect the shock lever assembly from the frame and leave all of the shock lever components attached to the swing arm.

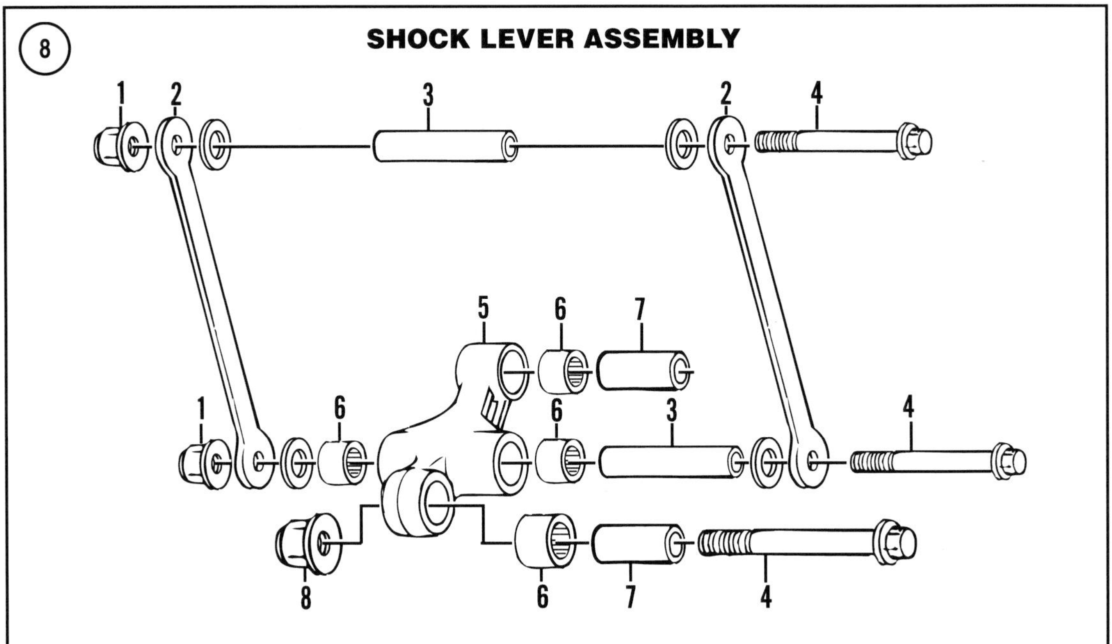

8

SHOCK LEVER ASSEMBLY

1. Nut
2. Tie rod
3. Collar
4. Through bolt
5. Shock lever
6. Needle bearing
7. Collar
8. Nut

1. Remove the rear wheel as described in Chapter Ten.

NOTE
Insert a piece of vinyl tubing or wood between the pads of the rear caliper once the caliper is removed. If the brake lever is inadvertently squeezed, the pistons will not be forced out of the cylinders. If this does happen, the caliper may have to be disassembled to reseat the pistons and the system will have to be bled. By using the wood, bleeding the brake is not necessary when installing the wheel.

2. Remove the muffler as described in Chapter Eight. Wrap a plastic bag around the exhaust pipe opening to keep out debris.
3. Place a box under the swing arm to support it and take the weight off the shock lever linkage.
4. Remove the left side foot peg and gearshift lever assembly as described in Chapter Fourteen.
5. Remove the right side foot peg and rear brake pedal assembly as described in Chapter Fourteen.

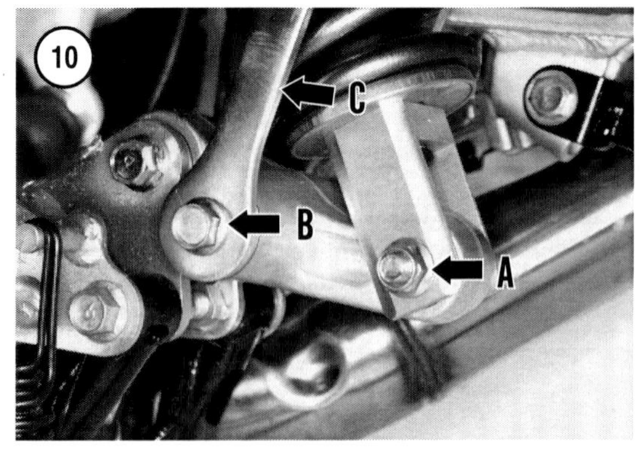

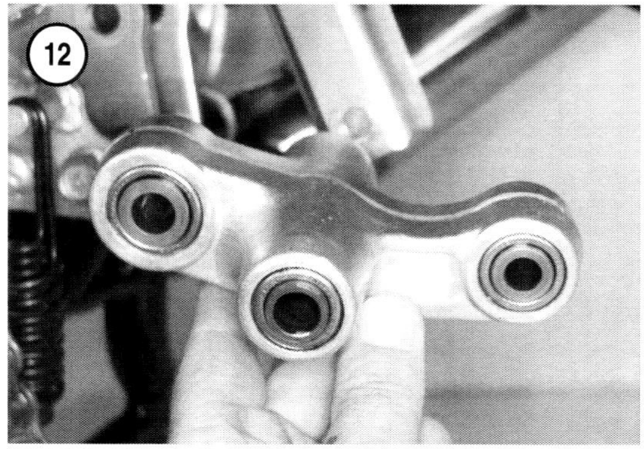

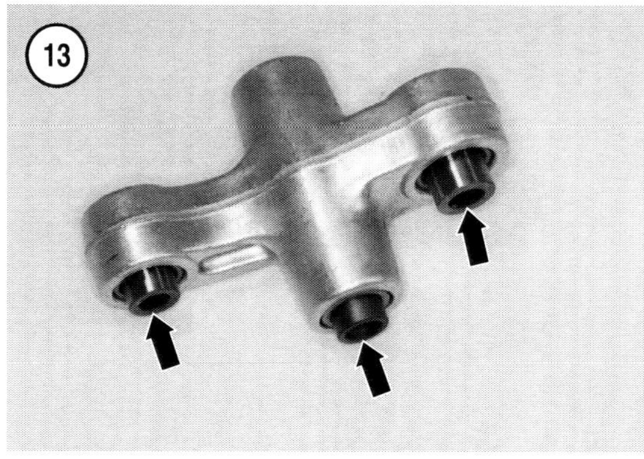

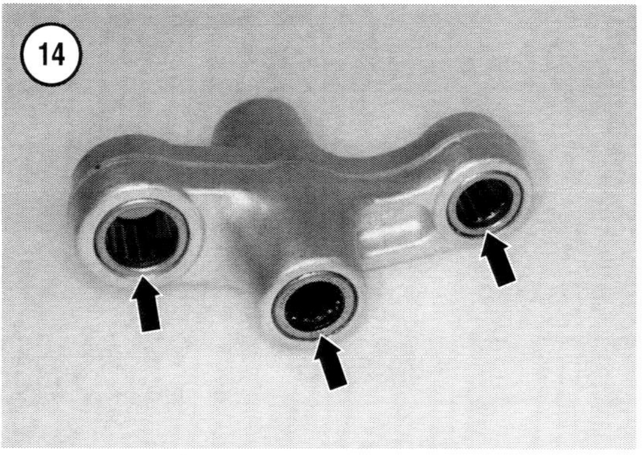

6. Remove the bolt and nut (**Figure 9**) securing the tie rods to the swing arm. On 2001-on models, do not lose the washer between each tie rod and the swing arm.
7. Remove the bolt and nut securing the shock absorber (A, **Figure 10**) to the shock lever.
8. Remove the bolt and nut (B, **Figure 10**) securing the tie rods to the shock lever.

NOTE
*On 2001-on models, do not lose the washer between each tie rod and the shock lever. Remove both tie rods (C, **Figure 10**).*

9. Remove the bolt and nut (**Figure 11**) securing the shock lever to the frame. Lower the shock lever and remove it from the frame and swing arm.
10. Inspect the shock lever as described in this chapter.
11. Install by reversing these removal steps while noting the following:
   a. Apply Suzuki Super Grease A or an equivalent waterproof grease to the bearings in the shock lever. Also apply grease to the pivot points on the lower shock mount and on the frame mounting boss.
   b. Position the shock lever as shown in **Figure 12** and install it.
   c. On 2001-on models, install a washer between each tie rod and the shock lever.
   d. Be sure the collars are in place on the shock lever and install the three pivot bolts from the left side.
   e. Install the three mounting nuts finger-tight.
   f. Tighten the mounting nuts to the specifications in **Table 2**. Tighten the nuts in the following order: First, torque the lower tie-rod mounting nut (B, **Figure 10**) to the shock lever, next the lower shock mounting nut (A) and finally, torque the shock lever upper mounting nut to the swing arm (**Figure 11**).
   g. After the right side footpeg has been installed, check that the electrical connector is still attached to the brake light switch.

Inspection

1. Inspect the shock lever pivot bearings as follows:
   a. Remove the pivot collars (**Figure 13**) from the shock lever.
   b. Use a clean lint-free rag and wipe off surface grease from the needle bearings (**Figure 14**) in the shock lever.

15

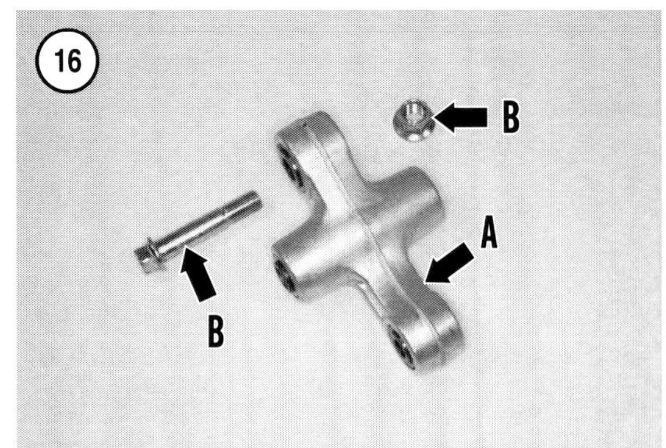

16

c. Turn each bearing by hand. The bearing should turn smoothly without excessive play or noise. Check the rollers for evidence of wear, pitting or rust.
d. Reinstall the pivot collars into the bearings and slowly rotate each pivot collar. Each collar must turn smoothly without excessive play or noise.
e. If the needle bearings must be replaced, refer to *Shock Lever Needle Bearing Replacement* in this chapter.

2. Inspect the pivot collars (**Figure 15**) for wear and damage. Replace each collar as necessary.
3. Inspect the shock lever (A, **Figure 16**) for cracks or damage. Replace as necessary.
4. Clean the pivot bolts and nuts (B, **Figure 16**) in solvent. Check the bolts for straightness. If a bolt is bent, it will restrict the movement of the rocker arm.
5. If removed, inspect the tie rods (A, **Figure 17**) for bending, cracks or damage. Replace as necessary. Check the bolt (B, **Figure 17**) for straightness. If a bolt is bent, it will restrict the movement of the rocker arm. Check the pivot collar (C, **Figure 17**) for wear or damage.
6. Prior to installing the pivot collars, coat the inner surface of the bearings with Suzuki Super Grease A or an equivalent waterproof bearing grease.

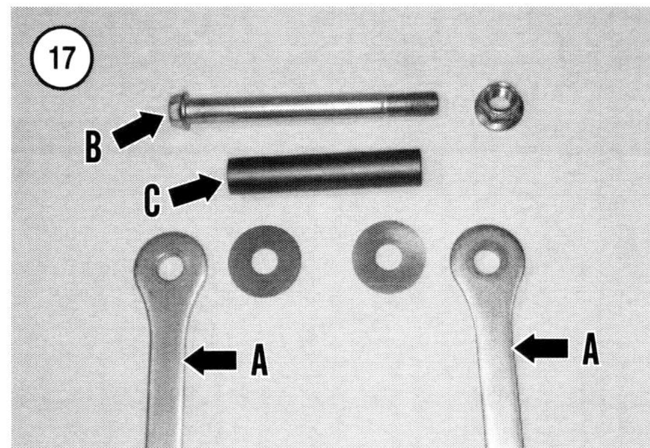

17

18

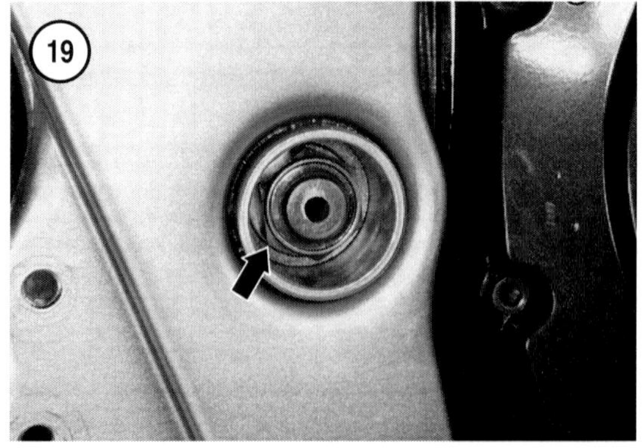
19

SWING ARM

Swing Arm Bearing Preliminary Inspection

The condition of the swing arm bearings can greatly affect the handling of the motorcycle. Worn bearings will cause wheel hop, pulling to one side under acceleration and pulling to the other side during braking. To check the condition of the swing arm bearings, perform the following procedure.

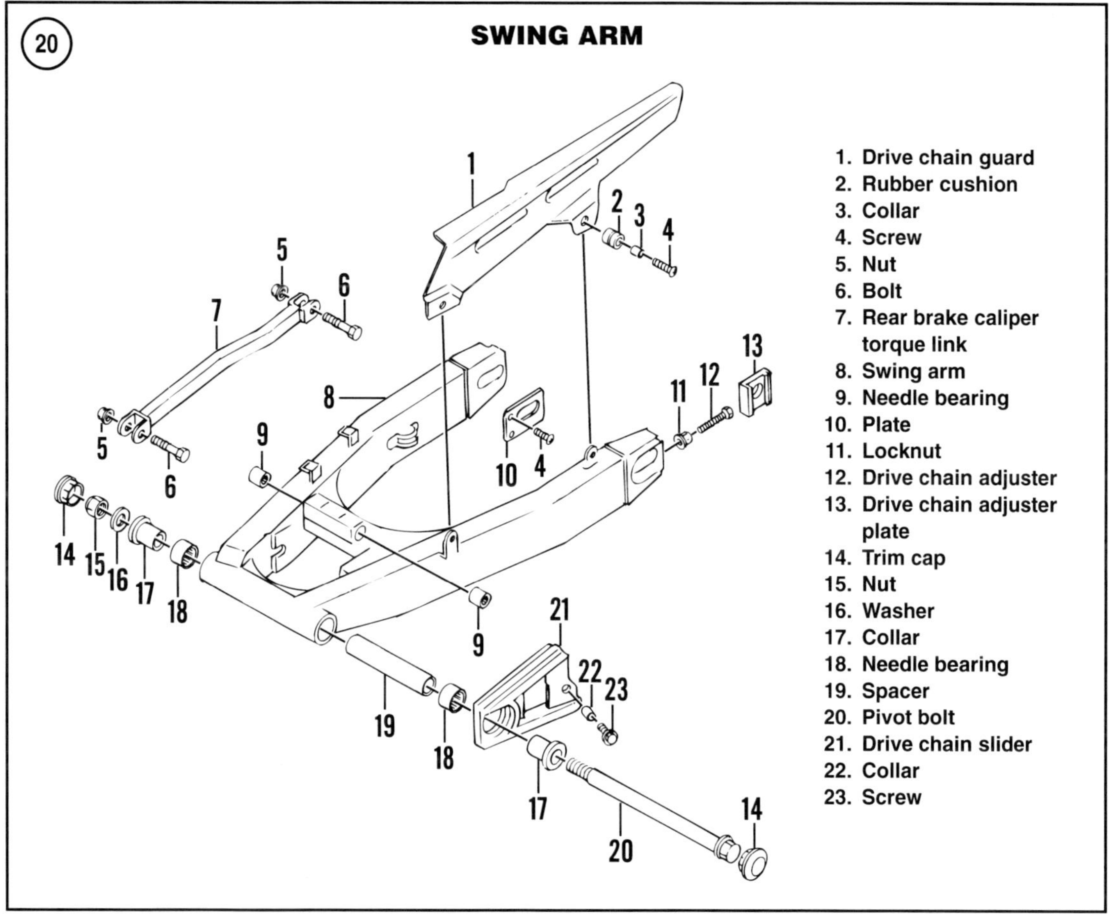

1. Remove the rear wheel as described in Chapter Ten.
2. Remove the tie rod mounting nut (**Figure 18**) and bolt and separate the tie rods from the shock lever. The tie rods do not have to be completely removed.

NOTE
On 2001-on models, do not lose the washer between each tie rod and the shock lever.

3. The swing arm is now free to move under its own weight.
4. The trim cap is flush with the frame. To prevent scratching the frame finish, insert a stiff flat feeler gauge (0.5 mm/0.020 in. or greater) between the end cap and the frame to remove the trim cap on the right side. Make sure the swing arm pivot nut (**Figure 19**) on the right side is tight.

NOTE
Have an assistant steady the motorcycle when performing Step 5 and Step 6.

5. Grasp both ends of the swing arm and attempt to move it from side to side in a horizontal arc. If more than a slight amount of movement is felt, the bearings are worn and must be replaced.
6. Grasp both ends of the swing arm and move it up and down. The swing arm should move smoothly with no binding or abnormal noise from the bearings. If there is binding or noise, the bearings are worn and must be replaced.
7. Move the swing arm and the tie rods into position. Install the rear tie rod bolt from the left side. Install the tie rod nut and tighten it to 78 N•m (57 ft.-lb.).
8. Install the rear wheel as described in Chapter Ten.

Removal

Refer to **Figure 20**.

1. Remove the banjo bolt and sealing washers (A, **Figure 21**) from the rear brake caliper. Place the

loose end of the brake hose in a reclosable plastic bag and close the bag.

2. Remove the rear bolt and washer (B, **Figure 21**) securing the torque link to the rear caliper. Set the rear brake caliper aside.

3. Remove the screws securing the drive chain guard (A, **Figure 22**) and remove the guard from the swing arm.

4. Remove the rear wheel (B, **Figure 22**) as described in Chapter Ten.

5. Remove the muffler as described in Chapter Eight. Wrap a plastic bag around the exhaust pipe opening to keep out debris.

6. Unhook the brake hose from the two clamps (A, **Figure 23**) on top of the swing arm.

7. Carefully pull the rear of the brake hose out from the guide (B, **Figure 23**) on the inner surface of the swing arm. Remove the brake hose.

8. Remove the left side foot peg and gearshift lever assembly (A, **Figure 24**) as described in Chapter Fourteen.

9. Remove the right side foot peg and rear brake pedal assembly as described in Chapter Fourteen.

10. Remove the shock lower mounting nut (**Figure 25**) and bolt.

11. Support the swing arm with a box or wooden blocks.

12. Remove the bolt and nut (**Figure 26**) securing the shock lever to the frame.

13. The trim cap is flush with the frame. To prevent scratching the frame finish, insert a stiff flat feeler gauge (0.5 mm/0.020 in. or greater) between the end cap and the frame to remove the trim cap on both sides.

14. Remove the pivot nut and washer (**Figure 19**) from the right side.

15. Carefully tap the pivot shaft into the right side of the frame and then pull the shaft (B, **Figure 24**) from the left side of the frame.

16. Lower the swing arm from the frame, disengage the drive chain and remove the swing arm.

17. If the swing arm bearings are not going to be serviced, place a strip of duct tape over each pivot. This will protect the bearing assemblies and prevent the loss of any small parts.

18. Inspect the swing arm as described in this chapter. Lubricate all bearings as described in this chapter.

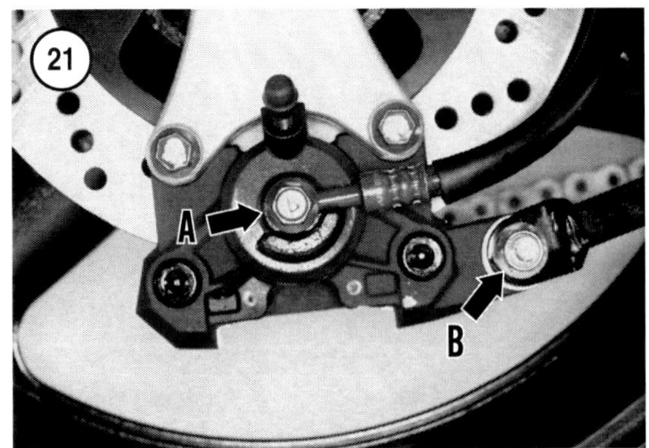

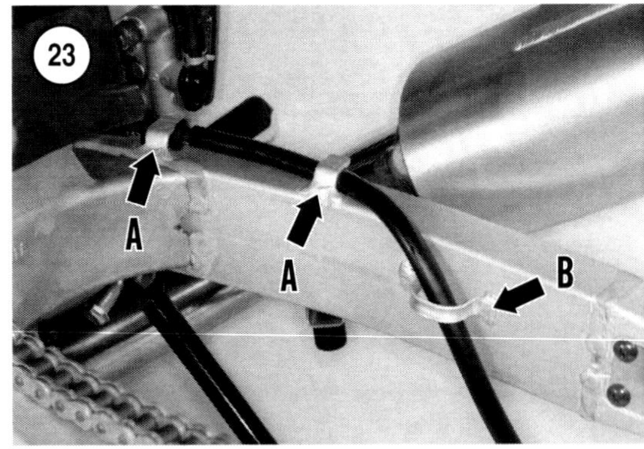

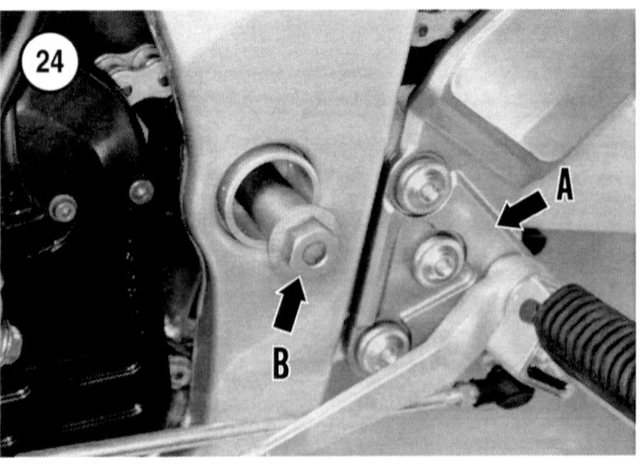

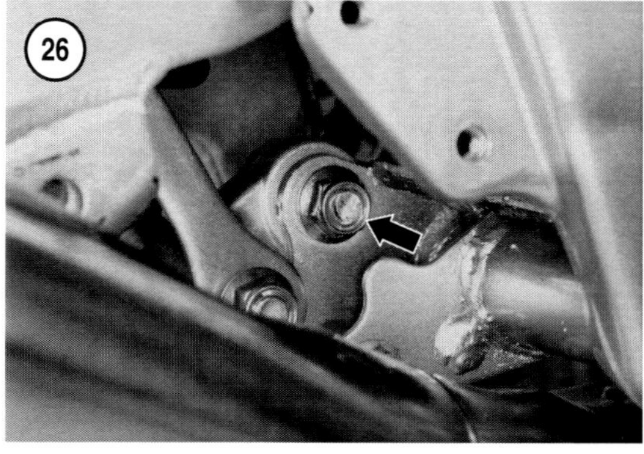

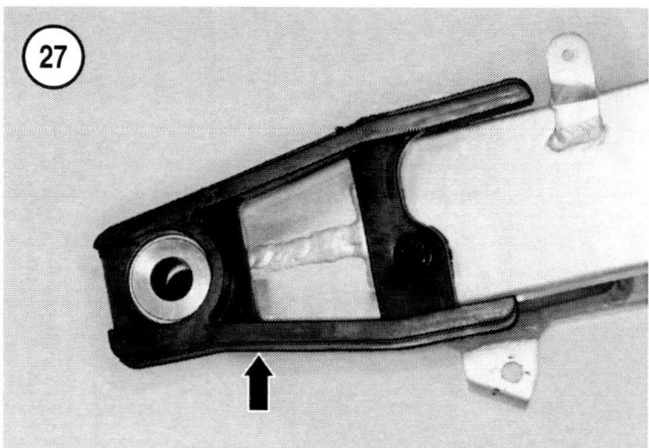

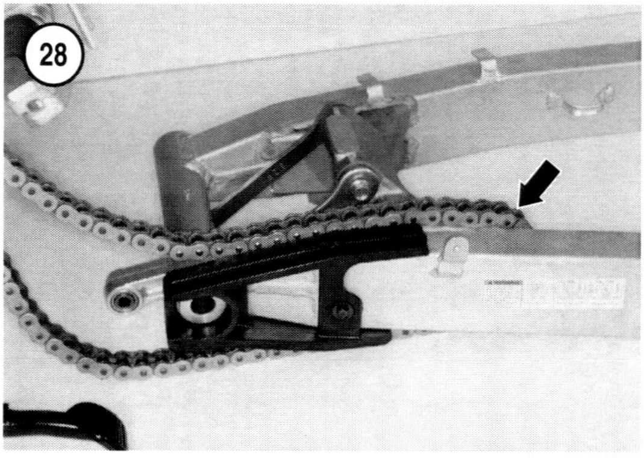

Installation

NOTE
Have an assistant available before starting swing arm installation. The swing arm can be installed by one person, but the job is much easier with two.

1. If removed, install the drive chain slider (**Figure 27**) onto the swing arm and tighten the bolt securely.
2. Lubricate the swing arm and shock lever bearings, the pivot bolts and collars with Suzuki Super Grease A or an equivalent waterproof grease prior to installation.
3. Engage the drive chain with the swing arm (**Figure 28**).
4. Secure the rear brake hose above the swing arm mount in the frame to prevent the brake hose from getting pinched by the swing arm.
5. Check that the drive chain is properly engaged with the engine sprocket.
6. Raise the swing arm so the shock absorber passes through the opening in the swing arm, then move the swing arm into position with the frame pivot point mounts.
7. From the left side of the frame, install the swing arm pivot shaft (B, **Figure 24**) through the swing arm pivot area and the right side of the frame.
8. Install the washer and pivot nut (**Figure 19**) onto the end of the pivot shaft. Tighten the swing arm pivot bolt nut to 100 N•m (74 ft.-lb.).
9. Grab the end of each arm and raise and lower the swing arm. The swing arm should pivot smoothly with no binding.
10. Align the front portion of the shock lever with the frame pivot area and install the pivot bolt and nut (**Figure 26**). Finger-tighten the nut.
11. Align the shock absorber lower pivot hole with the shock lever and install the pivot bolt and nut (**Figure 25**). Finger-tighten the nut.
12. Tighten the shock lever mounting nuts to 50 N•m (37 ft.-lb.).
13. Install the left side foot peg and gearshift lever assembly as described in Chapter Fourteen.

NOTE
After the right side footpeg has been installed, check that the electrical connector is still attached to the brake light switch.

14. Install the right side foot peg and rear brake pedal assembly as described in Chapter Fourteen.

15. Carefully feed the rear of the brake hose through the guide (B, **Figure 23**) on the inner surface of the swing arm. Secure the brake hose beneath the two clamps (A, **Figure 23**) on top of the swing arm.

16. Remove the plastic bag from the exhaust pipe and install the muffler as described in Chapter Eight.

17. Install the rear wheel (B, **Figure 22**) as described in Chapter Ten.

18. Install the drive chain guard (A, **Figure 22**) and tighten the screws securely.

19. Install the torque link onto the rear brake caliper and install the rear bolt and washer (B, **Figure 21**). Tighten the bolt and nut to 35 N•m (26 ft.-lb.).

20. Install the brake hose onto the rear caliper. Install the banjo bolt and *new* sealing washers. Tighten the banjo bolt to 23 N•m (17 ft.-lb.).

21. Adjust the chain as described in Chapter Three.

22. Bleed the brakes as described in Chapter Thirteen.

Disassembly

Refer to **Figure 20**.

1. Remove the swing arm as described in this chapter.

2. Remove the chain slider (A, **Figure 29**) from the swing arm.

NOTE
The tie rods are symmetrical and can be installed on either side of the shock lever. After prolonged use, they develop a unique wear pattern and should be reinstalled on the same side. Prior to removing the tie rods, mark them with an L (left) or R (right) so they can be reinstalled on the correct side of the shock lever.

3. Remove the tie rod mounting nut and bolt from the mounting boss. Remove the tie rods and shock lever (B, **Figure 29**) from the swing arm.

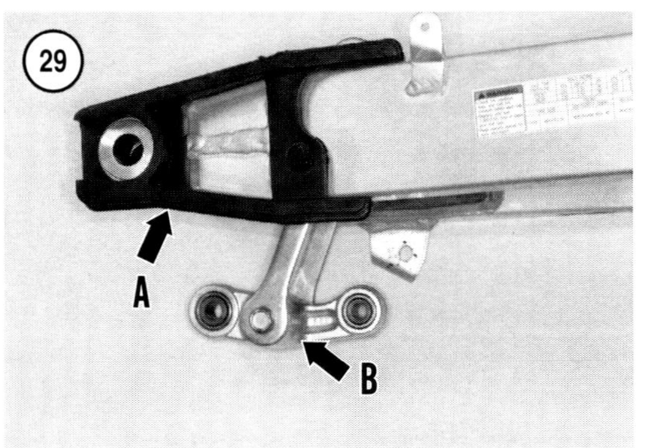

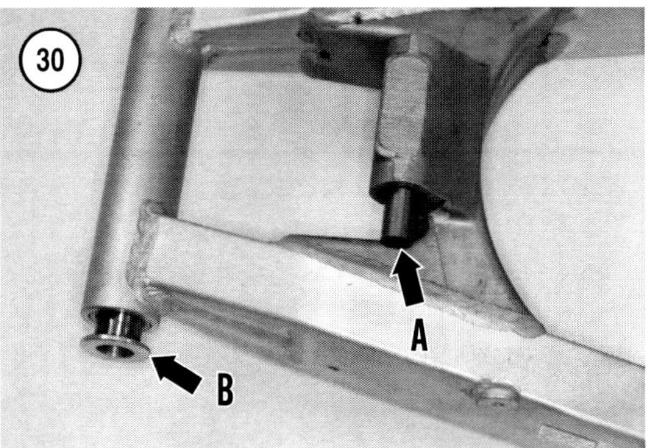

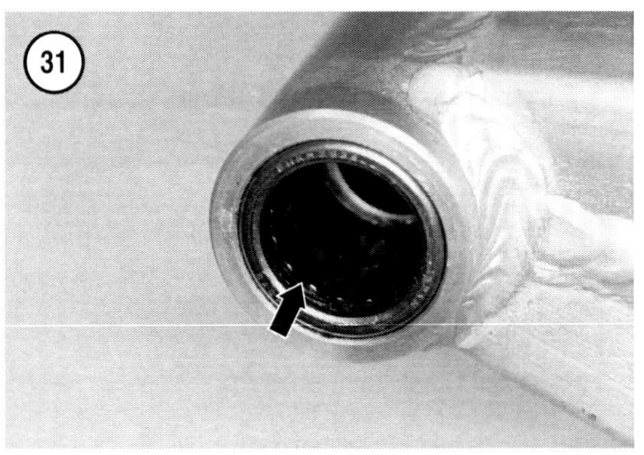

NOTE
On 2001-on models, do not lose the washer located between each tie rod and the mounting boss.

4. Remove the pivot collar (A, **Figure 30**) from the tie rod mounting boss.

5. Remove the pivot collar (B, **Figure 30**) from the needle bearing on each side of the swing arm pivot boss.

6. Inspect the swing arm as described in this chapter.

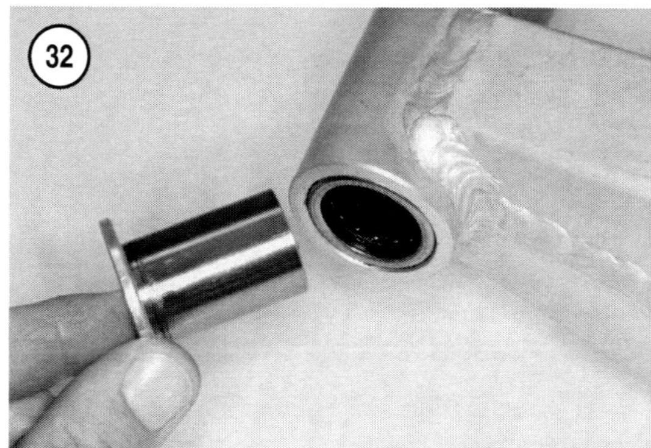
32

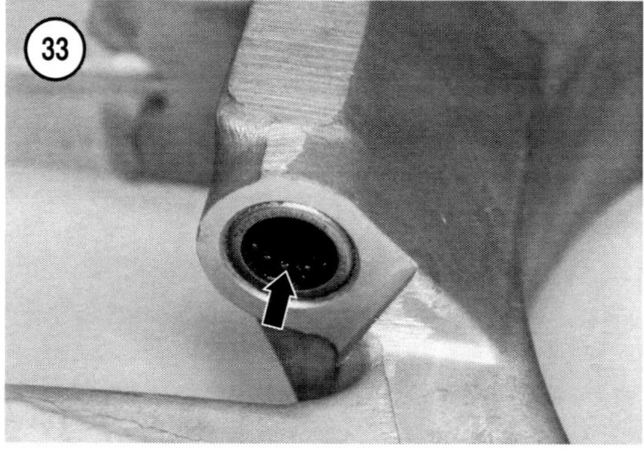
33

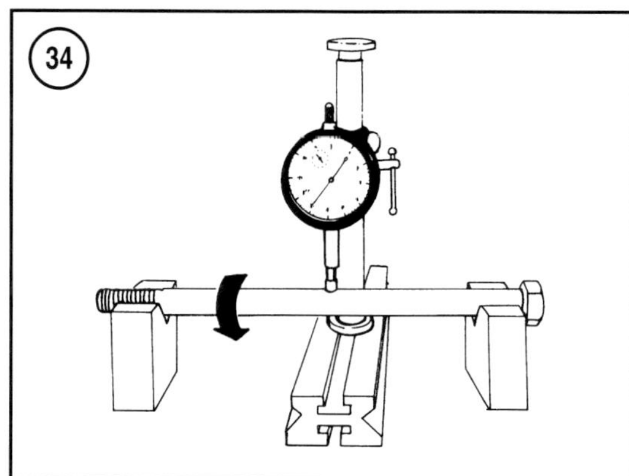
34

Assembly

1. Lubricate the needle bearings and collars with Suzuki Super Grease A or an equivalent waterproof bearing grease.
2. Install the pivot collar into the tie rod mounting boss (A, **Figure 30**) on the swing arm. Be sure the ends of the collar are flush with the end of each needle bearing.
3. Install the tie rods onto the swing arm by performing the following:
   a. Refer to marks made prior to removal to reinstall each tie rod onto its original side (left or right).
   b. Position the tie rods so they point down through the hole in the swing arm.

NOTE
On 2001-on models, install a washer between each tie rod and the swing arm pivot boss.

   c. Align the tie rods with the mounting boss on the swing arm and install the tie rod bolt from the left side of the swing arm.
   d. Install the tie rod mounting nut and tighten to 78 N•m (57 ft.-lb.).
4. Install the collar (B, **Figure 30**) into the needle bearing on each side of the swing arm pivot boss.
5. Install the chain slider onto the left side of the swing arm and tighten the screw securely.
6. Install the swing arm assembly as described in this chapter.

Inspection

1. Clean the bolts and collars in solvent, and thoroughly dry them.
2. Inspect the pivot collars (B, **Figure 30**) for wear, scratches or score marks.
3. Check the bolts for straightness. If a bolt is bent, it will restrict the movement of the swing arm.
4. Inspect the needle bearings by performing the following:
   a. Use a clean lint-free rag and wipe off surface grease from the pivot area of the needle bearing.
   b. Turn the bearing (**Figure 31**) by hand. The bearing should turn smoothly without excessive play or noise. Check the rollers for evidence of wear, pitting or rust.
   c. Insert the collar (**Figure 32**) into the bearings and slowly rotate the collar. The collars must turn smoothly without excessive play or noise.
   d. Repeat this procedure for each bearing in the swing arm pivot boss and in the tie rod mounting boss (**Figure 33**).
5. Replace any worn or damaged needle bearing as described in this chapter.
6. Check the swing arm for cracks or fractures and broken welds.
7. Check the pivot shaft for straightness with V-blocks and a dial indicator (**Figure 34**). Replace

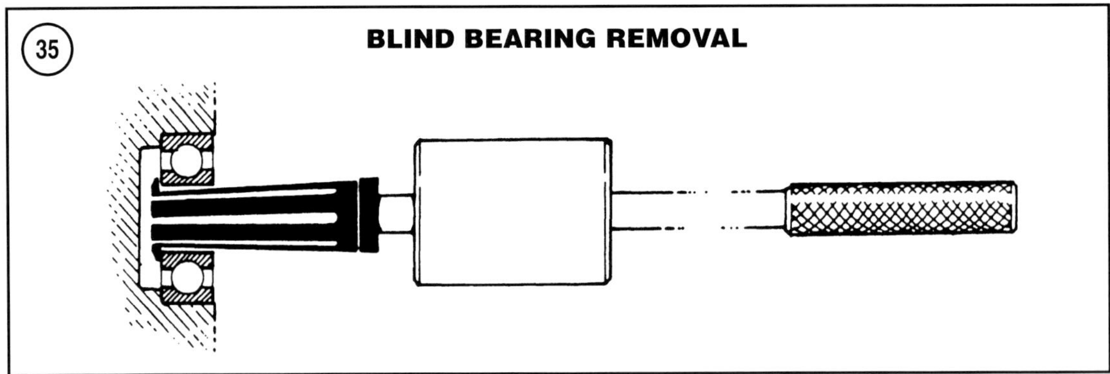

the pivot shaft if its runout is to the wear limit specified in **Table 1**.

8. Inspect the tie rods (A, **Figure 17**) for wear or damage.

9. Inspect the drive chain slider (**Figure 27**) for wear, cracks or other signs of damage.

BEARING REPLACEMENT

Swing Arm Needle Bearing Replacement

Do not remove the swing arm needle bearings unless they must be replaced. The needle bearings are pressed onto the swing arm. A blind bearing puller is required to remove the needle bearings. The needle bearings can be installed with a homemade tool.

Use Suzuki Super Grease A or an equivalent waterproof bearing grease when grease is called for in this procedure.

NOTE
If the needle bearings are replaced, replace the pivot collars at the same time. These parts should always be replaced as a set.

1. If still installed, remove the pivot collars from the needle bearings.
2. Insert the Suzuki bearing puller (part No. 09923-74510) or an equivalent blind bearing puller through the needle bearing and expand it behind the bearing.
3. Using sharp strokes of the slide hammer (**Figure 35**), withdraw the needle bearing from the pivot boss.
4. Remove the bearing puller and the bearing.
5. Withdraw the spacer located between the bearings in the swing arm pivot bore.

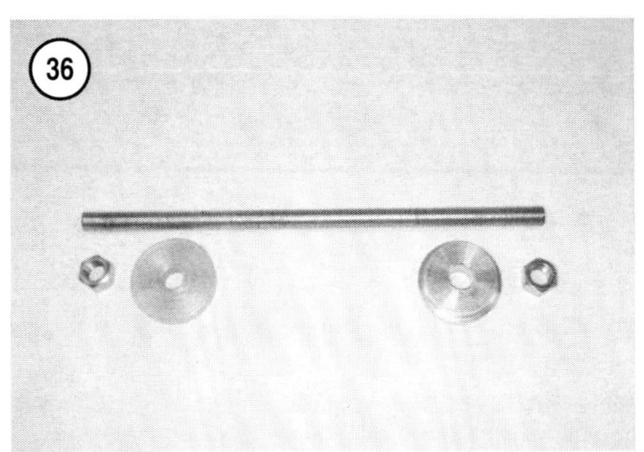

6. Repeat Steps 2-4 for the bearing on the other side.
7. Thoroughly clean out the inside of the pivot bore with solvent and dry it with compressed air.
8. Apply a light coat of grease to the exterior of the new bearings, the spacer and to the inner circumference of the pivot bore. This will make bearing installation easier.
9. Install the spacer into the pivot bore.

NOTE
Install one needle bearing at a time. Make sure the bearing enters the pivot boss squarely, otherwise the bearing and the pivot boss may be damaged.

10. Position the bearing with the manufacturer's marks facing out.

NOTE
*The bearing can be easily installed using a homemade tool consisting of a piece of threaded rod, two thick washers and two nuts (**Figure 36**).*

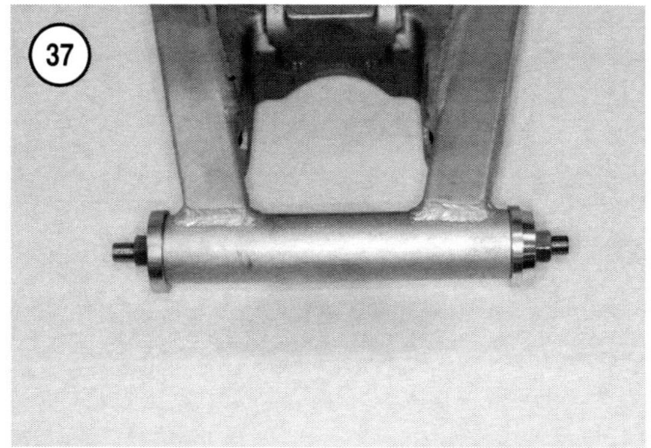
37

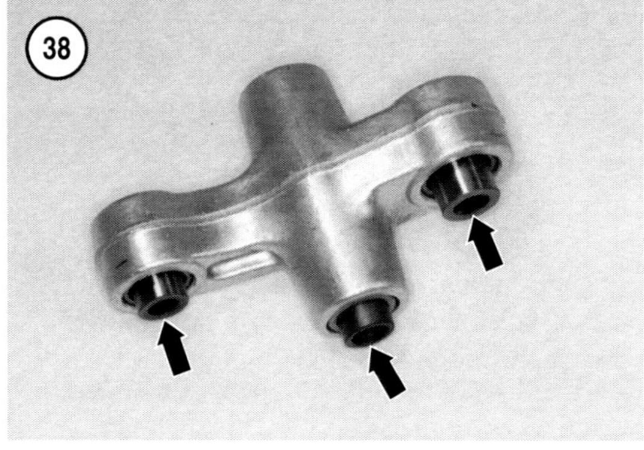
38

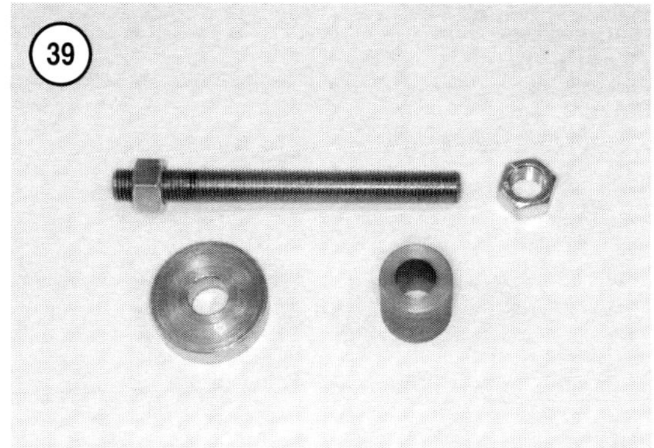
39

11. Locate and square the new bearing in the pivot bore. Assemble the homemade tool through the pivot bore so the large washer presses against the bearing (**Figure 37**).

12. Hold the nut next to the bearing being installed. Tighten the nut on the opposite side and slowly pull the bearing into the pivot bore until the bearing is flush with the outer surface of the bore (**Figure 31**).

13. Disassemble the tool.

14. Install the spacer into the swing arm pivot bore and against the just installed bearing.

15. Reinstall the tool on the opposite side and then repeat Steps 9-13 and install the other bearing.

16. Make sure the bearings are properly seated. Turn each bearing by hand. It should turn smoothly.

17. Lubricate the new bearings with grease.

18. If necessary, replace the bearings in the tie rod pivot boss on the top of the swing arm by repeating this procedure.

Shock Lever Needle Bearing Replacement

Do not remove the shock lever needle bearings unless they must be replaced. The needle bearings are pressed onto the shock lever. A blind bearing puller is required to remove the needle bearings. The needle bearings can be installed with a home-made tool, or socket and hammer.

Use Suzuki Super Grease A or an equivalent waterproof bearing grease when grease is called for in this procedure.

NOTE
If the needle bearings are replaced, replace the pivot collars at the same time. These parts should always be replaced as a set.

1. If still installed, remove the pivot collars (**Figure 38**).

NOTE
In the following steps, the bearing puller grabs the inner surface of the bearing and then withdraws it from the pivot areas of the shock lever.

2. Insert the Suzuki bearing puller (part No. 09923-73210) or equivalent through the needle bearing, and expand it behind the front bearing.

3. Using sharp strokes of the slide hammer (**Figure 35**), withdraw the needle bearing(s) from the front pivot bosses.

4. Thoroughly clean out the inside of the pivot bores with solvent. Dry with compressed air.

5. Apply a light coat of grease to the exterior of the new bearings and to the inner circumference of the pivot bores. This will make bearing installation easier.

NOTE
*Use the homemade tool shown in **Figure 39**, an appropriate size drift or a socket to install the bearings.*

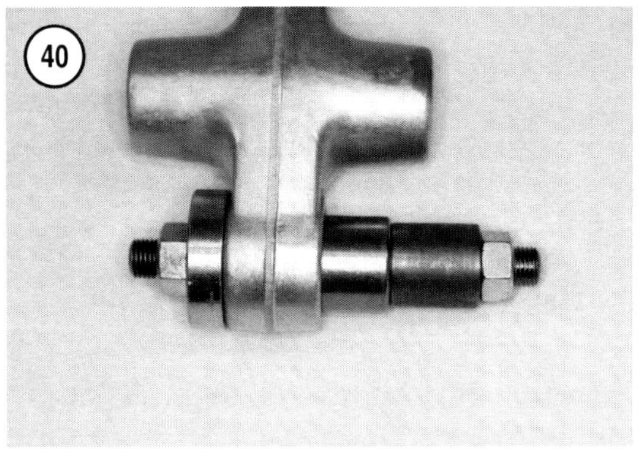

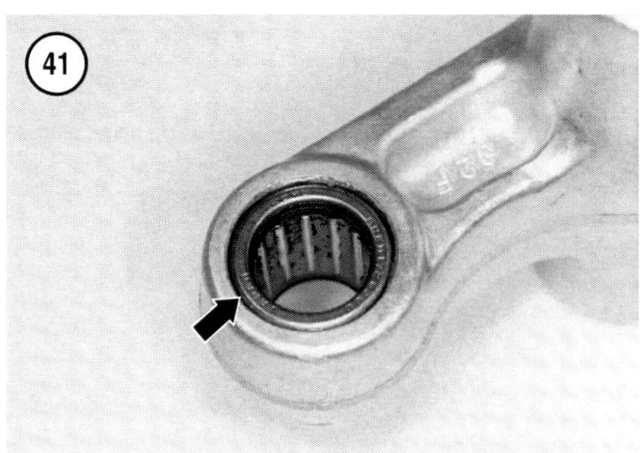

6. Locate and square the new bearing in the pivot bore. Assemble the homemade tool through the pivot bore so the socket presses against the bearing (**Figure 40**).
7. Hold the nut next to the bearing being installed. Tighten the nut on the opposite side and slowly pull the bearing into the pivot bore until the bearing is flush with the outer surface of the bore (**Figure 41**).
8. Disassemble the tool and repeat Step 6 and Step 7 for the remaining bearings.
9. Check that the bearing is properly seated in the bore. Turn each bearing by hand. The bearing should turn smoothly.

10. Lubricate the needles of the new bearing with grease.

11. Prior to installing the pivot collars, coat the inner surface of the bearings with grease. Install the pivot collars as described in this chapter.

Table 1 REAR SUSPENSION SPECIFICATIONS

Item	Specification
Rear wheel travel	134 mm (5.3 in.)
Swing-arm pivot-shaft runout wear limit	0.3 mm (0.012 in.)

Table 2 REAR SUSPENSION TORQUE SPECIFICATIONS

Item	N•m	in.-lb.	ft.-lb.
Brake hose banjo			
Front and rear	23	–	17
Shock absorber			
Mounting nut			
Upper and lower	50	–	37
Swing arm pivot nut	100	–	74
Shock lever			
To frame bolt and nut	78	–	57
To tie rod bolt and nut	78	–	57
Tie rod bolt and nut			
Lower (tie rod-to-shock lever mount)	78	–	57
Upper (tie rod-to-swing arm mount)	78	–	57
Torque link bolt/nut	35	–	26

CHAPTER THIRTEEN

BRAKES

This chapter describes repair and replacement procedures for the front and rear brake systems. Brake specifications are located in **Tables 1-3** at the end of this chapter.

The brake system consists of dual front disc brakes and a single disc brake on the rear wheel. There are two different front brake caliper assemblies. The 1996-2000 front caliper is equipped with four pistons while the 2001-on model has six. The rear caliper has two pistons and is the same on all years.

Anti-lock brakes (ABS) are optional on different years and in different countries. Unless otherwise specified in the service procedures, ABS-equipped motorcycles use the same components, such as the master cylinders and caliper assembles. Basic ABS operation and related unique service procedures are covered at the end of this chapter.

BRAKE SERVICE

The disc brake system transmits hydraulic pressure from the master cylinders to the brake calipers. This pressure is transmitted from the calipers to the brake pads. As the brake pads wear, the pistons move out of the caliper bores to automatically compensate for wear. As this occurs, the brake fluid level drops in the reservoir. This must be compensated for by occasionally adding brake fluid.

The proper operation of this system depends on a supply of clean brake fluid (DOT 4) and a clean work environment when any service is being performed. Any tiny particles of debris that enter the system can damage the components and cause poor brake performance.

Brake fluid is hygroscopic (easily absorbs moisture) and moisture in the system will reduce brake performance. Purchase new brake fluid in small containers and properly discard any small quantities that remain. Small quantities of fluid will quickly absorb the moisture in the container. Use only fluid clearly marked DOT 4. If possible, use the same brand of fluid. Do not replace the fluid with DOT 5 (silicone-base) fluid. Silicone-type fluids used in systems for which they were not designed will cause internal seals to swell and deteriorate. Do not reuse drained fluid and discard old fluid properly.

Proper service also includes carefully performed procedures. Do not use any sharp tools inside the master cylinders or calipers or on the pistons. Any damage to these components could cause a loss in the system's ability to maintain hydraulic pressure. If there is any doubt about having the ability to correctly and safely service the brake system, have a professional technician perform the task.

Consider the following when servicing the brake system:

1. The hydraulic components rarely require disassembly. Make sure it is necessary.
2. Keep the reservoir covers in place to prevent the entry of moisture and debris.
3. Clean parts with an aerosol brake part cleaner or isopropyl alcohol. Never use petroleum-based solvents on internal brake system components. They will cause seals to swell and distort.
4. Do not allow brake fluid to contact plastic, painted or plated parts. It will damage the surface.
5. Dispose of brake fluid properly.
6. If the hydraulic system has been opened (not including the reservoir cover), the system must be bled to remove air from the system. Refer to *Bleeding the Brakes* in this chapter.

WARNING
*Whenever working on the brake system, do **not** inhale brake dust. It may contain asbestos, which can cause lung injury and cancer. Wear a face mask that meets OSHA requirements for trapping asbestos particles, and wash hands and forearms thoroughly after completing the work.*

WARNING
***Never** use compressed air to clean any part of the brake system. This releases the harmful brake pad dust. Use an aerosol brake cleaner to clean parts when servicing any component still installed on the motorcycle.*

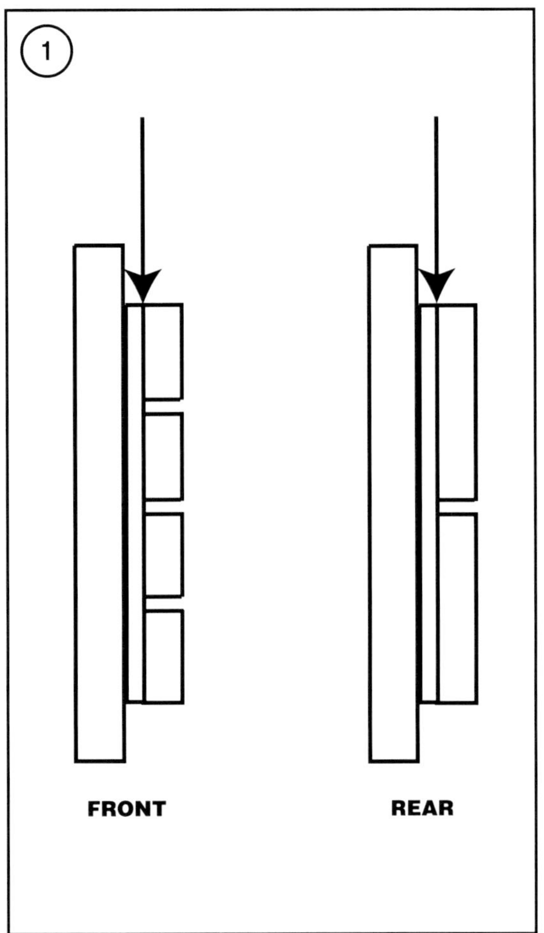

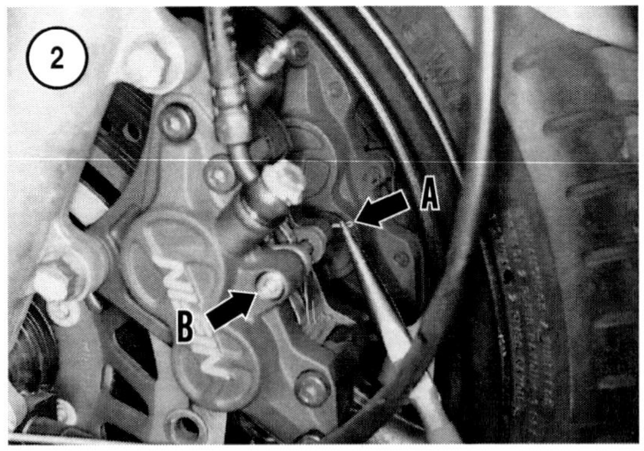

WARNING
Do not add to or replace the brake fluid with silicone (DOT 5) brake fluid. It is not compatible with the system and may cause brake failure.

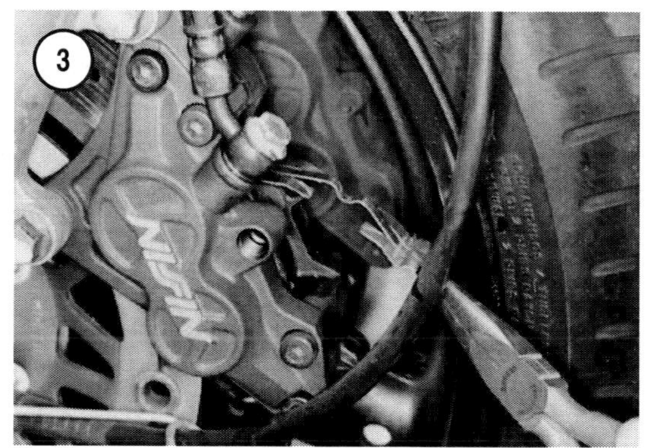

FRONT BRAKE PAD REPLACEMENT

Pad wear depends greatly on riding habits and conditions. Regularly check the pads for wear and replace them when the wear indicator reaches the edge of the brake disc. After removal, examine the pads. If either pad is worn to the wear limit (**Figure 1**, typical), replace the brake pads.

To maintain even brake pressure on the disc, always replace both pads in a caliper at the same time. When replacing the front brake pads, replace both pads in *both* front brake calipers at the same time. If any front brake pad is worn to the wear limit, replace all four front brake pads as a set.

CAUTION
Check the pads more frequently as the pad thickness approaches the wear limit. On some pads, the limit line is very close to the metal backing plate. If pad wear happens to be uneven for some reason, the backing plate could come in contact with the disc and cause damage.

NOTE
The brake hose does not have to be disconnected from the caliper during brake pad replacement. If the hose is disconnected, the brakes must be bled. Disconnect the hose only when servicing the brake caliper.

NOTE
This procedure is shown on a 2001-on model caliper equipped with six pistons. Where differences occur with the four-piston caliper, they are noted.

1. Read the *Brake Service* information in this chapter.
2. Securely support the motorcycle on level ground on the centerstand.
3. To prevent the front brake lever from being applied, place a spacer between the brake lever and the throttle grip and secure it in place. This will prevent the brake lever from moving if it is inadvertently squeezed, thus avoiding the possibility of the pistons being forced out of the cylinders.

4A. On 1996-2000 models, perform the following:
   a. Remove the clip (A, **Figure 2**) from the end of the pad pin bolt.
   b. Unscrew and remove the pad pin bolt (B, **Figure 2**) and spring (**Figure 3**).

4B. On 2001-on models, perform the following:
   a. Remove the screws securing the cover (**Figure 4**) and remove the cover.
   b. Remove the clip (**Figure 5**) from the inboard side of the pad pin and remove the pad pin (**Figure 6**) from the caliper.

5. Remove both brake pads from the caliper assembly (**Figure 7**).
6. Remove the bolts (**Figure 8**) securing the caliper to the fork slider and remove it.
7. Clean the pad recess and the end of both sets of pistons with a soft brush. Do not use solvent, or a wire brush or any hard tool that would damage the cylinders or pistons.
8. Carefully remove any rust or corrosion from the disc.
9. Thoroughly clean any corrosion or road dirt from the pad bolt or from the pad pin and clip.
10. Check the friction surface of the new pads for any foreign matter or manufacturing residue. If necessary, clean the pads with an aerosol brake cleaner.

NOTE
When installing new pads, make sure the friction compound of the new pad is compatible with the disc material. Remove any roughness from the metal backs of the new pads with a fine-cut file and clean them with an aerosol brake cleaner.

11. Repeat Steps 4-10 and remove the brake pads in the other caliper assembly.
12. When new pads are installed in the calipers, the master cylinder brake fluid level rises as the caliper pistons are repositioned. Perform the following:
   a. Clean all dirt and foreign matter from the top of the master cylinder.
   b. Drape a plastic drop cloth over the fairing and other parts sitting beneath the master cylinder to protect them from brake fluid spills.
   c. Remove the screws and the cover (A, **Figure 9**), diaphragm plate and diaphragm from the master cylinder reservoir.

CAUTION
Do not try to reseat the pistons with the caliper installed on the disc. Trying to reseat the pistons by prying against the thin brake disc will distort the disc.

   d. Insert a shop cloth (A, **Figure 10**) to protect the caliper, then use a tire iron (B) and reposition all pistons into the caliper housing.
   e. The pistons should move freely. If they do not, remove and service the caliper as described in this chapter.

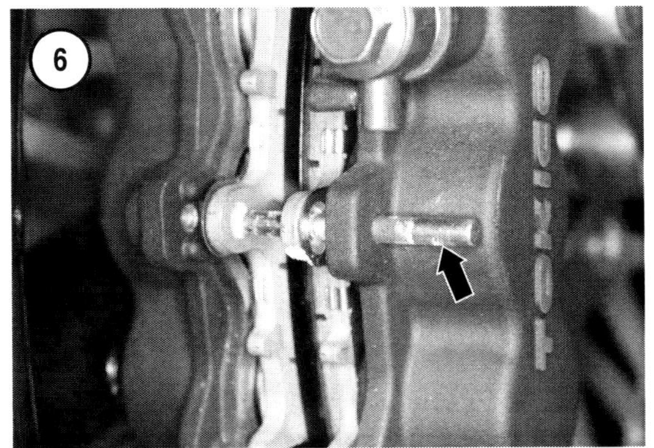

   f. Repeat this process for the other caliper.

13. Install the shim (**Figure 11**) onto the back of each brake pad.

14. Install the caliper onto the brake disc and fork slider. Install the mounting bolts (**Figure 8**) and tighten to 39 N•m (29 ft.-lb.).

15. Install both brake pads into the caliper (**Figure 7**) and carefully push them down until they bottom on the anti-rattle spring.

16A. On 1996-2000 models, perform the following:

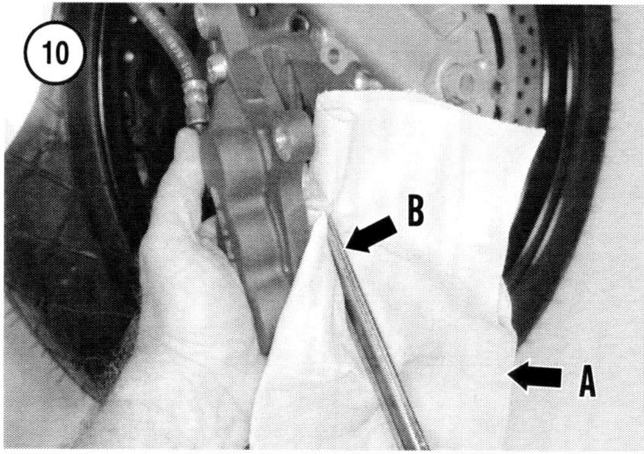

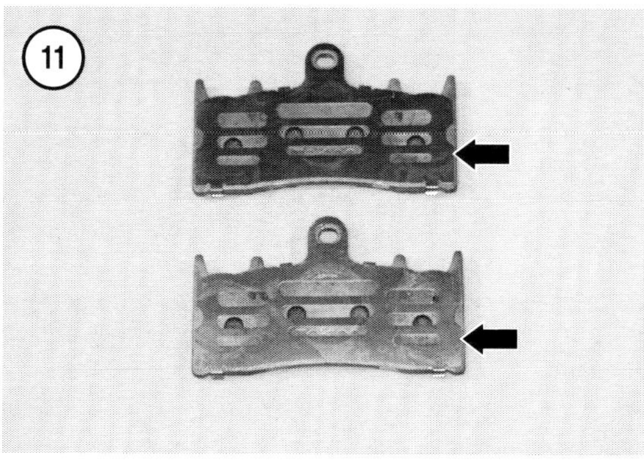

a. Install the spring (**Figure 3**), then install the pad pin bolt (B, **Figure 2**) and tighten to 18 N•m (13 ft.-lb.).
b. Install the clip (A, **Figure 2**) into the end of the pad pin bolt. Make sure it is seated correctly.

16B. On 2001-on models, perform the following:

a. Insert the pad pin (**Figure 6**) and push it in until it bottoms.
b. Install the clip (**Figure 5**) into the inboard side of the pad pin. Make sure it is seated correctly.
c. Install the cover (**Figure 4**) and tighten the screws securely.

17. Remove the spacer from the front brake lever.
18. Pump the front brake lever to reposition the brake pads against the brake disc. Roll the motorcycle back and forth and continue to pump the brake lever as many times as it takes to refill the cylinders in the calipers and correctly locate the brake pads against the disc.

WARNING
Use brake fluid clearly marked DOT 4 from a sealed container. Other types may vaporize and cause brake failure. Always use the same brand of brake fluid. Do not intermix brake fluid brands. Many brands are not compatible. Do not intermix silicone based (DOT 5) brake fluid, as it can cause brake component damage leading to brake system failure.

NOTE
To control the small flow of hydraulic fluid, punch a small hole into the seal of a new container of hydraulic (brake) fluid next to the edge of the pour spout. This will help eliminate fluid spillage, especially while adding fluid to the very small reservoir.

19. Refill the master cylinder reservoir, if necessary, to maintain the correct fluid level. Install the diaphragm and plate. Install the top cover, and tighten the screws securely.

WARNING
Do not ride the motorcycle before making sure the brakes are operating correctly with full hydraulic advantage. If necessary, bleed the brake as described in this chapter.

20. Bed the pads in gradually for the first two to three days of riding by using only light pressure as much as possible. Immediate hard application will glaze the new friction pads and greatly reduce the effectiveness of the brake.

FRONT CALIPER

Removal/Installation

1. On 1996-2000 models, perform the following:
   a. Remove the bolt (A, **Figure 12**) and remove the speedometer cable guide from the left side fork slider.

12
A
B

13
B
B
A

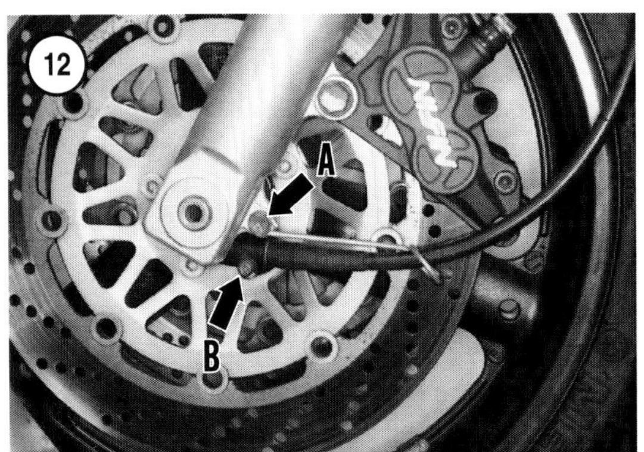

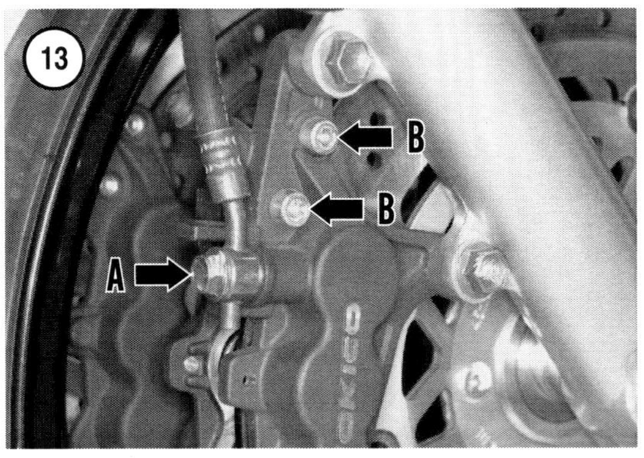

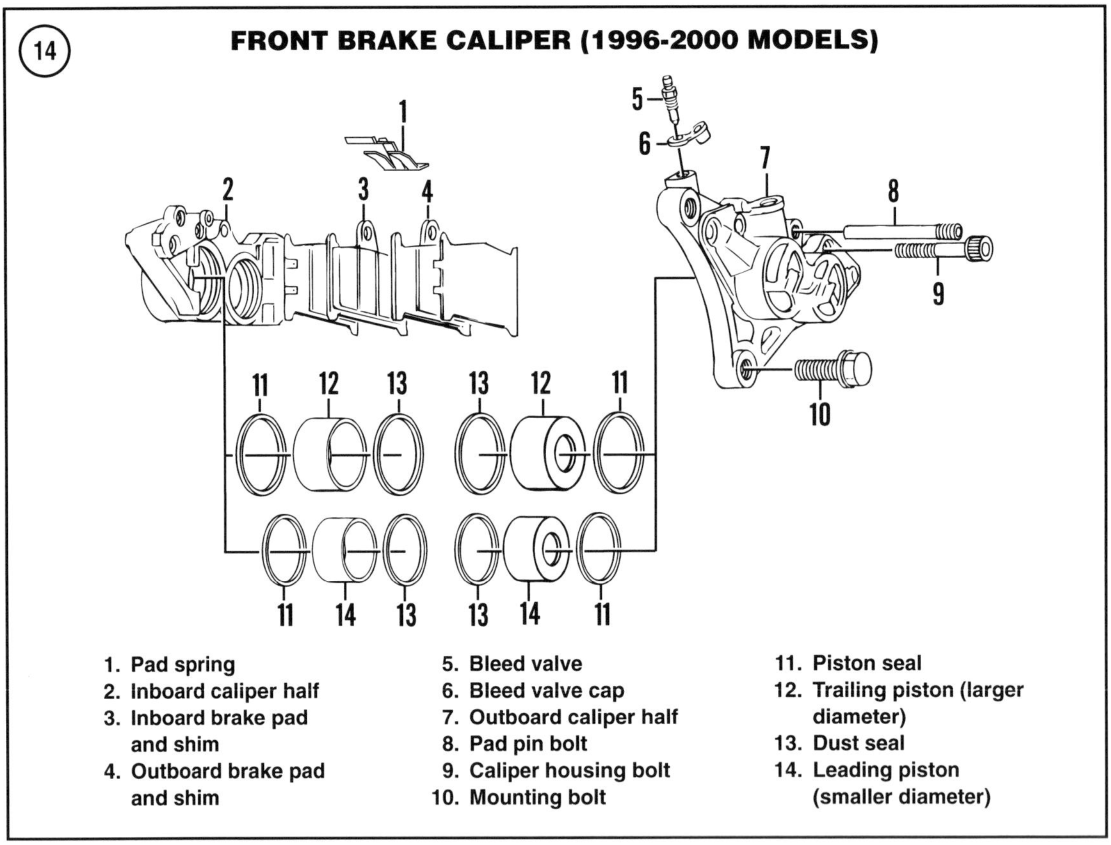

14
FRONT BRAKE CALIPER (1996-2000 MODELS)
1
2
3
4
5
6
7
8
9
10
11
12
13
14
1. Pad spring
2. Inboard caliper half
3. Inboard brake pad and shim
4. Outboard brake pad and shim
5. Bleed valve
6. Bleed valve cap
7. Outboard caliper half
8. Pad pin bolt
9. Caliper housing bolt
10. Mounting bolt
11. Piston seal
12. Trailing piston (larger diameter)
13. Dust seal
14. Leading piston (smaller diameter)

b. Remove the speedometer cable (B, **Figure 12**) from the speedometer gear and secure the cable out of the way.

CAUTION
Do not spill any brake fluid on the front fork or front wheel. Brake fluid is caustic and will damage the finish on any plastic, painted or plated surface. Immediately wash off spilled brake fluid from the motorcycle. Use soapy water, and rinse the area completely.

2. If the caliper assembly is going to be disassembled for service, perform the following:

NOTE
By performing Step 2c, compressed air may not be necessary for piston removal during caliper disassembly.

(15) **FRONT BRAKE CALIPER (2001-ON MODELS)**

1. Cover
2. Screw
3. Clip
4. Pad pin retainer
5. Brake pads and shims
6. Bleed valve cap
7. Bleed valve
8. Inboard caliper half
9. O-ring seal
10. Dust seal (larger diameter)
11. Trailing piston (larger diameter)
12. Piston seal (larger diameter)
13. Dust seal (smaller diameter)
14. Trailing piston (smaller diameter)
15. Piston seal (smaller diameter)
16. Outboard caliper half
17. Mounting bolt
18. Caliper housing bolt

a. Remove the brake pads as described in this chapter.

CAUTION
Do not allow the pistons to travel out far enough to come in contact with the brake disc. If this happens, the pistons may scratch or gouge the disc during caliper removal.

b. Slowly apply the brake lever to push the pistons partially out of the caliper assembly for ease of removal during caliper service.
c. Remove the banjo bolt (A, **Figure 13**) and sealing washers attaching the brake hose to the caliper assembly.
d. Place the loose end of the brake hose in a reclosable plastic bag to prevent residual brake fluid from dribbling onto the wheel or fork leg.
e. Loosen the four caliper housing bolts (B, **Figure 13**). Only two bolts are shown; loosen all four bolts.

3. Remove the two caliper mounting bolts (**Figure 8**) and carefully lift the brake caliper from the disc.
4. If necessary, disassemble and service the caliper assembly as described in this chapter.
5. Install by reversing these removal steps. Note the following:

a. Carefully install the caliper assembly onto the disc, being careful not to damage the leading edge of the brake pads.
b. Install the two caliper mounting bolts (**Figure 8**) and secure the brake caliper to the front fork. Tighten the caliper mounting bolts to 39 N•m (29 ft.-lb.).
c. If removed, install the brake hose onto the caliper. Install a *new* sealing washer on each side of the brake hose fitting and install the banjo bolt (A, **Figure 13**). Tighten the banjo bolt to 23 N•m (17 ft.-lb.).
d. If the caliper was disassembled, tighten the caliper housing bolts (B, **Figure 13**) to 30 N•m (22 ft.-lb.).
e. Bleed the brakes as described in this chapter.

WARNING
Do not ride the motorcycle before making sure the brakes are operating correctly with full hydraulic advantage. If necessary, bleed the brake as described in this chapter.

Disassembly

Refer to **Figure 14** and **Figure 15**.

1. Remove the caliper and brake pads as described in this chapter.
2. Remove the brake pad anti-rattle spring from the caliper.
3. Remove the caliper housing bolts (**Figure 16**) securing the caliper halves together.
4. Separate the caliper halves and remove the O-ring seals.

NOTE
If the pistons were partially forced out of the caliper body during removal, Steps 6-8 may not be necessary. If the pistons or caliper bores are corroded or very dirty, a small amount of compressed air may be necessary to completely remove the pistons from the bores.

5. Make sure the bleed valve is tight.

WARNING
In the next step, the piston may shoot out of the caliper body with considerable force. Keep hands and fingers out of the way. Wear shop gloves and safety goggles when using compressed air to remove the pistons.

6. On the *outboard caliper half*, pad the pistons with shop rags or wood blocks as shown in **Figure 17**. Apply compressed air through the caliper hose joint and blow the pistons out of the caliper.

NOTE
Since the compressed air must be applied to the inboard caliper half with the pistons facing up, the following tool should be used.

7. On the *inboard caliper half*, perform the following:
   a. Install two bolts into the caliper bolt holes as shown in A, **Figure 18**.
   b. Secure a piece of soft wood (B, **Figure 18**) to the open side of the caliper half and secure it with a C-clamp (C).
   c. Apply compressed air through the caliper joint hole and blow the pistons out of the caliper.
   d. Remove the C-clamp, wood and the two bolts.
8. If only one piston comes out of the caliper body, perform the following:

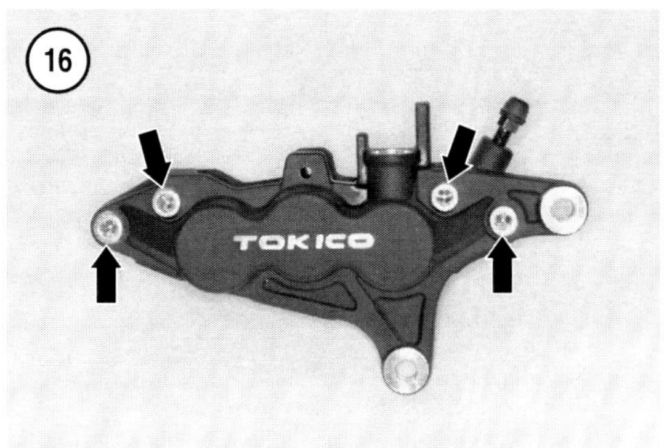

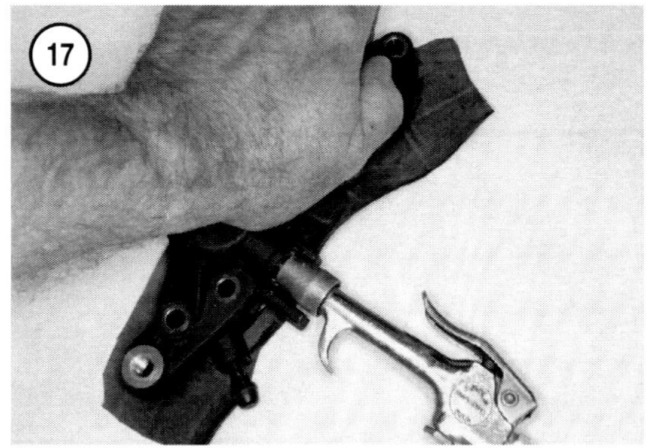

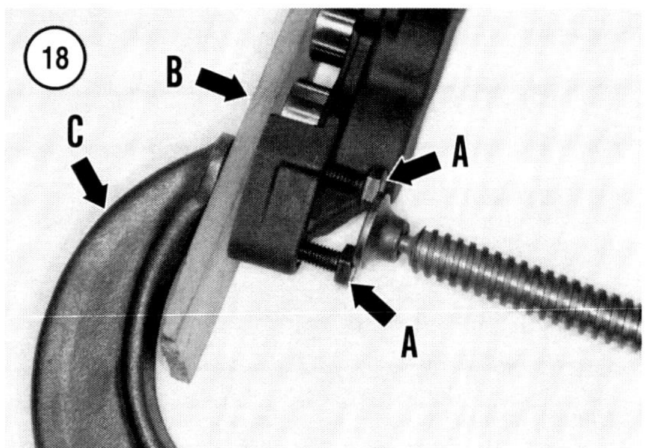

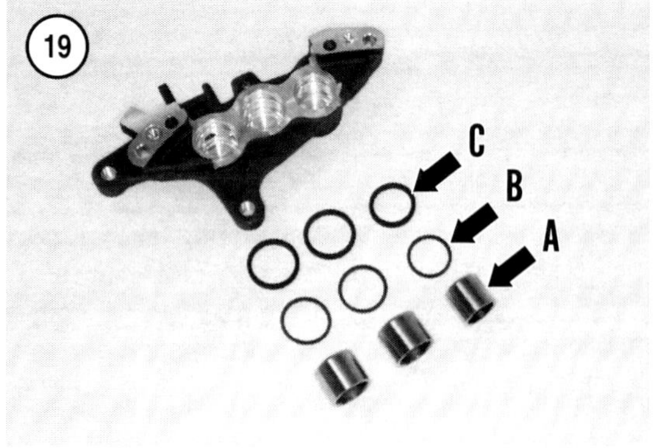

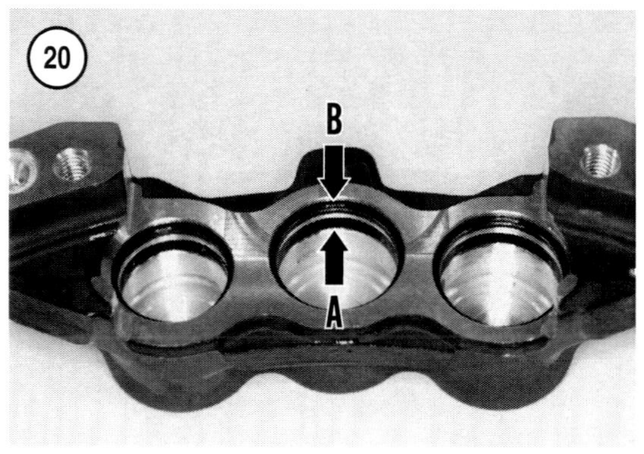

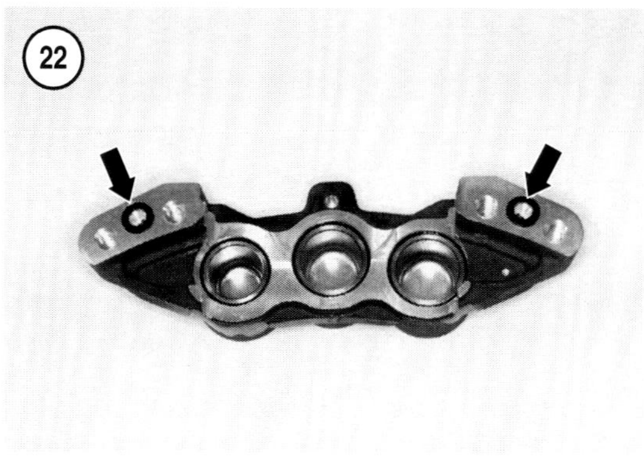

a. Push this piston back into the caliper body and set the caliper body face down on the mat.

b. Place a flat piece of plastic or a wooden shim over the piston that came out.

c. Pad the remaining piston and apply compressed air again. The shim will prevent the easy piston from coming out too far so that both pistons can be driven from their respective bores.

d. Remove each piston (A, **Figure 19**) by hand from its bore.

CAUTION
In the following step, do not use a sharp tool to remove the dust and piston seals from the caliper cylinders. Do not damage the cylinder surface.

9. Use a piece of wood or plastic scraper and carefully push the dust seal (B, **Figure 19**) and the piston seal (C) in toward the caliper cylinder and out of their grooves. Remove all dust and piston seals from the cylinders in each caliper half. Discard all seals.
10. If necessary, unscrew and remove the bleed valve assembly.
11. Inspect the caliper assembly as described in this section.

Assembly

WARNING
Never reuse old dust seals or piston seals. Very minor damage or age deterioration can make the seals useless.

NOTE
On 2001-on models, there are two different outer diameter pistons used in the brake caliper. Install the dust and piston seals and the pistons into the correct size cylinder bores.

1. Soak the new dust and piston seals in fresh DOT 4 brake fluid.
2. Coat the piston bores and pistons with clean DOT 4 brake fluid.
3. Carefully install the new piston seals (A, **Figure 20**) into the lower groove in each cylinder. Make sure the seals are properly seated in their respective grooves.
4. Carefully install the new dust seals (B, **Figure 20**) into the upper grooves. Make sure all seals are properly seated in their respective grooves.
5. Position the pistons with the open ends facing out and install the pistons into the caliper cylinders (**Figure 21**). Push the pistons into the bores until they bottom.
6. Repeat Steps 2-5 for the other caliper half.
7. Coat the new O-ring seals with DOT 4 brake fluid. Install the new O-rings (**Figure 22**) into the inboard caliper half.

8. Install two of the caliper mounting bolts (A, **Figure 23**) through the holes in the outboard caliper half and use them as a guide to install the outboard caliper half onto the inboard half.
9. Make sure the O-rings (B, **Figure 23**) are still in place and push the outboard caliper all the way down onto the inboard half.
10. Tighten the four caliper mounting bolts (**Figure 16**) finger-tight at this time. They will be tightened after the caliper assembly is mounted on the front fork slider.
11. If removed, install the bleed valve. Tighten it to 8 N•m (71 in.-lb.).
12. Install the brake pad anti-rattle spring into the caliper.
13. Install the brake pads and caliper as described in this chapter.
14. Bleed the brake as described in this chapter.

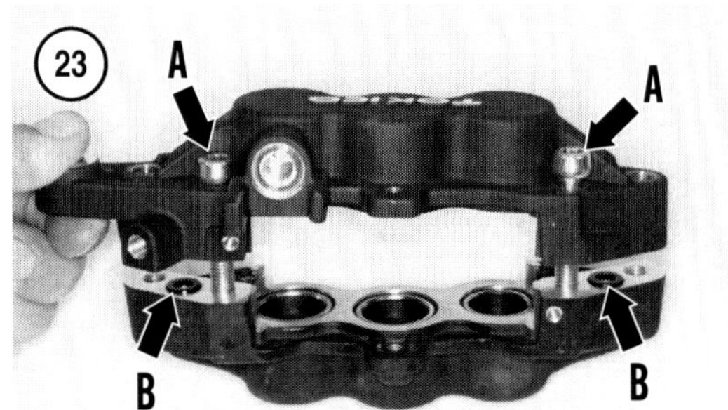

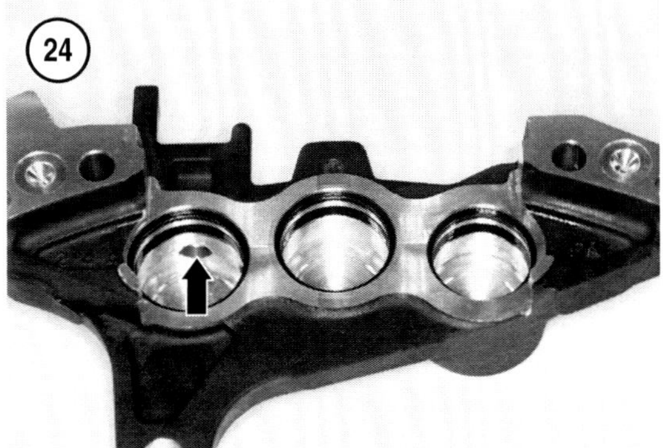

Inspection

When inspecting brake components, compare any measurements to the specifications in **Table 1** and **Table 2**. Replace any part that is damaged or out of specification.
1. Clean the caliper body and pistons in fresh DOT 4 brake fluid or isopropyl alcohol. Thoroughly dry the parts with compressed air.
2. Make sure the fluid passageways (**Figure 24**) in the base of the piston bores are clear. Apply compressed air to the openings to make sure they are clear. Clean out the passages, if necessary, with fresh brake fluid.
3. Make sure the fluid passageways (**Figure 25**) in both caliper body halves are clean. Apply compressed air to the openings to make sure they are clear. Clean them with fresh brake fluid, if necessary.
4. Inspect the piston and dust seal grooves (**Figure 26**) in both caliper cylinders for damage. If any groove is damaged or corroded, replace the caliper.
5. Inspect the banjo bolt threaded hole (A, **Figure 27**) in the outboard caliper body half. If worn or damaged, clean the threads with a metric thread tap or replace the caliper assembly.
6. Inspect the bleed valve threaded hole (B, **Figure 27**) in the caliper body. If worn or damaged, clean the threads with a metric tap or replace the caliper assembly.

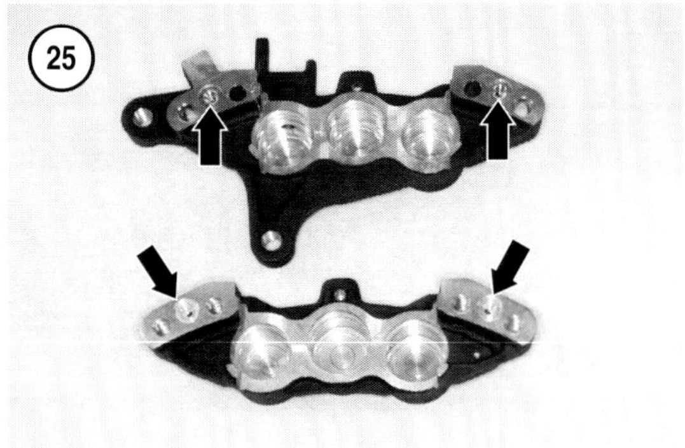

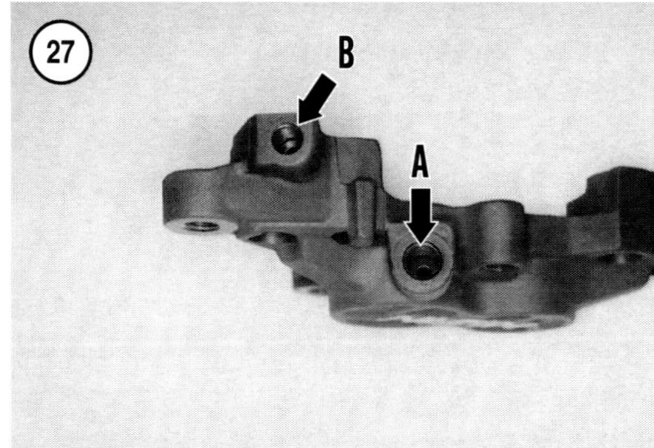

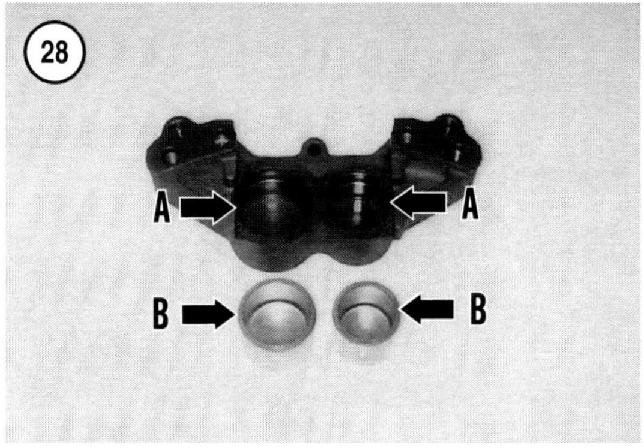

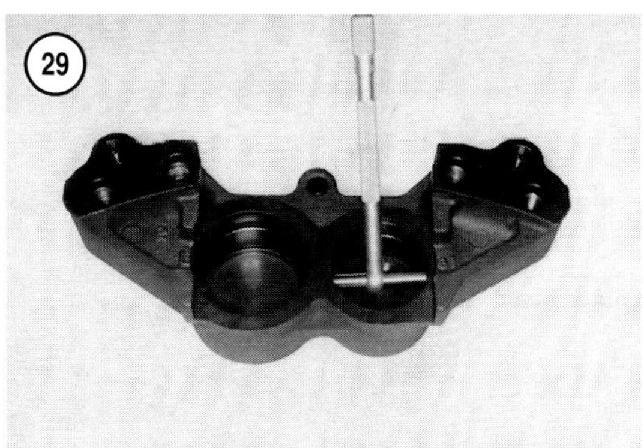

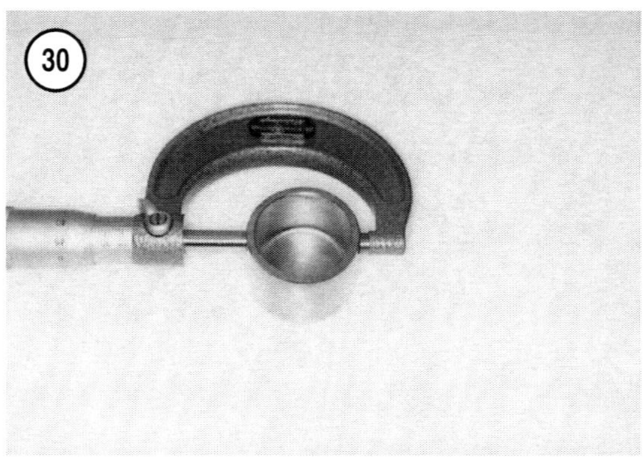

7. Inspect the bleed valve. Apply compressed air to the opening and make sure it is clear. Clean out if necessary with fresh brake fluid. Install the bleed valve, and tighten it to 8 N•m (71 in.-lb.).

8. Inspect the pad spring for cracks or other signs of damage.

9. Inspect the caliper body for damage. Check the caliper mounting bolt hole threads for wear or damage. Clean the threads with an appropriate size metric tap or replace the caliper assembly.

10. Inspect the cylinder walls (A, **Figure 28**) and pistons (B) for scratches, scoring or other damage.

11. Inspect the boots for tears or other damage. Replace any boot that is damaged or becoming hard.

12. Measure the cylinder bores with a bore gauge (**Figure 29**) or vernier caliper.

13. Measure the outside diameter of the pistons with a micrometer (**Figure 30**) or vernier caliper.

REAR BRAKE PAD REPLACEMENT

Pad wear depends greatly on riding habits and conditions. Regularly check the pads for wear and replace them when the wear indicator reaches the edge of the brake disc. To maintain even brake pressure on the disc, always replace both pads in the caliper at the same time.

NOTE
The brake hose does not have to be disconnected from the caliper during brake pad replacement. Disconnect the hose only when servicing the brake caliper.

1. Read the information listed in *Brake Service* in this chapter.

2. Place the motorcycle on the centerstand on level ground.

3. To prevent the rear brake pedal from being applied, tie the end of the pedal up to the frame. This will prevent the pedal from moving if it is inadvertently pressed, thus avoiding the possibility of the pistons being forced out of the cylinders.

4. Squeeze the sides of the pad cover and remove the cover.

5. Remove the clip (**Figure 31**).

6. Insert needlenose pliers (A, **Figure 32**) up into the caliper and move the pad pins (B) out of the caliper assembly.

7. Withdraw both pad pins from the caliper and remove the springs.

8. Withdraw both brake pads and shims from the caliper assembly.

9. Clean the pad recess and the end of both pistons with a soft brush. Do not use solvent, a wire brush or any hard tool that would damage the cylinders or pistons.

10. Carefully remove any rust or corrosion from the disc.

11. Thoroughly clean any corrosion or road dirt from the springs, pad pins and clip.

12. Check the friction surface of the new pads for any foreign matter or manufacturing residue. If necessary, clean the pads with an aerosol brake cleaner.

13. Remove the bolts (**Figure 33**) securing the caliper to the caliper carrier. Remove the caliper from the disc and the carrier.

14. When new pads are installed in the calipers, the rear master cylinder brake fluid level will rise as the caliper pistons are repositioned. Remove the hydraulic fluid from the master cylinder reservoir by performing the following:

a. Remove the rear frame cover as described in Chapter Fourteen.

b. Clean the top of the master cylinder reservoir of all dirt and foreign matter.

c. Remove the top cover mounting screws and remove the top cover (**Figure 34**) and diaphragm.

CAUTION

Do not try to reseat the pistons with the caliper installed on the disc. Trying to reseat the pistons by prying against the thin brake disc will distort the disc.

d. Insert a shop cloth to protect the caliper, then use a tire iron and reposition both pistons into the caliper housing.

e. The pistons should move freely. If they do not, remove and service the caliper as described in this chapter.

15. Install the shims onto the new brake pads so the closed end of the shim faces the rear of the motorcycle as shown in **Figure 35**.

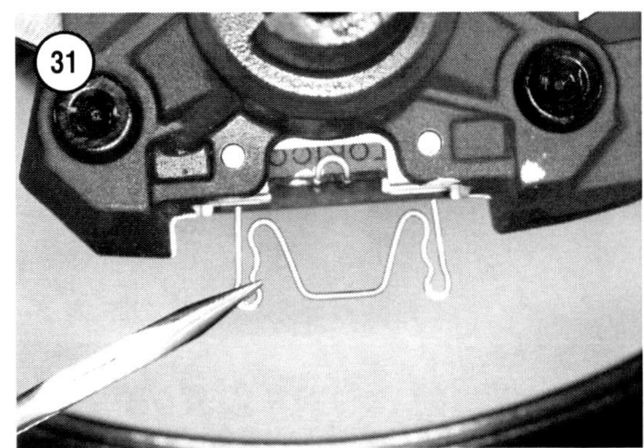

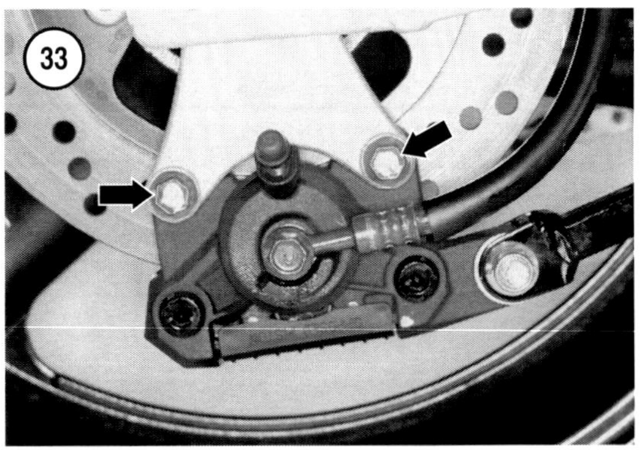

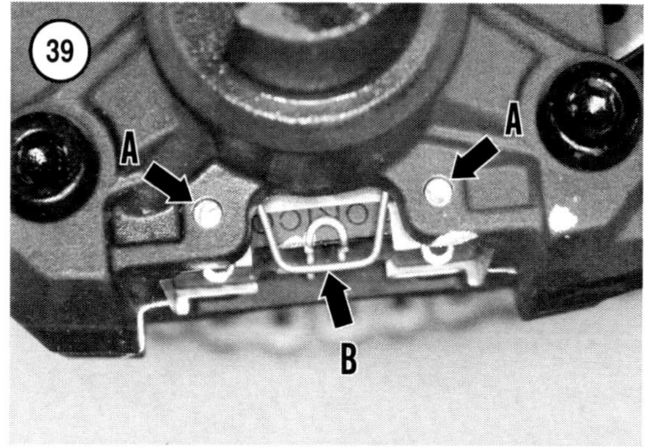

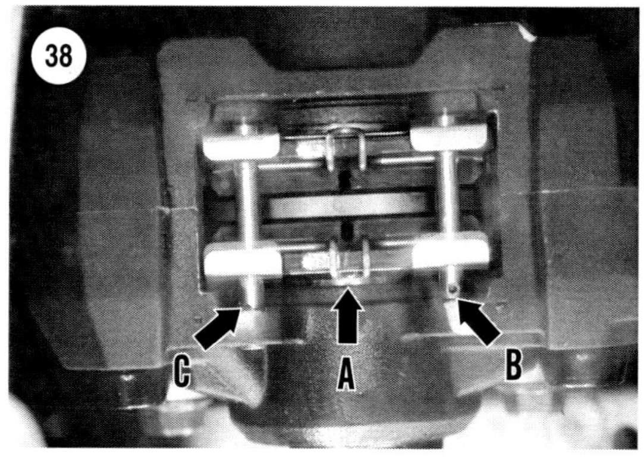

16. Install the caliper onto the brake disc and caliper carrier. Install the bolts (**Figure 33**) and tighten to 25 N•m (18 ft.-lb.).

17. Install the outboard brake pad (**Figure 36**) and the inboard pad (**Figure 37**) into the caliper.

18. Install the anti-rattle spring (A, **Figure 38**) into place on both brake pads.

19. Position the front pad pin (B, **Figure 38**) so its clip hole faces down and then insert the front pad pin through the caliper and into both pads. Make sure the pad pin is positioned above the anti-rattle spring in order to hold the pads in place.

20. Install the rear pad pin (C, **Figure 38**) through the caliper and into both pads. Make sure the pad pin is positioned above the anti-rattle springs and that the clip hole faces down.

21. Push the pins into the caliper until they bottom (A, **Figure 39**).

22. Slide the pin clip fingers through the hole in both pins. Push the clip into the caliper until the clip locks onto the pins (B, **Figure 39**).

23. Install the pad cover and make sure it is locked in place.

24. Untie the rear brake pedal.

25. Pump the rear brake pedal to reposition the brake pads against the brake disc. Roll the motorcycle back and forth and continue to pump the brake pedal as many times as it takes to refill the cylinders in the caliper and correctly locate the brake pads against the disc.

WARNING

Use brake fluid clearly marked DOT 4 from a sealed container. Other types may vaporize and cause brake failure. Always use the same brand of brake fluid. Do not intermix brands. They may not be compatible. Also do not in-

termix silicone based (DOT 5) brake fluid. It can cause brake component damage, leading to brake system failure.

NOTE

To control the small flow of hydraulic fluid, punch a small hole into the seal of a new container of hydraulic (brake) fluid next to the edge of the pour spout. This will help eliminate fluid spills especially while adding fluid to the very small reservoir.

26. Refill the master cylinder reservoir, if necessary, to maintain the correct fluid level as indicated on the side of the reservoir. Install the diaphragm and the top cover. Install the screws and tighten them securely.

WARNING

Do not ride the motorcycle before making sure the brakes are operating correctly with full hydraulic advantage. If necessary, bleed the brake as described in this chapter.

27. Bed the pads in gradually for the first two to three days of riding by using only light pressure as much as possible. Immediate hard application will glaze the new friction pads and greatly reduce the effectiveness of the brake.

REAR BRAKE CALIPER

Removal/Installation

CAUTION

Do not spill any brake fluid on the rear wheel or swing arm. Brake fluid will damage the finish on any plastic, painted or plated surface. Immediately wash off spilled brake fluid from the motorcycle. Use soapy water, and rinse the area completely.

1. If the caliper assembly is going to be disassembled for service, perform the following:
   a. Remove the brake pads as described in this chapter.

CAUTION

Do not allow the pistons to travel out far enough to contact the brake disc. If this happens the pistons may scratch or gouge the disc during caliper removal.

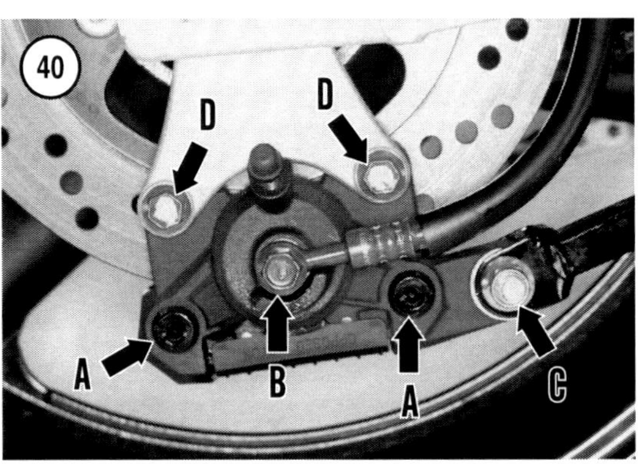

NOTE

By performing substep b, compressed air may not be necessary for piston removal during caliper disassembly.

   b. Apply the brake pedal to push the pistons partially out of the caliper assembly for ease of removal during caliper service.
   c. Loosen the caliper housing bolts (A, **Figure 40**).
   d. Place a drain pan under the rear caliper. Remove the banjo bolt and sealing washers (B, **Figure 40**) securing the brake hose to the caliper assembly.
   e. Place the loose end of the brake hose in a reclosable plastic bag to prevent the entry of foreign matter and prevent brake fluid from dribbling onto the motorcycle.
2. Remove the torque arm nut and bolt (C, **Figure 40**) and separate the torque arm from the caliper.
3. Remove the caliper mounting bolts (D, **Figure 40**) and lower the caliper from the caliper carrier and brake disc.
4. If necessary, disassemble and service the caliper assembly as described in this chapter.
5. Install by reversing these removal steps. Note the following:
   a. Install the caliper assembly onto the disc, being careful not to damage the leading edge of the brake pads.
   b. Install the caliper mounting bolts (D, **Figure 40**) and tighten them to 25 N•m (18 ft.-lb.).

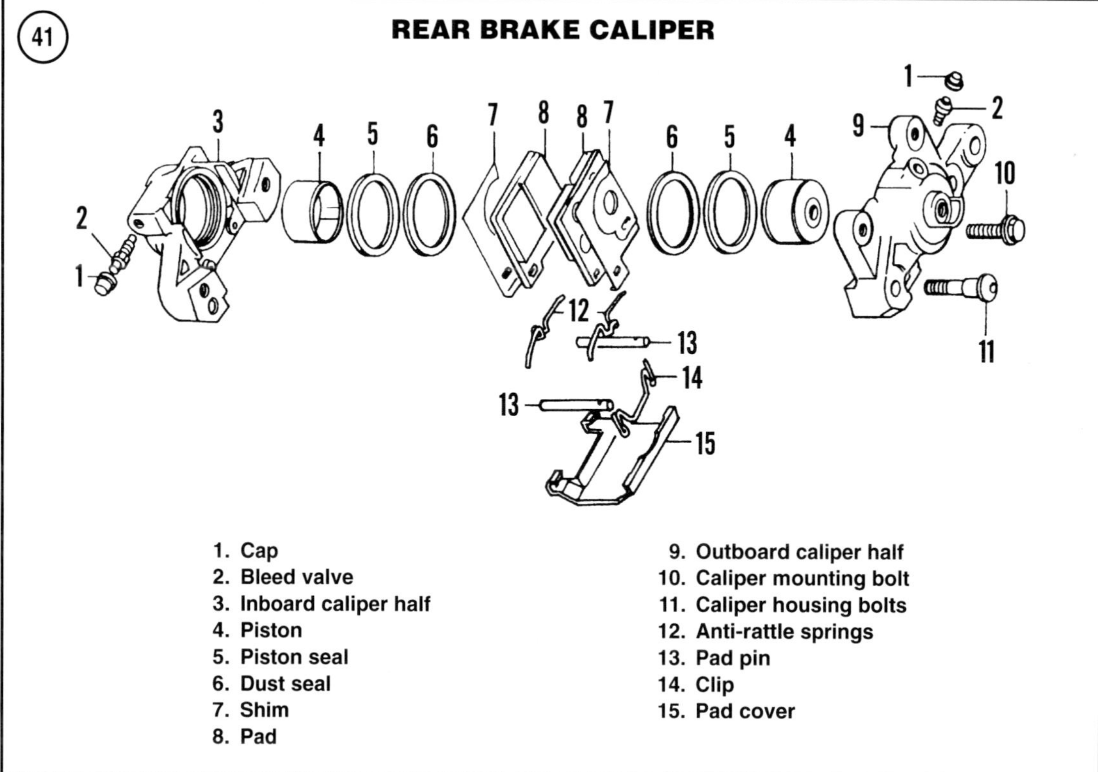

c. Secure the torque arm to the rear caliper. Tighten the torque arm nut (C, **Figure 40**) to 35 N•m (26 ft.-lb.).

d. Install a *new* sealing washer to each side of the brake hose fitting and install the banjo bolt (B, **Figure 40**). Torque the banjo bolt to 23 N•m (17 ft.-lb.).

e. If the caliper was serviced, tighten the rear caliper housing bolts (A, **Figure 40**) to 30 N•m (22 ft.-lb.).

f. Bleed the brake as described in this chapter.

WARNING
Do not ride the motorcycle before making sure the brakes are operating correctly with full hydraulic advantage.

Disassembly

Refer to **Figure 41**.

1. Remove the rear caliper and brake pads as described in this chapter.
2. Remove the two caliper housing bolts (**Figure 42**) loosened during the removal procedure.
3. Separate the caliper body halves. Remove the O-rings and discard them. New O-rings must be installed every time the caliper is disassembled.
4. Unscrew and remove the bleed valve.

NOTE
If the pistons were partially forced out of the caliper body during removal, Steps 5-7 may not be necessary. If the pistons or caliper bores are corroded or very dirty, a small amount of compressed air may be necessary to com-

pletely remove the pistons from the body bores.

5. Secure a piece of padded soft wood (A, **Figure 43**) to the open side of the caliper half with a C-clamp (B).

WARNING

In the next step, the piston may shoot out of the caliper body with considerable force. Keep hands and fingers out of the way. Wear shop gloves and safety goggles when using compressed air to remove the pistons.

6. Apply compressed air through the caliper bleed valve hole (C, **Figure 43**) or banjo bolt hole and blow the pistons out of the caliper. Use a service station air hose if compressor air is not available.
7. Remove the C-clamp and padded wood. Remove the piston from the bore.
8. Repeat for the other caliper half.

CAUTION

In the following step, do not use a sharp tool to remove the dust and piston seals from the caliper cylinders. Do not damage the cylinder surface.

9. Use a piece of wood or plastic scraper and carefully push the dust seal and the piston seal in toward the caliper cylinder and out of their grooves. Remove the dust and piston seals from the other caliper half and discard all seals.
10. If necessary, remove the bleed valve.
11. Inspect the caliper assembly as described in this section.

Assembly

WARNING

Never reuse old dust seals or piston seals. Very minor damage or age deterioration can make the seals useless.

1. Soak the new dust and piston seals in fresh DOT 4 brake fluid.
2. Coat the piston bores and pistons (**Figure 44**) with clean DOT 4 brake fluid.
3. Carefully install the *new* piston seal into the lower groove.

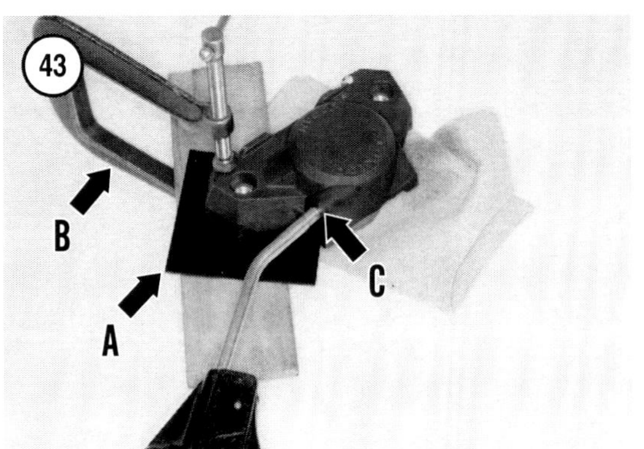

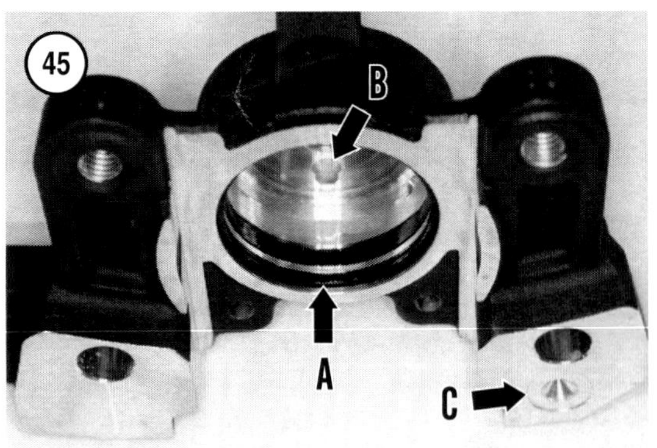

4. Carefully install the *new* dust seal into the upper groove. Make sure both seals are properly seated in their respective grooves (A, **Figure 45**).
5. Repeat Step 3 and Step 4 for the other caliper body half.
6. Position the piston with the open end facing out and install the piston into the caliper cylinder. Push the piston in until it bottoms (**Figure 46**).
7. Repeat Step 6 for the other caliper body half. Make sure both pistons are installed correctly.

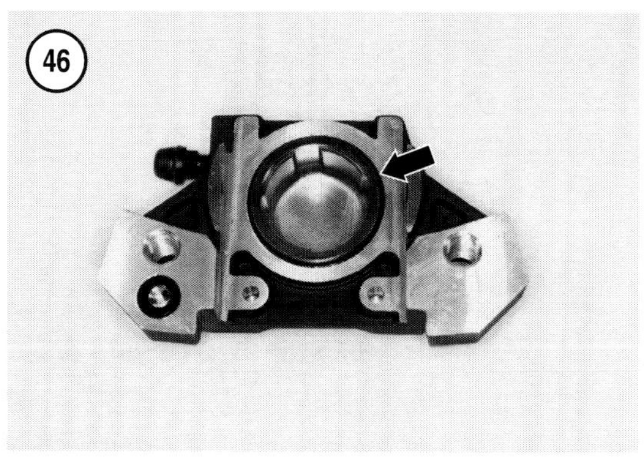
46

47

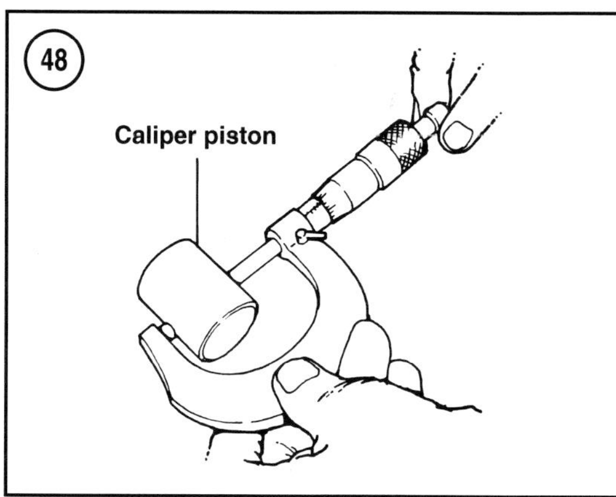
48

8. Coat the *new* O-ring with DOT 4 brake fluid and install the O-ring (**Figure 47**).

9. Make sure the O-ring is still in place and assemble the caliper body halves.

10. Install the two caliper housing bolts (**Figure 42**) and tighten them securely. Tighten the bolts to the final specification after the caliper is installed on the rear caliper bracket.

11. Install the bleed valve and tighten to 8 N•m (71 in.-lb.).

12. Install the caliper and brake pads as described in this chapter.

13. Tighten the two caliper housing bolts (**Figure 42**) to 30 N•m (22 ft.-lb.).

14. Bleed the brake as described in this chapter.

Inspection

Compare all measurements to the specifications in **Table 1** and **Table 2**. Replace any part that is damaged or out of specification.

1. Clean both caliper body halves and pistons in fresh DOT 4 brake fluid or isopropyl alcohol. Dry the parts with compressed air.

2. Make sure the fluid passageways (B, **Figure 45**) in the base of both cylinder bores are clean. Apply compressed air to the openings to make sure they are clear. Clean them with fresh brake fluid if necessary.

3. Make sure the fluid passageways (C, **Figure 45**) in the caliper body halves are clear. Apply compressed air to the openings to make sure they are clear. Clean them with fresh brake fluid if necessary.

4. Inspect the piston and dust seal grooves in both caliper bodies for damage. If damaged or corroded, replace the caliper assembly.

5. Inspect the banjo bolt threaded hole in the outboard caliper body. If worn or damaged, clean the threads with a metric tap or replace the caliper assembly.

6. Inspect the bleed valve threaded hole in the caliper body. If worn or damaged, clean the threads with a metric tap or replace the caliper assembly.

7. Inspect the bleed valves. Apply compressed air to the opening in each valve and make sure it is clear. Clean the valves with fresh brake fluid if necessary. Install the bleed valve into the caliper body and tighten to 8 N•m (71 in.-lb.).

8. Inspect both caliper bodies for damage. Check the threads of the caliper mounting hole for wear or damage. Clean the threads with an appropriate size metric tap or replace the caliper assembly.

9. Inspect the cylinder walls and pistons (**Figure 44**) for scratches, scoring or other damage.

10. Measure the cylinder bores with a bore gauge or vernier caliper.

11. Measure the outside diameter of the pistons with a micrometer (**Figure 48**) or vernier caliper.

FRONT MASTER CYLINDER

Removal

CAUTION
Cover the fuel tank and front fairing with a heavy cloth or plastic tarp to protect them from accidental brake fluid spills. Brake fluid will damage the finish on any plastic, painted or plated surfaces. Immediately wash off spilled brake fluid from the motorcycle. Use soapy water, and rinse the area completely.

Refer to **Figure 49**.

1. Clean all debris from the top of the master cylinder.
2. On models so equipped, unscrew and remove the rear view mirror (A, **Figure 50**).
3. Remove the top cover (B, **Figure 50**), diaphragm plate and diaphragm from the master cylinder reservoir.
4. Use a shop syringe and draw all of the brake fluid out of the master cylinder reservoir. Temporarily reinstall the plate, diaphragm and cover. Tighten the cover finger-tight.
5. Disconnect the brake light switch electrical connectors from the brake switch (A, **Figure 51**).
6. Place a rag beneath the banjo bolt (C, **Figure 50**), and remove the bolt. Separate the brake hose from the master cylinder. Do not lose the two sealing washers, one from each side of the brake hose fitting.
7. Place the loose end of the brake hose in a reclosable plastic bag to prevent brake fluid from leaking onto the motorcycle. Tie the loose end of the hose up to the handlebar.
8. Remove the master cylinder clamp bolts and the clamp (D, **Figure 50**).
9. Remove the master cylinder from the handlebar.
10. Drain any residual brake fluid from the master cylinder and reservoir. Dispose of fluid properly.
11. If the master cylinder is not going to be serviced, place it in a reclosable plastic bag to protect it from contamination.

Installation

1. Position the front master cylinder onto the right handlebar and align the mating surface of the master cylinder with the handlebar punch mark.

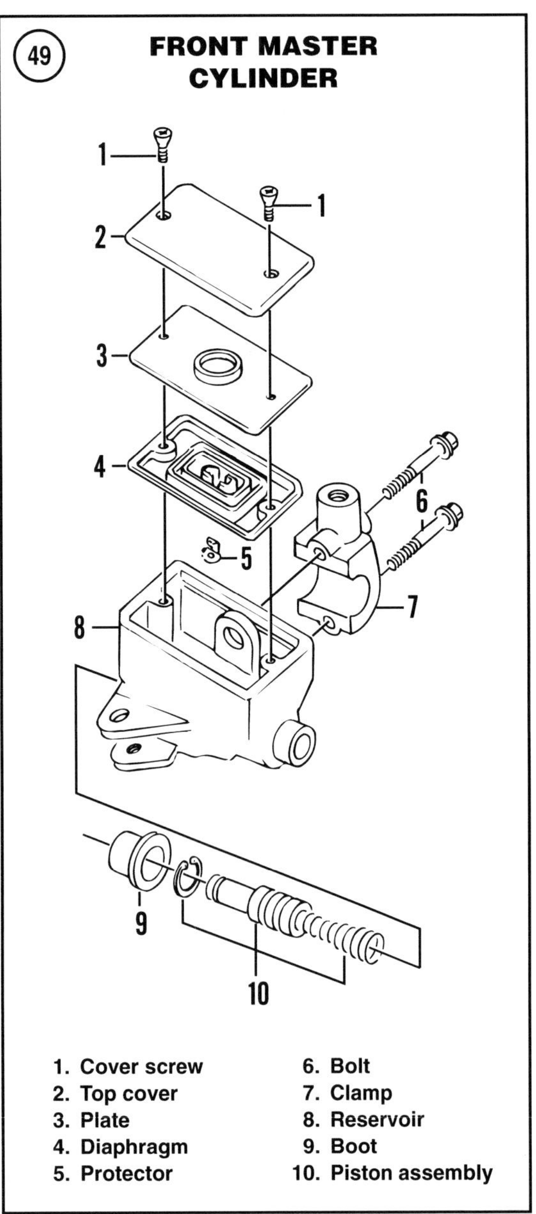

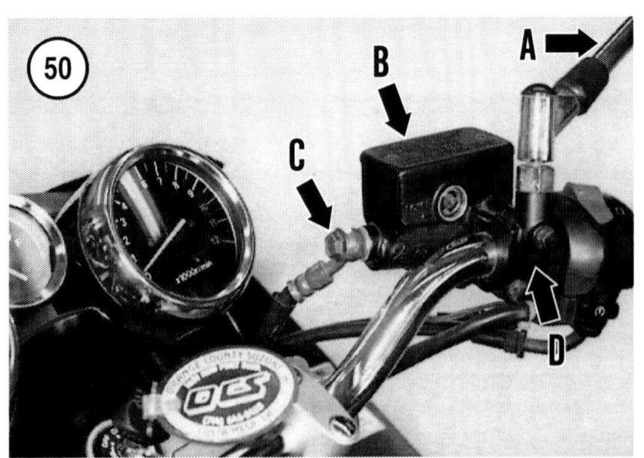

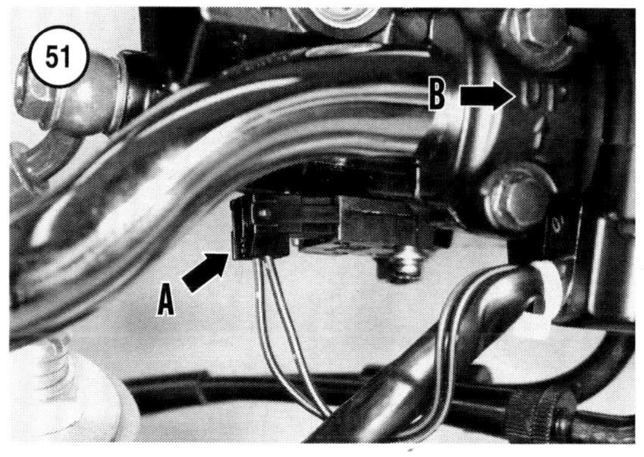

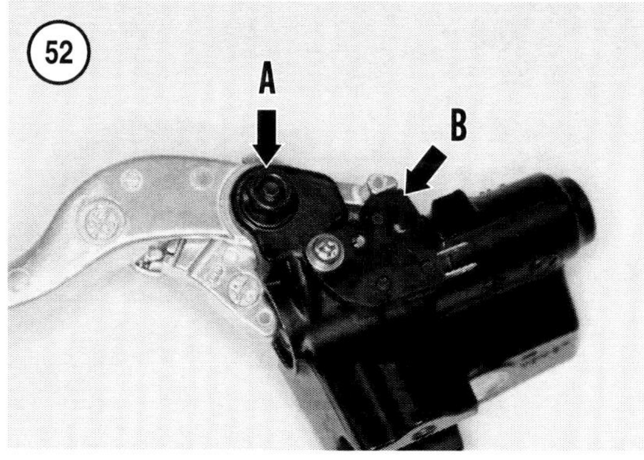

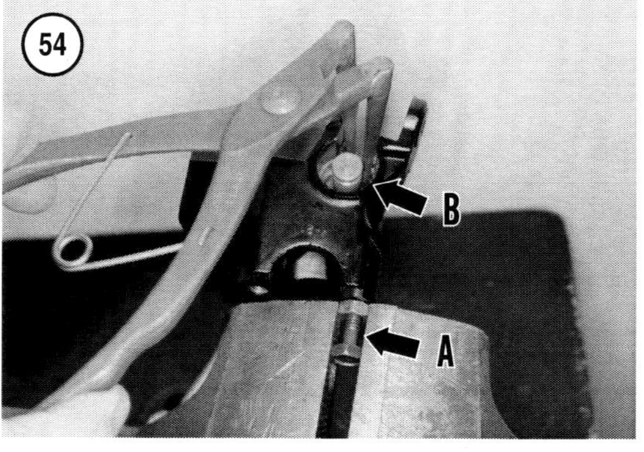

2. Position the clamp with the UP mark (B, **Figure 51**) facing up and install the master cylinder clamp bolts. Tighten the upper mounting bolt first and then the lower bolt, leaving a gap at the bottom. Tighten the bolts to 10 N•m (88 in.-lb.).
3. Install the brake hose onto the master cylinder. Install a *new* sealing washer onto each side of the hose fitting. Install the banjo bolt (C, **Figure 50**) and tighten to 23 N•m (17 ft.-lb.).
4. Reconnect the front brake light switch electrical connectors to the brake switch (**Figure 51**). Make sure the electrical connectors are free of corrosion and secure.
5. Refill the master cylinder and reservoir with fresh DOT 4 brake fluid and bleed the brake system as described in this chapter.
6. On models so equipped, install the rear view mirror (A, **Figure 50**) and adjust it correctly.

Disassembly

Refer to **Figure 49**.

1. Remove the master cylinder assembly as described in this chapter.
2. Remove the nut and pivot bolt (A, **Figure 52**) securing the hand lever to the master cylinder body. Remove the hand lever.
3. Remove the mounting screw and remove the brake light switch (B, **Figure 52**) from the master cylinder assembly.
4. Remove the rubber boot (**Figure 53**) from the cylinder bore on the master cylinder.

NOTE
To aid in the removal and installation of the snap ring, thread a bolt and nut into the clamp bolt fitting on the master cylinder. Tighten the nut, then secure the bolt in a vise (A, ***Figure 54****).*

5. Press the piston into the cylinder bore, then use snap ring pliers to remove the internal snap ring (B, **Figure 54**) from the bore.
6. Remove the piston assembly and the spring from the cylinder bore.
7. Inspect the components as described in this chapter.

Assembly

Refer to **Figure 49**.

13

1. Soak the new cups and the new piston assembly in fresh DOT 4 brake fluid for at least 15 minutes to make them pliable. Coat the inside of the cylinder bore with fresh brake fluid prior to the assembly of parts.
2. If removed, install the primary cup (A, **Figure 55**) onto the spring and install the secondary cup onto the piston (B). Position the spring (C, **Figure 55**) with its tapered end facing the piston.

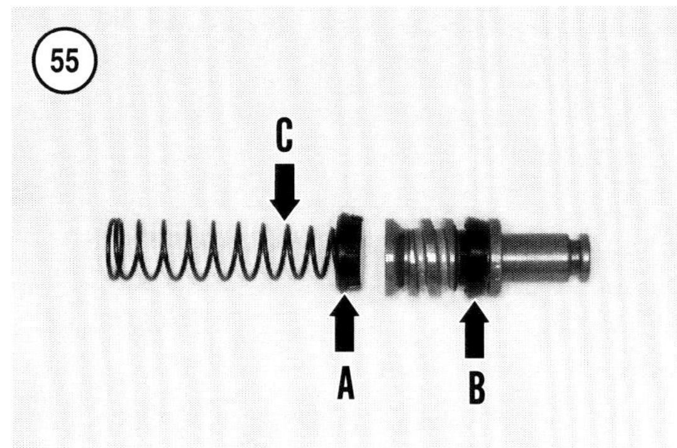

CAUTION
When installing the piston assembly, do not allow the cups to turn inside out. They will be damaged and allow brake fluid leakage within the cylinder bore.

3. Install the spring and piston assembly (**Figure 56**). Push them into the cylinder until they bottom in the bore.

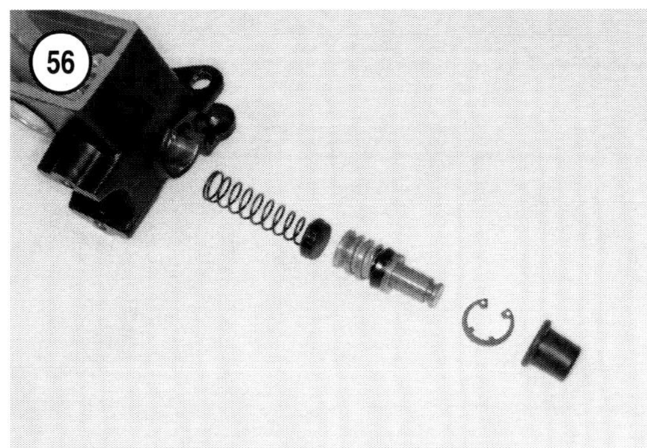

4. Press the piston assembly into the cylinder and install the snap ring (B, **Figure 54**). Make sure it is correctly seated in the snap ring groove.
5. Slide the rubber boot (**Figure 53**) into place in the cylinder bore. Make sure it is seated correctly in the master cylinder groove.
6. Install the hand lever, pivot bolt and nut (A, **Figure 52**). Tighten the bolt and nut securely. Make sure the hand lever operates freely within the master cylinder. There should be no binding.
7. Set the front brake switch (B, **Figure 52**) in place so the knob on the switch engages the dimple in the lever. Tighten the mounting screw securely.
8. Release the brake lever and make sure the switch plunger moves in and out with no binding.
9. Install the master cylinder as described in this chapter.

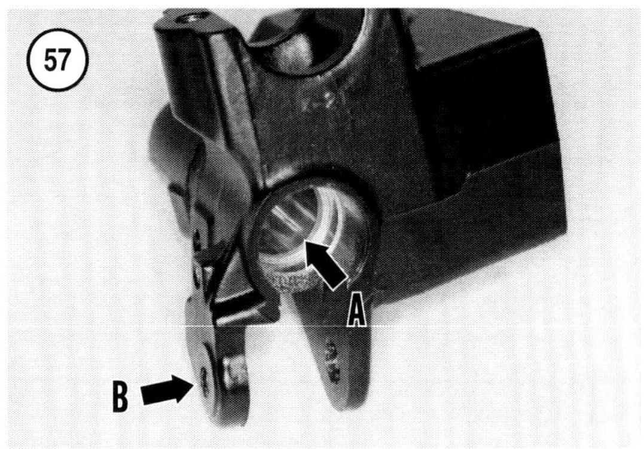

Inspection

Compare all measurements to the specifications in **Table 1** and **Table 2**. Replace any part that is damaged or out of specification.

1. Clean all parts in isopropyl alcohol or fresh DOT 4 brake fluid. Inspect the cylinder bore surface (A, **Figure 57**) for signs of wear or damage. If less than perfect, replace the master cylinder assembly. The body cannot be replaced separately.
2. Inspect the piston cups (A and B, **Figure 55**) for signs of wear and damage. If less than perfect, re-

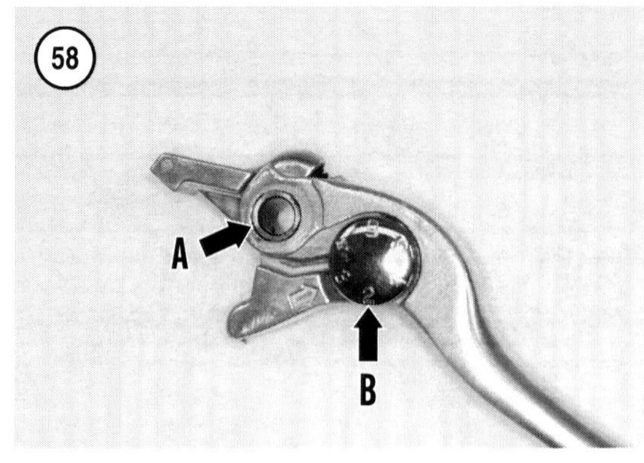

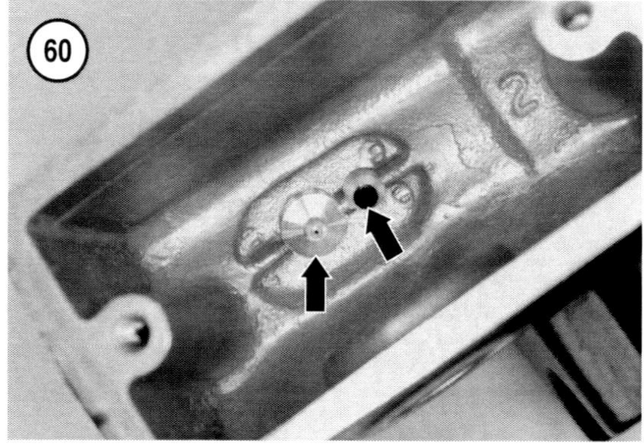

place the piston assembly. Individual cups cannot be replaced.

3. Inspect the piston contact surfaces for signs of wear and damage. If less than perfect, replace the piston assembly.

4. Check the end of the piston for wear caused by the hand lever. If worn, replace the piston assembly.

5. Inspect the pivot hole (A, **Figure 58**) in the hand lever. If worn or elongated, the lever must be replaced.

6. Inspect the pivot lugs (B, **Figure 57**) on the master cylinder for cracks or other signs of damage.

7. Remove the protector (**Figure 59**) from the bottom of the reservoir.

8. Make sure the fluid passages (**Figure 60**) in the bottom of the reservoir are clear. Clean them if necessary.

9. Inspect the threads in the cylinder bore. If worn or damaged, clean the threads with a metric thread tap or replace the master cylinder assembly.

10. Measure the cylinder bore with a bore gauge (**Figure 61**) or vernier caliper.

11. Measure the outside diameter of the piston with a micrometer (**Figure 62**).

12. Check the top cover, diaphragm and diaphragm plate for damage and deterioration; replace as necessary.

13. Inspect the adjuster (B, **Figure 58**) on the hand lever. If worn or damaged, replace the hand lever as an assembly.

REAR MASTER CYLINDER

Removal

CAUTION

Drape a heavy cloth or plastic tarp over the swing arm and rear wheel to protect them from accidental brake fluid spills. Brake fluid will damage the finish on any plastic, painted or plated surfaces. Immediately wash off spilled brake fluid from the motorcycle. Use soapy water, and rinse the area completely.

1. Remove the seat as described in Chapter Fourteen.

2. Remove the right side rear frame cover as described in Chapter Fourteen.

3. Clean all dirt and foreign matter from the top of the master cylinder reservoir.

4. Remove the reservoir top cover mounting screws and remove the top cover (A, **Figure 63**), plate and diaphragm.
5. Using a shop syringe, draw all of the brake fluid out of the master cylinder reservoir.
6. Attach a hose to the bleed valve (**Figure 64**) on the rear caliper and open the bleed valve.
7. Place the end of the hose over a container and let the brake fluid drain into the container. Slowly apply the rear brake pedal several times to expel most of the brake fluid from the rear hose and the master cylinder. Dispose of this brake fluid properly. Never reuse brake fluid.
8. Remove the hose and close the bleed valve.

NOTE
Do not disconnect any hoses from the rollover valve in Step 9.

9. On California models, remove the 6 mm bolt (B, **Figure 63**) securing the evaporation system rollover valve and bracket. Move the valve and bracket away from the master cylinder.
10. Remove the reservoir mounting bolt (C, **Figure 63**).
11. Loosen the two bolts (A, **Figure 65**) securing the master cylinder to the right side foot peg bracket.
12. Remove the three bolts (B, **Figure 65**) securing the right side foot peg bracket to the frame. Move the bracket away from the frame and turn it around.
13. Remove the cotter pin (**Figure 66**) from the end of the clevis pin. Withdraw the clevis pin that secures the master cylinder pushrod to the brake pedal. Do not lose the washer behind the pushrod yoke.
14. Place several rags under the banjo bolt and brake hose at the top of the master cylinder to catch any residual brake fluid.
15. Remove the banjo bolt (**Figure 67**) securing the brake hose to the top fitting on the master cylinder. Remove the sealing washer from each side of the hose fitting. Place the loose end of the hose in a reclosable plastic bag to keep moisture and debris out of the system. Tie the loose end of the hose up to the frame.
16. Remove the master cylinder mounting bolts loosened in Step 11. Remove the master cylinder from the footpeg bracket.
17. Remove the master cylinder and reservoir assembly from the frame.

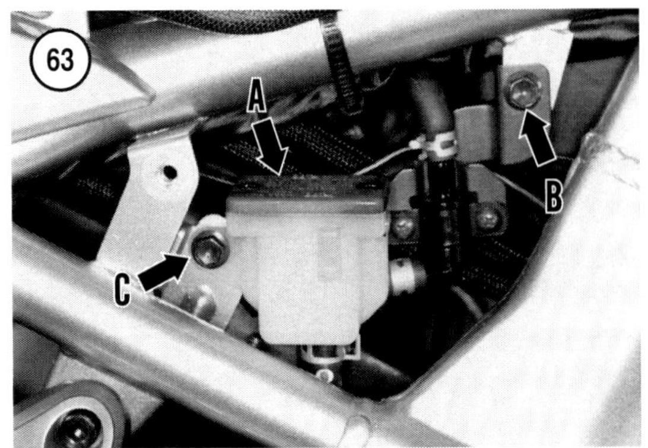

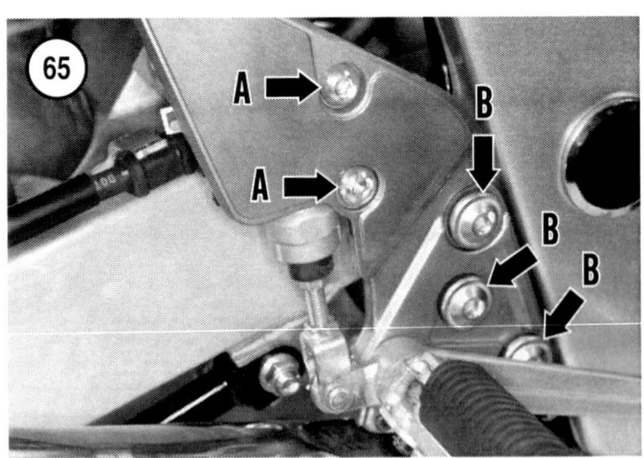

18. If the master cylinder and reservoir will not be serviced, place them in a reclosable plastic bag to protect them from contamination.
19. Clean up any spilled brake fluid immediately.

Installation

1. Install the master cylinder reservoir up through the frame and into position. Temporarily install the mounting bolt.

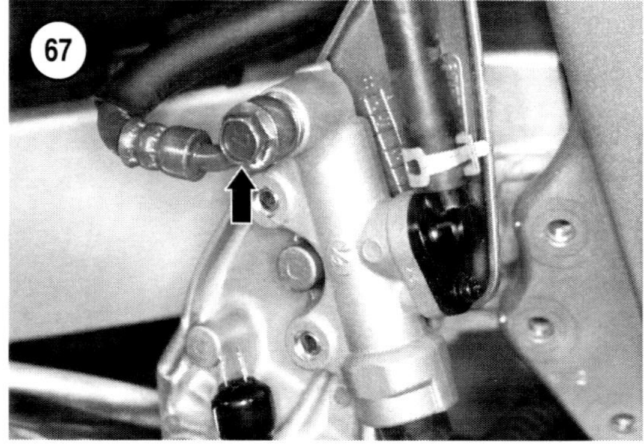

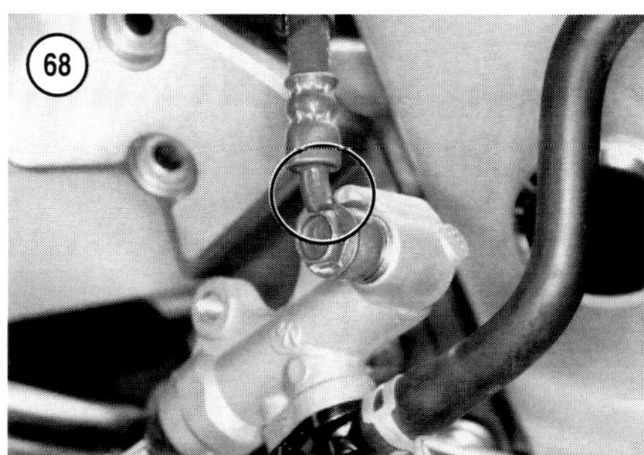

2. Install the master cylinder onto the backside of the right side footpeg bracket and loosely install the two mounting bolts (A, **Figure 65**).
3. Correctly position the brake hose onto the top of the master cylinder. Place a *new* sealing washer onto each side of the brake hose fitting and install the banjo bolt (**Figure 67**). Position the fitting between the two locating pins (**Figure 68**) on top of the master cylinder. Tighten the banjo bolt finger-tight.
4. Align the master cylinder pushrod yoke with the brake pedal and install the clevis pin through both parts. Slide the washer over the inboard end of the clevis pin. Install a *new* cotter pin (**Figure 66**) and bend the ends over completely.
5. Tighten the banjo bolt (**Figure 67**) to 23 N•m (17 ft.-lb.).
6. Move the right side footpeg bracket around and align it with the frame mounting area.
7. Install the three bolts (B, **Figure 65**) securing the right side footpeg bracket to the frame. Tighten the bolts to 39 N•m (29 ft.-lb.).
8. Tighten the two bolts (A, **Figure 65**) securing the master cylinder to the right side footpeg bracket to 23 N•m (17 ft.-lb.).
9. Tighten the reservoir mounting bolt (C, **Figure 63**) securely.
10. On California models, move the evaporation system rollover valve and bracket into position and install the 6 mm bolt (B, **Figure 63**). Tighten the bolt securely.
11. Fill the reservoir with fresh DOT 4 brake fluid, and bleed the rear brake as described in this chapter.
12. Install the right side frame cover and seat as described in Chapter Fifteen.

Disassembly

Refer to **Figure 69**.

1. Remove the rear master cylinder and reservoir assembly as described in this chapter.
2. Remove the screw on the fitting and disconnect the reservoir hose (A, **Figure 70**) from the side of the master cylinder.
3. Remove the O-ring (B, **Figure 70**) from the connector port on the master cylinder. Discard the O-ring.
4. Slide the rubber boot down the pushrod and out of the way.

NOTE

To aid in the removal and installation of the snap ring, thread a bolt and nut into the mounting bolt fitting on the master cylinder. Tighten the nut, then secure the bolt in a vise (A, ***Figure 71****).*

5. Using snap ring pliers, remove the internal snap ring (B, **Figure 71**) securing the pushrod assembly in the master cylinder body.
6. Withdraw the pushrod assembly, the piston assembly and spring from the master cylinder body.

69

REAR MASTER CYLINDER AND BRAKE HOSE

1. Screw
2. Cover
3. Diaphragm
4. Reservoir
5. Bolt
6. Hose clamp
7. Reservoir hose
8. Screw
9. Connector
10. O-ring
11. Screw
12. Nut
13. Body
14. Sealing washer
15. Brake hose
16. Banjo bolt
17. Spring
18. Primary cup
19. Piston
20. Pushrod
21. Snap ring
22. Rubber cap
23. Nut
24. Cotter pin
25. Washer
26. Yoke
27. Clevis pin

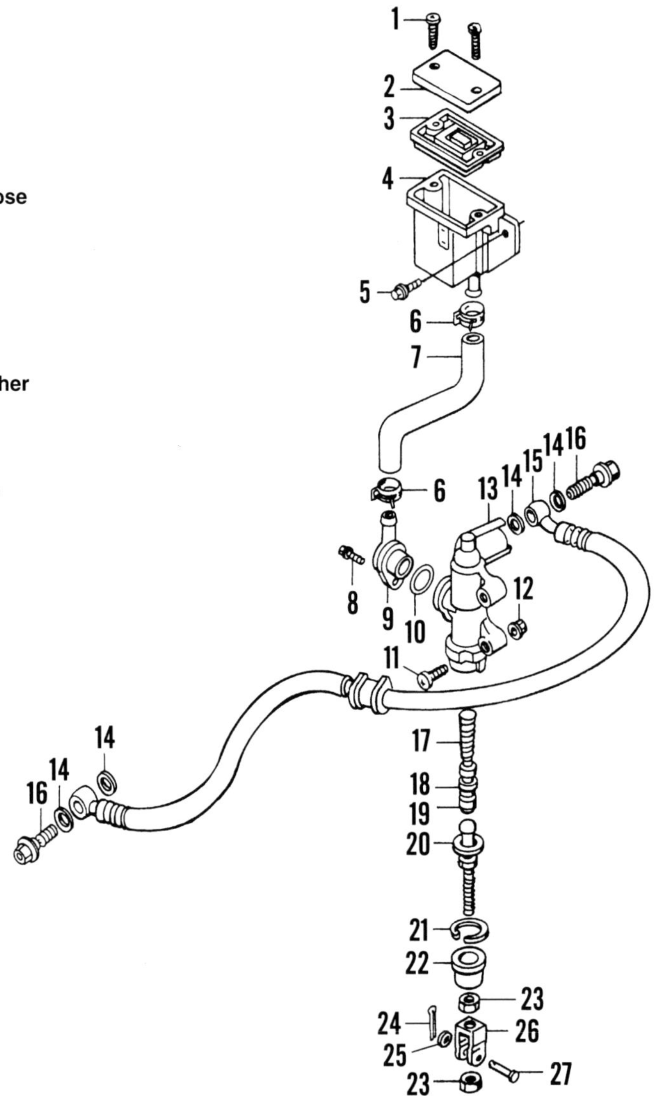

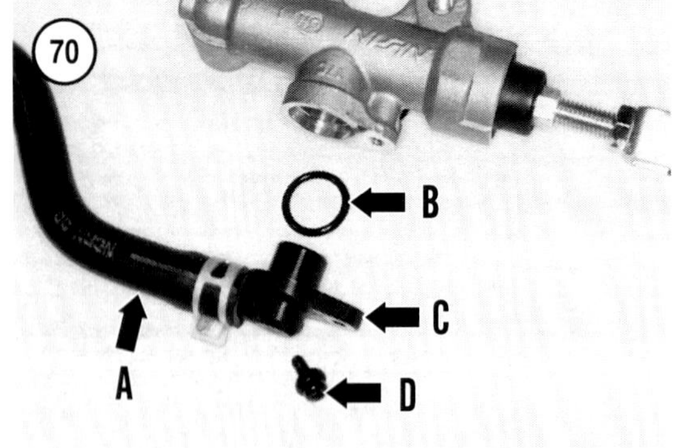

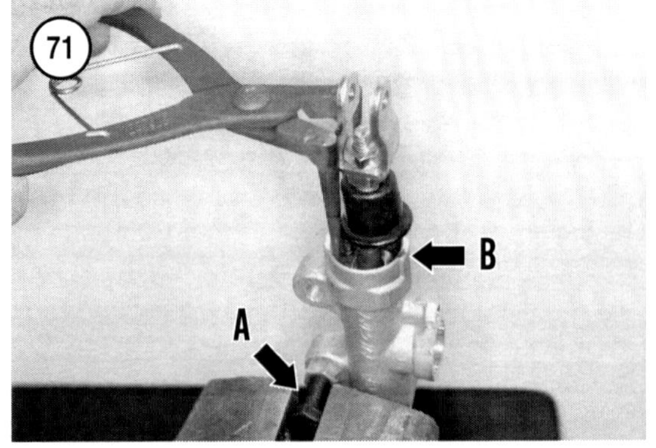

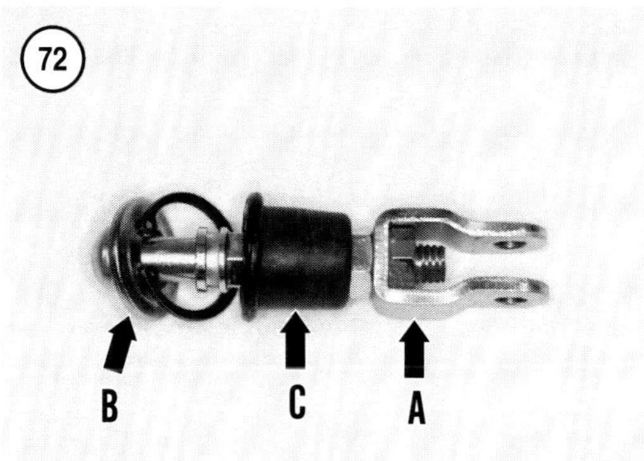

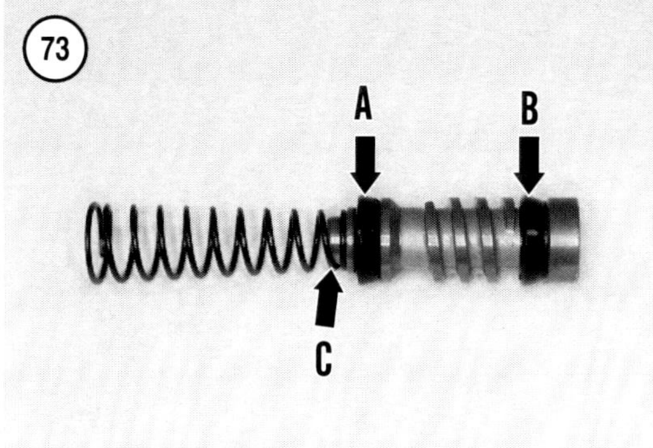

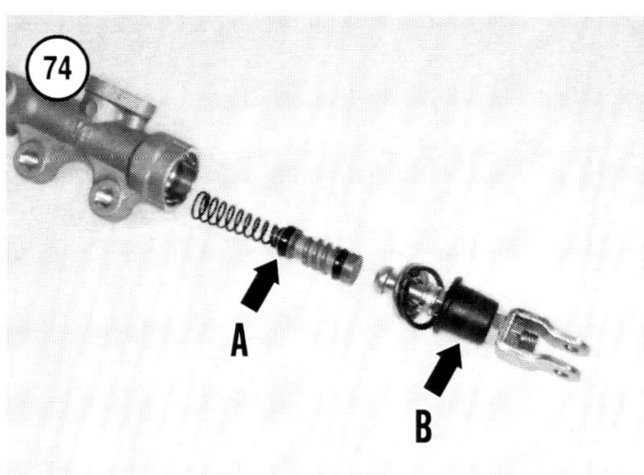

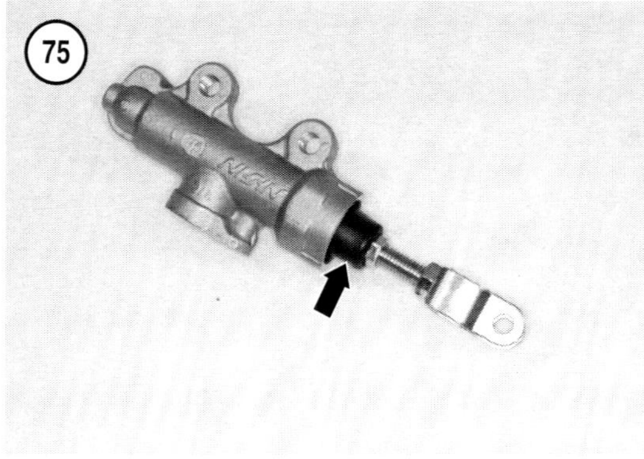

7. Pour out any residual brake fluid and discard it.
8. If necessary, loosen the master cylinder rod locknut and then remove the pushrod yoke and nut from the pushrod (A, **Figure 72**).
9. Inspect the master cylinder as described in this section.

Assembly

1. Soak the new cups and the new piston assembly in fresh DOT 4 brake fluid for at least 15 minutes to make them pliable. Coat the inside of the cylinder bore with fresh brake fluid prior to the assembly of parts.
2. If removed, install the yoke (A, **Figure 72**) and nut onto the pushrod. Do not tighten the locknut at this time as the brake pedal must be adjusted.
3. If removed, install the primary cup (A, **Figure 73**) onto the spring and install the secondary cup onto the piston (B). Position the spring (C, **Figure 73**) with its tapered end facing the piston.

WARNING
When installing the piston assembly, do not allow the cups to turn inside out. They will be damaged and allow brake fluid leakage within the cylinder bore.

4. Install the spring and piston assembly (A, **Figure 74**) into the cylinder together. Push the piston assembly all the way in until it bottoms in the cylinder.
5. Install the pushrod assembly (B, **Figure 74**) and push the piston cup assembly all the way into the cylinder.
6. Hold the pushrod assembly in this position and install the snap ring (B, **Figure 71**). Make sure the snap ring is correctly seated in the groove.
7. Slide the rubber boot (**Figure 75**) up into the body so it is completely seated in the cylinder. This is necessary to keep out dirt and moisture.
8. Install a new O-ring (B, **Figure 70**) onto the connector port in the master cylinder body. Apply a light coat of fresh brake fluid to the O-ring.
9. Make sure the O-ring is still in place and install the reservoir hose connector (C, **Figure 70**) onto the master cylinder. Secure the connector in place with the mounting screw (D, **Figure 70**) and tighten securely.
10. Install the master cylinder as described in this chapter.

11. Adjust the brake pedal height as described in Chapter Three.

Inspection

Compare all measurements to the specifications in **Table 1** and **Table 2**. Replace any part that is damaged, worn to the wear limit or out of specification.

1. Clean all parts in isopropyl alcohol or fresh DOT 4 hydraulic fluid.
2. Inspect the cylinder bore surface (A, **Figure 76**). If it is less than perfect, replace the master cylinder assembly. The body cannot be replaced separately.
3. Inspect the piston cups (A, **Figure 77**) for signs of wear and damage. If less than perfect, replace the piston assembly. The cups cannot be replaced separately.
4. Check the end of the piston (B, **Figure 77**) for wear caused by the pushrod. If worn, replace the piston assembly.
5. Make sure the fluid passageway (B, **Figure 76**) in the master cylinder body is clear. Clean it if necessary.
6. Measure the cylinder bore with a bore gauge (**Figure 78**) or vernier caliper.
7. Measure the outside diameter of the piston with a micrometer (**Figure 79**).
8. Check the entire master cylinder body for wear or damage. If damaged in any way, replace the master cylinder assembly.
9. Inspect the banjo bolt threads in the master cylinder body. If worn or damaged, clean the threads with a thread tap or replace the master cylinder assembly.
10. Inspect the piston push rod assembly (B, **Figure 72**) for wear or damage. Make sure the rubber boot (C, **Figure 72**) is in good condition. Replace the boot if necessary.
11. Inspect the banjo bolt threads for damage. If damaged, clean the threads with a metric thread die or replace the bolt. Make sure the brake fluid hole is clear. Clean out or replace if necessary.
12. Check the connector for damage.
13. Remove the cover and diaphragm from the reservoir. Check all components for damage and deterioration.
14. Inspect the reservoir and hose for wear or deterioration.

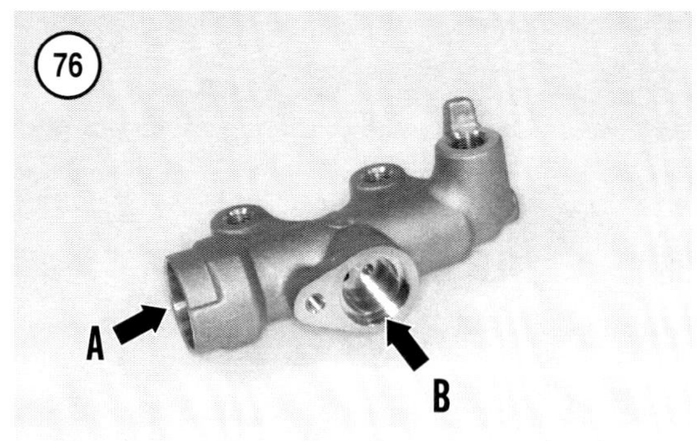

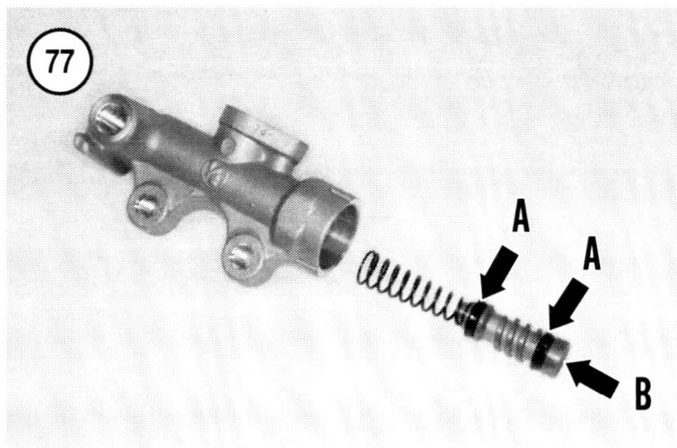

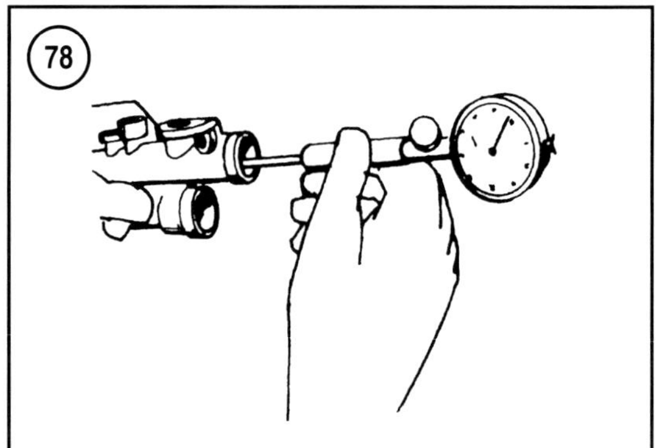

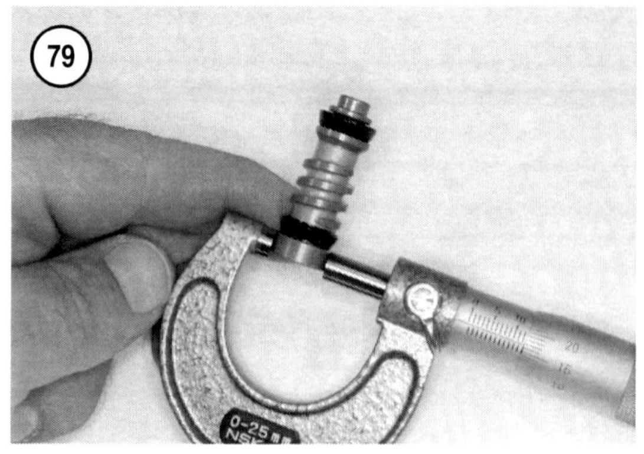

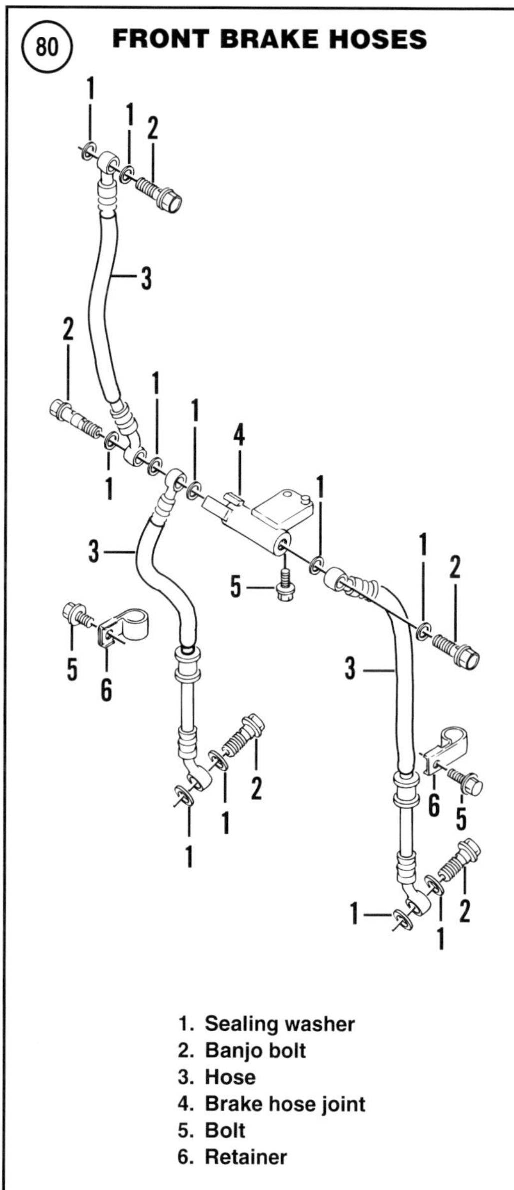

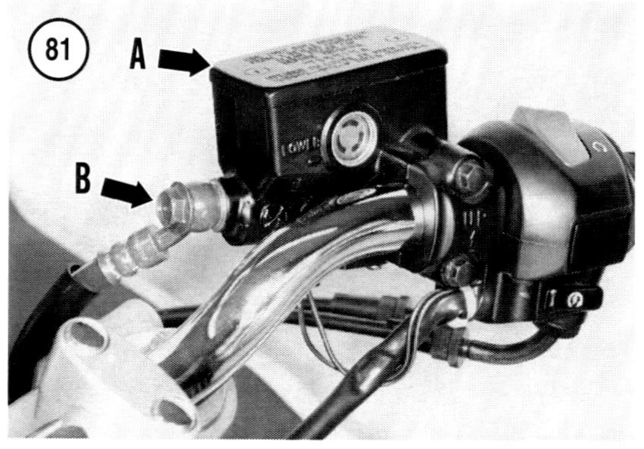

BRAKE HOSE REPLACEMENT (NON-ABS MODELS)

Suzuki recommends replacing all brake hoses every four years or when they show signs of cracking or damage.

Front Brake Hoses

Refer to **Figure 80**.

CAUTION
Drape a heavy cloth or plastic tarp over the front fender to protect it from accidental brake fluid spills. Brake fluid will damage the finish on plastic, painted or plated surfaces. Immediately wash off spilled brake fluid from the motorcycle. Use soapy water, and rinse the area completely.

1. On GSF1200S models, remove the front fairing as described in Chapter Fourteen.
2. Clean all dirt and foreign matter from the top of the master cylinder.
3. Remove the top cover (A, **Figure 81**), diaphragm plate and diaphragm from the master cylinder.

NOTE
Place a shop cloth under the banjo bolts and brake hose fittings to catch any spilled brake fluid that might leak out during this procedure.

4. Remove the banjo bolt (**Figure 82**) and sealing washers securing the brake hose to the left caliper.
5. Place the end of the brake hose over a container and let the brake fluid drain into the container. Apply the front brake lever several times to force the fluid out of the brake hose. Dispose of this brake fluid

properly. Never reuse brake fluid. Place the loose end of the brake hose in a reclosable plastic bag to prevent brake fluid from dribbling onto the motorcycle.

6. Remove the retainer bolt and release the hose from the retainer securing the brake hose to the fork slider.
7. Repeat Steps 4-6 for the right caliper.
8. Remove the banjo bolt and two sealing washers (A, **Figure 83**) from the left side of the brake hose joint and remove the left lower brake hose (B).
9. Disconnect the banjo bolt and the three sealing washers (C, **Figure 83**) from the right side of the brake hose joint and remove the right lower brake hose (D).
10. Remove the banjo bolt (B, **Figure 81**) and two sealing washers securing the upper brake hose to the master cylinder.
11. Carefully pull the upper end of the upper hose down and out from behind the throttle cables on the right side and remove the hose.
12. Wash off any spilled brake fluid that may have leaked out of the hoses during removal.
13. Install new hoses in the reverse order of removal. Note the following:
    a. Install *new* sealing washers on each side of the hose fittings.
    b. Be sure to use three sealing washers when securing the upper brake hose and the right lower brake hoses to the brake hose joint (C, **Figure 83**).
    c. Tighten the banjo bolts to 23 N•m (17 ft.-lb.).
    d. Refill the master cylinder reservoir and bleed the front brakes as described in this chapter.

Rear Brake Hose

Refer to **Figure 69**.

CAUTION
Cover the surrounding area with a heavy cloth or plastic tarp to protect the components from accidental brake fluid spills. Brake fluid will destroy the finish on any plastic, painted or plated surfaces. Immediately wash off spilled brake fluid from the motorcycle. Use soapy water, and rinse the area completely.

NOTE
*The reservoir hose replacement procedure is covered in **Rear Master Cylinder** in this chapter.*

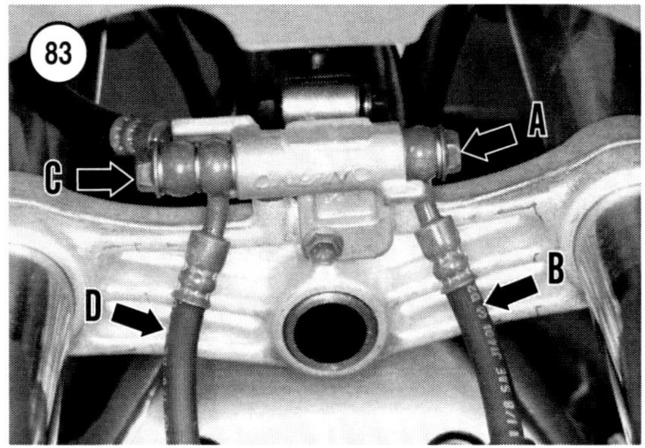

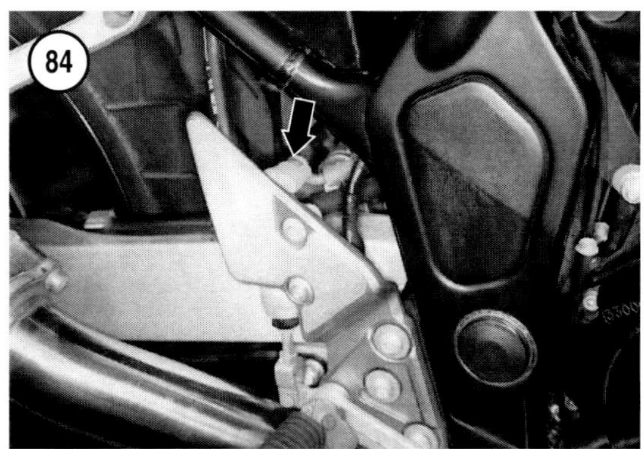

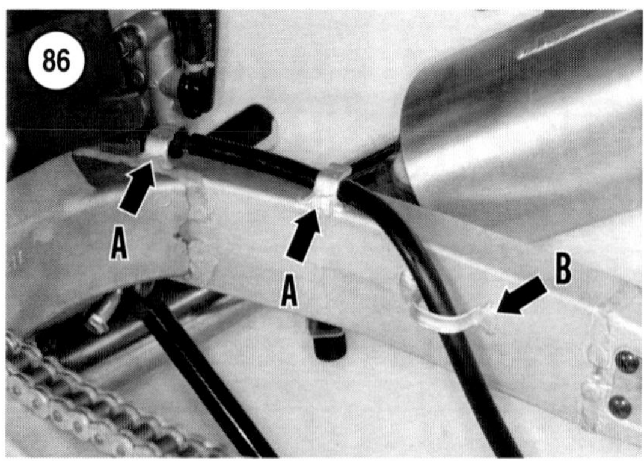

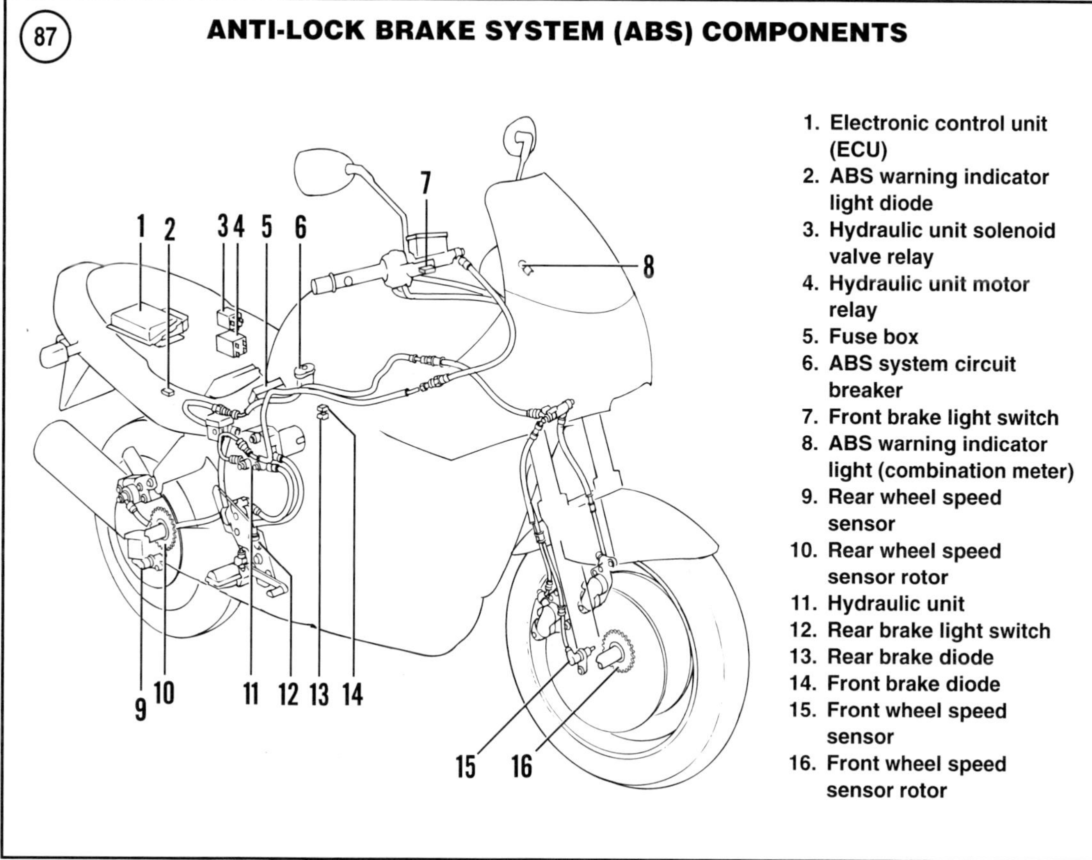

1. Remove the right side frame cover as described in Chapter Fourteen.

NOTE
Place a shop cloth under the banjo bolts and brake hose fittings to catch any spilled brake fluid that leaks out in the following steps.

2. Remove the banjo bolt (**Figure 84**) and sealing washers attaching the brake hose to the top of the rear master cylinder. Do not lose the sealing washer from each side of the hose fitting.

3. Remove the banjo bolt (**Figure 85**) and sealing washers attaching the brake hose to the rear caliper assembly. Do not lose the sealing washer from each side of the hose fitting.

4. Remove the rear wheel as described in Chapter Ten.

5. Unhook the brake hose from the two clamps (A, **Figure 86**) on top of the swing arm.

6. Carefully pull the rear of the brake hose out from the guide (B, **Figure 86**) on the inner surface of the swing arm and remove the brake hose.

7. Install the hose in the reverse order of removal. Note the following:
   a. Install *new* sealing washers on each side of the brake hose fittings.
   b. Tighten the banjo bolts to 23 N•m (17 ft.-lb.).
   c. Make sure the brake hose is correctly installed through the guide (B, **Figure 86**) on the swing arm so that it will not touch the rear wheel.
   d. Refill the master cylinder reservoir and bleed the rear brake system as described in this chapter.

BRAKE HOSE AND LINES REPLACEMENT (ABS EQUIPPED MODELS)

Suzuki recommends replacing all brake hoses every four years or when they show signs of cracking or damage. Refer to **Figure 87** for the layout of the ABS components.

13

The metal brake lines do not require routine replacement unless they are damaged or the end fittings are leaking. While replacing the flexible brake hoses, inspect the metal brake lines for damage. If they have been hit, the lines may be restricted, thus decreasing braking effectiveness.

WARNING
On ABS-equipped models, the brake system uses flexible brake hoses along with metal brake lines. Since brake pressure is critical in an ABS system, the Suzuki flexible brake hoses are designed to have the same minimal flexing characteristics as the steel lines. When replacing the flexible brake hoses, make sure to install authorized Suzuki replacement hoses specifically designed for use with the ABS system. Using a flexible brake hose of an alternate design will drastically change the characteristics of the brake system.

Front Brake Hoses and Lines

This procedure covers removal and installation of all of the front brake hoses and lines (**Figure 88** and **Figure 89**). If replacing only one hose, or line, refer to the steps relating to that specific hose or line.

CAUTION
Drape a heavy cloth or plastic tarp over the front fender and frame to protect it from accidental brake fluid spills. Brake fluid will damage the finish on plastic, painted or plated surfaces. Immediately wash spilled brake fluid off the motorcycle. Use soapy water, and rinse the area completely.

1. Refer to Chapter Fourteen and perform the following:
   a. Remove the front fairing.
   b. Remove the seat.
   c. Remove the frame right side cover.
   d. Remove the rear frame cover.
2. Drain the brake fluid from the front brake system as follows:
   a. Clean all debris from the top of the master cylinder.

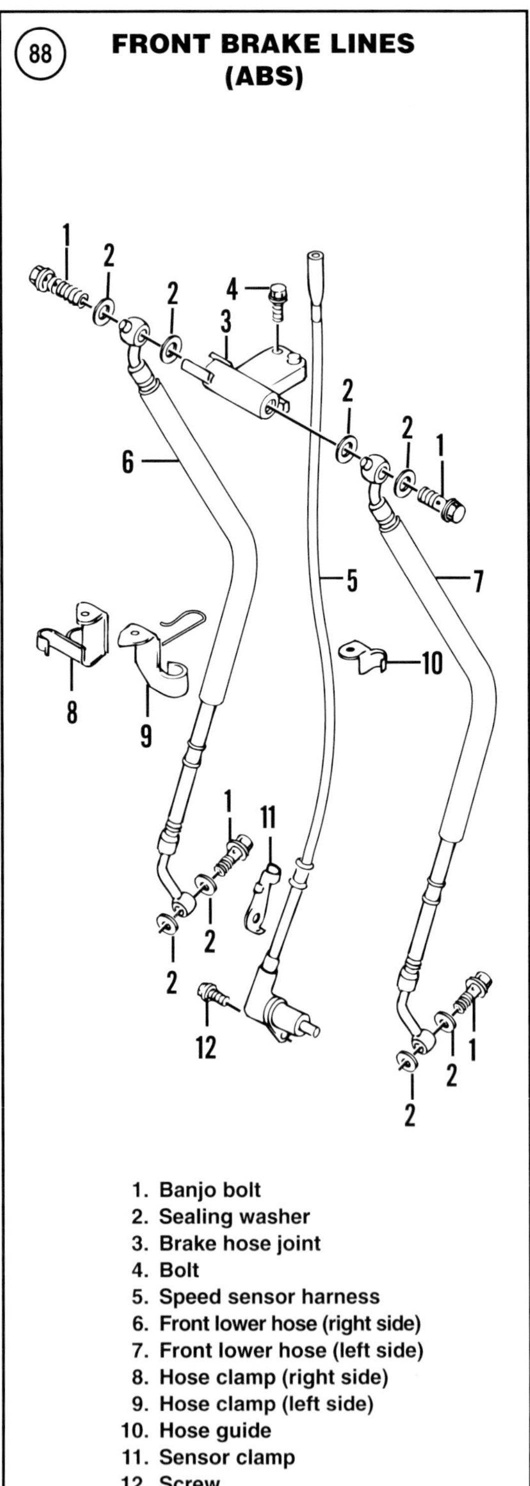

89

FRONT BRAKE LINES (ABS)

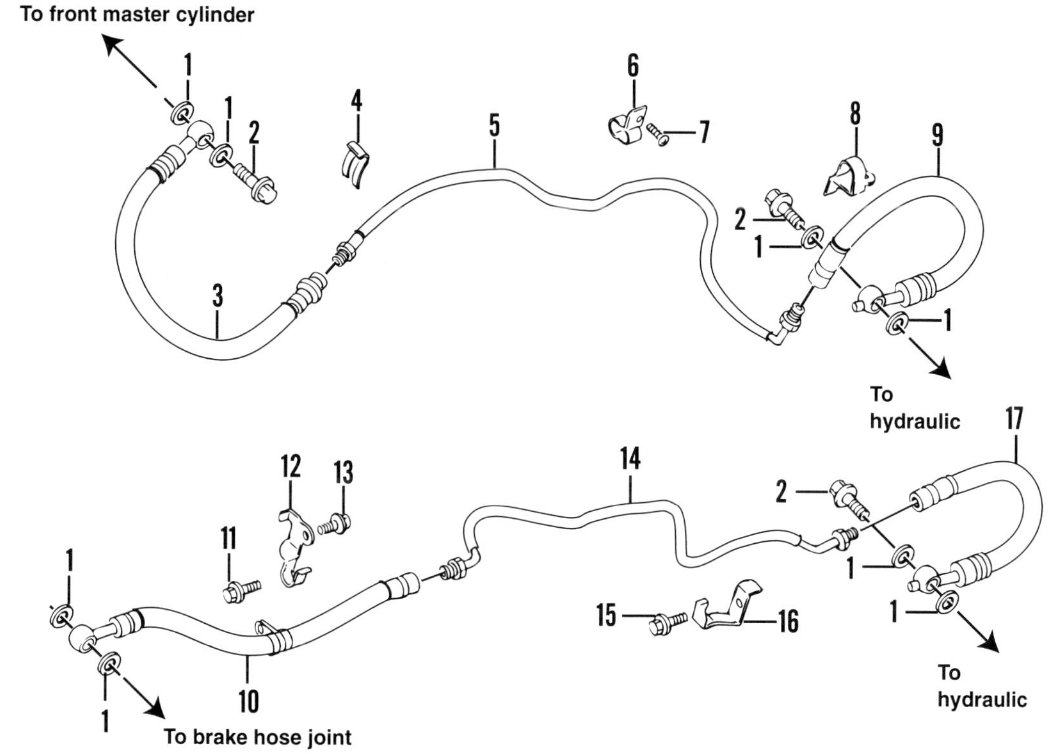

To front master cylinder

To hydraulic

To hydraulic

To brake hose joint

1. Sealing washers
2. Banjo bolt
3. Upper brake hose
4. Hose clip
5. Front brake pipe No. 1
6. Brake pipe clamp
7. Screw
8. Hose clamp
9. Inlet brake hose
10. Lower intermediate brake hose
11. Bolt
12. Hose joint clamp
13. Bolt
14. Front brake pipe No. 2
15. Bolt
16. Hose clamp
17. Inlet brake hose

b. Remove the top cover (A, **Figure 81**), diaphragm plate and diaphragm from the front master cylinder.

NOTE
Place a shop cloth under all banjo bolts and brake hose fittings to catch any spilled brake fluid that might leak out during this procedure.

c. Remove the banjo bolt (A, **Figure 90**) and sealing washers securing the brake hose to the left side caliper.

d. Place the end of the brake hose over a container and let the brake fluid drain out into the container. Apply the front brake lever several times to force the fluid out of the brake hose. Dispose of this brake fluid properly. Never reuse brake fluid. Place the loose end of the brake hose in a reclosable plastic bag to prevent brake fluid from leaking onto the motorcycle.

e. Repeat for the right side caliper.

3. To remove the upper brake hose, perform the following:

a. Remove the banjo bolt (B, **Figure 81**) and two sealing washers securing the upper brake hose to the front master cylinder.

b. Hold onto the fitting of the upper brake hose with a wrench. Use a flare nut wrench and loosen and unscrew the flare nut securing the upper hose to front brake pipe No. 1.

c. Disconnect the upper brake hose from the clip on the frame.

d. Remove the upper brake hose.

4. To remove the lower intermediate brake hose, perform the following:

a. Remove the banjo bolt and the three sealing washers (A, **Figure 91**) from the right side of the brake hose joint and remove the lower intermediate hose.

b. Hold onto the fitting of the lower intermediate brake hose with a wrench. Use a flare nut wrench and loosen and unscrew the flare nut securing the lower intermediate hose to front brake pipe No. 2.

c. Disconnect the hose from any clamps on the frame.

d. Remove the lower intermediate brake hose.

5. To remove the front lower brake lines, perform the following:

a. Remove the bolt and release the hose from the retainer securing the brake hose to the fork slider.

b. Remove the banjo bolt and two sealing washers (C, **Figure 90**) from the left side of the brake hose joint and remove the left lower brake hose (D).

c. Remove the banjo bolt and the three sealing washer (A, **Figure 91**) from the right side of the brake hose joint and remove the right lower hose (B).

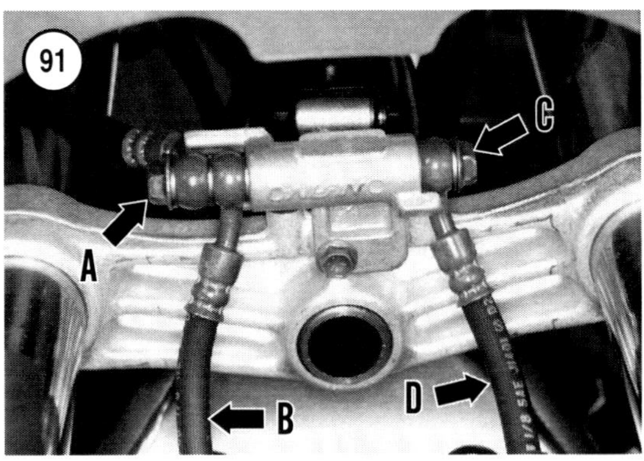

6. To remove the inlet and outlet brake hoses at the hydraulic unit, perform the following:

a. Remove the banjo bolt and two sealing washers securing the inlet brake hose to the hydraulic unit.

b. Hold onto the fitting of the inlet brake hose with a wrench. Use a flare nut wrench to loosen and unscrew the flare nut securing the inlet brake hose to front brake pipe No. 1.

c. Remove the inlet brake hose.

d. Remove the banjo bolt and two sealing washers securing the outlet brake hose to the hydraulic unit.

e. Hold onto the fitting of the inlet brake hose with a wrench. Use a flare nut wrench and loosen and unscrew the flare nut securing the outlet brake hose to front brake pipe No. 2.

f. Remove the outlet brake hose.

7. To remove front brake pipe No. 1 and/or No. 2, perform the following:

a. Disconnect the flexible brake hoses from each end of the brake pipe as previously described.

b. Disconnect the front brake pipe from any clamps and tie wraps securing the brake pipes to the frame.

c. Remove the front brake pipe(s) from the frame.

8. Wash off any spilled brake fluid that may have leaked out of the hoses during removal.

9. Install new hoses and/or brake pipes in the reverse order of removal. Note the following:

a. Install *new* sealing washers on each side of the hose fittings.

b. Be sure to use three sealing washers when securing the upper brake hose and the lower in-

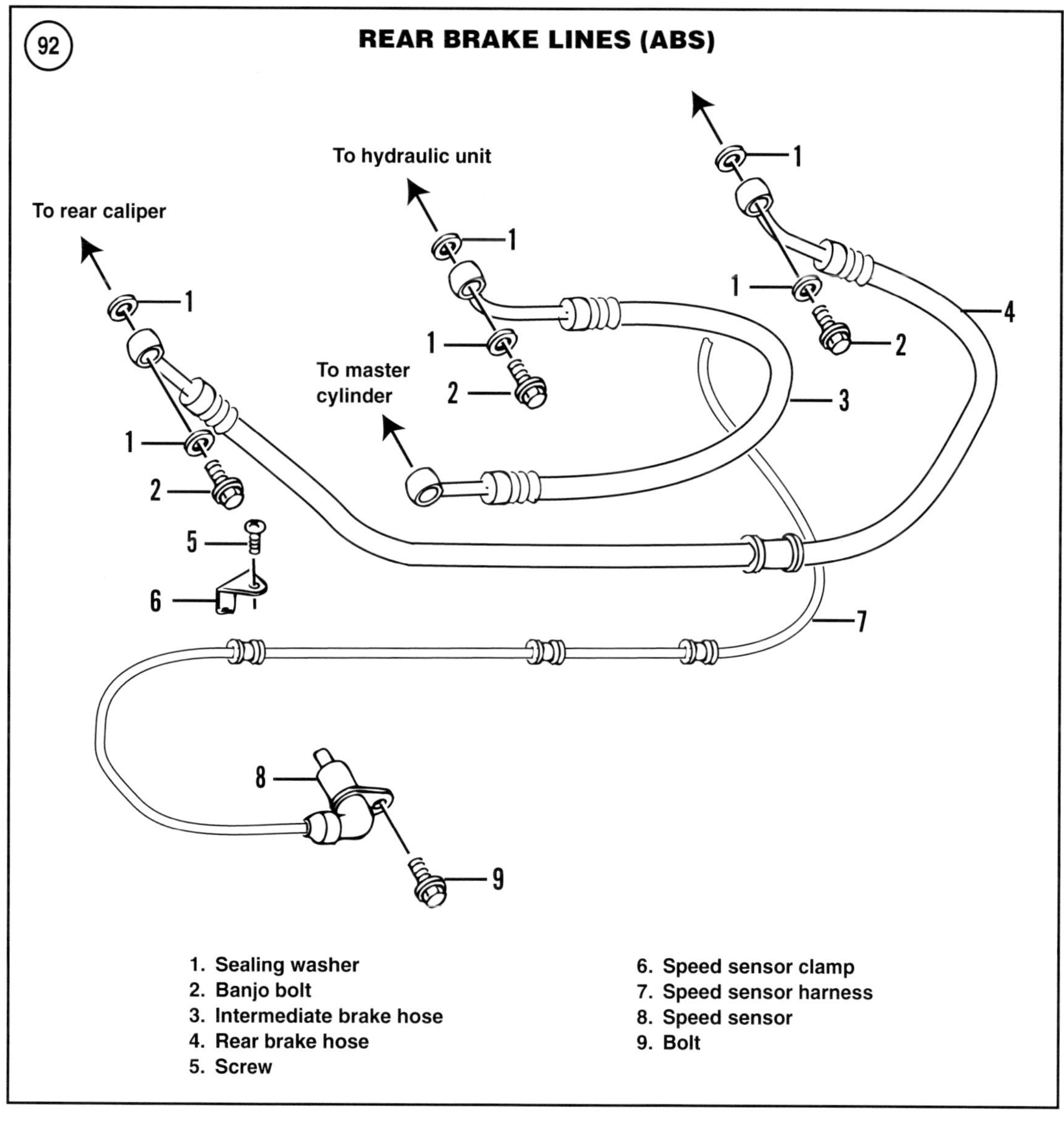

termediate brake hoses to the brake hose joint (A, **Figure 91**).

c. Tighten the banjo bolts to 23 N•m (17 ft.-lb.).

d. Tighten the brake pipe flare fittings securely.

e. Refill the master cylinder reservoir and bleed the front brakes as described in this chapter.

Rear Brake Hoses

This procedure covers removal and installation of all of the rear brake hoses. If replacing only one hose, refer to the steps relating to that specific hose.

Refer to **Figure 92**.

CAUTION

Drape a heavy cloth or plastic tarp over the rear wheel and frame to protect it from accidental brake fluid spills. Brake fluid will damage the finish on plastic, painted or plated surfaces. Immediately wash spilled brake fluid off the motorcycle. Use soapy water, and rinse the area completely.

1. Refer to Chapter Fourteen and perform the following:

a. Remove the seat.
b. Remove the frame right side cover.
c. Remove the rear frame cover.

2. Drain the brake fluid from the rear brake system as follows:
   a. Clean all debris from the top of the master cylinder.
   b. Remove the top cover (**Figure 93**), diaphragm plate and diaphragm from the rear master cylinder.

NOTE
Place a shop cloth under all banjo bolts and brake hose fittings to catch any spilled brake fluid that might leak out during this procedure.

   c. Remove the banjo bolt (**Figure 85**) and sealing washers attaching the brake hose to the rear caliper assembly. Do not lose the sealing washer from each side of the hose fitting.
   d. Place the end of the brake hose over a container and let the brake fluid drain out into the container. Apply the rear brake pedal several times to force the fluid out of the brake hoses. Dispose of this brake fluid properly. Never reuse brake fluid. Place the loose end of the brake hose in a reclosable plastic bag to prevent brake fluid from leaking onto the motorcycle.

3. To remove the rear brake hose, perform the following:
   a. Remove the banjo bolt and sealing washers attaching the rear brake hose to hydraulic unit. Do not lose the sealing washer from each side of the hose fitting.
   b. If still attached, remove the banjo bolt (**Figure 85**) and sealing washers attaching the rear brake hose to the rear caliper assembly. Do not lose the sealing washer from each side of the hose fitting.
   c. Remove the rear wheel as described in Chapter Ten.
   d. Unhook the brake hose from the two clamps (A, **Figure 86**) on top of the swing arm.
   e. Carefully pull the rear of the brake hose out from the guide (B, **Figure 86**) on the inner surface of the swing arm and remove the rear brake hose.

4. To remove the intermediate brake hose, perform the following:

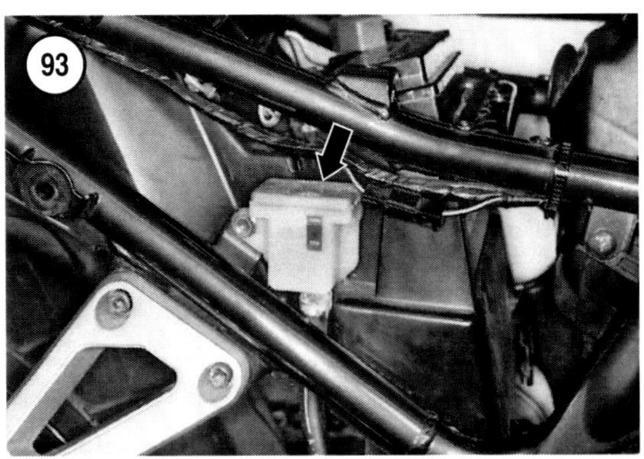
93

94

   a. Remove the banjo bolt (**Figure 84**) and sealing washers attaching the intermediate brake hose to the top of the rear master cylinder. Do not lose the sealing washer from each side of the hose fitting.
   b. Remove the banjo bolt and sealing washers attaching the intermediate brake hose to the hydraulic unit. Do not lose the sealing washer from each side of the hose fitting.
   c. Remove the intermediate brake hose from the frame.

5. Wash off any spilled brake fluid that may have leaked out of the hoses during removal.

6. Install new hoses and/or brake pipes in the reverse order of removal. Note the following:
   a. Install *new* sealing washers on each side of the hose fittings.
   b. Tighten the banjo bolts to 23 N•m (17 ft.-lb.).
   c. Refill the rear master cylinder reservoir and bleed the front brakes as described in this chapter.

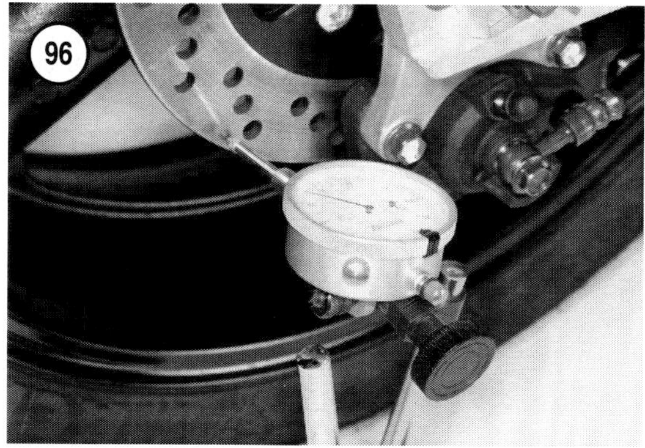

BRAKE DISC AND ABS ROTOR

The brake discs are separate from the wheel hubs and can be removed once the wheel is removed from the motorcycle.

Brake Disc Inspection

The brake disc can be inspected while it is installed on the wheel. Small nicks and marks on the disc are not important, but radial scratches deep enough to snag a fingernail reduce braking effectiveness and increase brake pad wear. If these grooves are evident and the brake pads are wearing rapidly, replace the disc.

The specifications for the standard thickness and wear limits are in **Table 1** and **Table 2**. A minimum (MIN) thickness is also stamped on the disc face (**Figure 94**). If the specification stamped on the disc differs from the wear limit in **Table 1** and **Table 2**, use the specification on the disc during inspection.

Do not have the discs machined to compensate for any warp. The discs are thin and grinding only makes them thinner, causing them to warp quite rapidly. If the disc is warped, the brake pads may be dragging on the disc due to a faulty caliper and causing the disc to overheat. Overheating can also be caused when there is unequal pad pressure on the sides of the disc.

NOTE
Disc thickness can be measured with the wheel installed or removed from the motorcycle.

1. Measure the thickness of the disc at several locations around the disc with a vernier caliper or a micrometer (**Figure 95**). Replace the disc if the thickness in any area is less than the specification in **Table 1** and **Table 2** or the MIN dimension stamped on the disc.
2. Check the disc runout with a dial indicator as shown in **Figure 96**. Make sure the disc mounting bolts are tight prior to running this check.

NOTE
When checking the front disc, turn the handlebar all the way to one side, then to the other side.

3. Slowly rotate the wheel and watch the dial indicator. Replace the disc if runout is out of specification.
4. Excessive runout usually causes the disc to overheat due to unequal brake pad pressure. Consider the following possibilities and determine the cause before installing a new brake disc:
   a. The brake caliper piston seals are worn and allowing the brake pads to drag on the brake disc.
   b. The master cylinder relief port is plugged.
   c. The master cylinder primary cup is worn or damaged.
5. Clean any rust or corrosion from the disc and wipe it clean with lacquer thinner. Never use an oil-based solvent that may leave an oil residue on the disc.
6. On the front brake discs, inspect the fasteners (**Figure 97**) between the outer and inner rings of the disc. If any are damaged, replace the disc.

Brake Disc Removal/Installation

1. Remove the front or rear wheel as described in Chapter Ten.

CAUTION
Set the sidewall on two wooden blocks. Do not set the wheel down on

13

the disc surface, as it may get scratched or warped.

NOTE

Insert a piece of wood or vinyl tube between the pads in the caliper(s). This way, if the brake lever or pedal is inadvertently applied, the pistons will not be forced out of the cylinders. If this does happen, the caliper might have to be disassembled to reseat the pistons and the system will have to be bled. By using the wood or vinyl tube in place of the disc, bleeding the system will not be necessary when installing the wheel.

2. Remove the bolts (**Figure 98**) securing the brake disc to the hub and remove the disc.
3. Install by reversing these removal steps while noting the following:
   a. On discs so marked, position the disc so the arrow points in the direction of tire rotation.

CAUTION

*The disc bolts are made from a harder material than similar bolts used on the motorcycle. When replacing the bolts, always use standard Suzuki brake disc bolts. Never compromise and use cheaper bolts. They will **not** properly secure the disc to the hub.*

   b. Use a small amount of a locking compound such as ThreeBond No. TB1360 on the brake disc bolts prior to installation.
   c. Tighten the disc mounting bolts to 23 N•m (17 ft.-lb.).

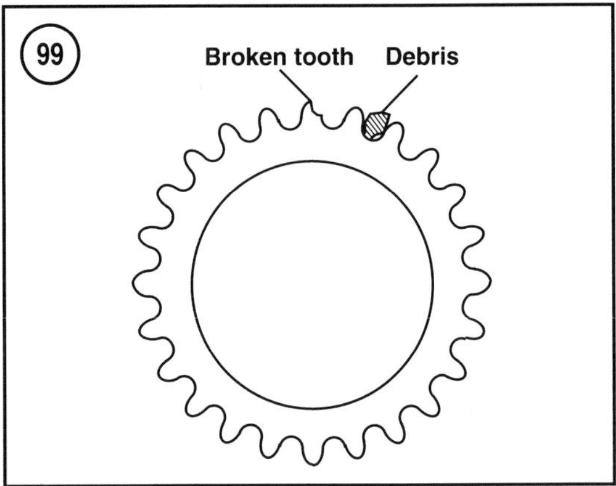

ABS Rotor Inspection

Inspect the ABS pulse generating rotor for damaged or broken teeth (**Figure 99**). Also check for any debris lodged into the teeth. Remove any debris.

Remove and replace the ABS rotor from the hub if damaged.

BLEEDING THE BRAKES

Bleeding the brakes removes air from the brake system. Air in the brakes increases brake lever or pedal travel and it makes the brakes feel soft or spongy. Under extreme circumstances, it can cause complete loss of brake pressure.

The brakes can be bled manually or with the use of a brake bleeding tool. Both methods are described here. When using a vacuum pump or other brake bleeding tool, follow the instructions that came with the tool. Only use fresh DOT 4 brake fluid when bleeding the brakes. Do not reuse old brake fluid and do not use DOT 5 (silicone-based) brake fluid.

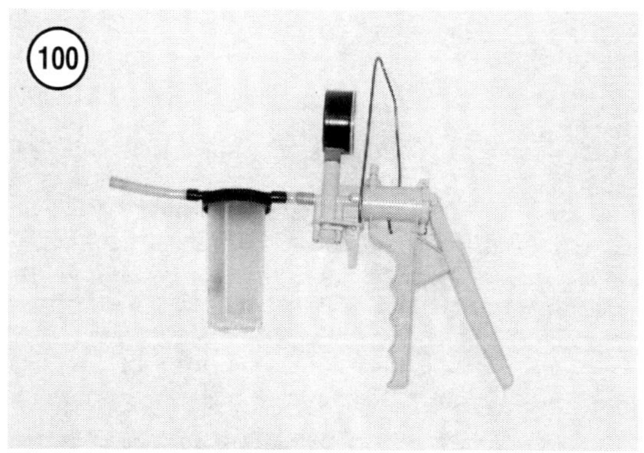

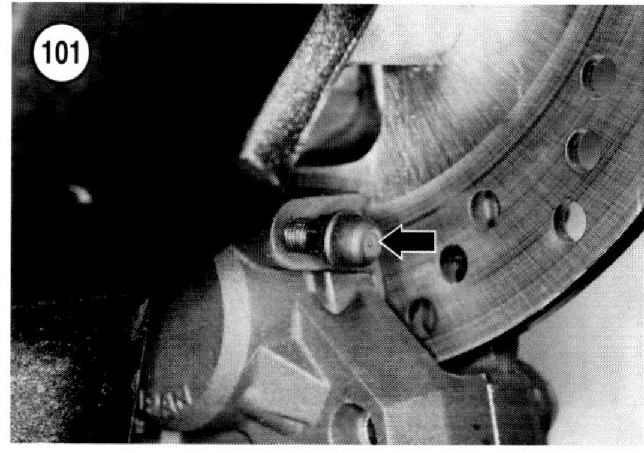

Protect the motorcycle from accidental spills by covering the areas beneath the calipers and master cylinders with a tarp. Brake fluid will damage the finish on most surfaces, so immediately clean up any spilled brake fluid. Wash the affected parts with soapy water and completely rinse the area with plenty of clean water.

Before bleeding the brake system, observe the following conditions:

1. Check the brake hoses and ABS brake pipes to make sure that all fittings are tight.
2. Check that the caliper piston does not stick or bind in its bore.
3. Check piston movement in each master cylinder. Operate the lever or brake pedal, making sure there is no binding or other abnormal conditions present.
4. When bleeding the front brakes, check the brake lever operation in each of the seven brake lever adjustment positions. The brakes may feel firm in the No. 1 position, but the lever may contact the throttle grip in the No. 7 position. If this occurs, continue to bleed the brakes until the lever is firm in all seven positions.

NOTE
On ABS-equipped models, this process will take longer due to the additional brake hoses and lines, therefore it is suggested that the brake bleeder procedure be used.

NOTE
The rear caliper is equipped with two bleed valves, one for each caliper body half. Bleed the inner caliper body first and then bleed the outer caliper half.

Brake Bleeder Process

This procedure uses the Mityvac hydraulic brake bleeding kit (**Figure 100**), which is available from automotive or motorcycle supply stores or from mail order outlets.

NOTE
This procedure is shown on the rear wheel and relates to the front wheel as well.

1. Remove the dust cap from the caliper bleed valve (**Figure 101**).
2. Place a clean shop cloth over the caliper to protect it from accidental brake fluid spills.
3. Clean the top of the master cylinder of all debris.

4A. On the front wheel, remove the screws securing the master cylinder top cover (**Figure 102**) and remove the cover, plate and diaphragm.

4B. On the rear wheel, perform the following:

a. Remove the seat and the right side frame cover as described in Chapter Fourteen.

b. Remove the screws securing the master cylinder top cover (**Figure 103**) and remove the cover, plate and diaphragm.

5. Add brake fluid to the reservoir until the fluid level is at the upper limit. Loosely install the plate, diaphragm and cover. Leave the cover in place during this procedure to prevent the entry of debris.

6. Assemble the brake bleeder according to its manufacturer's instructions. Secure it to the caliper bleed valve (**Figure 104**).

7A. On the front caliper, using a wrench, open the bleed screw approximately 1/2 turn.

7B. On the rear caliper, using a wrench, open the bleed screw approximately 1/2 turn. Refer to **Figure 105** for the inner bleed valve and **Figure 106** for the outer bleed valve.

8. Operate the pump several times to create a vacuum in the line. Brake fluid will quickly flow from the caliper into the pump's reservoir. Tighten the caliper bleed valve before the fluid stops flowing through the hose. To prevent air from being drawn through the master cylinder, add fluid to maintain its level at the top of the reservoir.

NOTE
Do not allow the master cylinder reservoir to empty during the bleeding operation or more air will enter the system. If this occurs, the procedure must be repeated.

9. Continue the bleeding process until the brake fluid flowing from the hose is clear and free of air. If the system is difficult to bleed, tap the master cylinder or caliper with a soft mallet to release trapped air bubbles.

10. When the brake fluid is free of bubbles, tighten the bleed valve and remove the brake bleeder assembly. Reinstall the bleed valve dust cap.

11. Test the feel of the brake lever or pedal. It must be firm and offer the same resistance each time it is operated. If the lever or pedal feels soft, air is still trapped in the system. Continue bleeding.

12. When bleeding is complete, disconnect the hose from the bleed valve. Tighten the caliper bleed valve to 8 N•m (71 in.-lb.).

13. If necessary, add brake fluid to the master cylinder to correct the fluid level.

14. Install the diaphragm, diaphragm plate (front reservoir only) and top cover. Be sure the top cover is secured in place.

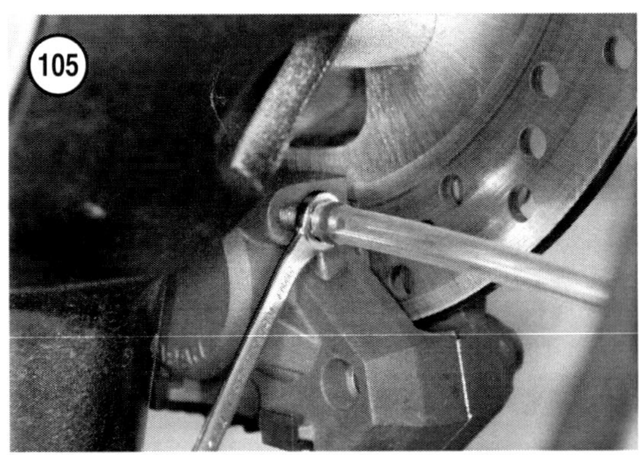

WARNING
Do not ride the motorcycle before making sure the brakes are working correctly with full hydraulic advantage. If necessary, bleed the brakes a second time.

Without a Brake Bleeder

1. Remove the dust cap from the caliper bleed valve (**Figure 101**).

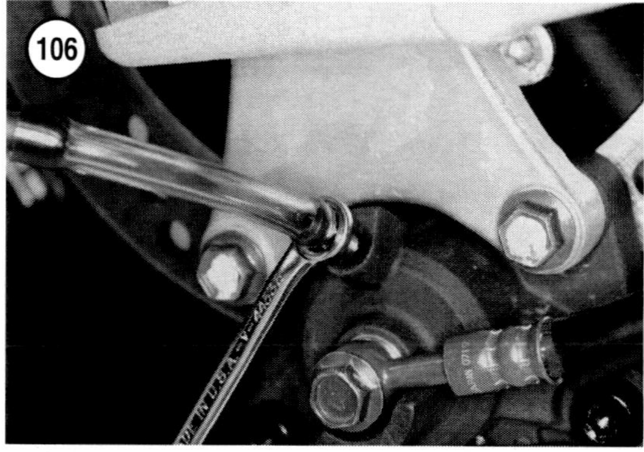

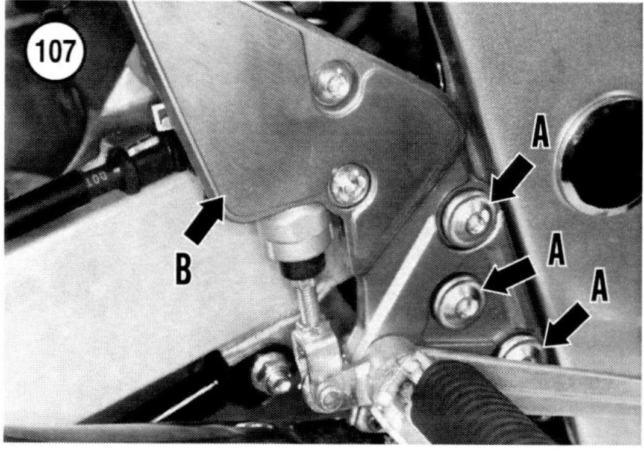

2. Place a clean shop cloth over the caliper to protect it from accidental brake fluid spills.

3. Clean the top of the master cylinder of all debris.

4A. On the front wheel, remove the screws securing the master cylinder top cover (**Figure 102**) and remove the cover, plate and diaphragm.

4B. On the rear wheel, perform the following:

a. Remove the seat and the right side frame cover as described in Chapter Fourteen.
b. Remove the screws securing the master cylinder top cover (**Figure 103**) and remove the cover, plate and diaphragm.

5. Add brake fluid to the reservoir until the fluid level is at the upper limit. Loosely install the plate, diaphragm and cover. Leave the cover in place during this procedure to prevent the entry of debris.

6. Pump the brake lever or pedal a few times and then release it.

7. Apply the front brake lever or the rear brake pedal until it stops and hold it in this position.

8A. On the front caliper, using a wrench, open the bleed screw approximately 1/2 turn.

8B. On the rear caliper, using a wrench, open the bleed screw approximately 1/2 turn. Refer to **Figure 105** for the inner bleed valve and **Figure 106** for the outer bleed valve.

9. Let the brake lever (or brake pedal) move to the limit of its travel and then close the bleed valve. Do not release the brake lever (or brake pedal) while the bleed valve is open.

NOTE

As brake fluid enters the system, the level in the reservoir drops. Add brake fluid as necessary to keep the fluid level 10 mm (3/8 in.) below the reservoir top so air will not be drawn into the system.

10. Repeat Steps 5-9 until the brake fluid flowing from the hose is clear and free of air. If the system is difficult to bleed, tap the master cylinder or caliper with a soft mallet to release trapped air bubbles.

11. Test the feel of the brake lever or pedal. It should feel firm and offer the same resistance each time it is operated. If the lever or pedal feels soft, air is still trapped in the system. Continue bleeding.

12. When bleeding is complete, disconnect the hose from the bleed valve. Tighten the caliper bleed valve to 8 N•m (71 in.-lb.).

13. If necessary, add brake fluid to the master cylinder to correct the fluid level.

14. Install the plate, diaphragm and top cover. Be sure the top cover is secured in place.

WARNING

Do not ride the motorcycle before making sure the brakes are working correctly with full hydraulic advantage. If necessary, bleed the brakes a second time.

REAR BRAKE PEDAL

Removal/Lubrication/Installation

1. Place the motorcycle on level ground on the centerstand.

2. Remove the three bolts (A, **Figure 107**) securing the right side footpeg assembly (B) to the frame. Pull the assembly away from the frame and turn it around.

3. Remove the cotter pin and remove the washer from the back end of the clevis pin (A, **Figure 108**) that secures the master cylinder pushrod to the brake pedal.

4. Withdraw the clevis pin and separate the pushrod yoke from the brake pedal.
5. Unhook the rear brake light switch spring (B, **Figure 108**) from the brake pedal.
6. Use vise grip pliers and disconnect the pedal return spring (C, **Figure 108**) from the brake pedal.
7. Remove the footpeg bolt (D, **Figure 108**) from the inboard side of the mounting bracket.
8. Remove the footpeg and rear brake pedal assembly. Do not lose the washer between the brake pedal and the footpeg mounting bracket.
9. Inspect the brake pedal for fractures or damage. Replace it if necessary.
10. Clean the footpeg bolt with solvent and inspect it for wear or damage. Replace if necessary.
11. Lubricate the footpeg bolt and bushing with waterproof grease.
12. Install the pedal by reversing these removal steps while noting the following:
   a. Tighten the footpeg bolt securely.
   b. Install a new cotter pin and bend the ends over completely.
   c. Adjust the rear brake pedal height as described in Chapter Three.

ANTI-LOCK BRAKE SYSTEM

The optional ABS (Anti-lock Braking System) is designed to eliminate brake lock-up and skidding under wet or slippery conditions and during panic stops. The system also provides for more stable braking by controlling the wheel braking speed to maximize the adhesion between the tire and the road surface.

The ABS components are shown in **Figure 87**. It consists of the front and rear wheel speed sensors and rotors, the ECU and the hydraulic unit. These three components work together to maximize safe braking.

The ABS components function as follows:

1. The ECU controls the functions of the entire system and is located under the seat.
2. The hydraulic unit controls the distribution of the brake fluid and is located under the seat below the battery.
3. The wheel speed sensors determine wheel rotational speed from the toothed pulse-generating rotor that is attached to each wheel hub.

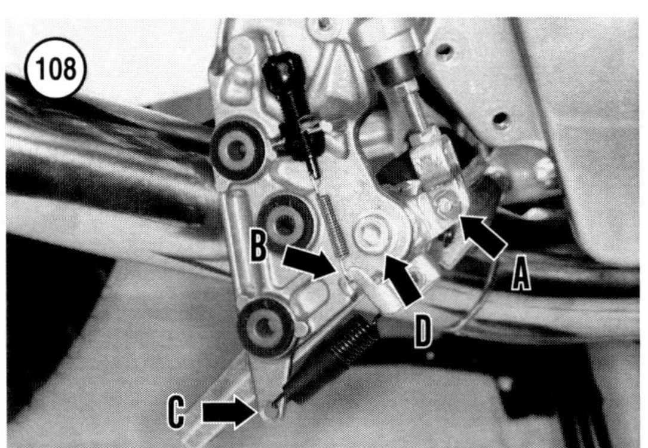

4. The ABS warning light notifies the rider that the ABS system is either working correctly, or there is a problem within the system that must be corrected.

NOTE
All of the ABS components are sealed and cannot be serviced. If any of the components are faulty, they must be replaced.

Self-Diagnosis Fault Codes

The ECU is a very complex and *expensive* piece of electronic hardware, therefore entrust all service work related to the control unit to a Suzuki dealership. Any applicable Suzuki warranty will be voided if the unit is serviced by anyone other than an authorized Suzuki dealership.

The ABS system has a self-diagnosis function incorporated into the ECU. This system informs the rider if there is a fault(s) within the system.

NOTE
If a fault code indication is shown, do not try to troubleshoot the system. Do

not disconnect the electrical connectors from the ECU, as this will erase the fault code held in the memory.

When there is a fault within the system, the ABS warning light located in the lower left side of the combination meter indicator panel (**Figure 109**) will illuminate and flash. This may occur while the motorcycle is being ridden or after a start-up. The motorcycle can still be ridden, but should be taken to a Suzuki dealership as soon as possible so they can evaluate and correct the problem.

When there is a fault within the system, the ABS portion of the brake system will not function. The brakes will still operate, but without ABS assist.

Table 1 BRAKE SPECIFICATIONS (NON-ABS MODELS)

Item	Standard mm (in.)	Wear limit mm (in.)
Brake fluid	DOT 4	–
Brake disc runout		
Front and rear	–	0.30 (0.012)
Brake disc thickness		
Front	4.3-4.7 (0.169-1.85)	4.0 (0.16)
Rear	4.8-5.2 (0.189-0.205)	4.5 (0.18)
Front master cylinder		
Cylinder bore	15.870-15.913 (0.6248-0.6265)	–
Piston diameter	15.827-15.854 (0.6231-0.6242)	–
Front caliper (1996-2000)		
Cylinder bore		
Leading bore	30.230-30.280 (1.1902-1.1921)	–
Trailing bore	33.960-34.010 (1.3370-1.3390)	–
Piston diameter		
Leading bore	30.160-30.180 (1.1874-1.1882)	–
Trailing bore	33.878-33.929 (1.3338-1.3357)	–
Front caliper (2001-on)		
Cylinder bore		
Leading bore	24.000-24.076 (0.9449-0.9479)	
Trailing bore	27.000-27.076 (1.0630-1.0660)	
Piston diameter		
Leading bore	23.925-23.975 (0.9419-0.9439)	
Trailing bore	26.920-26.970 (1.0598-1.0618)	
Rear master cylinder		
Cylinder bore	12.700-12.743 (0.5000-0.5017)	–
Piston diameter	12.657-12.684 (0.4983-0.4994)	–
Rear caliper		
Cylinder bore	38.180-38.256 (1.5031-1.5061)	–
Piston diameter	38.098-38.148 (1.4999-1.5019)	–
Brake pedal height	55 (2.2)	

Table 2 BRAKE SPECIFICATIONS (ABS MODELS)

Item	Standard mm (in.)	Wear limit mm (in.)
Brake fluid	DOT 4	–
Brake disc runout		
(front and rear)	–	0.30 (0.012)
Brake disc thickness		
Front	4.3-4.7 (0.169-1.85)	4.0 (0.16)
Rear	4.8-5.2 (0.189-0.205)	4.5 (0.18)

(continued)

Table 2 BRAKE SPECIFICATIONS (ABS MODELS) (continued)

Item	Standard mm (in.)	Wear limit mm (in.)
Front master cylinder		
Cylinder bore	15.870-15.913 (0.6248-0.6265)	–
Piston diameter	15.827-15.854 (0.6231-0.6242)	–
Front caliper		
Cylinder bore		
Leading bore	30.230-30.280 (1.1902-1.1921)	–
Trailing bore	32.030-32.080 (1.2610-1.2630)	–
Piston diameter		
Leading bore	30.160-30.180 (1.1874-1.1882)	–
Trailing bore	31.948-31.998 (1.2578-1.2598)	–
Rear master cylinder		
Cylinder bore	14.700-14.743 (0.5512-0.5529)	–
Piston diameter	13.959-13.984 (0.5496-0.5506)	–
Rear caliper		
Cylinder bore	38.180-38.256 (1.5031-1.5061)	–
Piston diameter	38.098-38.148 (1.4999-1.5019)	–
Brake pedal height	55 (2.2)	

Table 3 BRAKE TORQUE SPECIFICATIONS

Item	N•m	in.-lb.	ft.-lb.
Brake disc bolt			
(front and rear)	23	–	17
Brake hose banjo bolt			
(front and rear)	23	–	17
Caliper bleed valve			
(front and rear)	8	71	–
Front caliper housing bolt			
1996-2000 models	23	–	17
2001 models	30	–	22
Front caliper mounting bolts	39	–	29
Front caliper pad pin bolt			
1996-2000 models	18	–	13
Front master cylinder			
clamp bolt	10	88	–
Rear caliper housing bolts	30	–	22
Rear caliper			
mounting bolt	25	–	18
Rear footpeg			
mounting bolts	39	–	29
Rear master cylinder			
mounting bolts	23	–	17
Rear master cylinder			
rod locknut	18	–	13
Torque arm bolt/nut	35		26

CHAPTER FOURTEEN

BODY AND FRAME

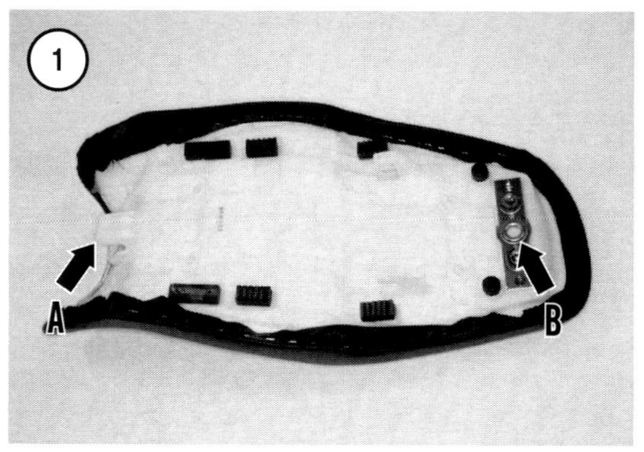

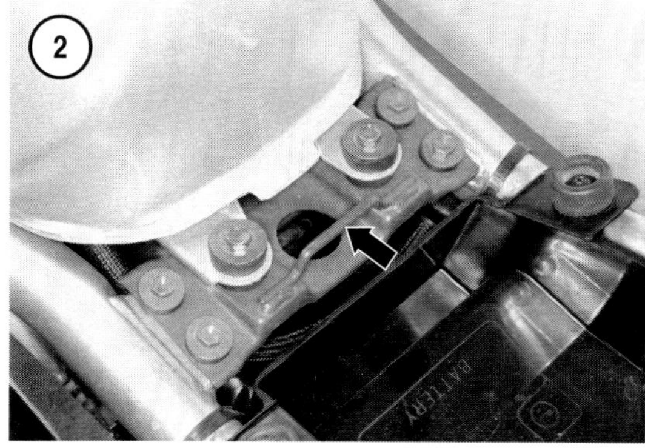

This chapter contains removal and installation procedures for the body panels, the sidestand and the centerstand.

Whenever removing a body or frame member, reinstall all mounting hardware (such as small brackets, bolts, nuts, rubber bushings and metal collars) onto the removed part so they will not be misplaced. Suzuki makes frequent changes during the model year, so a part and the way it attaches to the frame may differ slightly from the one used in the service procedures in this chapter.

The plastic fairing and frame cover parts are very expensive to replace. After each part is removed from the motorcycle, wrap it in a blanket or clean towels and place it a cardboard box. Store it in an area where it will not be damaged.

SEAT AND LOCK MECHANISM

Seat Removal/Installation

1. Insert the key into the seat lock on the left side and turn the lock clockwise.
2. Lift up the rear of the seat and pull the seat rearward.
3. To install the seat, slide the seat forward until the tang (A, **Figure 1**) on the seat engages the retainer (**Figure 2**) behind the fuel tank.

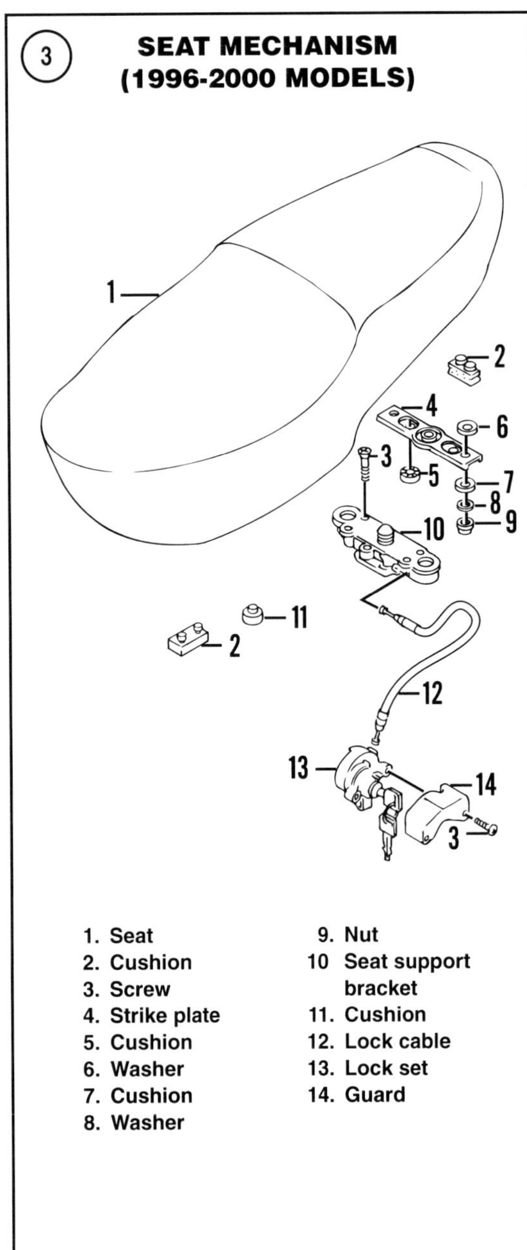

4. Press the seat down until the lock receptacle (B, **Figure 1**) at the back of the seat locks into the lock support bracket on the frame.
5. Pull up on the rear of the seat to ensure it is securely locked in place.

Seat Lock Mechanism Removal/Installation

Refer to **Figure 3** and **Figure 4**.

1. Remove the seat as previously described.

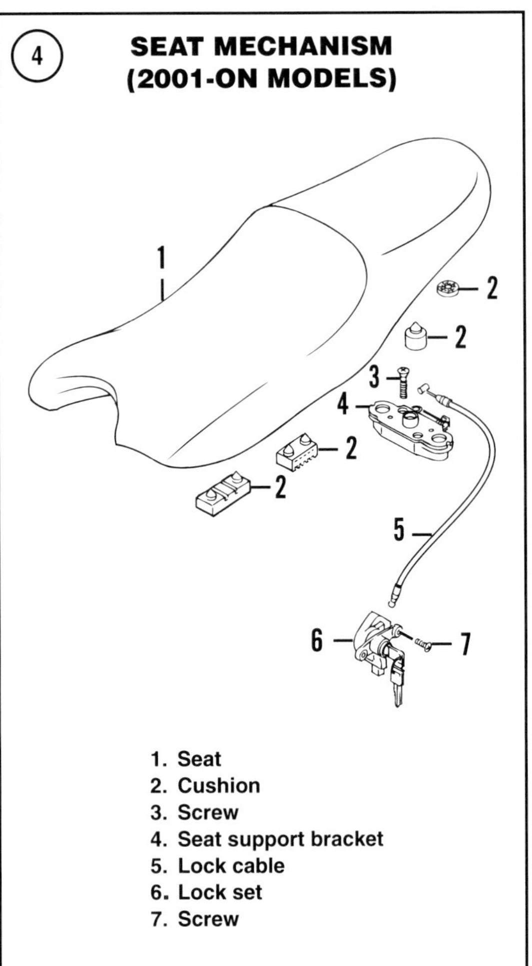

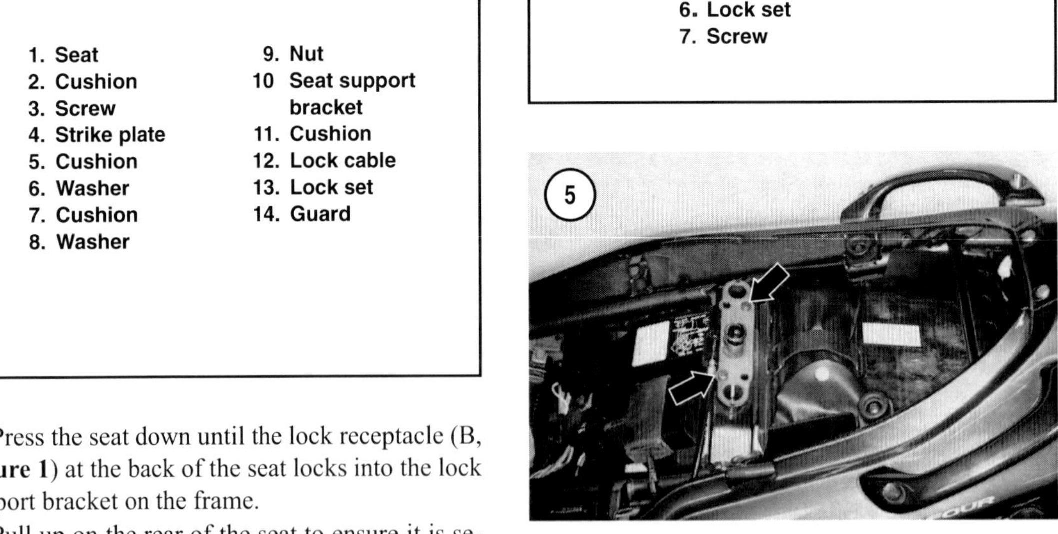

2. Remove the screws (**Figure 5**) securing the support bracket to the frame.
3. Disengage the lock cable from the support bracket and remove the support bracket.
4. If necessary, remove the screws securing the lock set to the frame.

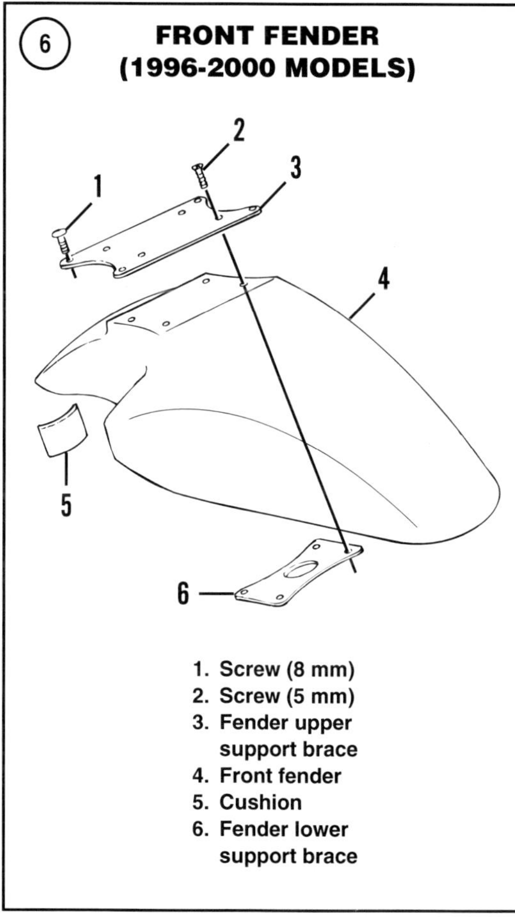

(6) FRONT FENDER (1996-2000 MODELS)

1. Screw (8 mm)
2. Screw (5 mm)
3. Fender upper support brace
4. Front fender
5. Cushion
6. Fender lower support brace

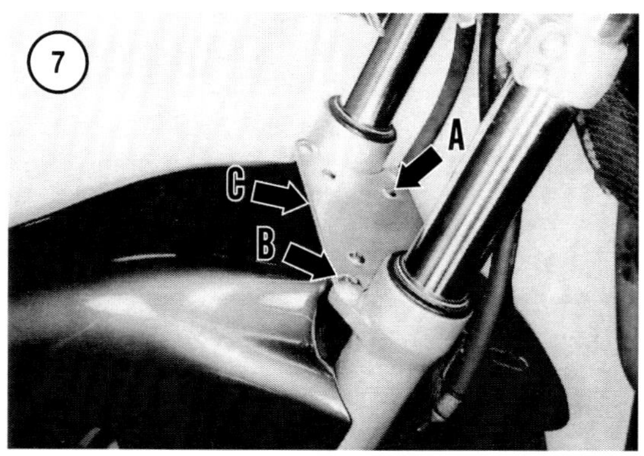

5. Disengage the lock cable from the lock set and remove the lock set.
6. Install by reversing these removal steps while noting the following:
   a. Apply a low strength locking compound to the to the support bracket screws prior to installation.
   b. Tighten all screws securely.

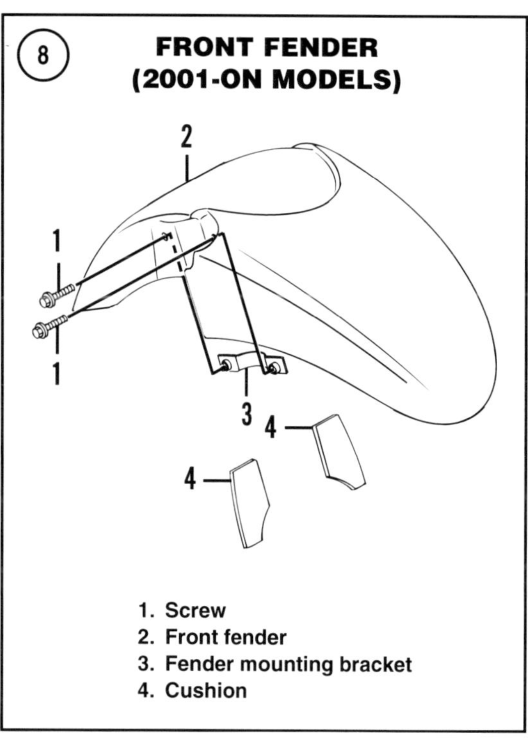

(8) FRONT FENDER (2001-ON MODELS)

1. Screw
2. Front fender
3. Fender mounting bracket
4. Cushion

FRONT FENDER

Removal/Installation (1996-2000 Models)

Refer to **Figure 6**.

1. Remove the front wheel and both brake calipers as described in Chapter Ten and Chapter Thirteen. Support the calipers with wire or bungee cords. Do not allow the calipers to hang from the hydraulic hoses.
2. Remove all fasteners securing the brake hoses to the fork slider and front fender.
3. Remove the four 5 mm inner screws (A, **Figure 7**) that secure the upper and lower brace panels to the front fender.
4. Remove the four 8 mm screws (B, **Figure 7**) securing the fender and fender brace to the fork sliders. Remove the upper brace (C, **Figure 7**).
5. Carefully slide the front fender down on the fork sliders, then pull the fender from between the fork legs.
6. Installation is the reverse of removal. Tighten the screws securely.

Removal and Installation (2001-on Models)

Refer to **Figure 8**.

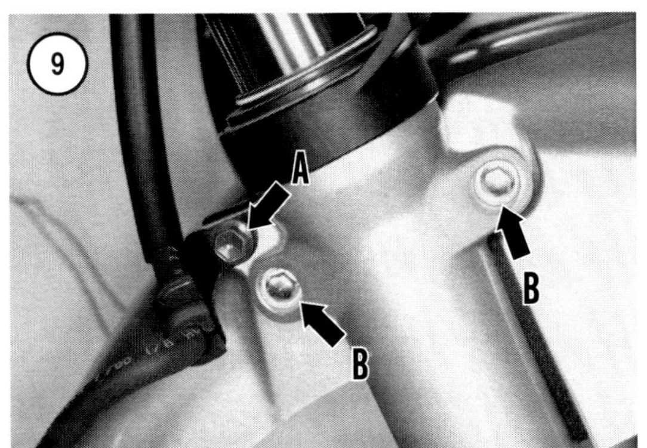

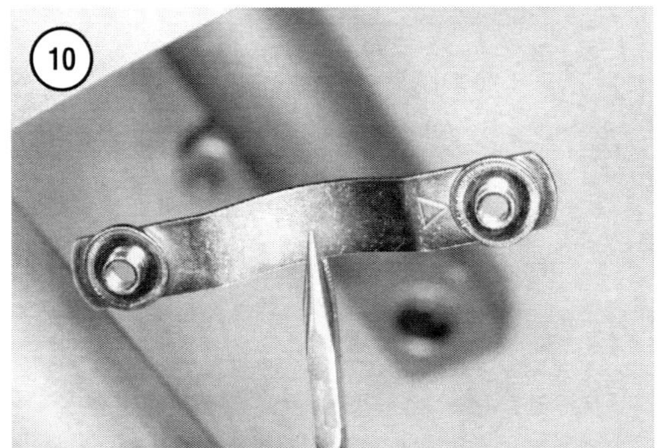

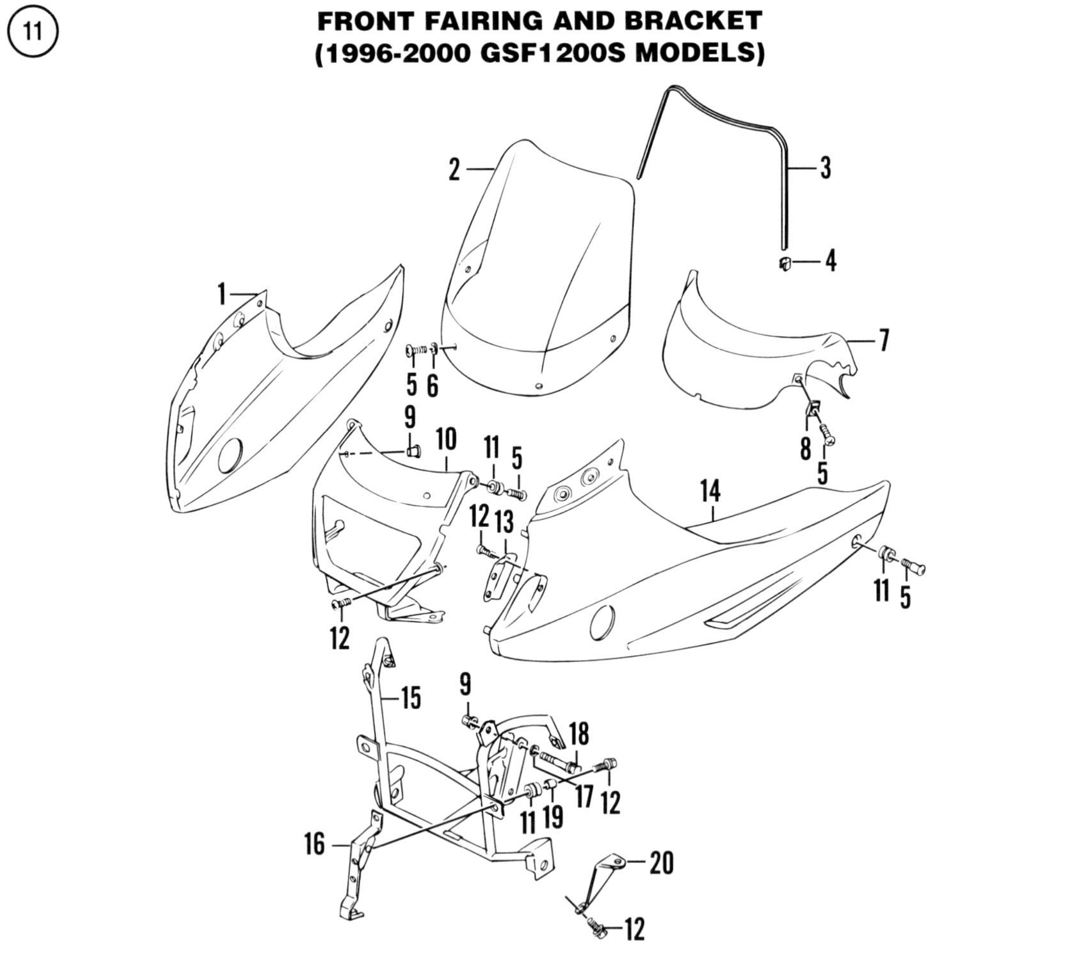

11

FRONT FAIRING AND BRACKET (1996-2000 GSF1200S MODELS)

1. Side fairing panel (right side)
2. Windshield
3. Trim
4. Cap
5. Screw
6. Washer
7. Inner panel
8. Special nut
9. Special nut
10. Center fairing
11. Grommet
12. Screw
13. Cover panel
14. Side fairing panel (left side)
15. Fairing mounting bracket
16. Headlight mounting bracket
17. Washer
18. Bolt
19. Collar
20. Side mounting bracket

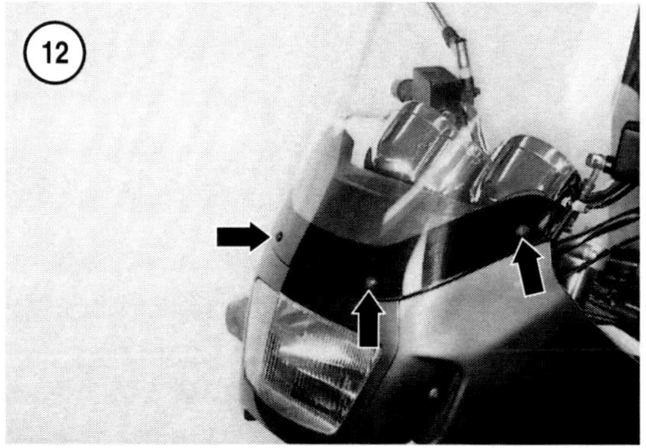

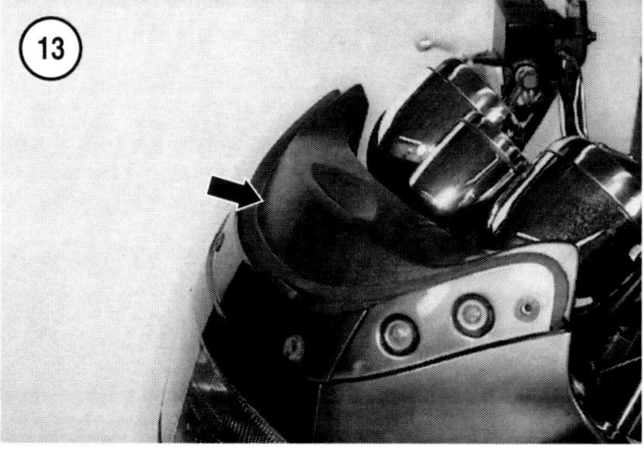

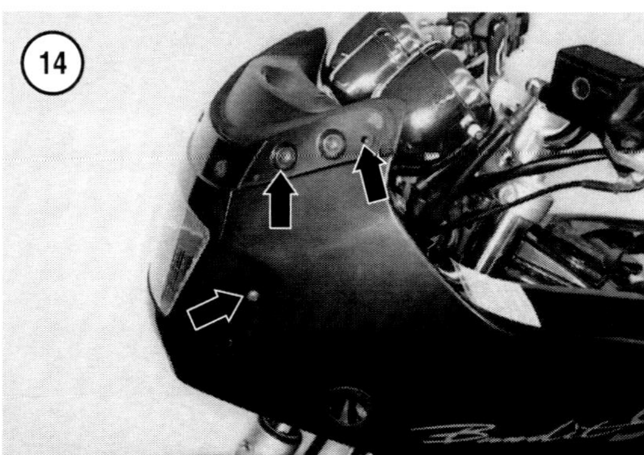

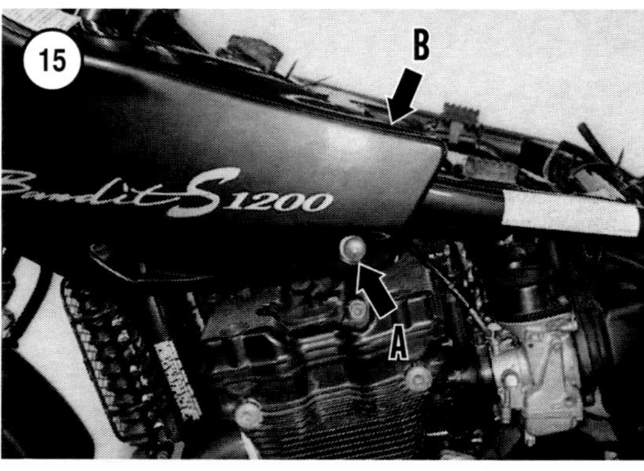

1. Remove the front wheel and both brake calipers as described in Chapter Ten and Chapter Thirteen. Support the calipers with wire or bungee cords. Do not allow the calipers to hang from the hydraulic hoses.
2. Remove the bolt (A, **Figure 9**) securing the brake hose to the fork slider. Repeat for the bolt on the other side.
3. Remove the two bolts (B, **Figure 9**) securing the front fender and mounting bracket to the fork slider. Repeat for the bolts on the other side.
4. Carefully slide the front fender down on the fork sliders, then pull the fender from between the fork legs.
5. Installation is the reverse of removal. Note the following:
   a. Install mounting bracket (**Figure 10**) onto the inside surface of the fork slider.
   b. Tighten the bolts securely.

FRONT FAIRING

Removal/Installation (1996-2000 GSF1200S Models)

Refer to **Figure 11**.

1. Remove the fuel tank as described in Chapter Eight.
2. Remove the windshield as follows:
   a. Remove the windshield mounting screws and washers (**Figure 12**).
   b. Lift the windshield from the fairing. Do not lose the rubber grommet at each screw location on the center fairing and both side fairings.
3. Remove the front turn signal assemblies as follows:
   a. Working within the side fairing, disconnect the two-pin electrical connector.
   b. Remove the nut securing the turn signal to the fairing mounting bracket. Remove the turn signal assembly.
   c. Repeat for the other side.
4. Remove the screws securing the inner panel and remove the inner panel (**Figure 13**).
5. Remove the screws securing the side fairing panel. Refer to **Figure 14** and A, **Figure 15**.
6. Remove the side fairing panel (B, **Figure 15**) from the mounting bracket and frame.
7. Repeat Step 5 and Step 6 for the other side fairing panel.
8. To remove the headlight and fairing mounting bracket, perform the following:
   a. Slide back the electrical connector cover.

16

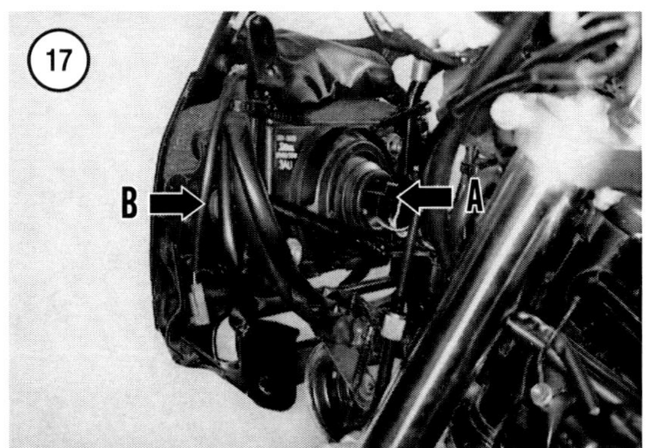

17

18

FRONT FAIRING (2001-ON GSF1200S MODELS)

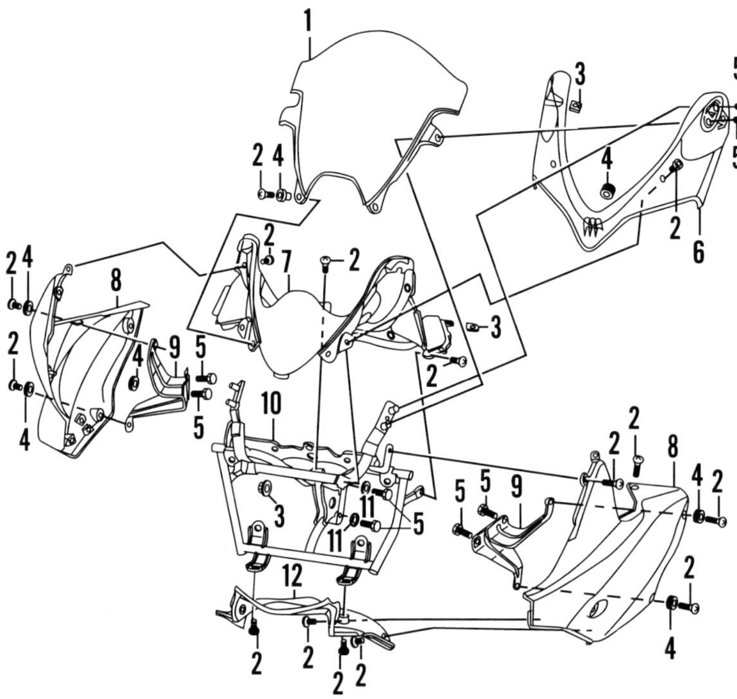

1. Windshield
2. Screw
3. Nut
4. Damper
5. Bolt
6. Upper fairing
7. Meter panel
8. Side fairing
9. Side fairing bracket
10. Brace
11. Washer
12. Lower fairing

b. Disconnect both handlebar switch connectors and the combination meter connector (**Figure 16**).

c. Disconnect the headlight electrical connector (A, **Figure 17**) from the backside of the headlight.

d. Disconnect the plastic ties holding the wiring harness in place.

e. Drape a thick towel over the front fender.

f. Remove the mounting bolts securing the fairing mounting bracket to the steering head.

g. Carefully pull the fairing mounting bracket and headlight assembly (B, **Figure 17**) forward and remove it from the frame.

9. Inspect the fairing as described in this chapter.

10. Install by reversing these removal steps. Note the following:

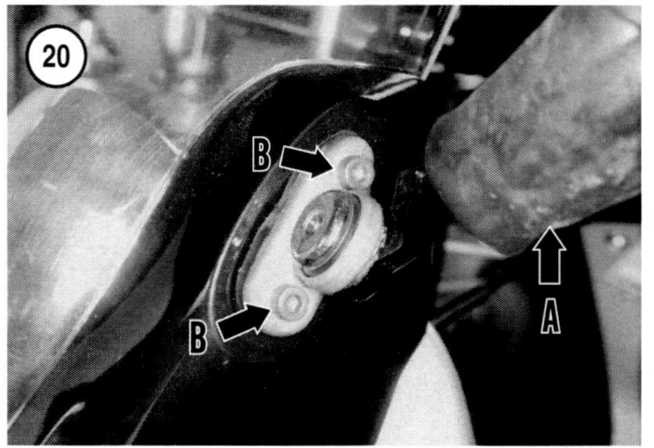

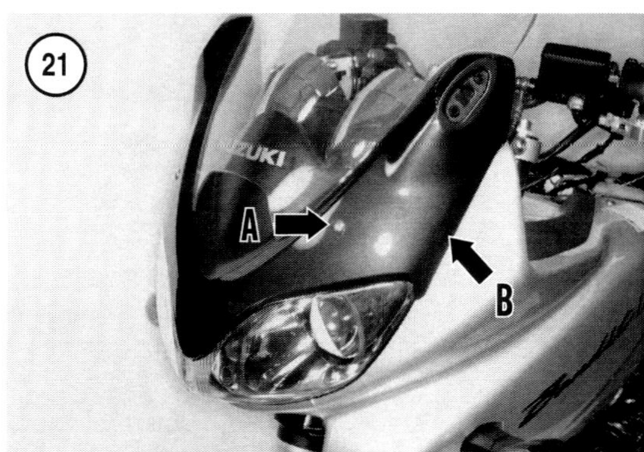

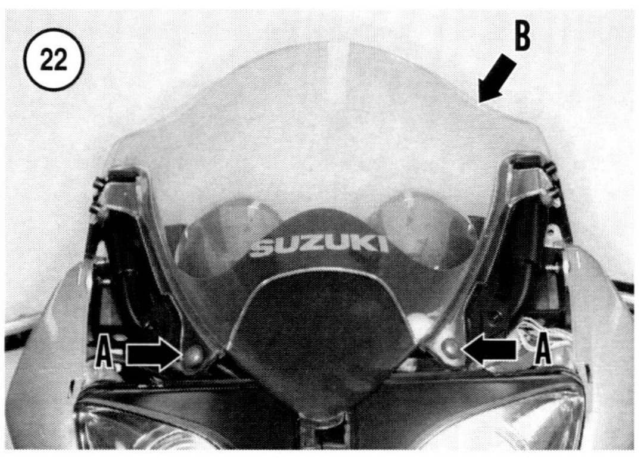

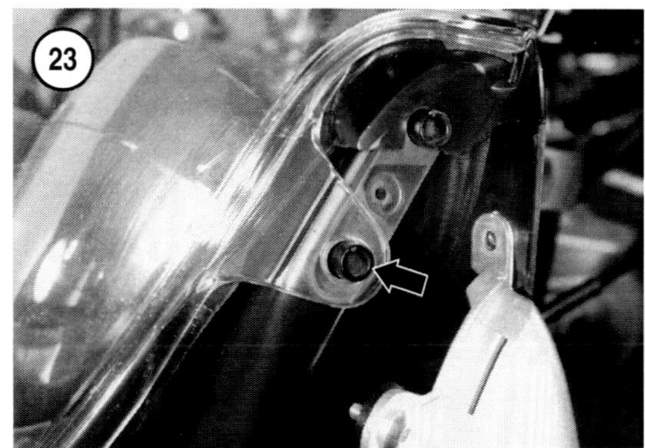

a. Do not overtighten the mounting screws, as plastic parts may fracture at the mounting location.

b. Make sure the electrical connector is corrosion-free and secure.

c. After installation is complete, turn the ignition switch to the ON position and check the operation of the combination meter, lights, each turn signal, horn and both handlebar switches.

Removal/Installation (2001-on GSF1200S Models)

Refer to **Figure 18**.

1. Remove the fuel tank as described in Chapter Eight.

2. Remove the rear view mirrors and the windshield as follows:

   a. Remove the two screws (**Figure 19**) securing the windshield to the upper fairing.

   b. Slide the rubber boot (A, **Figure 20**) away from the mount and remove the two bolts (B) securing the rear view mirror to the upper fairing and mounting bracket. Remove the mirror and repeat for the mirror on the other side.

   c. Remove the screw (A, **Figure 21**) on each side securing the upper faring (B) and remove the upper fairing.

   d. Remove the screw and damper (A, **Figure 22**) on each side securing the windshield.

CAUTION

Do not try to pry the windshield off both locating pins at the same time, as the windshield may crack. Release the windshield from one locating pin at a time.

   e. On one side, carefully lift the windshield up and off the locating pin (**Figure 23**). Lift the windshield off the other locating pin.

f. Lift the windshield (B, **Figure 22**) from the fairing and remove it. Do not lose the rubber grommet at each screw location on the center fairing and both side fairings.

NOTE
In the following step, to remove the push pins, push on the center part with a small punch and release the locking tension. Remove the push pin from the mounting hole of the lower fairing.

3. Remove the four push pins (A, **Figure 24**) and the two lower screws (B) securing the lower fairing to the mounting bracket.

4. Working within the side fairing, disconnect the turn signal two-pin electrical connector. Repeat for the other side.

5. Have an assistant secure the front fairing.

6. Remove the screws (**Figure 25**) securing the side fairing to the mounting bracket. Repeat for the other side and remove the lower fairing and both side fairings from the motorcycle.

7. To remove the fairing mounting bracket, perform the following:

a. Remove the headlight and combination meter as described in Chapter Nine.

b. Remove the screws securing the meter panel (**Figure 26**) to the mounting bracket and remove the meter panel.

c. Remove the two bolts (**Figure 27**) on each side securing the mounting bracket to the steering head.

d. Carefully pull the mounting bracket forward and from the frame.

8. Inspect the fairing as described in this chapter.

9. Install by reversing these removal steps. Note the following:

a. Do not overtighten the mounting screws, as the plastic parts may fracture at the mounting location.

b. Make sure the electrical connectors are corrosion-free and secure.

c. After installation is complete, turn the ignition switch to the ON position and check the operation of the combination meter, lights, each turn signal, horn and both handlebar switches.

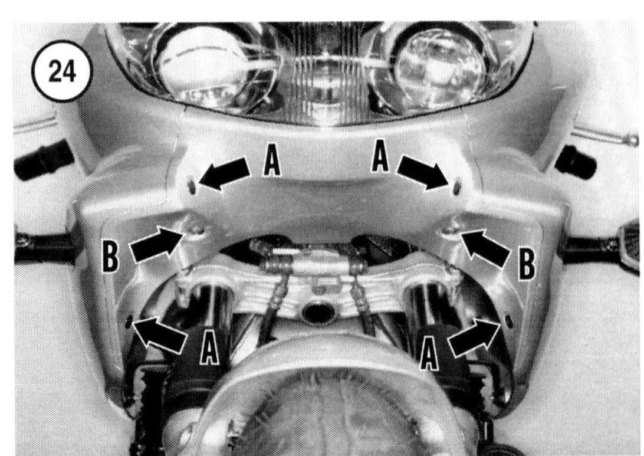

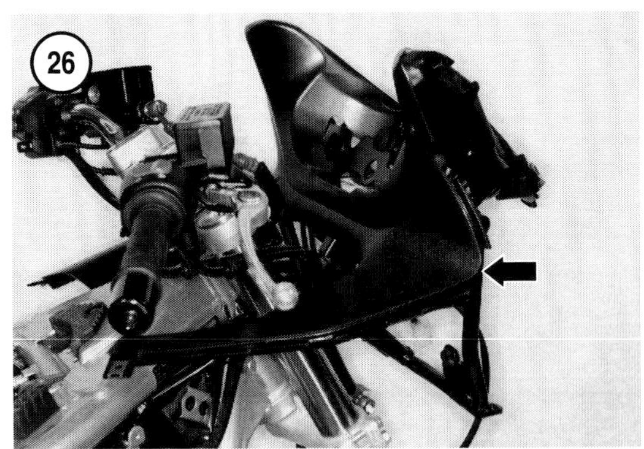

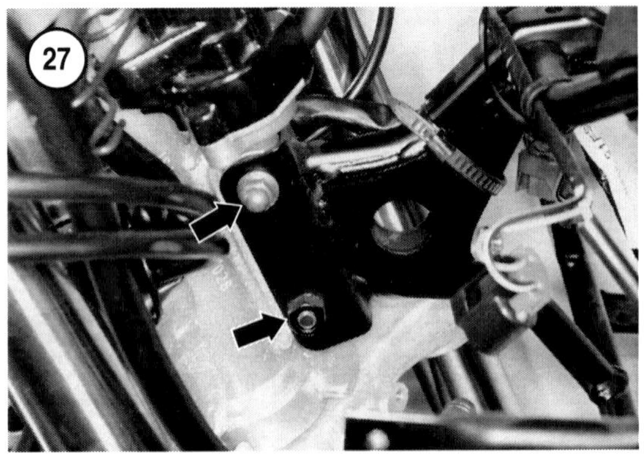

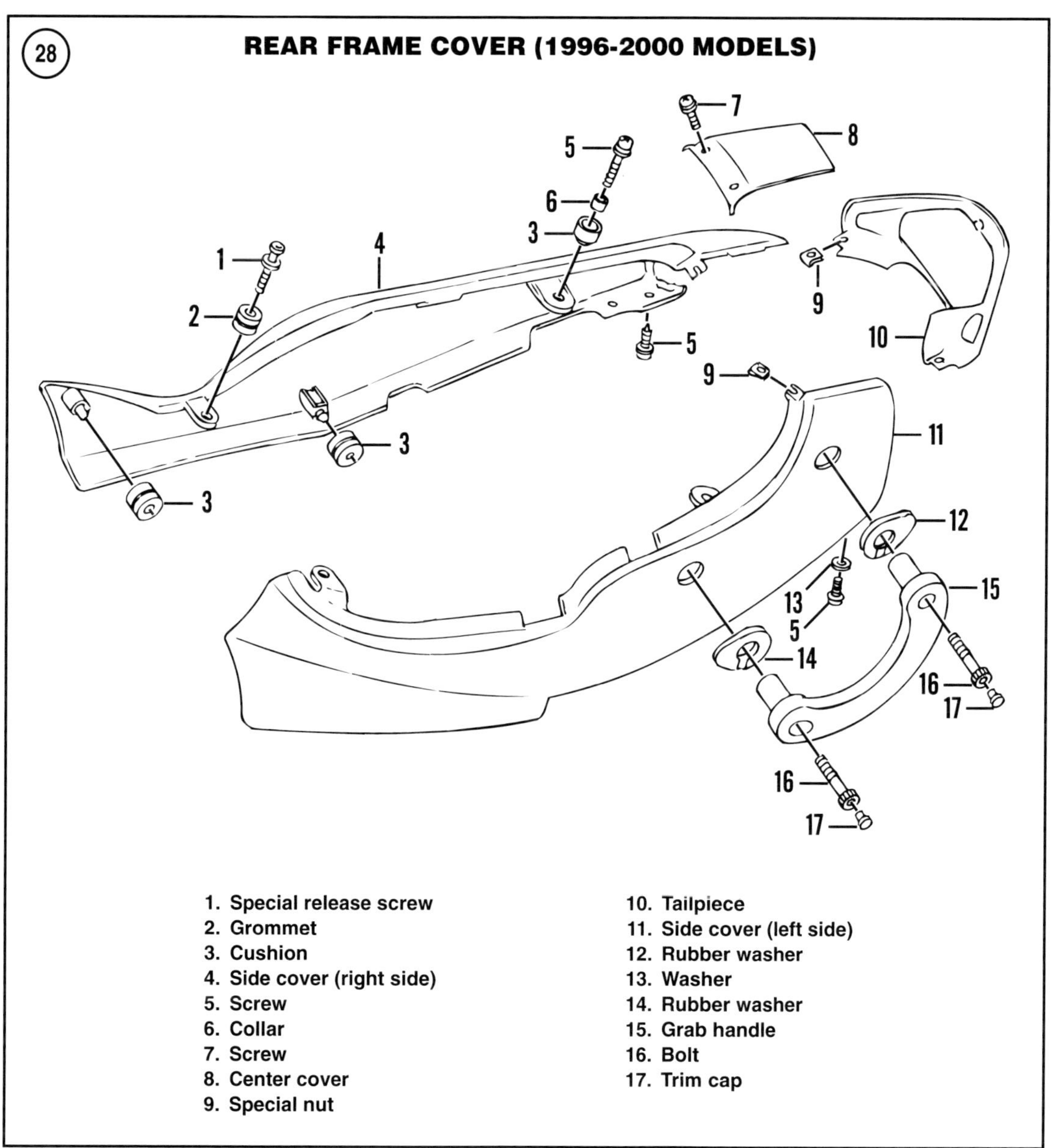

REAR FRAME COVER (1996-2000 MODELS)

Inspection (All Models)

1. Inspect all components for damage, cracks or fractures. Check each mounting hole for elongation or fractures from overtightening of fasteners.

2. Examine the raised post, on parts so equipped, for damage or cracks.

3. Repair or replace any damaged part.

4. If removed, inspect the mounting bracket for bending or other damage. Replace if necessary.

REAR FRAME COVER

Removal/Installation (1996-2000 Models)

Refer to **Figure 28**.

1. Remove the seat as described in this chapter.

2. Disconnect the taillight/brake light electrical connector (**Figure 29**).

3. Remove the forward mounting screw and washer (**Figure 30**) located next to the turn signal. Repeat for the other side.

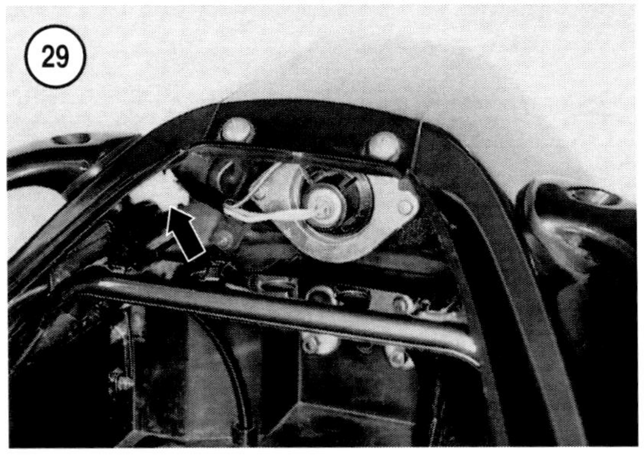

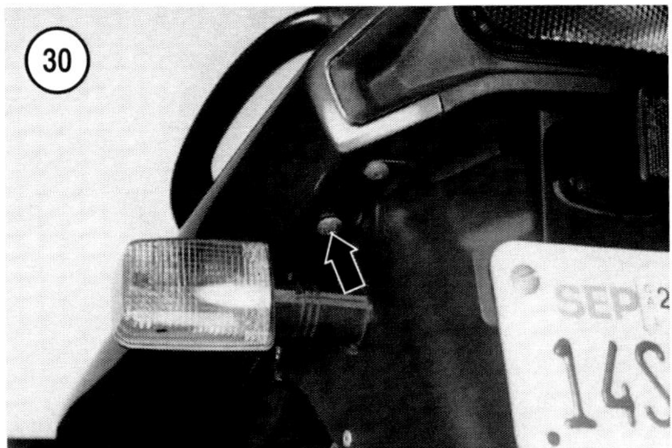

4. Remove the front mounting bolts and collars (**Figure 31**) securing the rear frame cover on each side. Do not lose the plastic insert on the frame mounting holes.
5. Remove the rear mounting bolts, collars and cushions (**Figure 32**) securing the rear frame cover on each side.
6. Remove the trim cap from the grab handle mounting screws.
7. Remove the mounting screws (**Figure 33**) and remove the grab handle.
8. Repeat Step 6 and Step 7 and remove the other grab handle.
9. Carefully pull out the two lower posts from the rubber grommets in the frame mounting tabs. Repeat for the other side.
10. Carefully pull the rear frame cover toward the rear and remove the assembly from the frame.
11. Install by reversing these removal steps. Note the following:
    a. Do not overtighten the mounting screws, as the plastic parts may fracture at the mounting location.
    b. Make sure the electrical connector is corrosion-free and secure.
    c. After installation is complete, turn the ignition switch to the ON position and check the operation of the taillight and brake lights.

Removal/Installation (2001-on Models)

Refer to **Figure 34**.

1. Remove the seat as described in this chapter.
2. Remove the caps from each side of the grab rail.
3. Remove the mounting bolts (A, **Figure 35**) from each side of the grab rail (B) and remove the grab

(34)

REAR FRAME COVER (2001-ON MODELS)

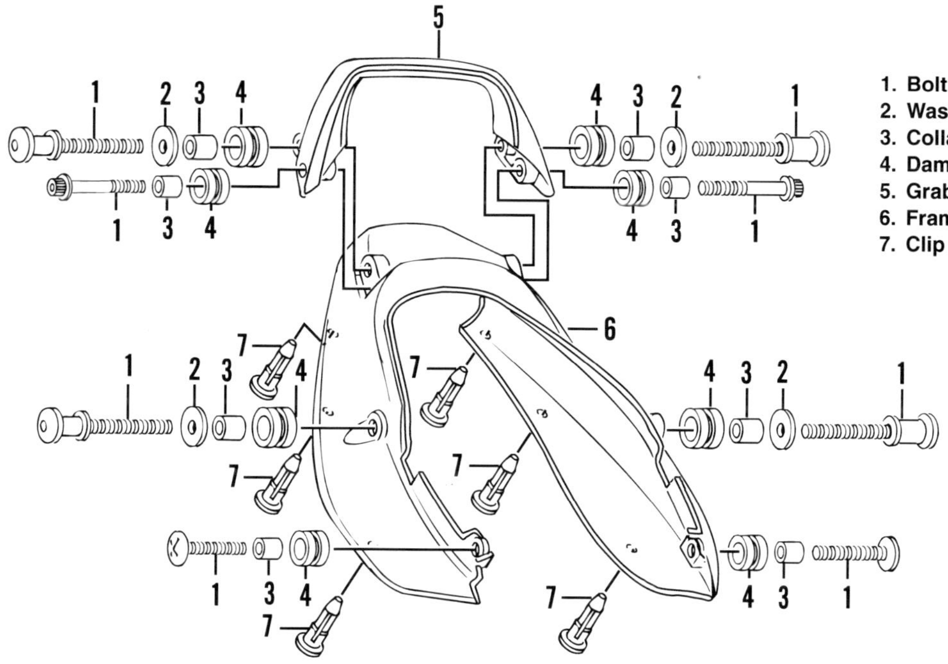

1. Bolt
2. Washer
3. Collar
4. Damper
5. Grab rail
6. Frame cover
7. Clip

(35)

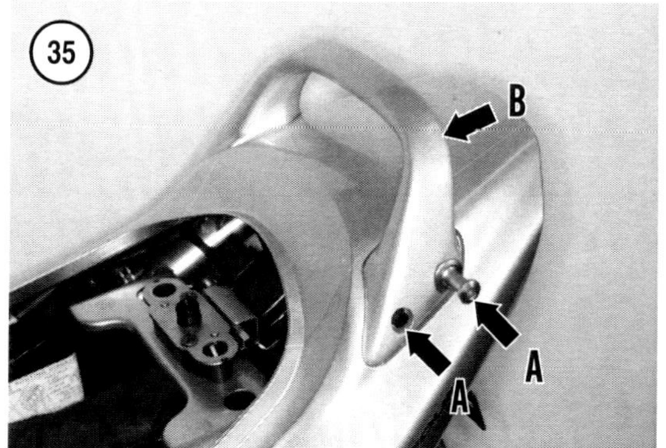

(36)

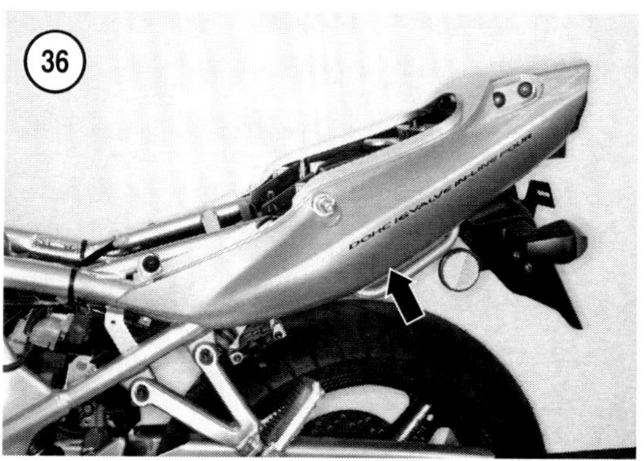

rail. Do not lose the damper and collar at each grab rail mount.

4. Disconnect the taillight/brake light connector from the wiring harness.

NOTE
In the following step, to remove the push pins, push on the center part with a small punch and release the locking tension. Remove the push pin from the lower mounting holes of the rear frame cover.

5. Remove the three push pins on each side of the rear frame cover.
6. Remove the mounting bolts from the mounts on each side of the cover. Do not lose the collar and damper from each mount.
7. Carefully pull the rear frame cover (**Figure 36**) toward the rear and remove the assembly from the frame.
8. Install by reversing these removal steps. Note the following:
   a. Do not overtighten the mounting screws, as the plastic parts may fracture at the mounting location.

b. Make sure the electrical connector is corrosion-free and secure.
c. After installation is complete, turn the ignition switch to the ON position and check the operation of the taillight and brake lights.

SIDE COVER

Removal/Installation (1996-2000 Models)

1. Remove the screw (A, **Figure 37**) and remove the side cover (B).
2. Install the side cover and tighten the screw securely.

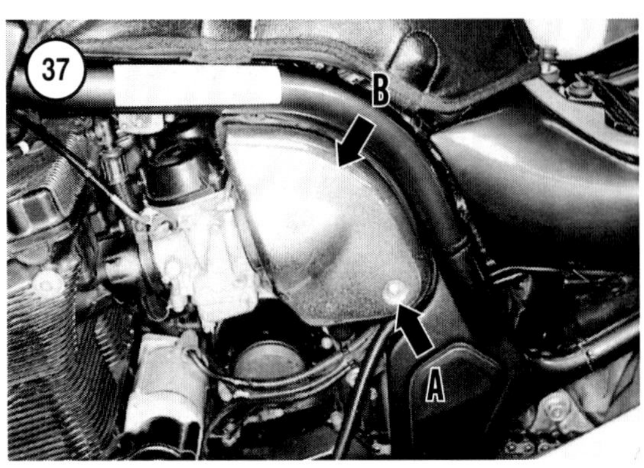

Removal/Installation (2001-on Models)

Refer to **Figure 38**.

1. Remove the front and rear mounting screws (A, **Figure 39**) from the side cover assembly. Do not lose the collar from the rear mount.
2. Gently pull the lower edge of the frame cover (B, **Figure 39**) until the post is freed from the damper in the frame. Remove the side cover assembly.
3. If necessary, disassemble the front cover from the rear cover.
4. Install by reversing these removal steps. Note the following:
   a. Make sure the post securely engages the damper in the frame and then reinstall the mounting screws.
   b. Make sure the collar is in place in the rear mount.

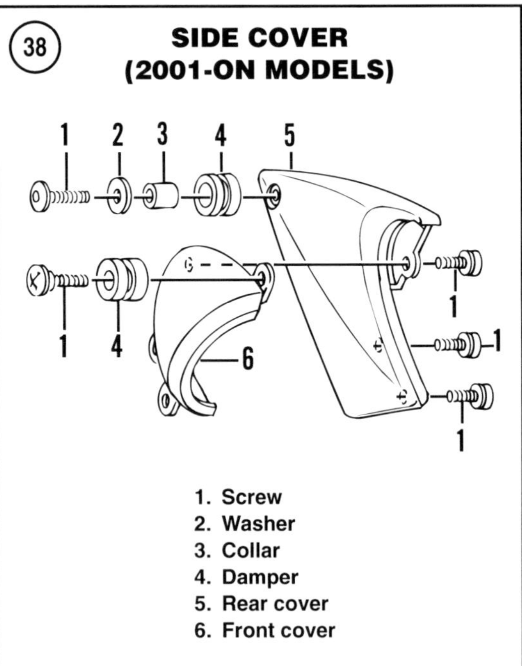

SIDESTAND

Removal/Installation

1. Securely support the motorcycle on level ground on the centerstand.
2. Disconnect both springs from the sidestand.
3. Remove the nut (**Figure 40**) from the bolt on the sidestand bracket and remove the sidestand.
4. Install by reversing these removal steps. Note the following:
   a. Lubricate the pivot and the springs with Suzuki Super Grease A or an equivalent waterproof bearing grease.
   b. Make sure the inner spring sits inside the outer spring and that both springs are connected to the post on the sidestand.
   c. Tighten the nut securely.

CENTERSTAND

Removal/Installation

1. Securely support the motorcycle on wooden blocks in an upright position.
2. Disconnect both springs from the centerstand.
3. Remove the bolt from each side of the centerstand mount and remove the centerstand from

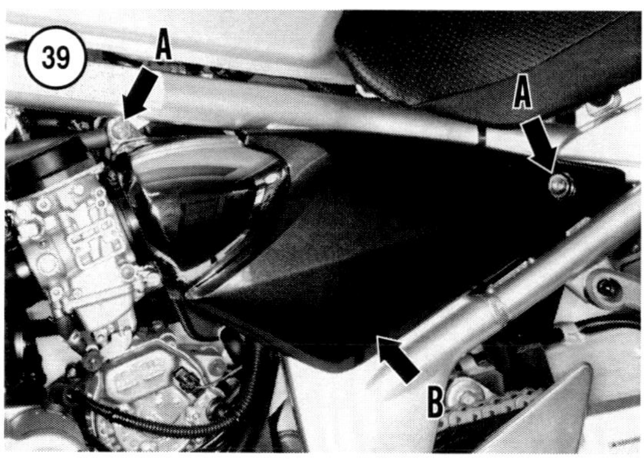

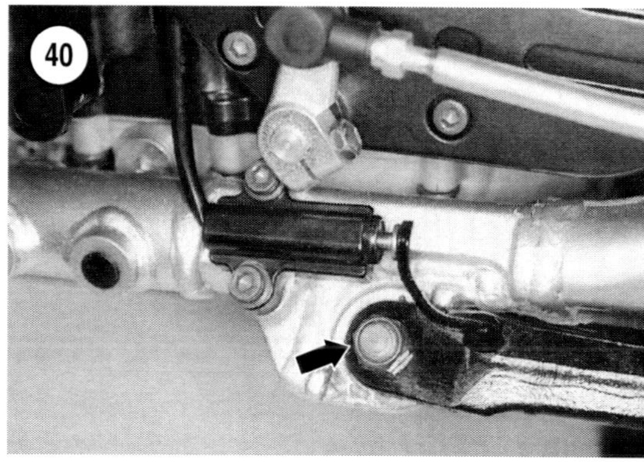

the frame. Do not lose the collar that sits inside each centerstand pivot.

4. Install by reversing the removal steps. Note the following:

a. Lubricate the pivots, collars and the springs with Suzuki Super Grease A or an equivalent waterproof bearing grease.
b. Tighten each bolt securely.

INDEX

A

B

C

15

M

O

P

R

S

T

15

V

W

WIRING DIAGRAMS

16

GSF 1200S U.S. AND CANADA MODELS (1997-2000)

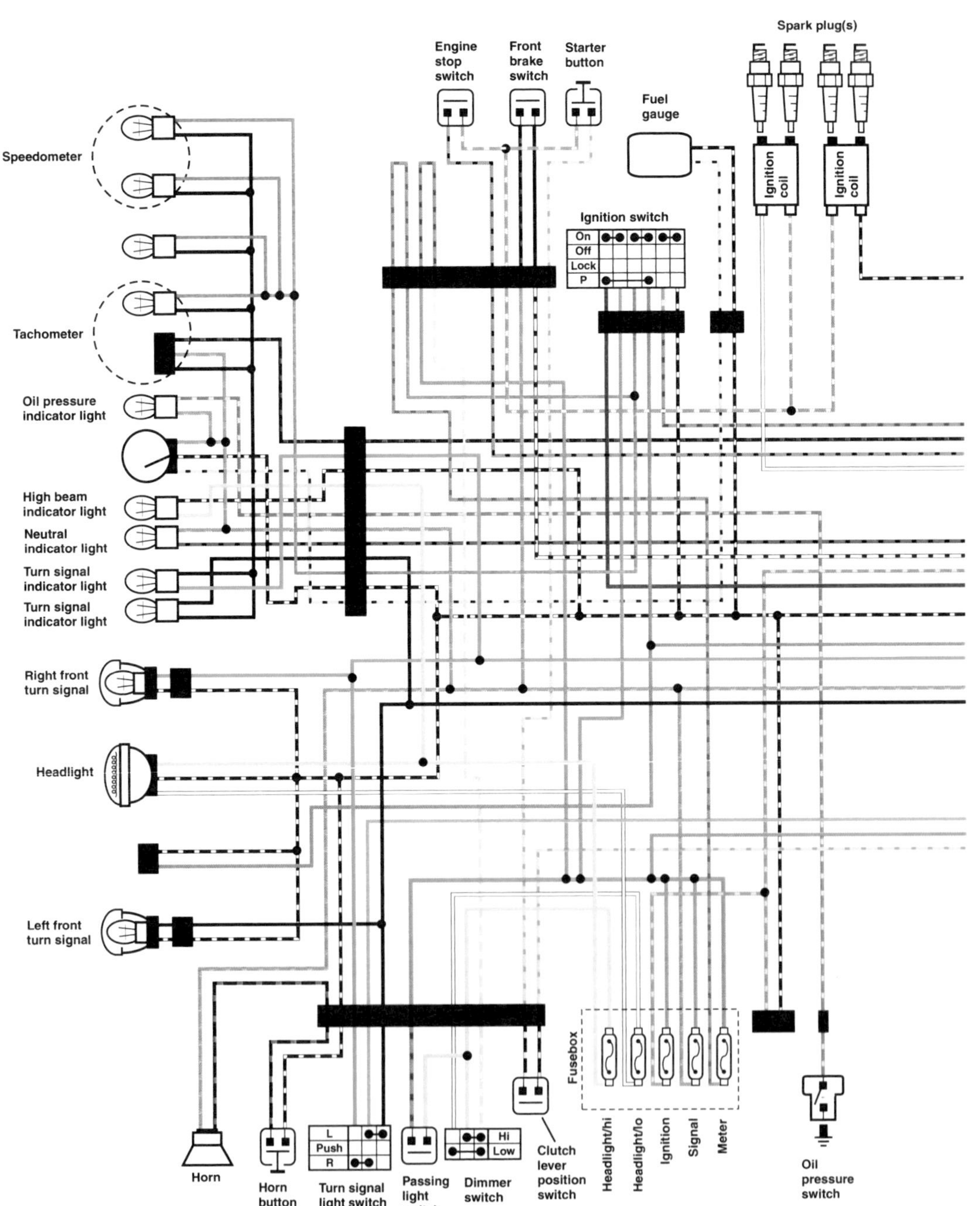

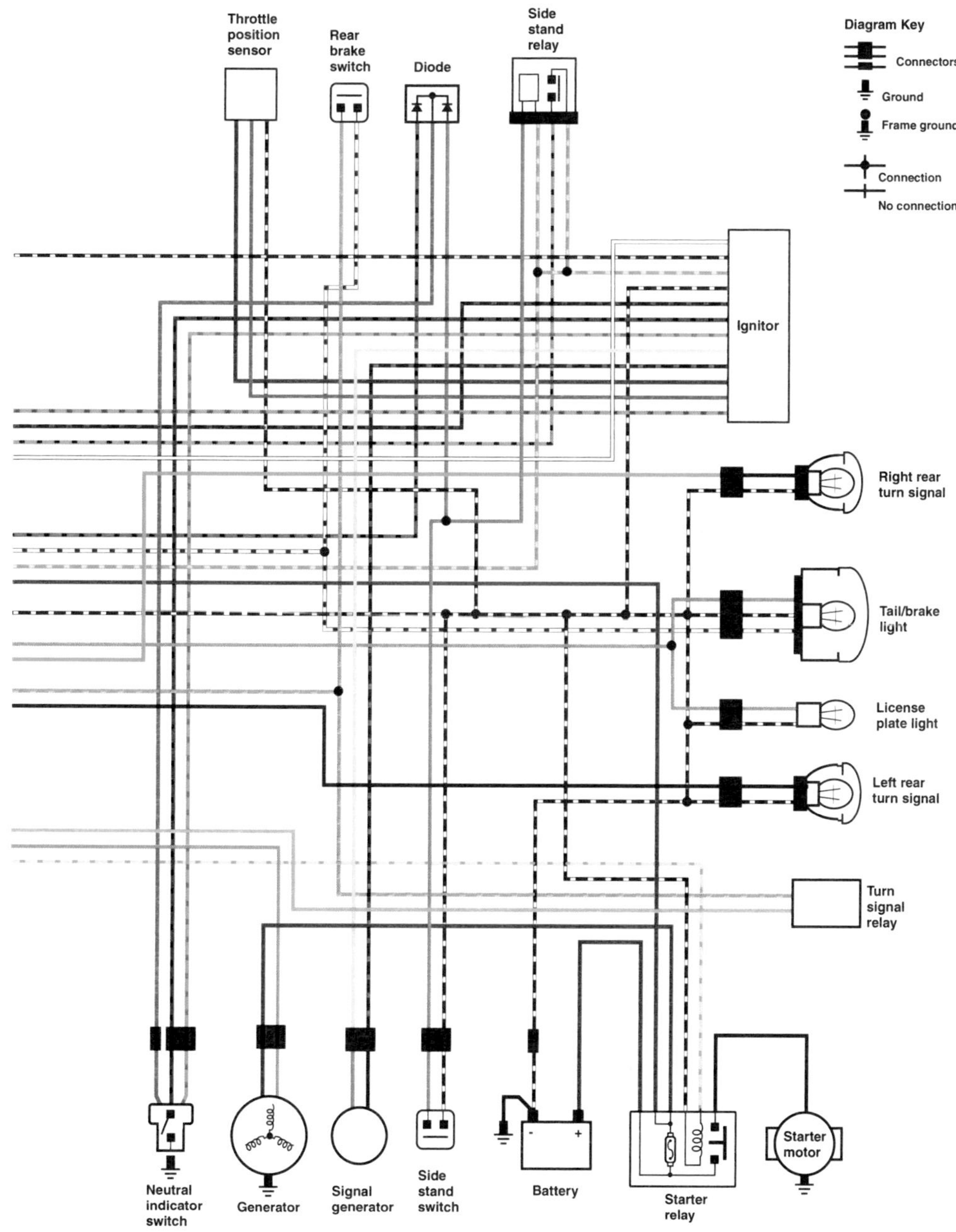
Throttle position sensor
Rear brake switch
Diode
Side stand relay
Diagram Key
Connectors
Ground
Frame ground
Connection
No connection
Ignitor
Right rear turn signal
Tail/brake light
License plate light
Left rear turn signal
Turn signal relay
Neutral indicator switch
Generator
Signal generator
Side stand switch
Battery
Starter relay
Starter motor

GSF 1200 U.K. MODELS (1996-2000)

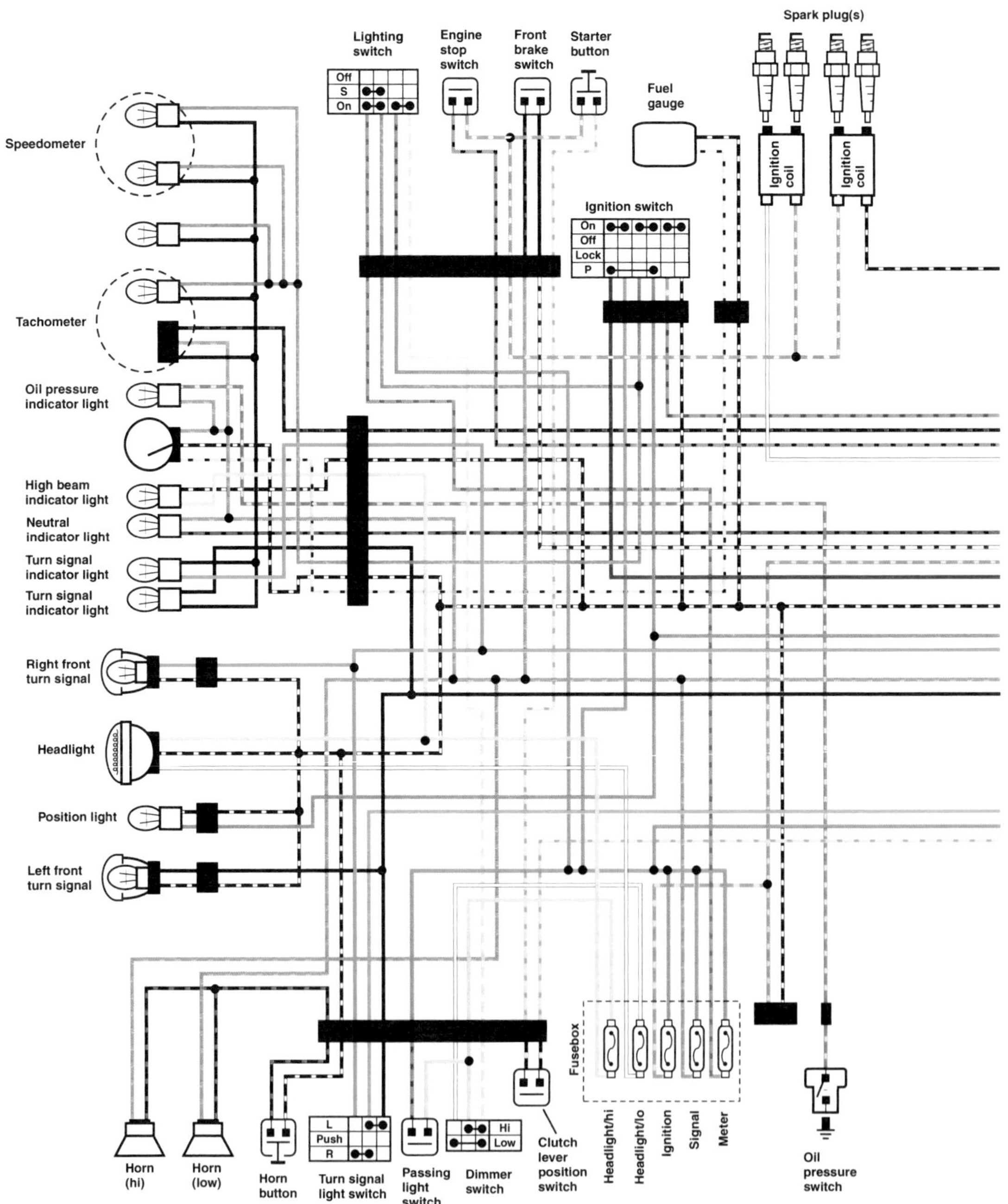

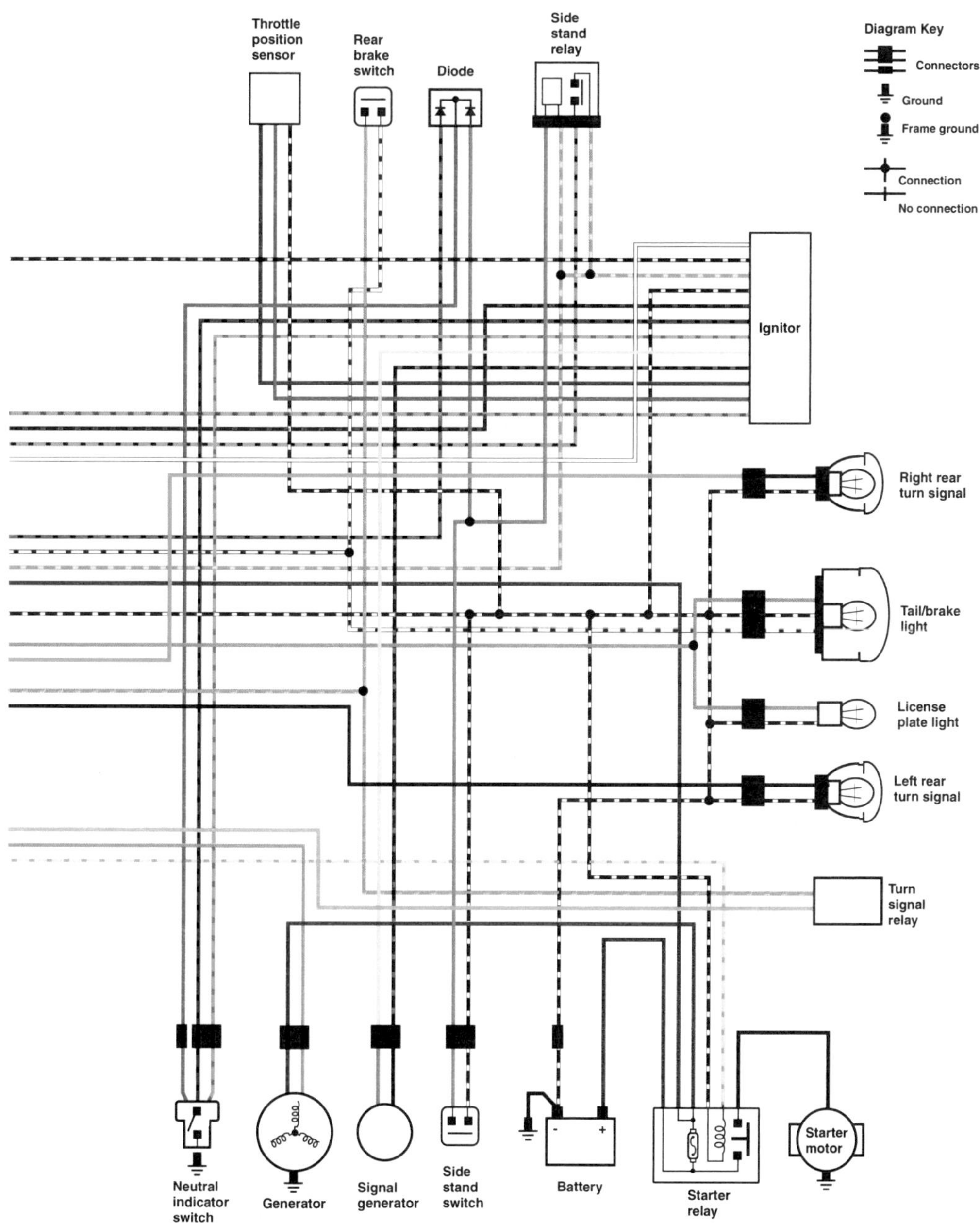
Throttle position sensor
Rear brake switch
Diode
Side stand relay
Diagram Key
Connectors
Ground
Frame ground
Connection
No connection
Ignitor
Right rear turn signal
Tail/brake light
License plate light
Left rear turn signal
Turn signal relay
Neutral indicator switch
Generator
Signal generator
Side stand switch
Battery
Starter relay
Starter motor

16

GSF 1200 AUSTRALIA MODELS (1996-2000)

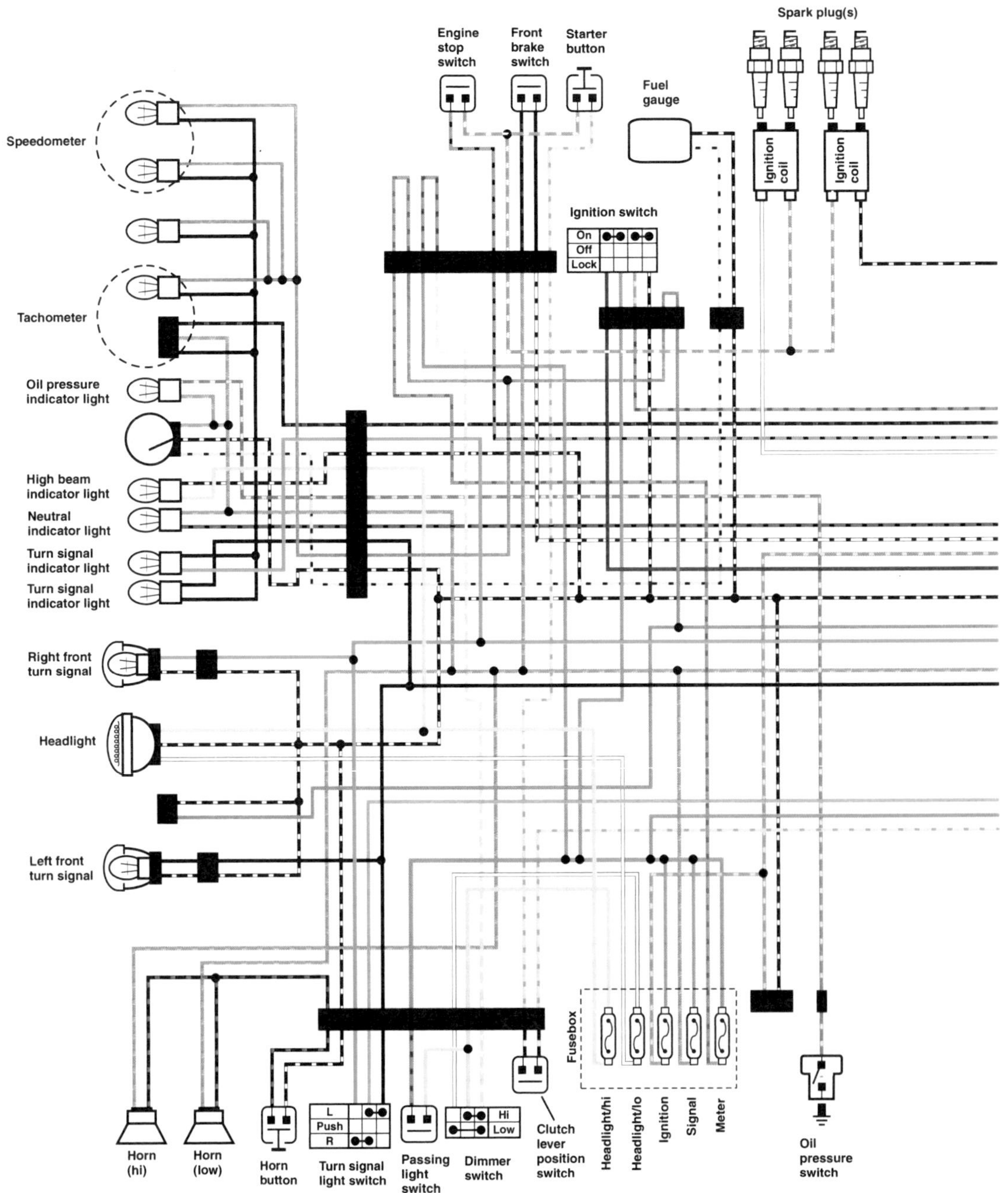

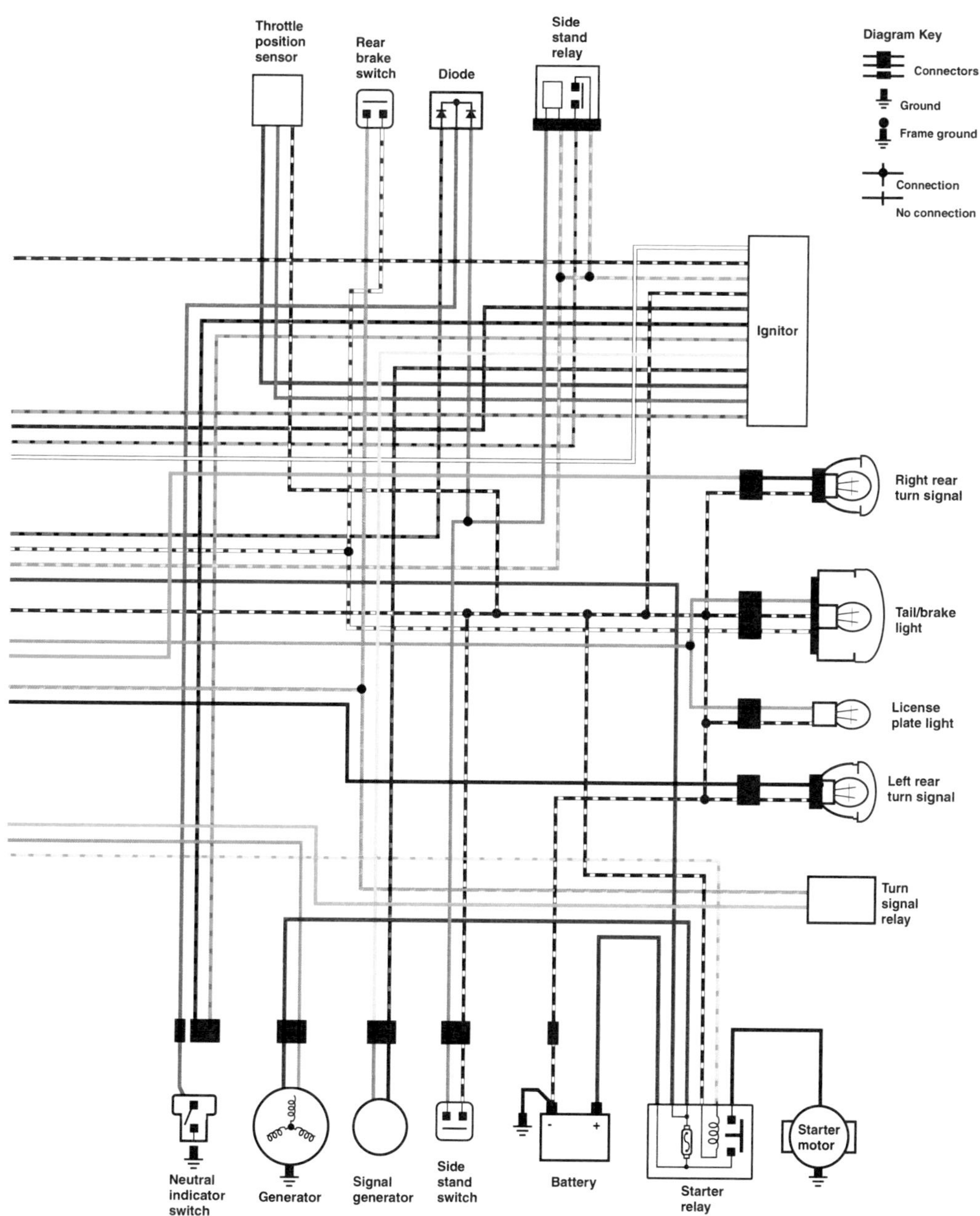
Throttle position sensor
Rear brake switch
Diode
Side stand relay
Diagram Key
Connectors
Ground
Frame ground
Connection
No connection
Ignitor
Right rear turn signal
Tail/brake light
License plate light
Left rear turn signal
Turn signal relay
Neutral indicator switch
Generator
Signal generator
Side stand switch
Battery
Starter relay
Starter motor

GSF 1200 CANADA MODELS (1997-2000)

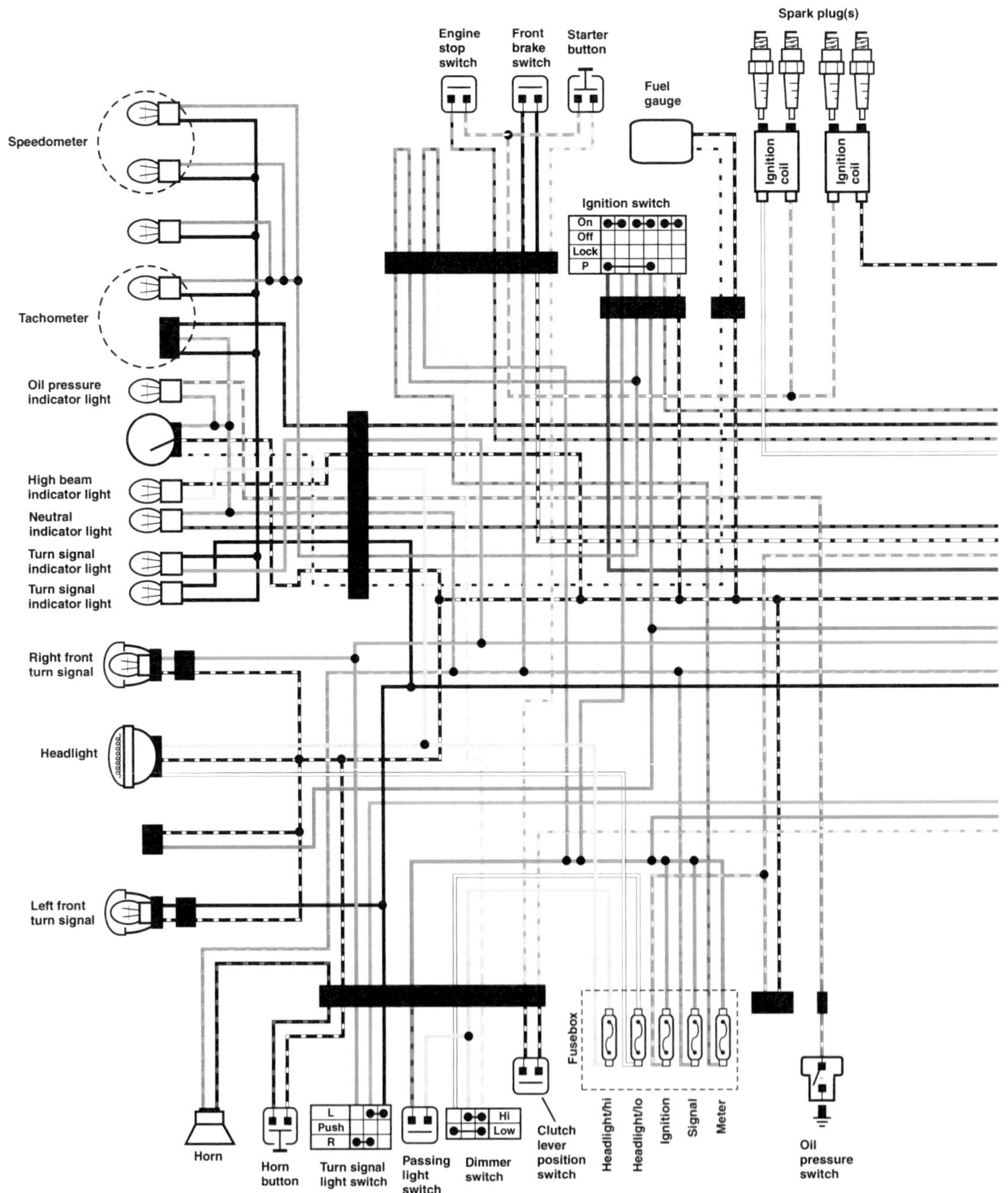

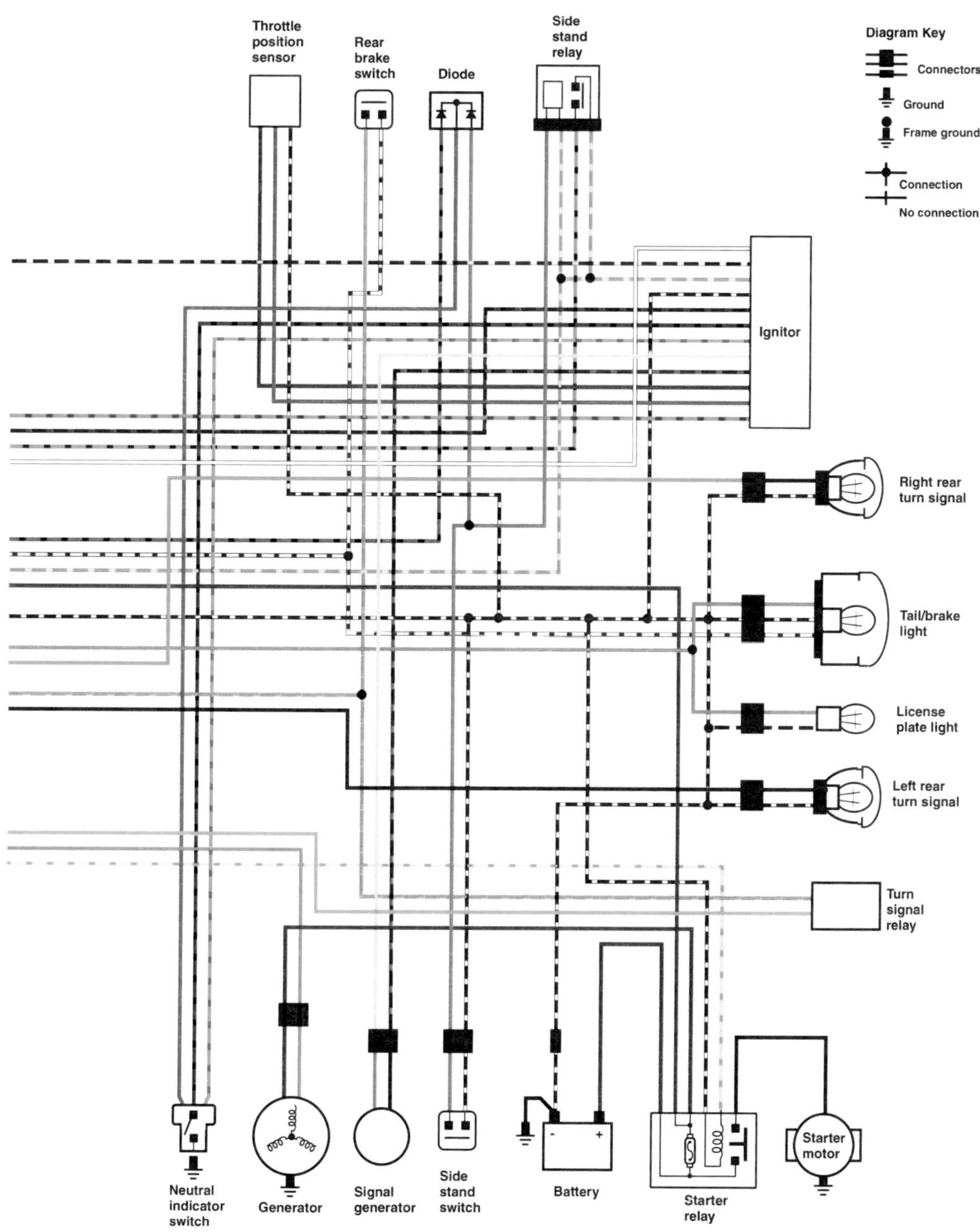
Throttle position sensor
Rear brake switch
Diode
Side stand relay
Diagram Key
Connectors
Ground
Frame ground
Connection
No connection
Ignitor
Right rear turn signal
Tail/brake light
License plate light
Left rear turn signal
Turn signal relay
Neutral indicator switch
Generator
Signal generator
Side stand switch
Battery
Starter relay
Starter motor

GSF 1200S AUSTRALIA MODELS (1996-2000)

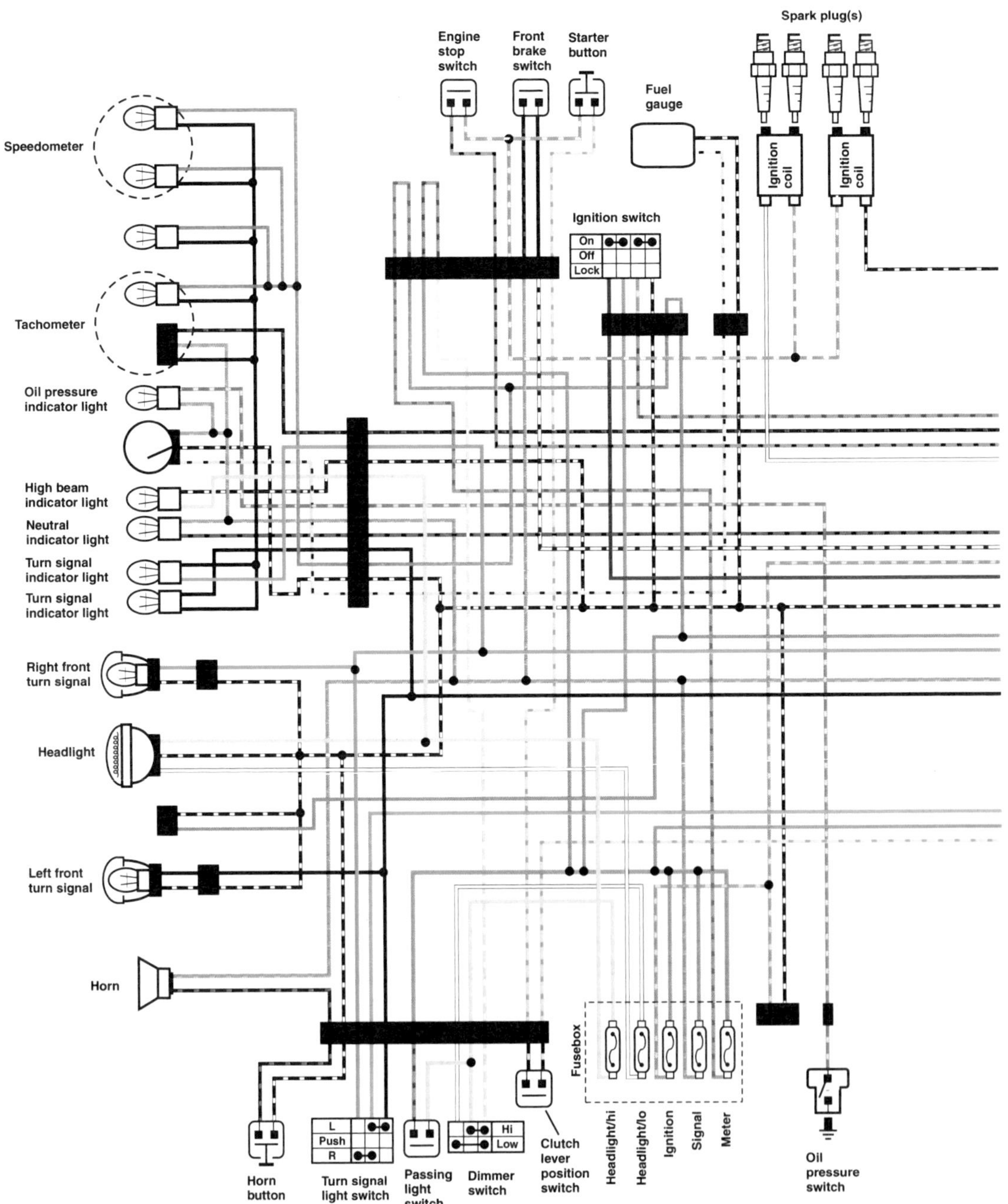

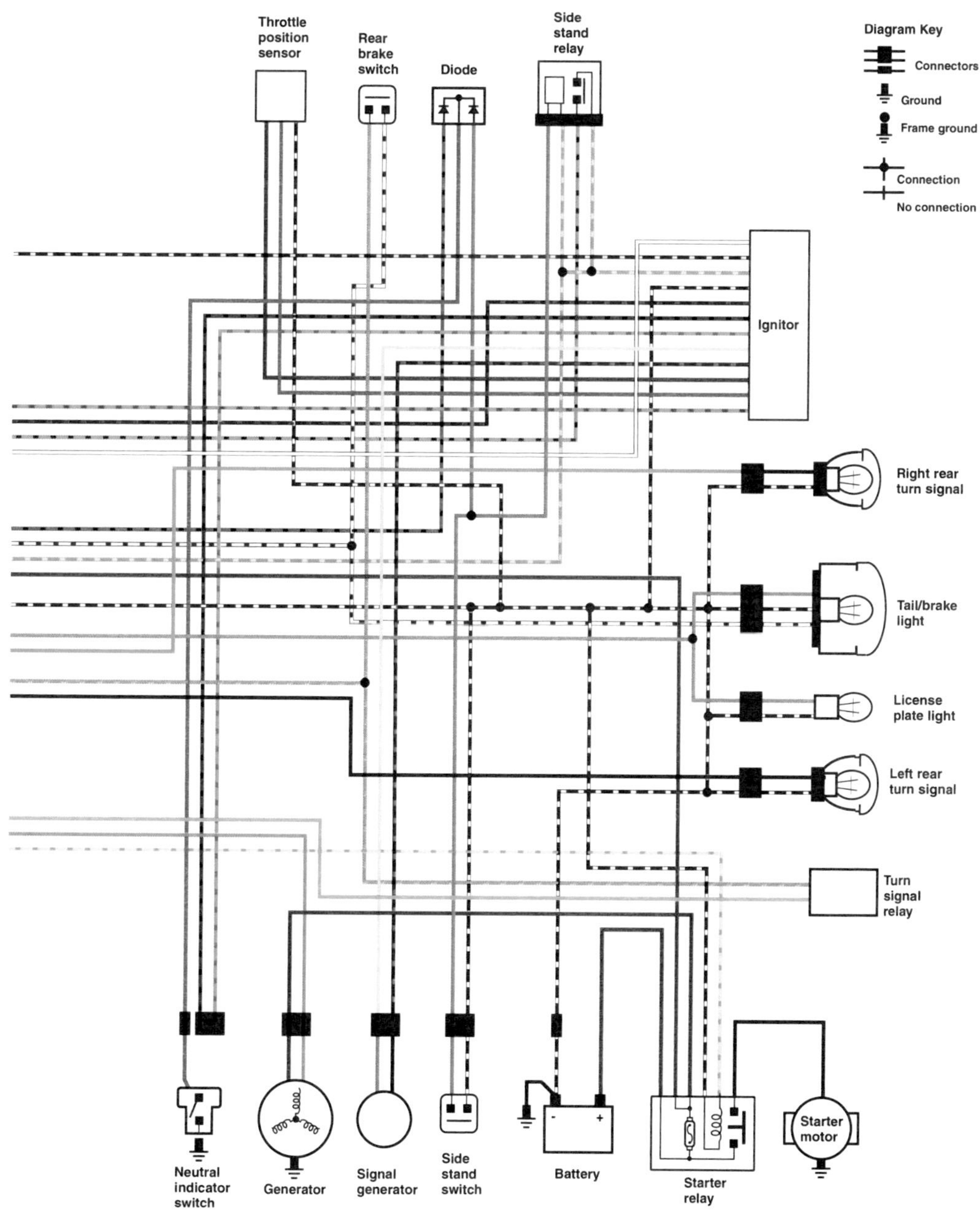
Throttle position sensor
Rear brake switch
Diode
Side stand relay
Diagram Key
Connectors
Ground
Frame ground
Connection
No connection
Ignitor
Right rear turn signal
Tail/brake light
License plate light
Left rear turn signal
Turn signal relay
Neutral indicator switch
Generator
Signal generator
Side stand switch
Battery
Starter relay
Starter motor

16

GSF 1200S MODELS EXCEPT U.S., CANADA AND AUSTRALIA (1996-2000)

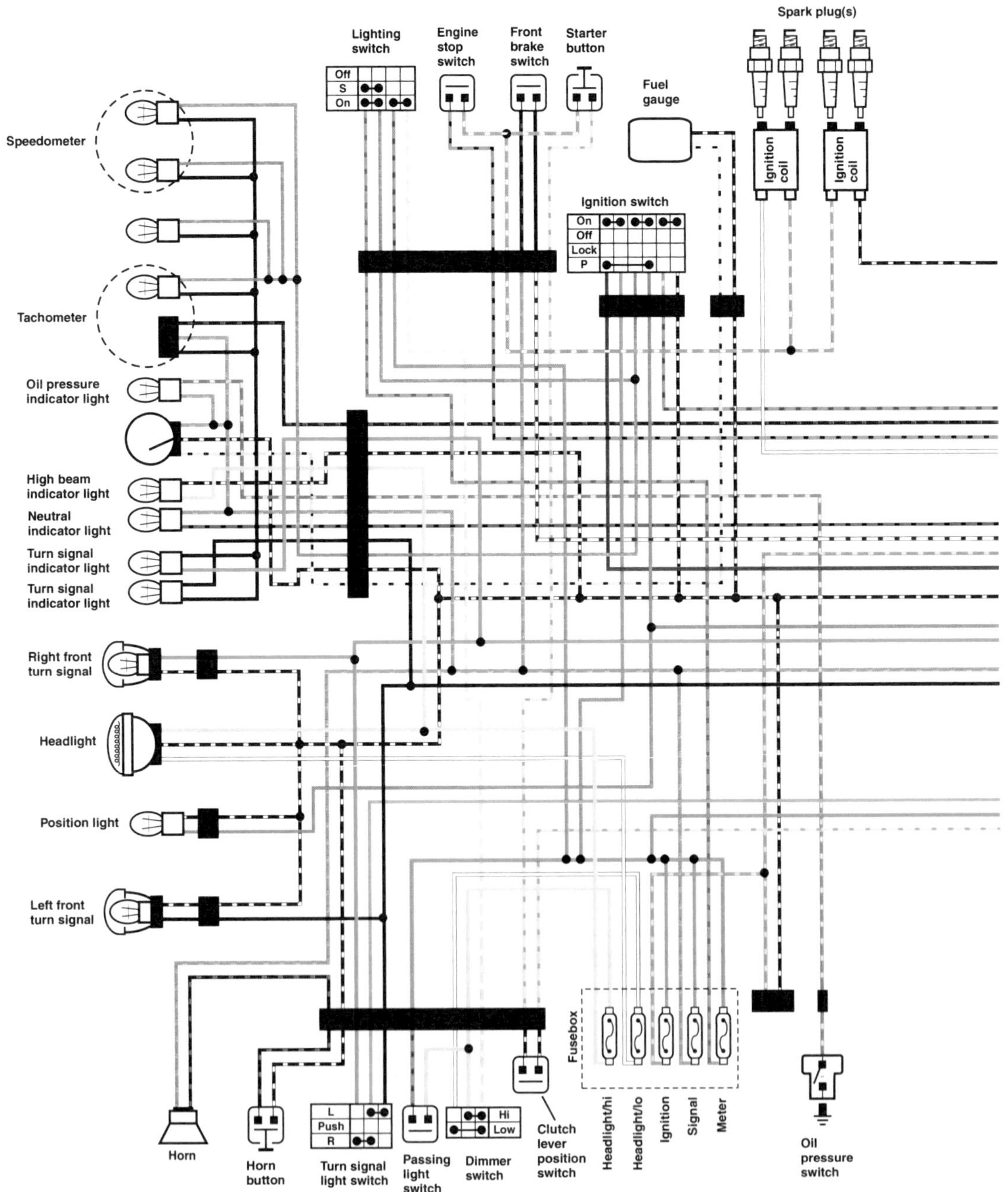

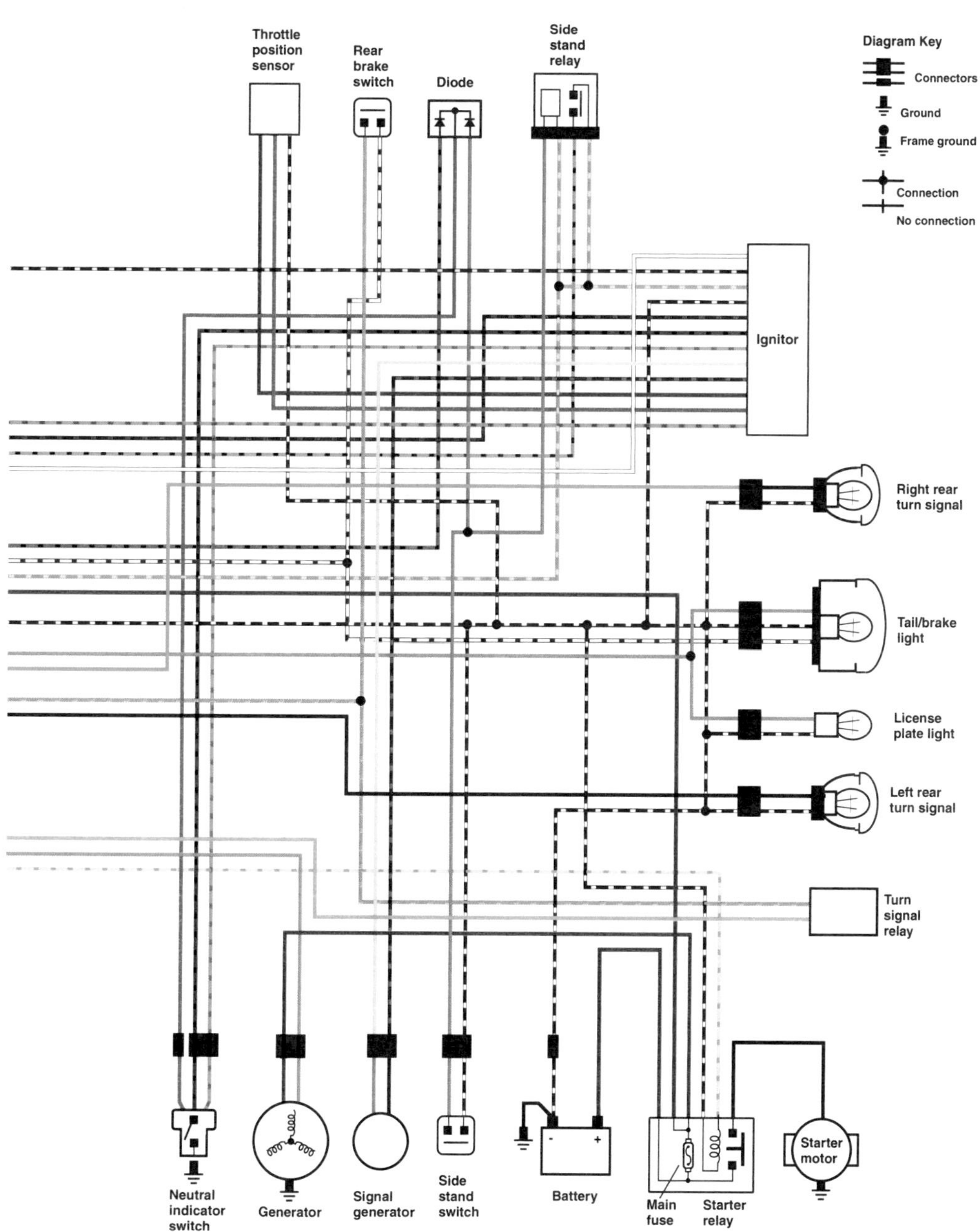
Throttle position sensor
Rear brake switch
Diode
Side stand relay
Diagram Key
Connectors
Ground
Frame ground
Connection
No connection
Ignitor
Right rear turn signal
Tail/brake light
License plate light
Left rear turn signal
Turn signal relay
Neutral indicator switch
Generator
Signal generator
Side stand switch
Battery
Main fuse
Starter relay
Starter motor

16

GSF 1200SA U.S. AND CANADA MODELS (1997) (ABS)

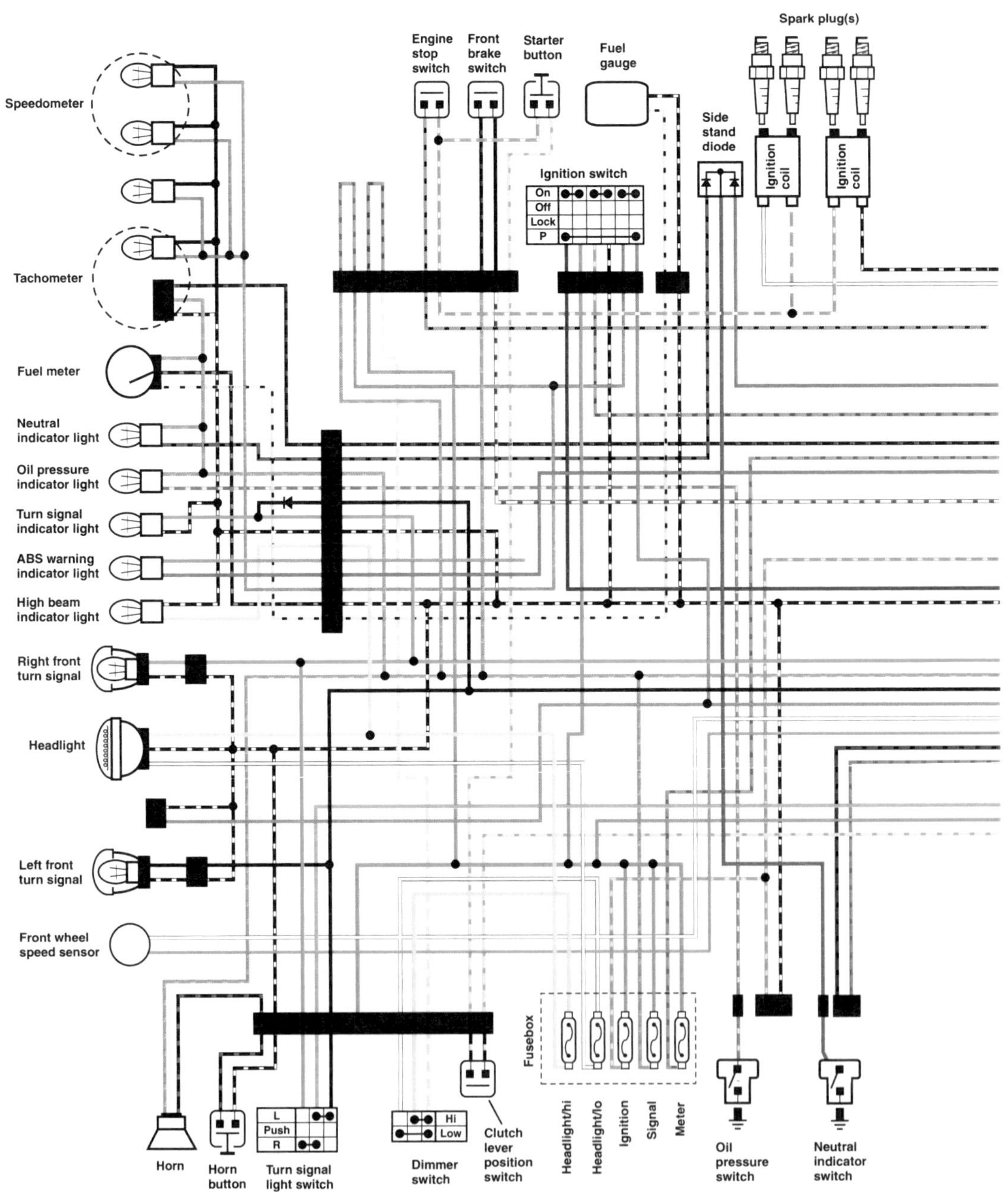

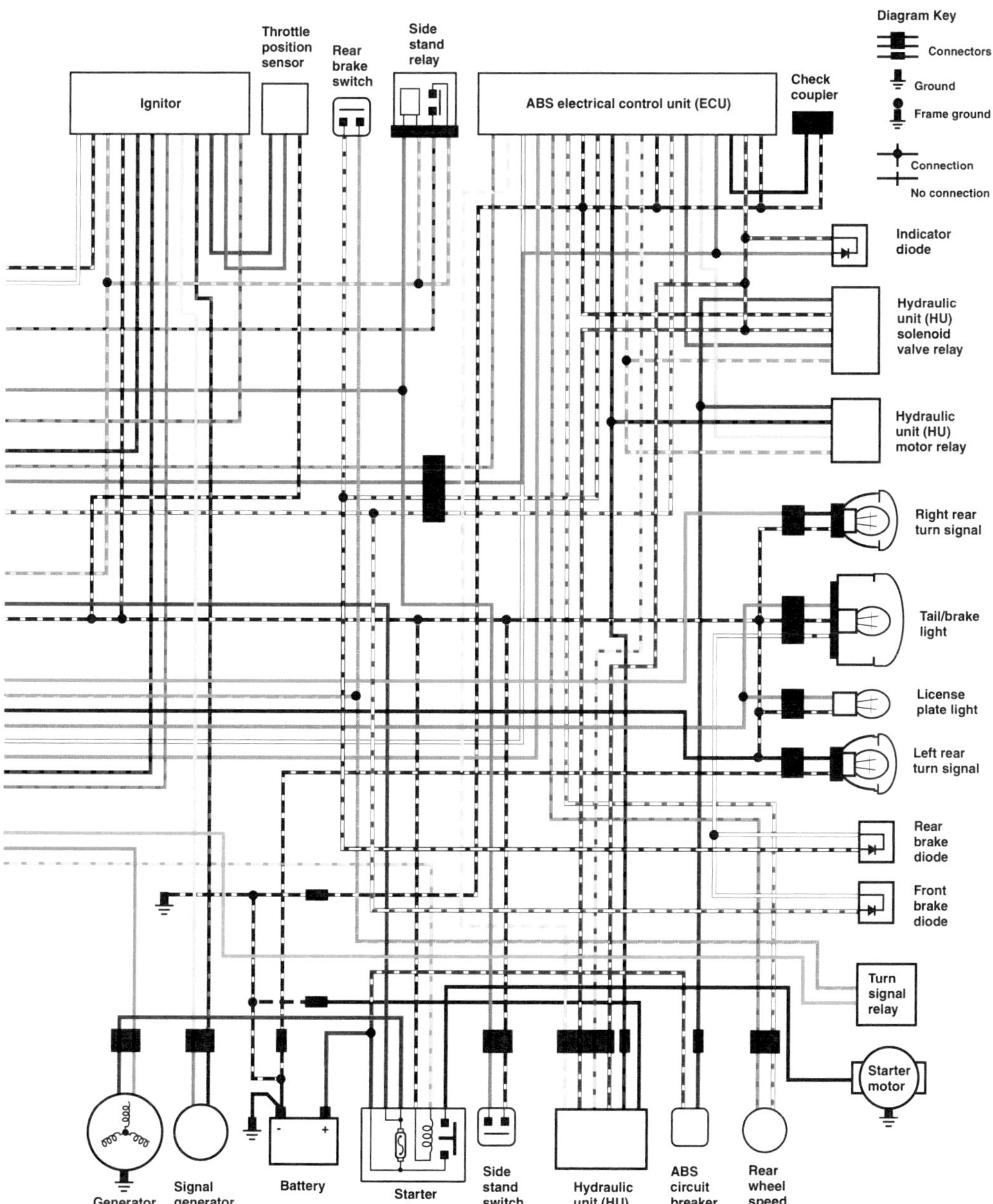
Diagram Key
Connectors
Ground
Frame ground
Connection
No connection
Ignitor
Throttle position sensor
Rear brake switch
Side stand relay
ABS electrical control unit (ECU)
Check coupler
Indicator diode
Hydraulic unit (HU) solenoid valve relay
Hydraulic unit (HU) motor relay
Right rear turn signal
Tail/brake light
License plate light
Left rear turn signal
Rear brake diode
Front brake diode
Turn signal relay
Starter motor
Generator
Signal generator
Battery
Starter relay
Side stand switch
Hydraulic unit (HU)
ABS circuit breaker
Rear wheel speed sensor

GSF 1200SA AUSTRALIA MODELS (1997-2000) (ABS)

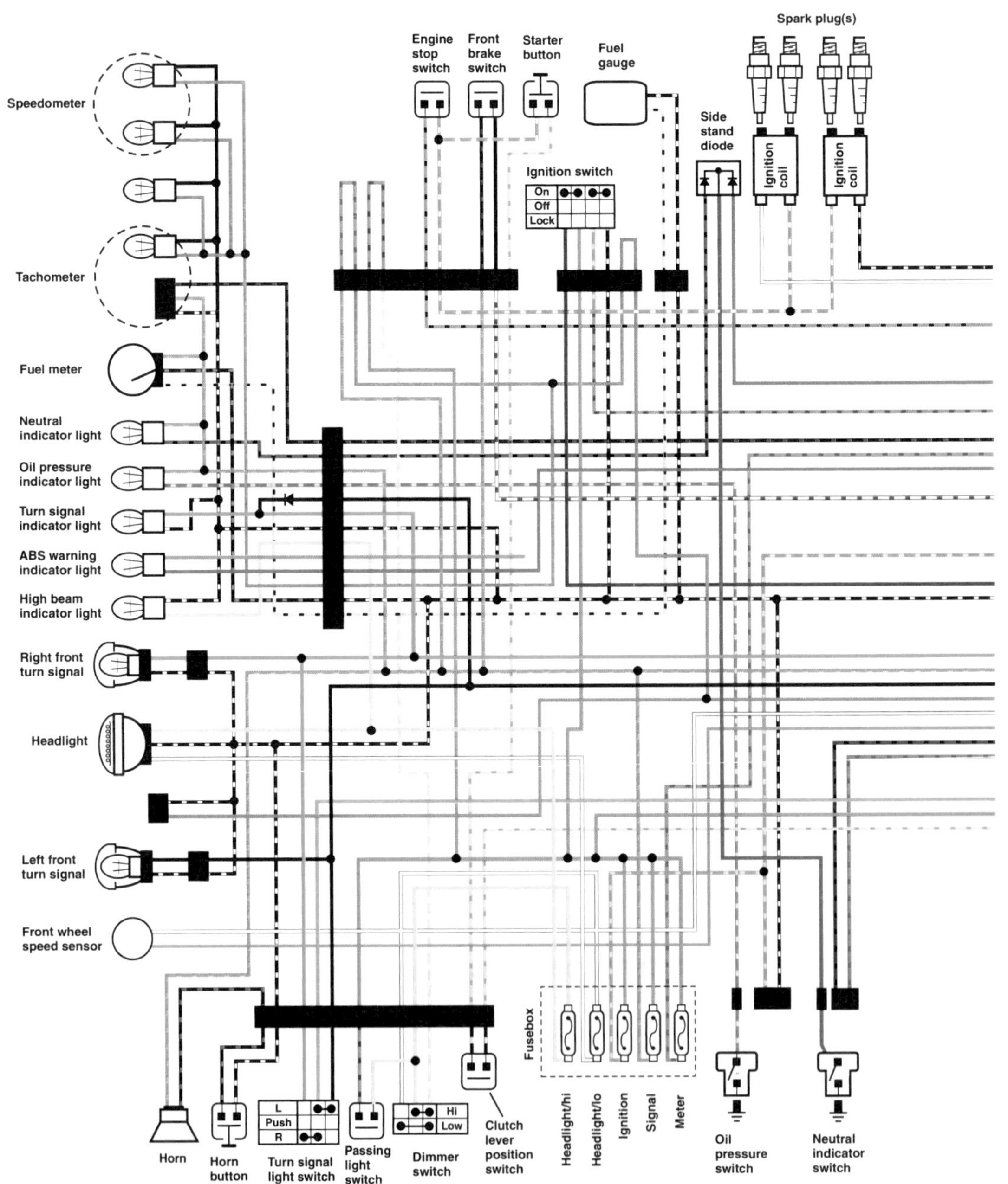

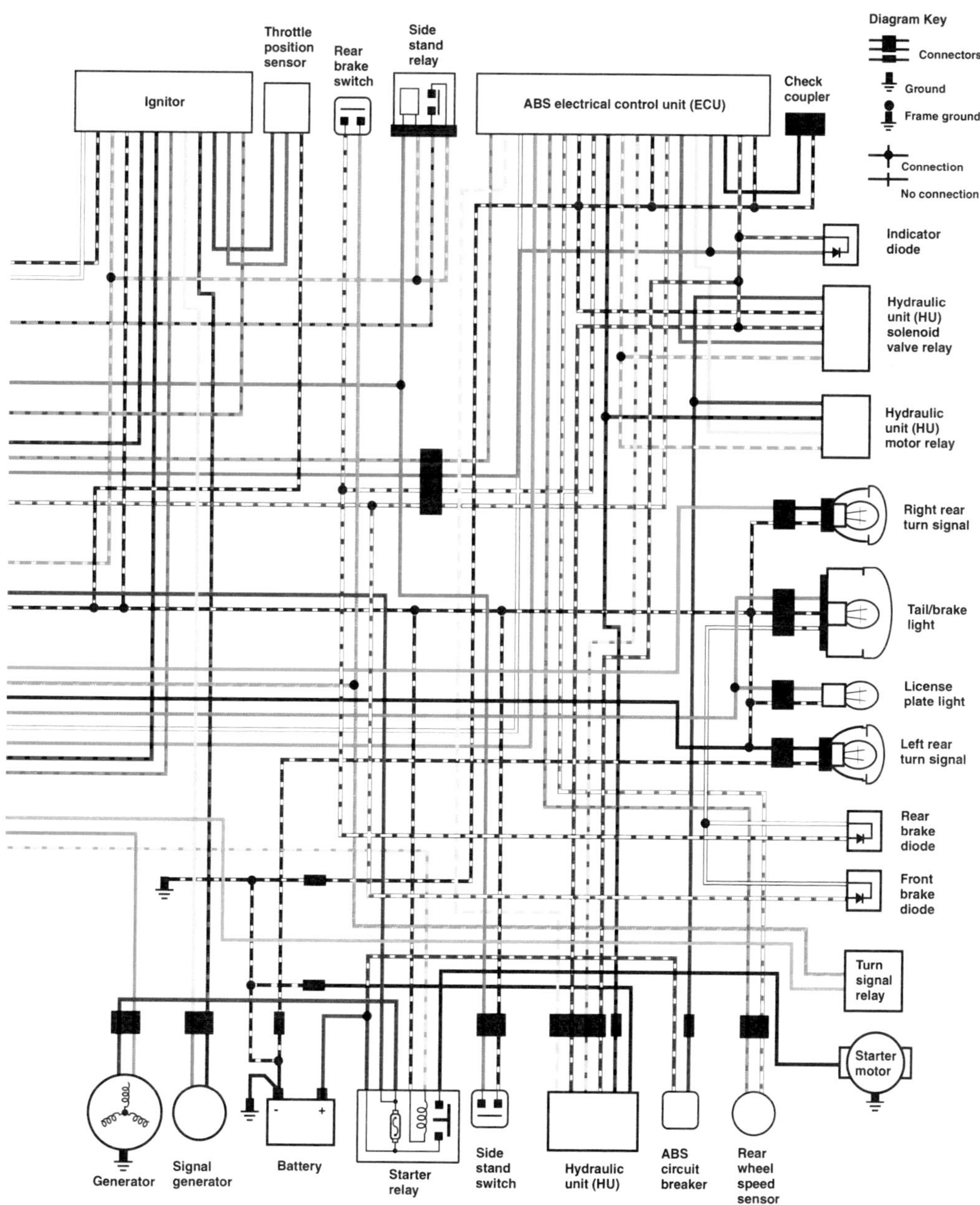
Throttle position sensor
Rear brake switch
Side stand relay
Diagram Key
Connectors
Ground
Frame ground
Connection
No connection
Ignitor
ABS electrical control unit (ECU)
Check coupler
Indicator diode
Hydraulic unit (HU) solenoid valve relay
Hydraulic unit (HU) motor relay
Right rear turn signal
Tail/brake light
License plate light
Left rear turn signal
Rear brake diode
Front brake diode
Turn signal relay
Starter motor
Generator
Signal generator
Battery
Starter relay
Side stand switch
Hydraulic unit (HU)
ABS circuit breaker
Rear wheel speed sensor

16

GSF 1200SA MODELS EXCEPT U.S., CANADA AND AUSTRALIA (1997-2000) (ABS)

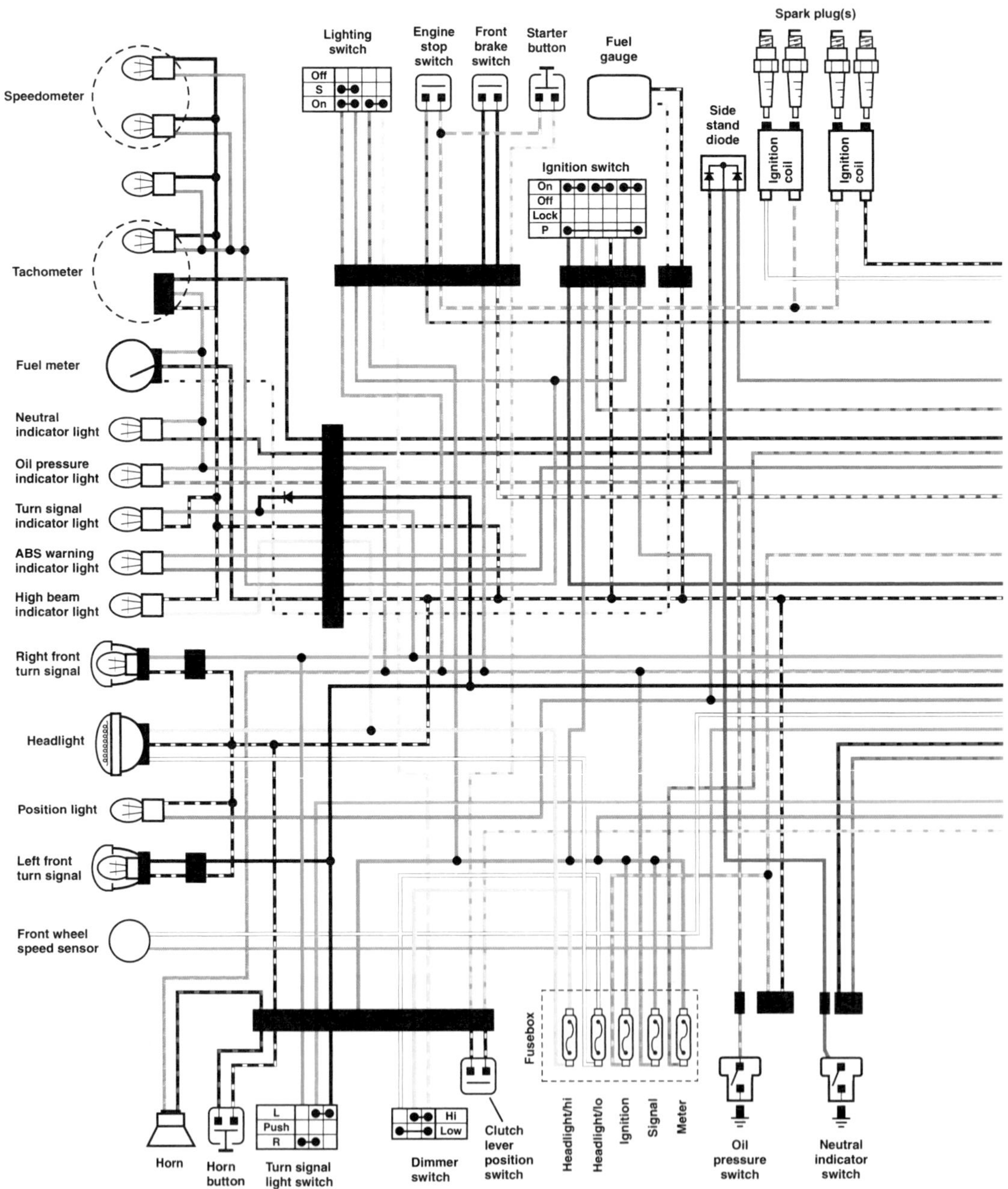

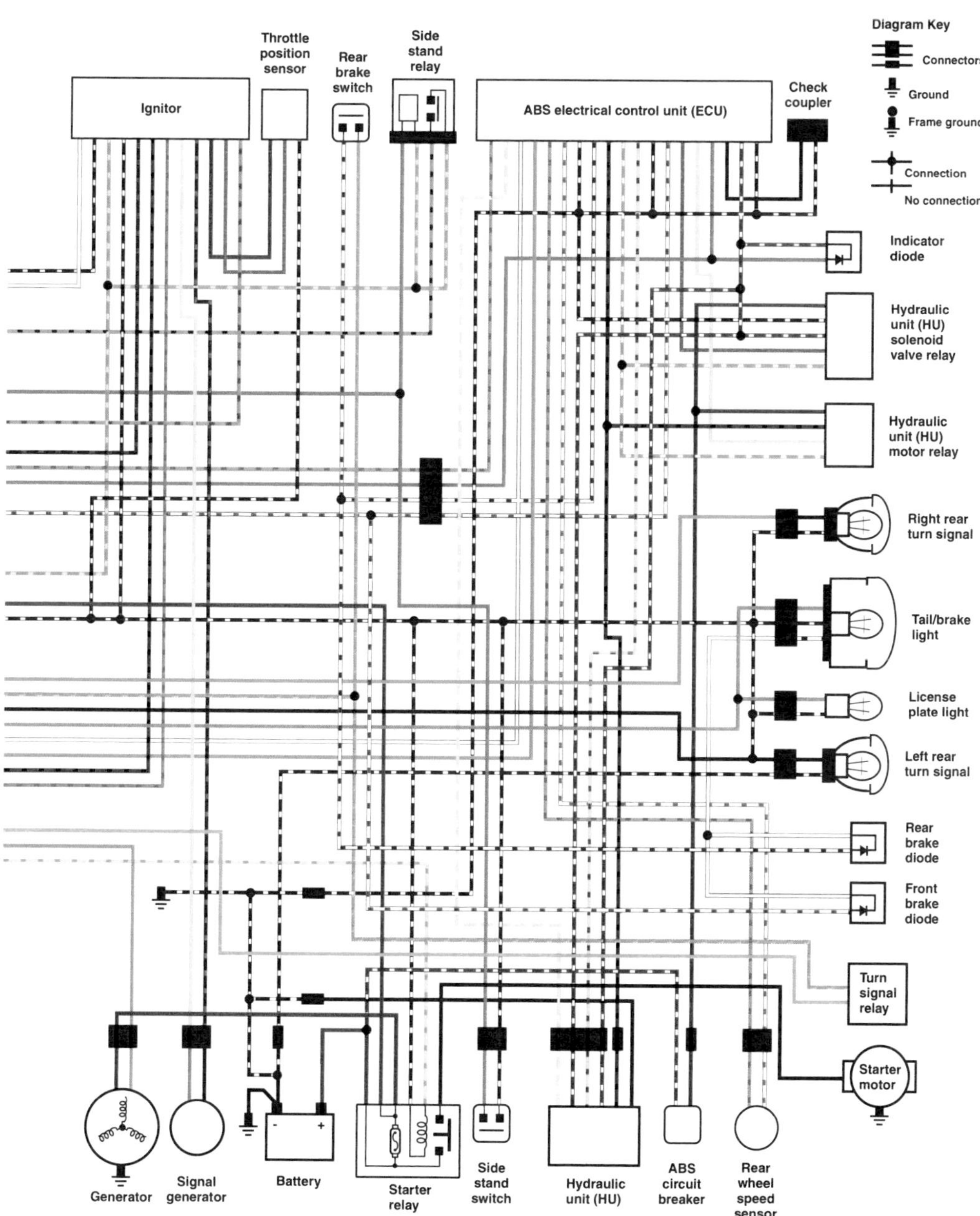
Diagram Key
Connectors
Ground
Frame ground
Connection
No connection
Ignitor
Throttle position sensor
Rear brake switch
Side stand relay
ABS electrical control unit (ECU)
Check coupler
Indicator diode
Hydraulic unit (HU) solenoid valve relay
Hydraulic unit (HU) motor relay
Right rear turn signal
Tail/brake light
License plate light
Left rear turn signal
Rear brake diode
Front brake diode
Turn signal relay
Starter motor
Generator
Signal generator
Battery
Starter relay
Side stand switch
Hydraulic unit (HU)
ABS circuit breaker
Rear wheel speed sensor

GSF 1200S U.S., CANADA AND AUSTRALIA MODELS (2001-ON)

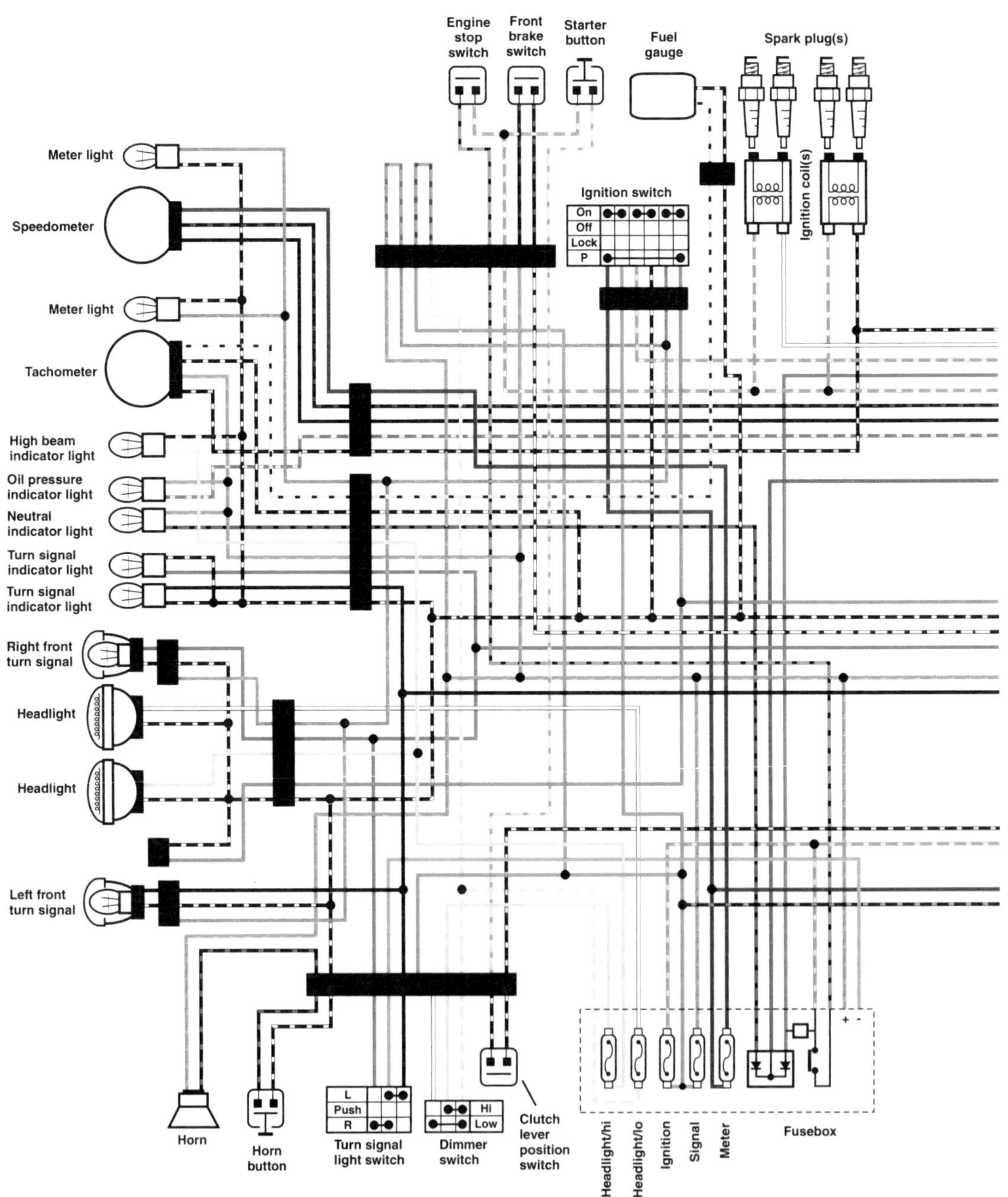

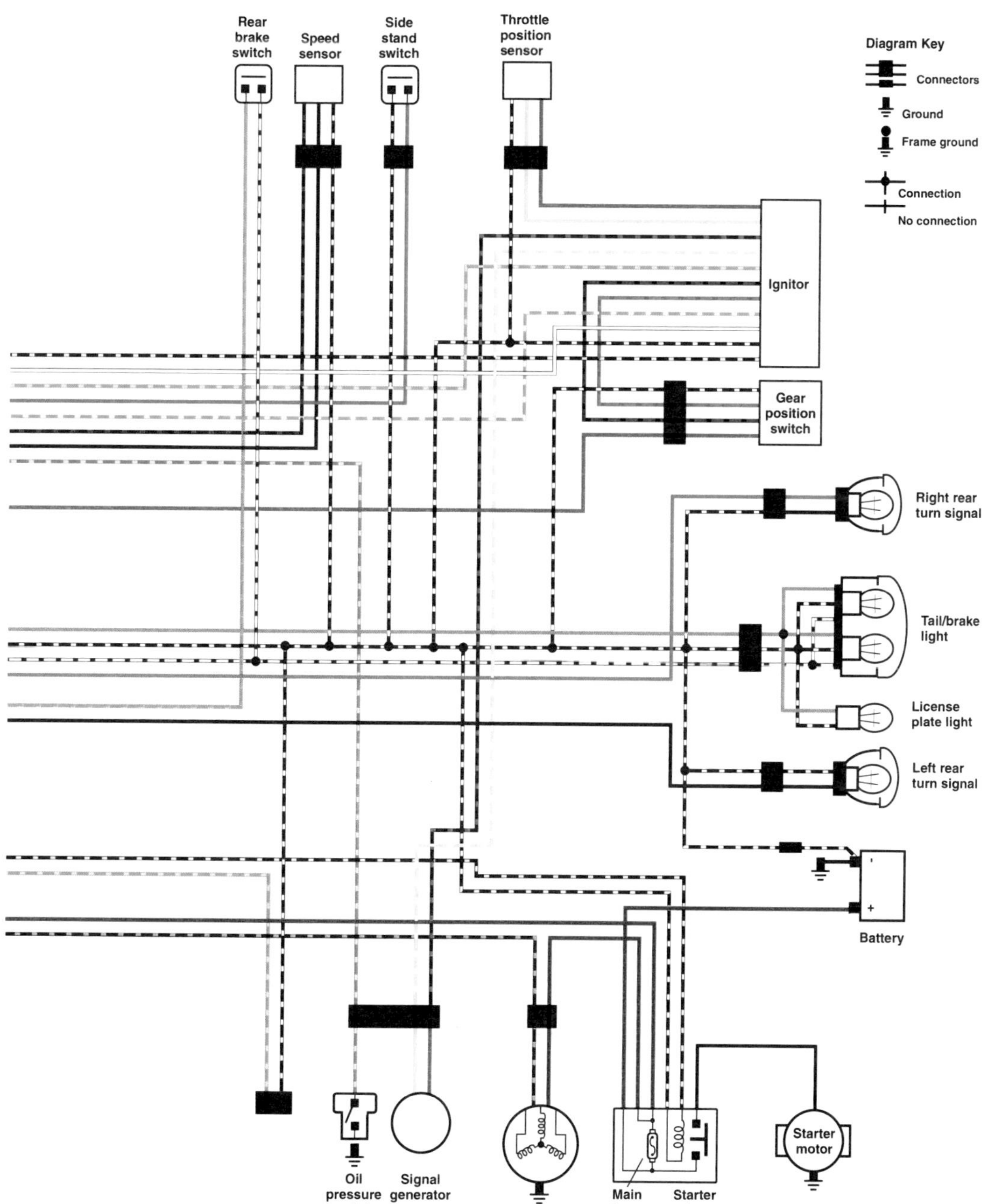

Rear brake switch
Speed sensor
Side stand switch
Throttle position sensor
Diagram Key
Connectors
Ground
Frame ground
Connection
No connection
Ignitor
Gear position switch
Right rear turn signal
Tail/brake light
License plate light
Left rear turn signal
Battery
Oil pressure switch
Signal generator
Generator
Main fuse
Starter relay
Starter motor

16

GSF 1200S EXCEPT U.S., CANADA AND AUSTRALIA MODELS (2001-ON)

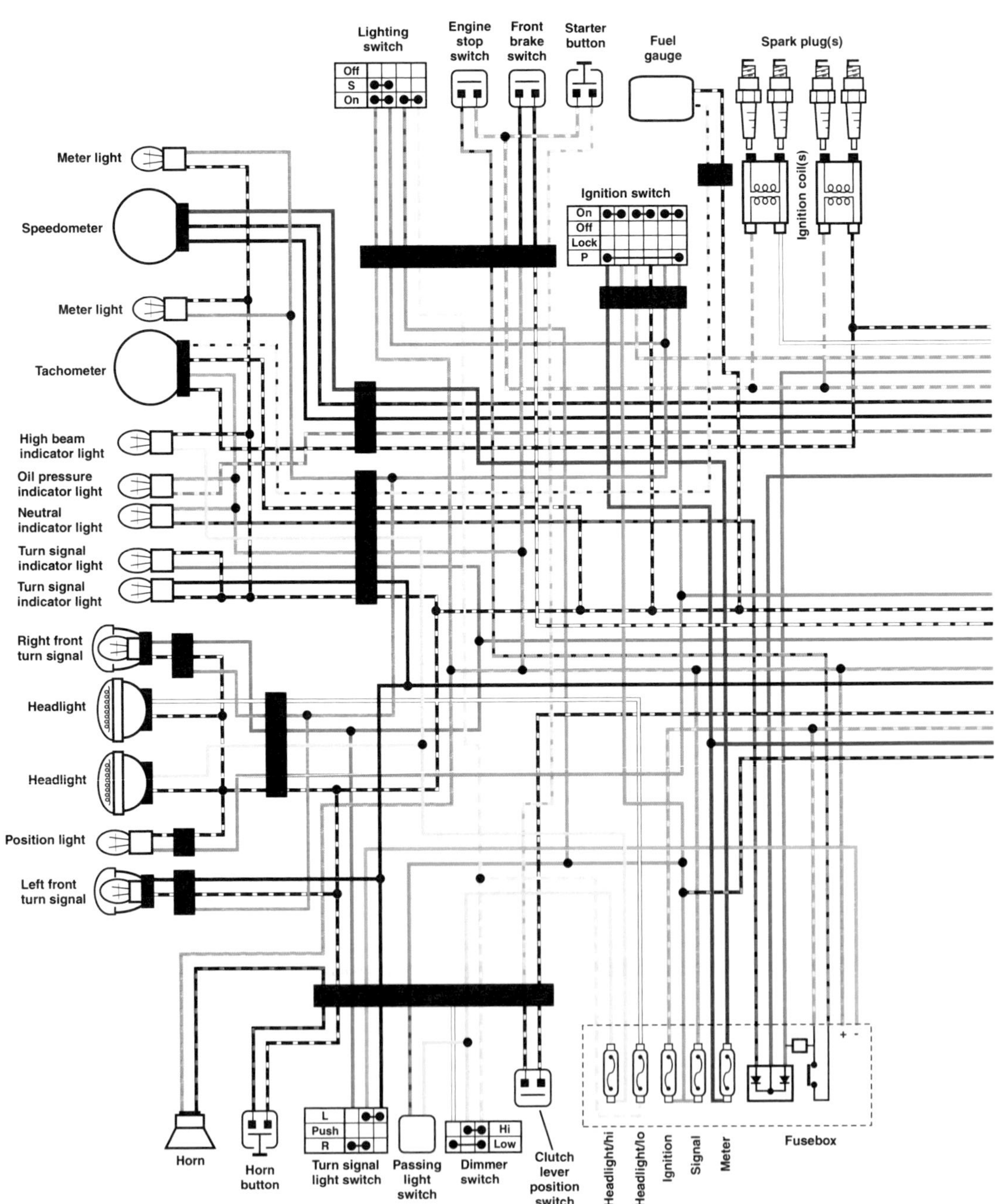

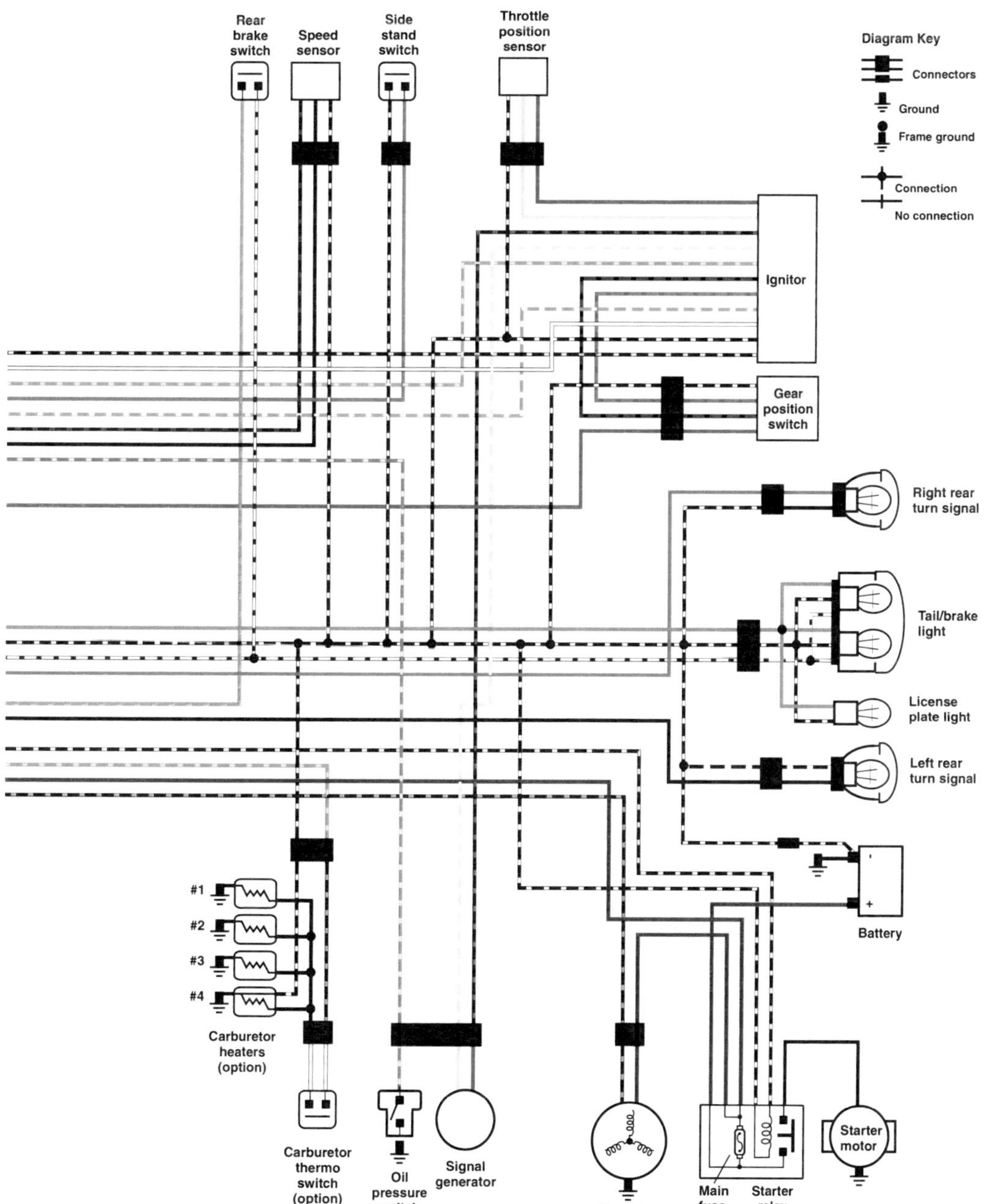
Rear brake switch
Speed sensor
Side stand switch
Throttle position sensor
Diagram Key
Connectors
Ground
Frame ground
Connection
No connection
Ignitor
Gear position switch
Right rear turn signal
Tail/brake light
License plate light
Left rear turn signal
Battery
#1
#2
#3
#4
Carburetor heaters (option)
Carburetor thermo switch (option)
Oil pressure switch
Signal generator
Generator
Main fuse
Starter relay
Starter motor

GSF 1200S U.K. MODELS (2001-ON)

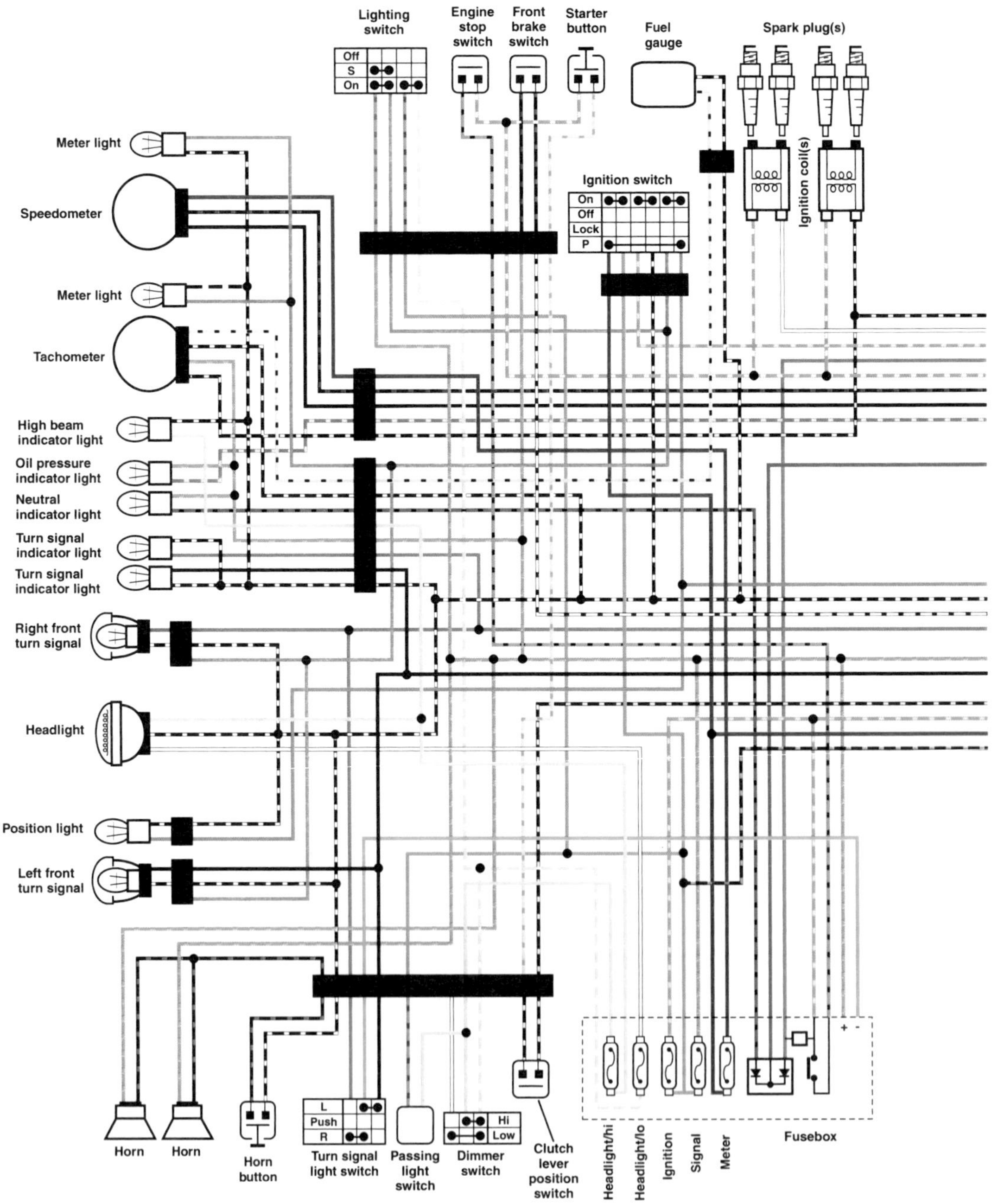

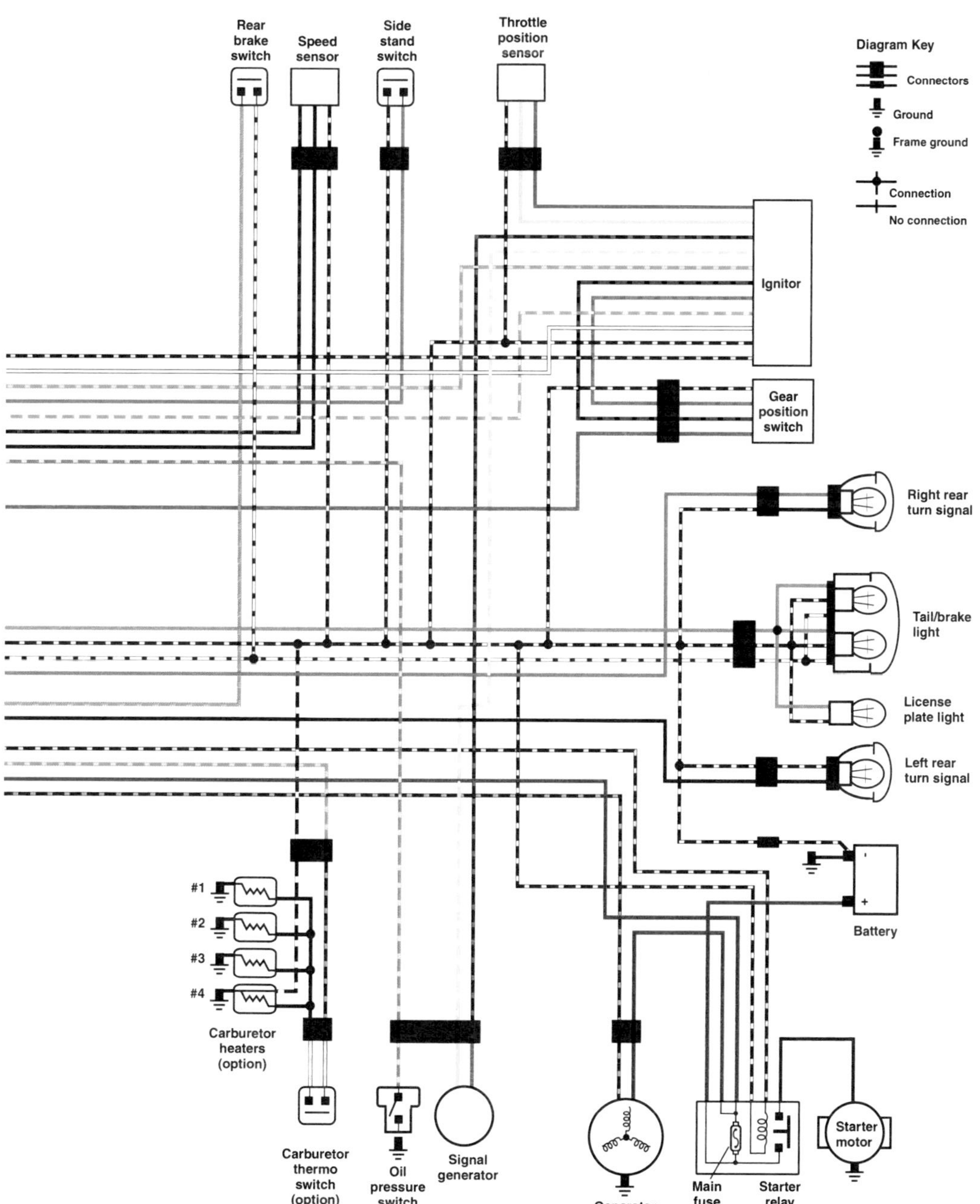

Rear brake switch
Speed sensor
Side stand switch
Throttle position sensor
Diagram Key
Connectors
Ground
Frame ground
Connection
No connection
Ignitor
Gear position switch
Right rear turn signal
Tail/brake light
License plate light
Left rear turn signal
Battery
#1
#2
#3
#4
Carburetor heaters (option)
Carburetor thermo switch (option)
Oil pressure switch
Signal generator
Generator
Main fuse
Starter relay
Starter motor

GSF 1200 U.S. AND CANADA MODELS (2001-ON)

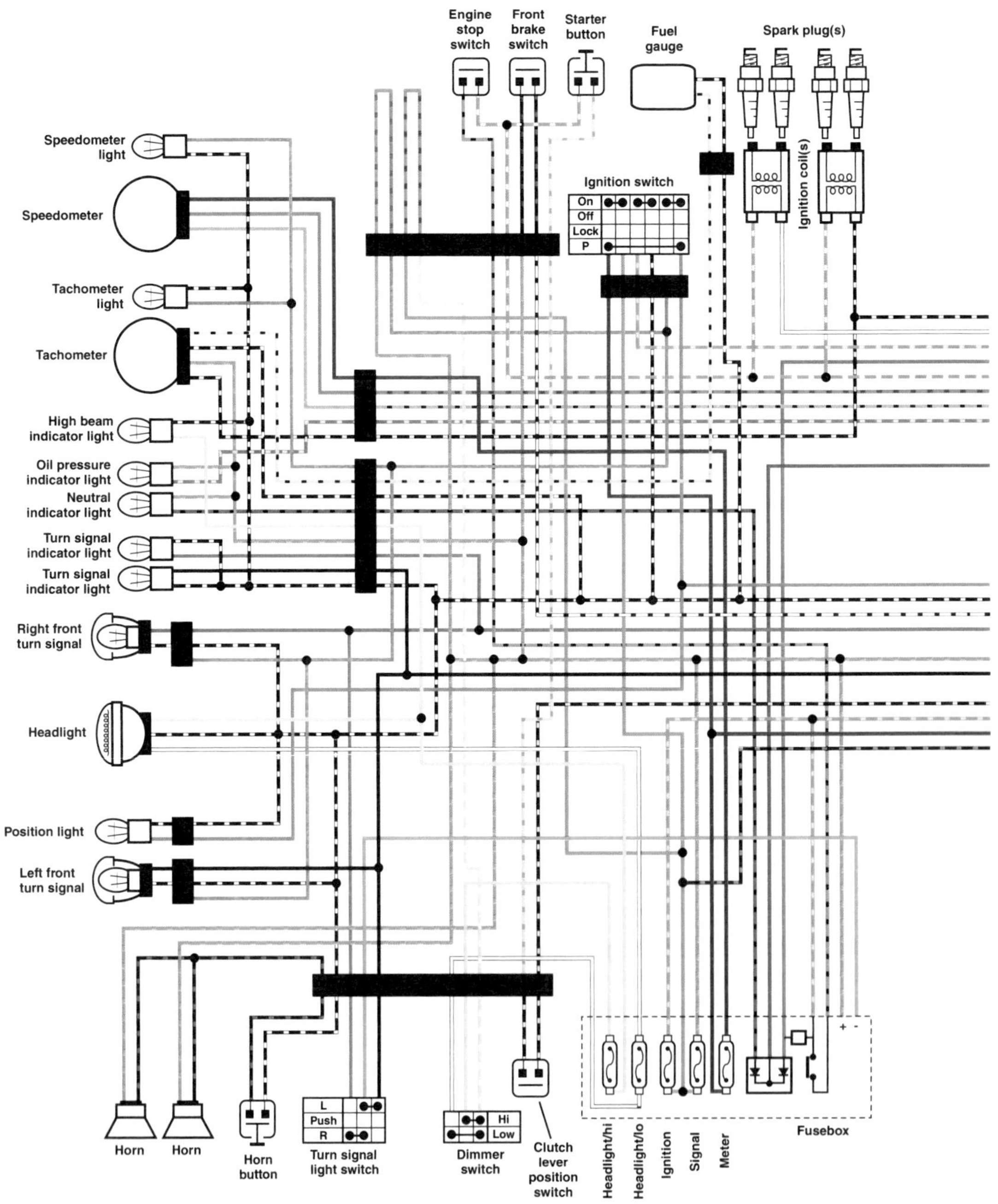

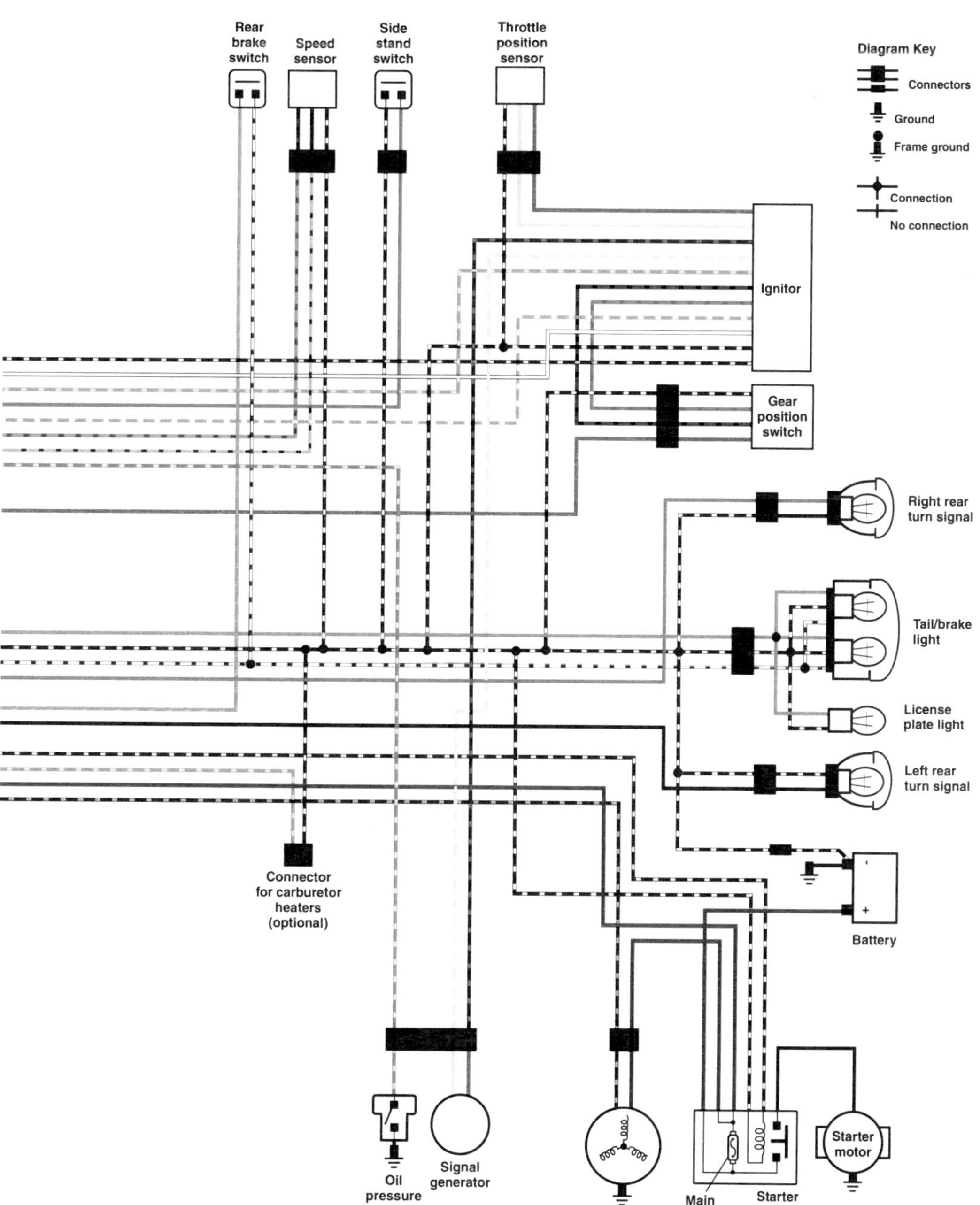
Rear brake switch
Speed sensor
Side stand switch
Throttle position sensor
Diagram Key
Connectors
Ground
Frame ground
Connection
No connection
Ignitor
Gear position switch
Right rear turn signal
Tail/brake light
License plate light
Left rear turn signal
Battery
Connector for carburetor heaters (optional)
Oil pressure switch
Signal generator
Generator
Main fuse
Starter relay
Starter motor

MAINTENANCE LOG

Date	Miles	Type of Service